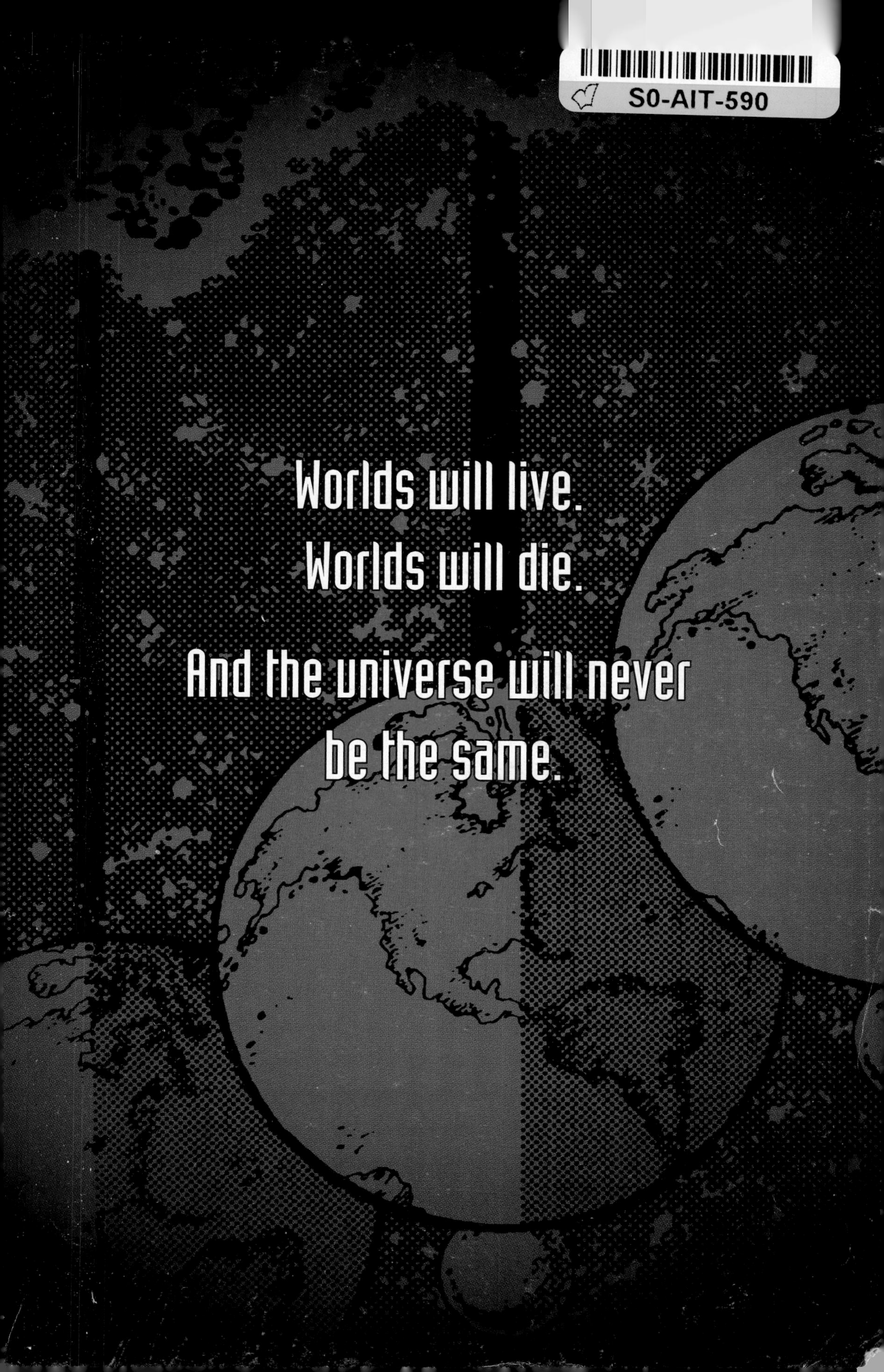
Worlds will live.
Worlds will die.
And the universe will never
be the same.

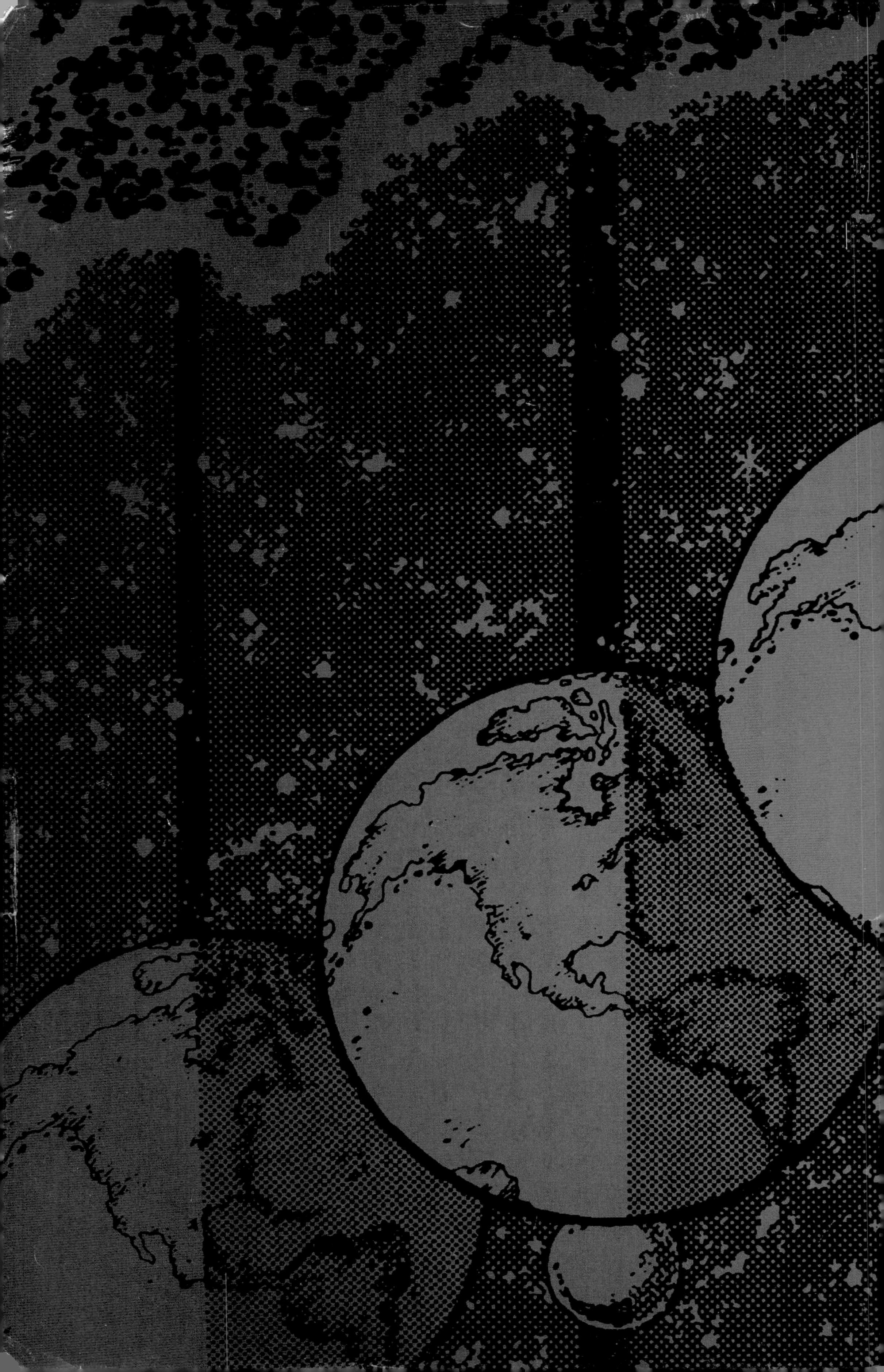

CRISIS
ON INFINITE EARTHS

MARV WOLFMAN
writer

GEORGE PÉREZ
penciller

DICK GIORDANO
MIKE DeCARLO
JERRY ORDWAY
inkers

ANTHONY TOLLIN
TOM ZIUKO
CARL GAFFORD
colorists - original series

TOM McCRAW
color reconstruction and enhancement

JOHN COSTANZA
letterer

original covers by
GEORGE PÉREZ

Marv Wolfman
Editor-original series

Robert Greenberger
Associate Editor-original series

Rick Taylor
Jim Spivey
Editors-collected edition

Bob Kahan
Consulting Editor-collected edition

Robbin Brosterman
Design Director – Books

Murphy Fogelnest
Publication Design

Bob Harras
Senior VP – Editor-in-Chief, DC Comics

Diane Nelson
President

Dan DiDio and Jim Lee
Co-Publishers

Geoff Johns
Chief Creative Officer

John Rood
Executive VP – Sales, Marketing &
Business Development

Amy Genkins
Senior VP – Business & Legal Affairs

Nairi Gardiner
Senior VP – Finance

Jeff Boison
VP – Publishing Planning

Mark Chiarello
VP – Art Direction & Design

John Cunningham
VP – Marketing

Terri Cunningham
VP – Editorial Administration

Alison Gill
Senior VP – Manufacturing & Operations

Hank Kanalz
Senior VP – Vertigo & Integrated Publishing

Jay Kogan
VP – Business & Legal Affairs, Publishing

Jack Mahan
VP – Business Affairs, Talent

Nick Napolitano
VP – Manufacturing Administration

Sue Pohja
VP – Book Sales

Courtney Simmons
Senior VP – Publicity

Bob Wayne
Senior VP – Sales

CRISIS ON INFINITE EARTHS

Published by DC Comics.
Compilation © 2000 DC Comics. All Rights Reserved.
Cover, introduction and afterword Copyright © 1998 DC Comics. All Rights Reserved.

Originally published in single magazine form as CRISIS ON INFINITE EARTHS 1-12.
Copyright © 1985 DC Comics. All Rights Reserved.
All characters, their distinctive likenesses and related elements featured in this publication
are trademarks of DC Comics. The stories, characters and incidents featured in this publication are
entirely fictional. DC Comics does not read or accept unsolicited submissions of ideas, stories or artwork.

DC Comics, 1700 Broadway, New York, NY 10019
A Warner Bros. Entertainment Company
Printed by RR Donnelley, Salem, VA, USA. 4/25/14. Tenth Printing.
ISBN: 978-1-5638-9750-4

Cover illustration by GEORGE PÉREZ AND ALEX ROSS.
Ink finishes on the "Monitor Tapes" by AL VEY.
Reproduction art assembly and reconstruction by NICK NAPOLITANO.
Black & white reconstruction on selected internal material by RICK KEENE.

SPECIAL THANKS TO KEVIN EASTMAN AND JONATHAN MANKUTA.

LIBRARY OF CONGRESS CATALOGING-IN-PUBLICATION DATA

WOLFMAN, MARV.
  CRISIS ON INFINITE EARTHS / MARV WOLFMAN, GEORGE PÉREZ, DICK GIORDANO,
MIKE DECARLO, JERRY ORDWAY.
    P. CM.
  "ORIGINALLY PUBLISHED IN SINGLE MAGAZINE FORM AS CRISIS ON INFINITE EARTHS 1-12."
  ISBN 978-1-5638-9750-4
  1. GRAPHIC NOVELS. I. PÉREZ, GEORGE, 1954- II. GIORDANO, DICK.
III. DE CARLO, MIKE. IV. ORDWAY, JERRY. V. TITLE.
  PN6728.C699W65 2012
  741.5'973 – DC23
                          2012032625

SUSTAINABLE FORESTRY INITIATIVE

Certified Chain of Custody
20% Certified Forest Content,
80% Certified Sourcing
www.sfiprogram.org
SFI-01042
APPLIES TO TEXT STOCK ONLY

Welcome to the collected CRISIS ON INFINITE EARTHS, a comic novel drawn by the always amazing George Pérez and written by me, originally published by DC Comics from January to December, 1985.

You can't possibly know how much this fully recolored, high quality hardcover printing means to me. You see, CRISIS ON INFINITE EARTHS was, in many ways, not just a job, but a calling; the story I had wanted to write ever since I was a kid reading comic books on my stoop under an unquestioning sun in Brooklyn, New York.

When I was growing up in the '60s, the super-hero team comic to read was the JUSTICE LEAGUE OF AMERICA, a book featuring seven or eight of DC's super-heroes. Occasionally, the JLA would meet THE JUSTICE SOCIETY OF AMERICA– their 1940's counterparts from Earth-Two, which was in another dimension – and we'd have maybe fifteen or sixteen heroes in a special two-part JLA/JSA story. But, being the greedy fan I was, I always wanted to see a single story featuring *all* the DC super-heroes from the past, present and future. I even came up with a villain for the saga and gave him the ever-so-awesome name of "The Librarian." Pretty scary, eh? What's he gonna do? Charge the heroes a nickel a day for overdue books?

Anyway, in my mind's eye, the Librarian, living in a satellite orbiting the Earth, observed all the heroes, and sold the information he obtained about the heroes to other villains. Eventually, the heroes would learn about the villain, team up and end his threat.

In the meantime, I'd become a fan of *The Prisoner* TV show. *The Prisoner* was, as far as I knew, the first intentional limited series with a beginning, middle and a definite end (even if it was cryptic). I loved the idea of a short-run series and wondered why it had never been done in comics. This format would be wonderful, I naively thought, for my Librarian series.

Once I became a professional writer I mentioned my "brilliant" idea to several editors at both DC and Marvel and was promptly told that limited series would be impossible to sell. Back in 1970, first issues of comics, I was informed, sold poorly. Readers were suspicious of comics with low numbers (as opposed to, say, ACTION COMICS #450, which indicated it had been around for a long time). Besides, it usually took six issues for readers to decide to give a new comic a try, therefore a limited series would be half over before sales could begin to improve. I felt like a fool for making the suggestion, shut up and went back to writing my little mystery stories for HOUSE OF SECRETS and WITCHING HOUR.

In the '70s, I went on to become an editor at Warren Publishing (*Creepy*, *Eerie* and *Vampirella* magazines), then editor for the Marvel Magazine line, and finally Editor-in-Chief of Marvel Comics.

At the same time, comics fandom exploded into creation. Comic book shops opened and the direct sales market was born. This meant for the first time there were stores that catered only to comic-book fans. These fans, like myself, didn't wait for issue ten to buy a new comic; they eagerly bought all first issues.

In 1980, I returned to DC Comics. George Pérez and I co-created THE NEW TEEN TITANS for DC, and it quickly became their number-one-selling book. George also drew JLA while I wrote SUPERMAN, BATMAN, GREEN LANTERN and others.

By this point I had given up on using the Librarian in a huge companywide crossover series and instead, with a name change to The Monitor, George and I made him a villain in THE TITANS.

While writing GREEN LANTERN I received a letter from a fan asking about a mixup in DC continuity. In my reply I said, "One day we (meaning the DC editorial we) will probably straighten out what is in the DC Universe…and what is outside." At this point in its history DC Comics had Earth-One, Earth-Two, Earth-Three, Earth-B, etc. There were super-heroes on each Earth and though old-time readers had no problem understanding DC continuity, it proved off-putting to new readers who suddenly discovered there was not one but three Supermans, Wonder Womans, Batmans, etc.

The letter to GREEN LANTERN made me wonder how DC could simplify its continuity and lure new readers to the fold. Suddenly, I thought of The Monitor and my original intent for the character. This would be the perfect vehicle in which to do the maxiseries. The ideas evolved quickly, and within four days DC approved a complete revamping of their entire universe to be done in a 12-part series. George signed on first as artist (then, by issue six, as co-plotter) and came up with the title, CRISIS ON INFINITE EARTHS, as an homage to the JLA/JSA team-ups of our youth.

We announced CRISIS in 1981 at a comics convention in New York City, but researching DC's long and convoluted history kept us busy for several years. We decided to hold off publishing CRISIS until 1985 – which was also DC's 50th Anniversary. What better gift to the company that began it all than to help restart its next 50 years.

When George and I began CRISIS we promised that worlds would live, worlds would die, and the DC Universe would never be the same.

It is now 1998, thirteen years later. In 1981, nobody could have predicted the effect CRISIS would have, not only at DC, but throughout the comics industry.

What began as one child's dream of doing a special series featuring all the heroes he knew has blossomed into a regular event at every company. After the astounding success of CRISIS – which was created only to simplify the DC universe for new readers – every publisher, even those who were brand-new, jumped onto the bandwagon with a company-changing series of their own, whether they needed to "clean house" or not. In many ways, I fear, the annual stunt has taken over comics publishing. If it isn't big, if heroes don't die, if worlds don't change, then, many feel, the stories aren't worth reading.

But CRISIS existed in its pure form only to bring DC back to an easy-to-read beginning before endless continuity took over. The idea was not to make comics accessible only to longtime fans, but to everyone.

Over the past decade and more, I've been asked many questions about CRISIS. Here's a chance to answer the most important ones.

• *Was* CRISIS ON INFINITE EARTHS *successful in its stated goal*? The answer is, partially. CRISIS brought readers to DC Comics, and that was, of course, its purpose. It allowed for the successful revamping of Superman and other series. It has also allowed for less successful relaunches, at DC and elsewhere.

• *Knowing what has happened in comics these past 13 years, would I do the Crisis all over again*? Yes. The idea was to simplify the universe, and we did so. After a few rough starts, I would like to think those who followed us understand the need to keep work-ing to broaden the reader base, not to shrink it by sticking with outdated continuity. My generation was lucky. The super-heroes began all over again in the late '50s and early '60s. We didn't worry about 1940s continuity. Most of us, in fact, didn't even know about the old heroes when we began reading comics. Every generation of comic-book readers deserves to have the comics belong to them, not to their older siblings and parents.

• *Why did we kill Supergirl?* Boy, I still get that at every convention I go to. Before CRISIS it seemed that half of Krypton survived its explosion. We had Superman, Supergirl, Krypto, the Phantom Zone criminals, the bottle city of Kandor and many others. Our goal was to make Superman unique. We went back to his origin and made Kal-El the only survivor of Krypton. That, sadly, was why Supergirl had to die. However, we are thrilled by all the letters we received saying Supergirl's death in CRISIS was the best Supergirl story they had read. Thank you. By the way, I miss Kara, too.

• *Did we have to kill the Barry Allen Flash?* We always liked Barry, so when we were asked to kill him we planted a secret plot device in the story that could bring him back if someone wanted to. Don't look for it; you won't find it — but if you corner me at a convention, and if I'm in a good mood, I'll tell you what it is.

• *Why did we kill all the JSA heroes?* We didn't. No JSA hero died in the Crisis. It was my policy not to kill any hero who was created before I was born. It was a silly rule, but I stuck with it for better or worse.

• *Did we have to kill so many heroes (do you sense a trend in the questions I've been asked)?* We actually didn't kill as many heroes as we're blamed for. Of course, we did kill about 3,000 universes filled with super-heroes, but I try not to think about them. Read through the series again, and you'll see that we're right.

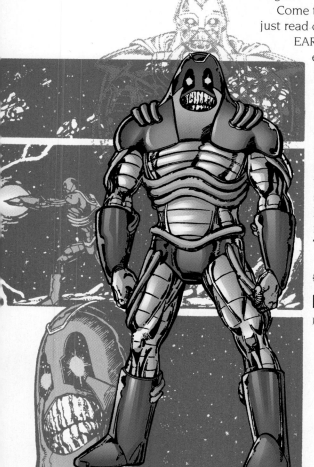

Come to think of it, ignore these words and just read or reread CRISIS ON INFINITE EARTHS. George and I have always been extremely proud of the work we did here. It was my childhood dream, and it came true. What more can one ask?

Before I sign off, I want to again thank George Pérez for his incredible work and his incredible cover for this collection. I've worked with some wonderful partners over the years, but George and I always seemed to anticipate each other, keep each other on track and make each other do our best. There is no one better.

Thanks to everyone for the good words over all these years.

Marv Wolfman

JULY 15, 1998

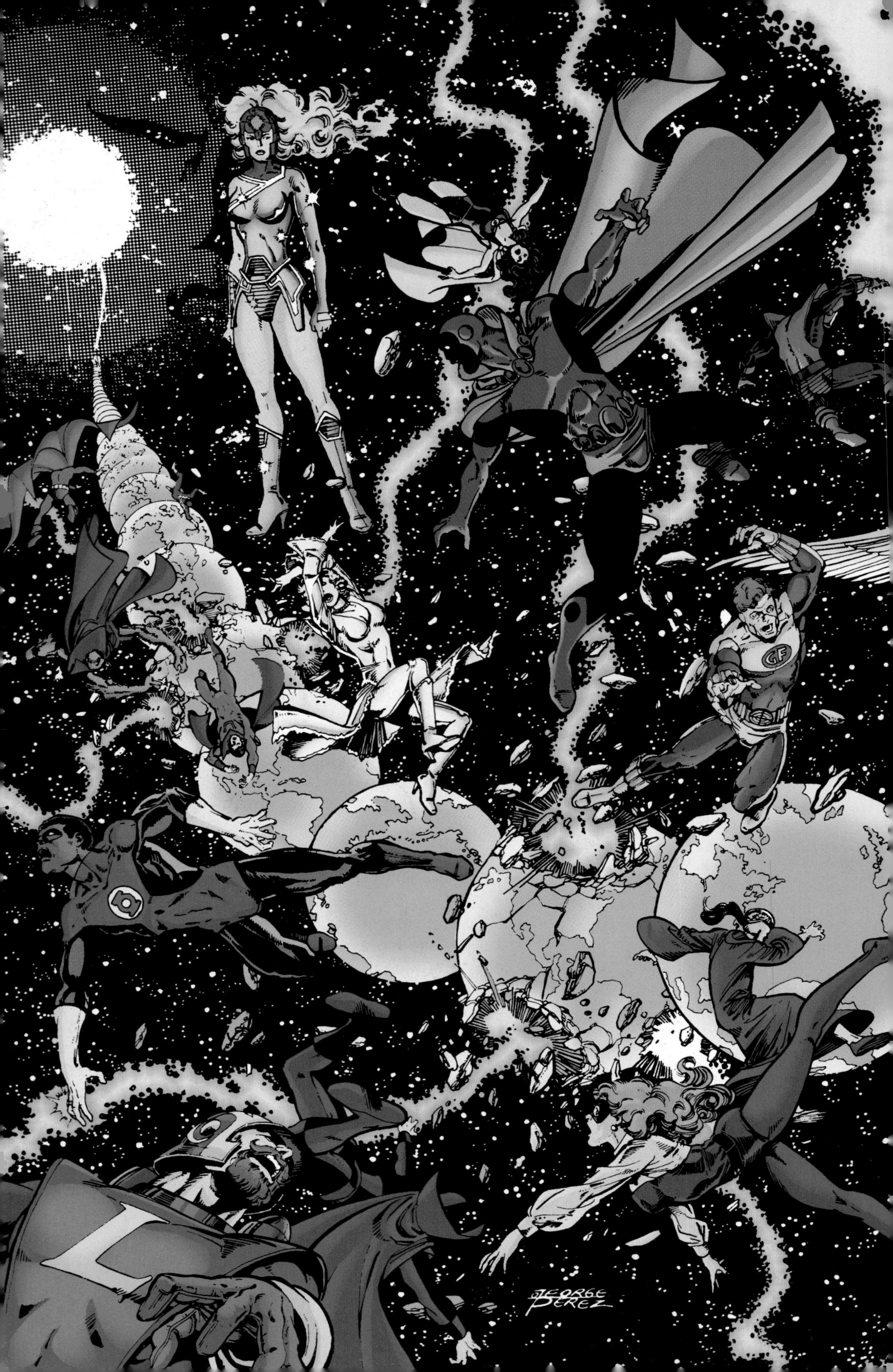
GEORGE PEREZ

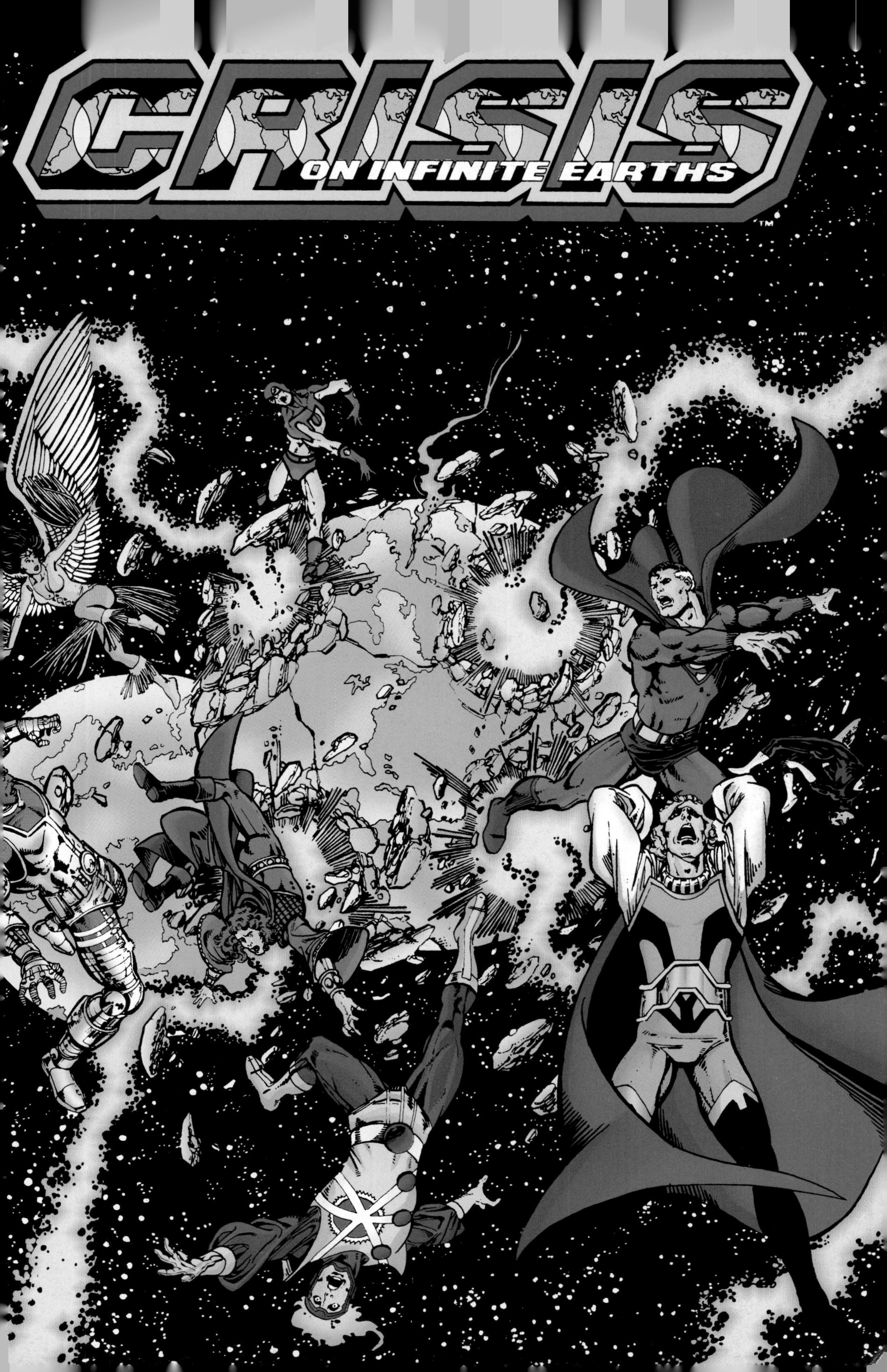
CRISIS
ON INFINITE EARTHS
™

IN THE BEGINNING THERE WAS ONLY ONE, A SINGLE BLACK INFINITUDE

...SO COLD AND DARK FOR SO VERY LONG...

...THAT EVEN THE BURNING LIGHT WAS IMPERCEPTIBLE.

BUT THE LIGHT GREW, AND THE INFINITUDE SHUDDERED...

...AND THE DARKNESS FINALLY... SCREAMED, AS MUCH IN PAIN AS IN RELIEF.

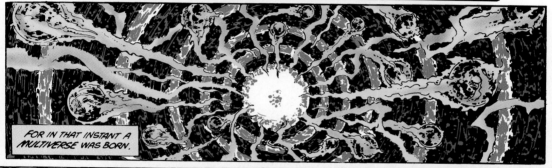

FOR IN THAT INSTANT A MULTIVERSE WAS BORN.

A MULTIVERSE OF WORLDS VIBRATING AND REPLICATING... AND A MULTIVERSE THAT SHOULD HAVE BEEN ONE, BECAME MANY!

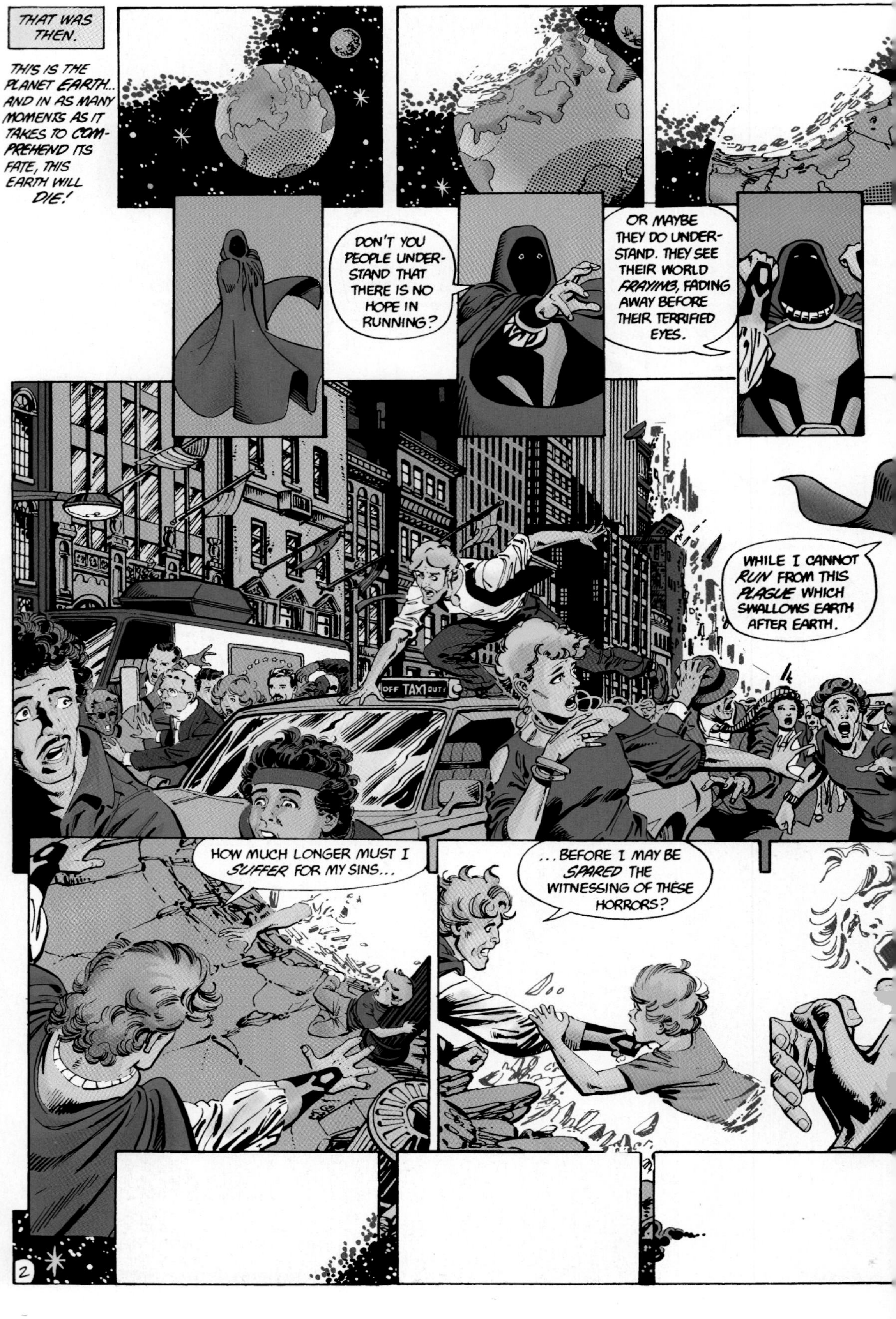
THAT WAS THEN.
THIS IS THE PLANET EARTH... AND IN AS MANY MOMENTS AS IT TAKES TO COMPREHEND ITS FATE, THIS EARTH WILL DIE!
DON'T YOU PEOPLE UNDERSTAND THAT THERE IS NO HOPE IN RUNNING?
OR MAYBE THEY DO UNDERSTAND. THEY SEE THEIR WORLD FRAYING, FADING AWAY BEFORE THEIR TERRIFIED EYES.
WHILE I CANNOT RUN FROM THIS PLAGUE WHICH SWALLOWS EARTH AFTER EARTH.
OFF TAXI DUTY
HOW MUCH LONGER MUST I SUFFER FOR MY SINS...
...BEFORE I MAY BE SPARED THE WITNESSING OF THESE HORRORS?
2

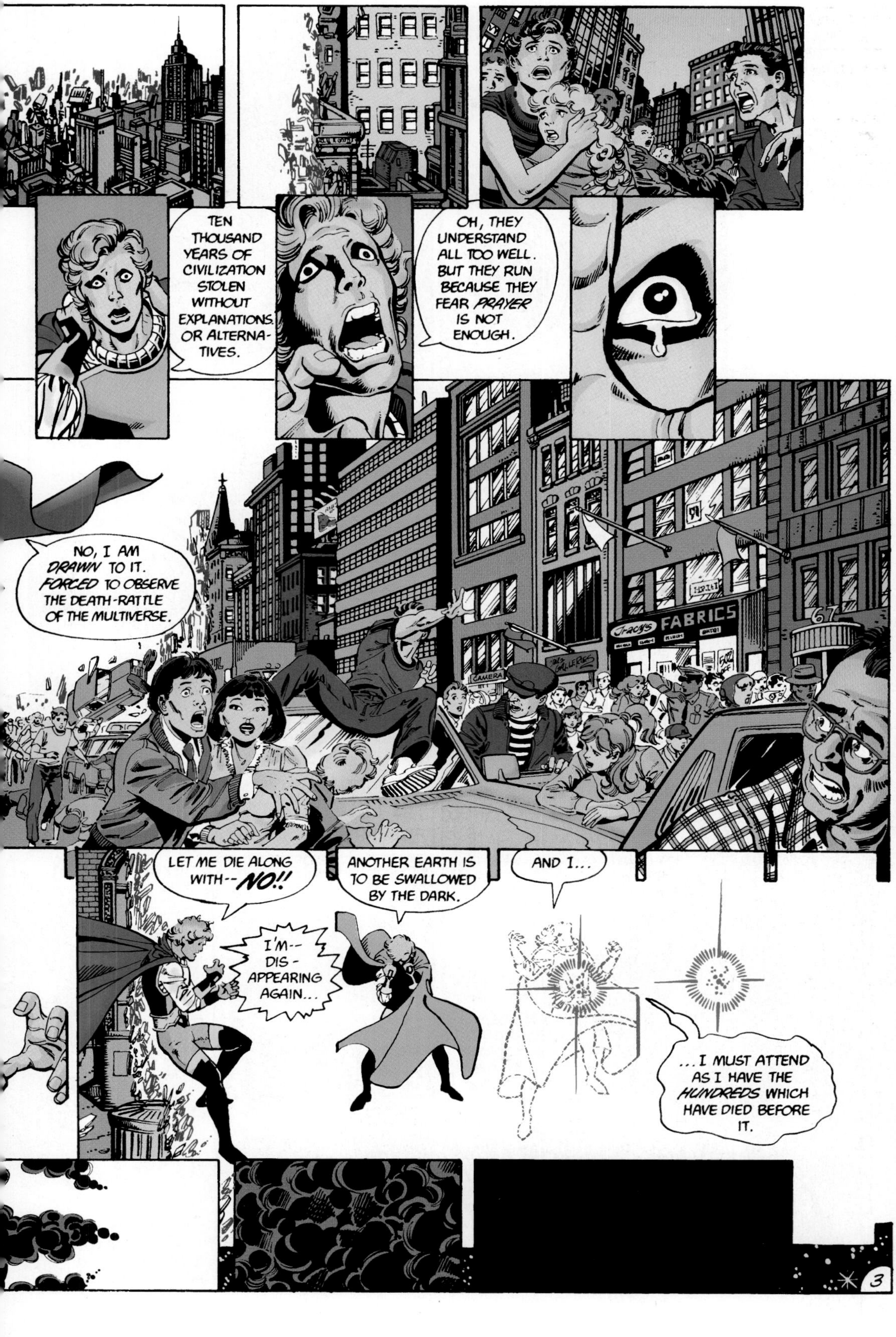
TEN THOUSAND YEARS OF CIVILIZATION STOLEN WITHOUT EXPLANATIONS. OR ALTERNATIVES.
OH, THEY UNDERSTAND ALL TOO WELL. BUT THEY RUN BECAUSE THEY FEAR PRAYER IS NOT ENOUGH.
NO, I AM DRAWN TO IT. FORCED TO OBSERVE THE DEATH-RATTLE OF THE MULTIVERSE.
FABRICS
67
LET ME DIE ALONG WITH--NO!!
I'M--DIS-APPEARING AGAIN...
ANOTHER EARTH IS TO BE SWALLOWED BY THE DARK.
AND I...
...I MUST ATTEND AS I HAVE THE HUNDREDS WHICH HAVE DIED BEFORE IT.
3

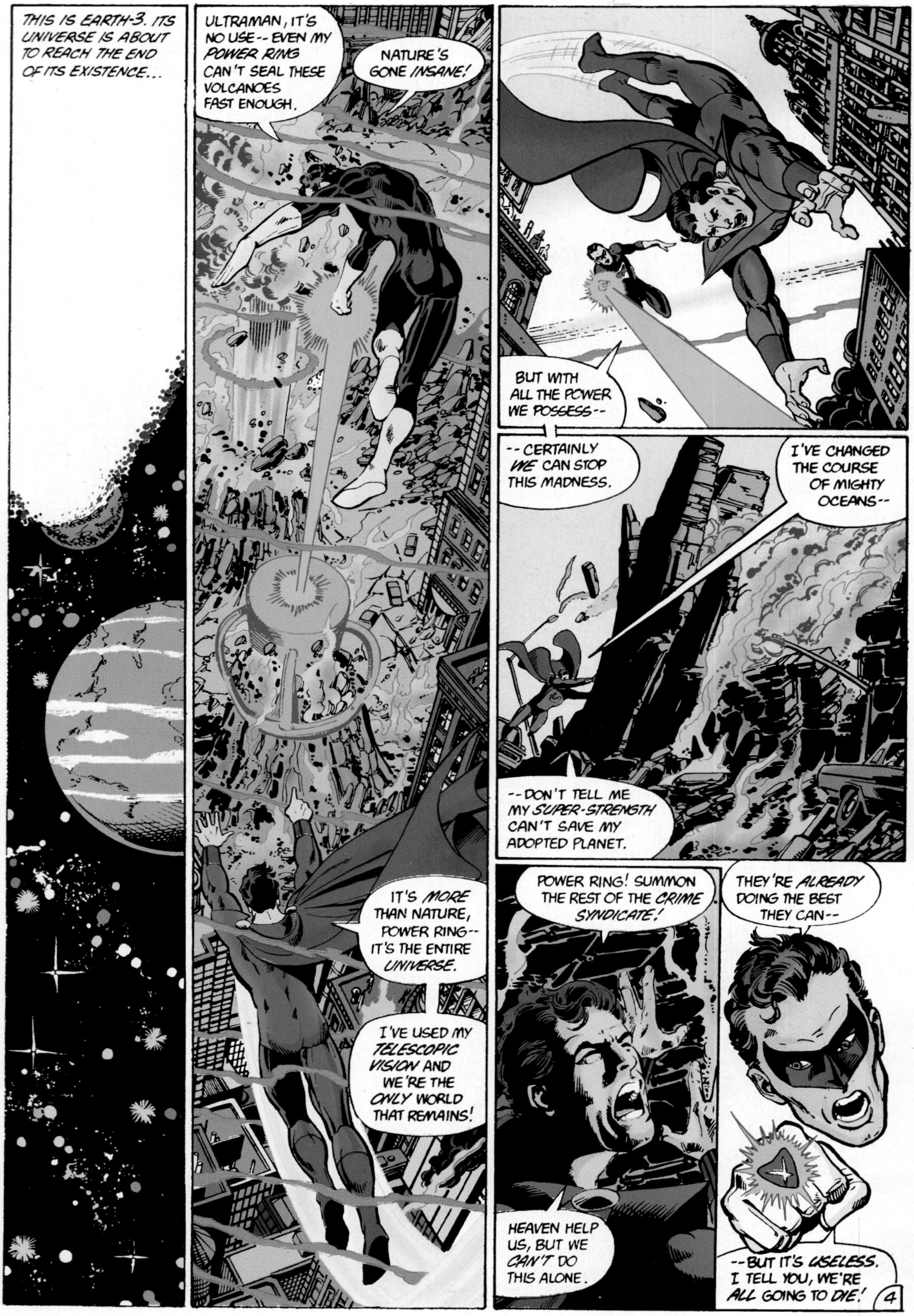
THIS IS EARTH-3. ITS UNIVERSE IS ABOUT TO REACH THE END OF ITS EXISTENCE...
ULTRAMAN, IT'S NO USE-- EVEN MY POWER RING CAN'T SEAL THESE VOLCANOES FAST ENOUGH.
NATURE'S GONE INSANE!
IT'S MORE THAN NATURE, POWER RING-- IT'S THE ENTIRE UNIVERSE.
I'VE USED MY TELESCOPIC VISION AND WE'RE THE ONLY WORLD THAT REMAINS!
BUT WITH ALL THE POWER WE POSSESS--
--CERTAINLY WE CAN STOP THIS MADNESS.
I'VE CHANGED THE COURSE OF MIGHTY OCEANS--
--DON'T TELL ME MY SUPER-STRENGTH CAN'T SAVE MY ADOPTED PLANET.
POWER RING! SUMMON THE REST OF THE CRIME SYNDICATE!
HEAVEN HELP US, BUT WE CAN'T DO THIS ALONE.
THEY'RE ALREADY DOING THE BEST THEY CAN--
--BUT IT'S USELESS. I TELL YOU, WE'RE ALL GOING TO DIE!
4

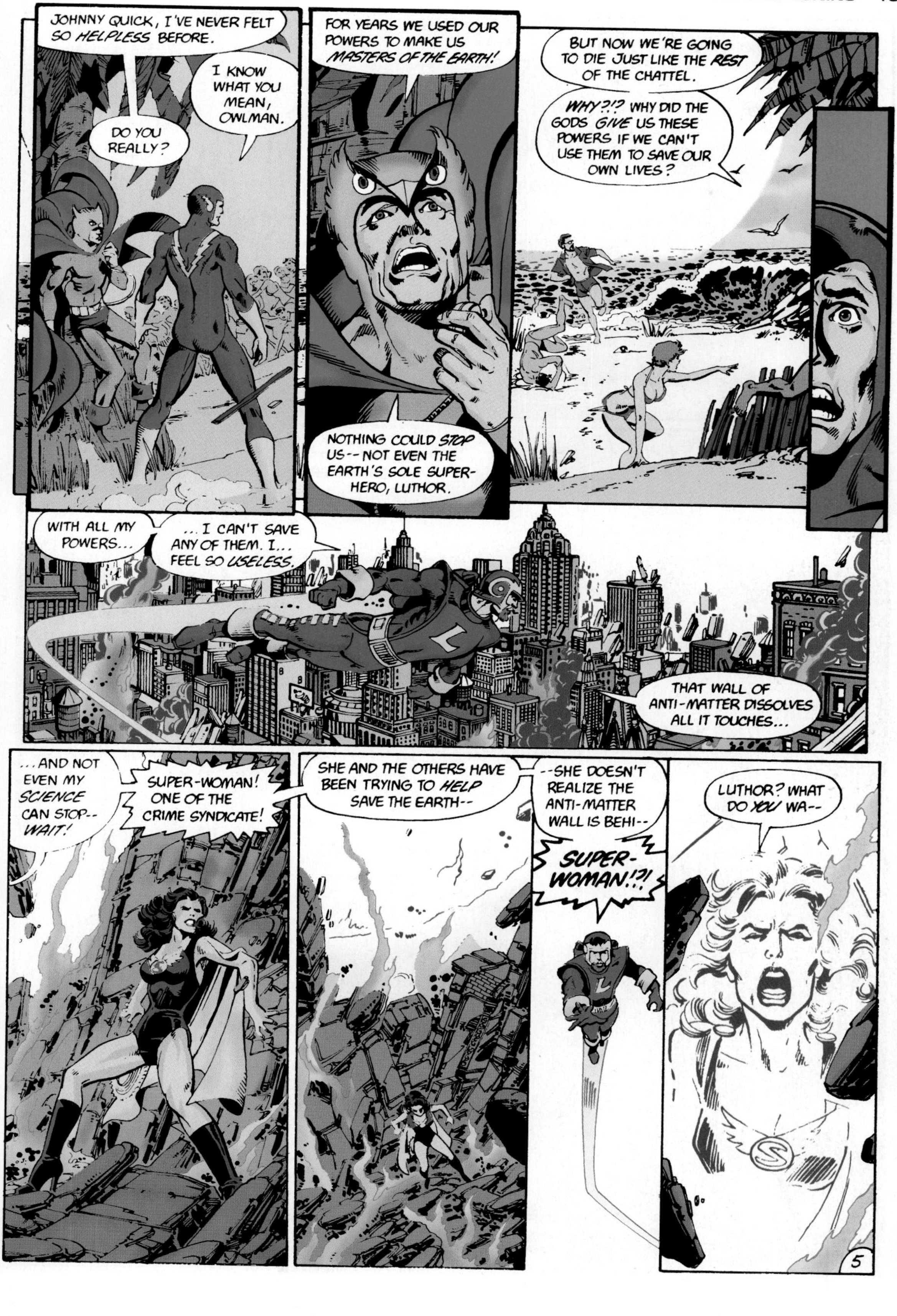
JOHNNY QUICK, I'VE NEVER FELT SO HELPLESS BEFORE.
I KNOW WHAT YOU MEAN, OWLMAN.
DO YOU REALLY?
FOR YEARS WE USED OUR POWERS TO MAKE US MASTERS OF THE EARTH!
NOTHING COULD STOP US-- NOT EVEN THE EARTH'S SOLE SUPER-HERO, LUTHOR.
BUT NOW WE'RE GOING TO DIE JUST LIKE THE REST OF THE CHATTEL.
WHY?!? WHY DID THE GODS GIVE US THESE POWERS IF WE CAN'T USE THEM TO SAVE OUR OWN LIVES?
WITH ALL MY POWERS...
...I CAN'T SAVE ANY OF THEM. I... FEEL SO USELESS.
THAT WALL OF ANTI-MATTER DISSOLVES ALL IT TOUCHES...
...AND NOT EVEN MY SCIENCE CAN STOP-- WAIT!
SUPER-WOMAN! ONE OF THE CRIME SYNDICATE!
SHE AND THE OTHERS HAVE BEEN TRYING TO HELP SAVE THE EARTH--
--SHE DOESN'T REALIZE THE ANTI-MATTER WALL IS BEHI--
SUPER-WOMAN!?!
LUTHOR? WHAT DO YOU WA--
5

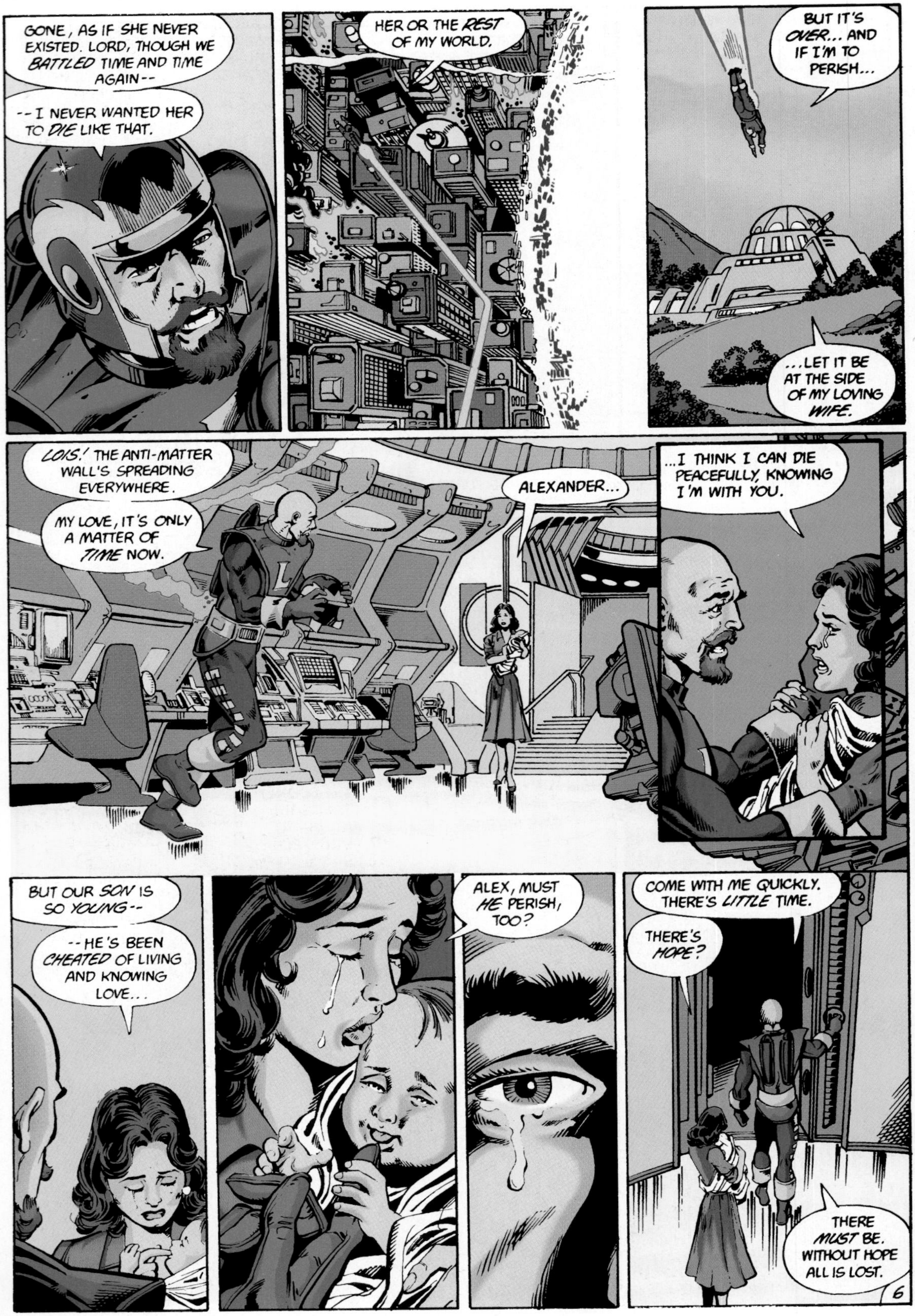
GONE, AS IF SHE NEVER EXISTED. LORD, THOUGH WE BATTLED TIME AND TIME AGAIN--
--I NEVER WANTED HER TO DIE LIKE THAT.
HER OR THE REST OF MY WORLD.
BUT IT'S OVER... AND IF I'M TO PERISH...
...LET IT BE AT THE SIDE OF MY LOVING WIFE.
LOIS! THE ANTI-MATTER WALL'S SPREADING EVERYWHERE.
MY LOVE, IT'S ONLY A MATTER OF TIME NOW.
ALEXANDER...
...I THINK I CAN DIE PEACEFULLY, KNOWING I'M WITH YOU.
BUT OUR SON IS SO YOUNG--
--HE'S BEEN CHEATED OF LIVING AND KNOWING LOVE...
ALEX, MUST HE PERISH, TOO?
COME WITH ME QUICKLY. THERE'S LITTLE TIME.
THERE'S HOPE?
THERE MUST BE. WITHOUT HOPE ALL IS LOST.
6

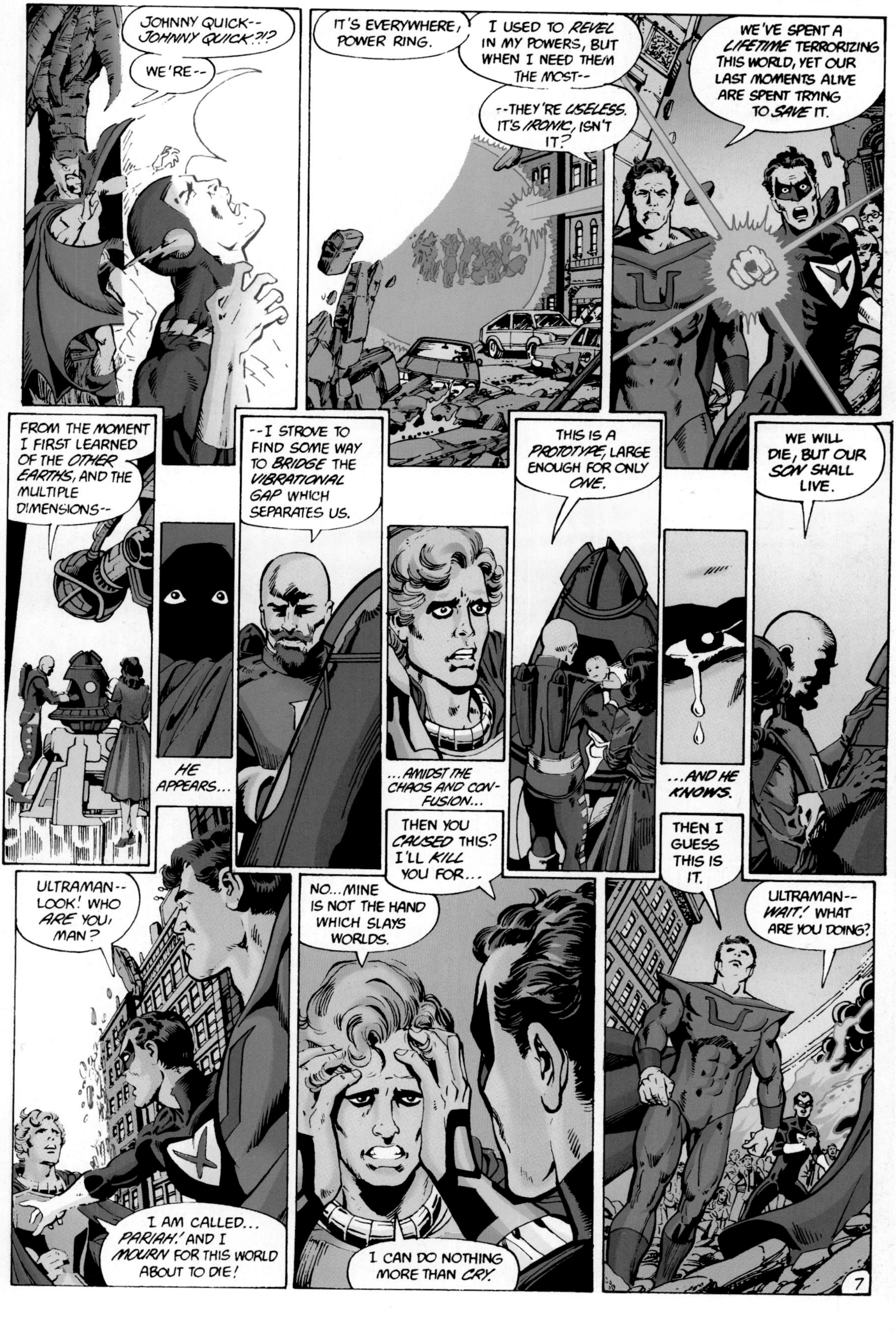
JOHNNY QUICK-- JOHNNY QUICK?!?
WE'RE--
IT'S EVERYWHERE, POWER RING.
I USED TO REVEL IN MY POWERS, BUT WHEN I NEED THEM THE MOST--
--THEY'RE USELESS. IT'S IRONIC, ISN'T IT?
WE'VE SPENT A LIFETIME TERRORIZING THIS WORLD, YET OUR LAST MOMENTS ALIVE ARE SPENT TRYING TO SAVE IT.
FROM THE MOMENT I FIRST LEARNED OF THE OTHER EARTHS, AND THE MULTIPLE DIMENSIONS--
HE APPEARS...
--I STROVE TO FIND SOME WAY TO BRIDGE THE VIBRATIONAL GAP WHICH SEPARATES US.
...AMIDST THE CHAOS AND CON-FUSION...
THIS IS A PROTOTYPE, LARGE ENOUGH FOR ONLY ONE.
...AND HE KNOWS.
WE WILL DIE, BUT OUR SON SHALL LIVE.
ULTRAMAN-- LOOK! WHO ARE YOU, MAN?
I AM CALLED... PARIAH! AND I MOURN FOR THIS WORLD ABOUT TO DIE!
THEN YOU CAUSED THIS? I'LL KILL YOU FOR...
NO...MINE IS NOT THE HAND WHICH SLAYS WORLDS.
I CAN DO NOTHING MORE THAN CRY.
THEN I GUESS THIS IS IT.
ULTRAMAN-- WAIT! WHAT ARE YOU DOING?
7

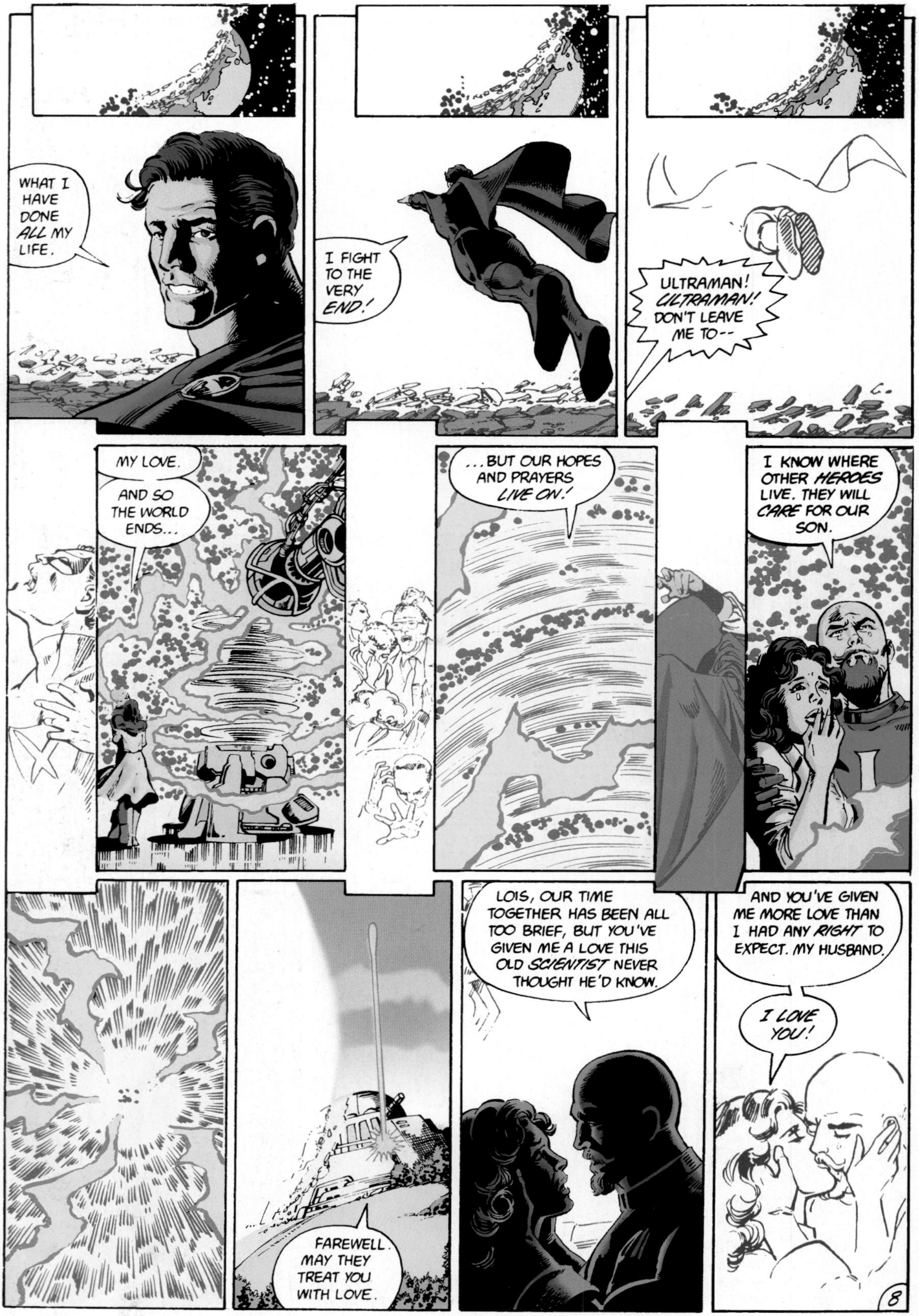
WHAT I HAVE DONE ALL MY LIFE.
I FIGHT TO THE VERY END!
ULTRAMAN! ULTRAMAN! DON'T LEAVE ME TO--
MY LOVE.
AND SO THE WORLD ENDS...
...BUT OUR HOPES AND PRAYERS LIVE ON!
I KNOW WHERE OTHER HEROES LIVE. THEY WILL CARE FOR OUR SON.
FAREWELL. MAY THEY TREAT YOU WITH LOVE.
LOIS, OUR TIME TOGETHER HAS BEEN ALL TOO BRIEF, BUT YOU'VE GIVEN ME A LOVE THIS OLD SCIENTIST NEVER THOUGHT HE'D KNOW.
AND YOU'VE GIVEN ME MORE LOVE THAN I HAD ANY RIGHT TO EXPECT. MY HUSBAND.
I LOVE YOU!
8

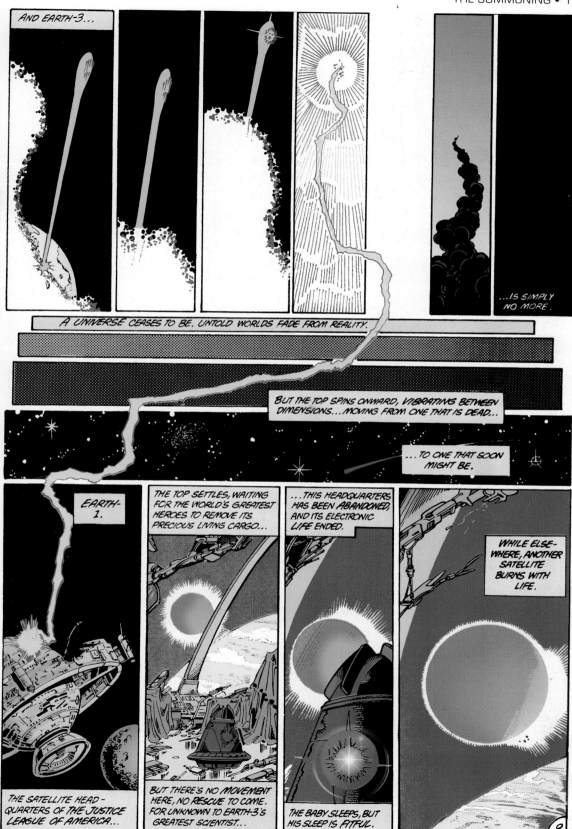

AND EARTH-3...

...IS SIMPLY NO MORE.

A UNIVERSE CEASES TO BE. UNTOLD WORLDS FADE FROM REALITY.

BUT THE TOP SPINS ONWARD, VIBRATING BETWEEN DIMENSIONS...MOVING FROM ONE THAT IS DEAD...

...TO ONE THAT SOON MIGHT BE.

EARTH-1.

THE TOP SETTLES, WAITING FOR THE WORLD'S GREATEST HEROES TO REMOVE ITS PRECIOUS LIVING CARGO...

...THIS HEADQUARTERS HAS BEEN ABANDONED, AND ITS ELECTRONIC LIFE ENDED.

WHILE ELSE-WHERE, ANOTHER SATELLITE BURNS WITH LIFE.

THE SATELLITE HEAD-QUARTERS OF THE JUSTICE LEAGUE OF AMERICA...

BUT THERE'S NO MOVEMENT HERE, NO RESCUE TO COME. FOR UNKNOWN TO EARTH-3'S GREATEST SCIENTIST...

THE BABY SLEEPS, BUT HIS SLEEP IS FITFUL.

9

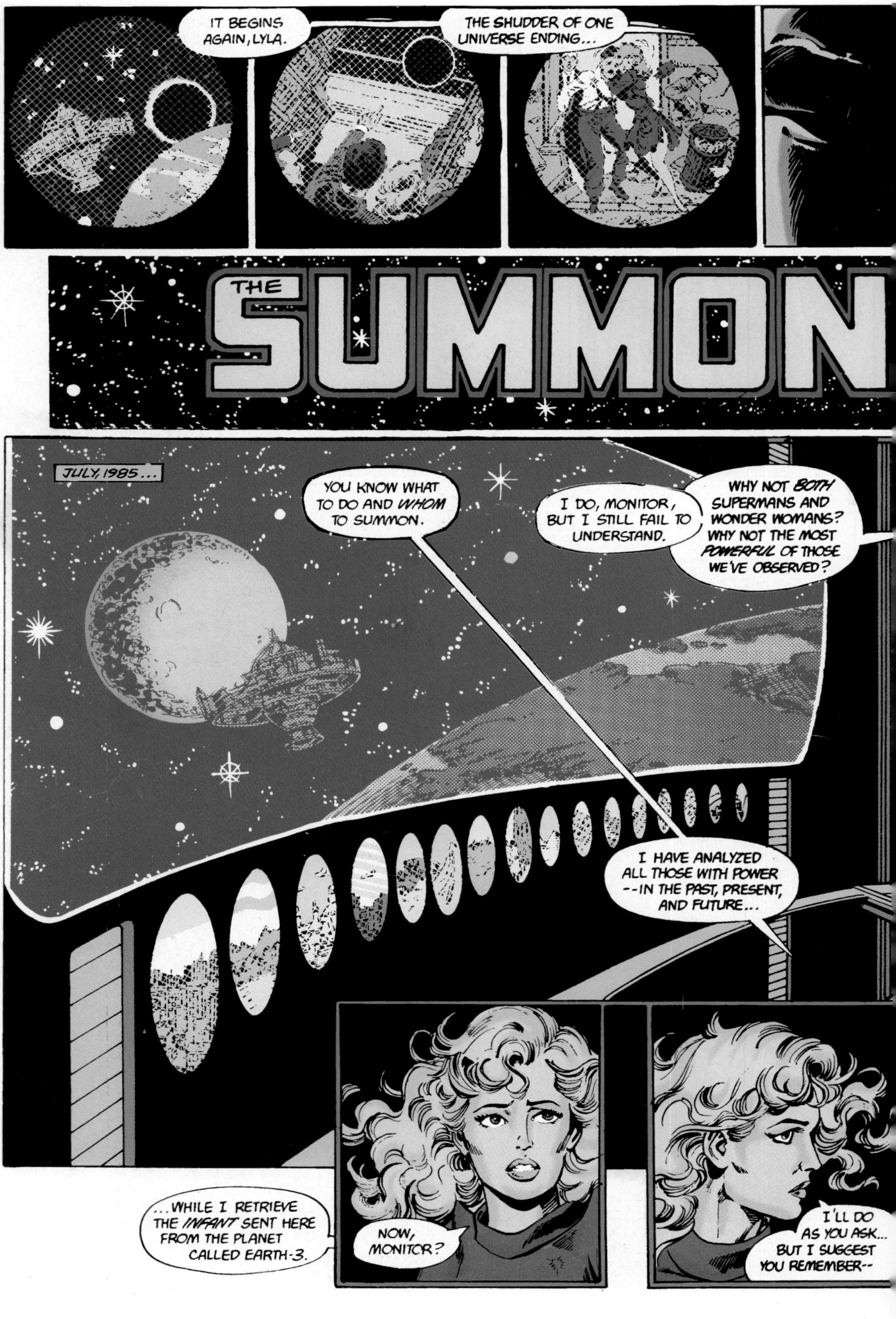

IT BEGINS AGAIN, LYLA.
THE SHUDDER OF ONE UNIVERSE ENDING...
THE SUMMON
JULY, 1985...
YOU KNOW WHAT TO DO AND *WHOM* TO SUMMON.
I DO, MONITOR, BUT I STILL FAIL TO UNDERSTAND.
WHY NOT *BOTH* SUPERMANS AND WONDER WOMANS? WHY NOT THE MOST *POWERFUL* OF THOSE WE'VE OBSERVED?
I HAVE ANALYZED ALL THOSE WITH POWER --IN THE PAST, PRESENT, AND FUTURE...
...WHILE I RETRIEVE THE *INFANT* SENT HERE FROM THE PLANET CALLED EARTH-3.
NOW, MONITOR?
I'LL DO AS YOU ASK... BUT I SUGGEST YOU REMEMBER--

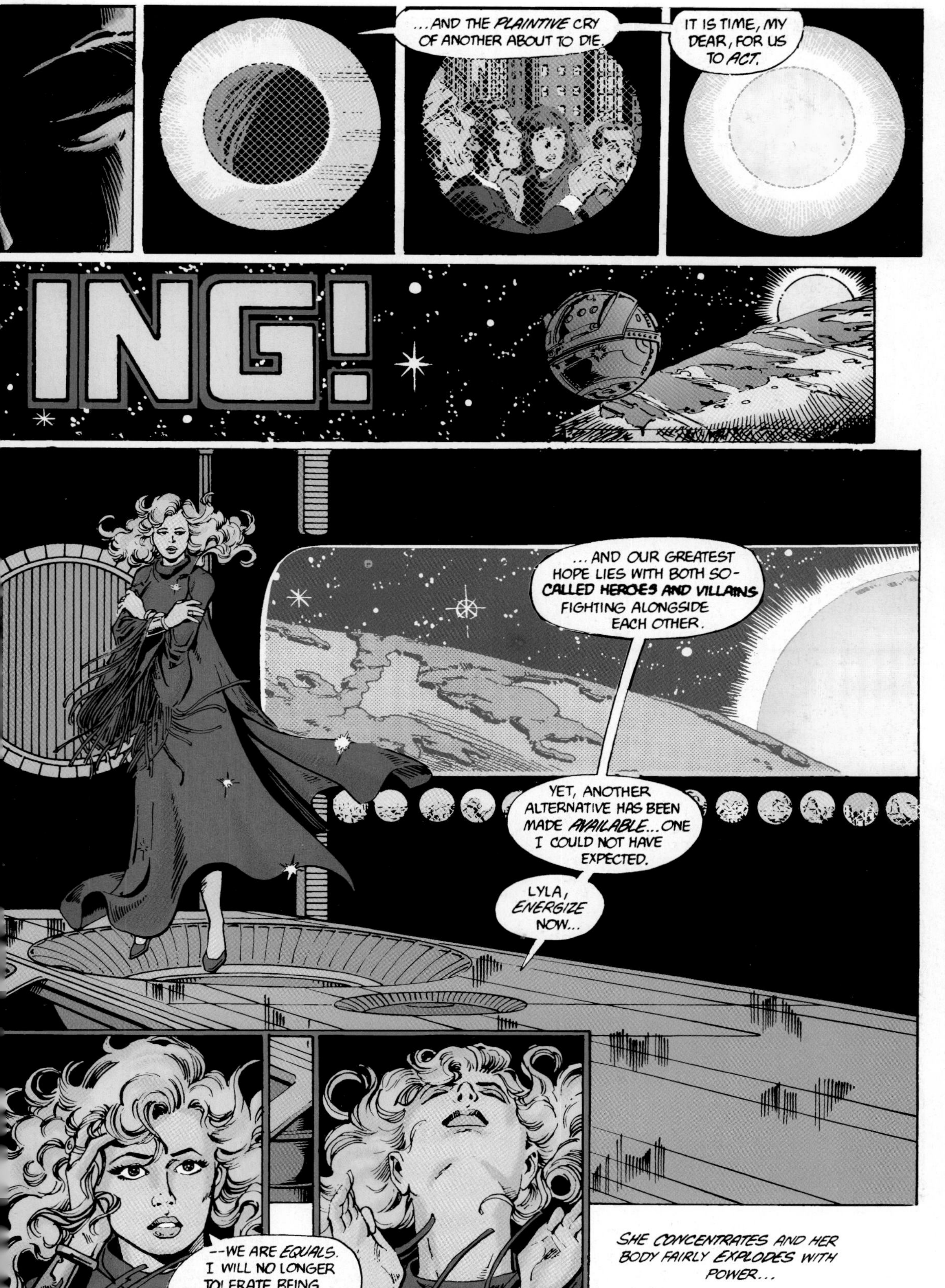
...AND THE PLAINTIVE CRY OF ANOTHER ABOUT TO DIE.
IT IS TIME, MY DEAR, FOR US TO ACT.
ING!
...AND OUR GREATEST HOPE LIES WITH BOTH SO-CALLED HEROES AND VILLAINS FIGHTING ALONGSIDE EACH OTHER.
YET, ANOTHER ALTERNATIVE HAS BEEN MADE AVAILABLE...ONE I COULD NOT HAVE EXPECTED.
LYLA, ENERGIZE NOW...
--WE ARE EQUALS. I WILL NO LONGER TOLERATE BEING TREATED AS YOUR SLAVE.
SHE CONCENTRATES AND HER BODY FAIRLY EXPLODES WITH POWER...

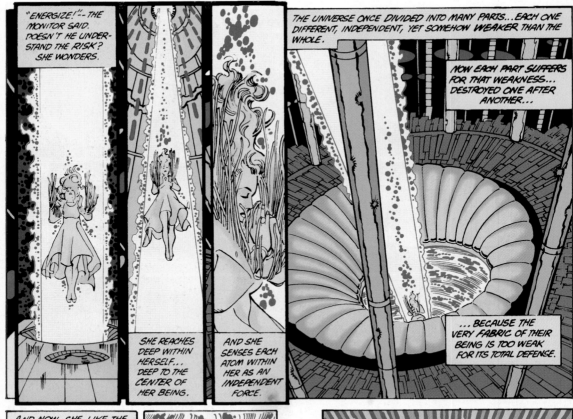

"ENERGIZE!"--THE MONITOR SAID. DOESN'T HE UNDERSTAND THE RISK? SHE WONDERS.

SHE REACHES DEEP WITHIN HERSELF... DEEP TO THE CENTER OF HER BEING.

AND SHE SENSES EACH ATOM WITHIN HER AS AN INDEPENDENT FORCE.

THE UNIVERSE ONCE DIVIDED INTO MANY PARTS...EACH ONE DIFFERENT, INDEPENDENT, YET SOMEHOW WEAKER THAN THE WHOLE.

NOW EACH PART SUFFERS FOR THAT WEAKNESS... DESTROYED ONE AFTER ANOTHER...

...BECAUSE THE VERY FABRIC OF THEIR BEING IS TOO WEAK FOR ITS TOTAL DEFENSE.

AND NOW SHE, LIKE THE UNIVERSE, MUST REPLICATE AS WELL...

SHE MUST DIVIDE HER POWER AMONG MANY.

EACH WITH POWER, YET EACH POWERLESS, AS WELL.

SHE IS NO LONGER THE WOMAN CALLED LYLA. WITH HER POWER AND MISSION, SHE BECOMES SOMEONE NEW.

SHE IS NOW-- HARBINGER!

AND SHE FEARS WHAT MAY COME NEXT.

12

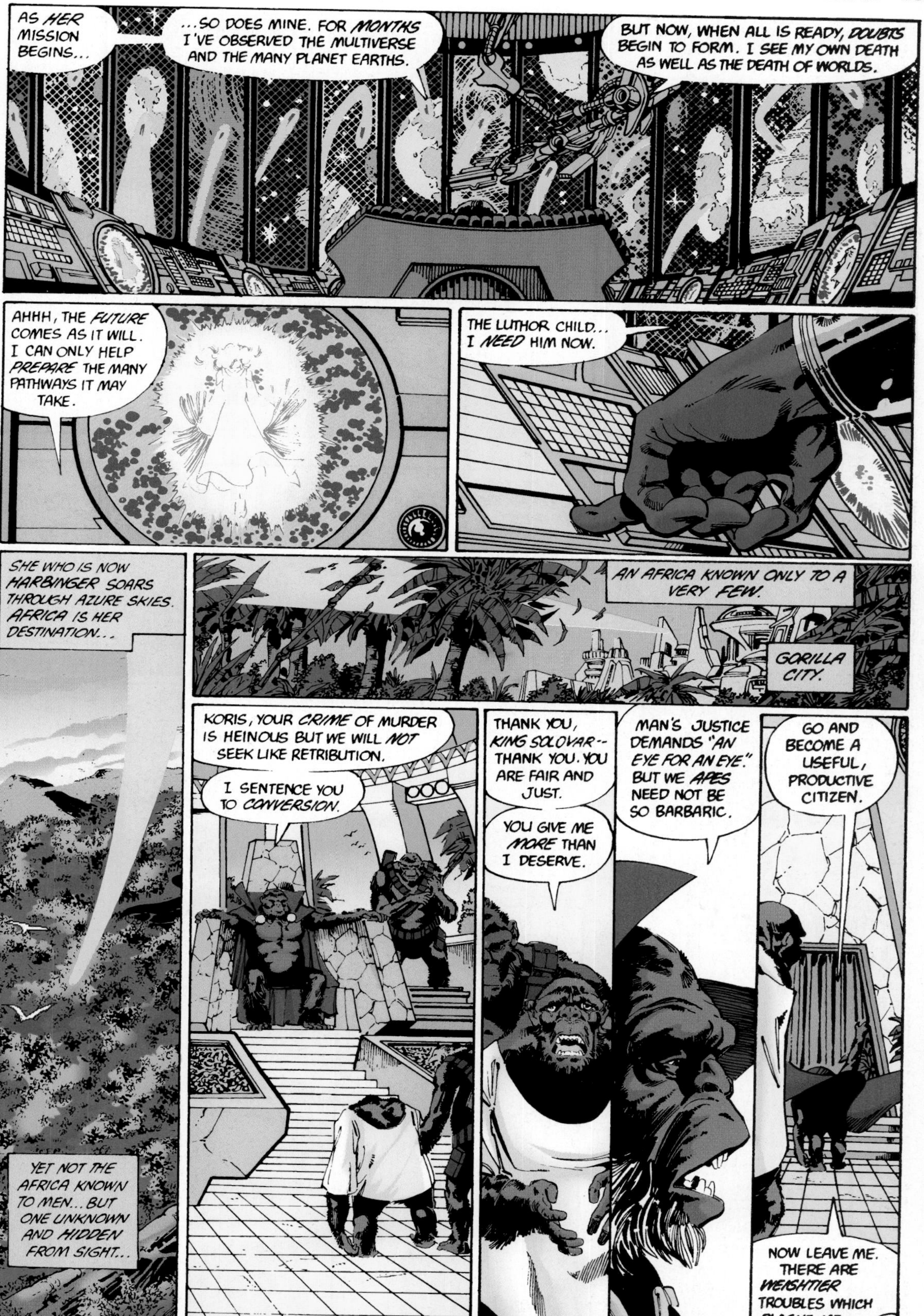
AS HER MISSION BEGINS...
...SO DOES MINE. FOR MONTHS I'VE OBSERVED THE MULTIVERSE AND THE MANY PLANET EARTHS.
BUT NOW, WHEN ALL IS READY, DOUBTS BEGIN TO FORM. I SEE MY OWN DEATH AS WELL AS THE DEATH OF WORLDS.
AHHH, THE FUTURE COMES AS IT WILL. I CAN ONLY HELP PREPARE THE MANY PATHWAYS IT MAY TAKE.
THE LUTHOR CHILD... I NEED HIM NOW.
SHE WHO IS NOW HARBINGER SOARS THROUGH AZURE SKIES. AFRICA IS HER DESTINATION...
YET NOT THE AFRICA KNOWN TO MEN... BUT ONE UNKNOWN AND HIDDEN FROM SIGHT...
AN AFRICA KNOWN ONLY TO A VERY FEW.
GORILLA CITY.
KORIS, YOUR CRIME OF MURDER IS HEINOUS BUT WE WILL NOT SEEK LIKE RETRIBUTION.
I SENTENCE YOU TO CONVERSION.
THANK YOU, KING SOLOVAR-- THANK YOU. YOU ARE FAIR AND JUST.
YOU GIVE ME MORE THAN I DESERVE.
MAN'S JUSTICE DEMANDS "AN EYE FOR AN EYE." BUT WE APES NEED NOT BE SO BARBARIC.
GO AND BECOME A USEFUL, PRODUCTIVE CITIZEN.
NOW LEAVE ME. THERE ARE WEIGHTIER TROUBLES WHICH PLAGUE ME.
13

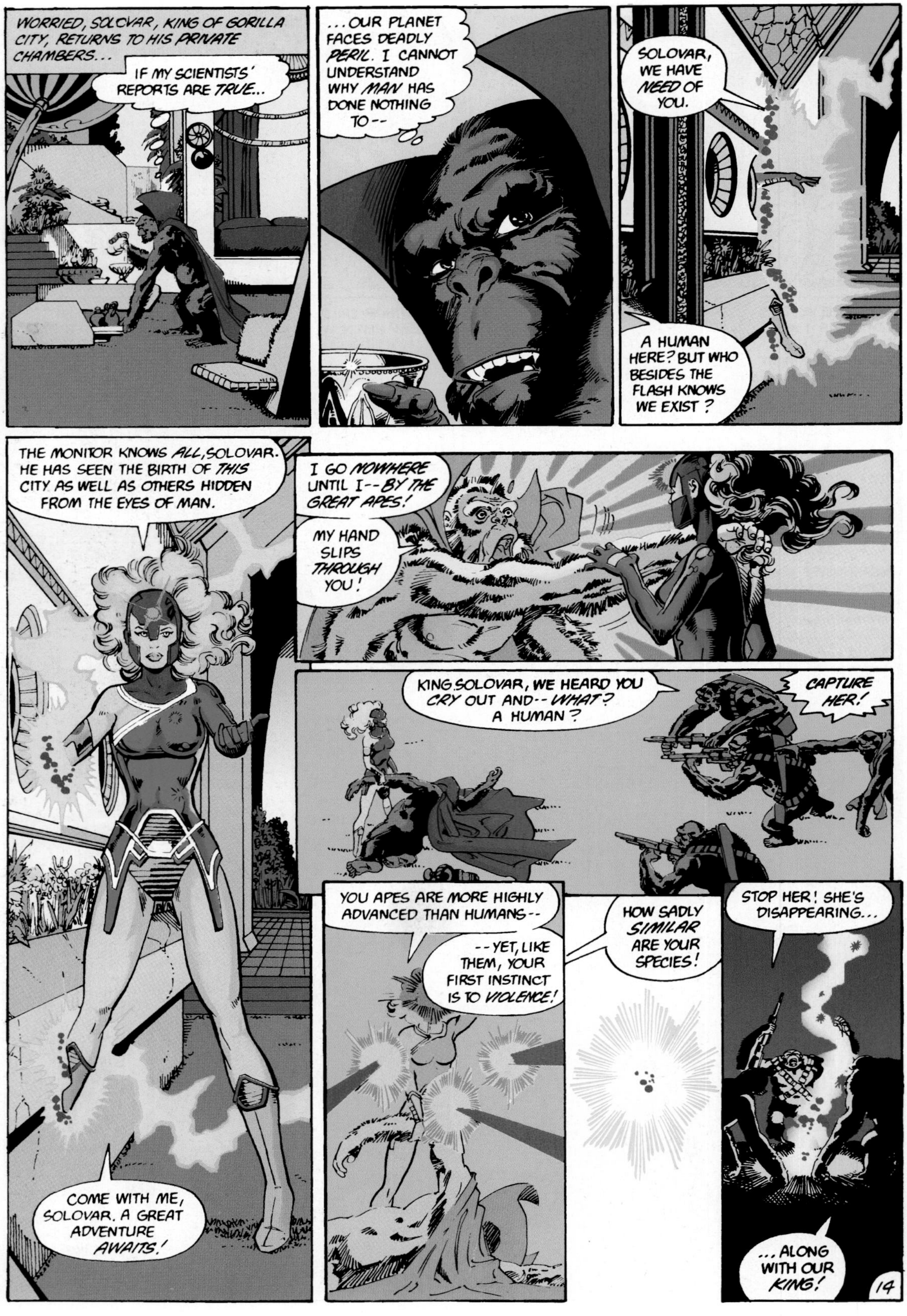
WORRIED, SOLOVAR, KING OF GORILLA CITY, RETURNS TO HIS PRIVATE CHAMBERS...
IF MY SCIENTISTS' REPORTS ARE TRUE...
...OUR PLANET FACES DEADLY PERIL. I CANNOT UNDERSTAND WHY MAN HAS DONE NOTHING TO--
SOLOVAR, WE HAVE NEED OF YOU.
A HUMAN HERE? BUT WHO BESIDES THE FLASH KNOWS WE EXIST?
THE MONITOR KNOWS ALL, SOLOVAR. HE HAS SEEN THE BIRTH OF THIS CITY AS WELL AS OTHERS HIDDEN FROM THE EYES OF MAN.
COME WITH ME, SOLOVAR. A GREAT ADVENTURE AWAITS!
I GO NOWHERE UNTIL I-- BY THE GREAT APES!
MY HAND SLIPS THROUGH YOU!
KING SOLOVAR, WE HEARD YOU CRY OUT AND-- WHAT? A HUMAN?
CAPTURE HER!
YOU APES ARE MORE HIGHLY ADVANCED THAN HUMANS--
--YET, LIKE THEM, YOUR FIRST INSTINCT IS TO VIOLENCE!
HOW SADLY SIMILAR ARE YOUR SPECIES!
STOP HER! SHE'S DISAPPEARING...
...ALONG WITH OUR KING!
14

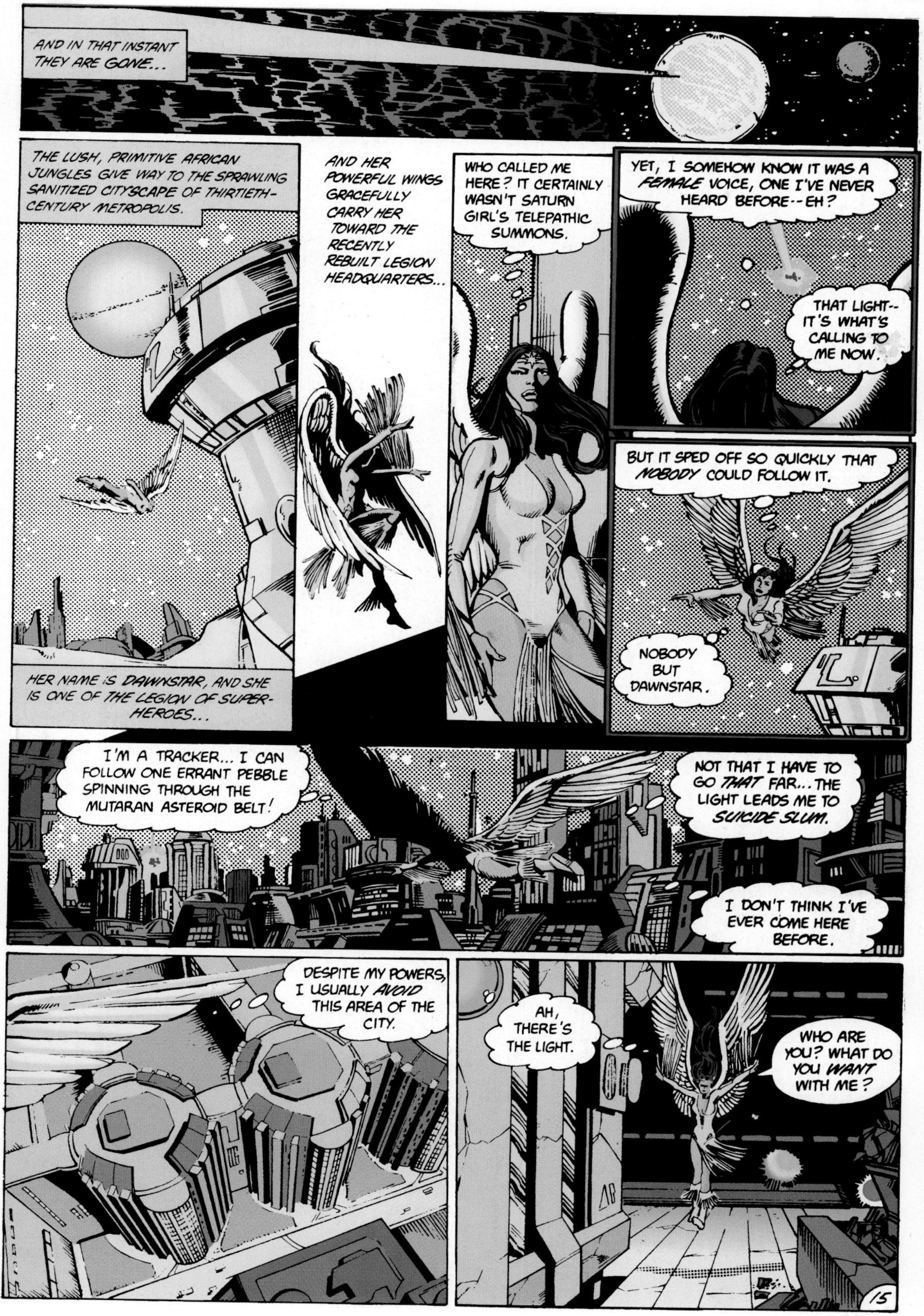
AND IN THAT INSTANT THEY ARE GONE...
THE LUSH, PRIMITIVE AFRICAN JUNGLES GIVE WAY TO THE SPRAWLING SANITIZED CITYSCAPE OF THIRTIETH-CENTURY METROPOLIS.
HER NAME IS DAWNSTAR, AND SHE IS ONE OF THE LEGION OF SUPER-HEROES...
AND HER POWERFUL WINGS GRACEFULLY CARRY HER TOWARD THE RECENTLY REBUILT LEGION HEADQUARTERS...
WHO CALLED ME HERE? IT CERTAINLY WASN'T SATURN GIRL'S TELEPATHIC SUMMONS.
YET, I SOMEHOW KNOW IT WAS A FEMALE VOICE, ONE I'VE NEVER HEARD BEFORE--EH?
THAT LIGHT--IT'S WHAT'S CALLING TO ME NOW.
BUT IT SPED OFF SO QUICKLY THAT NOBODY COULD FOLLOW IT.
NOBODY BUT DAWNSTAR.
I'M A TRACKER... I CAN FOLLOW ONE ERRANT PEBBLE SPINNING THROUGH THE MUTARAN ASTEROID BELT!
NOT THAT I HAVE TO GO THAT FAR... THE LIGHT LEADS ME TO SUICIDE SLUM.
I DON'T THINK I'VE EVER COME HERE BEFORE.
DESPITE MY POWERS, I USUALLY AVOID THIS AREA OF THE CITY.
AH, THERE'S THE LIGHT.
WHO ARE YOU? WHAT DO YOU WANT WITH ME?
15

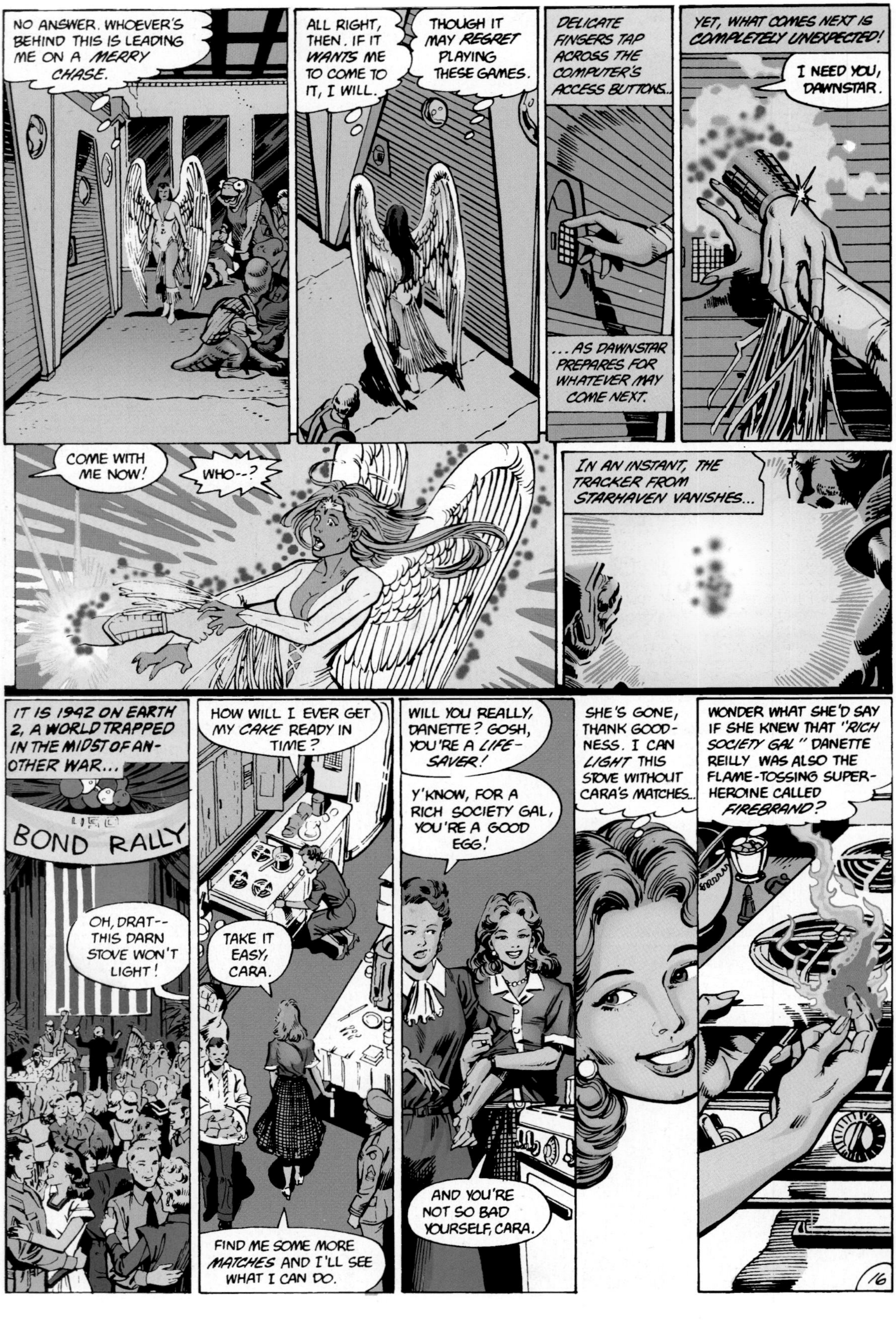
NO ANSWER. WHOEVER'S BEHIND THIS IS LEADING ME ON A MERRY CHASE.
ALL RIGHT, THEN. IF IT WANTS ME TO COME TO IT, I WILL.
THOUGH IT MAY REGRET PLAYING THESE GAMES.
DELICATE FINGERS TAP ACROSS THE COMPUTER'S ACCESS BUTTONS...
...AS DAWNSTAR PREPARES FOR WHATEVER MAY COME NEXT.
YET, WHAT COMES NEXT IS COMPLETELY UNEXPECTED!
I NEED YOU, DAWNSTAR.
COME WITH ME NOW!
WHO--?
IN AN INSTANT, THE TRACKER FROM STARHAVEN VANISHES...
IT IS 1942 ON EARTH 2, A WORLD TRAPPED IN THE MIDST OF ANOTHER WAR...
BOND RALLY
OH, DRAT-- THIS DARN STOVE WON'T LIGHT!
HOW WILL I EVER GET MY CAKE READY IN TIME?
TAKE IT EASY, CARA.
FIND ME SOME MORE MATCHES AND I'LL SEE WHAT I CAN DO.
WILL YOU REALLY, DANETTE? GOSH, YOU'RE A LIFE-SAVER!
Y'KNOW, FOR A RICH SOCIETY GAL, YOU'RE A GOOD EGG!
AND YOU'RE NOT SO BAD YOURSELF, CARA.
SHE'S GONE, THANK GOODNESS. I CAN LIGHT THIS STOVE WITHOUT CARA'S MATCHES...
WONDER WHAT SHE'D SAY IF SHE KNEW THAT "RICH SOCIETY GAL" DANETTE REILLY WAS ALSO THE FLAME-TOSSING SUPER-HEROINE CALLED FIREBRAND?
16

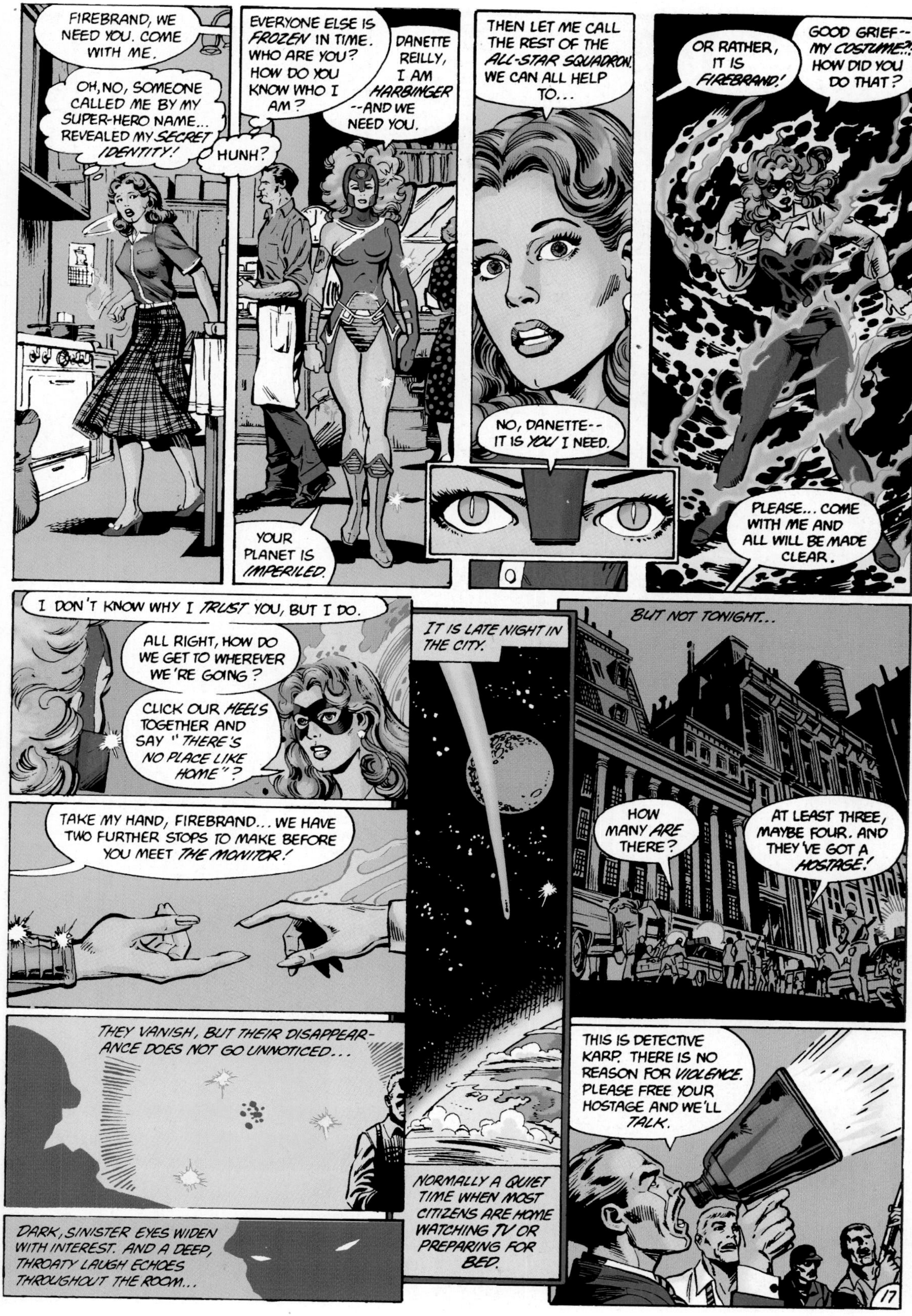
FIREBRAND, WE NEED YOU. COME WITH ME.
OH, NO, SOMEONE CALLED ME BY MY SUPER-HERO NAME... REVEALED MY SECRET IDENTITY!
HUNH?
EVERYONE ELSE IS FROZEN IN TIME. WHO ARE YOU? HOW DO YOU KNOW WHO I AM?
DANETTE REILLY, I AM HARBINGER --AND WE NEED YOU.
YOUR PLANET IS IMPERILED.
THEN LET ME CALL THE REST OF THE ALL-STAR SQUADRON. WE CAN ALL HELP TO...
NO, DANETTE-- IT IS YOU I NEED.
OR RATHER, IT IS FIREBRAND!
GOOD GRIEF-- MY COSTUME?!? HOW DID YOU DO THAT?
PLEASE... COME WITH ME AND ALL WILL BE MADE CLEAR.
I DON'T KNOW WHY I TRUST YOU, BUT I DO.
ALL RIGHT, HOW DO WE GET TO WHEREVER WE'RE GOING?
CLICK OUR HEELS TOGETHER AND SAY "THERE'S NO PLACE LIKE HOME"?
TAKE MY HAND, FIREBRAND... WE HAVE TWO FURTHER STOPS TO MAKE BEFORE YOU MEET THE MONITOR!
THEY VANISH, BUT THEIR DISAPPEARANCE DOES NOT GO UNNOTICED...
DARK, SINISTER EYES WIDEN WITH INTEREST. AND A DEEP, THROATY LAUGH ECHOES THROUGHOUT THE ROOM...
IT IS LATE NIGHT IN THE CITY.
NORMALLY A QUIET TIME WHEN MOST CITIZENS ARE HOME WATCHING TV OR PREPARING FOR BED.
BUT NOT TONIGHT...
HOW MANY ARE THERE?
AT LEAST THREE, MAYBE FOUR. AND THEY'VE GOT A HOSTAGE!
THIS IS DETECTIVE KARP. THERE IS NO REASON FOR VIOLENCE. PLEASE FREE YOUR HOSTAGE AND WE'LL TALK.
17

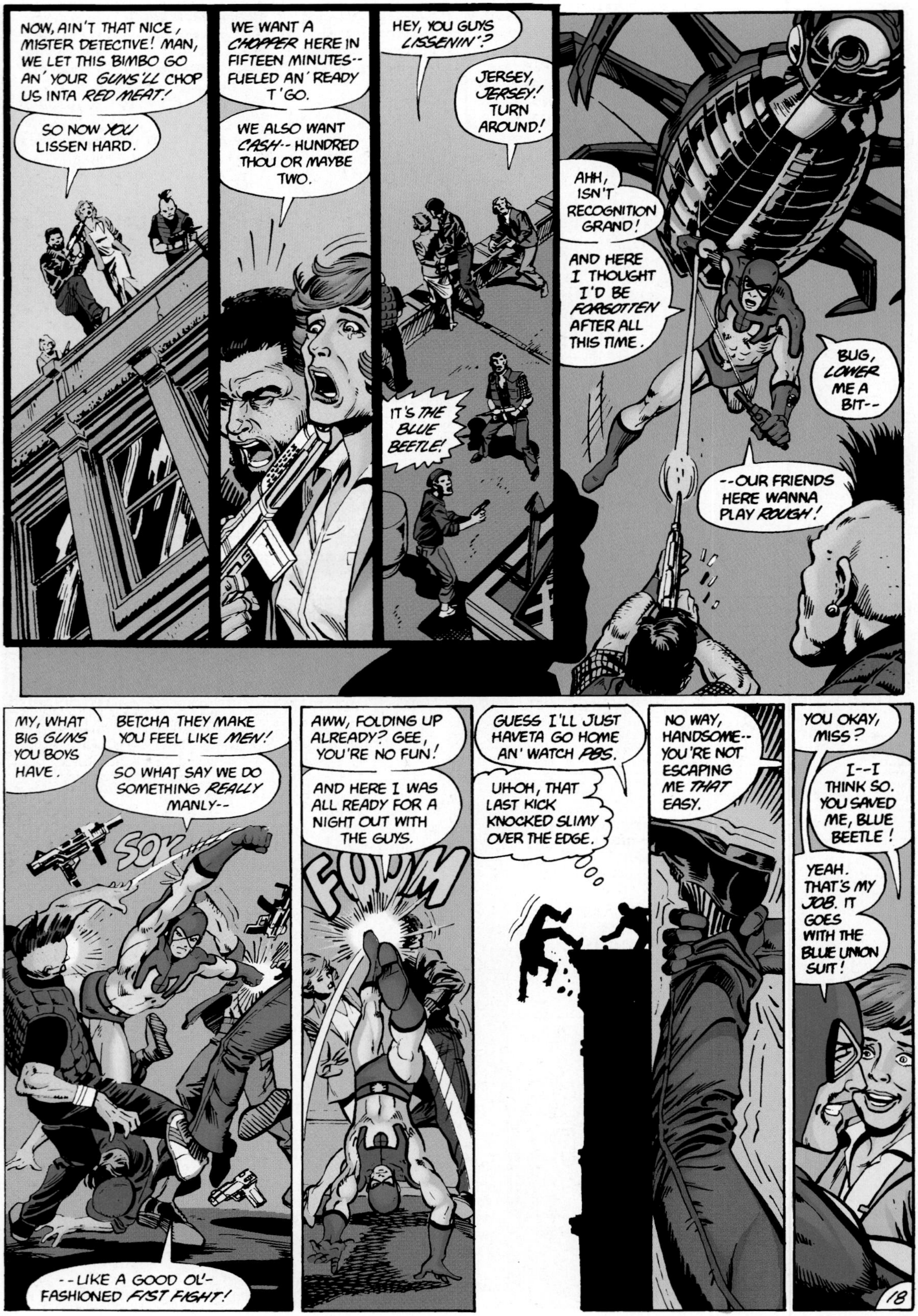
NOW, AIN'T THAT NICE, MISTER DETECTIVE! MAN, WE LET THIS BIMBO GO AN' YOUR GUNS'LL CHOP US INTA RED MEAT!
SO NOW YOU LISSEN HARD.
WE WANT A CHOPPER HERE IN FIFTEEN MINUTES-- FUELED AN' READY T'GO.
WE ALSO WANT CASH-- HUNDRED THOU OR MAYBE TWO.
HEY, YOU GUYS LISSENIN'?
JERSEY, JERSEY! TURN AROUND!
IT'S THE BLUE BEETLE!
AHH, ISN'T RECOGNITION GRAND!
AND HERE I THOUGHT I'D BE FORGOTTEN AFTER ALL THIS TIME.
BUG, LOWER ME A BIT--
--OUR FRIENDS HERE WANNA PLAY ROUGH!
MY, WHAT BIG GUNS YOU BOYS HAVE.
BETCHA THEY MAKE YOU FEEL LIKE MEN!
SO WHAT SAY WE DO SOMETHING REALLY MANLY--
SOK
--LIKE A GOOD OL'-FASHIONED FIST FIGHT!
AWW, FOLDING UP ALREADY? GEE, YOU'RE NO FUN!
AND HERE I WAS ALL READY FOR A NIGHT OUT WITH THE GUYS.
FOOM
GUESS I'LL JUST HAVETA GO HOME AN' WATCH PBS.
UH-OH, THAT LAST KICK KNOCKED SLIMY OVER THE EDGE.
NO WAY, HANDSOME-- YOU'RE NOT ESCAPING ME THAT EASY.
YOU OKAY, MISS?
I--I THINK SO. YOU SAVED ME, BLUE BEETLE!
YEAH. THAT'S MY JOB. IT GOES WITH THE BLUE UNION SUIT!
18

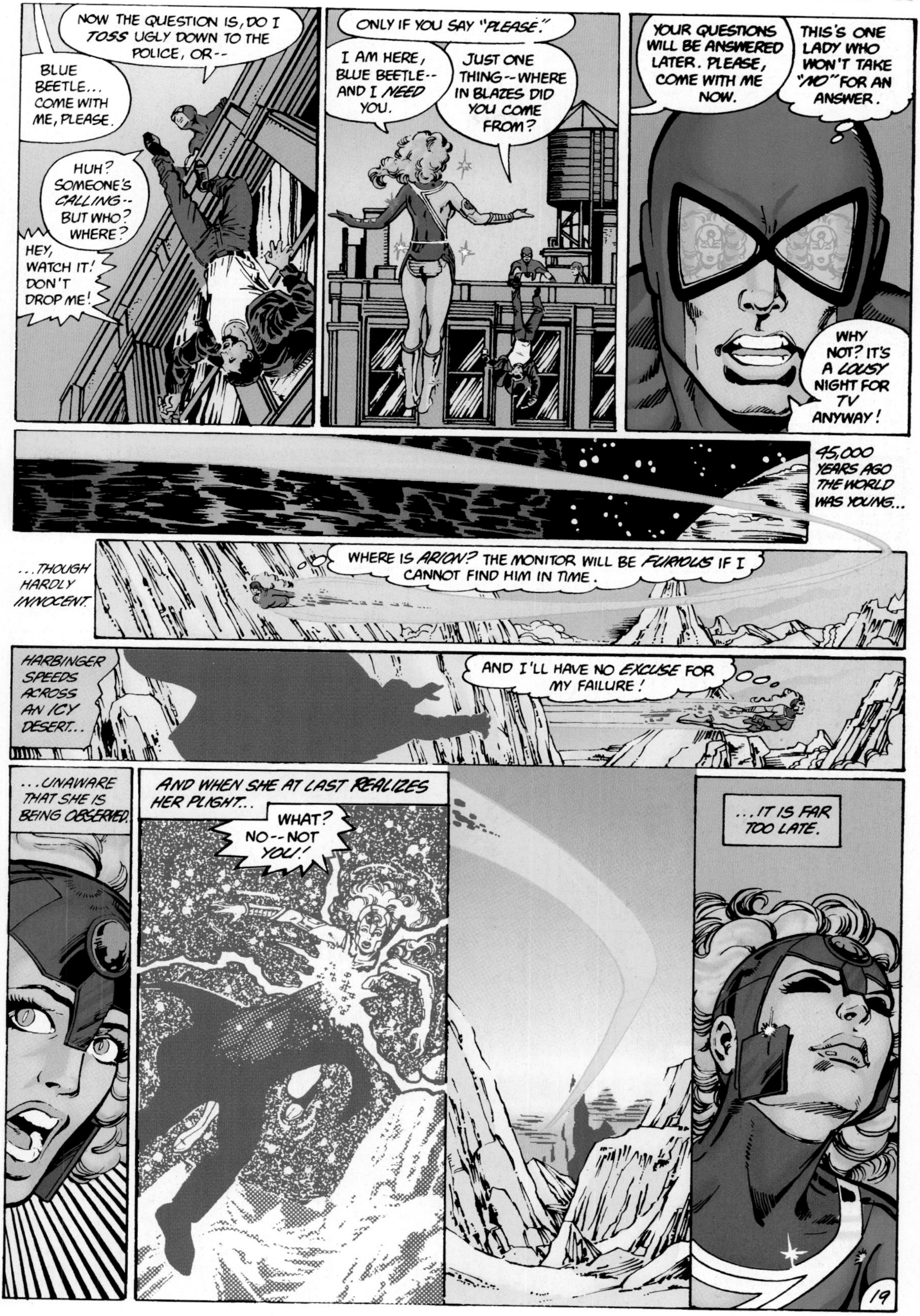
NOW THE QUESTION IS, DO I TOSS UGLY DOWN TO THE POLICE, OR--
BLUE BEETLE... COME WITH ME, PLEASE.
HUH? SOMEONE'S CALLING-- BUT WHO? WHERE?
HEY, WATCH IT! DON'T DROP ME!
ONLY IF YOU SAY "PLEASE."
I AM HERE, BLUE BEETLE-- AND I NEED YOU.
JUST ONE THING--WHERE IN BLAZES DID YOU COME FROM?
YOUR QUESTIONS WILL BE ANSWERED LATER. PLEASE, COME WITH ME NOW.
THIS'S ONE LADY WHO WON'T TAKE "NO" FOR AN ANSWER.
WHY NOT? IT'S A LOUSY NIGHT FOR TV ANYWAY!
45,000 YEARS AGO THE WORLD WAS YOUNG...
...THOUGH HARDLY INNOCENT.
WHERE IS ARION? THE MONITOR WILL BE FURIOUS IF I CANNOT FIND HIM IN TIME.
HARBINGER SPEEDS ACROSS AN ICY DESERT...
AND I'LL HAVE NO EXCUSE FOR MY FAILURE!
...UNAWARE THAT SHE IS BEING OBSERVED.
AND WHEN SHE AT LAST REALIZES HER PLIGHT...
WHAT? NO--NOT YOU!
...IT IS FAR TOO LATE.
19

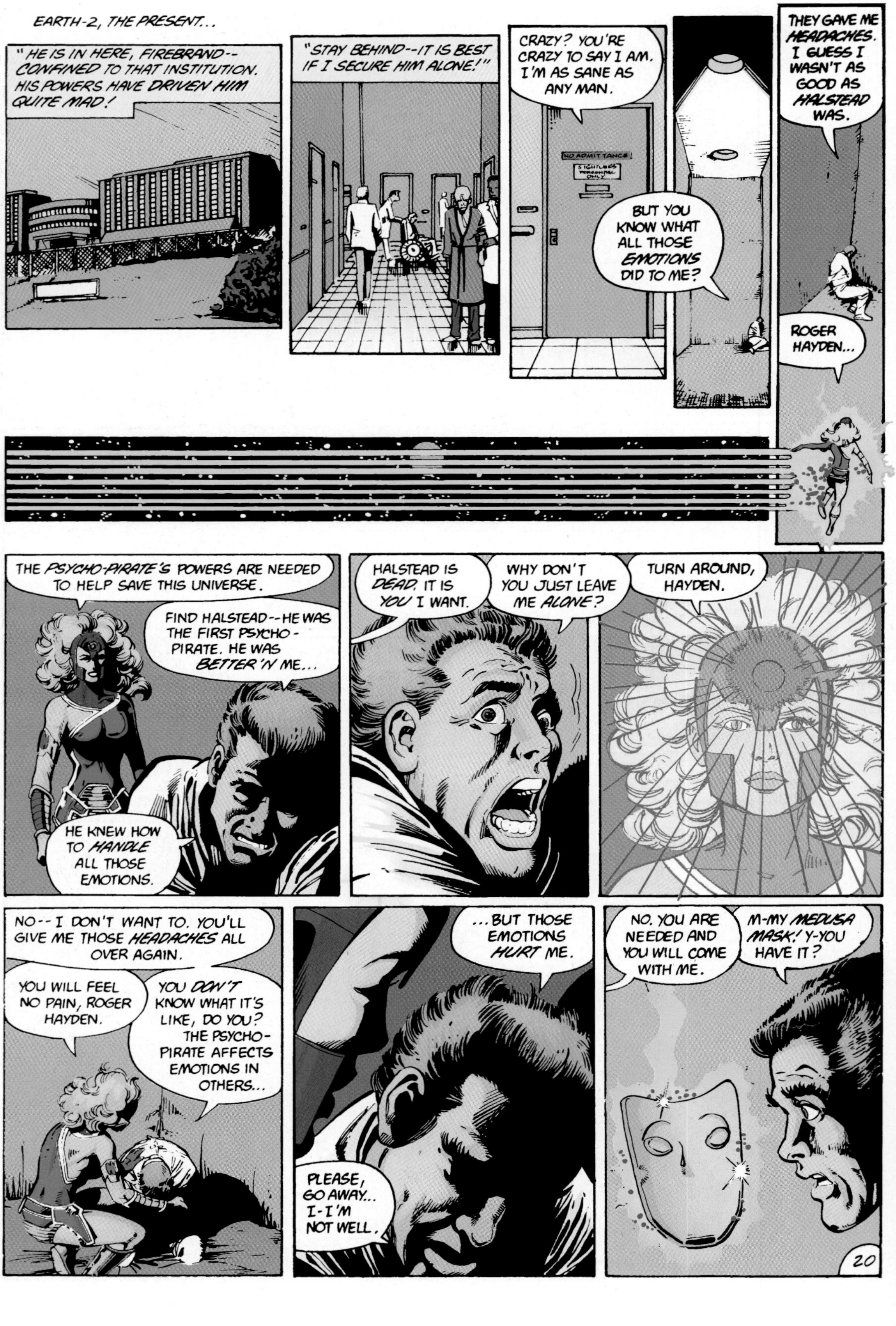
EARTH-2, THE PRESENT...
"HE IS IN HERE, FIREBRAND-- CONFINED TO THAT INSTITUTION. HIS POWERS HAVE DRIVEN HIM QUITE MAD!
"STAY BEHIND--IT IS BEST IF I SECURE HIM ALONE!"
CRAZY? YOU'RE CRAZY TO SAY I AM. I'M AS SANE AS ANY MAN.
NO ADMITTANCE
BUT YOU KNOW WHAT ALL THOSE EMOTIONS DID TO ME?
THEY GAVE ME HEADACHES. I GUESS I WASN'T AS GOOD AS HALSTEAD WAS.
ROGER HAYDEN...
THE PSYCHO-PIRATE'S POWERS ARE NEEDED TO HELP SAVE THIS UNIVERSE.
FIND HALSTEAD--HE WAS THE FIRST PSYCHO-PIRATE. HE WAS BETTER 'N ME...
HE KNEW HOW TO HANDLE ALL THOSE EMOTIONS.
HALSTEAD IS DEAD. IT IS YOU I WANT.
WHY DON'T YOU JUST LEAVE ME ALONE?
TURN AROUND, HAYDEN.
NO-- I DON'T WANT TO. YOU'LL GIVE ME THOSE HEADACHES ALL OVER AGAIN.
YOU WILL FEEL NO PAIN, ROGER HAYDEN.
YOU DON'T KNOW WHAT IT'S LIKE, DO YOU? THE PSYCHO-PIRATE AFFECTS EMOTIONS IN OTHERS...
...BUT THOSE EMOTIONS HURT ME.
PLEASE, GO AWAY... I-I'M NOT WELL.
NO. YOU ARE NEEDED AND YOU WILL COME WITH ME.
M-MY MEDUSA MASK! Y-YOU HAVE IT?
20

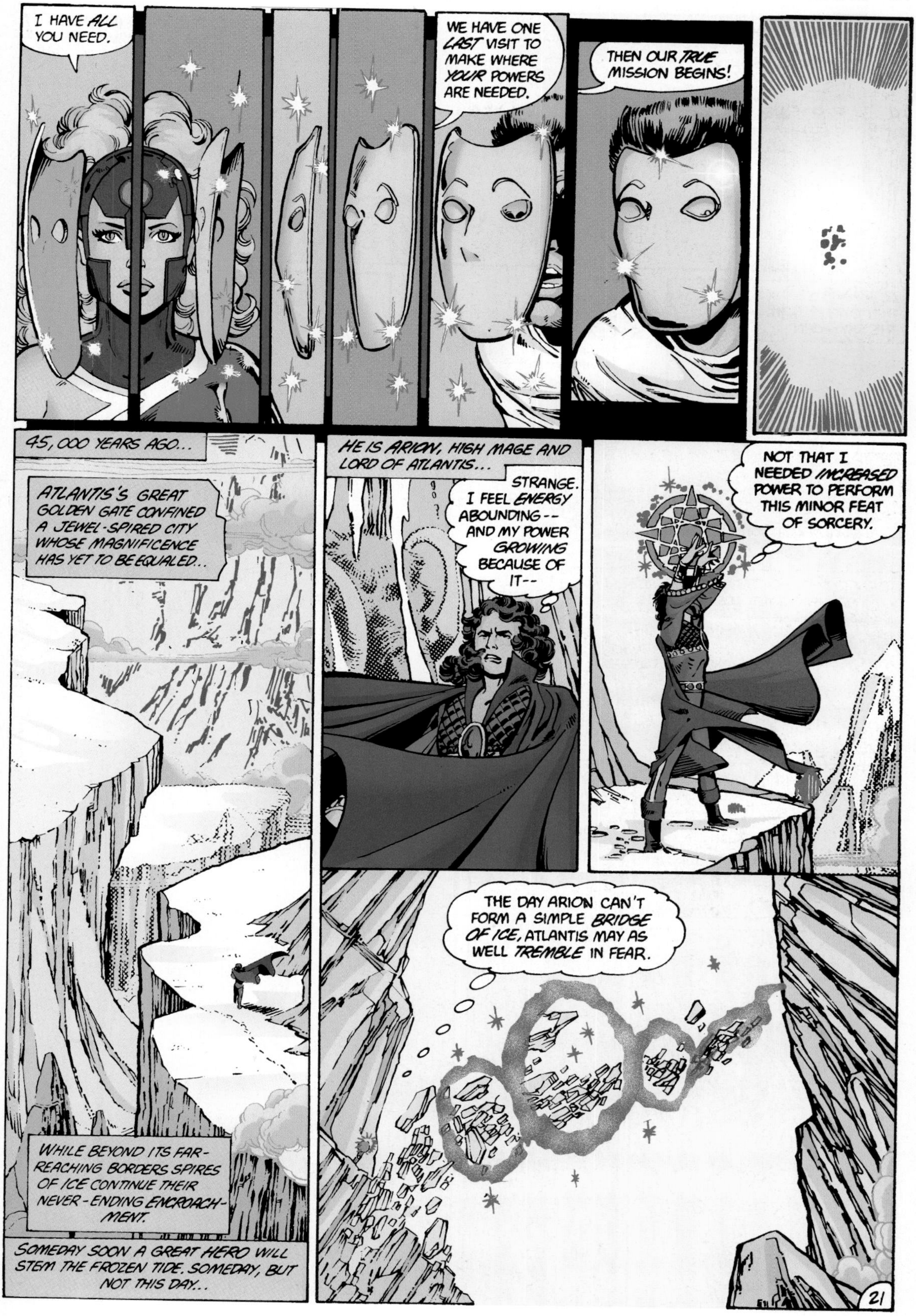
I HAVE ALL YOU NEED.
WE HAVE ONE LAST VISIT TO MAKE WHERE YOUR POWERS ARE NEEDED.
THEN OUR TRUE MISSION BEGINS!
45,000 YEARS AGO...
ATLANTIS'S GREAT GOLDEN GATE CONFINED A JEWEL-SPIRED CITY WHOSE MAGNIFICENCE HAS YET TO BE EQUALED...
WHILE BEYOND ITS FAR-REACHING BORDERS SPIRES OF ICE CONTINUE THEIR NEVER-ENDING ENCROACHMENT.
SOMEDAY SOON A GREAT HERO WILL STEM THE FROZEN TIDE. SOMEDAY, BUT NOT THIS DAY...
HE IS ARION, HIGH MAGE AND LORD OF ATLANTIS...
STRANGE. I FEEL ENERGY ABOUNDING--AND MY POWER GROWING BECAUSE OF IT--
NOT THAT I NEEDED INCREASED POWER TO PERFORM THIS MINOR FEAT OF SORCERY.
THE DAY ARION CAN'T FORM A SIMPLE BRIDGE OF ICE, ATLANTIS MAY AS WELL TREMBLE IN FEAR.
21

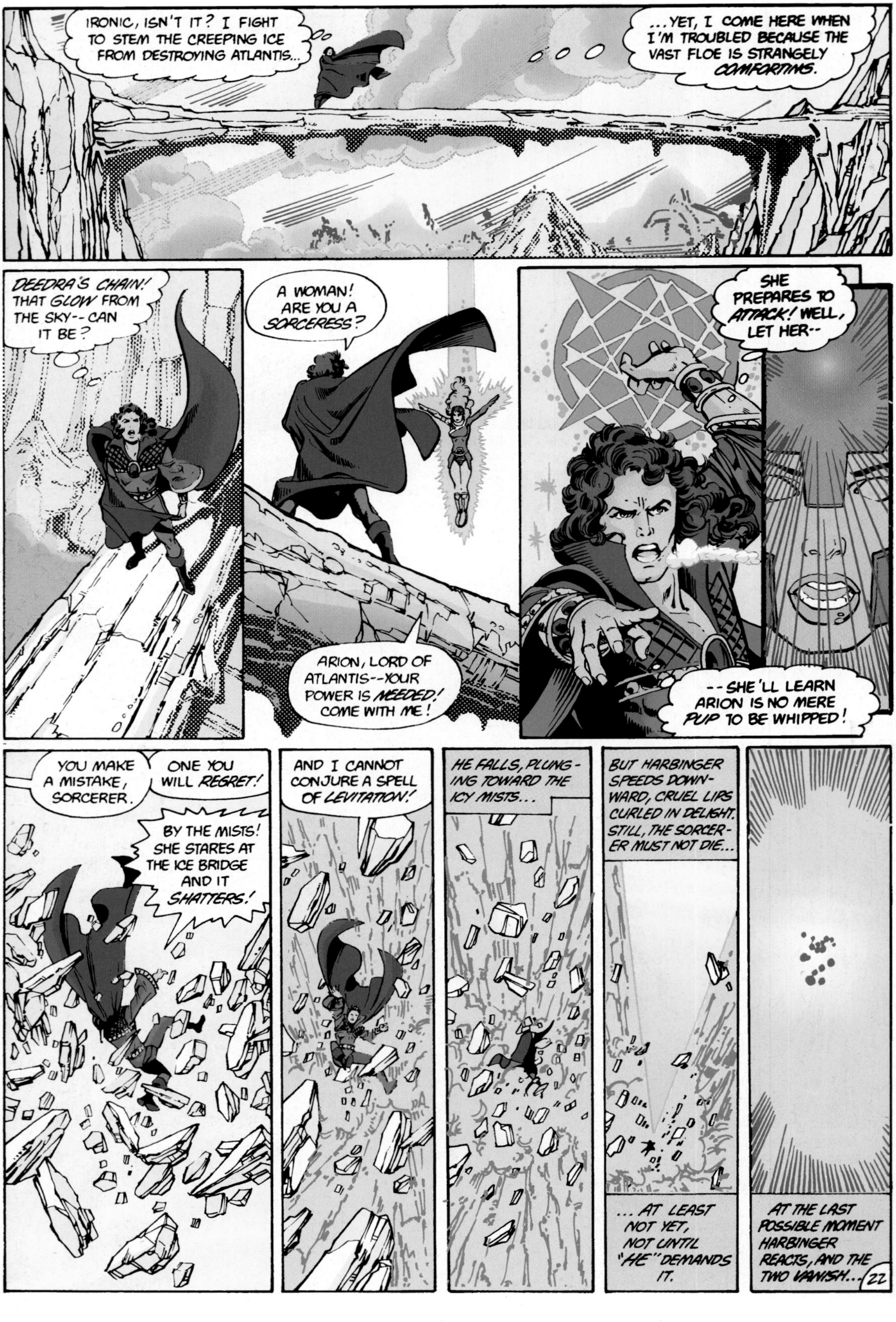
IRONIC, ISN'T IT? I FIGHT TO STEM THE CREEPING ICE FROM DESTROYING ATLANTIS...
...YET, I COME HERE WHEN I'M TROUBLED BECAUSE THE VAST FLOE IS STRANGELY COMFORTING.
DEEDRA'S CHAIN! THAT GLOW FROM THE SKY--CAN IT BE?
A WOMAN! ARE YOU A SORCERESS?
ARION, LORD OF ATLANTIS--YOUR POWER IS NEEDED! COME WITH ME!
SHE PREPARES TO ATTACK! WELL, LET HER--
--SHE'LL LEARN ARION IS NO MERE PUP TO BE WHIPPED!
YOU MAKE A MISTAKE, SORCERER.
ONE YOU WILL REGRET!
BY THE MISTS! SHE STARES AT THE ICE BRIDGE AND IT SHATTERS!
AND I CANNOT CONJURE A SPELL OF LEVITATION!
HE FALLS, PLUNGING TOWARD THE ICY MISTS...
BUT HARBINGER SPEEDS DOWNWARD, CRUEL LIPS CURLED IN DELIGHT. STILL, THE SORCERER MUST NOT DIE...
...AT LEAST NOT YET, NOT UNTIL "HE" DEMANDS IT.
AT THE LAST POSSIBLE MOMENT HARBINGER REACTS, AND THE TWO VANISH...
22

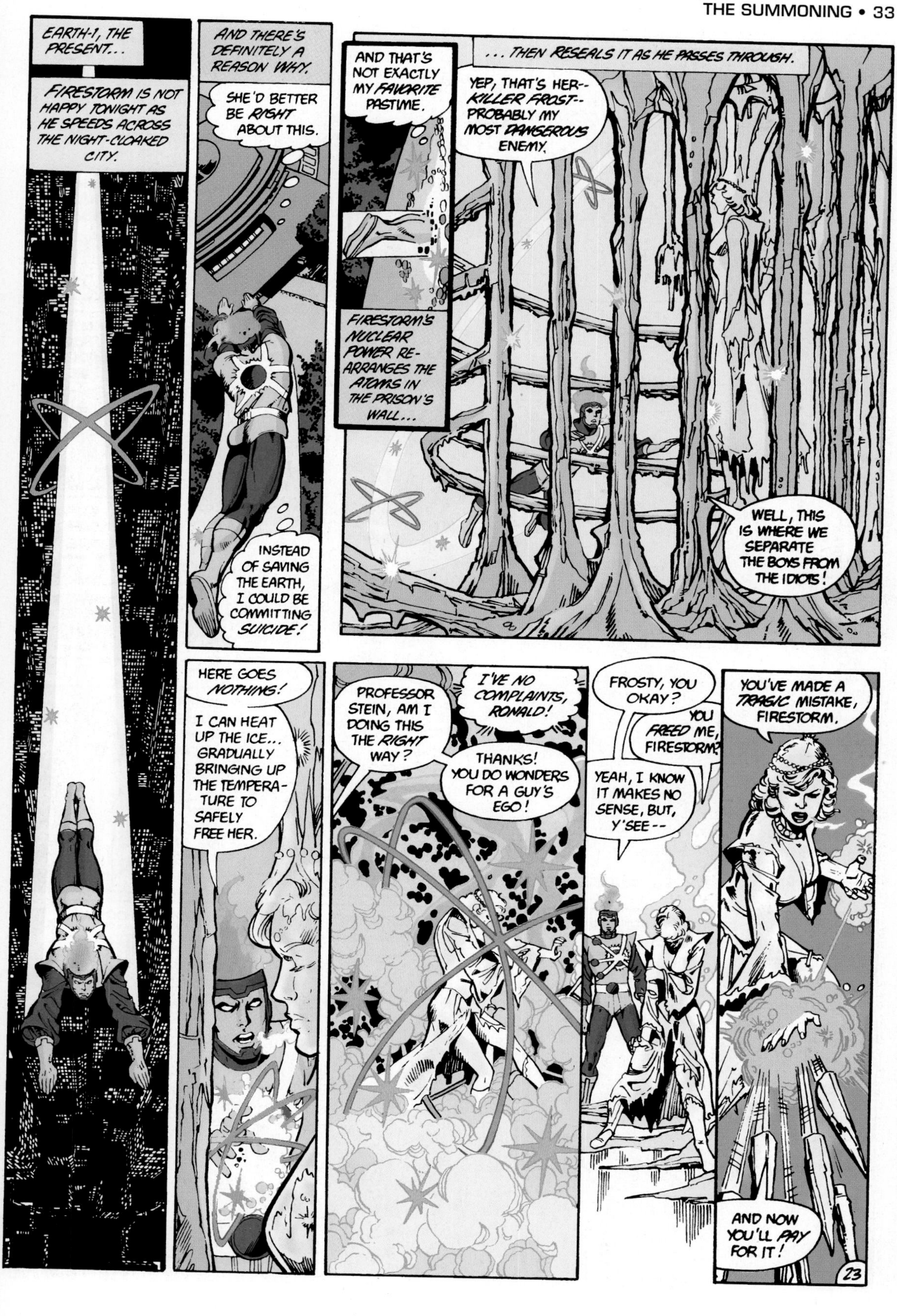
EARTH-1, THE PRESENT...
FIRESTORM IS NOT HAPPY TONIGHT AS HE SPEEDS ACROSS THE NIGHT-CLOAKED CITY.
AND THERE'S DEFINITELY A REASON WHY.
SHE'D BETTER BE RIGHT ABOUT THIS.
INSTEAD OF SAVING THE EARTH, I COULD BE COMMITTING SUICIDE!
AND THAT'S NOT EXACTLY MY FAVORITE PASTIME.
FIRESTORM'S NUCLEAR POWER RE-ARRANGES THE ATOMS IN THE PRISON'S WALL...
... THEN RESEALS IT AS HE PASSES THROUGH.
YEP, THAT'S HER-- KILLER FROST-- PROBABLY MY MOST DANGEROUS ENEMY.
WELL, THIS IS WHERE WE SEPARATE THE BOYS FROM THE IDIOTS!
HERE GOES NOTHING!
I CAN HEAT UP THE ICE... GRADUALLY BRINGING UP THE TEMPERA-TURE TO SAFELY FREE HER.
PROFESSOR STEIN, AM I DOING THIS THE RIGHT WAY?
I'VE NO COMPLAINTS, RONALD!
THANKS! YOU DO WONDERS FOR A GUY'S EGO!
FROSTY, YOU OKAY?
YOU FREED ME, FIRESTORM?
YEAH, I KNOW IT MAKES NO SENSE, BUT, Y'SEE --
YOU'VE MADE A TRAGIC MISTAKE, FIRESTORM.
AND NOW YOU'LL PAY FOR IT!
23

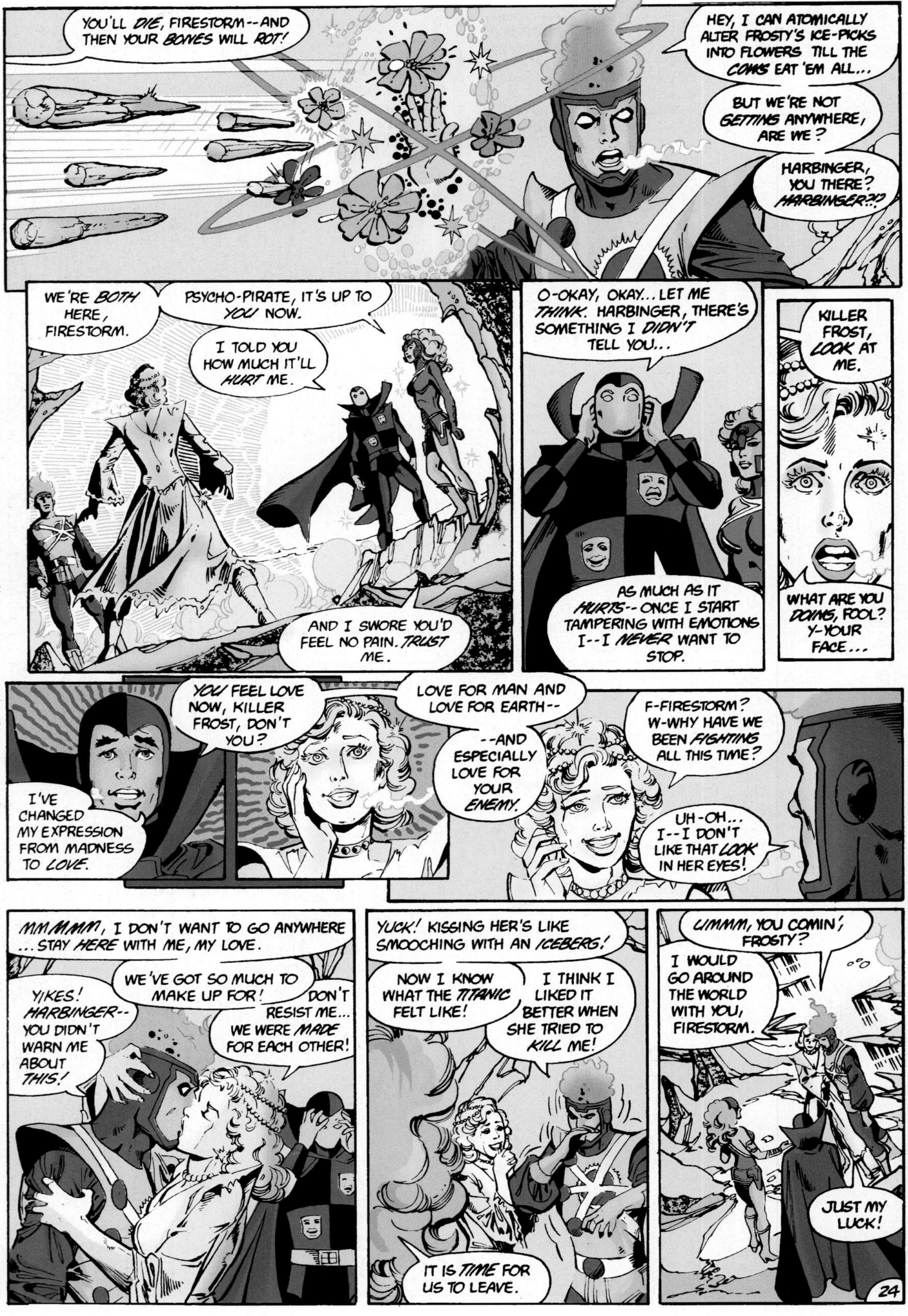
YOU'LL DIE, FIRESTORM--AND THEN YOUR BONES WILL ROT!
HEY, I CAN ATOMICALLY ALTER FROSTY'S ICE-PICKS INTO FLOWERS TILL THE COWS EAT 'EM ALL...
BUT WE'RE NOT GETTING ANYWHERE, ARE WE?
HARBINGER, YOU THERE? HARBINGER?!?
WE'RE BOTH HERE, FIRESTORM.
PSYCHO-PIRATE, IT'S UP TO YOU NOW.
I TOLD YOU HOW MUCH IT'LL HURT ME.
AND I SWORE YOU'D FEEL NO PAIN. TRUST ME.
O-OKAY, OKAY... LET ME THINK. HARBINGER, THERE'S SOMETHING I DIDN'T TELL YOU...
AS MUCH AS IT HURTS-- ONCE I START TAMPERING WITH EMOTIONS I--I NEVER WANT TO STOP.
KILLER FROST, LOOK AT ME.
WHAT ARE YOU DOING, FOOL? Y-YOUR FACE...
YOU FEEL LOVE NOW, KILLER FROST, DON'T YOU?
I'VE CHANGED MY EXPRESSION FROM MADNESS TO LOVE.
LOVE FOR MAN AND LOVE FOR EARTH--
--AND ESPECIALLY LOVE FOR YOUR ENEMY.
F-FIRESTORM? W-WHY HAVE WE BEEN FIGHTING ALL THIS TIME?
UH-OH... I--I DON'T LIKE THAT LOOK IN HER EYES!
MMMMM, I DON'T WANT TO GO ANYWHERE ...STAY HERE WITH ME, MY LOVE.
WE'VE GOT SO MUCH TO MAKE UP FOR! DON'T RESIST ME... WE WERE MADE FOR EACH OTHER!
YIKES! HARBINGER-- YOU DIDN'T WARN ME ABOUT THIS!
YUCK! KISSING HER'S LIKE SMOOCHING WITH AN ICEBERG!
NOW I KNOW WHAT THE TITANIC FELT LIKE!
I THINK I LIKED IT BETTER WHEN SHE TRIED TO KILL ME!
IT IS TIME FOR US TO LEAVE.
UMMM, YOU COMIN', FROSTY?
I WOULD GO AROUND THE WORLD WITH YOU, FIRESTORM.
JUST MY LUCK!
24

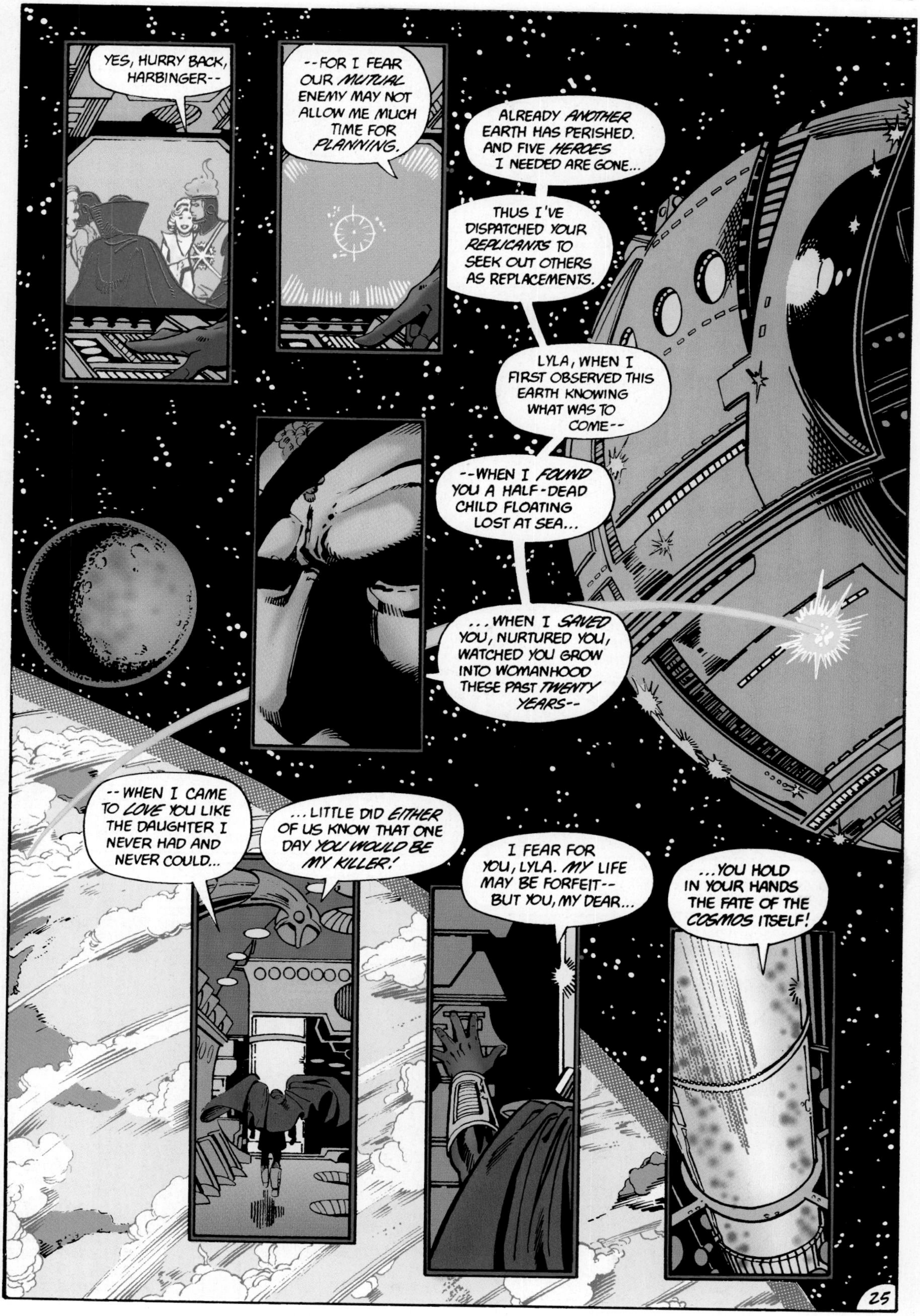
YES, HURRY BACK, HARBINGER--
--FOR I FEAR OUR MUTUAL ENEMY MAY NOT ALLOW ME MUCH TIME FOR PLANNING.
ALREADY ANOTHER EARTH HAS PERISHED. AND FIVE HEROES I NEEDED ARE GONE...
THUS I'VE DISPATCHED YOUR REPLICANTS TO SEEK OUT OTHERS AS REPLACEMENTS.
LYLA, WHEN I FIRST OBSERVED THIS EARTH KNOWING WHAT WAS TO COME--
--WHEN I FOUND YOU A HALF-DEAD CHILD FLOATING LOST AT SEA...
...WHEN I SAVED YOU, NURTURED YOU, WATCHED YOU GROW INTO WOMANHOOD THESE PAST TWENTY YEARS--
--WHEN I CAME TO LOVE YOU LIKE THE DAUGHTER I NEVER HAD AND NEVER COULD...
...LITTLE DID EITHER OF US KNOW THAT ONE DAY YOU WOULD BE MY KILLER!
I FEAR FOR YOU, LYLA. MY LIFE MAY BE FORFEIT--BUT YOU, MY DEAR...
...YOU HOLD IN YOUR HANDS THE FATE OF THE COSMOS ITSELF!
25

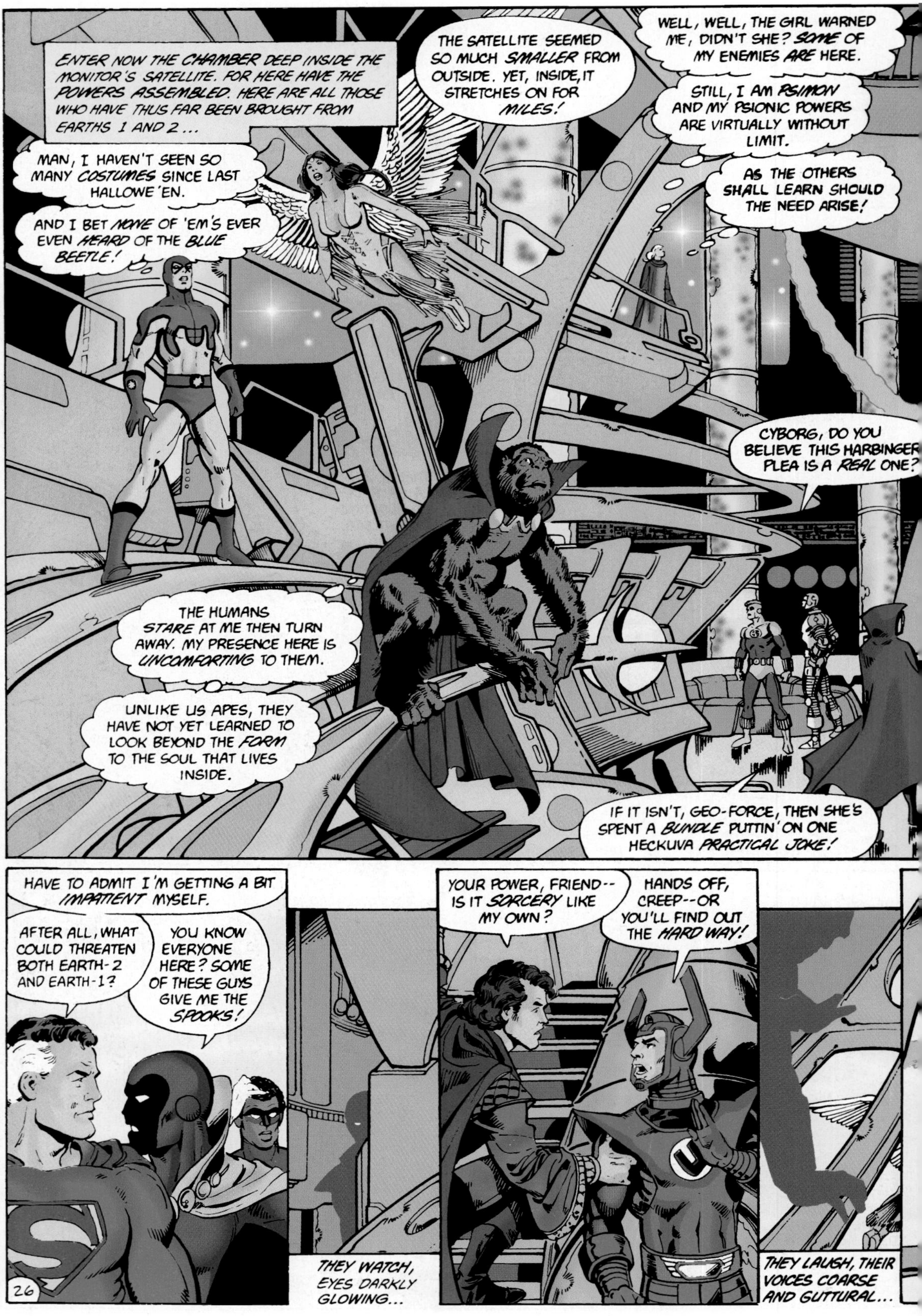
ENTER NOW THE CHAMBER DEEP INSIDE THE MONITOR'S SATELLITE. FOR HERE HAVE THE POWERS ASSEMBLED. HERE ARE ALL THOSE WHO HAVE THUS FAR BEEN BROUGHT FROM EARTHS 1 AND 2...
THE SATELLITE SEEMED SO MUCH SMALLER FROM OUTSIDE. YET, INSIDE, IT STRETCHES ON FOR MILES!
WELL, WELL, THE GIRL WARNED ME, DIDN'T SHE? SOME OF MY ENEMIES ARE HERE.
STILL, I AM PSIMON AND MY PSIONIC POWERS ARE VIRTUALLY WITHOUT LIMIT.
AS THE OTHERS SHALL LEARN SHOULD THE NEED ARISE!
MAN, I HAVEN'T SEEN SO MANY COSTUMES SINCE LAST HALLOWE'EN.
AND I BET NONE OF 'EM'S EVER EVEN HEARD OF THE BLUE BEETLE!
CYBORG, DO YOU BELIEVE THIS HARBINGER PLEA IS A REAL ONE?
THE HUMANS STARE AT ME THEN TURN AWAY. MY PRESENCE HERE IS UNCOMFORTING TO THEM.
UNLIKE US APES, THEY HAVE NOT YET LEARNED TO LOOK BEYOND THE FORM TO THE SOUL THAT LIVES INSIDE.
IF IT ISN'T, GEO-FORCE, THEN SHE'S SPENT A BUNDLE PUTTIN' ON ONE HECKUVA PRACTICAL JOKE!
HAVE TO ADMIT I'M GETTING A BIT IMPATIENT MYSELF.
AFTER ALL, WHAT COULD THREATEN BOTH EARTH-2 AND EARTH-1?
YOU KNOW EVERYONE HERE? SOME OF THESE GUYS GIVE ME THE SPOOKS!
26
THEY WATCH, EYES DARKLY GLOWING...
YOUR POWER, FRIEND-- IS IT SORCERY LIKE MY OWN?
HANDS OFF, CREEP--OR YOU'LL FIND OUT THE HARD WAY!
THEY LAUGH, THEIR VOICES COARSE AND GUTTURAL...

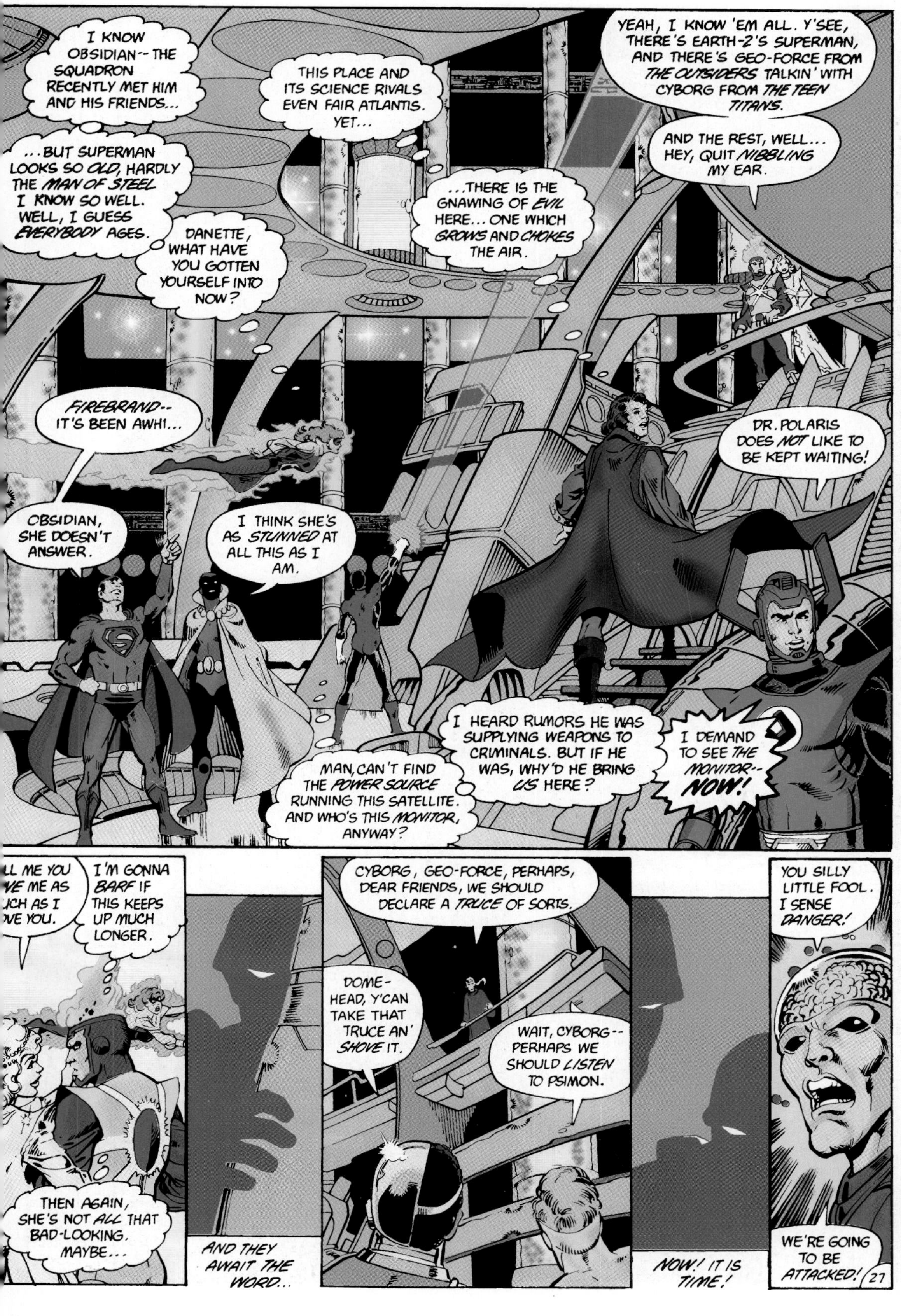
I KNOW OBSIDIAN-- THE SQUADRON RECENTLY MET HIM AND HIS FRIENDS...
...BUT SUPERMAN LOOKS SO OLD, HARDLY THE MAN OF STEEL I KNOW SO WELL. WELL, I GUESS EVERYBODY AGES.
THIS PLACE AND ITS SCIENCE RIVALS EVEN FAIR ATLANTIS. YET...
DANETTE, WHAT HAVE YOU GOTTEN YOURSELF INTO NOW?
...THERE IS THE GNAWING OF EVIL HERE... ONE WHICH GROWS AND CHOKES THE AIR.
YEAH, I KNOW 'EM ALL. Y'SEE, THERE'S EARTH-2'S SUPERMAN, AND THERE'S GEO-FORCE FROM THE OUTSIDERS TALKIN' WITH CYBORG FROM THE TEEN TITANS.
AND THE REST, WELL... HEY, QUIT NIBBLING MY EAR.
FIREBRAND-- IT'S BEEN AWHI...
DR. POLARIS DOES NOT LIKE TO BE KEPT WAITING!
OBSIDIAN, SHE DOESN'T ANSWER.
I THINK SHE'S AS STUNNED AT ALL THIS AS I AM.
MAN, CAN'T FIND THE POWER SOURCE RUNNING THIS SATELLITE. AND WHO'S THIS MONITOR, ANYWAY?
I HEARD RUMORS HE WAS SUPPLYING WEAPONS TO CRIMINALS. BUT IF HE WAS, WHY'D HE BRING US HERE?
I DEMAND TO SEE THE MONITOR-- NOW!
LL ME YOU VE ME AS UCH AS I OVE YOU.
I'M GONNA BARF IF THIS KEEPS UP MUCH LONGER.
THEN AGAIN, SHE'S NOT ALL THAT BAD-LOOKING. MAYBE...
AND THEY AWAIT THE WORD...
CYBORG, GEO-FORCE, PERHAPS, DEAR FRIENDS, WE SHOULD DECLARE A TRUCE OF SORTS.
DOME-HEAD, Y'CAN TAKE THAT TRUCE AN' SHOVE IT.
WAIT, CYBORG-- PERHAPS WE SHOULD LISTEN TO PSIMON.
NOW! IT IS TIME!
YOU SILLY LITTLE FOOL. I SENSE DANGER!
WE'RE GOING TO BE ATTACKED!
27

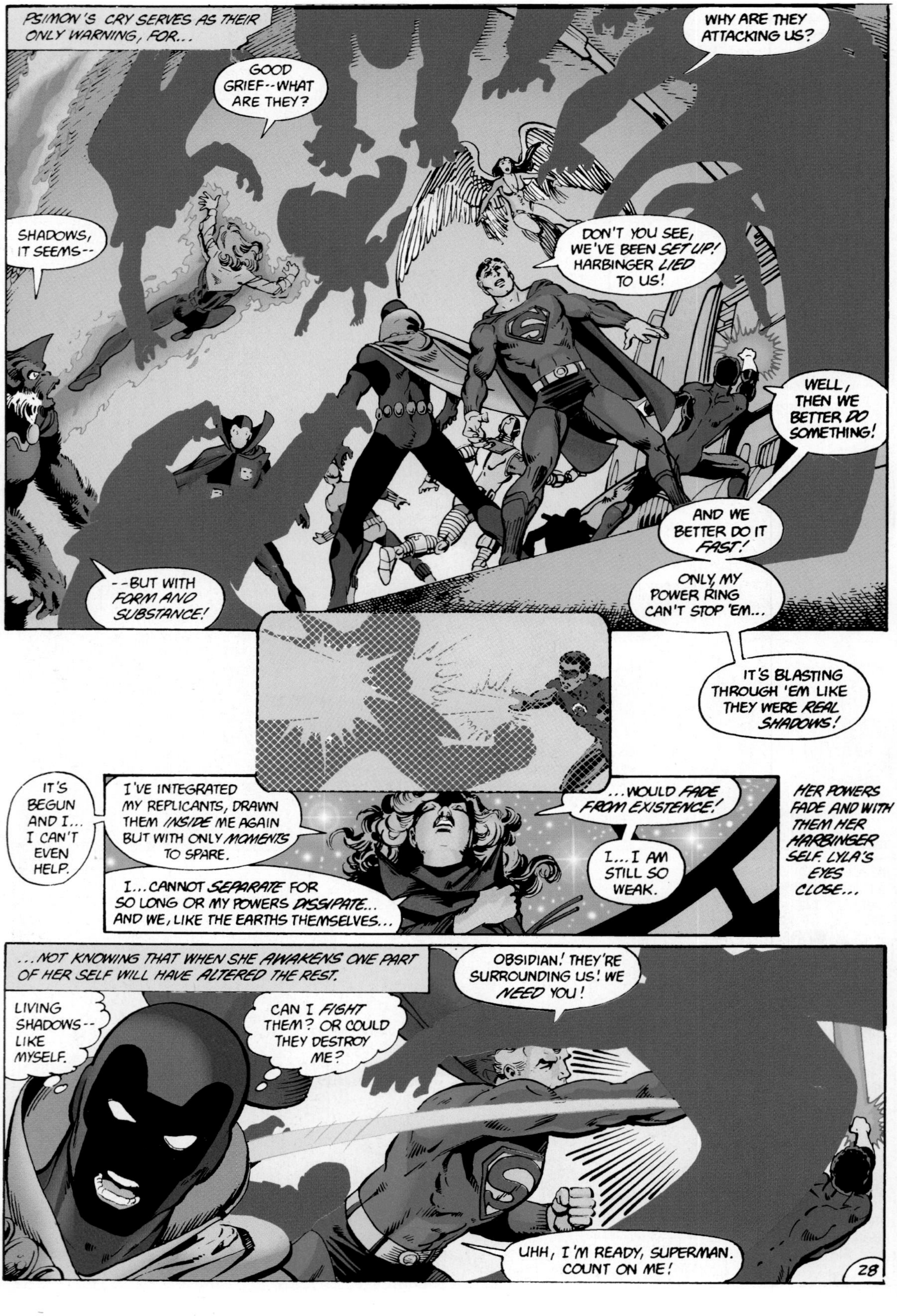
PSIMON'S CRY SERVES AS THEIR ONLY WARNING, FOR...
GOOD GRIEF--WHAT ARE THEY?
WHY ARE THEY ATTACKING US?
SHADOWS, IT SEEMS--
DON'T YOU SEE, WE'VE BEEN SET UP! HARBINGER LIED TO US!
WELL, THEN WE BETTER DO SOMETHING!
AND WE BETTER DO IT FAST!
--BUT WITH FORM AND SUBSTANCE!
ONLY, MY POWER RING CAN'T STOP 'EM...
IT'S BLASTING THROUGH 'EM LIKE THEY WERE REAL SHADOWS!
IT'S BEGUN AND I... I CAN'T EVEN HELP.
I'VE INTEGRATED MY REPLICANTS, DRAWN THEM INSIDE ME AGAIN BUT WITH ONLY MOMENTS TO SPARE.
I... CANNOT SEPARATE FOR SO LONG OR MY POWERS DISSIPATE... AND WE, LIKE THE EARTHS THEMSELVES...
...WOULD FADE FROM EXISTENCE!
I... I AM STILL SO WEAK.
HER POWERS FADE AND WITH THEM HER HARBINGER SELF. LYLA'S EYES CLOSE...
...NOT KNOWING THAT WHEN SHE AWAKENS ONE PART OF HER SELF WILL HAVE ALTERED THE REST.
OBSIDIAN! THEY'RE SURROUNDING US! WE NEED YOU!
LIVING SHADOWS--LIKE MYSELF.
CAN I FIGHT THEM? OR COULD THEY DESTROY ME?
UHH, I'M READY, SUPERMAN. COUNT ON ME!
28

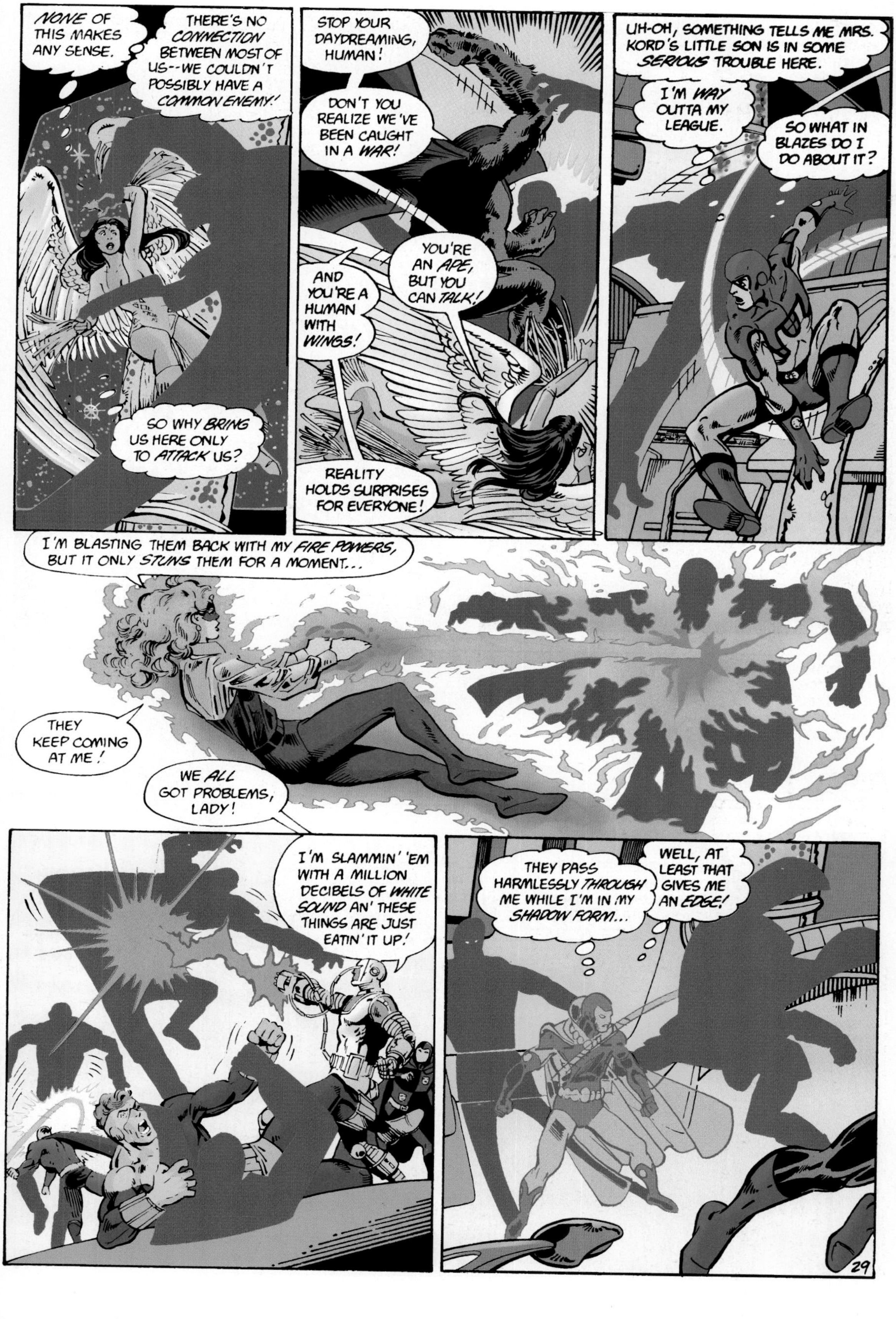
NONE OF THIS MAKES ANY SENSE.
THERE'S NO CONNECTION BETWEEN MOST OF US--WE COULDN'T POSSIBLY HAVE A COMMON ENEMY!
SO WHY BRING US HERE ONLY TO ATTACK US?
STOP YOUR DAYDREAMING, HUMAN!
DON'T YOU REALIZE WE'VE BEEN CAUGHT IN A WAR!
YOU'RE AN APE, BUT YOU CAN TALK!
AND YOU'RE A HUMAN WITH WINGS!
REALITY HOLDS SURPRISES FOR EVERYONE!
UH-OH, SOMETHING TELLS ME MRS. KORD'S LITTLE SON IS IN SOME SERIOUS TROUBLE HERE.
I'M WAY OUTTA MY LEAGUE.
SO WHAT IN BLAZES DO I DO ABOUT IT?
I'M BLASTING THEM BACK WITH MY FIRE POWERS, BUT IT ONLY STUNS THEM FOR A MOMENT...
THEY KEEP COMING AT ME!
WE ALL GOT PROBLEMS, LADY!
I'M SLAMMIN' 'EM WITH A MILLION DECIBELS OF WHITE SOUND AN' THESE THINGS ARE JUST EATIN' IT UP!
THEY PASS HARMLESSLY THROUGH ME WHILE I'M IN MY SHADOW FORM...
WELL, AT LEAST THAT GIVES ME AN EDGE!
29

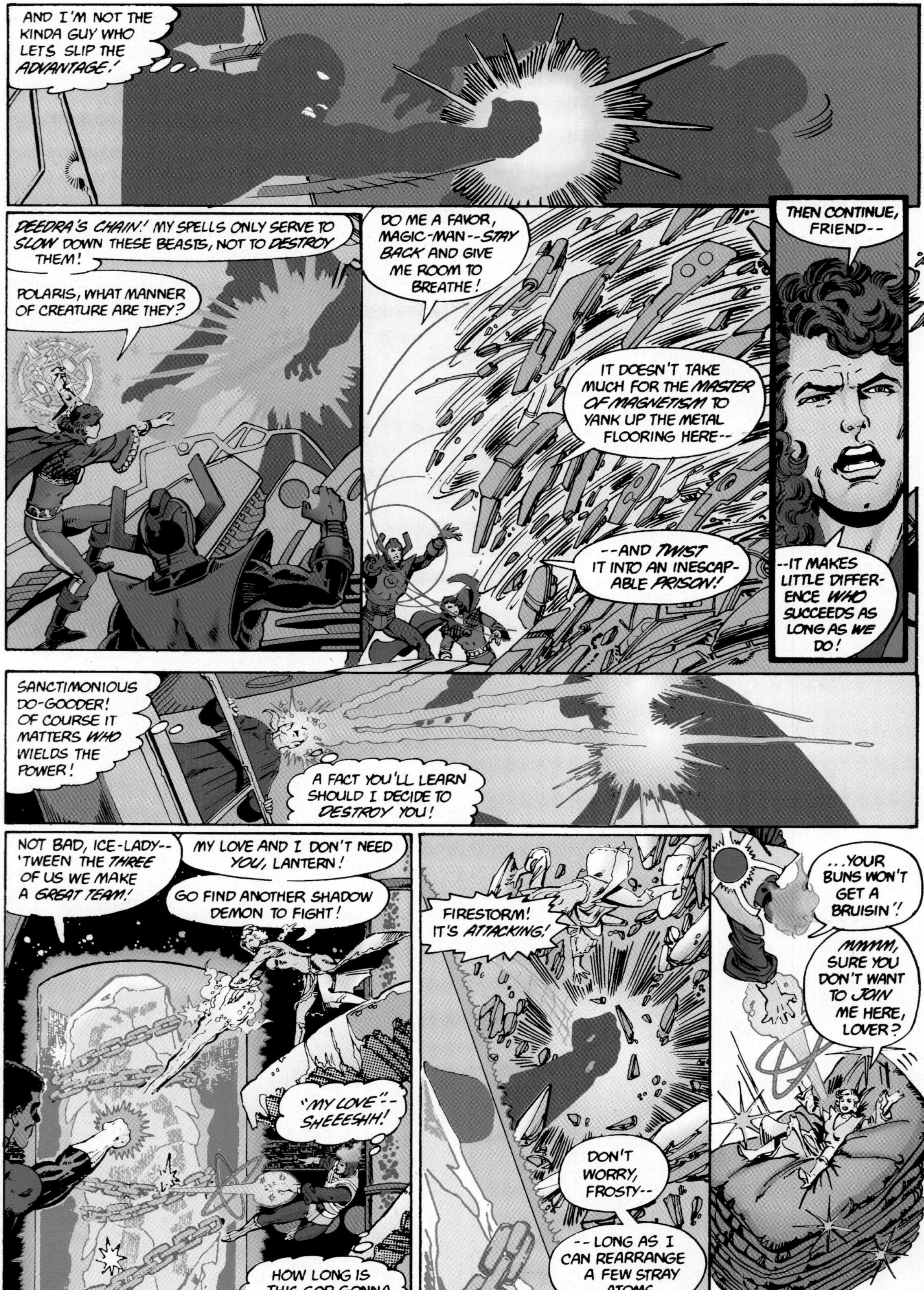
AND I'M NOT THE KINDA GUY WHO LETS SLIP THE ADVANTAGE!
DEEDRA'S CHAIN! MY SPELLS ONLY SERVE TO SLOW DOWN THESE BEASTS, NOT TO DESTROY THEM!
POLARIS, WHAT MANNER OF CREATURE ARE THEY?
DO ME A FAVOR, MAGIC-MAN--STAY BACK AND GIVE ME ROOM TO BREATHE!
IT DOESN'T TAKE MUCH FOR THE MASTER OF MAGNETISM TO YANK UP THE METAL FLOORING HERE--
--AND TWIST IT INTO AN INESCAPABLE PRISON!
THEN CONTINUE, FRIEND--
--IT MAKES LITTLE DIFFERENCE WHO SUCCEEDS AS LONG AS WE DO!
SANCTIMONIOUS DO-GOODER! OF COURSE IT MATTERS WHO WIELDS THE POWER!
A FACT YOU'LL LEARN SHOULD I DECIDE TO DESTROY YOU!
NOT BAD, ICE-LADY-- 'TWEEN THE THREE OF US WE MAKE A GREAT TEAM!
MY LOVE AND I DON'T NEED YOU, LANTERN!
GO FIND ANOTHER SHADOW DEMON TO FIGHT!
"MY LOVE"-- SHEEESHH!
HOW LONG IS THIS GOP GONNA GO ON?
FIRESTORM! IT'S ATTACKING!
DON'T WORRY, FROSTY--
--LONG AS I CAN REARRANGE A FEW STRAY ATOMS...
...YOUR BUNS WON'T GET A BRUISIN'!
MMMM, SURE YOU DON'T WANT TO JOIN ME HERE, LOVER?
30

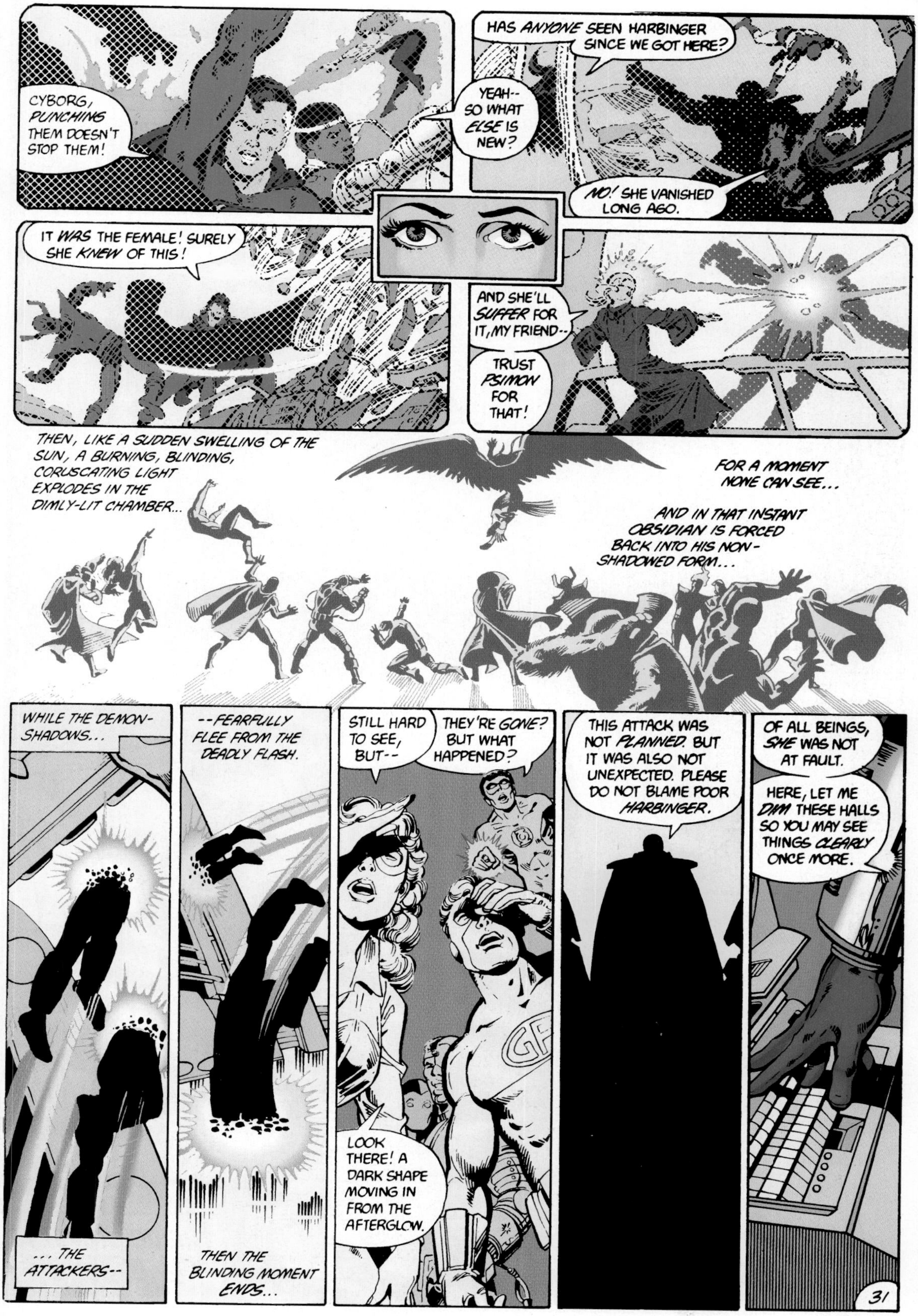
CYBORG, PUNCHING THEM DOESN'T STOP THEM!
YEAH-- SO WHAT ELSE IS NEW?
HAS ANYONE SEEN HARBINGER SINCE WE GOT HERE?
NO! SHE VANISHED LONG AGO.
IT WAS THE FEMALE! SURELY SHE KNEW OF THIS!
AND SHE'LL SUFFER FOR IT, MY FRIEND--
TRUST PSIMON FOR THAT!
THEN, LIKE A SUDDEN SWELLING OF THE SUN, A BURNING, BLINDING, CORUSCATING LIGHT EXPLODES IN THE DIMLY-LIT CHAMBER...
FOR A MOMENT NONE CAN SEE...
AND IN THAT INSTANT OBSIDIAN IS FORCED BACK INTO HIS NON-SHADOWED FORM...
WHILE THE DEMON-SHADOWS...
...THE ATTACKERS--
--FEARFULLY FLEE FROM THE DEADLY FLASH.
THEN THE BLINDING MOMENT ENDS...
STILL HARD TO SEE, BUT--
THEY'RE GONE? BUT WHAT HAPPENED?
LOOK THERE! A DARK SHAPE MOVING IN FROM THE AFTERGLOW.
THIS ATTACK WAS NOT PLANNED. BUT IT WAS ALSO NOT UNEXPECTED. PLEASE DO NOT BLAME POOR HARBINGER.
OF ALL BEINGS, SHE WAS NOT AT FAULT.
HERE, LET ME DIM THESE HALLS SO YOU MAY SEE THINGS CLEARLY ONCE MORE.
31

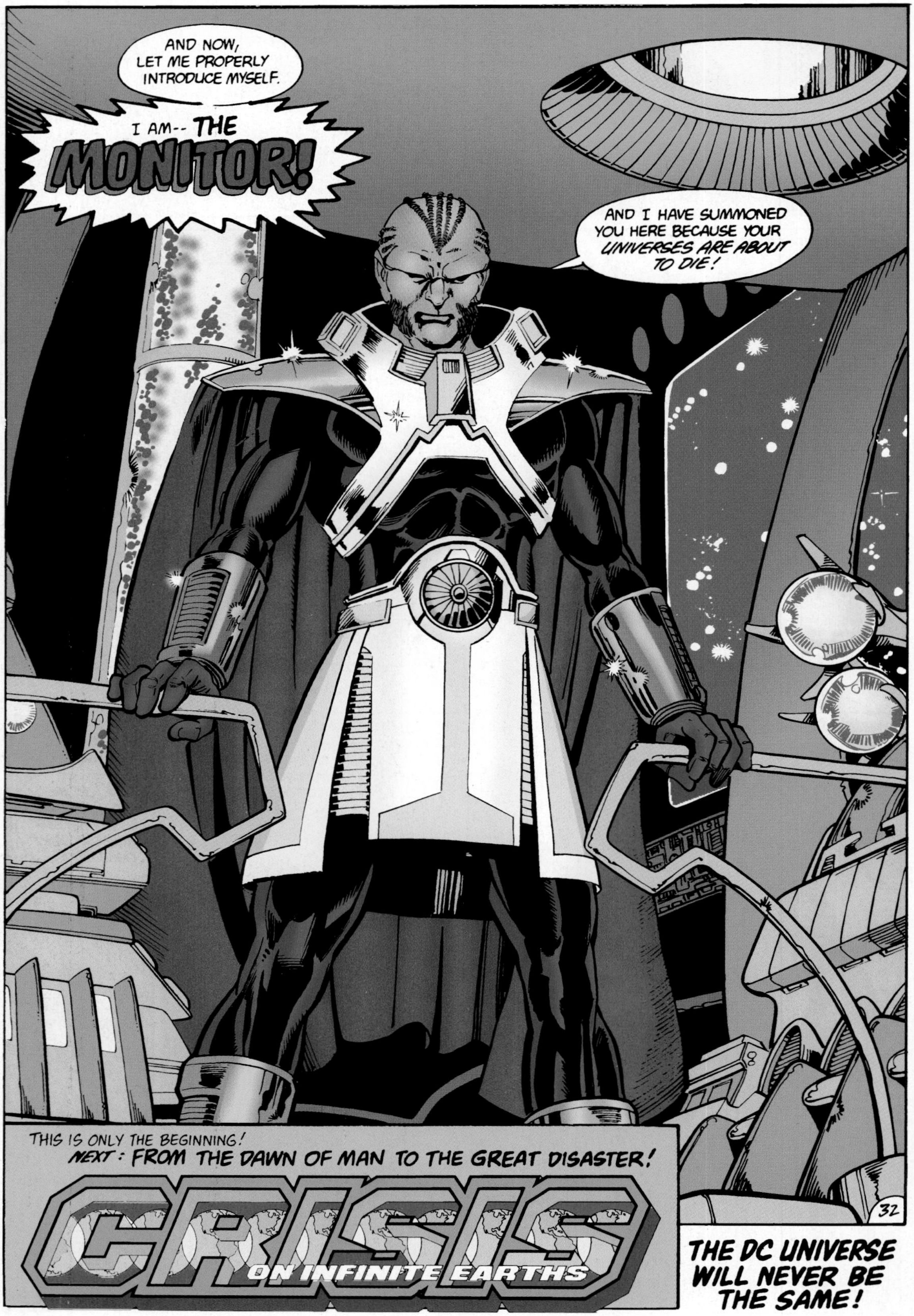
AND NOW, LET ME PROPERLY INTRODUCE MYSELF.
I AM-- THE MONITOR!
AND I HAVE SUMMONED YOU HERE BECAUSE YOUR UNIVERSES ARE ABOUT TO DIE!
THIS IS ONLY THE BEGINNING!
NEXT: FROM THE DAWN OF MAN TO THE GREAT DISASTER!
CRISIS ON INFINITE EARTHS
THE DC UNIVERSE WILL NEVER BE THE SAME!
32

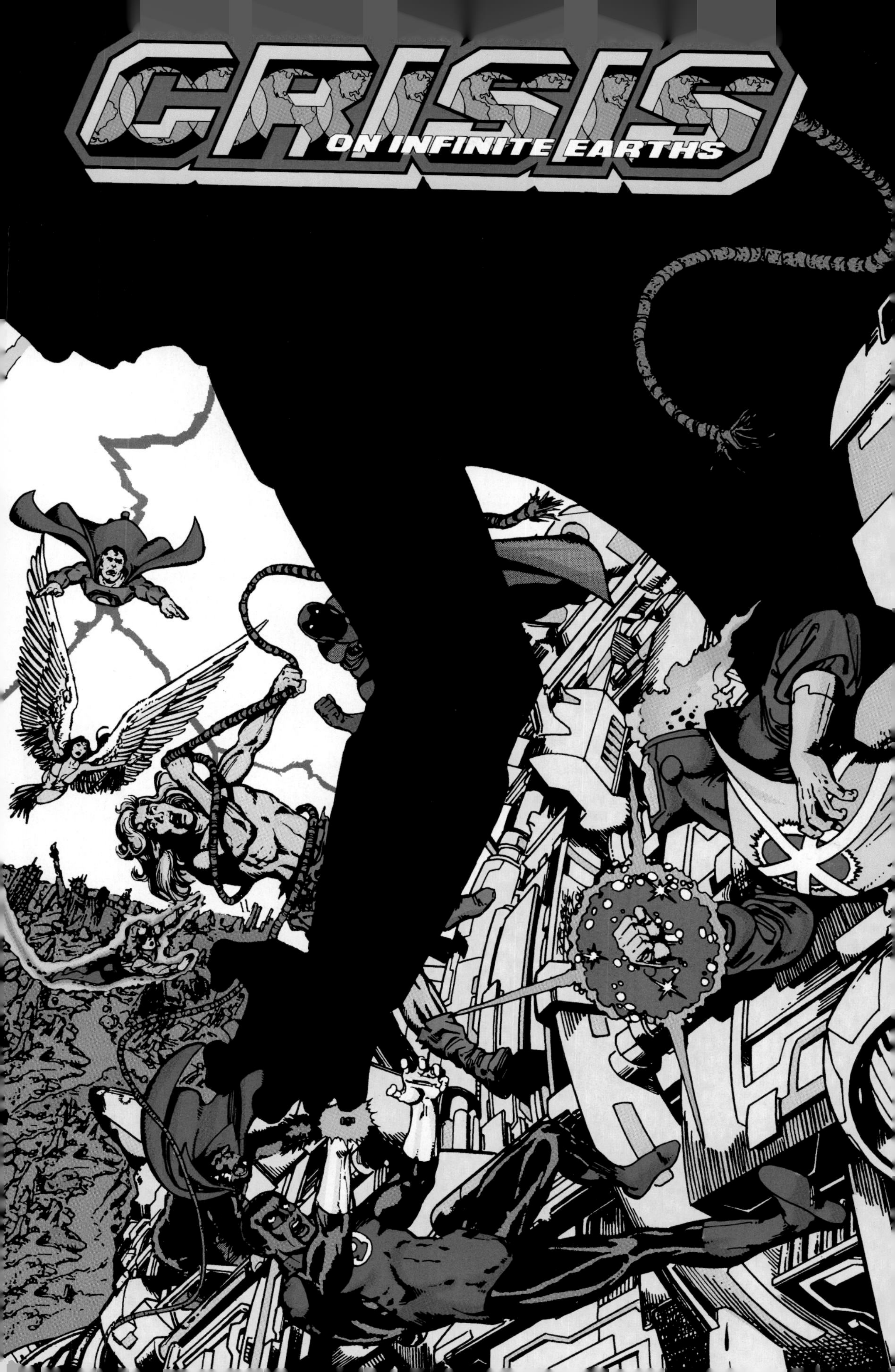
CRISIS
ON INFINITE EARTHS

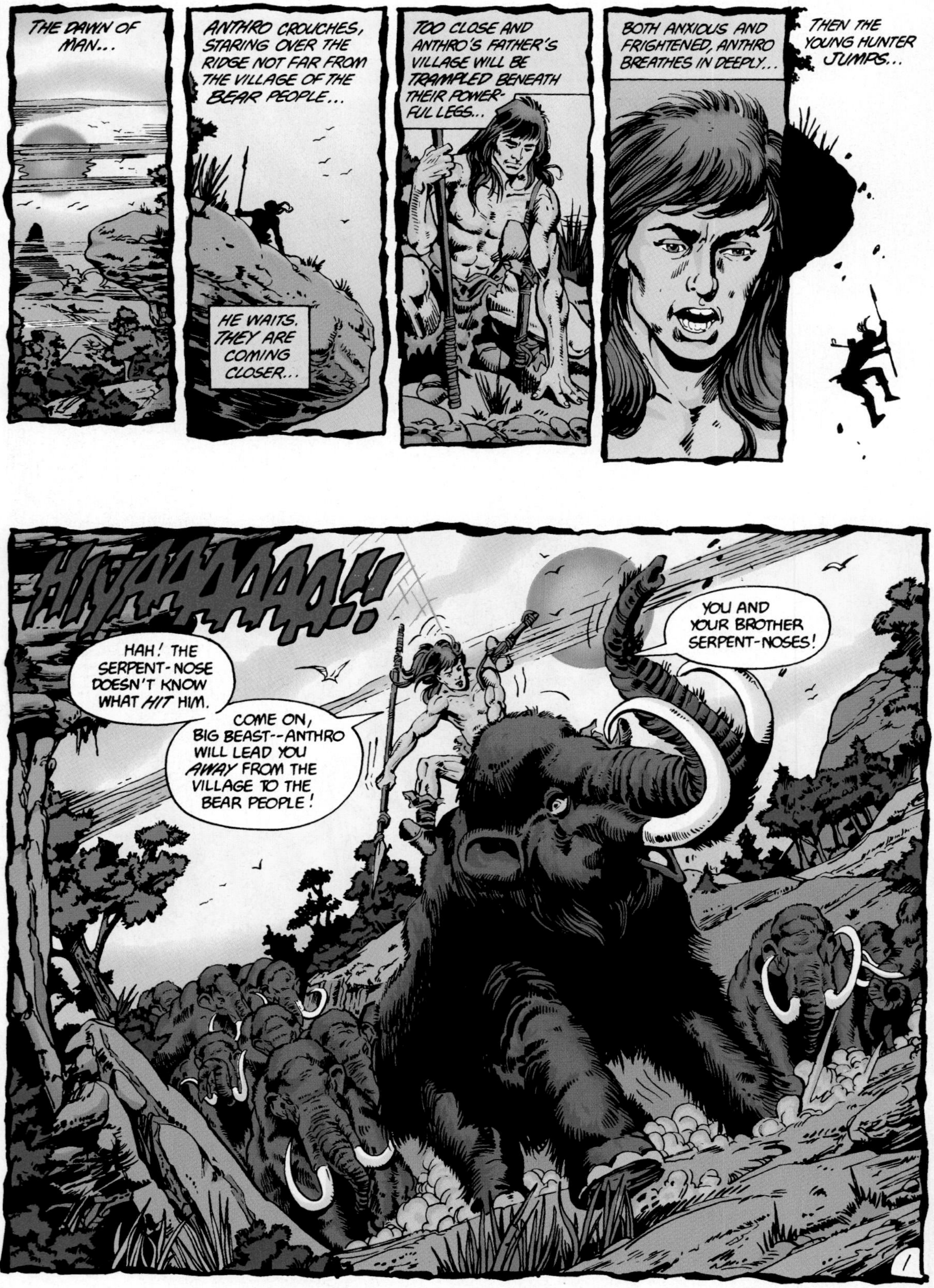
THE DAWN OF MAN...
ANTHRO CROUCHES, STARING OVER THE RIDGE NOT FAR FROM THE VILLAGE OF THE BEAR PEOPLE...
HE WAITS. THEY ARE COMING CLOSER...
TOO CLOSE AND ANTHRO'S FATHER'S VILLAGE WILL BE TRAMPLED BENEATH THEIR POWER-FUL LEGS...
BOTH ANXIOUS AND FRIGHTENED, ANTHRO BREATHES IN DEEPLY...
THEN THE YOUNG HUNTER JUMPS...
HIYAAAAAA!!
HAH! THE SERPENT-NOSE DOESN'T KNOW WHAT HIT HIM.
COME ON, BIG BEAST--ANTHRO WILL LEAD YOU AWAY FROM THE VILLAGE TO THE BEAR PEOPLE!
YOU AND YOUR BROTHER SERPENT-NOSES!

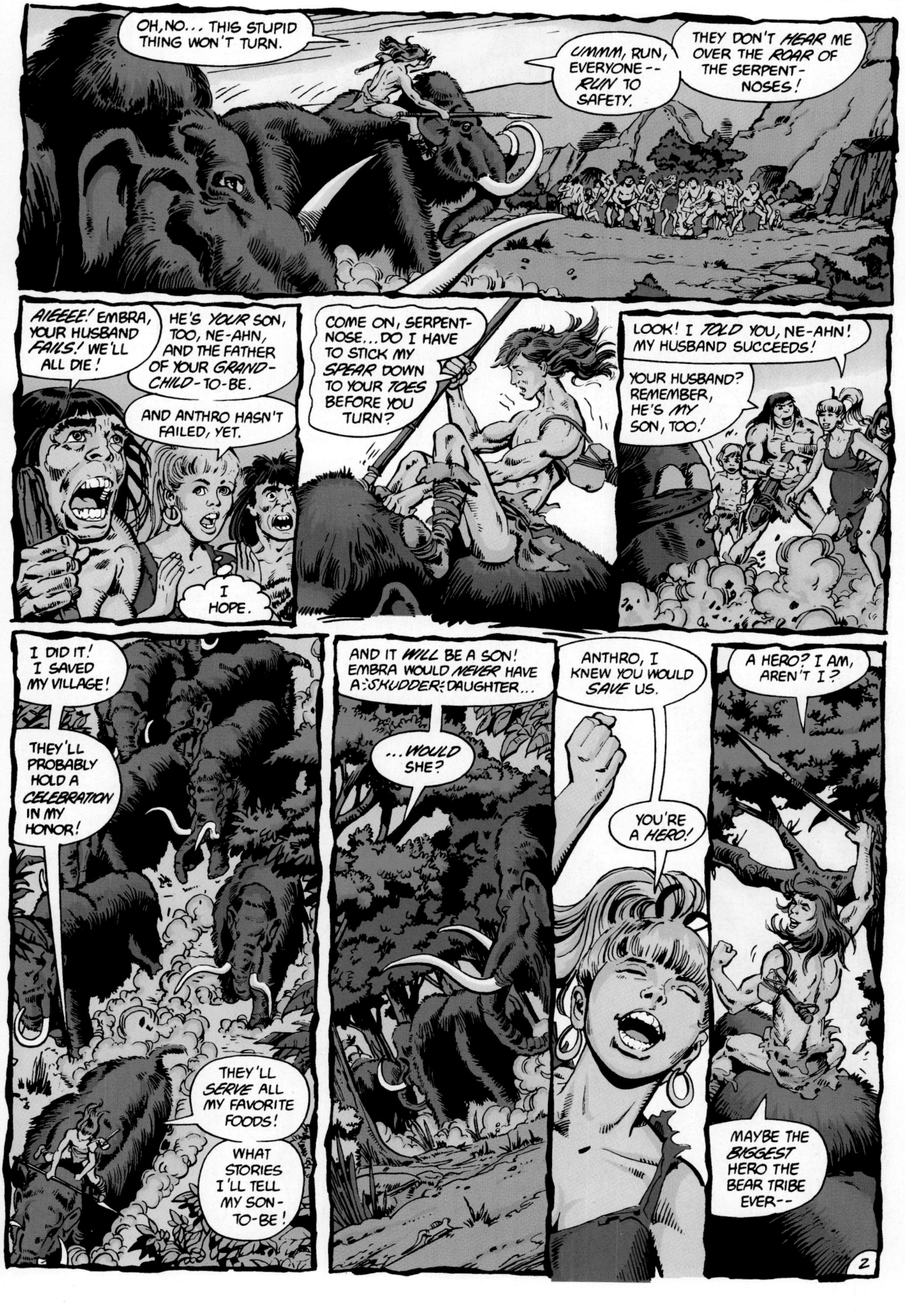
OH, NO... THIS STUPID THING WON'T TURN.
UMMM, RUN, EVERYONE-- RUN TO SAFETY.
THEY DON'T HEAR ME OVER THE ROAR OF THE SERPENT-NOSES!
AIEEEE! EMBRA, YOUR HUSBAND FAILS! WE'LL ALL DIE!
HE'S YOUR SON, TOO, NE-AHN, AND THE FATHER OF YOUR GRAND-CHILD-TO-BE.
AND ANTHRO HASN'T FAILED, YET.
I HOPE.
COME ON, SERPENT-NOSE... DO I HAVE TO STICK MY SPEAR DOWN TO YOUR TOES BEFORE YOU TURN?
LOOK! I TOLD YOU, NE-AHN! MY HUSBAND SUCCEEDS!
YOUR HUSBAND? REMEMBER, HE'S MY SON, TOO!
I DID IT! I SAVED MY VILLAGE!
THEY'LL PROBABLY HOLD A CELEBRATION IN MY HONOR!
THEY'LL SERVE ALL MY FAVORITE FOODS!
WHAT STORIES I'LL TELL MY SON-TO-BE!
AND IT WILL BE A SON! EMBRA WOULD NEVER HAVE A :SKUDDER: DAUGHTER...
...WOULD SHE?
ANTHRO, I KNEW YOU WOULD SAVE US.
YOU'RE A HERO!
A HERO? I AM, AREN'T I?
MAYBE THE BIGGEST HERO THE BEAR TRIBE EVER--
2

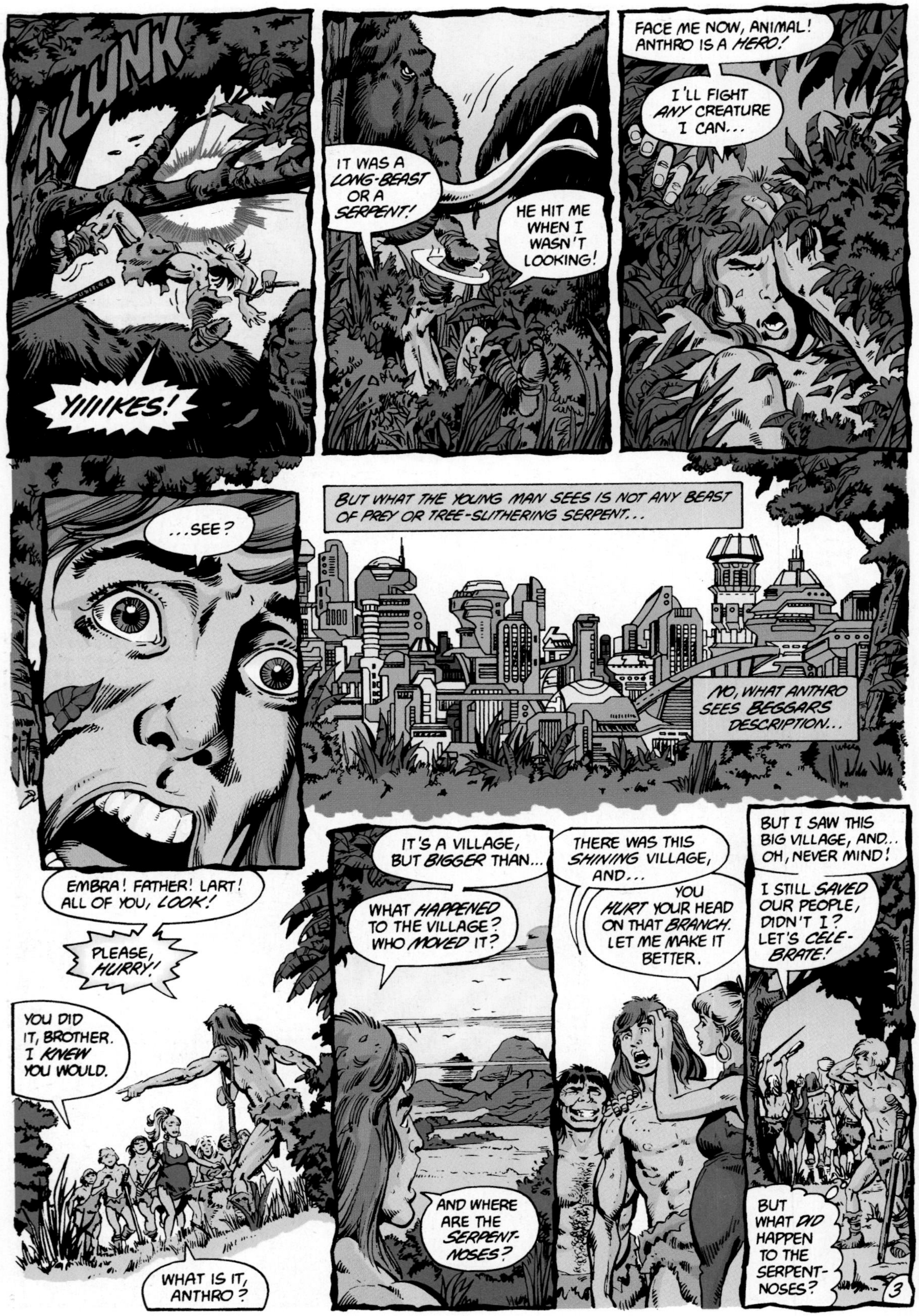
K-LUNK
YIIIIKES!
IT WAS A LONG-BEAST OR A SERPENT!
HE HIT ME WHEN I WASN'T LOOKING!
FACE ME NOW, ANIMAL! ANTHRO IS A HERO!
I'LL FIGHT ANY CREATURE I CAN...
...SEE?
BUT WHAT THE YOUNG MAN SEES IS NOT ANY BEAST OF PREY OR TREE-SLITHERING SERPENT...
NO, WHAT ANTHRO SEES BEGGARS DESCRIPTION...
EMBRA! FATHER! LART! ALL OF YOU, LOOK!
PLEASE, HURRY!
YOU DID IT, BROTHER. I KNEW YOU WOULD.
WHAT IS IT, ANTHRO?
IT'S A VILLAGE, BUT BIGGER THAN...
WHAT HAPPENED TO THE VILLAGE? WHO MOVED IT?
AND WHERE ARE THE SERPENT-NOSES?
THERE WAS THIS SHINING VILLAGE, AND...
YOU HURT YOUR HEAD ON THAT BRANCH. LET ME MAKE IT BETTER.
BUT I SAW THIS BIG VILLAGE, AND... OH, NEVER MIND!
I STILL SAVED OUR PEOPLE, DIDN'T I? LET'S CELE-BRATE!
BUT WHAT DID HAPPEN TO THE SERPENT-NOSES?
3

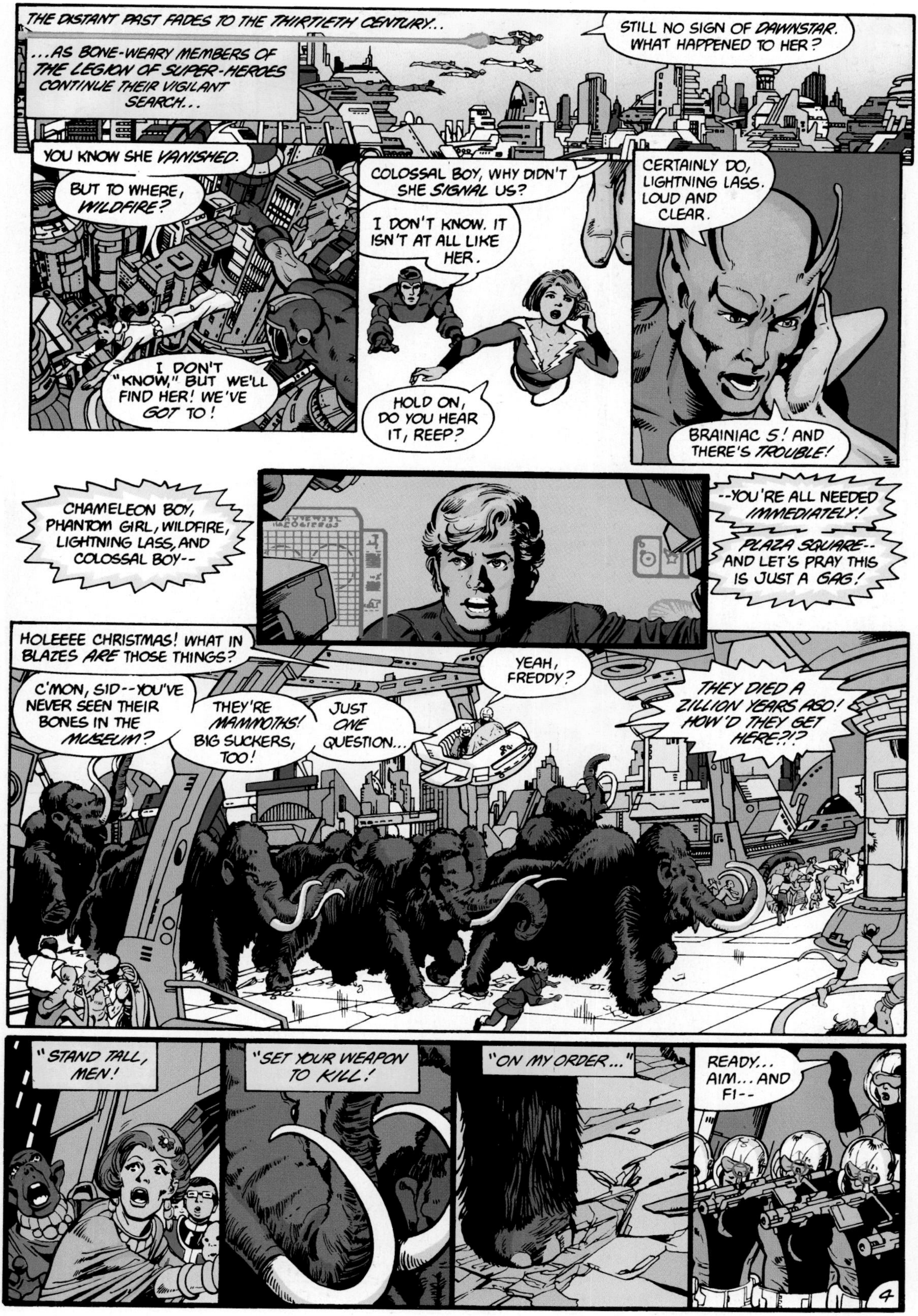
THE DISTANT PAST FADES TO THE THIRTIETH CENTURY...
...AS BONE-WEARY MEMBERS OF THE LEGION OF SUPER-HEROES CONTINUE THEIR VIGILANT SEARCH...
STILL NO SIGN OF DAWNSTAR. WHAT HAPPENED TO HER?
YOU KNOW SHE VANISHED.
BUT TO WHERE, WILDFIRE?
I DON'T "KNOW," BUT WE'LL FIND HER! WE'VE GOT TO!
COLOSSAL BOY, WHY DIDN'T SHE SIGNAL US?
I DON'T KNOW. IT ISN'T AT ALL LIKE HER.
HOLD ON, DO YOU HEAR IT, REEP?
CERTAINLY DO, LIGHTNING LASS. LOUD AND CLEAR.
BRAINIAC 5! AND THERE'S TROUBLE!
CHAMELEON BOY, PHANTOM GIRL, WILDFIRE, LIGHTNING LASS, AND COLOSSAL BOY--
--YOU'RE ALL NEEDED IMMEDIATELY!
PLAZA SQUARE-- AND LET'S PRAY THIS IS JUST A GAG!
HOLEEEE CHRISTMAS! WHAT IN BLAZES ARE THOSE THINGS?
C'MON, SID--YOU'VE NEVER SEEN THEIR BONES IN THE MUSEUM?
THEY'RE MAMMOTHS! BIG SUCKERS, TOO!
JUST ONE QUESTION...
YEAH, FREDDY?
THEY DIED A ZILLION YEARS AGO! HOW'D THEY GET HERE?!?
"STAND TALL, MEN!
"SET YOUR WEAPON TO KILL!
"ON MY ORDER..."
READY... AIM... AND FI--
4

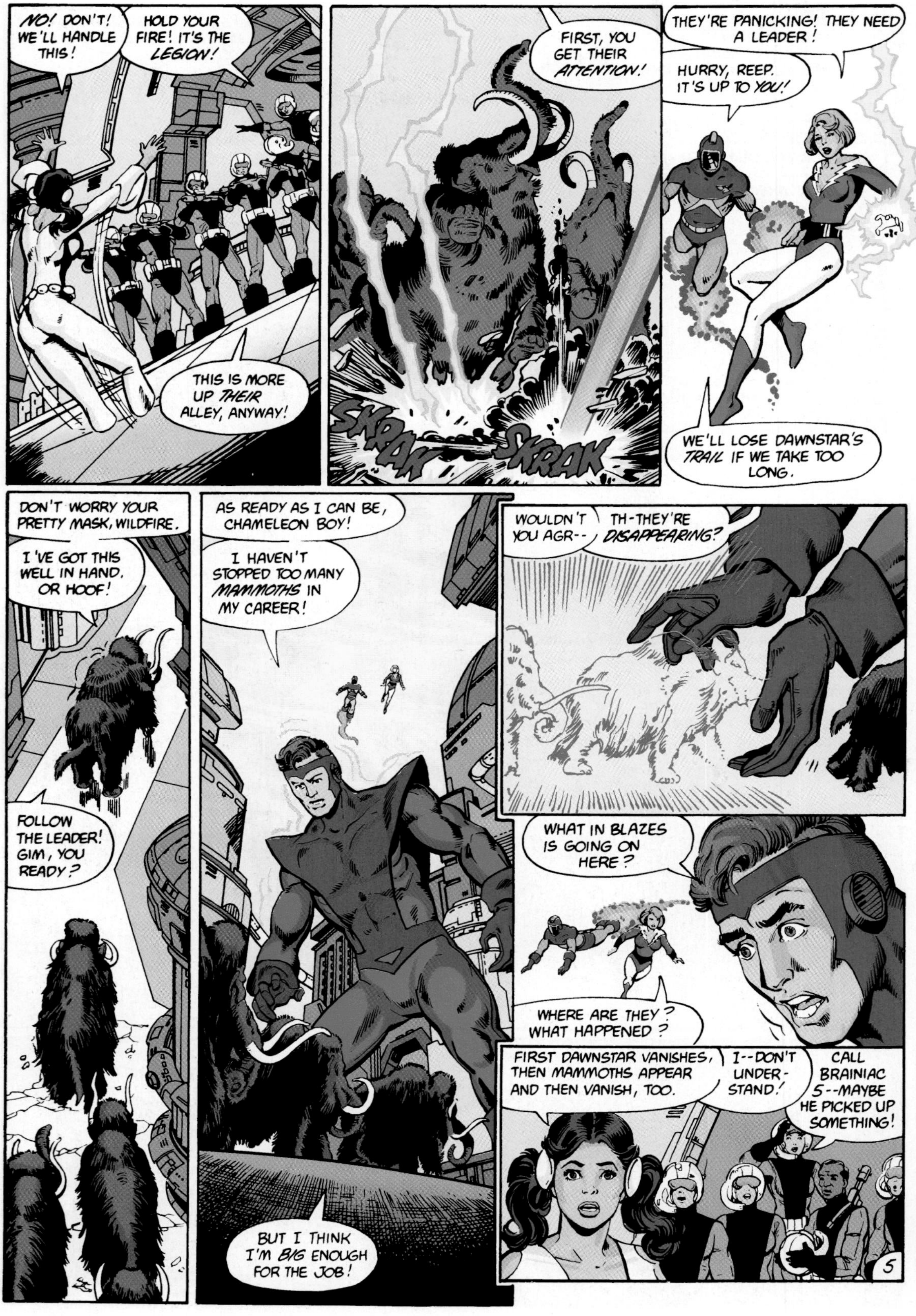
NO! DON'T! WE'LL HANDLE THIS!
HOLD YOUR FIRE! IT'S THE LEGION!
THIS IS MORE UP THEIR ALLEY, ANYWAY!
FIRST, YOU GET THEIR ATTENTION!
SKRAK
SKRAK
THEY'RE PANICKING! THEY NEED A LEADER!
HURRY, REEP. IT'S UP TO YOU!
WE'LL LOSE DAWNSTAR'S TRAIL IF WE TAKE TOO LONG.
DON'T WORRY YOUR PRETTY MASK, WILDFIRE.
I'VE GOT THIS WELL IN HAND, OR HOOF!
FOLLOW THE LEADER! GIM, YOU READY?
AS READY AS I CAN BE, CHAMELEON BOY!
I HAVEN'T STOPPED TOO MANY MAMMOTHS IN MY CAREER!
BUT I THINK I'M BIG ENOUGH FOR THE JOB!
WOULDN'T YOU AGR--
TH-THEY'RE DISAPPEARING?
WHAT IN BLAZES IS GOING ON HERE?
WHERE ARE THEY? WHAT HAPPENED?
FIRST DAWNSTAR VANISHES, THEN MAMMOTHS APPEAR AND THEN VANISH, TOO.
I--DON'T UNDER-STAND!
CALL BRAINIAC 5--MAYBE HE PICKED UP SOMETHING!
5

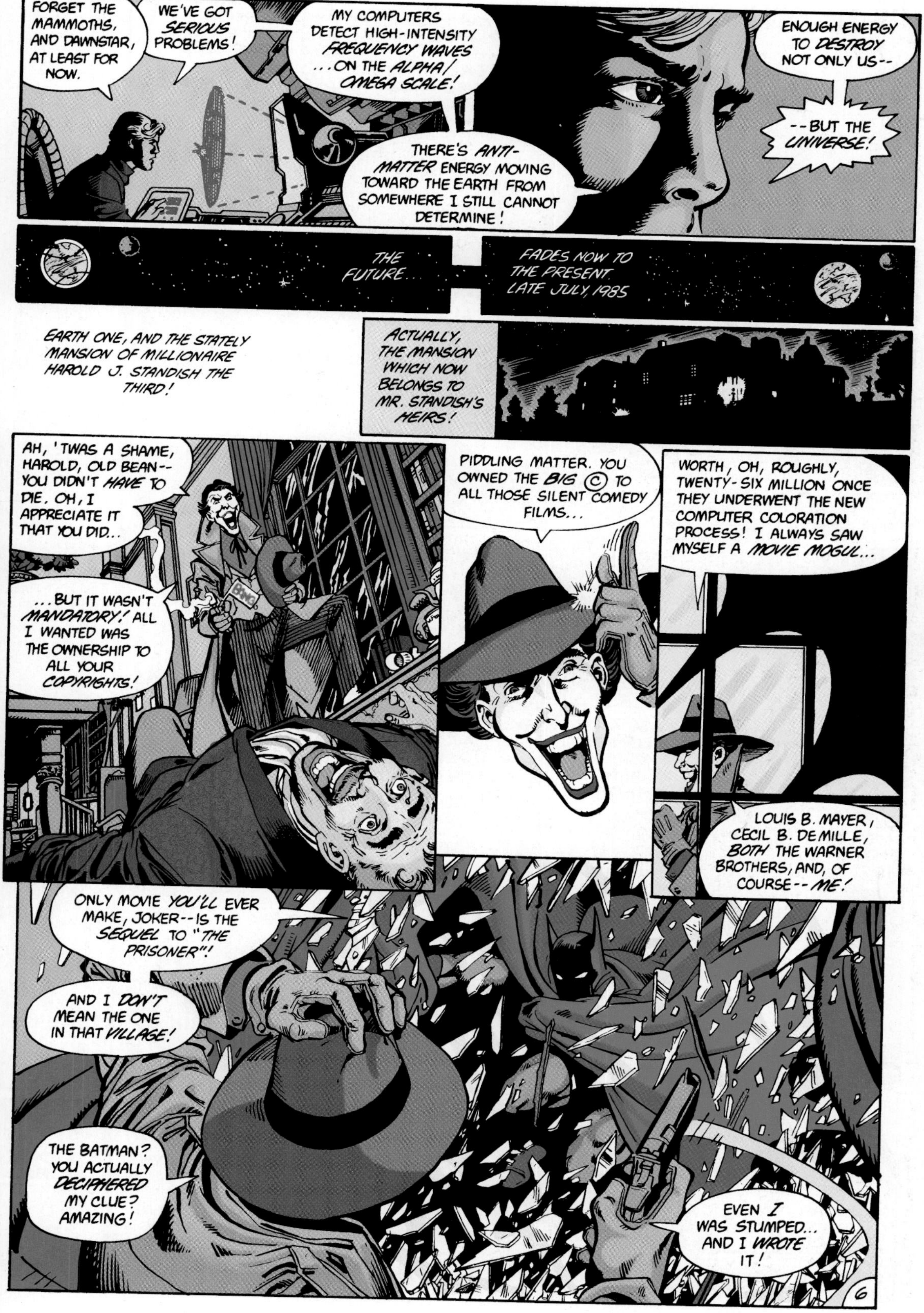
FORGET THE MAMMOTHS, AND DAWNSTAR, AT LEAST FOR NOW.
WE'VE GOT SERIOUS PROBLEMS!
MY COMPUTERS DETECT HIGH-INTENSITY FREQUENCY WAVES ...ON THE ALPHA/OMEGA SCALE!
THERE'S ANTI-MATTER ENERGY MOVING TOWARD THE EARTH FROM SOMEWHERE I STILL CANNOT DETERMINE!
ENOUGH ENERGY TO DESTROY NOT ONLY US--
--BUT THE UNIVERSE!
THE FUTURE...
FADES NOW TO THE PRESENT. LATE JULY, 1985
EARTH ONE, AND THE STATELY MANSION OF MILLIONAIRE HAROLD J. STANDISH THE THIRD!
ACTUALLY, THE MANSION WHICH NOW BELONGS TO MR. STANDISH'S HEIRS!
AH, 'TWAS A SHAME, HAROLD, OLD BEAN--YOU DIDN'T HAVE TO DIE. OH, I APPRECIATE IT THAT YOU DID...
...BUT IT WASN'T MANDATORY! ALL I WANTED WAS THE OWNERSHIP TO ALL YOUR COPYRIGHTS!
PIDDLING MATTER. YOU OWNED THE BIG © TO ALL THOSE SILENT COMEDY FILMS...
WORTH, OH, ROUGHLY, TWENTY-SIX MILLION ONCE THEY UNDERWENT THE NEW COMPUTER COLORATION PROCESS! I ALWAYS SAW MYSELF A MOVIE MOGUL...
LOUIS B. MAYER, CECIL B. DEMILLE, BOTH THE WARNER BROTHERS, AND, OF COURSE--ME!
ONLY MOVIE YOU'LL EVER MAKE, JOKER--IS THE SEQUEL TO "THE PRISONER"!
AND I DON'T MEAN THE ONE IN THAT VILLAGE!
THE BATMAN? YOU ACTUALLY DECIPHERED MY CLUE? AMAZING!
EVEN I WAS STUMPED... AND I WROTE IT!
6

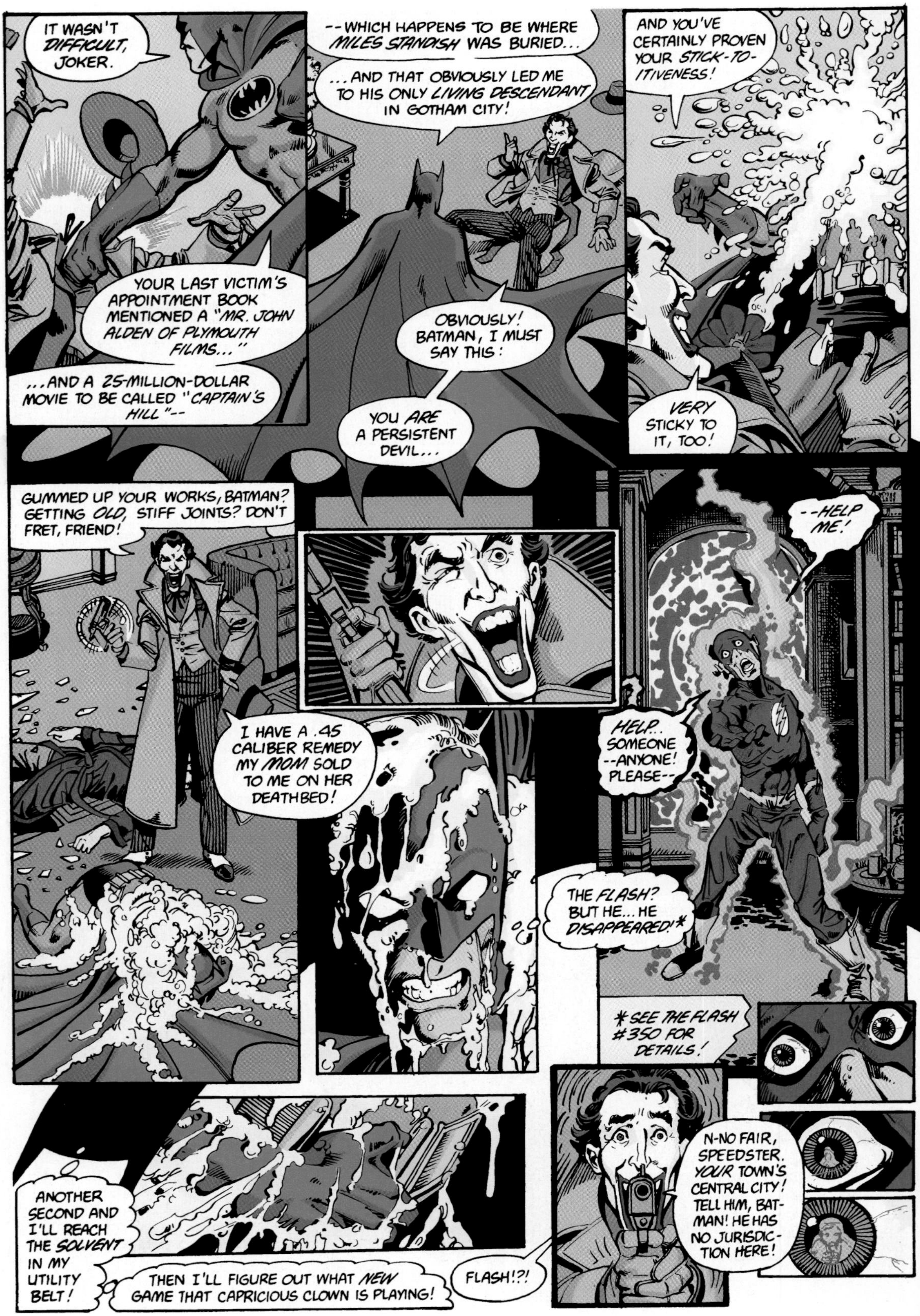
IT WASN'T DIFFICULT, JOKER.
YOUR LAST VICTIM'S APPOINTMENT BOOK MENTIONED A "MR. JOHN ALDEN OF PLYMOUTH FILMS..."
...AND A 25-MILLION-DOLLAR MOVIE TO BE CALLED "CAPTAIN'S HILL"--
--WHICH HAPPENS TO BE WHERE MILES STANDISH WAS BURIED...
...AND THAT OBVIOUSLY LED ME TO HIS ONLY LIVING DESCENDANT IN GOTHAM CITY!
OBVIOUSLY! BATMAN, I MUST SAY THIS:
YOU ARE A PERSISTENT DEVIL...
AND YOU'VE CERTAINLY PROVEN YOUR STICK-TO-ITIVENESS!
VERY STICKY TO IT, TOO!
GUMMED UP YOUR WORKS, BATMAN? GETTING OLD, STIFF JOINTS? DON'T FRET, FRIEND!
I HAVE A .45 CALIBER REMEDY MY MOM SOLD TO ME ON HER DEATHBED!
--HELP ME!
HELP... SOMEONE --ANYONE! PLEASE--
THE FLASH? BUT HE... HE DISAPPEARED!*
*SEE THE FLASH #350 FOR DETAILS!
ANOTHER SECOND AND I'LL REACH THE SOLVENT IN MY UTILITY BELT!
THEN I'LL FIGURE OUT WHAT NEW GAME THAT CAPRICIOUS CLOWN IS PLAYING!
FLASH!?!
N-NO FAIR, SPEEDSTER. YOUR TOWN'S CENTRAL CITY! TELL HIM, BATMAN! HE HAS NO JURISDICTION HERE!

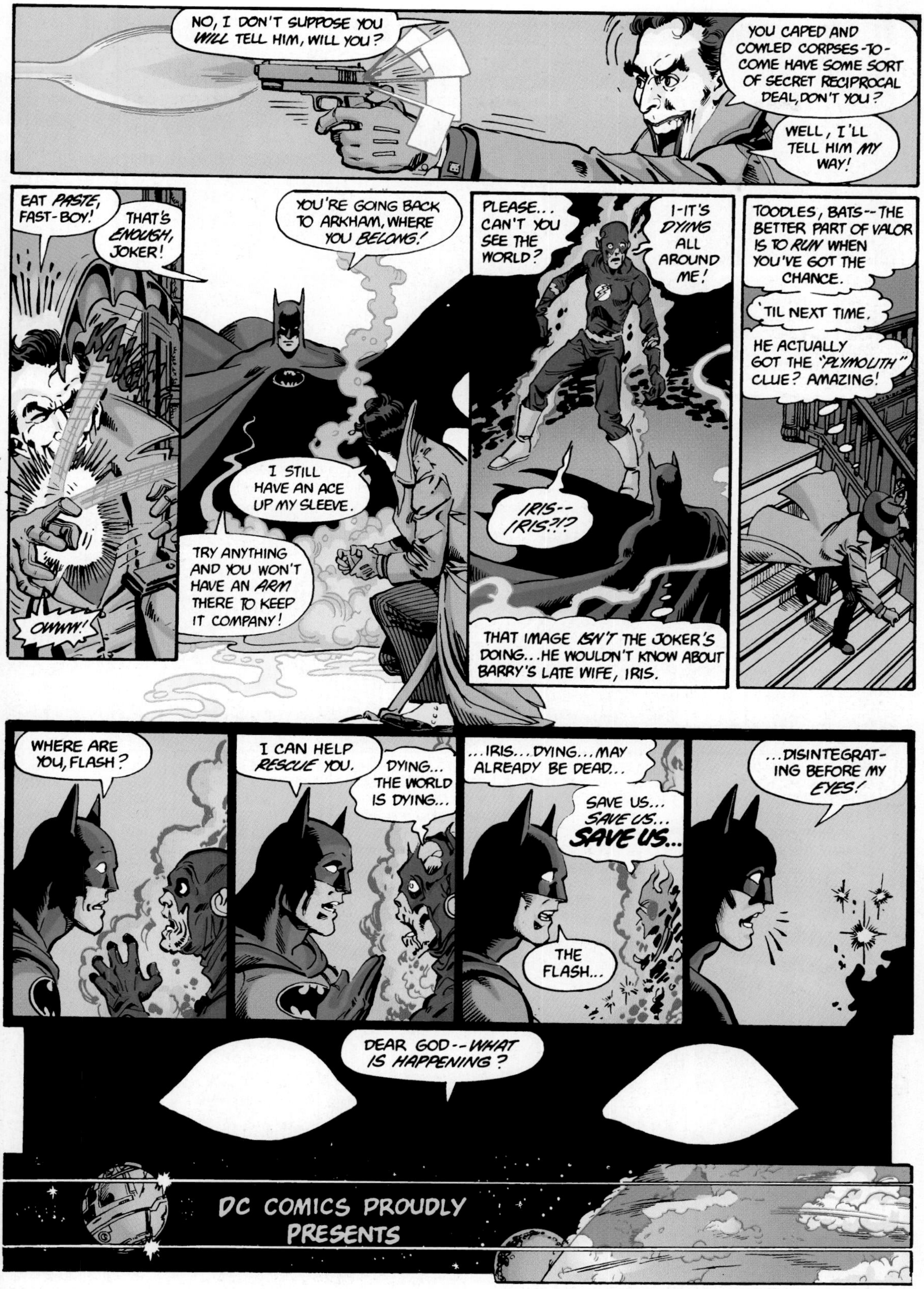
NO, I DON'T SUPPOSE YOU WILL TELL HIM, WILL YOU?
YOU CAPED AND COWLED CORPSES-TO-COME HAVE SOME SORT OF SECRET RECIPROCAL DEAL, DON'T YOU?
WELL, I'LL TELL HIM MY WAY!
EAT PASTE, FAST-BOY!
THAT'S ENOUGH, JOKER!
OWWW!
YOU'RE GOING BACK TO ARKHAM, WHERE YOU BELONG!
I STILL HAVE AN ACE UP MY SLEEVE.
TRY ANYTHING AND YOU WON'T HAVE AN ARM THERE TO KEEP IT COMPANY!
PLEASE... CAN'T YOU SEE THE WORLD?
I-IT'S DYING ALL AROUND ME!
IRIS--IRIS?!?
THAT IMAGE ISN'T THE JOKER'S DOING... HE WOULDN'T KNOW ABOUT BARRY'S LATE WIFE, IRIS.
TOODLES, BATS--THE BETTER PART OF VALOR IS TO RUN WHEN YOU'VE GOT THE CHANCE.
'TIL NEXT TIME.
HE ACTUALLY GOT THE "PLYMOUTH" CLUE? AMAZING!
WHERE ARE YOU, FLASH?
I CAN HELP RESCUE YOU.
DYING... THE WORLD IS DYING...
...IRIS... DYING... MAY ALREADY BE DEAD...
SAVE US... SAVE US... SAVE US...
THE FLASH...
...DISINTEGRATING BEFORE MY EYES!
DEAR GOD--WHAT IS HAPPENING?
DC COMICS PROUDLY PRESENTS

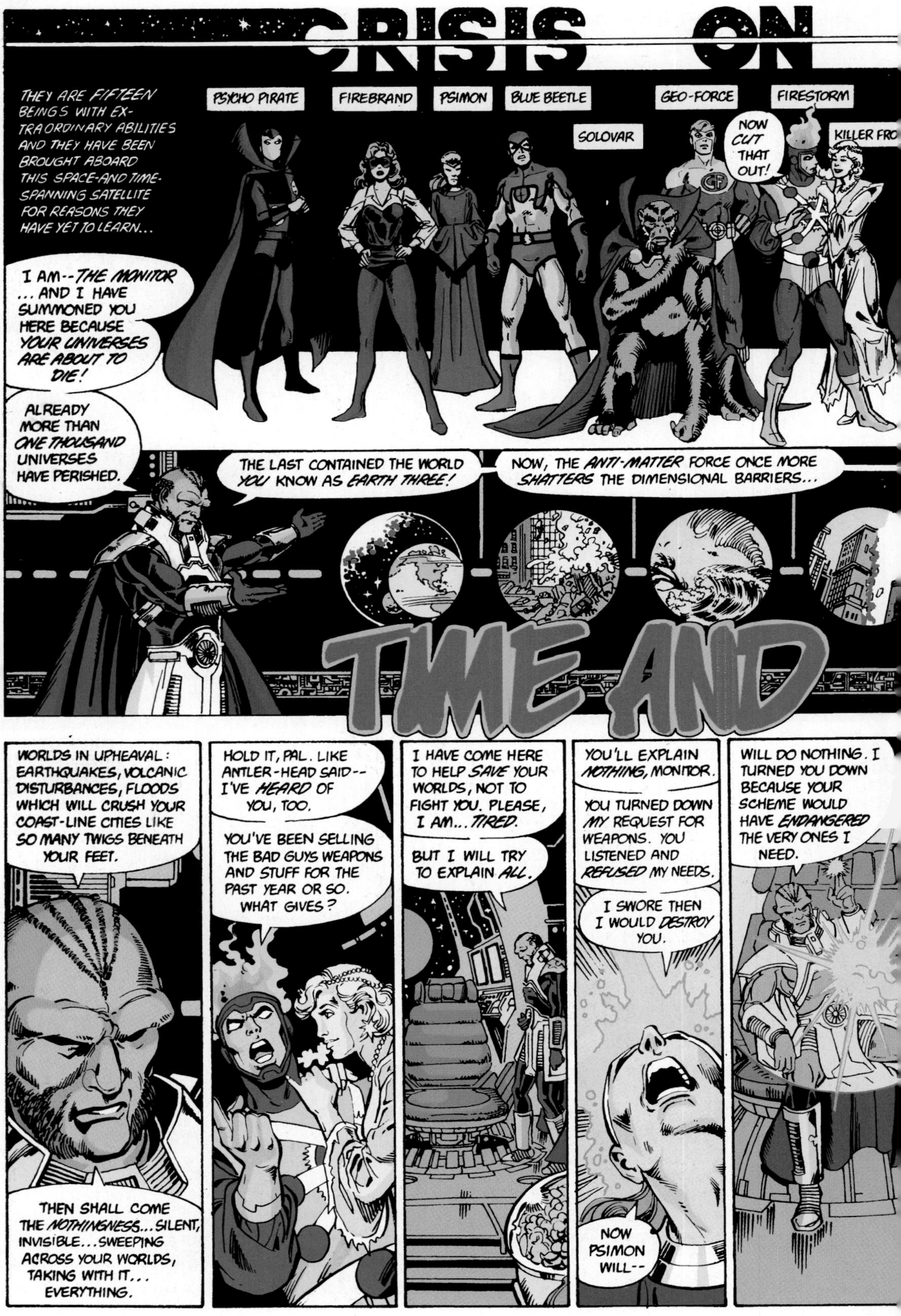
CRISIS ON
THEY ARE FIFTEEN BEINGS WITH EXTRAORDINARY ABILITIES AND THEY HAVE BEEN BROUGHT ABOARD THIS SPACE-AND TIME-SPANNING SATELLITE FOR REASONS THEY HAVE YET TO LEARN...
PSYCHO PIRATE
FIREBRAND
PSIMON
BLUE BEETLE
SOLOVAR
GEO-FORCE
FIRESTORM
KILLER FRO
NOW CUT THAT OUT!
I AM--THE MONITOR ...AND I HAVE SUMMONED YOU HERE BECAUSE YOUR UNIVERSES ARE ABOUT TO DIE!
ALREADY MORE THAN ONE THOUSAND UNIVERSES HAVE PERISHED.
THE LAST CONTAINED THE WORLD YOU KNOW AS EARTH THREE!
NOW, THE ANTI-MATTER FORCE ONCE MORE SHATTERS THE DIMENSIONAL BARRIERS...
TIME AND
WORLDS IN UPHEAVAL: EARTHQUAKES, VOLCANIC DISTURBANCES, FLOODS WHICH WILL CRUSH YOUR COAST-LINE CITIES LIKE SO MANY TWIGS BENEATH YOUR FEET.
THEN SHALL COME THE NOTHINGNESS... SILENT, INVISIBLE... SWEEPING ACROSS YOUR WORLDS, TAKING WITH IT... EVERYTHING.
HOLD IT, PAL. LIKE ANTLER-HEAD SAID-- I'VE HEARD OF YOU, TOO.
YOU'VE BEEN SELLING THE BAD GUYS WEAPONS AND STUFF FOR THE PAST YEAR OR SO. WHAT GIVES?
I HAVE COME HERE TO HELP SAVE YOUR WORLDS, NOT TO FIGHT YOU. PLEASE, I AM... TIRED.
BUT I WILL TRY TO EXPLAIN ALL.
YOU'LL EXPLAIN NOTHING, MONITOR.
YOU TURNED DOWN MY REQUEST FOR WEAPONS. YOU LISTENED AND REFUSED MY NEEDS.
I SWORE THEN I WOULD DESTROY YOU.
NOW PSIMON WILL--
WILL DO NOTHING. I TURNED YOU DOWN BECAUSE YOUR SCHEME WOULD HAVE ENDANGERED THE VERY ONES I NEED.

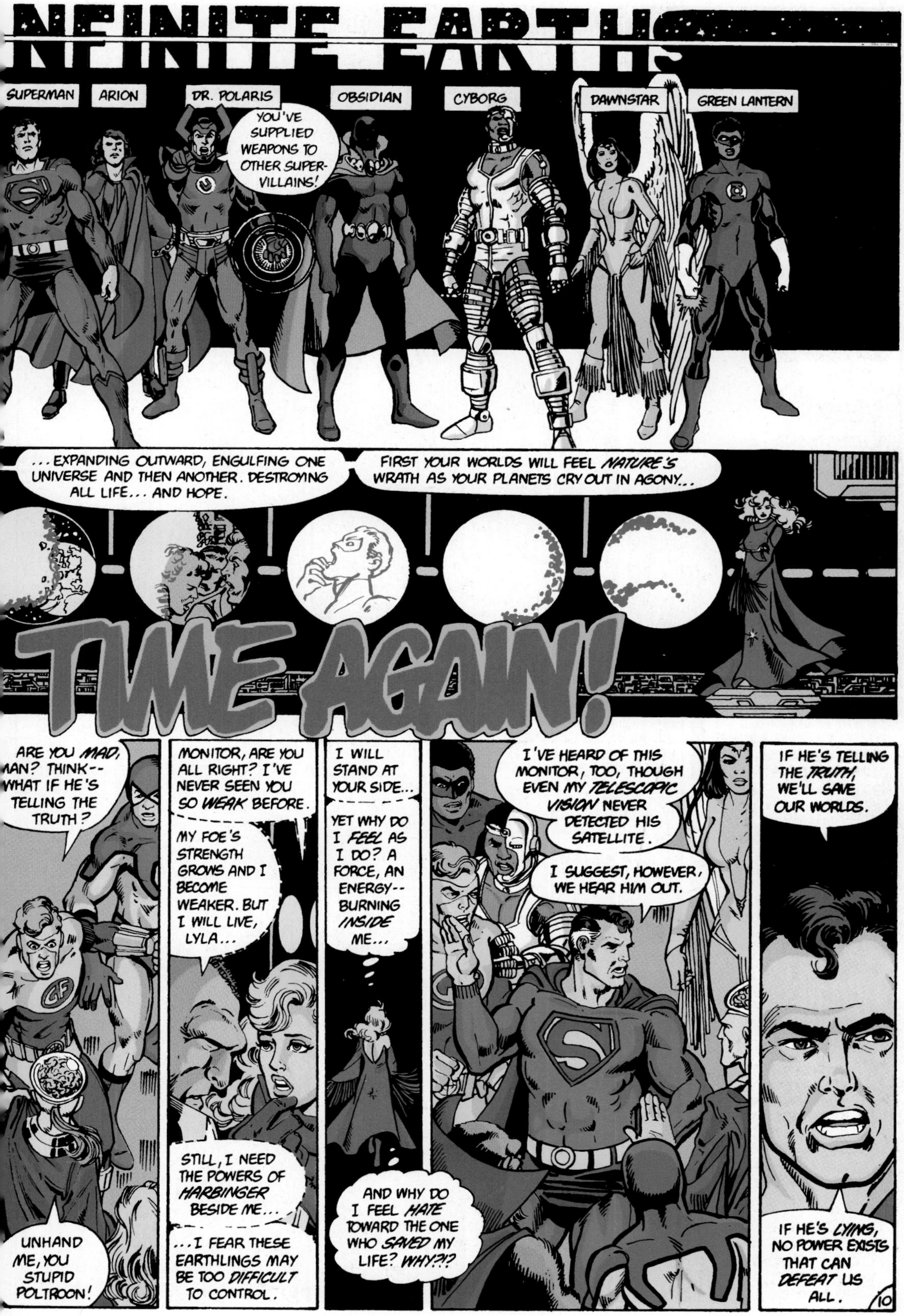
NFINITE EARTHS
SUPERMAN
ARION
DR. POLARIS
OBSIDIAN
CYBORG
DAWNSTAR
GREEN LANTERN
YOU'VE SUPPLIED WEAPONS TO OTHER SUPER-VILLAINS!
... EXPANDING OUTWARD, ENGULFING ONE UNIVERSE AND THEN ANOTHER. DESTROYING ALL LIFE... AND HOPE.
FIRST YOUR WORLDS WILL FEEL NATURE'S WRATH AS YOUR PLANETS CRY OUT IN AGONY...
TIME AGAIN!
ARE YOU MAD, MAN? THINK-- WHAT IF HE'S TELLING THE TRUTH?
UNHAND ME, YOU STUPID POLTROON!
MONITOR, ARE YOU ALL RIGHT? I'VE NEVER SEEN YOU SO WEAK BEFORE.
MY FOE'S STRENGTH GROWS AND I BECOME WEAKER. BUT I WILL LIVE, LYLA...
STILL, I NEED THE POWERS OF HARBINGER BESIDE ME...
...I FEAR THESE EARTHLINGS MAY BE TOO DIFFICULT TO CONTROL.
I WILL STAND AT YOUR SIDE...
YET WHY DO I FEEL AS I DO? A FORCE, AN ENERGY-- BURNING INSIDE ME...
AND WHY DO I FEEL HATE TOWARD THE ONE WHO SAVED MY LIFE? WHY?!?
I'VE HEARD OF THIS MONITOR, TOO, THOUGH EVEN MY TELESCOPIC VISION NEVER DETECTED HIS SATELLITE.
I SUGGEST, HOWEVER, WE HEAR HIM OUT.
IF HE'S TELLING THE TRUTH, WE'LL SAVE OUR WORLDS.
IF HE'S LYING, NO POWER EXISTS THAT CAN DEFEAT US ALL.
10

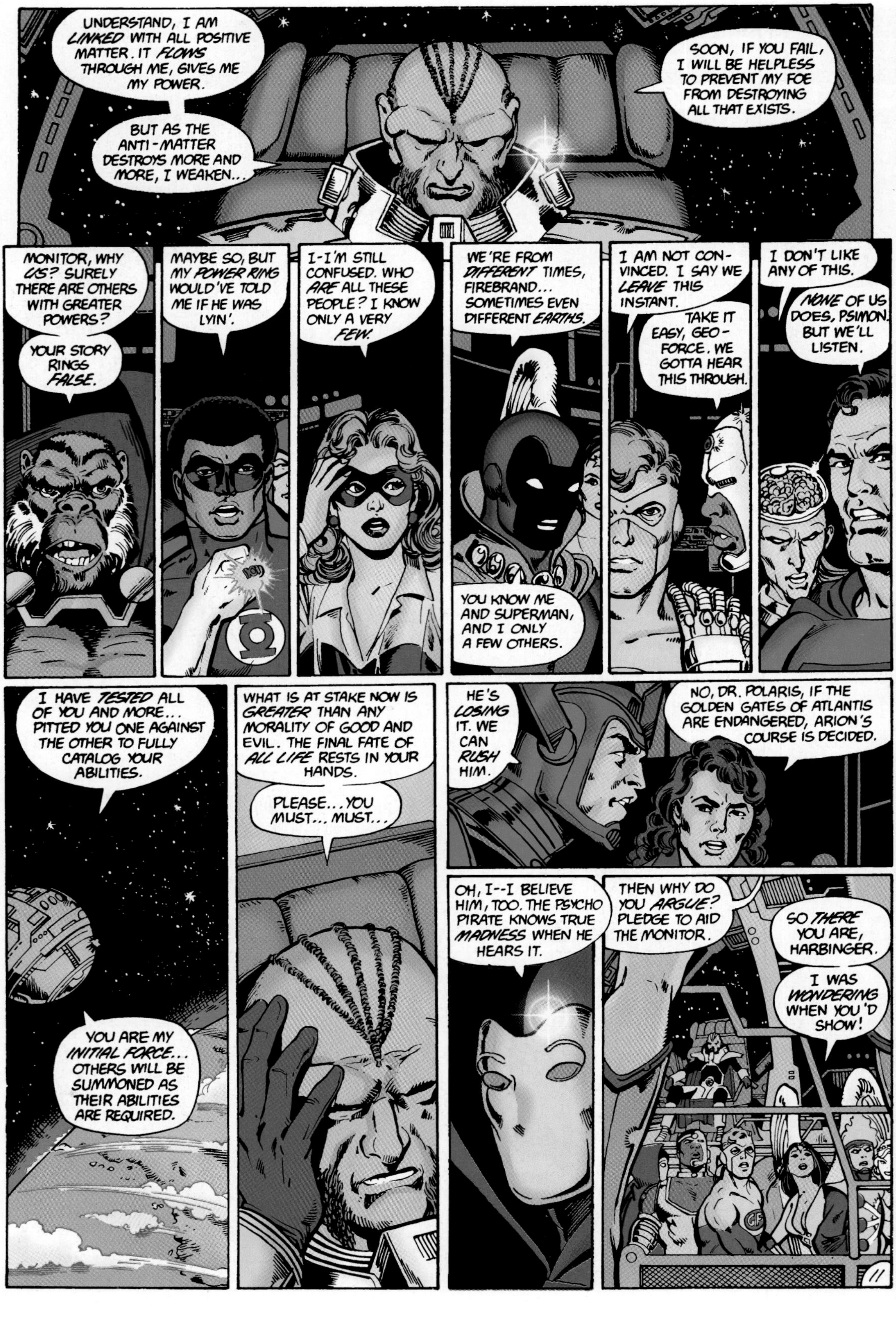
UNDERSTAND, I AM LINKED WITH ALL POSITIVE MATTER. IT FLOWS THROUGH ME, GIVES ME MY POWER.
BUT AS THE ANTI-MATTER DESTROYS MORE AND MORE, I WEAKEN...
SOON, IF YOU FAIL, I WILL BE HELPLESS TO PREVENT MY FOE FROM DESTROYING ALL THAT EXISTS.
MONITOR, WHY US? SURELY THERE ARE OTHERS WITH GREATER POWERS?
YOUR STORY RINGS FALSE.
MAYBE SO, BUT MY POWER RING WOULD'VE TOLD ME IF HE WAS LYIN'.
I-I'M STILL CONFUSED. WHO ARE ALL THESE PEOPLE? I KNOW ONLY A VERY FEW.
WE'RE FROM DIFFERENT TIMES, FIREBRAND... SOMETIMES EVEN DIFFERENT EARTHS.
YOU KNOW ME AND SUPERMAN, AND I ONLY A FEW OTHERS.
I AM NOT CONVINCED. I SAY WE LEAVE THIS INSTANT.
TAKE IT EASY, GEO-FORCE. WE GOTTA HEAR THIS THROUGH.
I DON'T LIKE ANY OF THIS.
NONE OF US DOES, PSIMON. BUT WE'LL LISTEN.
I HAVE TESTED ALL OF YOU AND MORE... PITTED YOU ONE AGAINST THE OTHER TO FULLY CATALOG YOUR ABILITIES.
YOU ARE MY INITIAL FORCE... OTHERS WILL BE SUMMONED AS THEIR ABILITIES ARE REQUIRED.
WHAT IS AT STAKE NOW IS GREATER THAN ANY MORALITY OF GOOD AND EVIL. THE FINAL FATE OF ALL LIFE RESTS IN YOUR HANDS.
PLEASE... YOU MUST... MUST...
HE'S LOSING IT. WE CAN RUSH HIM.
NO, DR. POLARIS, IF THE GOLDEN GATES OF ATLANTIS ARE ENDANGERED, ARION'S COURSE IS DECIDED.
OH, I--I BELIEVE HIM, TOO. THE PSYCHO PIRATE KNOWS TRUE MADNESS WHEN HE HEARS IT.
THEN WHY DO YOU ARGUE? PLEDGE TO AID THE MONITOR.
SO THERE YOU ARE, HARBINGER.
I WAS WONDERING WHEN YOU'D SHOW!
11

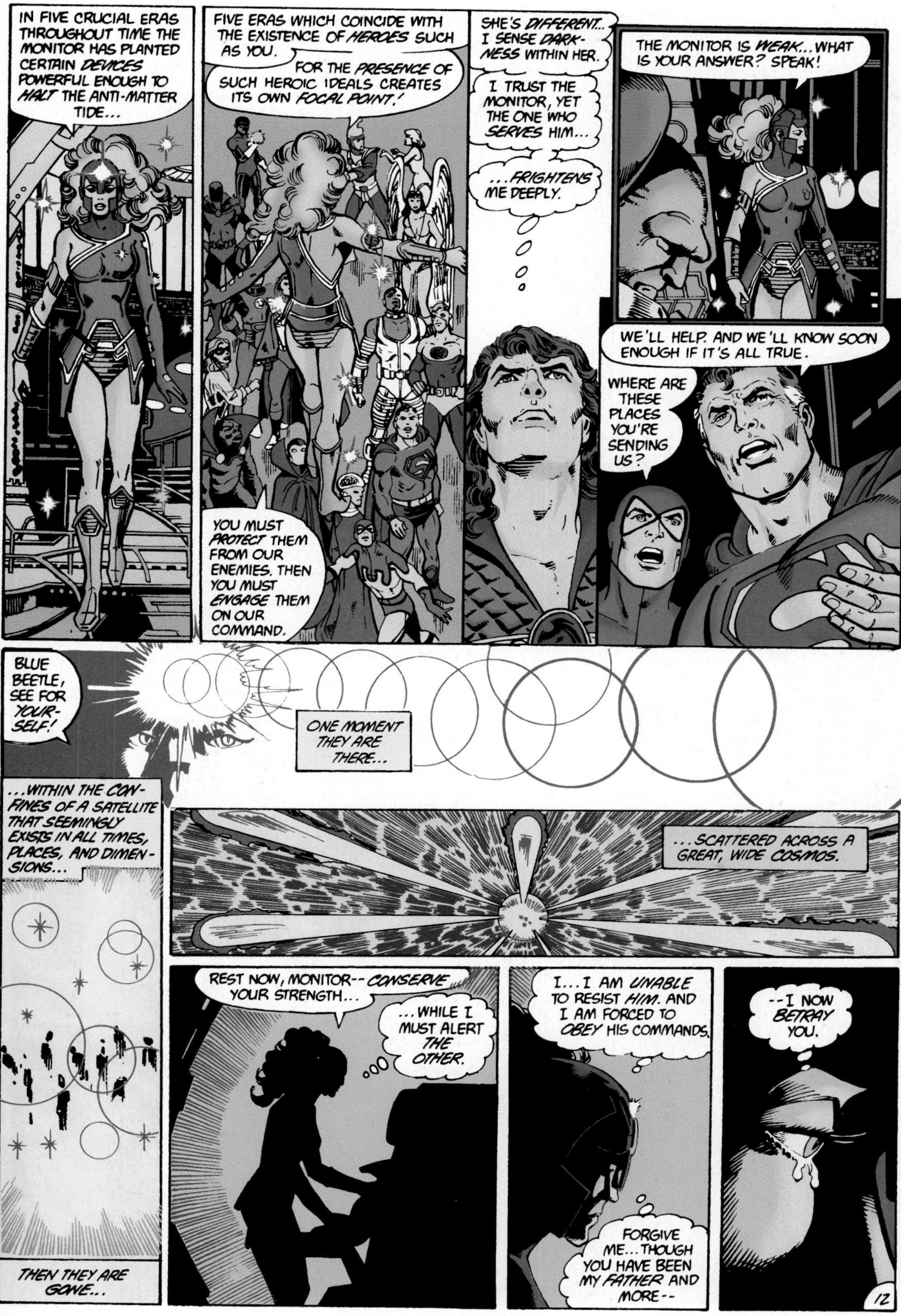
IN FIVE CRUCIAL ERAS THROUGHOUT TIME THE MONITOR HAS PLANTED CERTAIN DEVICES POWERFUL ENOUGH TO HALT THE ANTI-MATTER TIDE...
FIVE ERAS WHICH COINCIDE WITH THE EXISTENCE OF HEROES SUCH AS YOU.
FOR THE PRESENCE OF SUCH HEROIC IDEALS CREATES ITS OWN FOCAL POINT!
YOU MUST PROTECT THEM FROM OUR ENEMIES. THEN YOU MUST ENGAGE THEM ON OUR COMMAND.
SHE'S DIFFERENT... I SENSE DARKNESS WITHIN HER.
I TRUST THE MONITOR, YET THE ONE WHO SERVES HIM...
...FRIGHTENS ME DEEPLY.
THE MONITOR IS WEAK... WHAT IS YOUR ANSWER? SPEAK!
WE'LL HELP. AND WE'LL KNOW SOON ENOUGH IF IT'S ALL TRUE.
WHERE ARE THESE PLACES YOU'RE SENDING US?
BLUE BEETLE, SEE FOR YOURSELF!
ONE MOMENT THEY ARE THERE...
...WITHIN THE CONFINES OF A SATELLITE THAT SEEMINGLY EXISTS IN ALL TIMES, PLACES, AND DIMENSIONS...
...SCATTERED ACROSS A GREAT, WIDE COSMOS.
THEN THEY ARE GONE...
REST NOW, MONITOR--CONSERVE YOUR STRENGTH...
...WHILE I MUST ALERT THE OTHER.
I...I AM UNABLE TO RESIST HIM. AND I AM FORCED TO OBEY HIS COMMANDS.
FORGIVE ME... THOUGH YOU HAVE BEEN MY FATHER AND MORE--
--I NOW BETRAY YOU.
12

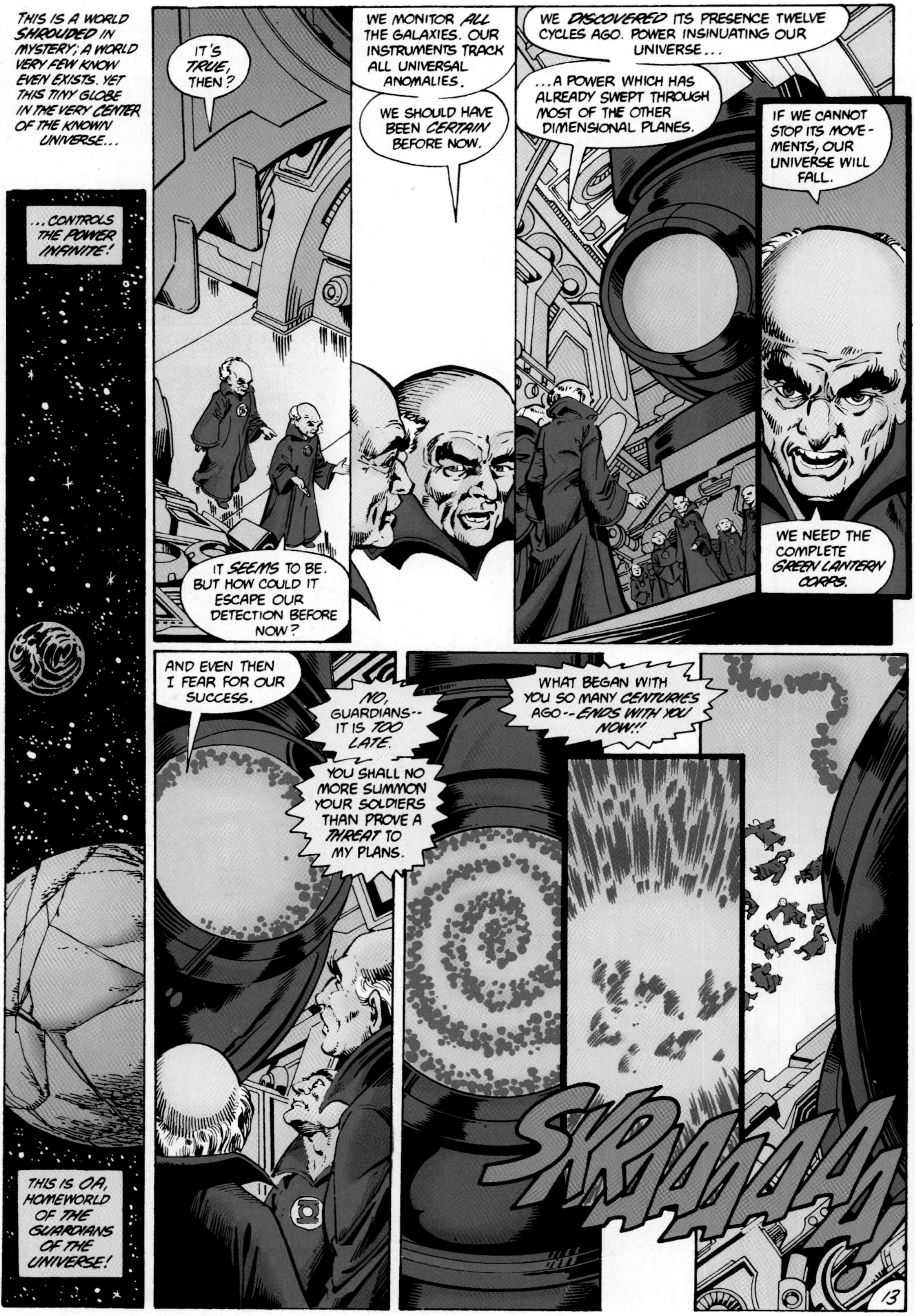

THIS IS A WORLD SHROUDED IN MYSTERY; A WORLD VERY FEW KNOW EVEN EXISTS. YET THIS TINY GLOBE IN THE VERY CENTER OF THE KNOWN UNIVERSE...
...CONTROLS THE POWER INFINITE!
IT'S TRUE, THEN?
IT SEEMS TO BE. BUT HOW COULD IT ESCAPE OUR DETECTION BEFORE NOW?
WE MONITOR ALL THE GALAXIES. OUR INSTRUMENTS TRACK ALL UNIVERSAL ANOMALIES.
WE SHOULD HAVE BEEN CERTAIN BEFORE NOW.
WE DISCOVERED ITS PRESENCE TWELVE CYCLES AGO. POWER INSINUATING OUR UNIVERSE...
...A POWER WHICH HAS ALREADY SWEPT THROUGH MOST OF THE OTHER DIMENSIONAL PLANES.
IF WE CANNOT STOP ITS MOVEMENTS, OUR UNIVERSE WILL FALL.
WE NEED THE COMPLETE GREEN LANTERN CORPS.
AND EVEN THEN I FEAR FOR OUR SUCCESS.
NO, GUARDIANS-- IT IS TOO LATE.
YOU SHALL NO MORE SUMMON YOUR SOLDIERS THAN PROVE A THREAT TO MY PLANS.
WHAT BEGAN WITH YOU SO MANY CENTURIES AGO-- ENDS WITH YOU NOW!!
SKRAAAAA
THIS IS OA, HOMEWORLD OF THE GUARDIANS OF THE UNIVERSE!
13

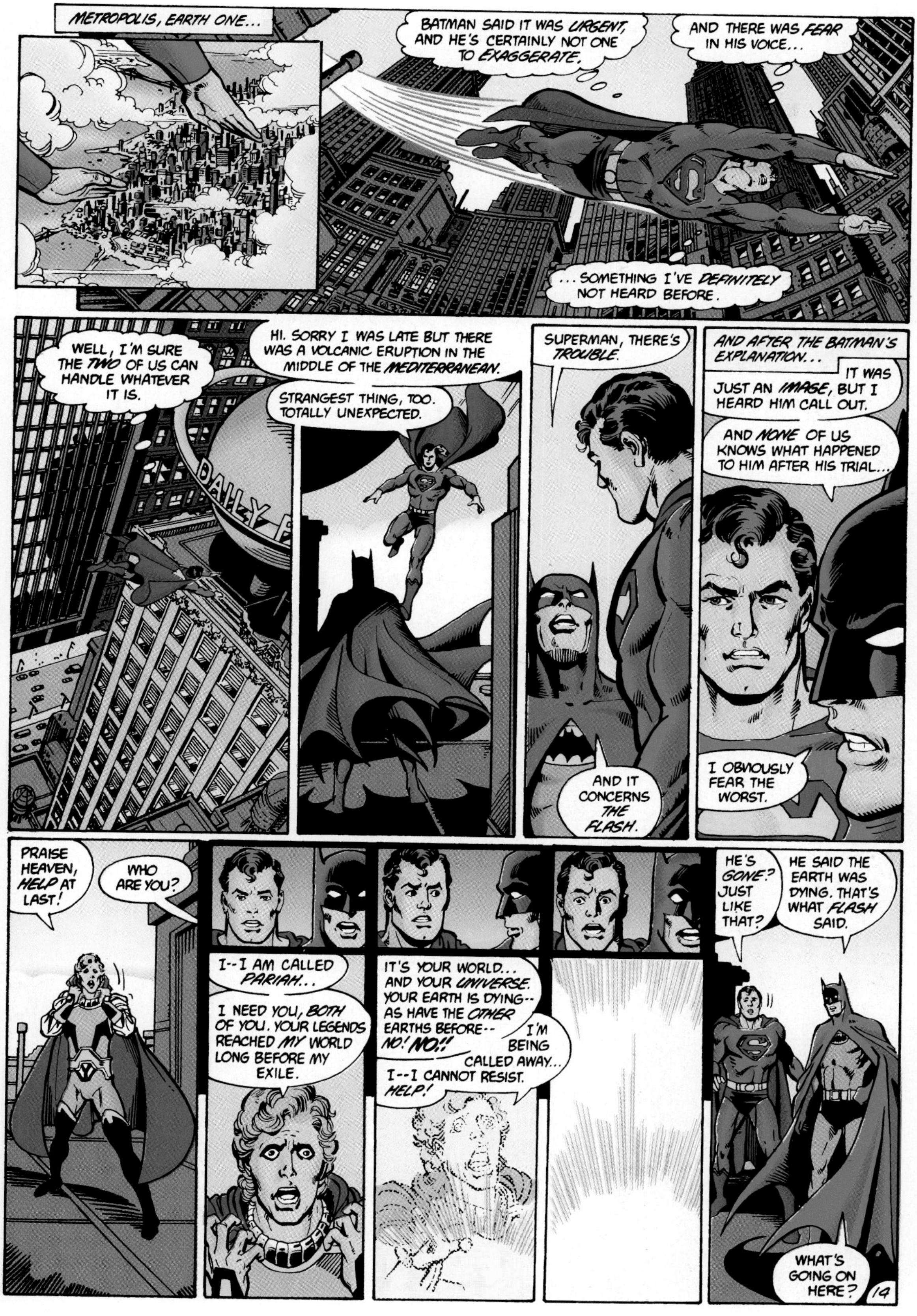

METROPOLIS, EARTH ONE...
BATMAN SAID IT WAS URGENT, AND HE'S CERTAINLY NOT ONE TO EXAGGERATE.
AND THERE WAS FEAR IN HIS VOICE...
...SOMETHING I'VE DEFINITELY NOT HEARD BEFORE.
WELL, I'M SURE THE TWO OF US CAN HANDLE WHATEVER IT IS.
HI. SORRY I WAS LATE BUT THERE WAS A VOLCANIC ERUPTION IN THE MIDDLE OF THE MEDITERRANEAN.
STRANGEST THING, TOO. TOTALLY UNEXPECTED.
SUPERMAN, THERE'S TROUBLE.
AND IT CONCERNS THE FLASH.
AND AFTER THE BATMAN'S EXPLANATION...
IT WAS JUST AN IMAGE, BUT I HEARD HIM CALL OUT.
AND NONE OF US KNOWS WHAT HAPPENED TO HIM AFTER HIS TRIAL...
I OBVIOUSLY FEAR THE WORST.
PRAISE HEAVEN, HELP AT LAST!
WHO ARE YOU?
I--I AM CALLED PARIAH...
I NEED YOU, BOTH OF YOU. YOUR LEGENDS REACHED MY WORLD LONG BEFORE MY EXILE.
IT'S YOUR WORLD... AND YOUR UNIVERSE. YOUR EARTH IS DYING-- AS HAVE THE OTHER EARTHS BEFORE-- NO! NO!!
I'M BEING CALLED AWAY...
I--I CANNOT RESIST. HELP!
HE'S GONE? JUST LIKE THAT?
HE SAID THE EARTH WAS DYING. THAT'S WHAT FLASH SAID.
WHAT'S GOING ON HERE?
14

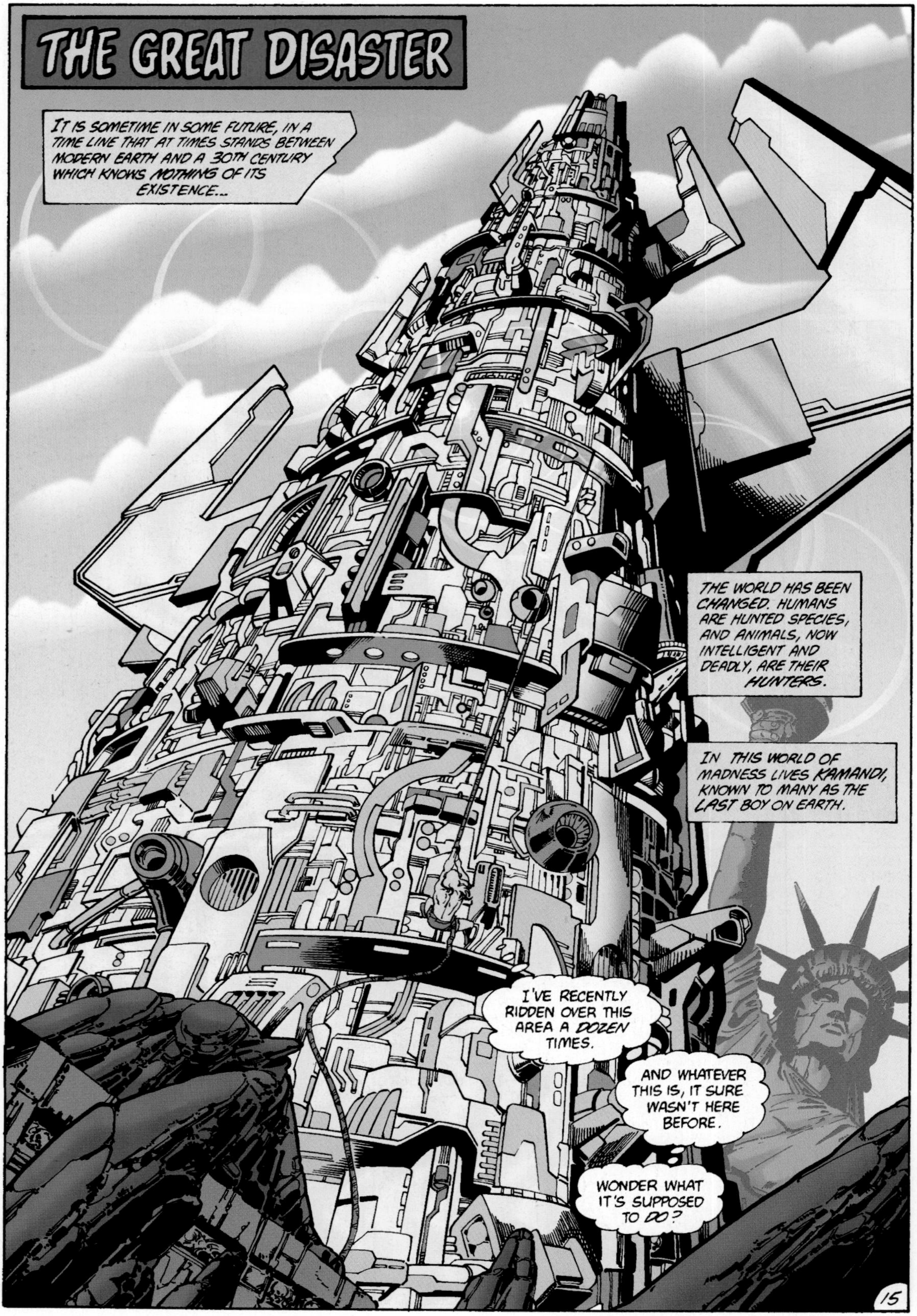
THE GREAT DISASTER
IT IS SOMETIME IN SOME FUTURE, IN A TIME LINE THAT AT TIMES STANDS BETWEEN MODERN EARTH AND A 30TH CENTURY WHICH KNOWS NOTHING OF ITS EXISTENCE...
THE WORLD HAS BEEN CHANGED. HUMANS ARE HUNTED SPECIES, AND ANIMALS, NOW INTELLIGENT AND DEADLY, ARE THEIR HUNTERS.
IN THIS WORLD OF MADNESS LIVES KAMANDI, KNOWN TO MANY AS THE LAST BOY ON EARTH.
I'VE RECENTLY RIDDEN OVER THIS AREA A DOZEN TIMES.
AND WHATEVER THIS IS, IT SURE WASN'T HERE BEFORE.
WONDER WHAT IT'S SUPPOSED TO DO?
15

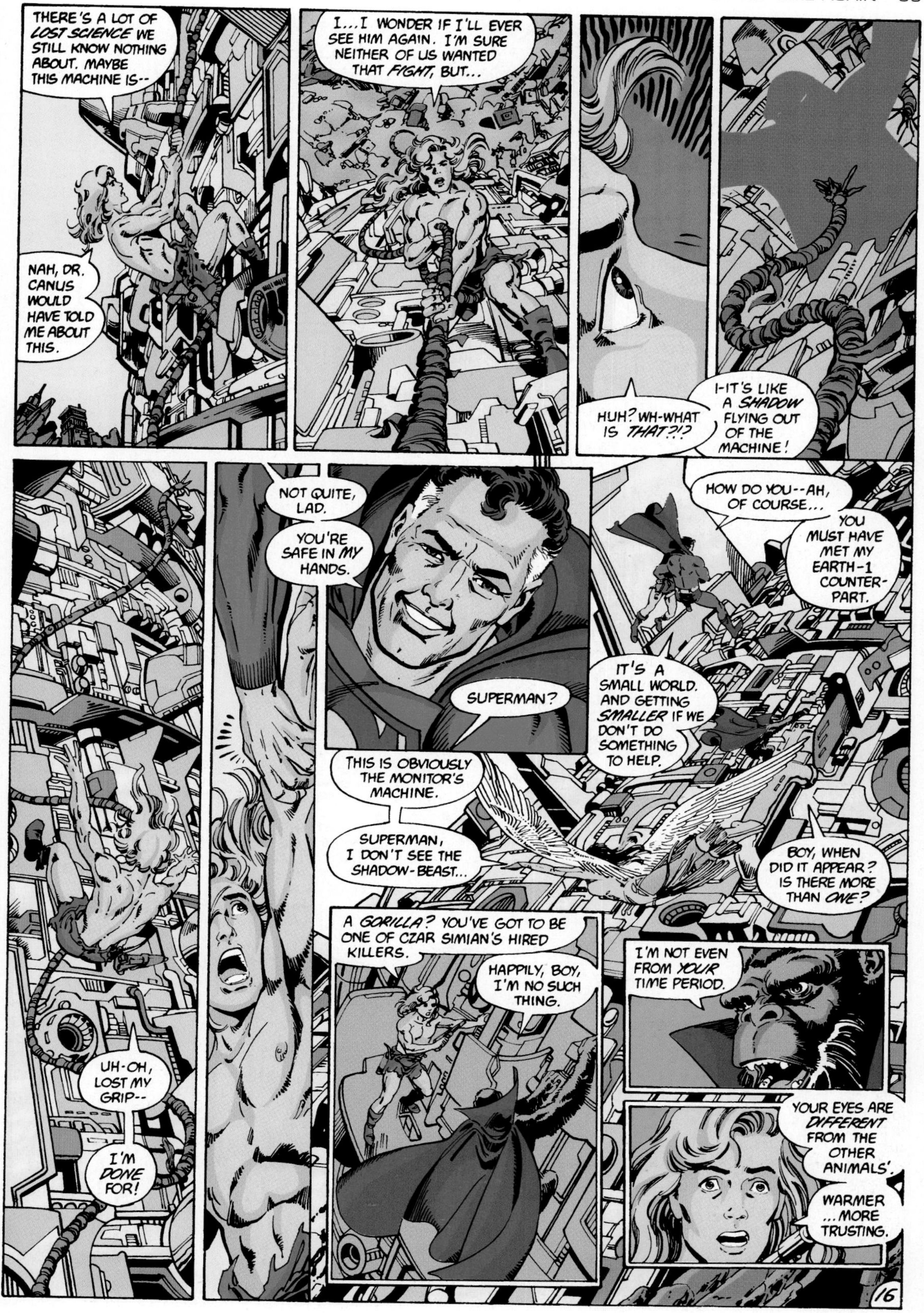
THERE'S A LOT OF LOST SCIENCE WE STILL KNOW NOTHING ABOUT. MAYBE THIS MACHINE IS--
NAH, DR. CANUS WOULD HAVE TOLD ME ABOUT THIS.
I...I WONDER IF I'LL EVER SEE HIM AGAIN. I'M SURE NEITHER OF US WANTED THAT FIGHT, BUT...
HUH? WH-WHAT IS THAT?!?
I-IT'S LIKE A SHADOW FLYING OUT OF THE MACHINE!
UH-OH, LOST MY GRIP--
I'M DONE FOR!
NOT QUITE, LAD.
YOU'RE SAFE IN MY HANDS.
SUPERMAN?
HOW DO YOU--AH, OF COURSE...
YOU MUST HAVE MET MY EARTH-1 COUNTER-PART.
IT'S A SMALL WORLD. AND GETTING SMALLER IF WE DON'T DO SOMETHING TO HELP.
THIS IS OBVIOUSLY THE MONITOR'S MACHINE.
SUPERMAN, I DON'T SEE THE SHADOW-BEAST...
BOY, WHEN DID IT APPEAR? IS THERE MORE THAN ONE?
A GORILLA? YOU'VE GOT TO BE ONE OF CZAR SIMIAN'S HIRED KILLERS.
HAPPILY, BOY, I'M NO SUCH THING.
I'M NOT EVEN FROM YOUR TIME PERIOD.
YOUR EYES ARE DIFFERENT FROM THE OTHER ANIMALS'.
WARMER ...MORE TRUSTING.
16

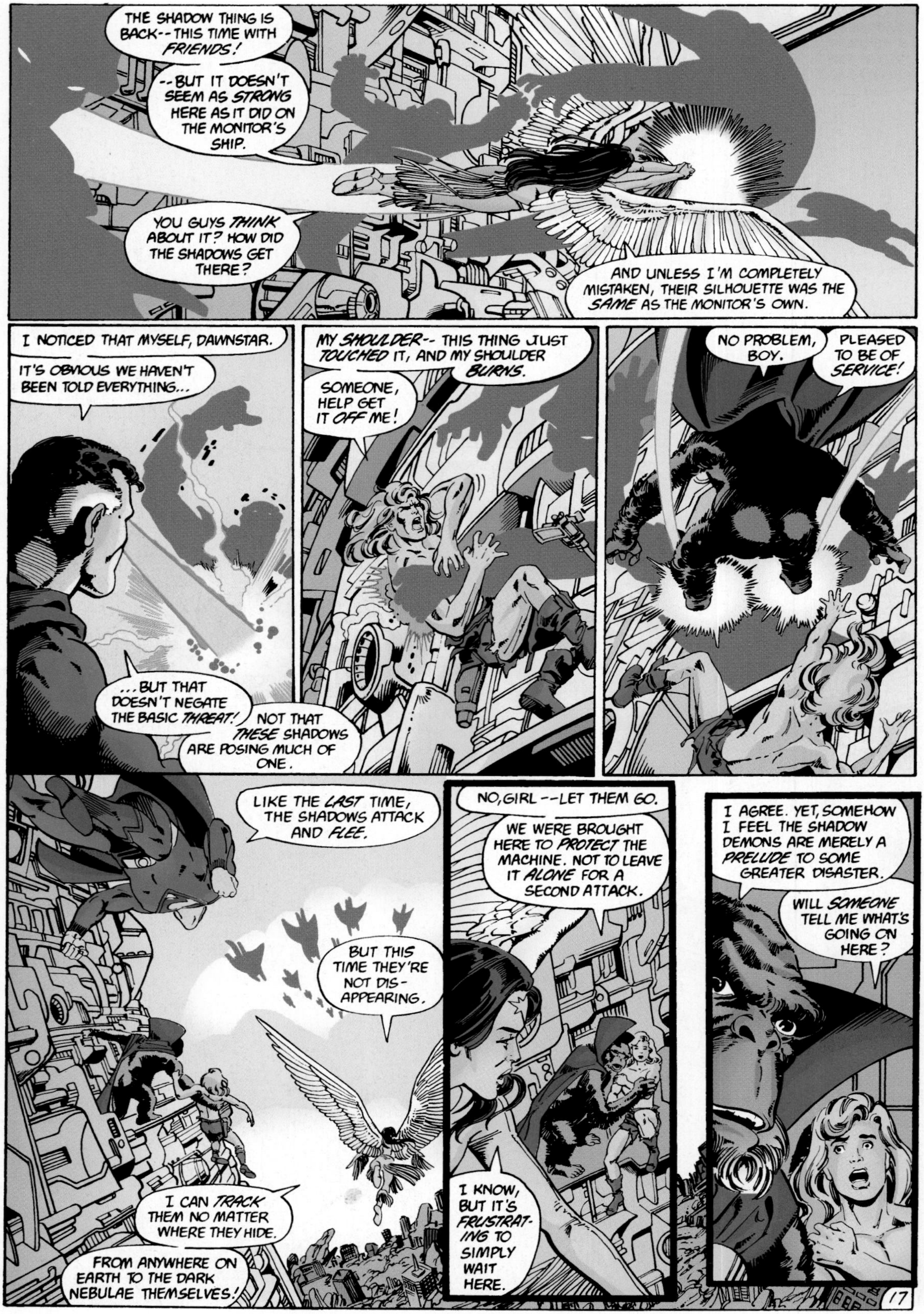
THE SHADOW THING IS BACK--THIS TIME WITH FRIENDS!
--BUT IT DOESN'T SEEM AS STRONG HERE AS IT DID ON THE MONITOR'S SHIP.
YOU GUYS THINK ABOUT IT? HOW DID THE SHADOWS GET THERE?
AND UNLESS I'M COMPLETELY MISTAKEN, THEIR SILHOUETTE WAS THE SAME AS THE MONITOR'S OWN.
I NOTICED THAT MYSELF, DAWNSTAR.
IT'S OBVIOUS WE HAVEN'T BEEN TOLD EVERYTHING...
...BUT THAT DOESN'T NEGATE THE BASIC THREAT!
NOT THAT THESE SHADOWS ARE POSING MUCH OF ONE.
MY SHOULDER-- THIS THING JUST TOUCHED IT, AND MY SHOULDER BURNS.
SOMEONE, HELP GET IT OFF ME!
NO PROBLEM, BOY.
PLEASED TO BE OF SERVICE!
LIKE THE LAST TIME, THE SHADOWS ATTACK AND FLEE.
BUT THIS TIME THEY'RE NOT DIS-APPEARING.
I CAN TRACK THEM NO MATTER WHERE THEY HIDE.
FROM ANYWHERE ON EARTH TO THE DARK NEBULAE THEMSELVES!
NO, GIRL--LET THEM GO.
WE WERE BROUGHT HERE TO PROTECT THE MACHINE. NOT TO LEAVE IT ALONE FOR A SECOND ATTACK.
I KNOW, BUT IT'S FRUSTRAT-ING TO SIMPLY WAIT HERE.
I AGREE. YET, SOMEHOW I FEEL THE SHADOW DEMONS ARE MERELY A PRELUDE TO SOME GREATER DISASTER.
WILL SOMEONE TELL ME WHAT'S GOING ON HERE?
17

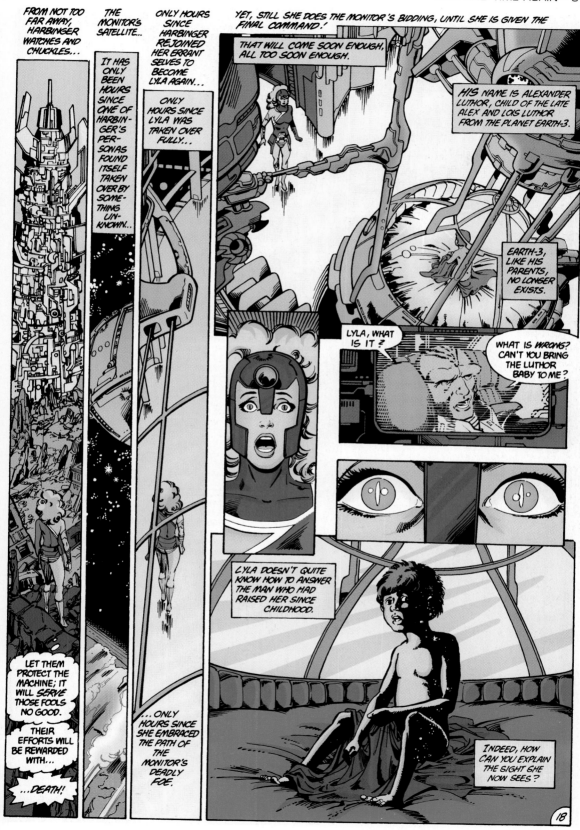

FROM NOT TOO FAR AWAY, HARBINGER WATCHES AND CHUCKLES...

LET THEM PROTECT THE MACHINE; IT WILL *SERVE* THOSE FOOLS NO GOOD.

THEIR EFFORTS WILL BE REWARDED WITH...

...*DEATH!*

THE MONITOR'S SATELLITE...

IT HAS ONLY BEEN HOURS SINCE ONE OF HARBINGER'S PERSONAS FOUND ITSELF TAKEN OVER BY SOMETHING UNKNOWN...

ONLY HOURS SINCE HARBINGER REJOINED HER ERRANT SELVES TO BECOME LYLA AGAIN...

ONLY HOURS SINCE LYLA WAS TAKEN OVER FULLY...

...ONLY HOURS SINCE SHE EMBRACED THE PATH OF THE MONITOR'S DEADLY FOE.

YET, STILL SHE DOES THE MONITOR'S BIDDING, UNTIL SHE IS GIVEN THE FINAL COMMAND.'

THAT WILL COME SOON ENOUGH, ALL TOO SOON ENOUGH.

HIS NAME IS ALEXANDER LUTHOR, CHILD OF THE LATE ALEX AND LOIS LUTHOR FROM THE PLANET EARTH-3.

EARTH-3, LIKE HIS PARENTS, NO LONGER EXISTS.

LYLA, WHAT IS IT?

WHAT IS *WRONG?* CAN'T YOU BRING THE LUTHOR BABY TO ME?

LYLA DOESN'T QUITE KNOW HOW TO ANSWER THE MAN WHO HAD RAISED HER SINCE CHILDHOOD.

INDEED, HOW CAN YOU EXPLAIN THE SIGHT SHE NOW SEES?

18

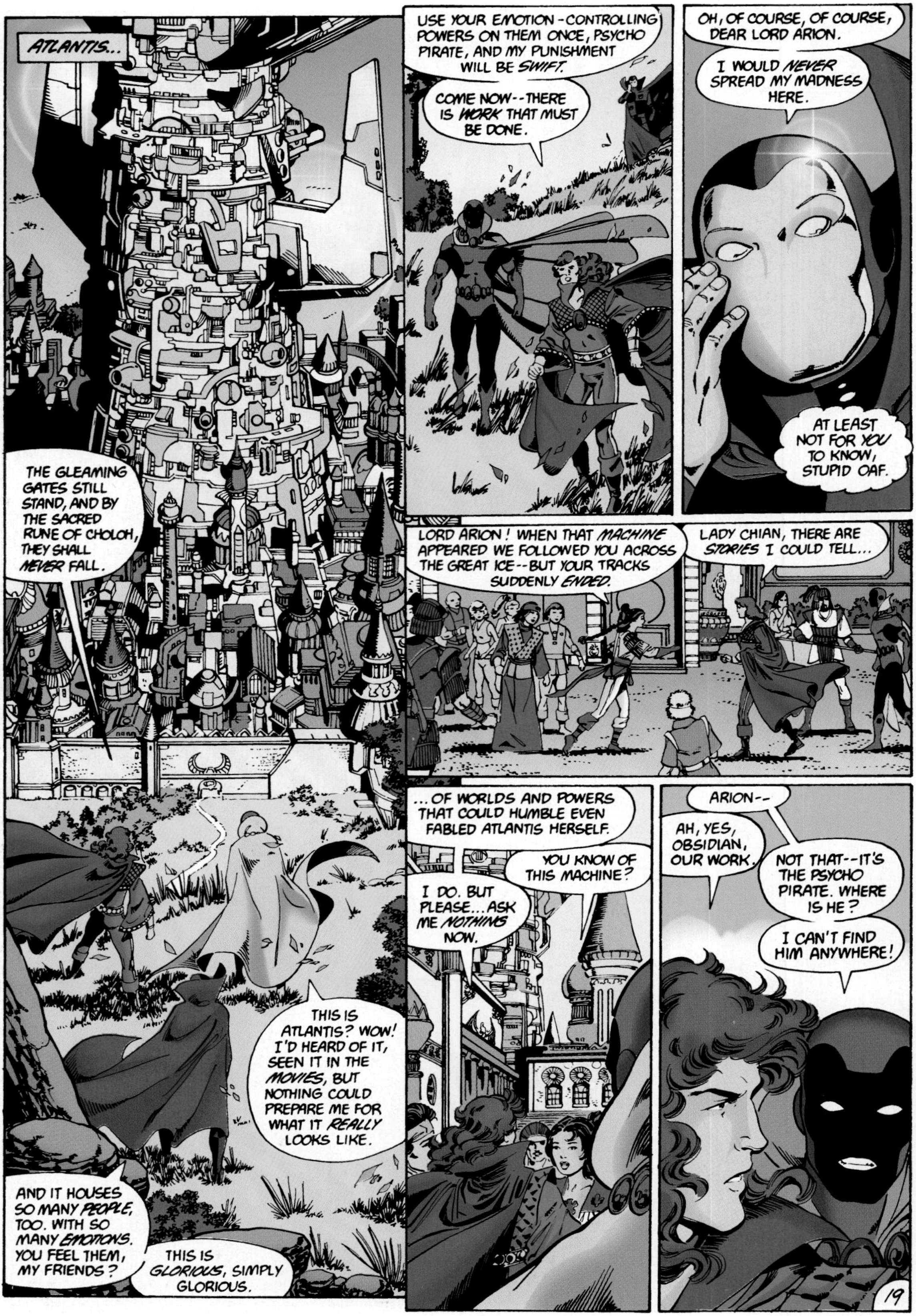
ATLANTIS...
THE GLEAMING GATES STILL STAND, AND BY THE SACRED RUNE OF CHOLOH, THEY SHALL NEVER FALL.
THIS IS ATLANTIS? WOW! I'D HEARD OF IT, SEEN IT IN THE MOVIES, BUT NOTHING COULD PREPARE ME FOR WHAT IT REALLY LOOKS LIKE.
AND IT HOUSES SO MANY PEOPLE, TOO. WITH SO MANY EMOTIONS. YOU FEEL THEM, MY FRIENDS?
THIS IS GLORIOUS, SIMPLY GLORIOUS.
USE YOUR EMOTION-CONTROLLING POWERS ON THEM ONCE, PSYCHO PIRATE, AND MY PUNISHMENT WILL BE SWIFT.
COME NOW--THERE IS WORK THAT MUST BE DONE.
OH, OF COURSE, OF COURSE, DEAR LORD ARION.
I WOULD NEVER SPREAD MY MADNESS HERE.
AT LEAST NOT FOR YOU TO KNOW, STUPID OAF.
LORD ARION! WHEN THAT MACHINE APPEARED WE FOLLOWED YOU ACROSS THE GREAT ICE--BUT YOUR TRACKS SUDDENLY ENDED.
LADY CHIAN, THERE ARE STORIES I COULD TELL...
...OF WORLDS AND POWERS THAT COULD HUMBLE EVEN FABLED ATLANTIS HERSELF.
YOU KNOW OF THIS MACHINE?
I DO. BUT PLEASE... ASK ME NOTHING NOW.
ARION--
AH, YES, OBSIDIAN, OUR WORK.
NOT THAT--IT'S THE PSYCHO PIRATE. WHERE IS HE?
I CAN'T FIND HIM ANYWHERE!
19

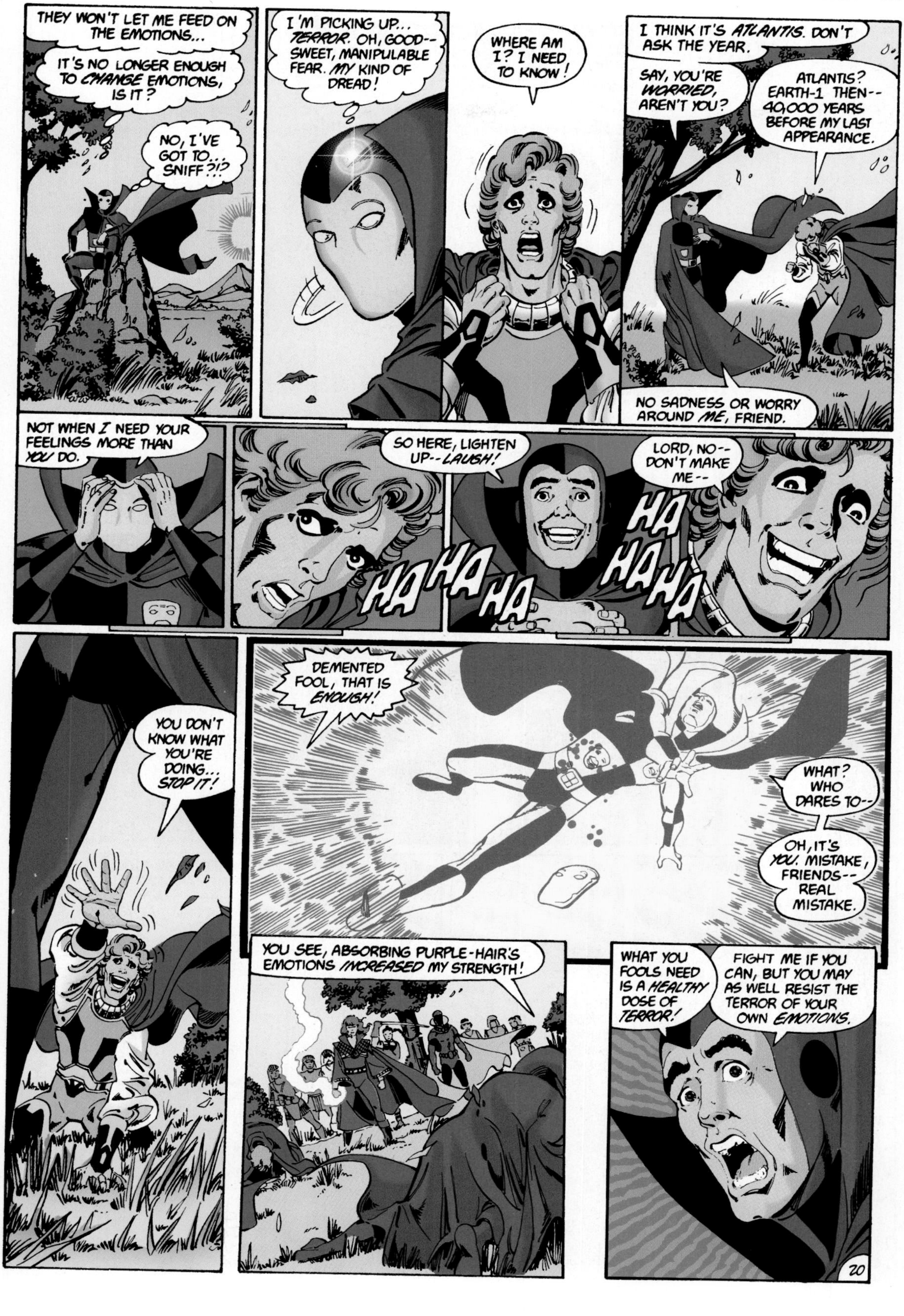
THEY WON'T LET ME FEED ON THE EMOTIONS...
IT'S NO LONGER ENOUGH TO CHANGE EMOTIONS, IS IT?
NO, I'VE GOT TO... SNIFF?!?
I'M PICKING UP... TERROR. OH, GOOD-- SWEET, MANIPULABLE FEAR. MY KIND OF DREAD!
WHERE AM I? I NEED TO KNOW!
I THINK IT'S ATLANTIS. DON'T ASK THE YEAR.
SAY, YOU'RE WORRIED, AREN'T YOU?
ATLANTIS? EARTH-1 THEN-- 40,000 YEARS BEFORE MY LAST APPEARANCE.
NO SADNESS OR WORRY AROUND ME, FRIEND.
NOT WHEN I NEED YOUR FEELINGS MORE THAN YOU DO.
SO HERE, LIGHTEN UP--LAUGH!
LORD, NO-- DON'T MAKE ME--
HAHAHAHA
HAHAHAHA
YOU DON'T KNOW WHAT YOU'RE DOING... STOP IT!
DEMENTED FOOL, THAT IS ENOUGH!
WHAT? WHO DARES TO--
OH, IT'S YOU. MISTAKE, FRIENDS-- REAL MISTAKE.
YOU SEE, ABSORBING PURPLE-HAIR'S EMOTIONS INCREASED MY STRENGTH!
WHAT YOU FOOLS NEED IS A HEALTHY DOSE OF TERROR!
FIGHT ME IF YOU CAN, BUT YOU MAY AS WELL RESIST THE TERROR OF YOUR OWN EMOTIONS.
20

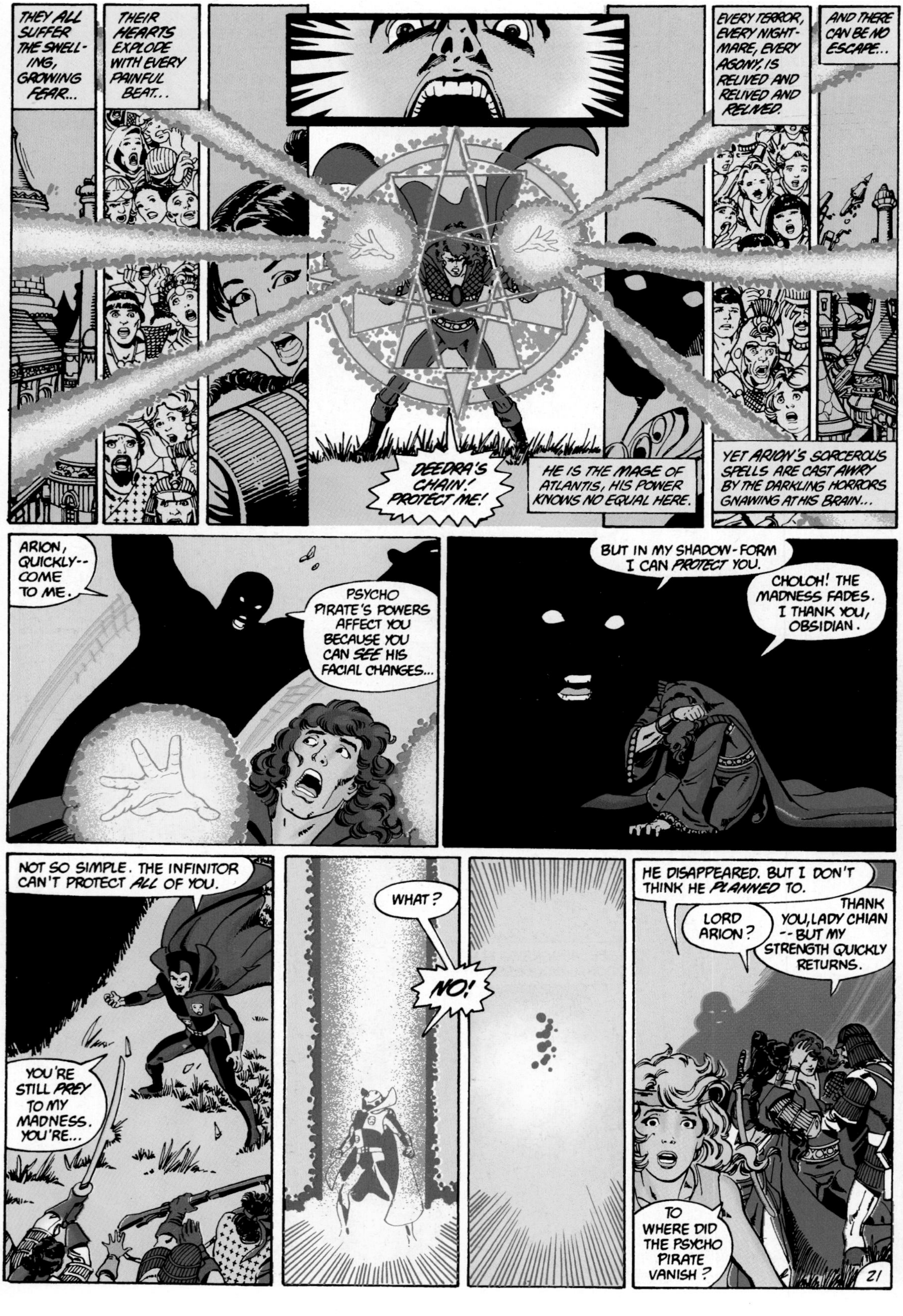

THEY ALL SUFFER THE SWELLING, GROWING FEAR...
THEIR HEARTS EXPLODE WITH EVERY PAINFUL BEAT...
EVERY TERROR, EVERY NIGHTMARE, EVERY AGONY, IS RELIVED AND RELIVED AND RELIVED.
AND THERE CAN BE NO ESCAPE...
DEEDRA'S CHAIN! PROTECT ME!
HE IS THE MAGE OF ATLANTIS, HIS POWER KNOWS NO EQUAL HERE.
YET ARION'S SORCEROUS SPELLS ARE CAST AWRY BY THE DARKLING HORRORS GNAWING AT HIS BRAIN...
ARION, QUICKLY-- COME TO ME.
PSYCHO PIRATE'S POWERS AFFECT YOU BECAUSE YOU CAN SEE HIS FACIAL CHANGES...
BUT IN MY SHADOW-FORM I CAN PROTECT YOU.
CHOLOH! THE MADNESS FADES. I THANK YOU, OBSIDIAN.
NOT SO SIMPLE. THE INFINITOR CAN'T PROTECT ALL OF YOU.
YOU'RE STILL PREY TO MY MADNESS. YOU'RE...
WHAT?
NO!
HE DISAPPEARED. BUT I DON'T THINK HE PLANNED TO.
LORD ARION?
THANK YOU, LADY CHIAN --BUT MY STRENGTH QUICKLY RETURNS.
TO WHERE DID THE PSYCHO PIRATE VANISH?

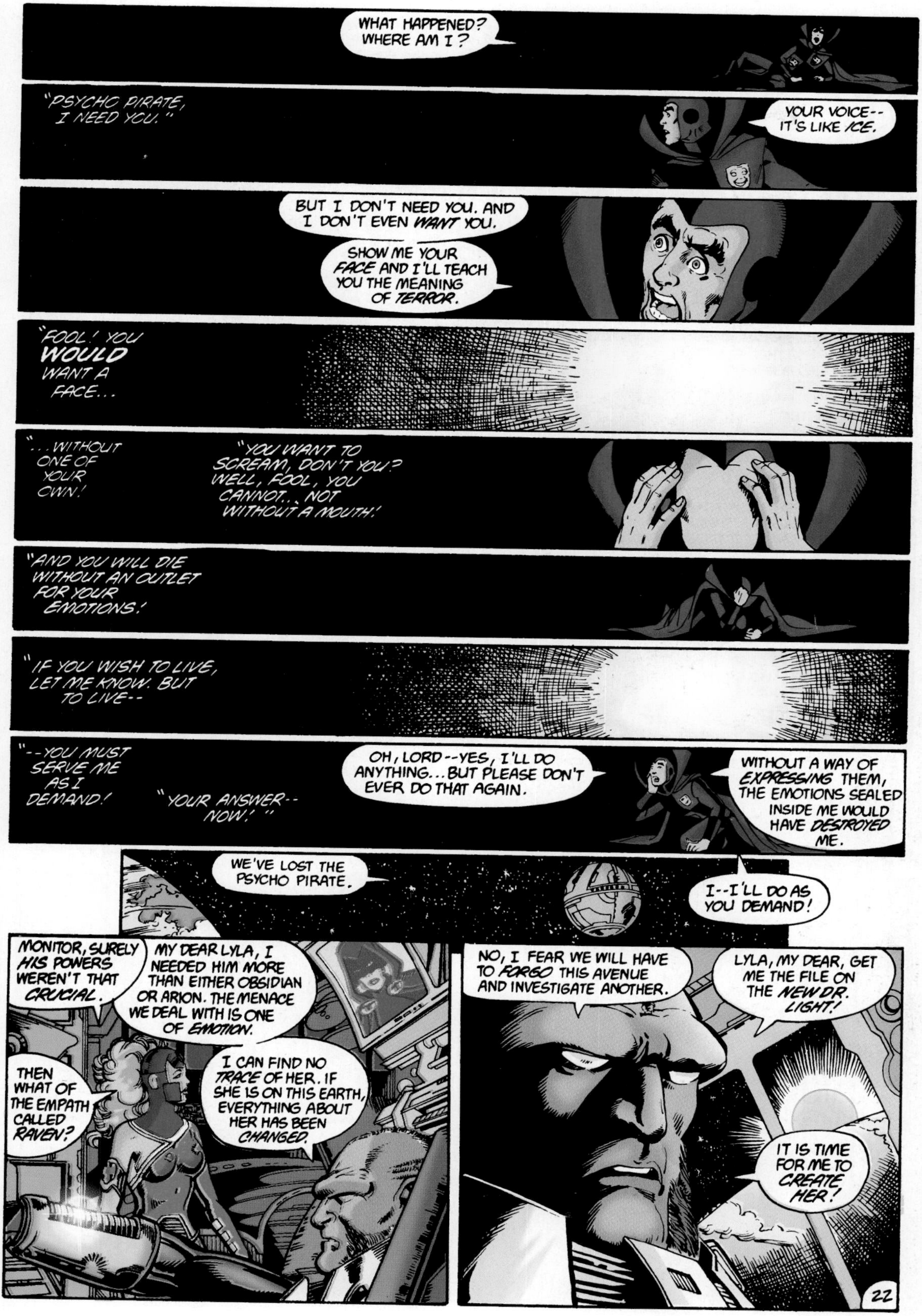
WHAT HAPPENED? WHERE AM I?
"PSYCHO PIRATE, I NEED YOU."
YOUR VOICE-- IT'S LIKE *ICE*.
BUT I DON'T NEED YOU. AND I DON'T EVEN *WANT* YOU.
SHOW ME YOUR *FACE* AND I'LL TEACH YOU THE MEANING OF *TERROR*.
"FOOL! YOU **WOULD** WANT A FACE...
"...WITHOUT ONE OF YOUR OWN!
"YOU WANT TO SCREAM, DON'T YOU? WELL, FOOL, YOU CANNOT... NOT WITHOUT A MOUTH!
"AND YOU WILL DIE WITHOUT AN OUTLET FOR YOUR EMOTIONS!
"IF YOU WISH TO LIVE, LET ME KNOW. BUT TO LIVE--
"--YOU MUST SERVE ME AS I DEMAND!
"YOUR ANSWER-- NOW!"
OH, LORD--YES, I'LL DO ANYTHING... BUT PLEASE DON'T EVER DO THAT AGAIN.
WITHOUT A WAY OF *EXPRESSING* THEM, THE EMOTIONS SEALED INSIDE ME WOULD HAVE *DESTROYED* ME.
I--I'LL DO AS YOU DEMAND!
WE'VE LOST THE PSYCHO PIRATE.
MONITOR, SURELY *HIS* POWERS WEREN'T THAT *CRUCIAL*.
MY DEAR LYLA, I NEEDED HIM MORE THAN EITHER OBSIDIAN OR ARION. THE MENACE WE DEAL WITH IS ONE OF *EMOTION*.
THEN WHAT OF THE EMPATH CALLED *RAVEN*?
I CAN FIND NO *TRACE* OF HER. IF SHE IS ON THIS EARTH, EVERYTHING ABOUT HER HAS BEEN *CHANGED*.
NO, I FEAR WE WILL HAVE TO *FORGO* THIS AVENUE AND INVESTIGATE ANOTHER.
LYLA, MY DEAR, GET ME THE FILE ON THE *NEW DR. LIGHT*!
IT IS TIME FOR ME TO *CREATE HER*!
22

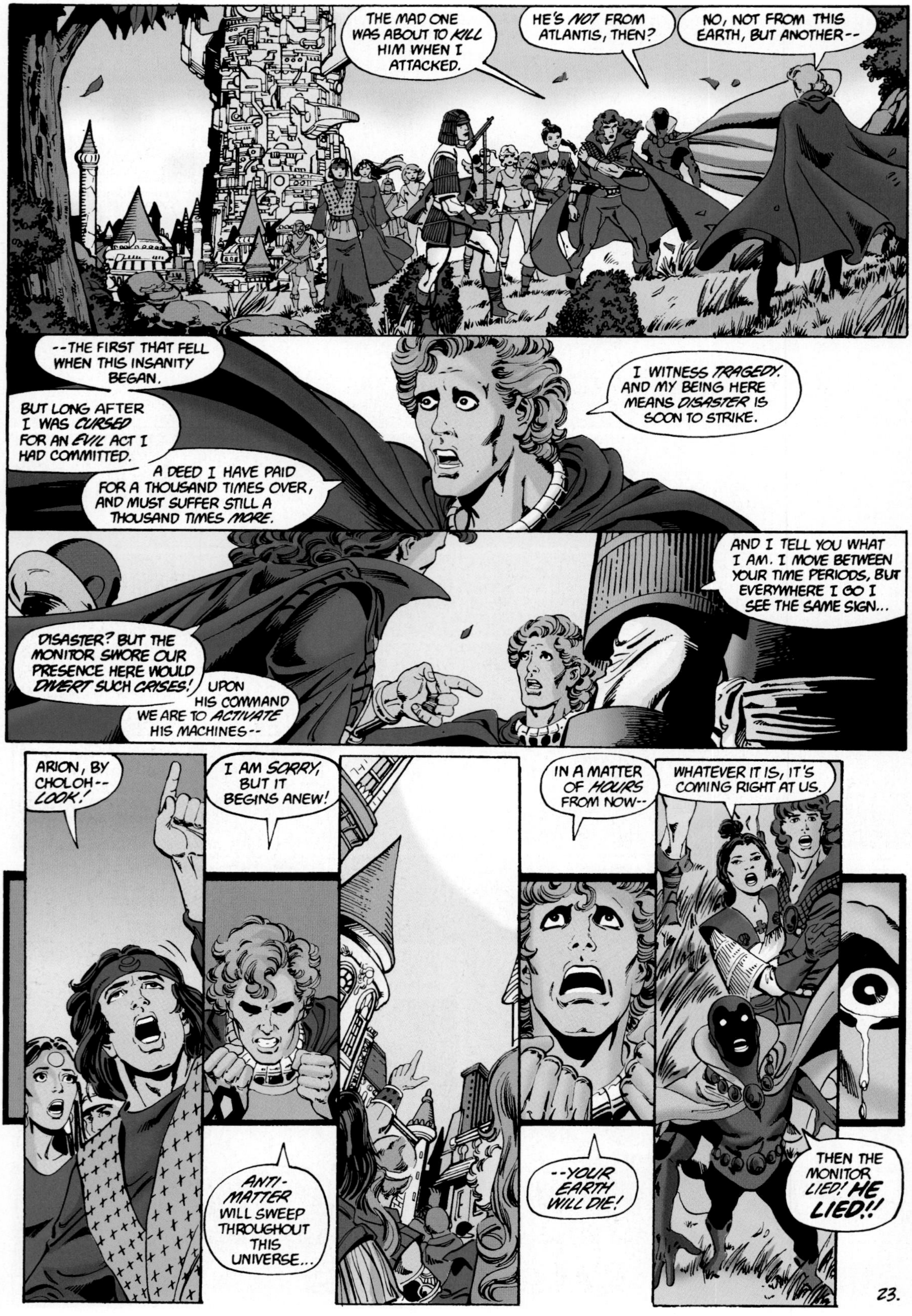
THE MAD ONE WAS ABOUT TO KILL HIM WHEN I ATTACKED.
HE'S NOT FROM ATLANTIS, THEN?
NO, NOT FROM THIS EARTH, BUT ANOTHER--
--THE FIRST THAT FELL WHEN THIS INSANITY BEGAN.
BUT LONG AFTER I WAS CURSED FOR AN EVIL ACT I HAD COMMITTED.
A DEED I HAVE PAID FOR A THOUSAND TIMES OVER, AND MUST SUFFER STILL A THOUSAND TIMES MORE.
I WITNESS TRAGEDY. AND MY BEING HERE MEANS DISASTER IS SOON TO STRIKE.
AND I TELL YOU WHAT I AM. I MOVE BETWEEN YOUR TIME PERIODS, BUT EVERYWHERE I GO I SEE THE SAME SIGN...
DISASTER? BUT THE MONITOR SWORE OUR PRESENCE HERE WOULD DIVERT SUCH CRISES!
UPON HIS COMMAND WE ARE TO ACTIVATE HIS MACHINES--
ARION, BY CHOLOH-- LOOK!
I AM SORRY, BUT IT BEGINS ANEW!
ANTI-MATTER WILL SWEEP THROUGHOUT THIS UNIVERSE...
IN A MATTER OF HOURS FROM NOW--
--YOUR EARTH WILL DIE!
WHATEVER IT IS, IT'S COMING RIGHT AT US.
THEN THE MONITOR LIED! HE LIED!!

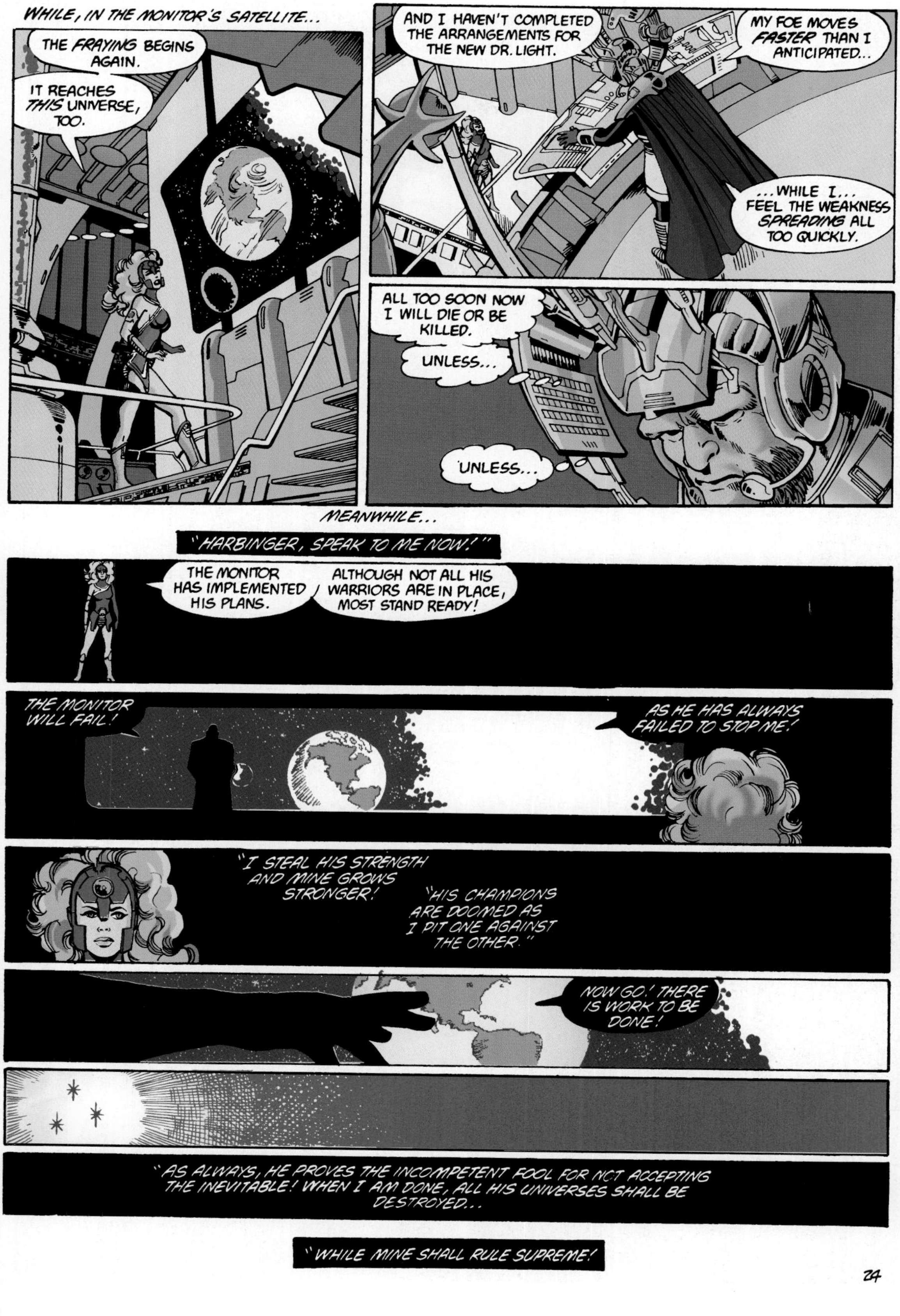
WHILE, IN THE MONITOR'S SATELLITE...
THE FRAYING BEGINS AGAIN.
IT REACHES THIS UNIVERSE, TOO.
AND I HAVEN'T COMPLETED THE ARRANGEMENTS FOR THE NEW DR. LIGHT.
MY FOE MOVES FASTER THAN I ANTICIPATED...
...WHILE I... FEEL THE WEAKNESS SPREADING ALL TOO QUICKLY.
ALL TOO SOON NOW I WILL DIE OR BE KILLED.
UNLESS...
UNLESS...
MEANWHILE...
"HARBINGER, SPEAK TO ME NOW!"
THE MONITOR HAS IMPLEMENTED HIS PLANS.
ALTHOUGH NOT ALL HIS WARRIORS ARE IN PLACE, MOST STAND READY!
THE MONITOR WILL FAIL!
AS HE HAS ALWAYS FAILED TO STOP ME!
"I STEAL HIS STRENGTH AND MINE GROWS STRONGER!
"HIS CHAMPIONS ARE DOOMED AS I PIT ONE AGAINST THE OTHER."
NOW GO! THERE IS WORK TO BE DONE!
"AS ALWAYS, HE PROVES THE INCOMPETENT FOOL FOR NOT ACCEPTING THE INEVITABLE! WHEN I AM DONE, ALL HIS UNIVERSES SHALL BE DESTROYED...
"WHILE MINE SHALL RULE SUPREME!
24

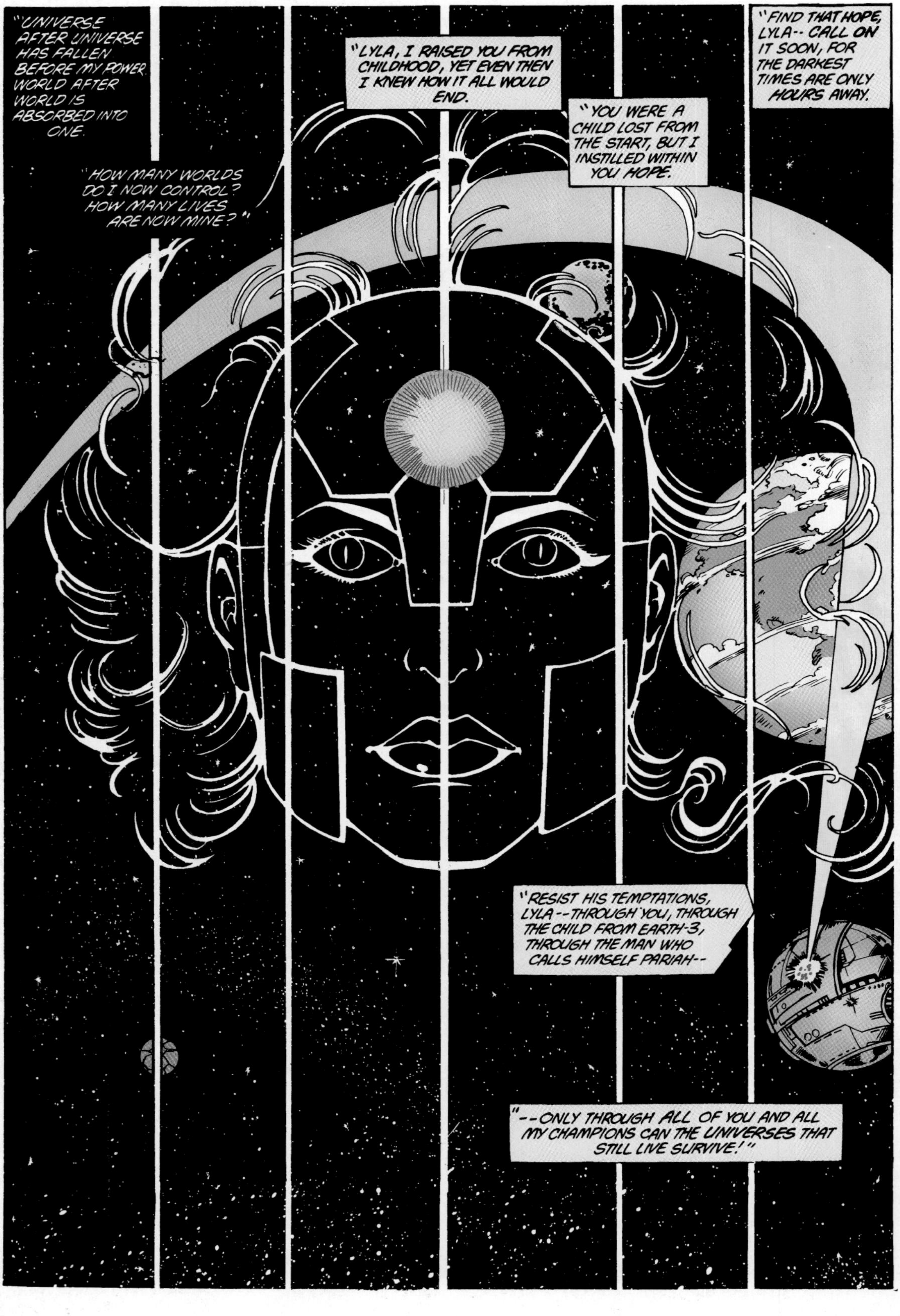
"UNIVERSE AFTER UNIVERSE HAS FALLEN BEFORE MY POWER. WORLD AFTER WORLD IS ABSORBED INTO ONE.
"HOW MANY WORLDS DO I NOW CONTROL? HOW MANY LIVES ARE NOW MINE?"
"LYLA, I RAISED YOU FROM CHILDHOOD, YET EVEN THEN I KNEW HOW IT ALL WOULD END.
"YOU WERE A CHILD LOST FROM THE START, BUT I INSTILLED WITHIN YOU HOPE.
"FIND THAT HOPE, LYLA-- CALL ON IT SOON, FOR THE DARKEST TIMES ARE ONLY HOURS AWAY.
"RESIST HIS TEMPTATIONS, LYLA--THROUGH YOU, THROUGH THE CHILD FROM EARTH-3, THROUGH THE MAN WHO CALLS HIMSELF PARIAH--
"--ONLY THROUGH ALL OF YOU AND ALL MY CHAMPIONS CAN THE UNIVERSES THAT STILL LIVE SURVIVE!"

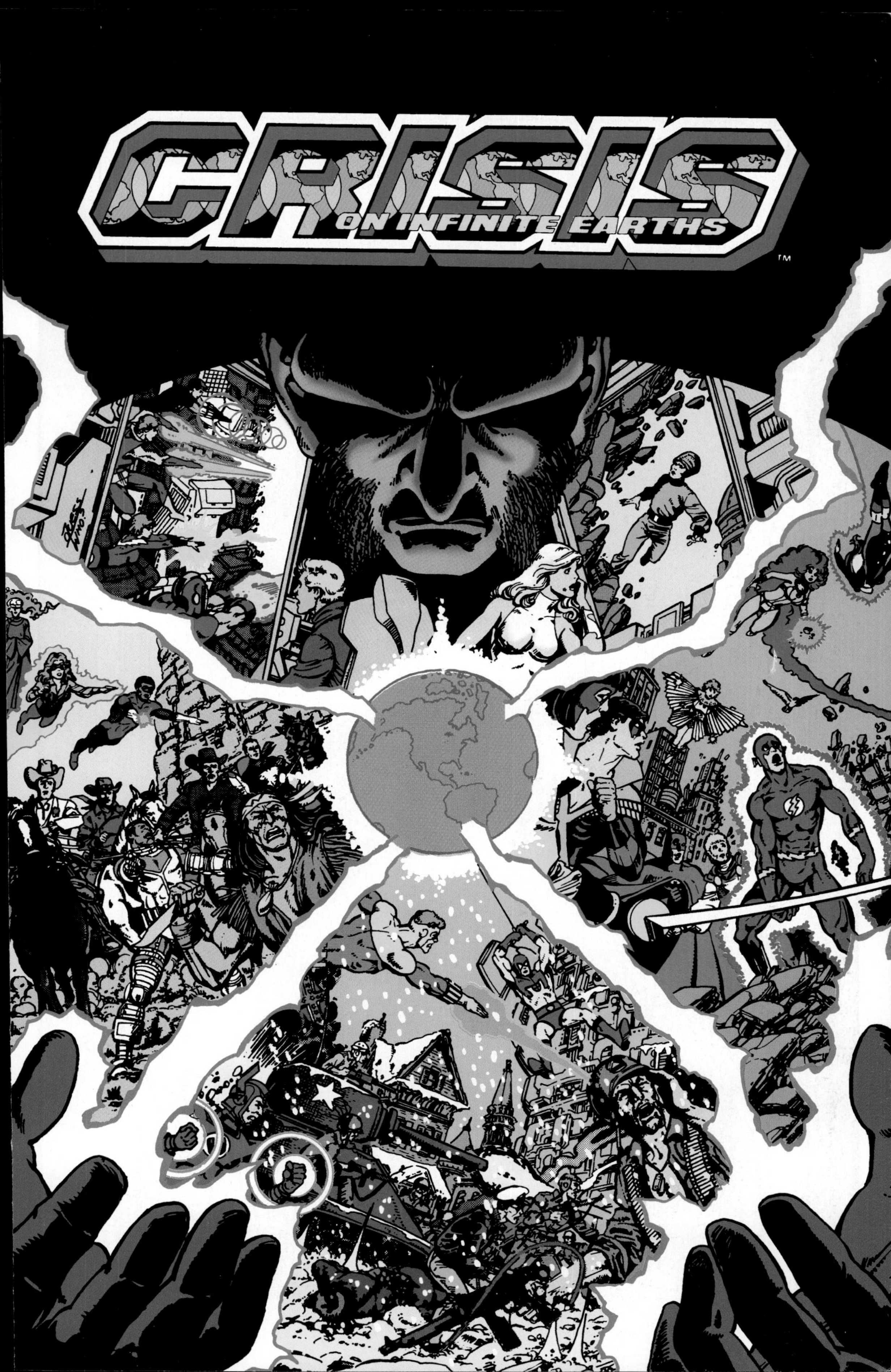
CRISIS
ON INFINITE EARTHS
TM

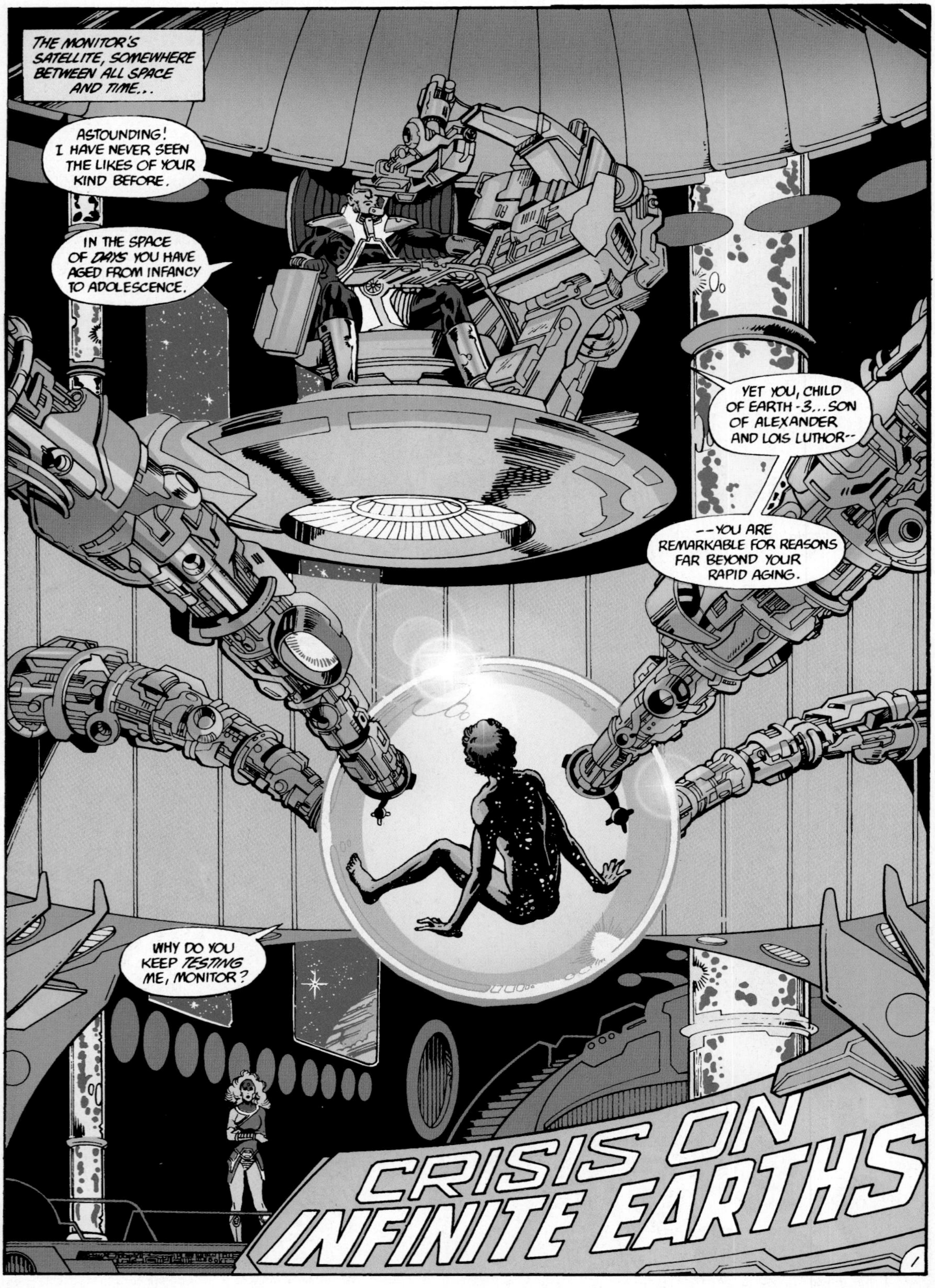
THE MONITOR'S SATELLITE, SOMEWHERE BETWEEN ALL SPACE AND TIME...
ASTOUNDING! I HAVE NEVER SEEN THE LIKES OF YOUR KIND BEFORE.
IN THE SPACE OF DAYS YOU HAVE AGED FROM INFANCY TO ADOLESCENCE.
YET YOU, CHILD OF EARTH-3,...SON OF ALEXANDER AND LOIS LUTHOR--
--YOU ARE REMARKABLE FOR REASONS FAR BEYOND YOUR RAPID AGING.
WHY DO YOU KEEP TESTING ME, MONITOR?
CRISIS ON INFINITE EARTHS
1

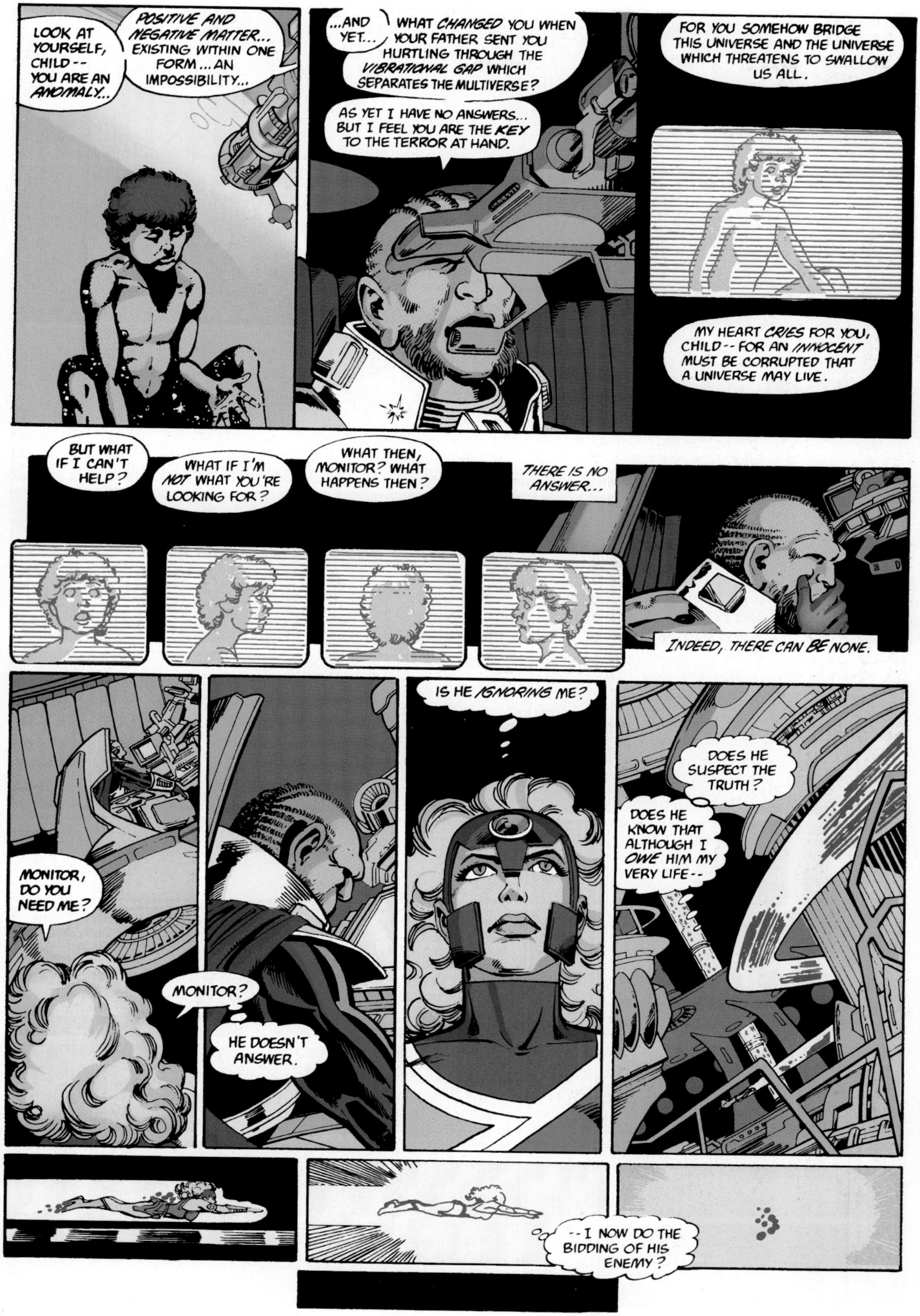
LOOK AT YOURSELF, CHILD-- YOU ARE AN ANOMALY...
POSITIVE AND NEGATIVE MATTER... EXISTING WITHIN ONE FORM... AN IMPOSSIBILITY...
...AND YET...
WHAT CHANGED YOU WHEN YOUR FATHER SENT YOU HURTLING THROUGH THE VIBRATIONAL GAP WHICH SEPARATES THE MULTIVERSE?
AS YET I HAVE NO ANSWERS... BUT I FEEL YOU ARE THE KEY TO THE TERROR AT HAND.
FOR YOU SOMEHOW BRIDGE THIS UNIVERSE AND THE UNIVERSE WHICH THREATENS TO SWALLOW US ALL.
MY HEART CRIES FOR YOU, CHILD-- FOR AN INNOCENT MUST BE CORRUPTED THAT A UNIVERSE MAY LIVE.
BUT WHAT IF I CAN'T HELP?
WHAT IF I'M NOT WHAT YOU'RE LOOKING FOR?
WHAT THEN, MONITOR? WHAT HAPPENS THEN?
THERE IS NO ANSWER...
INDEED, THERE CAN BE NONE.
MONITOR, DO YOU NEED ME?
MONITOR?
HE DOESN'T ANSWER.
IS HE IGNORING ME?
DOES HE SUSPECT THE TRUTH?
DOES HE KNOW THAT ALTHOUGH I OWE HIM MY VERY LIFE--
--I NOW DO THE BIDDING OF HIS ENEMY?

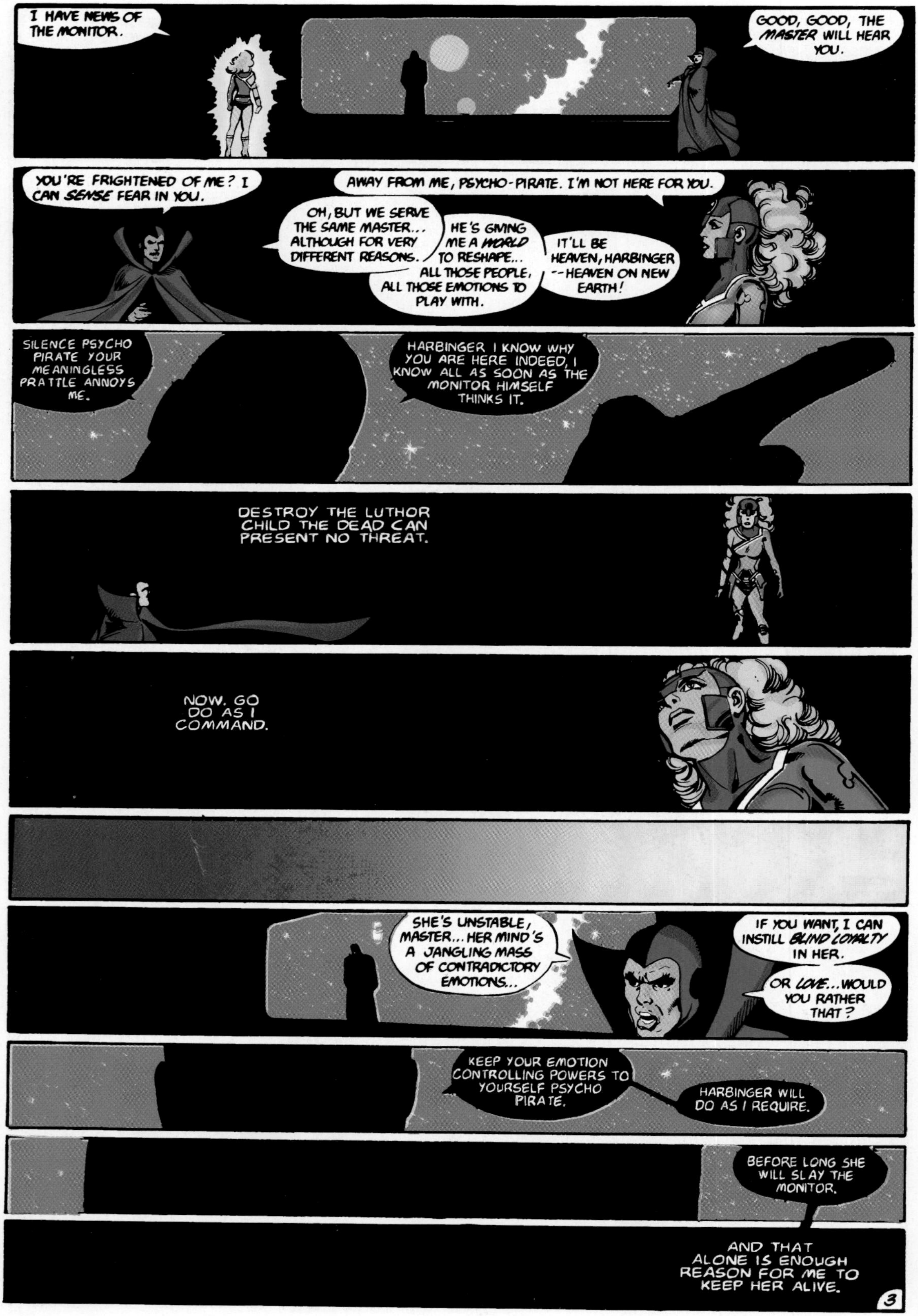

I HAVE NEWS OF THE MONITOR.
GOOD, GOOD, THE MASTER WILL HEAR YOU.
YOU'RE FRIGHTENED OF ME? I CAN SENSE FEAR IN YOU.
AWAY FROM ME, PSYCHO-PIRATE. I'M NOT HERE FOR YOU.
OH, BUT WE SERVE THE SAME MASTER... ALTHOUGH FOR VERY DIFFERENT REASONS.
HE'S GIVING ME A WORLD TO RESHAPE... ALL THOSE PEOPLE, ALL THOSE EMOTIONS TO PLAY WITH.
IT'LL BE HEAVEN, HARBINGER --HEAVEN ON NEW EARTH!
SILENCE PSYCHO PIRATE YOUR MEANINGLESS PRATTLE ANNOYS ME.
HARBINGER I KNOW WHY YOU ARE HERE INDEED, I KNOW ALL AS SOON AS THE MONITOR HIMSELF THINKS IT.
DESTROY THE LUTHOR CHILD THE DEAD CAN PRESENT NO THREAT.
NOW. GO DO AS I COMMAND.
SHE'S UNSTABLE, MASTER... HER MIND'S A JANGLING MASS OF CONTRADICTORY EMOTIONS...
IF YOU WANT, I CAN INSTILL BLIND LOYALTY IN HER.
OR LOVE... WOULD YOU RATHER THAT?
KEEP YOUR EMOTION CONTROLLING POWERS TO YOURSELF PSYCHO PIRATE.
HARBINGER WILL DO AS I REQUIRE.
BEFORE LONG SHE WILL SLAY THE MONITOR.
AND THAT ALONE IS ENOUGH REASON FOR ME TO KEEP HER ALIVE.
3

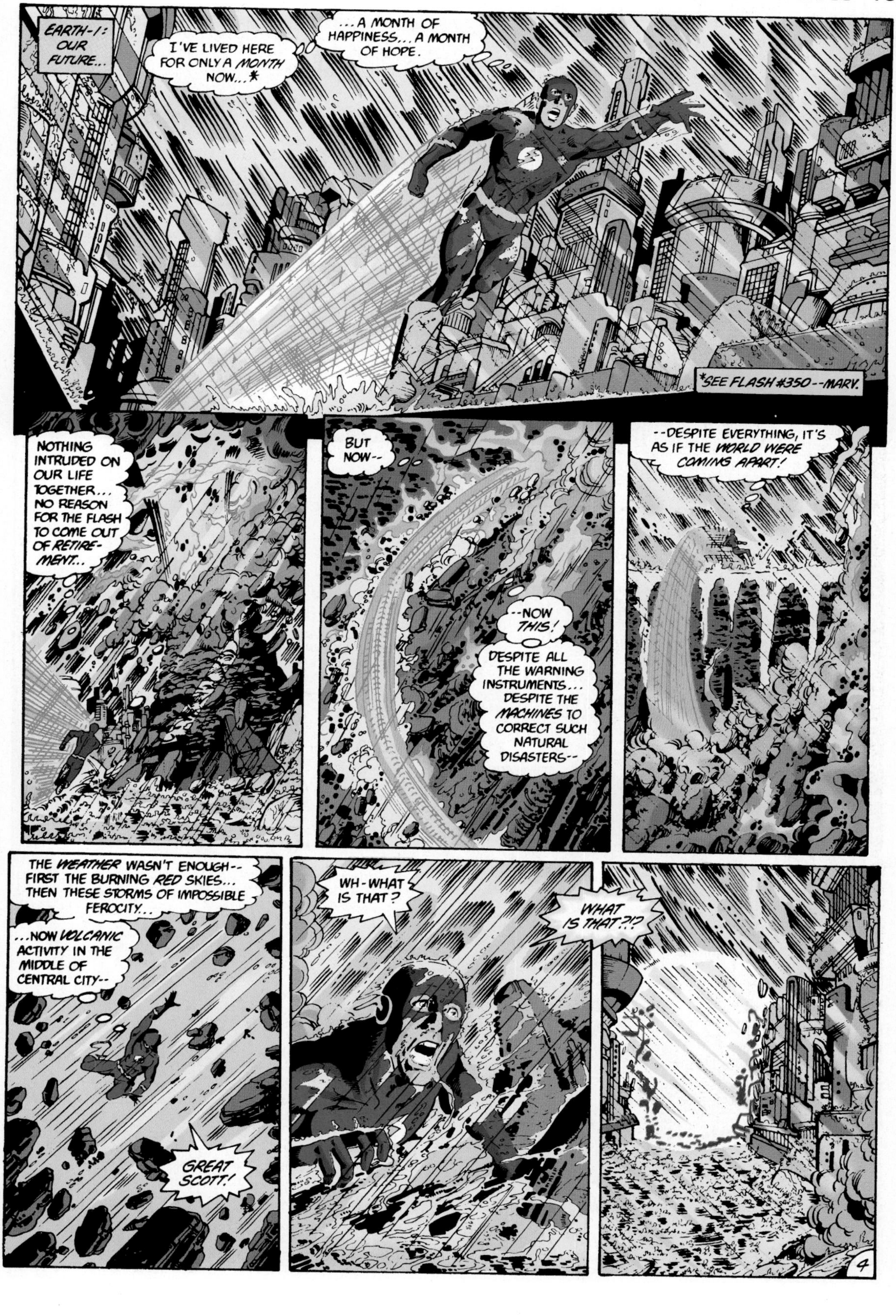
EARTH-1: OUR FUTURE...
I'VE LIVED HERE FOR ONLY A MONTH NOW...*
...A MONTH OF HAPPINESS... A MONTH OF HOPE.
*SEE FLASH #350--MARV.
NOTHING INTRUDED ON OUR LIFE TOGETHER... NO REASON FOR THE FLASH TO COME OUT OF RETIRE-MENT...
BUT NOW--
--NOW THIS!
DESPITE ALL THE WARNING INSTRUMENTS... DESPITE THE MACHINES TO CORRECT SUCH NATURAL DISASTERS--
--DESPITE EVERYTHING, IT'S AS IF THE WORLD WERE COMING APART!
THE WEATHER WASN'T ENOUGH-- FIRST THE BURNING RED SKIES... THEN THESE STORMS OF IMPOSSIBLE FEROCITY...
...NOW VOLCANIC ACTIVITY IN THE MIDDLE OF CENTRAL CITY--
GREAT SCOTT!
WH-WHAT IS THAT?
WHAT IS THAT?!?
4

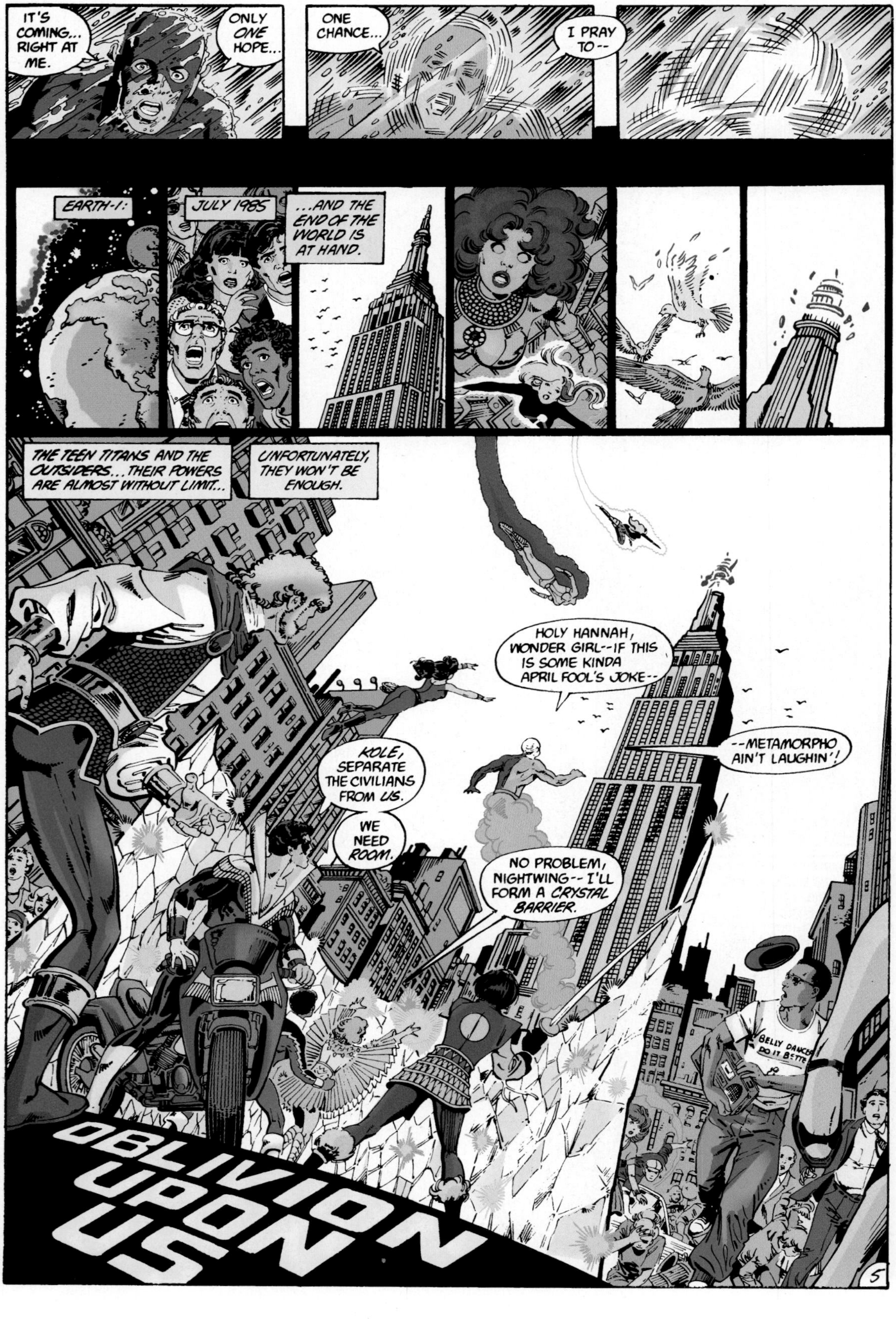
IT'S COMING... RIGHT AT ME.
ONLY ONE HOPE...
ONE CHANCE...
I PRAY TO--
EARTH-1:
JULY 1985
...AND THE END OF THE WORLD IS AT HAND.
THE TEEN TITANS AND THE OUTSIDERS... THEIR POWERS ARE ALMOST WITHOUT LIMIT...
UNFORTUNATELY, THEY WON'T BE ENOUGH.
HOLY HANNAH, WONDER GIRL--IF THIS IS SOME KINDA APRIL FOOL'S JOKE--
--METAMORPHO AIN'T LAUGHIN'!
KOLE, SEPARATE THE CIVILIANS FROM US.
WE NEED ROOM.
NO PROBLEM, NIGHTWING-- I'LL FORM A CRYSTAL BARRIER.
BELLY DANCERS DO IT BETTER
OBLIVION UPON US
5

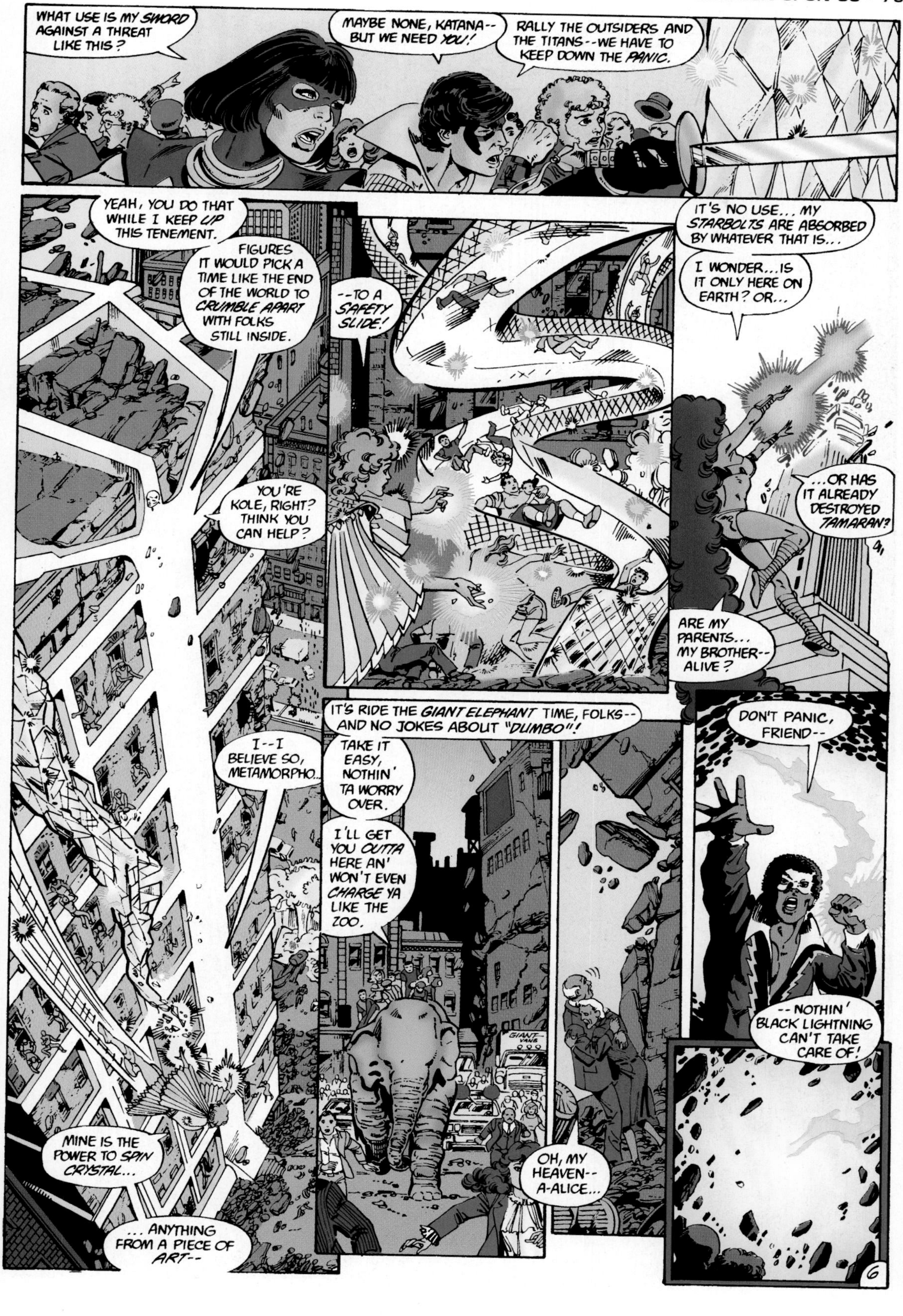
WHAT USE IS MY SWORD AGAINST A THREAT LIKE THIS?
MAYBE NONE, KATANA-- BUT WE NEED YOU!
RALLY THE OUTSIDERS AND THE TITANS--WE HAVE TO KEEP DOWN THE PANIC.
YEAH, YOU DO THAT WHILE I KEEP UP THIS TENEMENT.
FIGURES IT WOULD PICK A TIME LIKE THE END OF THE WORLD TO CRUMBLE APART WITH FOLKS STILL INSIDE.
YOU'RE KOLE, RIGHT? THINK YOU CAN HELP?
I--I BELIEVE SO, METAMORPHO...
MINE IS THE POWER TO SPIN CRYSTAL...
...ANYTHING FROM A PIECE OF ART--
--TO A SAFETY SLIDE!
IT'S NO USE... MY STARBOLTS ARE ABSORBED BY WHATEVER THAT IS...
I WONDER... IS IT ONLY HERE ON EARTH? OR...
...OR HAS IT ALREADY DESTROYED TAMARAN?
ARE MY PARENTS... MY BROTHER-- ALIVE?
IT'S RIDE THE GIANT ELEPHANT TIME, FOLKS-- AND NO JOKES ABOUT "DUMBO"!
TAKE IT EASY, NOTHIN' TA WORRY OVER.
I'LL GET YOU OUTTA HERE AN' WON'T EVEN CHARGE YA LIKE THE ZOO.
OH, MY HEAVEN-- A-ALICE...
DON'T PANIC, FRIEND--
--NOTHIN' BLACK LIGHTNING CAN'T TAKE CARE OF!
6

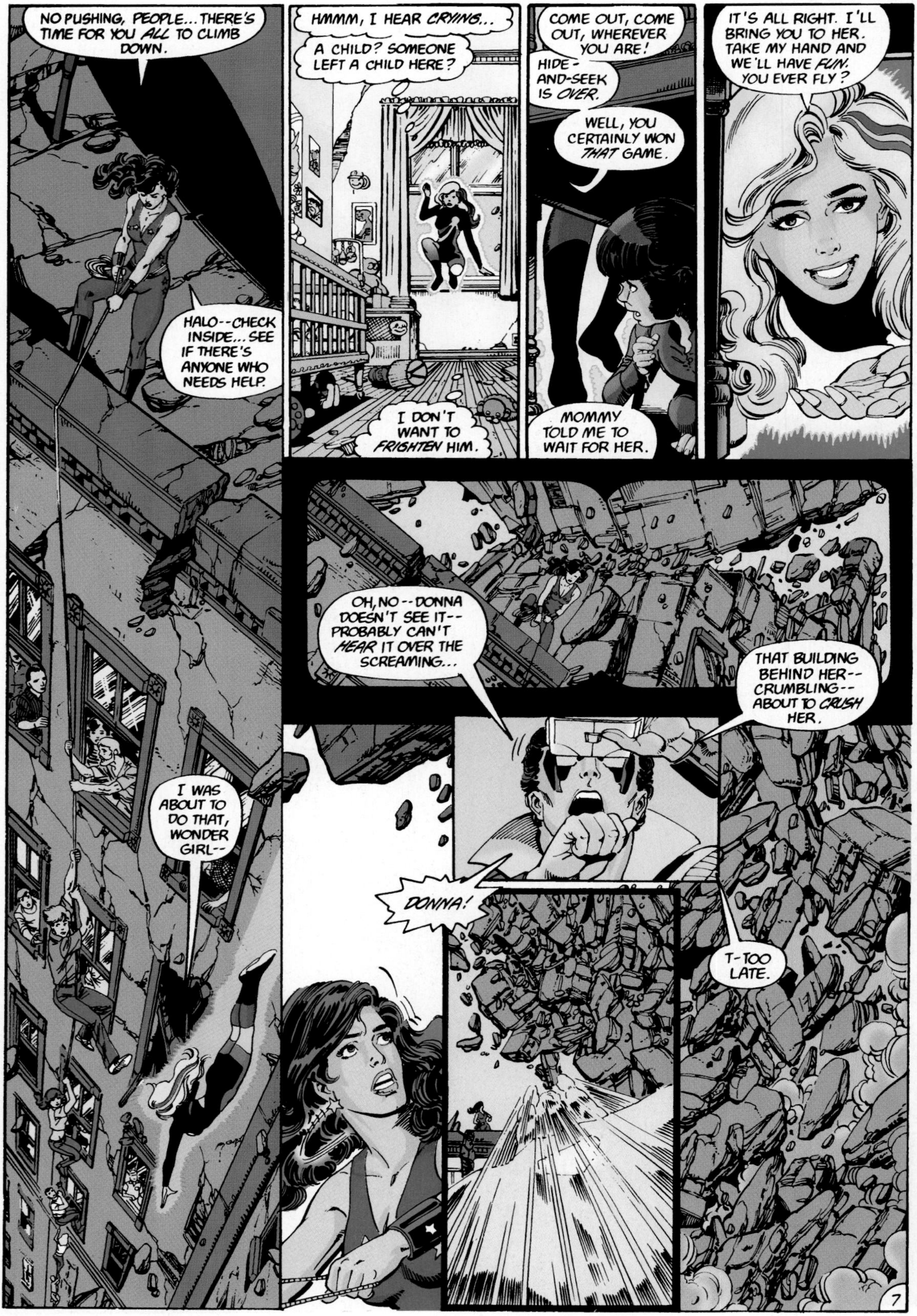
NO PUSHING, PEOPLE... THERE'S TIME FOR YOU ALL TO CLIMB DOWN.
HALO--CHECK INSIDE... SEE IF THERE'S ANYONE WHO NEEDS HELP.
I WAS ABOUT TO DO THAT, WONDER GIRL--
HMMM, I HEAR CRYING...
A CHILD? SOMEONE LEFT A CHILD HERE?
I DON'T WANT TO FRIGHTEN HIM.
COME OUT, COME OUT, WHEREVER YOU ARE!
HIDE-AND-SEEK IS OVER.
WELL, YOU CERTAINLY WON THAT GAME.
MOMMY TOLD ME TO WAIT FOR HER.
IT'S ALL RIGHT. I'LL BRING YOU TO HER. TAKE MY HAND AND WE'LL HAVE FUN. YOU EVER FLY?
OH, NO--DONNA DOESN'T SEE IT--PROBABLY CAN'T HEAR IT OVER THE SCREAMING...
THAT BUILDING BEHIND HER--CRUMBLING--ABOUT TO CRUSH HER.
DONNA!
T-TOO LATE.
7

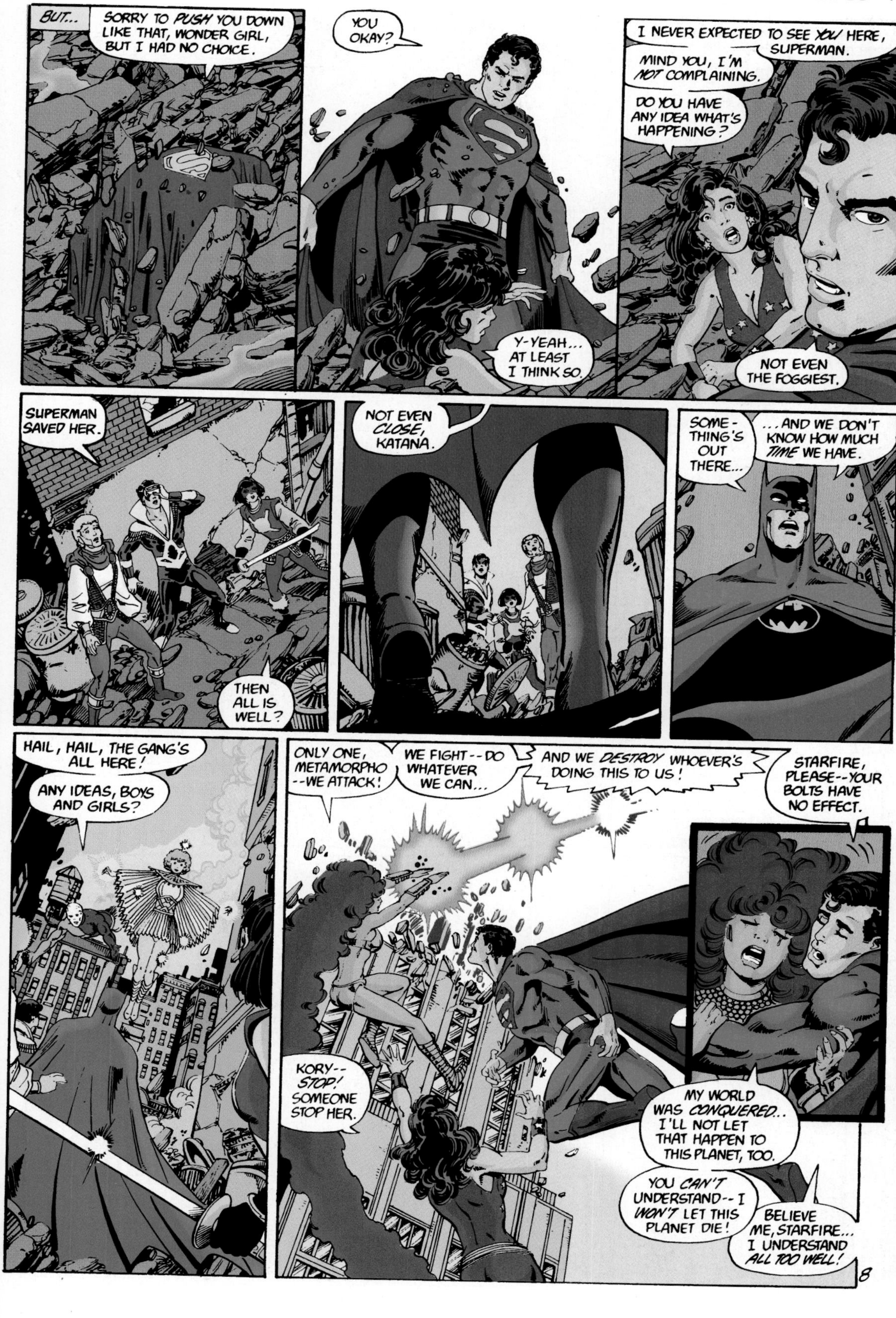
BUT...
SORRY TO PUSH YOU DOWN LIKE THAT, WONDER GIRL, BUT I HAD NO CHOICE.
YOU OKAY?
Y-YEAH... AT LEAST I THINK SO.
I NEVER EXPECTED TO SEE YOU HERE, SUPERMAN.
MIND YOU, I'M NOT COMPLAINING.
DO YOU HAVE ANY IDEA WHAT'S HAPPENING?
NOT EVEN THE FOGGIEST.
SUPERMAN SAVED HER.
THEN ALL IS WELL?
NOT EVEN CLOSE, KATANA.
SOME-THING'S OUT THERE...
...AND WE DON'T KNOW HOW MUCH TIME WE HAVE.
HAIL, HAIL, THE GANG'S ALL HERE!
ANY IDEAS, BOYS AND GIRLS?
ONLY ONE, METAMORPHO --WE ATTACK!
WE FIGHT--DO WHATEVER WE CAN...
AND WE DESTROY WHOEVER'S DOING THIS TO US!
STARFIRE, PLEASE--YOUR BOLTS HAVE NO EFFECT.
KORY--STOP! SOMEONE STOP HER.
MY WORLD WAS CONQUERED.. I'LL NOT LET THAT HAPPEN TO THIS PLANET, TOO.
YOU CAN'T UNDERSTAND--I WON'T LET THIS PLANET DIE!
BELIEVE ME, STARFIRE... I UNDERSTAND ALL TOO WELL!
8

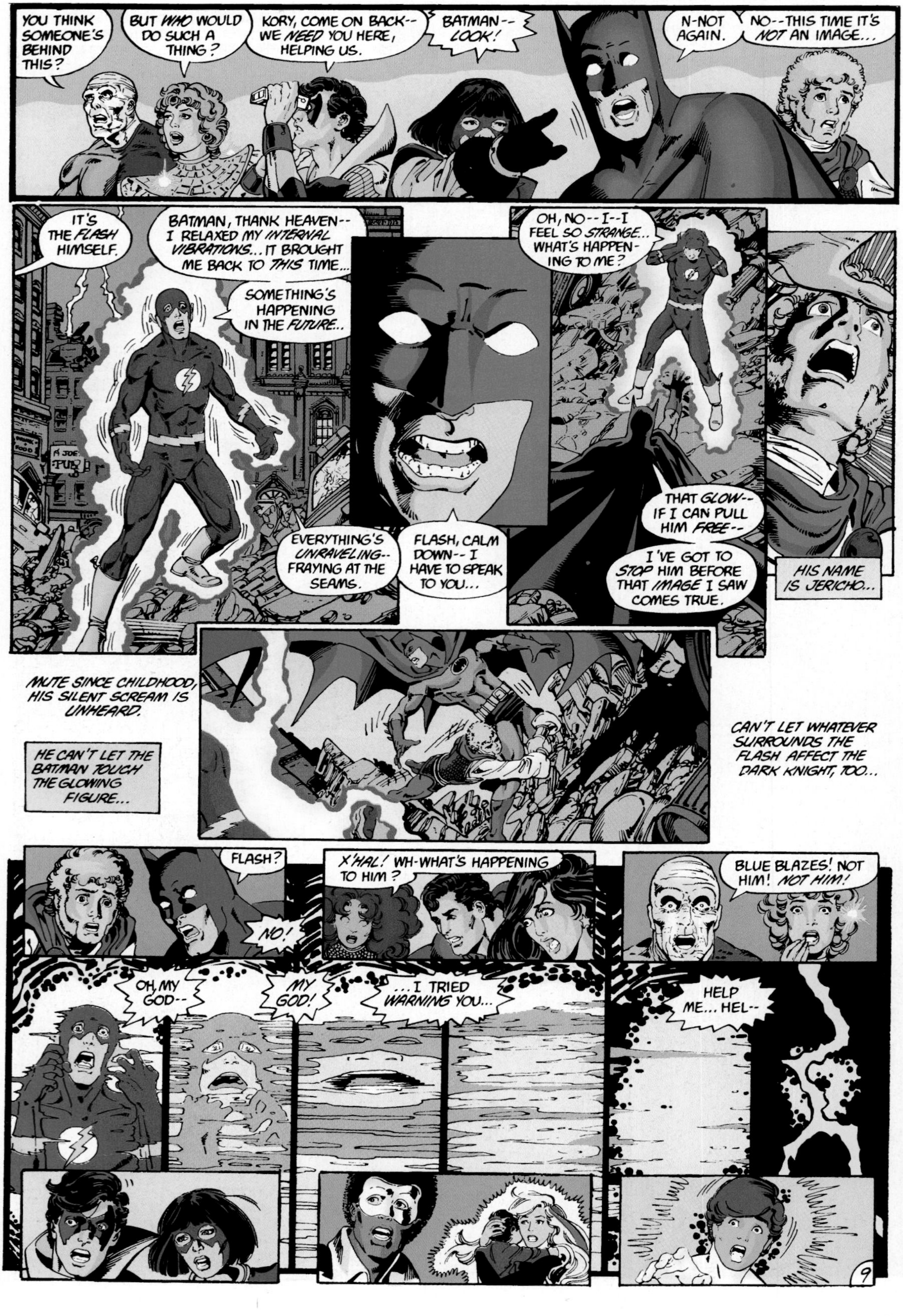
YOU THINK SOMEONE'S BEHIND THIS?
BUT WHO WOULD DO SUCH A THING?
KORY, COME ON BACK-- WE NEED YOU HERE, HELPING US.
BATMAN-- LOOK!
N-NOT AGAIN.
NO--THIS TIME IT'S NOT AN IMAGE...
IT'S THE FLASH HIMSELF.
BATMAN, THANK HEAVEN-- I RELAXED MY INTERNAL VIBRATIONS... IT BROUGHT ME BACK TO THIS TIME...
SOMETHING'S HAPPENING IN THE FUTURE...
EVERYTHING'S UNRAVELING-- FRAYING AT THE SEAMS.
FLASH, CALM DOWN-- I HAVE TO SPEAK TO YOU...
OH, NO-- I--I FEEL SO STRANGE... WHAT'S HAPPENING TO ME?
THAT GLOW-- IF I CAN PULL HIM FREE--
I'VE GOT TO STOP HIM BEFORE THAT IMAGE I SAW COMES TRUE.
HIS NAME IS JERICHO...
MUTE SINCE CHILDHOOD, HIS SILENT SCREAM IS UNHEARD.
HE CAN'T LET THE BATMAN TOUCH THE GLOWING FIGURE...
CAN'T LET WHATEVER SURROUNDS THE FLASH AFFECT THE DARK KNIGHT, TOO...
FLASH?
NO!
X'HAL! WH-WHAT'S HAPPENING TO HIM?
BLUE BLAZES! NOT HIM! NOT HIM!
OH, MY GOD--
MY GOD!
...I TRIED WARNING YOU...
HELP ME... HEL--
9

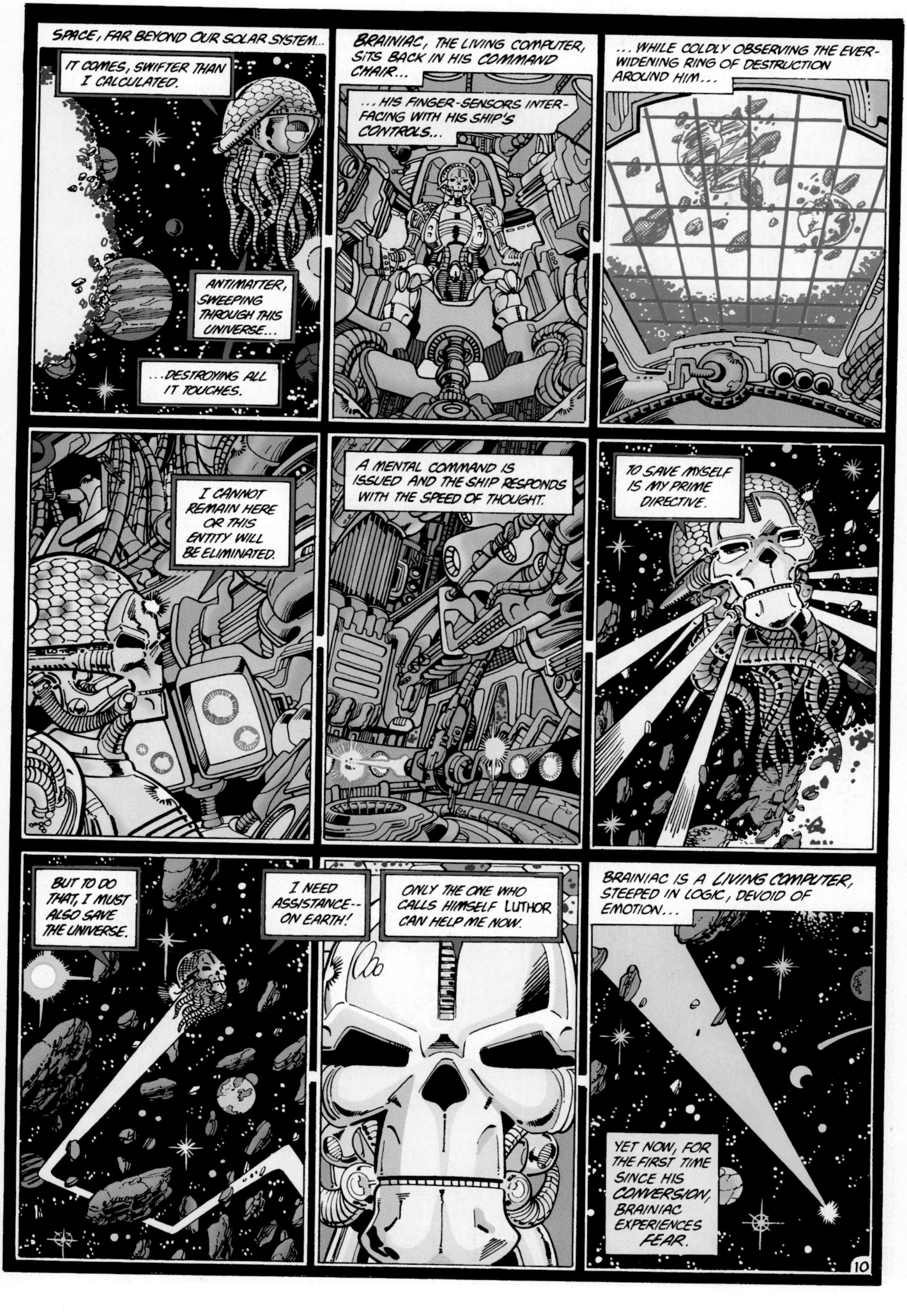
SPACE, FAR BEYOND OUR SOLAR SYSTEM...
IT COMES, SWIFTER THAN I CALCULATED.
ANTIMATTER, SWEEPING THROUGH THIS UNIVERSE...
...DESTROYING ALL IT TOUCHES.
BRAINIAC, THE LIVING COMPUTER, SITS BACK IN HIS COMMAND CHAIR...
...HIS FINGER-SENSORS INTERFACING WITH HIS SHIP'S CONTROLS...
...WHILE COLDLY OBSERVING THE EVER-WIDENING RING OF DESTRUCTION AROUND HIM...
I CANNOT REMAIN HERE OR THIS ENTITY WILL BE ELIMINATED.
A MENTAL COMMAND IS ISSUED AND THE SHIP RESPONDS WITH THE SPEED OF THOUGHT.
TO SAVE MYSELF IS MY PRIME DIRECTIVE.
BUT TO DO THAT, I MUST ALSO SAVE THE UNIVERSE.
I NEED ASSISTANCE-- ON EARTH!
ONLY THE ONE WHO CALLS HIMSELF LUTHOR CAN HELP ME NOW.
BRAINIAC IS A LIVING COMPUTER, STEEPED IN LOGIC, DEVOID OF EMOTION...
YET NOW, FOR THE FIRST TIME SINCE HIS CONVERSION, BRAINIAC EXPERIENCES FEAR.
10

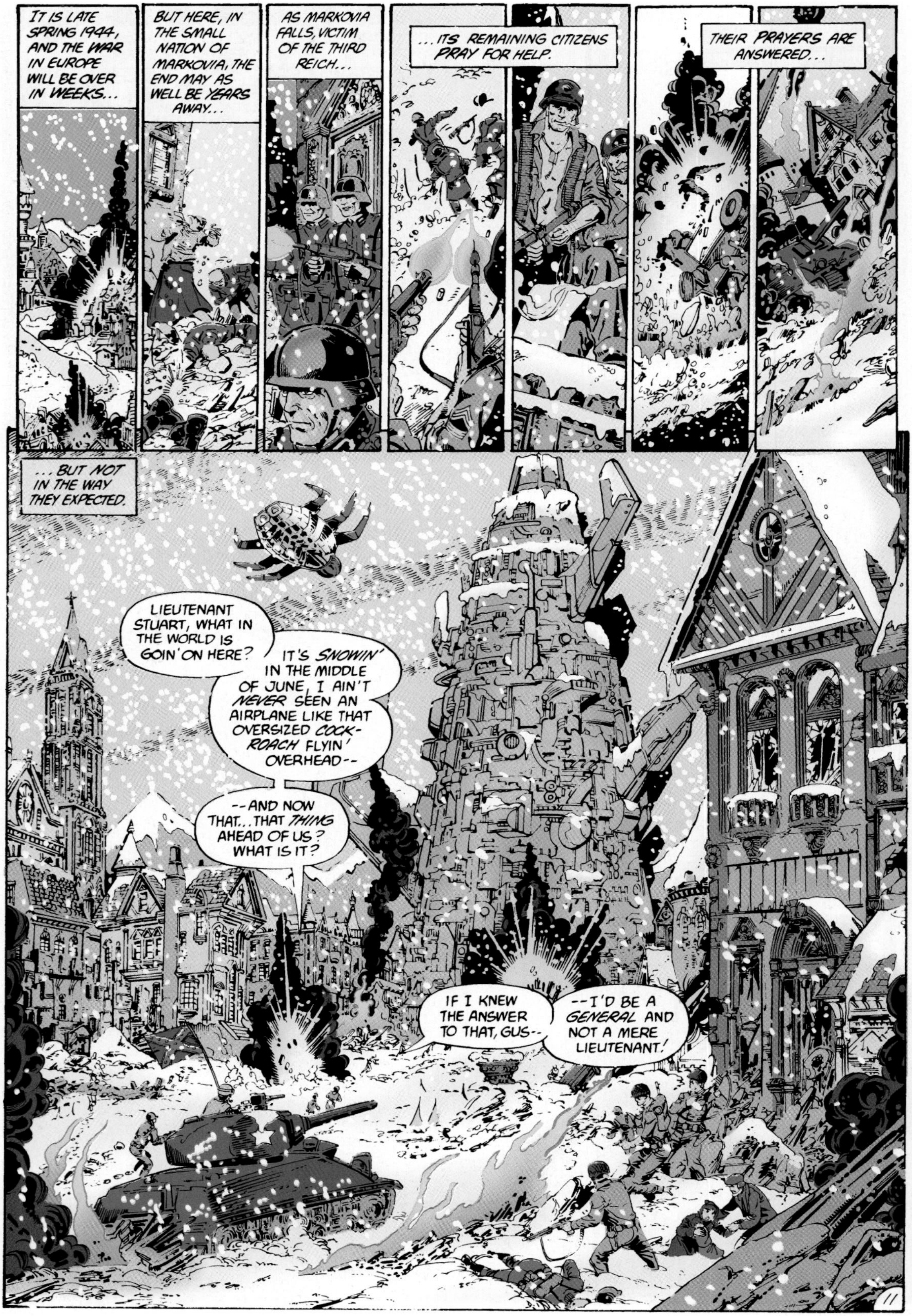
IT IS LATE SPRING 1944, AND THE WAR IN EUROPE WILL BE OVER IN WEEKS...
BUT HERE, IN THE SMALL NATION OF MARKOVIA, THE END MAY AS WELL BE YEARS AWAY...
AS MARKOVIA FALLS, VICTIM OF THE THIRD REICH...
...ITS REMAINING CITIZENS PRAY FOR HELP.
THEIR PRAYERS ARE ANSWERED...
...BUT NOT IN THE WAY THEY EXPECTED.
LIEUTENANT STUART, WHAT IN THE WORLD IS GOIN' ON HERE?
IT'S SNOWIN' IN THE MIDDLE OF JUNE, I AIN'T NEVER SEEN AN AIRPLANE LIKE THAT OVERSIZED COCK-ROACH FLYIN' OVERHEAD--
--AND NOW THAT...THAT THING AHEAD OF US? WHAT IS IT?
IF I KNEW THE ANSWER TO THAT, GUS--
--I'D BE A GENERAL AND NOT A MERE LIEUTENANT!
11

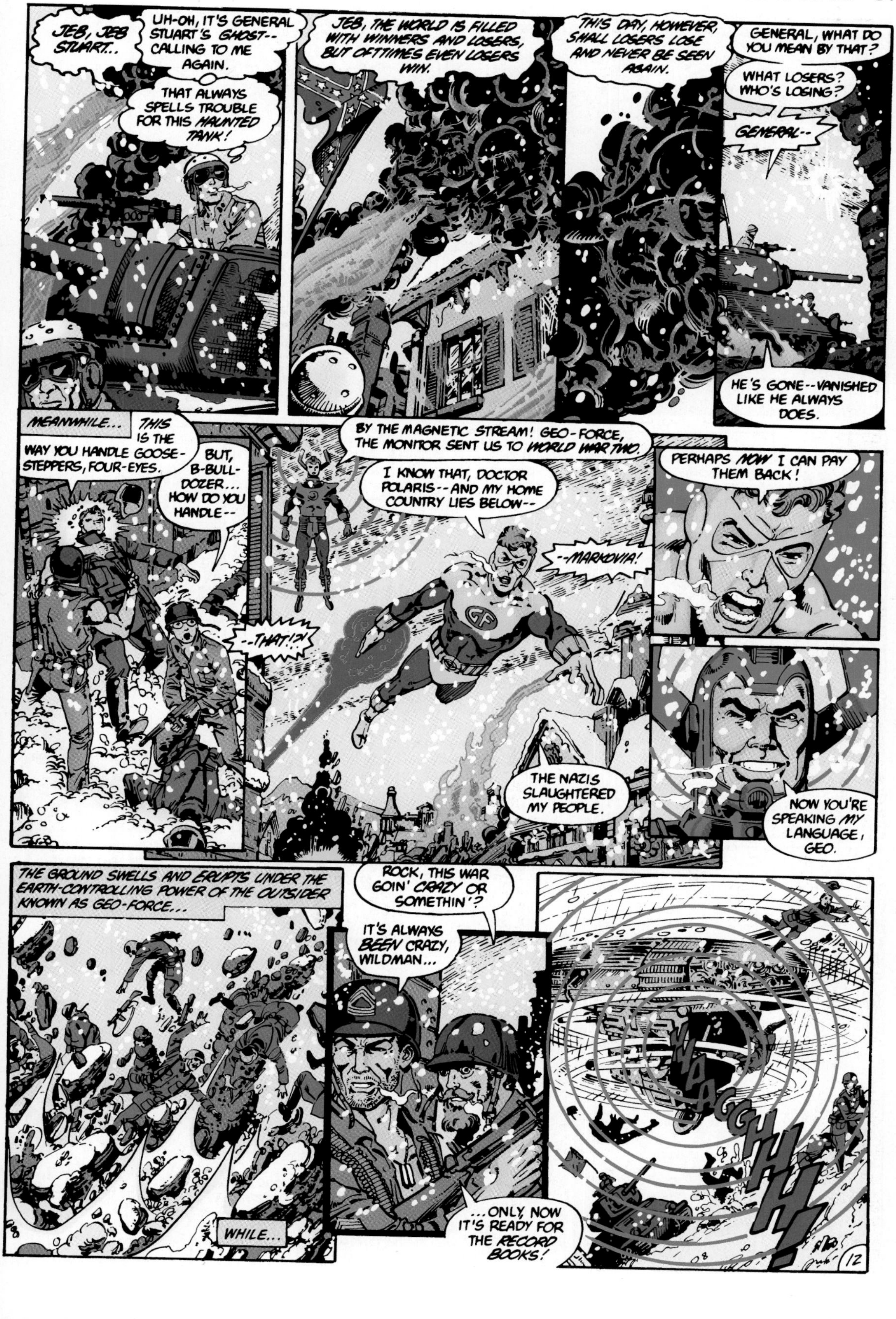
JEB, JEB STUART...
UH-OH, IT'S GENERAL STUART'S GHOST--CALLING TO ME AGAIN.
THAT ALWAYS SPELLS TROUBLE FOR THIS HAUNTED TANK!
JEB, THE WORLD IS FILLED WITH WINNERS AND LOSERS, BUT OFTTIMES EVEN LOSERS WIN.
THIS DAY, HOWEVER, SHALL LOSERS LOSE AND NEVER BE SEEN AGAIN.
GENERAL, WHAT DO YOU MEAN BY THAT?
WHAT LOSERS? WHO'S LOSING?
GENERAL--
HE'S GONE--VANISHED LIKE HE ALWAYS DOES.
MEANWHILE...
THIS IS THE WAY YOU HANDLE GOOSE-STEPPERS, FOUR-EYES.
BUT, B-BULL-DOZER... HOW DO YOU HANDLE--
--THAT!?!
BY THE MAGNETIC STREAM! GEO-FORCE, THE MONITOR SENT US TO WORLD WAR TWO.
I KNOW THAT, DOCTOR POLARIS--AND MY HOME COUNTRY LIES BELOW--
--MARKOVIA!
THE NAZIS SLAUGHTERED MY PEOPLE.
PERHAPS NOW I CAN PAY THEM BACK!
NOW YOU'RE SPEAKING MY LANGUAGE, GEO.
THE GROUND SWELLS AND ERUPTS UNDER THE EARTH-CONTROLLING POWER OF THE OUTSIDER KNOWN AS GEO-FORCE...
WHILE...
ROCK, THIS WAR GOIN' CRAZY OR SOMETHIN'?
IT'S ALWAYS BEEN CRAZY, WILDMAN...
...ONLY, NOW IT'S READY FOR THE RECORD BOOKS!
VAAGGHHH!
12

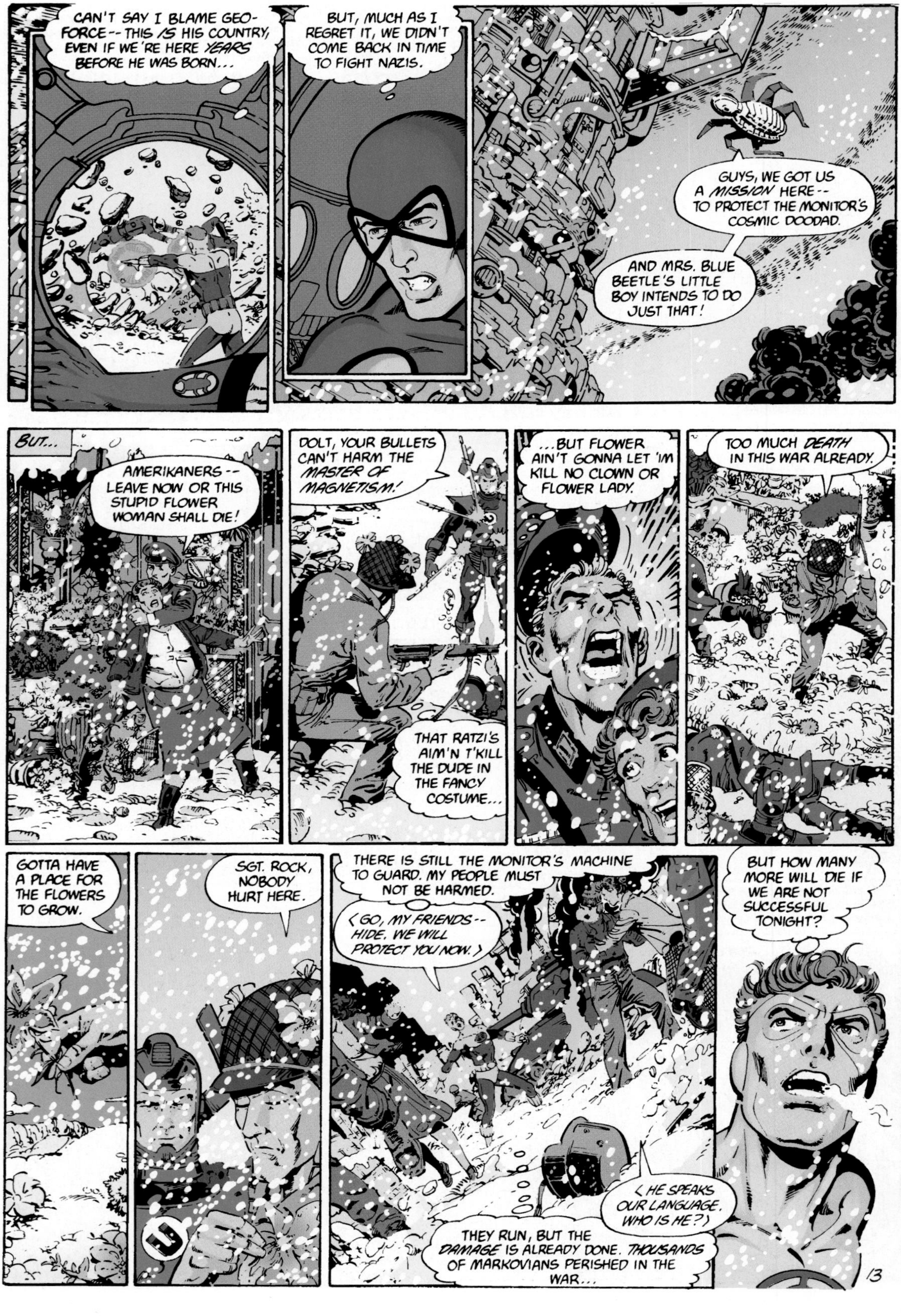
CAN'T SAY I BLAME GEO-FORCE -- THIS IS HIS COUNTRY, EVEN IF WE'RE HERE YEARS BEFORE HE WAS BORN...
BUT, MUCH AS I REGRET IT, WE DIDN'T COME BACK IN TIME TO FIGHT NAZIS.
GUYS, WE GOT US A MISSION HERE -- TO PROTECT THE MONITOR'S COSMIC DOODAD.
AND MRS. BLUE BEETLE'S LITTLE BOY INTENDS TO DO JUST THAT!
BUT...
AMERIKANERS -- LEAVE NOW OR THIS STUPID FLOWER WOMAN SHALL DIE!
DOLT, YOUR BULLETS CAN'T HARM THE MASTER OF MAGNETISM!
THAT RATZI'S AIM'N T'KILL THE DUDE IN THE FANCY COSTUME...
...BUT FLOWER AIN'T GONNA LET 'IM KILL NO CLOWN OR FLOWER LADY.
TOO MUCH DEATH IN THIS WAR ALREADY.
GOTTA HAVE A PLACE FOR THE FLOWERS TO GROW.
SGT. ROCK, NOBODY HURT HERE.
THERE IS STILL THE MONITOR'S MACHINE TO GUARD. MY PEOPLE MUST NOT BE HARMED.
< GO, MY FRIENDS -- HIDE. WE WILL PROTECT YOU NOW. >
< HE SPEAKS OUR LANGUAGE. WHO IS HE? >
THEY RUN, BUT THE DAMAGE IS ALREADY DONE. THOUSANDS OF MARKOVIANS PERISHED IN THE WAR...
BUT HOW MANY MORE WILL DIE IF WE ARE NOT SUCCESSFUL TONIGHT?
13

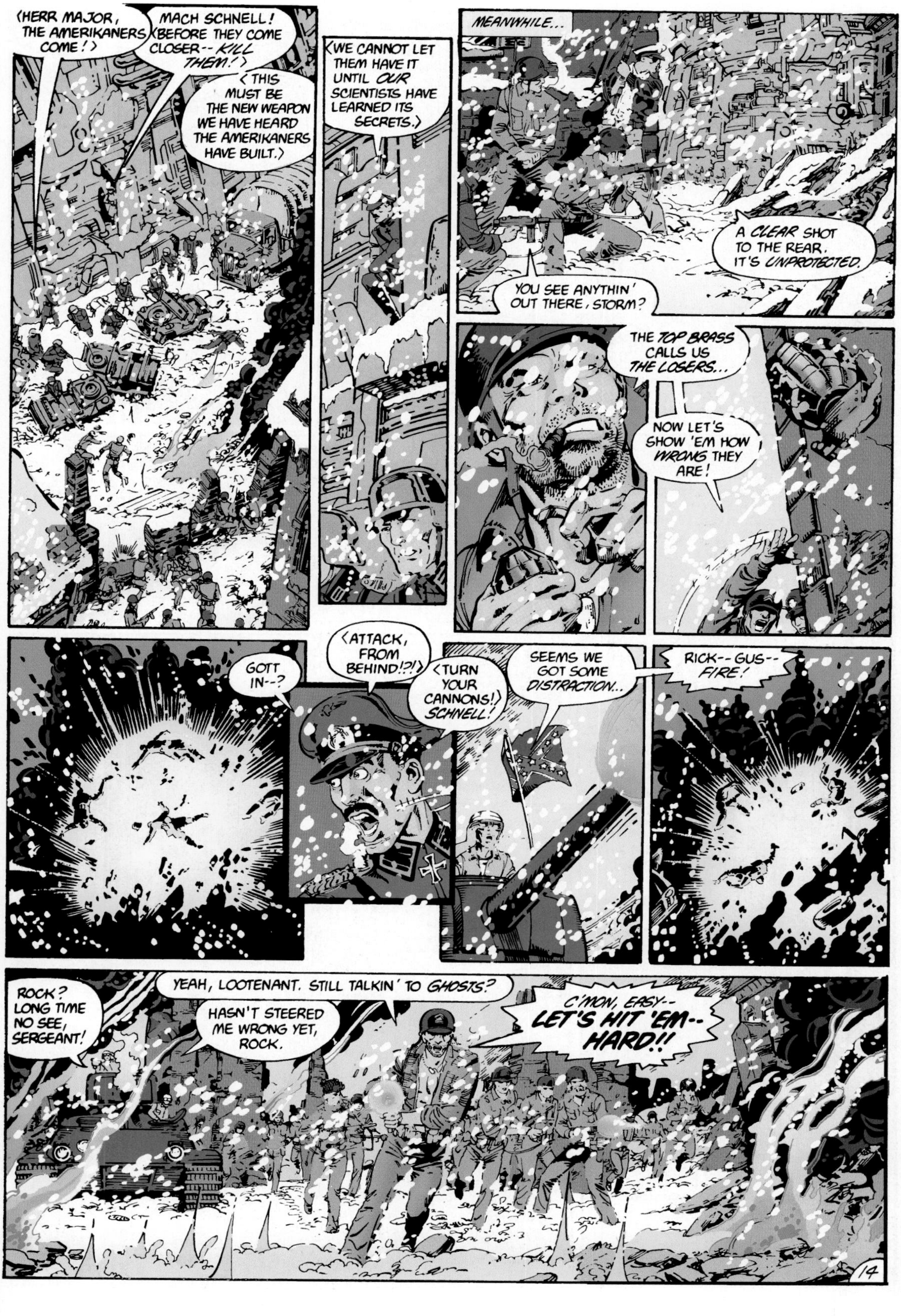

‹HERR MAJOR, THE AMERIKANERS COME!›
MACH SCHNELL! ‹BEFORE THEY COME CLOSER-- KILL THEM!›
‹THIS MUST BE THE NEW WEAPON WE HAVE HEARD THE AMERIKANERS HAVE BUILT.›
‹WE CANNOT LET THEM HAVE IT UNTIL OUR SCIENTISTS HAVE LEARNED ITS SECRETS.›
MEANWHILE...
YOU SEE ANYTHIN' OUT THERE, STORM?
A CLEAR SHOT TO THE REAR. IT'S UNPROTECTED.
THE TOP BRASS CALLS US THE LOSERS...
NOW LET'S SHOW 'EM HOW WRONG THEY ARE!
GOTT IN--?
‹ATTACK, FROM BEHIND!?!›
‹TURN YOUR CANNONS!› SCHNELL!
SEEMS WE GOT SOME DISTRACTION...
RICK-- GUS-- FIRE!
ROCK? LONG TIME NO SEE, SERGEANT!
YEAH, LOOTENANT. STILL TALKIN' TO GHOSTS?
HASN'T STEERED ME WRONG YET, ROCK.
C'MON, EASY-- LET'S HIT 'EM-- HARD!!
14

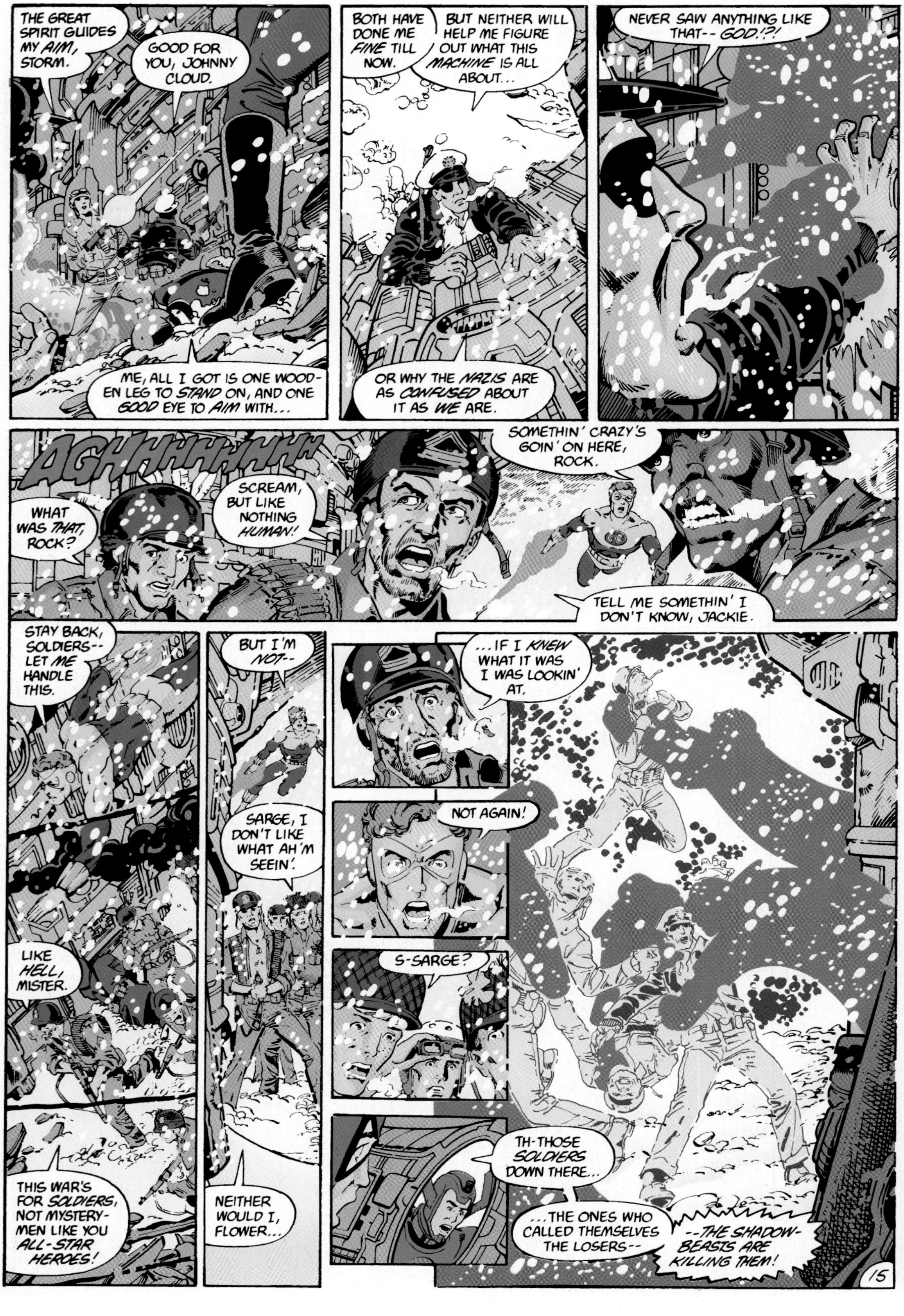

THE GREAT SPIRIT GUIDES MY AIM, STORM.
GOOD FOR YOU, JOHNNY CLOUD.
ME, ALL I GOT IS ONE WOODEN LEG TO STAND ON, AND ONE GOOD EYE TO AIM WITH...
BOTH HAVE DONE ME FINE TILL NOW.
BUT NEITHER WILL HELP ME FIGURE OUT WHAT THIS MACHINE IS ALL ABOUT...
OR WHY THE NAZIS ARE AS CONFUSED ABOUT IT AS WE ARE.
NEVER SAW ANYTHING LIKE THAT-- GOD!?!
AGHHHHHHHH
WHAT WAS THAT, ROCK?
SCREAM, BUT LIKE NOTHING HUMAN!
SOMETHIN' CRAZY'S GOIN' ON HERE, ROCK.
TELL ME SOMETHIN' I DON'T KNOW, JACKIE.
STAY BACK, SOLDIERS-- LET ME HANDLE THIS.
LIKE HELL, MISTER.
THIS WAR'S FOR SOLDIERS, NOT MYSTERY-MEN LIKE YOU ALL-STAR HEROES!
BUT I'M NOT--
SARGE, I DON'T LIKE WHAT AH'M SEEIN'.
NEITHER WOULD I, FLOWER...
...IF I KNEW WHAT IT WAS I WAS LOOKIN' AT.
NOT AGAIN!
S-SARGE?
TH-THOSE SOLDIERS DOWN THERE...
...THE ONES WHO CALLED THEMSELVES THE LOSERS--
--THE SHADOW-BEASTS ARE KILLING THEM!
15

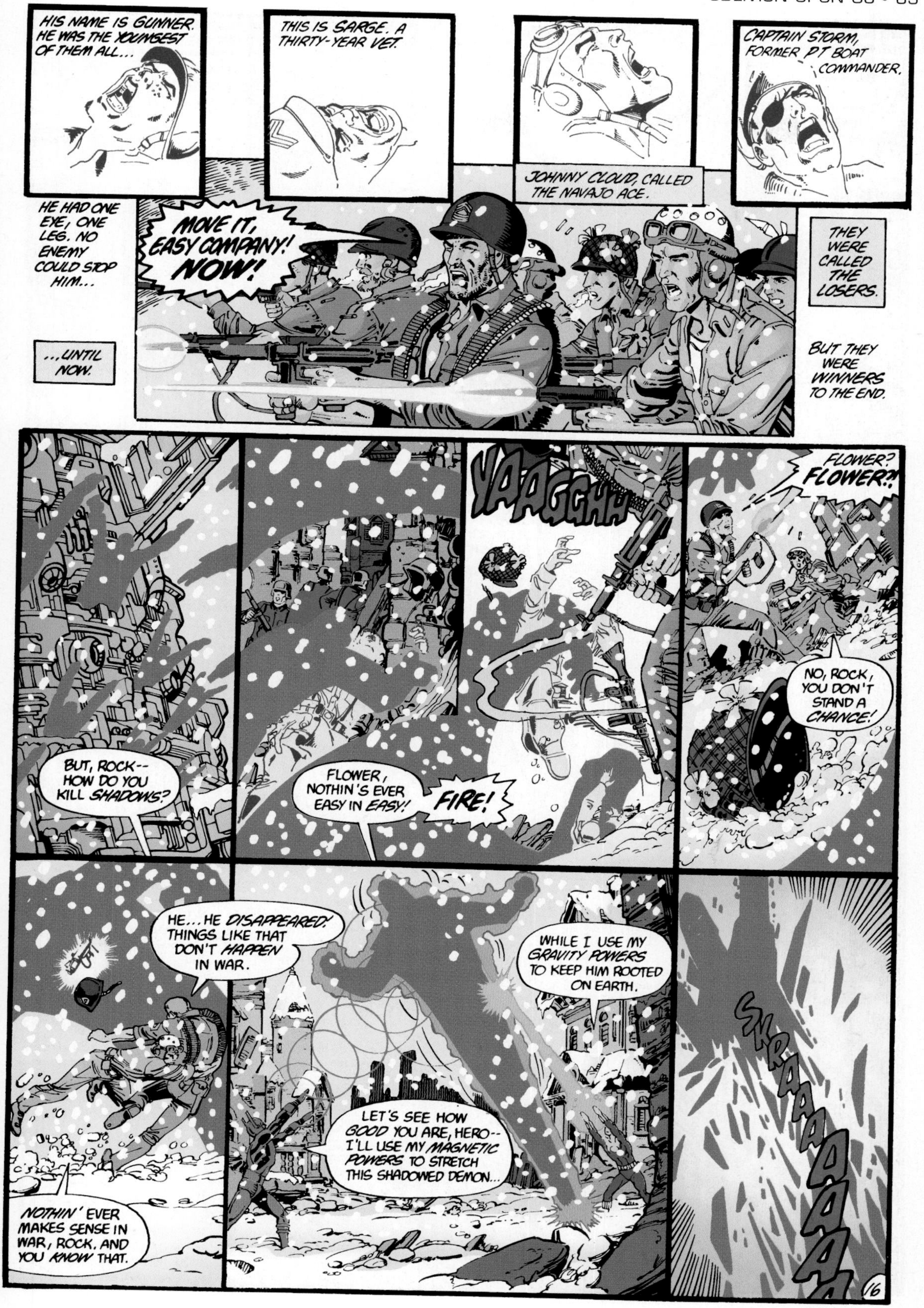
HIS NAME IS GUNNER. HE WAS THE YOUNGSEST OF THEM ALL...
THIS IS SARGE. A THIRTY-YEAR VET.
JOHNNY CLOUD, CALLED THE NAVAJO ACE.
CAPTAIN STORM, FORMER P.T. BOAT COMMANDER.
HE HAD ONE EYE, ONE LEG. NO ENEMY COULD STOP HIM...
...UNTIL NOW.
MOVE IT, EASY COMPANY! NOW!
THEY WERE CALLED THE LOSERS.
BUT THEY WERE WINNERS TO THE END.
BUT, ROCK-- HOW DO YOU KILL SHADOWS?
FLOWER, NOTHIN'S EVER EASY IN EASY!
FIRE!
YAAGGHH
FLOWER? FLOWER?!
NO, ROCK, YOU DON'T STAND A CHANCE!
HE... HE DISAPPEARED! THINGS LIKE THAT DON'T HAPPEN IN WAR.
NOTHIN' EVER MAKES SENSE IN WAR, ROCK, AND YOU KNOW THAT.
WHILE I USE MY GRAVITY POWERS TO KEEP HIM ROOTED ON EARTH.
LET'S SEE HOW GOOD YOU ARE, HERO-- I'LL USE MY MAGNETIC POWERS TO STRETCH THIS SHADOWED DEMON...
SKRAAAAAAAA
16

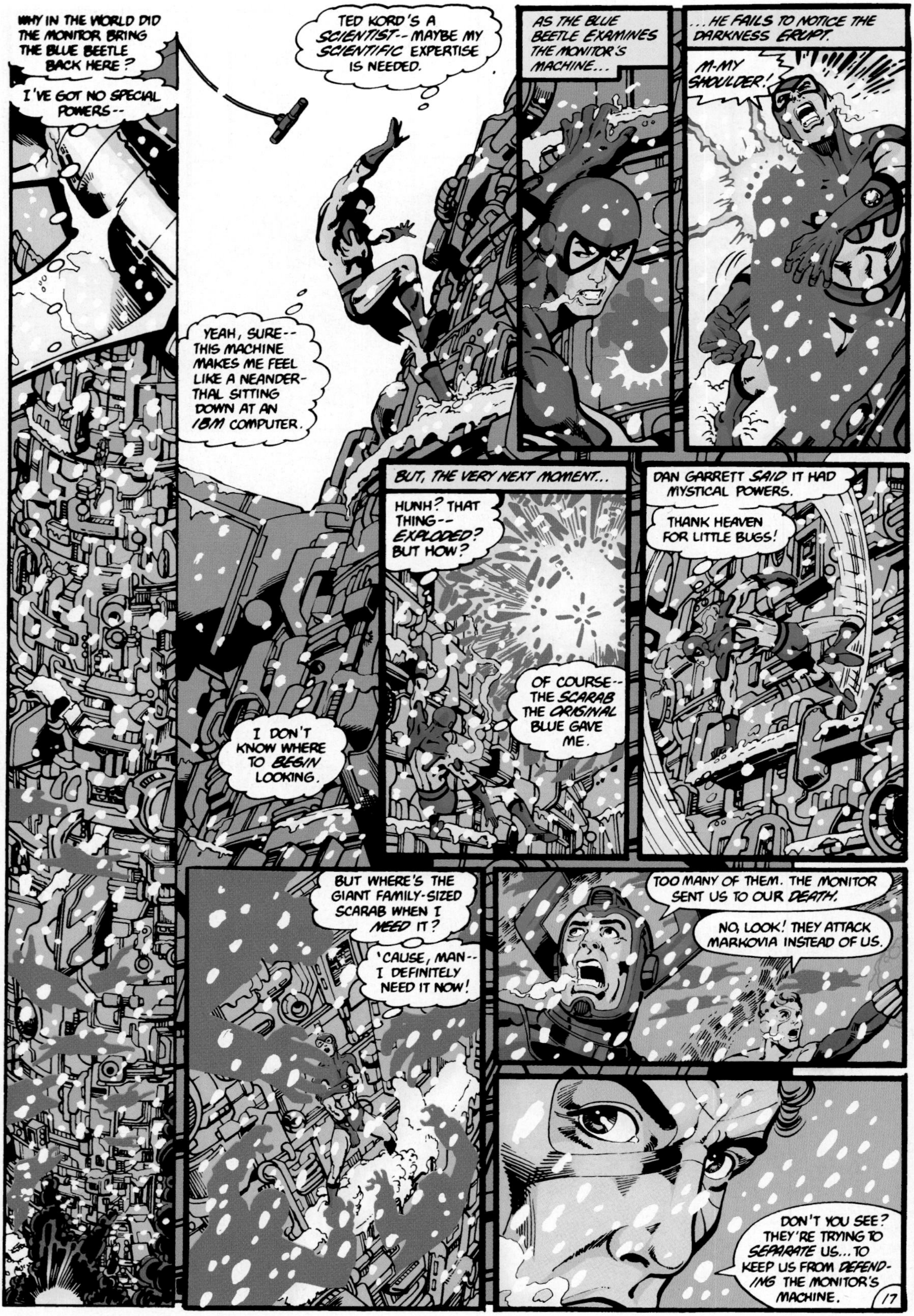
WHY IN THE WORLD DID THE MONITOR BRING THE BLUE BEETLE BACK HERE?
I'VE GOT NO SPECIAL POWERS--
TED KORD'S A SCIENTIST-- MAYBE MY SCIENTIFIC EXPERTISE IS NEEDED.
YEAH, SURE-- THIS MACHINE MAKES ME FEEL LIKE A NEANDERTHAL SITTING DOWN AT AN IBM COMPUTER.
I DON'T KNOW WHERE TO BEGIN LOOKING.
AS THE BLUE BEETLE EXAMINES THE MONITOR'S MACHINE...
...HE FAILS TO NOTICE THE DARKNESS ERUPT.
M-MY SHOULDER!
BUT, THE VERY NEXT MOMENT...
HUNH? THAT THING-- EXPLODED? BUT HOW?
OF COURSE-- THE SCARAB THE ORIGINAL BLUE GAVE ME.
DAN GARRETT SAID IT HAD MYSTICAL POWERS.
THANK HEAVEN FOR LITTLE BUGS!
BUT WHERE'S THE GIANT FAMILY-SIZED SCARAB WHEN I NEED IT?
'CAUSE, MAN-- I DEFINITELY NEED IT NOW!
TOO MANY OF THEM. THE MONITOR SENT US TO OUR DEATH.
NO, LOOK! THEY ATTACK MARKOVIA INSTEAD OF US.
DON'T YOU SEE? THEY'RE TRYING TO SEPARATE US... TO KEEP US FROM DEFENDING THE MONITOR'S MACHINE.
17

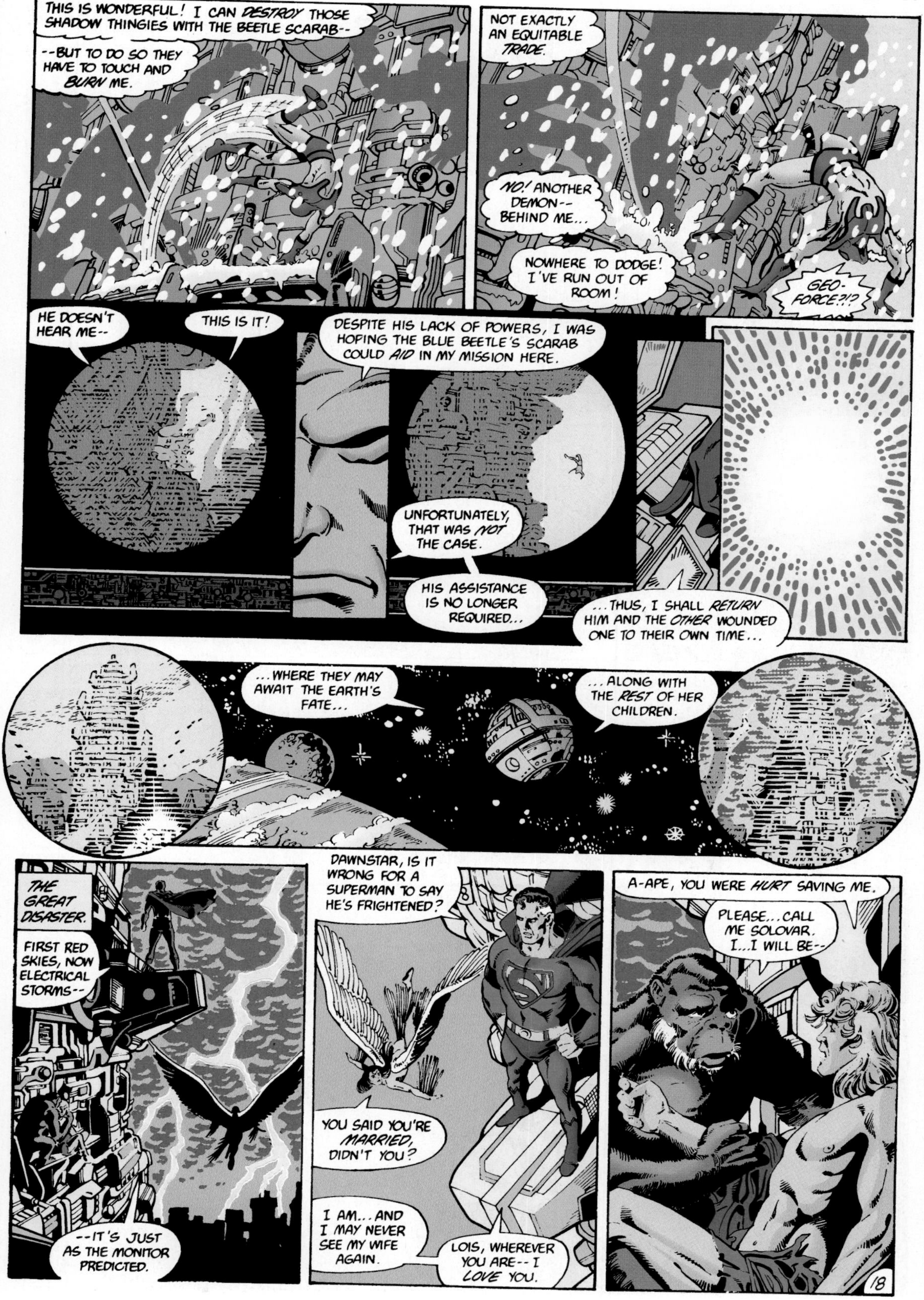
THIS IS WONDERFUL! I CAN DESTROY THOSE SHADOW THINGIES WITH THE BEETLE SCARAB--
--BUT TO DO SO THEY HAVE TO TOUCH AND BURN ME.
NOT EXACTLY AN EQUITABLE TRADE.
NO! ANOTHER DEMON-- BEHIND ME...
NOWHERE TO DODGE! I'VE RUN OUT OF ROOM!
GEO-FORCE?!?
HE DOESN'T HEAR ME--
THIS IS IT!
DESPITE HIS LACK OF POWERS, I WAS HOPING THE BLUE BEETLE'S SCARAB COULD AID IN MY MISSION HERE.
UNFORTUNATELY, THAT WAS NOT THE CASE.
HIS ASSISTANCE IS NO LONGER REQUIRED...
...THUS, I SHALL RETURN HIM AND THE OTHER WOUNDED ONE TO THEIR OWN TIME...
...WHERE THEY MAY AWAIT THE EARTH'S FATE...
...ALONG WITH THE REST OF HER CHILDREN.
THE GREAT DISASTER.
FIRST RED SKIES, NOW ELECTRICAL STORMS--
--IT'S JUST AS THE MONITOR PREDICTED.
DAWNSTAR, IS IT WRONG FOR A SUPERMAN TO SAY HE'S FRIGHTENED?
YOU SAID YOU'RE MARRIED, DIDN'T YOU?
I AM... AND I MAY NEVER SEE MY WIFE AGAIN.
LOIS, WHEREVER YOU ARE-- I LOVE YOU.
A-APE, YOU WERE HURT SAVING ME.
PLEASE... CALL ME SOLOVAR. I... I WILL BE--
18

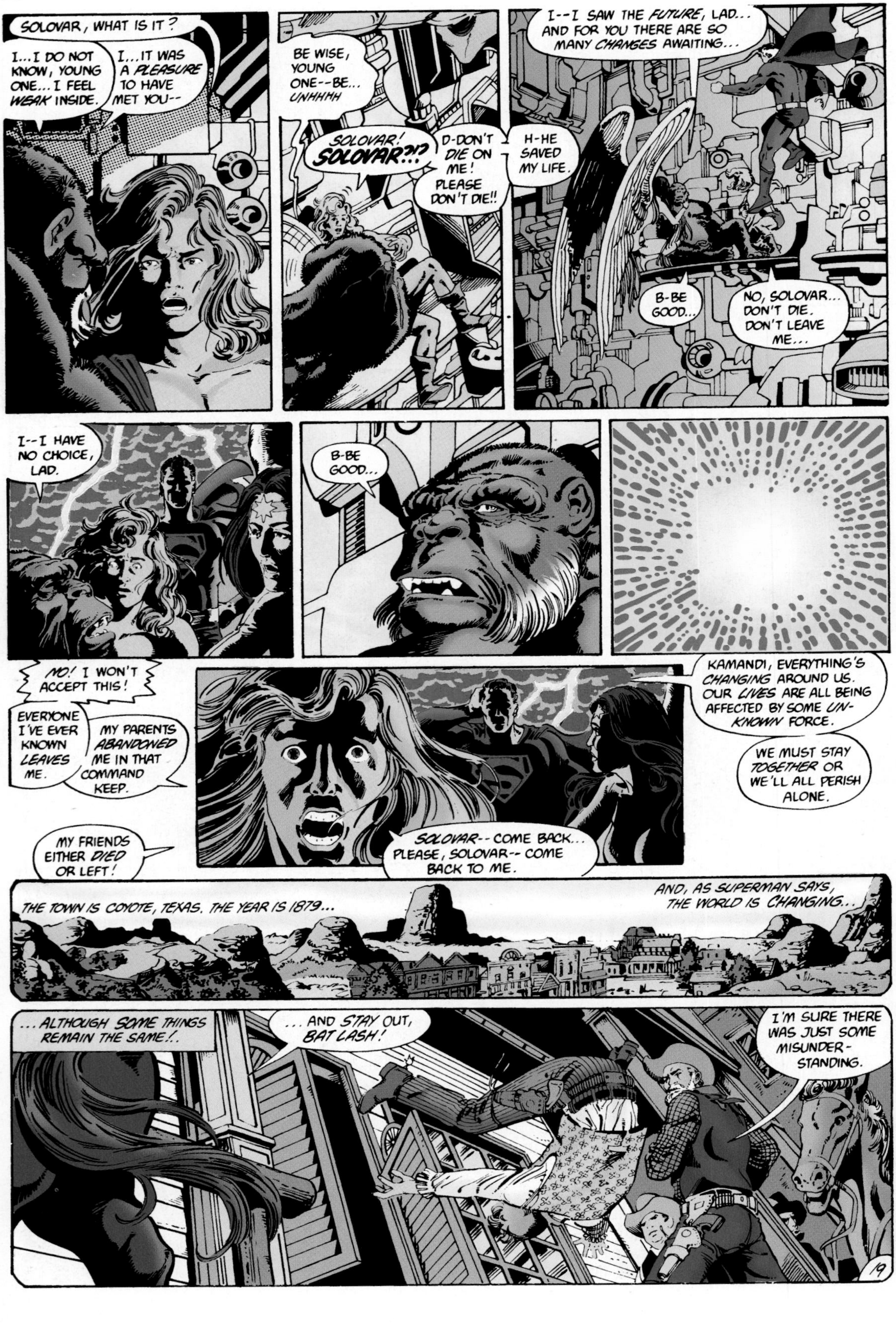
SOLOVAR, WHAT IS IT?
I...I DO NOT KNOW, YOUNG ONE... I FEEL WEAK INSIDE.
I...IT WAS A PLEASURE TO HAVE MET YOU--
BE WISE, YOUNG ONE--BE... UNHHHH
SOLOVAR! SOLOVAR?!?
D-DON'T DIE ON ME! PLEASE DON'T DIE!!
H-HE SAVED MY LIFE.
I--I SAW THE FUTURE, LAD... AND FOR YOU THERE ARE SO MANY CHANGES AWAITING...
B-BE GOOD...
NO, SOLOVAR... DON'T DIE. DON'T LEAVE ME...
I--I HAVE NO CHOICE, LAD.
B-BE GOOD...
NO! I WON'T ACCEPT THIS!
EVERYONE I'VE EVER KNOWN LEAVES ME.
MY PARENTS ABANDONED ME IN THAT COMMAND KEEP.
MY FRIENDS EITHER DIED OR LEFT!
SOLOVAR--COME BACK... PLEASE, SOLOVAR-- COME BACK TO ME.
KAMANDI, EVERYTHING'S CHANGING AROUND US. OUR LIVES ARE ALL BEING AFFECTED BY SOME UNKNOWN FORCE.
WE MUST STAY TOGETHER OR WE'LL ALL PERISH ALONE.
THE TOWN IS COYOTE, TEXAS. THE YEAR IS 1879...
AND, AS SUPERMAN SAYS, THE WORLD IS CHANGING...
...ALTHOUGH SOME THINGS REMAIN THE SAME!.
...AND STAY OUT, BAT LASH!
I'M SURE THERE WAS JUST SOME MISUNDERSTANDING.
19

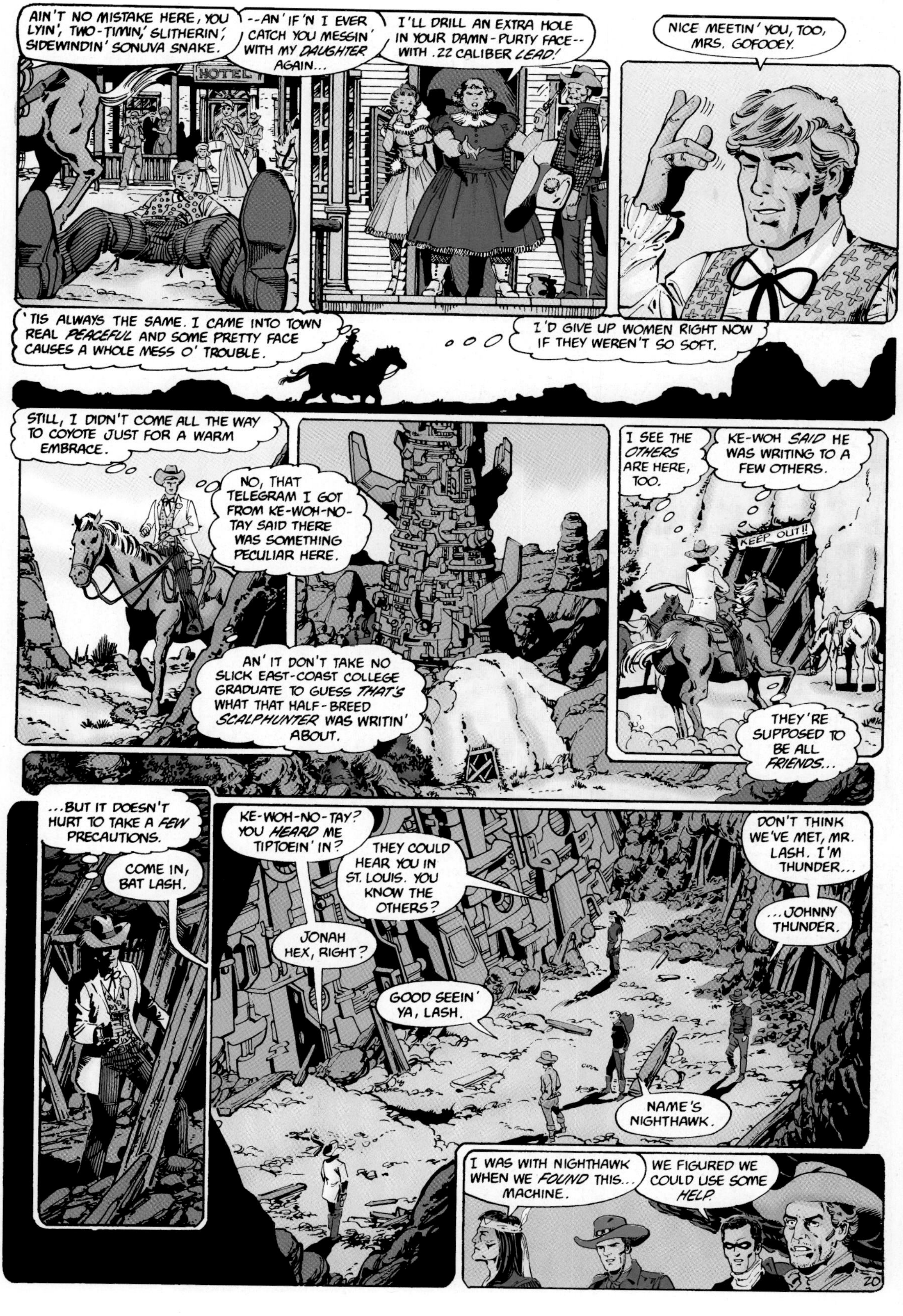
AIN'T NO MISTAKE HERE, YOU LYIN', TWO-TIMIN,' SLITHERIN,' SIDEWINDIN' SONUVA SNAKE.
--AN' IF 'N I EVER CATCH YOU MESSIN' WITH MY DAUGHTER AGAIN...
I'LL DRILL AN EXTRA HOLE IN YOUR DAMN-PURTY FACE-- WITH .22 CALIBER LEAD!
HOTEL
NICE MEETIN' YOU, TOO, MRS. GOFOOEY.
'TIS ALWAYS THE SAME. I CAME INTO TOWN REAL PEACEFUL AND SOME PRETTY FACE CAUSES A WHOLE MESS O' TROUBLE.
I'D GIVE UP WOMEN RIGHT NOW IF THEY WEREN'T SO SOFT.
STILL, I DIDN'T COME ALL THE WAY TO COYOTE JUST FOR A WARM EMBRACE.
NO, THAT TELEGRAM I GOT FROM KE-WOH-NO-TAY SAID THERE WAS SOMETHING PECULIAR HERE.
AN' IT DON'T TAKE NO SLICK EAST-COAST COLLEGE GRADUATE TO GUESS THAT'S WHAT THAT HALF-BREED SCALPHUNTER WAS WRITIN' ABOUT.
I SEE THE OTHERS ARE HERE, TOO.
KE-WOH SAID HE WAS WRITING TO A FEW OTHERS.
KEEP OUT!!
THEY'RE SUPPOSED TO BE ALL FRIENDS...
...BUT IT DOESN'T HURT TO TAKE A FEW PRECAUTIONS.
COME IN, BAT LASH.
KE-WOH-NO-TAY? YOU HEARD ME TIPTOEIN' IN?
THEY COULD HEAR YOU IN ST. LOUIS. YOU KNOW THE OTHERS?
JONAH HEX, RIGHT?
GOOD SEEIN' YA, LASH.
DON'T THINK WE'VE MET, MR. LASH. I'M THUNDER...
...JOHNNY THUNDER.
NAME'S NIGHTHAWK.
I WAS WITH NIGHTHAWK WHEN WE FOUND THIS... MACHINE.
WE FIGURED WE COULD USE SOME HELP.
20

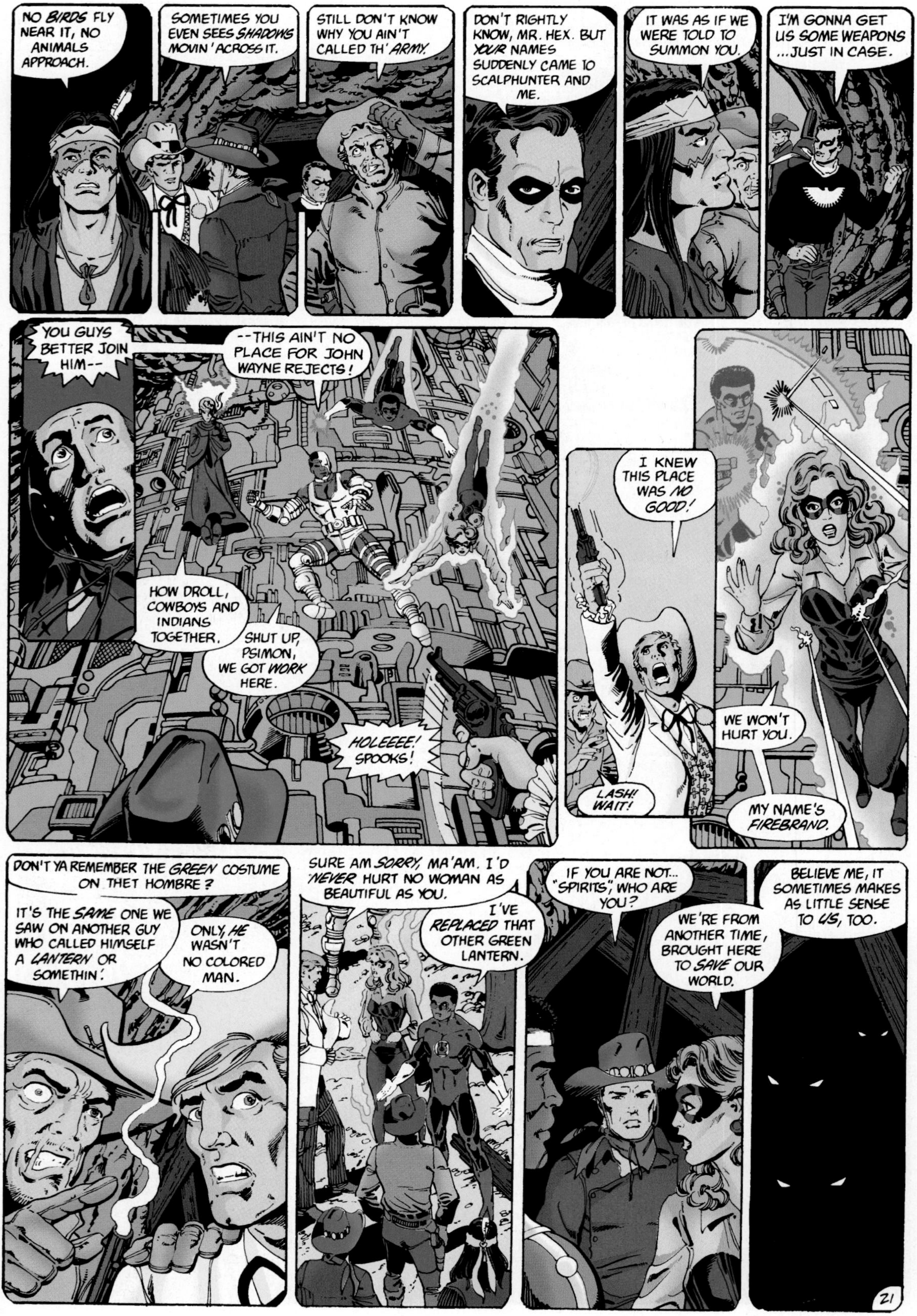
NO BIRDS FLY NEAR IT, NO ANIMALS APPROACH.
SOMETIMES YOU EVEN SEES SHADOWS MOVIN' ACROSS IT.
STILL DON'T KNOW WHY YOU AIN'T CALLED TH' ARMY.
DON'T RIGHTLY KNOW, MR. HEX. BUT YOUR NAMES SUDDENLY CAME TO SCALPHUNTER AND ME.
IT WAS AS IF WE WERE TOLD TO SUMMON YOU.
I'M GONNA GET US SOME WEAPONS ...JUST IN CASE.
YOU GUYS BETTER JOIN HIM--
--THIS AIN'T NO PLACE FOR JOHN WAYNE REJECTS!
HOW DROLL, COWBOYS AND INDIANS TOGETHER.
SHUT UP, PSIMON, WE GOT WORK HERE.
HOLEEEE! SPOOKS!
I KNEW THIS PLACE WAS NO GOOD!
LASH! WAIT!
WE WON'T HURT YOU.
MY NAME'S FIREBRAND.
DON'T YA REMEMBER THE GREEN COSTUME ON THET HOMBRE?
IT'S THE SAME ONE WE SAW ON ANOTHER GUY WHO CALLED HIMSELF A LANTERN OR SOMETHIN'.
ONLY, HE WASN'T NO COLORED MAN.
SURE AM SORRY, MA'AM. I'D NEVER HURT NO WOMAN AS BEAUTIFUL AS YOU.
I'VE REPLACED THAT OTHER GREEN LANTERN.
IF YOU ARE NOT... "SPIRITS," WHO ARE YOU?
WE'RE FROM ANOTHER TIME, BROUGHT HERE TO SAVE OUR WORLD.
BELIEVE ME, IT SOMETIMES MAKES AS LITTLE SENSE TO US, TOO.
21

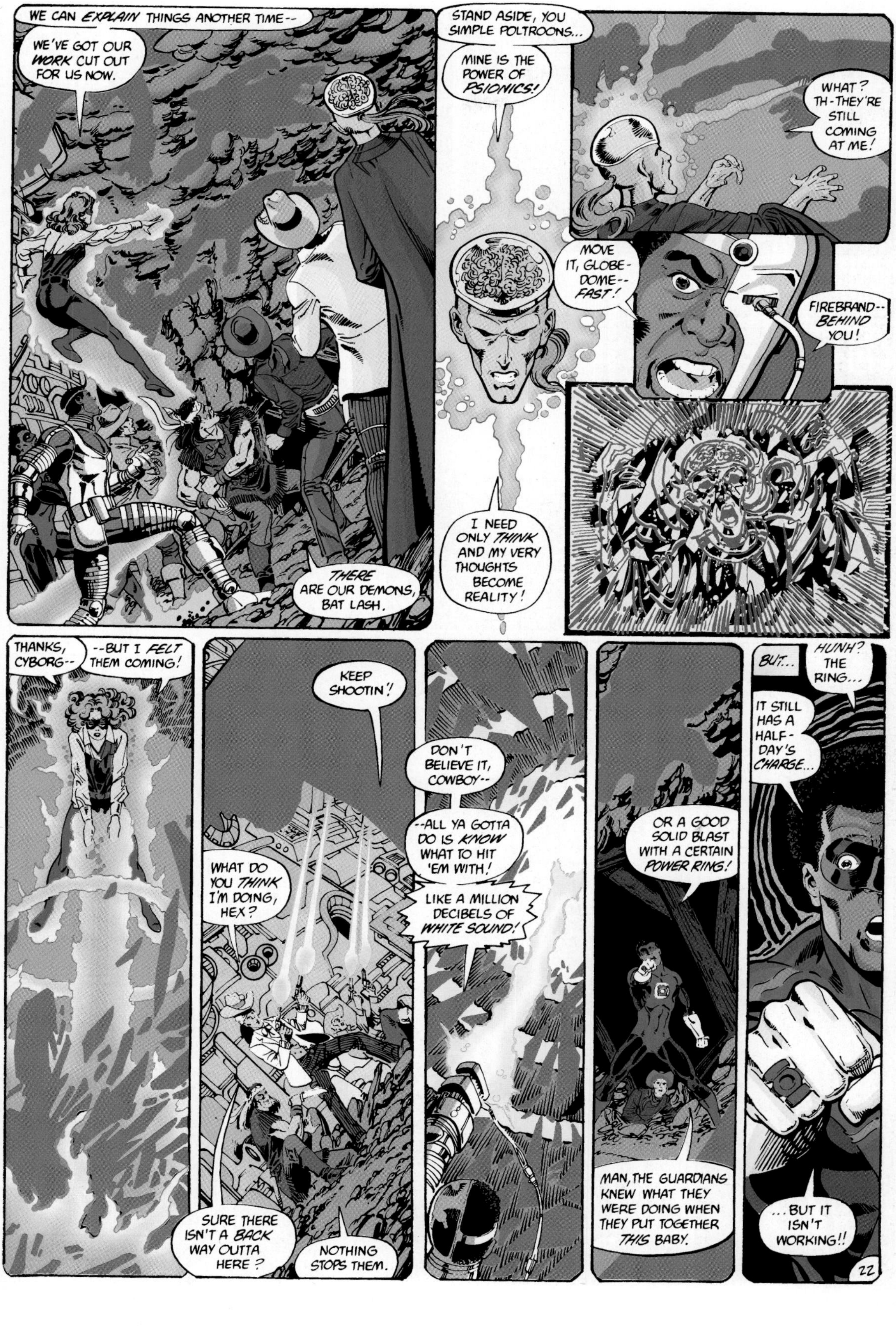
WE CAN EXPLAIN THINGS ANOTHER TIME--
WE'VE GOT OUR WORK CUT OUT FOR US NOW.
THERE ARE OUR DEMONS, BAT LASH.
STAND ASIDE, YOU SIMPLE POLTROONS...
MINE IS THE POWER OF PSIONICS!
I NEED ONLY THINK AND MY VERY THOUGHTS BECOME REALITY!
WHAT? TH-THEY'RE STILL COMING AT ME!
MOVE IT, GLOBE-DOME-- FAST!
FIREBRAND-- BEHIND YOU!
THANKS, CYBORG--
--BUT I FELT THEM COMING!
KEEP SHOOTIN'!
WHAT DO YOU THINK I'M DOING, HEX?
SURE THERE ISN'T A BACK WAY OUTTA HERE?
NOTHING STOPS THEM.
DON'T BELIEVE IT, COWBOY--
--ALL YA GOTTA DO IS KNOW WHAT TO HIT 'EM WITH!
LIKE A MILLION DECIBELS OF WHITE SOUND!
OR A GOOD SOLID BLAST WITH A CERTAIN POWER RING!
MAN, THE GUARDIANS KNEW WHAT THEY WERE DOING WHEN THEY PUT TOGETHER THIS BABY.
BUT...
HUNH? THE RING...
IT STILL HAS A HALF-DAY'S CHARGE...
...BUT IT ISN'T WORKING!!
22

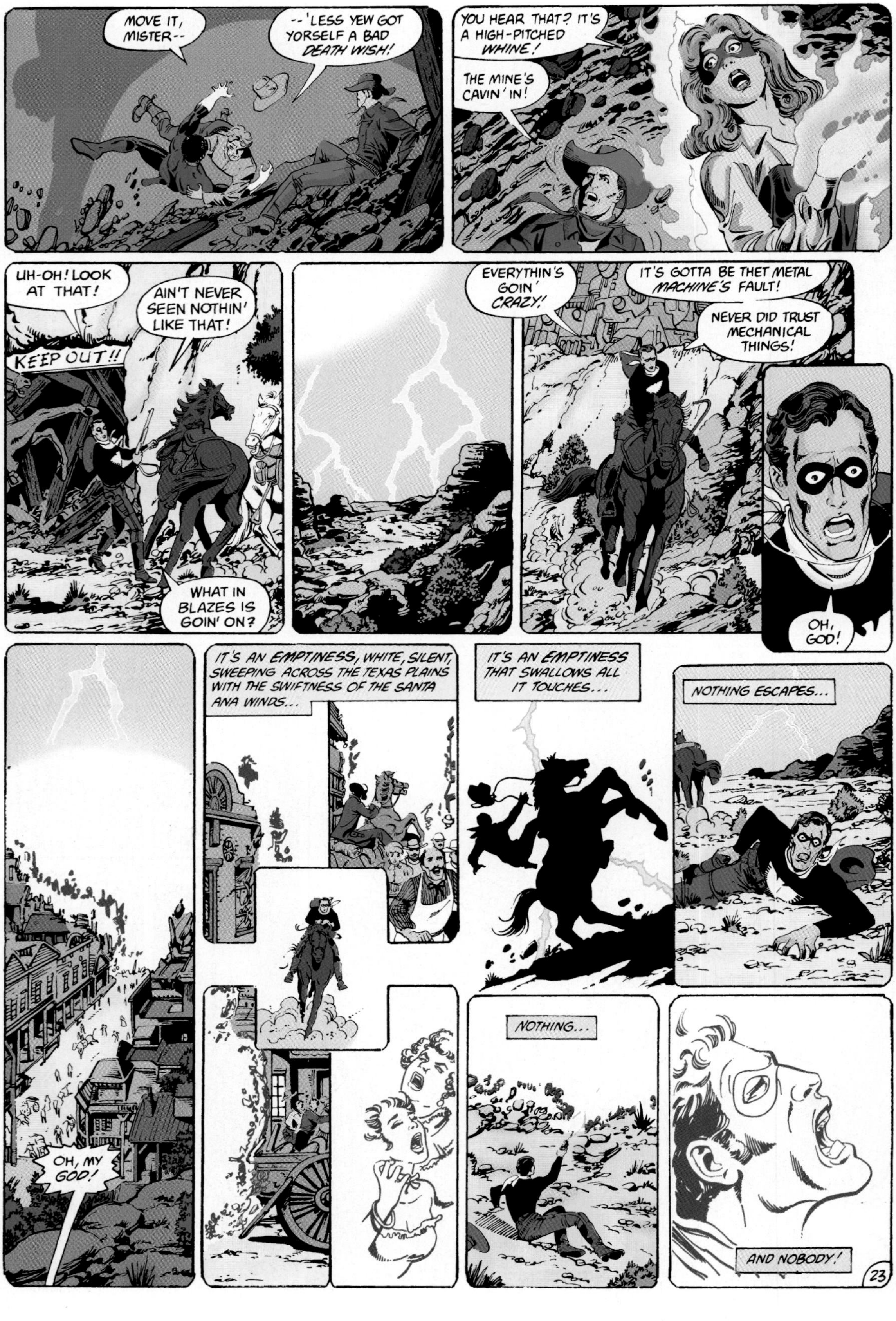
MOVE IT, MISTER--
--'LESS YEW GOT YORSELF A BAD DEATH WISH!
YOU HEAR THAT? IT'S A HIGH-PITCHED WHINE!
THE MINE'S CAVIN' IN!
UH-OH! LOOK AT THAT!
AIN'T NEVER SEEN NOTHIN' LIKE THAT!
KEEP OUT!!
WHAT IN BLAZES IS GOIN' ON?
EVERYTHIN'S GOIN' CRAZY!
IT'S GOTTA BE THET METAL MACHINE'S FAULT!
NEVER DID TRUST MECHANICAL THINGS!
OH, GOD!
OH, MY GOD!
IT'S AN EMPTINESS, WHITE, SILENT, SWEEPING ACROSS THE TEXAS PLAINS WITH THE SWIFTNESS OF THE SANTA ANA WINDS...
IT'S AN EMPTINESS THAT SWALLOWS ALL IT TOUCHES...
NOTHING ESCAPES...
NOTHING...
AND NOBODY!
23

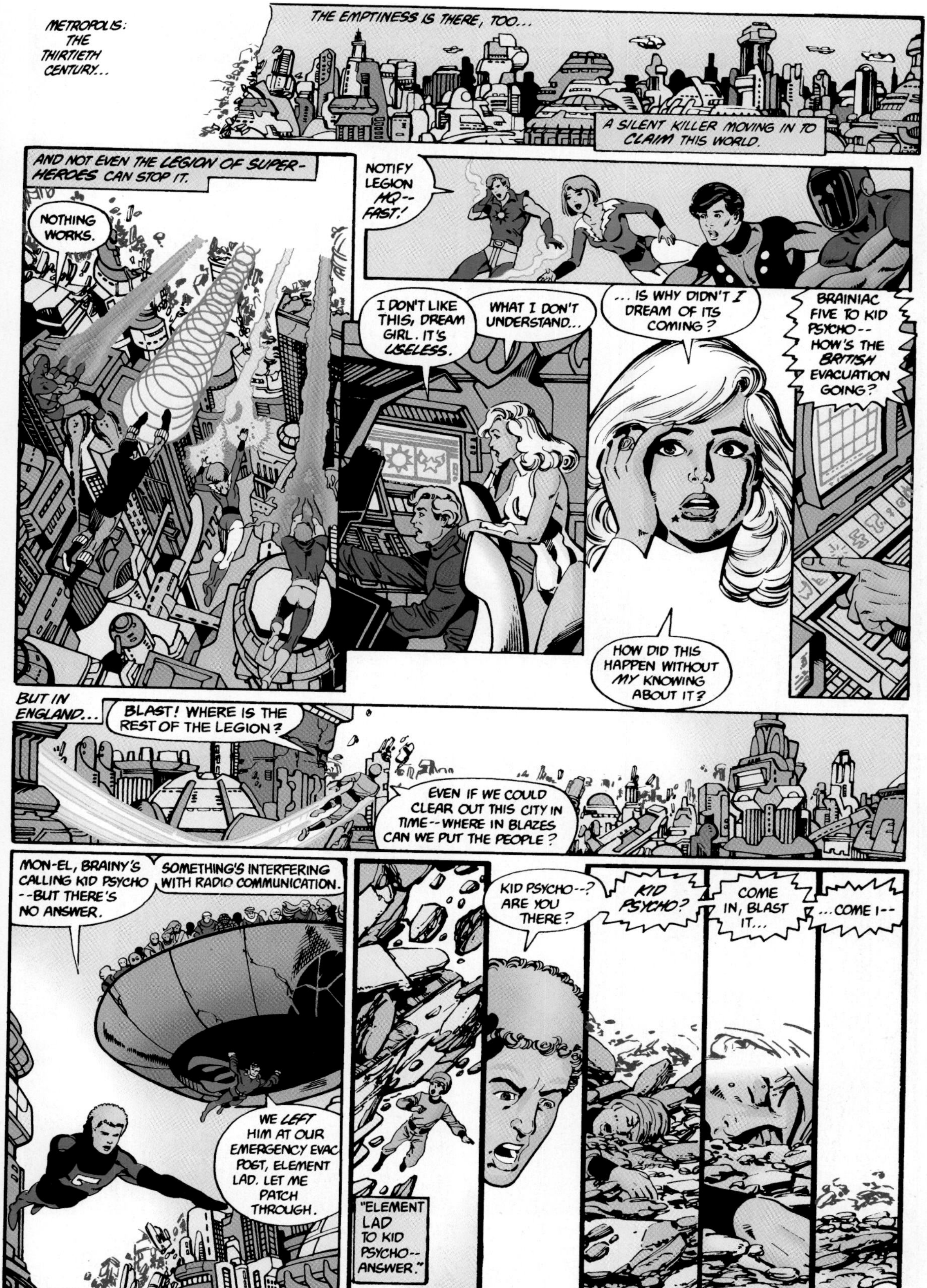
METROPOLIS: THE THIRTIETH CENTURY...
THE EMPTINESS IS THERE, TOO...
A SILENT KILLER MOVING IN TO CLAIM THIS WORLD.
AND NOT EVEN THE LEGION OF SUPER-HEROES CAN STOP IT.
NOTHING WORKS.
NOTIFY LEGION HQ--FAST!
I DON'T LIKE THIS, DREAM GIRL. IT'S USELESS.
WHAT I DON'T UNDERSTAND...
...IS WHY DIDN'T I DREAM OF ITS COMING?
HOW DID THIS HAPPEN WITHOUT MY KNOWING ABOUT IT?
BRAINIAC FIVE TO KID PSYCHO--HOW'S THE BRITISH EVACUATION GOING?
BUT IN ENGLAND...
BLAST! WHERE IS THE REST OF THE LEGION?
EVEN IF WE COULD CLEAR OUT THIS CITY IN TIME--WHERE IN BLAZES CAN WE PUT THE PEOPLE?
MON-EL, BRAINY'S CALLING KID PSYCHO --BUT THERE'S NO ANSWER.
SOMETHING'S INTERFERING WITH RADIO COMMUNICATION.
WE LEFT HIM AT OUR EMERGENCY EVAC POST, ELEMENT LAD. LET ME PATCH THROUGH.
"ELEMENT LAD TO KID PSYCHO--ANSWER."
KID PSYCHO--? ARE YOU THERE?
KID PSYCHO?
COME IN, BLAST IT...
...COME I--
24

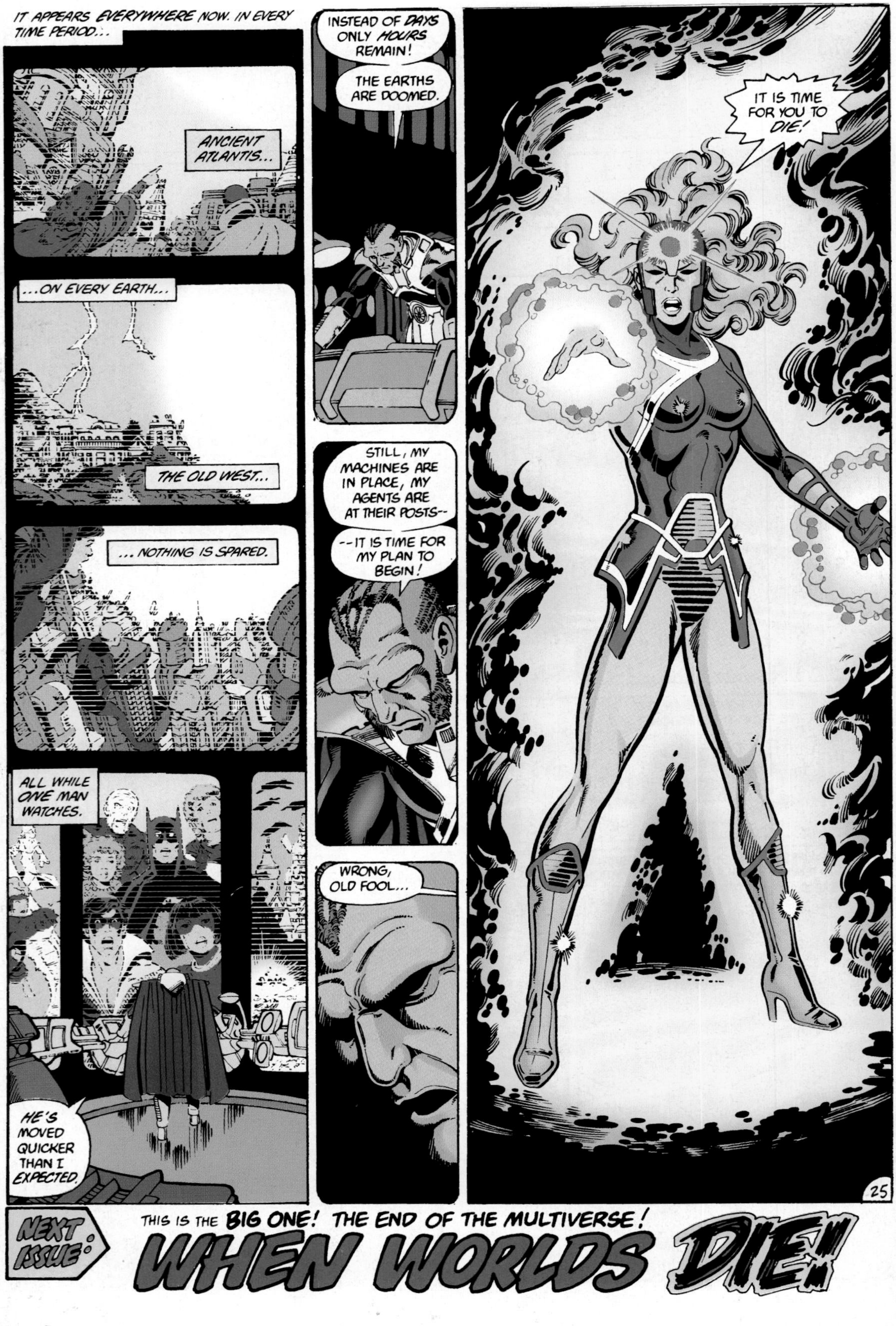
IT APPEARS EVERYWHERE NOW. IN EVERY TIME PERIOD...
ANCIENT ATLANTIS...
...ON EVERY EARTH...
THE OLD WEST...
...NOTHING IS SPARED.
ALL WHILE ONE MAN WATCHES.
HE'S MOVED QUICKER THAN I EXPECTED.
INSTEAD OF DAYS ONLY HOURS REMAIN!
THE EARTHS ARE DOOMED.
STILL, MY MACHINES ARE IN PLACE, MY AGENTS ARE AT THEIR POSTS--
--IT IS TIME FOR MY PLAN TO BEGIN!
WRONG, OLD FOOL...
IT IS TIME FOR YOU TO DIE!
25
NEXT ISSUE:
THIS IS THE BIG ONE! THE END OF THE MULTIVERSE!
WHEN WORLDS DIE!

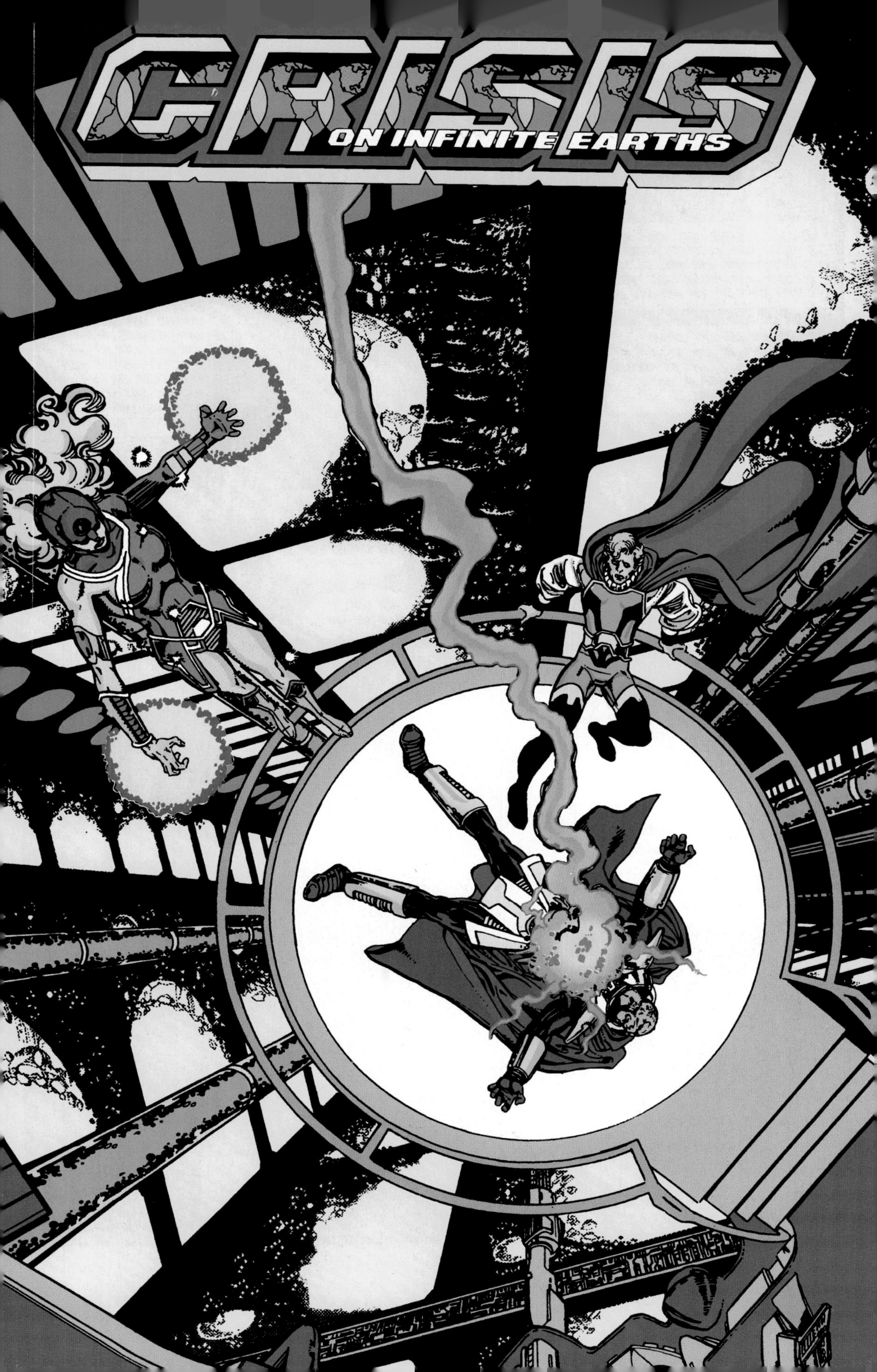
CRISIS
ON INFINITE EARTHS

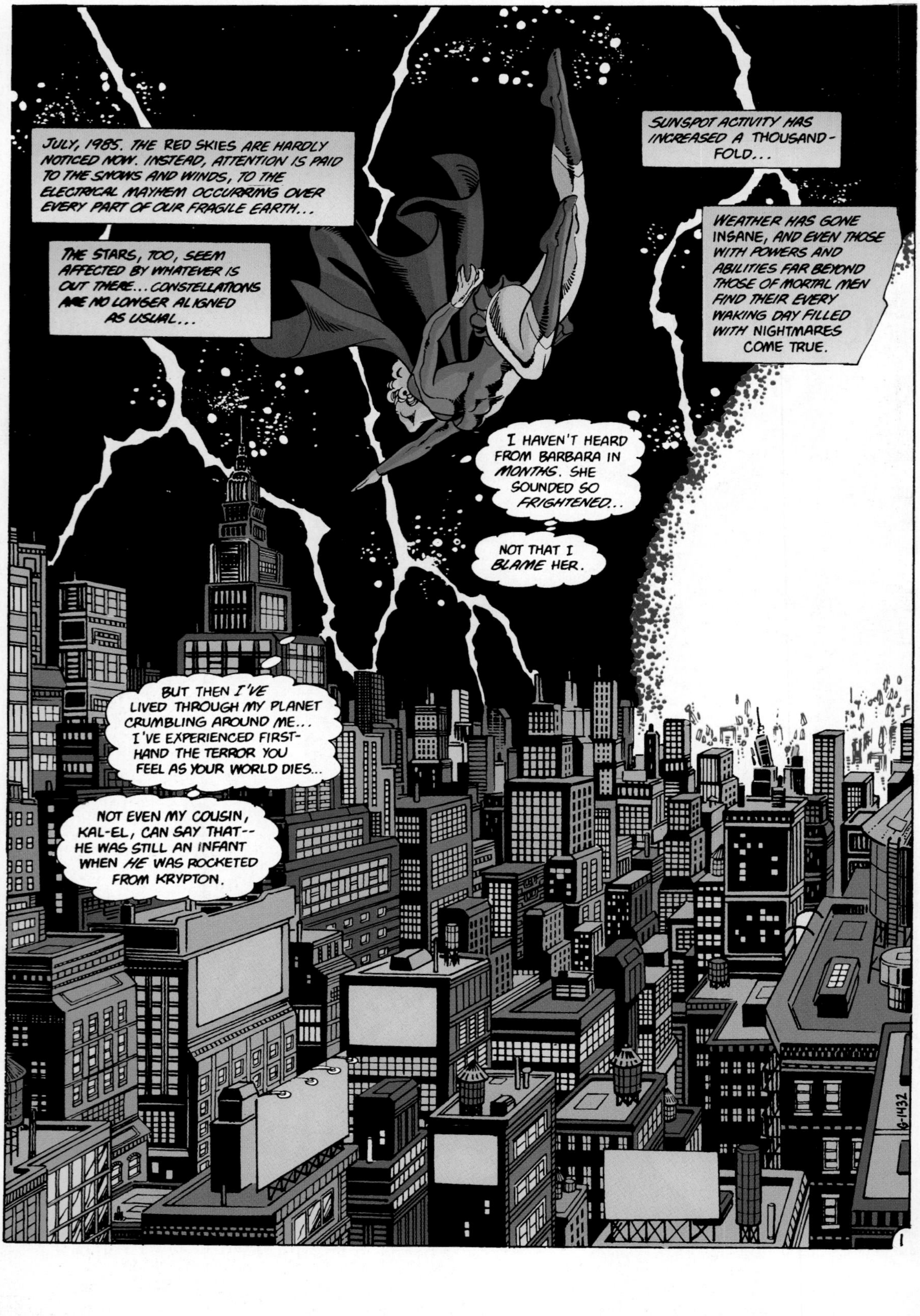
JULY, 1985. THE RED SKIES ARE HARDLY NOTICED NOW. INSTEAD, ATTENTION IS PAID TO THE SNOWS AND WINDS, TO THE ELECTRICAL MAYHEM OCCURRING OVER EVERY PART OF OUR FRAGILE EARTH...
THE STARS, TOO, SEEM AFFECTED BY WHATEVER IS OUT THERE... CONSTELLATIONS ARE NO LONGER ALIGNED AS USUAL...
SUNSPOT ACTIVITY HAS INCREASED A THOUSAND-FOLD...
WEATHER HAS GONE INSANE, AND EVEN THOSE WITH POWERS AND ABILITIES FAR BEYOND THOSE OF MORTAL MEN FIND THEIR EVERY WAKING DAY FILLED WITH NIGHTMARES COME TRUE.
I HAVEN'T HEARD FROM BARBARA IN MONTHS. SHE SOUNDED SO FRIGHTENED...
NOT THAT I BLAME HER.
BUT THEN I'VE LIVED THROUGH MY PLANET CRUMBLING AROUND ME... I'VE EXPERIENCED FIRST-HAND THE TERROR YOU FEEL AS YOUR WORLD DIES...
NOT EVEN MY COUSIN, KAL-EL, CAN SAY THAT-- HE WAS STILL AN INFANT WHEN HE WAS ROCKETED FROM KRYPTON.
G-1432
1

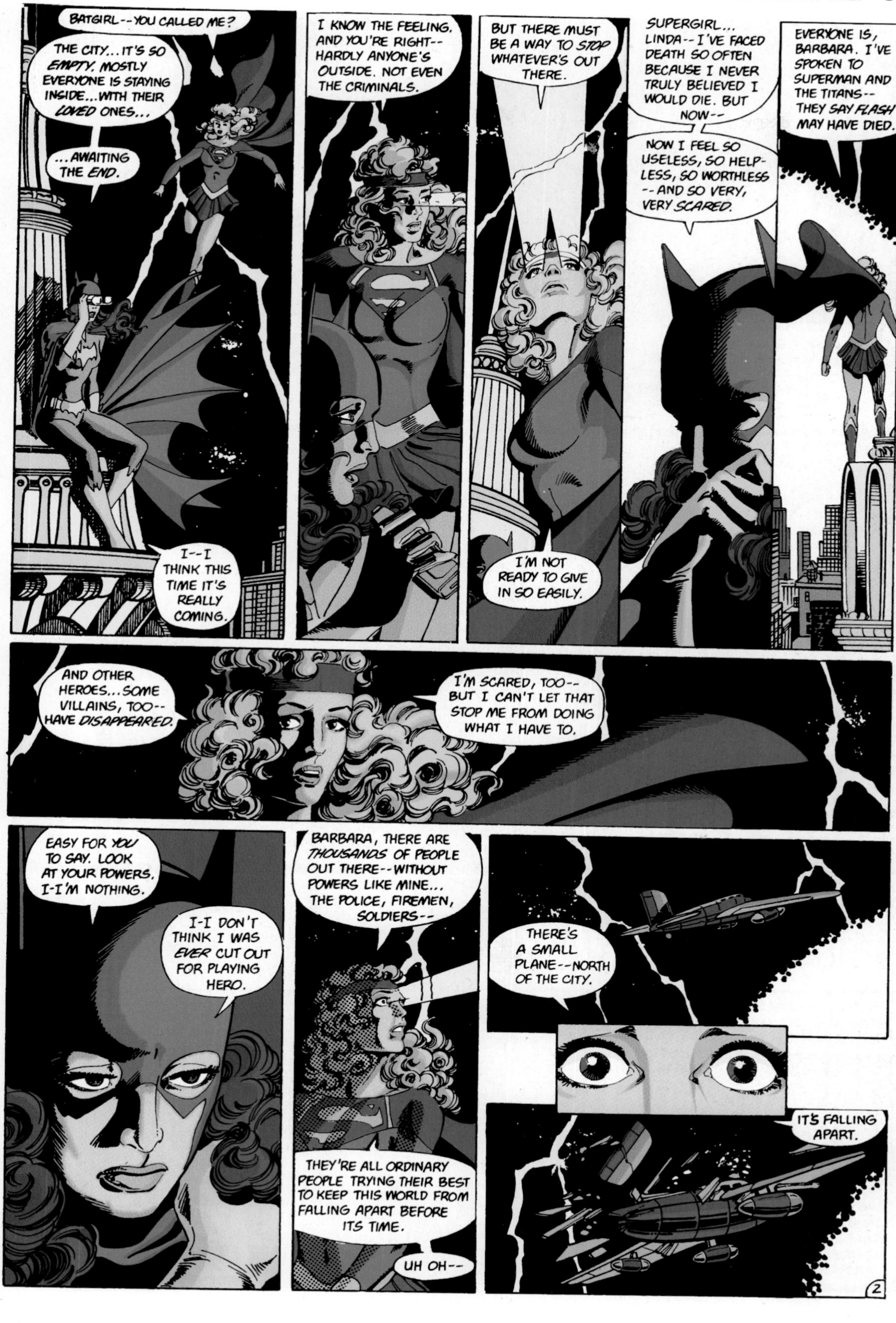
BATGIRL--YOU CALLED ME?
THE CITY... IT'S SO EMPTY. MOSTLY EVERYONE IS STAYING INSIDE... WITH THEIR LOVED ONES...
...AWAITING THE END.
I--I THINK THIS TIME IT'S REALLY COMING.
I KNOW THE FEELING. AND YOU'RE RIGHT-- HARDLY ANYONE'S OUTSIDE. NOT EVEN THE CRIMINALS.
BUT THERE MUST BE A WAY TO STOP WHATEVER'S OUT THERE.
I'M NOT READY TO GIVE IN SO EASILY.
SUPERGIRL... LINDA-- I'VE FACED DEATH SO OFTEN BECAUSE I NEVER TRULY BELIEVED I WOULD DIE. BUT NOW--
NOW I FEEL SO USELESS, SO HELP-LESS, SO WORTHLESS --AND SO VERY, VERY SCARED.
EVERYONE IS, BARBARA. I'VE SPOKEN TO SUPERMAN AND THE TITANS-- THEY SAY FLASH MAY HAVE DIED.
AND OTHER HEROES... SOME VILLAINS, TOO-- HAVE DISAPPEARED.
I'M SCARED, TOO-- BUT I CAN'T LET THAT STOP ME FROM DOING WHAT I HAVE TO.
EASY FOR YOU TO SAY. LOOK AT YOUR POWERS. I-I'M NOTHING.
I-I DON'T THINK I WAS EVER CUT OUT FOR PLAYING HERO.
BARBARA, THERE ARE THOUSANDS OF PEOPLE OUT THERE--WITHOUT POWERS LIKE MINE... THE POLICE, FIREMEN, SOLDIERS--
THEY'RE ALL ORDINARY PEOPLE TRYING THEIR BEST TO KEEP THIS WORLD FROM FALLING APART BEFORE ITS TIME.
UH OH--
THERE'S A SMALL PLANE--NORTH OF THE CITY.
IT'S FALLING APART.
2

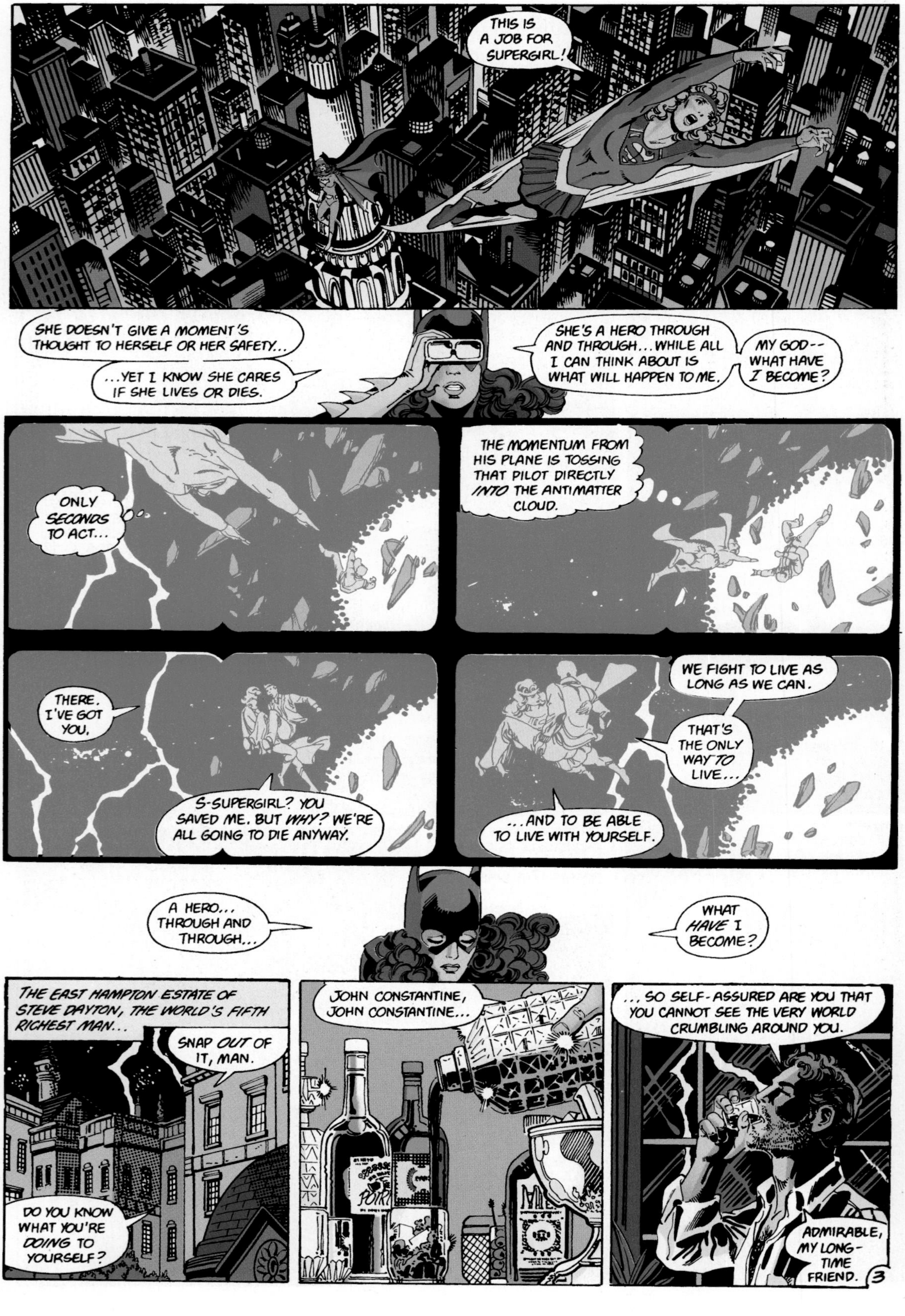
THIS IS A JOB FOR SUPERGIRL!
SHE DOESN'T GIVE A MOMENT'S THOUGHT TO HERSELF OR HER SAFETY...
...YET I KNOW SHE CARES IF SHE LIVES OR DIES.
SHE'S A HERO THROUGH AND THROUGH...WHILE ALL I CAN THINK ABOUT IS WHAT WILL HAPPEN TO ME.
MY GOD-- WHAT HAVE I BECOME?
ONLY SECONDS TO ACT...
THE MOMENTUM FROM HIS PLANE IS TOSSING THAT PILOT DIRECTLY INTO THE ANTIMATTER CLOUD.
THERE. I'VE GOT YOU.
S-SUPERGIRL? YOU SAVED ME. BUT WHY? WE'RE ALL GOING TO DIE ANYWAY.
WE FIGHT TO LIVE AS LONG AS WE CAN.
THAT'S THE ONLY WAY TO LIVE...
...AND TO BE ABLE TO LIVE WITH YOURSELF.
A HERO... THROUGH AND THROUGH...
WHAT HAVE I BECOME?
THE EAST HAMPTON ESTATE OF STEVE DAYTON, THE WORLD'S FIFTH RICHEST MAN...
SNAP OUT OF IT, MAN.
DO YOU KNOW WHAT YOU'RE DOING TO YOURSELF?
JOHN CONSTANTINE, JOHN CONSTANTINE...
...SO SELF-ASSURED ARE YOU THAT YOU CANNOT SEE THE VERY WORLD CRUMBLING AROUND YOU.
ADMIRABLE, MY LONG-TIME FRIEND.
3

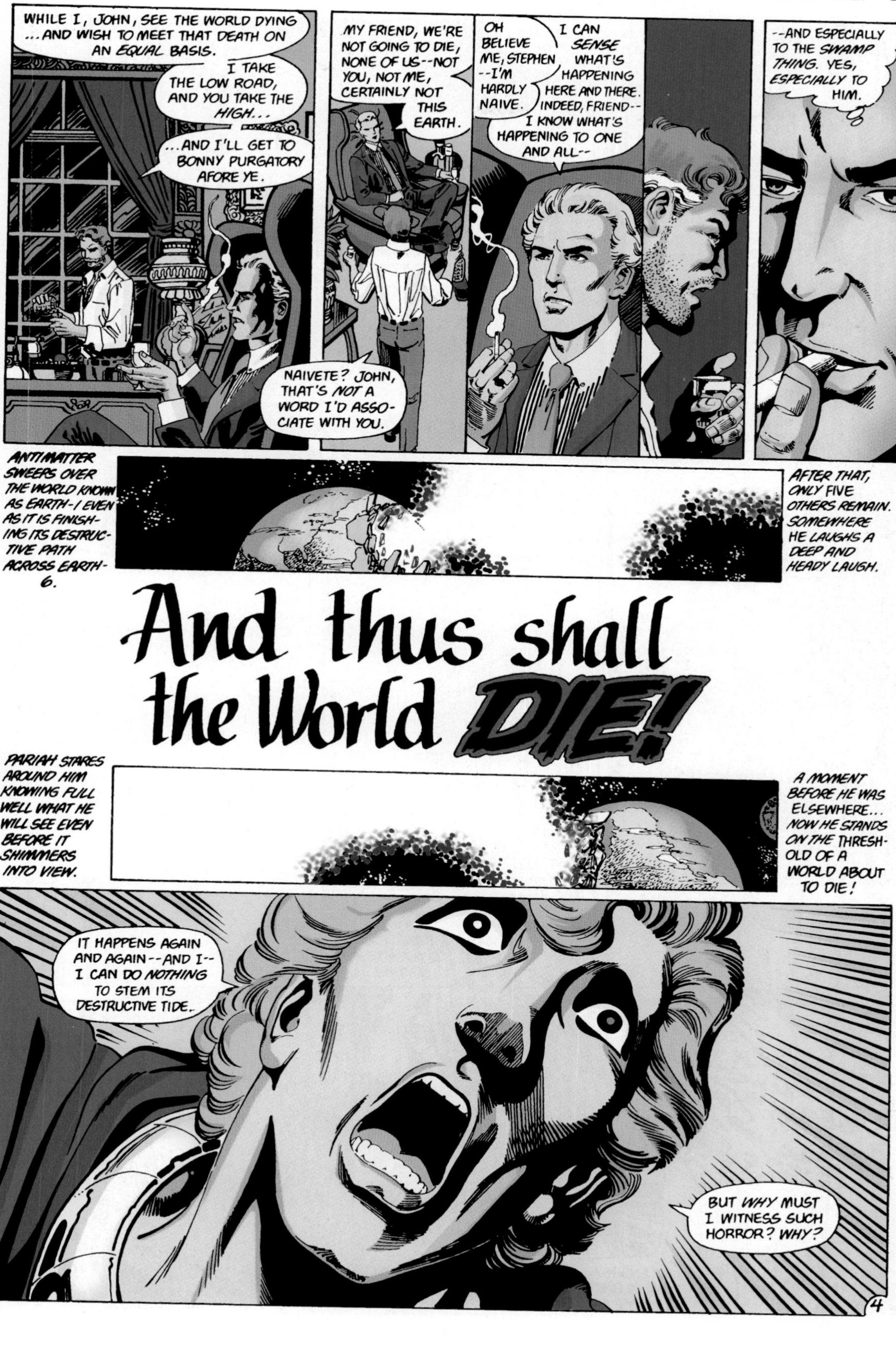
WHILE I, JOHN, SEE THE WORLD DYING ...AND WISH TO MEET THAT DEATH ON AN EQUAL BASIS.
I TAKE THE LOW ROAD, AND YOU TAKE THE HIGH...
...AND I'LL GET TO BONNY PURGATORY AFORE YE.
MY FRIEND, WE'RE NOT GOING TO DIE, NONE OF US--NOT YOU, NOT ME, CERTAINLY NOT THIS EARTH.
NAIVETE? JOHN, THAT'S NOT A WORD I'D ASSOCIATE WITH YOU.
OH BELIEVE ME, STEPHEN --I'M HARDLY NAIVE.
I CAN SENSE WHAT'S HAPPENING HERE AND THERE. INDEED, FRIEND-- I KNOW WHAT'S HAPPENING TO ONE AND ALL--
--AND ESPECIALLY TO THE SWAMP THING. YES, ESPECIALLY TO HIM.
ANTIMATTER SWEEPS OVER THE WORLD KNOWN AS EARTH-I EVEN AS IT IS FINISHING ITS DESTRUCTIVE PATH ACROSS EARTH-6.
AFTER THAT, ONLY FIVE OTHERS REMAIN. SOMEWHERE HE LAUGHS A DEEP AND HEADY LAUGH.
And thus shall the World DIE!
PARIAH STARES AROUND HIM KNOWING FULL WELL WHAT HE WILL SEE EVEN BEFORE IT SHIMMERS INTO VIEW.
A MOMENT BEFORE HE WAS ELSEWHERE... NOW HE STANDS ON THE THRESHOLD OF A WORLD ABOUT TO DIE!
IT HAPPENS AGAIN AND AGAIN--AND I-- I CAN DO NOTHING TO STEM ITS DESTRUCTIVE TIDE.
BUT WHY MUST I WITNESS SUCH HORROR? WHY?
4

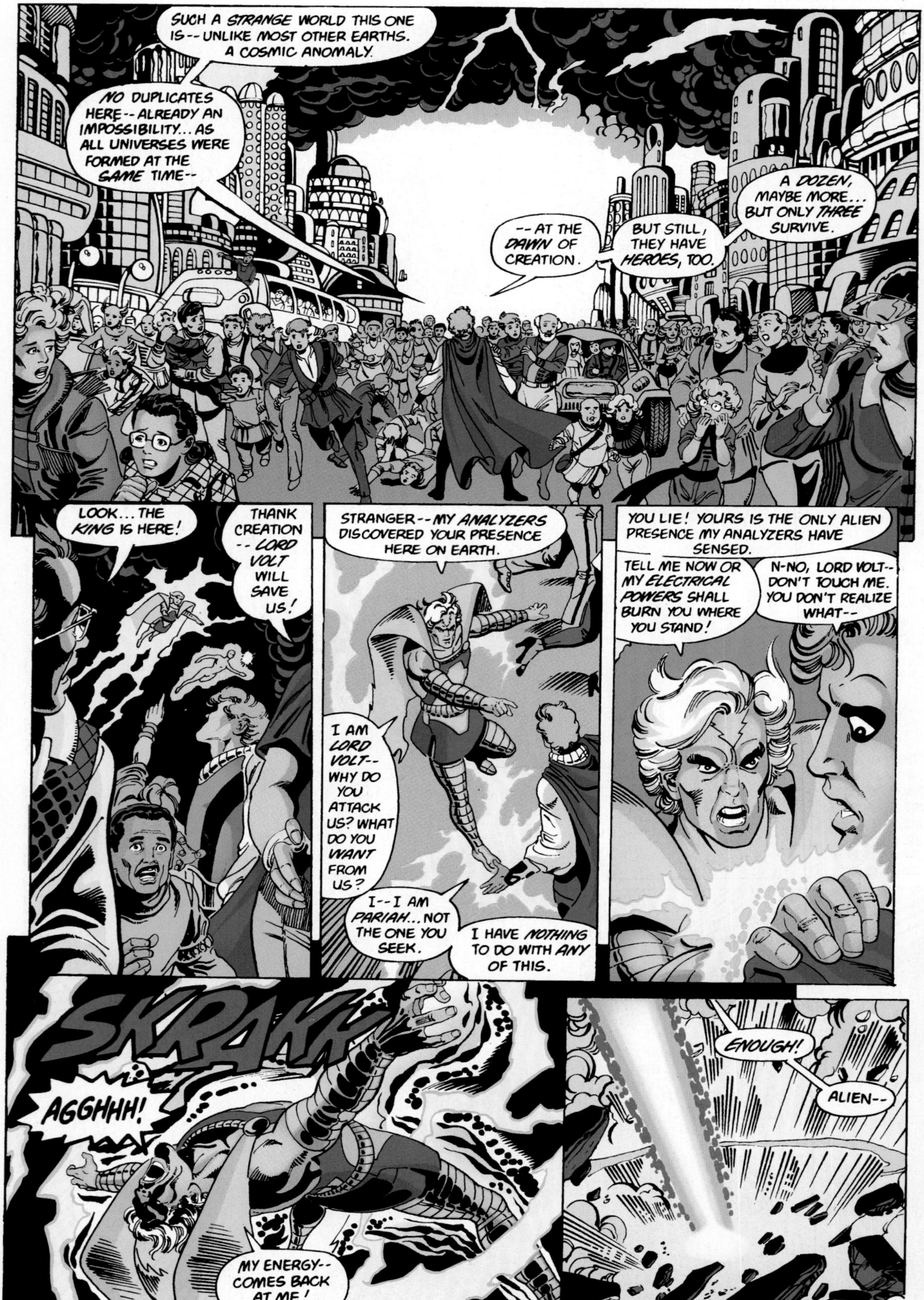
SUCH A STRANGE WORLD THIS ONE IS--UNLIKE MOST OTHER EARTHS. A COSMIC ANOMALY.
NO DUPLICATES HERE--ALREADY AN IMPOSSIBILITY... AS ALL UNIVERSES WERE FORMED AT THE SAME TIME--
--AT THE DAWN OF CREATION.
BUT STILL, THEY HAVE HEROES, TOO.
A DOZEN, MAYBE MORE... BUT ONLY THREE SURVIVE.
LOOK... THE KING IS HERE!
THANK CREATION--LORD VOLT WILL SAVE US!
STRANGER--MY ANALYZERS DISCOVERED YOUR PRESENCE HERE ON EARTH.
I AM LORD VOLT--WHY DO YOU ATTACK US? WHAT DO YOU WANT FROM US?
I--I AM PARIAH... NOT THE ONE YOU SEEK.
I HAVE NOTHING TO DO WITH ANY OF THIS.
YOU LIE! YOURS IS THE ONLY ALIEN PRESENCE MY ANALYZERS HAVE SENSED.
TELL ME NOW OR MY ELECTRICAL POWERS SHALL BURN YOU WHERE YOU STAND!
N-NO, LORD VOLT--DON'T TOUCH ME. YOU DON'T REALIZE WHAT--
SKRAKK
AGGHHH!
MY ENERGY--COMES BACK AT ME!
ENOUGH!
ALIEN--
5

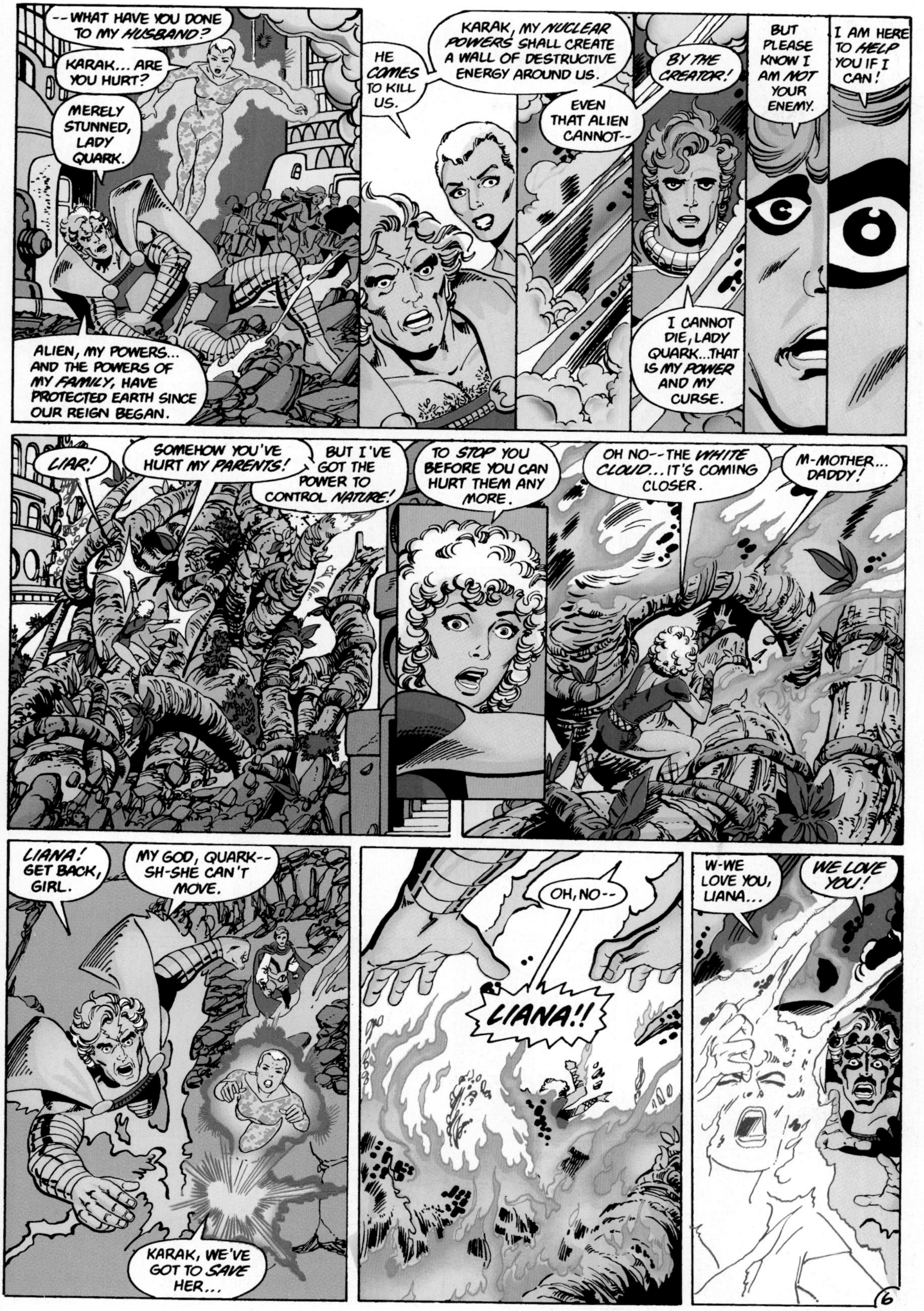
--WHAT HAVE YOU DONE TO MY HUSBAND?
KARAK... ARE YOU HURT?
MERELY STUNNED, LADY QUARK.
ALIEN, MY POWERS... AND THE POWERS OF MY FAMILY, HAVE PROTECTED EARTH SINCE OUR REIGN BEGAN.
HE COMES TO KILL US.
KARAK, MY NUCLEAR POWERS SHALL CREATE A WALL OF DESTRUCTIVE ENERGY AROUND US.
EVEN THAT ALIEN CANNOT--
BY THE CREATOR!
I CANNOT DIE, LADY QUARK...THAT IS MY POWER AND MY CURSE.
BUT PLEASE KNOW I AM NOT YOUR ENEMY.
I AM HERE TO HELP YOU IF I CAN!
LIAR!
SOMEHOW YOU'VE HURT MY PARENTS!
BUT I'VE GOT THE POWER TO CONTROL NATURE!
TO STOP YOU BEFORE YOU CAN HURT THEM ANY MORE.
OH NO--THE WHITE CLOUD...IT'S COMING CLOSER.
M-MOTHER... DADDY!
LIANA! GET BACK, GIRL.
MY GOD, QUARK--SH-SHE CAN'T MOVE.
KARAK, WE'VE GOT TO SAVE HER...
OH, NO--
LIANA!!
W-WE LOVE YOU, LIANA...
WE LOVE YOU!
6

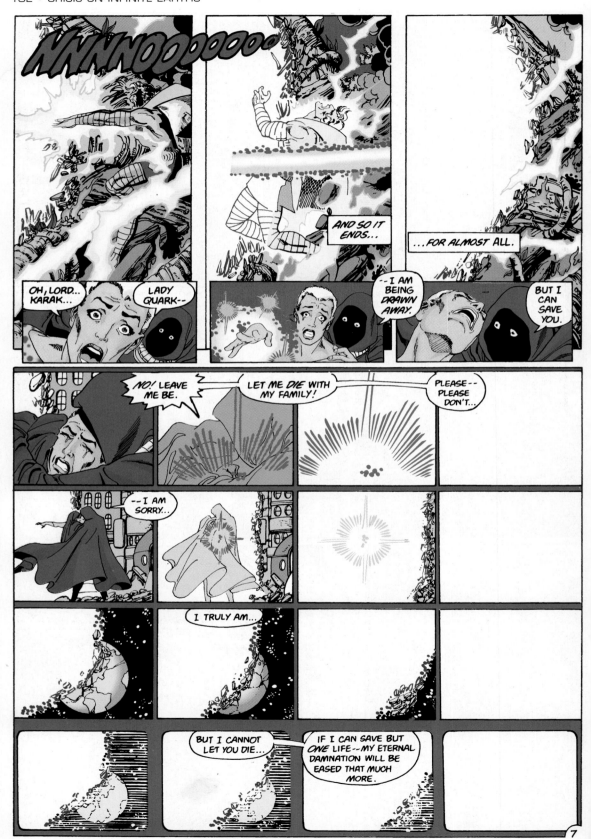

NNNNOOOOOOO

AND SO IT ENDS...

...FOR ALMOST ALL.

OH, LORD... KARAK...

LADY QUARK--

--I AM BEING *DRAWN* AWAY.

BUT I CAN SAVE YOU.

NO! LEAVE ME BE.

LET ME *DIE* WITH MY FAMILY!

PLEASE-- PLEASE DON'T...

--I AM SORRY...

I TRULY AM...

BUT I CANNOT LET YOU DIE...

IF I CAN SAVE BUT *ONE* LIFE--MY ETERNAL DAMNATION WILL BE EASED THAT MUCH MORE.

7

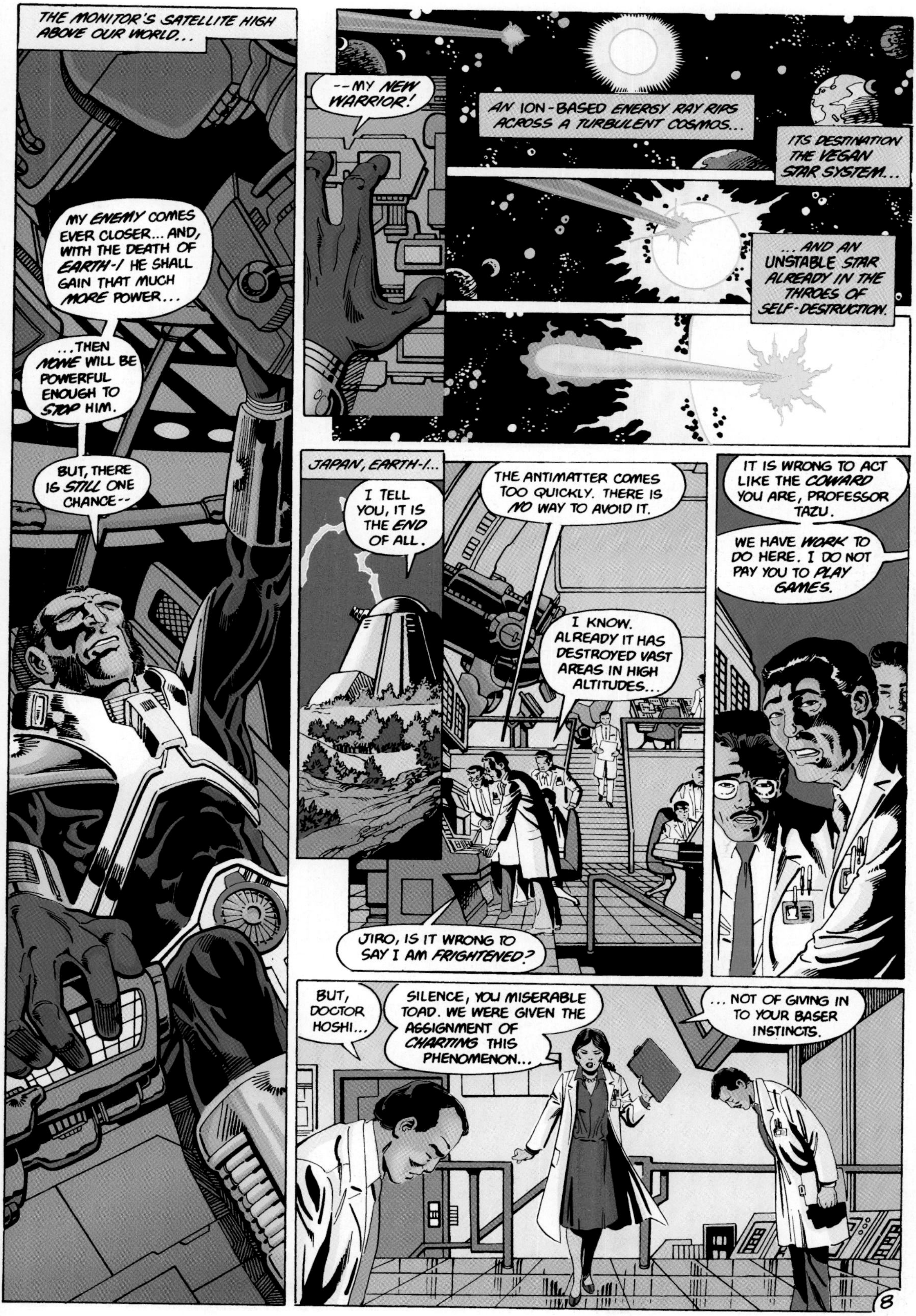
THE MONITOR'S SATELLITE HIGH ABOVE OUR WORLD...
MY ENEMY COMES EVER CLOSER... AND, WITH THE DEATH OF EARTH-1 HE SHALL GAIN THAT MUCH MORE POWER...
...THEN NONE WILL BE POWERFUL ENOUGH TO STOP HIM.
BUT, THERE IS STILL ONE CHANCE--
--MY NEW WARRIOR!
AN ION-BASED ENERGY RAY RIPS ACROSS A TURBULENT COSMOS...
ITS DESTINATION THE VEGAN STAR SYSTEM...
...AND AN UNSTABLE STAR ALREADY IN THE THROES OF SELF-DESTRUCTION.
JAPAN, EARTH-1...
I TELL YOU, IT IS THE END OF ALL.
THE ANTIMATTER COMES TOO QUICKLY. THERE IS NO WAY TO AVOID IT.
I KNOW. ALREADY IT HAS DESTROYED VAST AREAS IN HIGH ALTITUDES...
JIRO, IS IT WRONG TO SAY I AM FRIGHTENED?
IT IS WRONG TO ACT LIKE THE COWARD YOU ARE, PROFESSOR TAZU.
WE HAVE WORK TO DO HERE. I DO NOT PAY YOU TO PLAY GAMES.
BUT, DOCTOR HOSHI...
SILENCE, YOU MISERABLE TOAD. WE WERE GIVEN THE ASSIGNMENT OF CHARTING THIS PHENOMENON...
...NOT OF GIVING IN TO YOUR BASER INSTINCTS.
8

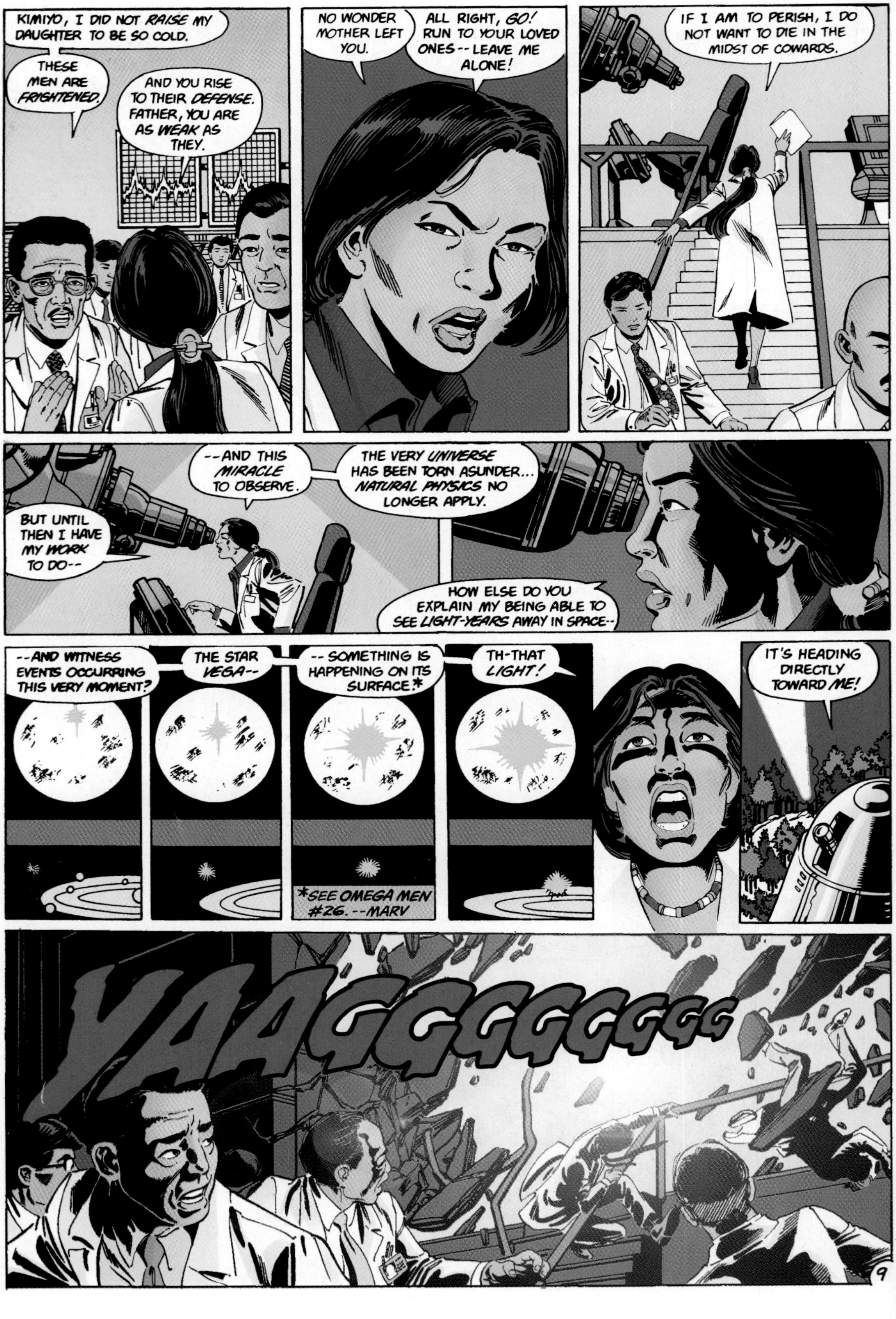
KIMIYO, I DID NOT RAISE MY DAUGHTER TO BE SO COLD.
THESE MEN ARE FRIGHTENED.
AND YOU RISE TO THEIR DEFENSE. FATHER, YOU ARE AS WEAK AS THEY.
NO WONDER MOTHER LEFT YOU.
ALL RIGHT, GO! RUN TO YOUR LOVED ONES -- LEAVE ME ALONE!
IF I AM TO PERISH, I DO NOT WANT TO DIE IN THE MIDST OF COWARDS.
BUT UNTIL THEN I HAVE MY WORK TO DO--
--AND THIS MIRACLE TO OBSERVE.
THE VERY UNIVERSE HAS BEEN TORN ASUNDER... NATURAL PHYSICS NO LONGER APPLY.
HOW ELSE DO YOU EXPLAIN MY BEING ABLE TO SEE LIGHT-YEARS AWAY IN SPACE--
--AND WITNESS EVENTS OCCURRING THIS VERY MOMENT?
THE STAR VEGA--
-- SOMETHING IS HAPPENING ON ITS SURFACE.*
*SEE OMEGA MEN #26. --MARV
TH-THAT LIGHT!
IT'S HEADING DIRECTLY TOWARD ME!
YAAGGGGGGGG
9

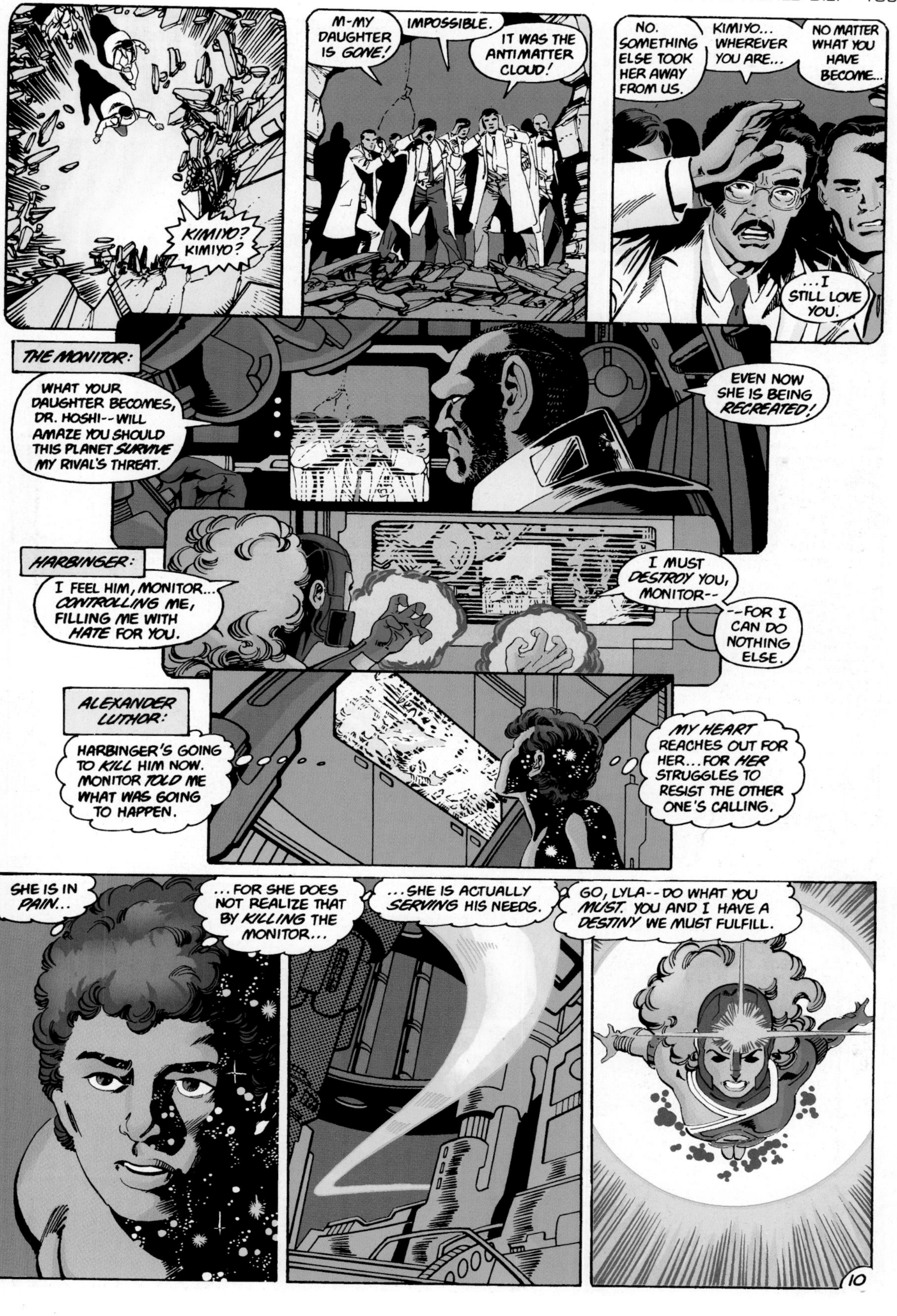
KIMIYO? KIMIYO?
M-MY DAUGHTER IS GONE!
IMPOSSIBLE.
IT WAS THE ANTIMATTER CLOUD!
NO. SOMETHING ELSE TOOK HER AWAY FROM US.
KIMIYO... WHEREVER YOU ARE...
NO MATTER WHAT YOU HAVE BECOME...
...I STILL LOVE YOU.
THE MONITOR:
WHAT YOUR DAUGHTER BECOMES, DR. HOSHI--WILL AMAZE YOU SHOULD THIS PLANET SURVIVE MY RIVAL'S THREAT.
EVEN NOW SHE IS BEING RECREATED!
HARBINGER:
I FEEL HIM, MONITOR... CONTROLLING ME, FILLING ME WITH HATE FOR YOU.
I MUST DESTROY YOU, MONITOR--
--FOR I CAN DO NOTHING ELSE.
ALEXANDER LUTHOR:
HARBINGER'S GOING TO KILL HIM NOW. MONITOR TOLD ME WHAT WAS GOING TO HAPPEN.
MY HEART REACHES OUT FOR HER... FOR HER STRUGGLES TO RESIST THE OTHER ONE'S CALLING.
SHE IS IN PAIN...
...FOR SHE DOES NOT REALIZE THAT BY KILLING THE MONITOR...
...SHE IS ACTUALLY SERVING HIS NEEDS.
GO, LYLA--DO WHAT YOU MUST. YOU AND I HAVE A DESTINY WE MUST FULFILL.
10

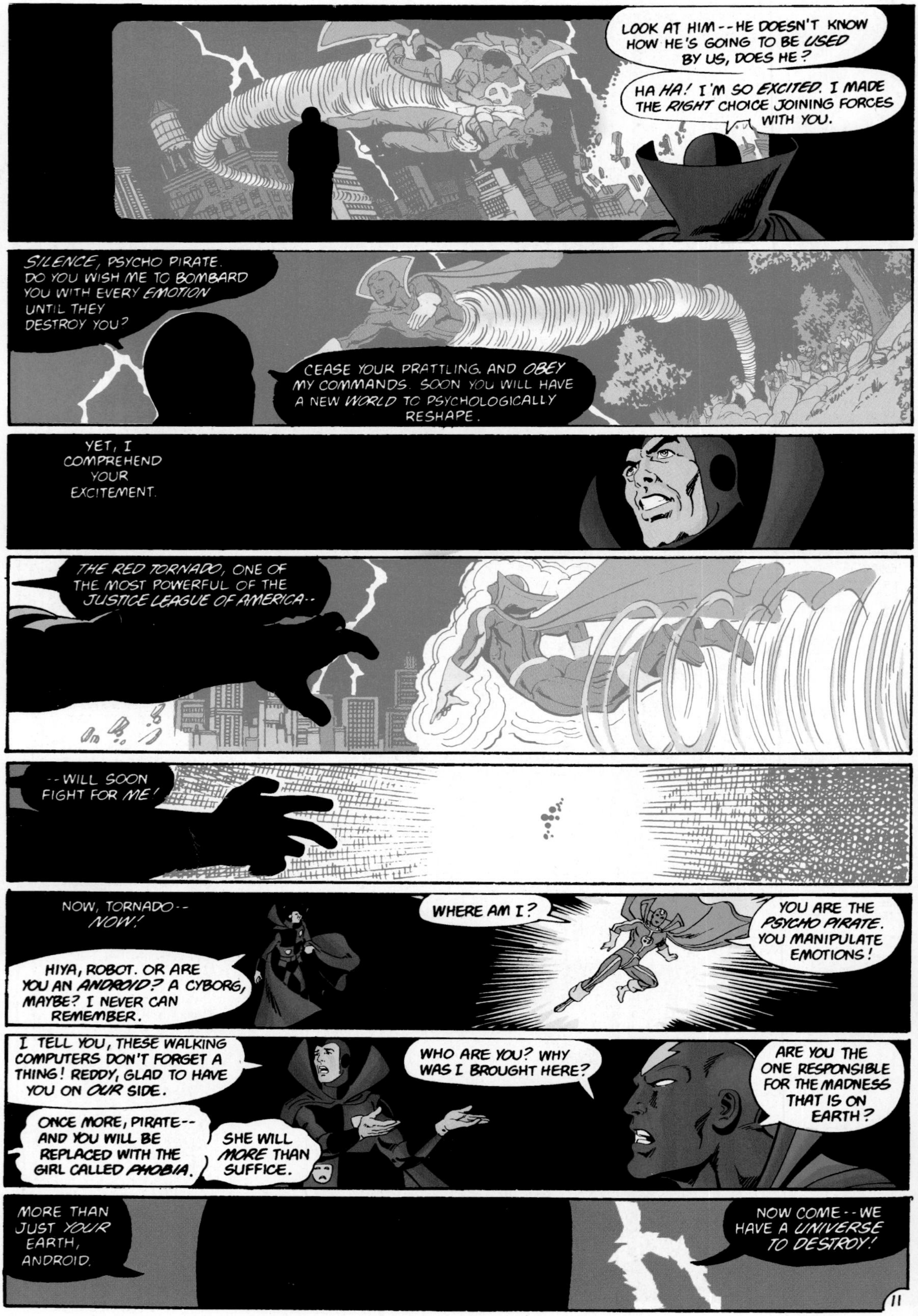
LOOK AT HIM -- HE DOESN'T KNOW HOW HE'S GOING TO BE USED BY US, DOES HE?
HA HA! I'M SO EXCITED. I MADE THE RIGHT CHOICE JOINING FORCES WITH YOU.
SILENCE, PSYCHO PIRATE. DO YOU WISH ME TO BOMBARD YOU WITH EVERY EMOTION UNTIL THEY DESTROY YOU?
CEASE YOUR PRATTLING. AND OBEY MY COMMANDS. SOON YOU WILL HAVE A NEW WORLD TO PSYCHOLOGICALLY RESHAPE.
YET, I COMPREHEND YOUR EXCITEMENT.
THE RED TORNADO, ONE OF THE MOST POWERFUL OF THE JUSTICE LEAGUE OF AMERICA--
--WILL SOON FIGHT FOR ME!
NOW, TORNADO-- NOW!
HIYA, ROBOT. OR ARE YOU AN ANDROID? A CYBORG, MAYBE? I NEVER CAN REMEMBER.
WHERE AM I?
YOU ARE THE PSYCHO PIRATE. YOU MANIPULATE EMOTIONS!
I TELL YOU, THESE WALKING COMPUTERS DON'T FORGET A THING! REDDY, GLAD TO HAVE YOU ON OUR SIDE.
ONCE MORE, PIRATE-- AND YOU WILL BE REPLACED WITH THE GIRL CALLED PHOBIA.
SHE WILL MORE THAN SUFFICE.
WHO ARE YOU? WHY WAS I BROUGHT HERE?
ARE YOU THE ONE RESPONSIBLE FOR THE MADNESS THAT IS ON EARTH?
MORE THAN JUST YOUR EARTH, ANDROID.
NOW COME--WE HAVE A UNIVERSE TO DESTROY!
11

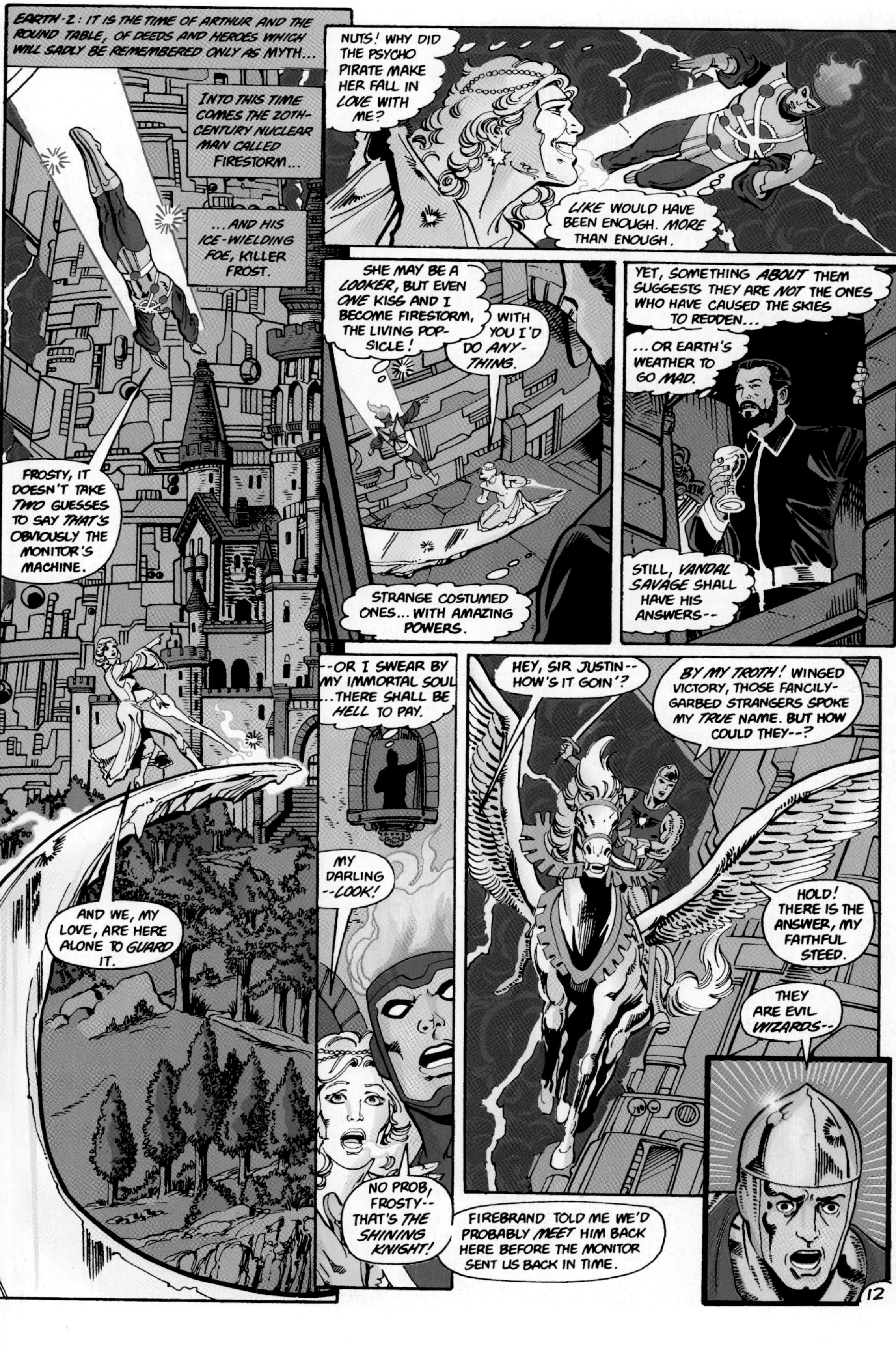
EARTH-2: IT IS THE TIME OF ARTHUR AND THE ROUND TABLE, OF DEEDS AND HEROES WHICH WILL SADLY BE REMEMBERED ONLY AS MYTH...
INTO THIS TIME COMES THE 20TH-CENTURY NUCLEAR MAN CALLED FIRESTORM...
...AND HIS ICE-WIELDING FOE, KILLER FROST.
FROSTY, IT DOESN'T TAKE TWO GUESSES TO SAY THAT'S OBVIOUSLY THE MONITOR'S MACHINE.
AND WE, MY LOVE, ARE HERE ALONE TO GUARD IT.
NUTS! WHY DID THE PSYCHO PIRATE MAKE HER FALL IN LOVE WITH ME?
LIKE WOULD HAVE BEEN ENOUGH. MORE THAN ENOUGH.
SHE MAY BE A LOOKER, BUT EVEN ONE KISS AND I BECOME FIRESTORM, THE LIVING POP-SICLE!
WITH YOU I'D DO ANY-THING.
STRANGE COSTUMED ONES... WITH AMAZING POWERS.
YET, SOMETHING ABOUT THEM SUGGESTS THEY ARE NOT THE ONES WHO HAVE CAUSED THE SKIES TO REDDEN...
...OR EARTH'S WEATHER TO GO MAD.
STILL, VANDAL SAVAGE SHALL HAVE HIS ANSWERS--
--OR I SWEAR BY MY IMMORTAL SOUL ...THERE SHALL BE HELL TO PAY.
MY DARLING --LOOK!
HEY, SIR JUSTIN-- HOW'S IT GOIN'?
BY MY TROTH! WINGED VICTORY, THOSE FANCILY-GARBED STRANGERS SPOKE MY TRUE NAME. BUT HOW COULD THEY--?
HOLD! THERE IS THE ANSWER, MY FAITHFUL STEED.
THEY ARE EVIL WIZARDS--
NO PROB, FROSTY-- THAT'S THE SHINING KNIGHT!
FIREBRAND TOLD ME WE'D PROBABLY MEET HIM BACK HERE BEFORE THE MONITOR SENT US BACK IN TIME.
12

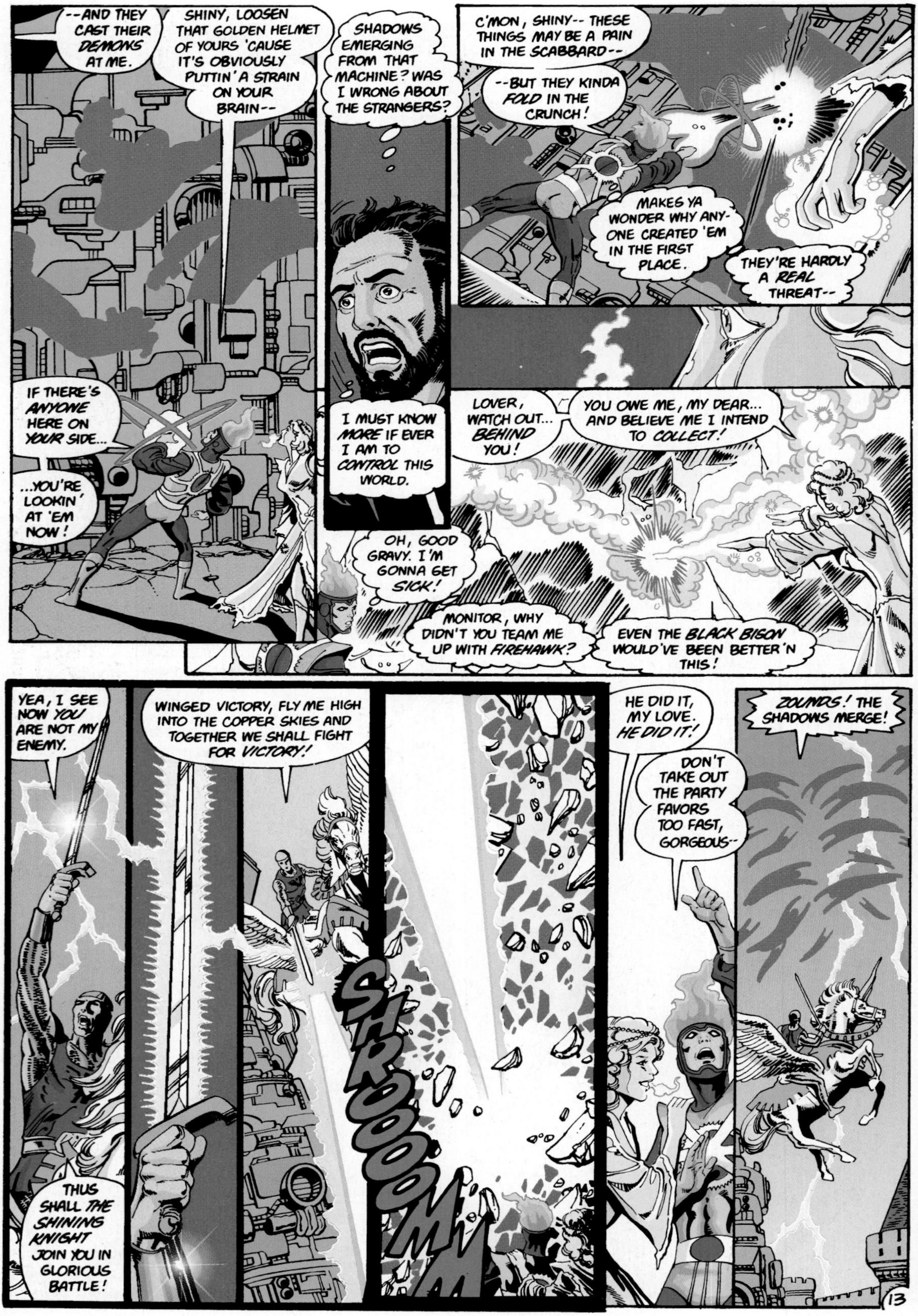
--AND THEY CAST THEIR DEMONS AT ME.
SHINY, LOOSEN THAT GOLDEN HELMET OF YOURS 'CAUSE IT'S OBVIOUSLY PUTTIN' A STRAIN ON YOUR BRAIN--
IF THERE'S ANYONE HERE ON YOUR SIDE...
...YOU'RE LOOKIN' AT 'EM NOW!
SHADOWS EMERGING FROM THAT MACHINE? WAS I WRONG ABOUT THE STRANGERS?
I MUST KNOW MORE IF EVER I AM TO CONTROL THIS WORLD.
C'MON, SHINY-- THESE THINGS MAY BE A PAIN IN THE SCABBARD--
--BUT THEY KINDA FOLD IN THE CRUNCH!
MAKES YA WONDER WHY ANY-ONE CREATED 'EM IN THE FIRST PLACE.
THEY'RE HARDLY A REAL THREAT--
LOVER, WATCH OUT... BEHIND YOU!
YOU OWE ME, MY DEAR... AND BELIEVE ME I INTEND TO COLLECT!
OH, GOOD GRAVY. I'M GONNA GET SICK!
MONITOR, WHY DIDN'T YOU TEAM ME UP WITH FIREHAWK?
EVEN THE BLACK BISON WOULD'VE BEEN BETTER'N THIS!
YEA, I SEE NOW YOU ARE NOT MY ENEMY.
THUS SHALL THE SHINING KNIGHT JOIN YOU IN GLORIOUS BATTLE!
WINGED VICTORY, FLY ME HIGH INTO THE COPPER SKIES AND TOGETHER WE SHALL FIGHT FOR VICTORY!
SHROOOOOMM
HE DID IT, MY LOVE. HE DID IT!
DON'T TAKE OUT THE PARTY FAVORS TOO FAST, GORGEOUS--
ZOUNDS! THE SHADOWS MERGE!
13

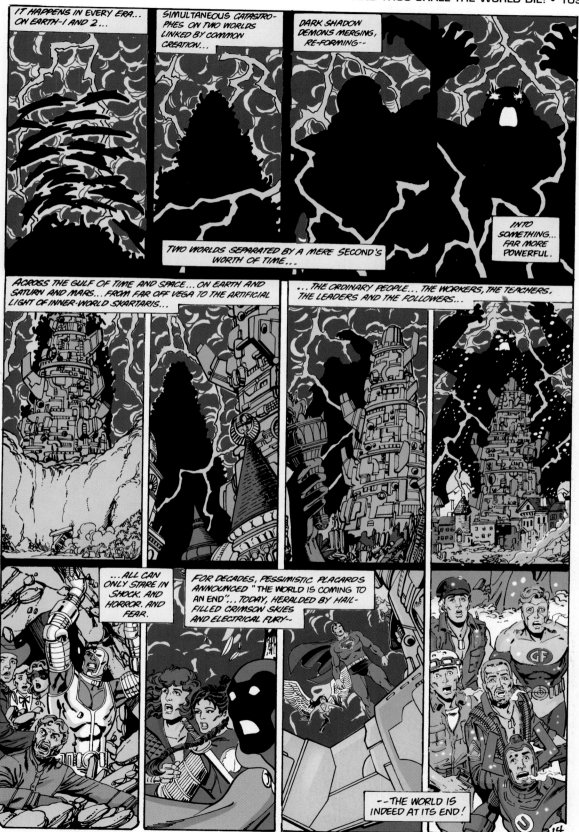

IT HAPPENS IN EVERY ERA... ON EARTH-1 AND 2...

SIMULTANEOUS CATASTROPHES ON TWO WORLDS LINKED BY COMMON CREATION...

DARK SHADOW DEMONS MERGING, RE-FORMING--

INTO SOMETHING... FAR MORE POWERFUL.

TWO WORLDS SEPARATED BY A MERE SECOND'S WORTH OF TIME...

ACROSS THE GULF OF TIME AND SPACE... ON EARTH AND SATURN AND MARS... FROM FAR OFF VEGA TO THE ARTIFICIAL LIGHT OF INNER-WORLD SKARTARIS...

...THE ORDINARY PEOPLE... THE WORKERS, THE TEACHERS, THE LEADERS AND THE FOLLOWERS...

...ALL CAN ONLY STARE IN SHOCK. AND HORROR. AND FEAR.

FOR DECADES, PESSIMISTIC PLACARDS ANNOUNCED "THE WORLD IS COMING TO AN END"... TODAY, HERALDED BY HAIL-FILLED CRIMSON SKIES AND ELECTRICAL FURY--

--THE WORLD IS INDEED AT ITS END!

14

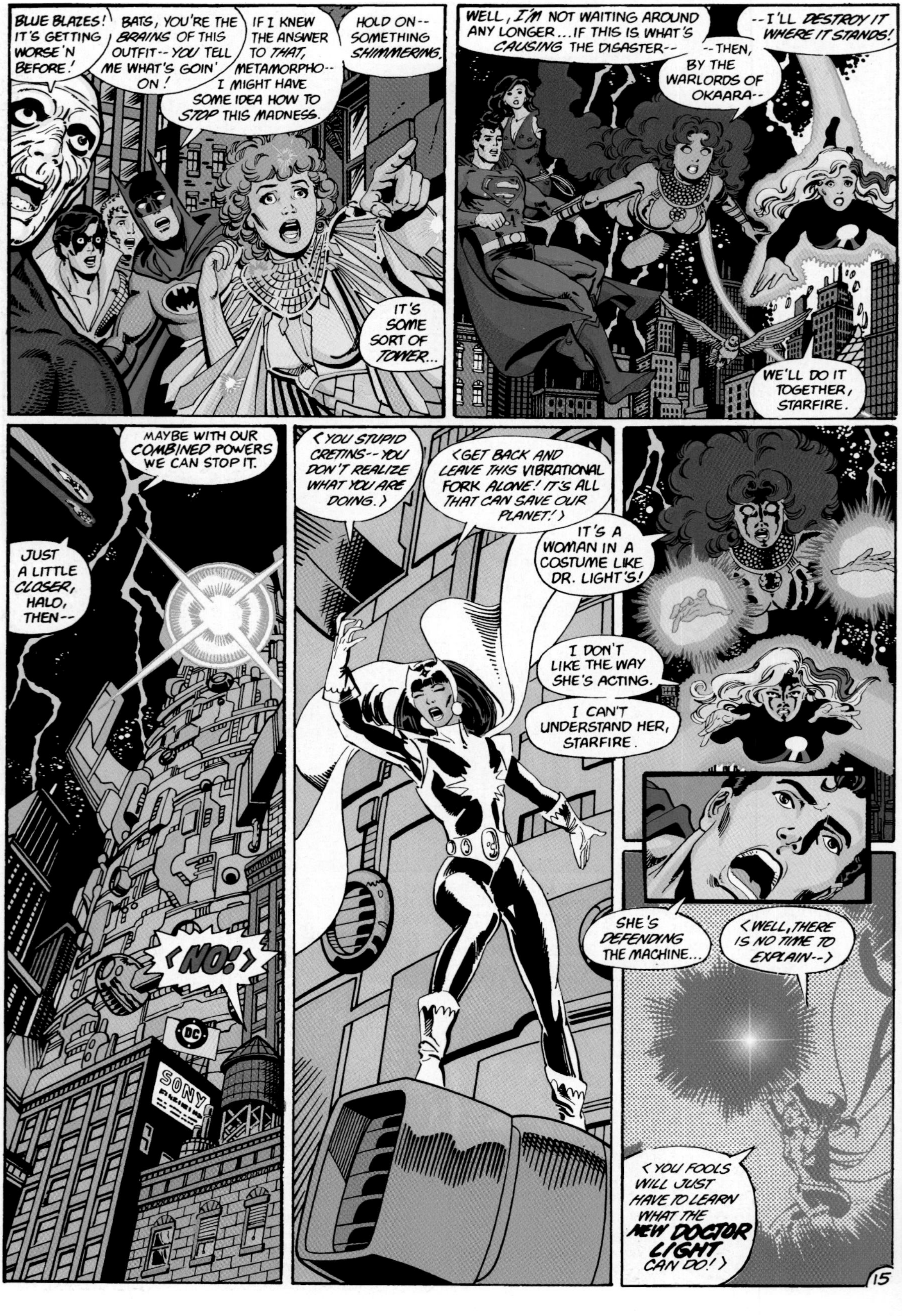
BLUE BLAZES! IT'S GETTING WORSE 'N BEFORE!
BATS, YOU'RE THE BRAINS OF THIS OUTFIT-- YOU TELL ME WHAT'S GOIN' ON!
IF I KNEW THE ANSWER TO THAT, METAMORPHO-- I MIGHT HAVE SOME IDEA HOW TO STOP THIS MADNESS.
HOLD ON-- SOMETHING SHIMMERING.
IT'S SOME SORT OF TOWER...
WELL, I'M NOT WAITING AROUND ANY LONGER... IF THIS IS WHAT'S CAUSING THE DISASTER--
--THEN, BY THE WARLORDS OF OKAARA--
--I'LL DESTROY IT WHERE IT STANDS!
WE'LL DO IT TOGETHER, STARFIRE.
MAYBE WITH OUR COMBINED POWERS WE CAN STOP IT.
JUST A LITTLE CLOSER, HALO, THEN--
‹NO!›
SONY
‹YOU STUPID CRETINS-- YOU DON'T REALIZE WHAT YOU ARE DOING.›
‹GET BACK AND LEAVE THIS VIBRATIONAL FORK ALONE! IT'S ALL THAT CAN SAVE OUR PLANET!›
IT'S A WOMAN IN A COSTUME LIKE DR. LIGHT'S!
I DON'T LIKE THE WAY SHE'S ACTING.
I CAN'T UNDERSTAND HER, STARFIRE.
SHE'S DEFENDING THE MACHINE...
‹WELL, THERE IS NO TIME TO EXPLAIN--›
‹YOU FOOLS WILL JUST HAVE TO LEARN WHAT THE NEW DOCTOR LIGHT CAN DO!›
15

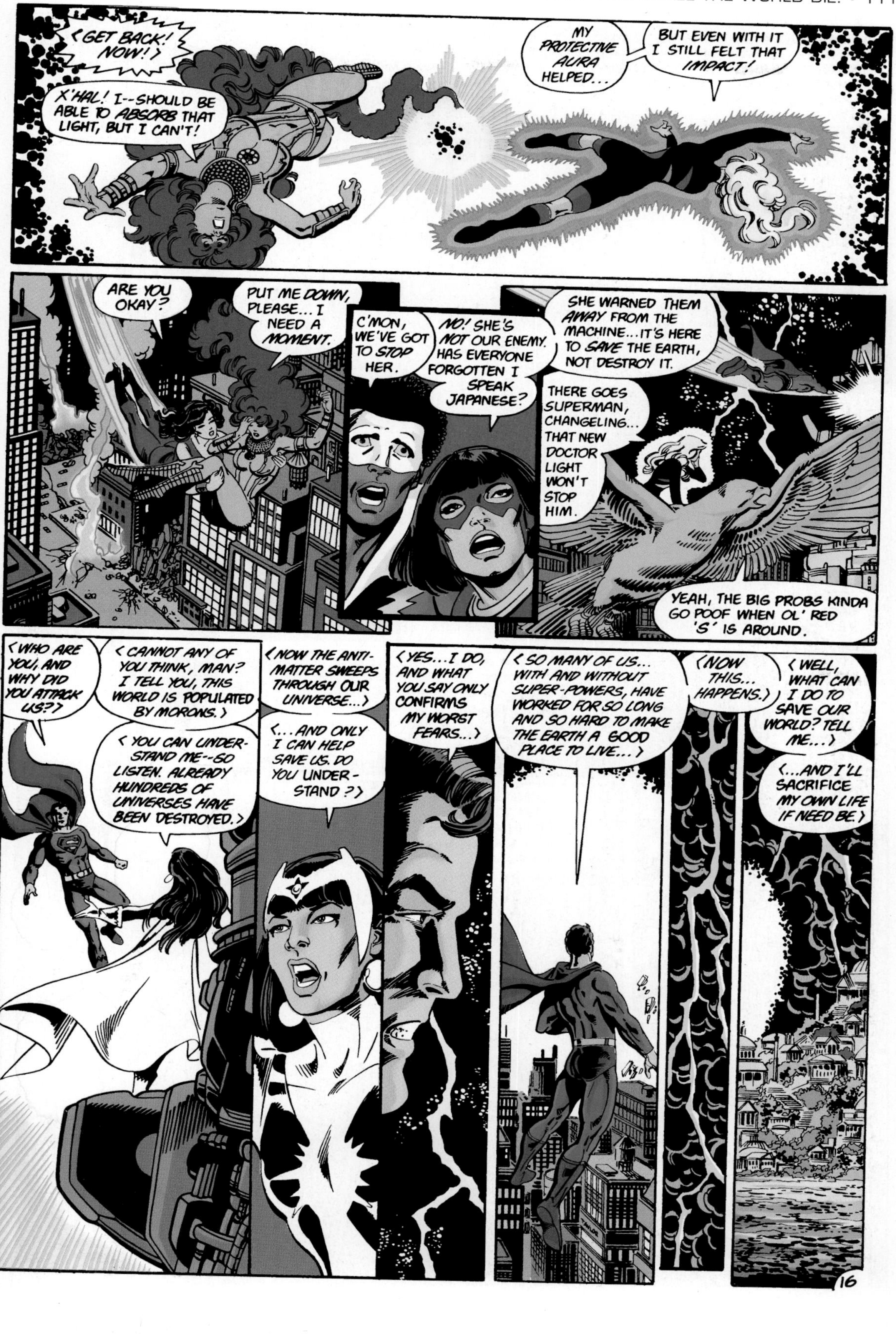

‹GET BACK! NOW!›
X'HAL! I--SHOULD BE ABLE TO ABSORB THAT LIGHT, BUT I CAN'T!
MY PROTECTIVE AURA HELPED...
BUT EVEN WITH IT I STILL FELT THAT IMPACT!
ARE YOU OKAY?
PUT ME DOWN, PLEASE... I NEED A MOMENT.
C'MON, WE'VE GOT TO STOP HER.
NO! SHE'S NOT OUR ENEMY. HAS EVERYONE FORGOTTEN I SPEAK JAPANESE?
SHE WARNED THEM AWAY FROM THE MACHINE... IT'S HERE TO SAVE THE EARTH, NOT DESTROY IT.
THERE GOES SUPERMAN, CHANGELING... THAT NEW DOCTOR LIGHT WON'T STOP HIM.
YEAH, THE BIG PROBS KINDA GO POOF WHEN OL' RED 'S' IS AROUND.
‹WHO ARE YOU, AND WHY DID YOU ATTACK US?›
‹CANNOT ANY OF YOU THINK, MAN? I TELL YOU, THIS WORLD IS POPULATED BY MORONS.›
‹YOU CAN UNDERSTAND ME--SO LISTEN. ALREADY HUNDREDS OF UNIVERSES HAVE BEEN DESTROYED.›
‹NOW THE ANTI-MATTER SWEEPS THROUGH OUR UNIVERSE...›
‹...AND ONLY I CAN HELP SAVE US. DO YOU UNDERSTAND?›
‹YES... I DO, AND WHAT YOU SAY ONLY CONFIRMS MY WORST FEARS...›
‹SO MANY OF US... WITH AND WITHOUT SUPER-POWERS, HAVE WORKED FOR SO LONG AND SO HARD TO MAKE THE EARTH A GOOD PLACE TO LIVE...›
‹NOW THIS... HAPPENS.›
‹WELL, WHAT CAN I DO TO SAVE OUR WORLD? TELL ME...›
‹...AND I'LL SACRIFICE MY OWN LIFE IF NEED BE.›
16

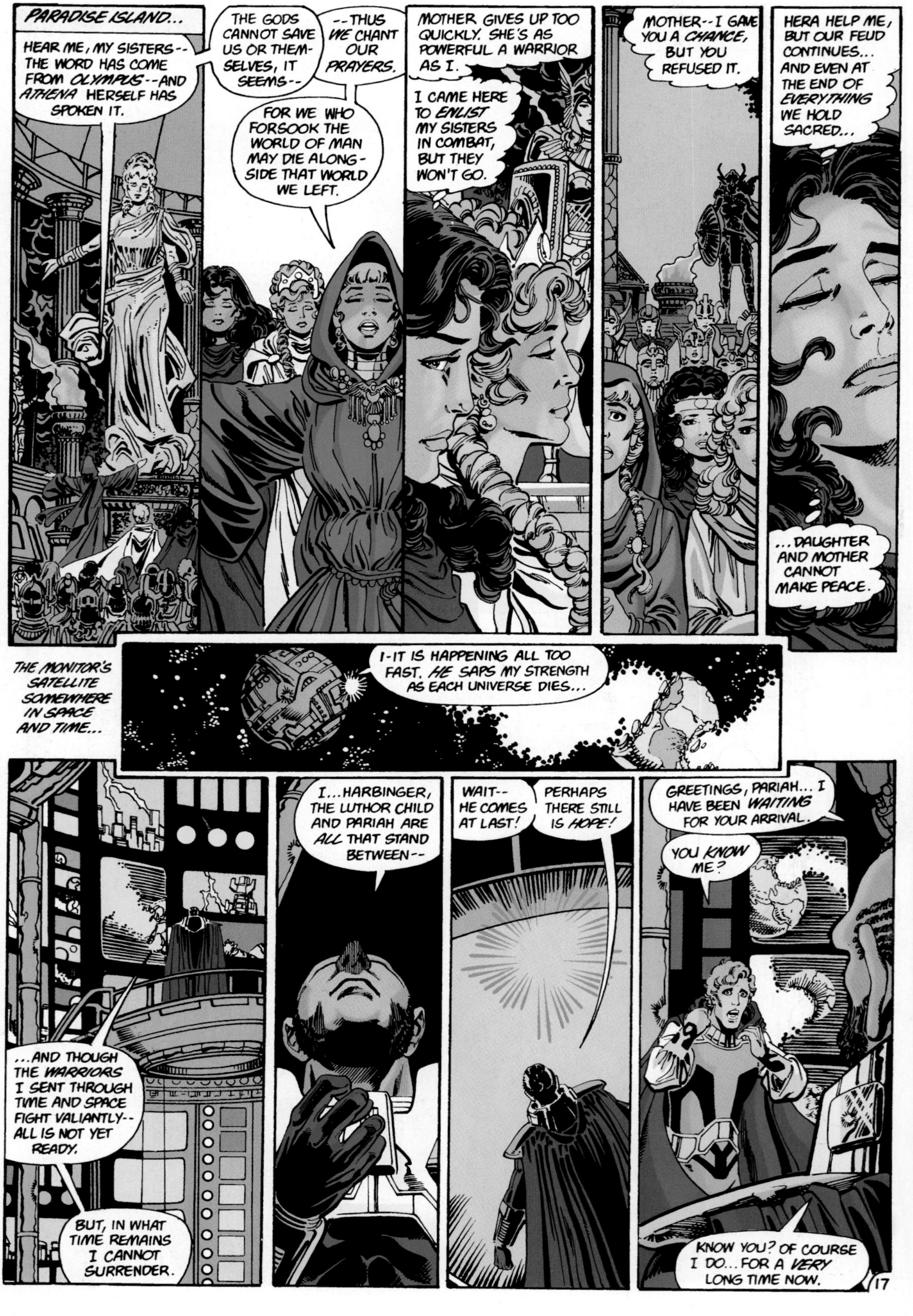
PARADISE ISLAND...
HEAR ME, MY SISTERS-- THE WORD HAS COME FROM OLYMPUS--AND ATHENA HERSELF HAS SPOKEN IT.
THE GODS CANNOT SAVE US OR THEMSELVES, IT SEEMS--
--THUS WE CHANT OUR PRAYERS.
FOR WE WHO FORSOOK THE WORLD OF MAN MAY DIE ALONGSIDE THAT WORLD WE LEFT.
MOTHER GIVES UP TOO QUICKLY. SHE'S AS POWERFUL A WARRIOR AS I.
I CAME HERE TO ENLIST MY SISTERS IN COMBAT, BUT THEY WON'T GO.
MOTHER--I GAVE YOU A CHANCE, BUT YOU REFUSED IT.
HERA HELP ME, BUT OUR FEUD CONTINUES... AND EVEN AT THE END OF EVERYTHING WE HOLD SACRED...
...DAUGHTER AND MOTHER CANNOT MAKE PEACE.
THE MONITOR'S SATELLITE SOMEWHERE IN SPACE AND TIME...
I-IT IS HAPPENING ALL TOO FAST. HE SAPS MY STRENGTH AS EACH UNIVERSE DIES...
...AND THOUGH THE WARRIORS I SENT THROUGH TIME AND SPACE FIGHT VALIANTLY-- ALL IS NOT YET READY.
BUT, IN WHAT TIME REMAINS I CANNOT SURRENDER.
I...HARBINGER, THE LUTHOR CHILD AND PARIAH ARE ALL THAT STAND BETWEEN--
WAIT-- HE COMES AT LAST!
PERHAPS THERE STILL IS HOPE!
GREETINGS, PARIAH... I HAVE BEEN WAITING FOR YOUR ARRIVAL.
YOU KNOW ME?
KNOW YOU? OF COURSE I DO... FOR A VERY LONG TIME NOW.
17

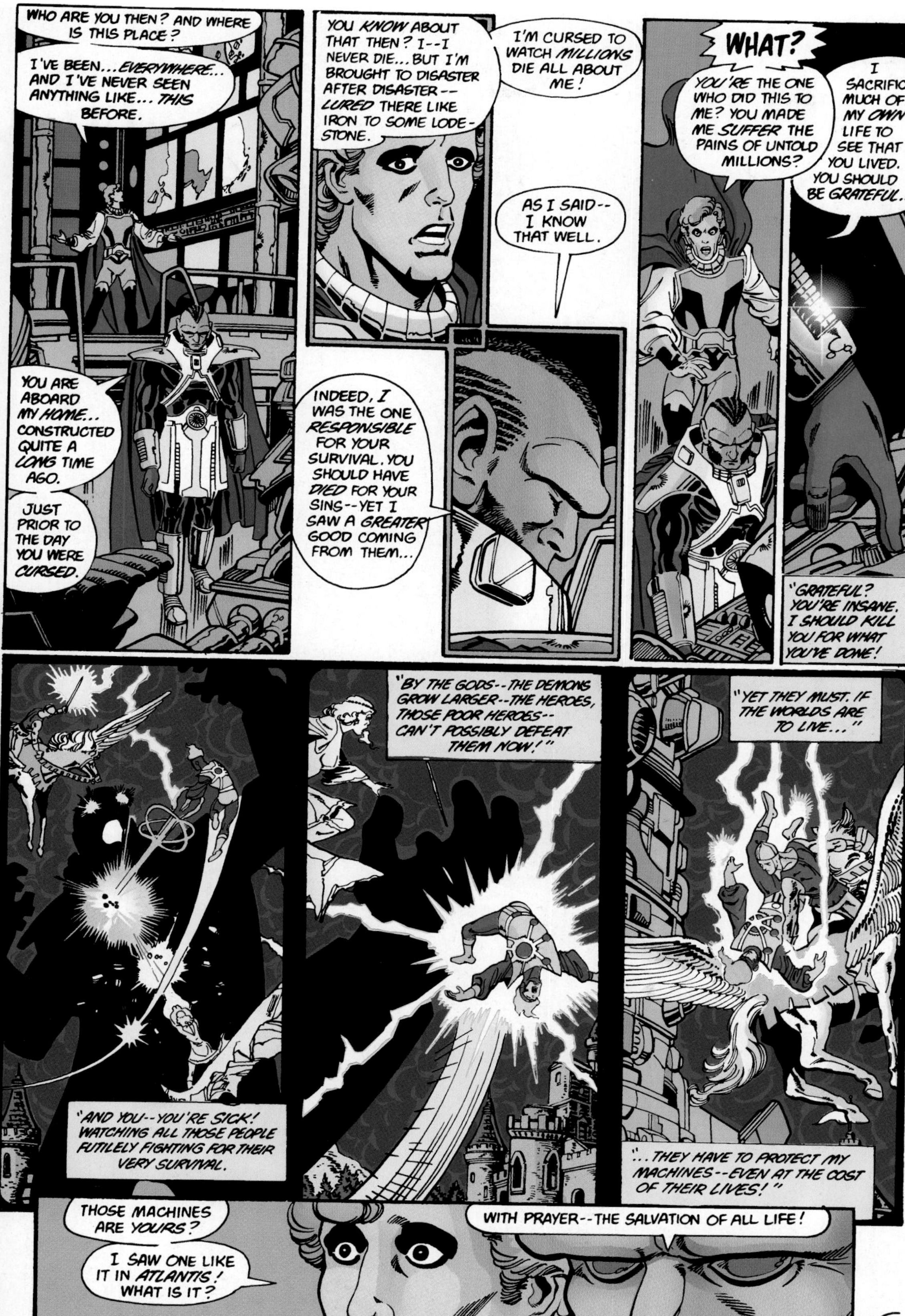
WHO ARE YOU THEN? AND WHERE IS THIS PLACE?
I'VE BEEN... EVERYWHERE... AND I'VE NEVER SEEN ANYTHING LIKE... THIS BEFORE.
YOU ARE ABOARD MY HOME... CONSTRUCTED QUITE A LONG TIME AGO.
JUST PRIOR TO THE DAY YOU WERE CURSED.
YOU KNOW ABOUT THAT THEN? I--I NEVER DIE... BUT I'M BROUGHT TO DISASTER AFTER DISASTER-- LURED THERE LIKE IRON TO SOME LODE-STONE.
I'M CURSED TO WATCH MILLIONS DIE ALL ABOUT ME!
AS I SAID-- I KNOW THAT WELL.
INDEED, I WAS THE ONE RESPONSIBLE FOR YOUR SURVIVAL. YOU SHOULD HAVE DIED FOR YOUR SINS--YET I SAW A GREATER GOOD COMING FROM THEM...
WHAT?
YOU'RE THE ONE WHO DID THIS TO ME? YOU MADE ME SUFFER THE PAINS OF UNTOLD MILLIONS?
I SACRIFICED MUCH OF MY OWN LIFE TO SEE THAT YOU LIVED. YOU SHOULD BE GRATEFUL...
"GRATEFUL? YOU'RE INSANE. I SHOULD KILL YOU FOR WHAT YOU'VE DONE!
"AND YOU--YOU'RE SICK! WATCHING ALL THOSE PEOPLE FUTILELY FIGHTING FOR THEIR VERY SURVIVAL.
"BY THE GODS--THE DEMONS GROW LARGER--THE HEROES, THOSE POOR HEROES-- CAN'T POSSIBLY DEFEAT THEM NOW!"
"YET THEY MUST, IF THE WORLDS ARE TO LIVE..."
"...THEY HAVE TO PROTECT MY MACHINES--EVEN AT THE COST OF THEIR LIVES!"
THOSE MACHINES ARE YOURS?
I SAW ONE LIKE IT IN ATLANTIS! WHAT IS IT?
WITH PRAYER--THE SALVATION OF ALL LIFE!
18

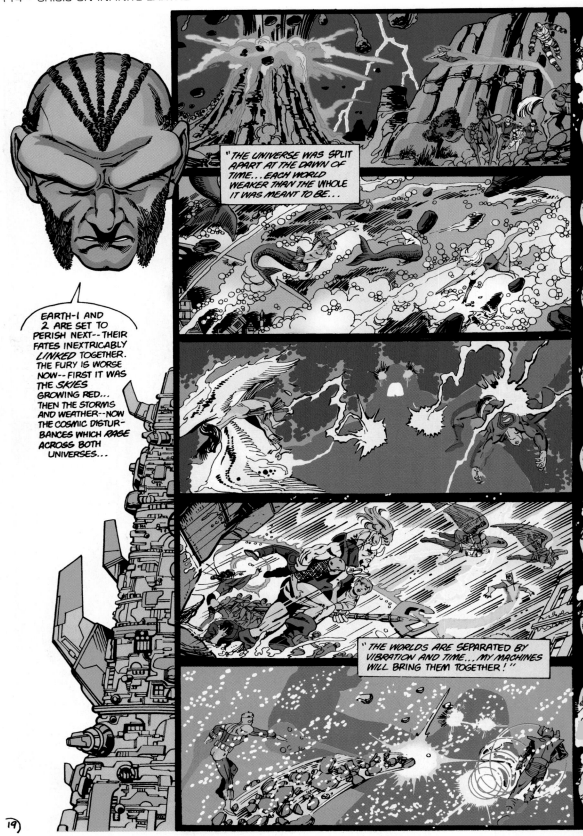

"THE UNIVERSE WAS SPLIT APART AT THE DAWN OF TIME... EACH WORLD WEAKER THAN THE WHOLE IT WAS MEANT TO BE..."

EARTH-1 AND 2 ARE SET TO PERISH NEXT-- THEIR FATES INEXTRICABLY *LINKED* TOGETHER. THE FURY IS WORSE NOW-- FIRST IT WAS THE *SKIES* GROWING RED... THEN THE STORMS AND WEATHER--NOW THE COSMIC DISTUR- BANCES WHICH *RAGE* ACROSS BOTH UNIVERSES...

"THE WORLDS ARE SEPARATED BY VIBRATION AND TIME... MY MACHINES WILL BRING THEM TOGETHER!"

19)

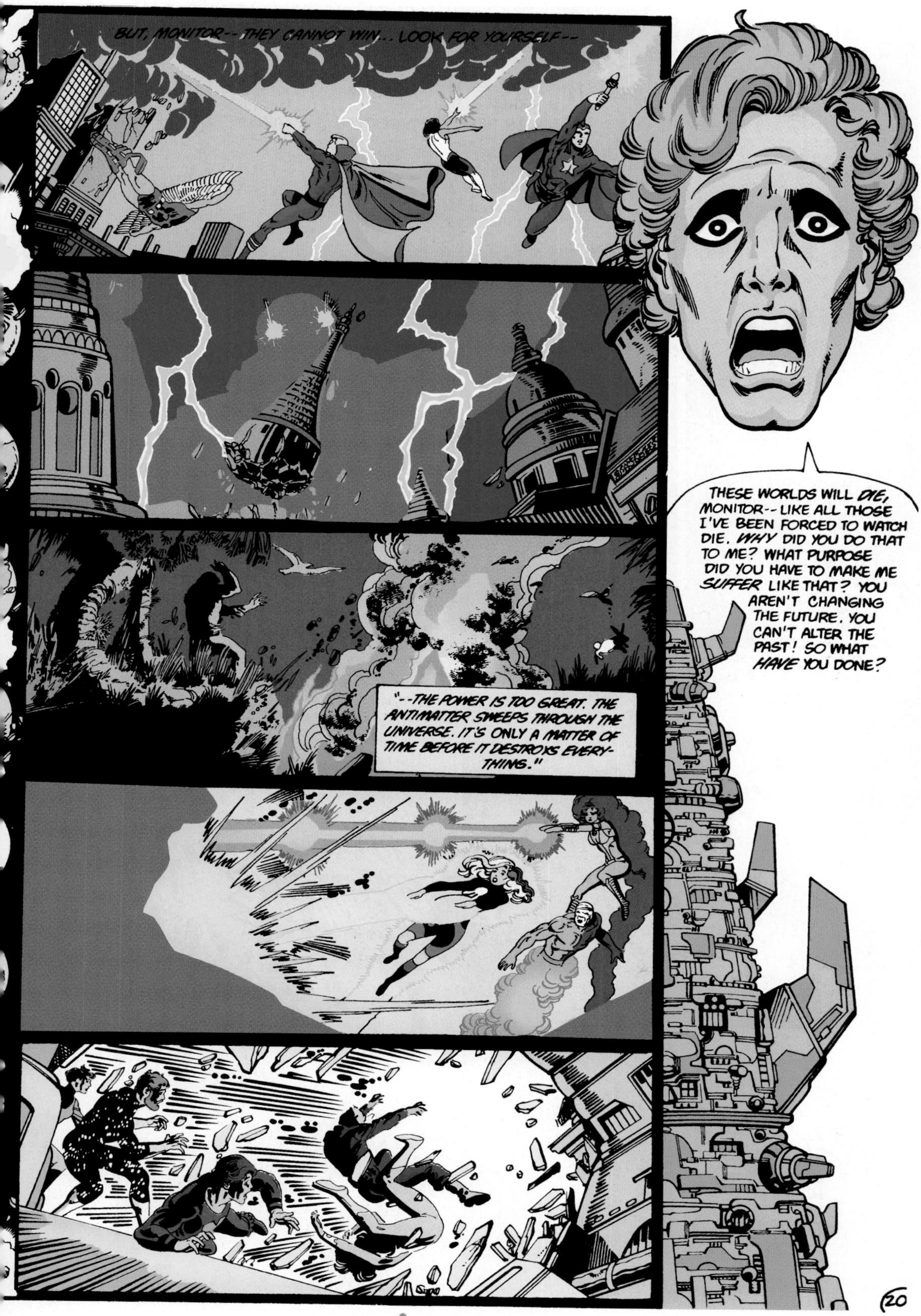
BUT, MONITOR-- THEY CANNOT WIN... LOOK FOR YOURSELF--
THESE WORLDS WILL DIE, MONITOR-- LIKE ALL THOSE I'VE BEEN FORCED TO WATCH DIE. WHY DID YOU DO THAT TO ME? WHAT PURPOSE DID YOU HAVE TO MAKE ME SUFFER LIKE THAT? YOU AREN'T CHANGING THE FUTURE. YOU CAN'T ALTER THE PAST! SO WHAT HAVE YOU DONE?
"--THE POWER IS TOO GREAT. THE ANTIMATTER SWEEPS THROUGH THE UNIVERSE. IT'S ONLY A MATTER OF TIME BEFORE IT DESTROYS EVERYTHING."
20

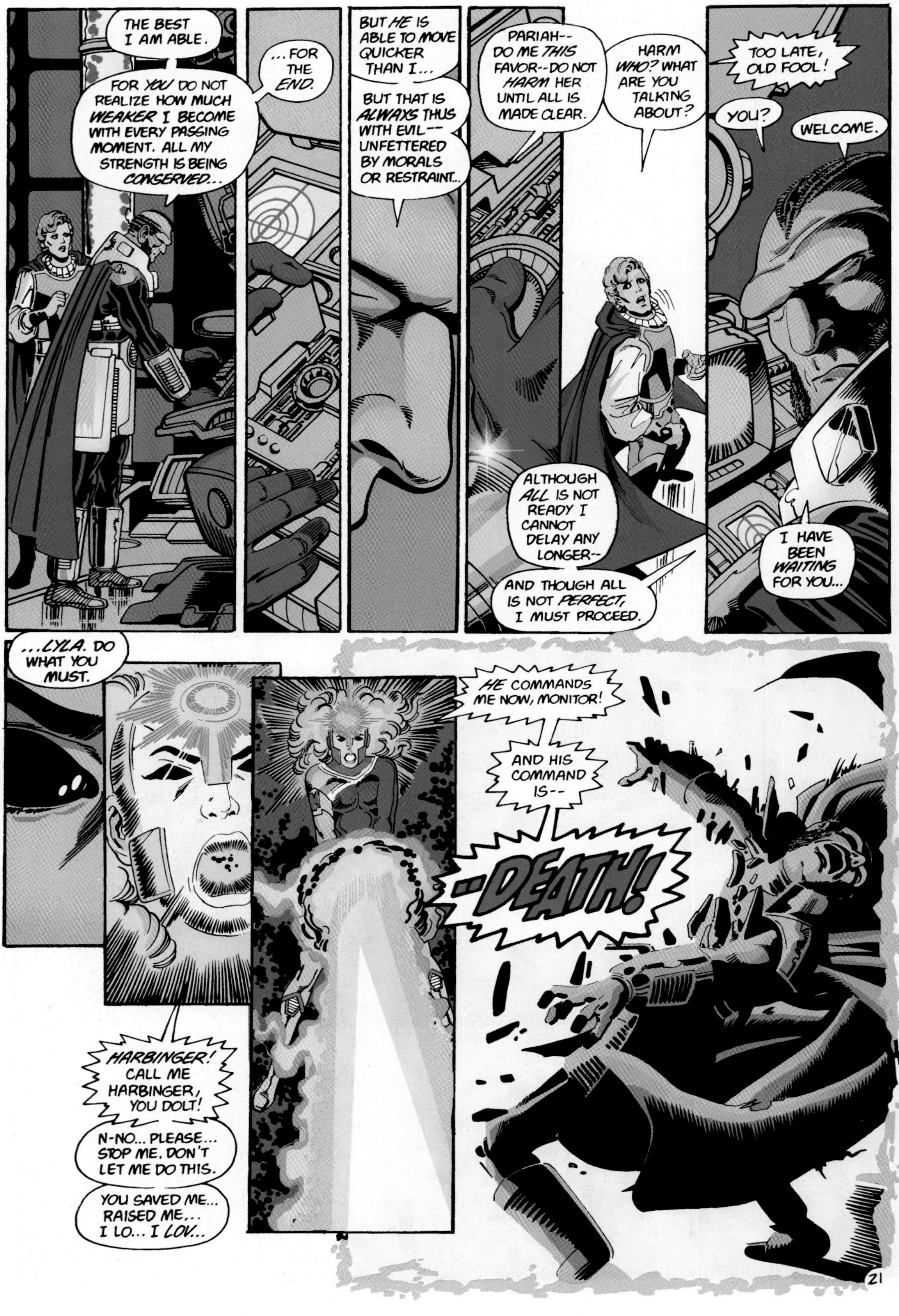
THE BEST I AM ABLE.
FOR YOU DO NOT REALIZE HOW MUCH WEAKER I BECOME WITH EVERY PASSING MOMENT. ALL MY STRENGTH IS BEING CONSERVED...
...FOR THE END.
BUT HE IS ABLE TO MOVE QUICKER THAN I...
BUT THAT IS ALWAYS THUS WITH EVIL-- UNFETTERED BY MORALS OR RESTRAINT...
PARIAH-- DO ME THIS FAVOR--DO NOT HARM HER UNTIL ALL IS MADE CLEAR.
HARM WHO? WHAT ARE YOU TALKING ABOUT?
ALTHOUGH ALL IS NOT READY I CANNOT DELAY ANY LONGER--
AND THOUGH ALL IS NOT PERFECT, I MUST PROCEED.
TOO LATE, OLD FOOL!
YOU?
WELCOME.
I HAVE BEEN WAITING FOR YOU...
...LYLA. DO WHAT YOU MUST.
HARBINGER! CALL ME HARBINGER, YOU DOLT!
N-NO... PLEASE... STOP ME. DON'T LET ME DO THIS.
YOU SAVED ME... RAISED ME... I LO... I LOV...
HE COMMANDS ME NOW, MONITOR!
AND HIS COMMAND IS--
--DEATH!
21

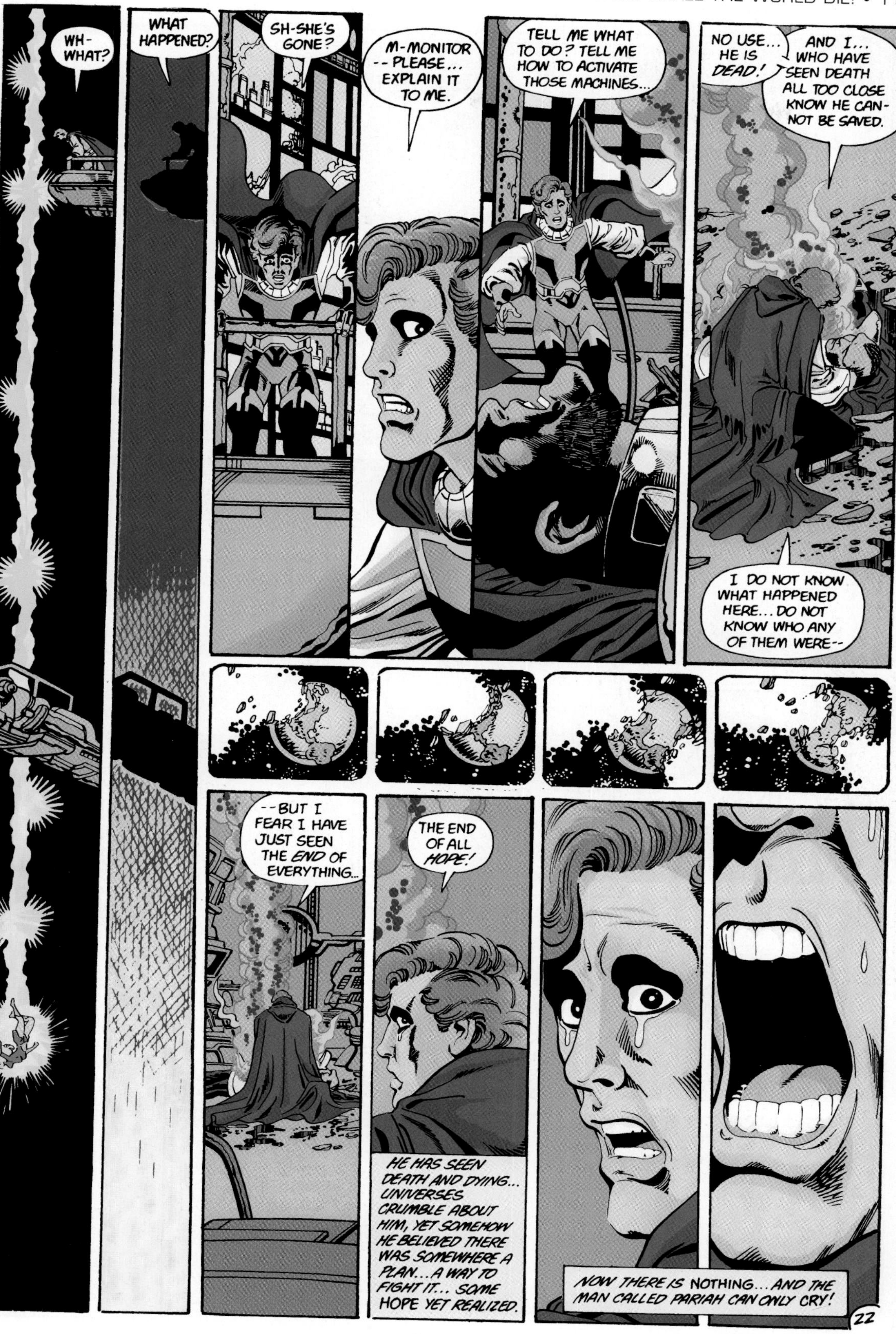
WH-WHAT?
WHAT HAPPENED?
SH-SHE'S GONE?
M-MONITOR --PLEASE... EXPLAIN IT TO ME.
TELL ME WHAT TO DO? TELL ME HOW TO ACTIVATE THOSE MACHINES...
NO USE... HE IS DEAD!
AND I... WHO HAVE SEEN DEATH ALL TOO CLOSE KNOW HE CAN-NOT BE SAVED.
I DO NOT KNOW WHAT HAPPENED HERE... DO NOT KNOW WHO ANY OF THEM WERE--
--BUT I FEAR I HAVE JUST SEEN THE END OF EVERYTHING...
THE END OF ALL HOPE!
HE HAS SEEN DEATH AND DYING... UNIVERSES CRUMBLE ABOUT HIM, YET SOMEHOW HE BELIEVED THERE WAS SOMEWHERE A PLAN... A WAY TO FIGHT IT... SOME HOPE YET REALIZED.
NOW THERE IS NOTHING... AND THE MAN CALLED PARIAH CAN ONLY CRY!
22

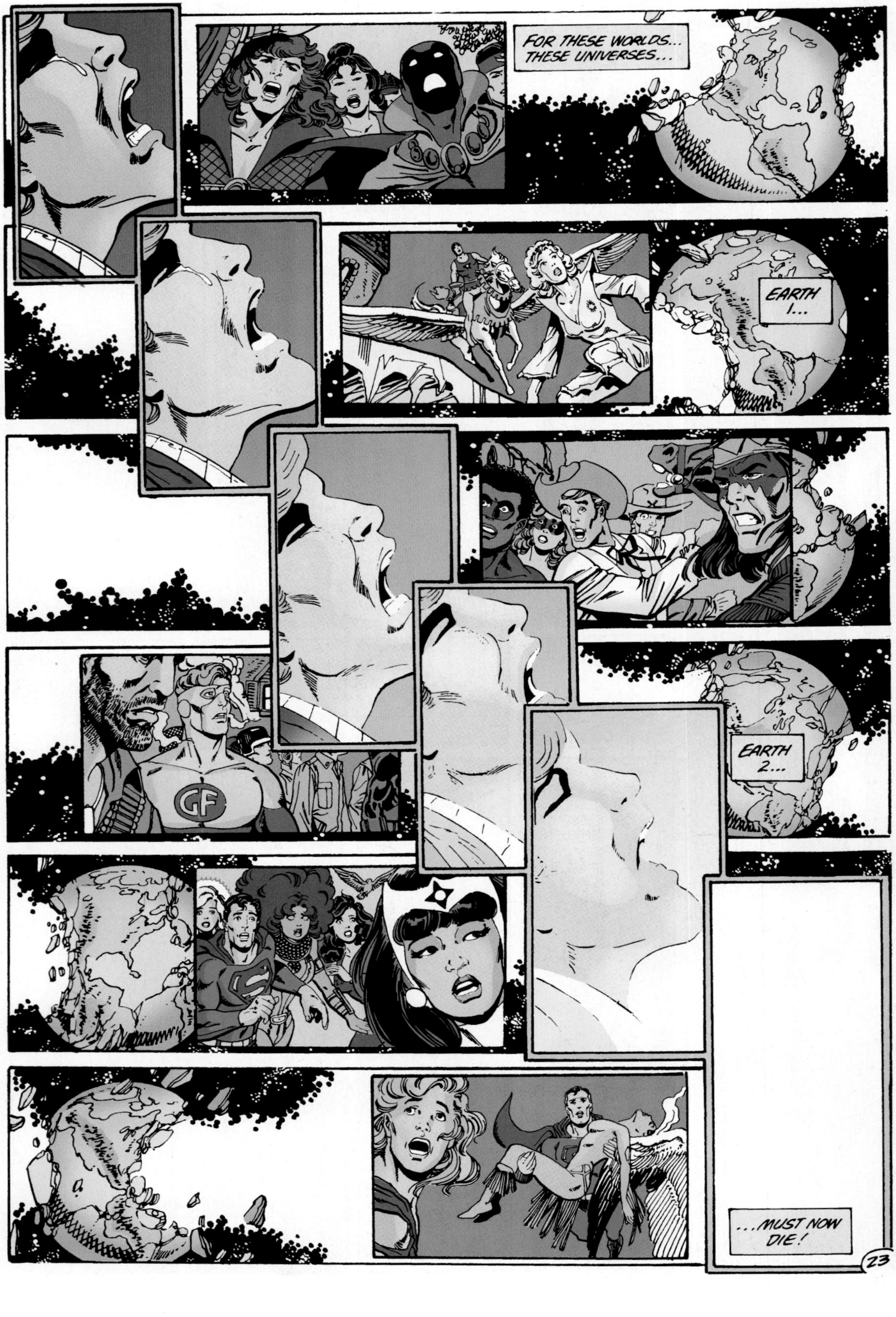
FOR THESE WORLDS...
THESE UNIVERSES...
EARTH 1...
EARTH 2...
...MUST NOW DIE!
23

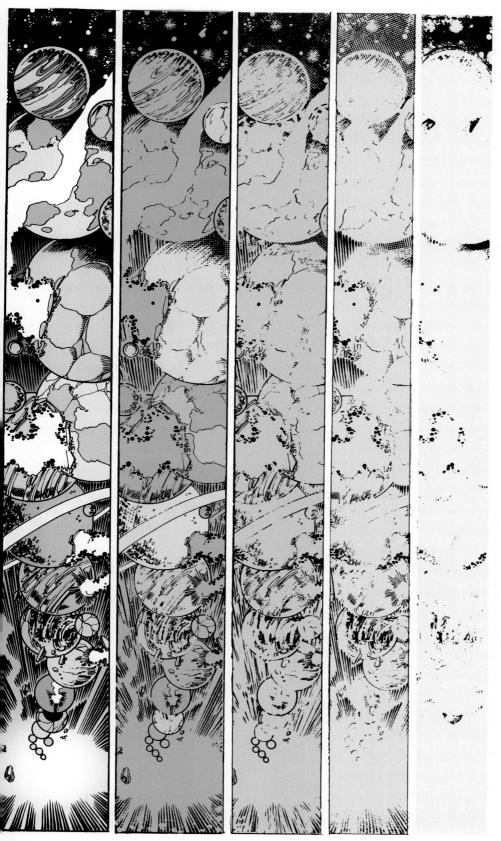

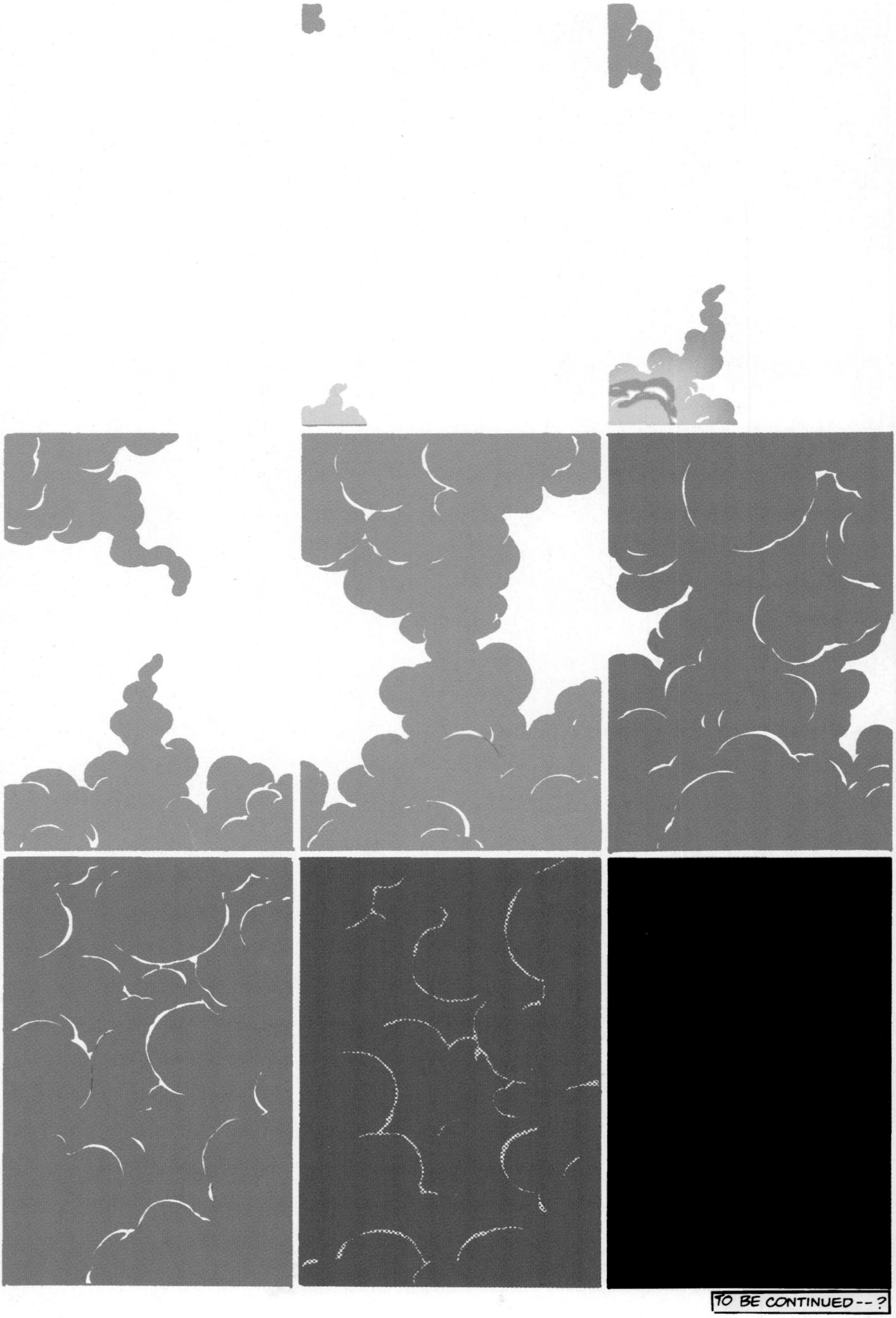
TO BE CONTINUED--?

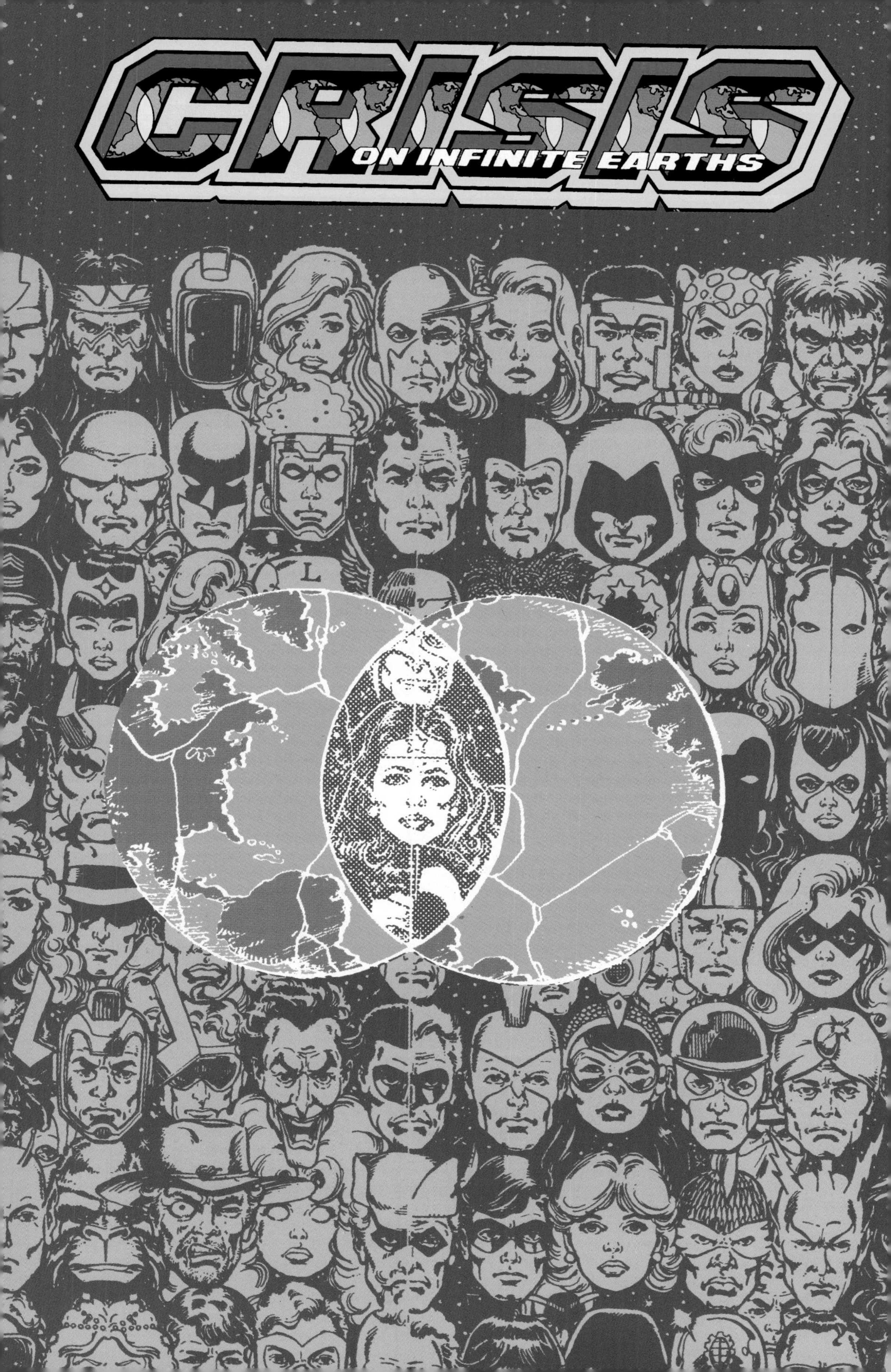
CRISIS
ON INFINITE EARTHS

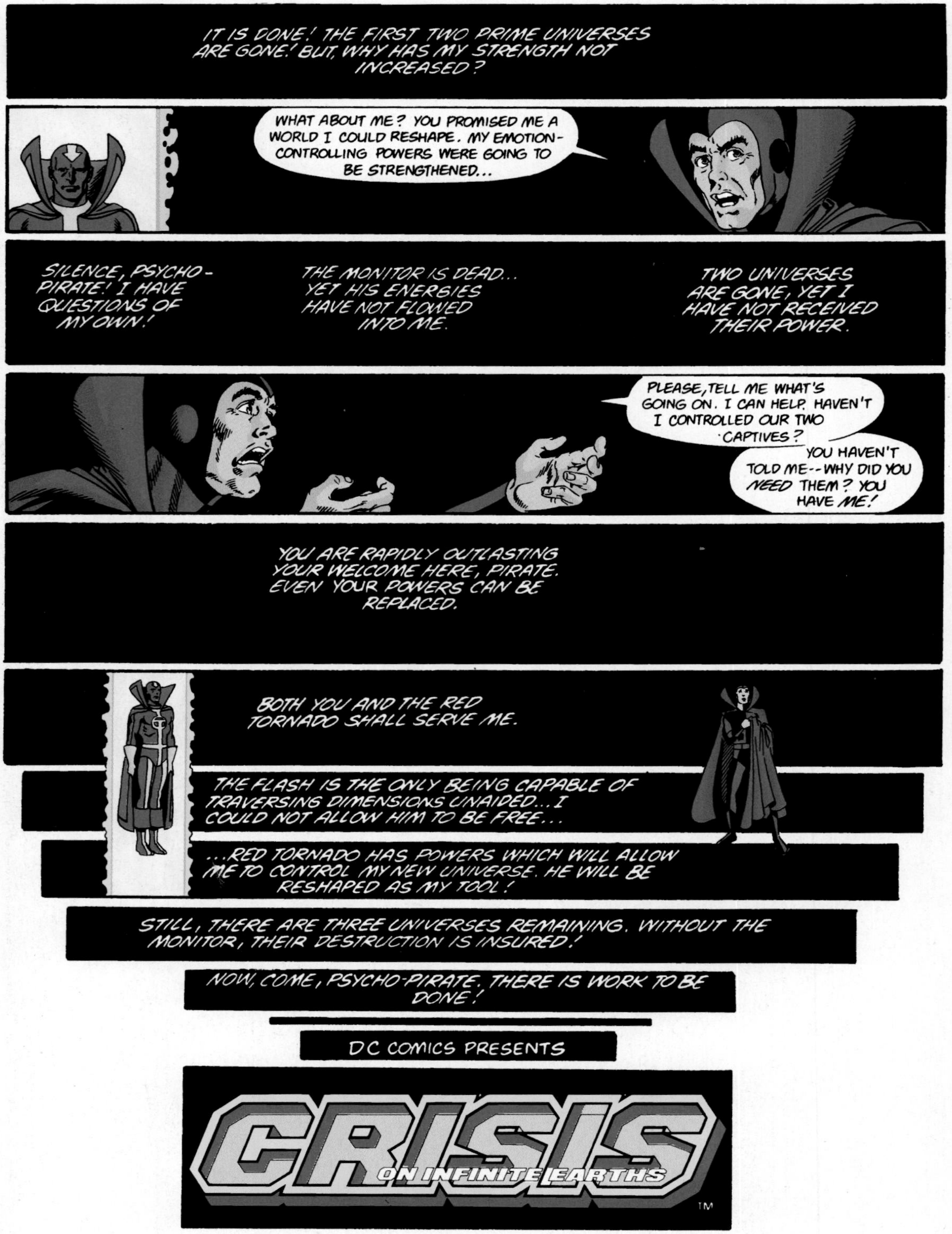
IT IS DONE! THE FIRST TWO PRIME UNIVERSES ARE GONE! BUT, WHY HAS MY STRENGTH NOT INCREASED?
WHAT ABOUT ME? YOU PROMISED ME A WORLD I COULD RESHAPE. MY EMOTION-CONTROLLING POWERS WERE GOING TO BE STRENGTHENED...
SILENCE, PSYCHO-PIRATE! I HAVE QUESTIONS OF MY OWN!
THE MONITOR IS DEAD... YET HIS ENERGIES HAVE NOT FLOWED INTO ME.
TWO UNIVERSES ARE GONE, YET I HAVE NOT RECEIVED THEIR POWER.
PLEASE, TELL ME WHAT'S GOING ON. I CAN HELP. HAVEN'T I CONTROLLED OUR TWO CAPTIVES?
YOU HAVEN'T TOLD ME--WHY DID YOU NEED THEM? YOU HAVE ME!
YOU ARE RAPIDLY OUTLASTING YOUR WELCOME HERE, PIRATE. EVEN YOUR POWERS CAN BE REPLACED.
BOTH YOU AND THE RED TORNADO SHALL SERVE ME.
THE FLASH IS THE ONLY BEING CAPABLE OF TRAVERSING DIMENSIONS UNAIDED... I COULD NOT ALLOW HIM TO BE FREE...
...RED TORNADO HAS POWERS WHICH WILL ALLOW ME TO CONTROL MY NEW UNIVERSE. HE WILL BE RESHAPED AS MY TOOL!
STILL, THERE ARE THREE UNIVERSES REMAINING. WITHOUT THE MONITOR, THEIR DESTRUCTION IS INSURED!
NOW, COME, PSYCHO-PIRATE. THERE IS WORK TO BE DONE!
DC COMICS PRESENTS
CRISIS
ON INFINITE EARTHS
TM

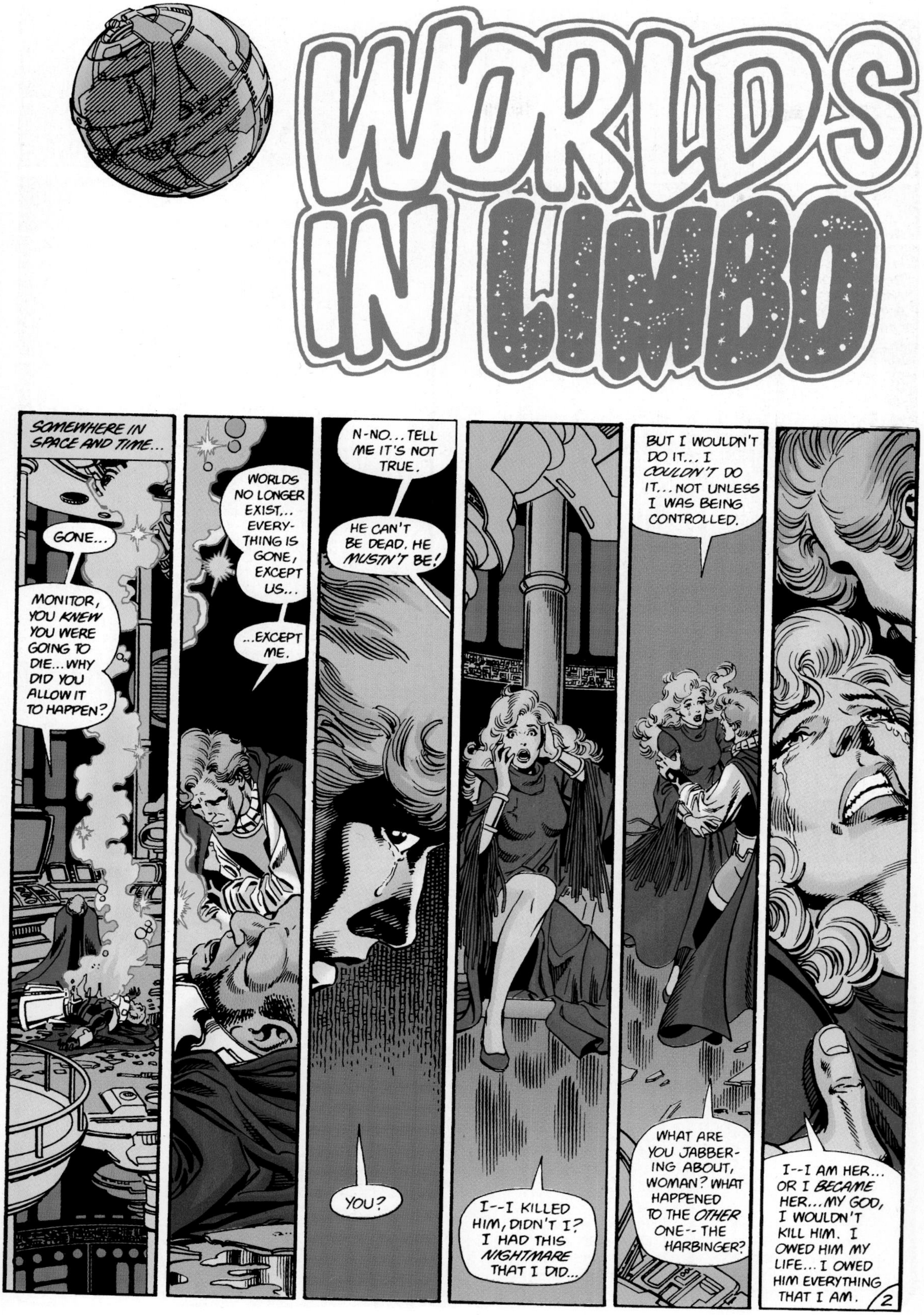
WORLDS IN LIMBO
SOMEWHERE IN SPACE AND TIME...
GONE...
MONITOR, YOU KNEW YOU WERE GOING TO DIE... WHY DID YOU ALLOW IT TO HAPPEN?
WORLDS NO LONGER EXIST... EVERY-THING IS GONE, EXCEPT US...
...EXCEPT ME.
N-NO... TELL ME IT'S NOT TRUE.
HE CAN'T BE DEAD. HE MUSTN'T BE!
YOU?
I--I KILLED HIM, DIDN'T I? I HAD THIS NIGHTMARE THAT I DID...
BUT I WOULDN'T DO IT... I COULDN'T DO IT... NOT UNLESS I WAS BEING CONTROLLED.
WHAT ARE YOU JABBER-ING ABOUT, WOMAN? WHAT HAPPENED TO THE OTHER ONE-- THE HARBINGER?
I--I AM HER... OR I BECAME HER... MY GOD, I WOULDN'T KILL HIM. I OWED HIM MY LIFE... I OWED HIM EVERYTHING THAT I AM.
2

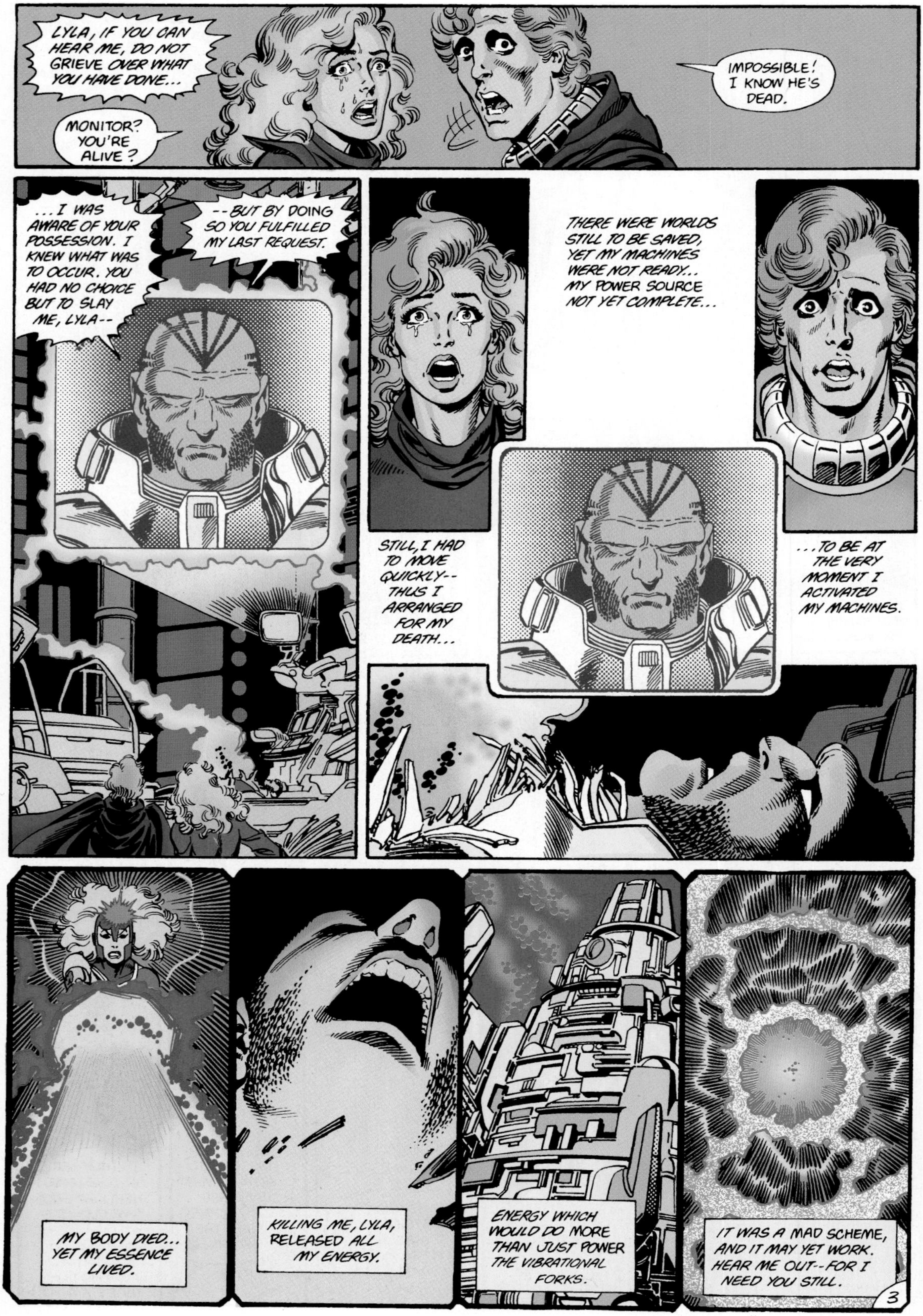
LYLA, IF YOU CAN HEAR ME, DO NOT GRIEVE OVER WHAT YOU HAVE DONE...
MONITOR? YOU'RE ALIVE?
IMPOSSIBLE! I KNOW HE'S DEAD.
...I WAS AWARE OF YOUR POSSESSION. I KNEW WHAT WAS TO OCCUR. YOU HAD NO CHOICE BUT TO SLAY ME, LYLA--
--BUT BY DOING SO YOU FULFILLED MY LAST REQUEST.
THERE WERE WORLDS STILL TO BE SAVED, YET MY MACHINES WERE NOT READY... MY POWER SOURCE NOT YET COMPLETE...
STILL, I HAD TO MOVE QUICKLY-- THUS I ARRANGED FOR MY DEATH...
...TO BE AT THE VERY MOMENT I ACTIVATED MY MACHINES.
MY BODY DIED... YET MY ESSENCE LIVED.
KILLING ME, LYLA, RELEASED ALL MY ENERGY.
ENERGY WHICH WOULD DO MORE THAN JUST POWER THE VIBRATIONAL FORKS.
IT WAS A MAD SCHEME, AND IT MAY YET WORK. HEAR ME OUT--FOR I NEED YOU STILL.
3

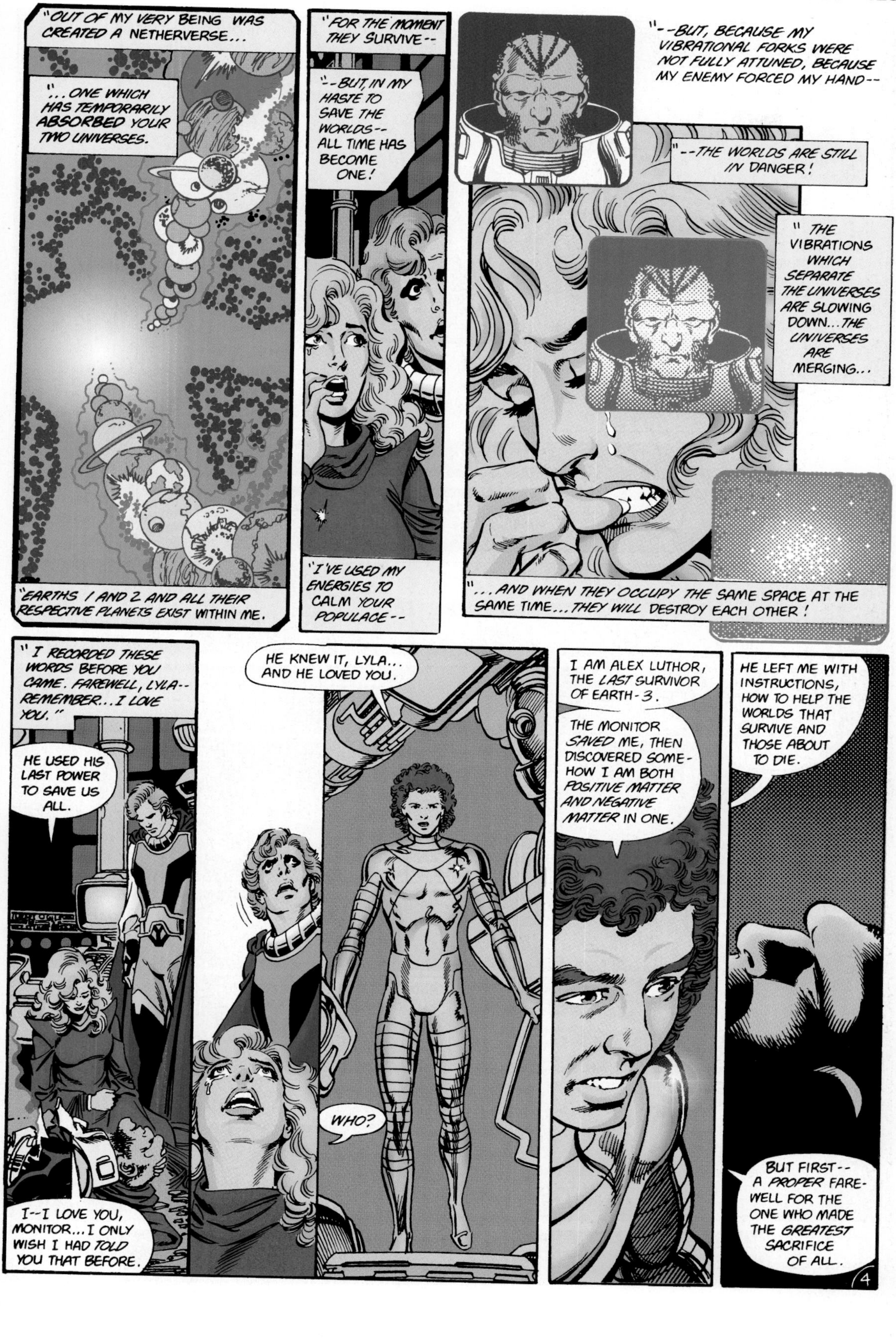
"OUT OF MY VERY BEING WAS CREATED A NETHERVERSE...
"...ONE WHICH HAS TEMPORARILY ABSORBED YOUR TWO UNIVERSES.
"EARTHS 1 AND 2 AND ALL THEIR RESPECTIVE PLANETS EXIST WITHIN ME.
"FOR THE MOMENT THEY SURVIVE--
"--BUT, IN MY HASTE TO SAVE THE WORLDS--ALL TIME HAS BECOME ONE!
"I'VE USED MY ENERGIES TO CALM YOUR POPULACE--
"--BUT, BECAUSE MY VIBRATIONAL FORKS WERE NOT FULLY ATTUNED, BECAUSE MY ENEMY FORCED MY HAND--
"--THE WORLDS ARE STILL IN DANGER!
" THE VIBRATIONS WHICH SEPARATE THE UNIVERSES ARE SLOWING DOWN...THE UNIVERSES ARE MERGING...
"...AND WHEN THEY OCCUPY THE SAME SPACE AT THE SAME TIME...THEY WILL DESTROY EACH OTHER!
"I RECORDED THESE WORDS BEFORE YOU CAME. FAREWELL, LYLA--REMEMBER...I LOVE YOU."
HE USED HIS LAST POWER TO SAVE US ALL.
I--I LOVE YOU, MONITOR...I ONLY WISH I HAD TOLD YOU THAT BEFORE.
HE KNEW IT, LYLA... AND HE LOVED YOU.
WHO?
I AM ALEX LUTHOR, THE LAST SURVIVOR OF EARTH-3.
THE MONITOR SAVED ME, THEN DISCOVERED SOMEHOW I AM BOTH POSITIVE MATTER AND NEGATIVE MATTER IN ONE.
HE LEFT ME WITH INSTRUCTIONS, HOW TO HELP THE WORLDS THAT SURVIVE AND THOSE ABOUT TO DIE.
BUT FIRST--A PROPER FAREWELL FOR THE ONE WHO MADE THE GREATEST SACRIFICE OF ALL.
4

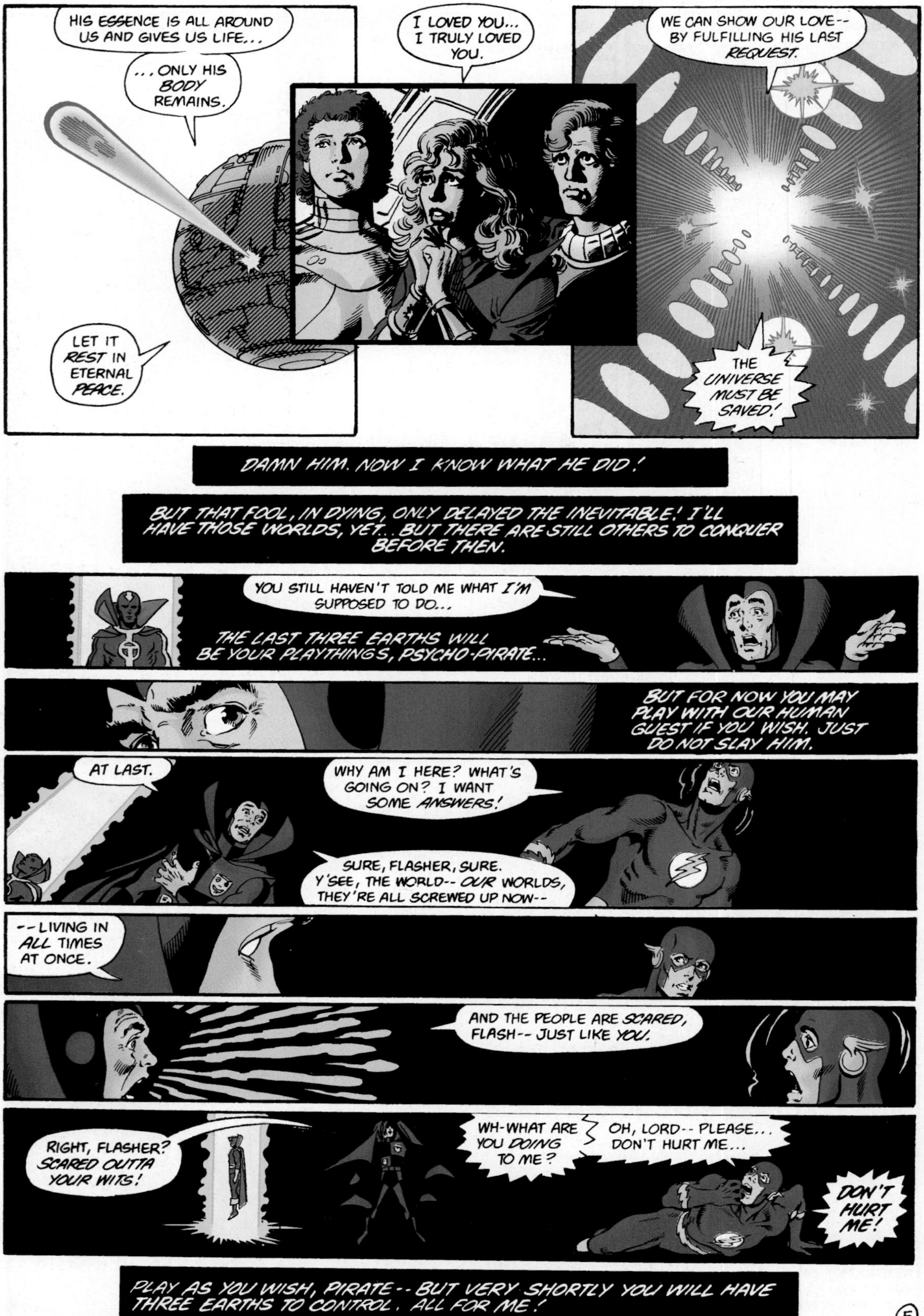
HIS ESSENCE IS ALL AROUND US AND GIVES US LIFE...
...ONLY HIS BODY REMAINS.
LET IT REST IN ETERNAL PEACE.
I LOVED YOU... I TRULY LOVED YOU.
WE CAN SHOW OUR LOVE-- BY FULFILLING HIS LAST REQUEST.
THE UNIVERSE MUST BE SAVED!
DAMN HIM. NOW I KNOW WHAT HE DID!
BUT THAT FOOL, IN DYING, ONLY DELAYED THE INEVITABLE! I'LL HAVE THOSE WORLDS, YET... BUT THERE ARE STILL OTHERS TO CONQUER BEFORE THEN.
YOU STILL HAVEN'T TOLD ME WHAT I'M SUPPOSED TO DO...
THE LAST THREE EARTHS WILL BE YOUR PLAYTHINGS, PSYCHO-PIRATE...
BUT FOR NOW YOU MAY PLAY WITH OUR HUMAN GUEST IF YOU WISH. JUST DO NOT SLAY HIM.
AT LAST.
WHY AM I HERE? WHAT'S GOING ON? I WANT SOME ANSWERS!
SURE, FLASHER, SURE. Y'SEE, THE WORLD-- OUR WORLDS, THEY'RE ALL SCREWED UP NOW--
--LIVING IN ALL TIMES AT ONCE.
AND THE PEOPLE ARE SCARED, FLASH-- JUST LIKE YOU.
RIGHT, FLASHER? SCARED OUTTA YOUR WITS!
WH-WHAT ARE YOU DOING TO ME?
OH, LORD-- PLEASE... DON'T HURT ME...
DON'T HURT ME!
PLAY AS YOU WISH, PIRATE-- BUT VERY SHORTLY YOU WILL HAVE THREE EARTHS TO CONTROL. ALL FOR ME!
5

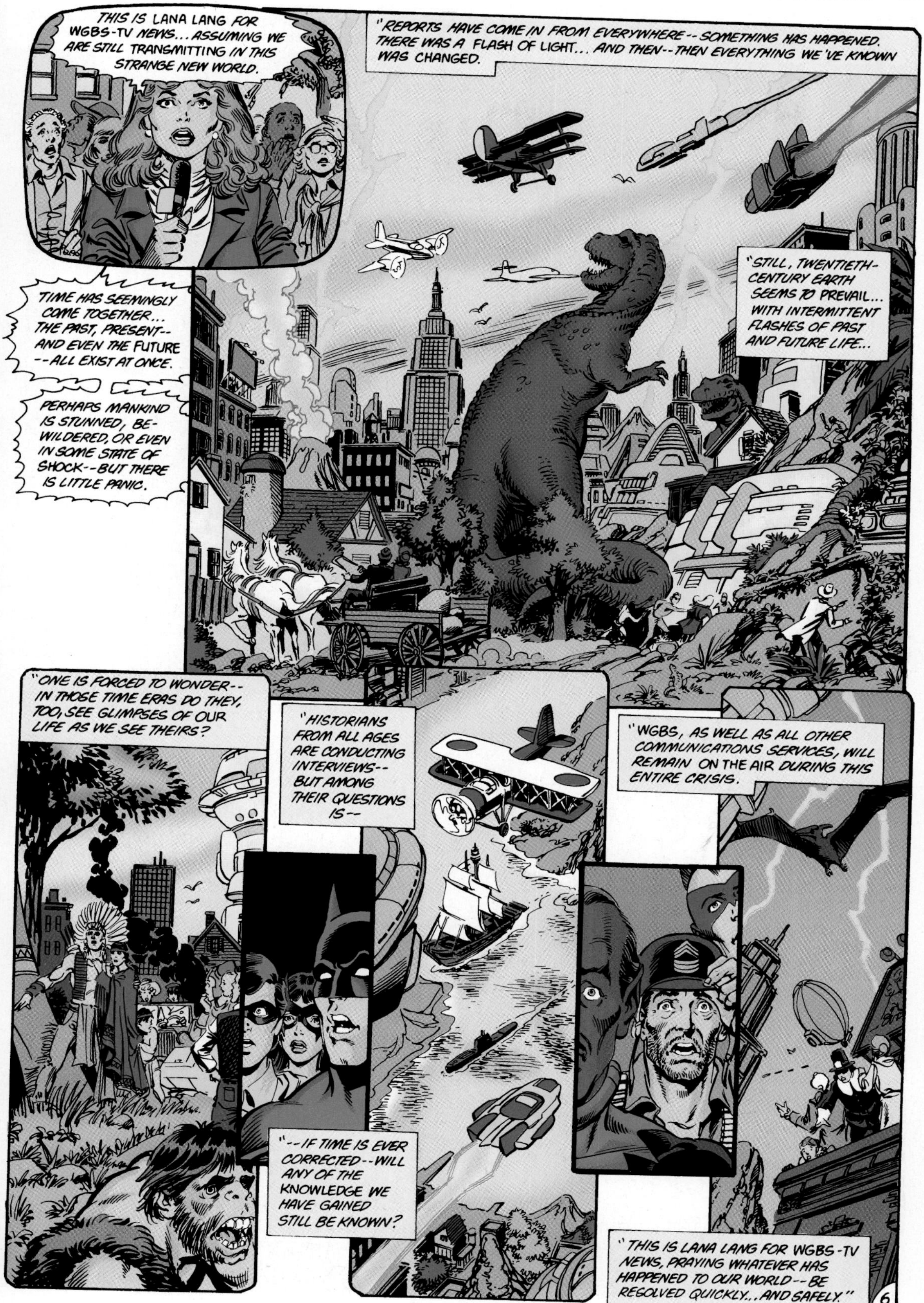
THIS IS LANA LANG FOR WGBS-TV NEWS... ASSUMING WE ARE STILL TRANSMITTING IN THIS STRANGE NEW WORLD.
"REPORTS HAVE COME IN FROM EVERYWHERE--SOMETHING HAS HAPPENED. THERE WAS A FLASH OF LIGHT... AND THEN--THEN EVERYTHING WE'VE KNOWN WAS CHANGED.
TIME HAS SEEMINGLY COME TOGETHER... THE PAST, PRESENT--AND EVEN THE FUTURE--ALL EXIST AT ONCE.
PERHAPS MANKIND IS STUNNED, BEWILDERED, OR EVEN IN SOME STATE OF SHOCK--BUT THERE IS LITTLE PANIC.
"STILL, TWENTIETH-CENTURY EARTH SEEMS TO PREVAIL... WITH INTERMITTENT FLASHES OF PAST AND FUTURE LIFE...
"ONE IS FORCED TO WONDER--IN THOSE TIME ERAS DO THEY, TOO, SEE GLIMPSES OF OUR LIFE AS WE SEE THEIRS?
"HISTORIANS FROM ALL AGES ARE CONDUCTING INTERVIEWS--BUT AMONG THEIR QUESTIONS IS--
"--IF TIME IS EVER CORRECTED--WILL ANY OF THE KNOWLEDGE WE HAVE GAINED STILL BE KNOWN?
"WGBS, AS WELL AS ALL OTHER COMMUNICATIONS SERVICES, WILL REMAIN ON THE AIR DURING THIS ENTIRE CRISIS.
"THIS IS LANA LANG FOR WGBS-TV NEWS, PRAYING WHATEVER HAS HAPPENED TO OUR WORLD--BE RESOLVED QUICKLY... AND SAFELY."
6

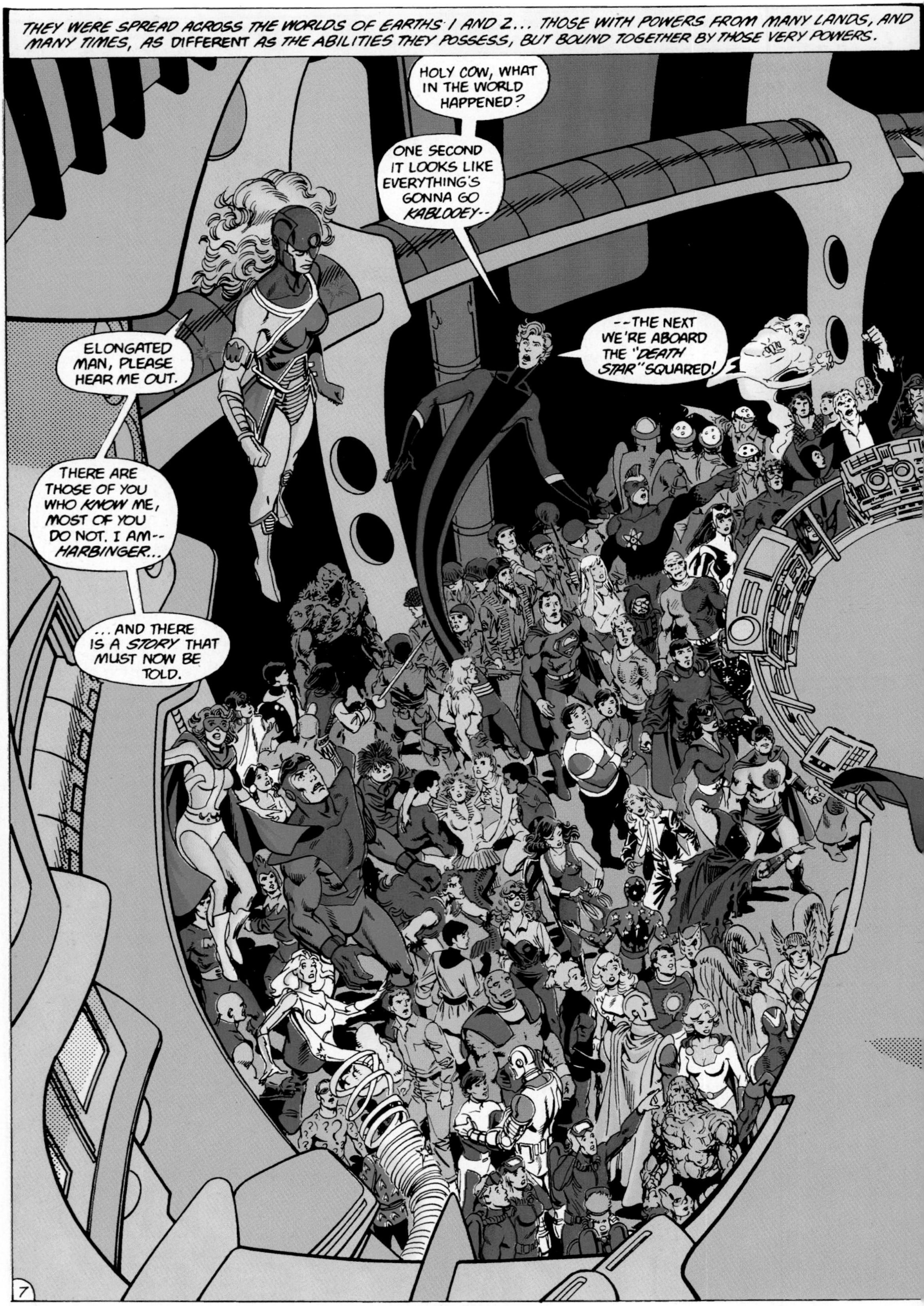
THEY WERE SPREAD ACROSS THE WORLDS OF EARTHS 1 AND 2... THOSE WITH POWERS FROM MANY LANDS, AND MANY TIMES, AS DIFFERENT AS THE ABILITIES THEY POSSESS, BUT BOUND TOGETHER BY THOSE VERY POWERS.
HOLY COW, WHAT IN THE WORLD HAPPENED?
ONE SECOND IT LOOKS LIKE EVERYTHING'S GONNA GO KABLOOEY--
--THE NEXT WE'RE ABOARD THE "DEATH STAR" SQUARED!
ELONGATED MAN, PLEASE HEAR ME OUT.
THERE ARE THOSE OF YOU WHO KNOW ME, MOST OF YOU DO NOT. I AM--HARBINGER...
...AND THERE IS A STORY THAT MUST NOW BE TOLD.
7

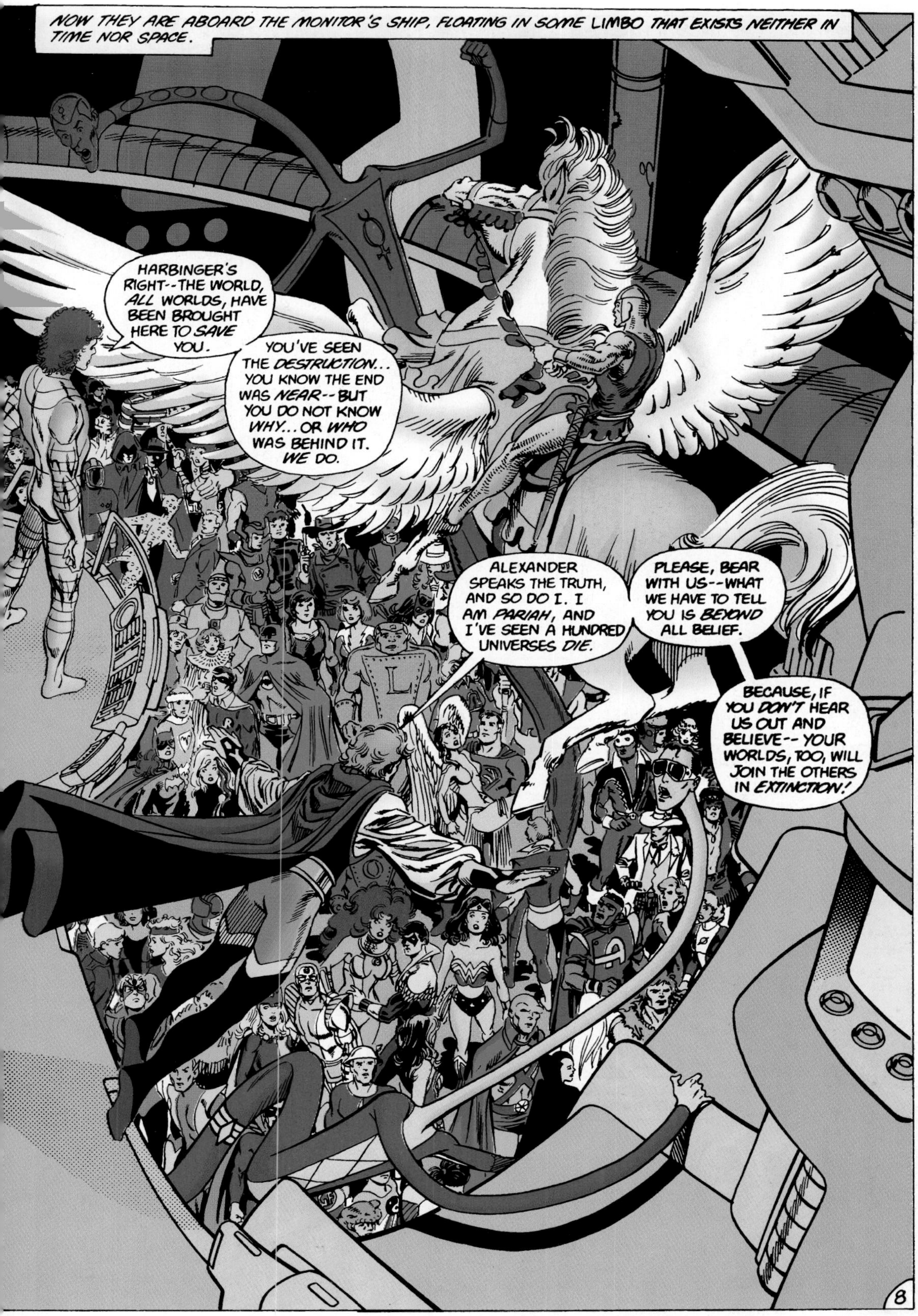
NOW THEY ARE ABOARD THE MONITOR'S SHIP, FLOATING IN SOME LIMBO THAT EXISTS NEITHER IN TIME NOR SPACE.
HARBINGER'S RIGHT--THE WORLD, ALL WORLDS, HAVE BEEN BROUGHT HERE TO SAVE YOU.
YOU'VE SEEN THE DESTRUCTION... YOU KNOW THE END WAS NEAR--BUT YOU DO NOT KNOW WHY... OR WHO WAS BEHIND IT. WE DO.
ALEXANDER SPEAKS THE TRUTH, AND SO DO I. I AM PARIAH, AND I'VE SEEN A HUNDRED UNIVERSES DIE.
PLEASE, BEAR WITH US--WHAT WE HAVE TO TELL YOU IS BEYOND ALL BELIEF.
BECAUSE, IF YOU DON'T HEAR US OUT AND BELIEVE--YOUR WORLDS, TOO, WILL JOIN THE OTHERS IN EXTINCTION!
8

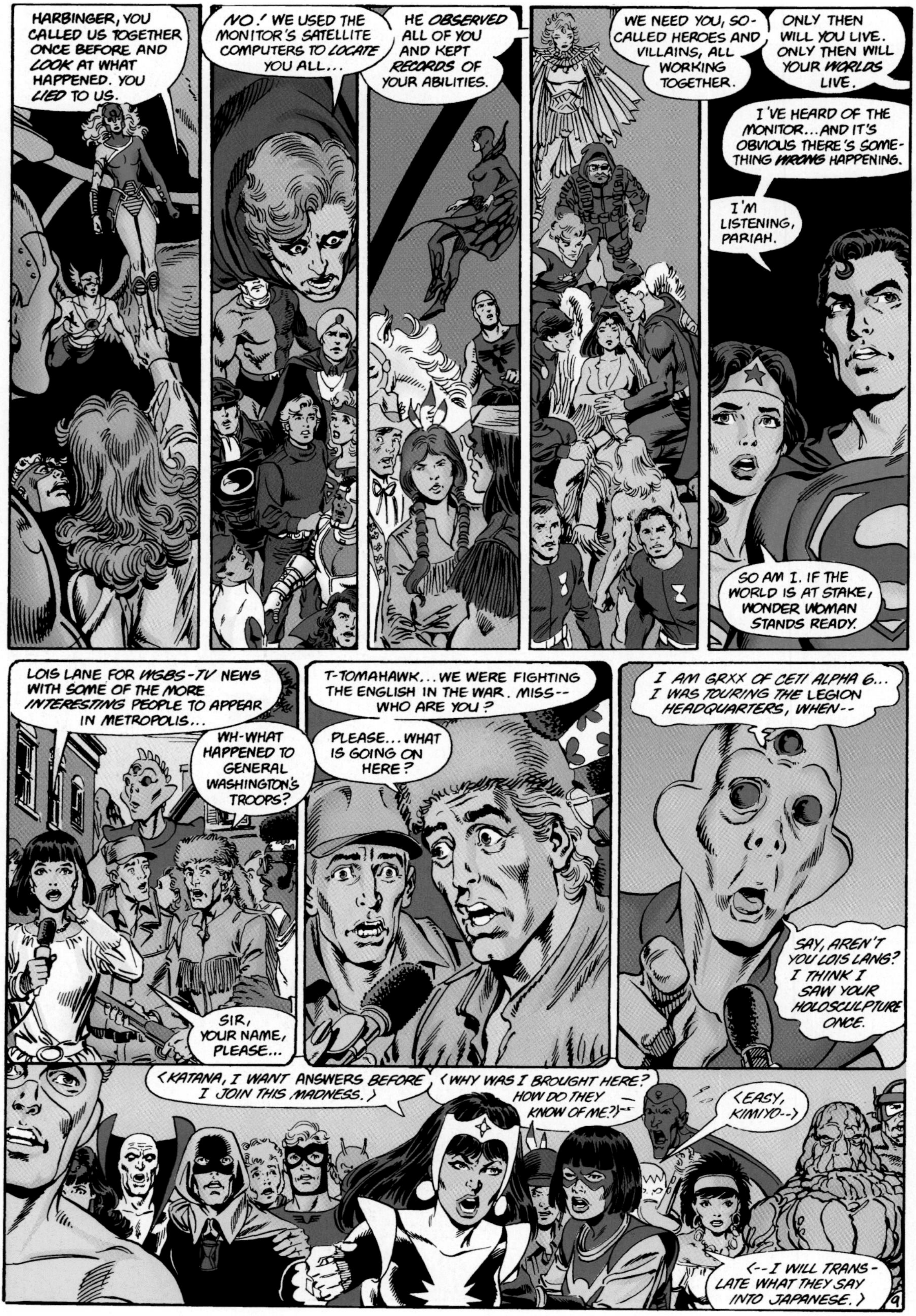
HARBINGER, YOU CALLED US TOGETHER ONCE BEFORE AND LOOK AT WHAT HAPPENED. YOU LIED TO US.
NO! WE USED THE MONITOR'S SATELLITE COMPUTERS TO LOCATE YOU ALL...
HE OBSERVED ALL OF YOU AND KEPT RECORDS OF YOUR ABILITIES.
WE NEED YOU, SO-CALLED HEROES AND VILLAINS, ALL WORKING TOGETHER.
ONLY THEN WILL YOU LIVE. ONLY THEN WILL YOUR WORLDS LIVE.
I'VE HEARD OF THE MONITOR...AND IT'S OBVIOUS THERE'S SOMETHING WRONG HAPPENING.
I'M LISTENING, PARIAH.
SO AM I. IF THE WORLD IS AT STAKE, WONDER WOMAN STANDS READY.
LOIS LANE FOR WGBS-TV NEWS WITH SOME OF THE MORE INTERESTING PEOPLE TO APPEAR IN METROPOLIS...
WH-WHAT HAPPENED TO GENERAL WASHINGTON'S TROOPS?
SIR, YOUR NAME, PLEASE...
T-TOMAHAWK...WE WERE FIGHTING THE ENGLISH IN THE WAR. MISS-- WHO ARE YOU?
PLEASE...WHAT IS GOING ON HERE?
I AM GRXX OF CETI ALPHA 6... I WAS TOURING THE LEGION HEADQUARTERS, WHEN--
SAY, AREN'T YOU LOIS LANG? I THINK I SAW YOUR HOLOSCULPTURE ONCE.
<KATANA, I WANT ANSWERS BEFORE I JOIN THIS MADNESS.>
<WHY WAS I BROUGHT HERE? HOW DO THEY KNOW OF ME?>
<EASY, KIMIYO-->
<--I WILL TRANSLATE WHAT THEY SAY INTO JAPANESE.>
9

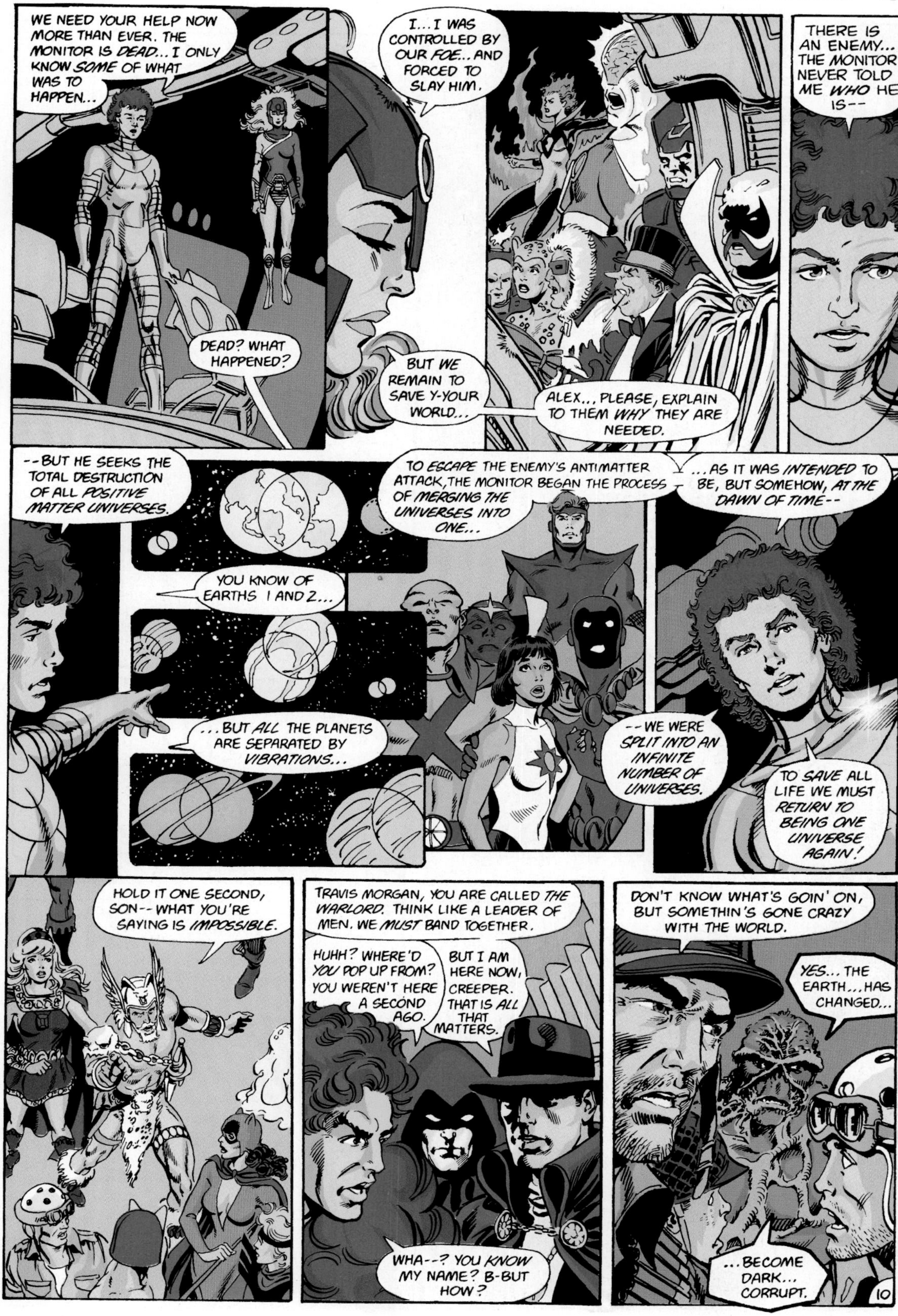
WE NEED YOUR HELP NOW MORE THAN EVER. THE MONITOR IS DEAD... I ONLY KNOW SOME OF WHAT WAS TO HAPPEN...
DEAD? WHAT HAPPENED?
I... I WAS CONTROLLED BY OUR FOE... AND FORCED TO SLAY HIM.
BUT WE REMAIN TO SAVE Y-YOUR WORLD...
ALEX..., PLEASE, EXPLAIN TO THEM WHY THEY ARE NEEDED.
THERE IS AN ENEMY... THE MONITOR NEVER TOLD ME WHO HE IS--
--BUT HE SEEKS THE TOTAL DESTRUCTION OF ALL POSITIVE MATTER UNIVERSES.
YOU KNOW OF EARTHS 1 AND 2...
...BUT ALL THE PLANETS ARE SEPARATED BY VIBRATIONS...
TO ESCAPE THE ENEMY'S ANTIMATTER ATTACK, THE MONITOR BEGAN THE PROCESS OF MERGING THE UNIVERSES INTO ONE...
...AS IT WAS INTENDED TO BE, BUT SOMEHOW, AT THE DAWN OF TIME--
--WE WERE SPLIT INTO AN INFINITE NUMBER OF UNIVERSES.
TO SAVE ALL LIFE WE MUST RETURN TO BEING ONE UNIVERSE AGAIN!
HOLD IT ONE SECOND, SON-- WHAT YOU'RE SAYING IS IMPOSSIBLE.
TRAVIS MORGAN, YOU ARE CALLED THE WARLORD. THINK LIKE A LEADER OF MEN. WE MUST BAND TOGETHER.
HUHH? WHERE'D YOU POP UP FROM? YOU WEREN'T HERE A SECOND AGO.
BUT I AM HERE NOW, CREEPER. THAT IS ALL THAT MATTERS.
WHA--? YOU KNOW MY NAME? B-BUT HOW?
DON'T KNOW WHAT'S GOIN' ON, BUT SOMETHIN'S GONE CRAZY WITH THE WORLD.
YES... THE EARTH... HAS CHANGED...
...BECOME DARK... CORRUPT.
10

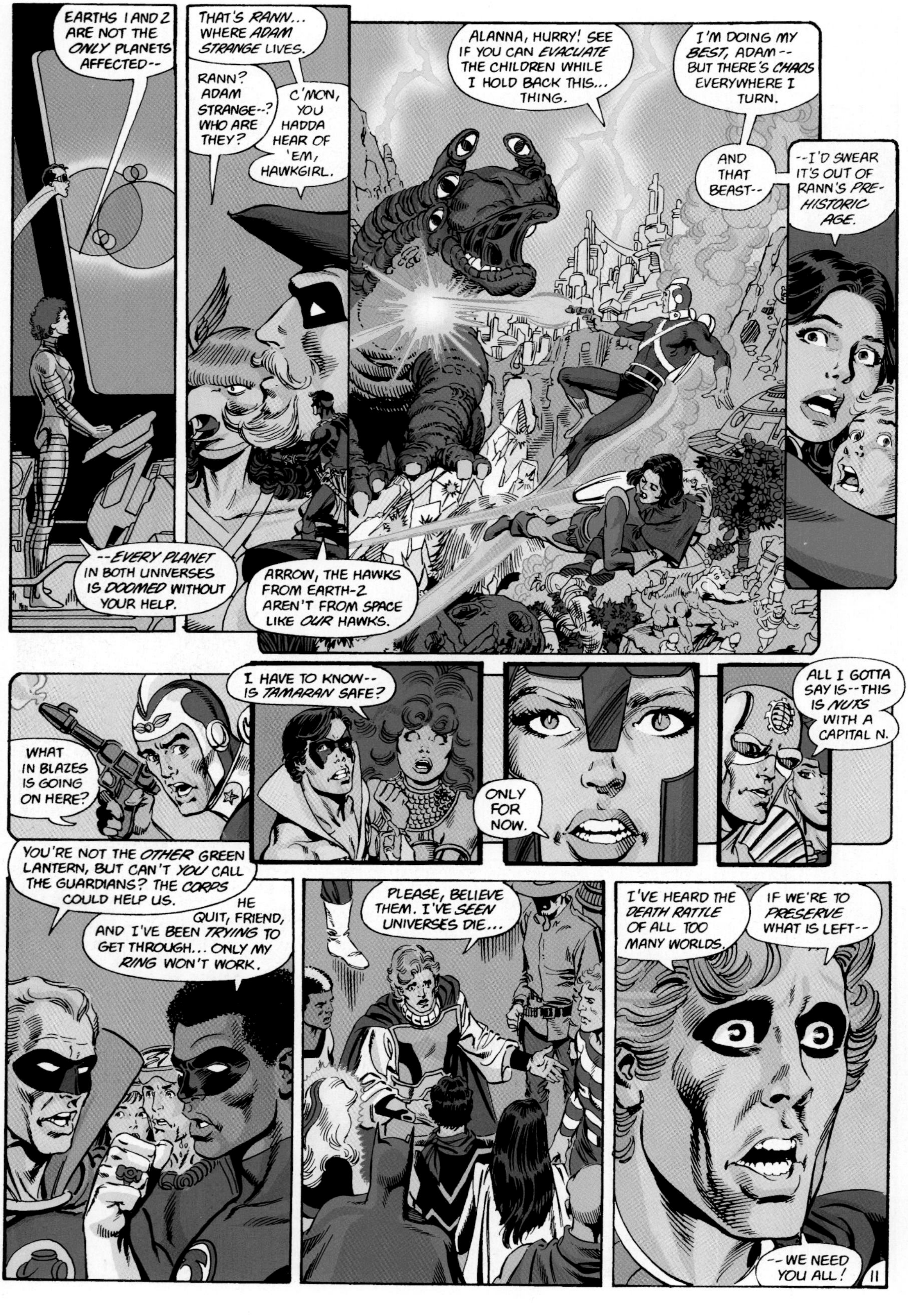
EARTHS 1 AND 2 ARE NOT THE ONLY PLANETS AFFECTED--
--EVERY PLANET IN BOTH UNIVERSES IS DOOMED WITHOUT YOUR HELP.
THAT'S RANN... WHERE ADAM STRANGE LIVES.
RANN? ADAM STRANGE--? WHO ARE THEY?
C'MON, YOU HADDA HEAR OF 'EM, HAWKGIRL.
ARROW, THE HAWKS FROM EARTH-2 AREN'T FROM SPACE LIKE OUR HAWKS.
ALANNA, HURRY! SEE IF YOU CAN EVACUATE THE CHILDREN WHILE I HOLD BACK THIS... THING.
I'M DOING MY BEST, ADAM -- BUT THERE'S CHAOS EVERYWHERE I TURN.
AND THAT BEAST--
--I'D SWEAR IT'S OUT OF RANN'S PRE-HISTORIC AGE.
WHAT IN BLAZES IS GOING ON HERE?
I HAVE TO KNOW-- IS TAMARAN SAFE?
ONLY FOR NOW.
ALL I GOTTA SAY IS--THIS IS NUTS WITH A CAPITAL N.
YOU'RE NOT THE OTHER GREEN LANTERN, BUT CAN'T YOU CALL THE GUARDIANS? THE CORPS COULD HELP US.
HE QUIT, FRIEND, AND I'VE BEEN TRYING TO GET THROUGH... ONLY MY RING WON'T WORK.
PLEASE, BELIEVE THEM. I'VE SEEN UNIVERSES DIE...
I'VE HEARD THE DEATH RATTLE OF ALL TOO MANY WORLDS.
IF WE'RE TO PRESERVE WHAT IS LEFT--
--WE NEED YOU ALL!
11

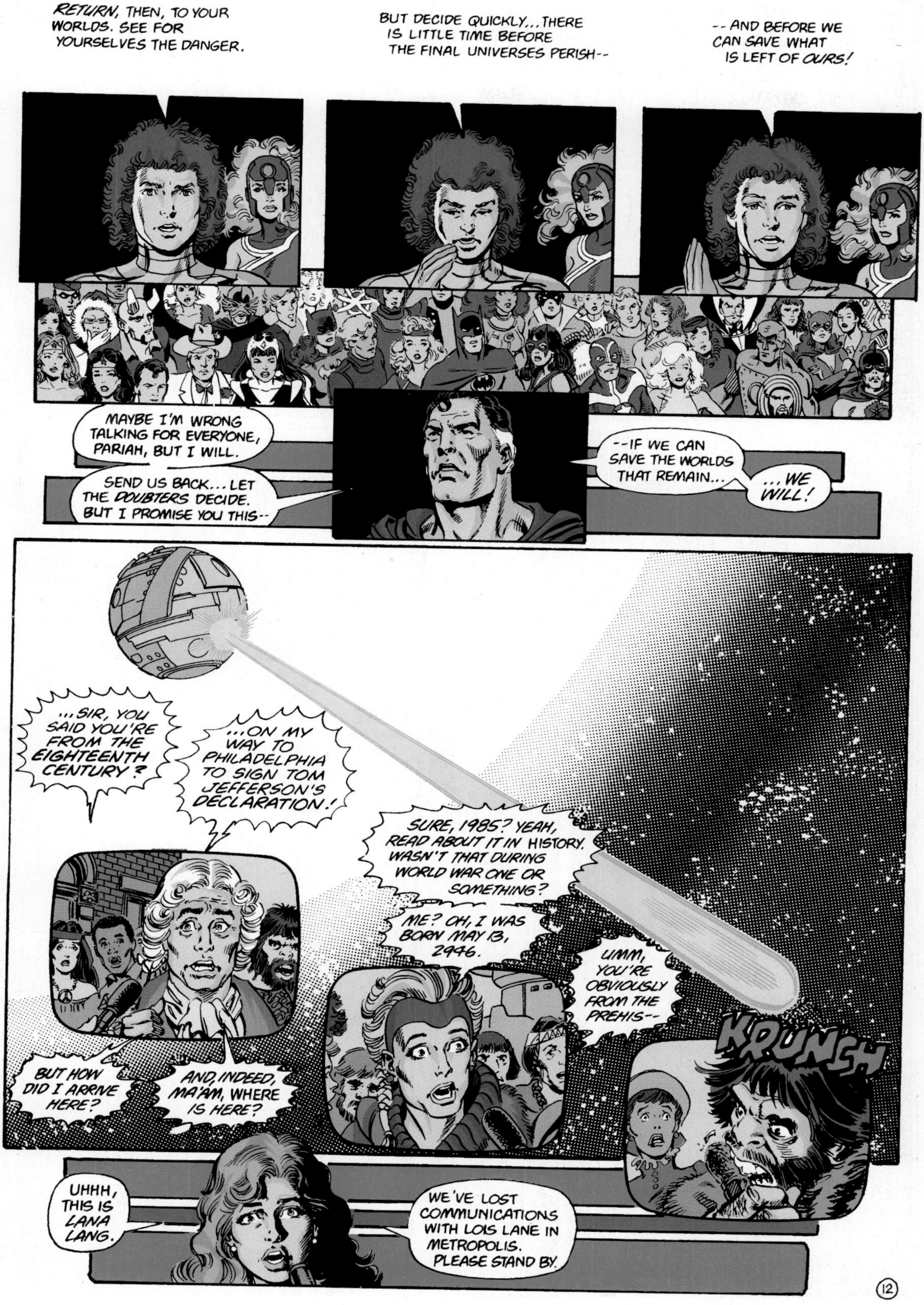
RETURN, THEN, TO YOUR WORLDS. SEE FOR YOURSELVES THE DANGER.
BUT DECIDE QUICKLY... THERE IS LITTLE TIME BEFORE THE FINAL UNIVERSES PERISH--
--AND BEFORE WE CAN SAVE WHAT IS LEFT OF OURS!
MAYBE I'M WRONG TALKING FOR EVERYONE, PARIAH, BUT I WILL.
SEND US BACK... LET THE DOUBTERS DECIDE. BUT I PROMISE YOU THIS--
--IF WE CAN SAVE THE WORLDS THAT REMAIN...
...WE WILL!
...SIR, YOU SAID YOU'RE FROM THE EIGHTEENTH CENTURY?
...ON MY WAY TO PHILADELPHIA TO SIGN TOM JEFFERSON'S DECLARATION!
SURE, 1985? YEAH, READ ABOUT IT IN HISTORY. WASN'T THAT DURING WORLD WAR ONE OR SOMETHING?
ME? OH, I WAS BORN MAY 13, 2946.
UMM, YOU'RE OBVIOUSLY FROM THE PREHIS--
BUT HOW DID I ARRIVE HERE?
AND, INDEED, MA'AM, WHERE IS HERE?
KRUNSH
UHHH, THIS IS LANA LANG.
WE'VE LOST COMMUNICATIONS WITH LOIS LANE IN METROPOLIS. PLEASE STAND BY.
12

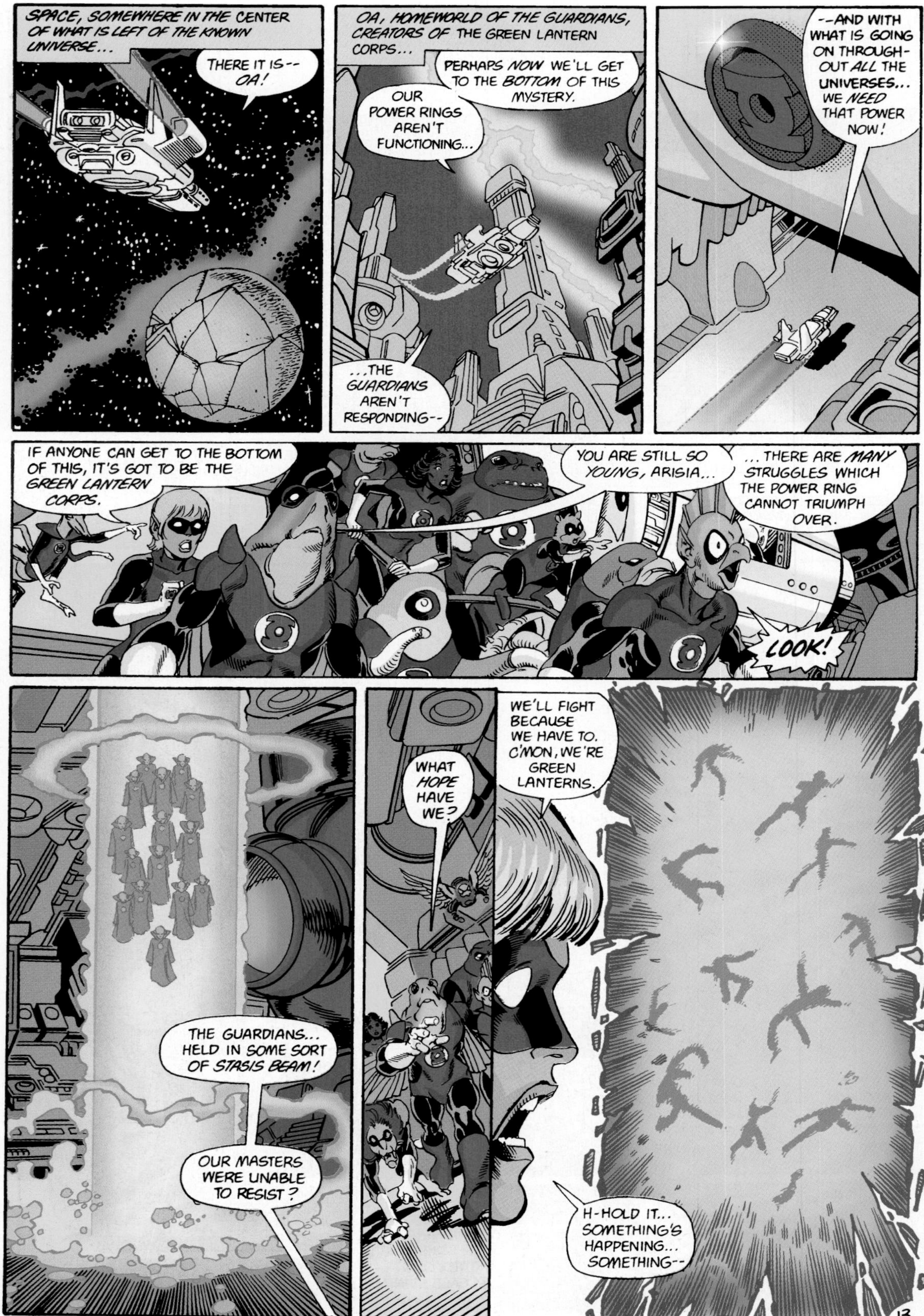
SPACE, SOMEWHERE IN THE CENTER OF WHAT IS LEFT OF THE KNOWN UNIVERSE...
THERE IT IS-- OA!
OA, HOMEWORLD OF THE GUARDIANS, CREATORS OF THE GREEN LANTERN CORPS...
PERHAPS NOW WE'LL GET TO THE BOTTOM OF THIS MYSTERY.
OUR POWER RINGS AREN'T FUNCTIONING...
...THE GUARDIANS AREN'T RESPONDING--
--AND WITH WHAT IS GOING ON THROUGHOUT ALL THE UNIVERSES... WE NEED THAT POWER NOW!
IF ANYONE CAN GET TO THE BOTTOM OF THIS, IT'S GOT TO BE THE GREEN LANTERN CORPS.
YOU ARE STILL SO YOUNG, ARISIA...
...THERE ARE MANY STRUGGLES WHICH THE POWER RING CANNOT TRIUMPH OVER.
LOOK!
THE GUARDIANS... HELD IN SOME SORT OF STASIS BEAM!
OUR MASTERS WERE UNABLE TO RESIST?
WHAT HOPE HAVE WE?
WE'LL FIGHT BECAUSE WE HAVE TO. C'MON, WE'RE GREEN LANTERNS.
H-HOLD IT... SOMETHING'S HAPPENING... SOMETHING--
13

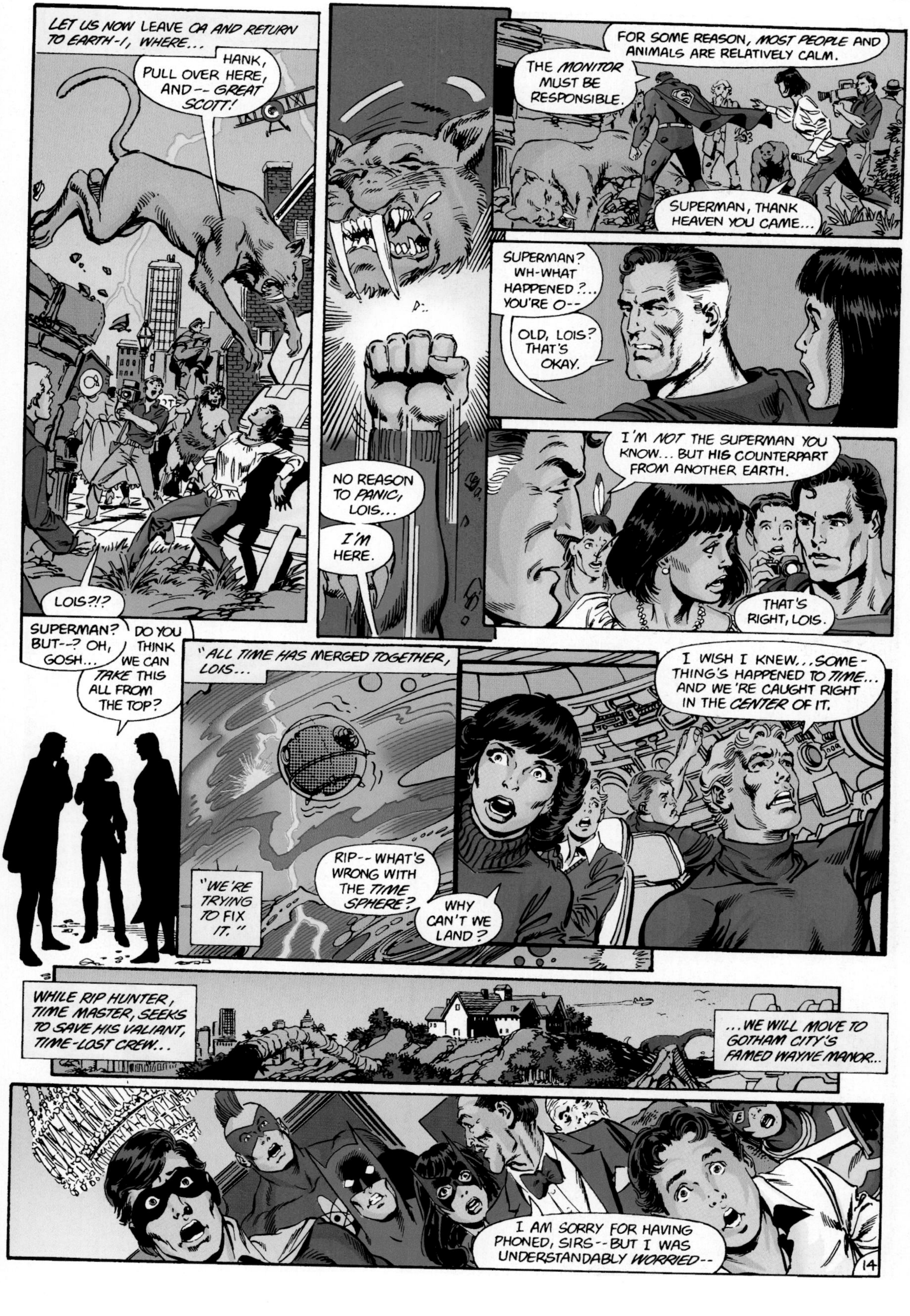
LET US NOW LEAVE OA AND RETURN TO EARTH-1, WHERE...
HANK, PULL OVER HERE, AND-- GREAT SCOTT!
LOIS?!?
NO REASON TO PANIC, LOIS...
I'M HERE.
FOR SOME REASON, MOST PEOPLE AND ANIMALS ARE RELATIVELY CALM.
THE MONITOR MUST BE RESPONSIBLE.
SUPERMAN, THANK HEAVEN YOU CAME...
SUPERMAN? WH-WHAT HAPPENED?... YOU'RE O--
OLD, LOIS? THAT'S OKAY.
I'M NOT THE SUPERMAN YOU KNOW... BUT HIS COUNTERPART FROM ANOTHER EARTH.
THAT'S RIGHT, LOIS.
SUPERMAN? BUT--? OH, GOSH...
DO YOU THINK WE CAN TAKE THIS ALL FROM THE TOP?
"ALL TIME HAS MERGED TOGETHER, LOIS...
"WE'RE TRYING TO FIX IT."
RIP-- WHAT'S WRONG WITH THE TIME SPHERE?
WHY CAN'T WE LAND?
I WISH I KNEW... SOME-THING'S HAPPENED TO TIME... AND WE'RE CAUGHT RIGHT IN THE CENTER OF IT.
WHILE RIP HUNTER, TIME MASTER, SEEKS TO SAVE HIS VALIANT, TIME-LOST CREW...
...WE WILL MOVE TO GOTHAM CITY'S FAMED WAYNE MANOR...
I AM SORRY FOR HAVING PHONED, SIRS--BUT I WAS UNDERSTANDABLY WORRIED--
14

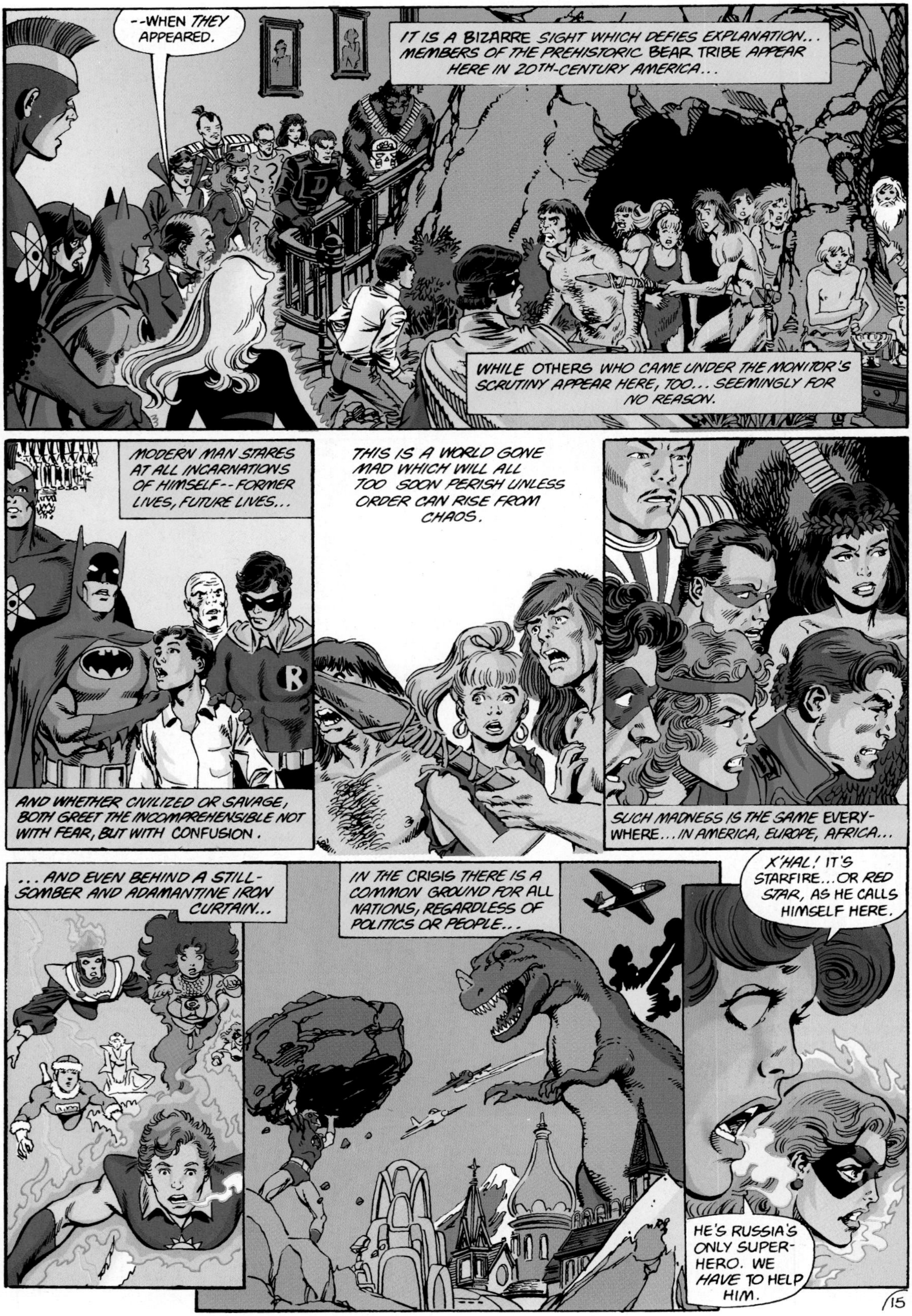
--WHEN THEY APPEARED.
IT IS A BIZARRE SIGHT WHICH DEFIES EXPLANATION... MEMBERS OF THE PREHISTORIC BEAR TRIBE APPEAR HERE IN 20TH-CENTURY AMERICA...
WHILE OTHERS WHO CAME UNDER THE MONITOR'S SCRUTINY APPEAR HERE, TOO... SEEMINGLY FOR NO REASON.
MODERN MAN STARES AT ALL INCARNATIONS OF HIMSELF--FORMER LIVES, FUTURE LIVES...
AND WHETHER CIVILIZED OR SAVAGE, BOTH GREET THE INCOMPREHENSIBLE NOT WITH FEAR, BUT WITH CONFUSION.
THIS IS A WORLD GONE MAD WHICH WILL ALL TOO SOON PERISH UNLESS ORDER CAN RISE FROM CHAOS.
SUCH MADNESS IS THE SAME EVERYWHERE... IN AMERICA, EUROPE, AFRICA...
...AND EVEN BEHIND A STILL-SOMBER AND ADAMANTINE IRON CURTAIN...
IN THE CRISIS THERE IS A COMMON GROUND FOR ALL NATIONS, REGARDLESS OF POLITICS OR PEOPLE...
X'HAL! IT'S STARFIRE...OR RED STAR, AS HE CALLS HIMSELF HERE.
HE'S RUSSIA'S ONLY SUPER-HERO. WE HAVE TO HELP HIM.
15

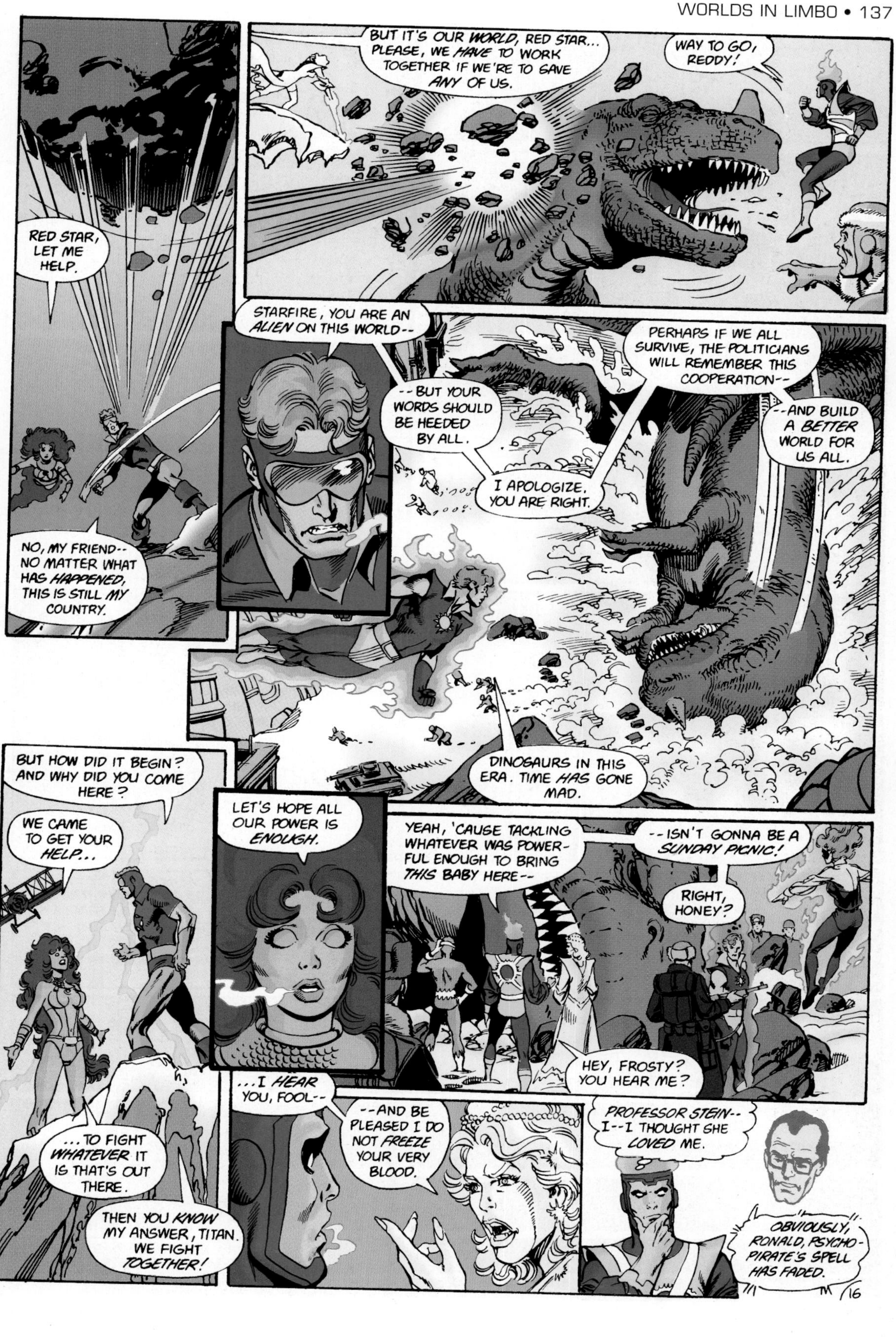
RED STAR, LET ME HELP.
NO, MY FRIEND-- NO MATTER WHAT HAS HAPPENED, THIS IS STILL MY COUNTRY.
BUT IT'S OUR WORLD, RED STAR... PLEASE, WE HAVE TO WORK TOGETHER IF WE'RE TO SAVE ANY OF US.
WAY TO GO, REDDY!
STARFIRE, YOU ARE AN ALIEN ON THIS WORLD--
--BUT YOUR WORDS SHOULD BE HEEDED BY ALL.
I APOLOGIZE. YOU ARE RIGHT.
PERHAPS IF WE ALL SURVIVE, THE POLITICIANS WILL REMEMBER THIS COOPERATION--
--AND BUILD A BETTER WORLD FOR US ALL.
DINOSAURS IN THIS ERA. TIME HAS GONE MAD.
BUT HOW DID IT BEGIN? AND WHY DID YOU COME HERE?
WE CAME TO GET YOUR HELP...
...TO FIGHT WHATEVER IT IS THAT'S OUT THERE.
THEN YOU KNOW MY ANSWER, TITAN. WE FIGHT TOGETHER!
LET'S HOPE ALL OUR POWER IS ENOUGH.
YEAH, 'CAUSE TACKLING WHATEVER WAS POWERFUL ENOUGH TO BRING THIS BABY HERE--
--ISN'T GONNA BE A SUNDAY PICNIC!
RIGHT, HONEY?
HEY, FROSTY? YOU HEAR ME?
...I HEAR YOU, FOOL--
--AND BE PLEASED I DO NOT FREEZE YOUR VERY BLOOD.
PROFESSOR STEIN-- I--I THOUGHT SHE LOVED ME.
OBVIOUSLY, RONALD, PSYCHO-PIRATE'S SPELL HAS FADED.
16

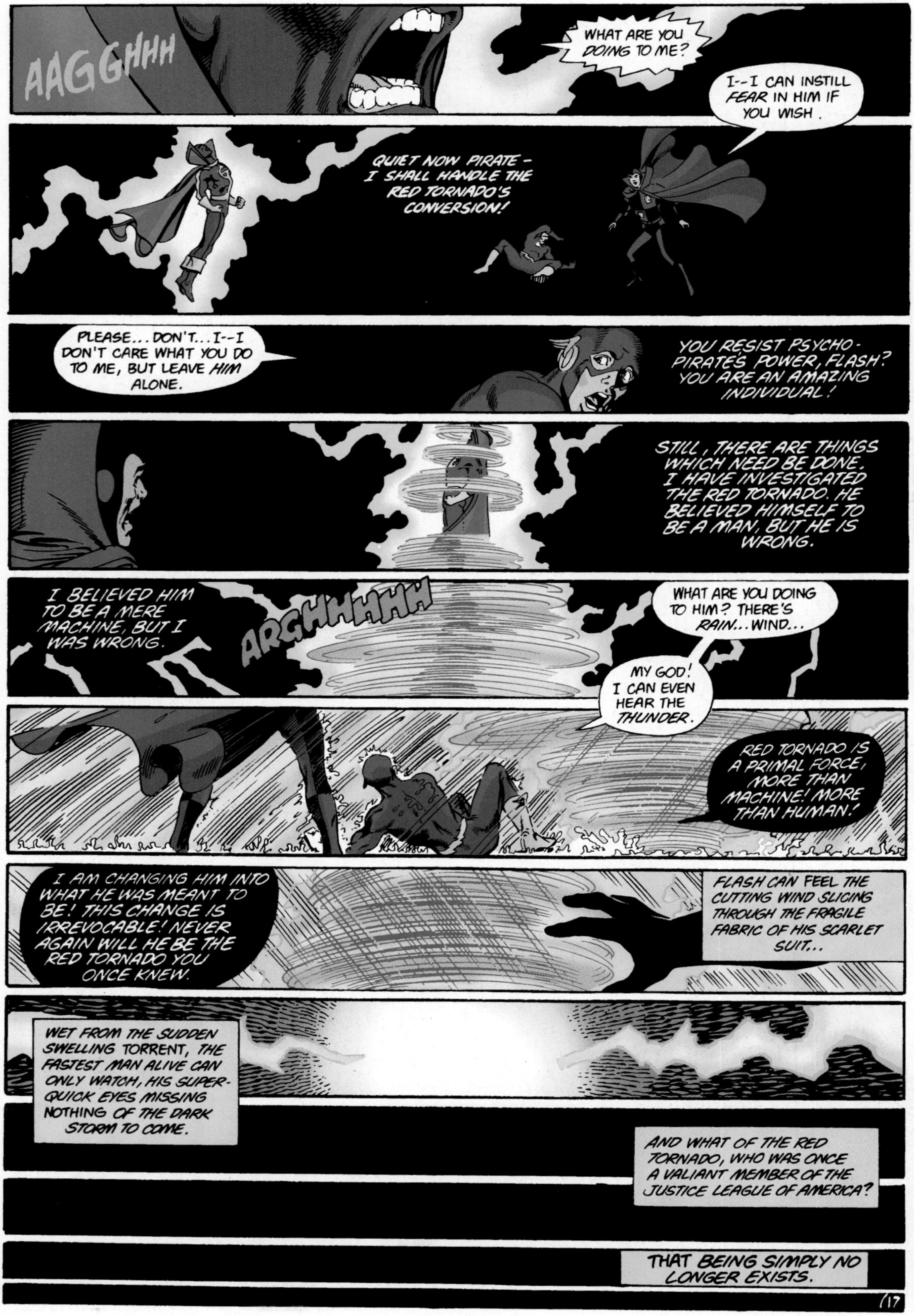
AAGGHHH
WHAT ARE YOU DOING TO ME?
I--I CAN INSTILL FEAR IN HIM IF YOU WISH.
QUIET NOW PIRATE - I SHALL HANDLE THE RED TORNADO'S CONVERSION!
PLEASE... DON'T... I--I DON'T CARE WHAT YOU DO TO ME, BUT LEAVE HIM ALONE.
YOU RESIST PSYCHO-PIRATE'S POWER, FLASH? YOU ARE AN AMAZING INDIVIDUAL!
STILL, THERE ARE THINGS WHICH NEED BE DONE. I HAVE INVESTIGATED THE RED TORNADO. HE BELIEVED HIMSELF TO BE A MAN, BUT HE IS WRONG.
I BELIEVED HIM TO BE A MERE MACHINE, BUT I WAS WRONG.
ARGHHHHHH
WHAT ARE YOU DOING TO HIM? THERE'S RAIN... WIND...
MY GOD! I CAN EVEN HEAR THE THUNDER.
RED TORNADO IS A PRIMAL FORCE, MORE THAN MACHINE! MORE THAN HUMAN!
I AM CHANGING HIM INTO WHAT HE WAS MEANT TO BE! THIS CHANGE IS IRREVOCABLE! NEVER AGAIN WILL HE BE THE RED TORNADO YOU ONCE KNEW.
FLASH CAN FEEL THE CUTTING WIND SLICING THROUGH THE FRAGILE FABRIC OF HIS SCARLET SUIT...
WET FROM THE SUDDEN SWELLING TORRENT, THE FASTEST MAN ALIVE CAN ONLY WATCH, HIS SUPER-QUICK EYES MISSING NOTHING OF THE DARK STORM TO COME.
AND WHAT OF THE RED TORNADO, WHO WAS ONCE A VALIANT MEMBER OF THE JUSTICE LEAGUE OF AMERICA?
THAT BEING SIMPLY NO LONGER EXISTS.
17

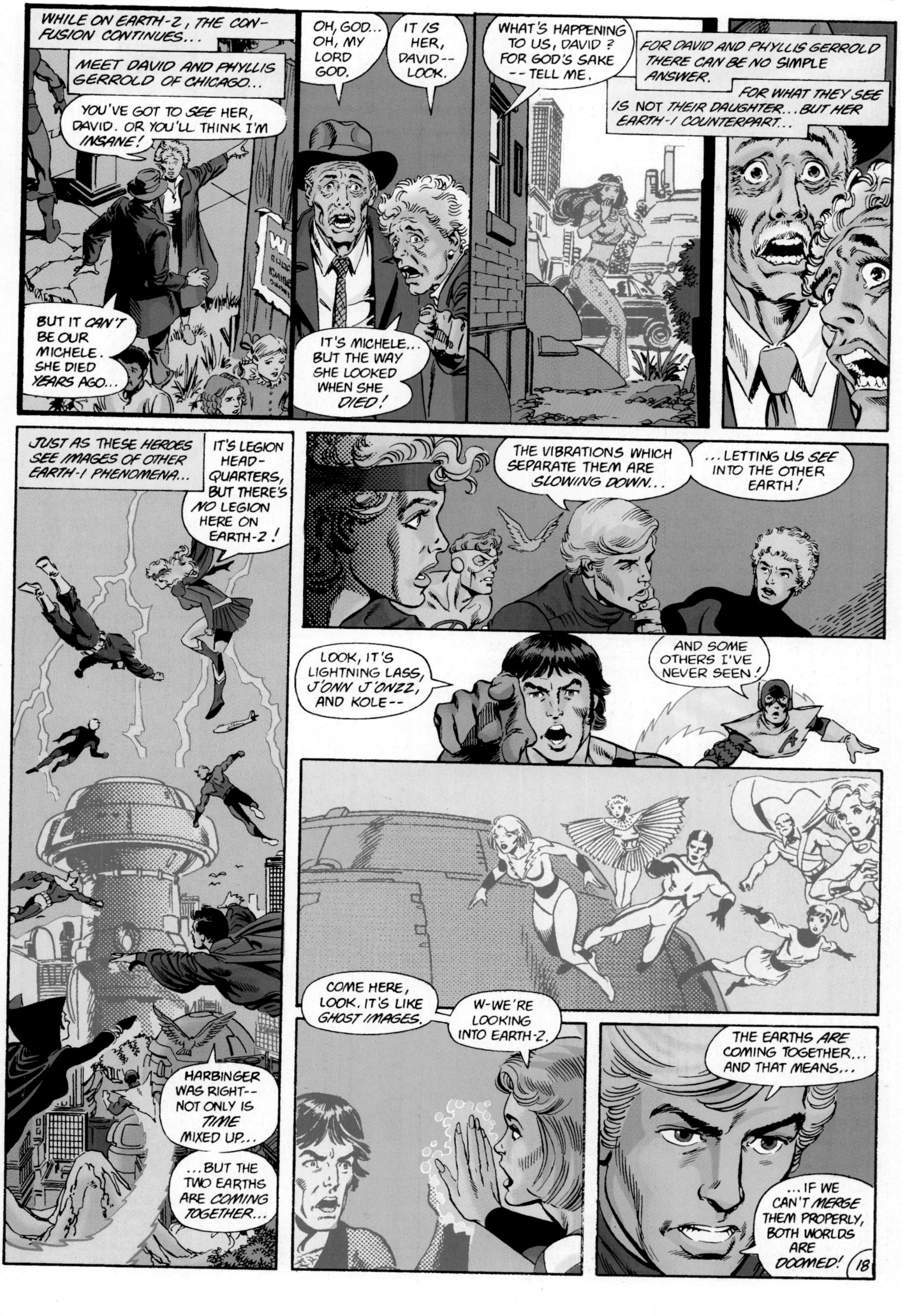
WHILE ON EARTH-2, THE CONFUSION CONTINUES...
MEET DAVID AND PHYLLIS GERROLD OF CHICAGO...
YOU'VE GOT TO SEE HER, DAVID. OR YOU'LL THINK I'M INSANE!
BUT IT CAN'T BE OUR MICHELE. SHE DIED YEARS AGO...
OH, GOD... OH, MY LORD GOD.
IT IS HER, DAVID-- LOOK.
IT'S MICHELE... BUT THE WAY SHE LOOKED WHEN SHE DIED!
WHAT'S HAPPENING TO US, DAVID? FOR GOD'S SAKE --TELL ME.
FOR DAVID AND PHYLLIS GERROLD THERE CAN BE NO SIMPLE ANSWER.
FOR WHAT THEY SEE IS NOT THEIR DAUGHTER... BUT HER EARTH-1 COUNTERPART...
JUST AS THESE HEROES SEE IMAGES OF OTHER EARTH-1 PHENOMENA...
IT'S LEGION HEAD-QUARTERS, BUT THERE'S NO LEGION HERE ON EARTH-2!
HARBINGER WAS RIGHT-- NOT ONLY IS TIME MIXED UP...
...BUT THE TWO EARTHS ARE COMING TOGETHER...
THE VIBRATIONS WHICH SEPARATE THEM ARE SLOWING DOWN...
...LETTING US SEE INTO THE OTHER EARTH!
LOOK, IT'S LIGHTNING LASS, J'ONN J'ONZZ, AND KOLE--
AND SOME OTHERS I'VE NEVER SEEN!
COME HERE, LOOK. IT'S LIKE GHOST IMAGES.
W-WE'RE LOOKING INTO EARTH-2.
THE EARTHS ARE COMING TOGETHER... AND THAT MEANS...
...IF WE CAN'T MERGE THEM PROPERLY, BOTH WORLDS ARE DOOMED!
18

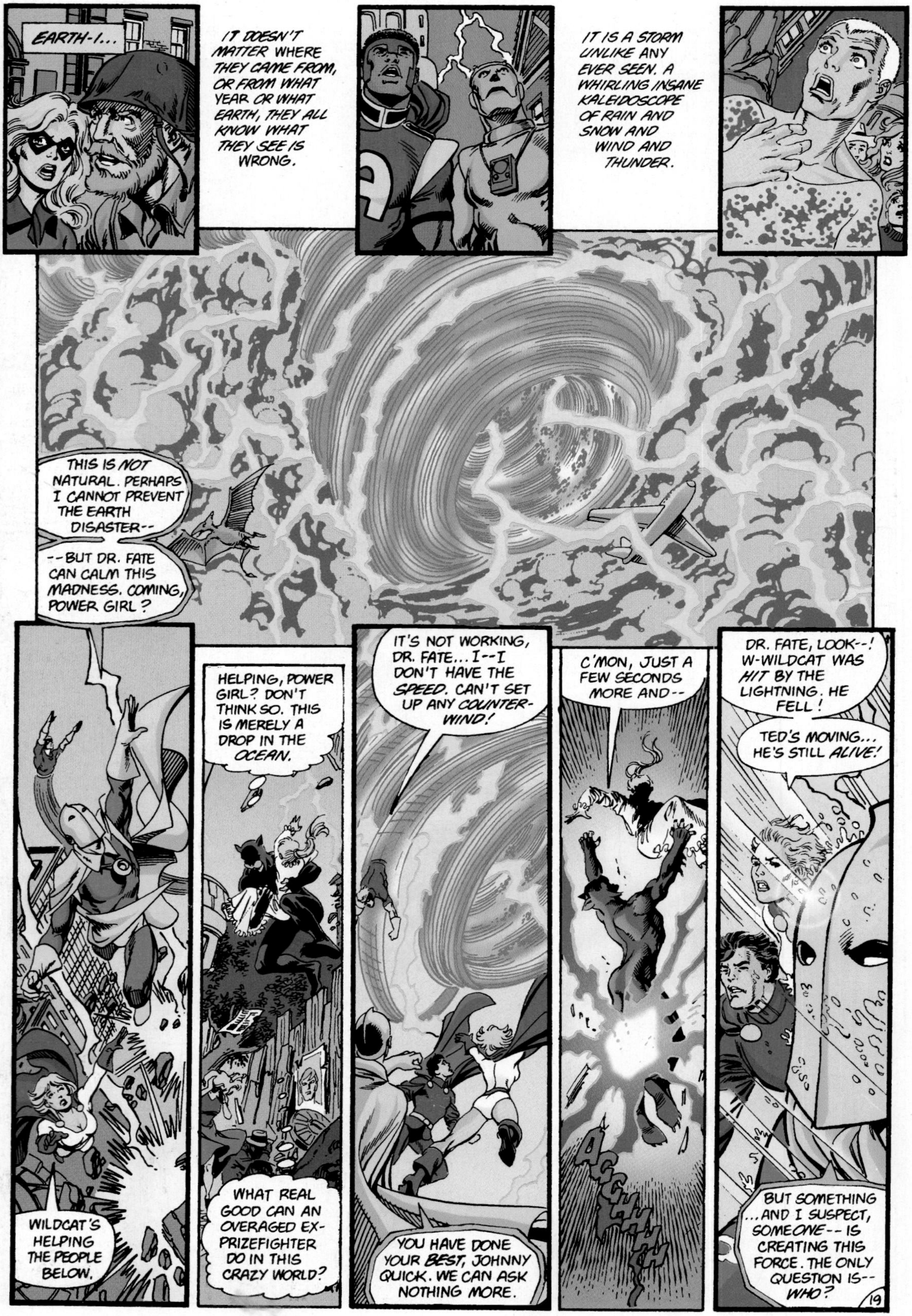
EARTH-1...
IT DOESN'T MATTER WHERE THEY CAME FROM, OR FROM WHAT YEAR OR WHAT EARTH, THEY ALL KNOW WHAT THEY SEE IS WRONG.
IT IS A STORM UNLIKE ANY EVER SEEN. A WHIRLING INSANE KALEIDOSCOPE OF RAIN AND SNOW AND WIND AND THUNDER.
THIS IS NOT NATURAL. PERHAPS I CANNOT PREVENT THE EARTH DISASTER--
--BUT DR. FATE CAN CALM THIS MADNESS. COMING, POWER GIRL?
WILDCAT'S HELPING THE PEOPLE BELOW.
HELPING, POWER GIRL? DON'T THINK SO. THIS IS MERELY A DROP IN THE OCEAN.
WHAT REAL GOOD CAN AN OVERAGED EX-PRIZEFIGHTER DO IN THIS CRAZY WORLD?
IT'S NOT WORKING, DR. FATE... I--I DON'T HAVE THE SPEED. CAN'T SET UP ANY COUNTER-WIND!
YOU HAVE DONE YOUR BEST, JOHNNY QUICK. WE CAN ASK NOTHING MORE.
C'MON, JUST A FEW SECONDS MORE AND--
AGHHHH
DR. FATE, LOOK--! W-WILDCAT WAS HIT BY THE LIGHTNING. HE FELL!
TED'S MOVING... HE'S STILL ALIVE!
BUT SOMETHING ...AND I SUSPECT, SOMEONE-- IS CREATING THIS FORCE. THE ONLY QUESTION IS-- WHO?
19

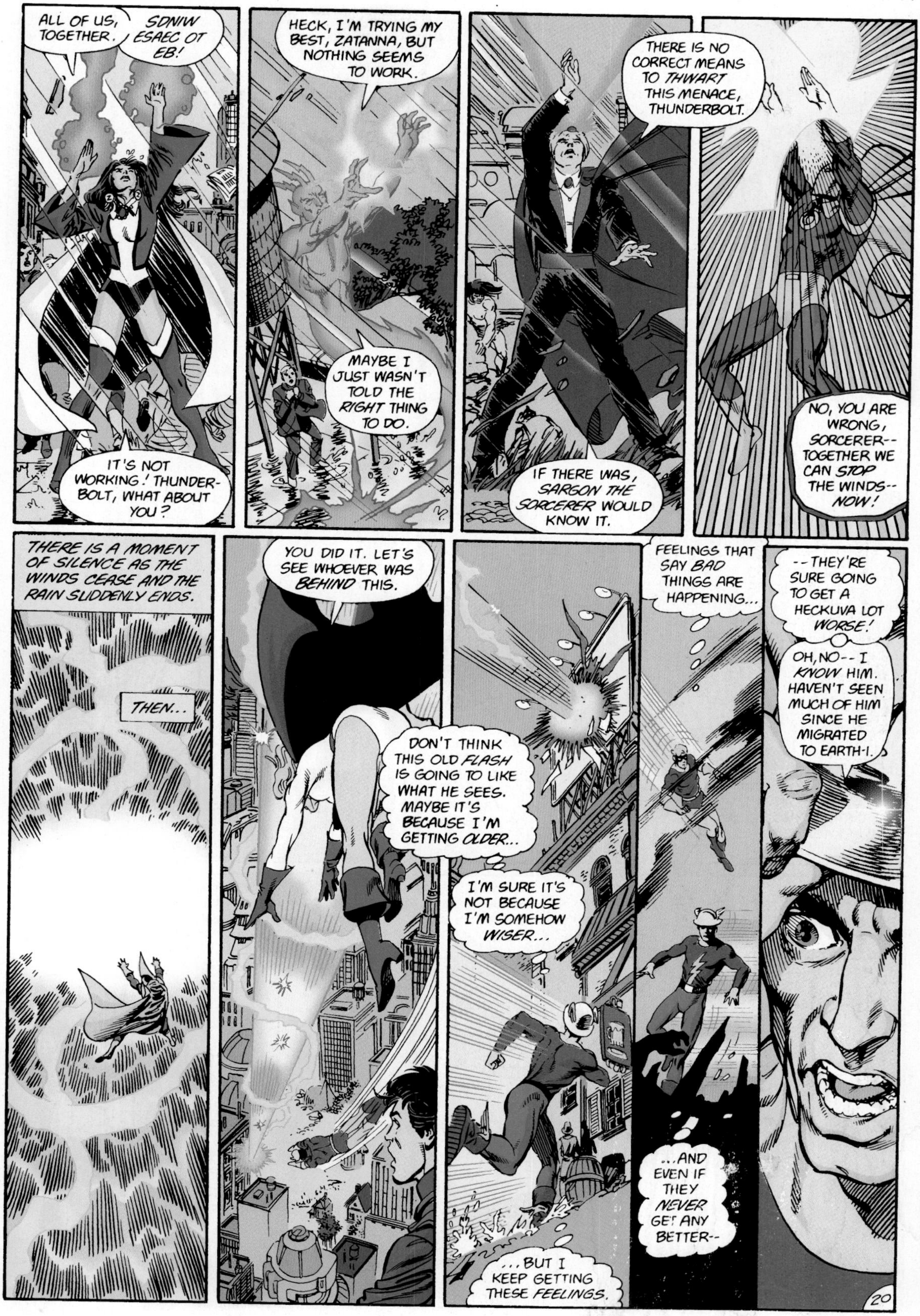
ALL OF US, TOGETHER.
SDNIW ESAEC OT EB!
IT'S NOT WORKING! THUNDER-BOLT, WHAT ABOUT YOU?
HECK, I'M TRYING MY BEST, ZATANNA, BUT NOTHING SEEMS TO WORK.
MAYBE I JUST WASN'T TOLD THE RIGHT THING TO DO.
THERE IS NO CORRECT MEANS TO THWART THIS MENACE, THUNDERBOLT.
IF THERE WAS, SARGON THE SORCERER WOULD KNOW IT.
NO, YOU ARE WRONG, SORCERER-- TOGETHER WE CAN STOP THE WINDS-- NOW!
THERE IS A MOMENT OF SILENCE AS THE WINDS CEASE AND THE RAIN SUDDENLY ENDS.
THEN...
YOU DID IT. LET'S SEE WHOEVER WAS BEHIND THIS.
DON'T THINK THIS OLD FLASH IS GOING TO LIKE WHAT HE SEES. MAYBE IT'S BECAUSE I'M GETTING OLDER...
I'M SURE IT'S NOT BECAUSE I'M SOMEHOW WISER...
...BUT I KEEP GETTING THESE FEELINGS.
FEELINGS THAT SAY BAD THINGS ARE HAPPENING...
...AND EVEN IF THEY NEVER GET ANY BETTER--
--THEY'RE SURE GOING TO GET A HECKUVA LOT WORSE!
OH, NO-- I KNOW HIM. HAVEN'T SEEN MUCH OF HIM SINCE HE MIGRATED TO EARTH-1.
20

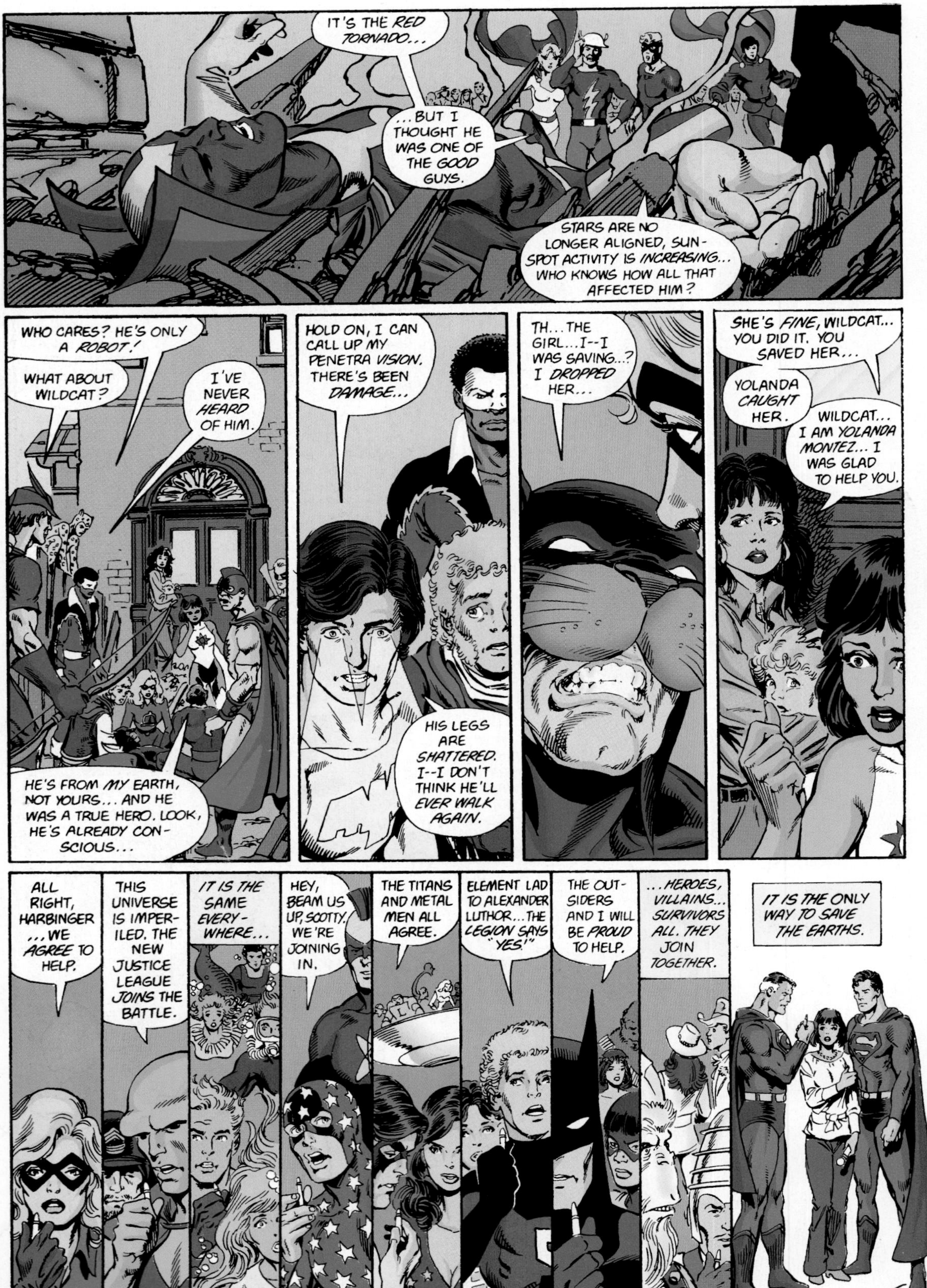
IT'S THE *RED TORNADO*...
...BUT I THOUGHT HE WAS ONE OF THE *GOOD* GUYS.
STARS ARE NO LONGER ALIGNED, SUN-SPOT ACTIVITY IS *INCREASING*... WHO KNOWS HOW ALL THAT AFFECTED HIM?
WHO CARES? HE'S ONLY A *ROBOT*!
WHAT ABOUT WILDCAT?
I'VE NEVER *HEARD* OF HIM.
HE'S FROM *MY EARTH*, NOT YOURS... AND HE WAS A TRUE HERO. LOOK, HE'S ALREADY CON-SCIOUS...
HOLD ON, I CAN CALL UP MY PENETRA *VISION*. THERE'S BEEN *DAMAGE*...
HIS LEGS ARE *SHATTERED*. I--I DON'T THINK HE'LL *EVER WALK AGAIN*.
TH... THE GIRL... I--I WAS SAVING...? I *DROPPED* HER...
SHE'S *FINE*, WILDCAT... YOU DID IT. YOU SAVED HER...
YOLANDA *CAUGHT* HER.
WILDCAT... I AM *YOLANDA MONTEZ*... I WAS GLAD TO HELP YOU.
ALL RIGHT, HARBINGER ...WE *AGREE* TO HELP.
THIS UNIVERSE IS IMPER-ILED. THE NEW JUSTICE LEAGUE *JOINS* THE BATTLE.
IT IS THE SAME EVERY-WHERE...
HEY, BEAM US UP, SCOTTY. WE'RE JOINING IN.
THE TITANS AND METAL MEN ALL AGREE.
ELEMENT LAD TO ALEXANDER LUTHOR... THE *LEGION* SAYS *"YES!"*
THE OUT-SIDERS AND I WILL BE *PROUD* TO HELP.
...HEROES, VILLAINS... SURVIVORS ALL. THEY JOIN TOGETHER.
IT IS THE ONLY WAY TO SAVE THE EARTHS.
21

PLEASE...UNDERSTAND. I PURPOSELY *DIDN'T* BRING ALL OF YOU UP HERE... YOU'RE NEEDED FOR *ANOTHER MISSION.*

ONE THE MONITOR HIMSELF WAS SETTING UP *AFTER* YOU SAVED EARTHS I AND Z.

THE ANTI-MATTER CLOUD IS MOVING THROUGH THE FINAL *THREE* UNIVERSES... AND THERE, AS BEFORE-- THE *CRUX POINT* IS THE *INFINITE EARTHS!*

I'VE BROUGHT YOU HERE TO HELP *SAVE* THE FIRST OF THOSE UNIVERSES.

BUT OUR *OWN* WORLDS ARE STILL IN DANGER... YOU SAID SO YOURSELF.

I *KNOW* THAT, STARFIRE, BUT YOU MUST UNDERSTAND...

ONLY BY SAVING ALL FIVE UNIVERSES WILL WE HAVE ENOUGH POWER TO *RESIST* HIM.

< I DON'T LIKE THIS, LUTHOR. I DON'T WANT TO BE INVOLVED. >

< UNDERSTAND THIS, DR. LIGHT-- IF YOU FAIL TO HELP US... YOUR EARTH... ALL EARTHS-- WILL BE DESTROYED. >

"AS ANTIMATTER DESTROYS EACH UNIVERSE, OUR ENEMY'S UNIVERSE GROWS MORE POWERFUL.

ALEXANDER LUTHOR--WAIT!

WHAT IS IT, PARIAH?

S-SOMETHING'S HAPPENING TO THE MONITOR'S SATELLITE.

NOW, LET ME SEND YOU THROUGH THE VORTEX BETWEEN ALL--

I SENSE... DISASTER!

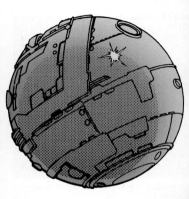

22

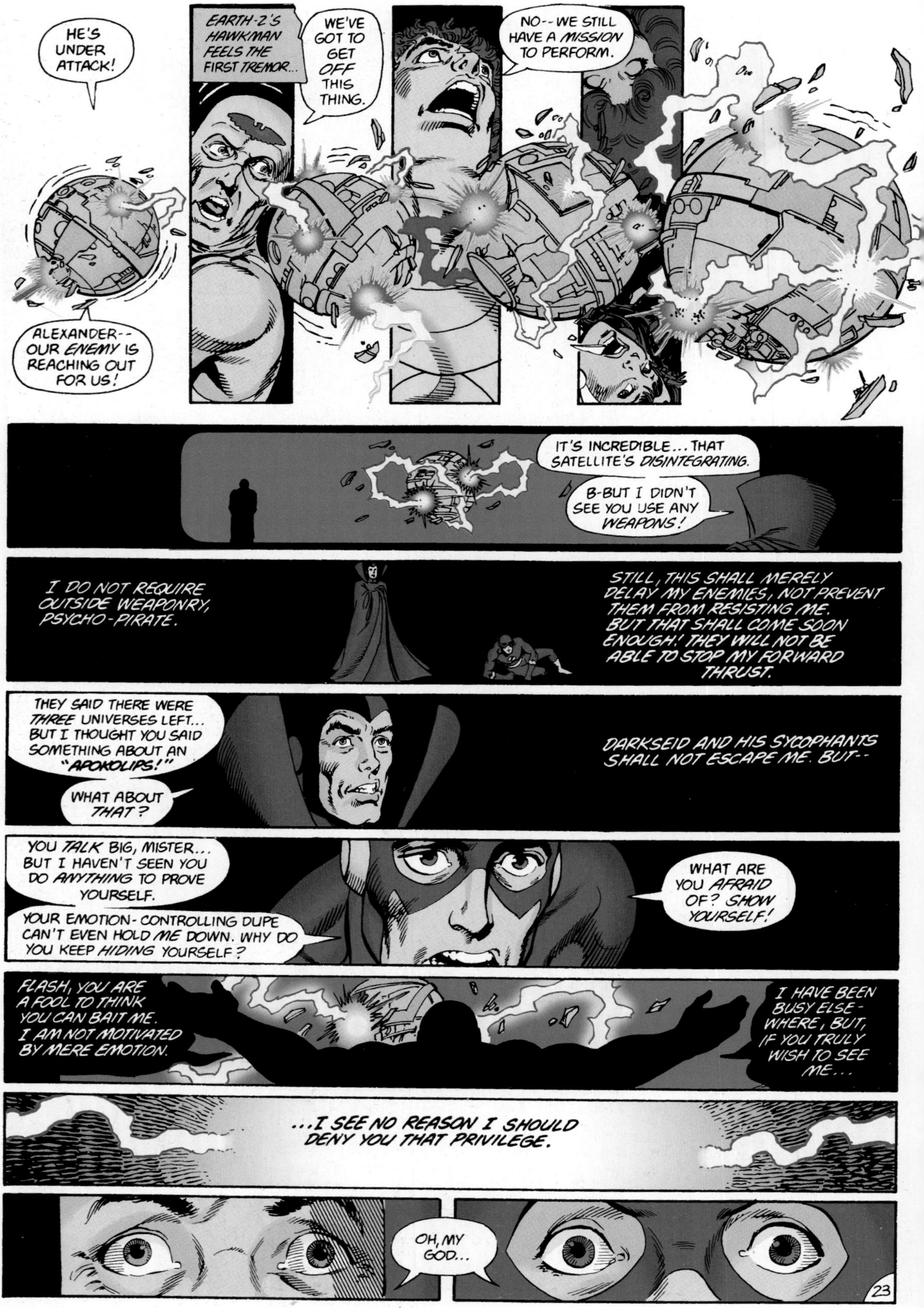
HE'S UNDER ATTACK!
ALEXANDER-- OUR ENEMY IS REACHING OUT FOR US!
EARTH-2'S HAWKMAN FEELS THE FIRST TREMOR...
WE'VE GOT TO GET OFF THIS THING.
NO--WE STILL HAVE A MISSION TO PERFORM.
IT'S INCREDIBLE... THAT SATELLITE'S DISINTEGRATING.
B-BUT I DIDN'T SEE YOU USE ANY WEAPONS!
I DO NOT REQUIRE OUTSIDE WEAPONRY, PSYCHO-PIRATE.
STILL, THIS SHALL MERELY DELAY MY ENEMIES, NOT PREVENT THEM FROM RESISTING ME. BUT THAT SHALL COME SOON ENOUGH! THEY WILL NOT BE ABLE TO STOP MY FORWARD THRUST.
THEY SAID THERE WERE THREE UNIVERSES LEFT... BUT I THOUGHT YOU SAID SOMETHING ABOUT AN "APOKOLIPS!"
WHAT ABOUT THAT?
DARKSEID AND HIS SYCOPHANTS SHALL NOT ESCAPE ME. BUT--
YOU TALK BIG, MISTER... BUT I HAVEN'T SEEN YOU DO ANYTHING TO PROVE YOURSELF.
YOUR EMOTION-CONTROLLING DUPE CAN'T EVEN HOLD ME DOWN. WHY DO YOU KEEP HIDING YOURSELF?
WHAT ARE YOU AFRAID OF? SHOW YOURSELF!
FLASH, YOU ARE A FOOL TO THINK YOU CAN BAIT ME. I AM NOT MOTIVATED BY MERE EMOTION.
I HAVE BEEN BUSY ELSE-WHERE, BUT, IF YOU TRULY WISH TO SEE ME...
...I SEE NO REASON I SHOULD DENY YOU THAT PRIVILEGE.
OH, MY GOD...
23

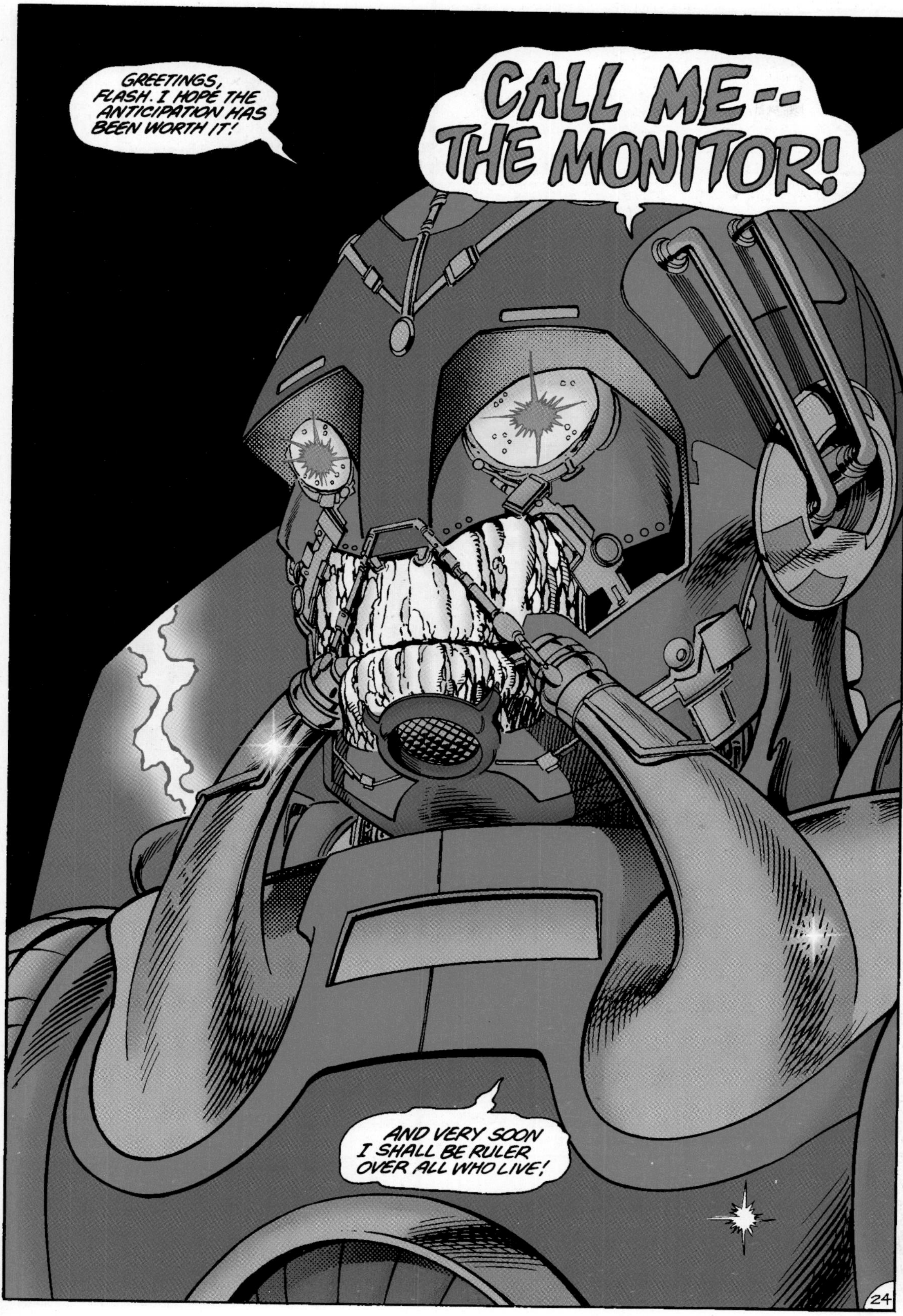
GREETINGS, FLASH. I HOPE THE ANTICIPATION HAS BEEN WORTH IT!
CALL ME-- THE MONITOR!
AND VERY SOON I SHALL BE RULER OVER ALL WHO LIVE!
24

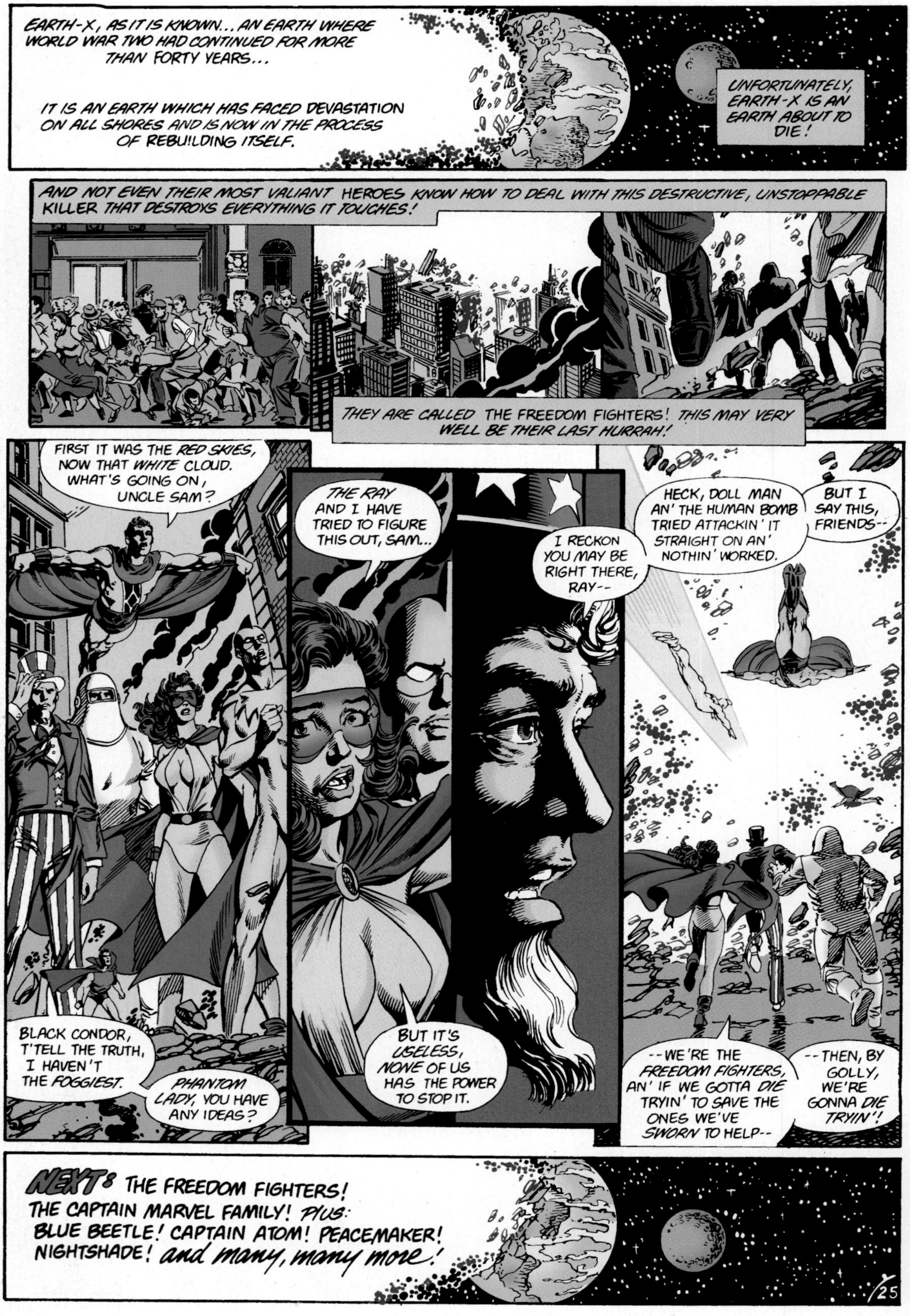
EARTH-X, AS IT IS KNOWN... AN EARTH WHERE WORLD WAR TWO HAD CONTINUED FOR MORE THAN FORTY YEARS...
IT IS AN EARTH WHICH HAS FACED DEVASTATION ON ALL SHORES AND IS NOW IN THE PROCESS OF REBUILDING ITSELF.
UNFORTUNATELY, EARTH-X IS AN EARTH ABOUT TO DIE!
AND NOT EVEN THEIR MOST VALIANT HEROES KNOW HOW TO DEAL WITH THIS DESTRUCTIVE, UNSTOPPABLE KILLER THAT DESTROYS EVERYTHING IT TOUCHES!
THEY ARE CALLED THE FREEDOM FIGHTERS! THIS MAY VERY WELL BE THEIR LAST HURRAH!
FIRST IT WAS THE RED SKIES, NOW THAT WHITE CLOUD. WHAT'S GOING ON, UNCLE SAM?
BLACK CONDOR, T'TELL THE TRUTH, I HAVEN'T THE FOGGIEST.
PHANTOM LADY, YOU HAVE ANY IDEAS?
THE RAY AND I HAVE TRIED TO FIGURE THIS OUT, SAM...
BUT IT'S USELESS, NONE OF US HAS THE POWER TO STOP IT.
I RECKON YOU MAY BE RIGHT THERE, RAY--
HECK, DOLL MAN AN' THE HUMAN BOMB TRIED ATTACKIN' IT STRAIGHT ON AN' NOTHIN' WORKED.
BUT I SAY THIS, FRIENDS--
--WE'RE THE FREEDOM FIGHTERS, AN' IF WE GOTTA DIE TRYIN' TO SAVE THE ONES WE'VE SWORN TO HELP--
--THEN, BY GOLLY, WE'RE GONNA DIE TRYIN'!
NEXT: THE FREEDOM FIGHTERS! THE CAPTAIN MARVEL FAMILY! PLUS: BLUE BEETLE! CAPTAIN ATOM! PEACEMAKER! NIGHTSHADE! and many, many more!
25

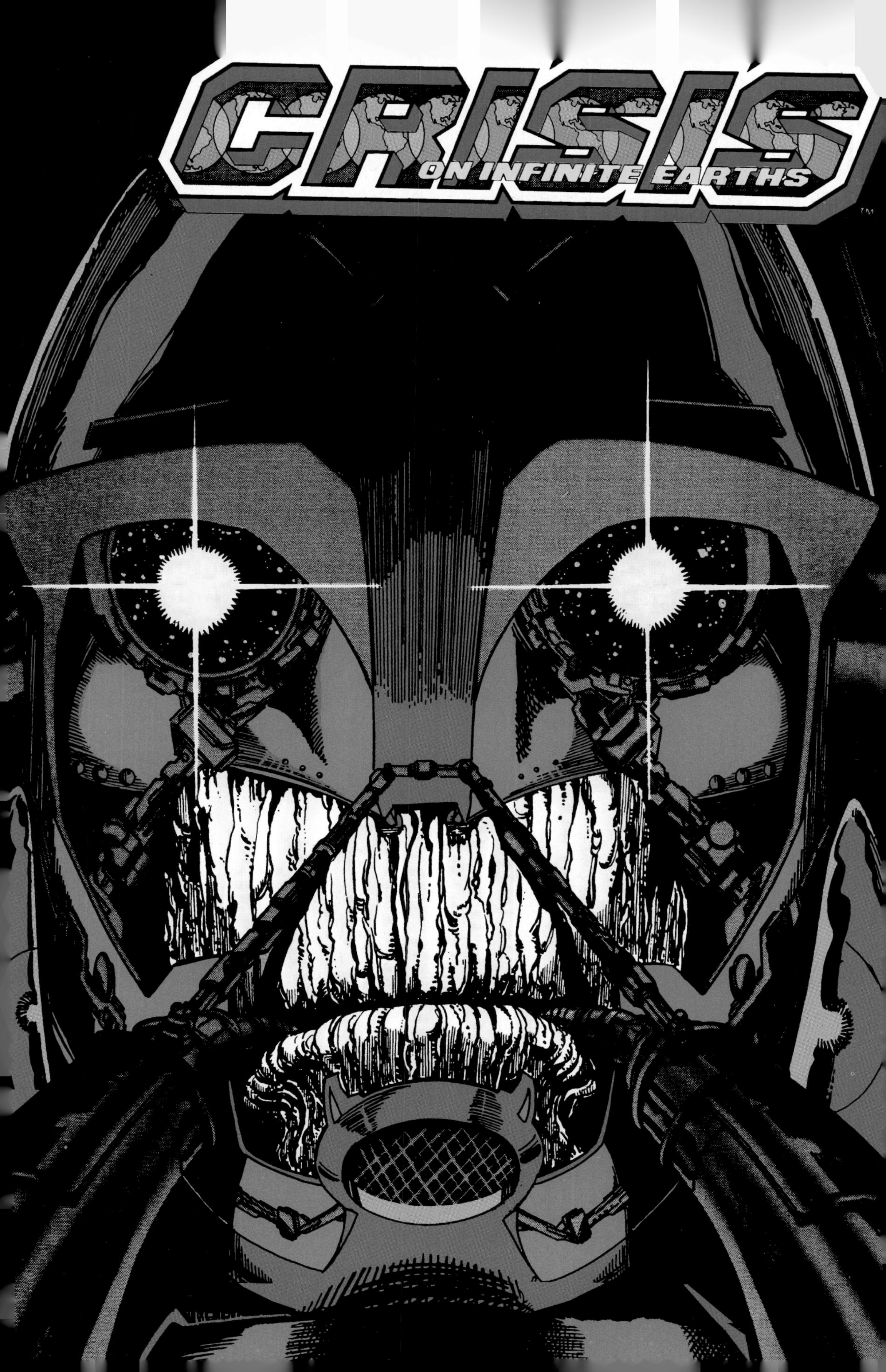
CRISIS
ON INFINITE EARTHS
TM

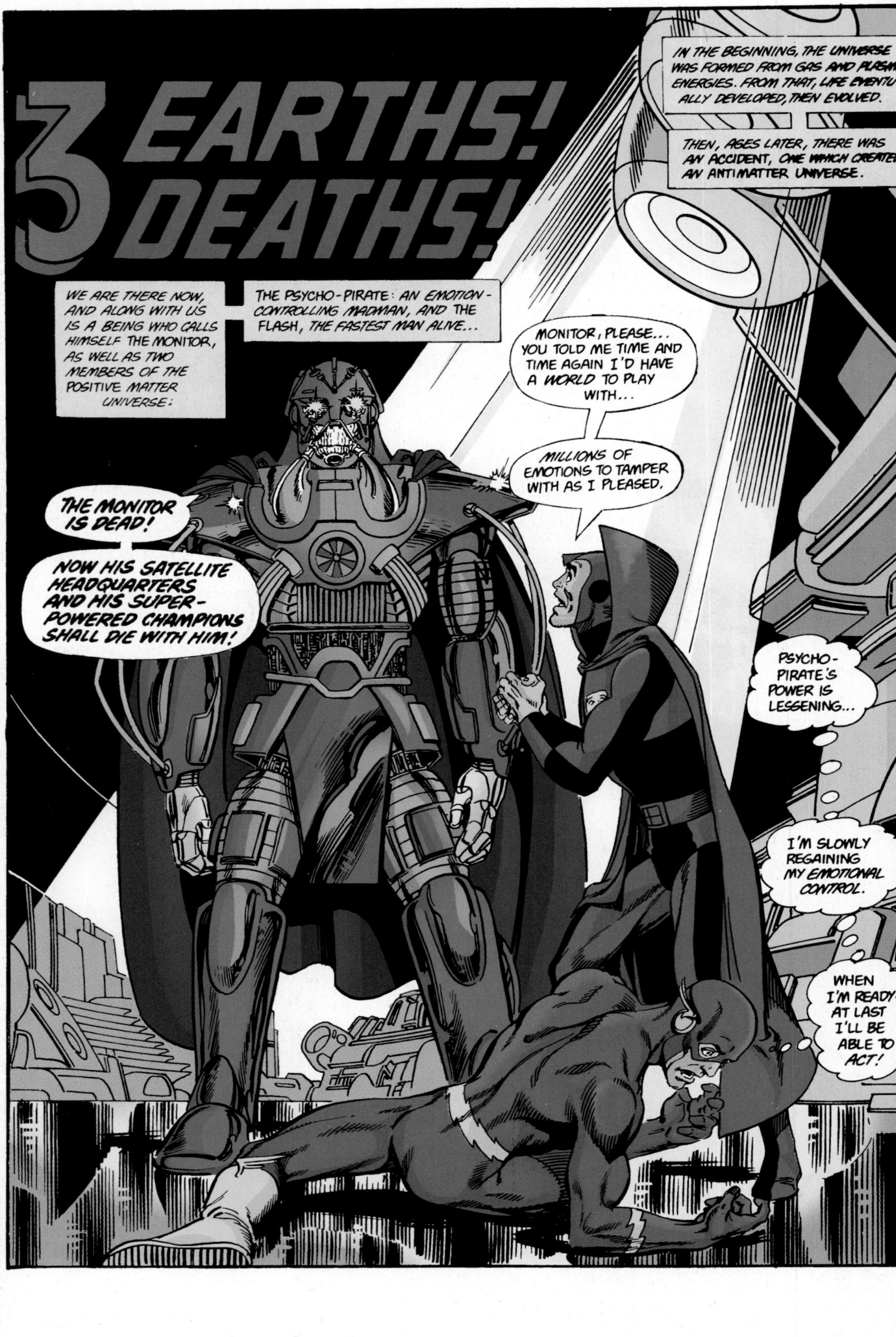
3 EARTHS! DEATHS!
IN THE BEGINNING, THE UNIVERSE WAS FORMED FROM GAS AND PLASMIC ENERGIES. FROM THAT, LIFE EVENTUALLY DEVELOPED, THEN EVOLVED.
THEN, AGES LATER, THERE WAS AN ACCIDENT, ONE WHICH CREATED AN ANTIMATTER UNIVERSE.
WE ARE THERE NOW, AND ALONG WITH US IS A BEING WHO CALLS HIMSELF THE MONITOR, AS WELL AS TWO MEMBERS OF THE POSITIVE MATTER UNIVERSE:
THE PSYCHO-PIRATE: AN EMOTION-CONTROLLING MADMAN, AND THE FLASH, THE FASTEST MAN ALIVE...
MONITOR, PLEASE... YOU TOLD ME TIME AND TIME AGAIN I'D HAVE A WORLD TO PLAY WITH...
MILLIONS OF EMOTIONS TO TAMPER WITH AS I PLEASED.
THE MONITOR IS DEAD!
NOW HIS SATELLITE HEADQUARTERS AND HIS SUPER-POWERED CHAMPIONS SHALL DIE WITH HIM!
PSYCHO-PIRATE'S POWER IS LESSENING...
I'M SLOWLY REGAINING MY EMOTIONAL CONTROL.
WHEN I'M READY-- AT LAST I'LL BE ABLE TO ACT!
G-2006

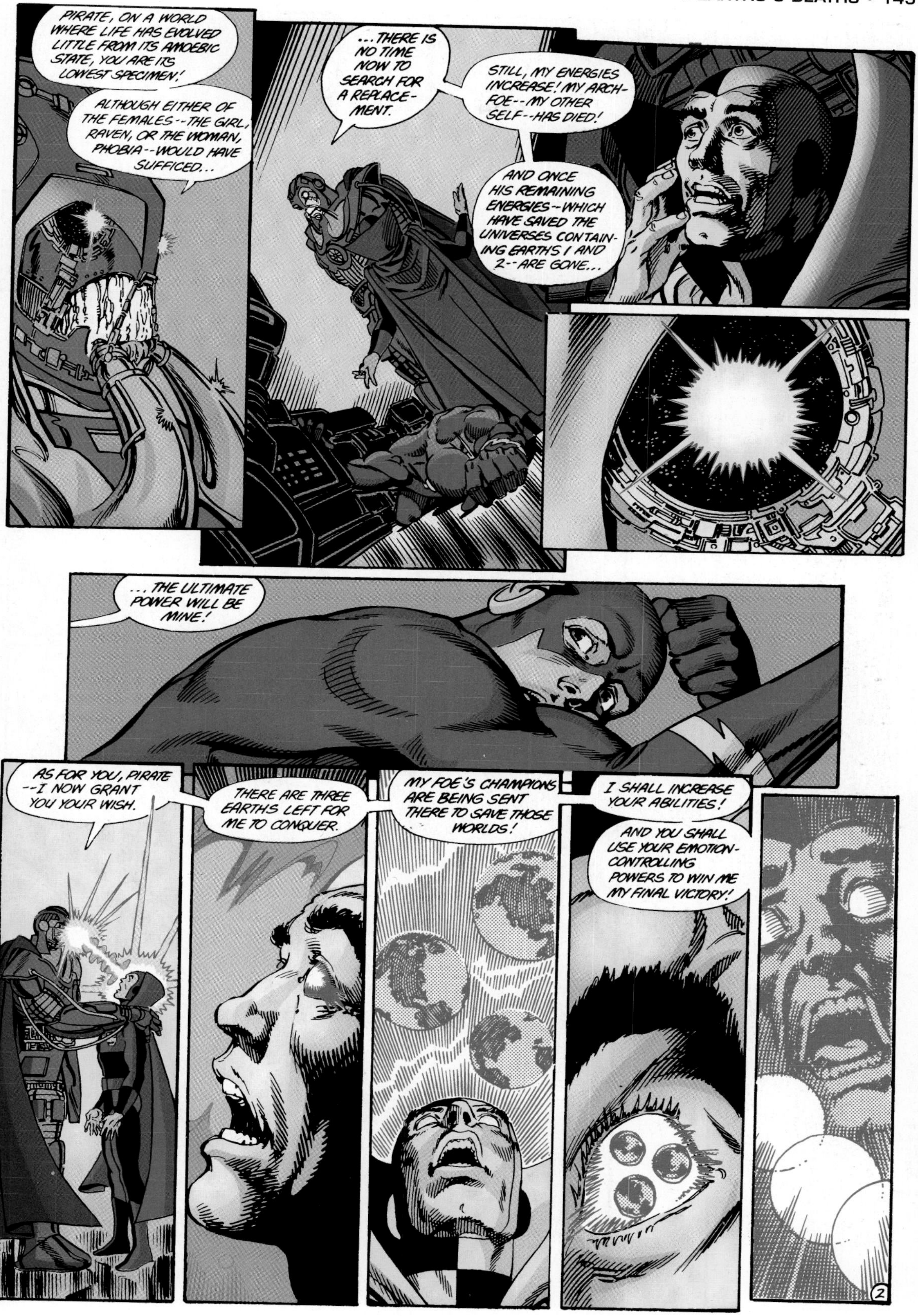
PIRATE, ON A WORLD WHERE LIFE HAS EVOLVED LITTLE FROM ITS AMOEBIC STATE, YOU ARE ITS LOWEST SPECIMEN!
ALTHOUGH EITHER OF THE FEMALES--THE GIRL, RAVEN, OR THE WOMAN, PHOBIA--WOULD HAVE SUFFICED...
...THERE IS NO TIME NOW TO SEARCH FOR A REPLACE-MENT.
STILL, MY ENERGIES INCREASE! MY ARCH-FOE--MY OTHER SELF--HAS DIED!
AND ONCE HIS REMAINING ENERGIES--WHICH HAVE SAVED THE UNIVERSES CONTAIN-ING EARTH'S 1 AND 2--ARE GONE...
...THE ULTIMATE POWER WILL BE MINE!
AS FOR YOU, PIRATE --I NOW GRANT YOU YOUR WISH.
THERE ARE THREE EARTHS LEFT FOR ME TO CONQUER.
MY FOE'S CHAMPIONS ARE BEING SENT THERE TO SAVE THOSE WORLDS!
I SHALL INCREASE YOUR ABILITIES!
AND YOU SHALL USE YOUR EMOTION-CONTROLLING POWERS TO WIN ME MY FINAL VICTORY!
2

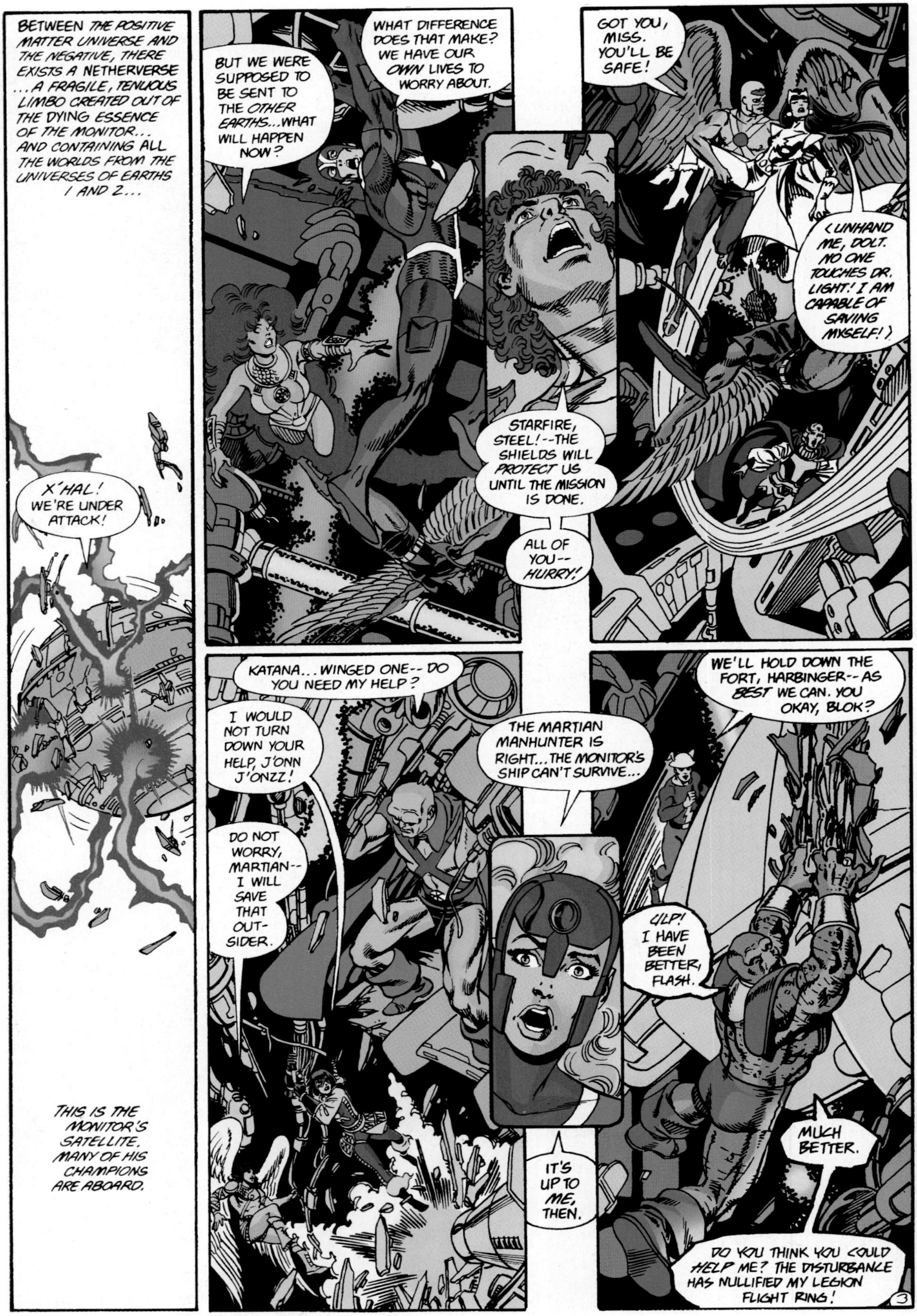
BETWEEN THE POSITIVE MATTER UNIVERSE AND THE NEGATIVE, THERE EXISTS A NETHERVERSE ...A FRAGILE, TENUOUS LIMBO CREATED OUT OF THE DYING ESSENCE OF THE MONITOR... AND CONTAINING ALL THE WORLDS FROM THE UNIVERSES OF EARTHS 1 AND 2...
X'HAL! WE'RE UNDER ATTACK!
THIS IS THE MONITOR'S SATELLITE. MANY OF HIS CHAMPIONS ARE ABOARD.
BUT WE WERE SUPPOSED TO BE SENT TO THE OTHER EARTHS...WHAT WILL HAPPEN NOW?
WHAT DIFFERENCE DOES THAT MAKE? WE HAVE OUR OWN LIVES TO WORRY ABOUT.
STARFIRE, STEEL!--THE SHIELDS WILL PROTECT US UNTIL THE MISSION IS DONE.
ALL OF YOU--HURRY!
GOT YOU, MISS. YOU'LL BE SAFE!
(UNHAND ME, DOLT. NO ONE TOUCHES DR. LIGHT! I AM CAPABLE OF SAVING MYSELF!)
KATANA...WINGED ONE--DO YOU NEED MY HELP?
I WOULD NOT TURN DOWN YOUR HELP, J'ONN J'ONZZ!
DO NOT WORRY, MARTIAN--I WILL SAVE THAT OUT-SIDER.
THE MARTIAN MANHUNTER IS RIGHT...THE MONITOR'S SHIP CAN'T SURVIVE...
IT'S UP TO ME, THEN.
WE'LL HOLD DOWN THE FORT, HARBINGER--AS BEST WE CAN. YOU OKAY, BLOK?
ULP! I HAVE BEEN BETTER, FLASH.
MUCH BETTER.
DO YOU THINK YOU COULD HELP ME? THE DISTURBANCE HAS NULLIFIED MY LEGION FLIGHT RING!
3

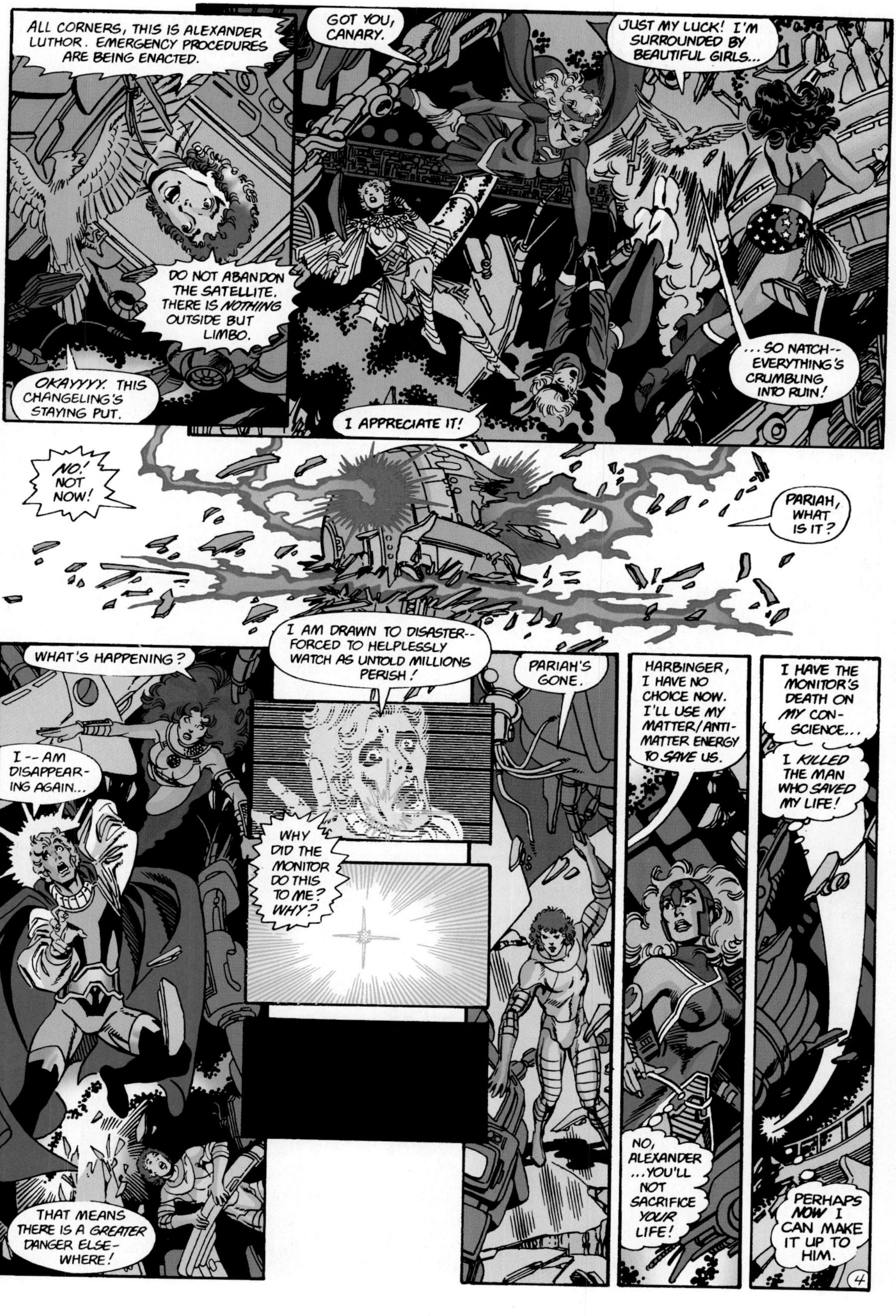
ALL CORNERS, THIS IS ALEXANDER LUTHOR. EMERGENCY PROCEDURES ARE BEING ENACTED.
DO NOT ABANDON THE SATELLITE. THERE IS NOTHING OUTSIDE BUT LIMBO.
OKAYYYY. THIS CHANGELING'S STAYING PUT.
GOT YOU, CANARY.
I APPRECIATE IT!
JUST MY LUCK! I'M SURROUNDED BY BEAUTIFUL GIRLS...
...SO NATCH--EVERYTHING'S CRUMBLING INTO RUIN!
NO! NOT NOW!
PARIAH, WHAT IS IT?
WHAT'S HAPPENING?
I--AM DISAPPEARING AGAIN...
THAT MEANS THERE IS A GREATER DANGER ELSEWHERE!
I AM DRAWN TO DISASTER--FORCED TO HELPLESSLY WATCH AS UNTOLD MILLIONS PERISH!
WHY DID THE MONITOR DO THIS TO ME? WHY?
PARIAH'S GONE.
HARBINGER, I HAVE NO CHOICE NOW. I'LL USE MY MATTER/ANTI-MATTER ENERGY TO SAVE US.
NO, ALEXANDER ...YOU'LL NOT SACRIFICE YOUR LIFE!
I HAVE THE MONITOR'S DEATH ON MY CONSCIENCE...
I KILLED THE MAN WHO SAVED MY LIFE!
PERHAPS NOW I CAN MAKE IT UP TO HIM.
4

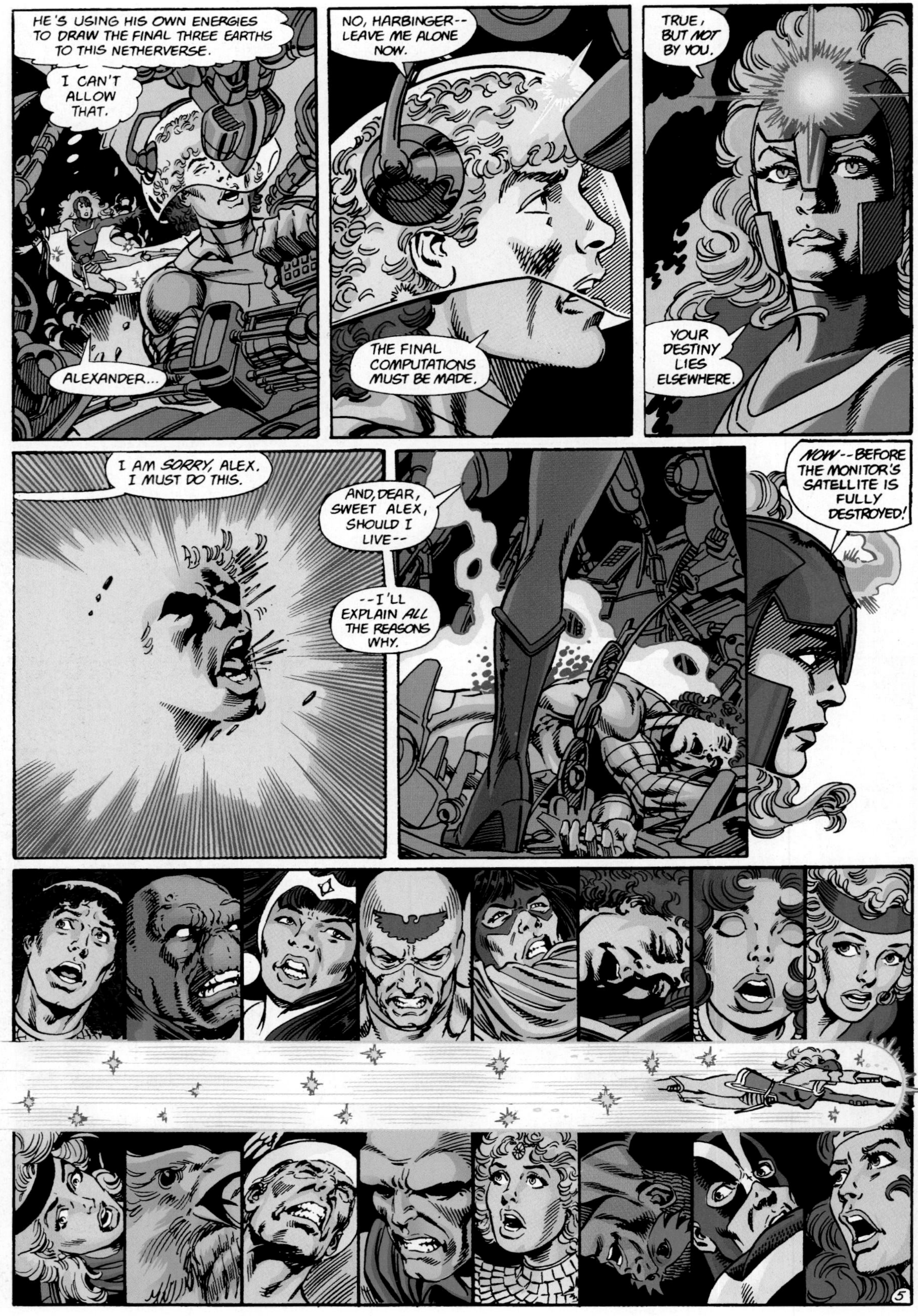
HE'S USING HIS OWN ENERGIES TO DRAW THE FINAL THREE EARTHS TO THIS NETHERVERSE.
I CAN'T ALLOW THAT.
ALEXANDER...
NO, HARBINGER-- LEAVE ME ALONE NOW.
THE FINAL COMPUTATIONS MUST BE MADE.
TRUE, BUT NOT BY YOU.
YOUR DESTINY LIES ELSEWHERE.
I AM SORRY, ALEX. I MUST DO THIS.
AND, DEAR, SWEET ALEX, SHOULD I LIVE--
--I'LL EXPLAIN ALL THE REASONS WHY.
NOW--BEFORE THE MONITOR'S SATELLITE IS FULLY DESTROYED!
5

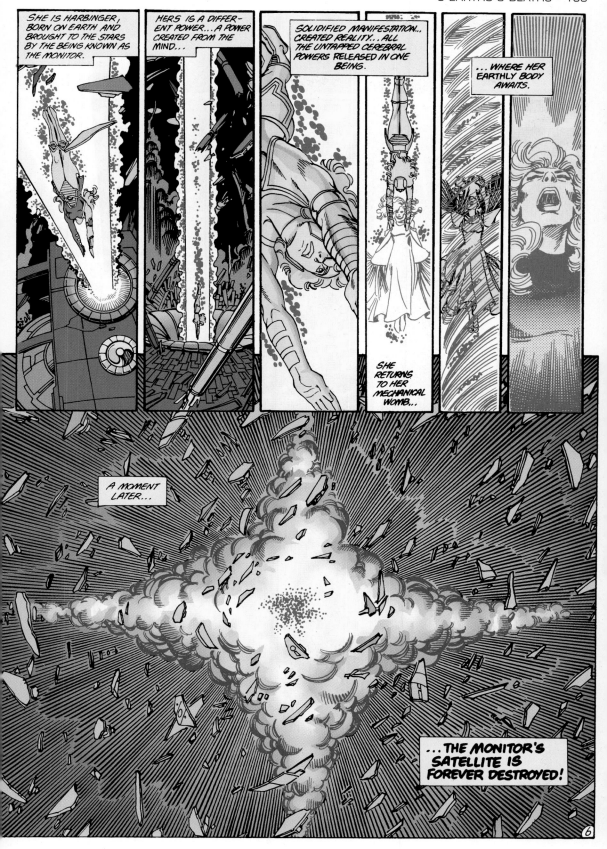

SHE IS HARBINGER, BORN ON EARTH AND BROUGHT TO THE STARS BY THE BEING KNOWN AS THE MONITOR.

HERS IS A DIFFER-ENT POWER... A POWER CREATED FROM THE MIND...

SOLIDIFIED MANIFESTATION... CREATED REALITY... ALL THE UNTAPPED CEREBRAL POWERS RELEASED IN ONE BEING.

...WHERE HER EARTHLY BODY AWAITS.

SHE RETURNS TO HER MECHANICAL WOMB...

A MOMENT LATER...

...THE MONITOR'S SATELLITE IS FOREVER DESTROYED!

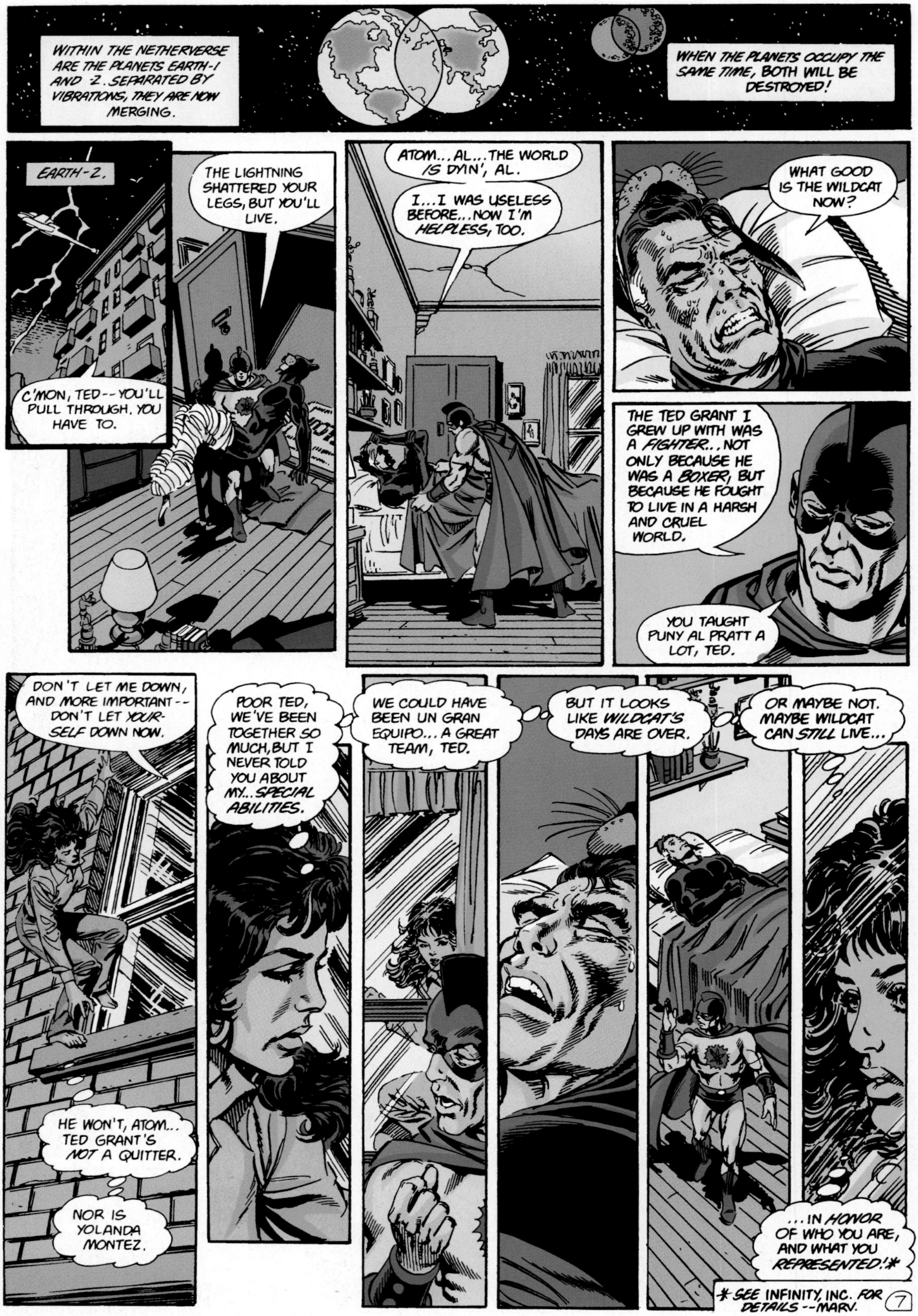
WITHIN THE NETHERVERSE ARE THE PLANETS EARTH-1 AND -2. SEPARATED BY VIBRATIONS, THEY ARE NOW MERGING.
WHEN THE PLANETS OCCUPY THE SAME TIME, BOTH WILL BE DESTROYED!
EARTH-2.
THE LIGHTNING SHATTERED YOUR LEGS, BUT YOU'LL LIVE.
C'MON, TED--YOU'LL PULL THROUGH. YOU HAVE TO.
ATOM... AL... THE WORLD IS DYIN', AL.
I...I WAS USELESS BEFORE...NOW I'M HELPLESS, TOO.
WHAT GOOD IS THE WILDCAT NOW?
THE TED GRANT I GREW UP WITH WAS A FIGHTER.. NOT ONLY BECAUSE HE WAS A BOXER, BUT BECAUSE HE FOUGHT TO LIVE IN A HARSH AND CRUEL WORLD.
YOU TAUGHT PUNY AL PRATT A LOT, TED.
DON'T LET ME DOWN, AND MORE IMPORTANT-- DON'T LET YOURSELF DOWN NOW.
HE WON'T, ATOM.. TED GRANT'S NOT A QUITTER.
NOR IS YOLANDA MONTEZ.
POOR TED, WE'VE BEEN TOGETHER SO MUCH, BUT I NEVER TOLD YOU ABOUT MY...SPECIAL ABILITIES.
WE COULD HAVE BEEN UN GRAN EQUIPO... A GREAT TEAM, TED.
BUT IT LOOKS LIKE WILDCAT'S DAYS ARE OVER.
OR MAYBE NOT. MAYBE WILDCAT CAN STILL LIVE...
...IN HONOR OF WHO YOU ARE, AND WHAT YOU REPRESENTED!*
*SEE INFINITY, INC. FOR DETAILS--MARV.
7

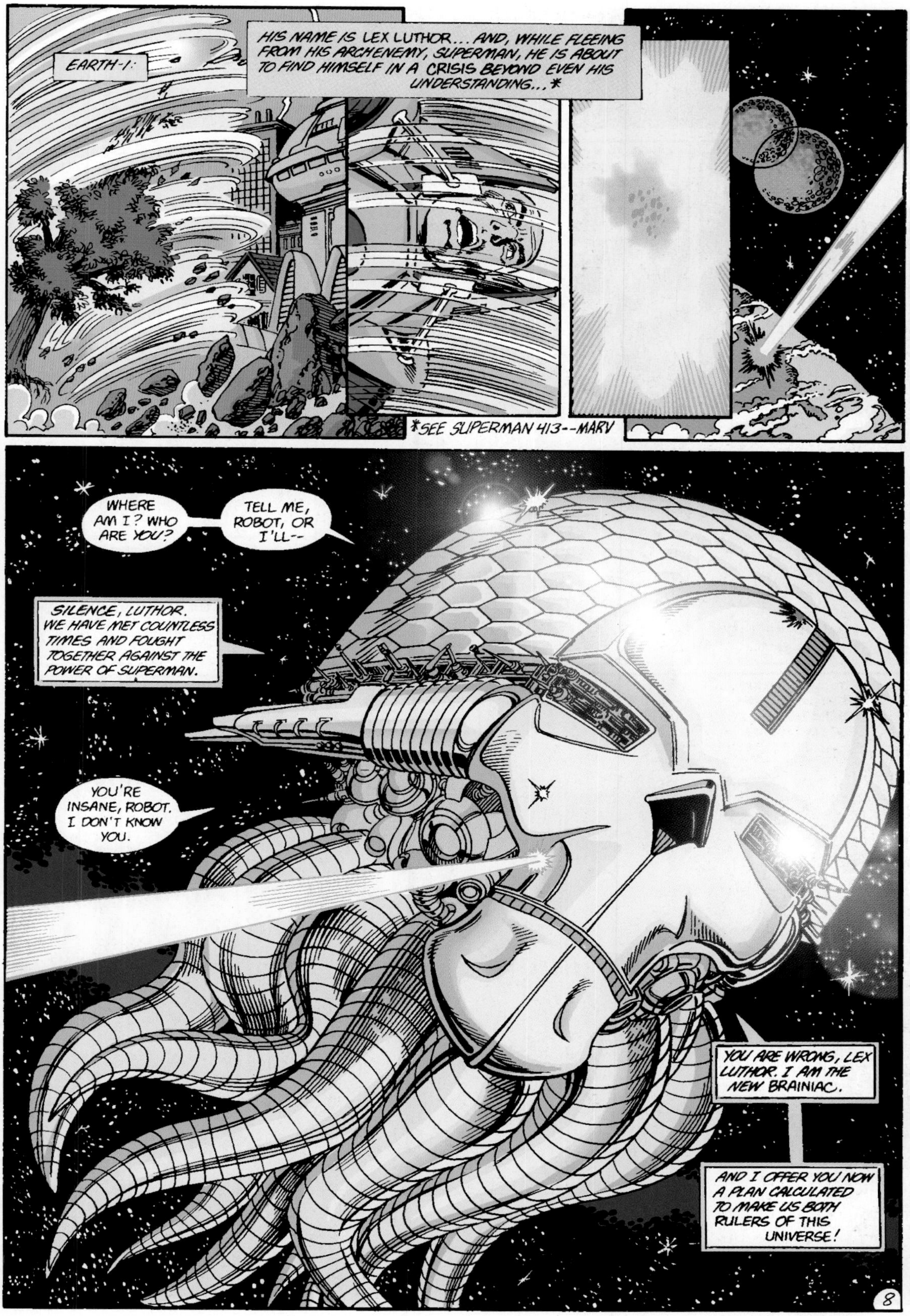
EARTH-1:
HIS NAME IS LEX LUTHOR... AND, WHILE FLEEING FROM HIS ARCHENEMY, SUPERMAN, HE IS ABOUT TO FIND HIMSELF IN A CRISIS BEYOND EVEN HIS UNDERSTANDING...*
*SEE SUPERMAN 413--MARV
WHERE AM I? WHO ARE YOU?
TELL ME, ROBOT, OR I'LL--
SILENCE, LUTHOR. WE HAVE MET COUNTLESS TIMES AND FOUGHT TOGETHER AGAINST THE POWER OF SUPERMAN.
YOU'RE INSANE, ROBOT. I DON'T KNOW YOU.
YOU ARE WRONG, LEX LUTHOR. I AM THE NEW BRAINIAC.
AND I OFFER YOU NOW A PLAN CALCULATED TO MAKE US BOTH RULERS OF THIS UNIVERSE!
8

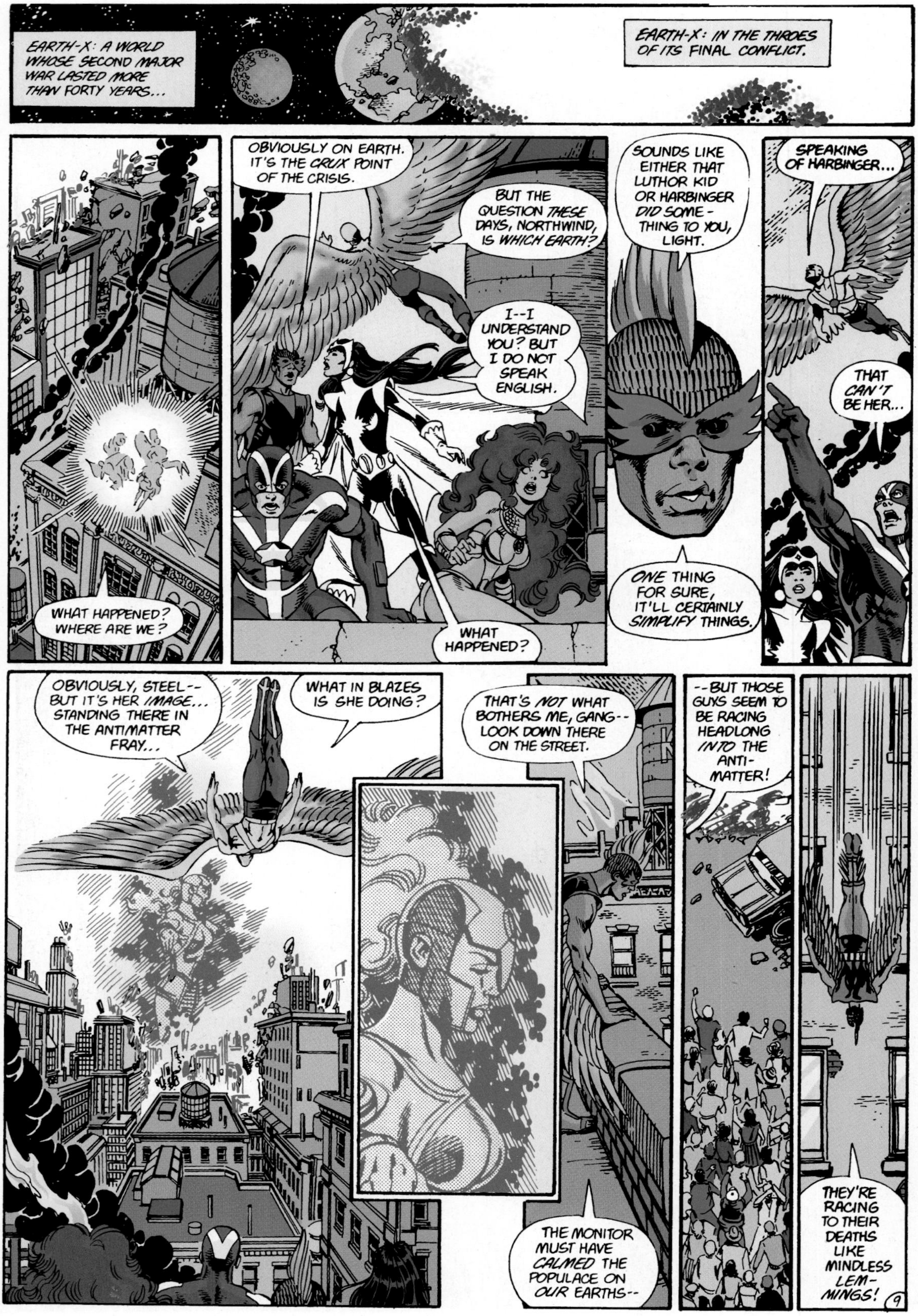
EARTH-X: A WORLD WHOSE SECOND MAJOR WAR LASTED MORE THAN FORTY YEARS...
EARTH-X: IN THE THROES OF ITS FINAL CONFLICT.
WHAT HAPPENED? WHERE ARE WE?
OBVIOUSLY ON EARTH. IT'S THE CRUX POINT OF THE CRISIS.
BUT THE QUESTION THESE DAYS, NORTHWIND, IS WHICH EARTH?
I--I UNDERSTAND YOU? BUT I DO NOT SPEAK ENGLISH.
WHAT HAPPENED?
SOUNDS LIKE EITHER THAT LUTHOR KID OR HARBINGER DID SOME-THING TO YOU, LIGHT.
ONE THING FOR SURE, IT'LL CERTAINLY SIMPLIFY THINGS.
SPEAKING OF HARBINGER...
THAT CAN'T BE HER...
OBVIOUSLY, STEEL--BUT IT'S HER IMAGE... STANDING THERE IN THE ANTI-MATTER FRAY...
WHAT IN BLAZES IS SHE DOING?
THAT'S NOT WHAT BOTHERS ME, GANG--LOOK DOWN THERE ON THE STREET.
THE MONITOR MUST HAVE CALMED THE POPULACE ON OUR EARTHS--
--BUT THOSE GUYS SEEM TO BE RACING HEADLONG INTO THE ANTI-MATTER!
THEY'RE RACING TO THEIR DEATHS LIKE MINDLESS LEM-MINGS!
9

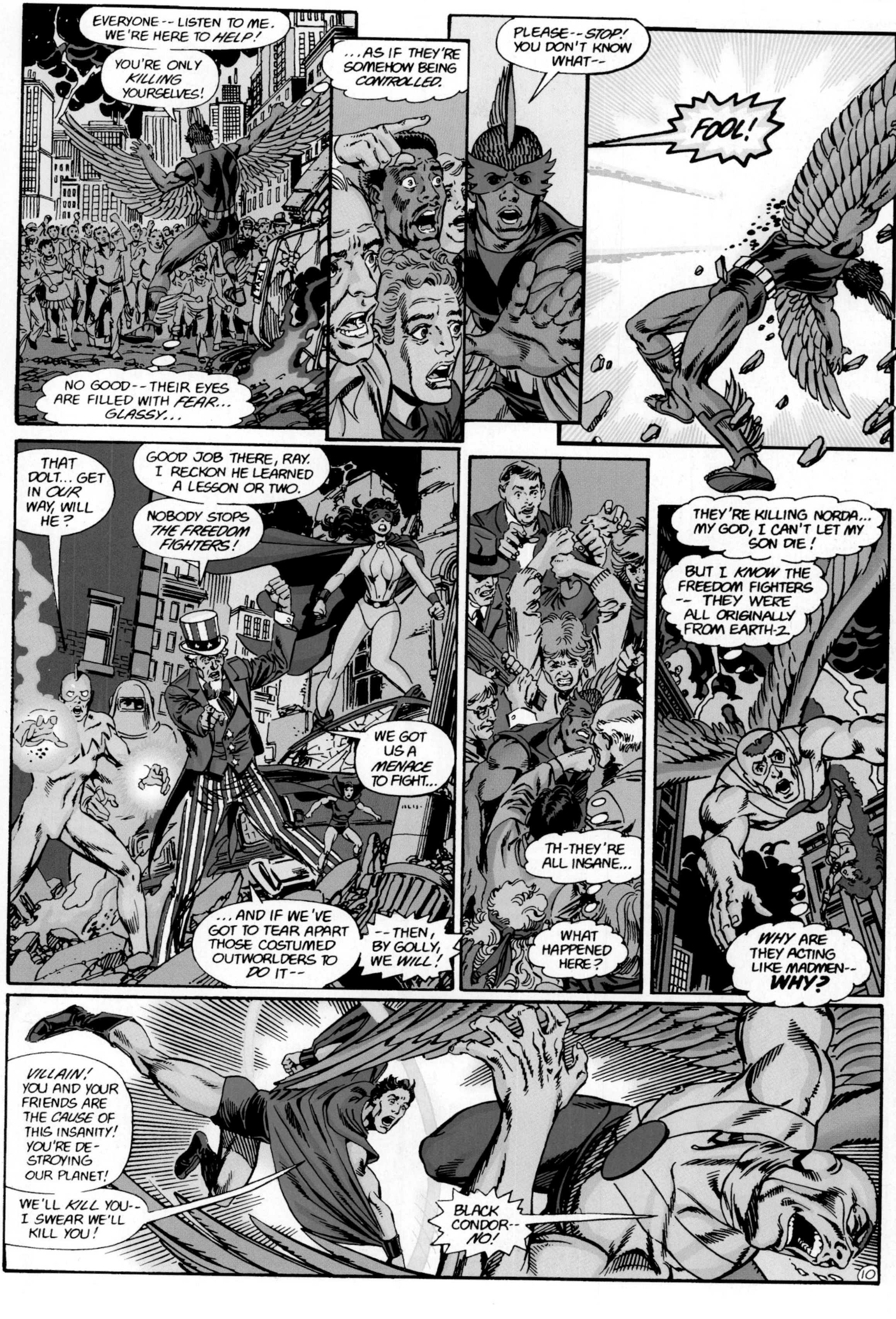
EVERYONE -- LISTEN TO ME. WE'RE HERE TO HELP!
YOU'RE ONLY KILLING YOURSELVES!
NO GOOD -- THEIR EYES ARE FILLED WITH FEAR... GLASSY...
...AS IF THEY'RE SOMEHOW BEING CONTROLLED.
PLEASE -- STOP! YOU DON'T KNOW WHAT--
FOOL!
THAT DOLT... GET IN OUR WAY, WILL HE?
GOOD JOB THERE, RAY. I RECKON HE LEARNED A LESSON OR TWO.
NOBODY STOPS THE FREEDOM FIGHTERS!
WE GOT US A MENACE TO FIGHT...
...AND IF WE'VE GOT TO TEAR APART THOSE COSTUMED OUTWORLDERS TO DO IT--
--THEN, BY GOLLY, WE WILL!
TH-THEY'RE ALL INSANE...
WHAT HAPPENED HERE?
THEY'RE KILLING NORDA... MY GOD, I CAN'T LET MY SON DIE!
BUT I KNOW THE FREEDOM FIGHTERS -- THEY WERE ALL ORIGINALLY FROM EARTH-2
WHY ARE THEY ACTING LIKE MADMEN-- WHY?
VILLAIN! YOU AND YOUR FRIENDS ARE THE CAUSE OF THIS INSANITY! YOU'RE DE-STROYING OUR PLANET!
WE'LL KILL YOU-- I SWEAR WE'LL KILL YOU!
BLACK CONDOR-- NO!
10

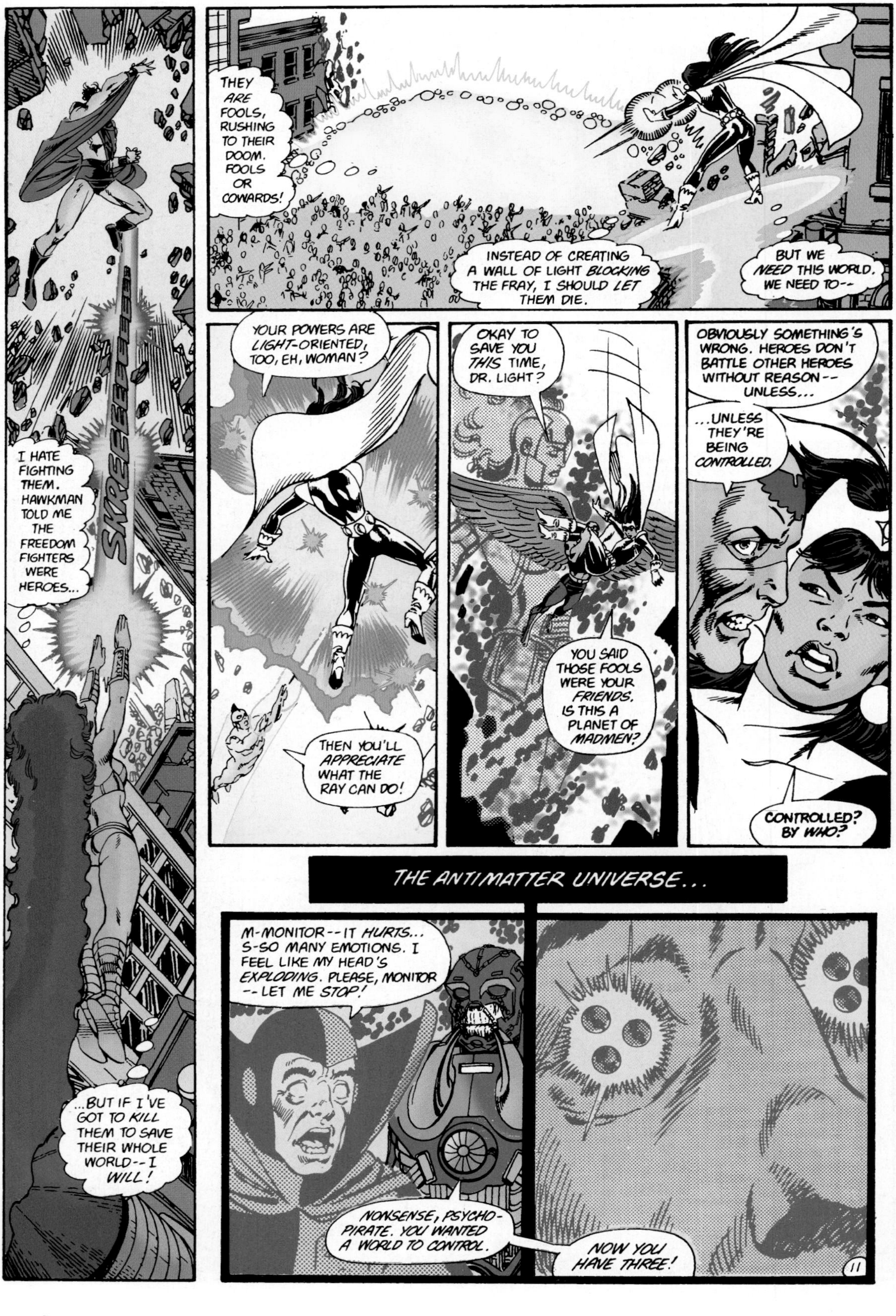
THEY ARE FOOLS, RUSHING TO THEIR DOOM. FOOLS OR COWARDS!
INSTEAD OF CREATING A WALL OF LIGHT BLOCKING THE FRAY, I SHOULD LET THEM DIE.
BUT WE NEED THIS WORLD. WE NEED TO--
SKREEEEEEEEE
I HATE FIGHTING THEM. HAWKMAN TOLD ME THE FREEDOM FIGHTERS WERE HEROES...
...BUT IF I'VE GOT TO KILL THEM TO SAVE THEIR WHOLE WORLD--I WILL!
YOUR POWERS ARE LIGHT-ORIENTED, TOO, EH, WOMAN?
THEN YOU'LL APPRECIATE WHAT THE RAY CAN DO!
OKAY TO SAVE YOU THIS TIME, DR. LIGHT?
YOU SAID THOSE FOOLS WERE YOUR FRIENDS. IS THIS A PLANET OF MADMEN?
OBVIOUSLY SOMETHING'S WRONG. HEROES DON'T BATTLE OTHER HEROES WITHOUT REASON-- UNLESS...
...UNLESS THEY'RE BEING CONTROLLED.
CONTROLLED? BY WHO?
THE ANTIMATTER UNIVERSE...
M-MONITOR--IT HURTS... S-SO MANY EMOTIONS. I FEEL LIKE MY HEAD'S EXPLODING. PLEASE, MONITOR --LET ME STOP!
NONSENSE, PSYCHO-PIRATE. YOU WANTED A WORLD TO CONTROL.
NOW YOU HAVE THREE!
11

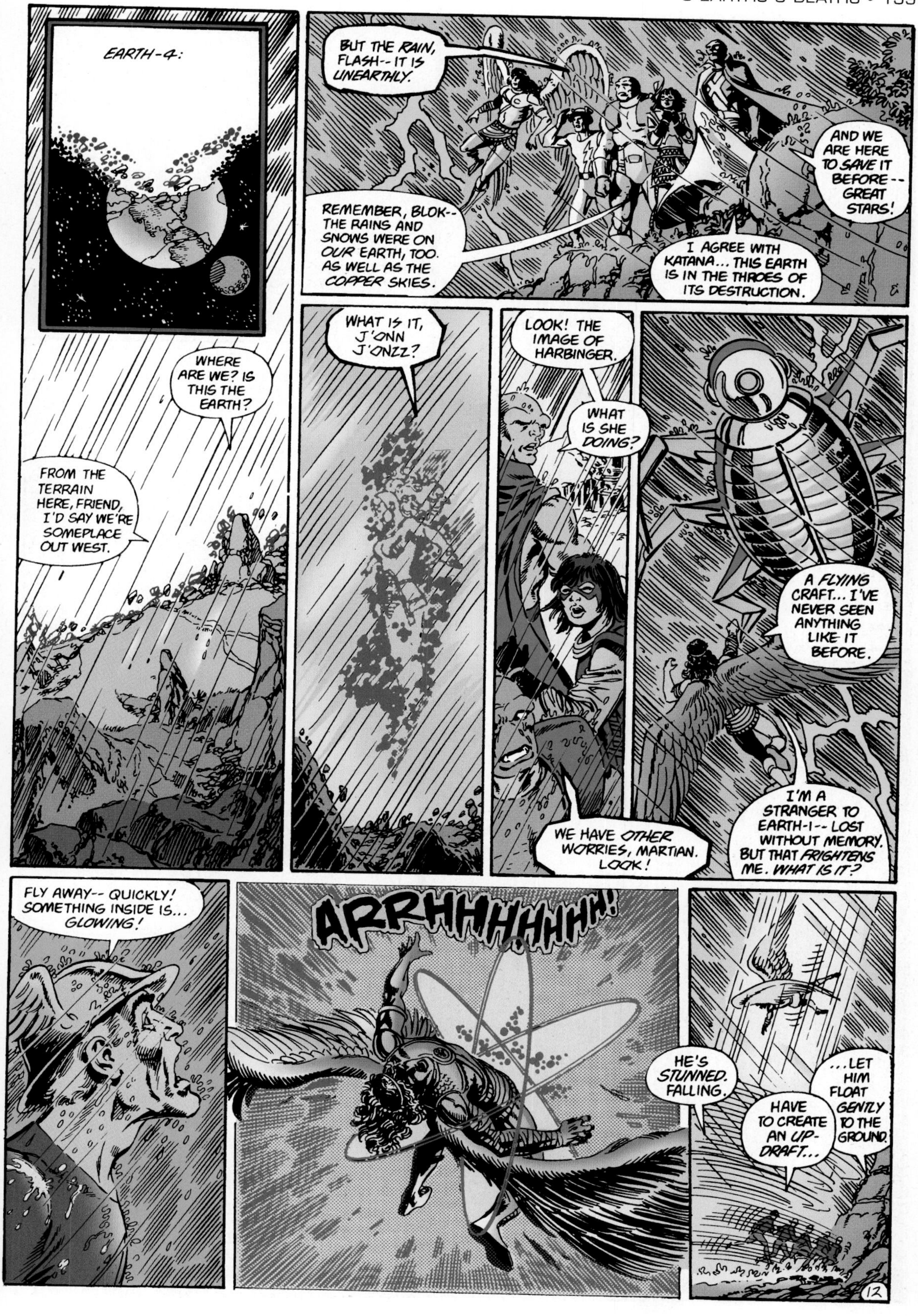
EARTH-4:
BUT THE RAIN, FLASH-- IT IS UNEARTHLY.
REMEMBER, BLOK-- THE RAINS AND SNOWS WERE ON OUR EARTH, TOO. AS WELL AS THE COPPER SKIES.
I AGREE WITH KATANA... THIS EARTH IS IN THE THROES OF ITS DESTRUCTION.
AND WE ARE HERE TO SAVE IT BEFORE-- GREAT STARS!
WHERE ARE WE? IS THIS THE EARTH?
FROM THE TERRAIN HERE, FRIEND, I'D SAY WE'RE SOMEPLACE OUT WEST.
WHAT IS IT, J'ONN J'ONZZ?
LOOK! THE IMAGE OF HARBINGER.
WHAT IS SHE DOING?
WE HAVE OTHER WORRIES, MARTIAN. LOOK!
A FLYING CRAFT... I'VE NEVER SEEN ANYTHING LIKE IT BEFORE.
I'M A STRANGER TO EARTH-1-- LOST WITHOUT MEMORY. BUT THAT FRIGHTENS ME. WHAT IS IT?
FLY AWAY-- QUICKLY! SOMETHING INSIDE IS... GLOWING!
ARRHHHHHHHH!
HE'S STUNNED. FALLING.
HAVE TO CREATE AN UP-DRAFT...
...LET HIM FLOAT GENTLY TO THE GROUND.
12

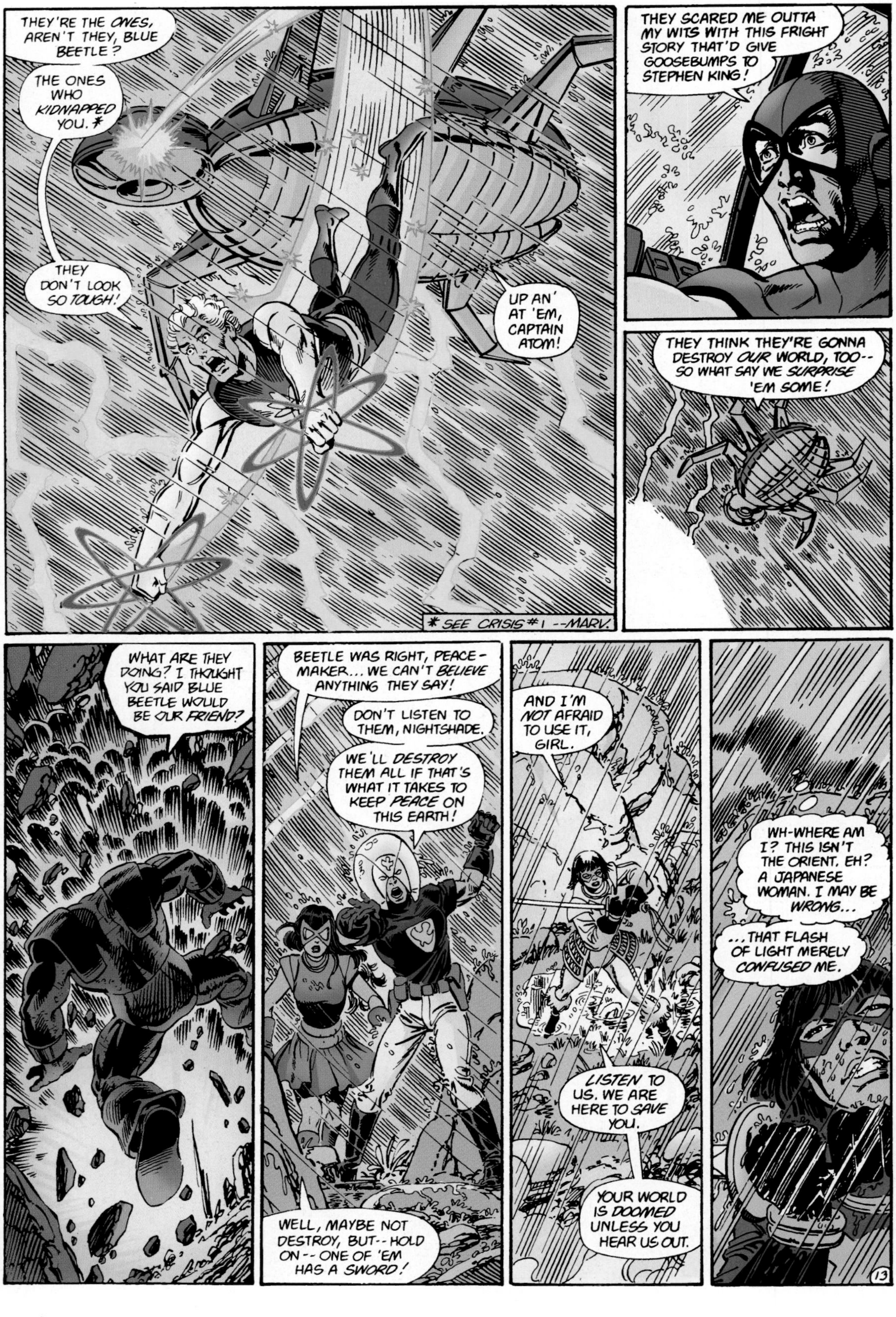

THEY'RE THE ONES, AREN'T THEY, BLUE BEETLE?
THE ONES WHO KIDNAPPED YOU.*
THEY DON'T LOOK SO TOUGH!
UP AN' AT 'EM, CAPTAIN ATOM!
* SEE CRISIS #1 --MARV.
THEY SCARED ME OUTTA MY WITS WITH THIS FRIGHT STORY THAT'D GIVE GOOSEBUMPS TO STEPHEN KING!
THEY THINK THEY'RE GONNA DESTROY OUR WORLD, TOO-- SO WHAT SAY WE SURPRISE 'EM SOME!
WHAT ARE THEY DOING? I THOUGHT YOU SAID BLUE BEETLE WOULD BE OUR FRIEND?
BEETLE WAS RIGHT, PEACE-MAKER... WE CAN'T BELIEVE ANYTHING THEY SAY!
DON'T LISTEN TO THEM, NIGHTSHADE.
WE'LL DESTROY THEM ALL IF THAT'S WHAT IT TAKES TO KEEP PEACE ON THIS EARTH!
WELL, MAYBE NOT DESTROY, BUT--HOLD ON -- ONE OF 'EM HAS A SWORD!
AND I'M NOT AFRAID TO USE IT, GIRL.
LISTEN TO US. WE ARE HERE TO SAVE YOU.
YOUR WORLD IS DOOMED UNLESS YOU HEAR US OUT.
WH-WHERE AM I? THIS ISN'T THE ORIENT, EH? A JAPANESE WOMAN. I MAY BE WRONG...
...THAT FLASH OF LIGHT MERELY CONFUSED ME.
13

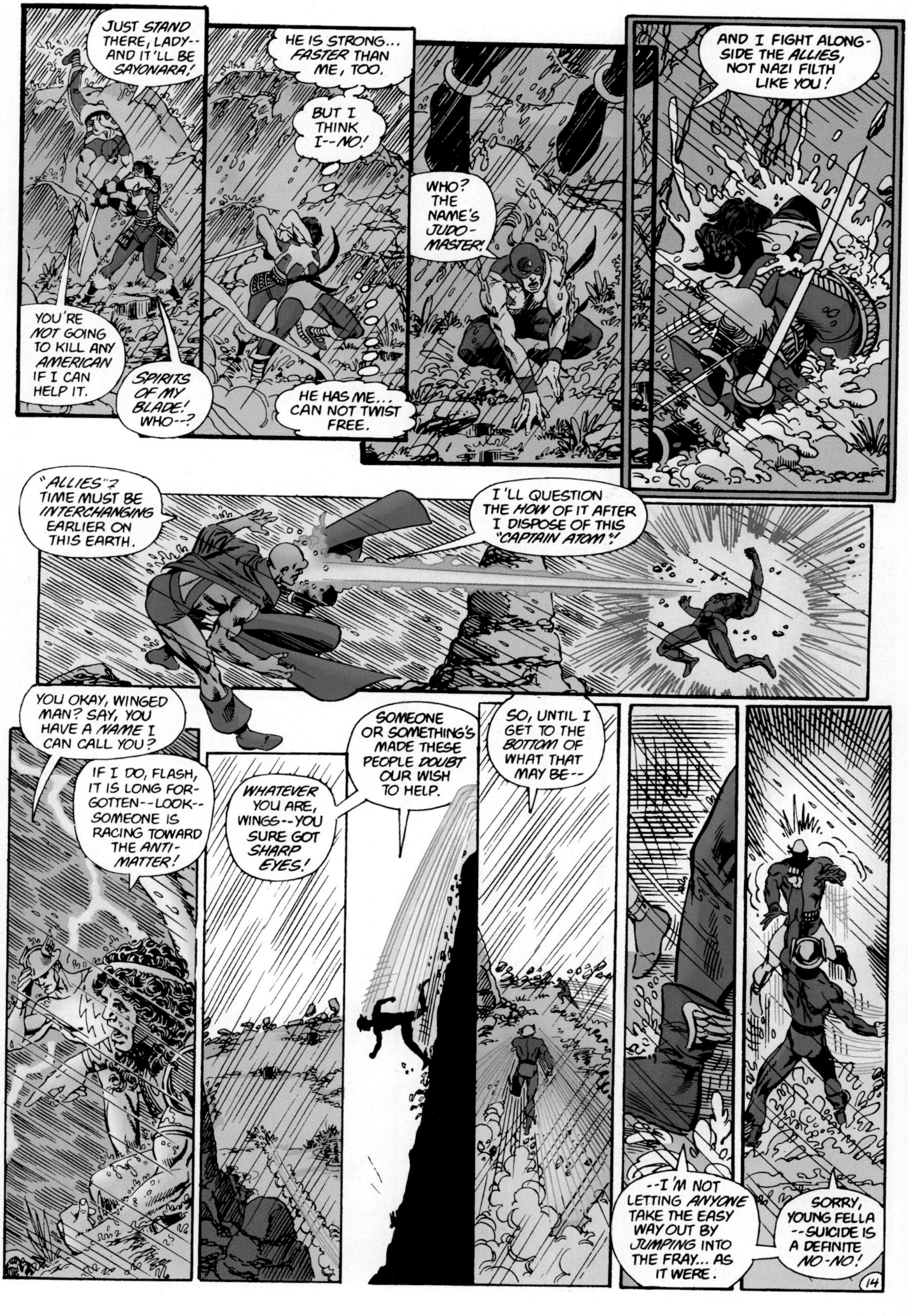
JUST STAND THERE, LADY-- AND IT'LL BE SAYONARA!
YOU'RE NOT GOING TO KILL ANY AMERICAN IF I CAN HELP IT.
SPIRITS OF MY BLADE! WHO--?
HE IS STRONG... FASTER THAN ME, TOO.
BUT I THINK I--NO!
HE HAS ME... CAN NOT TWIST FREE.
WHO? THE NAME'S JUDO-MASTER!
AND I FIGHT ALONG-SIDE THE ALLIES, NOT NAZI FILTH LIKE YOU!
"ALLIES"? TIME MUST BE INTERCHANGING EARLIER ON THIS EARTH.
I'LL QUESTION THE HOW OF IT AFTER I DISPOSE OF THIS "CAPTAIN ATOM"!
YOU OKAY, WINGED MAN? SAY, YOU HAVE A NAME I CAN CALL YOU?
IF I DO, FLASH, IT IS LONG FOR-GOTTEN--LOOK-- SOMEONE IS RACING TOWARD THE ANTI-MATTER!
WHATEVER YOU ARE, WINGS--YOU SURE GOT SHARP EYES!
SOMEONE OR SOMETHING'S MADE THESE PEOPLE DOUBT OUR WISH TO HELP.
SO, UNTIL I GET TO THE BOTTOM OF WHAT THAT MAY BE--
--I'M NOT LETTING ANYONE TAKE THE EASY WAY OUT BY JUMPING INTO THE FRAY... AS IT WERE.
SORRY, YOUNG FELLA --SUICIDE IS A DEFINITE NO-NO!
14

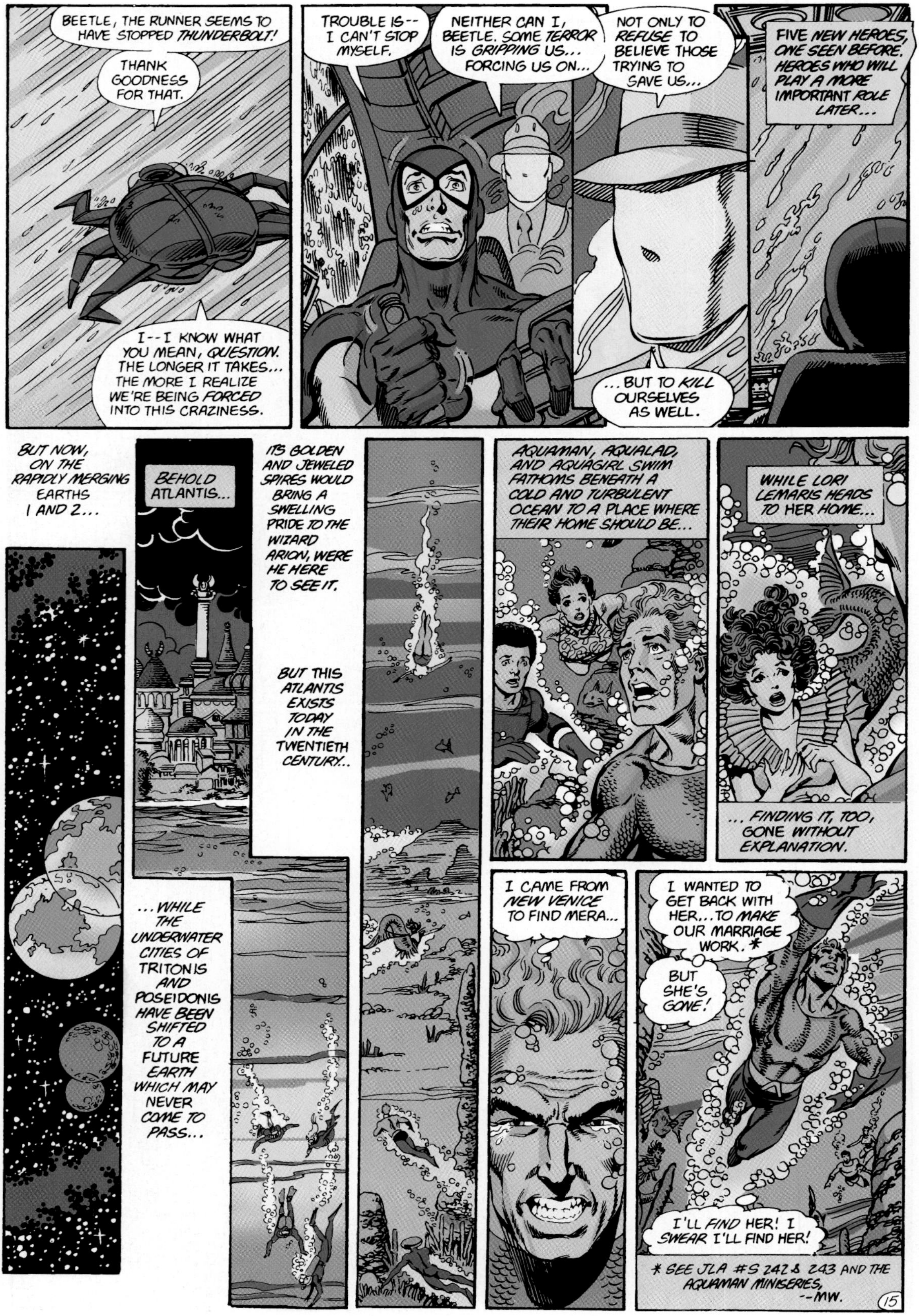
BEETLE, THE RUNNER SEEMS TO HAVE STOPPED THUNDERBOLT!
THANK GOODNESS FOR THAT.
I--I KNOW WHAT YOU MEAN, QUESTION. THE LONGER IT TAKES... THE MORE I REALIZE WE'RE BEING FORCED INTO THIS CRAZINESS.
TROUBLE IS-- I CAN'T STOP MYSELF.
NEITHER CAN I, BEETLE. SOME TERROR IS GRIPPING US... FORCING US ON...
NOT ONLY TO REFUSE TO BELIEVE THOSE TRYING TO SAVE US...
...BUT TO KILL OURSELVES AS WELL.
FIVE NEW HEROES, ONE SEEN BEFORE. HEROES WHO WILL PLAY A MORE IMPORTANT ROLE LATER...
BUT NOW, ON THE RAPIDLY MERGING EARTHS 1 AND 2...
BEHOLD ATLANTIS...
ITS GOLDEN AND JEWELED SPIRES WOULD BRING A SWELLING PRIDE TO THE WIZARD ARION, WERE HE HERE TO SEE IT.
BUT THIS ATLANTIS EXISTS TODAY IN THE TWENTIETH CENTURY...
...WHILE THE UNDERWATER CITIES OF TRITONIS AND POSEIDONIS HAVE BEEN SHIFTED TO A FUTURE EARTH WHICH MAY NEVER COME TO PASS...
AQUAMAN, AQUALAD, AND AQUAGIRL SWIM FATHOMS BENEATH A COLD AND TURBULENT OCEAN TO A PLACE WHERE THEIR HOME SHOULD BE...
WHILE LORI LEMARIS HEADS TO HER HOME...
...FINDING IT, TOO, GONE WITHOUT EXPLANATION.
I CAME FROM NEW VENICE TO FIND MERA...
I WANTED TO GET BACK WITH HER... TO MAKE OUR MARRIAGE WORK. *
BUT SHE'S GONE!
I'LL FIND HER! I SWEAR I'LL FIND HER!
* SEE JLA #S 242 & 243 AND THE AQUAMAN MINISERIES. --MW.
15

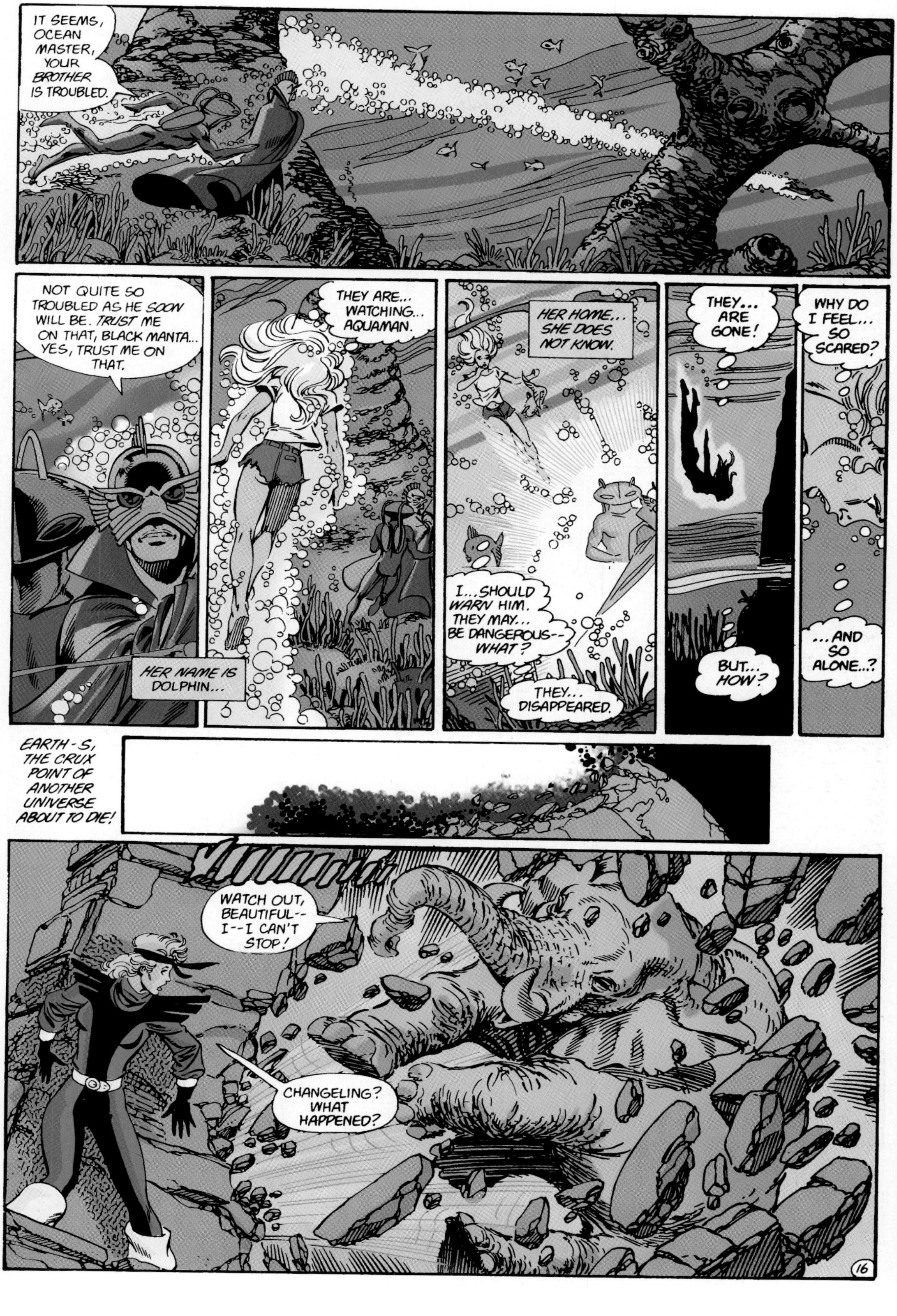
IT SEEMS, OCEAN MASTER, YOUR BROTHER IS TROUBLED.
NOT QUITE SO TROUBLED AS HE SOON WILL BE. TRUST ME ON THAT, BLACK MANTA... YES, TRUST ME ON THAT.
HER NAME IS DOLPHIN...
THEY ARE... WATCHING... AQUAMAN.
HER HOME... SHE DOES NOT KNOW.
I...SHOULD WARN HIM. THEY MAY... BE DANGEROUS-- WHAT?
THEY... DISAPPEARED.
THEY... ARE GONE!
BUT... HOW?
WHY DO I FEEL... SO SCARED?
...AND SO ALONE...?
EARTH-S, THE CRUX POINT OF ANOTHER UNIVERSE ABOUT TO DIE!
WATCH OUT, BEAUTIFUL-- I--I CAN'T STOP!
CHANGELING? WHAT HAPPENED?
16

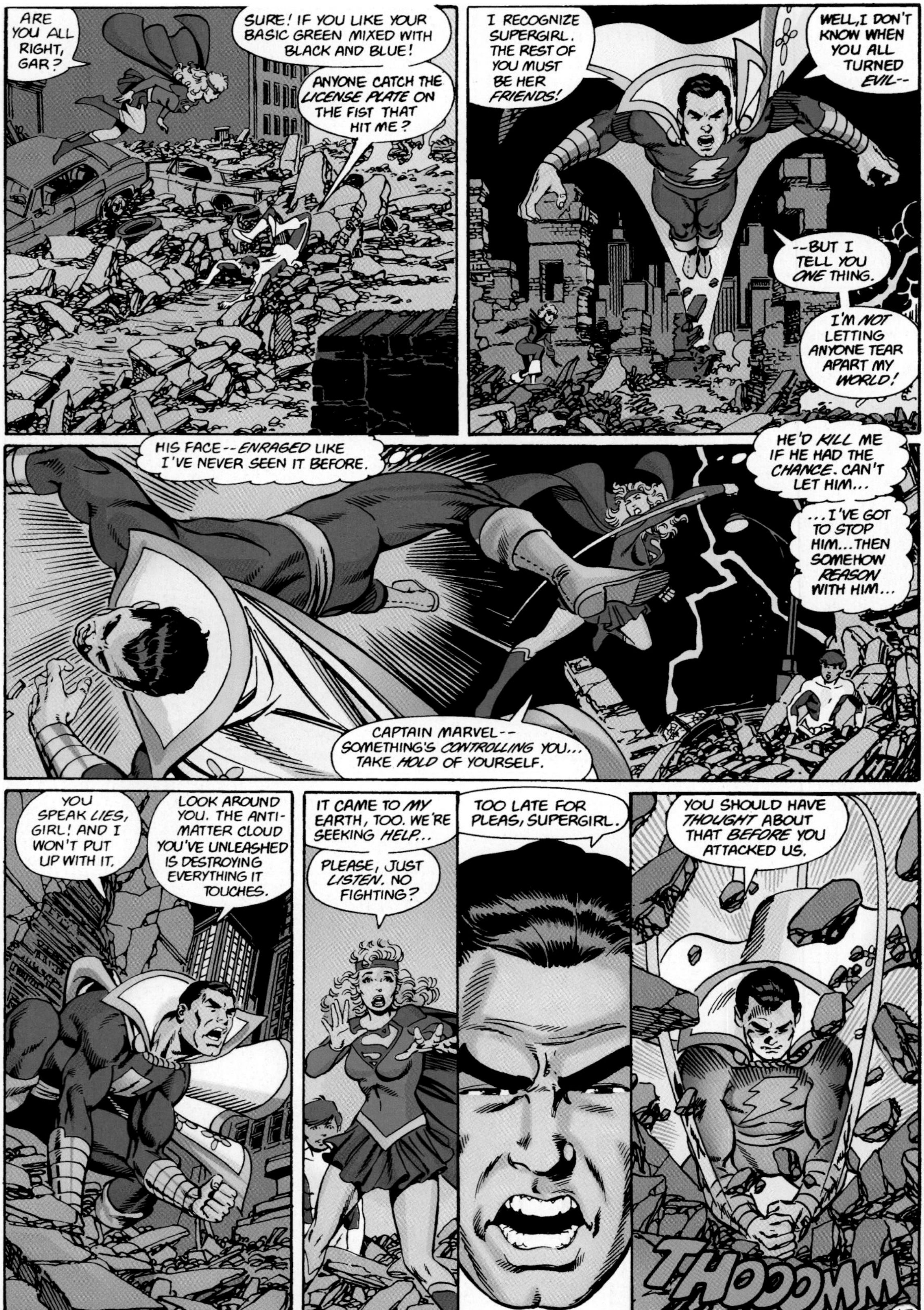
ARE YOU ALL RIGHT, GAR?
SURE! IF YOU LIKE YOUR BASIC GREEN MIXED WITH BLACK AND BLUE!
ANYONE CATCH THE LICENSE PLATE ON THE FIST THAT HIT ME?
I RECOGNIZE SUPERGIRL. THE REST OF YOU MUST BE HER FRIENDS!
WELL, I DON'T KNOW WHEN YOU ALL TURNED EVIL--
--BUT I TELL YOU ONE THING.
I'M NOT LETTING ANYONE TEAR APART MY WORLD!
HIS FACE--ENRAGED LIKE I'VE NEVER SEEN IT BEFORE.
HE'D KILL ME IF HE HAD THE CHANCE. CAN'T LET HIM...
...I'VE GOT TO STOP HIM...THEN SOMEHOW REASON WITH HIM...
CAPTAIN MARVEL--SOMETHING'S CONTROLLING YOU... TAKE HOLD OF YOURSELF.
YOU SPEAK LIES, GIRL! AND I WON'T PUT UP WITH IT.
LOOK AROUND YOU. THE ANTI-MATTER CLOUD YOU'VE UNLEASHED IS DESTROYING EVERYTHING IT TOUCHES.
IT CAME TO MY EARTH, TOO. WE'RE SEEKING HELP...
PLEASE, JUST LISTEN. NO FIGHTING?
TOO LATE FOR PLEAS, SUPERGIRL.
YOU SHOULD HAVE THOUGHT ABOUT THAT BEFORE YOU ATTACKED US.
THOOOMM
17

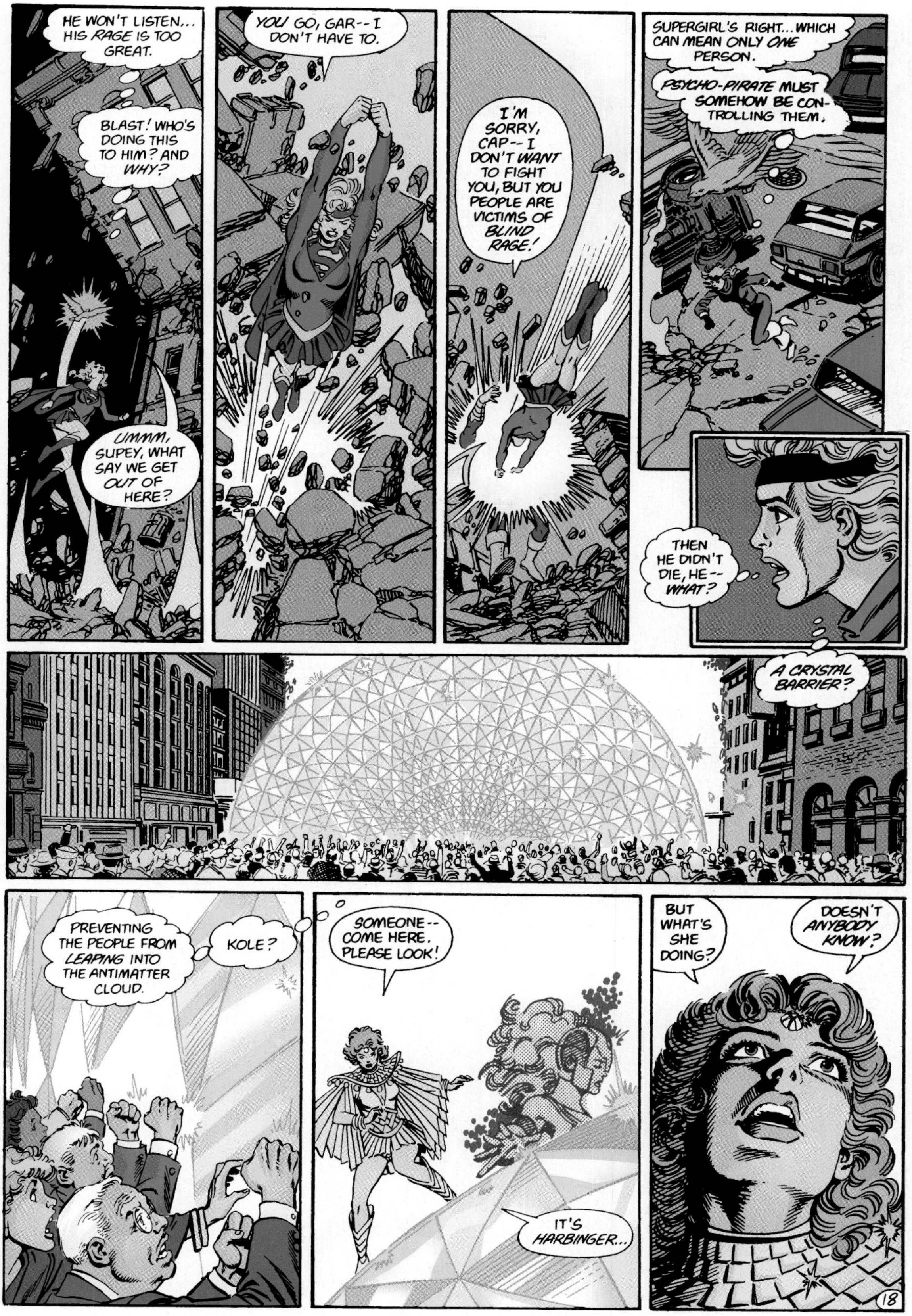
HE WON'T LISTEN... HIS RAGE IS TOO GREAT.
BLAST! WHO'S DOING THIS TO HIM? AND WHY?
UMMM, SUPEY, WHAT SAY WE GET OUT OF HERE?
YOU GO, GAR-- I DON'T HAVE TO.
I'M SORRY, CAP-- I DON'T WANT TO FIGHT YOU, BUT YOU PEOPLE ARE VICTIMS OF BLIND RAGE!
SUPERGIRL'S RIGHT... WHICH CAN MEAN ONLY ONE PERSON.
PSYCHO-PIRATE MUST SOMEHOW BE CONTROLLING THEM.
THEN HE DIDN'T DIE, HE-- WHAT?
A CRYSTAL BARRIER?
PREVENTING THE PEOPLE FROM LEAPING INTO THE ANTIMATTER CLOUD.
KOLE?
SOMEONE-- COME HERE. PLEASE LOOK!
IT'S HARBINGER...
BUT WHAT'S SHE DOING?
DOESN'T ANYBODY KNOW?
18

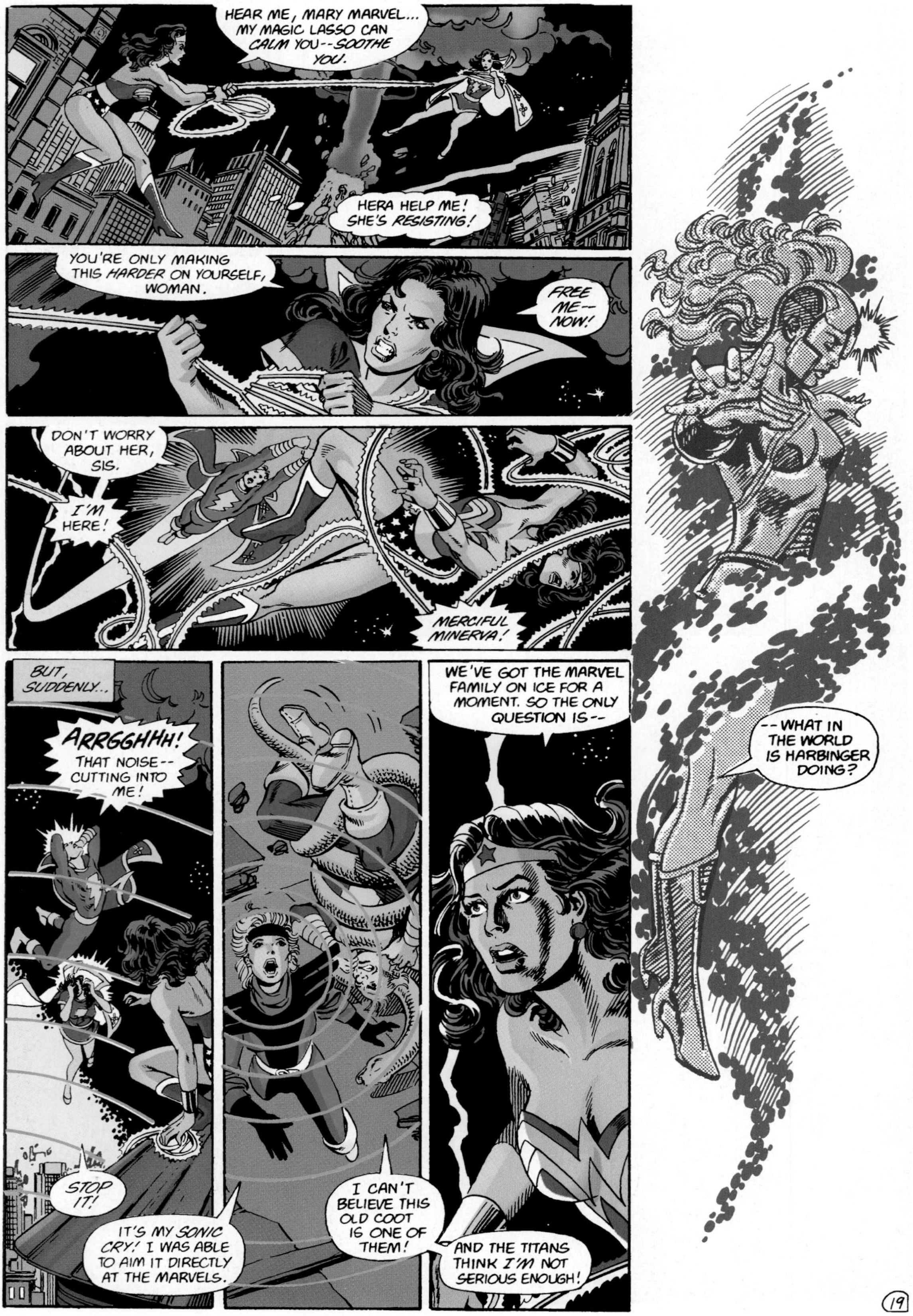
HEAR ME, MARY MARVEL... MY MAGIC LASSO CAN CALM YOU--SOOTHE YOU.
HERA HELP ME! SHE'S RESISTING!
YOU'RE ONLY MAKING THIS HARDER ON YOURSELF, WOMAN.
FREE ME--NOW!
DON'T WORRY ABOUT HER, SIS.
I'M HERE!
MERCIFUL MINERVA!
BUT, SUDDENLY...
ARRGGHHH! THAT NOISE--CUTTING INTO ME!
STOP IT!
IT'S MY SONIC CRY! I WAS ABLE TO AIM IT DIRECTLY AT THE MARVELS.
I CAN'T BELIEVE THIS OLD COOT IS ONE OF THEM!
WE'VE GOT THE MARVEL FAMILY ON ICE FOR A MOMENT. SO THE ONLY QUESTION IS--
AND THE TITANS THINK I'M NOT SERIOUS ENOUGH!
--WHAT IN THE WORLD IS HARBINGER DOING?
19

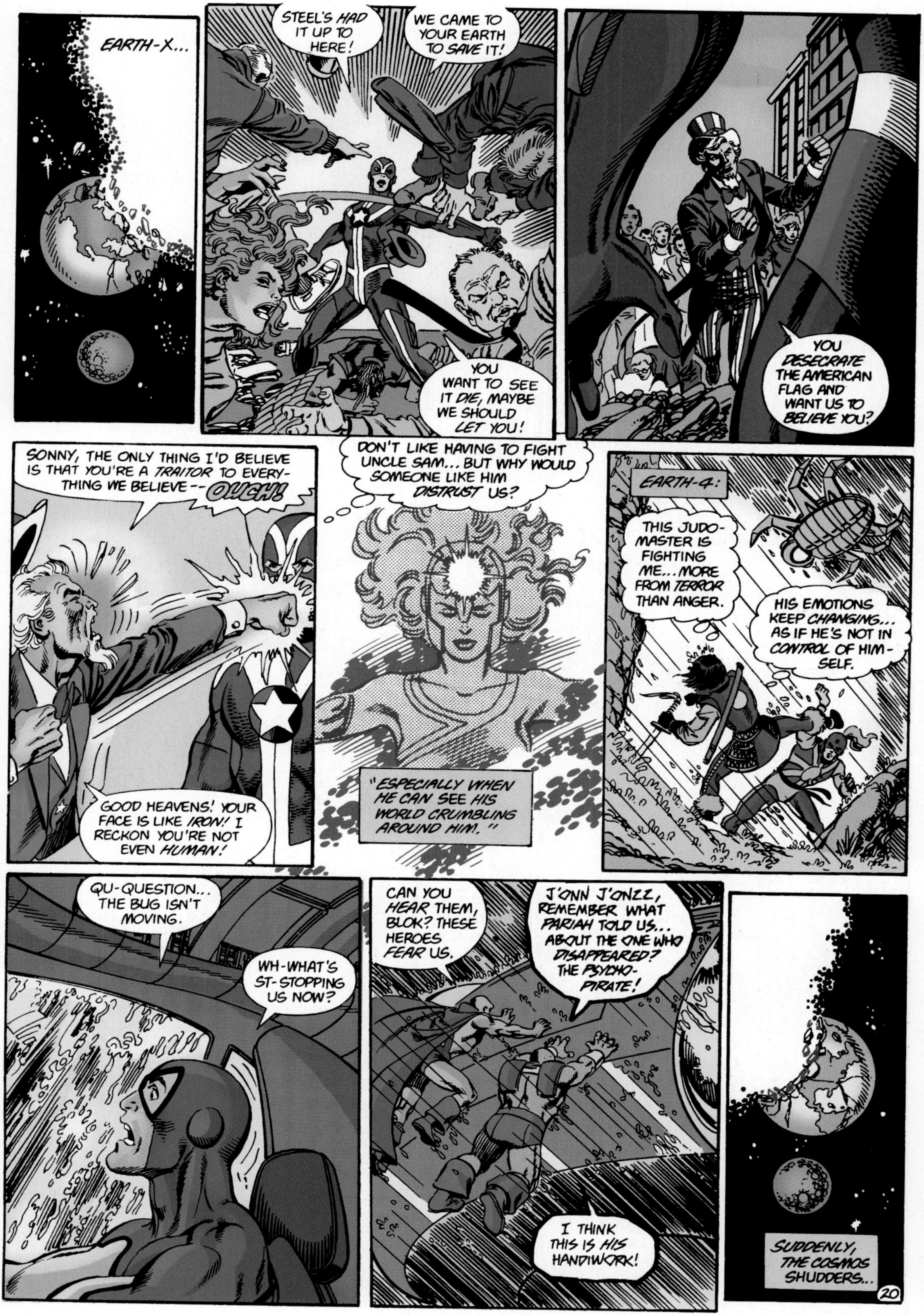
EARTH-X...
STEEL'S HAD IT UP TO HERE!
WE CAME TO YOUR EARTH TO SAVE IT!
YOU WANT TO SEE IT DIE, MAYBE WE SHOULD LET YOU!
YOU DESECRATE THE AMERICAN FLAG AND WANT US TO BELIEVE YOU?
SONNY, THE ONLY THING I'D BELIEVE IS THAT YOU'RE A TRAITOR TO EVERYTHING WE BELIEVE-- OUCH!
GOOD HEAVENS! YOUR FACE IS LIKE IRON! I RECKON YOU'RE NOT EVEN HUMAN!
DON'T LIKE HAVING TO FIGHT UNCLE SAM... BUT WHY WOULD SOMEONE LIKE HIM DISTRUST US?
"ESPECIALLY WHEN HE CAN SEE HIS WORLD CRUMBLING AROUND HIM."
EARTH-4:
THIS JUDOMASTER IS FIGHTING ME... MORE FROM TERROR THAN ANGER.
HIS EMOTIONS KEEP CHANGING... AS IF HE'S NOT IN CONTROL OF HIMSELF.
QU-QUESTION... THE BUG ISN'T MOVING.
WH-WHAT'S ST-STOPPING US NOW?
CAN YOU HEAR THEM, BLOK? THESE HEROES FEAR US.
J'ONN J'ONZZ, REMEMBER WHAT PARIAH TOLD US... ABOUT THE ONE WHO DISAPPEARED? THE PSYCHO-PIRATE!
I THINK THIS IS HIS HANDIWORK!
SUDDENLY, THE COSMOS SHUDDERS...
20

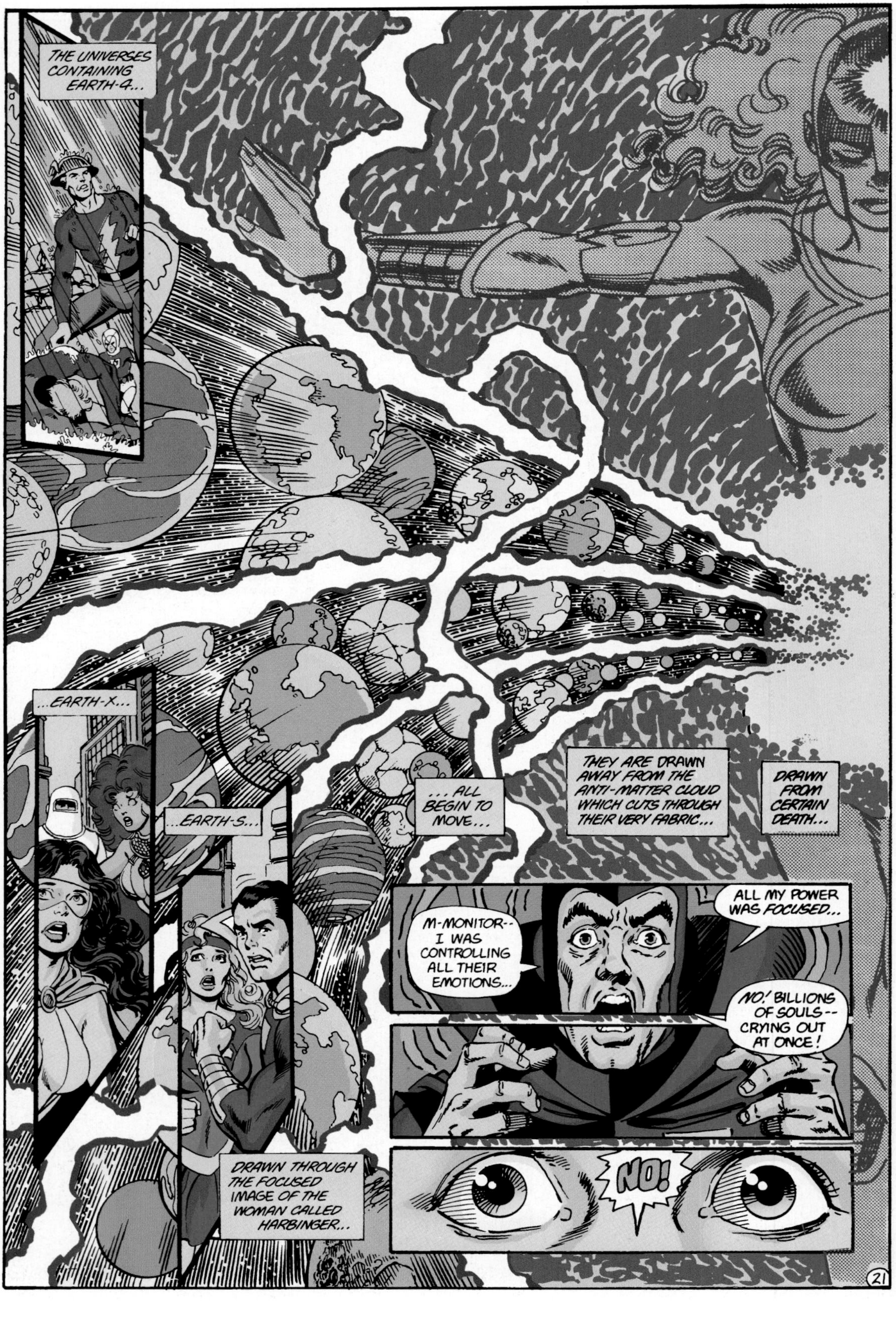
THE UNIVERSES CONTAINING EARTH-4...
...EARTH-X...
...EARTH-S...
...ALL BEGIN TO MOVE...
THEY ARE DRAWN AWAY FROM THE ANTI-MATTER CLOUD WHICH CUTS THROUGH THEIR VERY FABRIC...
DRAWN FROM CERTAIN DEATH...
M-MONITOR-- I WAS CONTROLLING ALL THEIR EMOTIONS...
ALL MY POWER WAS FOCUSED...
NO! BILLIONS OF SOULS-- CRYING OUT AT ONCE!
NO!
DRAWN THROUGH THE FOCUSED IMAGE OF THE WOMAN CALLED HARBINGER...
21

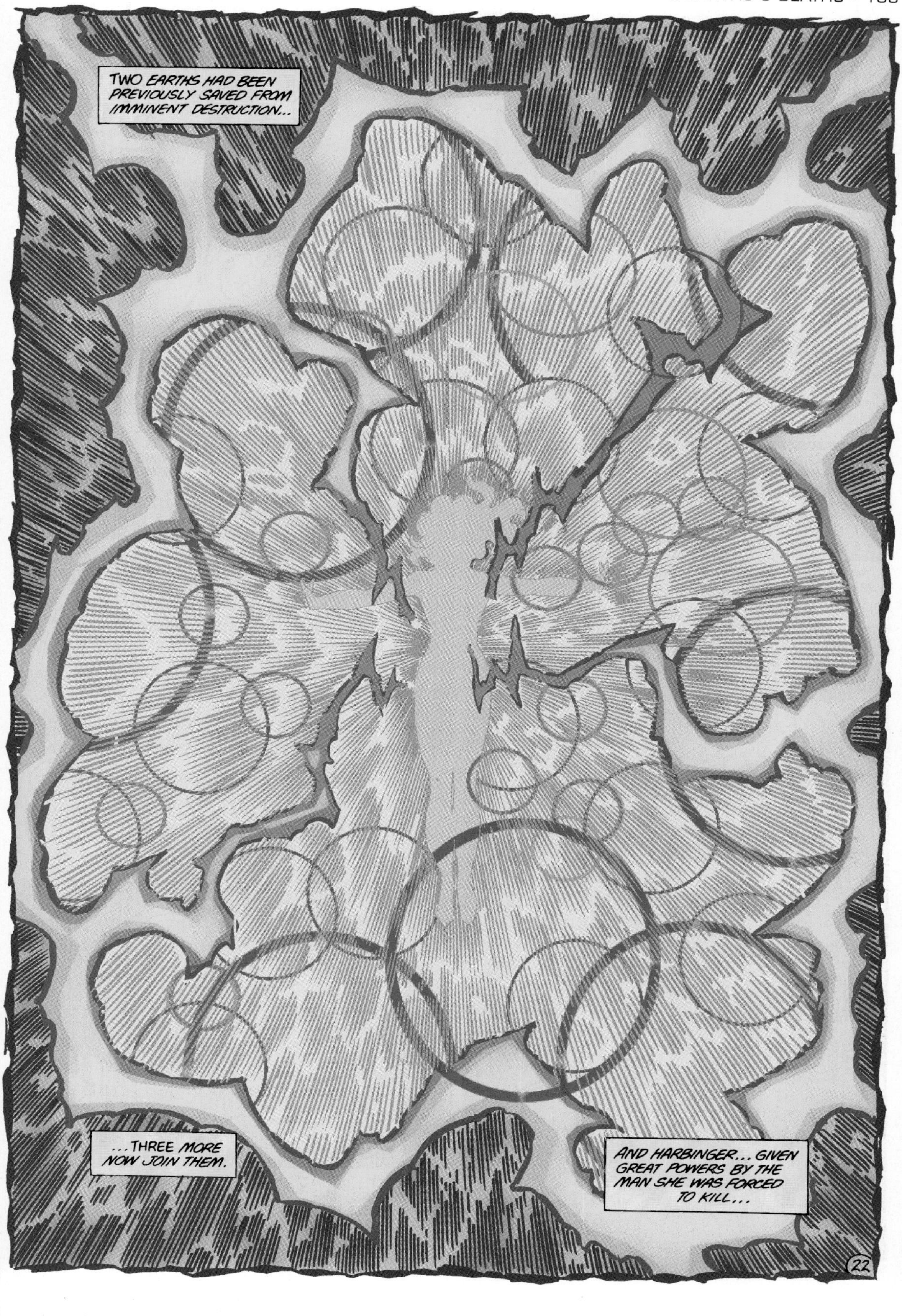
TWO EARTHS HAD BEEN PREVIOUSLY SAVED FROM IMMINENT DESTRUCTION...
...THREE MORE NOW JOIN THEM.
AND HARBINGER... GIVEN GREAT POWERS BY THE MAN SHE WAS FORCED TO KILL...
22

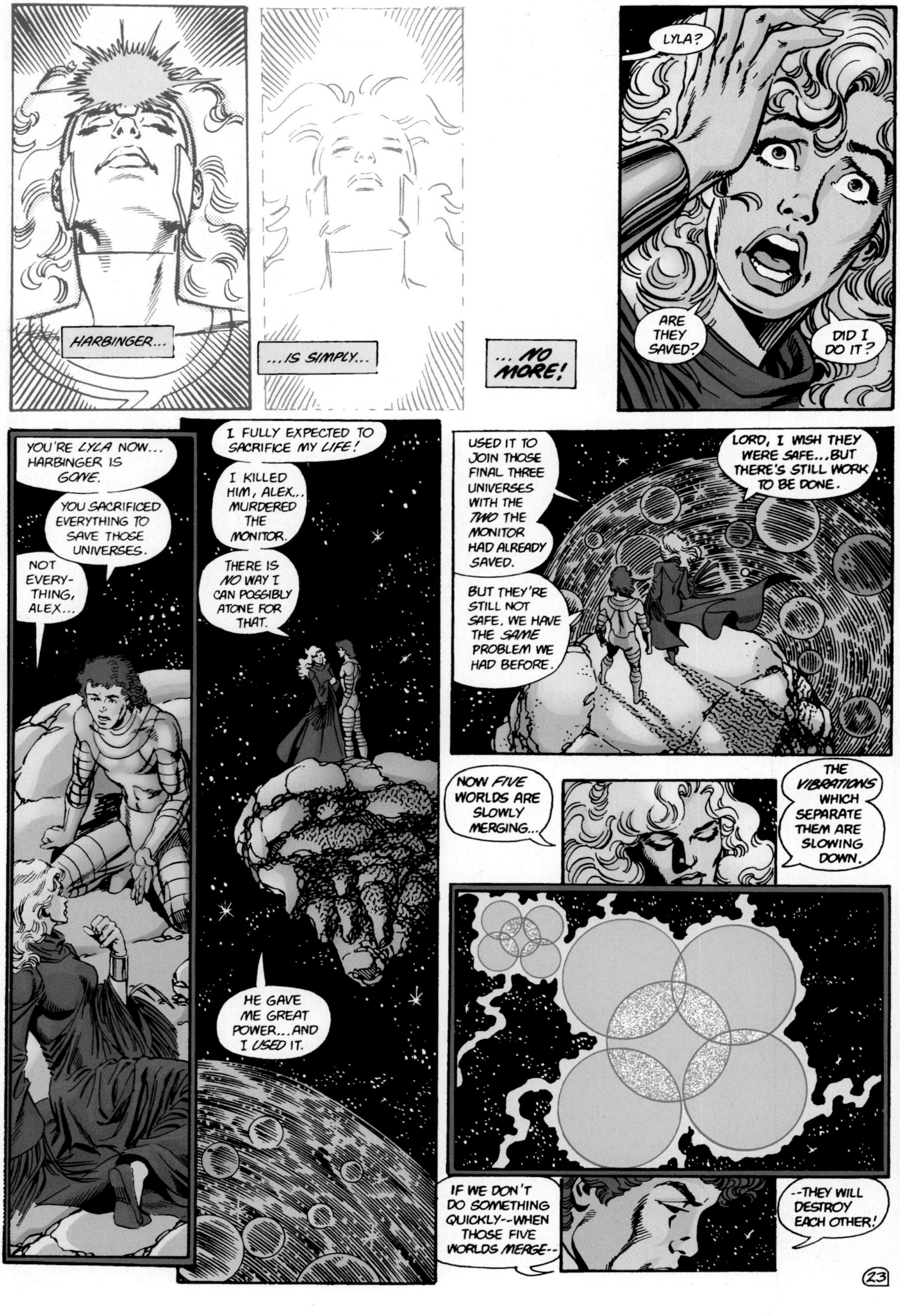
HARBINGER...
...IS SIMPLY...
...NO MORE!
LYLA?
ARE THEY SAVED?
DID I DO IT?
YOU'RE LYLA NOW... HARBINGER IS GONE.
YOU SACRIFICED EVERYTHING TO SAVE THOSE UNIVERSES.
NOT EVERY-THING, ALEX...
I FULLY EXPECTED TO SACRIFICE MY LIFE!
I KILLED HIM, ALEX... MURDERED THE MONITOR.
THERE IS NO WAY I CAN POSSIBLY ATONE FOR THAT.
HE GAVE ME GREAT POWER...AND I USED IT.
USED IT TO JOIN THOSE FINAL THREE UNIVERSES WITH THE TWO THE MONITOR HAD ALREADY SAVED.
BUT THEY'RE STILL NOT SAFE. WE HAVE THE SAME PROBLEM WE HAD BEFORE.
LORD, I WISH THEY WERE SAFE...BUT THERE'S STILL WORK TO BE DONE.
NOW FIVE WORLDS ARE SLOWLY MERGING...
THE VIBRATIONS WHICH SEPARATE THEM ARE SLOWING DOWN.
IF WE DON'T DO SOMETHING QUICKLY--WHEN THOSE FIVE WORLDS MERGE--
--THEY WILL DESTROY EACH OTHER!
23

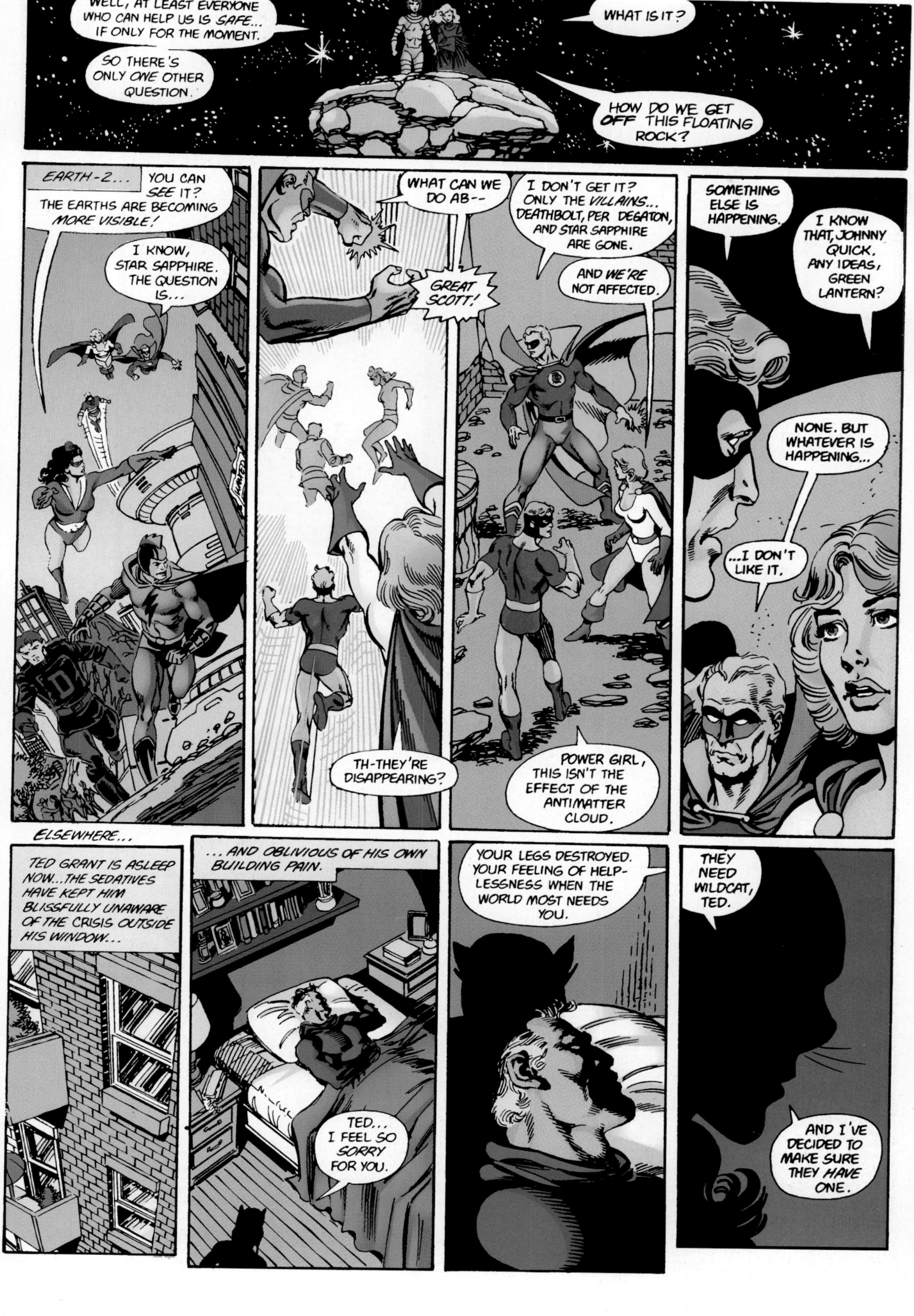
WELL, AT LEAST EVERYONE WHO CAN HELP US IS SAFE... IF ONLY FOR THE MOMENT.
SO THERE'S ONLY ONE OTHER QUESTION.
WHAT IS IT?
HOW DO WE GET OFF THIS FLOATING ROCK?
EARTH-2...
YOU CAN SEE IT? THE EARTHS ARE BECOMING MORE VISIBLE!
I KNOW, STAR SAPPHIRE. THE QUESTION IS...
WHAT CAN WE DO AB--
GREAT SCOTT!
TH-THEY'RE DISAPPEARING?
I DON'T GET IT? ONLY THE VILLAINS... DEATHBOLT, PER DEGATON, AND STAR SAPPHIRE ARE GONE.
AND WE'RE NOT AFFECTED.
POWER GIRL, THIS ISN'T THE EFFECT OF THE ANTIMATTER CLOUD.
SOMETHING ELSE IS HAPPENING.
I KNOW THAT, JOHNNY QUICK. ANY IDEAS, GREEN LANTERN?
NONE. BUT WHATEVER IS HAPPENING...
...I DON'T LIKE IT.
ELSEWHERE...
TED GRANT IS ASLEEP NOW...THE SEDATIVES HAVE KEPT HIM BLISSFULLY UNAWARE OF THE CRISIS OUTSIDE HIS WINDOW...
...AND OBLIVIOUS OF HIS OWN BUILDING PAIN.
TED... I FEEL SO SORRY FOR YOU.
YOUR LEGS DESTROYED. YOUR FEELING OF HELP-LESSNESS WHEN THE WORLD MOST NEEDS YOU.
THEY NEED WILDCAT, TED.
AND I'VE DECIDED TO MAKE SURE THEY HAVE ONE.

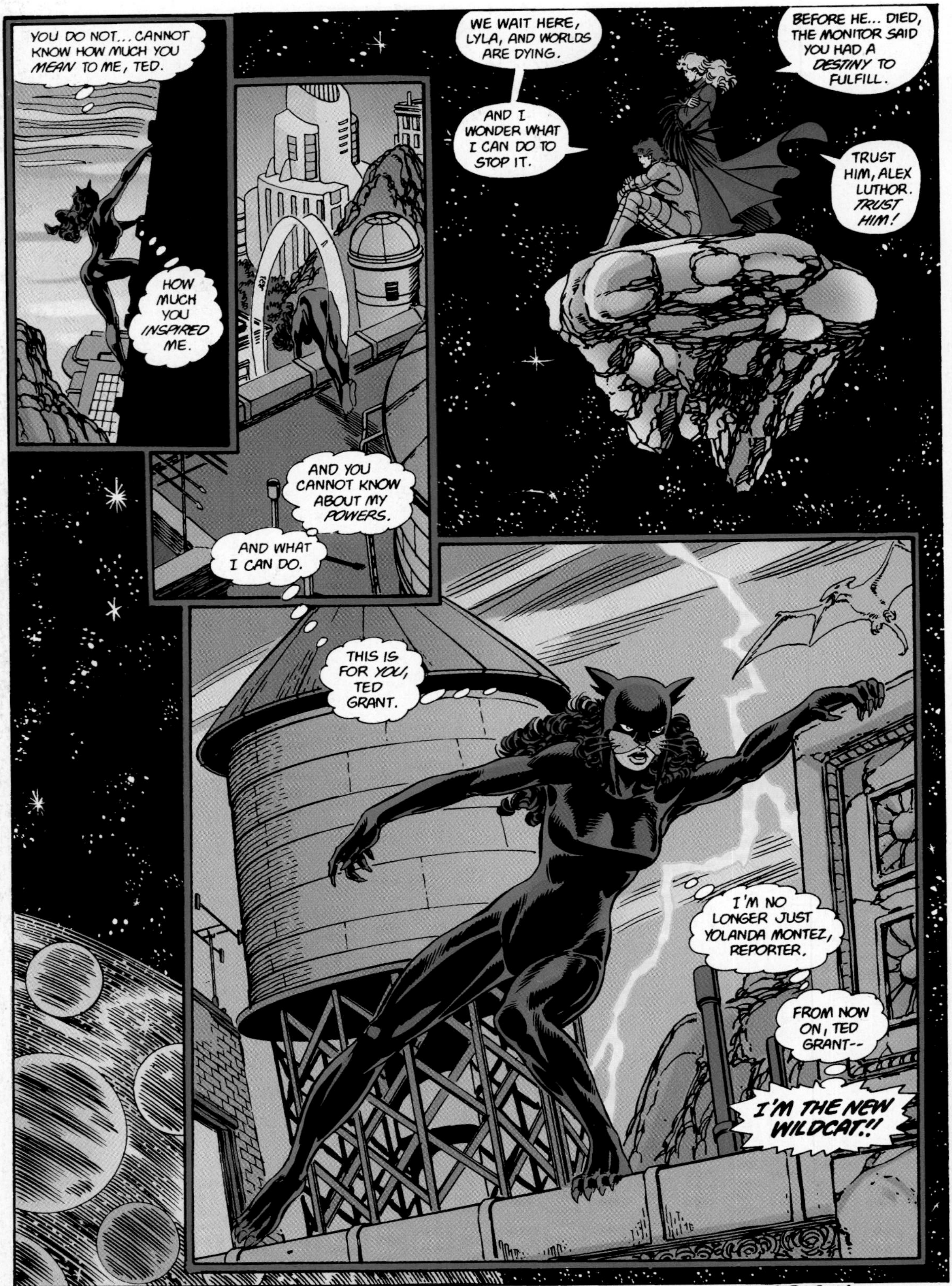
YOU DO NOT... CANNOT KNOW HOW MUCH YOU MEAN TO ME, TED.
HOW MUCH YOU INSPIRED ME.
WE WAIT HERE, LYLA, AND WORLDS ARE DYING.
AND I WONDER WHAT I CAN DO TO STOP IT.
BEFORE HE... DIED, THE MONITOR SAID YOU HAD A DESTINY TO FULFILL.
TRUST HIM, ALEX LUTHOR. TRUST HIM!
AND YOU CANNOT KNOW ABOUT MY POWERS.
AND WHAT I CAN DO.
THIS IS FOR YOU, TED GRANT.
I'M NO LONGER JUST YOLANDA MONTEZ, REPORTER.
FROM NOW ON, TED GRANT--
I'M THE NEW WILDCAT!!

NEXT: DOUBLE-SIZED DYNAMITE! THE ONE YOU'VE BEEN DEMANDING! THE *ORIGIN OF THE MONITOR!* THE *ORIGIN OF PARIAH!* THE *ORIGIN OF HARBINGER!* *PLUS*... THE SHOCKING ENDING OF THE CENTURY! *BE HERE!*

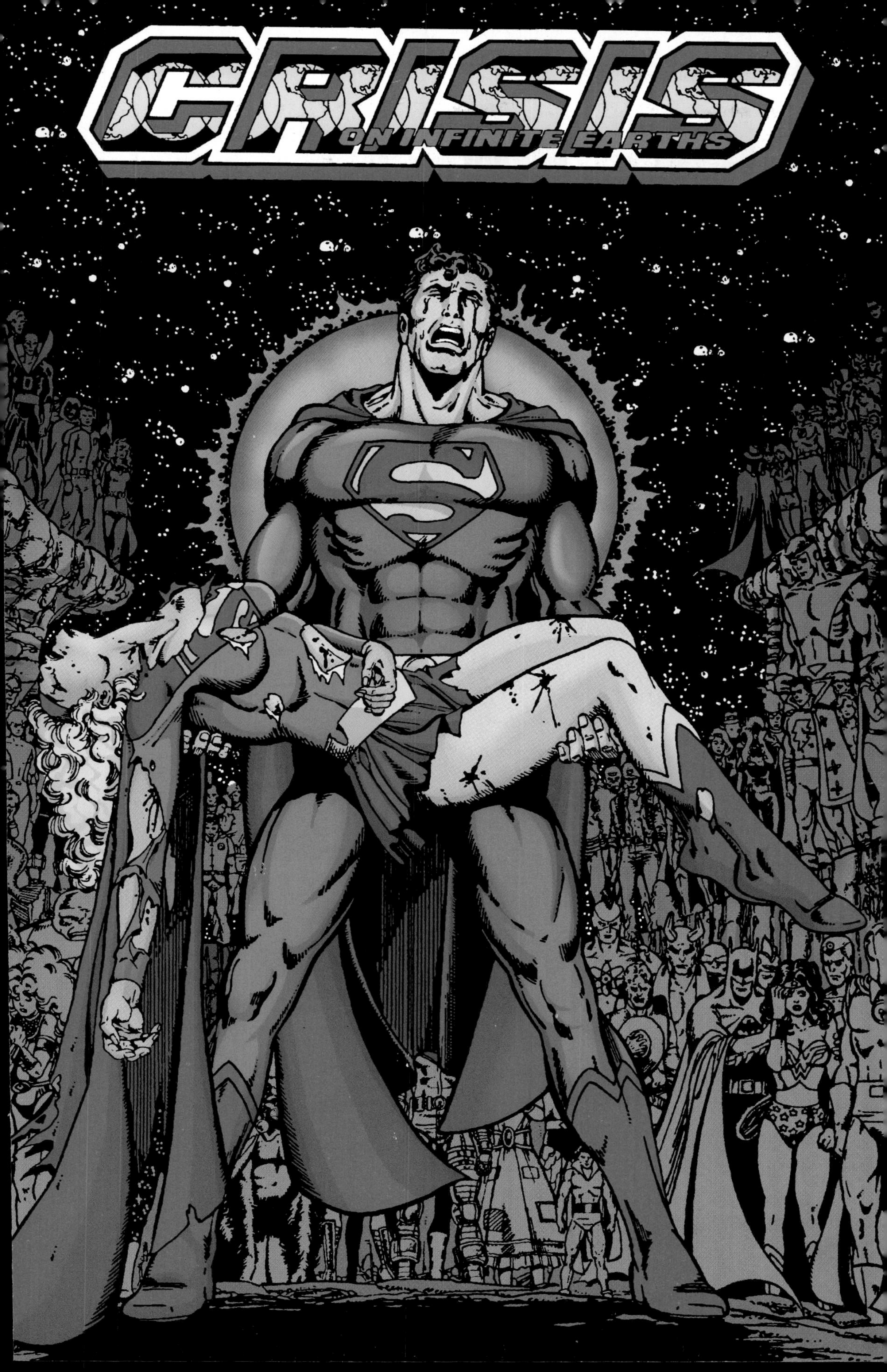
CRISIS
ON INFINITE EARTHS

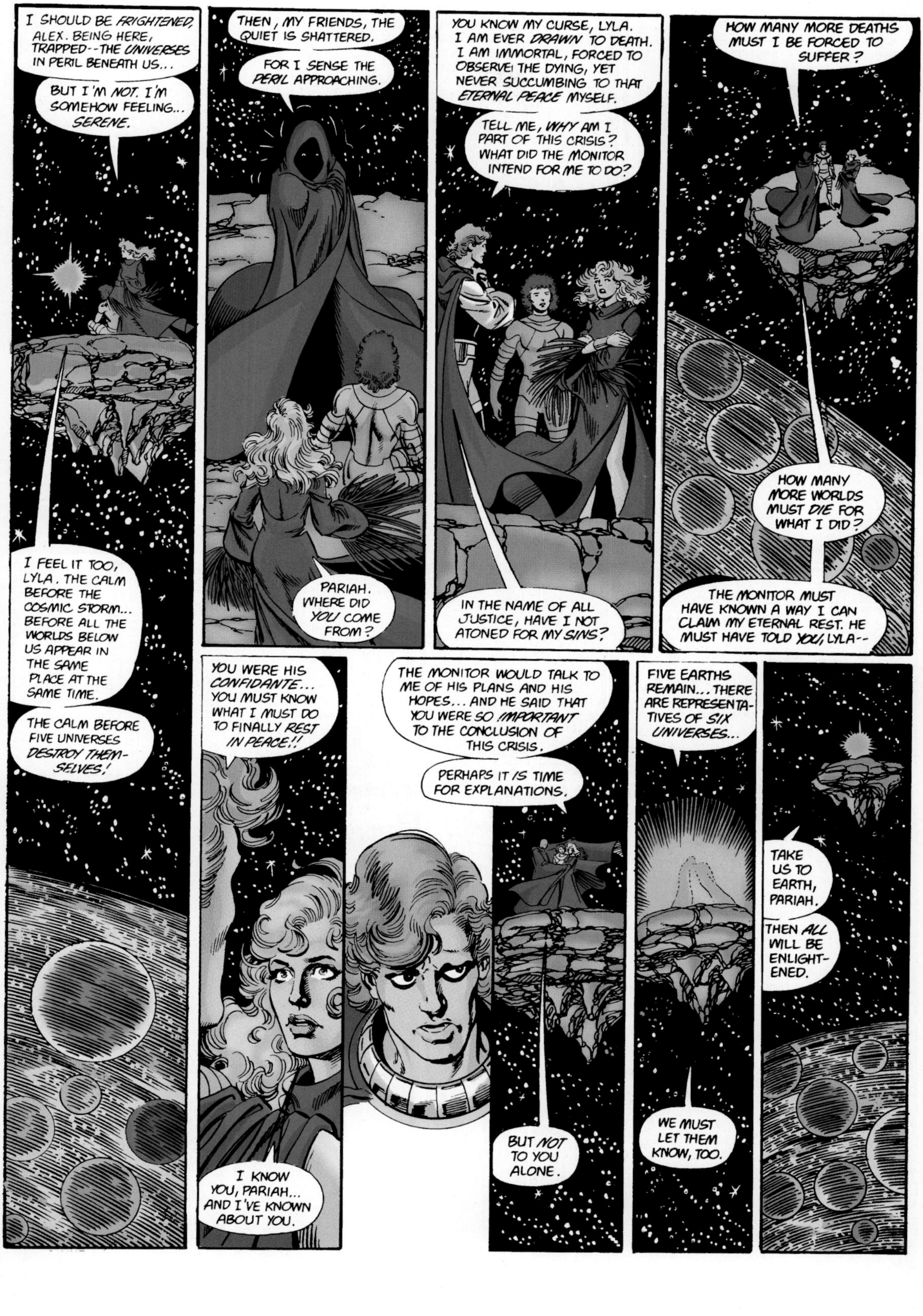

I SHOULD BE FRIGHTENED, ALEX. BEING HERE, TRAPPED--THE UNIVERSES IN PERIL BENEATH US...
BUT I'M NOT. I'M SOMEHOW FEELING... SERENE.
I FEEL IT TOO, LYLA. THE CALM BEFORE THE COSMIC STORM... BEFORE ALL THE WORLDS BELOW US APPEAR IN THE SAME PLACE AT THE SAME TIME.
THE CALM BEFORE FIVE UNIVERSES DESTROY THEMSELVES!
THEN, MY FRIENDS, THE QUIET IS SHATTERED.
FOR I SENSE THE PERIL APPROACHING.
PARIAH. WHERE DID YOU COME FROM?
YOU KNOW MY CURSE, LYLA. I AM EVER DRAWN TO DEATH. I AM IMMORTAL, FORCED TO OBSERVE THE DYING, YET NEVER SUCCUMBING TO THAT ETERNAL PEACE MYSELF.
TELL ME, WHY AM I PART OF THIS CRISIS? WHAT DID THE MONITOR INTEND FOR ME TO DO?
IN THE NAME OF ALL JUSTICE, HAVE I NOT ATONED FOR MY SINS?
HOW MANY MORE DEATHS MUST I BE FORCED TO SUFFER?
HOW MANY MORE WORLDS MUST DIE FOR WHAT I DID?
THE MONITOR MUST HAVE KNOWN A WAY I CAN CLAIM MY ETERNAL REST. HE MUST HAVE TOLD YOU, LYLA--
YOU WERE HIS CONFIDANTE... YOU MUST KNOW WHAT I MUST DO TO FINALLY REST IN PEACE!!
I KNOW YOU, PARIAH... AND I'VE KNOWN ABOUT YOU.
THE MONITOR WOULD TALK TO ME OF HIS PLANS AND HIS HOPES... AND HE SAID THAT YOU WERE SO IMPORTANT TO THE CONCLUSION OF THIS CRISIS.
PERHAPS IT IS TIME FOR EXPLANATIONS.
BUT NOT TO YOU ALONE.
FIVE EARTHS REMAIN... THERE ARE REPRESENTATIVES OF SIX UNIVERSES...
WE MUST LET THEM KNOW, TOO.
TAKE US TO EARTH, PARIAH.
THEN ALL WILL BE ENLIGHTENED.

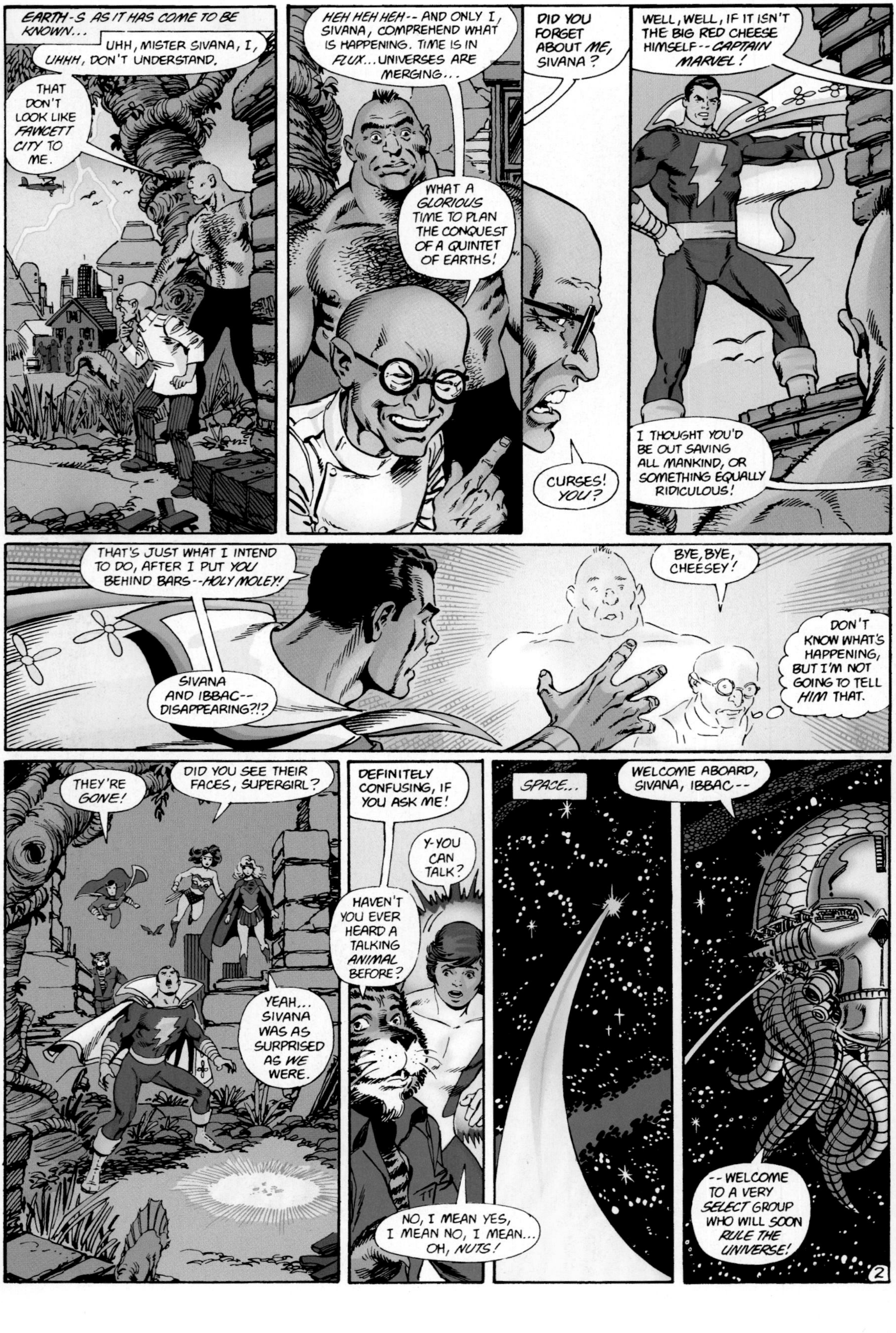
EARTH-S AS IT HAS COME TO BE KNOWN...
UHH, MISTER SIVANA, I, UHHH, DON'T UNDERSTAND.
THAT DON'T LOOK LIKE FAWCETT CITY TO ME.
HEH HEH HEH-- AND ONLY I, SIVANA, COMPREHEND WHAT IS HAPPENING. TIME IS IN FLUX... UNIVERSES ARE MERGING...
WHAT A GLORIOUS TIME TO PLAN THE CONQUEST OF A QUINTET OF EARTHS!
DID YOU FORGET ABOUT ME, SIVANA?
CURSES! YOU?
WELL, WELL, IF IT ISN'T THE BIG RED CHEESE HIMSELF--CAPTAIN MARVEL!
I THOUGHT YOU'D BE OUT SAVING ALL MANKIND, OR SOMETHING EQUALLY RIDICULOUS!
THAT'S JUST WHAT I INTEND TO DO, AFTER I PUT YOU BEHIND BARS--HOLY MOLEY!
SIVANA AND IBBAC-- DISAPPEARING?!?
BYE, BYE, CHEESEY!
DON'T KNOW WHAT'S HAPPENING, BUT I'M NOT GOING TO TELL HIM THAT.
THEY'RE GONE!
DID YOU SEE THEIR FACES, SUPERGIRL?
YEAH... SIVANA WAS AS SURPRISED AS WE WERE.
DEFINITELY CONFUSING, IF YOU ASK ME!
Y-YOU CAN TALK?
HAVEN'T YOU EVER HEARD A TALKING ANIMAL BEFORE?
NO, I MEAN YES, I MEAN NO, I MEAN... OH, NUTS!
SPACE...
WELCOME ABOARD, SIVANA, IBBAC--
--WELCOME TO A VERY SELECT GROUP WHO WILL SOON RULE THE UNIVERSE!
2

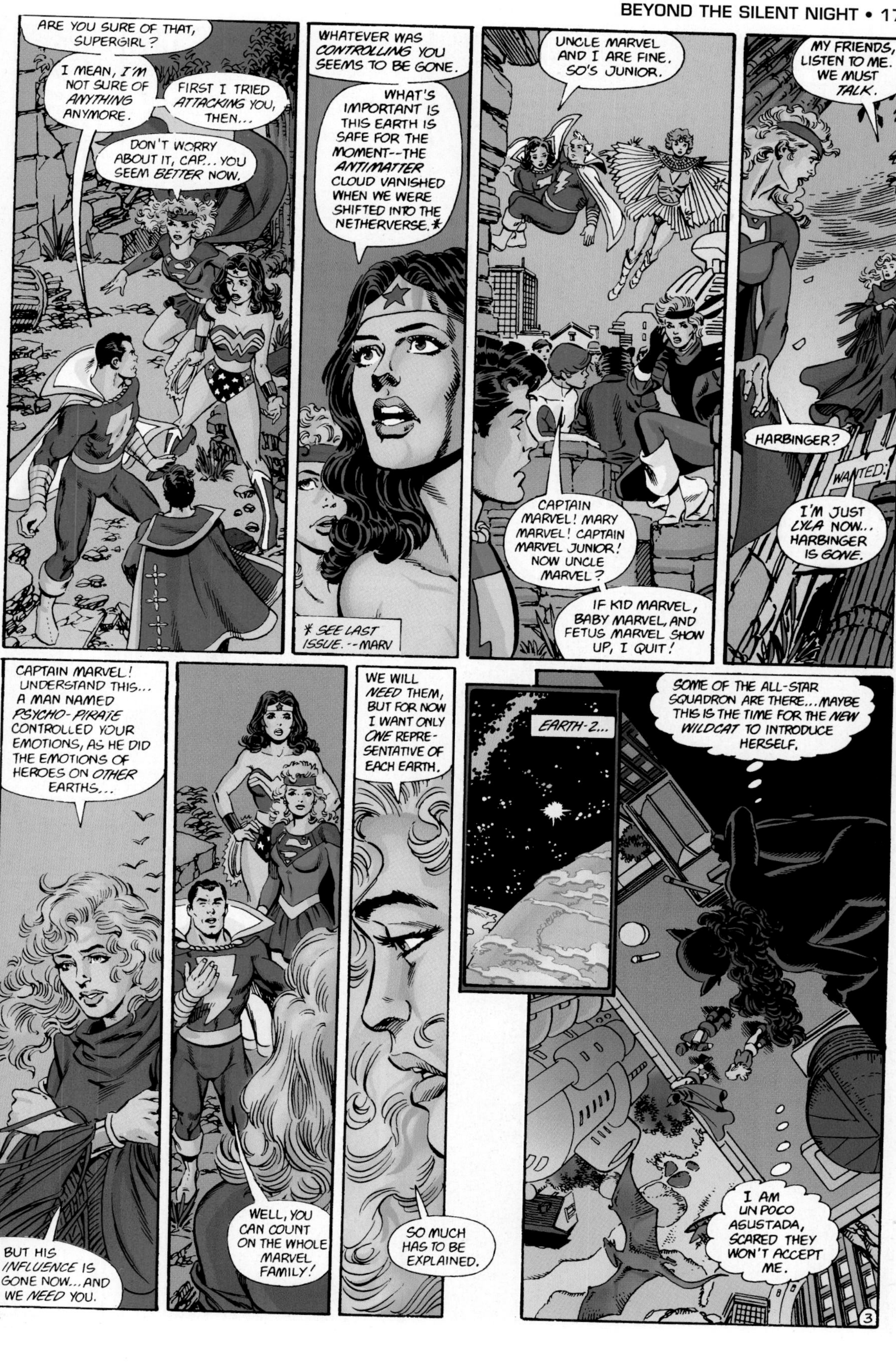
ARE YOU SURE OF THAT, SUPERGIRL?
I MEAN, I'M NOT SURE OF ANYTHING ANYMORE.
FIRST I TRIED ATTACKING YOU, THEN...
DON'T WORRY ABOUT IT, CAP... YOU SEEM BETTER NOW.
WHATEVER WAS CONTROLLING YOU SEEMS TO BE GONE.
WHAT'S IMPORTANT IS THIS EARTH IS SAFE FOR THE MOMENT--THE ANTIMATTER CLOUD VANISHED WHEN WE WERE SHIFTED INTO THE NETHERVERSE.*
* SEE LAST ISSUE. --MARV
UNCLE MARVEL AND I ARE FINE. SO'S JUNIOR.
CAPTAIN MARVEL! MARY MARVEL! CAPTAIN MARVEL JUNIOR! NOW UNCLE MARVEL?
IF KID MARVEL, BABY MARVEL, AND FETUS MARVEL SHOW UP, I QUIT!
MY FRIENDS, LISTEN TO ME. WE MUST TALK.
HARBINGER?
WANTED:
I'M JUST LYLA NOW... HARBINGER IS GONE.
CAPTAIN MARVEL! UNDERSTAND THIS... A MAN NAMED PSYCHO-PIRATE CONTROLLED YOUR EMOTIONS, AS HE DID THE EMOTIONS OF HEROES ON OTHER EARTHS...
BUT HIS INFLUENCE IS GONE NOW... AND WE NEED YOU.
WELL, YOU CAN COUNT ON THE WHOLE MARVEL FAMILY!
WE WILL NEED THEM, BUT FOR NOW I WANT ONLY ONE REPRESENTATIVE OF EACH EARTH.
SO MUCH HAS TO BE EXPLAINED.
EARTH-2...
SOME OF THE ALL-STAR SQUADRON ARE THERE... MAYBE THIS IS THE TIME FOR THE NEW WILDCAT TO INTRODUCE HERSELF.
I AM UN POCO ASUSTADA, SCARED THEY WON'T ACCEPT ME.
3

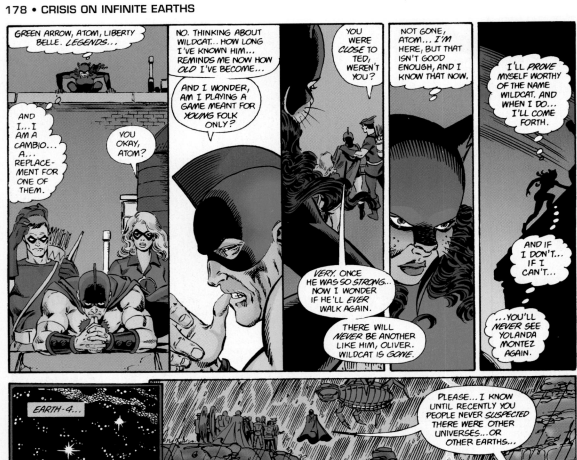

GREEN ARROW, ATOM, LIBERTY BELLE. *LEGENDS...*

AND I...I AM A *CAMBIO*... A...*REPLACEMENT* FOR ONE OF THEM.

YOU OKAY, ATOM?

NO. THINKING ABOUT *WILDCAT*... HOW LONG I'VE KNOWN HIM... REMINDS ME NOW HOW *OLD* I'VE BECOME...

AND I WONDER, AM I PLAYING A GAME MEANT FOR *YOUNG* FOLK ONLY?

YOU WERE *CLOSE* TO TED, WEREN'T YOU?

VERY. ONCE HE WAS SO *STRONG*... NOW I WONDER IF HE'LL *EVER* WALK AGAIN.

THERE WILL *NEVER* BE ANOTHER LIKE HIM, OLIVER. WILDCAT IS *GONE*.

NOT GONE, ATOM... *I'M* HERE, BUT THAT ISN'T GOOD ENOUGH, AND I KNOW THAT NOW.

I'LL *PROVE* MYSELF *WORTHY* OF THE NAME WILDCAT. AND WHEN I DO... I'LL COME FORTH.

AND IF I DON'T... IF I *CAN'T*...

...YOU'LL *NEVER* SEE YOLANDA MONTEZ AGAIN.

EARTH-4...

PLEASE... I KNOW UNTIL RECENTLY YOU PEOPLE NEVER *SUSPECTED* THERE WERE OTHER UNIVERSES...OR OTHER EARTHS...

...BUT THERE ARE ...AND THEIR FATE AND YOURS ARE CONNECTED BY SO MANY FRAGILE *THREADS*.

YOU HAVE MET *SOME* OF THE HEROES FROM THE OTHER EARTHS...

BLUE BEETLE TOLD YOU HE WAS WITH US... AND NOW THAT YOU ARE *FREE* OF THE *PSYCHO-PIRATE'S* INFLUENCE...

...YOU MUST *BELIEVE* I AM SPEAK-ING THE *TRUTH*.

CAN THE TELETHON, PAL-- YOU GOT OUR DONATION.

I'LL *JOIN* YOUR GABFEST.

THE FINAL FATE OF FIVE UNIVERSES MAY REST WITH WHAT WE DECIDE.

4

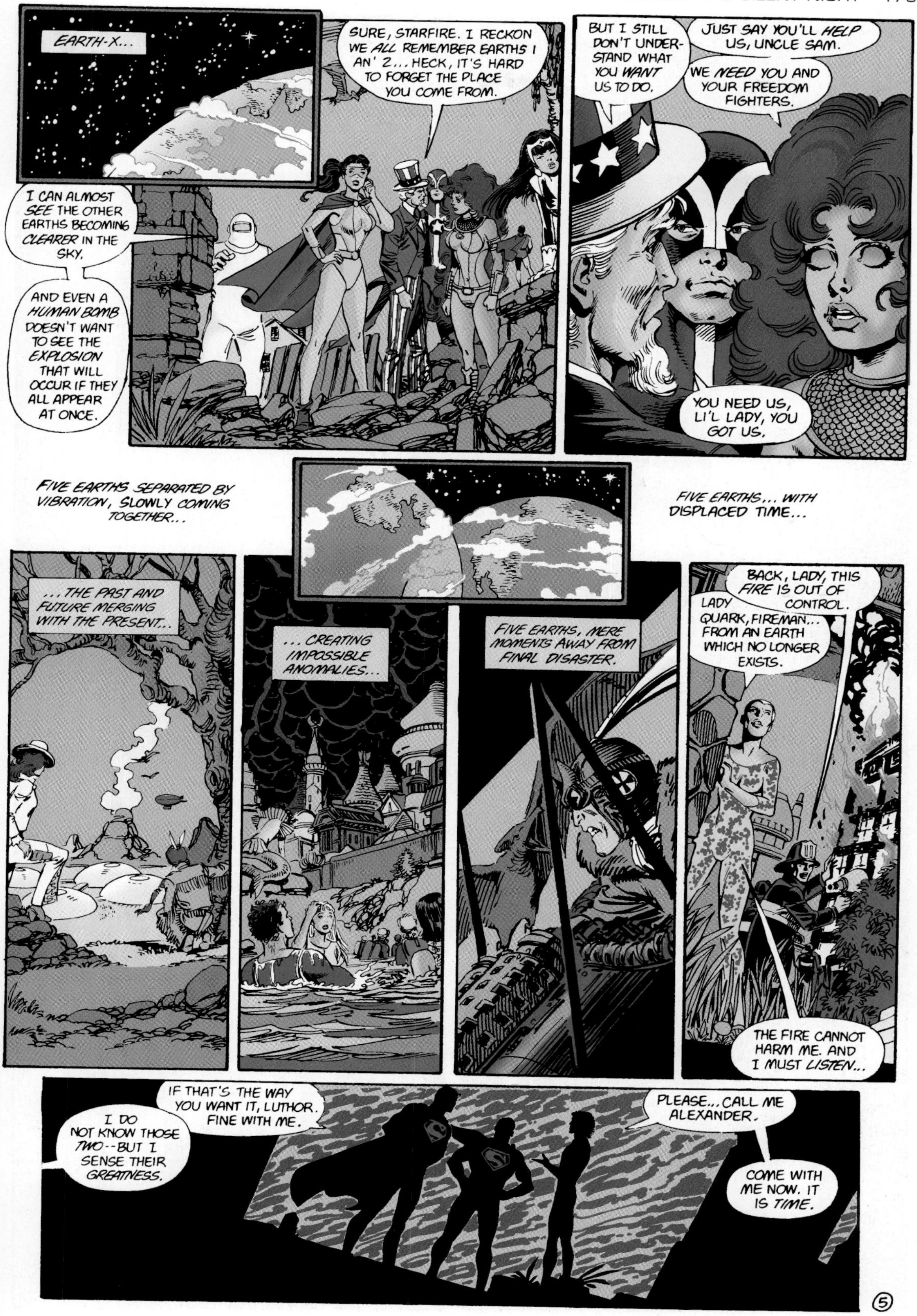
EARTH-X...
SURE, STARFIRE. I RECKON WE ALL REMEMBER EARTHS 1 AN' 2... HECK, IT'S HARD TO FORGET THE PLACE YOU COME FROM.
I CAN ALMOST SEE THE OTHER EARTHS BECOMING CLEARER IN THE SKY.
AND EVEN A HUMAN BOMB DOESN'T WANT TO SEE THE EXPLOSION THAT WILL OCCUR IF THEY ALL APPEAR AT ONCE.
BUT I STILL DON'T UNDERSTAND WHAT YOU WANT US TO DO.
JUST SAY YOU'LL HELP US, UNCLE SAM.
WE NEED YOU AND YOUR FREEDOM FIGHTERS.
YOU NEED US, LI'L LADY, YOU GOT US.
FIVE EARTHS SEPARATED BY VIBRATION, SLOWLY COMING TOGETHER...
FIVE EARTHS... WITH DISPLACED TIME...
...THE PAST AND FUTURE MERGING WITH THE PRESENT...
...CREATING IMPOSSIBLE ANOMALIES...
FIVE EARTHS, MERE MOMENTS AWAY FROM FINAL DISASTER.
BACK, LADY, THIS FIRE IS OUT OF CONTROL.
LADY QUARK, FIREMAN... FROM AN EARTH WHICH NO LONGER EXISTS.
THE FIRE CANNOT HARM ME. AND I MUST LISTEN...
I DO NOT KNOW THOSE TWO--BUT I SENSE THEIR GREATNESS.
IF THAT'S THE WAY YOU WANT IT, LUTHOR. FINE WITH ME.
PLEASE... CALL ME ALEXANDER.
COME WITH ME NOW. IT IS TIME.

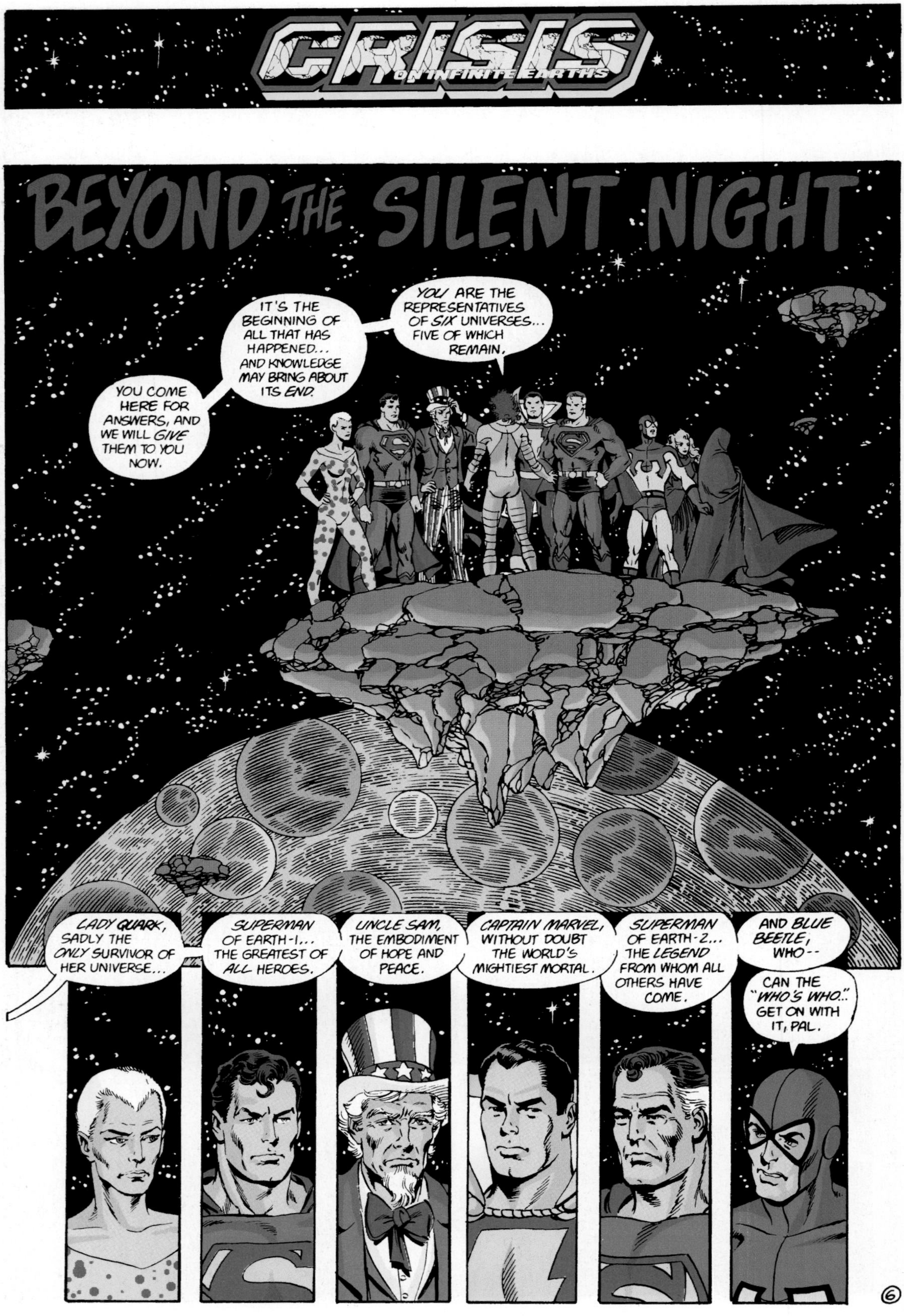
CRISIS ON INFINITE EARTHS
BEYOND THE SILENT NIGHT
YOU COME HERE FOR ANSWERS, AND WE WILL GIVE THEM TO YOU NOW.
IT'S THE BEGINNING OF ALL THAT HAS HAPPENED... AND KNOWLEDGE MAY BRING ABOUT ITS END.
YOU ARE THE REPRESENTATIVES OF SIX UNIVERSES... FIVE OF WHICH REMAIN.
LADY QUARK, SADLY THE ONLY SURVIVOR OF HER UNIVERSE...
SUPERMAN OF EARTH-1... THE GREATEST OF ALL HEROES.
UNCLE SAM, THE EMBODIMENT OF HOPE AND PEACE.
CAPTAIN MARVEL, WITHOUT DOUBT THE WORLD'S MIGHTIEST MORTAL.
SUPERMAN OF EARTH-2... THE LEGEND FROM WHOM ALL OTHERS HAVE COME.
AND BLUE BEETLE, WHO--
CAN THE "WHO'S WHO.." GET ON WITH IT, PAL.
6

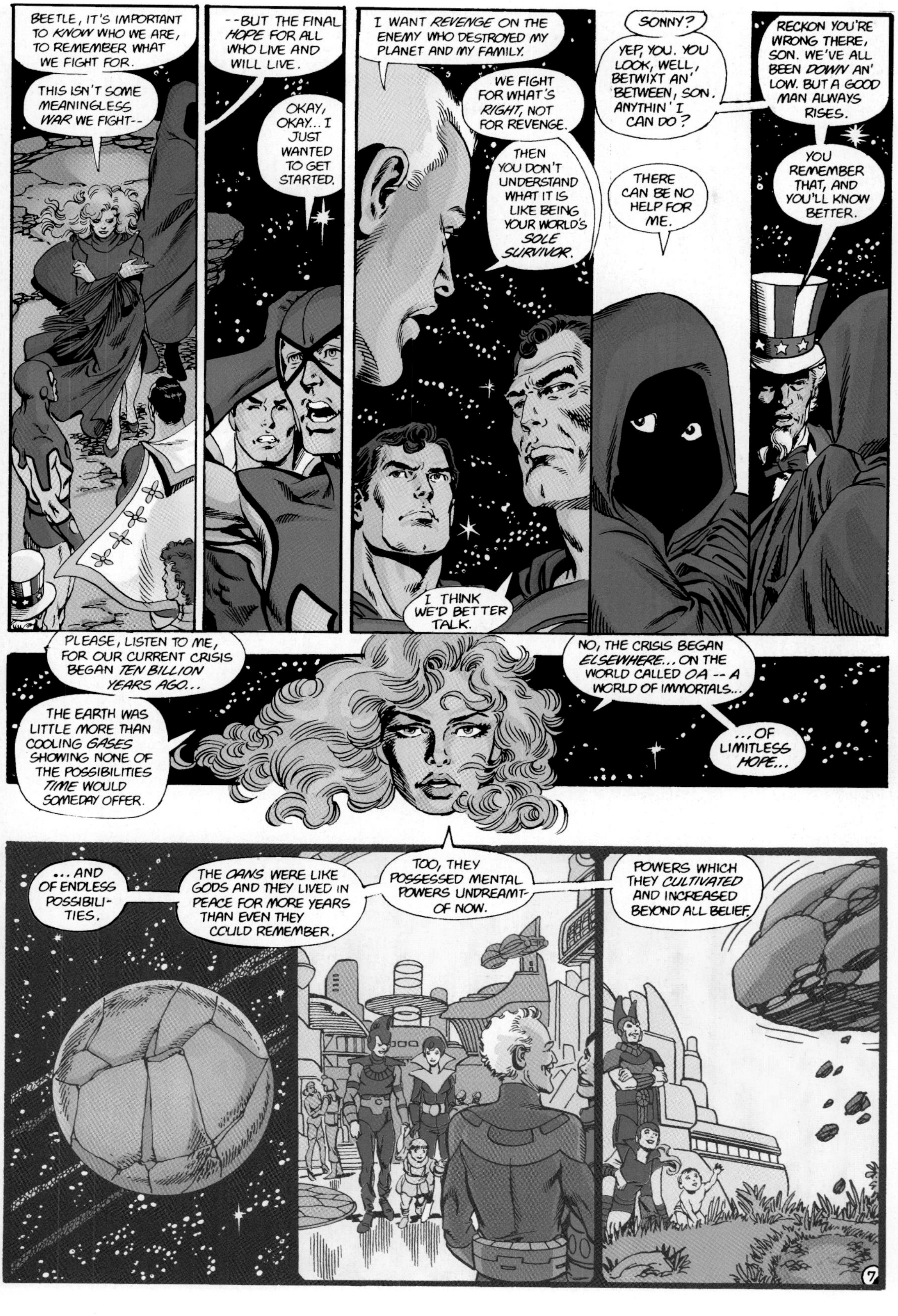
BEETLE, IT'S IMPORTANT TO KNOW WHO WE ARE, TO REMEMBER WHAT WE FIGHT FOR.
THIS ISN'T SOME MEANINGLESS WAR WE FIGHT--
--BUT THE FINAL HOPE FOR ALL WHO LIVE AND WILL LIVE.
OKAY, OKAY... I JUST WANTED TO GET STARTED.
I WANT REVENGE ON THE ENEMY WHO DESTROYED MY PLANET AND MY FAMILY.
WE FIGHT FOR WHAT'S RIGHT, NOT FOR REVENGE.
THEN YOU DON'T UNDERSTAND WHAT IT IS LIKE BEING YOUR WORLD'S SOLE SURVIVOR.
I THINK WE'D BETTER TALK.
SONNY?
YEP, YOU. YOU LOOK, WELL, BETWIXT AN' BETWEEN, SON. ANYTHIN' I CAN DO?
THERE CAN BE NO HELP FOR ME.
RECKON YOU'RE WRONG THERE, SON. WE'VE ALL BEEN DOWN AN' LOW. BUT A GOOD MAN ALWAYS RISES.
YOU REMEMBER THAT, AND YOU'LL KNOW BETTER.
PLEASE, LISTEN TO ME, FOR OUR CURRENT CRISIS BEGAN TEN BILLION YEARS AGO...
THE EARTH WAS LITTLE MORE THAN COOLING GASES SHOWING NONE OF THE POSSIBILITIES TIME WOULD SOMEDAY OFFER.
NO, THE CRISIS BEGAN ELSEWHERE... ON THE WORLD CALLED OA -- A WORLD OF IMMORTALS...
..., OF LIMITLESS HOPE...
... AND OF ENDLESS POSSIBILITIES.
THE OANS WERE LIKE GODS AND THEY LIVED IN PEACE FOR MORE YEARS THAN EVEN THEY COULD REMEMBER.
TOO, THEY POSSESSED MENTAL POWERS UNDREAMT-OF NOW.
POWERS WHICH THEY CULTIVATED AND INCREASED BEYOND ALL BELIEF.
7

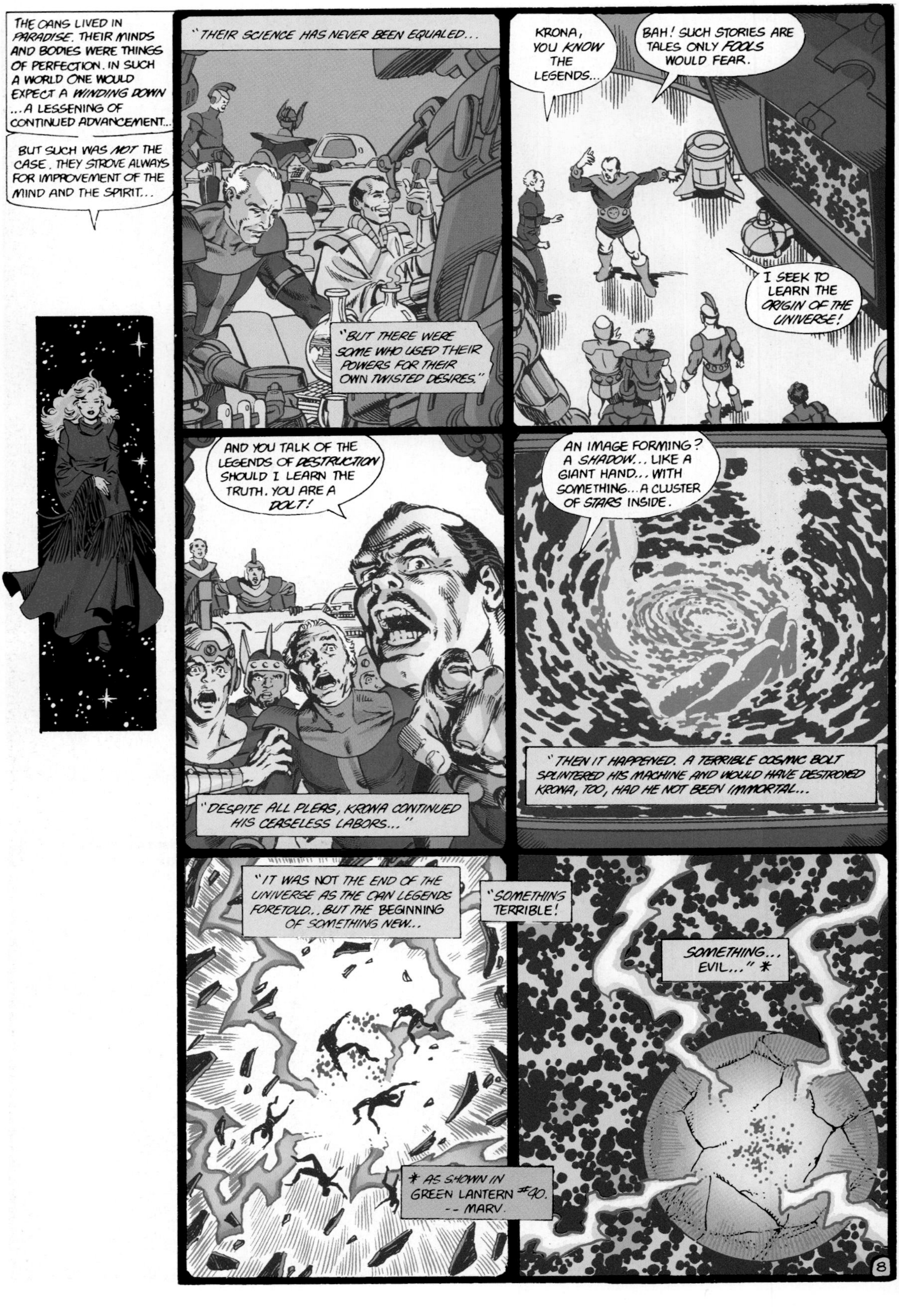
THE OANS LIVED IN PARADISE. THEIR MINDS AND BODIES WERE THINGS OF PERFECTION. IN SUCH A WORLD ONE WOULD EXPECT A WINDING DOWN ...A LESSENING OF CONTINUED ADVANCEMENT...
BUT SUCH WAS NOT THE CASE. THEY STROVE ALWAYS FOR IMPROVEMENT OF THE MIND AND THE SPIRIT...
"THEIR SCIENCE HAS NEVER BEEN EQUALED...
"BUT THERE WERE SOME WHO USED THEIR POWERS FOR THEIR OWN TWISTED DESIRES."
KRONA, YOU KNOW THE LEGENDS...
BAH! SUCH STORIES ARE TALES ONLY FOOLS WOULD FEAR.
I SEEK TO LEARN THE ORIGIN OF THE UNIVERSE!
AND YOU TALK OF THE LEGENDS OF DESTRUCTION SHOULD I LEARN THE TRUTH. YOU ARE A DOLT!
"DESPITE ALL PLEAS, KRONA CONTINUED HIS CEASELESS LABORS..."
AN IMAGE FORMING? A SHADOW... LIKE A GIANT HAND... WITH SOMETHING... A CLUSTER OF STARS INSIDE.
"THEN IT HAPPENED. A TERRIBLE COSMIC BOLT SPLINTERED HIS MACHINE AND WOULD HAVE DESTROYED KRONA, TOO, HAD HE NOT BEEN IMMORTAL...
"IT WAS NOT THE END OF THE UNIVERSE AS THE OAN LEGENDS FORETOLD... BUT THE BEGINNING OF SOMETHING NEW...
"SOMETHING TERRIBLE!
SOMETHING... EVIL..." *
* AS SHOWN IN GREEN LANTERN #40. -- MARV.
8

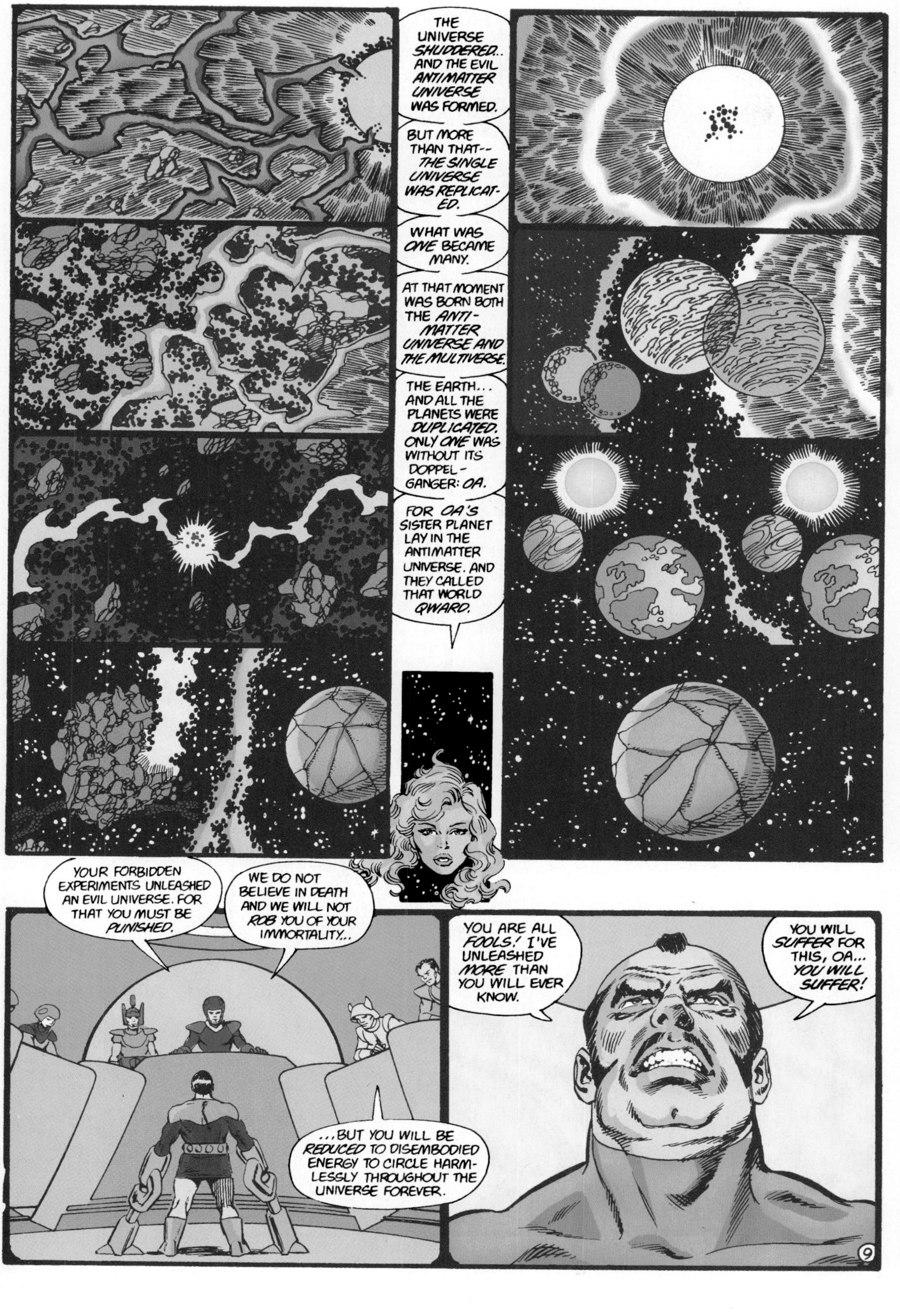
THE UNIVERSE SHUDDERED.. AND THE EVIL ANTIMATTER UNIVERSE WAS FORMED.
BUT MORE THAN THAT-- THE SINGLE UNIVERSE WAS REPLICATED.
WHAT WAS ONE BECAME MANY.
AT THAT MOMENT WAS BORN BOTH THE ANTI-MATTER UNIVERSE AND THE MULTIVERSE.
THE EARTH... AND ALL THE PLANETS WERE DUPLICATED. ONLY ONE WAS WITHOUT ITS DOPPEL-GANGER: OA.
FOR OA'S SISTER PLANET LAY IN THE ANTIMATTER UNIVERSE. AND THEY CALLED THAT WORLD QWARD.
YOUR FORBIDDEN EXPERIMENTS UNLEASHED AN EVIL UNIVERSE. FOR THAT YOU MUST BE PUNISHED.
WE DO NOT BELIEVE IN DEATH AND WE WILL NOT ROB YOU OF YOUR IMMORTALITY...
...BUT YOU WILL BE REDUCED TO DISEMBODIED ENERGY TO CIRCLE HARMLESSLY THROUGHOUT THE UNIVERSE FOREVER.
YOU ARE ALL FOOLS! I'VE UNLEASHED MORE THAN YOU WILL EVER KNOW.
YOU WILL SUFFER FOR THIS, OA... YOU WILL SUFFER!
9

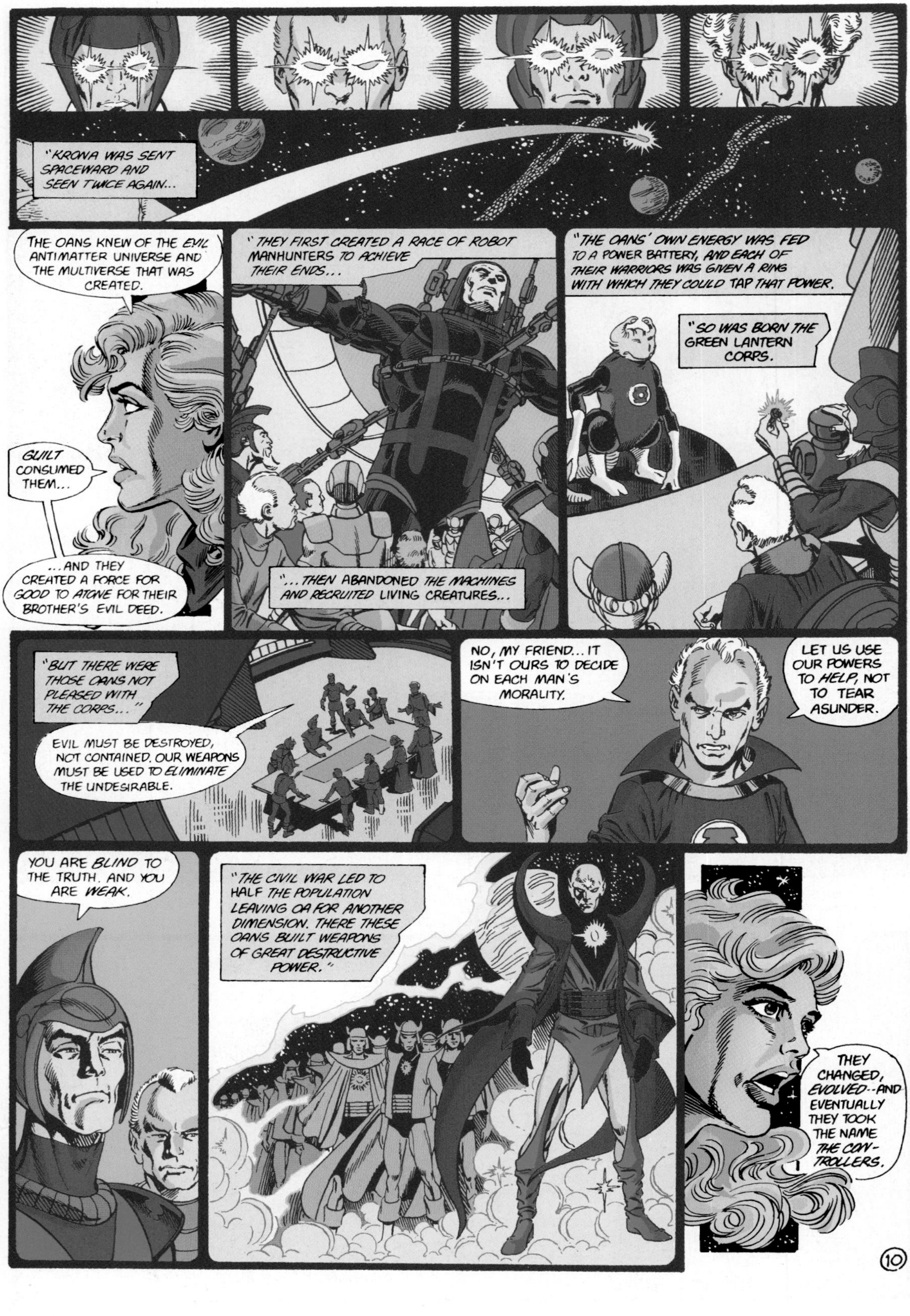
"KRONA WAS SENT SPACEWARD AND SEEN TWICE AGAIN...
THE OANS KNEW OF THE EVIL ANTIMATTER UNIVERSE AND THE MULTIVERSE THAT WAS CREATED.
GUILT CONSUMED THEM...
...AND THEY CREATED A FORCE FOR GOOD TO ATONE FOR THEIR BROTHER'S EVIL DEED.
"THEY FIRST CREATED A RACE OF ROBOT MANHUNTERS TO ACHIEVE THEIR ENDS...
"...THEN ABANDONED THE MACHINES AND RECRUITED LIVING CREATURES...
"THE OANS' OWN ENERGY WAS FED TO A POWER BATTERY, AND EACH OF THEIR WARRIORS WAS GIVEN A RING WITH WHICH THEY COULD TAP THAT POWER.
"SO WAS BORN THE GREEN LANTERN CORPS.
"BUT THERE WERE THOSE OANS NOT PLEASED WITH THE CORPS..."
EVIL MUST BE DESTROYED, NOT CONTAINED. OUR WEAPONS MUST BE USED TO ELIMINATE THE UNDESIRABLE.
NO, MY FRIEND... IT ISN'T OURS TO DECIDE ON EACH MAN'S MORALITY.
LET US USE OUR POWERS TO HELP, NOT TO TEAR ASUNDER.
YOU ARE BLIND TO THE TRUTH. AND YOU ARE WEAK.
"THE CIVIL WAR LED TO HALF THE POPULATION LEAVING OA FOR ANOTHER DIMENSION. THERE THESE OANS BUILT WEAPONS OF GREAT DESTRUCTIVE POWER."
THEY CHANGED, EVOLVED--AND EVENTUALLY THEY TOOK THE NAME THE CONTROLLERS.
10

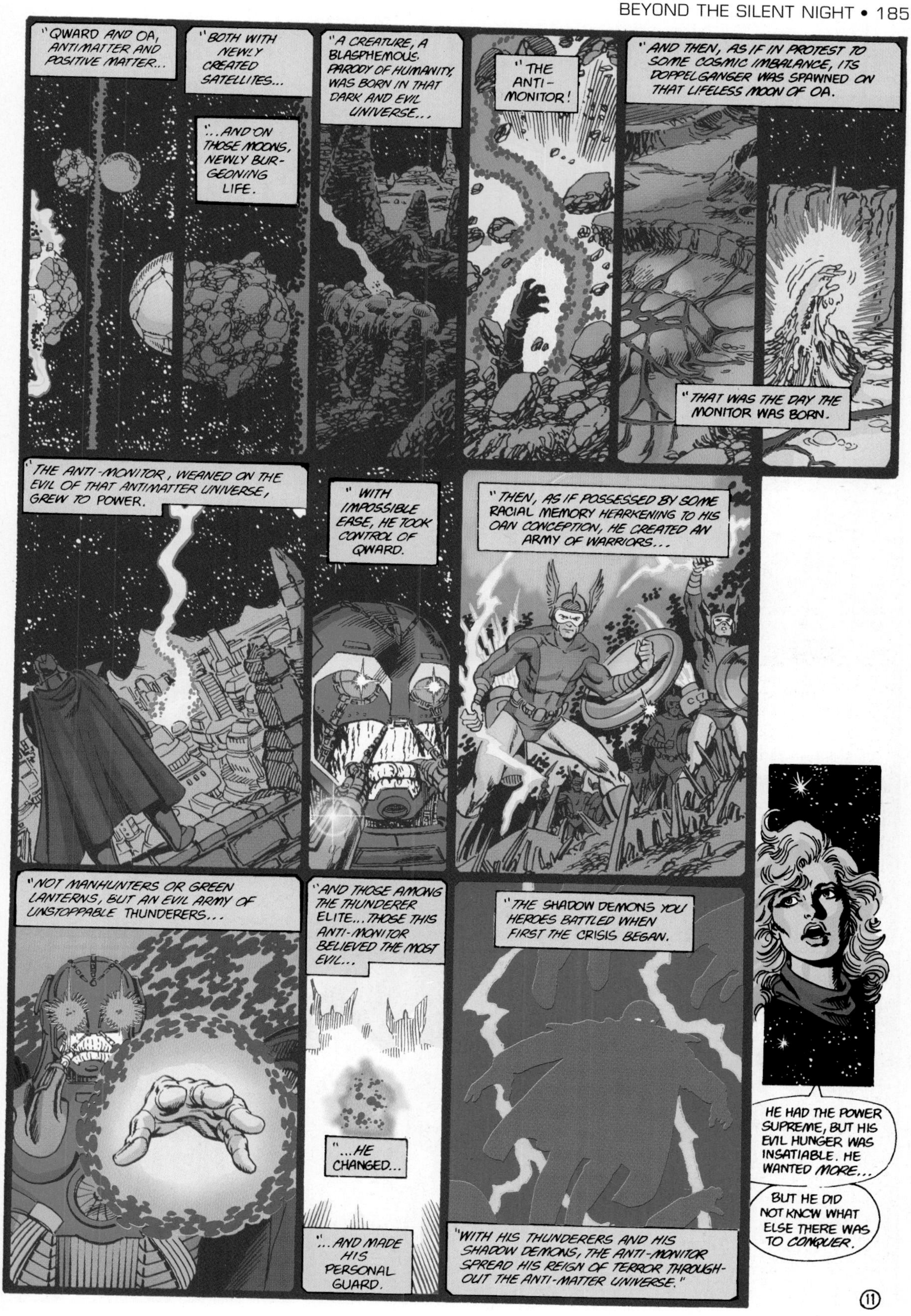
"QWARD AND OA, ANTIMATTER AND POSITIVE MATTER...
"BOTH WITH NEWLY CREATED SATELLITES...
"...AND ON THOSE MOONS, NEWLY BUR-GEONING LIFE.
"A CREATURE, A BLASPHEMOUS PARODY OF HUMANITY, WAS BORN IN THAT DARK AND EVIL UNIVERSE...
"THE ANTI-MONITOR!
"AND THEN, AS IF IN PROTEST TO SOME COSMIC IMBALANCE, ITS DOPPELGANGER WAS SPAWNED ON THAT LIFELESS MOON OF OA.
"THAT WAS THE DAY THE MONITOR WAS BORN.
"THE ANTI-MONITOR, WEANED ON THE EVIL OF THAT ANTIMATTER UNIVERSE, GREW TO POWER.
"WITH IMPOSSIBLE EASE, HE TOOK CONTROL OF QWARD.
"THEN, AS IF POSSESSED BY SOME RACIAL MEMORY HEARKENING TO HIS OAN CONCEPTION, HE CREATED AN ARMY OF WARRIORS...
"NOT MANHUNTERS OR GREEN LANTERNS, BUT AN EVIL ARMY OF UNSTOPPABLE THUNDERERS...
"AND THOSE AMONG THE THUNDERER ELITE...THOSE THIS ANTI-MONITOR BELIEVED THE MOST EVIL...
"...HE CHANGED...
"...AND MADE HIS PERSONAL GUARD.
"THE SHADOW DEMONS YOU HEROES BATTLED WHEN FIRST THE CRISIS BEGAN.
"WITH HIS THUNDERERS AND HIS SHADOW DEMONS, THE ANTI-MONITOR SPREAD HIS REIGN OF TERROR THROUGH-OUT THE ANTI-MATTER UNIVERSE."
HE HAD THE POWER SUPREME, BUT HIS EVIL HUNGER WAS INSATIABLE. HE WANTED MORE...
BUT HE DID NOT KNOW WHAT ELSE THERE WAS TO CONQUER.
11

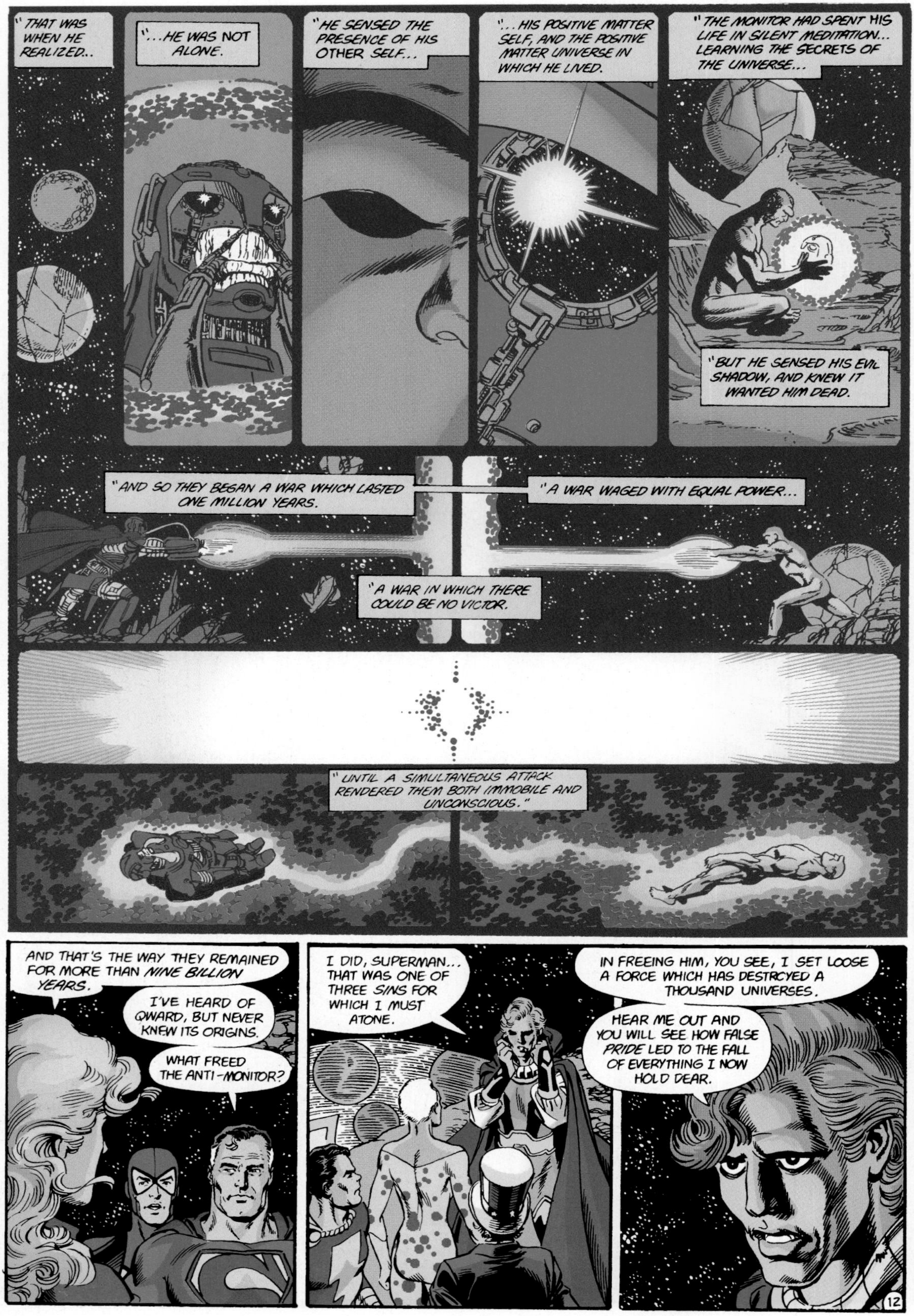
"THAT WAS WHEN HE REALIZED...
"...HE WAS NOT ALONE.
"HE SENSED THE PRESENCE OF HIS OTHER SELF...
"...HIS POSITIVE MATTER SELF, AND THE POSITIVE MATTER UNIVERSE IN WHICH HE LIVED.
"THE MONITOR HAD SPENT HIS LIFE IN SILENT MEDITATION... LEARNING THE SECRETS OF THE UNIVERSE...
"BUT HE SENSED HIS EVIL SHADOW, AND KNEW IT WANTED HIM DEAD.
"AND SO THEY BEGAN A WAR WHICH LASTED ONE MILLION YEARS.
"A WAR WAGED WITH EQUAL POWER...
"A WAR IN WHICH THERE COULD BE NO VICTOR.
"UNTIL A SIMULTANEOUS ATTACK RENDERED THEM BOTH IMMOBILE AND UNCONSCIOUS."
AND THAT'S THE WAY THEY REMAINED FOR MORE THAN NINE BILLION YEARS.
I'VE HEARD OF QWARD, BUT NEVER KNEW ITS ORIGINS.
WHAT FREED THE ANTI-MONITOR?
I DID, SUPERMAN... THAT WAS ONE OF THREE SINS FOR WHICH I MUST ATONE.
IN FREEING HIM, YOU SEE, I SET LOOSE A FORCE WHICH HAS DESTROYED A THOUSAND UNIVERSES.
HEAR ME OUT AND YOU WILL SEE HOW FALSE PRIDE LED TO THE FALL OF EVERYTHING I NOW HOLD DEAR.
12

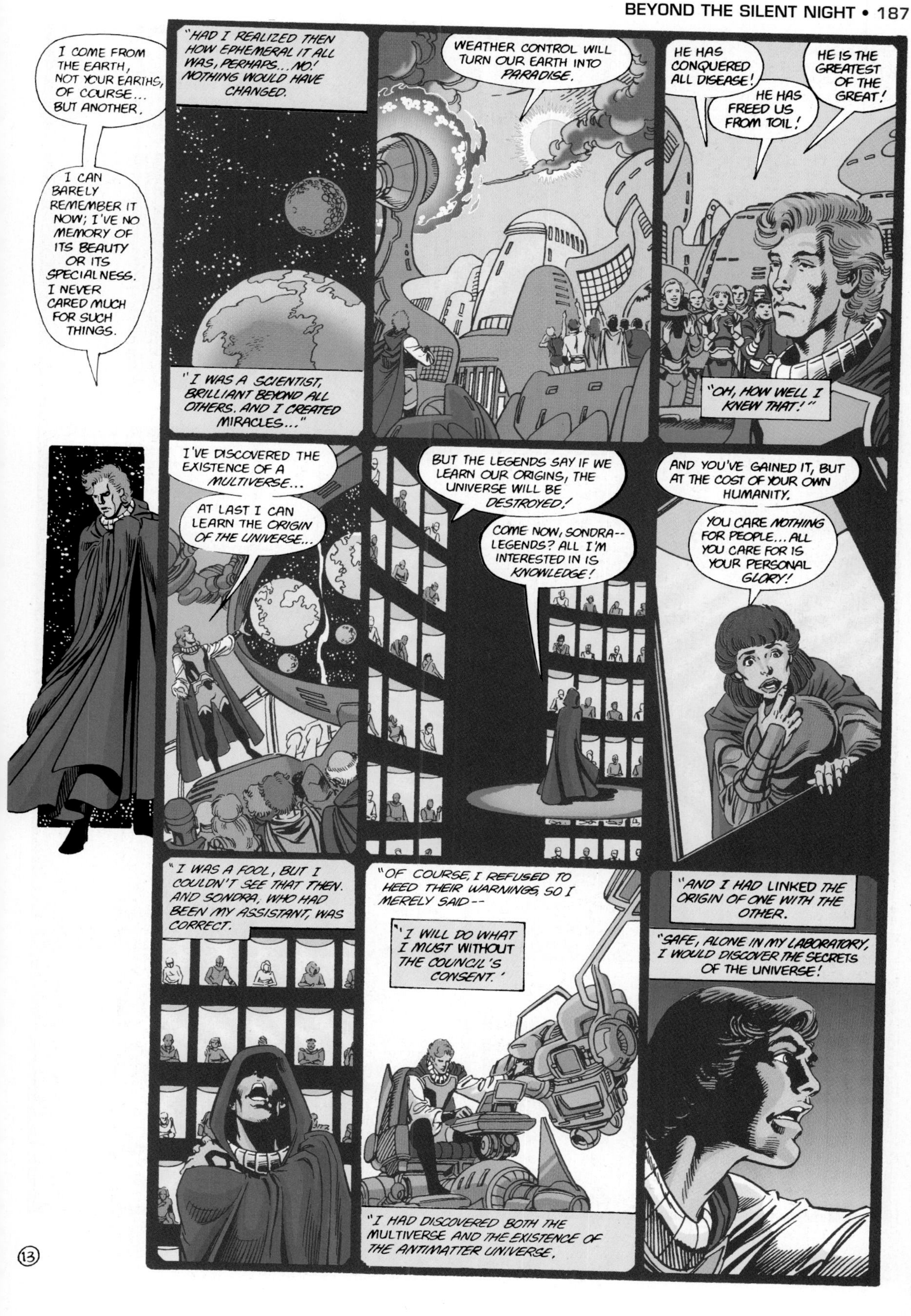
I COME FROM THE EARTH, NOT YOUR EARTHS, OF COURSE... BUT ANOTHER.
I CAN BARELY REMEMBER IT NOW; I'VE NO MEMORY OF ITS BEAUTY OR ITS SPECIALNESS. I NEVER CARED MUCH FOR SUCH THINGS.
"HAD I REALIZED THEN HOW EPHEMERAL IT ALL WAS, PERHAPS... NO! NOTHING WOULD HAVE CHANGED.
"I WAS A SCIENTIST, BRILLIANT BEYOND ALL OTHERS. AND I CREATED MIRACLES..."
WEATHER CONTROL WILL TURN OUR EARTH INTO PARADISE.
HE HAS CONQUERED ALL DISEASE!
HE HAS FREED US FROM TOIL!
HE IS THE GREATEST OF THE GREAT!
"OH, HOW WELL I KNEW THAT!"
I'VE DISCOVERED THE EXISTENCE OF A MULTIVERSE...
AT LAST I CAN LEARN THE ORIGIN OF THE UNIVERSE...
BUT THE LEGENDS SAY IF WE LEARN OUR ORIGINS, THE UNIVERSE WILL BE DESTROYED!
COME NOW, SONDRA-- LEGENDS? ALL I'M INTERESTED IN IS KNOWLEDGE!
AND YOU'VE GAINED IT, BUT AT THE COST OF YOUR OWN HUMANITY.
YOU CARE NOTHING FOR PEOPLE... ALL YOU CARE FOR IS YOUR PERSONAL GLORY!
"I WAS A FOOL, BUT I COULDN'T SEE THAT THEN. AND SONDRA, WHO HAD BEEN MY ASSISTANT, WAS CORRECT.
"OF COURSE, I REFUSED TO HEED THEIR WARNINGS, SO I MERELY SAID--
"'I WILL DO WHAT I MUST WITHOUT THE COUNCIL'S CONSENT.'
"I HAD DISCOVERED BOTH THE MULTIVERSE AND THE EXISTENCE OF THE ANTIMATTER UNIVERSE,
"AND I HAD LINKED THE ORIGIN OF ONE WITH THE OTHER.
"SAFE, ALONE IN MY LABORATORY, I WOULD DISCOVER THE SECRETS OF THE UNIVERSE!
13

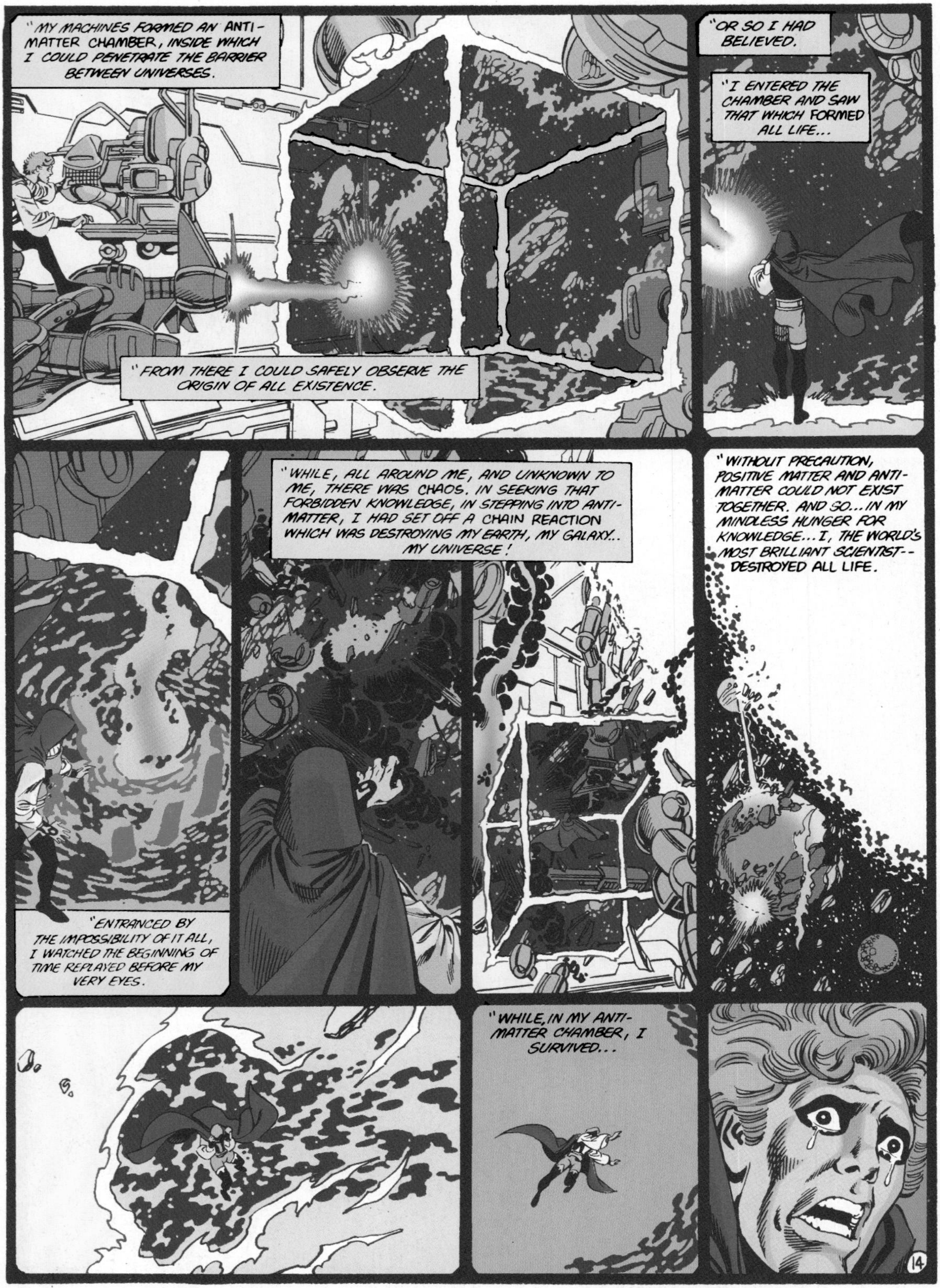
"MY MACHINES FORMED AN ANTI-MATTER CHAMBER, INSIDE WHICH I COULD PENETRATE THE BARRIER BETWEEN UNIVERSES.
"FROM THERE I COULD SAFELY OBSERVE THE ORIGIN OF ALL EXISTENCE.
"OR SO I HAD BELIEVED.
"I ENTERED THE CHAMBER AND SAW THAT WHICH FORMED ALL LIFE...
"ENTRANCED BY THE IMPOSSIBILITY OF IT ALL, I WATCHED THE BEGINNING OF TIME REPLAYED BEFORE MY VERY EYES.
"WHILE, ALL AROUND ME, AND UNKNOWN TO ME, THERE WAS CHAOS. IN SEEKING THAT FORBIDDEN KNOWLEDGE, IN STEPPING INTO ANTI-MATTER, I HAD SET OFF A CHAIN REACTION WHICH WAS DESTROYING MY EARTH, MY GALAXY... MY UNIVERSE!
"WITHOUT PRECAUTION, POSITIVE MATTER AND ANTI-MATTER COULD NOT EXIST TOGETHER. AND SO... IN MY MINDLESS HUNGER FOR KNOWLEDGE... I, THE WORLD'S MOST BRILLIANT SCIENTIST-- DESTROYED ALL LIFE.
"WHILE, IN MY ANTI-MATTER CHAMBER, I SURVIVED...
14

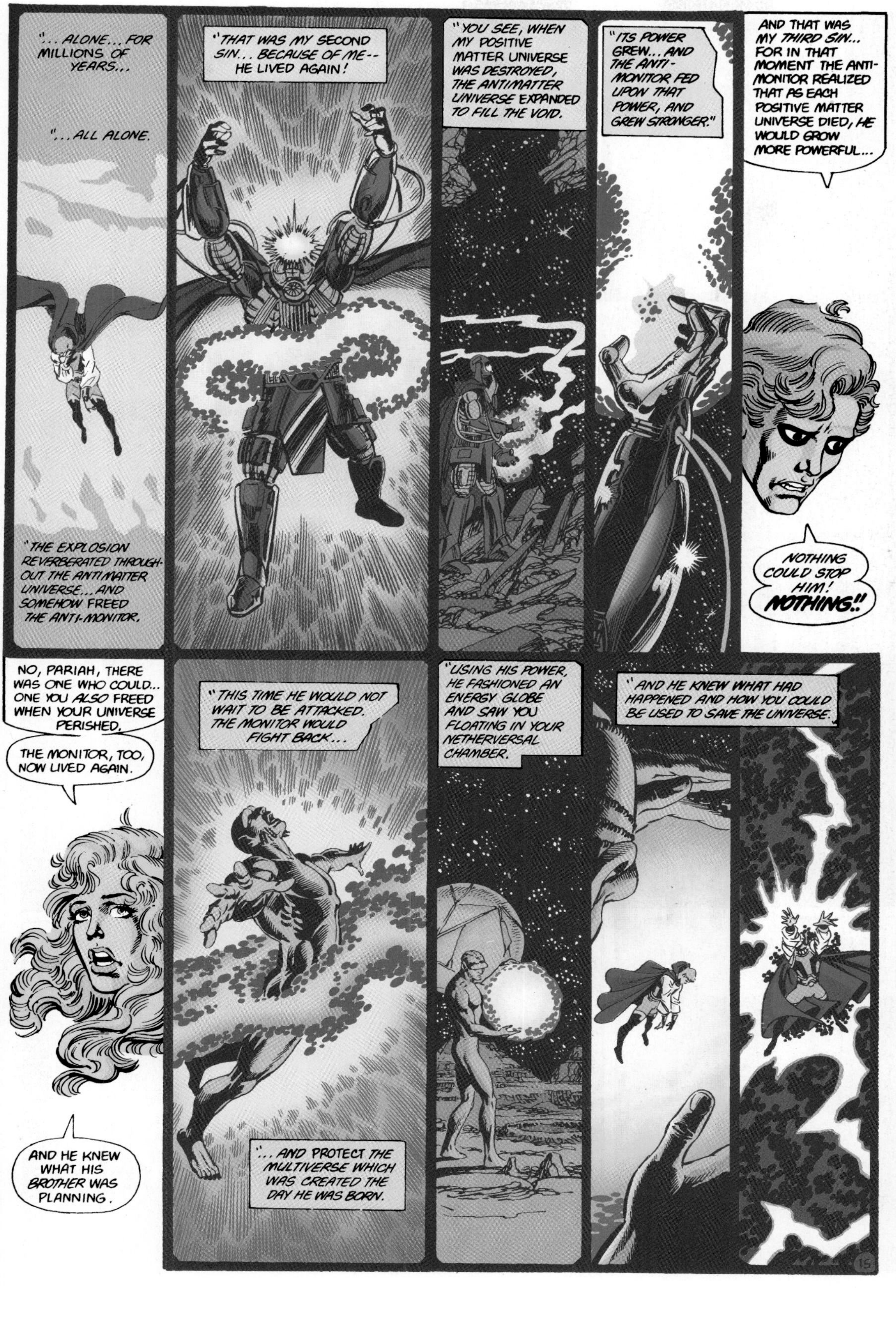
"... ALONE... FOR MILLIONS OF YEARS...
"... ALL ALONE.
"THE EXPLOSION REVERBERATED THROUGH-OUT THE ANTIMATTER UNIVERSE... AND SOMEHOW FREED THE ANTI-MONITOR.
"THAT WAS MY SECOND SIN... BECAUSE OF ME-- HE LIVED AGAIN!
"YOU SEE, WHEN MY POSITIVE MATTER UNIVERSE WAS DESTROYED, THE ANTIMATTER UNIVERSE EXPANDED TO FILL THE VOID.
"ITS POWER GREW... AND THE ANTI-MONITOR FED UPON THAT POWER, AND GREW STRONGER."
AND THAT WAS MY THIRD SIN... FOR IN THAT MOMENT THE ANTI-MONITOR REALIZED THAT AS EACH POSITIVE MATTER UNIVERSE DIED, HE WOULD GROW MORE POWERFUL...
NOTHING COULD STOP HIM! NOTHING!!
NO, PARIAH, THERE WAS ONE WHO COULD... ONE YOU ALSO FREED WHEN YOUR UNIVERSE PERISHED.
THE MONITOR, TOO, NOW LIVED AGAIN.
AND HE KNEW WHAT HIS BROTHER WAS PLANNING.
"THIS TIME HE WOULD NOT WAIT TO BE ATTACKED. THE MONITOR WOULD FIGHT BACK...
"... AND PROTECT THE MULTIVERSE WHICH WAS CREATED THE DAY HE WAS BORN.
"USING HIS POWER, HE FASHIONED AN ENERGY GLOBE AND SAW YOU FLOATING IN YOUR NETHERVERSAL CHAMBER.
"AND HE KNEW WHAT HAD HAPPENED AND HOW YOU COULD BE USED TO SAVE THE UNIVERSE.
15

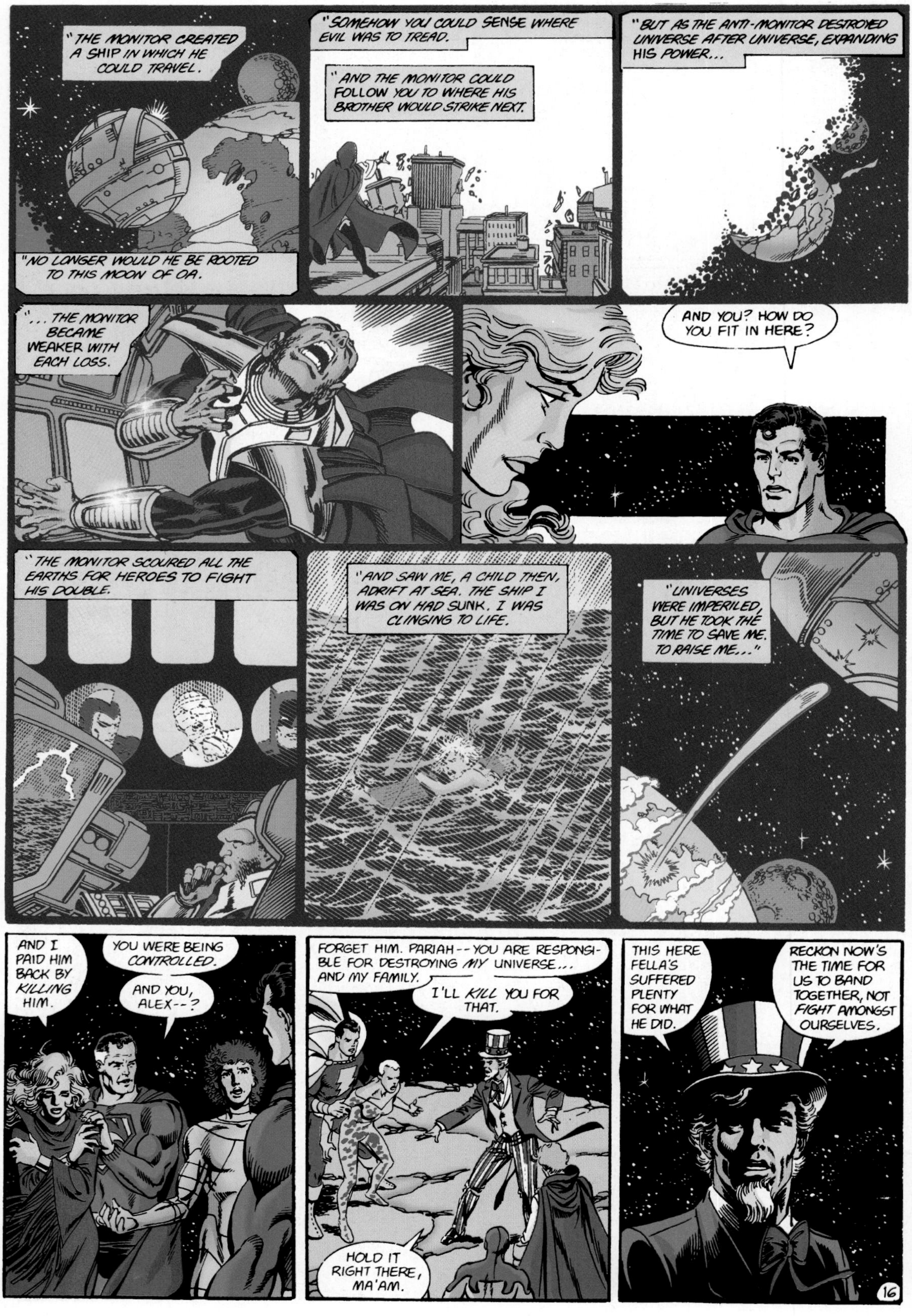
"THE MONITOR CREATED A SHIP IN WHICH HE COULD TRAVEL.
"NO LONGER WOULD HE BE ROOTED TO THIS MOON OF OA.
"SOMEHOW YOU COULD SENSE WHERE EVIL WAS TO TREAD.
"AND THE MONITOR COULD FOLLOW YOU TO WHERE HIS BROTHER WOULD STRIKE NEXT.
"BUT AS THE ANTI-MONITOR DESTROYED UNIVERSE AFTER UNIVERSE, EXPANDING HIS POWER...
"...THE MONITOR BECAME WEAKER WITH EACH LOSS.
AND YOU? HOW DO YOU FIT IN HERE?
"THE MONITOR SCOURED ALL THE EARTHS FOR HEROES TO FIGHT HIS DOUBLE.
"AND SAW ME, A CHILD THEN, ADRIFT AT SEA. THE SHIP I WAS ON HAD SUNK. I WAS CLINGING TO LIFE.
"UNIVERSES WERE IMPERILED, BUT HE TOOK THE TIME TO SAVE ME. TO RAISE ME..."
AND I PAID HIM BACK BY KILLING HIM.
YOU WERE BEING CONTROLLED.
AND YOU, ALEX--?
FORGET HIM. PARIAH--YOU ARE RESPONSIBLE FOR DESTROYING MY UNIVERSE... AND MY FAMILY.
I'LL KILL YOU FOR THAT.
HOLD IT RIGHT THERE, MA'AM.
THIS HERE FELLA'S SUFFERED PLENTY FOR WHAT HE DID.
RECKON NOW'S THE TIME FOR US TO BAND TOGETHER, NOT FIGHT AMONGST OURSELVES.
16

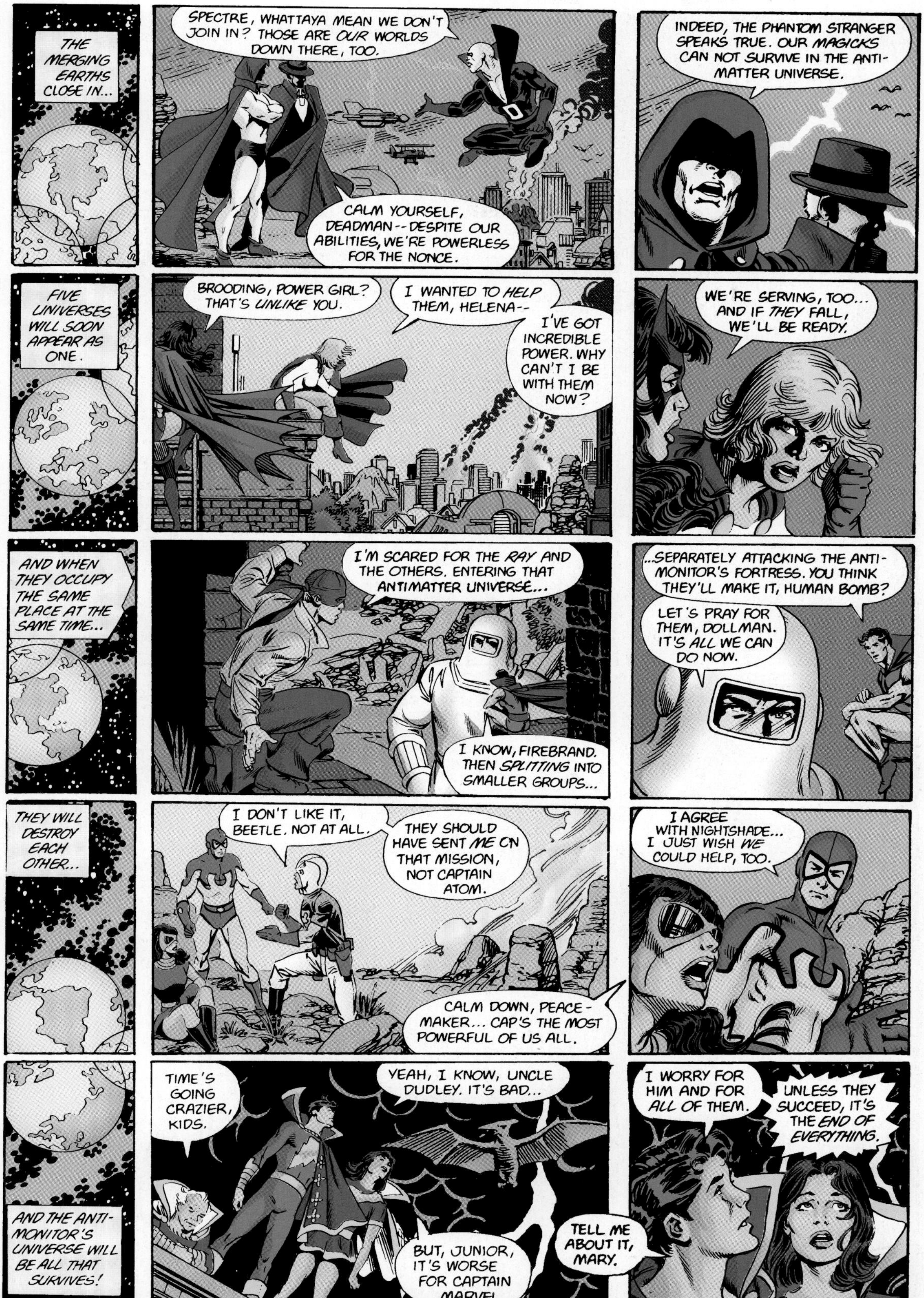
THE MERGING EARTHS CLOSE IN...
SPECTRE, WHATTAYA MEAN WE DON'T JOIN IN? THOSE ARE OUR WORLDS DOWN THERE, TOO.
CALM YOURSELF, DEADMAN--DESPITE OUR ABILITIES, WE'RE POWERLESS FOR THE NONCE.
INDEED, THE PHANTOM STRANGER SPEAKS TRUE. OUR MAGICKS CAN NOT SURVIVE IN THE ANTI-MATTER UNIVERSE.
FIVE UNIVERSES WILL SOON APPEAR AS ONE.
BROODING, POWER GIRL? THAT'S UNLIKE YOU.
I WANTED TO HELP THEM, HELENA--
I'VE GOT INCREDIBLE POWER. WHY CAN'T I BE WITH THEM NOW?
WE'RE SERVING, TOO... AND IF THEY FALL, WE'LL BE READY.
AND WHEN THEY OCCUPY THE SAME PLACE AT THE SAME TIME...
I'M SCARED FOR THE RAY AND THE OTHERS. ENTERING THAT ANTIMATTER UNIVERSE...
I KNOW, FIREBRAND. THEN SPLITTING INTO SMALLER GROUPS...
...SEPARATELY ATTACKING THE ANTI-MONITOR'S FORTRESS. YOU THINK THEY'LL MAKE IT, HUMAN BOMB?
LET'S PRAY FOR THEM, DOLLMAN. IT'S ALL WE CAN DO NOW.
THEY WILL DESTROY EACH OTHER...
I DON'T LIKE IT, BEETLE. NOT AT ALL.
THEY SHOULD HAVE SENT ME ON THAT MISSION, NOT CAPTAIN ATOM.
CALM DOWN, PEACE-MAKER... CAP'S THE MOST POWERFUL OF US ALL.
I AGREE WITH NIGHTSHADE... I JUST WISH WE COULD HELP, TOO.
AND THE ANTI-MONITOR'S UNIVERSE WILL BE ALL THAT SURVIVES!
TIME'S GOING CRAZIER, KIDS.
YEAH, I KNOW, UNCLE DUDLEY. IT'S BAD...
BUT, JUNIOR, IT'S WORSE FOR CAPTAIN MARVEL.
TELL ME ABOUT IT, MARY.
I WORRY FOR HIM AND FOR ALL OF THEM.
UNLESS THEY SUCCEED, IT'S THE END OF EVERYTHING.
17

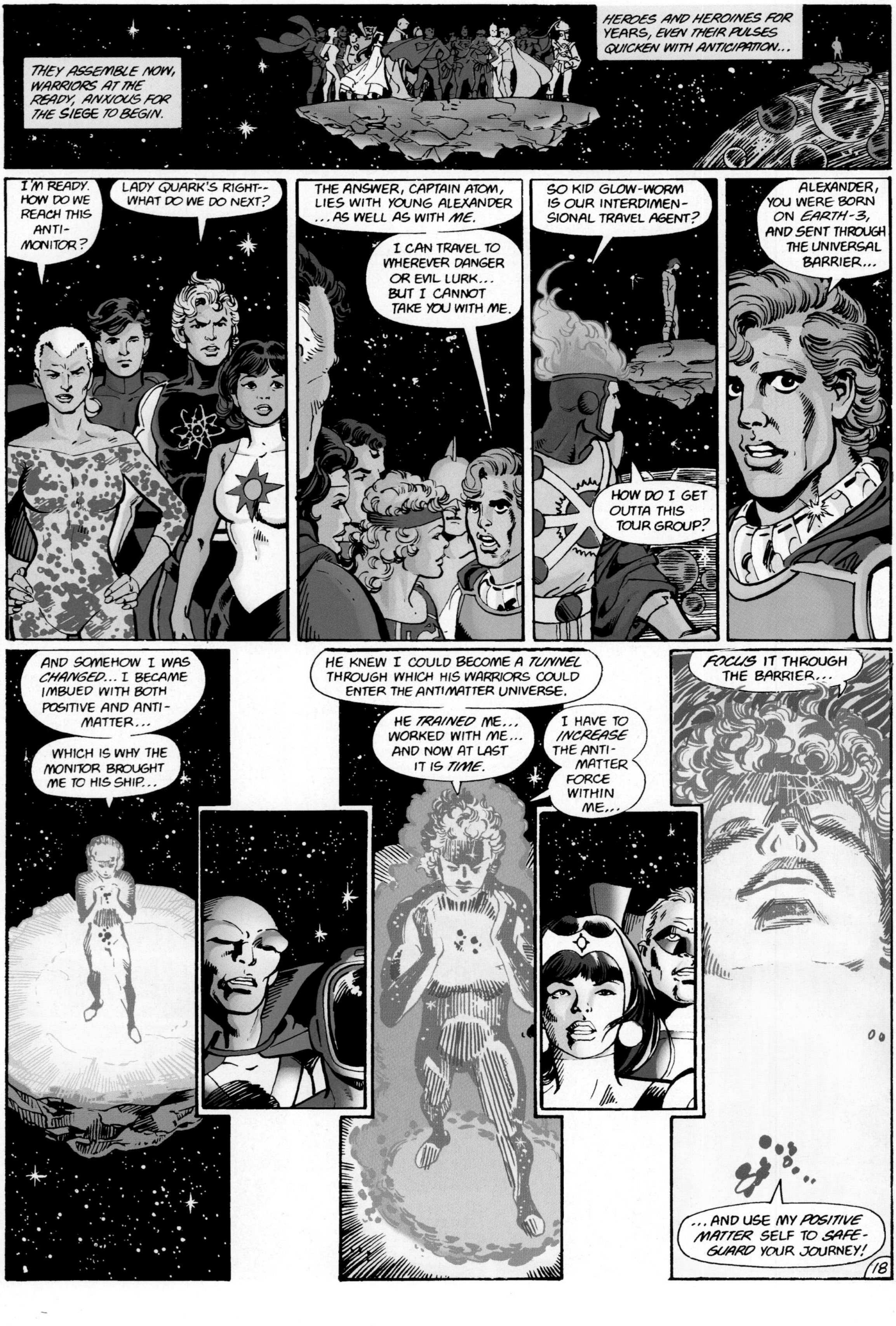
THEY ASSEMBLE NOW, WARRIORS AT THE READY, ANXIOUS FOR THE SIEGE TO BEGIN.
HEROES AND HEROINES FOR YEARS, EVEN THEIR PULSES QUICKEN WITH ANTICIPATION...
I'M READY. HOW DO WE REACH THIS ANTI-MONITOR?
LADY QUARK'S RIGHT-- WHAT DO WE DO NEXT?
THE ANSWER, CAPTAIN ATOM, LIES WITH YOUNG ALEXANDER ...AS WELL AS WITH ME.
I CAN TRAVEL TO WHEREVER DANGER OR EVIL LURK... BUT I CANNOT TAKE YOU WITH ME.
SO KID GLOW-WORM IS OUR INTERDIMENSIONAL TRAVEL AGENT?
HOW DO I GET OUTTA THIS TOUR GROUP?
ALEXANDER, YOU WERE BORN ON EARTH-3, AND SENT THROUGH THE UNIVERSAL BARRIER...
AND SOMEHOW I WAS CHANGED... I BECAME IMBUED WITH BOTH POSITIVE AND ANTI-MATTER...
WHICH IS WHY THE MONITOR BROUGHT ME TO HIS SHIP...
HE KNEW I COULD BECOME A TUNNEL THROUGH WHICH HIS WARRIORS COULD ENTER THE ANTIMATTER UNIVERSE.
HE TRAINED ME... WORKED WITH ME... AND NOW AT LAST IT IS TIME.
I HAVE TO INCREASE THE ANTI-MATTER FORCE WITHIN ME...
FOCUS IT THROUGH THE BARRIER...
...AND USE MY POSITIVE MATTER SELF TO SAFE-GUARD YOUR JOURNEY!
18

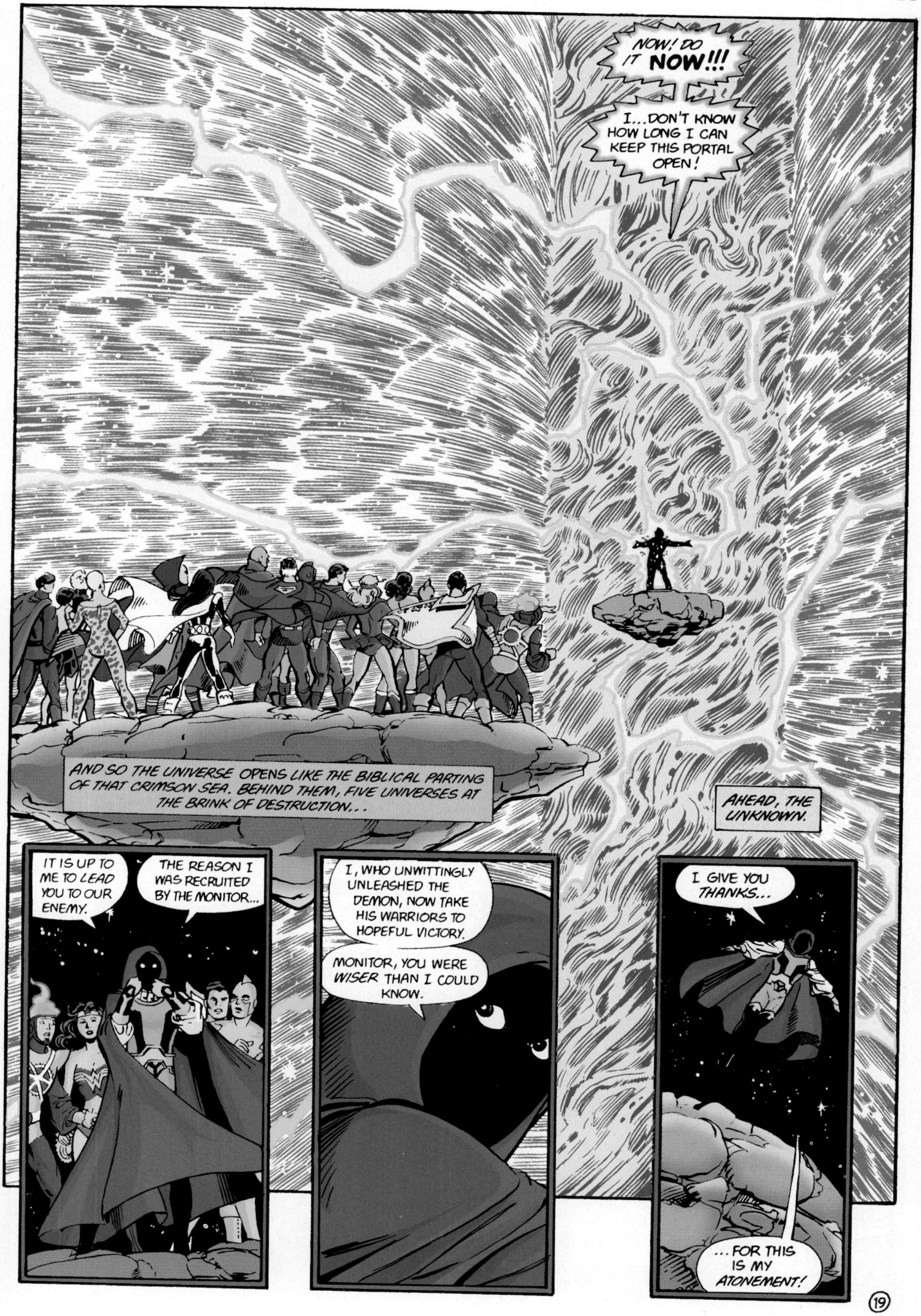
NOW! DO IT NOW!!!
I...DON'T KNOW HOW LONG I CAN KEEP THIS PORTAL OPEN!
AND SO THE UNIVERSE OPENS LIKE THE BIBLICAL PARTING OF THAT CRIMSON SEA. BEHIND THEM, FIVE UNIVERSES AT THE BRINK OF DESTRUCTION...
AHEAD, THE UNKNOWN.
IT IS UP TO ME TO LEAD YOU TO OUR ENEMY.
THE REASON I WAS RECRUITED BY THE MONITOR...
I, WHO UNWITTINGLY UNLEASHED THE DEMON, NOW TAKE HIS WARRIORS TO HOPEFUL VICTORY.
MONITOR, YOU WERE WISER THAN I COULD KNOW.
I GIVE YOU THANKS...
...FOR THIS IS MY ATONEMENT!

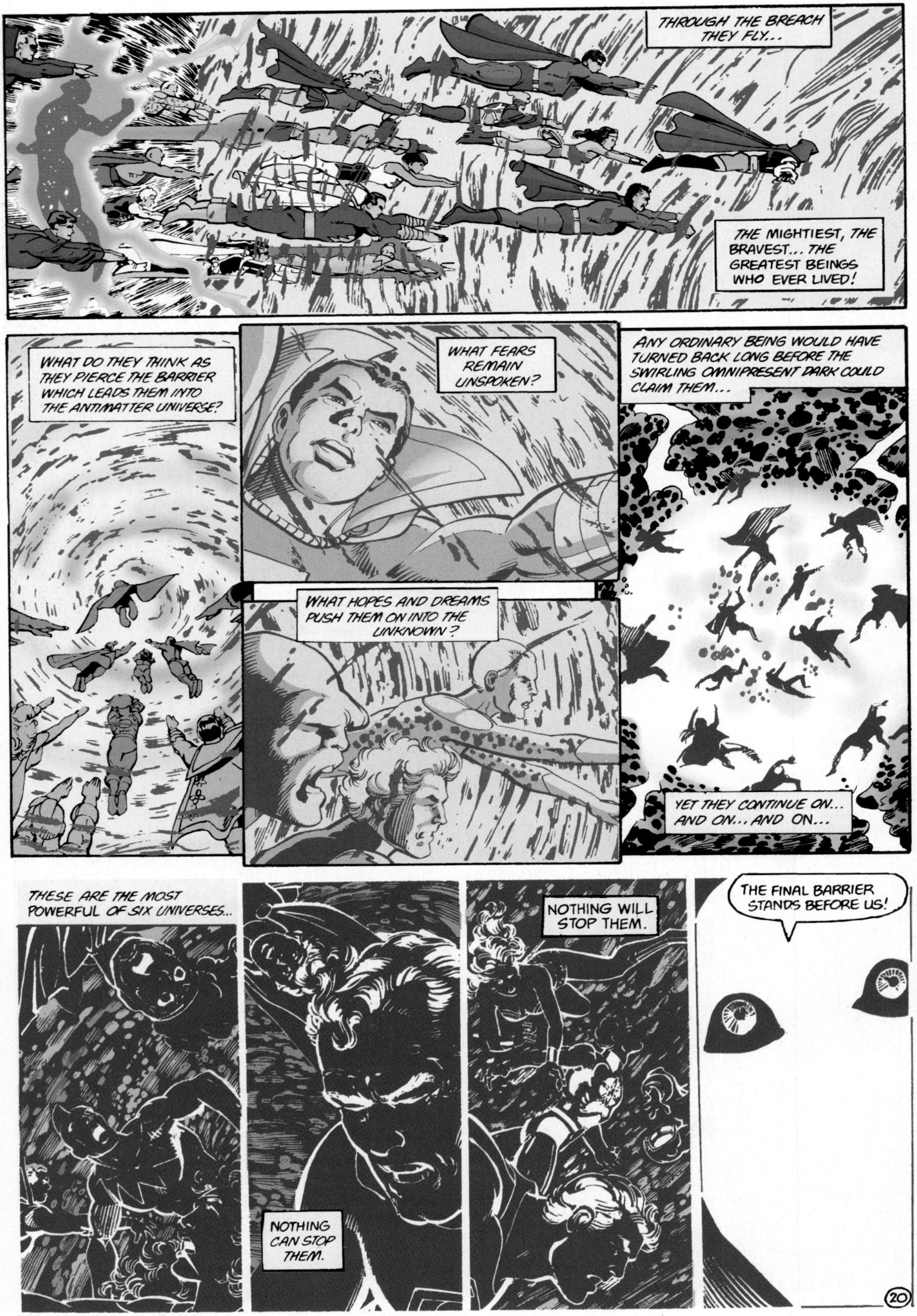
THROUGH THE BREACH THEY FLY...
THE MIGHTIEST, THE BRAVEST... THE GREATEST BEINGS WHO EVER LIVED!
WHAT DO THEY THINK AS THEY PIERCE THE BARRIER WHICH LEADS THEM INTO THE ANTIMATTER UNIVERSE?
WHAT FEARS REMAIN UNSPOKEN?
WHAT HOPES AND DREAMS PUSH THEM ON INTO THE UNKNOWN?
ANY ORDINARY BEING WOULD HAVE TURNED BACK LONG BEFORE THE SWIRLING OMNIPRESENT DARK COULD CLAIM THEM...
YET THEY CONTINUE ON... AND ON... AND ON...
THESE ARE THE MOST POWERFUL OF SIX UNIVERSES...
NOTHING CAN STOP THEM.
NOTHING WILL STOP THEM.
THE FINAL BARRIER STANDS BEFORE US!
20

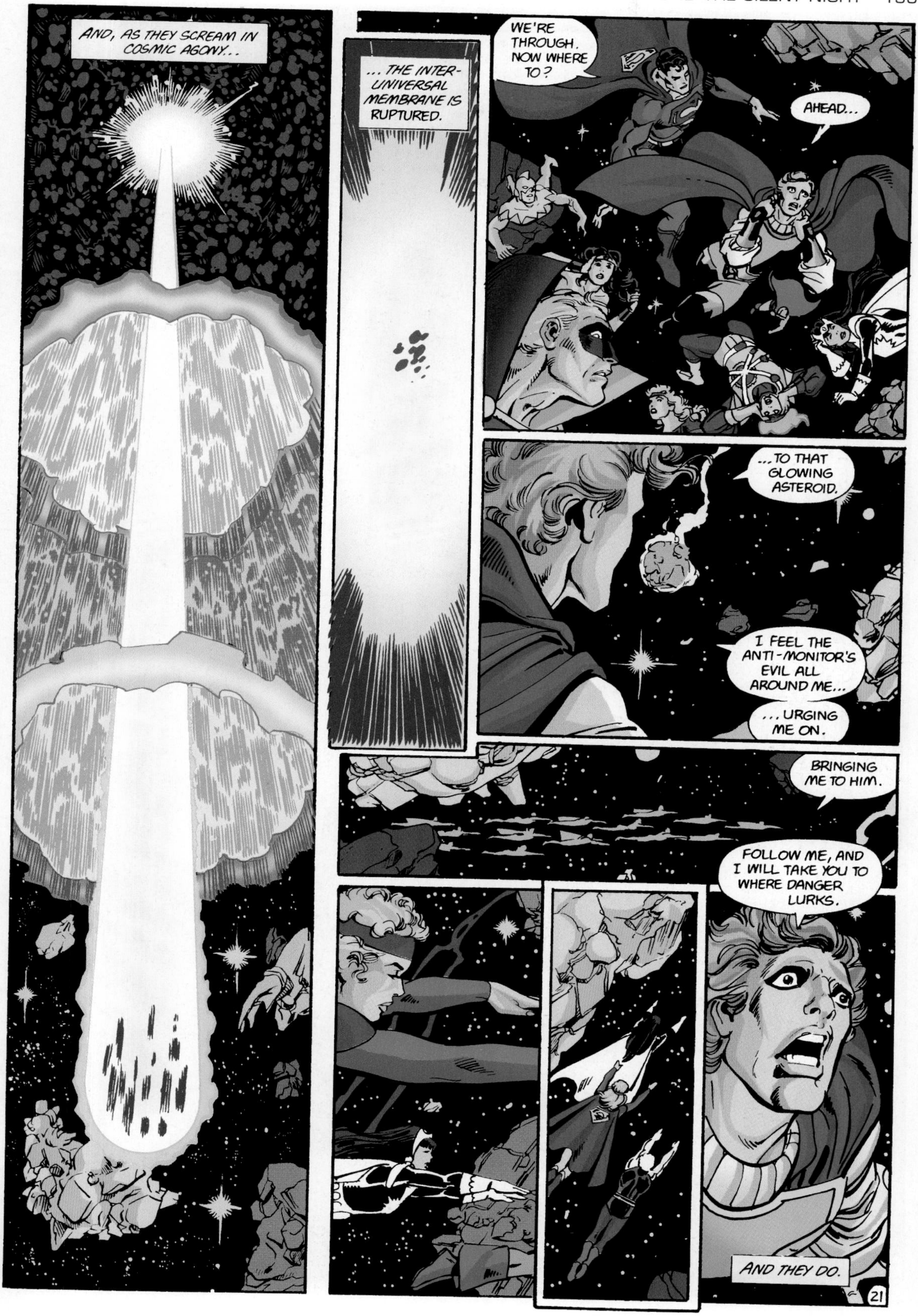
AND, AS THEY SCREAM IN COSMIC AGONY...
...THE INTER-UNIVERSAL MEMBRANE IS RUPTURED.
WE'RE THROUGH. NOW WHERE TO?
AHEAD...
...TO THAT GLOWING ASTEROID.
I FEEL THE ANTI-MONITOR'S EVIL ALL AROUND ME...
...URGING ME ON.
BRINGING ME TO HIM.
FOLLOW ME, AND I WILL TAKE YOU TO WHERE DANGER LURKS.
AND THEY DO.
21

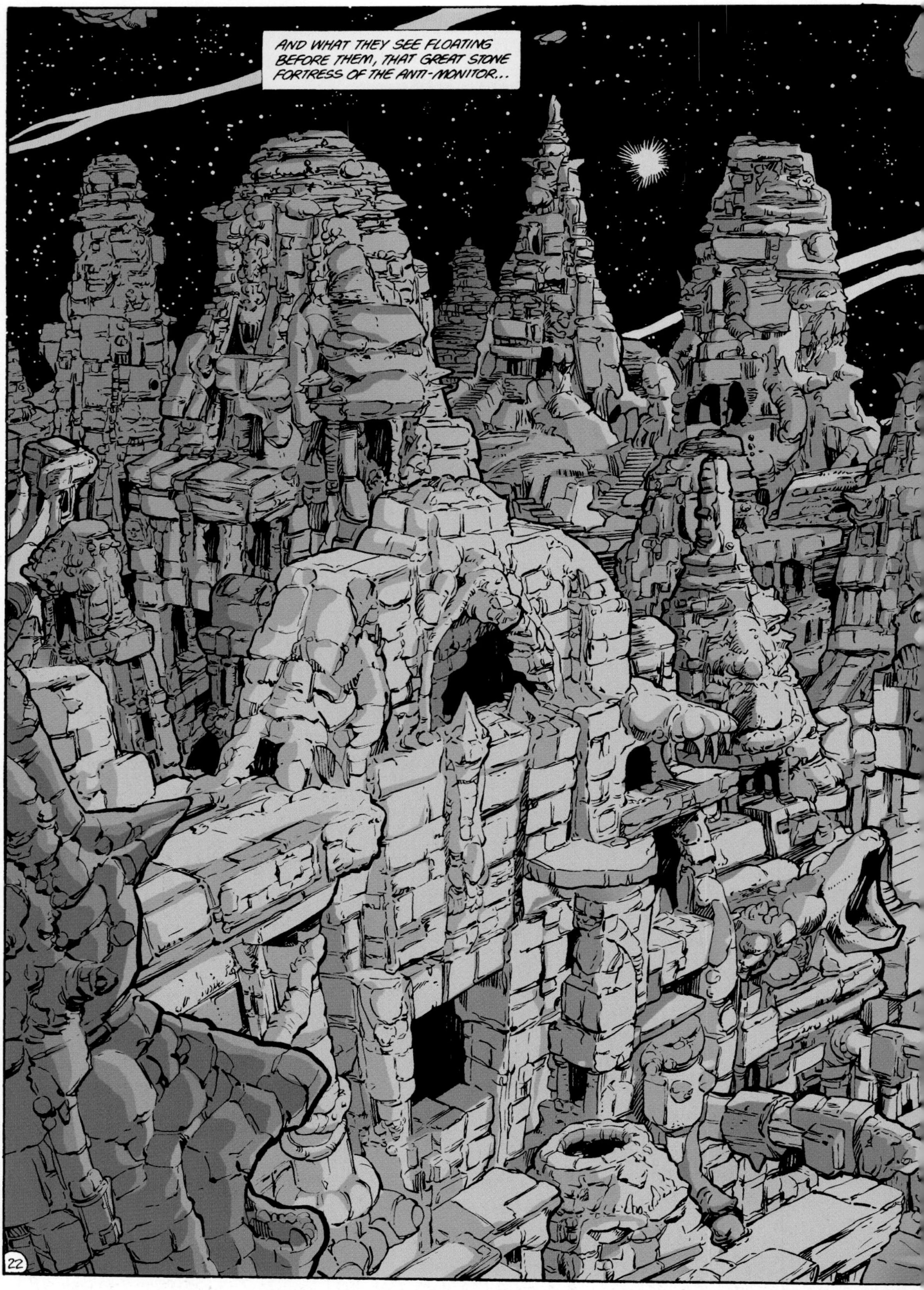
AND WHAT THEY SEE FLOATING BEFORE THEM, THAT GREAT STONE FORTRESS OF THE ANTI-MONITOR...
22

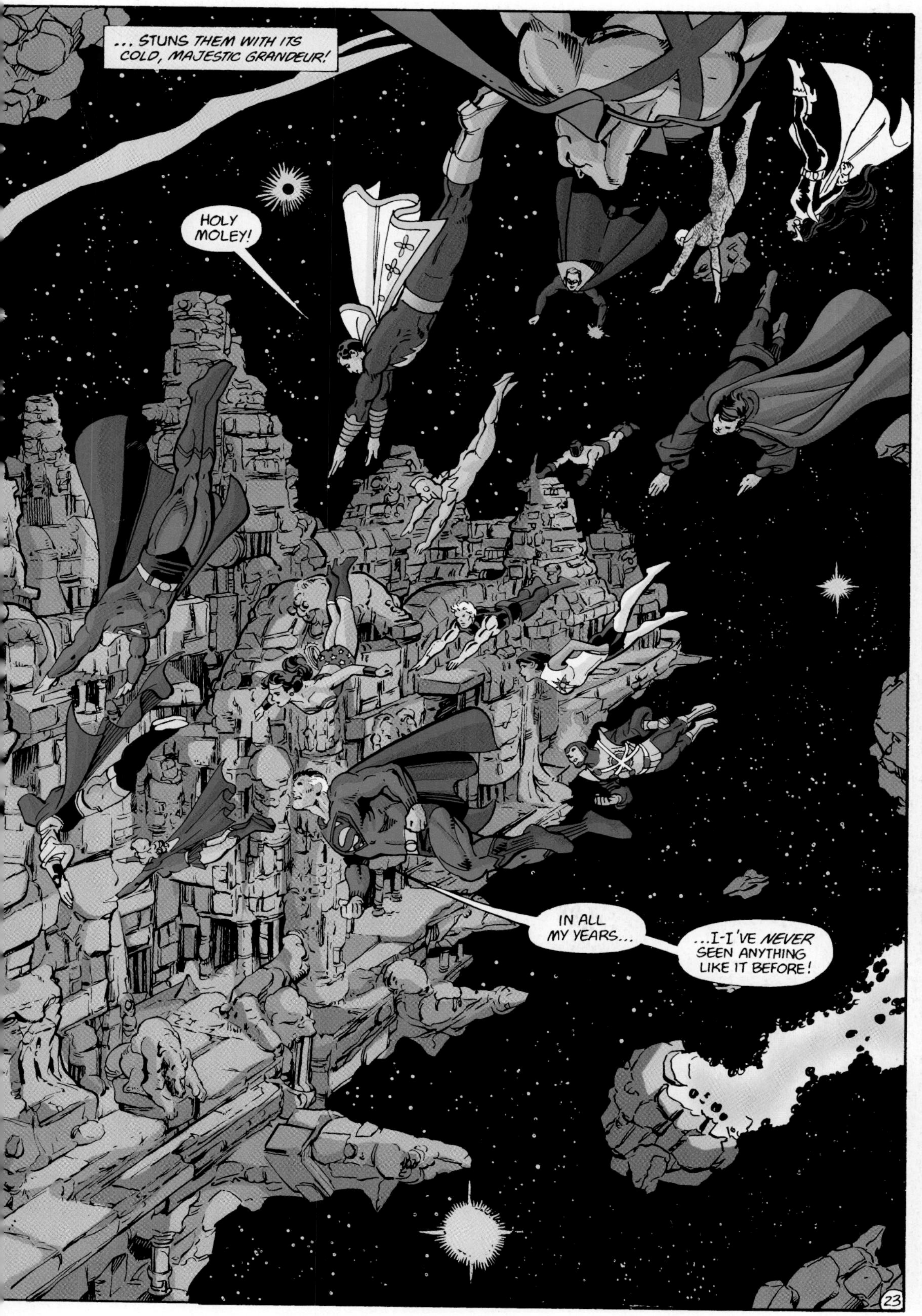
...STUNS THEM WITH ITS COLD, MAJESTIC GRANDEUR!
HOLY MOLEY!
IN ALL MY YEARS...
...I-I'VE NEVER SEEN ANYTHING LIKE IT BEFORE!
23

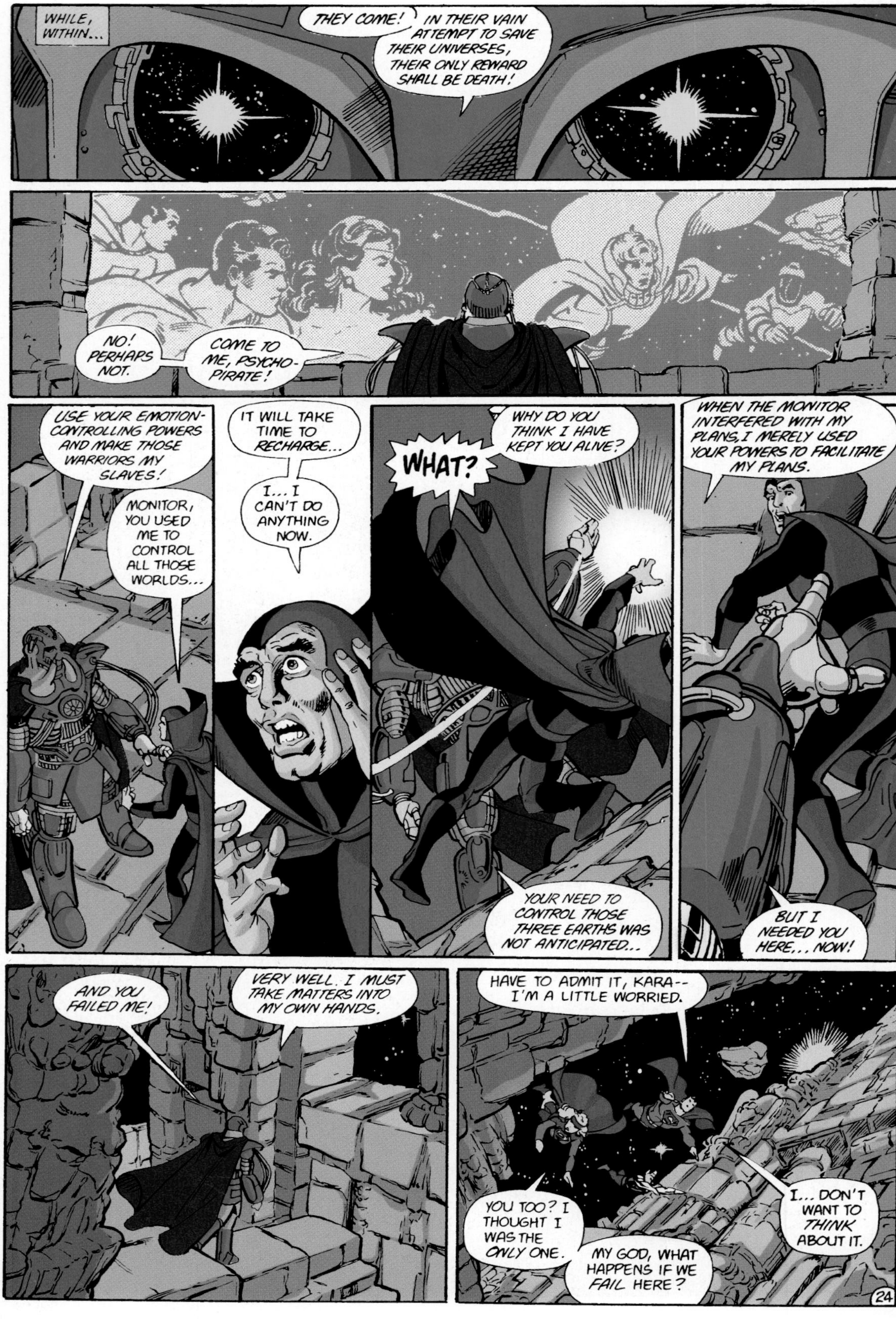
WHILE, WITHIN...
THEY COME!
IN THEIR VAIN ATTEMPT TO SAVE THEIR UNIVERSES, THEIR ONLY REWARD SHALL BE DEATH!
NO! PERHAPS NOT.
COME TO ME, PSYCHO-PIRATE!
USE YOUR EMOTION-CONTROLLING POWERS AND MAKE THOSE WARRIORS MY SLAVES!
MONITOR, YOU USED ME TO CONTROL ALL THOSE WORLDS...
IT WILL TAKE TIME TO RECHARGE...
I... I CAN'T DO ANYTHING NOW.
WHAT?
WHY DO YOU THINK I HAVE KEPT YOU ALIVE?
YOUR NEED TO CONTROL THOSE THREE EARTHS WAS NOT ANTICIPATED...
WHEN THE MONITOR INTERFERED WITH MY PLANS, I MERELY USED YOUR POWERS TO FACILITATE MY PLANS.
BUT I NEEDED YOU HERE,.. NOW!
AND YOU FAILED ME!
VERY WELL. I MUST TAKE MATTERS INTO MY OWN HANDS.
HAVE TO ADMIT IT, KARA-- I'M A LITTLE WORRIED.
YOU TOO? I THOUGHT I WAS THE ONLY ONE.
MY GOD, WHAT HAPPENS IF WE FAIL HERE?
I... DON'T WANT TO THINK ABOUT IT.
24

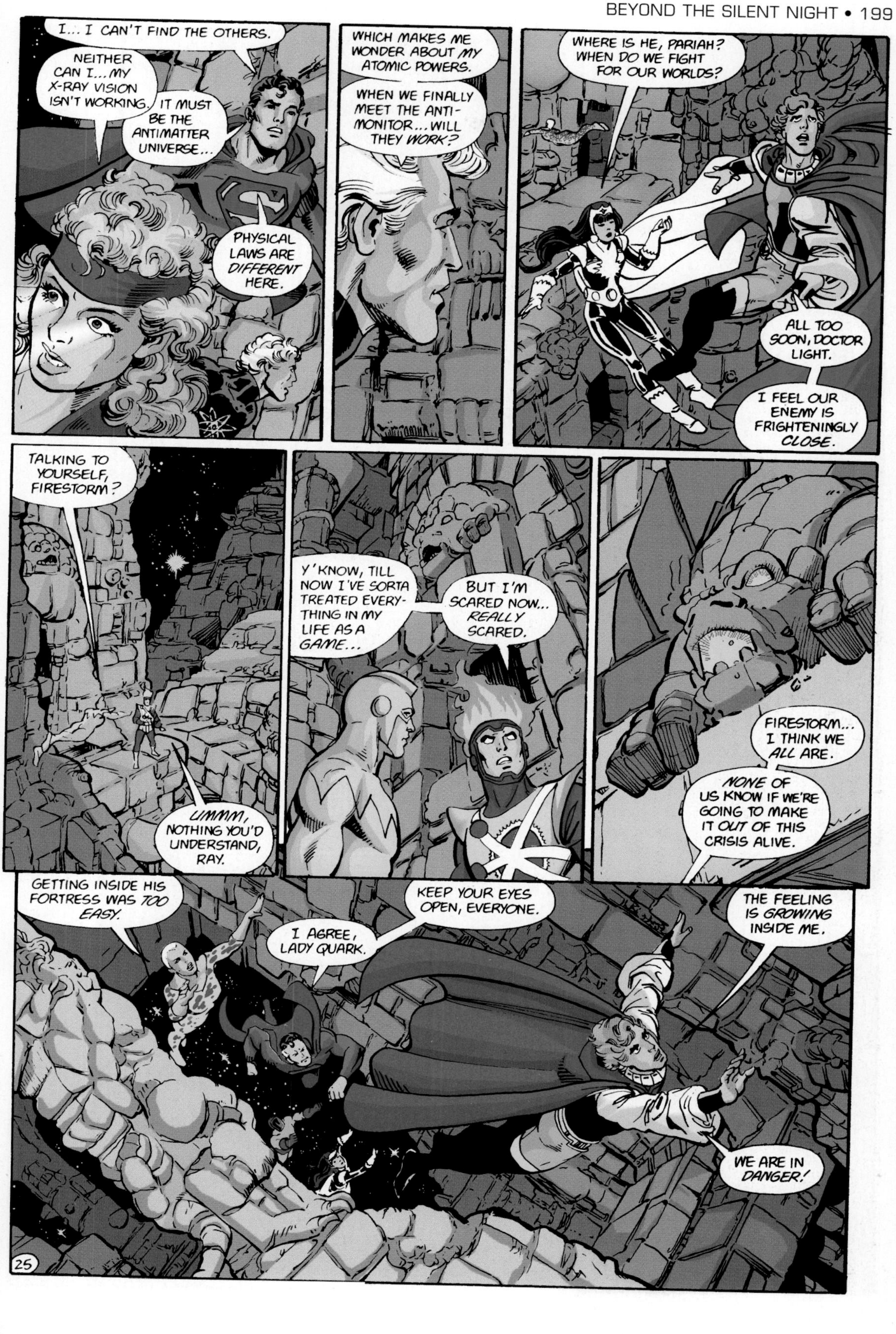
I... I CAN'T FIND THE OTHERS.
NEITHER CAN I... MY X-RAY VISION ISN'T WORKING.
IT MUST BE THE ANTIMATTER UNIVERSE...
PHYSICAL LAWS ARE *DIFFERENT* HERE.
WHICH MAKES ME WONDER ABOUT *MY* ATOMIC POWERS.
WHEN WE FINALLY MEET THE ANTI-MONITOR... WILL THEY *WORK?*
WHERE IS HE, PARIAH? WHEN DO WE FIGHT FOR OUR WORLDS?
ALL TOO SOON, DOCTOR LIGHT.
I FEEL OUR ENEMY IS FRIGHTENINGLY *CLOSE.*
TALKING TO YOURSELF, FIRESTORM?
UMMM, NOTHING YOU'D UNDERSTAND, RAY.
Y'KNOW, TILL NOW I'VE SORTA TREATED EVERY-THING IN MY LIFE AS A *GAME...*
BUT I'M SCARED NOW... *REALLY* SCARED.
FIRESTORM... I THINK WE *ALL* ARE.
NONE OF US KNOW IF WE'RE GOING TO MAKE IT *OUT* OF THIS CRISIS ALIVE.
GETTING INSIDE HIS FORTRESS WAS *TOO EASY.*
KEEP YOUR EYES OPEN, EVERYONE.
I AGREE, LADY QUARK.
THE FEELING IS *GROWING* INSIDE ME.
WE ARE IN *DANGER!*
25

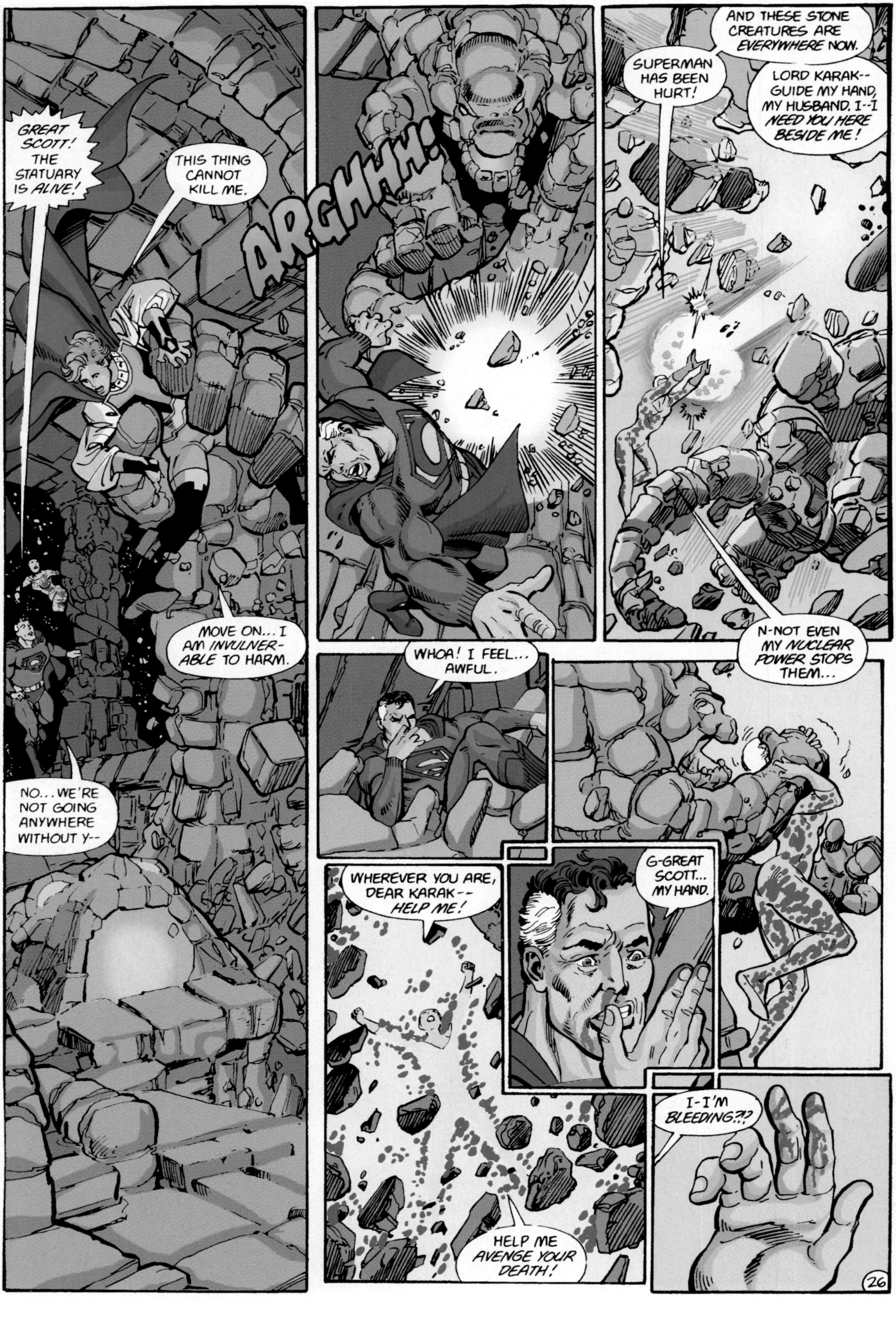
GREAT SCOTT! THE STATUARY IS ALIVE!
THIS THING CANNOT KILL ME.
MOVE ON... I AM INVULNERABLE TO HARM.
NO... WE'RE NOT GOING ANYWHERE WITHOUT Y--
ARGHHH!
AND THESE STONE CREATURES ARE EVERYWHERE NOW.
SUPERMAN HAS BEEN HURT!
LORD KARAK-- GUIDE MY HAND, MY HUSBAND. I--I NEED YOU HERE BESIDE ME!
N-NOT EVEN MY NUCLEAR POWER STOPS THEM...
WHOA! I FEEL... AWFUL.
WHEREVER YOU ARE, DEAR KARAK-- HELP ME!
HELP ME AVENGE YOUR DEATH!
G-GREAT SCOTT... MY HAND.
I-I'M BLEEDING?!?
26

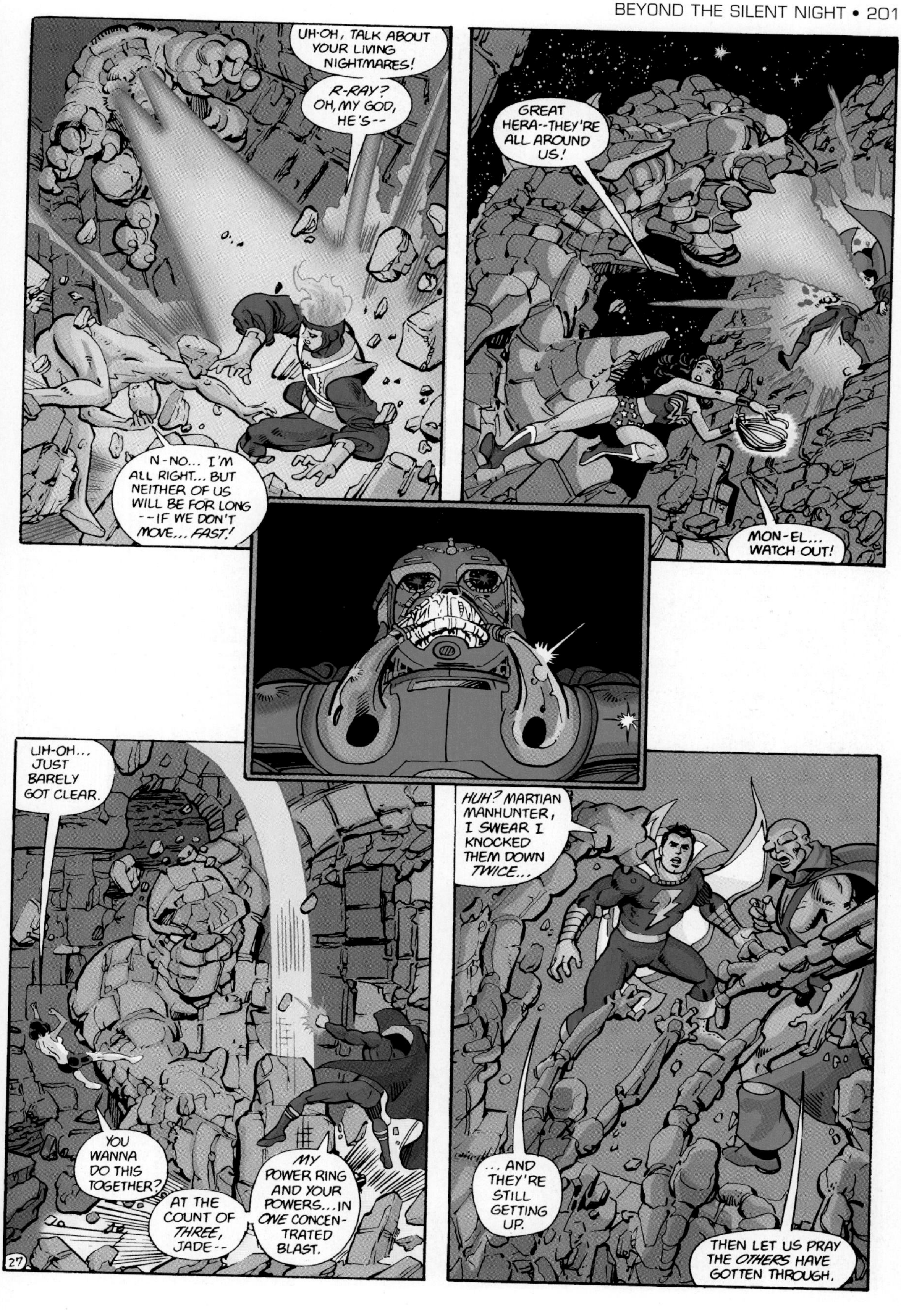
UH-OH, TALK ABOUT YOUR LIVING NIGHTMARES!
R-RAY? OH, MY GOD, HE'S--
N-NO... I'M ALL RIGHT... BUT NEITHER OF US WILL BE FOR LONG --IF WE DON'T MOVE... FAST!
GREAT HERA--THEY'RE ALL AROUND US!
MON-EL... WATCH OUT!
UH-OH... JUST BARELY GOT CLEAR.
YOU WANNA DO THIS TOGETHER?
AT THE COUNT OF THREE, JADE--
MY POWER RING AND YOUR POWERS... IN ONE CONCENTRATED BLAST.
27
HUH? MARTIAN MANHUNTER, I SWEAR I KNOCKED THEM DOWN TWICE...
...AND THEY'RE STILL GETTING UP.
THEN LET US PRAY THE OTHERS HAVE GOTTEN THROUGH.

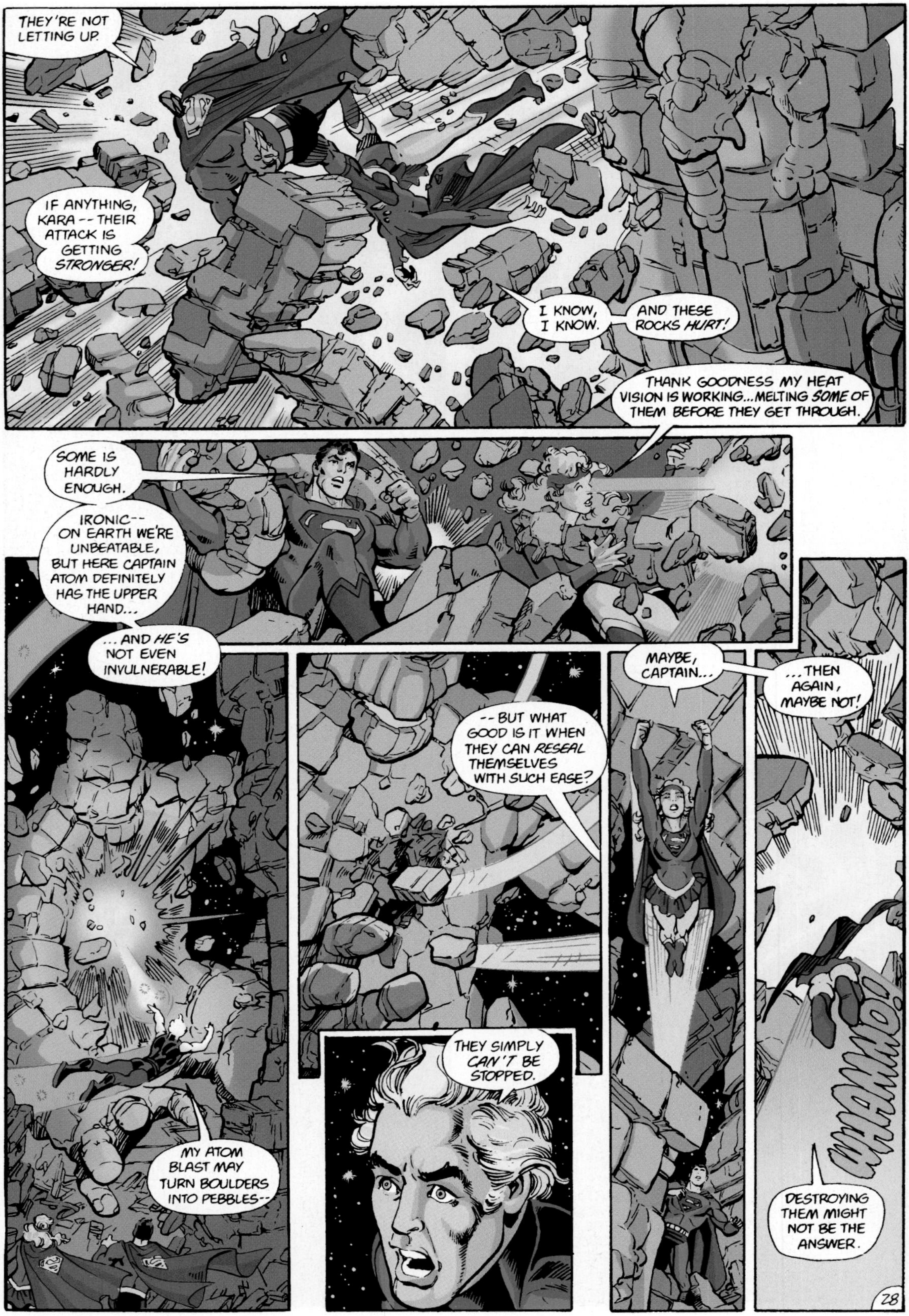
THEY'RE NOT LETTING UP.
IF ANYTHING, KARA -- THEIR ATTACK IS GETTING STRONGER!
I KNOW, I KNOW.
AND THESE ROCKS HURT!
THANK GOODNESS MY HEAT VISION IS WORKING...MELTING SOME OF THEM BEFORE THEY GET THROUGH.
SOME IS HARDLY ENOUGH.
IRONIC-- ON EARTH WE'RE UNBEATABLE, BUT HERE CAPTAIN ATOM DEFINITELY HAS THE UPPER HAND...
...AND HE'S NOT EVEN INVULNERABLE!
MY ATOM BLAST MAY TURN BOULDERS INTO PEBBLES--
--BUT WHAT GOOD IS IT WHEN THEY CAN RESEAL THEMSELVES WITH SUCH EASE?
THEY SIMPLY CAN'T BE STOPPED.
MAYBE, CAPTAIN...
...THEN AGAIN, MAYBE NOT!
WHAMMOO!
DESTROYING THEM MIGHT NOT BE THE ANSWER.
28

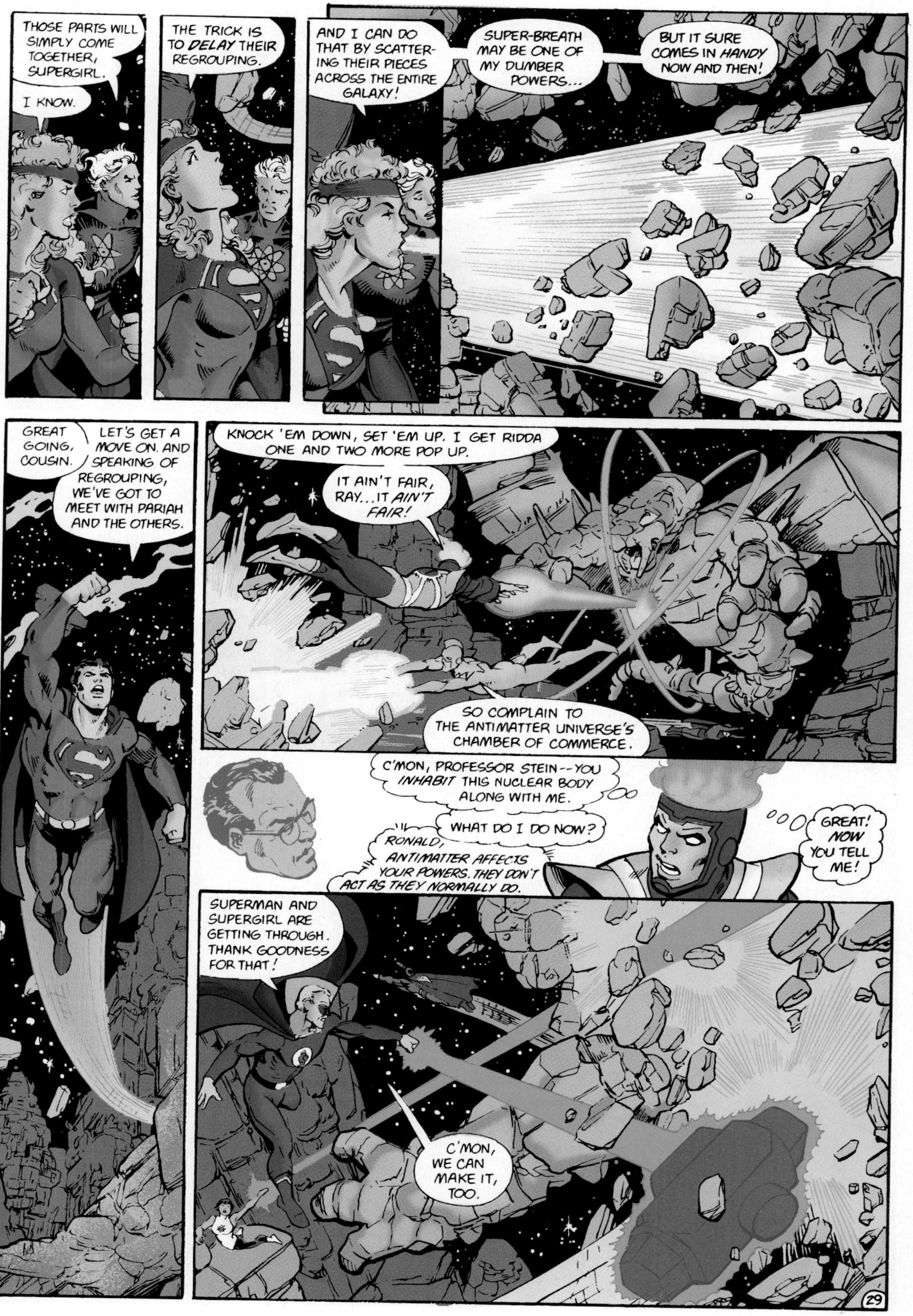
THOSE PARTS WILL SIMPLY COME TOGETHER, SUPERGIRL.
I KNOW.
THE TRICK IS TO *DELAY* THEIR REGROUPING.
AND I CAN DO THAT BY SCATTERING THEIR PIECES ACROSS THE ENTIRE GALAXY!
SUPER-BREATH MAY BE ONE OF MY DUMBER POWERS...
BUT IT SURE COMES IN *HANDY* NOW AND THEN!
GREAT GOING, COUSIN.
LET'S GET A MOVE ON. AND SPEAKING OF REGROUPING, WE'VE GOT TO MEET WITH PARIAH AND THE OTHERS.
KNOCK 'EM DOWN, SET 'EM UP. I GET RIDDA ONE AND TWO MORE POP UP.
IT AIN'T FAIR, RAY... IT *AIN'T FAIR!*
SO COMPLAIN TO THE ANTIMATTER UNIVERSE'S CHAMBER OF COMMERCE.
C'MON, PROFESSOR STEIN--YOU *INHABIT* THIS NUCLEAR BODY ALONG WITH ME.
WHAT DO I DO NOW?
RONALD, ANTIMATTER AFFECTS YOUR POWERS. THEY DON'T ACT AS THEY NORMALLY DO.
GREAT! *NOW* YOU TELL ME!
SUPERMAN AND SUPERGIRL ARE GETTING THROUGH. THANK GOODNESS FOR THAT!
C'MON, WE CAN MAKE IT, TOO.
29

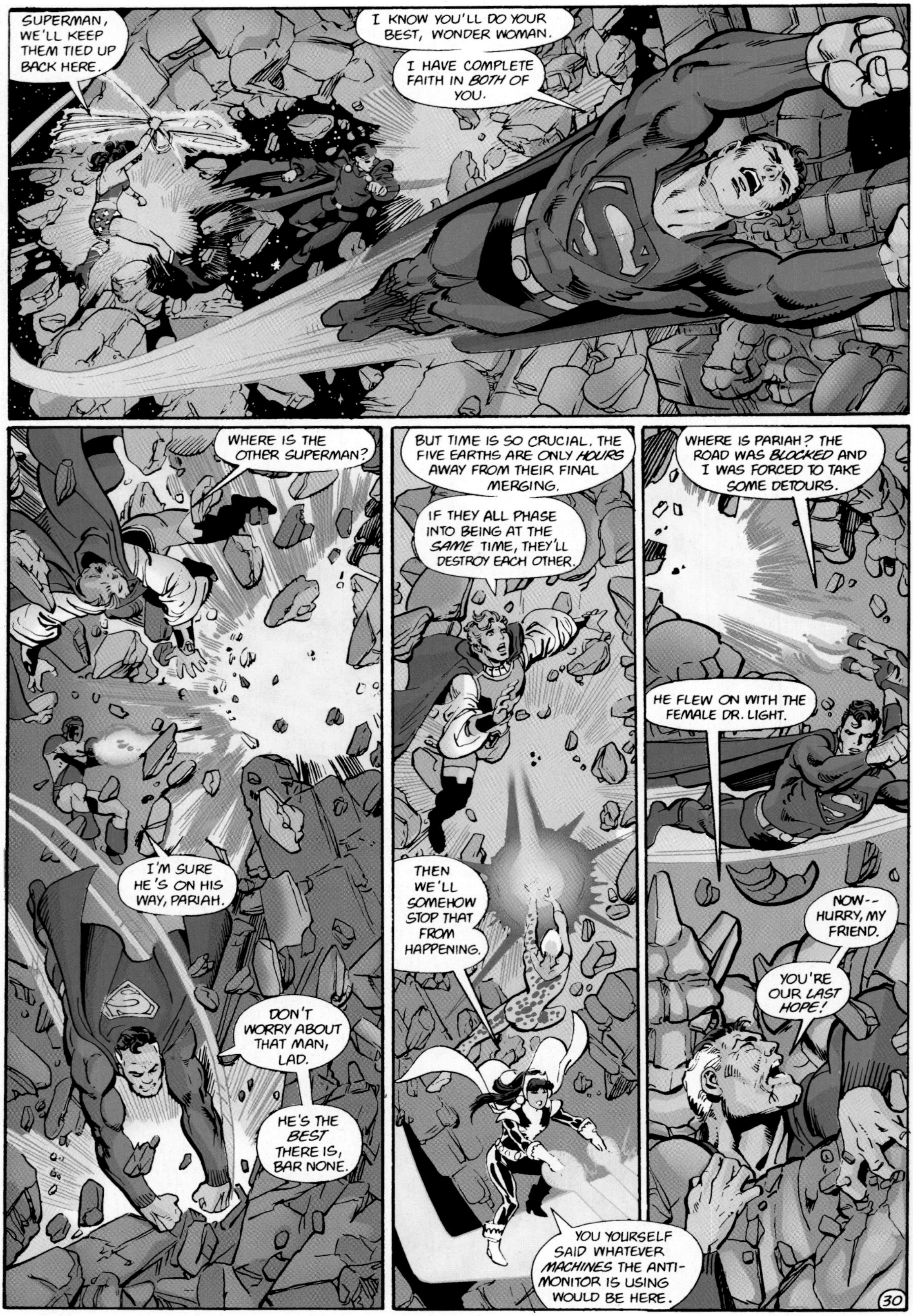
SUPERMAN, WE'LL KEEP THEM TIED UP BACK HERE.
I KNOW YOU'LL DO YOUR BEST, WONDER WOMAN.
I HAVE COMPLETE FAITH IN BOTH OF YOU.
WHERE IS THE OTHER SUPERMAN?
I'M SURE HE'S ON HIS WAY, PARIAH.
DON'T WORRY ABOUT THAT MAN, LAD.
HE'S THE BEST THERE IS, BAR NONE.
BUT TIME IS SO CRUCIAL. THE FIVE EARTHS ARE ONLY HOURS AWAY FROM THEIR FINAL MERGING.
IF THEY ALL PHASE INTO BEING AT THE SAME TIME, THEY'LL DESTROY EACH OTHER.
THEN WE'LL SOMEHOW STOP THAT FROM HAPPENING.
YOU YOURSELF SAID WHATEVER MACHINES THE ANTI-MONITOR IS USING WOULD BE HERE.
WHERE IS PARIAH? THE ROAD WAS BLOCKED AND I WAS FORCED TO TAKE SOME DETOURS.
HE FLEW ON WITH THE FEMALE DR. LIGHT.
NOW--HURRY, MY FRIEND.
YOU'RE OUR LAST HOPE!
30

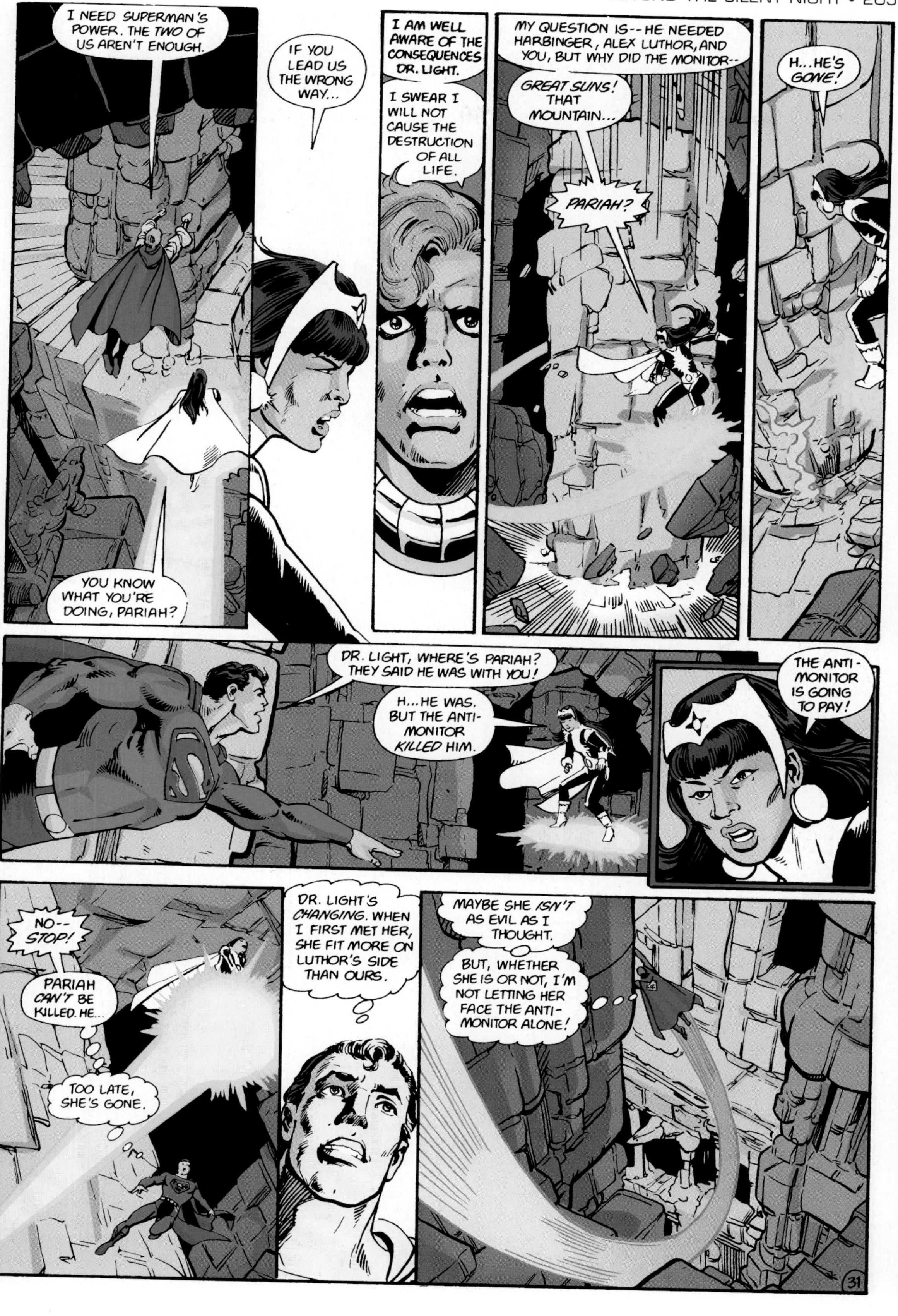
I NEED SUPERMAN'S POWER. THE TWO OF US AREN'T ENOUGH.
YOU KNOW WHAT YOU'RE DOING, PARIAH?
IF YOU LEAD US THE WRONG WAY...
I AM WELL AWARE OF THE CONSEQUENCES DR. LIGHT.
I SWEAR I WILL NOT CAUSE THE DESTRUCTION OF ALL LIFE.
MY QUESTION IS-- HE NEEDED HARBINGER, ALEX LUTHOR, AND YOU, BUT WHY DID THE MONITOR--
GREAT SUNS! THAT MOUNTAIN...
PARIAH?
H...HE'S GONE!
DR. LIGHT, WHERE'S PARIAH? THEY SAID HE WAS WITH YOU!
H...HE WAS. BUT THE ANTI-MONITOR KILLED HIM.
THE ANTI-MONITOR IS GOING TO PAY!
NO-- STOP!
PARIAH CAN'T BE KILLED. HE...
TOO LATE, SHE'S GONE.
DR. LIGHT'S CHANGING. WHEN I FIRST MET HER, SHE FIT MORE ON LUTHOR'S SIDE THAN OURS.
MAYBE SHE ISN'T AS EVIL AS I THOUGHT.
BUT, WHETHER SHE IS OR NOT, I'M NOT LETTING HER FACE THE ANTI-MONITOR ALONE!
31

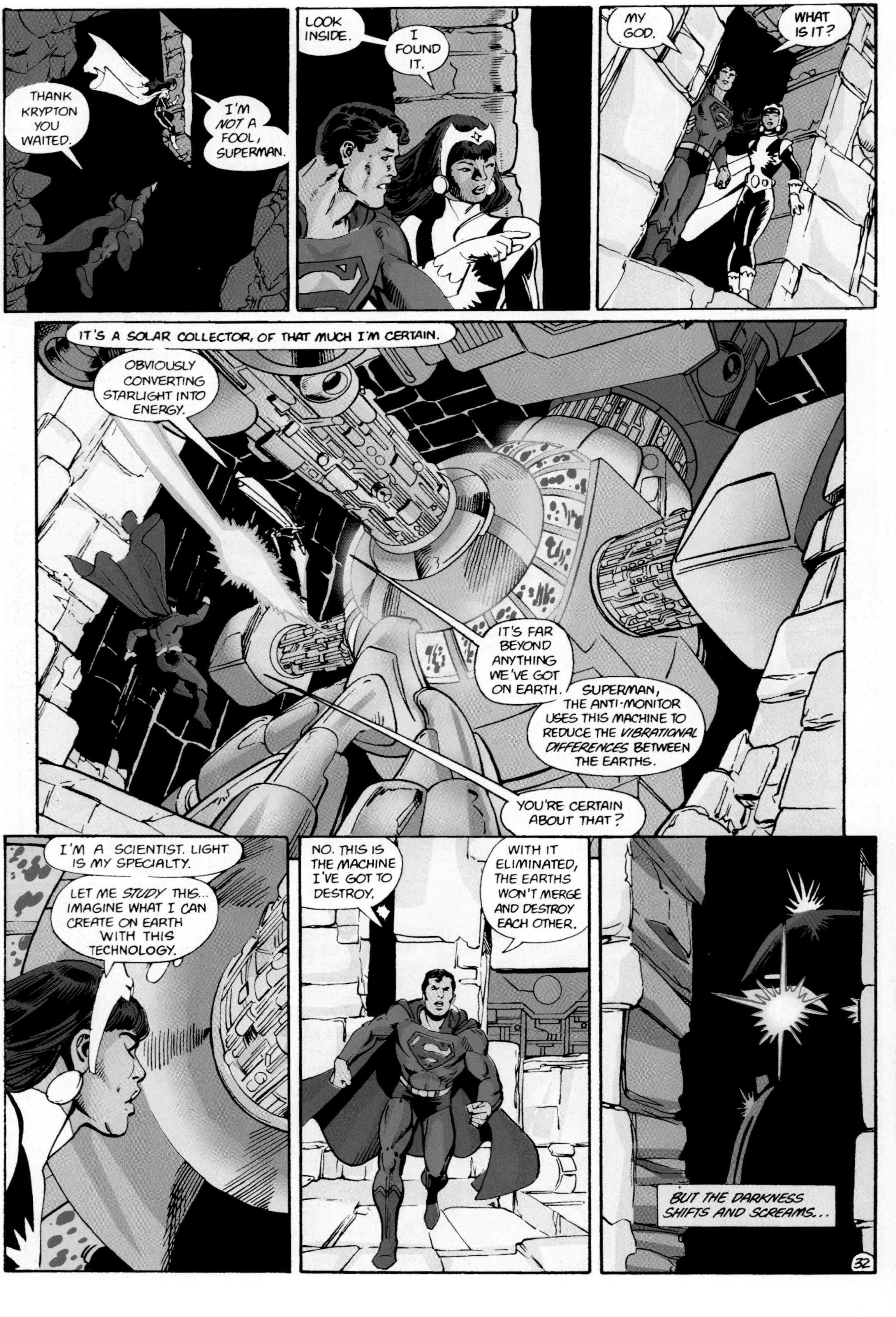
THANK KRYPTON YOU WAITED.
I'M NOT A FOOL, SUPERMAN.
LOOK INSIDE.
I FOUND IT.
MY GOD.
WHAT IS IT?
IT'S A SOLAR COLLECTOR, OF THAT MUCH I'M CERTAIN.
OBVIOUSLY CONVERTING STARLIGHT INTO ENERGY.
IT'S FAR BEYOND ANYTHING WE'VE GOT ON EARTH.
SUPERMAN, THE ANTI-MONITOR USES THIS MACHINE TO REDUCE THE VIBRATIONAL DIFFERENCES BETWEEN THE EARTHS.
YOU'RE CERTAIN ABOUT THAT?
I'M A SCIENTIST. LIGHT IS MY SPECIALTY.
LET ME STUDY THIS... IMAGINE WHAT I CAN CREATE ON EARTH WITH THIS TECHNOLOGY.
NO. THIS IS THE MACHINE I'VE GOT TO DESTROY.
WITH IT ELIMINATED, THE EARTHS WON'T MERGE AND DESTROY EACH OTHER.
BUT THE DARKNESS SHIFTS AND SCREAMS...
32

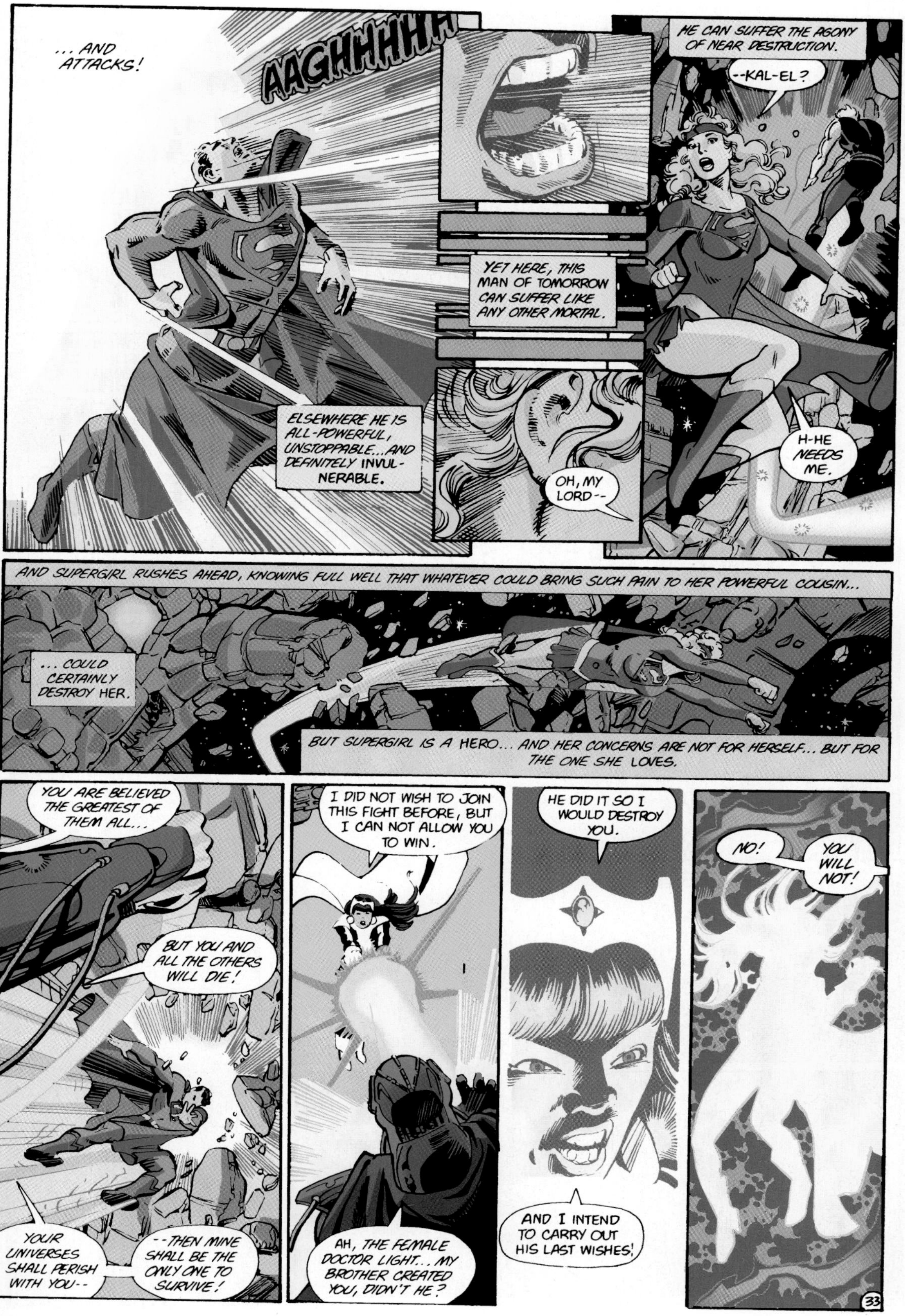
...AND ATTACKS!
AAGHHHHH
ELSEWHERE HE IS ALL-POWERFUL, UNSTOPPABLE...AND DEFINITELY INVULNERABLE.
YET HERE, THIS MAN OF TOMORROW CAN SUFFER LIKE ANY OTHER MORTAL.
OH, MY LORD--
HE CAN SUFFER THE AGONY OF NEAR DESTRUCTION.
--KAL-EL?
H-HE NEEDS ME.
AND SUPERGIRL RUSHES AHEAD, KNOWING FULL WELL THAT WHATEVER COULD BRING SUCH PAIN TO HER POWERFUL COUSIN...
...COULD CERTAINLY DESTROY HER.
BUT SUPERGIRL IS A HERO... AND HER CONCERNS ARE NOT FOR HERSELF... BUT FOR THE ONE SHE LOVES.
YOU ARE BELIEVED THE GREATEST OF THEM ALL...
BUT YOU AND ALL THE OTHERS WILL DIE!
YOUR UNIVERSES SHALL PERISH WITH YOU--
--THEN MINE SHALL BE THE ONLY ONE TO SURVIVE!
I DID NOT WISH TO JOIN THIS FIGHT BEFORE, BUT I CAN NOT ALLOW YOU TO WIN.
AH, THE FEMALE DOCTOR LIGHT... MY BROTHER CREATED YOU, DIDN'T HE?
HE DID IT SO I WOULD DESTROY YOU.
AND I INTEND TO CARRY OUT HIS LAST WISHES!
NO!
YOU WILL NOT!
33

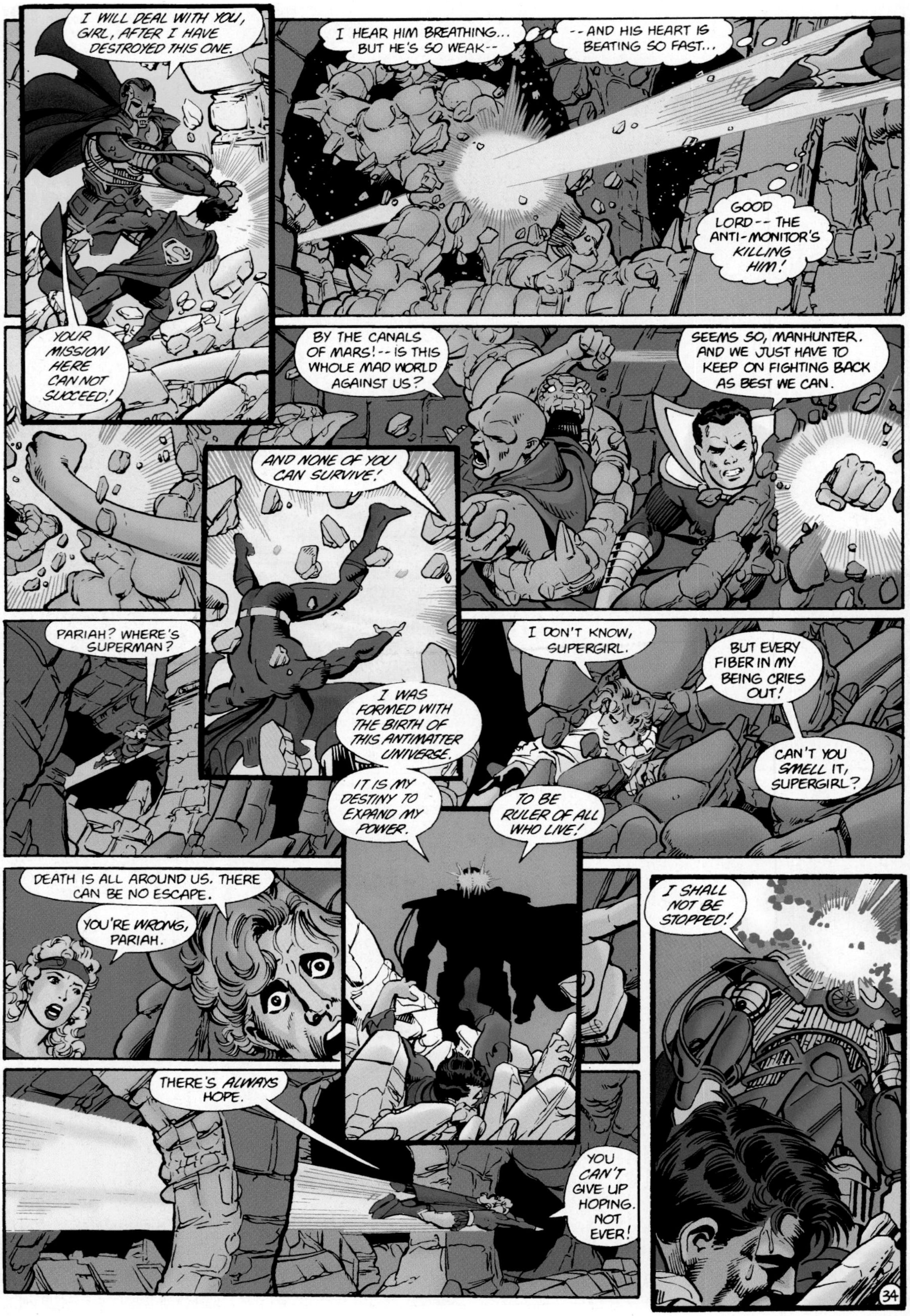
I WILL DEAL WITH YOU, GIRL, AFTER I HAVE DESTROYED THIS ONE.
YOUR MISSION HERE CAN NOT SUCCEED!
I HEAR HIM BREATHING... BUT HE'S SO WEAK--
--AND HIS HEART IS BEATING SO FAST...
GOOD LORD-- THE ANTI-MONITOR'S KILLING HIM!
BY THE CANALS OF MARS!--IS THIS WHOLE MAD WORLD AGAINST US?
SEEMS SO, MANHUNTER. AND WE JUST HAVE TO KEEP ON FIGHTING BACK AS BEST WE CAN.
AND NONE OF YOU CAN SURVIVE!
I WAS FORMED WITH THE BIRTH OF THIS ANTIMATTER UNIVERSE.
PARIAH? WHERE'S SUPERMAN?
I DON'T KNOW, SUPERGIRL.
BUT EVERY FIBER IN MY BEING CRIES OUT!
CAN'T YOU SMELL IT, SUPERGIRL?
IT IS MY DESTINY TO EXPAND MY POWER.
TO BE RULER OF ALL WHO LIVE!
DEATH IS ALL AROUND US. THERE CAN BE NO ESCAPE.
YOU'RE WRONG, PARIAH.
THERE'S ALWAYS HOPE.
YOU CAN'T GIVE UP HOPING. NOT EVER!
I SHALL NOT BE STOPPED!
34

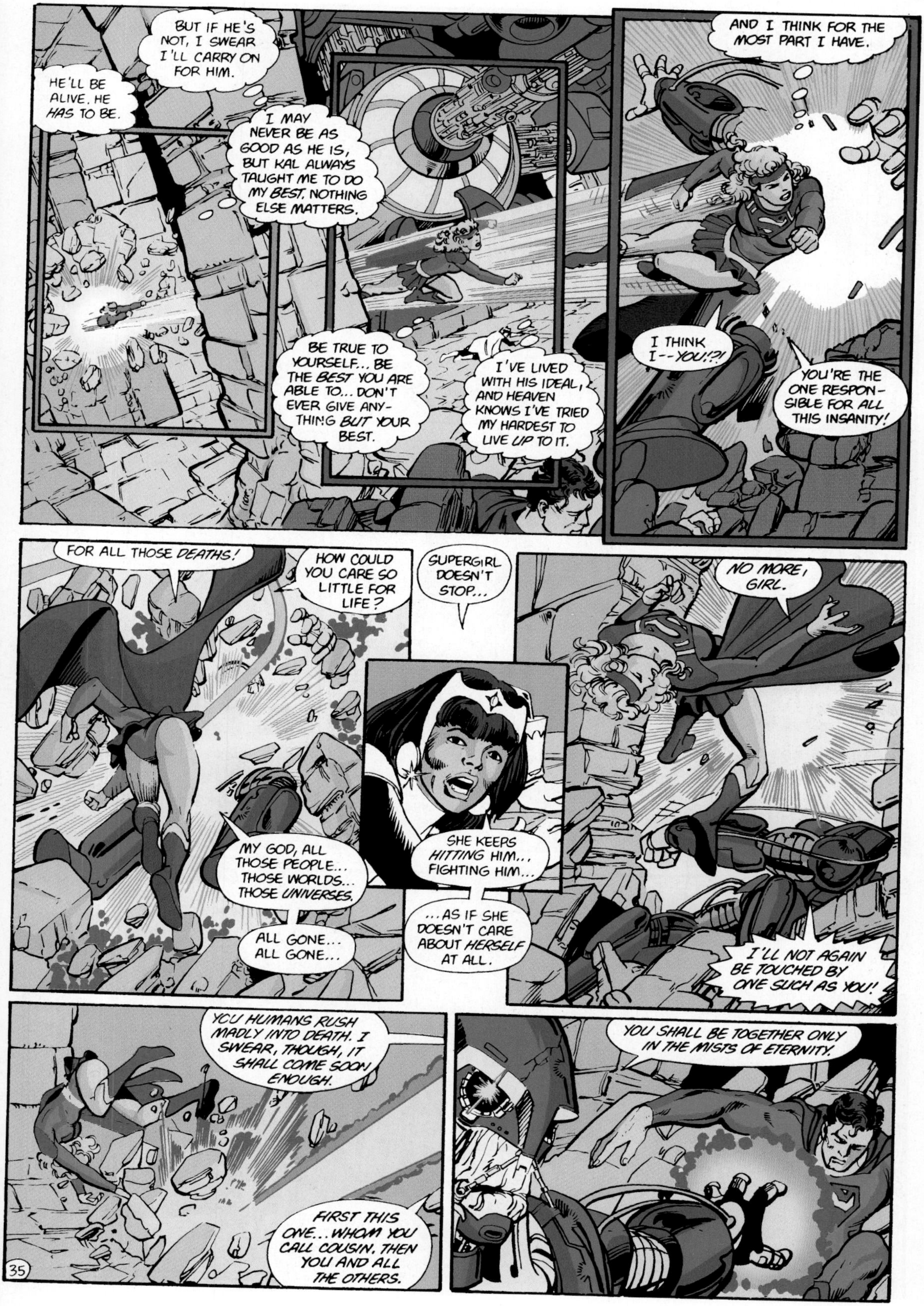
HE'LL BE ALIVE. HE *HAS* TO BE.
BUT IF HE'S NOT, I SWEAR I'LL CARRY ON FOR HIM.
I MAY NEVER BE AS GOOD AS HE IS, BUT KAL ALWAYS TAUGHT ME TO DO MY *BEST*. NOTHING ELSE MATTERS.
BE TRUE TO YOURSELF... BE THE *BEST* YOU ARE ABLE TO... DON'T EVER GIVE ANY-THING *BUT* YOUR BEST.
I'VE LIVED WITH HIS IDEAL, AND HEAVEN KNOWS I'VE TRIED MY HARDEST TO LIVE *UP* TO IT.
AND I THINK FOR THE MOST PART I HAVE.
I THINK I--*YOU!?!*
YOU'RE THE ONE RESPON-SIBLE FOR *ALL* THIS INSANITY!
FOR ALL THOSE *DEATHS!*
HOW COULD YOU CARE SO LITTLE FOR LIFE?
MY GOD, ALL THOSE PEOPLE... THOSE WORLDS... THOSE *UNIVERSES*.
ALL GONE... ALL GONE...
SUPERGIRL DOESN'T STOP...
SHE KEEPS *HITTING* HIM... FIGHTING HIM...
...AS IF SHE DOESN'T CARE ABOUT *HERSELF* AT ALL.
NO MORE, GIRL.
I'LL NOT AGAIN BE TOUCHED BY ONE SUCH AS YOU!
YOU HUMANS RUSH MADLY INTO DEATH. I SWEAR, THOUGH, IT SHALL COME SOON ENOUGH.
FIRST THIS ONE... WHOM YOU CALL COUSIN. THEN YOU AND ALL THE OTHERS.
YOU SHALL BE TOGETHER ONLY IN THE MISTS OF ETERNITY.
35

NO! YOU'RE NOT GOING TO KILL SUPERMAN.

I WON'T ALLOW IT!

YOU HEAR ME?!?

WHAT?

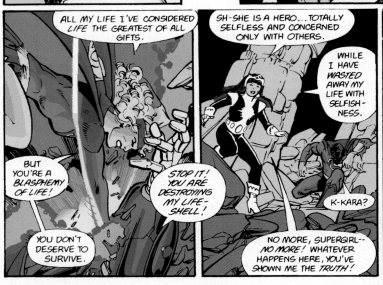

ALL MY LIFE I'VE CONSIDERED LIFE THE GREATEST OF ALL GIFTS.

BUT YOU'RE A BLASPHEMY OF LIFE!

YOU DON'T DESERVE TO SURVIVE.

SH-SHE IS A HERO...TOTALLY SELFLESS AND CONCERNED ONLY WITH OTHERS.

WHILE I HAVE WASTED AWAY MY LIFE WITH SELFISH-NESS.

STOP IT! YOU ARE DESTROYING MY LIFE-SHELL!

K-KARA?

NO MORE, SUPERGIRL-- NO MORE! WHATEVER HAPPENS HERE, YOU'VE SHOWN ME THE TRUTH!

IT IS OVER, SUPER-GIRL!

YOU HAVE DESTROYED MOST OF MY BODY!

I FEEL MY ENERGIES WANING!

THUS I CAN WAIT NO LONGER.

YOU ARE DEAD!

36

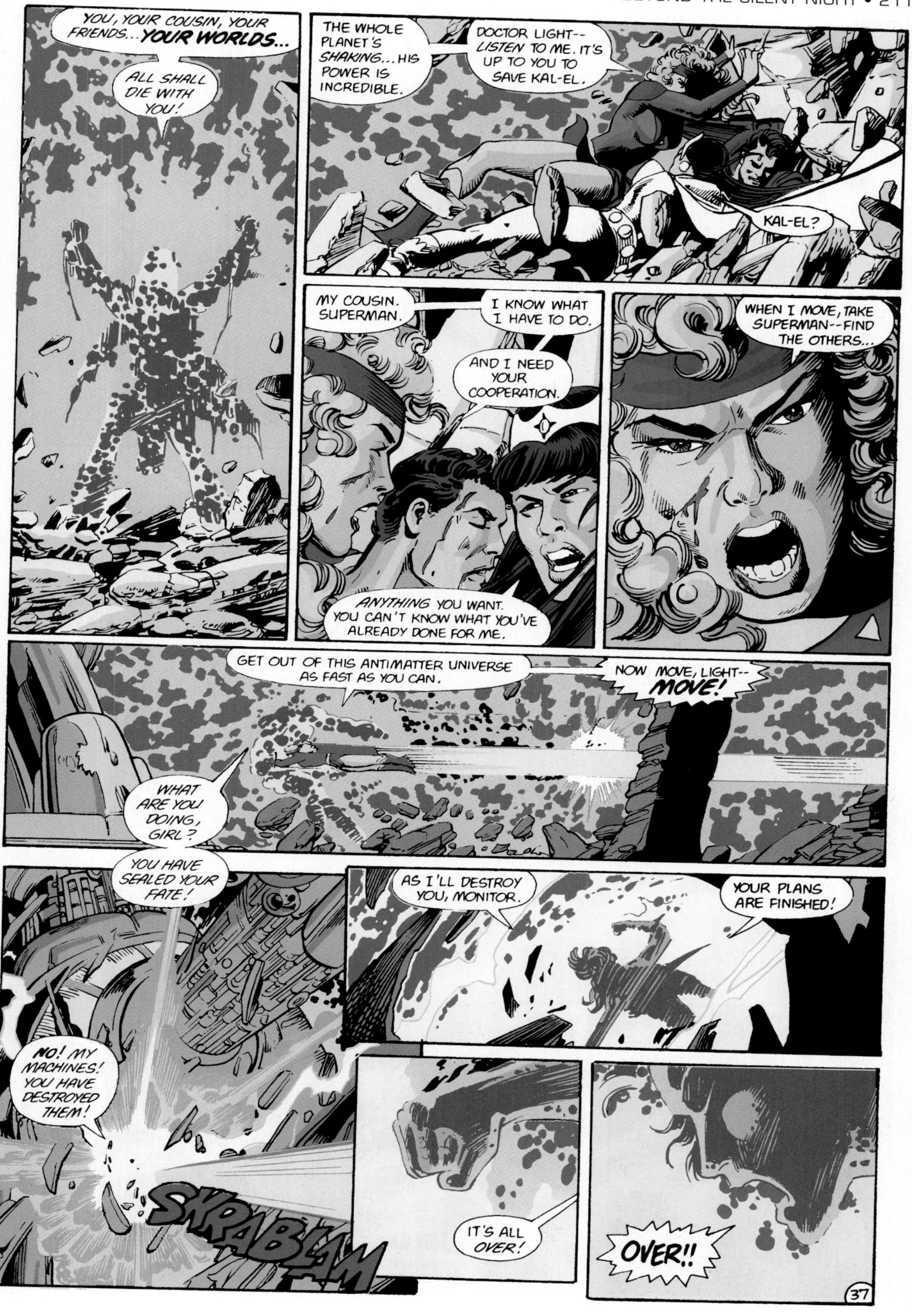
YOU, YOUR COUSIN, YOUR FRIENDS... YOUR WORLDS...
ALL SHALL DIE WITH YOU!
THE WHOLE PLANET'S SHAKING... HIS POWER IS INCREDIBLE.
DOCTOR LIGHT-- LISTEN TO ME. IT'S UP TO YOU TO SAVE KAL-EL.
KAL-EL?
MY COUSIN. SUPERMAN.
I KNOW WHAT I HAVE TO DO.
AND I NEED YOUR COOPERATION.
ANYTHING YOU WANT. YOU CAN'T KNOW WHAT YOU'VE ALREADY DONE FOR ME.
WHEN I MOVE, TAKE SUPERMAN--FIND THE OTHERS...
GET OUT OF THIS ANTIMATTER UNIVERSE AS FAST AS YOU CAN.
NOW MOVE, LIGHT-- MOVE!
WHAT ARE YOU DOING, GIRL?
YOU HAVE SEALED YOUR FATE!
AS I'LL DESTROY YOU, MONITOR.
YOUR PLANS ARE FINISHED!
NO! MY MACHINES! YOU HAVE DESTROYED THEM!
SKRABLAM
IT'S ALL OVER!
OVER!!
37

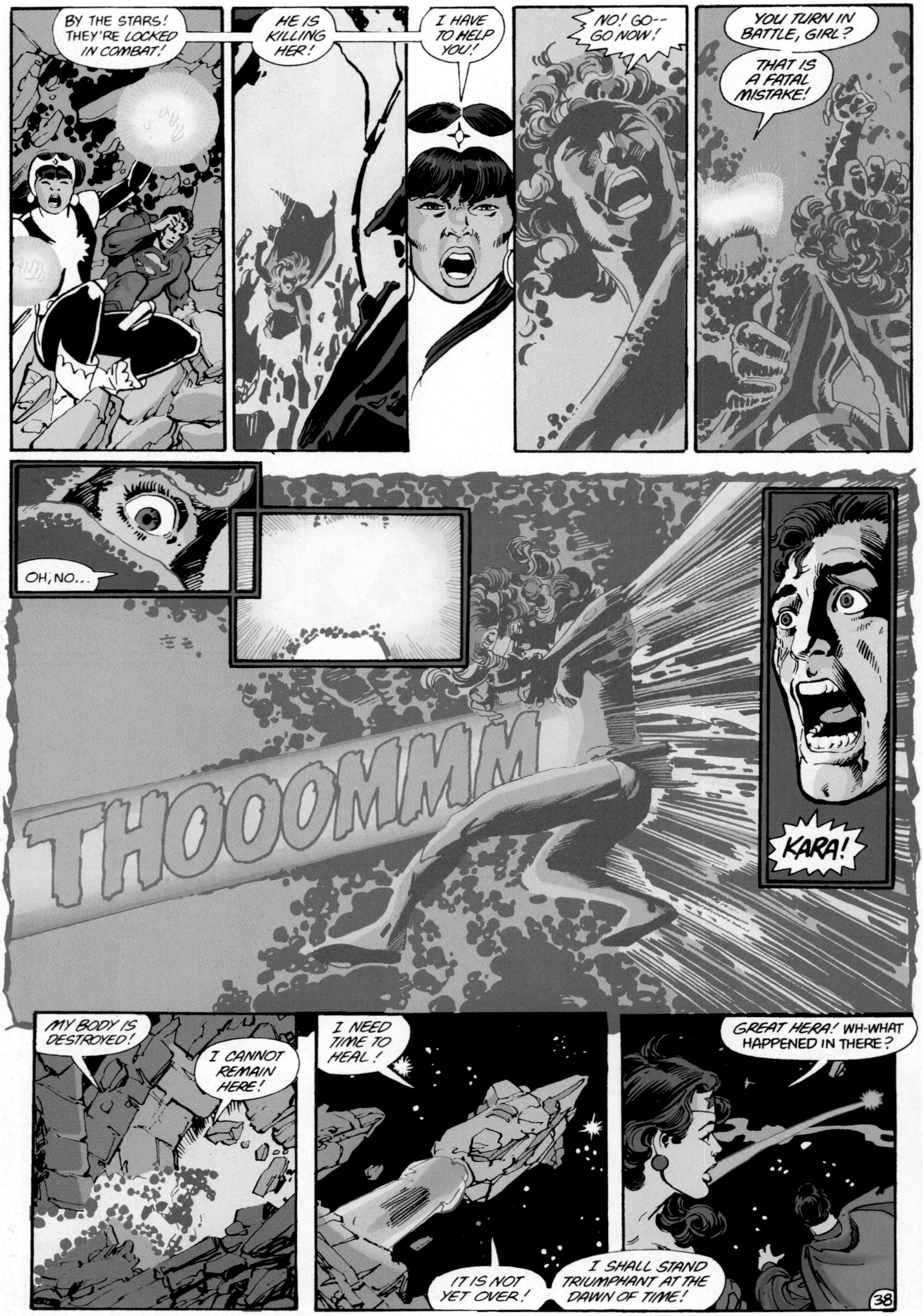
BY THE STARS! THEY'RE LOCKED IN COMBAT!
HE IS KILLING HER!
I HAVE TO HELP YOU!
NO! GO-- GO NOW!
YOU TURN IN BATTLE, GIRL?
THAT IS A FATAL MISTAKE!
OH, NO...
THOOOMMM
KARA!
MY BODY IS DESTROYED!
I CANNOT REMAIN HERE!
I NEED TIME TO HEAL!
IT IS NOT YET OVER!
I SHALL STAND TRIUMPHANT AT THE DAWN OF TIME!
GREAT HERA! WH-WHAT HAPPENED IN THERE?
38

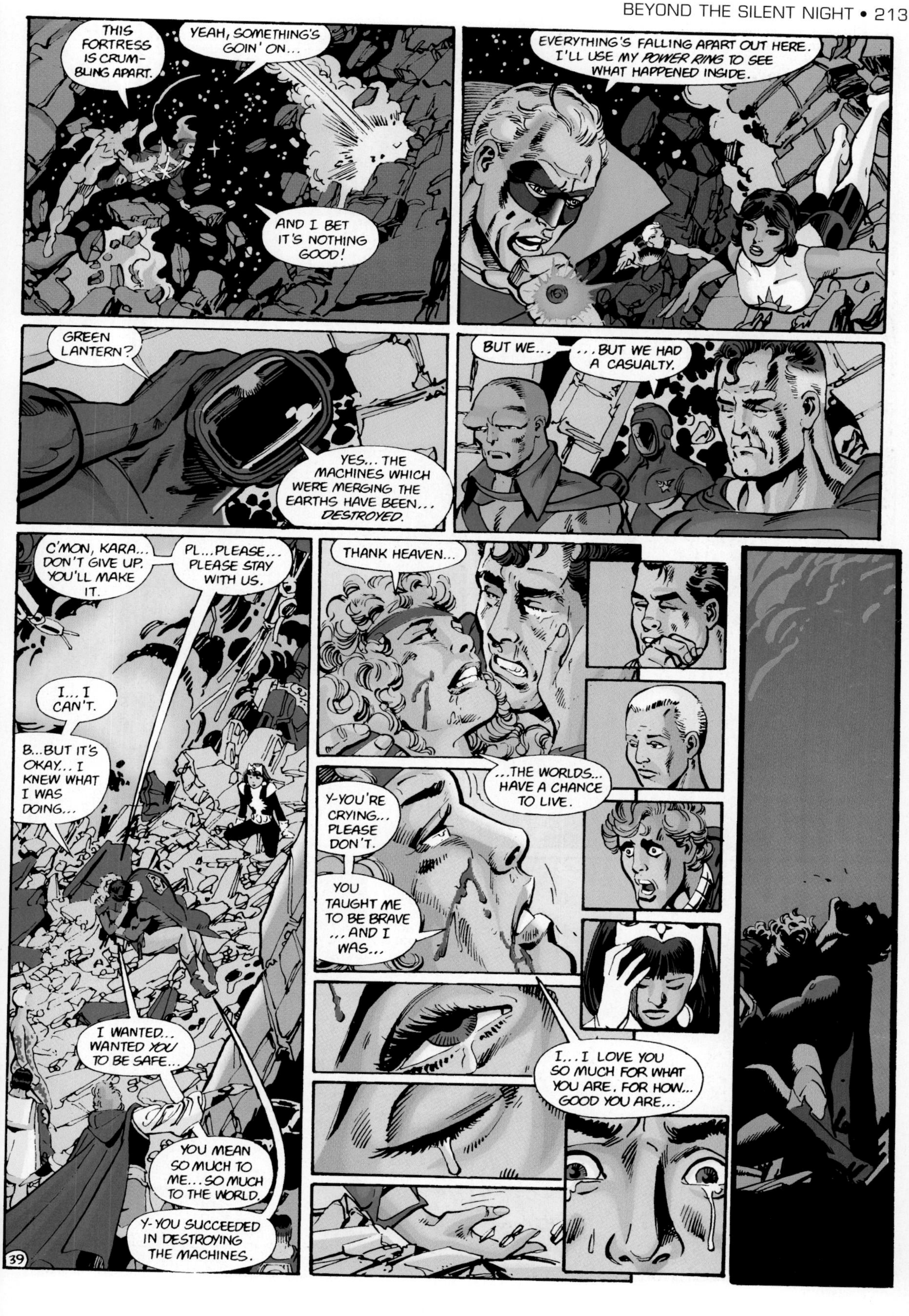
THIS FORTRESS IS CRUM-BLING APART.
YEAH, SOMETHING'S GOIN' ON...
AND I BET IT'S NOTHING GOOD!
EVERYTHING'S FALLING APART OUT HERE. I'LL USE MY POWER RING TO SEE WHAT HAPPENED INSIDE.
GREEN LANTERN?
YES... THE MACHINES WHICH WERE MERGING THE EARTHS HAVE BEEN... DESTROYED.
BUT WE...
...BUT WE HAD A CASUALTY.
C'MON, KARA... DON'T GIVE UP. YOU'LL MAKE IT.
PL...PLEASE... PLEASE STAY WITH US.
I... I CAN'T.
B...BUT IT'S OKAY... I KNEW WHAT I WAS DOING...
I WANTED... WANTED YOU TO BE SAFE...
YOU MEAN SO MUCH TO ME... SO MUCH TO THE WORLD.
Y-YOU SUCCEEDED IN DESTROYING THE MACHINES.
39
THANK HEAVEN...
...THE WORLDS... HAVE A CHANCE TO LIVE.
Y-YOU'RE CRYING... PLEASE DON'T.
YOU TAUGHT ME TO BE BRAVE ...AND I WAS...
I... I LOVE YOU SO MUCH FOR WHAT YOU ARE. FOR HOW... GOOD YOU ARE...

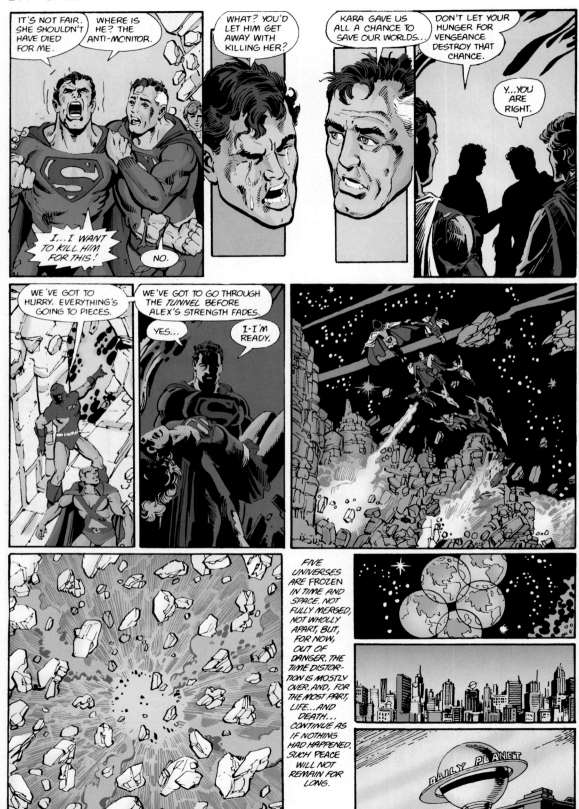

IT'S NOT FAIR. SHE SHOULDN'T HAVE DIED FOR ME.

WHERE IS HE? THE ANTI-MONITOR.

WHAT? YOU'D LET HIM GET AWAY WITH KILLING HER?

KARA GAVE US ALL A CHANCE TO SAVE OUR WORLDS...

DON'T LET YOUR HUNGER FOR VENGEANCE DESTROY THAT CHANCE.

Y...YOU ARE RIGHT.

I...I WANT TO KILL HIM FOR THIS!

NO.

WE'VE GOT TO HURRY. EVERYTHING'S GOING TO PIECES.

WE'VE GOT TO GO THROUGH THE TUNNEL BEFORE ALEX'S STRENGTH FADES.

YES...

I-I'M READY.

FIVE UNIVERSES ARE FROZEN IN TIME AND SPACE, NOT FULLY MERGED, NOT WHOLLY APART, BUT, FOR NOW, OUT OF DANGER. THE TIME DISTORTION IS MOSTLY OVER. AND, FOR THE MOST PART, LIFE...AND DEATH... CONTINUE AS IF NOTHING HAD HAPPENED. SUCH PEACE WILL NOT REMAIN FOR LONG.

DAILY PLANET

40

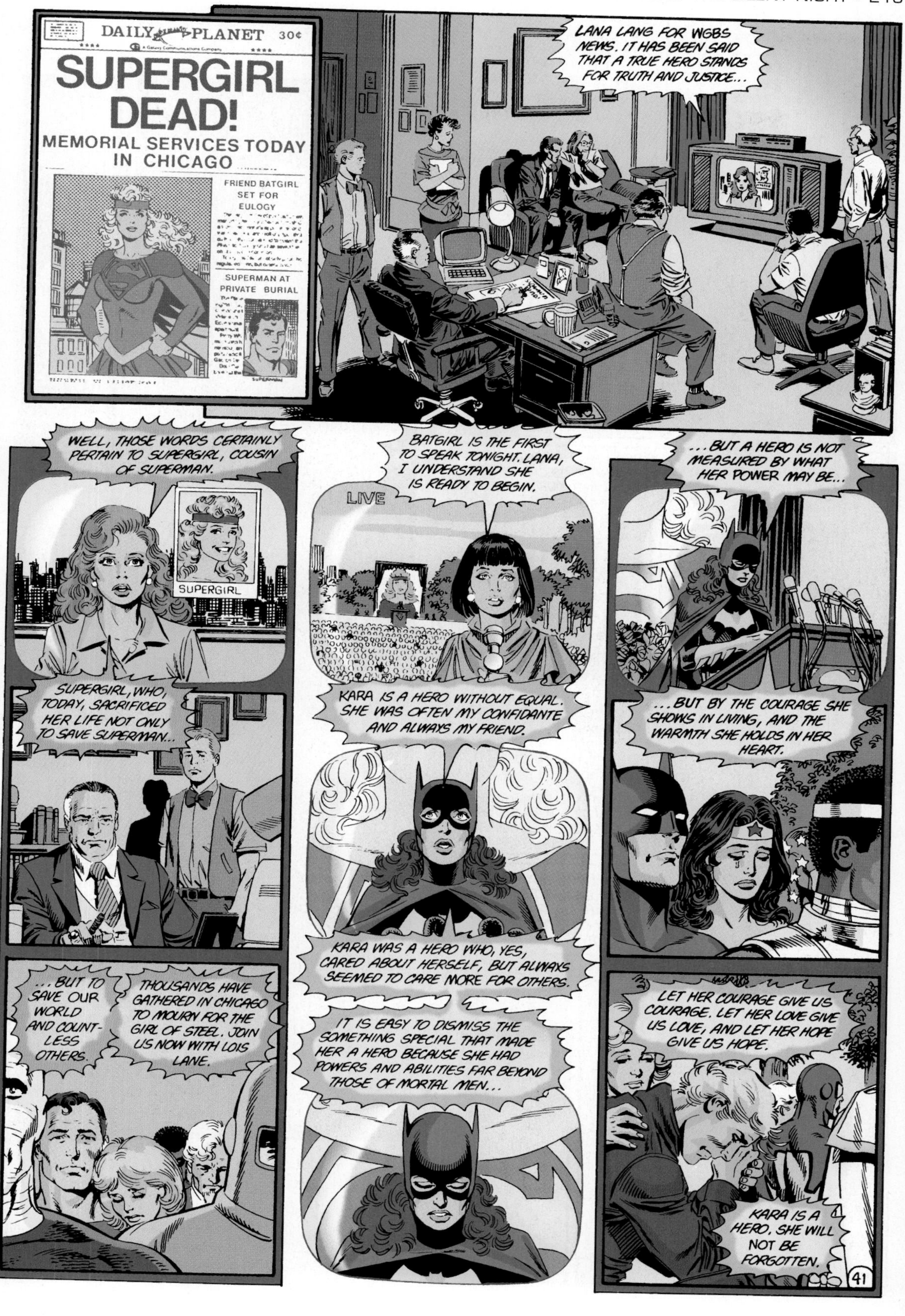
DAILY PLANET 30¢
SUPERGIRL DEAD!
MEMORIAL SERVICES TODAY IN CHICAGO
FRIEND BATGIRL SET FOR EULOGY
SUPERMAN AT PRIVATE BURIAL
LANA LANG FOR WGBS NEWS. IT HAS BEEN SAID THAT A TRUE HERO STANDS FOR TRUTH AND JUSTICE...
WELL, THOSE WORDS CERTAINLY PERTAIN TO SUPERGIRL, COUSIN OF SUPERMAN.
SUPERGIRL
SUPERGIRL, WHO, TODAY, SACRIFICED HER LIFE NOT ONLY TO SAVE SUPERMAN...
...BUT TO SAVE OUR WORLD AND COUNT-LESS OTHERS.
THOUSANDS HAVE GATHERED IN CHICAGO TO MOURN FOR THE GIRL OF STEEL. JOIN US NOW WITH LOIS LANE.
BATGIRL IS THE FIRST TO SPEAK TONIGHT. LANA, I UNDERSTAND SHE IS READY TO BEGIN.
LIVE
KARA IS A HERO WITHOUT EQUAL. SHE WAS OFTEN MY CONFIDANTE AND ALWAYS MY FRIEND.
KARA WAS A HERO WHO, YES, CARED ABOUT HERSELF, BUT ALWAYS SEEMED TO CARE MORE FOR OTHERS.
IT IS EASY TO DISMISS THE SOMETHING SPECIAL THAT MADE HER A HERO BECAUSE SHE HAD POWERS AND ABILITIES FAR BEYOND THOSE OF MORTAL MEN...
...BUT A HERO IS NOT MEASURED BY WHAT HER POWER MAY BE...
...BUT BY THE COURAGE SHE SHOWS IN LIVING, AND THE WARMTH SHE HOLDS IN HER HEART.
LET HER COURAGE GIVE US COURAGE. LET HER LOVE GIVE US LOVE, AND LET HER HOPE GIVE US HOPE.
KARA IS A HERO. SHE WILL NOT BE FORGOTTEN.
41

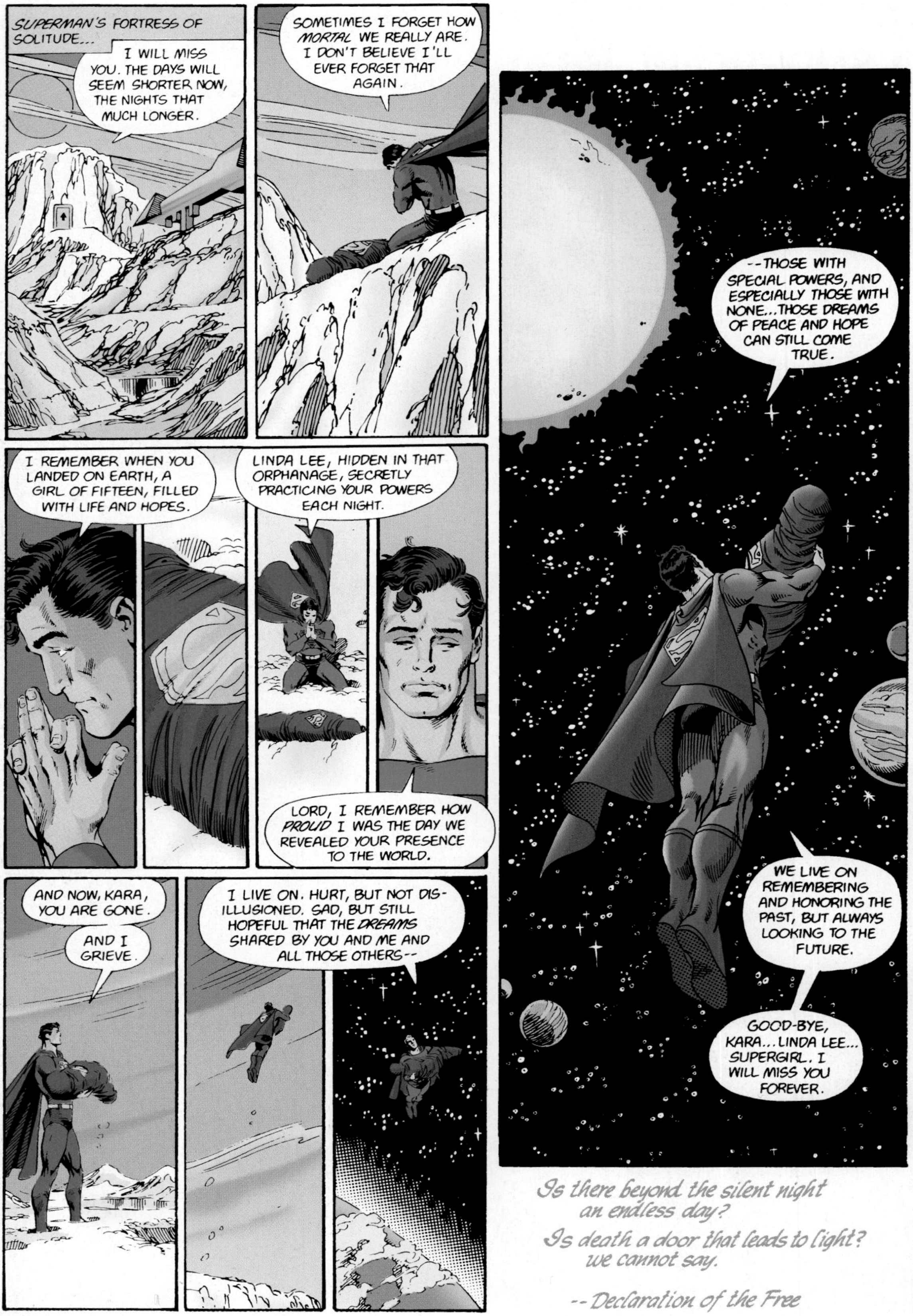
SUPERMAN'S FORTRESS OF SOLITUDE...
I WILL MISS YOU. THE DAYS WILL SEEM SHORTER NOW, THE NIGHTS THAT MUCH LONGER.
SOMETIMES I FORGET HOW MORTAL WE REALLY ARE. I DON'T BELIEVE I'LL EVER FORGET THAT AGAIN.
I REMEMBER WHEN YOU LANDED ON EARTH, A GIRL OF FIFTEEN, FILLED WITH LIFE AND HOPES.
LINDA LEE, HIDDEN IN THAT ORPHANAGE, SECRETLY PRACTICING YOUR POWERS EACH NIGHT.
LORD, I REMEMBER HOW PROUD I WAS THE DAY WE REVEALED YOUR PRESENCE TO THE WORLD.
AND NOW, KARA, YOU ARE GONE.
AND I GRIEVE.
I LIVE ON. HURT, BUT NOT DIS-ILLUSIONED. SAD, BUT STILL HOPEFUL THAT THE DREAMS SHARED BY YOU AND ME AND ALL THOSE OTHERS--
--THOSE WITH SPECIAL POWERS, AND ESPECIALLY THOSE WITH NONE...THOSE DREAMS OF PEACE AND HOPE CAN STILL COME TRUE.
WE LIVE ON REMEMBERING AND HONORING THE PAST, BUT ALWAYS LOOKING TO THE FUTURE.
GOOD-BYE, KARA...LINDA LEE... SUPERGIRL. I WILL MISS YOU FOREVER.

Is there beyond the silent night
an endless day?
Is death a door that leads to light?
we cannot say.

--Declaration of the Free

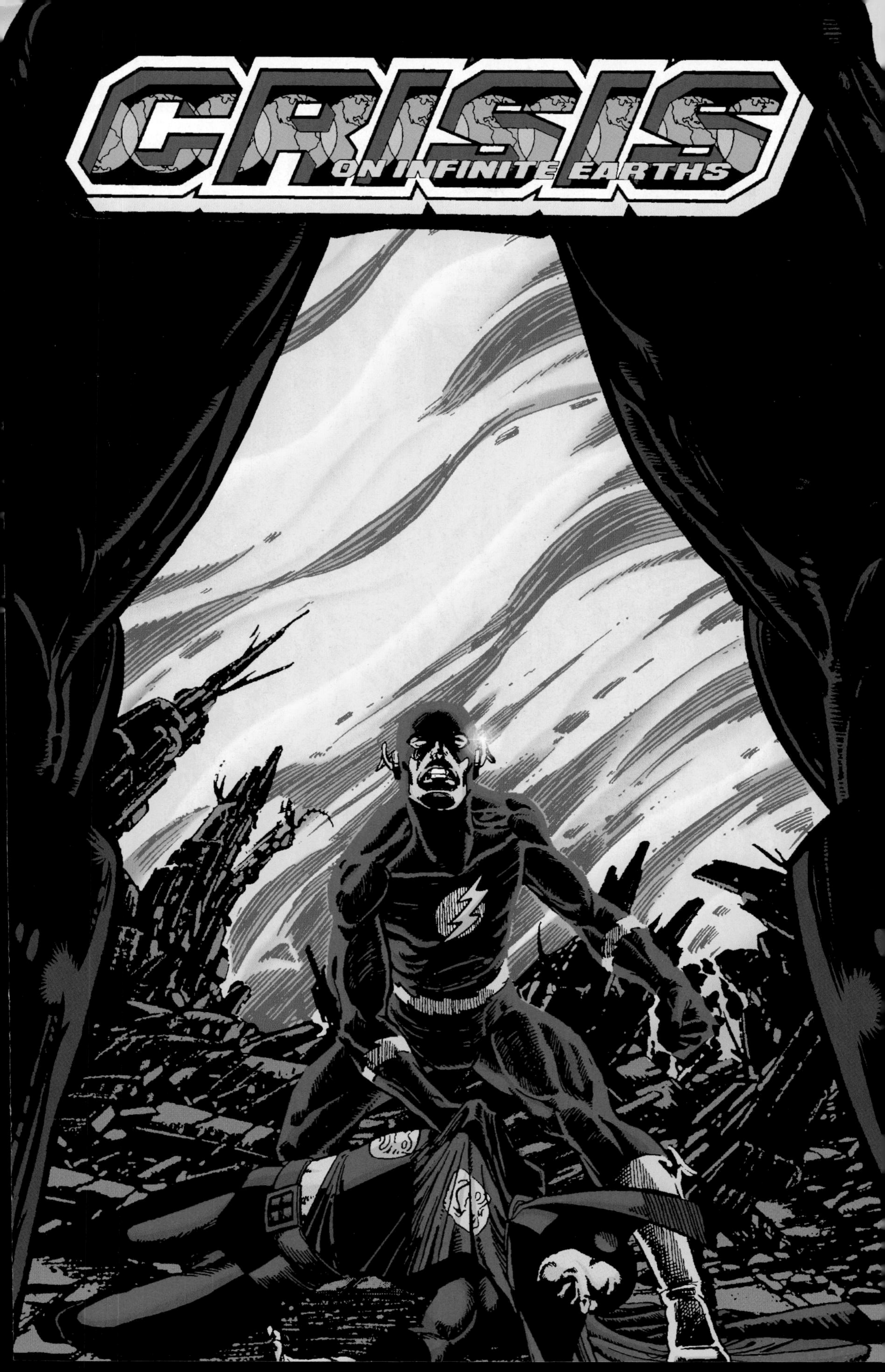
CRISIS
ON INFINITE EARTHS

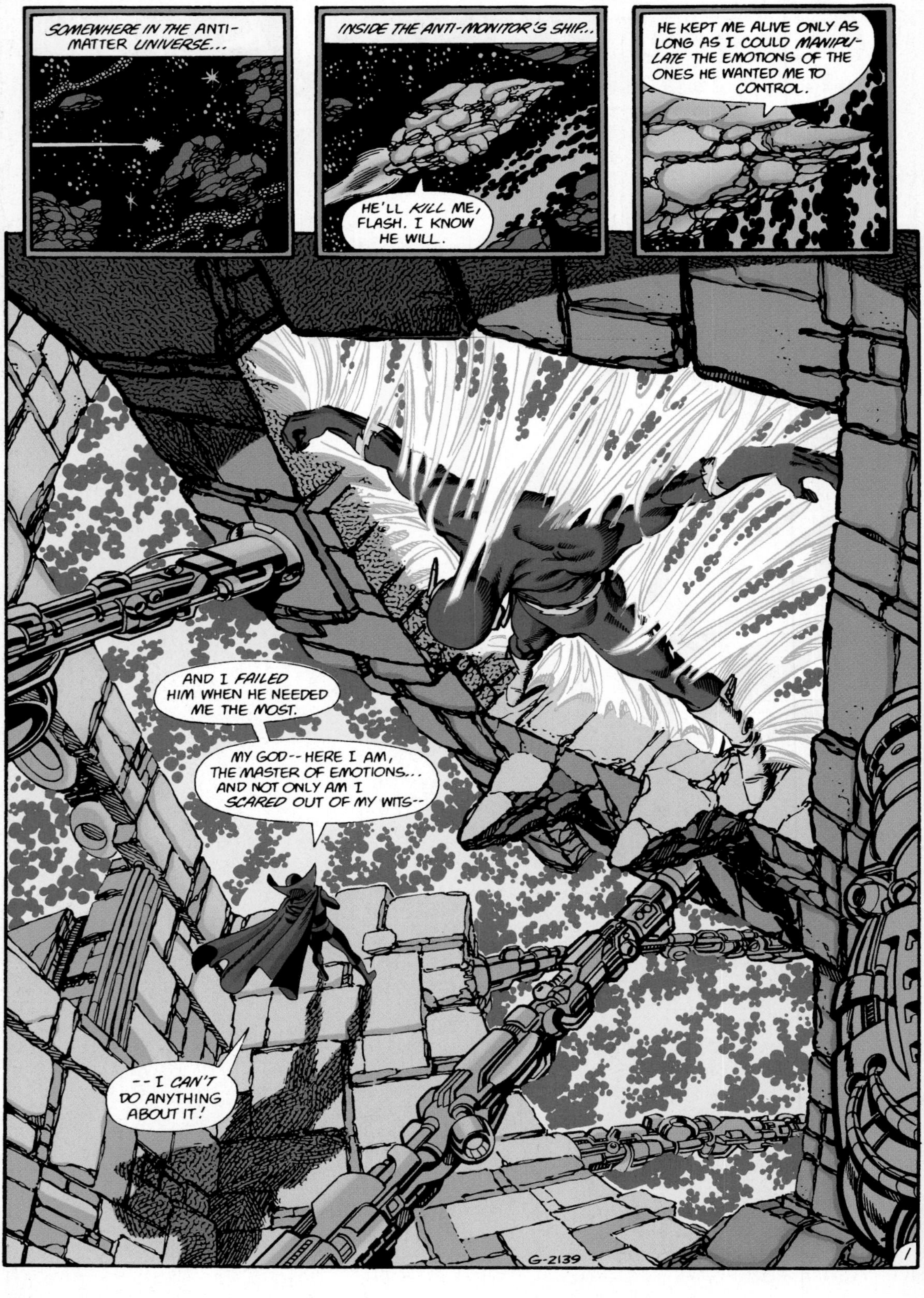
SOMEWHERE IN THE ANTI-MATTER UNIVERSE...
INSIDE THE ANTI-MONITOR'S SHIP...
HE'LL KILL ME, FLASH. I KNOW HE WILL.
HE KEPT ME ALIVE ONLY AS LONG AS I COULD MANIPULATE THE EMOTIONS OF THE ONES HE WANTED ME TO CONTROL.
AND I FAILED HIM WHEN HE NEEDED ME THE MOST.
MY GOD--HERE I AM, THE MASTER OF EMOTIONS... AND NOT ONLY AM I SCARED OUT OF MY WITS-
--I CAN'T DO ANYTHING ABOUT IT!
G-2139
1

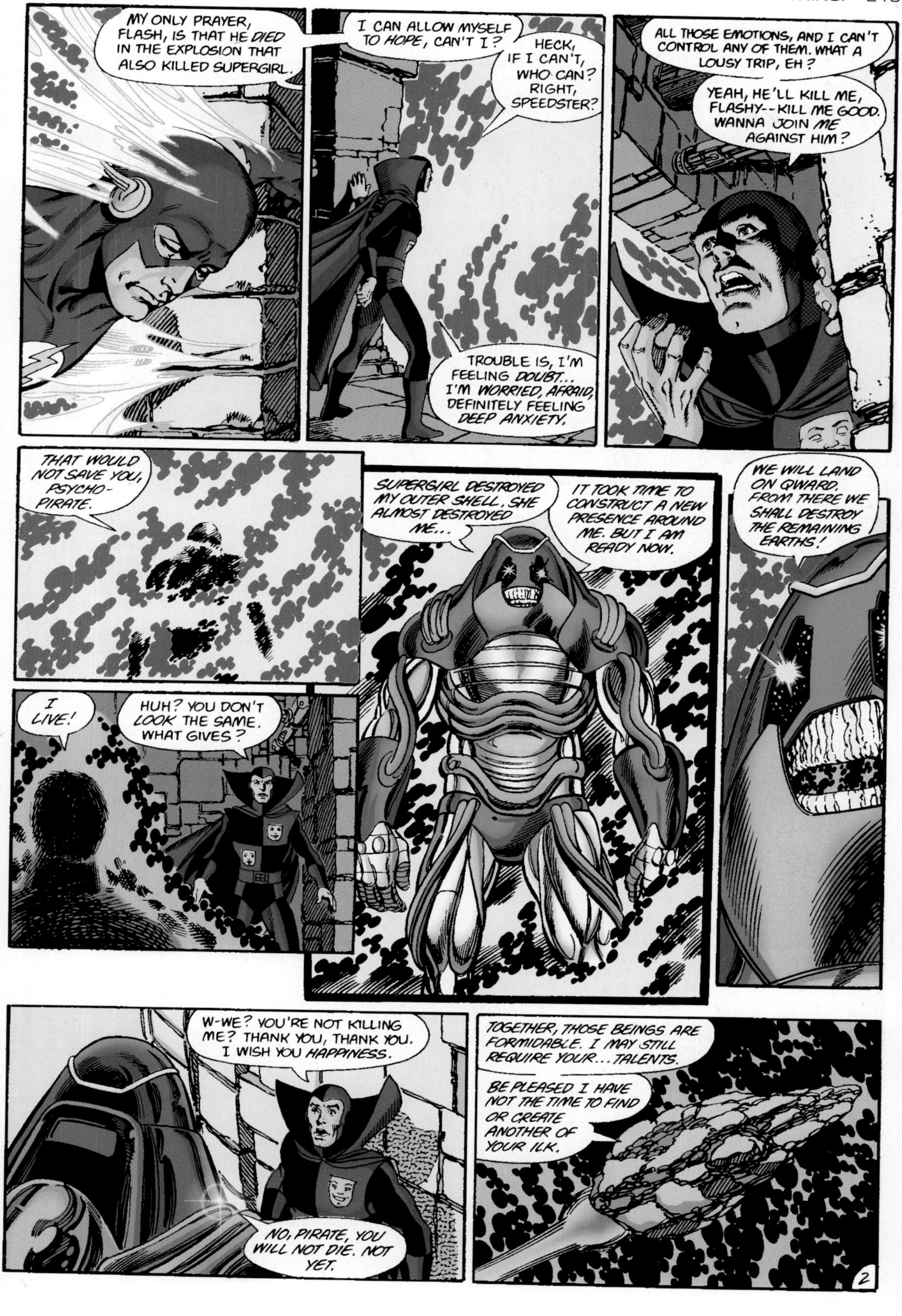
MY ONLY PRAYER, FLASH, IS THAT HE DIED IN THE EXPLOSION THAT ALSO KILLED SUPERGIRL.
I CAN ALLOW MYSELF TO HOPE, CAN'T I?
HECK, IF I CAN'T, WHO CAN? RIGHT, SPEEDSTER?
TROUBLE IS, I'M FEELING DOUBT... I'M WORRIED, AFRAID, DEFINITELY FEELING DEEP ANXIETY.
ALL THOSE EMOTIONS, AND I CAN'T CONTROL ANY OF THEM. WHAT A LOUSY TRIP, EH?
YEAH, HE'LL KILL ME, FLASHY--KILL ME GOOD. WANNA JOIN ME AGAINST HIM?
THAT WOULD NOT SAVE YOU, PSYCHO-PIRATE.
I LIVE!
HUH? YOU DON'T LOOK THE SAME. WHAT GIVES?
SUPERGIRL DESTROYED MY OUTER SHELL. SHE ALMOST DESTROYED ME...
IT TOOK TIME TO CONSTRUCT A NEW PRESENCE AROUND ME. BUT I AM READY NOW.
WE WILL LAND ON QWARD. FROM THERE WE SHALL DESTROY THE REMAINING EARTHS!
W-WE? YOU'RE NOT KILLING ME? THANK YOU, THANK YOU. I WISH YOU HAPPINESS.
NO, PIRATE, YOU WILL NOT DIE. NOT YET.
TOGETHER, THOSE BEINGS ARE FORMIDABLE. I MAY STILL REQUIRE YOUR... TALENTS.
BE PLEASED I HAVE NOT THE TIME TO FIND OR CREATE ANOTHER OF YOUR ILK.
2

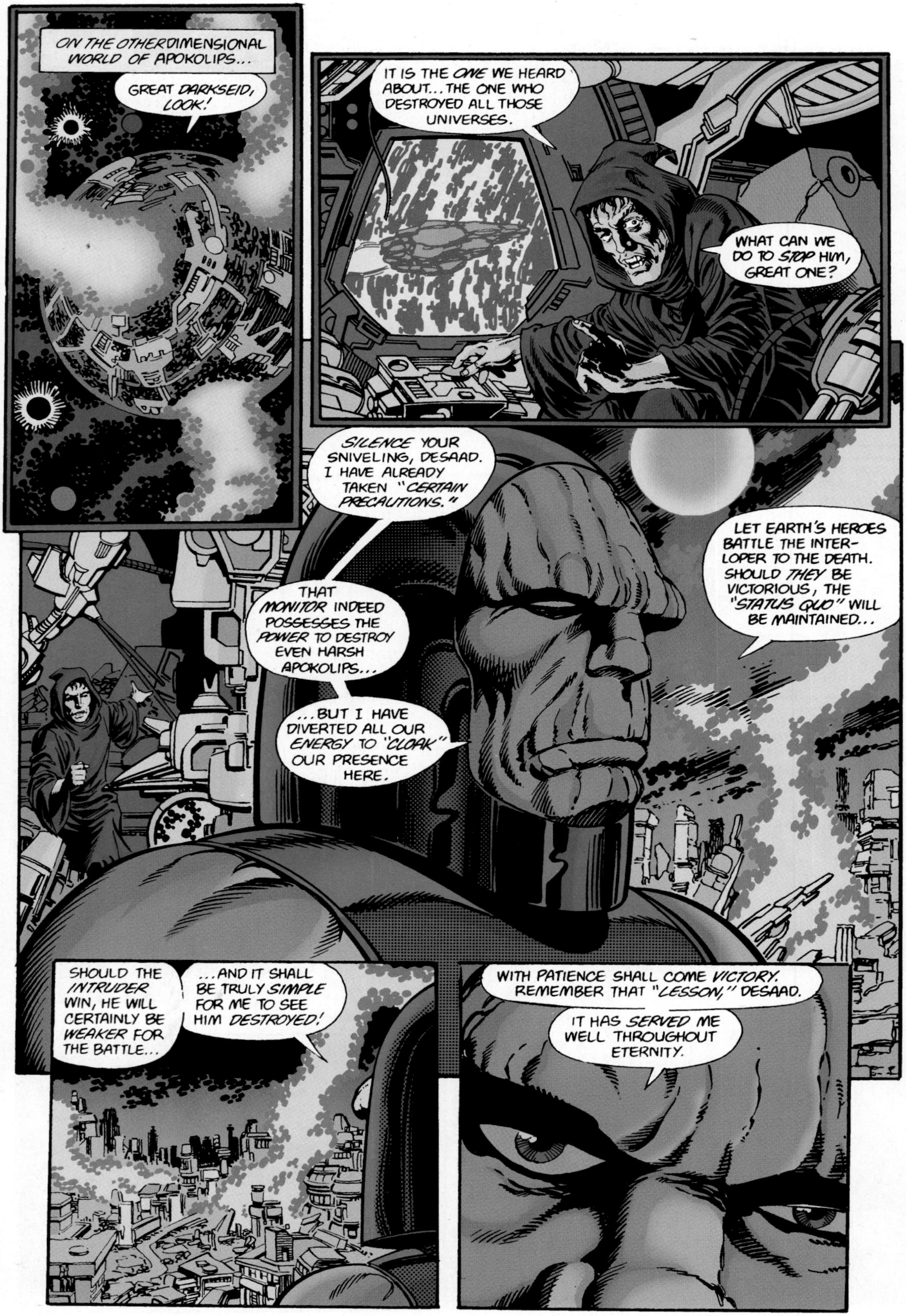
ON THE OTHERDIMENSIONAL WORLD OF APOKOLIPS...
GREAT DARKSEID, LOOK!
IT IS THE ONE WE HEARD ABOUT... THE ONE WHO DESTROYED ALL THOSE UNIVERSES.
WHAT CAN WE DO TO STOP HIM, GREAT ONE?
SILENCE YOUR SNIVELING, DESAAD. I HAVE ALREADY TAKEN "CERTAIN PRECAUTIONS."
THAT MONITOR INDEED POSSESSES THE POWER TO DESTROY EVEN HARSH APOKOLIPS...
...BUT I HAVE DIVERTED ALL OUR ENERGY TO "CLOAK" OUR PRESENCE HERE.
LET EARTH'S HEROES BATTLE THE INTER-LOPER TO THE DEATH. SHOULD THEY BE VICTORIOUS, THE "STATUS QUO" WILL BE MAINTAINED...
SHOULD THE INTRUDER WIN, HE WILL CERTAINLY BE WEAKER FOR THE BATTLE...
...AND IT SHALL BE TRULY SIMPLE FOR ME TO SEE HIM DESTROYED!
WITH PATIENCE SHALL COME VICTORY. REMEMBER THAT "LESSON," DESAAD.
IT HAS SERVED ME WELL THROUGHOUT ETERNITY.

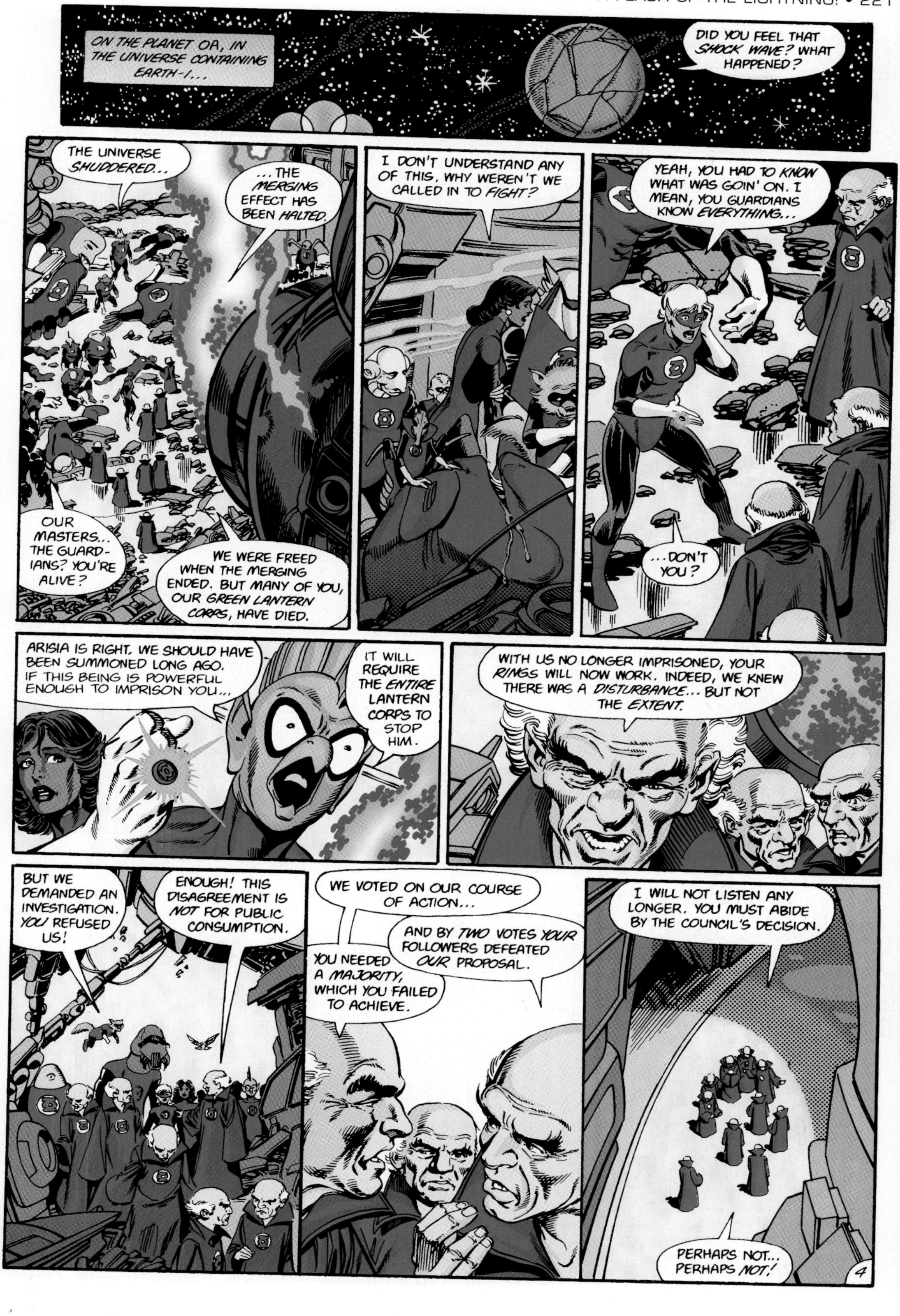
ON THE PLANET OA, IN THE UNIVERSE CONTAINING EARTH-1...
DID YOU FEEL THAT SHOCK WAVE? WHAT HAPPENED?
THE UNIVERSE SHUDDERED...
...THE MERGING EFFECT HAS BEEN HALTED.
OUR MASTERS... THE GUARDIANS? YOU'RE ALIVE?
WE WERE FREED WHEN THE MERGING ENDED. BUT MANY OF YOU, OUR GREEN LANTERN CORPS, HAVE DIED.
I DON'T UNDERSTAND ANY OF THIS. WHY WEREN'T WE CALLED IN TO FIGHT?
YEAH, YOU HAD TO KNOW WHAT WAS GOIN' ON. I MEAN, YOU GUARDIANS KNOW EVERYTHING...
...DON'T YOU?
ARISIA IS RIGHT. WE SHOULD HAVE BEEN SUMMONED LONG AGO. IF THIS BEING IS POWERFUL ENOUGH TO IMPRISON YOU...
IT WILL REQUIRE THE ENTIRE LANTERN CORPS TO STOP HIM.
WITH US NO LONGER IMPRISONED, YOUR RINGS WILL NOW WORK. INDEED, WE KNEW THERE WAS A DISTURBANCE... BUT NOT THE EXTENT.
BUT WE DEMANDED AN INVESTIGATION. YOU REFUSED US!
ENOUGH! THIS DISAGREEMENT IS NOT FOR PUBLIC CONSUMPTION.
WE VOTED ON OUR COURSE OF ACTION...
AND BY TWO VOTES YOUR FOLLOWERS DEFEATED OUR PROPOSAL.
YOU NEEDED A MAJORITY, WHICH YOU FAILED TO ACHIEVE.
I WILL NOT LISTEN ANY LONGER. YOU MUST ABIDE BY THE COUNCIL'S DECISION.
PERHAPS NOT... PERHAPS NOT!
4

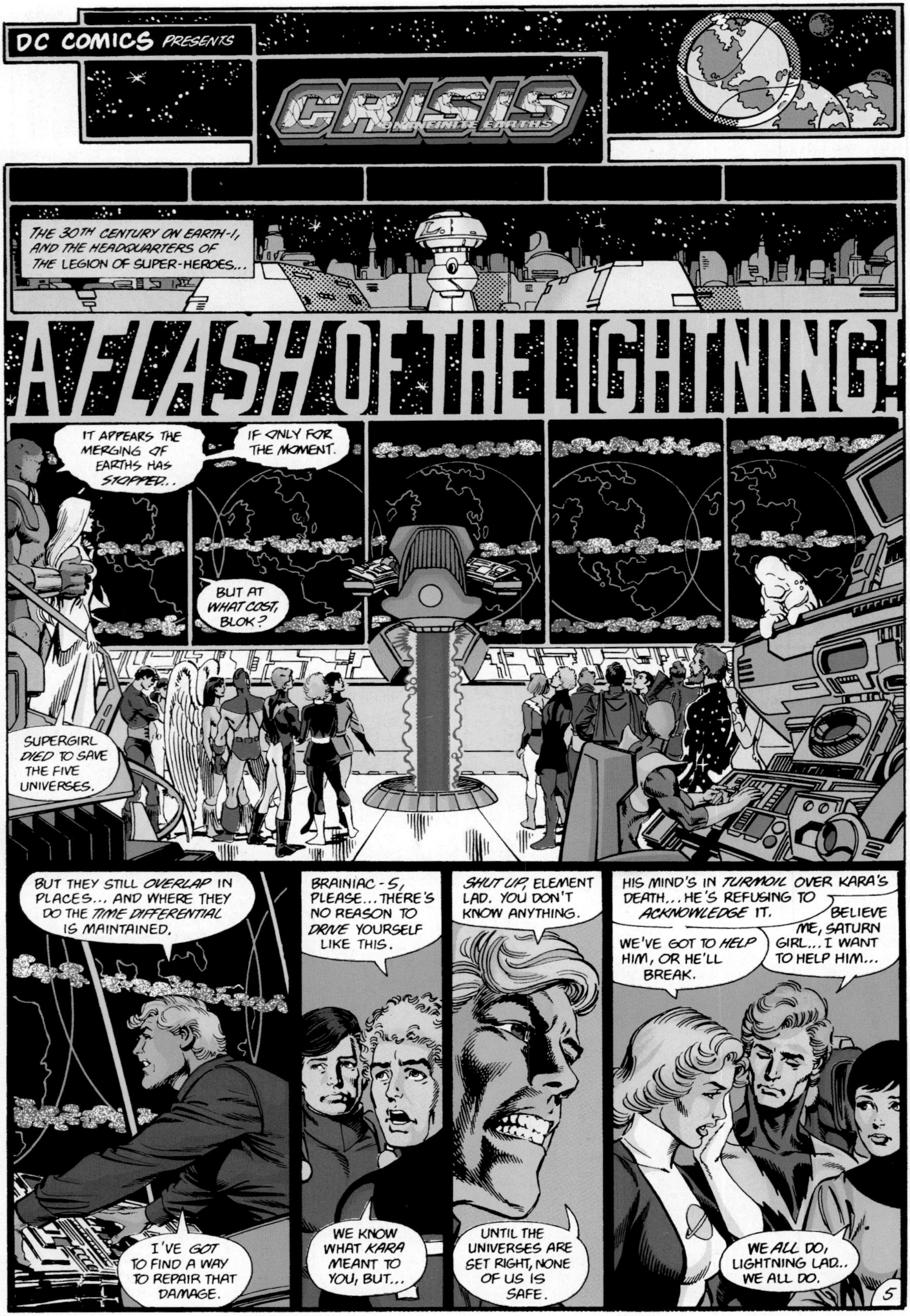
DC COMICS PRESENTS
CRISIS ON INFINITE EARTHS
THE 30TH CENTURY ON EARTH-1, AND THE HEADQUARTERS OF THE LEGION OF SUPER-HEROES...
A FLASH OF THE LIGHTNING!
IT APPEARS THE MERGING OF EARTHS HAS STOPPED..
IF ONLY FOR THE MOMENT.
BUT AT WHAT COST, BLOK?
SUPERGIRL DIED TO SAVE THE FIVE UNIVERSES.
BUT THEY STILL OVERLAP IN PLACES... AND WHERE THEY DO THE TIME DIFFERENTIAL IS MAINTAINED.
I'VE GOT TO FIND A WAY TO REPAIR THAT DAMAGE.
BRAINIAC-5, PLEASE... THERE'S NO REASON TO DRIVE YOURSELF LIKE THIS.
WE KNOW WHAT KARA MEANT TO YOU, BUT...
SHUT UP, ELEMENT LAD. YOU DON'T KNOW ANYTHING.
UNTIL THE UNIVERSES ARE SET RIGHT, NONE OF US IS SAFE.
HIS MIND'S IN TURMOIL OVER KARA'S DEATH... HE'S REFUSING TO ACKNOWLEDGE IT.
WE'VE GOT TO HELP HIM, OR HE'LL BREAK.
BELIEVE ME, SATURN GIRL... I WANT TO HELP HIM...
WE ALL DO, LIGHTNING LAD.. WE ALL DO.
5

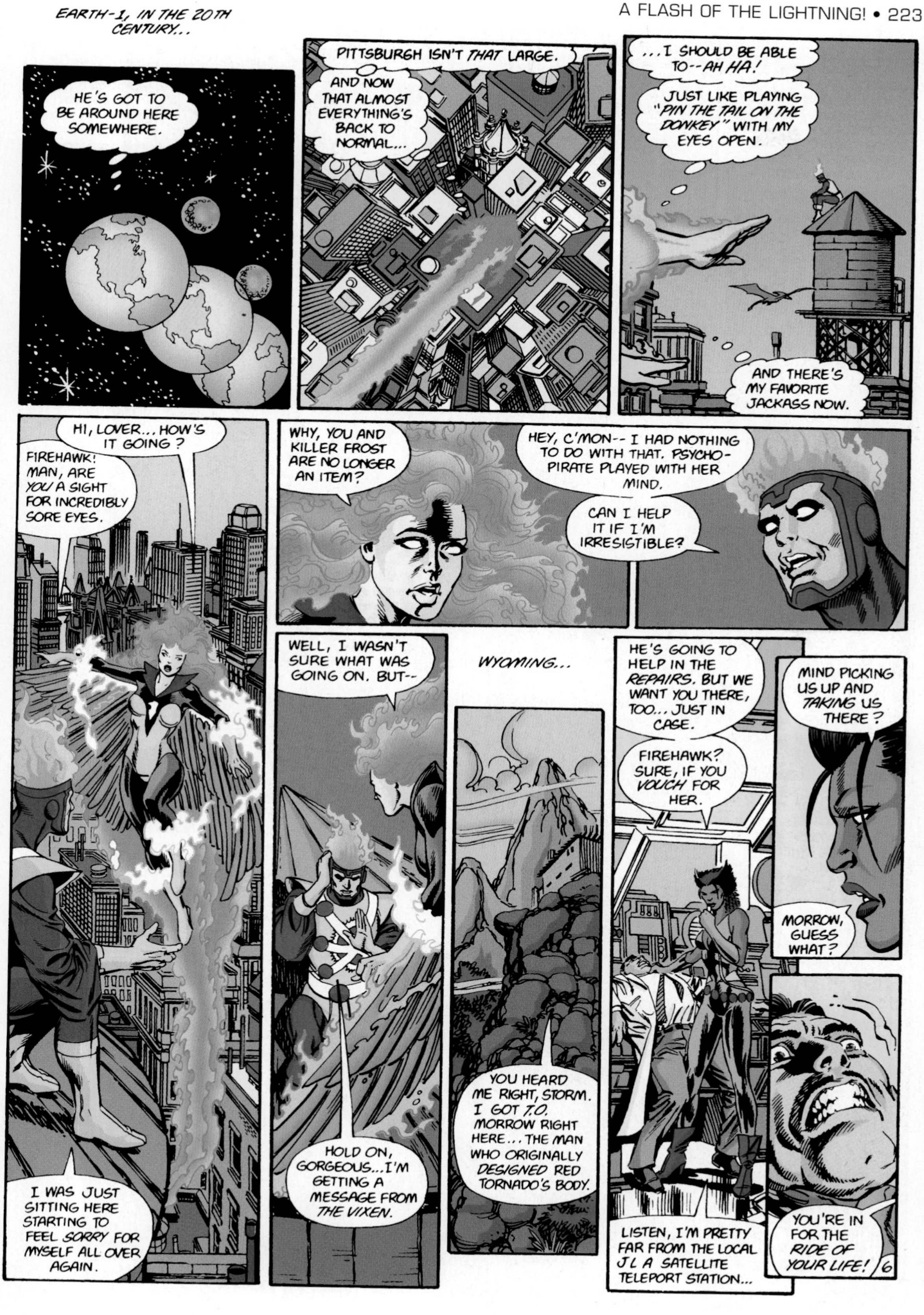
EARTH-1, IN THE 20TH CENTURY...
HE'S GOT TO BE AROUND HERE SOMEWHERE.
PITTSBURGH ISN'T THAT LARGE.
AND NOW THAT ALMOST EVERYTHING'S BACK TO NORMAL...
...I SHOULD BE ABLE TO--AH HA!
JUST LIKE PLAYING "PIN THE TAIL ON THE DONKEY" WITH MY EYES OPEN.
AND THERE'S MY FAVORITE JACKASS NOW.
HI, LOVER... HOW'S IT GOING?
FIREHAWK! MAN, ARE YOU A SIGHT FOR INCREDIBLY SORE EYES.
I WAS JUST SITTING HERE STARTING TO FEEL SORRY FOR MYSELF ALL OVER AGAIN.
WHY, YOU AND KILLER FROST ARE NO LONGER AN ITEM?
HEY, C'MON-- I HAD NOTHING TO DO WITH THAT. PSYCHO-PIRATE PLAYED WITH HER MIND.
CAN I HELP IT IF I'M IRRESISTIBLE?
WELL, I WASN'T SURE WHAT WAS GOING ON. BUT--
HOLD ON, GORGEOUS...I'M GETTING A MESSAGE FROM THE VIXEN.
WYOMING...
YOU HEARD ME RIGHT, STORM. I GOT T.O. MORROW RIGHT HERE... THE MAN WHO ORIGINALLY DESIGNED RED TORNADO'S BODY.
HE'S GOING TO HELP IN THE REPAIRS. BUT WE WANT YOU THERE, TOO... JUST IN CASE.
FIREHAWK? SURE, IF YOU VOUCH FOR HER.
LISTEN, I'M PRETTY FAR FROM THE LOCAL JLA SATELLITE TELEPORT STATION...
MIND PICKING US UP AND TAKING US THERE?
MORROW, GUESS WHAT?
YOU'RE IN FOR THE RIDE OF YOUR LIFE!
6

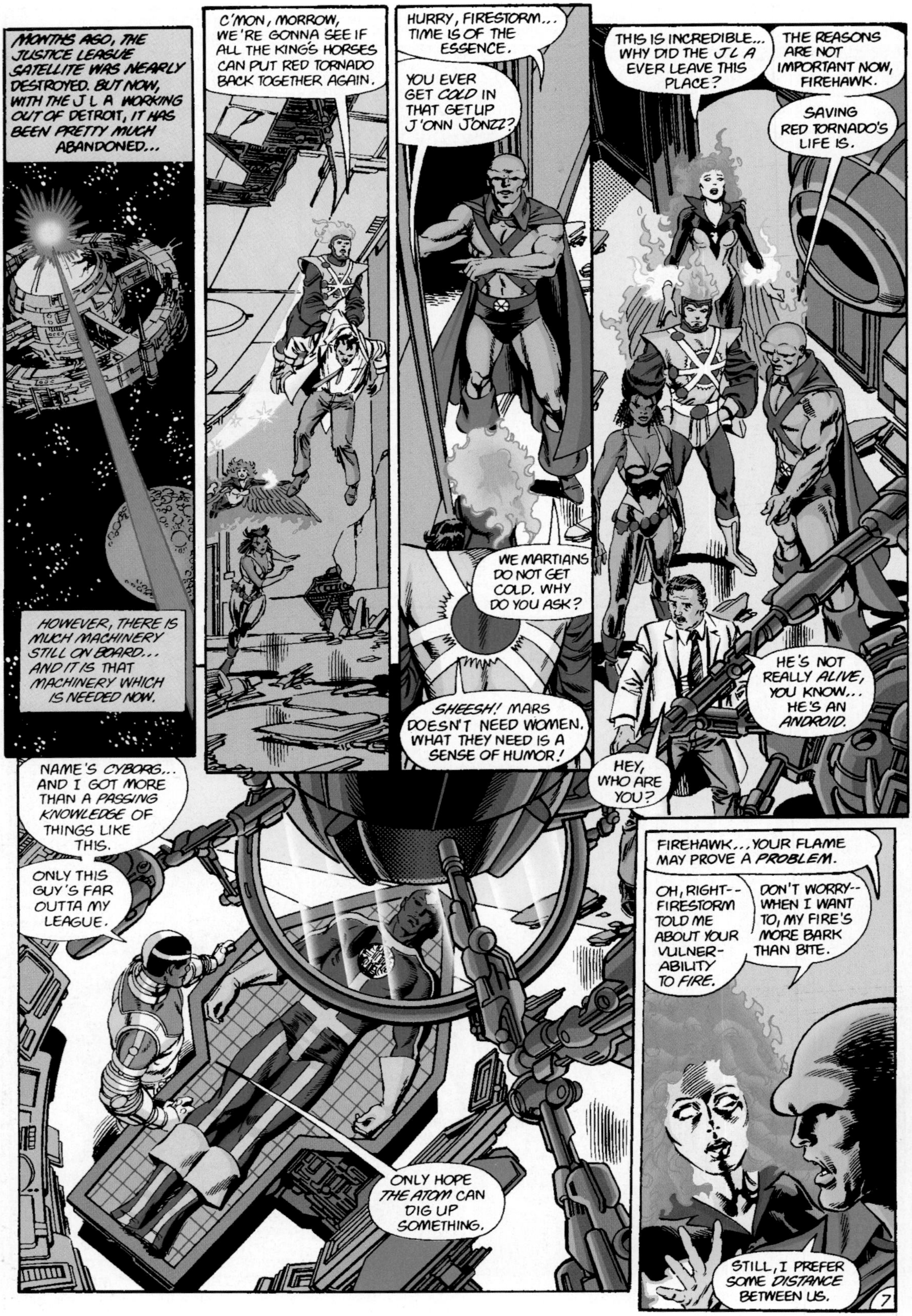
MONTHS AGO, THE JUSTICE LEAGUE SATELLITE WAS NEARLY DESTROYED. BUT NOW, WITH THE J L A WORKING OUT OF DETROIT, IT HAS BEEN PRETTY MUCH ABANDONED...
HOWEVER, THERE IS MUCH MACHINERY STILL ON BOARD... AND IT IS THAT MACHINERY WHICH IS NEEDED NOW.
C'MON, MORROW, WE'RE GONNA SEE IF ALL THE KING'S HORSES CAN PUT RED TORNADO BACK TOGETHER AGAIN.
HURRY, FIRESTORM... TIME IS OF THE ESSENCE.
YOU EVER GET COLD IN THAT GETUP J'ONN J'ONZZ?
WE MARTIANS DO NOT GET COLD. WHY DO YOU ASK?
SHEESH! MARS DOESN'T NEED WOMEN. WHAT THEY NEED IS A SENSE OF HUMOR!
THIS IS INCREDIBLE... WHY DID THE J L A EVER LEAVE THIS PLACE?
THE REASONS ARE NOT IMPORTANT NOW, FIREHAWK.
SAVING RED TORNADO'S LIFE IS.
HE'S NOT REALLY ALIVE, YOU KNOW... HE'S AN ANDROID.
HEY, WHO ARE YOU?
NAME'S CYBORG... AND I GOT MORE THAN A PASSING KNOWLEDGE OF THINGS LIKE THIS.
ONLY THIS GUY'S FAR OUTTA MY LEAGUE.
ONLY HOPE THE ATOM CAN DIG UP SOMETHING.
FIREHAWK... YOUR FLAME MAY PROVE A PROBLEM.
OH, RIGHT-- FIRESTORM TOLD ME ABOUT YOUR VULNER-ABILITY TO FIRE.
DON'T WORRY-- WHEN I WANT TO, MY FIRE'S MORE BARK THAN BITE.
STILL, I PREFER SOME DISTANCE BETWEEN US.
7

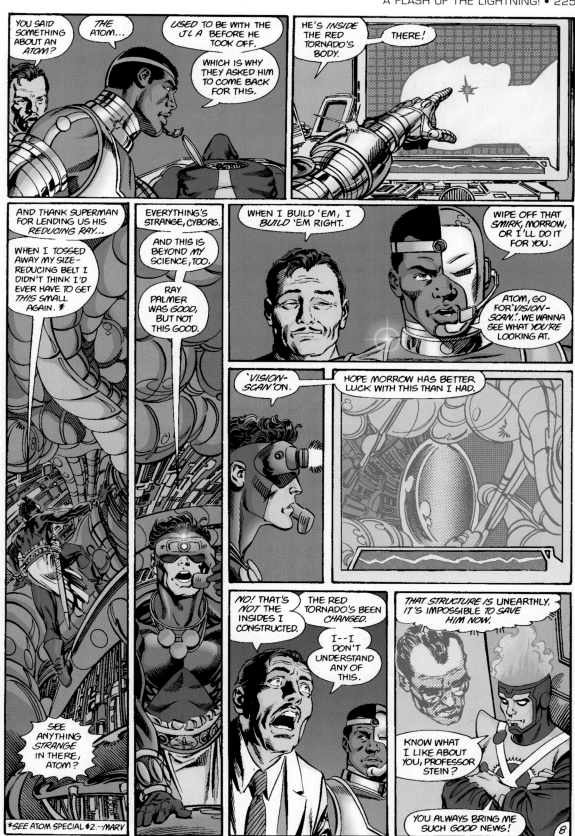

YOU SAID SOMETHING ABOUT AN ATOM?

THE ATOM...

USED TO BE WITH THE JLA BEFORE HE TOOK OFF.

WHICH IS WHY THEY ASKED HIM TO COME BACK FOR THIS.

HE'S INSIDE THE RED TORNADO'S BODY.

THERE!

AND THANK SUPERMAN FOR LENDING US HIS REDUCING RAY...

WHEN I TOSSED AWAY MY SIZE-REDUCING BELT I DIDN'T THINK I'D EVER HAVE TO GET THIS SMALL AGAIN. *

EVERYTHING'S STRANGE, CYBORG.

AND THIS IS BEYOND MY SCIENCE, TOO.

RAY PALMER WAS GOOD, BUT NOT THIS GOOD.

WHEN I BUILD 'EM, I BUILD 'EM RIGHT.

WIPE OFF THAT SMIRK, MORROW, OR I'LL DO IT FOR YOU.

ATOM, GO FOR 'VISION-SCAN'... WE WANNA SEE WHAT YOU'RE LOOKING AT.

'VISION-SCAN' ON.

HOPE MORROW HAS BETTER LUCK WITH THIS THAN I HAD.

SEE ANYTHING STRANGE IN THERE, ATOM?

NO! THAT'S NOT THE INSIDES I CONSTRUCTED.

THE RED TORNADO'S BEEN CHANGED.

I--I DON'T UNDERSTAND ANY OF THIS.

THAT STRUCTURE IS UNEARTHLY. IT'S IMPOSSIBLE TO SAVE HIM NOW.

KNOW WHAT I LIKE ABOUT YOU, PROFESSOR STEIN?

YOU ALWAYS BRING ME SUCH GOOD NEWS!

*SEE ATOM SPECIAL #2.--MARV

8

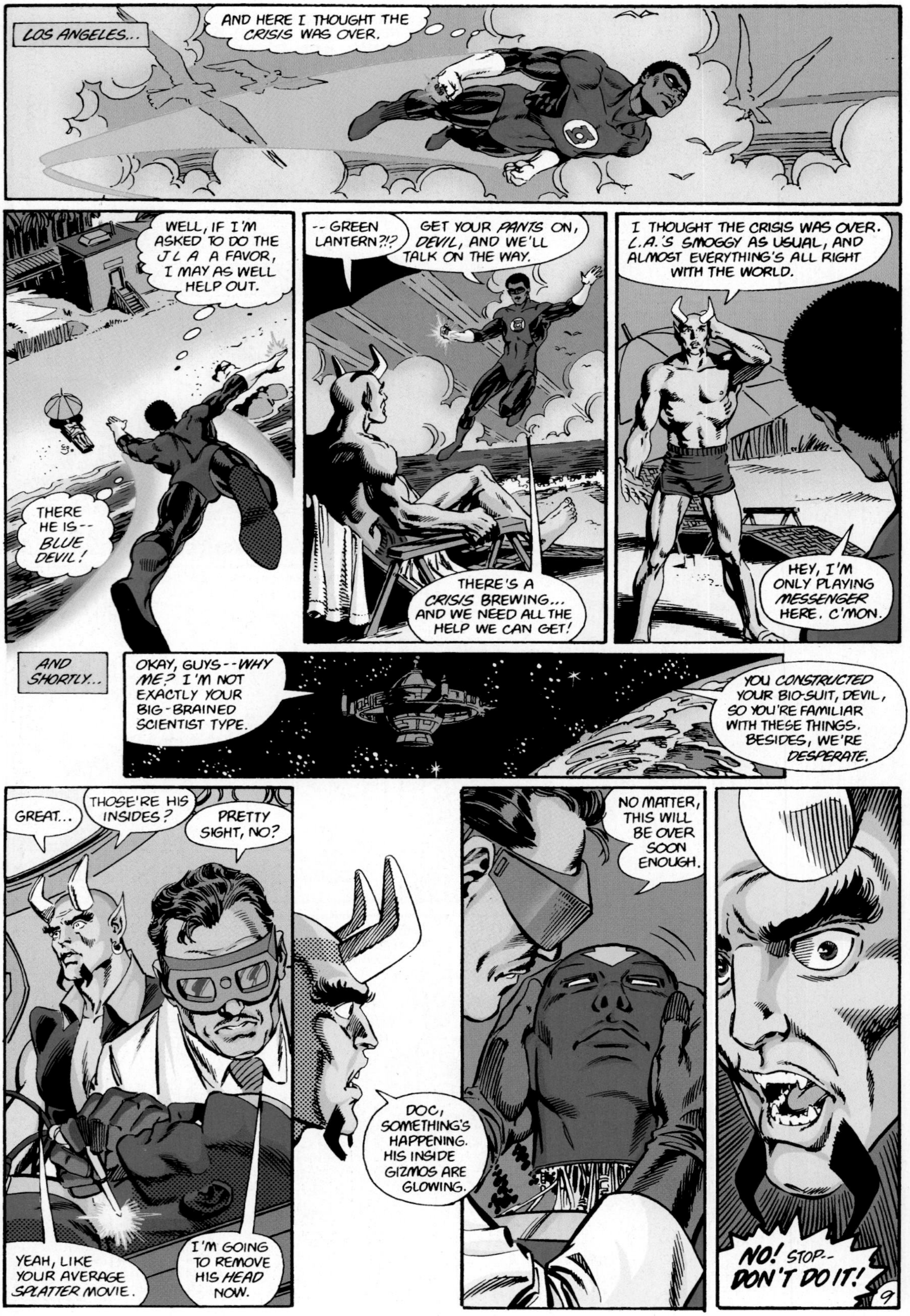
LOS ANGELES...
AND HERE I THOUGHT THE CRISIS WAS OVER.
WELL, IF I'M ASKED TO DO THE J L A A FAVOR, I MAY AS WELL HELP OUT.
THERE HE IS-- BLUE DEVIL!
--GREEN LANTERN?!?
GET YOUR PANTS ON, DEVIL, AND WE'LL TALK ON THE WAY.
THERE'S A CRISIS BREWING... AND WE NEED ALL THE HELP WE CAN GET!
I THOUGHT THE CRISIS WAS OVER. L.A.'S SMOGGY AS USUAL, AND ALMOST EVERYTHING'S ALL RIGHT WITH THE WORLD.
HEY, I'M ONLY PLAYING MESSENGER HERE. C'MON.
AND SHORTLY...
OKAY, GUYS--WHY ME? I'M NOT EXACTLY YOUR BIG-BRAINED SCIENTIST TYPE.
YOU CONSTRUCTED YOUR BIO-SUIT, DEVIL, SO YOU'RE FAMILIAR WITH THESE THINGS. BESIDES, WE'RE DESPERATE.
GREAT...
THOSE'RE HIS INSIDES?
PRETTY SIGHT, NO?
YEAH, LIKE YOUR AVERAGE SPLATTER MOVIE.
I'M GOING TO REMOVE HIS HEAD NOW.
DOC, SOMETHING'S HAPPENING. HIS INSIDE GIZMOS ARE GLOWING.
NO MATTER, THIS WILL BE OVER SOON ENOUGH.
NO! STOP-- DON'T DO IT!
9

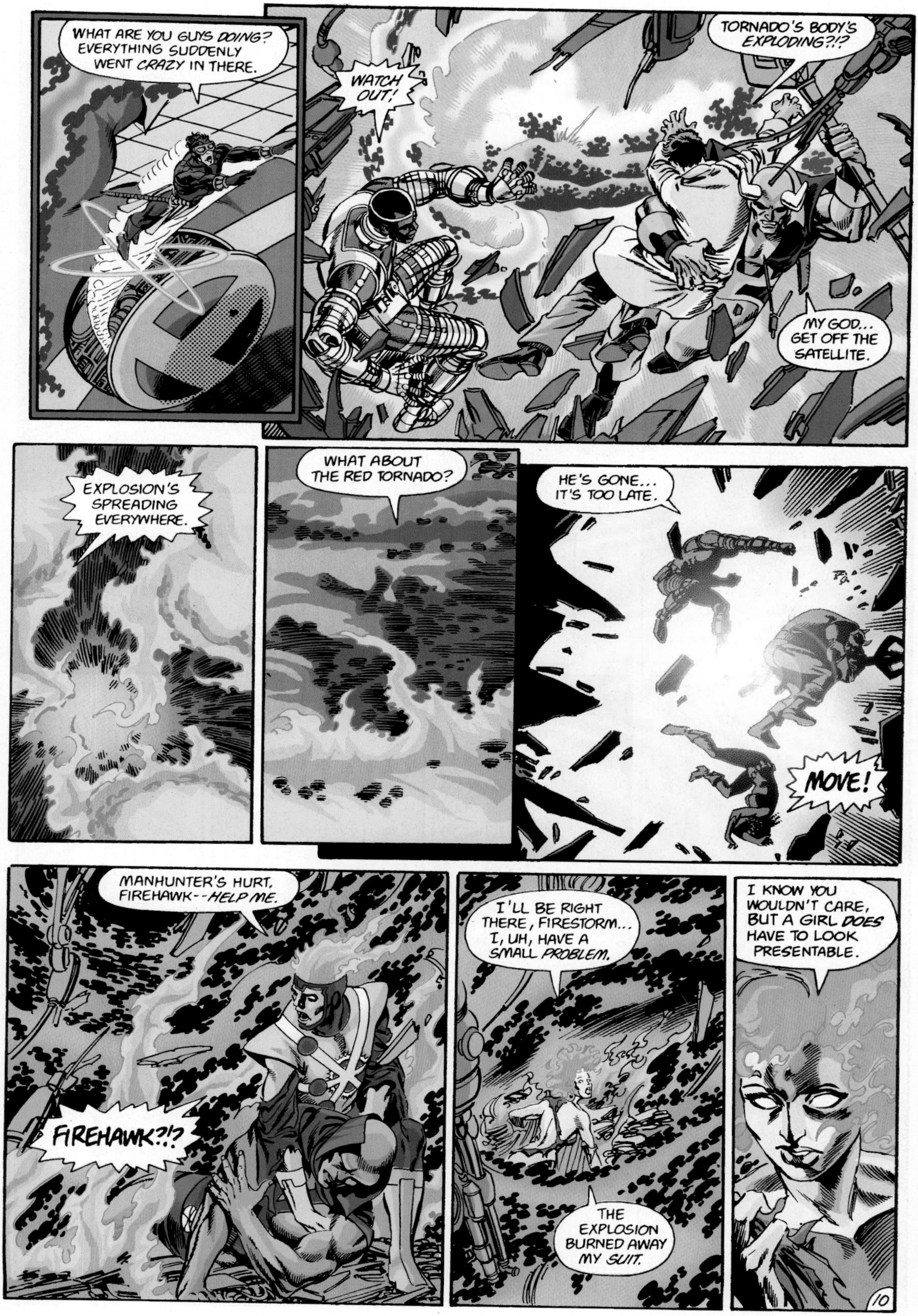
WHAT ARE YOU GUYS DOING? EVERYTHING SUDDENLY WENT CRAZY IN THERE.
WATCH OUT!
TORNADO'S BODY'S EXPLODING?!?
MY GOD... GET OFF THE SATELLITE.
EXPLOSION'S SPREADING EVERYWHERE.
WHAT ABOUT THE RED TORNADO?
HE'S GONE... IT'S TOO LATE.
MOVE!
MANHUNTER'S HURT, FIREHAWK--HELP ME.
FIREHAWK?!?
I'LL BE RIGHT THERE, FIRESTORM... I, UH, HAVE A SMALL PROBLEM.
THE EXPLOSION BURNED AWAY MY SUIT.
I KNOW YOU WOULDN'T CARE, BUT A GIRL DOES HAVE TO LOOK PRESENTABLE.
10

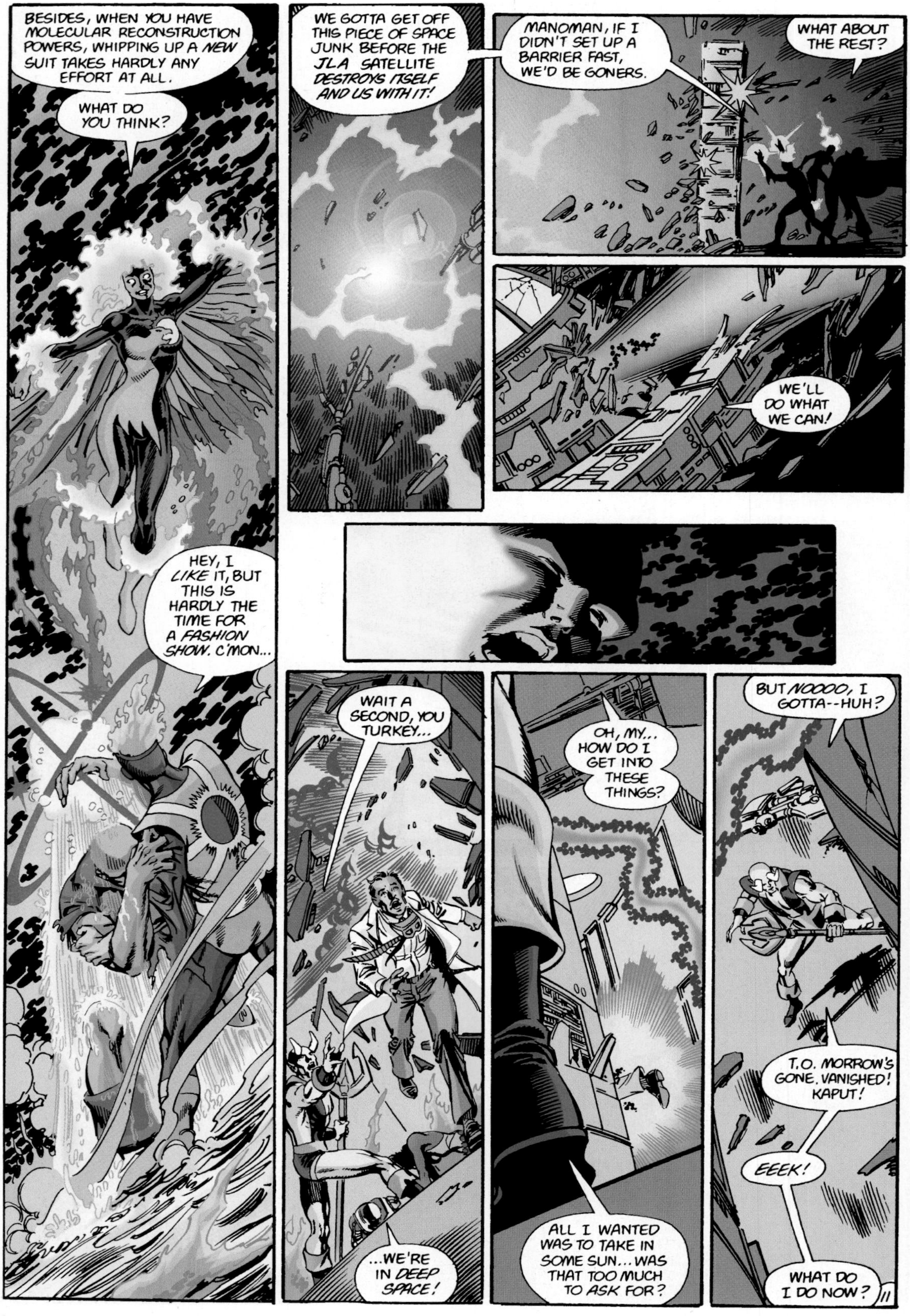
BESIDES, WHEN YOU HAVE MOLECULAR RECONSTRUCTION POWERS, WHIPPING UP A *NEW* SUIT TAKES HARDLY ANY EFFORT AT ALL.
WHAT DO YOU THINK?
HEY, I *LIKE* IT, BUT THIS IS HARDLY THE TIME FOR A *FASHION SHOW*. C'MON...
WE GOTTA GET OFF THIS PIECE OF SPACE JUNK BEFORE THE *JLA* SATELLITE *DESTROYS ITSELF AND US WITH IT!*
MANOMAN, IF I DIDN'T SET UP A BARRIER FAST, WE'D BE GONERS.
WHAT ABOUT THE REST?
WE'LL DO WHAT WE CAN!
WAIT A SECOND, YOU TURKEY...
...WE'RE IN *DEEP SPACE!*
OH, MY... HOW DO I GET INTO THESE THINGS?
ALL I WANTED WAS TO TAKE IN SOME SUN... WAS THAT TOO MUCH TO *ASK* FOR?
BUT *NOOOO*, I GOTTA--HUH?
T.O. MORROW'S GONE. VANISHED! KAPUT!
EEEK!
WHAT DO I DO NOW?
11

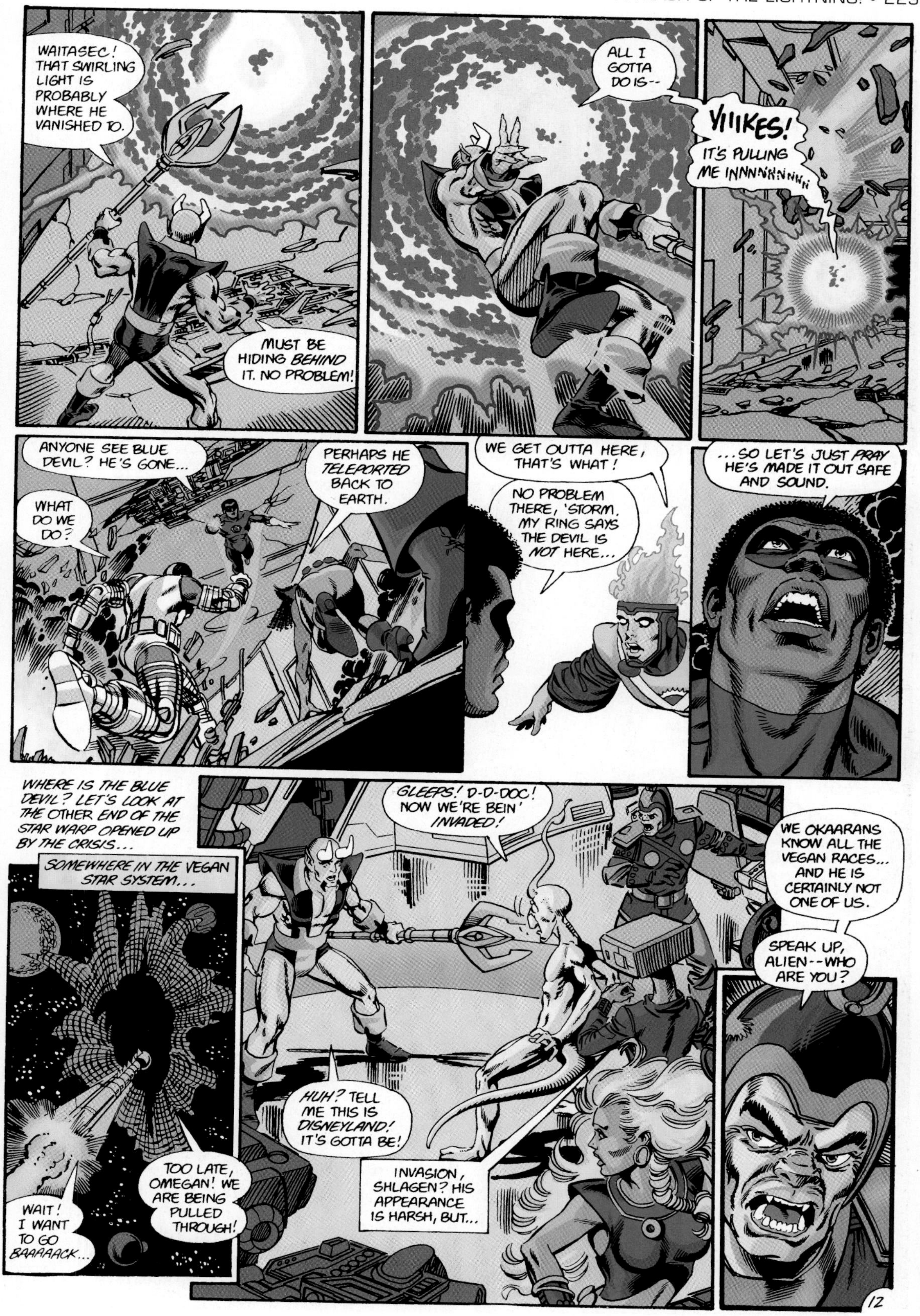
WAITASEC! THAT SWIRLING LIGHT IS PROBABLY WHERE HE VANISHED TO.
MUST BE HIDING BEHIND IT. NO PROBLEM!
ALL I GOTTA DO IS--
YIIIKES! IT'S PULLING ME INNNNNNNNN
ANYONE SEE BLUE DEVIL? HE'S GONE...
WHAT DO WE DO?
PERHAPS HE TELEPORTED BACK TO EARTH.
WE GET OUTTA HERE, THAT'S WHAT!
NO PROBLEM THERE, 'STORM. MY RING SAYS THE DEVIL IS NOT HERE...
...SO LET'S JUST PRAY HE'S MADE IT OUT SAFE AND SOUND.
WHERE IS THE BLUE DEVIL? LET'S LOOK AT THE OTHER END OF THE STAR WARP OPENED UP BY THE CRISIS...
SOMEWHERE IN THE VEGAN STAR SYSTEM...
WAIT! I WANT TO GO BAAAAACK...
TOO LATE, OMEGAN! WE ARE BEING PULLED THROUGH!
GLEEPS! D-D-DOC! NOW WE'RE BEIN' INVADED!
HUH? TELL ME THIS IS DISNEYLAND! IT'S GOTTA BE!
INVASION, SHLAGEN? HIS APPEARANCE IS HARSH, BUT...
WE OKAARANS KNOW ALL THE VEGAN RACES... AND HE IS CERTAINLY NOT ONE OF US.
SPEAK UP, ALIEN--WHO ARE YOU?
12

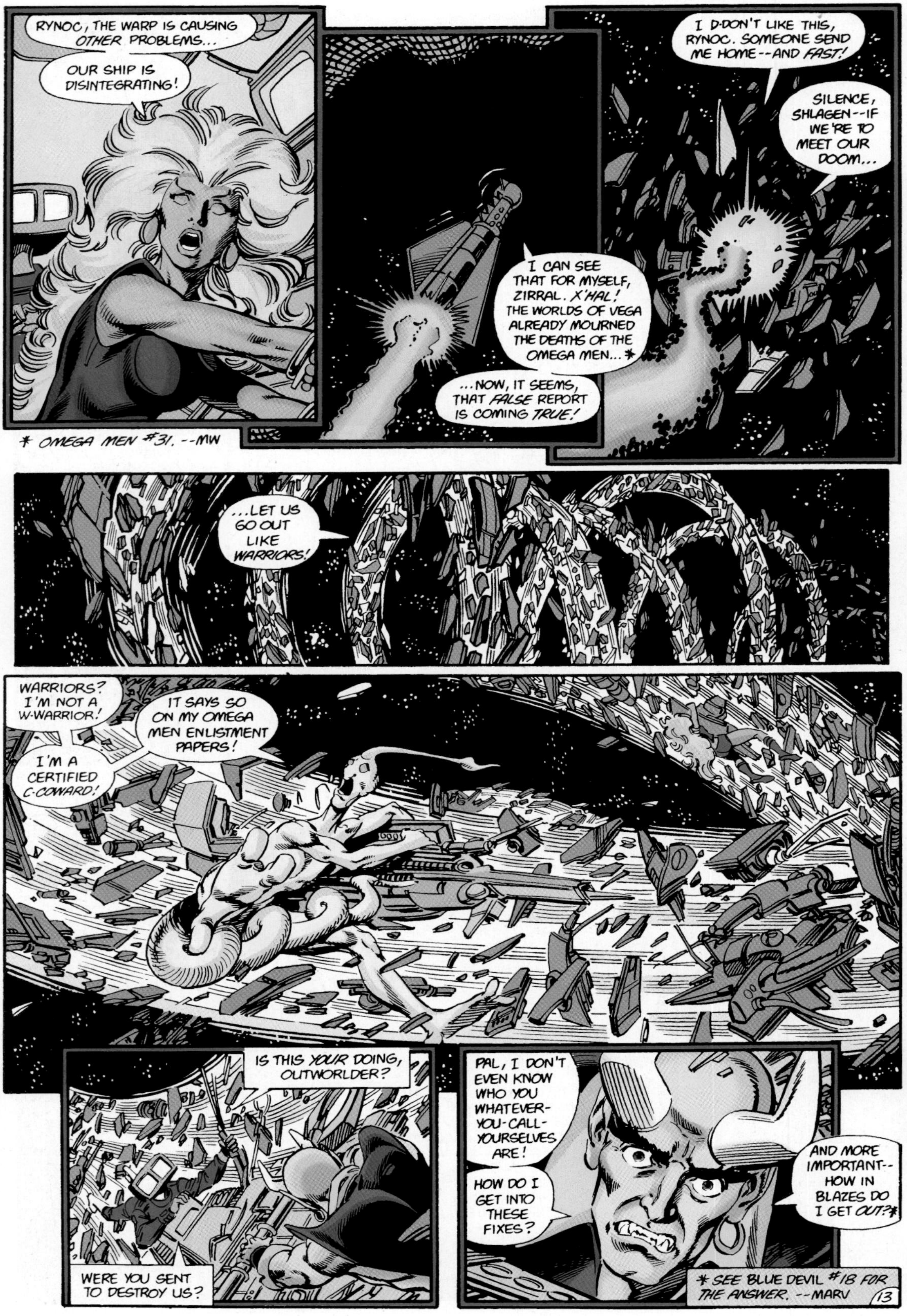

RYNOC, THE WARP IS CAUSING OTHER PROBLEMS...
OUR SHIP IS DISINTEGRATING!
I CAN SEE THAT FOR MYSELF, ZIRRAL. X'HAL! THE WORLDS OF VEGA ALREADY MOURNED THE DEATHS OF THE OMEGA MEN...*
...NOW, IT SEEMS, THAT FALSE REPORT IS COMING TRUE!
* OMEGA MEN #31. --MW
I D-DON'T LIKE THIS, RYNOC. SOMEONE SEND ME HOME--AND FAST!
SILENCE, SHLAGEN--IF WE'RE TO MEET OUR DOOM...
...LET US GO OUT LIKE WARRIORS!
WARRIORS? I'M NOT A W-WARRIOR!
IT SAYS SO ON MY OMEGA MEN ENLISTMENT PAPERS!
I'M A CERTIFIED C-COWARD!
IS THIS YOUR DOING, OUTWORLDER?
WERE YOU SENT TO DESTROY US?
PAL, I DON'T EVEN KNOW WHO YOU WHATEVER-YOU-CALL-YOURSELVES ARE!
HOW DO I GET INTO THESE FIXES?
AND MORE IMPORTANT--HOW IN BLAZES DO I GET OUT?*
* SEE BLUE DEVIL #18 FOR THE ANSWER. --MARV
13

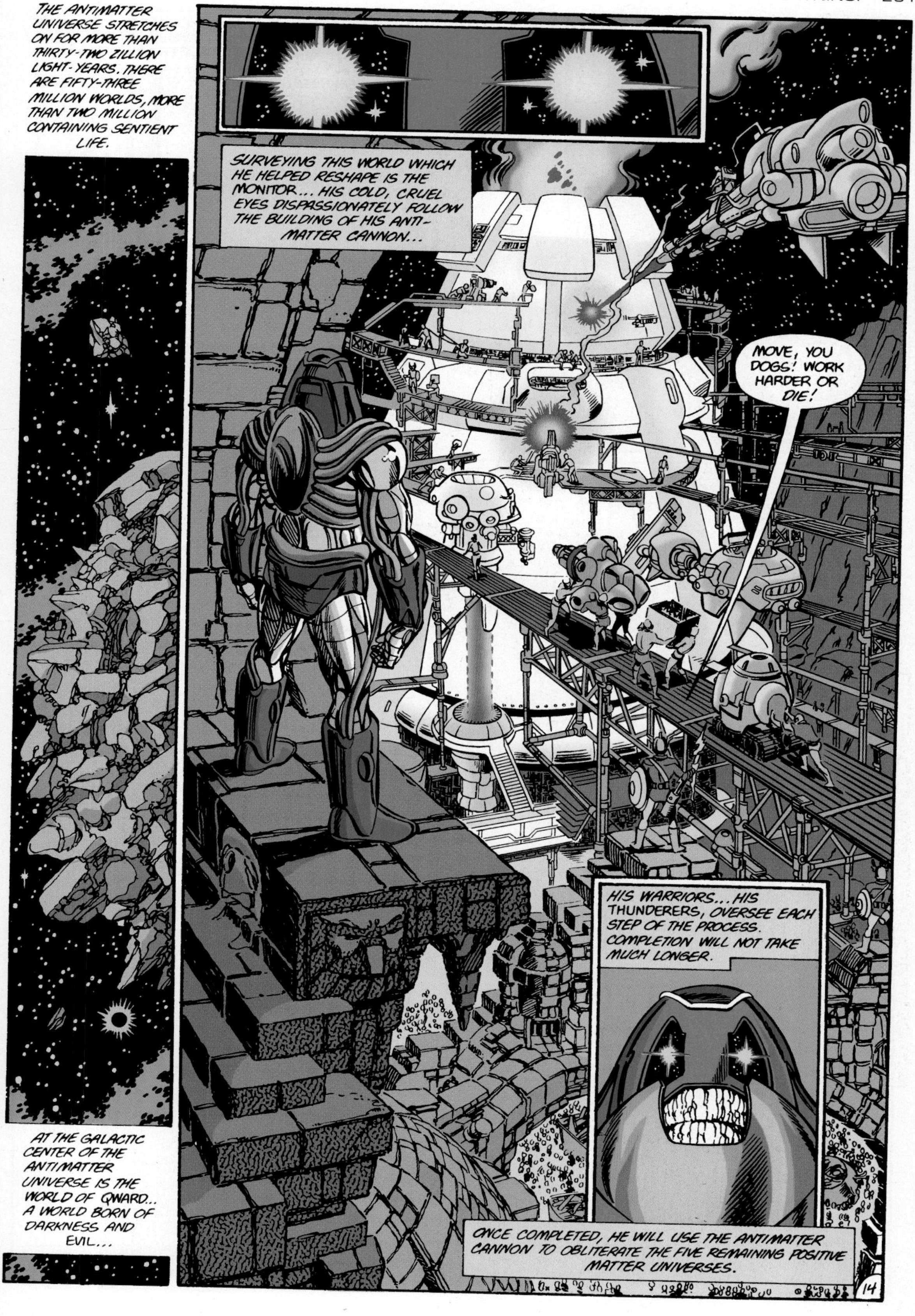
THE ANTIMATTER UNIVERSE STRETCHES ON FOR MORE THAN THIRTY-TWO ZILLION LIGHT-YEARS. THERE ARE FIFTY-THREE MILLION WORLDS, MORE THAN TWO MILLION CONTAINING SENTIENT LIFE.
AT THE GALACTIC CENTER OF THE ANTIMATTER UNIVERSE IS THE WORLD OF QWARD... A WORLD BORN OF DARKNESS AND EVIL...
SURVEYING THIS WORLD WHICH HE HELPED RESHAPE IS THE MONITOR... HIS COLD, CRUEL EYES DISPASSIONATELY FOLLOW THE BUILDING OF HIS ANTI-MATTER CANNON...
MOVE, YOU DOGS! WORK HARDER OR DIE!
HIS WARRIORS... HIS THUNDERERS, OVERSEE EACH STEP OF THE PROCESS. COMPLETION WILL NOT TAKE MUCH LONGER.
ONCE COMPLETED, HE WILL USE THE ANTIMATTER CANNON TO OBLITERATE THE FIVE REMAINING POSITIVE MATTER UNIVERSES.
14

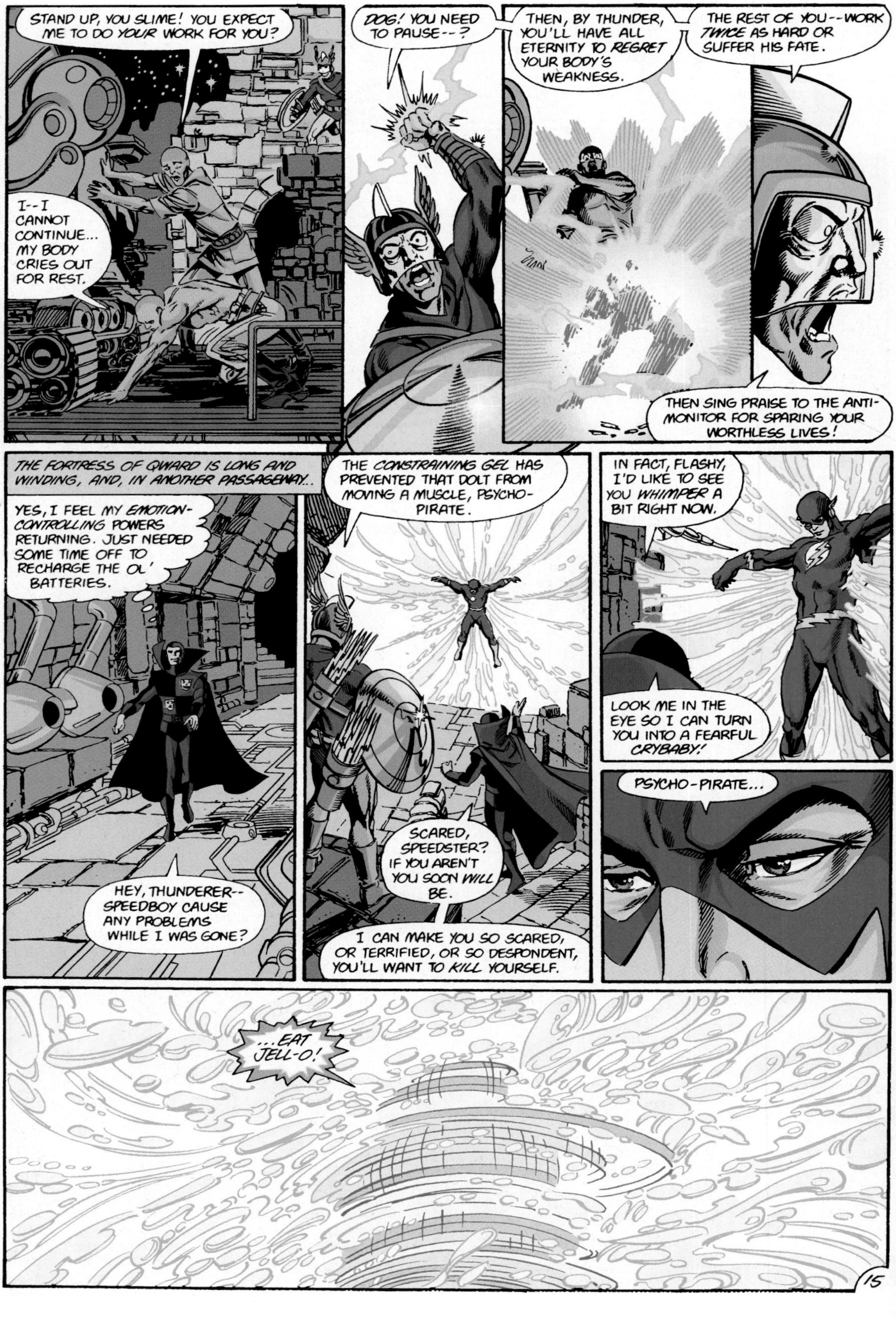
STAND UP, YOU SLIME! YOU EXPECT ME TO DO YOUR WORK FOR YOU?
I--I CANNOT CONTINUE... MY BODY CRIES OUT FOR REST.
DOG! YOU NEED TO PAUSE--?
THEN, BY THUNDER, YOU'LL HAVE ALL ETERNITY TO REGRET YOUR BODY'S WEAKNESS.
THE REST OF YOU--WORK TWICE AS HARD OR SUFFER HIS FATE.
THEN SING PRAISE TO THE ANTI-MONITOR FOR SPARING YOUR WORTHLESS LIVES!
THE FORTRESS OF QWARD IS LONG AND WINDING, AND, IN ANOTHER PASSAGEWAY...
YES, I FEEL MY EMOTION-CONTROLLING POWERS RETURNING. JUST NEEDED SOME TIME OFF TO RECHARGE THE OL' BATTERIES.
HEY, THUNDERER-- SPEEDBOY CAUSE ANY PROBLEMS WHILE I WAS GONE?
THE CONSTRAINING GEL HAS PREVENTED THAT DOLT FROM MOVING A MUSCLE, PSYCHO-PIRATE.
SCARED, SPEEDSTER? IF YOU AREN'T YOU SOON WILL BE.
I CAN MAKE YOU SO SCARED, OR TERRIFIED, OR SO DESPONDENT, YOU'LL WANT TO KILL YOURSELF.
IN FACT, FLASHY, I'D LIKE TO SEE YOU WHIMPER A BIT RIGHT NOW.
LOOK ME IN THE EYE SO I CAN TURN YOU INTO A FEARFUL CRYBABY!
PSYCHO-PIRATE...
...EAT JELL-O!
15

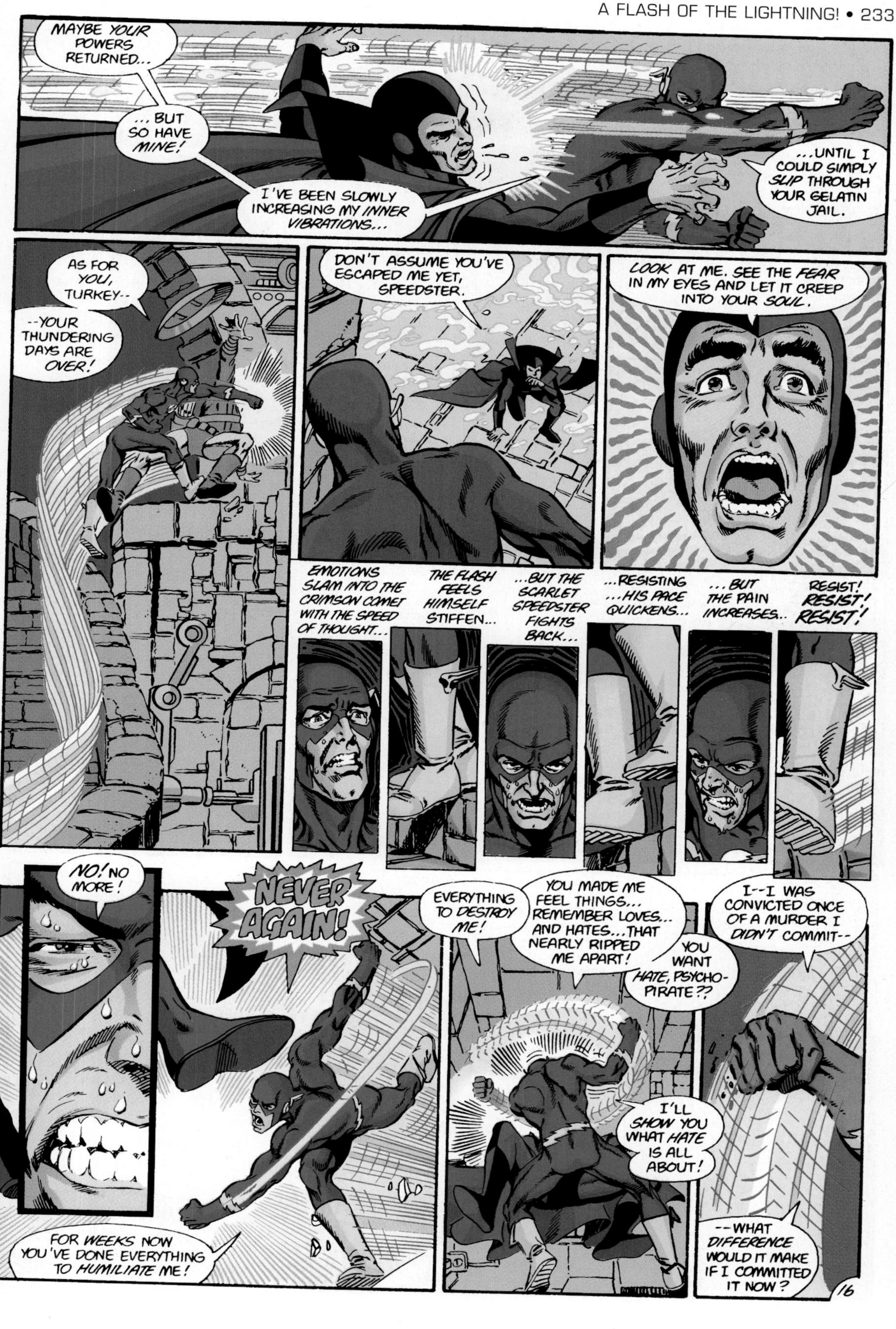
MAYBE YOUR POWERS RETURNED...
..., BUT SO HAVE MINE!
I'VE BEEN SLOWLY INCREASING MY INNER VIBRATIONS...
...UNTIL I COULD SIMPLY SLIP THROUGH YOUR GELATIN JAIL.
AS FOR YOU, TURKEY--
--YOUR THUNDERING DAYS ARE OVER!
DON'T ASSUME YOU'VE ESCAPED ME YET, SPEEDSTER.
LOOK AT ME. SEE THE FEAR IN MY EYES AND LET IT CREEP INTO YOUR SOUL.
EMOTIONS SLAM INTO THE CRIMSON COMET WITH THE SPEED OF THOUGHT...
THE FLASH FEELS HIMSELF STIFFEN...
...BUT THE SCARLET SPEEDSTER FIGHTS BACK...
...RESISTING ...HIS PACE QUICKENS...
...BUT THE PAIN INCREASES...
RESIST! RESIST! RESIST!
NO! NO MORE!
FOR WEEKS NOW YOU'VE DONE EVERYTHING TO HUMILIATE ME!
NEVER AGAIN!
EVERYTHING TO DESTROY ME!
YOU MADE ME FEEL THINGS... REMEMBER LOVES... AND HATES... THAT NEARLY RIPPED ME APART!
YOU WANT HATE, PSYCHO-PIRATE??
I'LL SHOW YOU WHAT HATE IS ALL ABOUT!
I--I WAS CONVICTED ONCE OF A MURDER I DIDN'T COMMIT--
--WHAT DIFFERENCE WOULD IT MAKE IF I COMMITTED IT NOW?
16

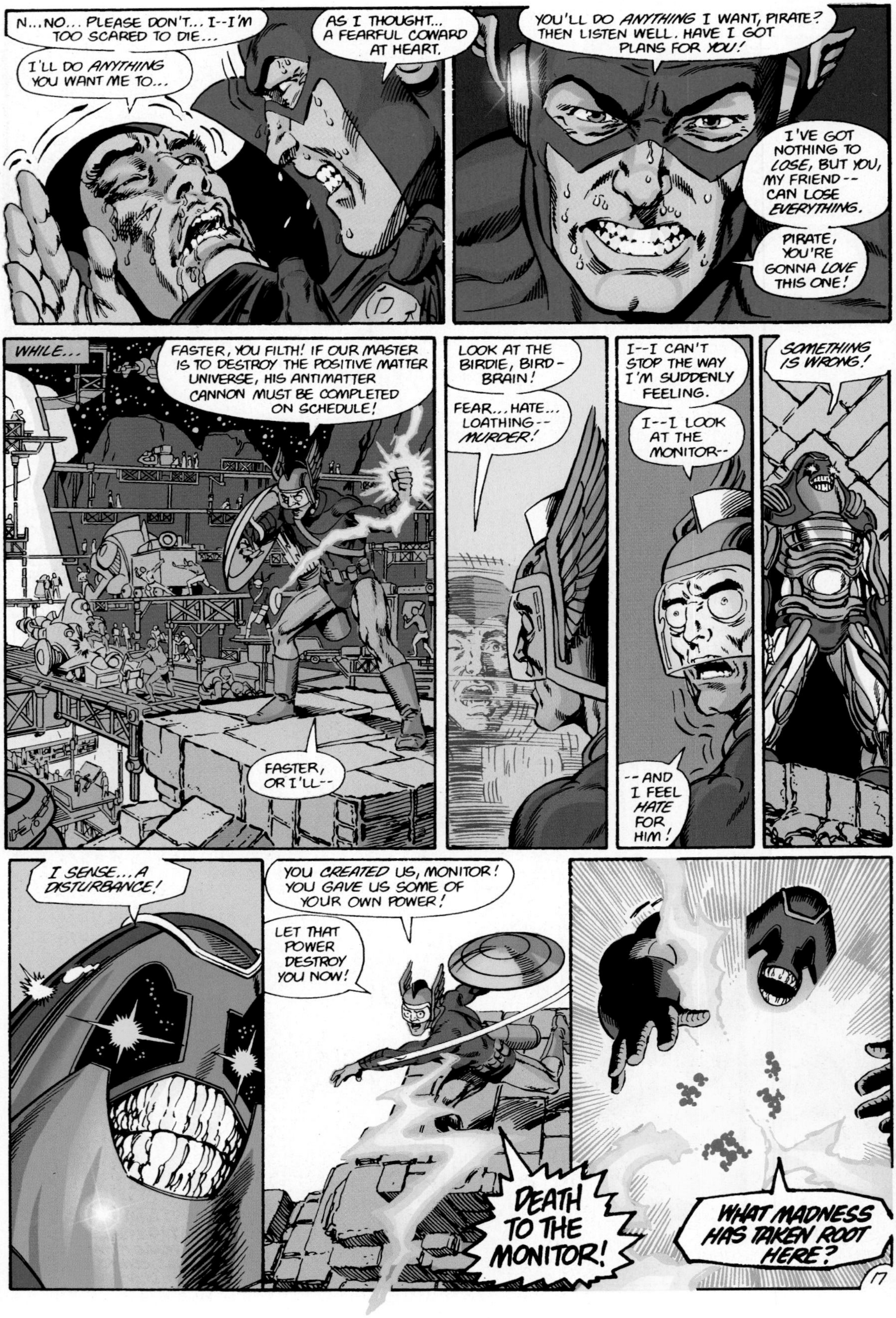
N...NO... PLEASE DON'T... I--I'M TOO SCARED TO DIE...
I'LL DO ANYTHING YOU WANT ME TO...
AS I THOUGHT... A FEARFUL COWARD AT HEART.
YOU'LL DO ANYTHING I WANT, PIRATE? THEN LISTEN WELL. HAVE I GOT PLANS FOR YOU!
I'VE GOT NOTHING TO LOSE, BUT YOU, MY FRIEND-- CAN LOSE EVERYTHING.
PIRATE, YOU'RE GONNA LOVE THIS ONE!
WHILE...
FASTER, YOU FILTH! IF OUR MASTER IS TO DESTROY THE POSITIVE MATTER UNIVERSE, HIS ANTIMATTER CANNON MUST BE COMPLETED ON SCHEDULE!
FASTER, OR I'LL--
LOOK AT THE BIRDIE, BIRD-BRAIN!
FEAR... HATE... LOATHING-- MURDER!
I--I CAN'T STOP THE WAY I'M SUDDENLY FEELING.
I--I LOOK AT THE MONITOR--
--AND I FEEL HATE FOR HIM!
SOMETHING IS WRONG!
I SENSE... A DISTURBANCE!
YOU CREATED US, MONITOR! YOU GAVE US SOME OF YOUR OWN POWER!
LET THAT POWER DESTROY YOU NOW!
DEATH TO THE MONITOR!
WHAT MADNESS HAS TAKEN ROOT HERE?
17

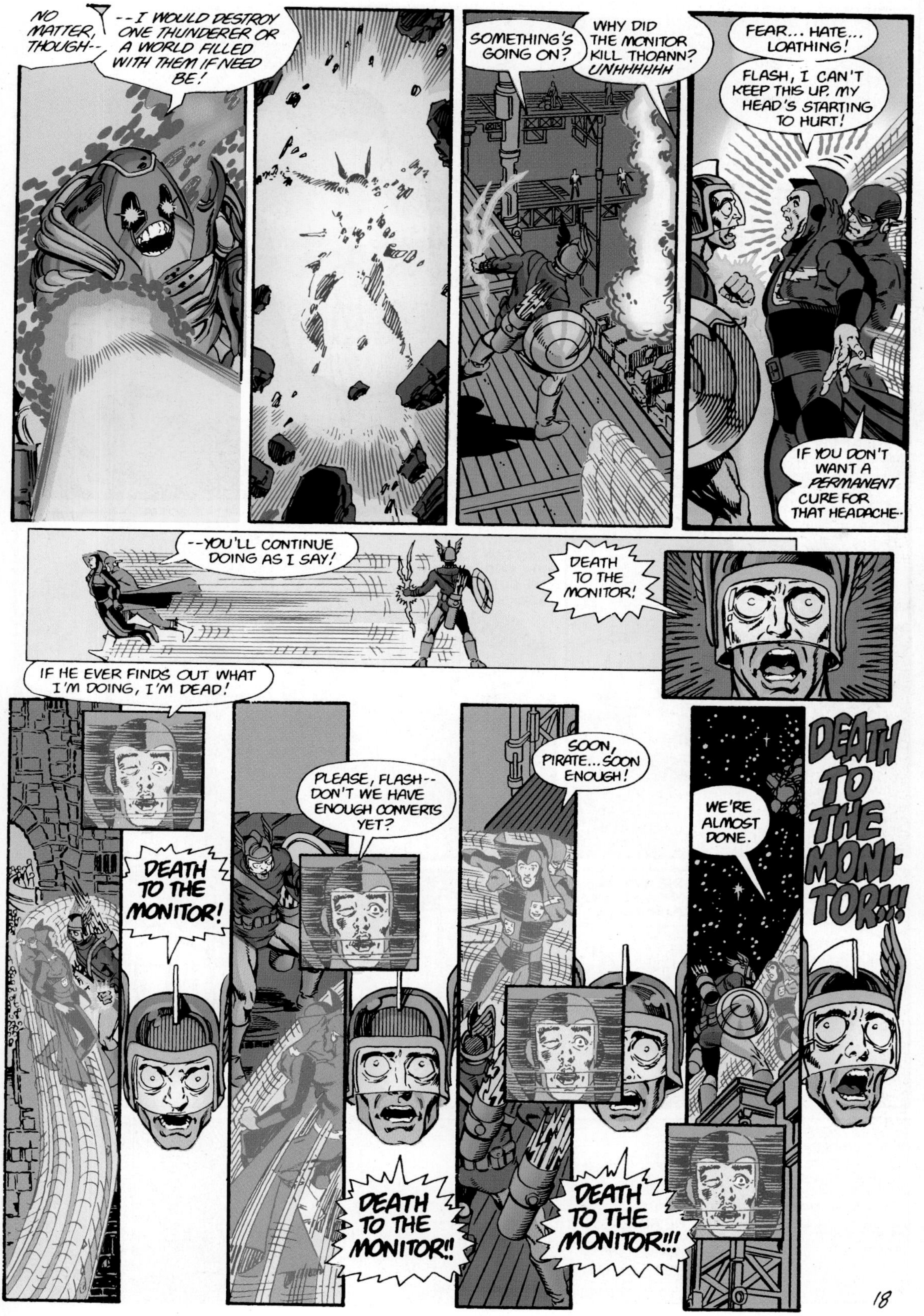
NO MATTER, THOUGH--
--I WOULD DESTROY ONE THUNDERER OR A WORLD FILLED WITH THEM IF NEED BE!
SOMETHING'S GOING ON?
WHY DID THE MONITOR KILL THOANN? UNHHHHHH
FEAR... HATE... LOATHING!
FLASH, I CAN'T KEEP THIS UP. MY HEAD'S STARTING TO HURT!
IF YOU DON'T WANT A PERMANENT CURE FOR THAT HEADACHE--
--YOU'LL CONTINUE DOING AS I SAY!
DEATH TO THE MONITOR!
IF HE EVER FINDS OUT WHAT I'M DOING, I'M DEAD!
DEATH TO THE MONITOR!
PLEASE, FLASH-- DON'T WE HAVE ENOUGH CONVERTS YET?
DEATH TO THE MONITOR!!
SOON, PIRATE... SOON ENOUGH!
DEATH TO THE MONITOR!!!
WE'RE ALMOST DONE.
DEATH TO THE MONI-TOR!!!

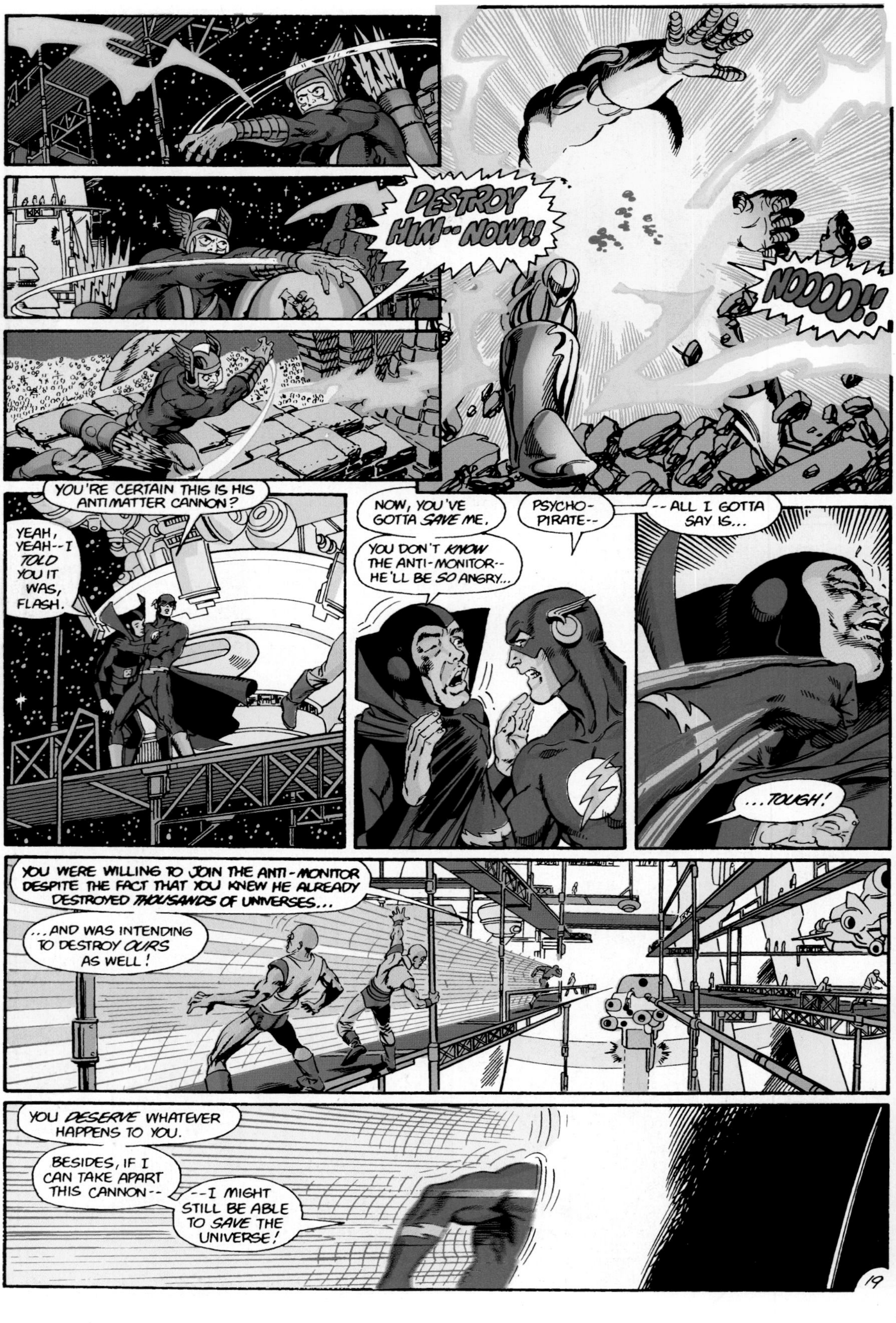
DESTROY HIM--NOW!!
NOOOOO!!
YOU'RE CERTAIN THIS IS HIS ANTIMATTER CANNON?
YEAH, YEAH--I TOLD YOU IT WAS, FLASH.
NOW, YOU'VE GOTTA SAVE ME.
YOU DON'T KNOW THE ANTI-MONITOR-- HE'LL BE SO ANGRY...
PSYCHO-PIRATE--
--ALL I GOTTA SAY IS...
...TOUGH!
YOU WERE WILLING TO JOIN THE ANTI-MONITOR DESPITE THE FACT THAT YOU KNEW HE ALREADY DESTROYED THOUSANDS OF UNIVERSES...
...AND WAS INTENDING TO DESTROY OURS AS WELL!
YOU DESERVE WHATEVER HAPPENS TO YOU.
BESIDES, IF I CAN TAKE APART THIS CANNON--
--I MIGHT STILL BE ABLE TO SAVE THE UNIVERSE!
19

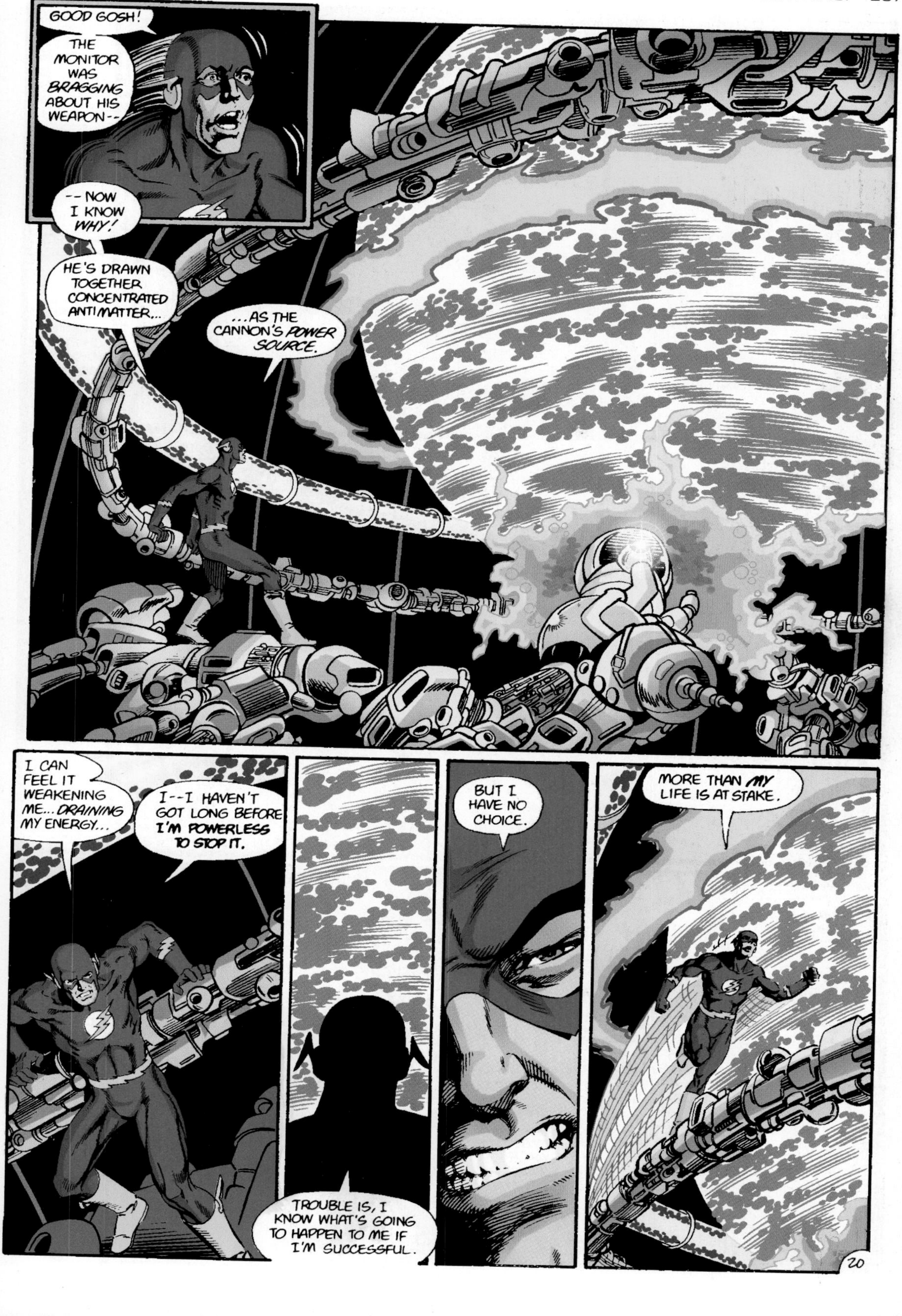
GOOD GOSH!
THE MONITOR WAS BRAGGING ABOUT HIS WEAPON--
--NOW I KNOW WHY!
HE'S DRAWN TOGETHER CONCENTRATED ANTIMATTER...
...AS THE CANNON'S POWER SOURCE.
I CAN FEEL IT WEAKENING ME... DRAINING MY ENERGY...
I--I HAVEN'T GOT LONG BEFORE I'M POWERLESS TO STOP IT.
TROUBLE IS, I KNOW WHAT'S GOING TO HAPPEN TO ME IF I'M SUCCESSFUL.
BUT I HAVE NO CHOICE.
MORE THAN MY LIFE IS AT STAKE.
20

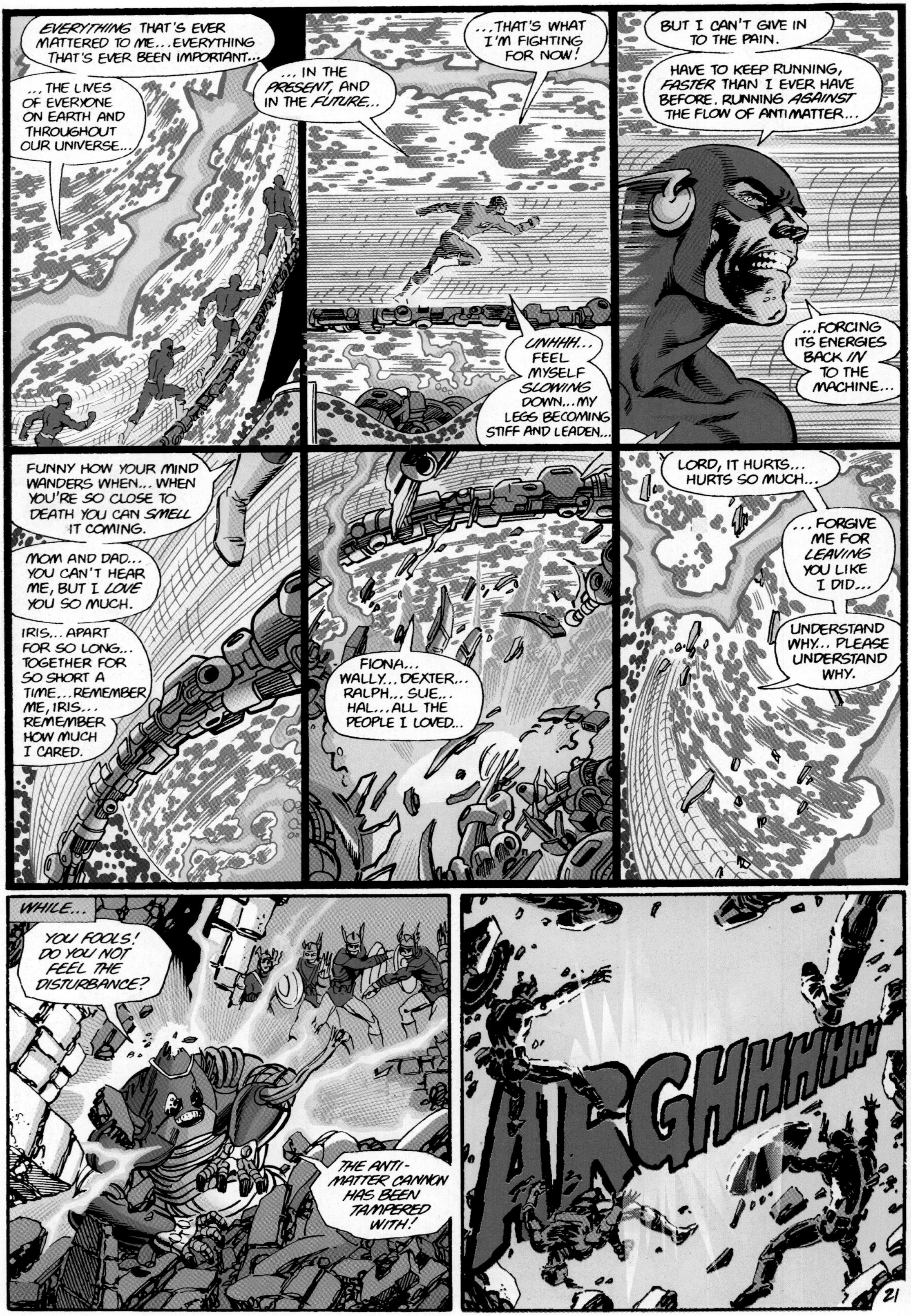
EVERYTHING THAT'S EVER MATTERED TO ME... EVERYTHING THAT'S EVER BEEN IMPORTANT...
...THE LIVES OF EVERYONE ON EARTH AND THROUGHOUT OUR UNIVERSE...
...IN THE PRESENT, AND IN THE FUTURE...
...THAT'S WHAT I'M FIGHTING FOR NOW!
UNHHH... FEEL MYSELF SLOWING DOWN... MY LEGS BECOMING STIFF AND LEADEN...
BUT I CAN'T GIVE IN TO THE PAIN.
HAVE TO KEEP RUNNING, FASTER THAN I EVER HAVE BEFORE. RUNNING AGAINST THE FLOW OF ANTIMATTER...
...FORCING ITS ENERGIES BACK IN TO THE MACHINE...
FUNNY HOW YOUR MIND WANDERS WHEN... WHEN YOU'RE SO CLOSE TO DEATH YOU CAN SMELL IT COMING.
MOM AND DAD... YOU CAN'T HEAR ME, BUT I LOVE YOU SO MUCH.
IRIS... APART FOR SO LONG... TOGETHER FOR SO SHORT A TIME... REMEMBER ME, IRIS... REMEMBER HOW MUCH I CARED.
FIONA... WALLY... DEXTER... RALPH... SUE... HAL... ALL THE PEOPLE I LOVED...
LORD, IT HURTS... HURTS SO MUCH...
...FORGIVE ME FOR LEAVING YOU LIKE I DID...
UNDERSTAND WHY... PLEASE UNDERSTAND WHY.
WHILE...
YOU FOOLS! DO YOU NOT FEEL THE DISTURBANCE?
THE ANTI-MATTER CANNON HAS BEEN TAMPERED WITH!
ARGHHHHHH!
21

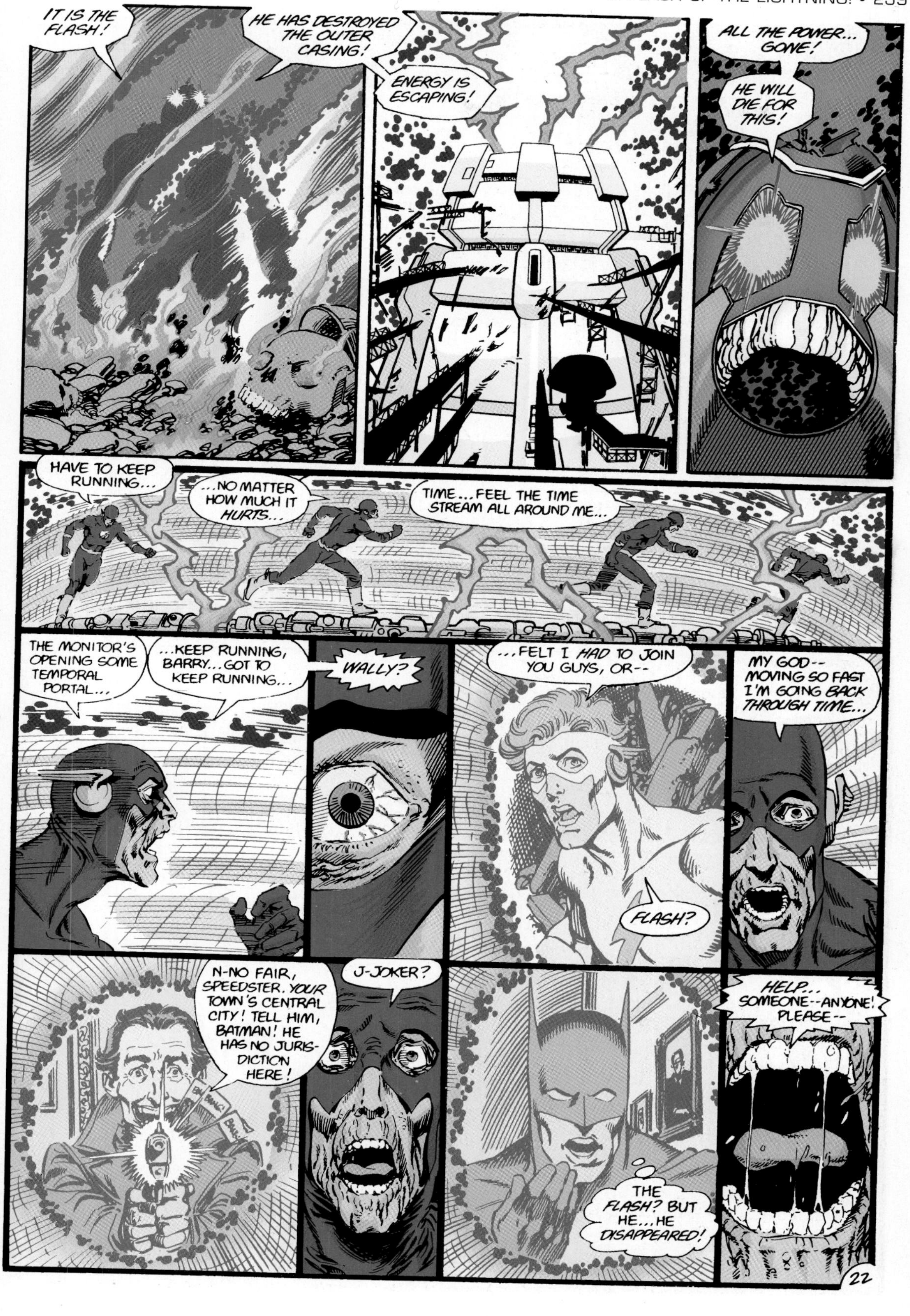
IT IS THE FLASH!
HE HAS DESTROYED THE OUTER CASING!
ENERGY IS ESCAPING!
ALL THE POWER... GONE!
HE WILL DIE FOR THIS!
HAVE TO KEEP RUNNING...
...NO MATTER HOW MUCH IT HURTS...
TIME... FEEL THE TIME STREAM ALL AROUND ME...
THE MONITOR'S OPENING SOME TEMPORAL PORTAL...
...KEEP RUNNING, BARRY... GOT TO KEEP RUNNING...
WALLY?
...FELT I HAD TO JOIN YOU GUYS, OR--
FLASH?
MY GOD-- MOVING SO FAST I'M GOING BACK THROUGH TIME...
N-NO FAIR, SPEEDSTER. YOUR TOWN'S CENTRAL CITY! TELL HIM, BATMAN! HE HAS NO JURIS-DICTION HERE!
J-JOKER?
THE FLASH? BUT HE... HE DISAPPEARED!
HELP... SOMEONE--ANYONE! PLEASE--

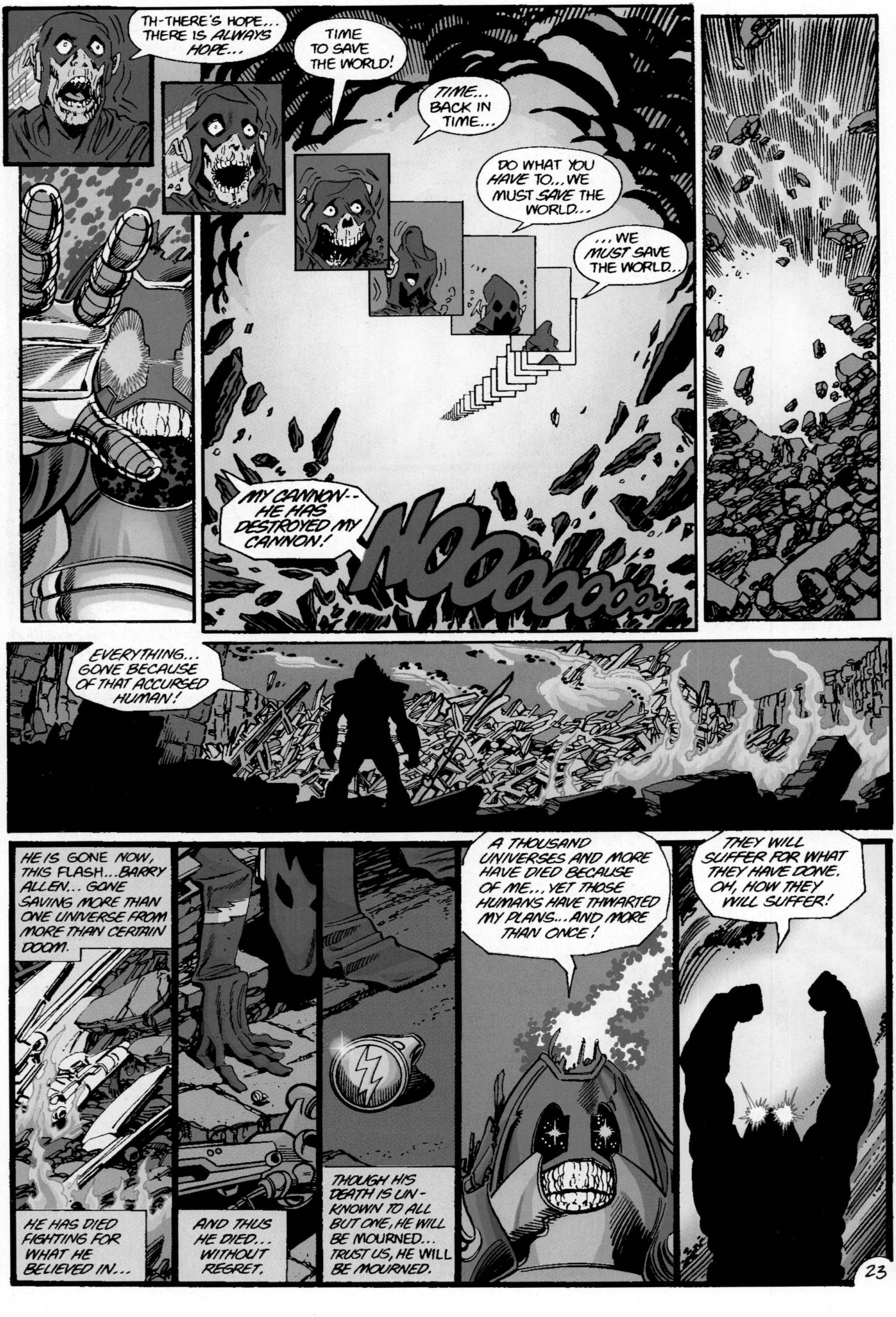
TH-THERE'S HOPE... THERE IS ALWAYS HOPE...
TIME TO SAVE THE WORLD!
TIME... BACK IN TIME...
DO WHAT YOU HAVE TO... WE MUST SAVE THE WORLD...
...WE MUST SAVE THE WORLD...
MY CANNON-- HE HAS DESTROYED MY CANNON!
NOOOOOOOO...
EVERYTHING... GONE BECAUSE OF THAT ACCURSED HUMAN!
HE IS GONE NOW, THIS FLASH... BARRY ALLEN... GONE SAVING MORE THAN ONE UNIVERSE FROM MORE THAN CERTAIN DOOM.
HE HAS DIED FIGHTING FOR WHAT HE BELIEVED IN...
AND THUS HE DIED... WITHOUT REGRET.
THOUGH HIS DEATH IS UN-KNOWN TO ALL BUT ONE, HE WILL BE MOURNED... TRUST US, HE WILL BE MOURNED.
A THOUSAND UNIVERSES AND MORE HAVE DIED BECAUSE OF ME... YET THOSE HUMANS HAVE THWARTED MY PLANS... AND MORE THAN ONCE!
THEY WILL SUFFER FOR WHAT THEY HAVE DONE. OH, HOW THEY WILL SUFFER!
23

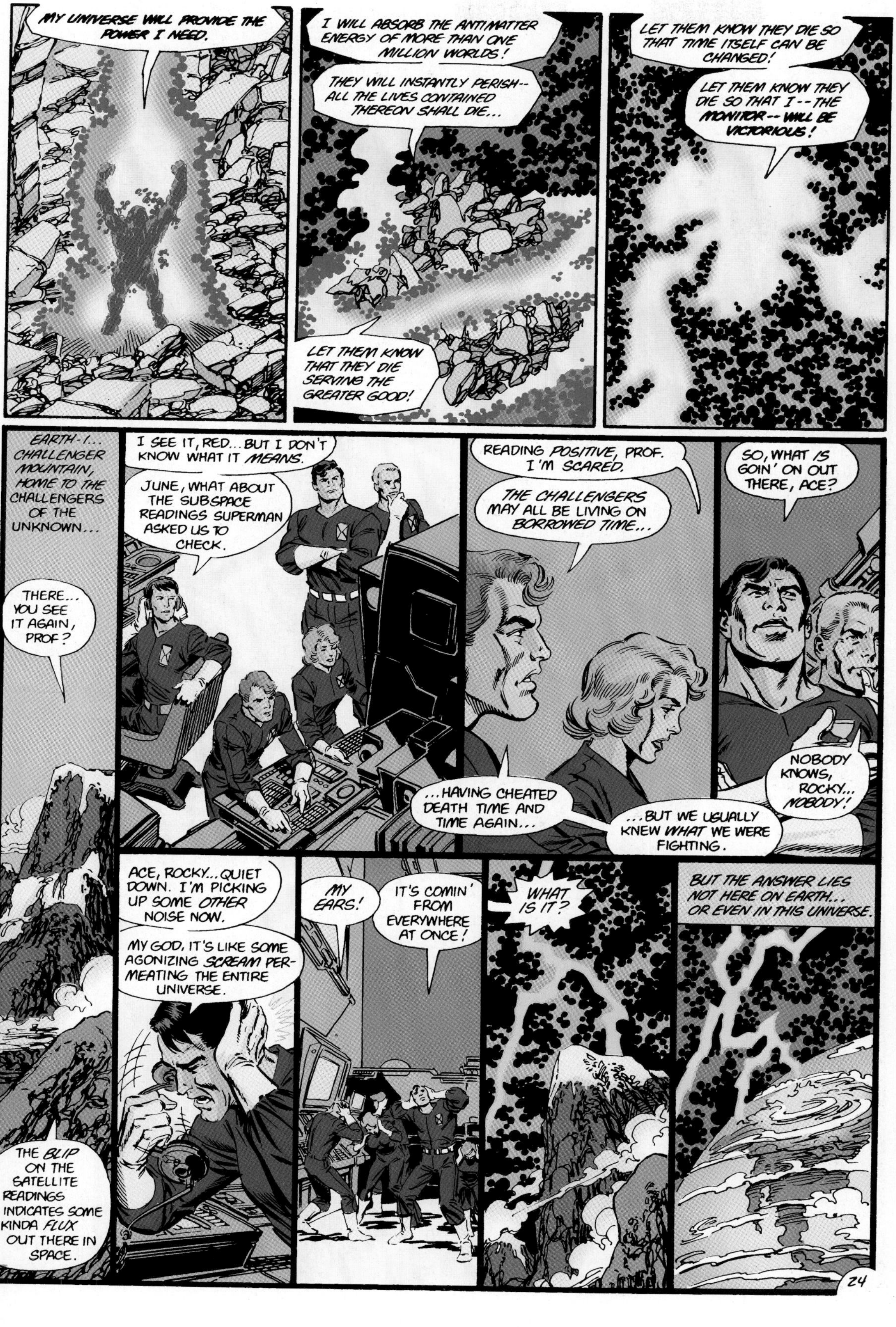
MY UNIVERSE WILL PROVIDE THE POWER I NEED.
I WILL ABSORB THE ANTIMATTER ENERGY OF MORE THAN ONE MILLION WORLDS!
THEY WILL INSTANTLY PERISH-- ALL THE LIVES CONTAINED THEREON SHALL DIE...
LET THEM KNOW THAT THEY DIE SERVING THE GREATER GOOD!
LET THEM KNOW THEY DIE SO THAT TIME ITSELF CAN BE CHANGED!
LET THEM KNOW THEY DIE SO THAT I--THE MONITOR--WILL BE VICTORIOUS!
EARTH-1... CHALLENGER MOUNTAIN, HOME TO THE CHALLENGERS OF THE UNKNOWN...
THERE... YOU SEE IT AGAIN, PROF?
I SEE IT, RED... BUT I DON'T KNOW WHAT IT MEANS.
JUNE, WHAT ABOUT THE SUBSPACE READINGS SUPERMAN ASKED US TO CHECK.
READING POSITIVE, PROF. I'M SCARED.
THE CHALLENGERS MAY ALL BE LIVING ON BORROWED TIME...
...HAVING CHEATED DEATH TIME AND TIME AGAIN...
SO, WHAT IS GOIN' ON OUT THERE, ACE?
NOBODY KNOWS, ROCKY... NOBODY!
...BUT WE USUALLY KNEW WHAT WE WERE FIGHTING.
THE BLIP ON THE SATELLITE READINGS INDICATES SOME KINDA FLUX OUT THERE IN SPACE.
ACE, ROCKY... QUIET DOWN. I'M PICKING UP SOME OTHER NOISE NOW.
MY GOD, IT'S LIKE SOME AGONIZING SCREAM PER-MEATING THE ENTIRE UNIVERSE.
MY EARS!
IT'S COMIN' FROM EVERYWHERE AT ONCE!
WHAT IS IT?
BUT THE ANSWER LIES NOT HERE ON EARTH... OR EVEN IN THIS UNIVERSE.
24

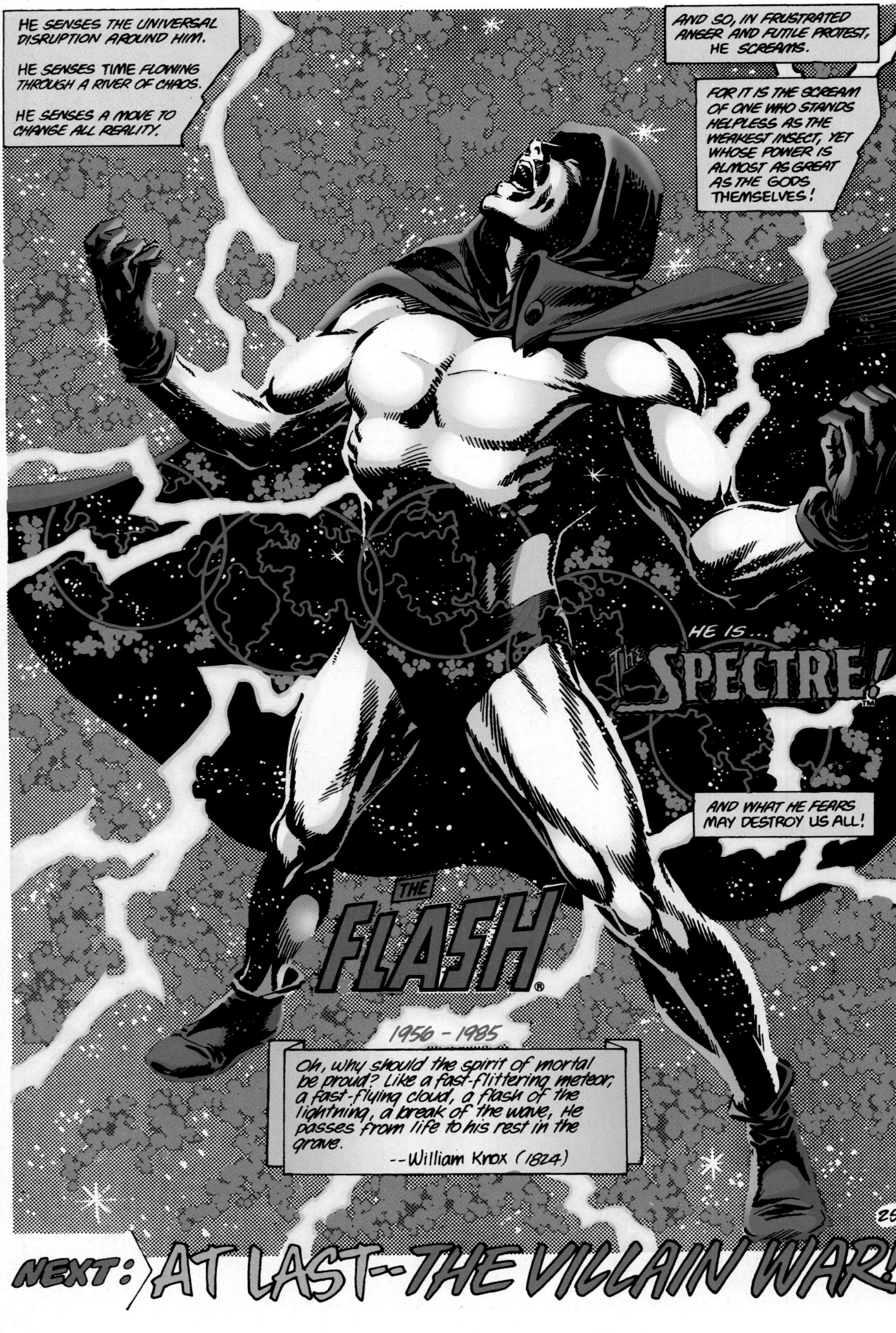
HE SENSES THE UNIVERSAL DISRUPTION AROUND HIM.
HE SENSES TIME FLOWING THROUGH A RIVER OF CHAOS.
HE SENSES A MOVE TO CHANGE ALL REALITY.
AND SO, IN FRUSTRATED ANGER AND FUTILE PROTEST, HE SCREAMS.
FOR IT IS THE SCREAM OF ONE WHO STANDS HELPLESS AS THE WEAKEST INSECT, YET WHOSE POWER IS ALMOST AS GREAT AS THE GODS THEMSELVES!
HE IS... The SPECTRE!™
AND WHAT HE FEARS MAY DESTROY US ALL!
THE FLASH®
1956 - 1985
Oh, why should the spirit of mortal be proud? Like a fast-flittering meteor, a fast-flying cloud, a flash of the lightning, a break of the wave, He passes from life to his rest in the grave.
--William Knox (1824)
25
NEXT: AT LAST--THE VILLAIN WAR!

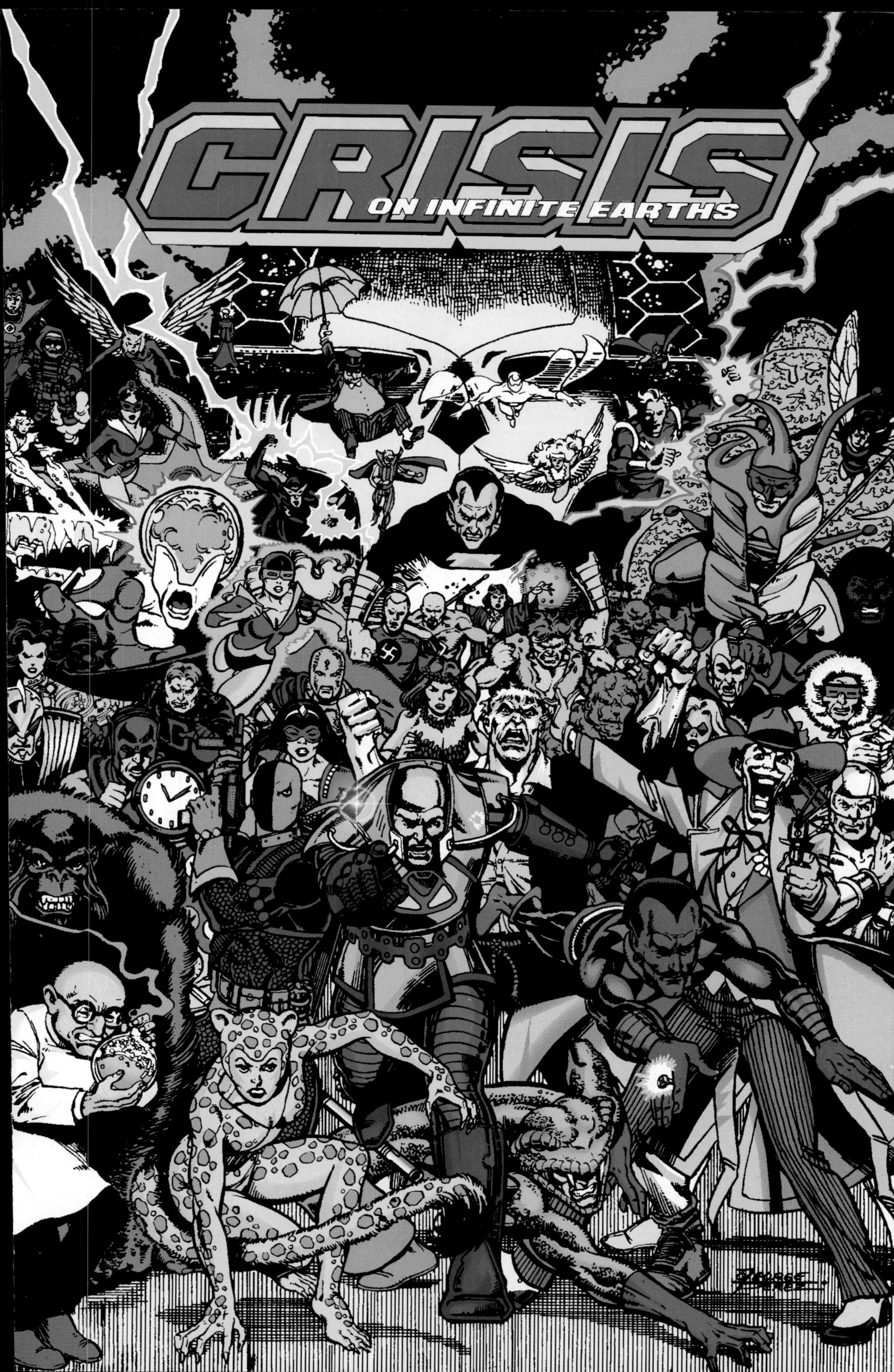
CRISIS
ON INFINITE EARTHS

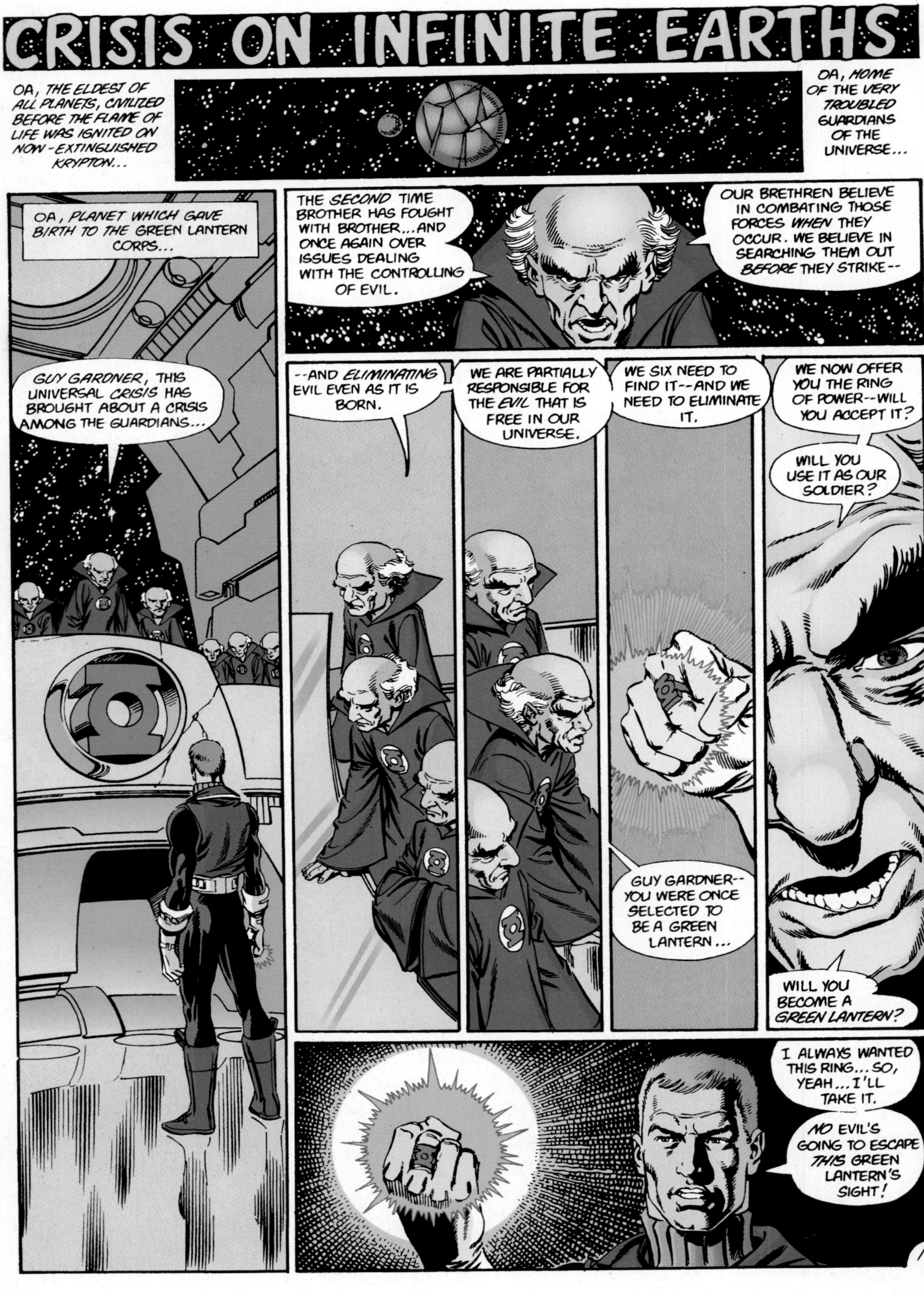
CRISIS ON INFINITE EARTHS
OA, THE ELDEST OF ALL PLANETS, CIVILIZED BEFORE THE FLAME OF LIFE WAS IGNITED ON NOW-EXTINGUISHED KRYPTON...
OA, HOME OF THE VERY TROUBLED GUARDIANS OF THE UNIVERSE...
OA, PLANET WHICH GAVE BIRTH TO THE GREEN LANTERN CORPS...
GUY GARDNER, THIS UNIVERSAL CRISIS HAS BROUGHT ABOUT A CRISIS AMONG THE GUARDIANS...
THE SECOND TIME BROTHER HAS FOUGHT WITH BROTHER...AND ONCE AGAIN OVER ISSUES DEALING WITH THE CONTROLLING OF EVIL.
OUR BRETHREN BELIEVE IN COMBATING THOSE FORCES WHEN THEY OCCUR. WE BELIEVE IN SEARCHING THEM OUT BEFORE THEY STRIKE--
--AND ELIMINATING EVIL EVEN AS IT IS BORN.
WE ARE PARTIALLY RESPONSIBLE FOR THE EVIL THAT IS FREE IN OUR UNIVERSE.
WE SIX NEED TO FIND IT--AND WE NEED TO ELIMINATE IT.
GUY GARDNER--YOU WERE ONCE SELECTED TO BE A GREEN LANTERN...
WE NOW OFFER YOU THE RING OF POWER--WILL YOU ACCEPT IT?
WILL YOU USE IT AS OUR SOLDIER?
WILL YOU BECOME A GREEN LANTERN?
I ALWAYS WANTED THIS RING... SO, YEAH... I'LL TAKE IT.
NO EVIL'S GOING TO ESCAPE THIS GREEN LANTERN'S SIGHT!
1

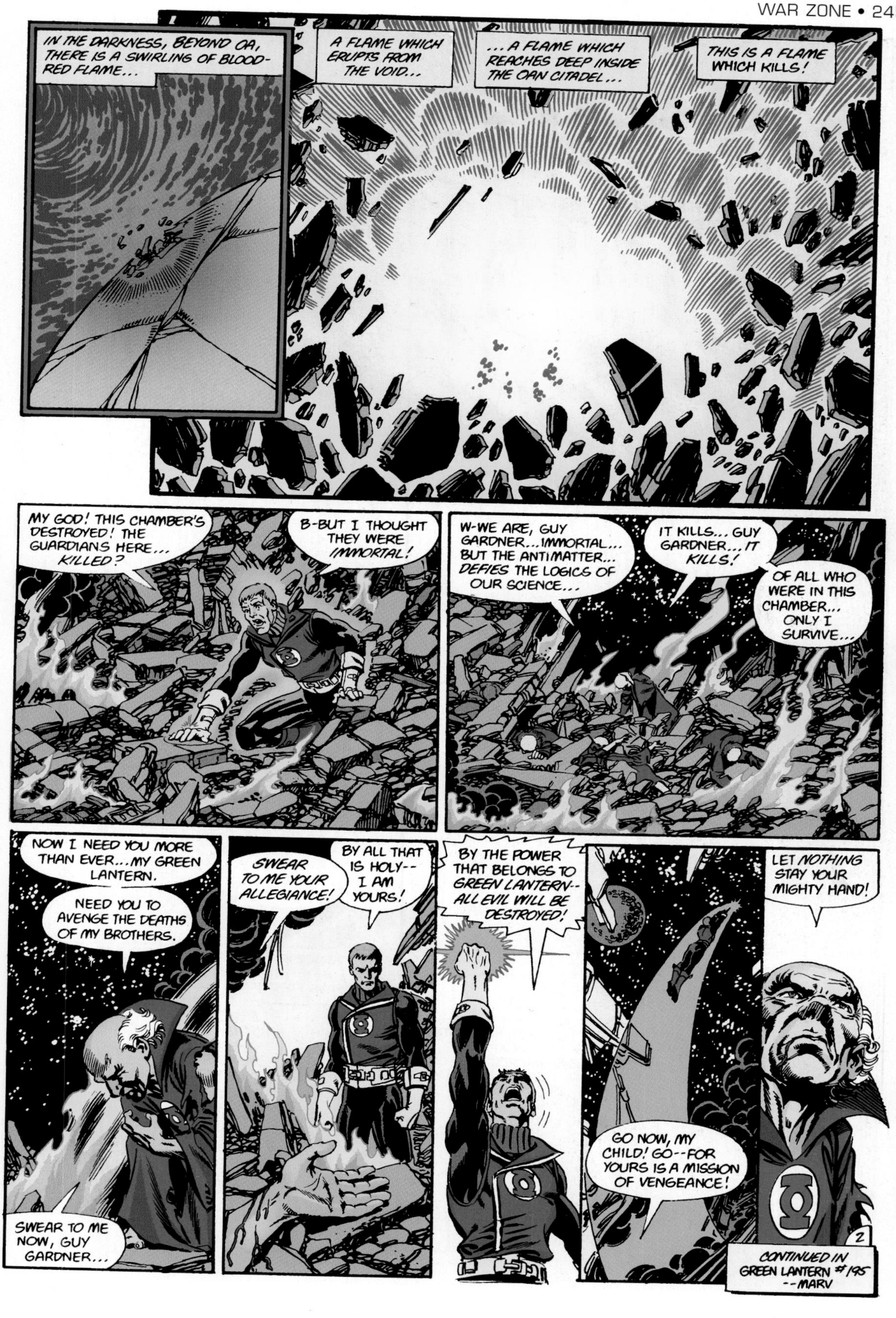

IN THE DARKNESS, BEYOND OA, THERE IS A SWIRLING OF BLOOD-RED FLAME...
A FLAME WHICH ERUPTS FROM THE VOID...
...A FLAME WHICH REACHES DEEP INSIDE THE OAN CITADEL...
THIS IS A FLAME WHICH KILLS!
MY GOD! THIS CHAMBER'S DESTROYED! THE GUARDIANS HERE... KILLED?
B-BUT I THOUGHT THEY WERE IMMORTAL!
W-WE ARE, GUY GARDNER... IMMORTAL... BUT THE ANTIMATTER... DEFIES THE LOGICS OF OUR SCIENCE...
IT KILLS... GUY GARDNER... IT KILLS!
OF ALL WHO WERE IN THIS CHAMBER... ONLY I SURVIVE...
NOW I NEED YOU MORE THAN EVER... MY GREEN LANTERN.
NEED YOU TO AVENGE THE DEATHS OF MY BROTHERS.
SWEAR TO ME NOW, GUY GARDNER...
SWEAR TO ME YOUR ALLEGIANCE!
BY ALL THAT IS HOLY-- I AM YOURS!
BY THE POWER THAT BELONGS TO GREEN LANTERN-- ALL EVIL WILL BE DESTROYED!
LET NOTHING STAY YOUR MIGHTY HAND!
GO NOW, MY CHILD! GO--FOR YOURS IS A MISSION OF VENGEANCE!
2
CONTINUED IN GREEN LANTERN #195 --MARV

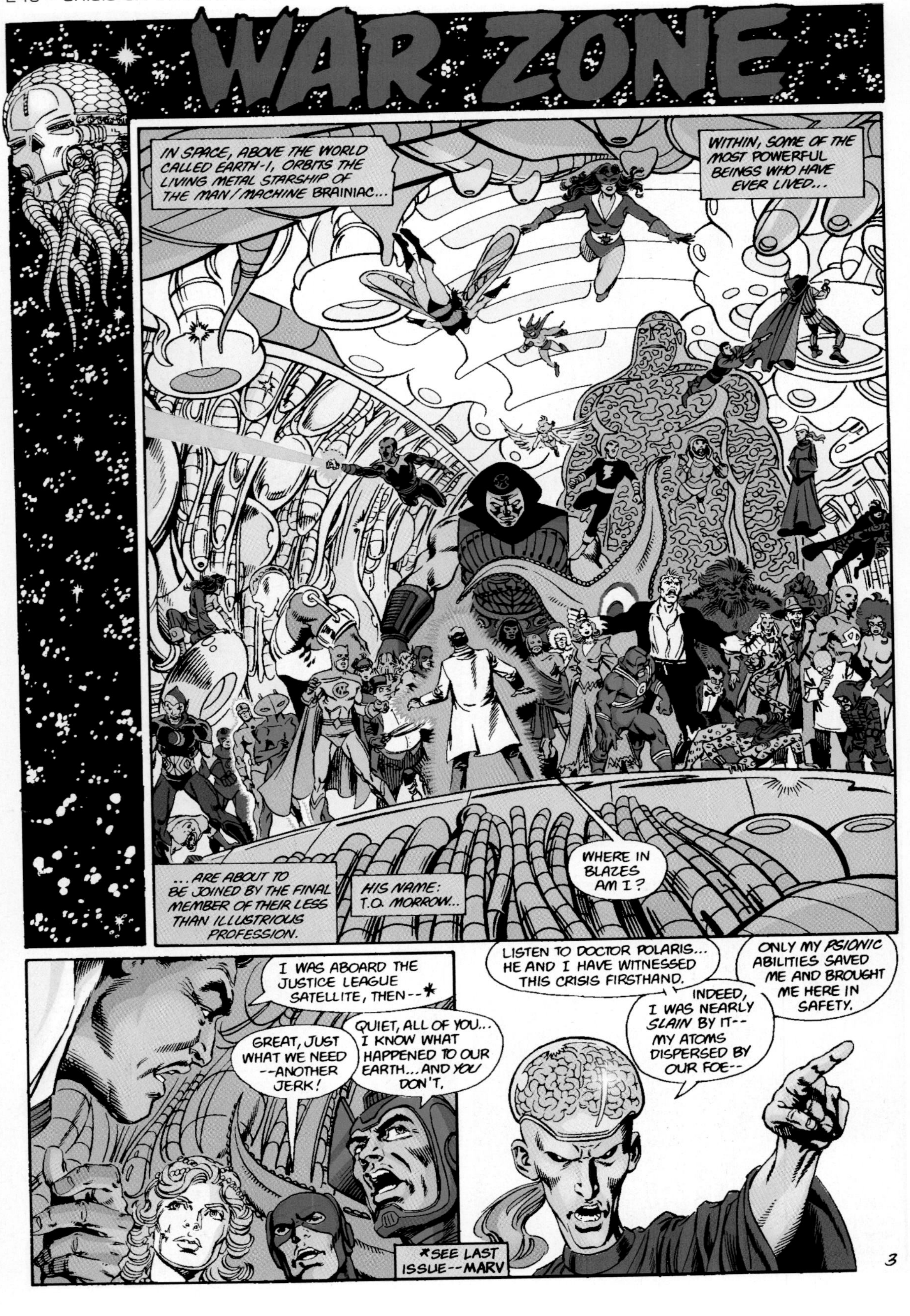
WAR ZONE
IN SPACE, ABOVE THE WORLD CALLED EARTH-1, ORBITS THE LIVING METAL STARSHIP OF THE MAN/MACHINE BRAINIAC...
WITHIN, SOME OF THE MOST POWERFUL BEINGS WHO HAVE EVER LIVED...
... ARE ABOUT TO BE JOINED BY THE FINAL MEMBER OF THEIR LESS THAN ILLUSTRIOUS PROFESSION.
HIS NAME: T.O. MORROW...
WHERE IN BLAZES AM I?
I WAS ABOARD THE JUSTICE LEAGUE SATELLITE, THEN--*
GREAT, JUST WHAT WE NEED --ANOTHER JERK!
QUIET, ALL OF YOU... I KNOW WHAT HAPPENED TO OUR EARTH... AND YOU DON'T.
LISTEN TO DOCTOR POLARIS... HE AND I HAVE WITNESSED THIS CRISIS FIRSTHAND.
INDEED, I WAS NEARLY SLAIN BY IT-- MY ATOMS DISPERSED BY OUR FOE--
ONLY MY PSIONIC ABILITIES SAVED ME AND BROUGHT ME HERE IN SAFETY.
*SEE LAST ISSUE--MARV
3

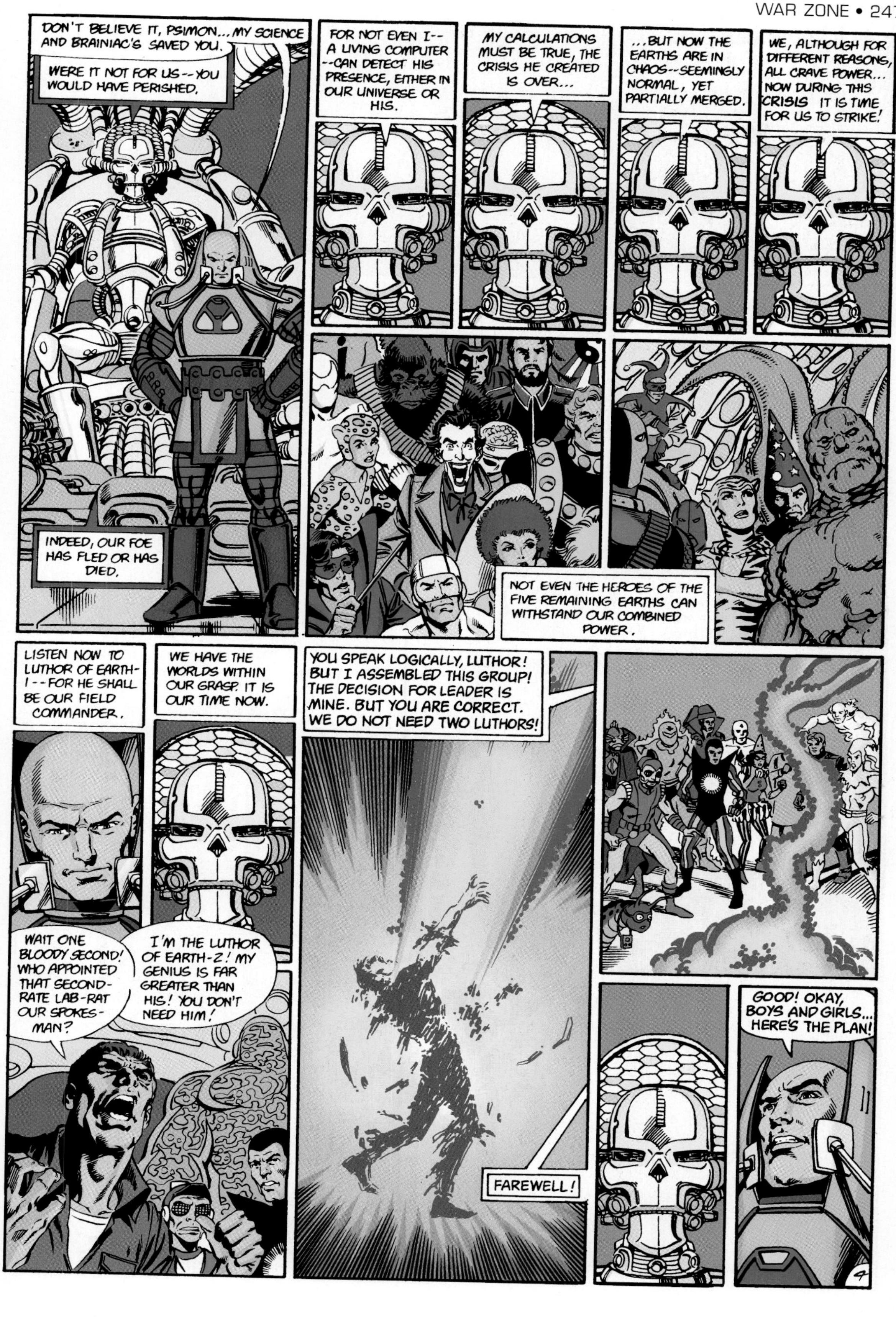
DON'T BELIEVE IT, PSIMON... MY SCIENCE AND BRAINIAC'S SAVED YOU.
WERE IT NOT FOR US--YOU WOULD HAVE PERISHED.
INDEED, OUR FOE HAS FLED OR HAS DIED.
FOR NOT EVEN I-- A LIVING COMPUTER --CAN DETECT HIS PRESENCE, EITHER IN OUR UNIVERSE OR HIS.
MY CALCULATIONS MUST BE TRUE, THE CRISIS HE CREATED IS OVER...
...BUT NOW THE EARTHS ARE IN CHAOS--SEEMINGLY NORMAL, YET PARTIALLY MERGED.
WE, ALTHOUGH FOR DIFFERENT REASONS, ALL CRAVE POWER... NOW DURING THIS CRISIS IT IS TIME FOR US TO STRIKE!
NOT EVEN THE HEROES OF THE FIVE REMAINING EARTHS CAN WITHSTAND OUR COMBINED POWER.
LISTEN NOW TO LUTHOR OF EARTH-1--FOR HE SHALL BE OUR FIELD COMMANDER.
WE HAVE THE WORLDS WITHIN OUR GRASP. IT IS OUR TIME NOW.
WAIT ONE BLOODY SECOND! WHO APPOINTED THAT SECOND-RATE LAB-RAT OUR SPOKES-MAN?
I'M THE LUTHOR OF EARTH-2! MY GENIUS IS FAR GREATER THAN HIS! YOU DON'T NEED HIM!
YOU SPEAK LOGICALLY, LUTHOR! BUT I ASSEMBLED THIS GROUP! THE DECISION FOR LEADER IS MINE. BUT YOU ARE CORRECT. WE DO NOT NEED TWO LUTHORS!
FAREWELL!
GOOD! OKAY, BOYS AND GIRLS... HERE'S THE PLAN!
4

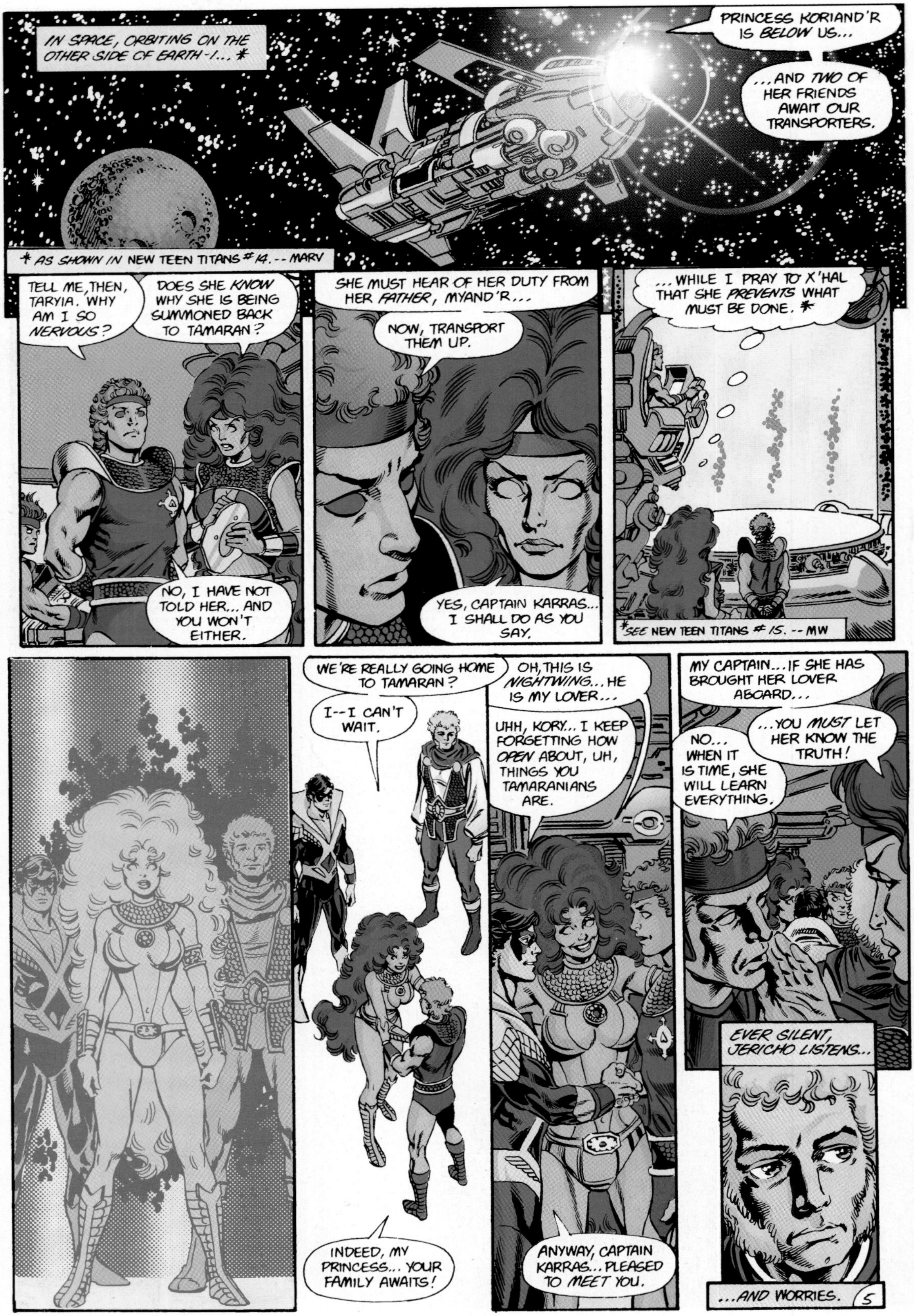
IN SPACE, ORBITING ON THE OTHER SIDE OF EARTH-1... *
PRINCESS KORIAND'R IS BELOW US...
...AND TWO OF HER FRIENDS AWAIT OUR TRANSPORTERS.
* AS SHOWN IN NEW TEEN TITANS # 14. -- MARV
TELL ME, THEN, TARYIA. WHY AM I SO NERVOUS?
DOES SHE KNOW WHY SHE IS BEING SUMMONED BACK TO TAMARAN?
NO, I HAVE NOT TOLD HER... AND YOU WON'T EITHER.
SHE MUST HEAR OF HER DUTY FROM HER FATHER, MYAND'R...
NOW, TRANSPORT THEM UP.
YES, CAPTAIN KARRAS... I SHALL DO AS YOU SAY.
...WHILE I PRAY TO X'HAL THAT SHE PREVENTS WHAT MUST BE DONE. *
* SEE NEW TEEN TITANS # 15. -- MW
WE'RE REALLY GOING HOME TO TAMARAN?
I--I CAN'T WAIT.
INDEED, MY PRINCESS... YOUR FAMILY AWAITS!
OH, THIS IS NIGHTWING... HE IS MY LOVER...
UHH, KORY... I KEEP FORGETTING HOW OPEN ABOUT, UH, THINGS YOU TAMARANIANS ARE.
ANYWAY, CAPTAIN KARRAS... PLEASED TO MEET YOU.
MY CAPTAIN... IF SHE HAS BROUGHT HER LOVER ABOARD...
...YOU MUST LET HER KNOW THE TRUTH!
NO... WHEN IT IS TIME, SHE WILL LEARN EVERYTHING.
EVER SILENT, JERICHO LISTENS...
...AND WORRIES.
5

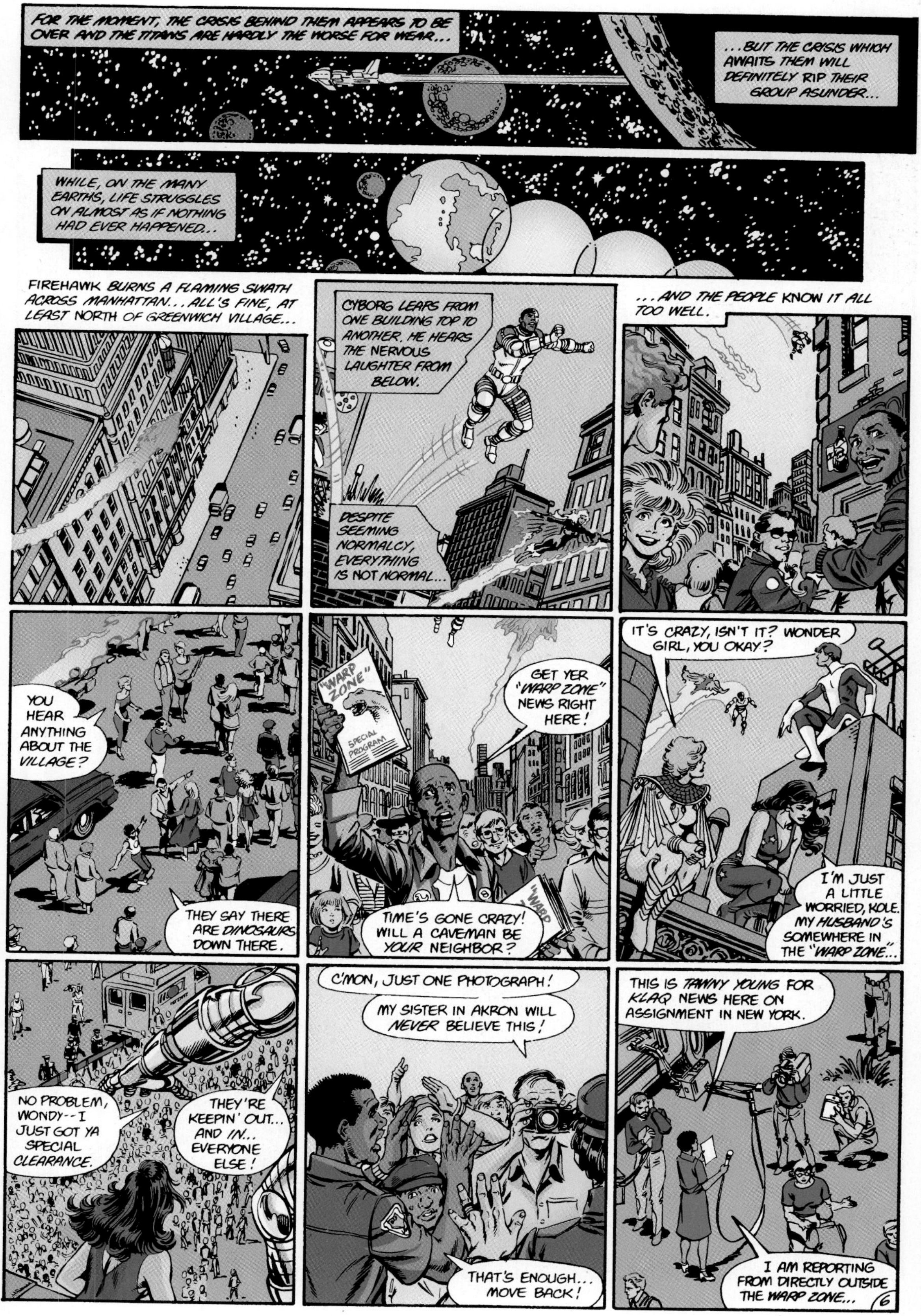

FOR THE MOMENT, THE CRISIS BEHIND THEM APPEARS TO BE OVER AND THE TITANS ARE HARDLY THE WORSE FOR WEAR...
...BUT THE CRISIS WHICH AWAITS THEM WILL DEFINITELY RIP THEIR GROUP ASUNDER...
WHILE, ON THE MANY EARTHS, LIFE STRUGGLES ON ALMOST AS IF NOTHING HAD EVER HAPPENED...
FIREHAWK BURNS A FLAMING SWATH ACROSS MANHATTAN... ALL'S FINE, AT LEAST NORTH OF GREENWICH VILLAGE...
CYBORG LEAPS FROM ONE BUILDING TOP TO ANOTHER. HE HEARS THE NERVOUS LAUGHTER FROM BELOW.
DESPITE SEEMING NORMALCY, EVERYTHING IS NOT NORMAL...
...AND THE PEOPLE KNOW IT ALL TOO WELL.
YOU HEAR ANYTHING ABOUT THE VILLAGE?
THEY SAY THERE ARE DINOSAURS DOWN THERE.
"WARP ZONE"
SPECIAL PROGRAM
GET YER "WARP ZONE" NEWS RIGHT HERE!
TIME'S GONE CRAZY! WILL A CAVEMAN BE YOUR NEIGHBOR?
IT'S CRAZY, ISN'T IT? WONDER GIRL, YOU OKAY?
I'M JUST A LITTLE WORRIED, KOLE. MY HUSBAND'S SOMEWHERE IN THE "WARP ZONE"...
NO PROBLEM, WONDY-- I JUST GOT YA SPECIAL CLEARANCE.
THEY'RE KEEPIN' OUT... AND IN... EVERYONE ELSE!
C'MON, JUST ONE PHOTOGRAPH!
MY SISTER IN AKRON WILL NEVER BELIEVE THIS!
THAT'S ENOUGH... MOVE BACK!
THIS IS TAWNY YOUNG FOR KLAQ NEWS HERE ON ASSIGNMENT IN NEW YORK.
I AM REPORTING FROM DIRECTLY OUTSIDE THE WARP ZONE...
6

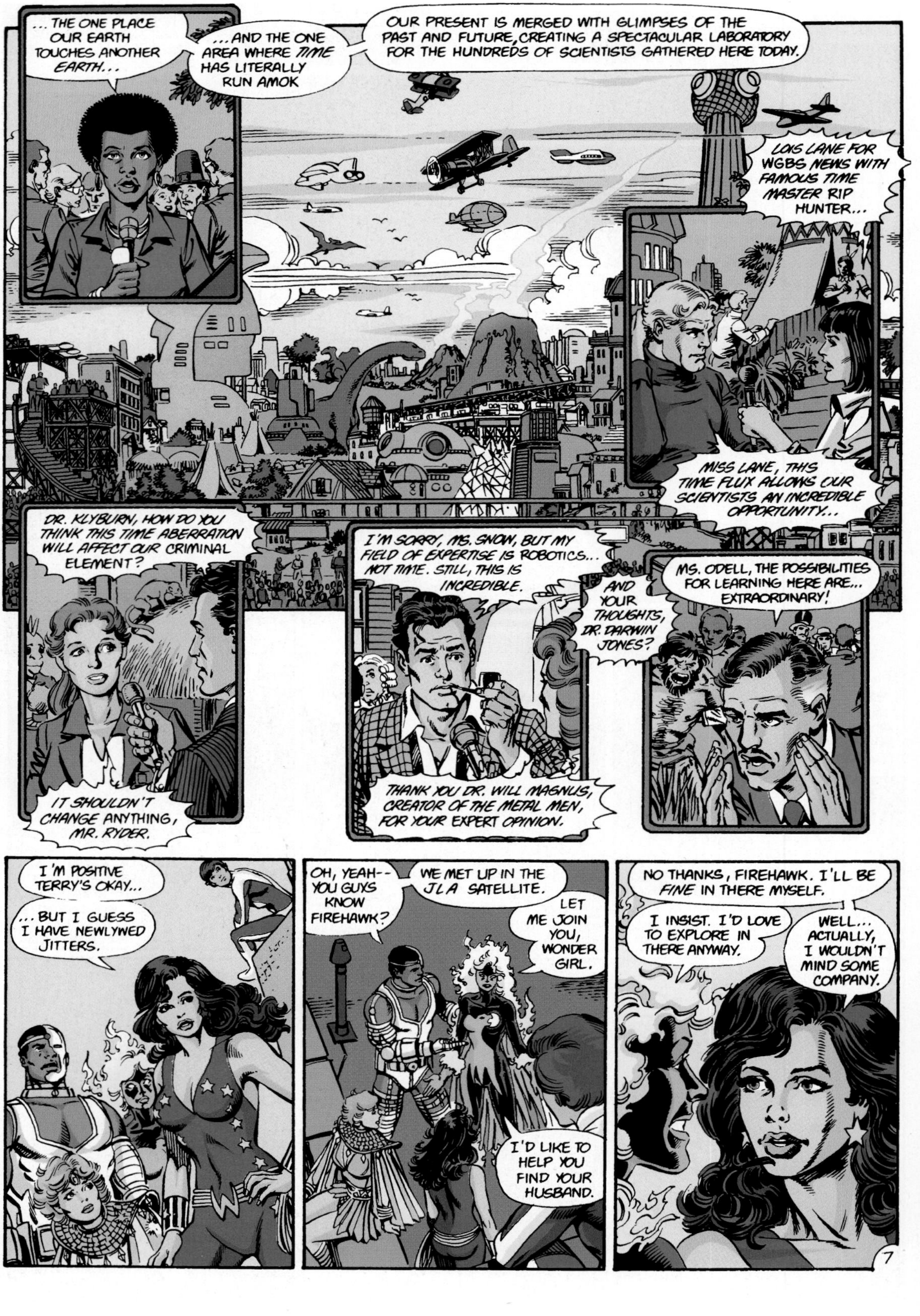
...THE ONE PLACE OUR EARTH TOUCHES ANOTHER EARTH...
...AND THE ONE AREA WHERE TIME HAS LITERALLY RUN AMOK
OUR PRESENT IS MERGED WITH GLIMPSES OF THE PAST AND FUTURE, CREATING A SPECTACULAR LABORATORY FOR THE HUNDREDS OF SCIENTISTS GATHERED HERE TODAY.
LOIS LANE FOR WGBS NEWS WITH FAMOUS TIME MASTER RIP HUNTER...
MISS LANE, THIS TIME FLUX ALLOWS OUR SCIENTISTS AN INCREDIBLE OPPORTUNITY...
DR. KLYBURN, HOW DO YOU THINK THIS TIME ABERRATION WILL AFFECT OUR CRIMINAL ELEMENT?
IT SHOULDN'T CHANGE ANYTHING, MR. RYDER.
I'M SORRY, MS. SNOW, BUT MY FIELD OF EXPERTISE IS ROBOTICS... NOT TIME. STILL, THIS IS INCREDIBLE.
THANK YOU DR. WILL MAGNUS, CREATOR OF THE METAL MEN, FOR YOUR EXPERT OPINION.
AND YOUR THOUGHTS, DR. DARWIN JONES?
MS. ODELL, THE POSSIBILITIES FOR LEARNING HERE ARE... EXTRAORDINARY!
I'M POSITIVE TERRY'S OKAY...
...BUT I GUESS I HAVE NEWLYWED JITTERS.
OH, YEAH-- YOU GUYS KNOW FIREHAWK?
WE MET UP IN THE JLA SATELLITE.
LET ME JOIN YOU, WONDER GIRL.
I'D LIKE TO HELP YOU FIND YOUR HUSBAND.
NO THANKS, FIREHAWK. I'LL BE FINE IN THERE MYSELF.
I INSIST. I'D LOVE TO EXPLORE IN THERE ANYWAY.
WELL... ACTUALLY, I WOULDN'T MIND SOME COMPANY.
7

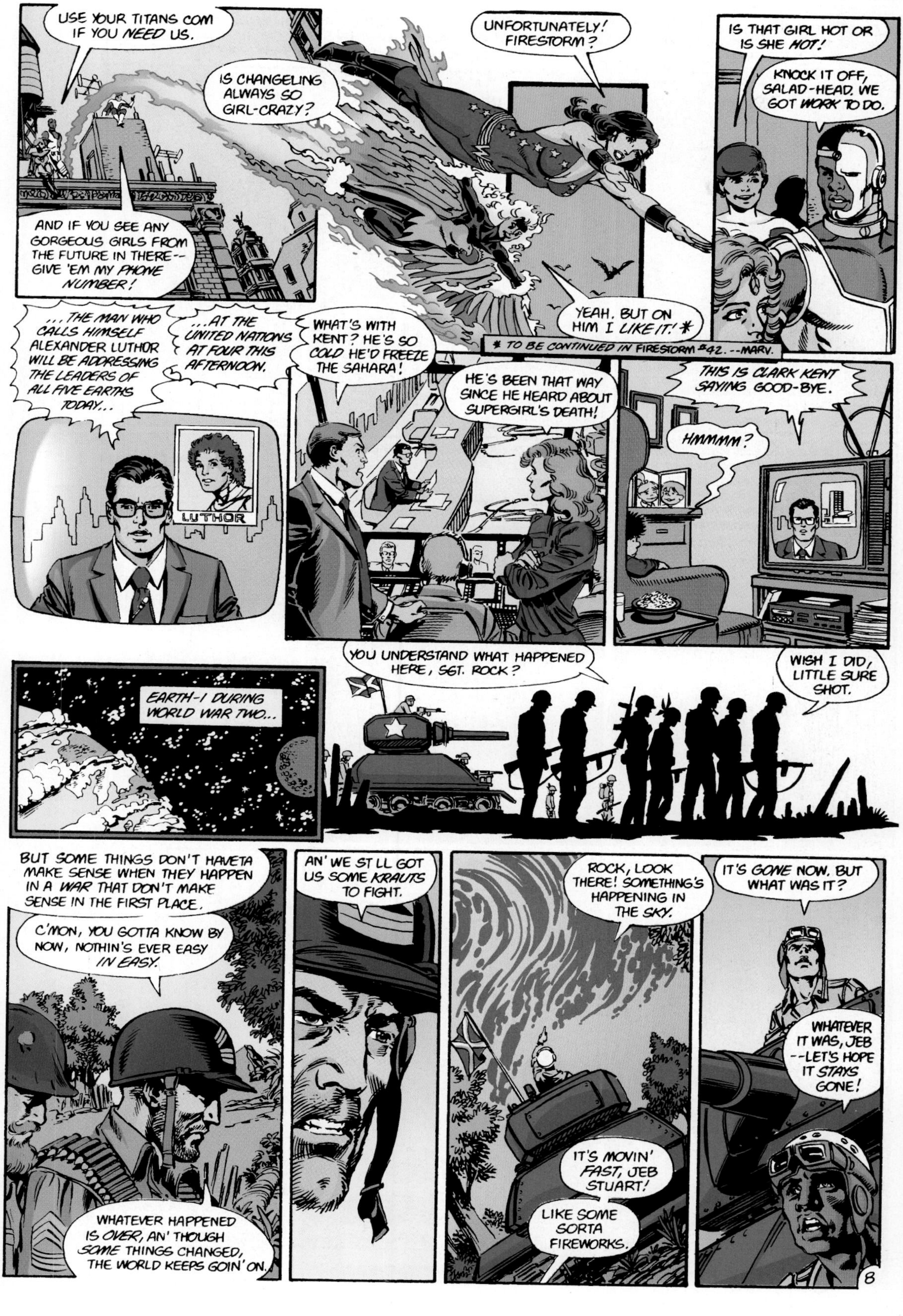
USE YOUR TITANS COM IF YOU NEED US.
AND IF YOU SEE ANY GORGEOUS GIRLS FROM THE FUTURE IN THERE-- GIVE 'EM MY PHONE NUMBER!
IS CHANGELING ALWAYS SO GIRL-CRAZY?
UNFORTUNATELY! FIRESTORM?
YEAH. BUT ON HIM I LIKE IT! *
IS THAT GIRL HOT OR IS SHE NOT!
KNOCK IT OFF, SALAD-HEAD. WE GOT WORK TO DO.
* TO BE CONTINUED IN FIRESTORM #42. --MARV.
...THE MAN WHO CALLS HIMSELF ALEXANDER LUTHOR WILL BE ADDRESSING THE LEADERS OF ALL FIVE EARTHS TODAY...
...AT THE UNITED NATIONS AT FOUR THIS AFTERNOON.
LUTHOR
WHAT'S WITH KENT? HE'S SO COLD HE'D FREEZE THE SAHARA!
HE'S BEEN THAT WAY SINCE HE HEARD ABOUT SUPERGIRL'S DEATH!
THIS IS CLARK KENT SAYING GOOD-BYE.
HMMMM?
EARTH-1 DURING WORLD WAR TWO...
YOU UNDERSTAND WHAT HAPPENED HERE, SGT. ROCK?
WISH I DID, LITTLE SURE SHOT.
BUT SOME THINGS DON'T HAVETA MAKE SENSE WHEN THEY HAPPEN IN A WAR THAT DON'T MAKE SENSE IN THE FIRST PLACE.
C'MON, YOU GOTTA KNOW BY NOW, NOTHIN'S EVER EASY IN EASY.
WHATEVER HAPPENED IS OVER, AN' THOUGH SOME THINGS CHANGED, THE WORLD KEEPS GOIN' ON.
AN' WE ST LL GOT US SOME KRAUTS TO FIGHT.
ROCK, LOOK THERE! SOMETHING'S HAPPENING IN THE SKY.
IT'S MOVIN' FAST, JEB STUART!
LIKE SOME SORTA FIREWORKS.
IT'S GONE NOW. BUT WHAT WAS IT?
WHATEVER IT WAS, JEB --LET'S HOPE IT STAYS GONE!
8

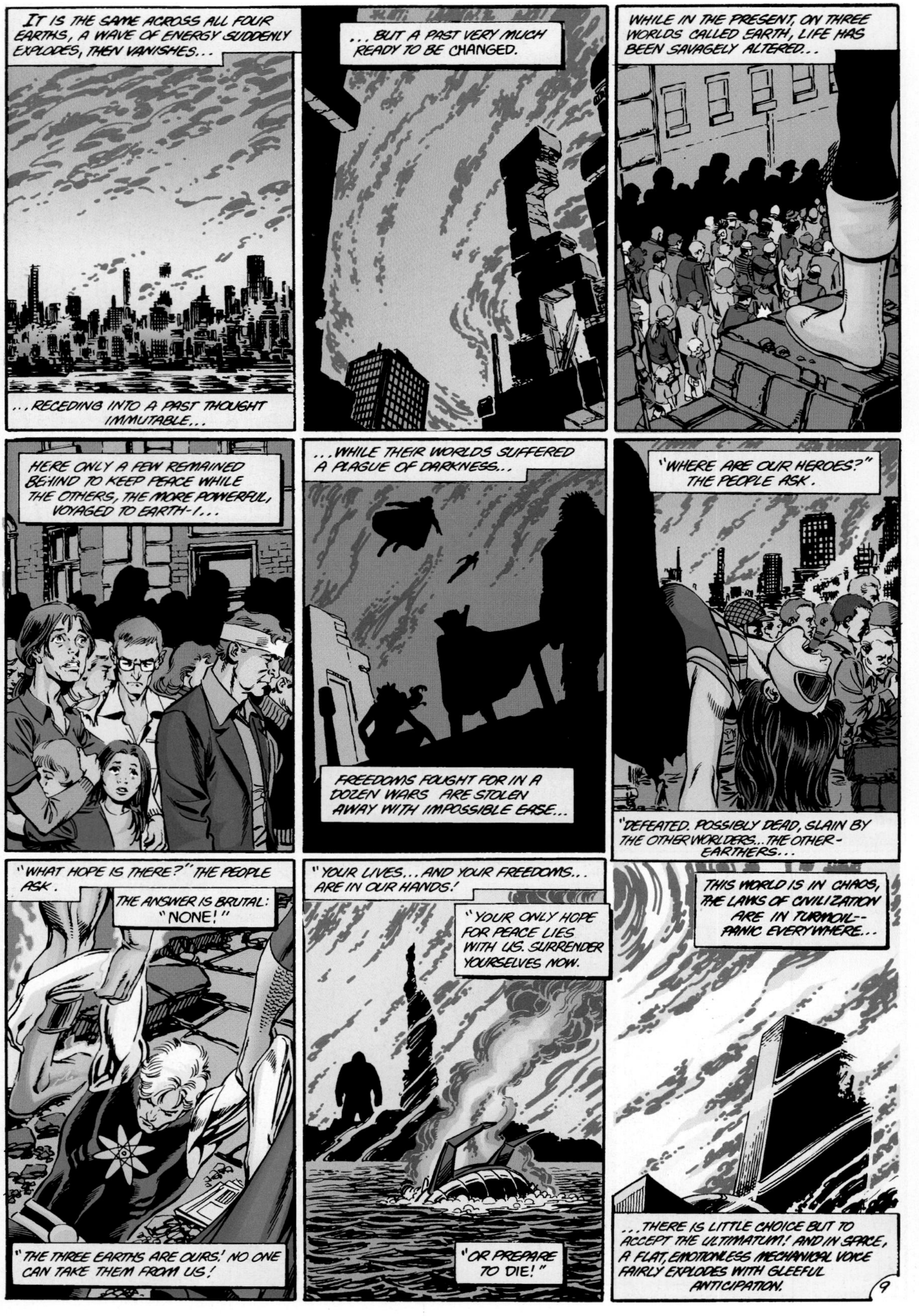
IT IS THE SAME ACROSS ALL FOUR EARTHS, A WAVE OF ENERGY SUDDENLY EXPLODES, THEN VANISHES...
...RECEDING INTO A PAST THOUGHT IMMUTABLE...
...BUT A PAST VERY MUCH READY TO BE CHANGED.
WHILE IN THE PRESENT, ON THREE WORLDS CALLED EARTH, LIFE HAS BEEN SAVAGELY ALTERED...
HERE ONLY A FEW REMAINED BEHIND TO KEEP PEACE WHILE THE OTHERS, THE MORE POWERFUL, VOYAGED TO EARTH-1...
...WHILE THEIR WORLDS SUFFERED A PLAGUE OF DARKNESS...
FREEDOMS FOUGHT FOR IN A DOZEN WARS ARE STOLEN AWAY WITH IMPOSSIBLE EASE...
"WHERE ARE OUR HEROES?" THE PEOPLE ASK.
"DEFEATED. POSSIBLY DEAD, SLAIN BY THE OTHER WORLDERS... THE OTHER-EARTHERS...
"WHAT HOPE IS THERE?" THE PEOPLE ASK.
THE ANSWER IS BRUTAL: "NONE!"
"THE THREE EARTHS ARE OURS! NO ONE CAN TAKE THEM FROM US!
"YOUR LIVES... AND YOUR FREEDOMS... ARE IN OUR HANDS!
"YOUR ONLY HOPE FOR PEACE LIES WITH US. SURRENDER YOURSELVES NOW.
"OR PREPARE TO DIE!"
THIS WORLD IS IN CHAOS, THE LAWS OF CIVILIZATION ARE IN TURMOIL-- PANIC EVERYWHERE...
...THERE IS LITTLE CHOICE BUT TO ACCEPT THE ULTIMATUM! AND IN SPACE, A FLAT, EMOTIONLESS MECHANICAL VOICE FAIRLY EXPLODES WITH GLEEFUL ANTICIPATION.
9

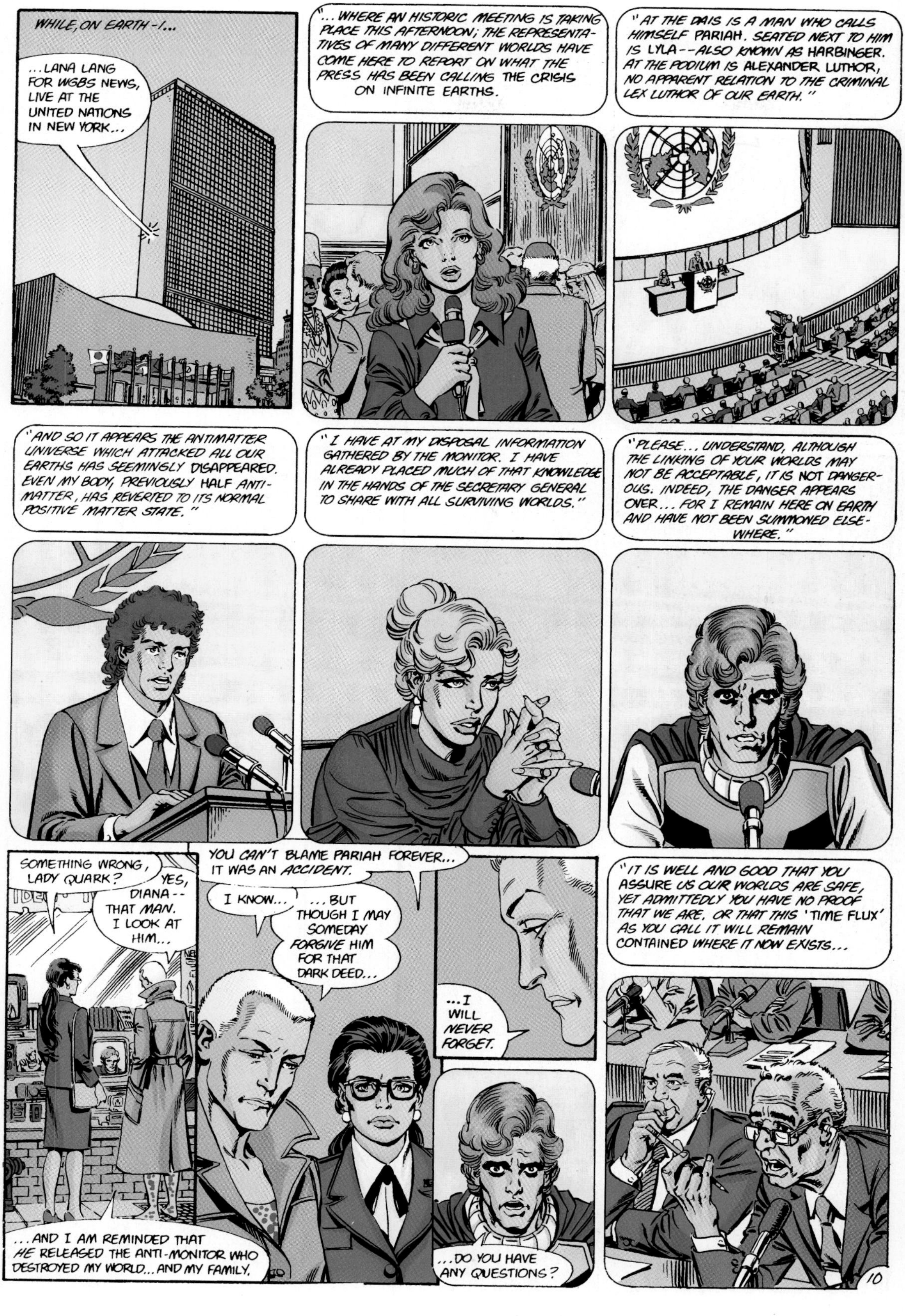
WHILE, ON EARTH-1...
...LANA LANG FOR WGBS NEWS, LIVE AT THE UNITED NATIONS IN NEW YORK...
"...WHERE AN HISTORIC MEETING IS TAKING PLACE THIS AFTERNOON; THE REPRESENTATIVES OF MANY DIFFERENT WORLDS HAVE COME HERE TO REPORT ON WHAT THE PRESS HAS BEEN CALLING THE CRISIS ON INFINITE EARTHS.
"AT THE DAIS IS A MAN WHO CALLS HIMSELF PARIAH. SEATED NEXT TO HIM IS LYLA--ALSO KNOWN AS HARBINGER. AT THE PODIUM IS ALEXANDER LUTHOR, NO APPARENT RELATION TO THE CRIMINAL LEX LUTHOR OF OUR EARTH."
"AND SO IT APPEARS THE ANTIMATTER UNIVERSE WHICH ATTACKED ALL OUR EARTHS HAS SEEMINGLY DISAPPEARED. EVEN MY BODY, PREVIOUSLY HALF ANTI-MATTER, HAS REVERTED TO ITS NORMAL POSITIVE MATTER STATE."
"I HAVE AT MY DISPOSAL INFORMATION GATHERED BY THE MONITOR. I HAVE ALREADY PLACED MUCH OF THAT KNOWLEDGE IN THE HANDS OF THE SECRETARY GENERAL TO SHARE WITH ALL SURVIVING WORLDS."
"PLEASE... UNDERSTAND, ALTHOUGH THE LINKING OF YOUR WORLDS MAY NOT BE ACCEPTABLE, IT IS NOT DANGEROUS. INDEED, THE DANGER APPEARS OVER... FOR I REMAIN HERE ON EARTH AND HAVE NOT BEEN SUMMONED ELSEWHERE."
SOMETHING WRONG, LADY QUARK?
YES, DIANA--THAT MAN. I LOOK AT HIM...
...AND I AM REMINDED THAT HE RELEASED THE ANTI-MONITOR WHO DESTROYED MY WORLD... AND MY FAMILY.
YOU CAN'T BLAME PARIAH FOREVER... IT WAS AN ACCIDENT.
I KNOW...
...BUT THOUGH I MAY SOMEDAY FORGIVE HIM FOR THAT DARK DEED...
...I WILL NEVER FORGET.
...DO YOU HAVE ANY QUESTIONS?
"IT IS WELL AND GOOD THAT YOU ASSURE US OUR WORLDS ARE SAFE, YET ADMITTEDLY YOU HAVE NO PROOF THAT WE ARE, OR THAT THIS 'TIME FLUX' AS YOU CALL IT WILL REMAIN CONTAINED WHERE IT NOW EXISTS...
10

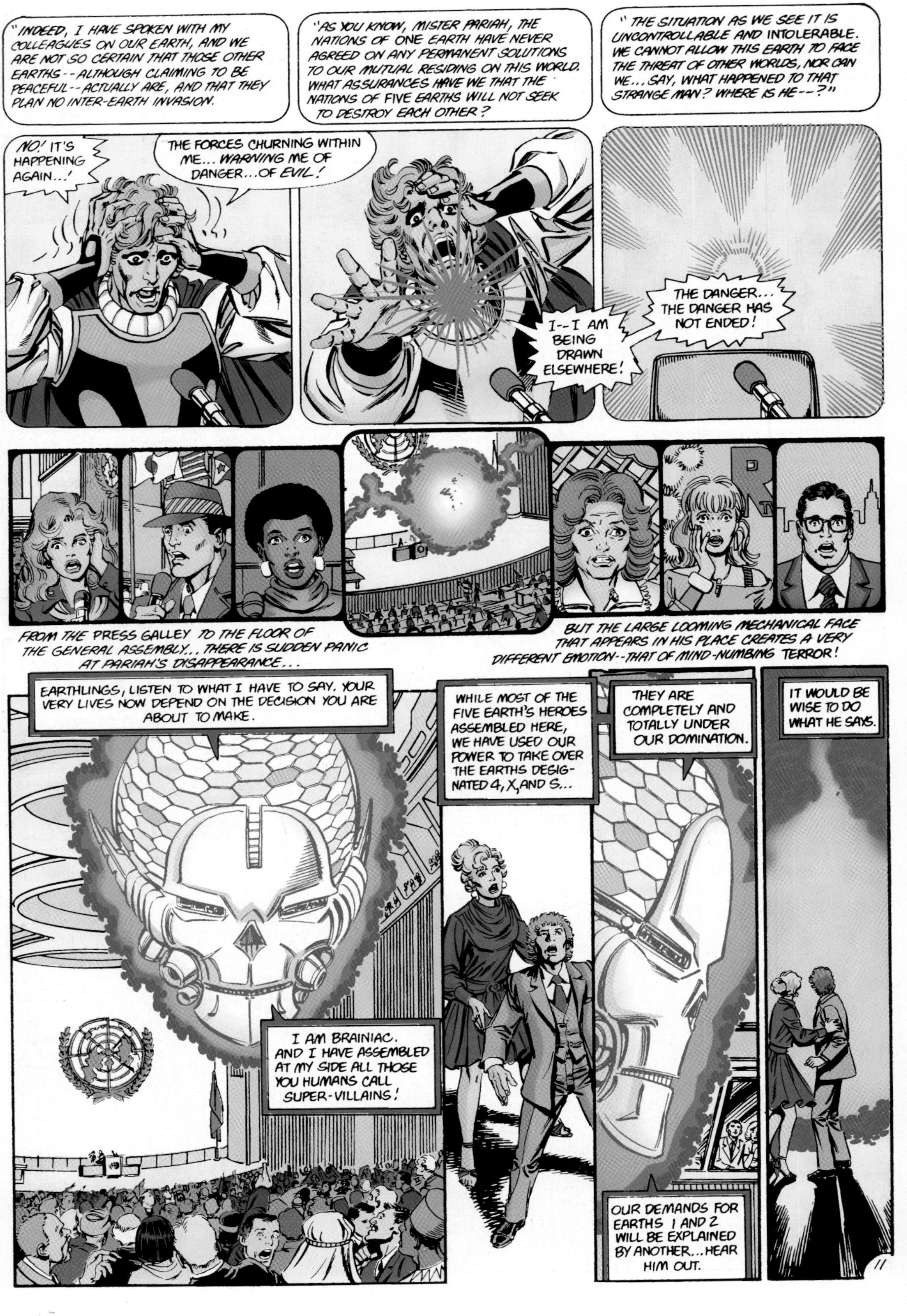
"INDEED, I HAVE SPOKEN WITH MY COLLEAGUES ON OUR EARTH, AND WE ARE NOT SO CERTAIN THAT THOSE OTHER EARTHS--ALTHOUGH CLAIMING TO BE PEACEFUL--ACTUALLY ARE, AND THAT THEY PLAN NO INTER-EARTH INVASION.
"AS YOU KNOW, MISTER PARIAH, THE NATIONS OF ONE EARTH HAVE NEVER AGREED ON ANY PERMANENT SOLUTIONS TO OUR MUTUAL RESIDING ON THIS WORLD. WHAT ASSURANCES HAVE WE THAT THE NATIONS OF FIVE EARTHS WILL NOT SEEK TO DESTROY EACH OTHER?
" THE SITUATION AS WE SEE IT IS UNCONTROLLABLE AND INTOLERABLE. WE CANNOT ALLOW THIS EARTH TO FACE THE THREAT OF OTHER WORLDS, NOR CAN WE..., SAY, WHAT HAPPENED TO THAT STRANGE MAN? WHERE IS HE--?"
NO! IT'S HAPPENING AGAIN...!
THE FORCES CHURNING WITHIN ME... WARNING ME OF DANGER...OF EVIL!
I--I AM BEING DRAWN ELSEWHERE!
THE DANGER... THE DANGER HAS NOT ENDED!
FROM THE PRESS GALLEY TO THE FLOOR OF THE GENERAL ASSEMBLY... THERE IS SUDDEN PANIC AT PARIAH'S DISAPPEARANCE...
BUT THE LARGE LOOMING MECHANICAL FACE THAT APPEARS IN HIS PLACE CREATES A VERY DIFFERENT EMOTION--THAT OF MIND-NUMBING TERROR!
EARTHLINGS, LISTEN TO WHAT I HAVE TO SAY. YOUR VERY LIVES NOW DEPEND ON THE DECISION YOU ARE ABOUT TO MAKE.
I AM BRAINIAC. AND I HAVE ASSEMBLED AT MY SIDE ALL THOSE YOU HUMANS CALL SUPER-VILLAINS!
WHILE MOST OF THE FIVE EARTH'S HEROES ASSEMBLED HERE, WE HAVE USED OUR POWER TO TAKE OVER THE EARTHS DESIGNATED 4, X, AND S...
THEY ARE COMPLETELY AND TOTALLY UNDER OUR DOMINATION.
OUR DEMANDS FOR EARTHS 1 AND 2 WILL BE EXPLAINED BY ANOTHER...HEAR HIM OUT.
IT WOULD BE WISE TO DO WHAT HE SAYS.
11

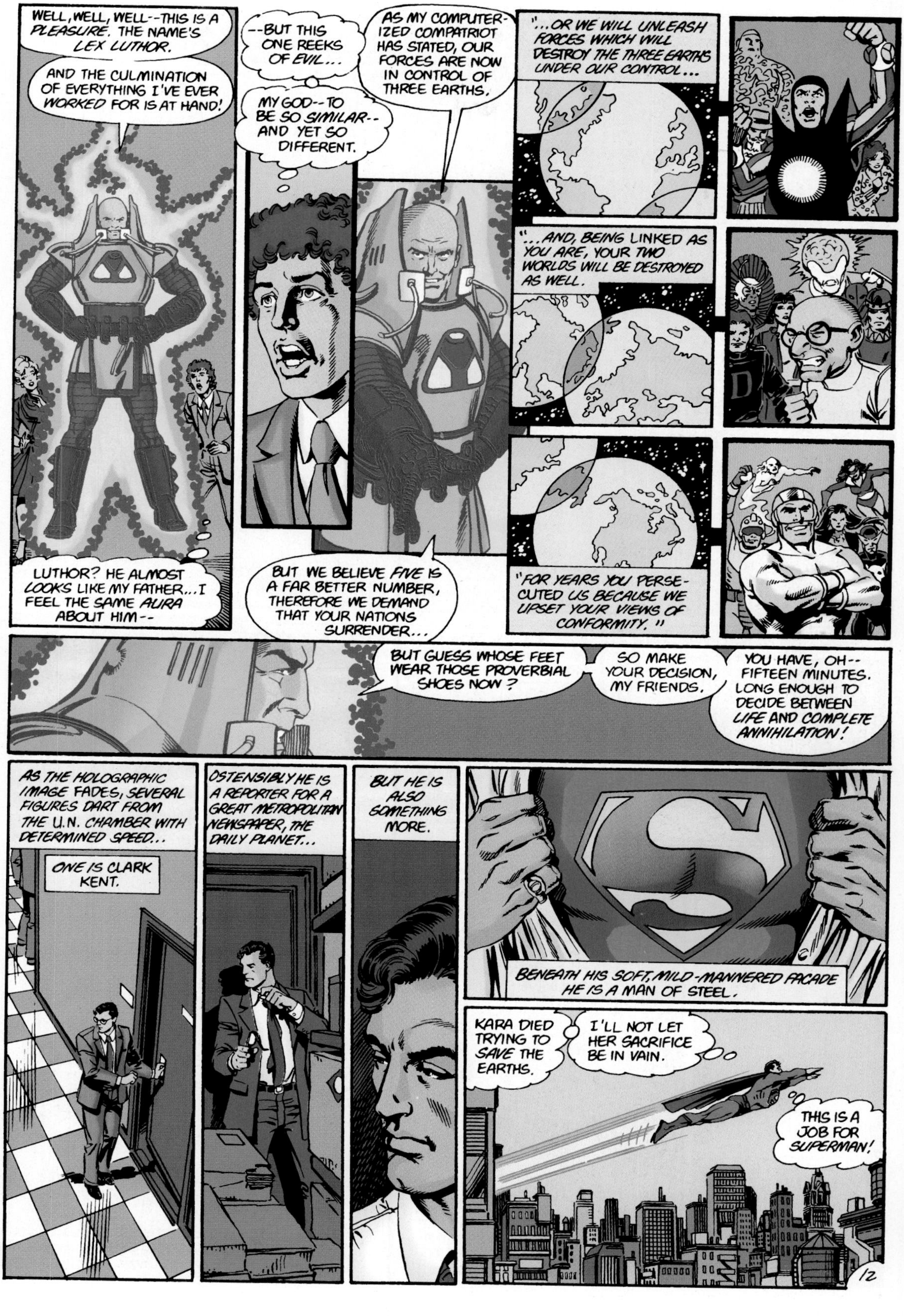
WELL, WELL, WELL--THIS IS A PLEASURE. THE NAME'S LEX LUTHOR.
AND THE CULMINATION OF EVERYTHING I'VE EVER WORKED FOR IS AT HAND!
LUTHOR? HE ALMOST LOOKS LIKE MY FATHER... I FEEL THE SAME AURA ABOUT HIM--
--BUT THIS ONE REEKS OF EVIL...
MY GOD--TO BE SO SIMILAR--AND YET SO DIFFERENT.
AS MY COMPUTERIZED COMPATRIOT HAS STATED, OUR FORCES ARE NOW IN CONTROL OF THREE EARTHS.
BUT WE BELIEVE FIVE IS A FAR BETTER NUMBER, THEREFORE WE DEMAND THAT YOUR NATIONS SURRENDER...
"...OR WE WILL UNLEASH FORCES WHICH WILL DESTROY THE THREE EARTHS UNDER OUR CONTROL...
"...AND, BEING LINKED AS YOU ARE, YOUR TWO WORLDS WILL BE DESTROYED AS WELL.
"FOR YEARS YOU PERSECUTED US BECAUSE WE UPSET YOUR VIEWS OF CONFORMITY."
BUT GUESS WHOSE FEET WEAR THOSE PROVERBIAL SHOES NOW?
SO MAKE YOUR DECISION, MY FRIENDS.
YOU HAVE, OH--FIFTEEN MINUTES. LONG ENOUGH TO DECIDE BETWEEN LIFE AND COMPLETE ANNIHILATION!
AS THE HOLOGRAPHIC IMAGE FADES, SEVERAL FIGURES DART FROM THE U.N. CHAMBER WITH DETERMINED SPEED...
ONE IS CLARK KENT.
OSTENSIBLY HE IS A REPORTER FOR A GREAT METROPOLITAN NEWSPAPER, THE DAILY PLANET...
BUT HE IS ALSO SOMETHING MORE.
BENEATH HIS SOFT, MILD-MANNERED FACADE HE IS A MAN OF STEEL.
KARA DIED TRYING TO SAVE THE EARTHS.
I'LL NOT LET HER SACRIFICE BE IN VAIN.
THIS IS A JOB FOR SUPERMAN!
12

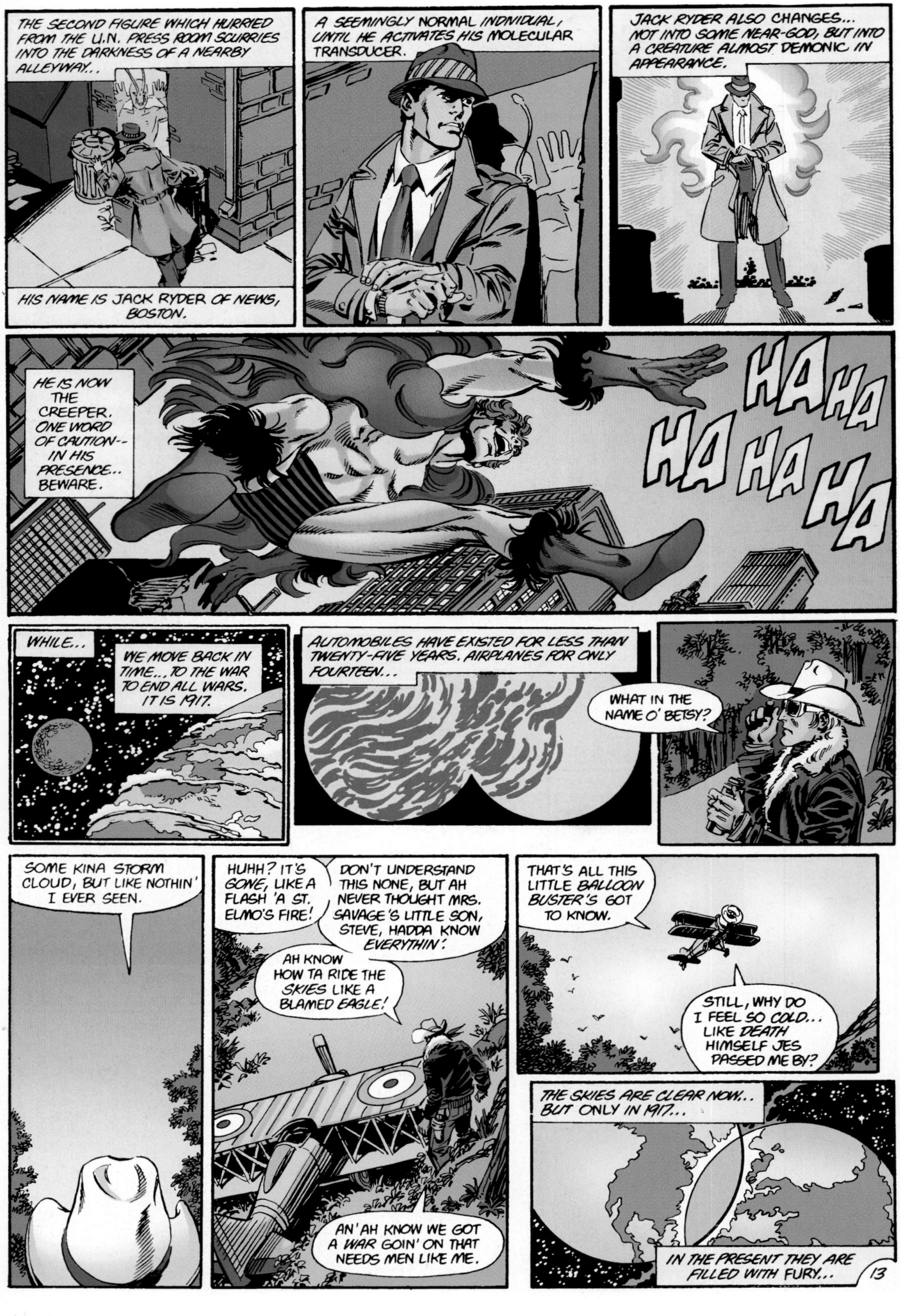
THE SECOND FIGURE WHICH HURRIED FROM THE U.N. PRESS ROOM SCURRIES INTO THE DARKNESS OF A NEARBY ALLEYWAY...
HIS NAME IS JACK RYDER OF NEWS, BOSTON.
A SEEMINGLY NORMAL INDIVIDUAL, UNTIL HE ACTIVATES HIS MOLECULAR TRANSDUCER.
JACK RYDER ALSO CHANGES... NOT INTO SOME NEAR-GOD, BUT INTO A CREATURE ALMOST DEMONIC IN APPEARANCE.
HE IS NOW THE CREEPER. ONE WORD OF CAUTION-- IN HIS PRESENCE... BEWARE.
HAHAHA HAHAHA HAHA
WHILE...
WE MOVE BACK IN TIME... TO THE WAR TO END ALL WARS. IT IS 1917.
AUTOMOBILES HAVE EXISTED FOR LESS THAN TWENTY-FIVE YEARS. AIRPLANES FOR ONLY FOURTEEN...
WHAT IN THE NAME O' BETSY?
SOME KINA STORM CLOUD, BUT LIKE NOTHIN' I EVER SEEN.
HUHH? IT'S GONE, LIKE A FLASH 'A ST. ELMO'S FIRE!
DON'T UNDERSTAND THIS NONE, BUT AH NEVER THOUGHT MRS. SAVAGE'S LITTLE SON, STEVE, HADDA KNOW EVERYTHIN'.
AH KNOW HOW TA RIDE THE SKIES LIKE A BLAMED EAGLE!
AN' AH KNOW WE GOT A WAR GOIN' ON THAT NEEDS MEN LIKE ME.
THAT'S ALL THIS LITTLE BALLOON BUSTER'S GOT TO KNOW.
STILL, WHY DO I FEEL SO COLD... LIKE DEATH HIMSELF JES PASSED ME BY?
THE SKIES ARE CLEAR NOW... BUT ONLY IN 1917...
IN THE PRESENT THEY ARE FILLED WITH FURY...
13

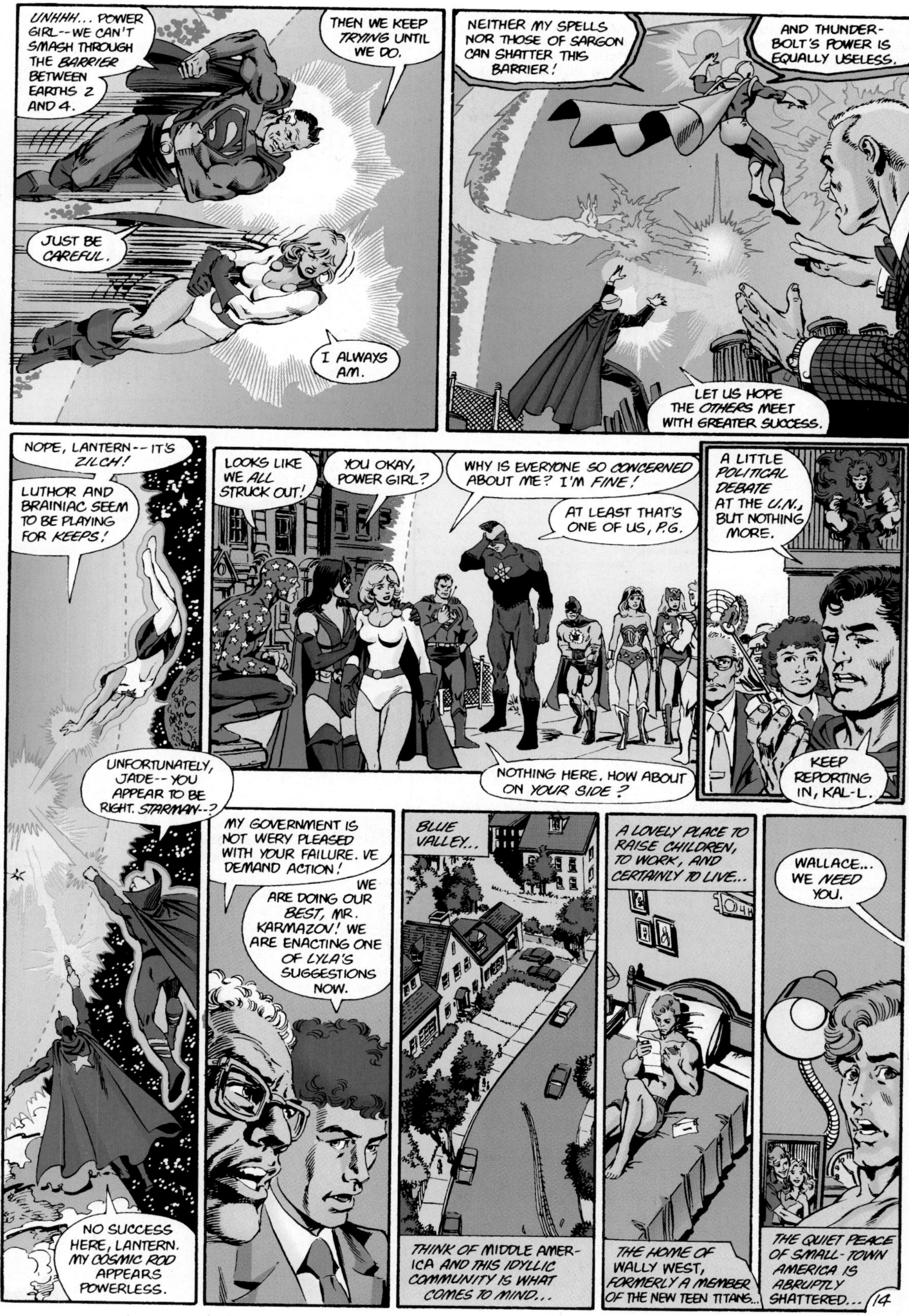
UNHHH... POWER GIRL--WE CAN'T SMASH THROUGH THE BARRIER BETWEEN EARTHS 2 AND 4.
THEN WE KEEP TRYING UNTIL WE DO.
JUST BE CAREFUL.
I ALWAYS AM.
NEITHER MY SPELLS NOR THOSE OF SARGON CAN SHATTER THIS BARRIER!
AND THUNDER-BOLT'S POWER IS EQUALLY USELESS.
LET US HOPE THE OTHERS MEET WITH GREATER SUCCESS.
NOPE, LANTERN--IT'S ZILCH!
LUTHOR AND BRAINIAC SEEM TO BE PLAYING FOR KEEPS!
UNFORTUNATELY, JADE--YOU APPEAR TO BE RIGHT. STARMAN--?
NO SUCCESS HERE, LANTERN. MY COSMIC ROD APPEARS POWERLESS.
LOOKS LIKE WE ALL STRUCK OUT!
YOU OKAY, POWER GIRL?
WHY IS EVERYONE SO CONCERNED ABOUT ME? I'M FINE!
AT LEAST THAT'S ONE OF US, P.G.
NOTHING HERE. HOW ABOUT ON YOUR SIDE?
A LITTLE POLITICAL DEBATE AT THE U.N., BUT NOTHING MORE.
KEEP REPORTING IN, KAL-L.
MY GOVERNMENT IS NOT WERY PLEASED WITH YOUR FAILURE. VE DEMAND ACTION!
WE ARE DOING OUR BEST, MR. KARMAZOV! WE ARE ENACTING ONE OF LYLA'S SUGGESTIONS NOW.
BLUE VALLEY...
THINK OF MIDDLE AMERICA AND THIS IDYLLIC COMMUNITY IS WHAT COMES TO MIND...
A LOVELY PLACE TO RAISE CHILDREN, TO WORK, AND CERTAINLY TO LIVE...
THE HOME OF WALLY WEST, FORMERLY A MEMBER OF THE NEW TEEN TITANS...
WALLACE... WE NEED YOU.
THE QUIET PEACE OF SMALL-TOWN AMERICA IS ABRUPTLY SHATTERED...
14

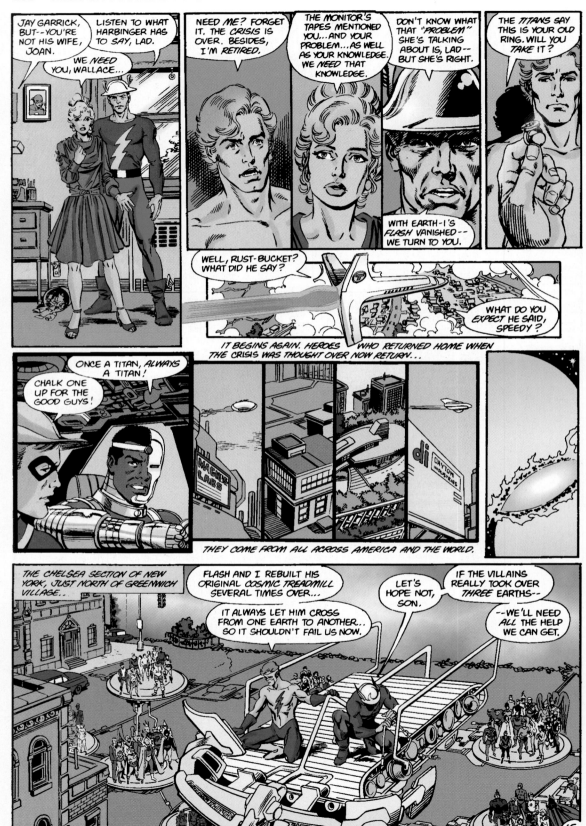

JAY GARRICK, BUT--YOU'RE NOT HIS WIFE, JOAN.

LISTEN TO WHAT HARBINGER HAS TO SAY, LAD.

WE *NEED* YOU, WALLACE...

NEED *ME?* FORGET IT. THE *CRISIS* IS OVER. BESIDES, I'M *RETIRED.*

THE MONITOR'S TAPES MENTIONED YOU...AND YOUR PROBLEM...AS WELL AS YOUR KNOWLEDGE. WE *NEED* THAT KNOWLEDGE.

DON'T KNOW WHAT THAT "*PROBLEM*" SHE'S TALKING ABOUT IS, LAD-- BUT SHE'S RIGHT.

WITH EARTH-1'S *FLASH* VANISHED-- WE TURN TO YOU.

THE *TITANS* SAY THIS IS YOUR OLD RING. WILL YOU *TAKE* IT?

WELL, RUST-BUCKET? WHAT DID HE SAY?

WHAT DO YOU EXPECT HE SAID, SPEEDY?

IT BEGINS AGAIN. HEROES WHO RETURNED HOME WHEN THE CRISIS WAS THOUGHT OVER NOW RETURN...

ONCE A TITAN, *ALWAYS* A TITAN!

CHALK ONE UP FOR THE GOOD GUYS!

MAGNIS LABS

DAYTON INDUSTRIES

THEY COME FROM ALL ACROSS AMERICA AND THE WORLD.

THE CHELSEA SECTION OF NEW YORK, JUST NORTH OF GREENWICH VILLAGE...

FLASH AND I REBUILT HIS ORIGINAL *COSMIC TREADMILL* SEVERAL TIMES OVER...

IT ALWAYS LET HIM CROSS FROM ONE EARTH TO ANOTHER... SO IT SHOULDN'T FAIL US NOW.

LET'S HOPE NOT, SON.

IF THE VILLAINS REALLY TOOK OVER *THREE EARTHS*--

--WE'LL NEED *ALL* THE HELP WE CAN GET.

15

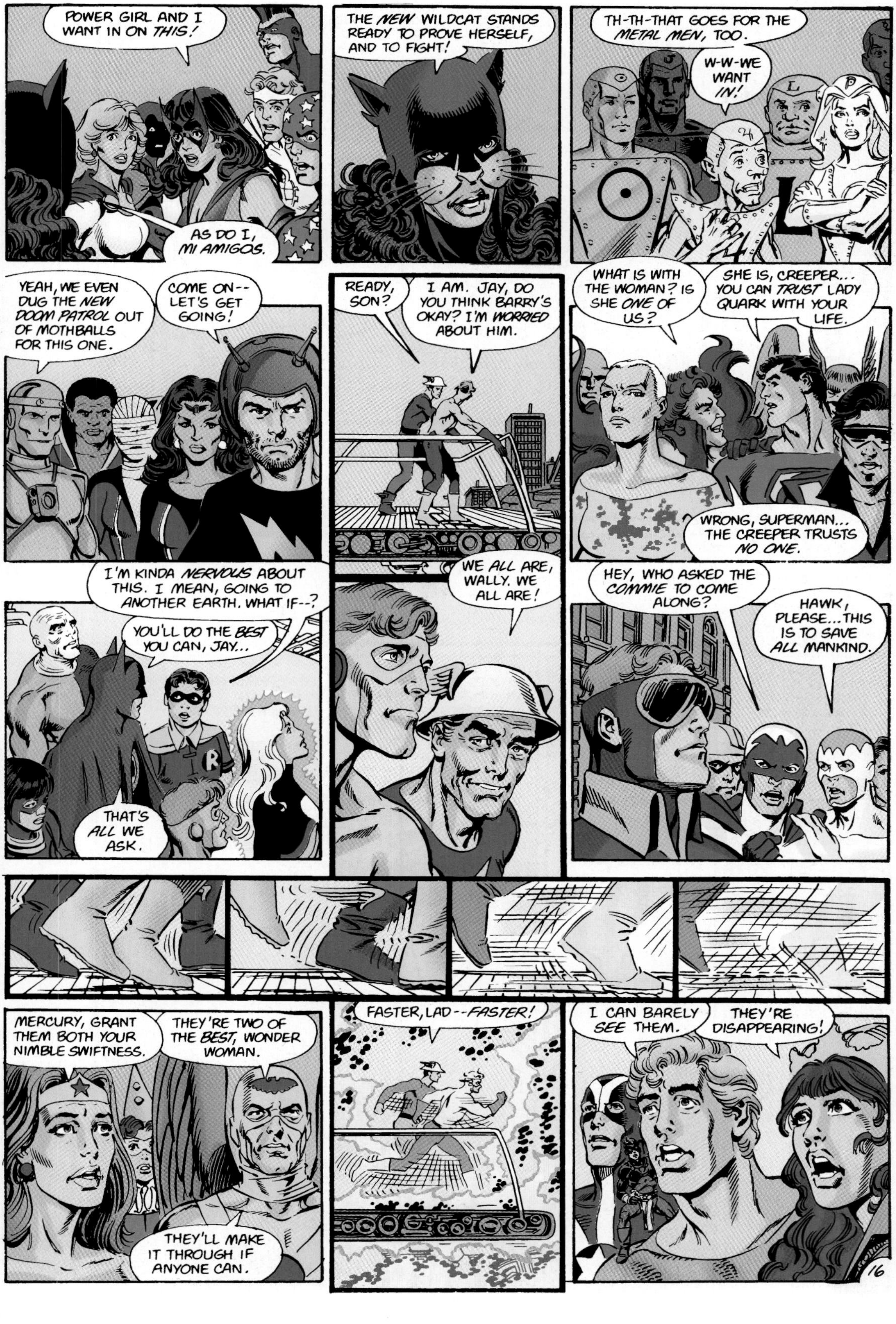
POWER GIRL AND I WANT IN ON THIS!
AS DO I, MI AMIGOS.
THE NEW WILDCAT STANDS READY TO PROVE HERSELF, AND TO FIGHT!
TH-TH-THAT GOES FOR THE METAL MEN, TOO.
W-W-WE WANT IN!
YEAH, WE EVEN DUG THE NEW DOOM PATROL OUT OF MOTHBALLS FOR THIS ONE.
COME ON-- LET'S GET GOING!
READY, SON?
I AM. JAY, DO YOU THINK BARRY'S OKAY? I'M WORRIED ABOUT HIM.
WHAT IS WITH THE WOMAN? IS SHE ONE OF US?
SHE IS, CREEPER... YOU CAN TRUST LADY QUARK WITH YOUR LIFE.
WRONG, SUPERMAN... THE CREEPER TRUSTS NO ONE.
I'M KINDA NERVOUS ABOUT THIS. I MEAN, GOING TO ANOTHER EARTH. WHAT IF--?
YOU'LL DO THE BEST YOU CAN, JAY...
THAT'S ALL WE ASK.
WE ALL ARE, WALLY. WE ALL ARE!
HEY, WHO ASKED THE COMMIE TO COME ALONG?
HAWK, PLEASE... THIS IS TO SAVE ALL MANKIND.
MERCURY, GRANT THEM BOTH YOUR NIMBLE SWIFTNESS.
THEY'RE TWO OF THE BEST, WONDER WOMAN.
THEY'LL MAKE IT THROUGH IF ANYONE CAN.
FASTER, LAD--FASTER!
I CAN BARELY SEE THEM.
THEY'RE DISAPPEARING!
16

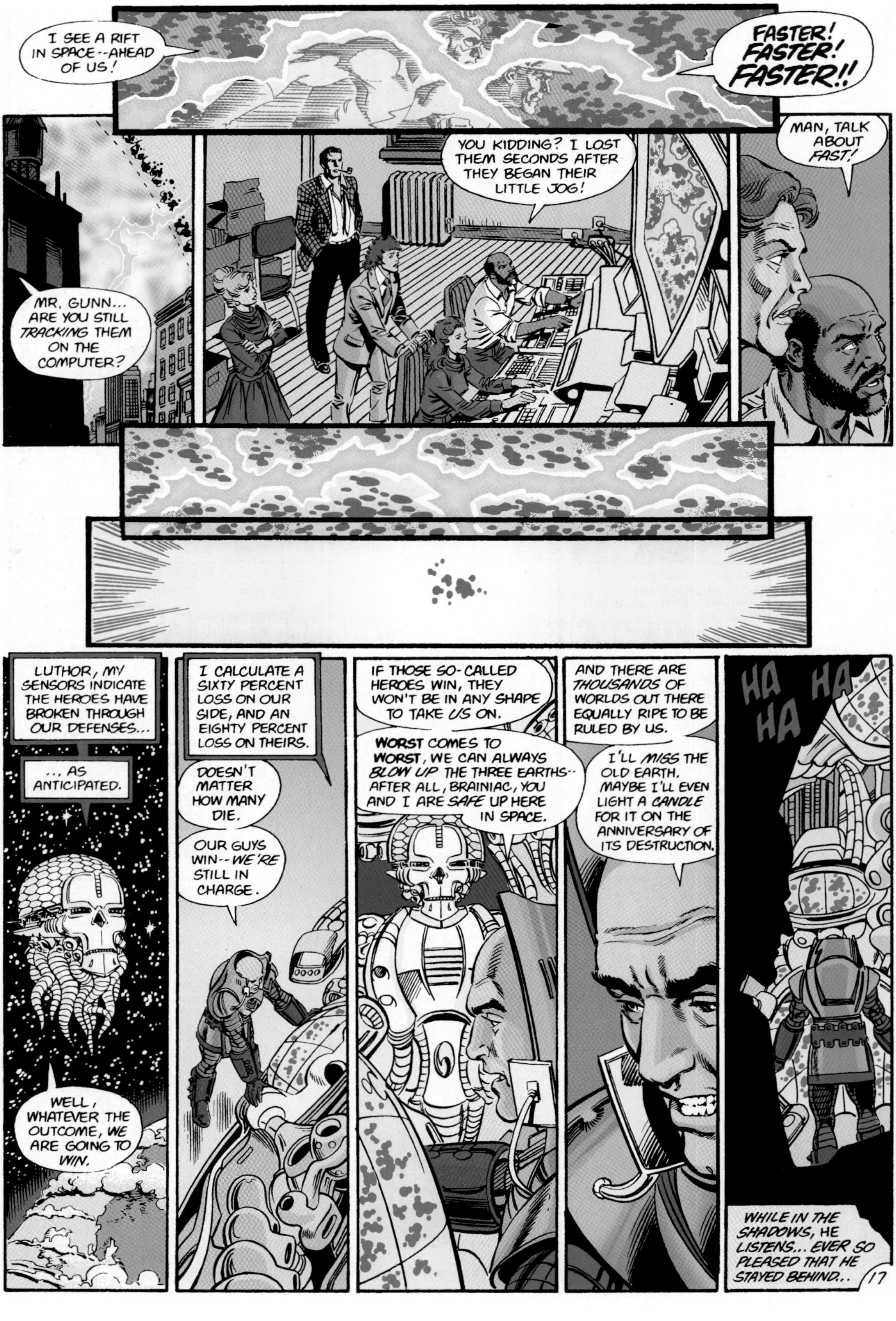

I SEE A RIFT IN SPACE--AHEAD OF US!
FASTER! FASTER! FASTER!!
MR. GUNN... ARE YOU STILL TRACKING THEM ON THE COMPUTER?
YOU KIDDING? I LOST THEM SECONDS AFTER THEY BEGAN THEIR LITTLE JOG!
MAN, TALK ABOUT FAST!
LUTHOR, MY SENSORS INDICATE THE HEROES HAVE BROKEN THROUGH OUR DEFENSES...
..., AS ANTICIPATED.
WELL, WHATEVER THE OUTCOME, WE ARE GOING TO WIN.
I CALCULATE A SIXTY PERCENT LOSS ON OUR SIDE, AND AN EIGHTY PERCENT LOSS ON THEIRS.
DOESN'T MATTER HOW MANY DIE.
OUR GUYS WIN--WE'RE STILL IN CHARGE.
IF THOSE SO-CALLED HEROES WIN, THEY WON'T BE IN ANY SHAPE TO TAKE US ON.
WORST COMES TO WORST, WE CAN ALWAYS BLOW UP THE THREE EARTHS--AFTER ALL, BRAINIAC, YOU AND I ARE SAFE UP HERE IN SPACE.
AND THERE ARE THOUSANDS OF WORLDS OUT THERE EQUALLY RIPE TO BE RULED BY US.
I'LL MISS THE OLD EARTH. MAYBE I'LL EVEN LIGHT A CANDLE FOR IT ON THE ANNIVERSARY OF ITS DESTRUCTION.
HA HA HA HA
WHILE IN THE SHADOWS, HE LISTENS... EVER SO PLEASED THAT HE STAYED BEHIND..
17

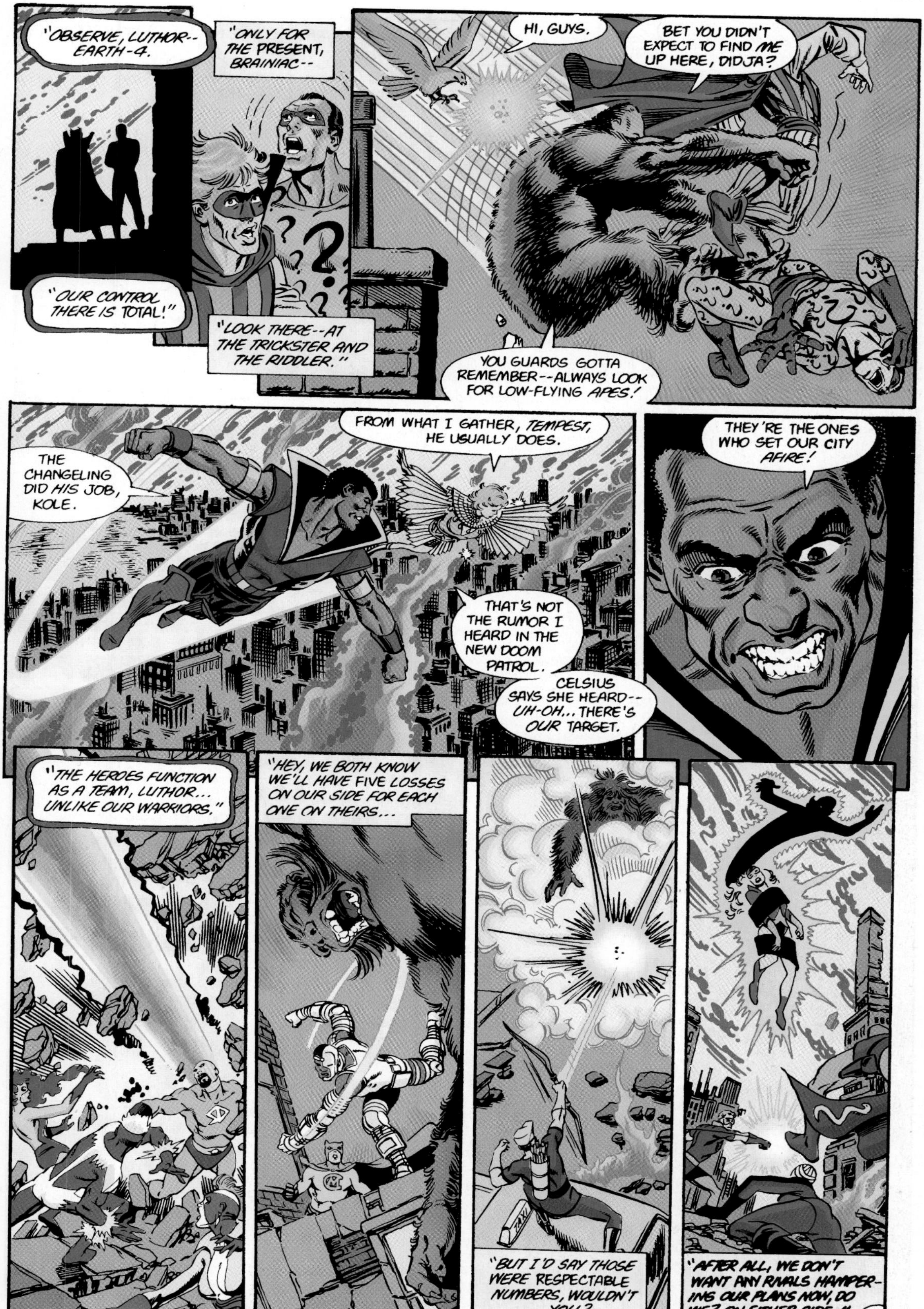
"OBSERVE, LUTHOR-- EARTH-4.
"OUR CONTROL THERE IS TOTAL!"
"ONLY FOR THE PRESENT, BRAINIAC--
"LOOK THERE--AT THE TRICKSTER AND THE RIDDLER."
HI, GUYS.
BET YOU DIDN'T EXPECT TO FIND ME UP HERE, DIDJA?
YOU GUARDS GOTTA REMEMBER--ALWAYS LOOK FOR LOW-FLYING APES!
THE CHANGELING DID HIS JOB, KOLE.
FROM WHAT I GATHER, TEMPEST, HE USUALLY DOES.
THAT'S NOT THE RUMOR I HEARD IN THE NEW DOOM PATROL.
CELSIUS SAYS SHE HEARD-- UH-OH... THERE'S OUR TARGET.
THEY'RE THE ONES WHO SET OUR CITY AFIRE!
"THE HEROES FUNCTION AS A TEAM, LUTHOR... UNLIKE OUR WARRIORS."
"HEY, WE BOTH KNOW WE'LL HAVE FIVE LOSSES ON OUR SIDE FOR EACH ONE ON THEIRS...
"BUT I'D SAY THOSE WERE RESPECTABLE NUMBERS, WOULDN'T YOU?
"AFTER ALL, WE DON'T WANT ANY RIVALS HAMPERING OUR PLANS NOW, DO WE? ON EITHER SIDE."
18

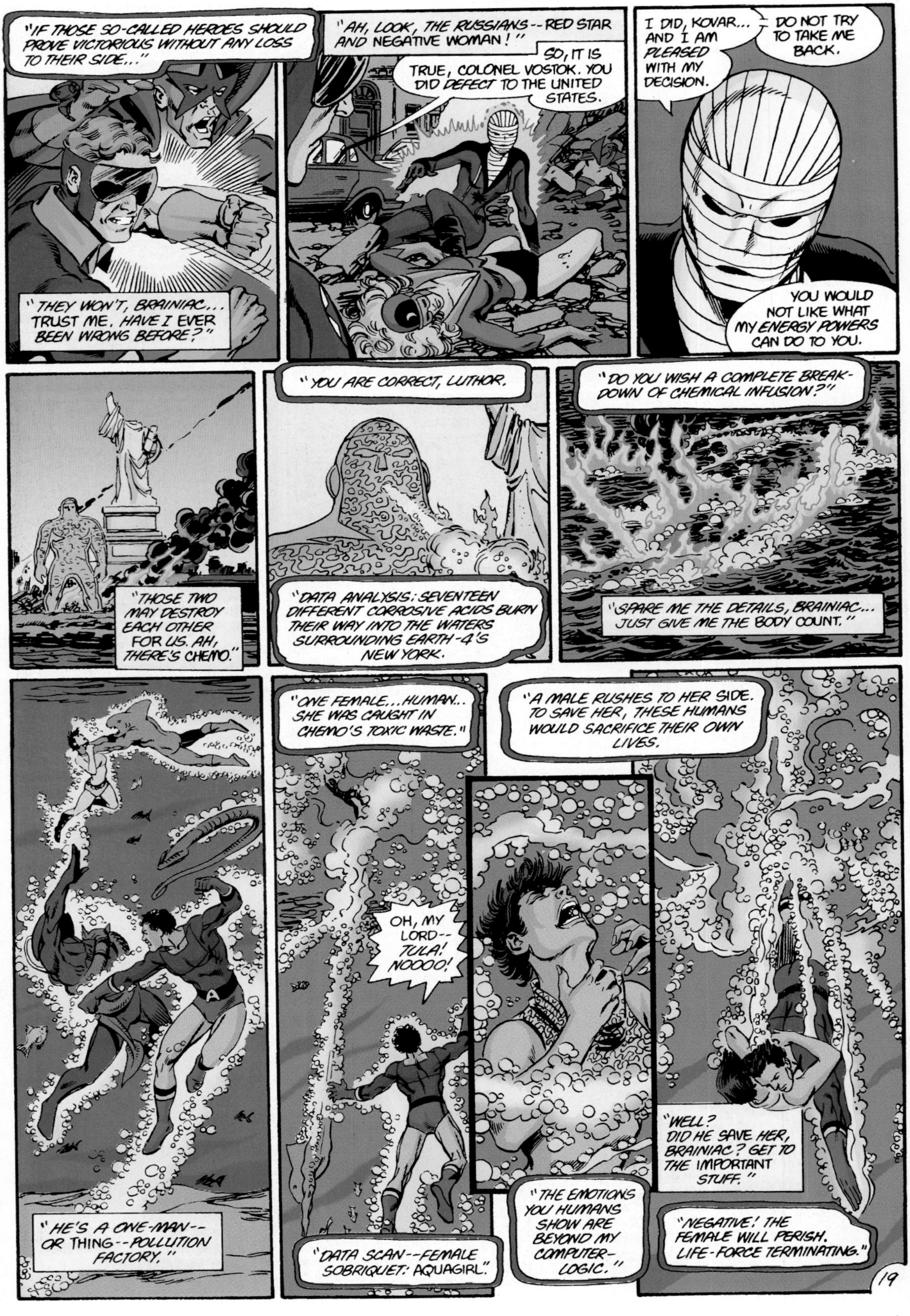
"IF THOSE SO-CALLED HEROES SHOULD PROVE VICTORIOUS WITHOUT ANY LOSS TO THEIR SIDE..."
"THEY WON'T, BRAINIAC... TRUST ME. HAVE I EVER BEEN WRONG BEFORE?"
"AH, LOOK, THE RUSSIANS--RED STAR AND NEGATIVE WOMAN!"
SO, IT IS TRUE, COLONEL VOSTOK. YOU DID DEFECT TO THE UNITED STATES.
I DID, KOVAR... AND I AM PLEASED WITH MY DECISION.
DO NOT TRY TO TAKE ME BACK.
YOU WOULD NOT LIKE WHAT MY ENERGY POWERS CAN DO TO YOU.
"THOSE TWO MAY DESTROY EACH OTHER FOR US. AH, THERE'S CHEMO."
"YOU ARE CORRECT, LUTHOR.
DATA ANALYSIS: SEVENTEEN DIFFERENT CORROSIVE ACIDS BURN THEIR WAY INTO THE WATERS SURROUNDING EARTH-4'S NEW YORK.
"DO YOU WISH A COMPLETE BREAK-DOWN OF CHEMICAL INFUSION?"
"SPARE ME THE DETAILS, BRAINIAC... JUST GIVE ME THE BODY COUNT."
"HE'S A ONE-MAN--OR THING--POLLUTION FACTORY."
"ONE FEMALE... HUMAN... SHE WAS CAUGHT IN CHEMO'S TOXIC WASTE."
OH, MY LORD-- TULA! NOOOO!
"DATA SCAN--FEMALE SOBRIQUET: AQUAGIRL."
"A MALE RUSHES TO HER SIDE. TO SAVE HER, THESE HUMANS WOULD SACRIFICE THEIR OWN LIVES.
"THE EMOTIONS YOU HUMANS SHOW ARE BEYOND MY COMPUTER-LOGIC."
"WELL? DID HE SAVE HER, BRAINIAC? GET TO THE IMPORTANT STUFF."
"NEGATIVE! THE FEMALE WILL PERISH. LIFE-FORCE TERMINATING."
19

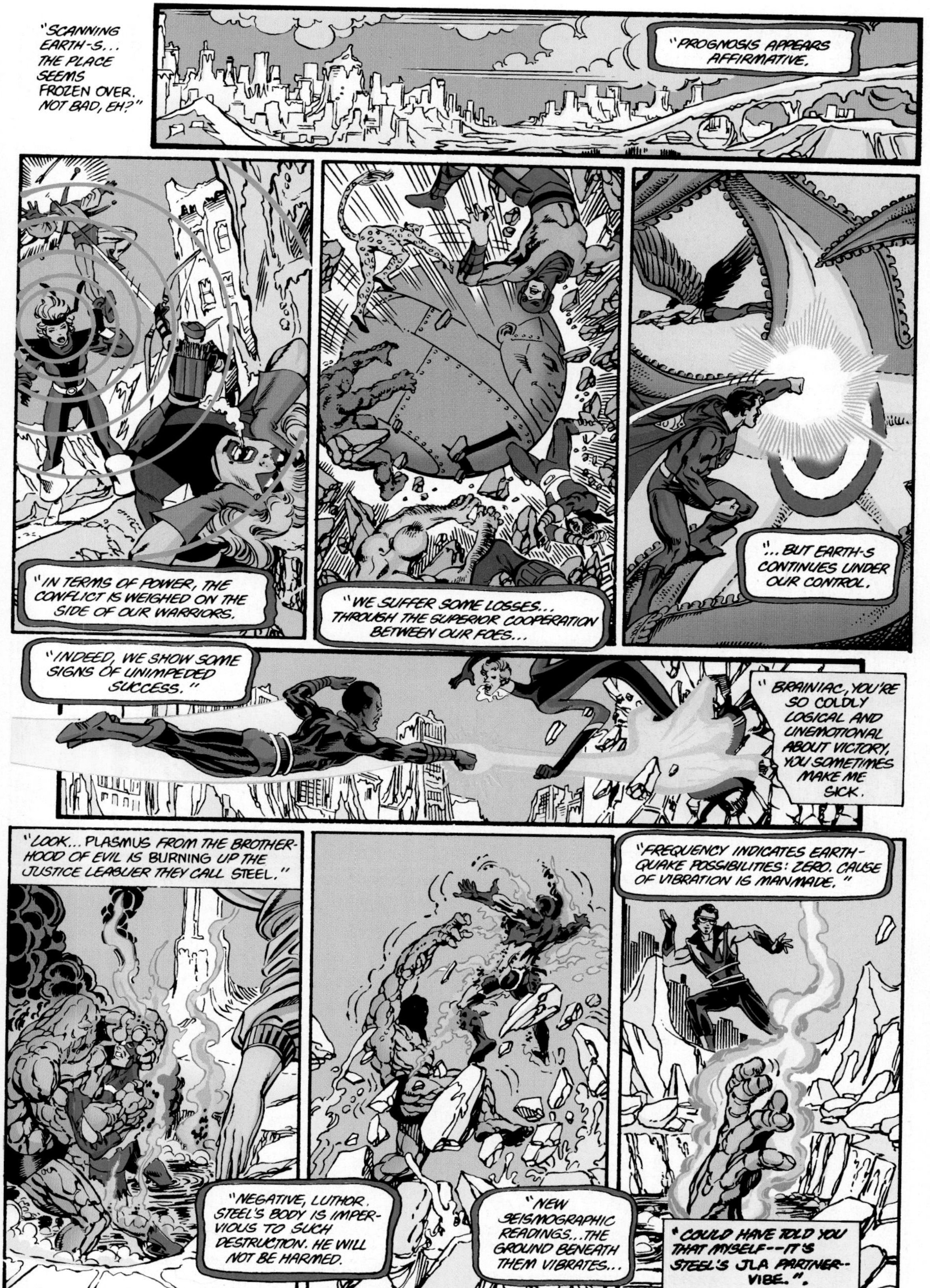
"SCANNING EARTH-S... THE PLACE SEEMS FROZEN OVER. NOT BAD, EH?"
"PROGNOSIS APPEARS AFFIRMATIVE.
"IN TERMS OF POWER, THE CONFLICT IS WEIGHED ON THE SIDE OF OUR WARRIORS.
"WE SUFFER SOME LOSSES... THROUGH THE SUPERIOR COOPERATION BETWEEN OUR FOES...
"...BUT EARTH-S CONTINUES UNDER OUR CONTROL.
"INDEED, WE SHOW SOME SIGNS OF UNIMPEDED SUCCESS."
"BRAINIAC, YOU'RE SO COLDLY LOGICAL AND UNEMOTIONAL ABOUT VICTORY, YOU SOMETIMES MAKE ME SICK.
"LOOK... PLASMUS FROM THE BROTHERHOOD OF EVIL IS BURNING UP THE JUSTICE LEAGUER THEY CALL STEEL."
"NEGATIVE, LUTHOR. STEEL'S BODY IS IMPERVIOUS TO SUCH DESTRUCTION. HE WILL NOT BE HARMED.
"NEW SEISMOGRAPHIC READINGS...THE GROUND BENEATH THEM VIBRATES...
"FREQUENCY INDICATES EARTHQUAKE POSSIBILITIES: ZERO. CAUSE OF VIBRATION IS MANMADE."
"COULD HAVE TOLD YOU THAT MYSELF--IT'S STEEL'S JLA PARTNER-VIBE.".
20

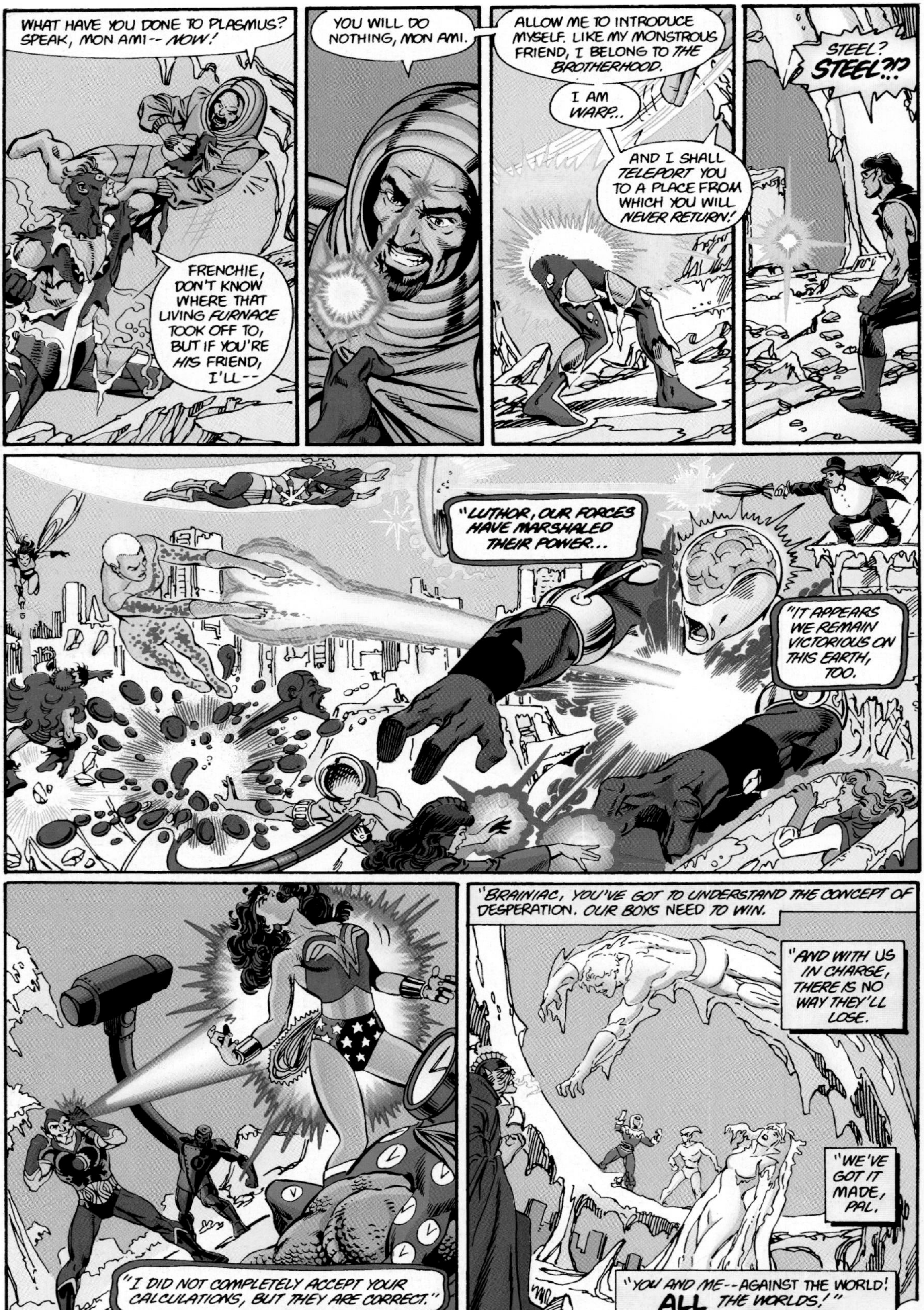
WHAT HAVE YOU DONE TO PLASMUS? SPEAK, MON AMI-- NOW!
FRENCHIE, DON'T KNOW WHERE THAT LIVING FURNACE TOOK OFF TO, BUT IF YOU'RE HIS FRIEND, I'LL--
YOU WILL DO NOTHING, MON AMI.
ALLOW ME TO INTRODUCE MYSELF. LIKE MY MONSTROUS FRIEND, I BELONG TO THE BROTHERHOOD.
I AM WARP...
AND I SHALL TELEPORT YOU TO A PLACE FROM WHICH YOU WILL NEVER RETURN!
STEEL? STEEL?!?
"LUTHOR, OUR FORCES HAVE MARSHALED THEIR POWER...
"IT APPEARS WE REMAIN VICTORIOUS ON THIS EARTH, TOO.
"I DID NOT COMPLETELY ACCEPT YOUR CALCULATIONS, BUT THEY ARE CORRECT."
"BRAINIAC, YOU'VE GOT TO UNDERSTAND THE CONCEPT OF DESPERATION. OUR BOYS NEED TO WIN.
"AND WITH US IN CHARGE, THERE IS NO WAY THEY'LL LOSE.
"WE'VE GOT IT MADE, PAL.
"YOU AND ME--AGAINST THE WORLD! ALL THE WORLDS!"
21

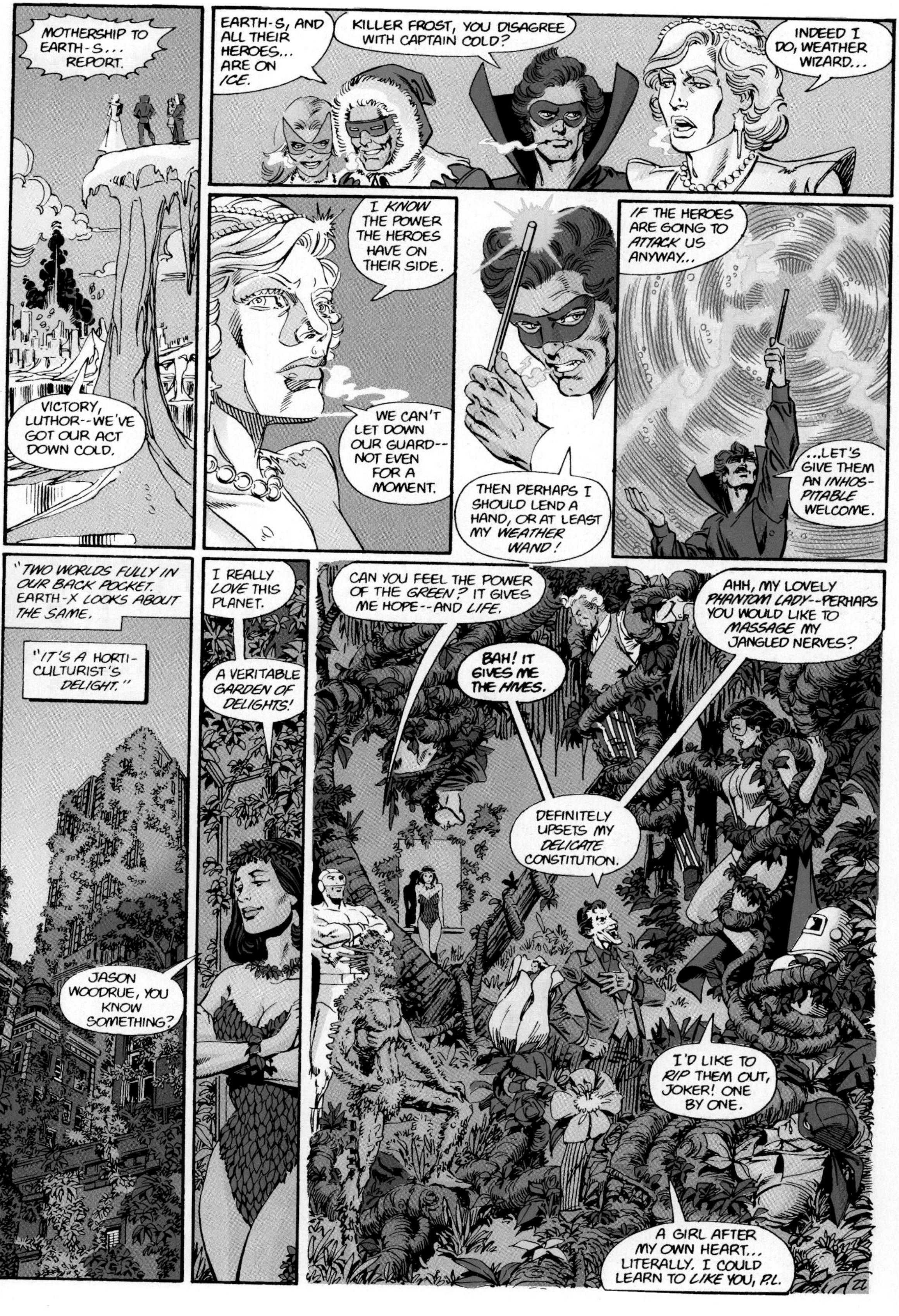
MOTHERSHIP TO EARTH-S... REPORT.
VICTORY, LUTHOR--WE'VE GOT OUR ACT DOWN COLD.
EARTH-S, AND ALL THEIR HEROES... ARE ON ICE.
KILLER FROST, YOU DISAGREE WITH CAPTAIN COLD?
INDEED I DO, WEATHER WIZARD...
I KNOW THE POWER THE HEROES HAVE ON THEIR SIDE.
WE CAN'T LET DOWN OUR GUARD--NOT EVEN FOR A MOMENT.
THEN PERHAPS I SHOULD LEND A HAND, OR AT LEAST MY WEATHER WAND!
IF THE HEROES ARE GOING TO ATTACK US ANYWAY...
...LET'S GIVE THEM AN INHOSPITABLE WELCOME.
"TWO WORLDS FULLY IN OUR BACK POCKET. EARTH-X LOOKS ABOUT THE SAME.
"IT'S A HORTICULTURIST'S DELIGHT."
I REALLY LOVE THIS PLANET.
A VERITABLE GARDEN OF DELIGHTS!
JASON WOODRUE, YOU KNOW SOMETHING?
CAN YOU FEEL THE POWER OF THE GREEN? IT GIVES ME HOPE--AND LIFE.
BAH! IT GIVES ME THE HIVES.
DEFINITELY UPSETS MY DELICATE CONSTITUTION.
AHH, MY LOVELY PHANTOM LADY--PERHAPS YOU WOULD LIKE TO MASSAGE MY JANGLED NERVES?
I'D LIKE TO RIP THEM OUT, JOKER! ONE BY ONE.
A GIRL AFTER MY OWN HEART... LITERALLY. I COULD LEARN TO LIKE YOU, P.L.
22

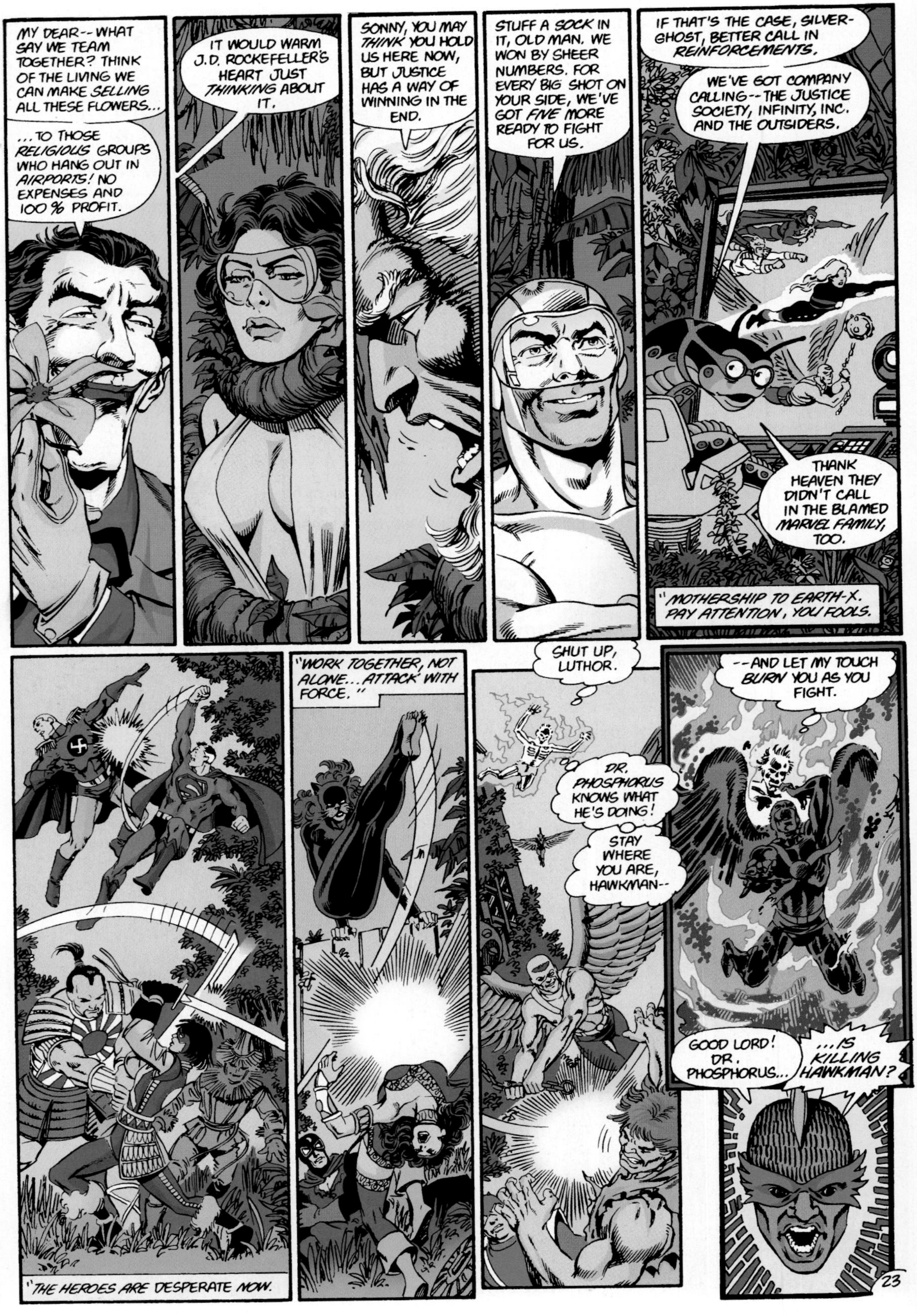
MY DEAR-- WHAT SAY WE TEAM TOGETHER? THINK OF THE LIVING WE CAN MAKE SELLING ALL THESE FLOWERS...
...TO THOSE RELIGIOUS GROUPS WHO HANG OUT IN AIRPORTS! NO EXPENSES AND 100% PROFIT.
IT WOULD WARM J.D. ROCKEFELLER'S HEART JUST THINKING ABOUT IT.
SONNY, YOU MAY THINK YOU HOLD US HERE NOW, BUT JUSTICE HAS A WAY OF WINNING IN THE END.
STUFF A SOCK IN IT, OLD MAN. WE WON BY SHEER NUMBERS. FOR EVERY BIG SHOT ON YOUR SIDE, WE'VE GOT FIVE MORE READY TO FIGHT FOR US.
IF THAT'S THE CASE, SILVER-GHOST, BETTER CALL IN REINFORCEMENTS.
WE'VE GOT COMPANY CALLING-- THE JUSTICE SOCIETY, INFINITY, INC. AND THE OUTSIDERS.
THANK HEAVEN THEY DIDN'T CALL IN THE BLAMED MARVEL FAMILY, TOO.
"MOTHERSHIP TO EARTH-X. PAY ATTENTION, YOU FOOLS.
"THE HEROES ARE DESPERATE NOW.
"WORK TOGETHER, NOT ALONE... ATTACK WITH FORCE."
SHUT UP, LUTHOR.
DR. PHOSPHORUS KNOWS WHAT HE'S DOING!
STAY WHERE YOU ARE, HAWKMAN--
--AND LET MY TOUCH BURN YOU AS YOU FIGHT.
GOOD LORD! DR. PHOSPHORUS...
...IS KILLING HAWKMAN?
23

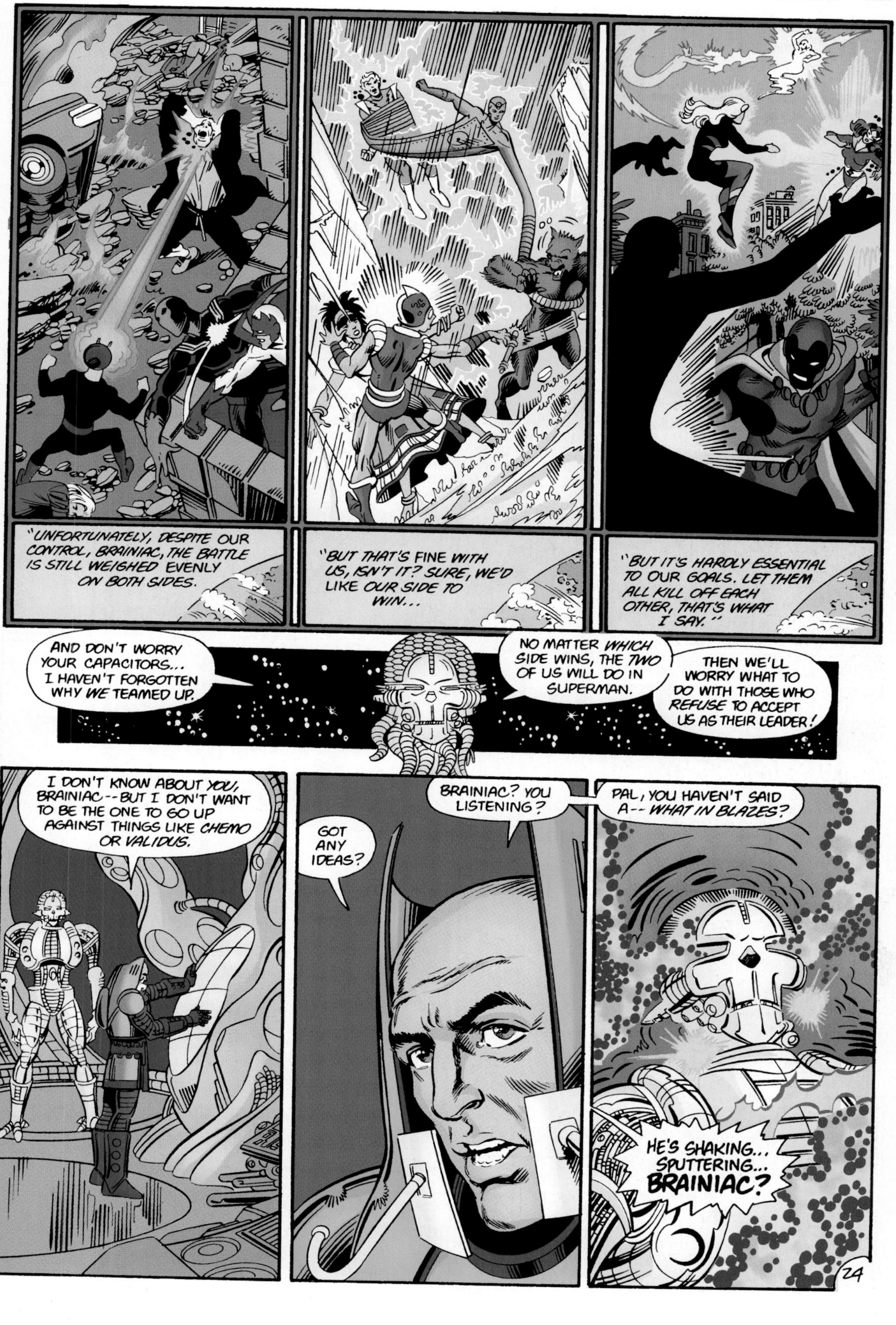
"UNFORTUNATELY, DESPITE OUR CONTROL, BRAINIAC, THE BATTLE IS STILL WEIGHED EVENLY ON BOTH SIDES.
"BUT THAT'S FINE WITH US, ISN'T IT? SURE, WE'D LIKE OUR SIDE TO WIN...
"BUT IT'S HARDLY ESSENTIAL TO OUR GOALS. LET THEM ALL KILL OFF EACH OTHER, THAT'S WHAT I SAY."
AND DON'T WORRY YOUR CAPACITORS... I HAVEN'T FORGOTTEN WHY WE TEAMED UP.
NO MATTER WHICH SIDE WINS, THE TWO OF US WILL DO IN SUPERMAN.
THEN WE'LL WORRY WHAT TO DO WITH THOSE WHO REFUSE TO ACCEPT US AS THEIR LEADER!
I DON'T KNOW ABOUT YOU, BRAINIAC--BUT I DON'T WANT TO BE THE ONE TO GO UP AGAINST THINGS LIKE CHEMO OR VALIDUS.
GOT ANY IDEAS?
BRAINIAC? YOU LISTENING?
PAL, YOU HAVEN'T SAID A-- WHAT IN BLAZES?
HE'S SHAKING... SPUTTERING... BRAINIAC?
24

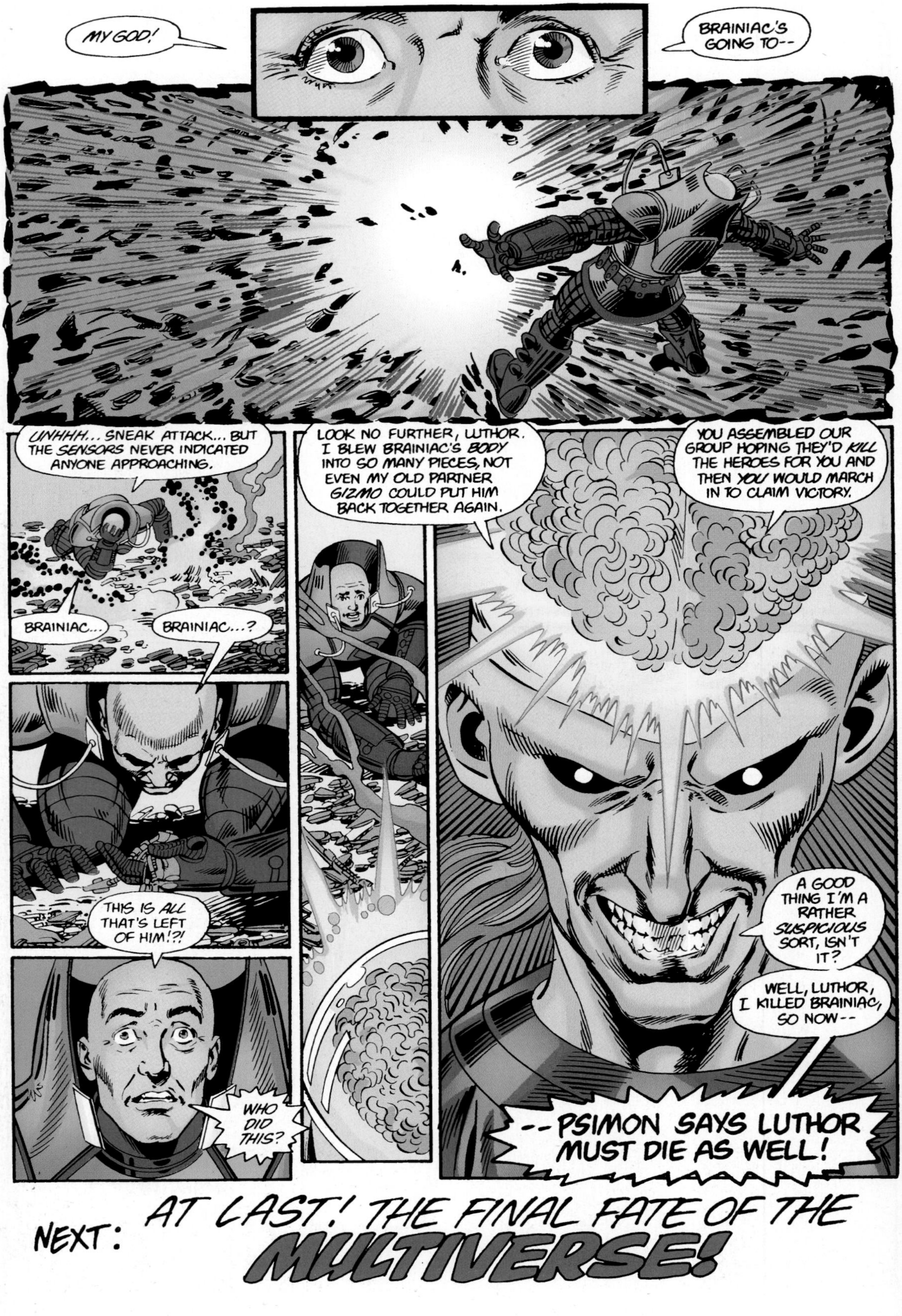
MY GOD!
BRAINIAC'S GOING TO--
UNHHH... SNEAK ATTACK... BUT THE SENSORS NEVER INDICATED ANYONE APPROACHING.
BRAINIAC...
BRAINIAC...?
THIS IS ALL THAT'S LEFT OF HIM!?!
WHO DID THIS?
LOOK NO FURTHER, LUTHOR. I BLEW BRAINIAC'S BODY INTO SO MANY PIECES, NOT EVEN MY OLD PARTNER GIZMO COULD PUT HIM BACK TOGETHER AGAIN.
YOU ASSEMBLED OUR GROUP HOPING THEY'D KILL THE HEROES FOR YOU AND THEN YOU WOULD MARCH IN TO CLAIM VICTORY.
A GOOD THING I'M A RATHER SUSPICIOUS SORT, ISN'T IT?
WELL, LUTHOR, I KILLED BRAINIAC, SO NOW--
--PSIMON SAYS LUTHOR MUST DIE AS WELL!
NEXT: AT LAST! THE FINAL FATE OF THE MULTIVERSE!

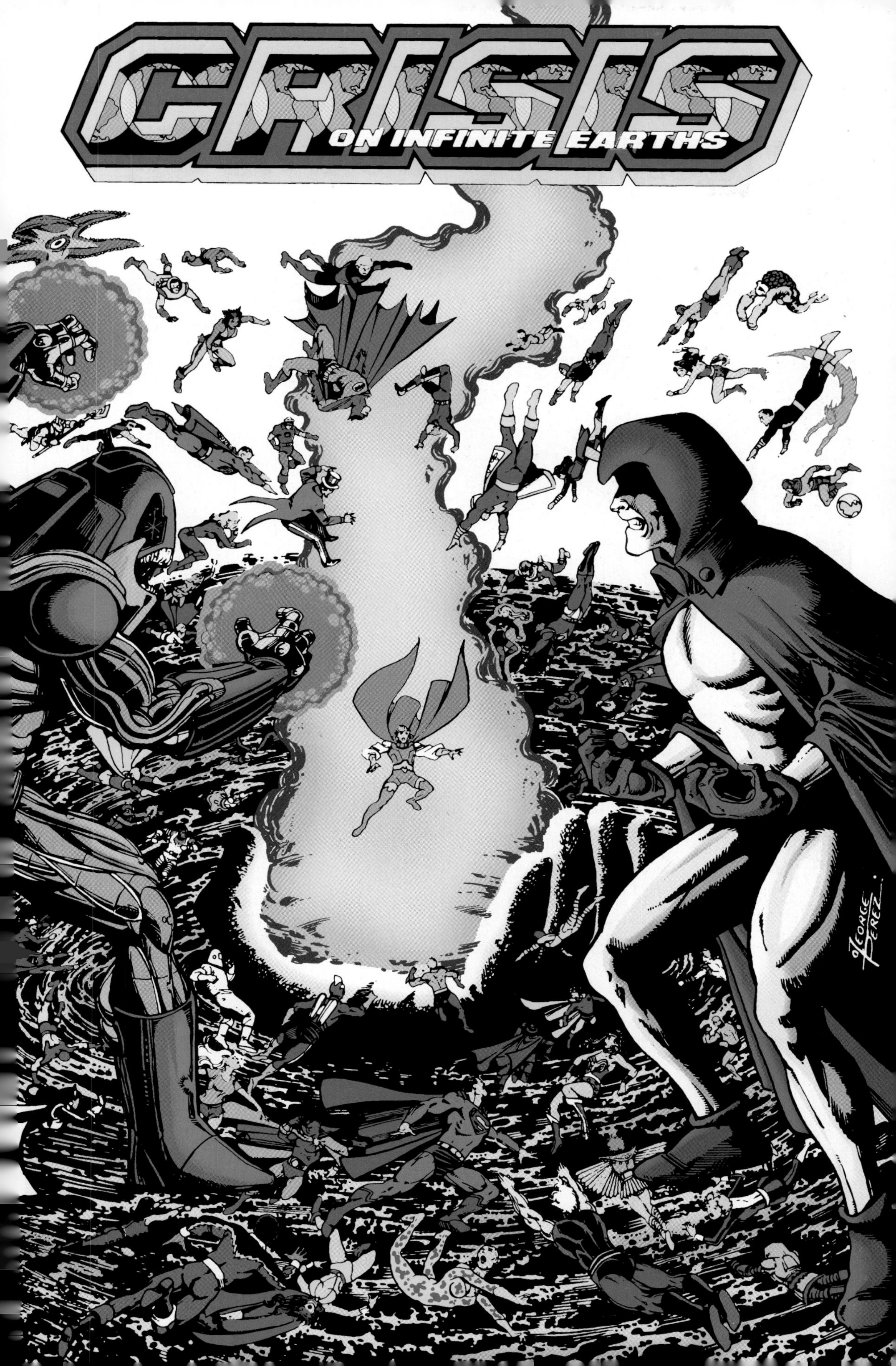
CRISIS
ON INFINITE EARTHS
George Perez

CRISIS ON INFINITE EARTHS

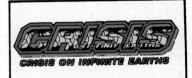

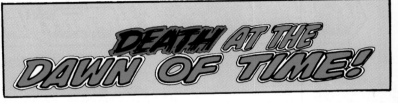

DEATH AT THE DAWN OF TIME!

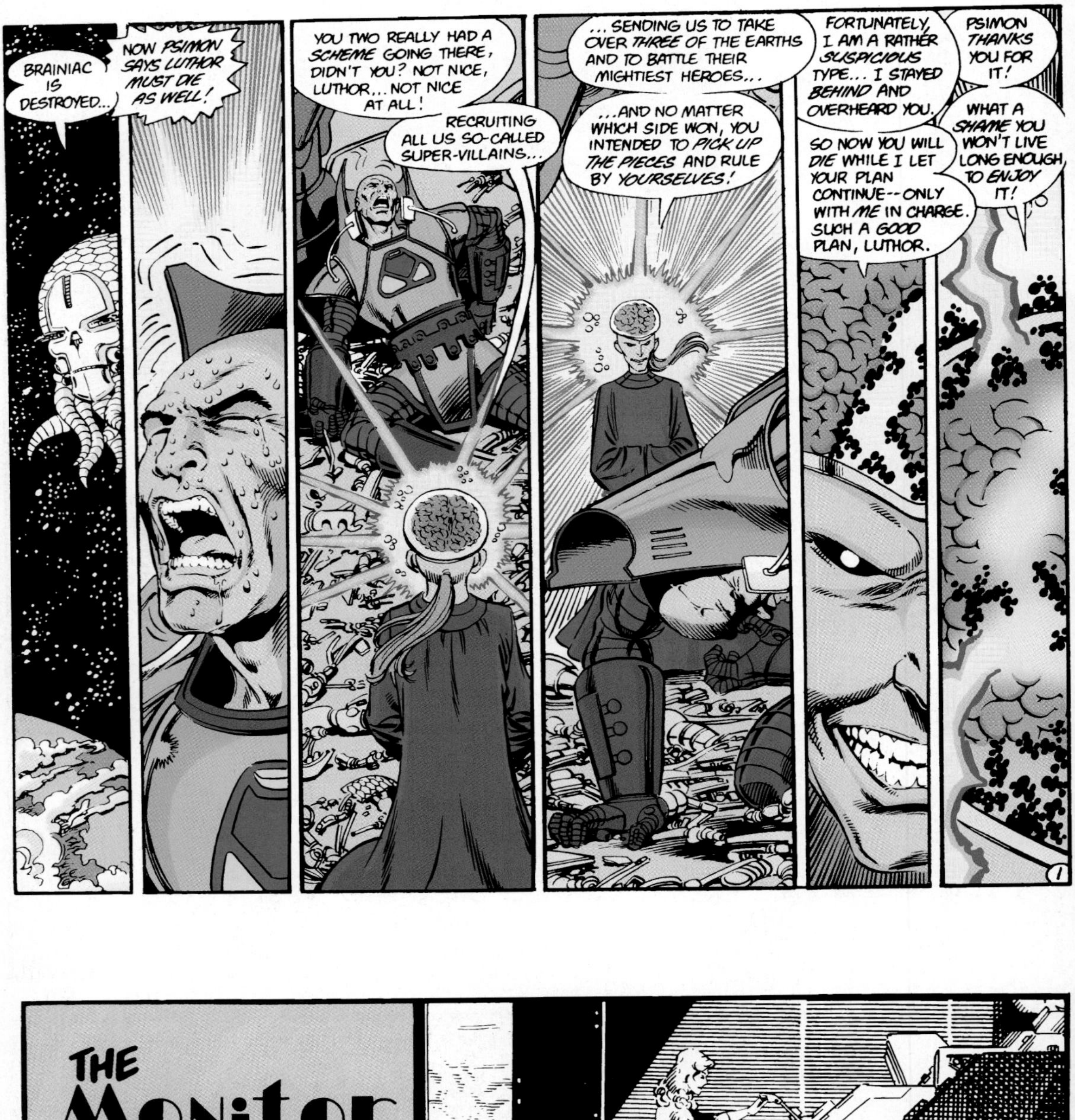
BRAINIAC IS DESTROYED...
NOW PSIMON SAYS LUTHOR MUST DIE AS WELL!
YOU TWO REALLY HAD A SCHEME GOING THERE, DIDN'T YOU? NOT NICE, LUTHOR... NOT NICE AT ALL!
RECRUITING ALL US SO-CALLED SUPER-VILLAINS...
... SENDING US TO TAKE OVER THREE OF THE EARTHS AND TO BATTLE THEIR MIGHTIEST HEROES...
...AND NO MATTER WHICH SIDE WON, YOU INTENDED TO PICK UP THE PIECES AND RULE BY YOURSELVES!
FORTUNATELY, I AM A RATHER SUSPICIOUS TYPE... I STAYED BEHIND AND OVERHEARD YOU.
SO NOW YOU WILL DIE WHILE I LET YOUR PLAN CONTINUE--ONLY WITH ME IN CHARGE. SUCH A GOOD PLAN, LUTHOR.
PSIMON THANKS YOU FOR IT!
WHAT A SHAME YOU WON'T LIVE LONG ENOUGH TO ENJOY IT!
1

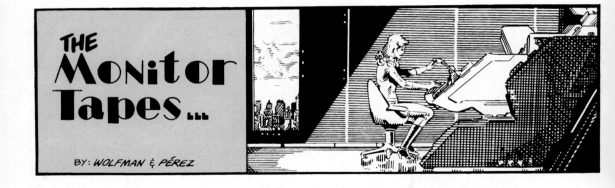

THE Monitor Tapes...

BY: WOLFMAN & PÉREZ

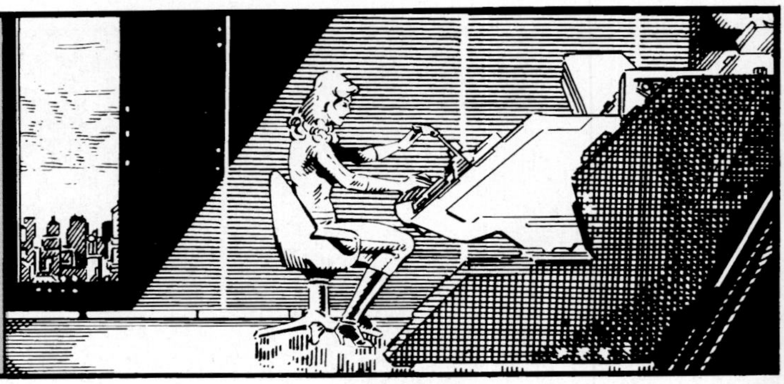

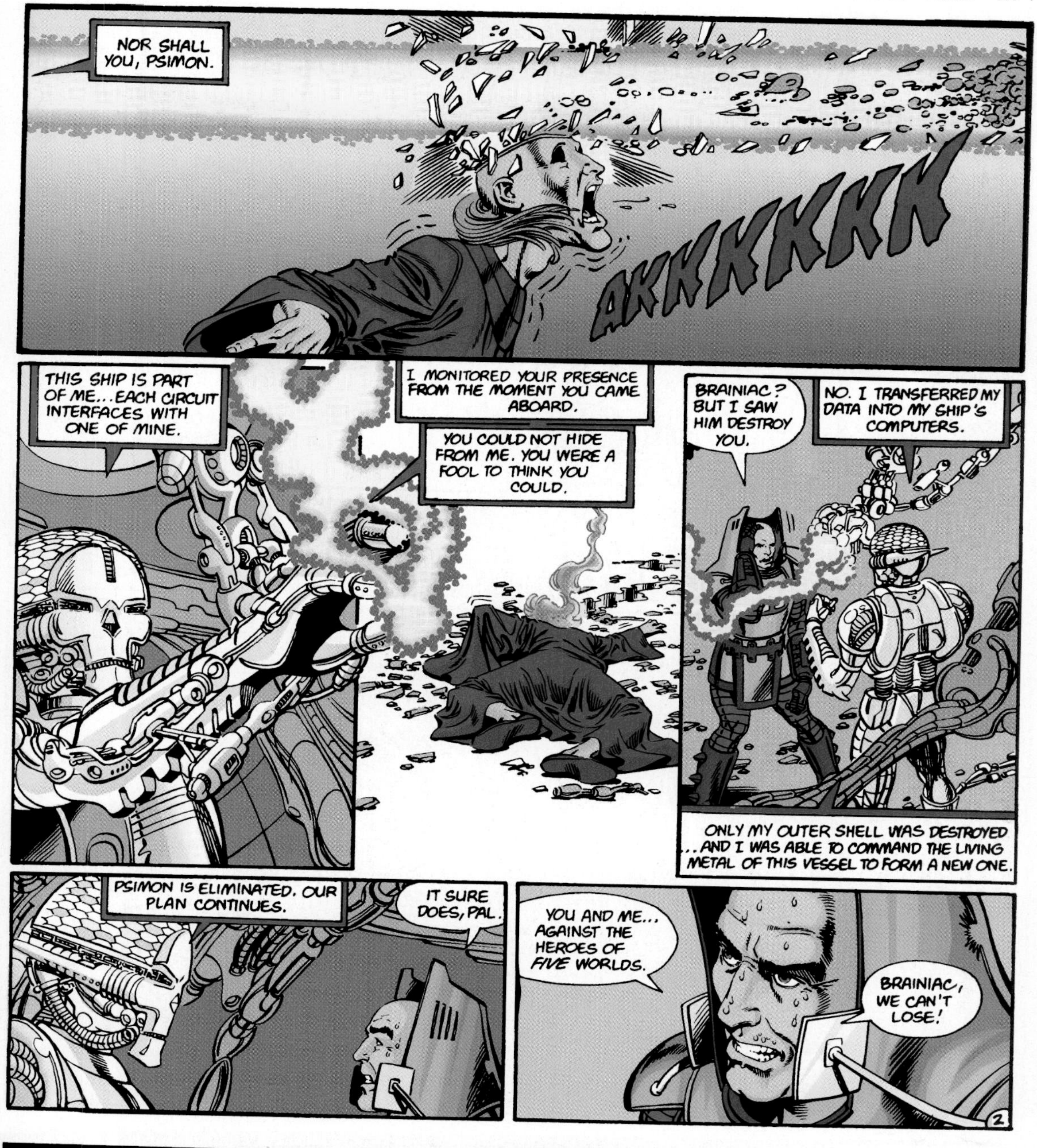
NOR SHALL YOU, PSIMON.
AKKKKKKK
THIS SHIP IS PART OF ME... EACH CIRCUIT INTERFACES WITH ONE OF MINE.
I MONITORED YOUR PRESENCE FROM THE MOMENT YOU CAME ABOARD.
YOU COULD NOT HIDE FROM ME. YOU WERE A FOOL TO THINK YOU COULD.
BRAINIAC? BUT I SAW HIM DESTROY YOU.
NO. I TRANSFERRED MY DATA INTO MY SHIP'S COMPUTERS.
ONLY MY OUTER SHELL WAS DESTROYED ...AND I WAS ABLE TO COMMAND THE LIVING METAL OF THIS VESSEL TO FORM A NEW ONE.
PSIMON IS ELIMINATED. OUR PLAN CONTINUES.
IT SURE DOES, PAL.
YOU AND ME... AGAINST THE HEROES OF FIVE WORLDS.
BRAINIAC, WE CAN'T LOSE!
2

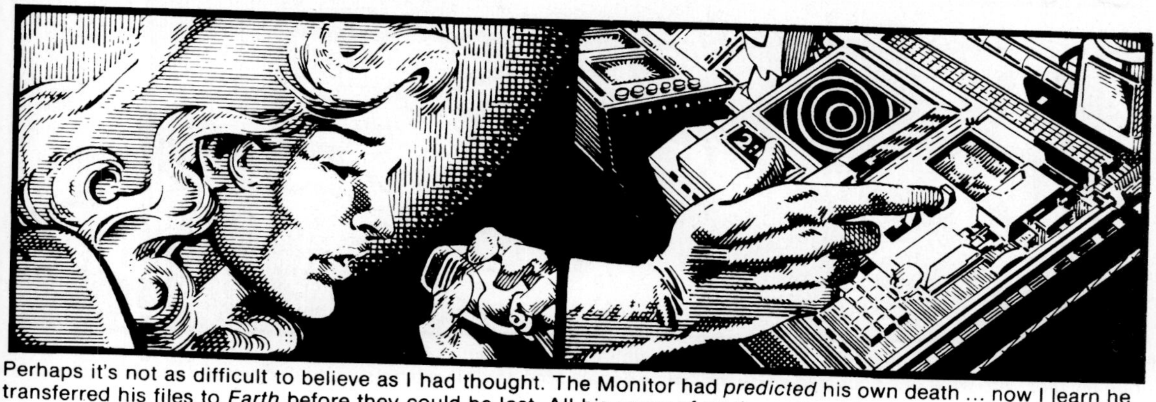

Perhaps it's not as difficult to believe as I had thought. The Monitor had *predicted* his own death ... now I learn he transferred his files to *Earth* before they could be lost. All his years of work must not be in vain.

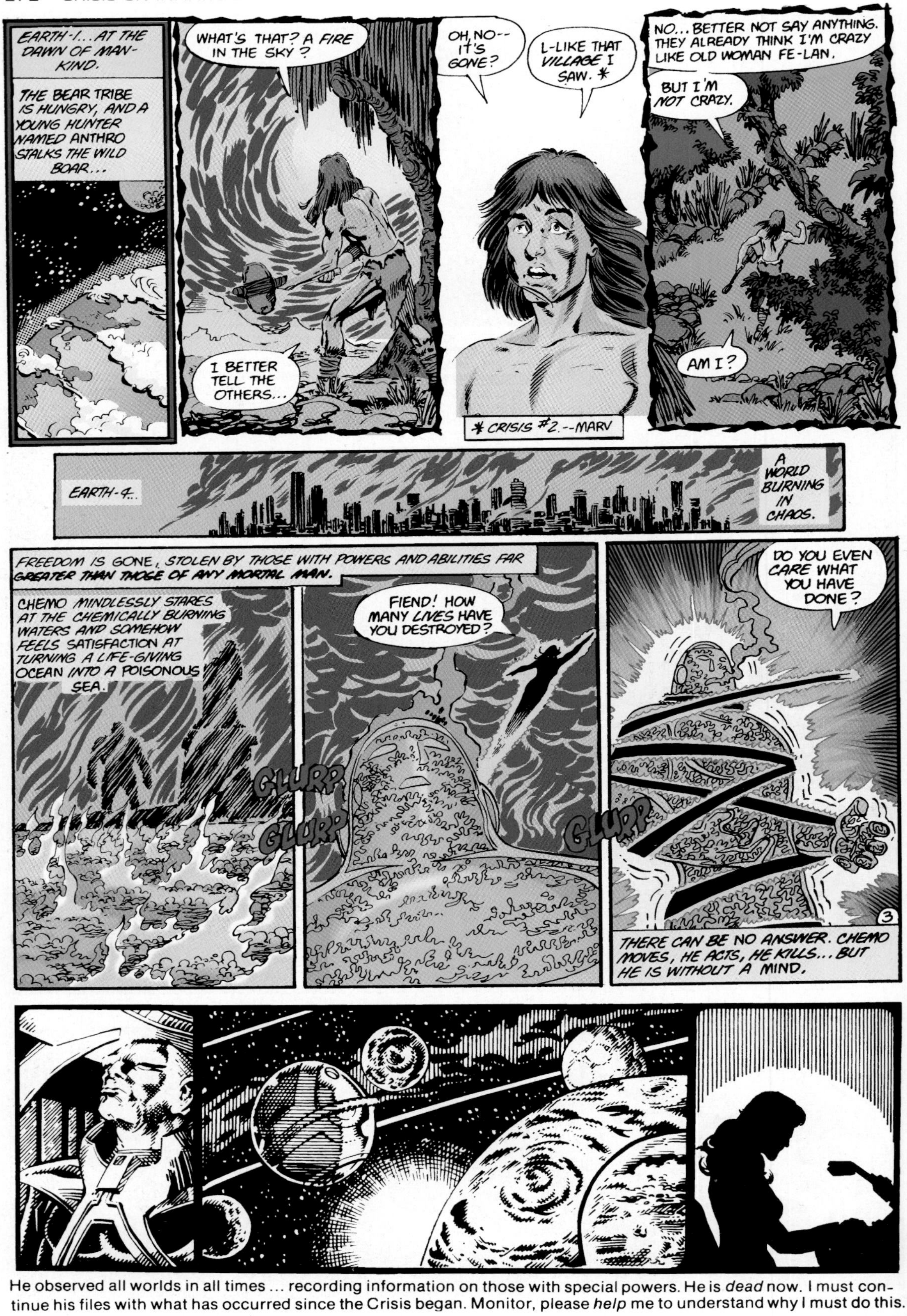
EARTH-1... AT THE DAWN OF MAN-KIND.
THE BEAR TRIBE IS HUNGRY, AND A YOUNG HUNTER NAMED ANTHRO STALKS THE WILD BOAR...
WHAT'S THAT? A FIRE IN THE SKY?
I BETTER TELL THE OTHERS...
OH, NO-- IT'S GONE?
L-LIKE THAT VILLAGE I SAW. *
* CRISIS #2.--MARV
NO... BETTER NOT SAY ANYTHING. THEY ALREADY THINK I'M CRAZY LIKE OLD WOMAN FE-LAN.
BUT I'M NOT CRAZY.
AM I?
EARTH-4...
A WORLD BURNING IN CHAOS.
FREEDOM IS GONE, STOLEN BY THOSE WITH POWERS AND ABILITIES FAR GREATER THAN THOSE OF ANY MORTAL MAN.
CHEMO MINDLESSLY STARES AT THE CHEMICALLY BURNING WATERS AND SOMEHOW FEELS SATISFACTION AT TURNING A LIFE-GIVING OCEAN INTO A POISONOUS SEA.
GLURP GLURP
FIEND! HOW MANY LIVES HAVE YOU DESTROYED?
GLURP
DO YOU EVEN CARE WHAT YOU HAVE DONE?
3
THERE CAN BE NO ANSWER. CHEMO MOVES, HE ACTS, HE KILLS... BUT HE IS WITHOUT A MIND.

He observed all worlds in all times ... recording information on those with special powers. He is *dead* now. I must continue his files with what has occurred since the Crisis began. Monitor, please *help* me to understand why I must do this.

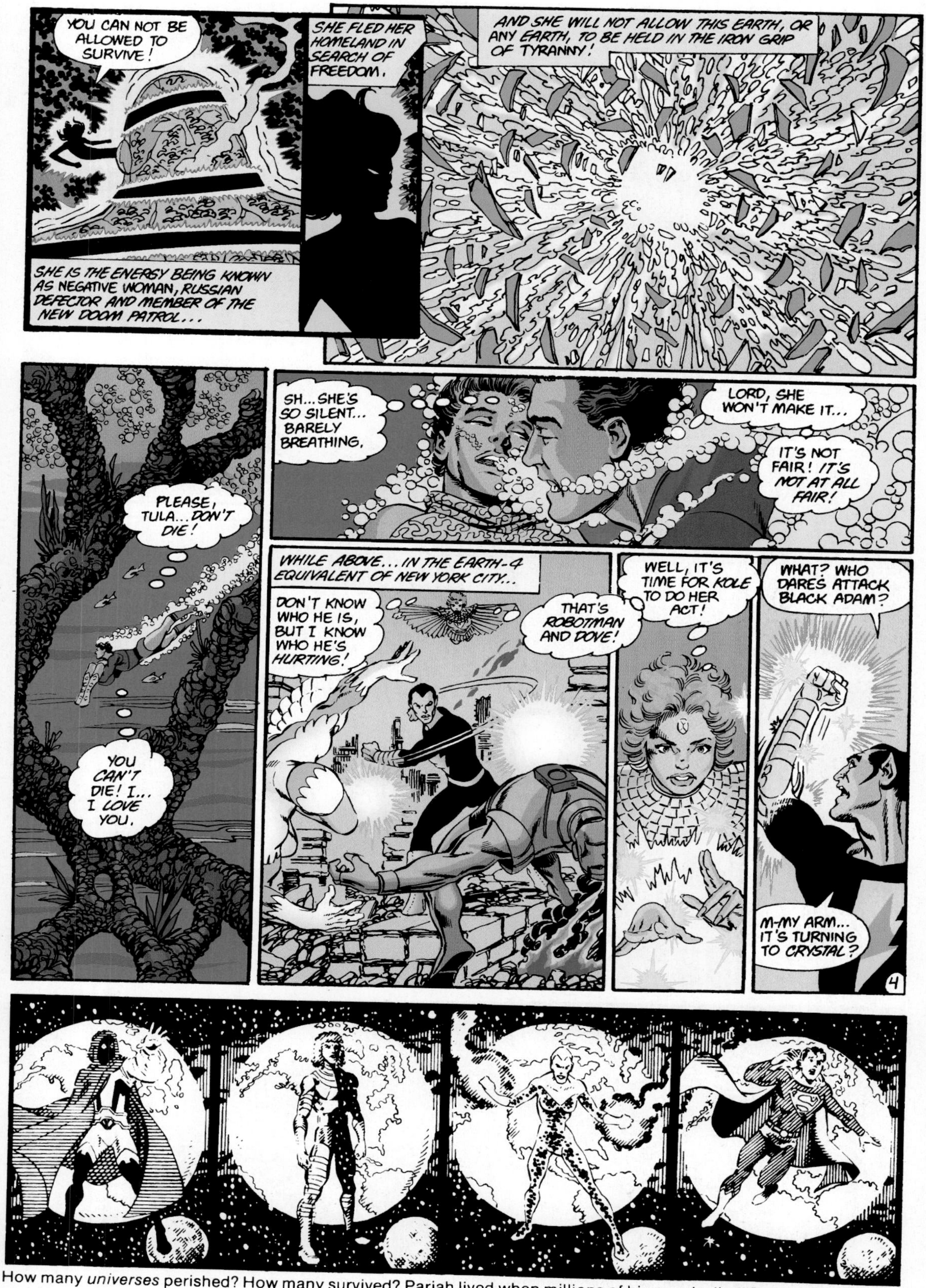
YOU CAN NOT BE ALLOWED TO SURVIVE!
SHE IS THE ENERGY BEING KNOWN AS NEGATIVE WOMAN, RUSSIAN DEFECTOR AND MEMBER OF THE NEW DOOM PATROL...
SHE FLED HER HOMELAND IN SEARCH OF FREEDOM.
AND SHE WILL NOT ALLOW THIS EARTH, OR ANY EARTH, TO BE HELD IN THE IRON GRIP OF TYRANNY!
PLEASE, TULA... DON'T DIE!
YOU CAN'T DIE! I... I LOVE YOU.
SH...SHE'S SO SILENT... BARELY BREATHING.
LORD, SHE WON'T MAKE IT...
IT'S NOT FAIR! IT'S NOT AT ALL FAIR!
WHILE ABOVE... IN THE EARTH-4 EQUIVALENT OF NEW YORK CITY...
DON'T KNOW WHO HE IS, BUT I KNOW WHO HE'S HURTING!
THAT'S ROBOTMAN AND DOVE!
WELL, IT'S TIME FOR KOLE TO DO HER ACT!
WHAT? WHO DARES ATTACK BLACK ADAM?
M-MY ARM... IT'S TURNING TO CRYSTAL?
4

How many *universes* perished? How many survived? Pariah lived when millions of his people died. So did Lady Quark and Alexander Luthor ... and the *boy* ... from Earth-Prime as they called it ... he survived ... where has *he* gone?

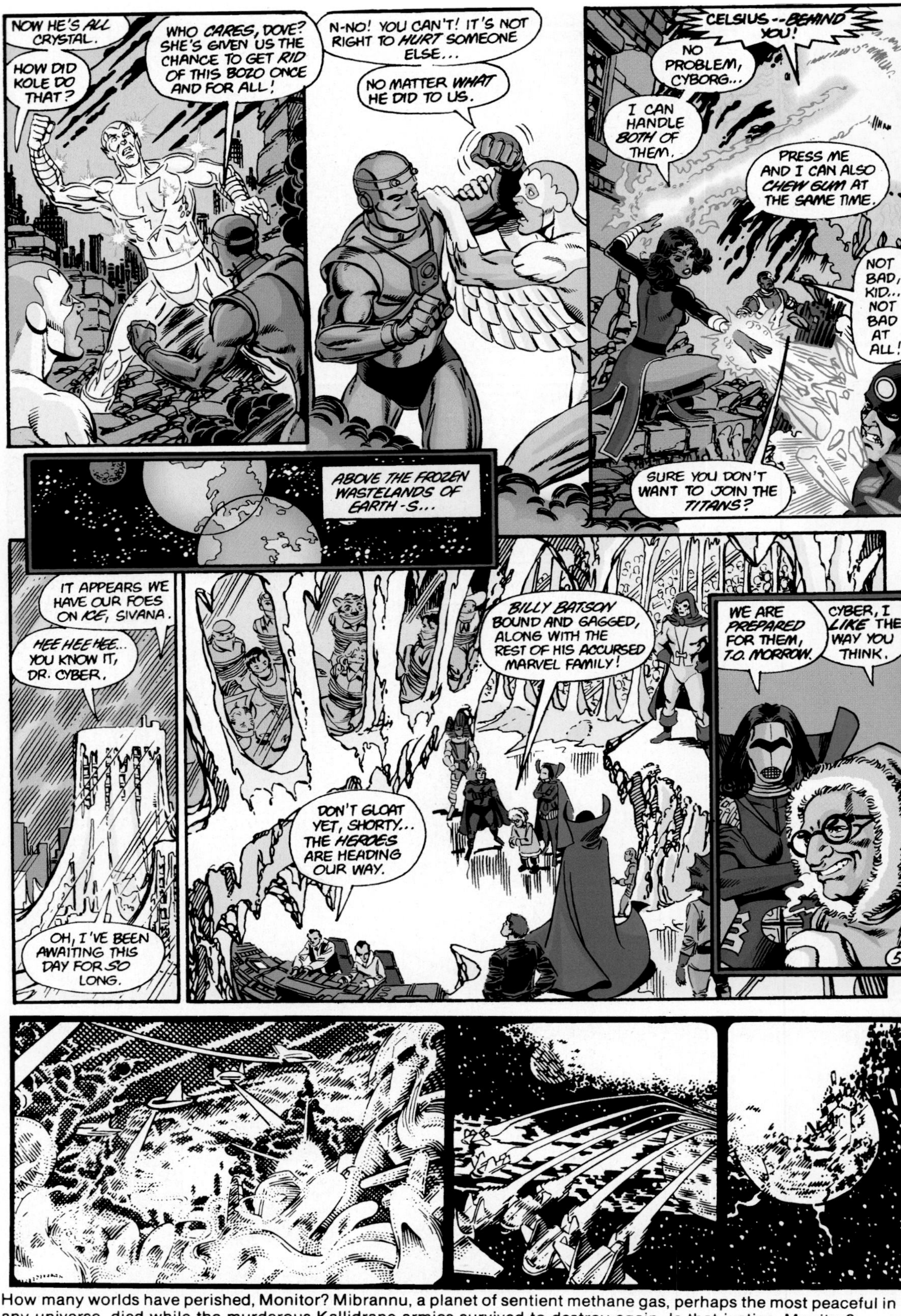
NOW HE'S ALL CRYSTAL.
HOW DID KOLE DO THAT?
WHO CARES, DOVE? SHE'S GIVEN US THE CHANCE TO GET RID OF THIS BOZO ONCE AND FOR ALL!
N-NO! YOU CAN'T! IT'S NOT RIGHT TO HURT SOMEONE ELSE...
NO MATTER WHAT HE DID TO US.
CELSIUS--BEHIND YOU!
NO PROBLEM, CYBORG...
I CAN HANDLE BOTH OF THEM.
PRESS ME AND I CAN ALSO CHEW GUM AT THE SAME TIME.
NOT BAD, KID... NOT BAD AT ALL!
SURE YOU DON'T WANT TO JOIN THE TITANS?
ABOVE THE FROZEN WASTELANDS OF EARTH-S...
IT APPEARS WE HAVE OUR FOES ON ICE, SIVANA.
HEE HEE HEE... YOU KNOW IT, DR. CYBER.
OH, I'VE BEEN AWAITING THIS DAY FOR SO LONG.
BILLY BATSON BOUND AND GAGGED, ALONG WITH THE REST OF HIS ACCURSED MARVEL FAMILY!
DON'T GLOAT YET, SHORTY... THE HEROES ARE HEADING OUR WAY.
WE ARE PREPARED FOR THEM, T.O. MORROW.
CYBER, I LIKE THE WAY YOU THINK.
5

How many worlds have perished, Monitor? Mibrannu, a planet of sentient methane gas, perhaps the most peaceful in any universe, died while the murderous Kallidrane armies survived to destroy again. Is that justice, Monitor?

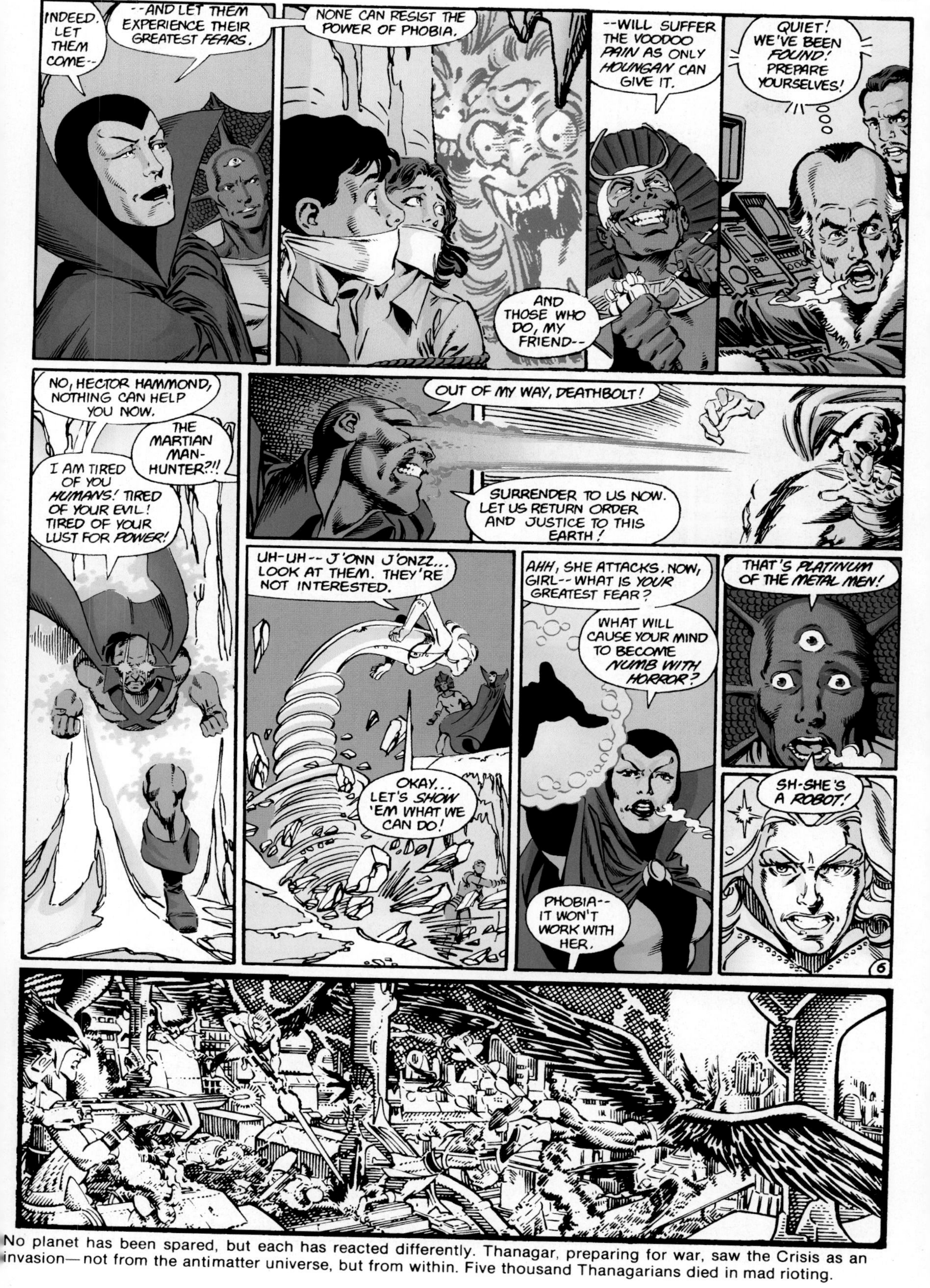
INDEED. LET THEM COME--
--AND LET THEM EXPERIENCE THEIR GREATEST FEARS.
NONE CAN RESIST THE POWER OF PHOBIA.
AND THOSE WHO DO, MY FRIEND--
--WILL SUFFER THE VOODOO PAIN AS ONLY HOUNGAN CAN GIVE IT.
QUIET! WE'VE BEEN FOUND! PREPARE YOURSELVES!
NO, HECTOR HAMMOND, NOTHING CAN HELP YOU NOW.
THE MARTIAN MAN-HUNTER?!!
I AM TIRED OF YOU HUMANS! TIRED OF YOUR EVIL! TIRED OF YOUR LUST FOR POWER!
OUT OF MY WAY, DEATHBOLT!
SURRENDER TO US NOW. LET US RETURN ORDER AND JUSTICE TO THIS EARTH!
UH-UH-- J'ONN J'ONZZ... LOOK AT THEM. THEY'RE NOT INTERESTED.
OKAY... LET'S SHOW 'EM WHAT WE CAN DO!
AHH, SHE ATTACKS. NOW, GIRL-- WHAT IS YOUR GREATEST FEAR?
WHAT WILL CAUSE YOUR MIND TO BECOME NUMB WITH HORROR?
PHOBIA-- IT WON'T WORK WITH HER.
THAT'S PLATINUM OF THE METAL MEN!
SH-SHE'S A ROBOT!
6

No planet has been spared, but each has reacted differently. Thanagar, preparing for war, saw the Crisis as an invasion—not from the antimatter universe, but from within. Five thousand Thanagarians died in mad rioting.

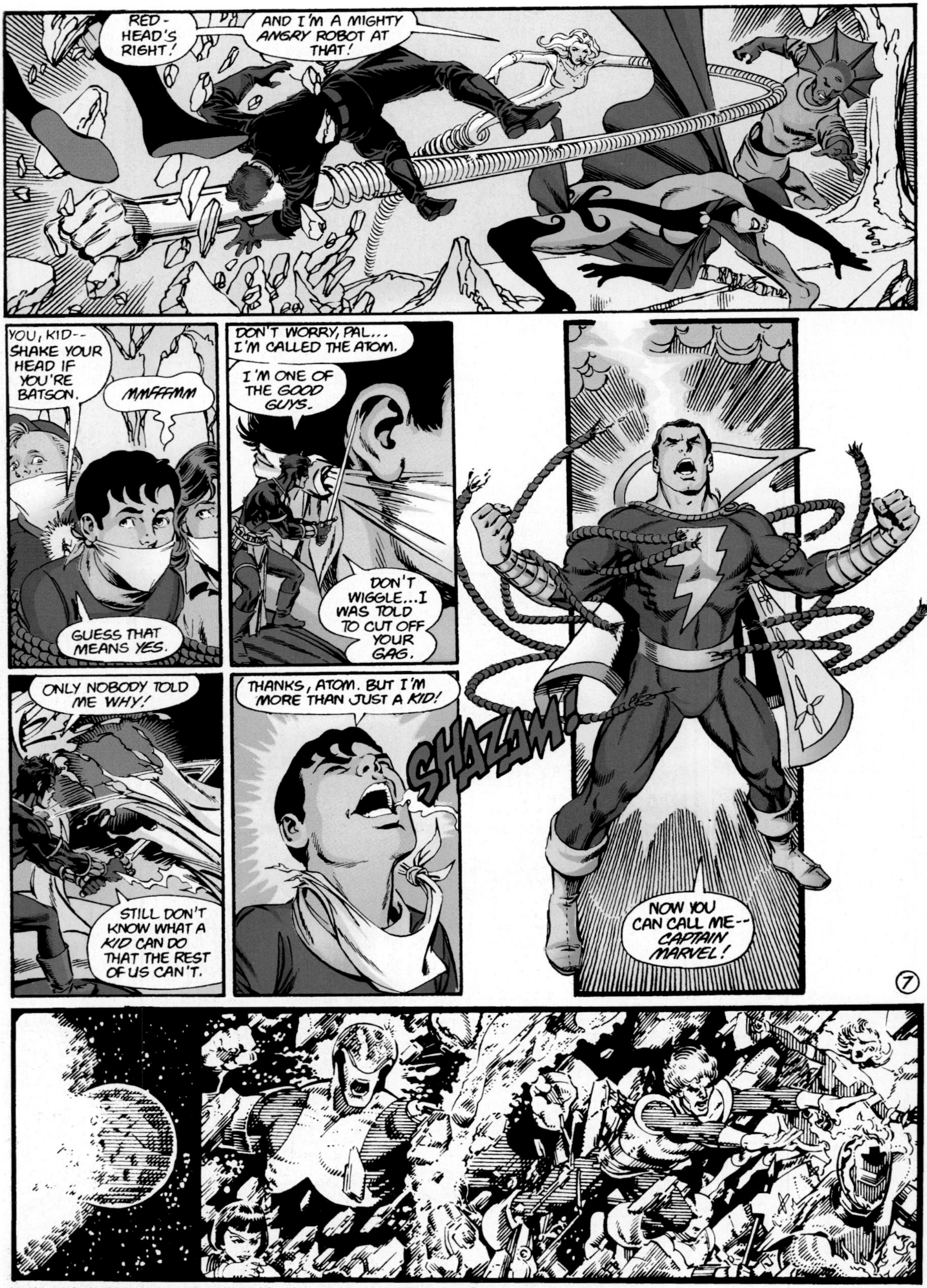
RED-HEAD'S RIGHT!
AND I'M A MIGHTY ANGRY ROBOT AT THAT!
YOU, KID-- SHAKE YOUR HEAD IF YOU'RE BATSON.
MMFFFMM
GUESS THAT MEANS YES.
DON'T WORRY, PAL... I'M CALLED THE ATOM.
I'M ONE OF THE GOOD GUYS.
DON'T WIGGLE...I WAS TOLD TO CUT OFF YOUR GAG.
ONLY NOBODY TOLD ME WHY!
STILL DON'T KNOW WHAT A KID CAN DO THAT THE REST OF US CAN'T.
THANKS, ATOM. BUT I'M MORE THAN JUST A KID!
SHAZAM!
NOW YOU CAN CALL ME-- CAPTAIN MARVEL!
7

In the thirtieth century, the *Anti-Monitor* destroyed *Takron-Galtos*, the prison planet. Into a universe already doomed were unleashed the most evil of evils. The Legion of Super-Heroes couldn't stop them. Nobody could. *Is that justice?*

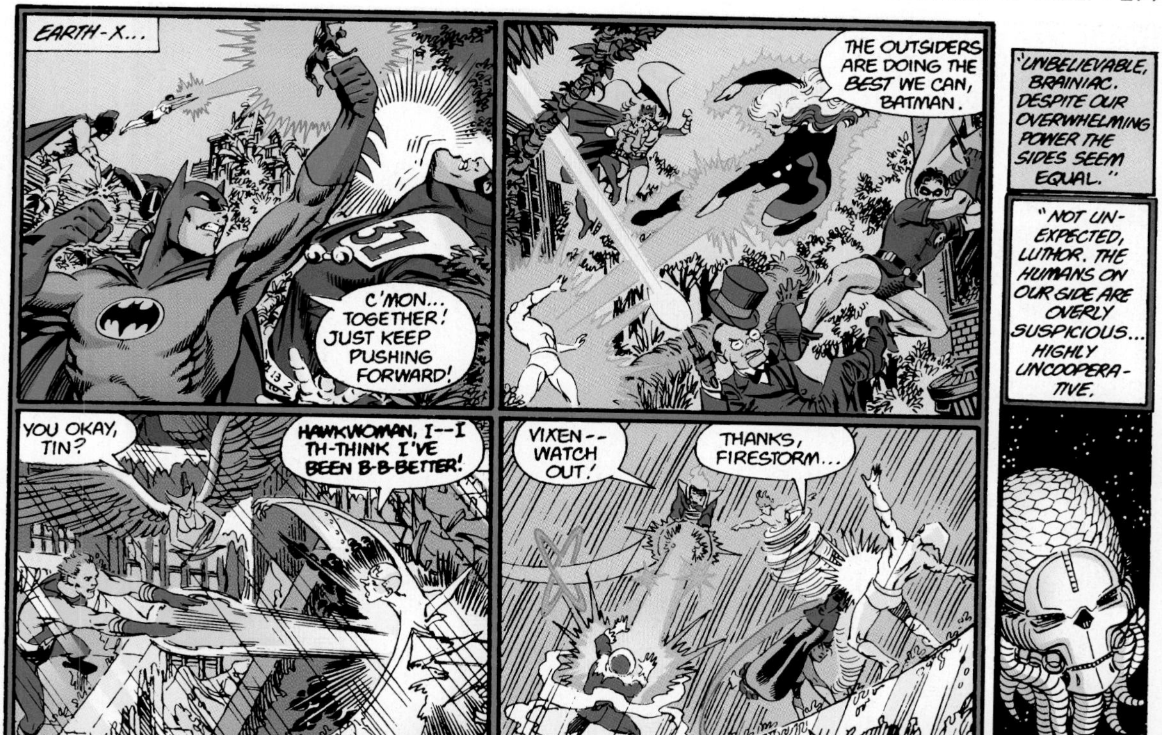
EARTH-X...
C'MON... TOGETHER! JUST KEEP PUSHING FORWARD!
THE OUTSIDERS ARE DOING THE BEST WE CAN, BATMAN.
"UNBELIEVABLE, BRAINIAC. DESPITE OUR OVERWHELMING POWER THE SIDES SEEM EQUAL."
"NOT UN-EXPECTED, LUTHOR. THE HUMANS ON OUR SIDE ARE OVERLY SUSPICIOUS... HIGHLY UNCOOPERA-TIVE.
YOU OKAY, TIN?
HAWKWOMAN, I--I TH-THINK I'VE BEEN B-B-BETTER!
VIXEN-- WATCH OUT!
THANKS, FIRESTORM...
...BUT I SMELLED THIS CREEP COMING A MILE AWAY!
I CAN'T STOP HIM. THE SHAGGY MAN'S NOT EVEN ALIVE.
GREAT!
THEN I DON'T MIND USING MY EXPLOSIVE ARROW!
WAY TO GO, SPEEDY!
SCRATCH ONE SHAGGY MAN! OVER AND OUT!
8
"THEY FIGHT ALONE... DISDAINING THE AID OF OTHERS. OUR FOES WORK IN TEAMS... ONLY IN UNITY IS THERE STRENGTH."
"I KNOW... I KNOW. BUT I EXPECTED A BETTER SHOWING.
I WANTED THOSE SO-CALLED HEROES DEAD AND BURIED!"

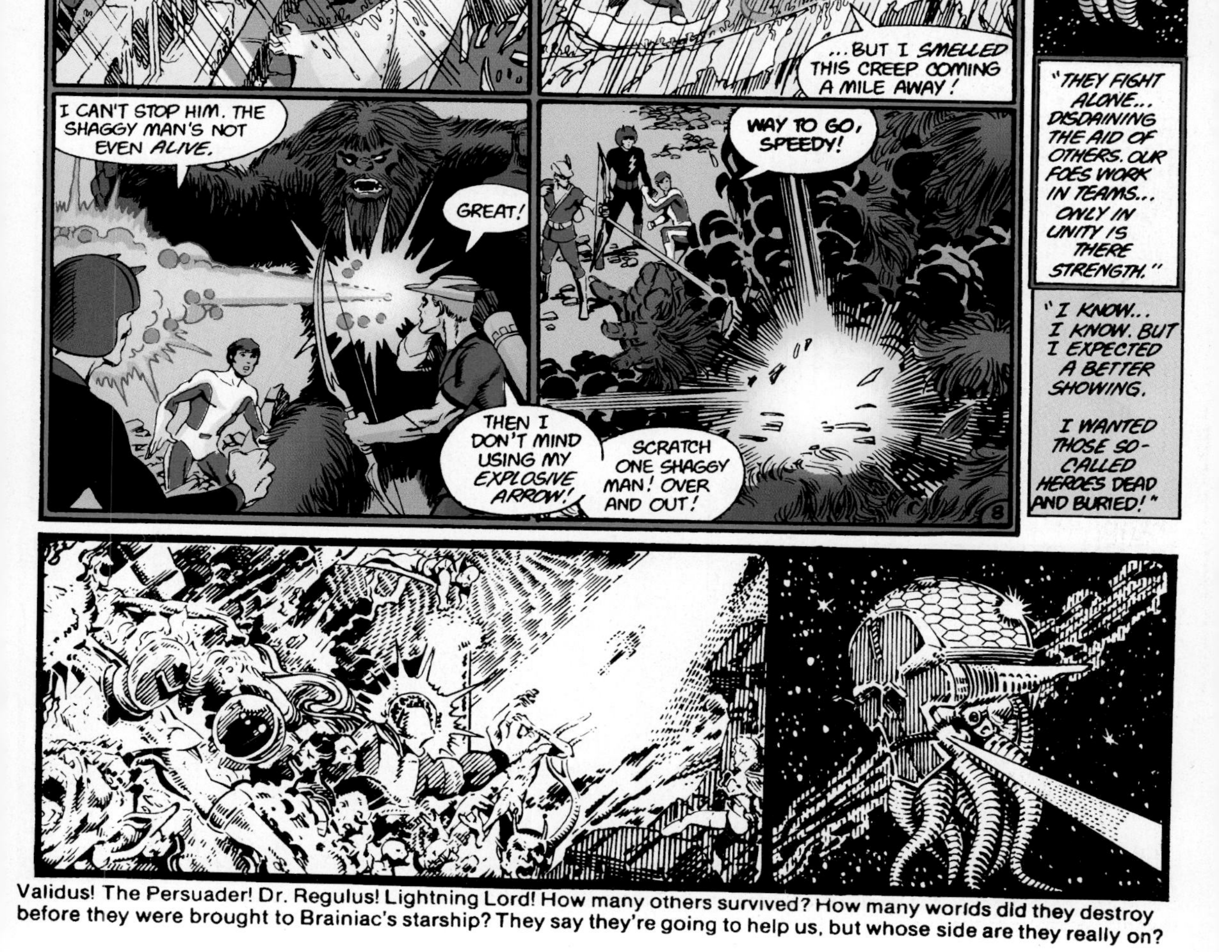

Validus! The Persuader! Dr. Regulus! Lightning Lord! How many others survived? How many worlds did they destroy before they were brought to Brainiac's starship? They say they're going to help us, but whose side are they really on?

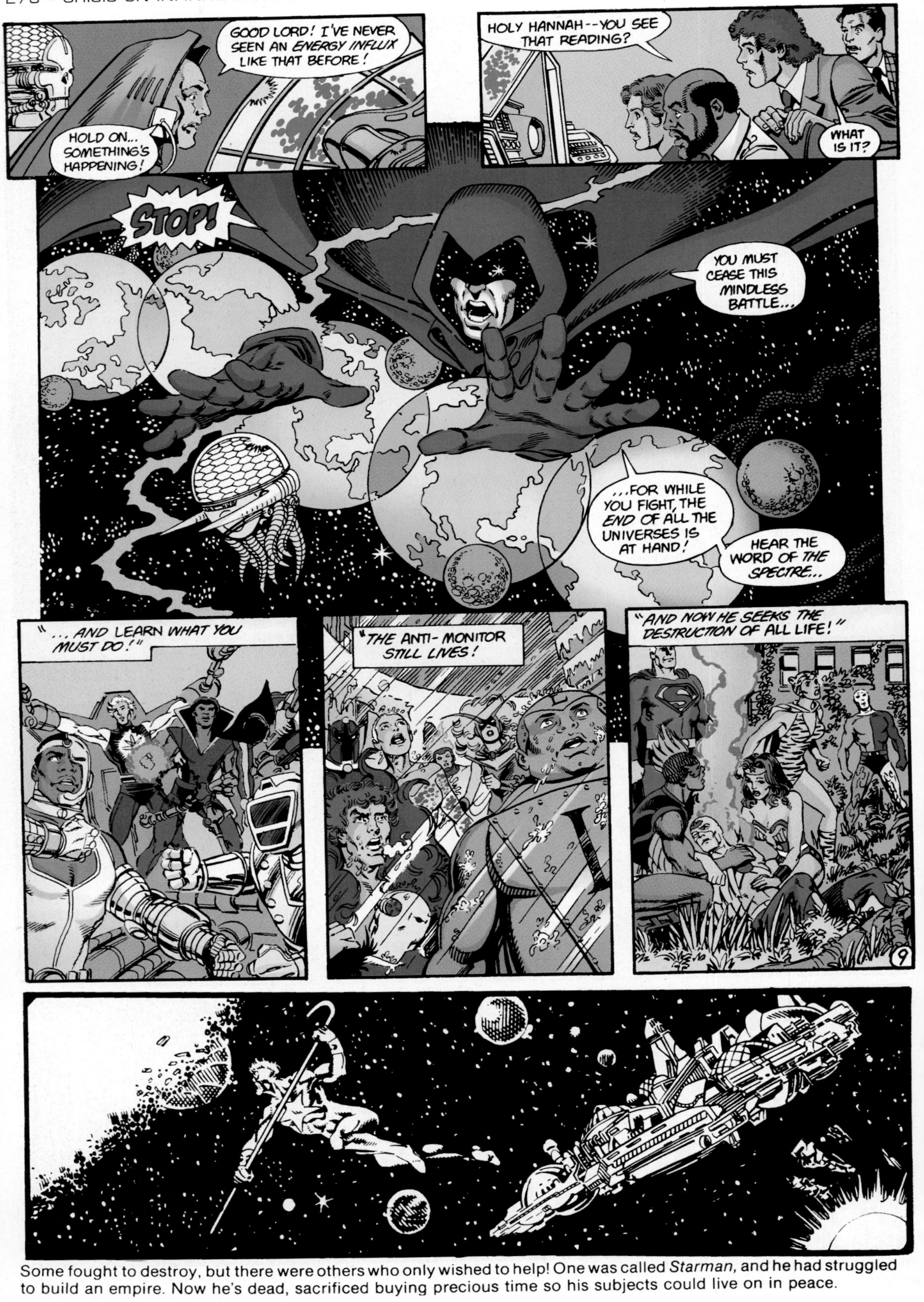
GOOD LORD! I'VE NEVER SEEN AN *ENERGY INFLUX* LIKE THAT BEFORE!
HOLD ON... SOMETHING'S HAPPENING!
HOLY HANNAH--YOU SEE THAT READING?
WHAT IS IT?
STOP!
YOU MUST CEASE THIS MINDLESS BATTLE...
...FOR WHILE YOU FIGHT, THE *END OF ALL THE UNIVERSES* IS AT HAND!
HEAR THE WORD OF *THE SPECTRE*...
"...AND LEARN WHAT YOU MUST DO!"
"THE ANTI-MONITOR STILL LIVES!
"AND NOW HE SEEKS THE DESTRUCTION OF ALL LIFE!"
9

Some fought to destroy, but there were others who only wished to help! One was called *Starman,* and he had struggled to build an empire. Now he's dead, sacrificed buying precious time so his subjects could live on in peace.

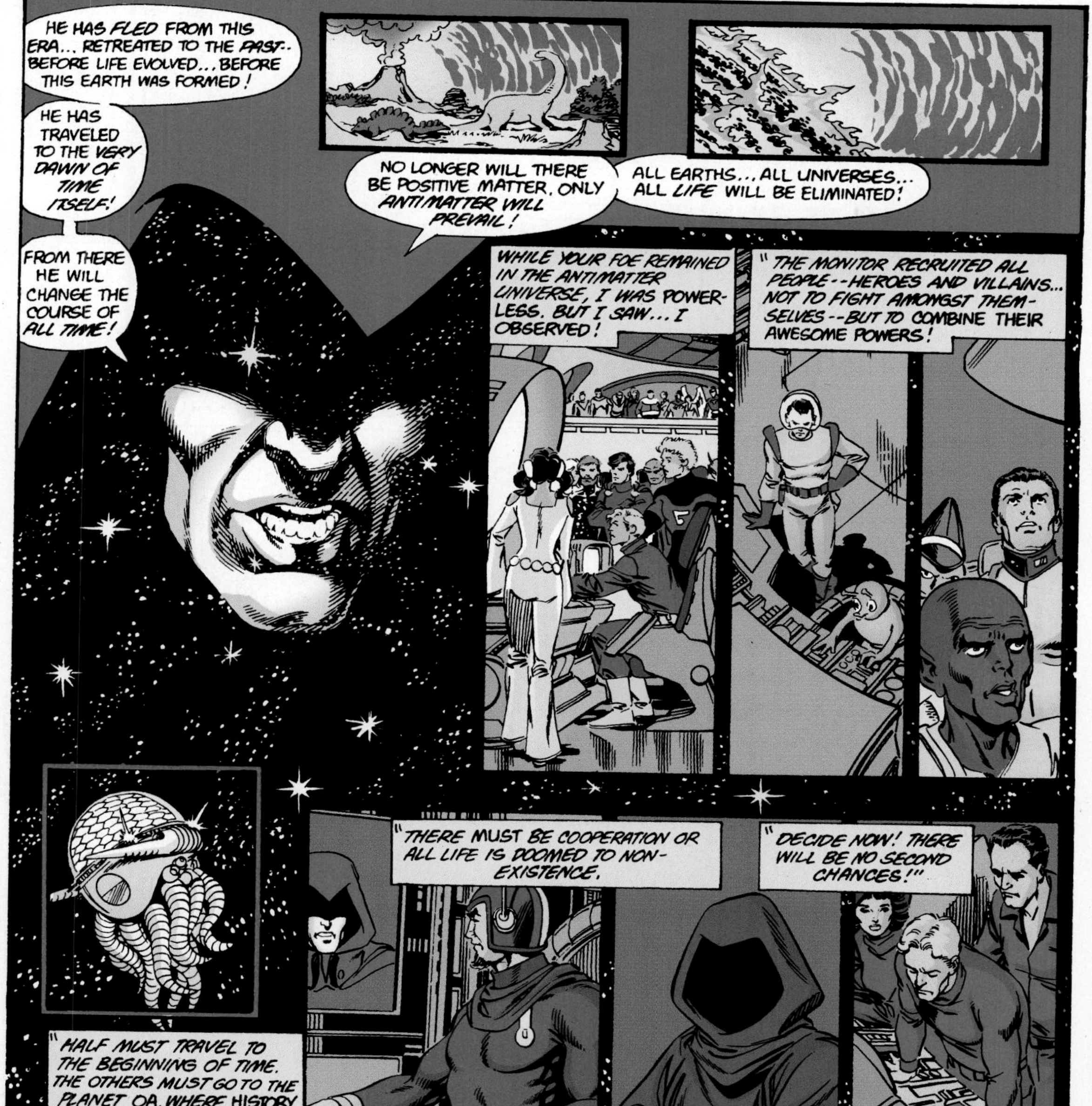
HE HAS FLED FROM THIS ERA... RETREATED TO THE PAST-- BEFORE LIFE EVOLVED... BEFORE THIS EARTH WAS FORMED!
HE HAS TRAVELED TO THE VERY DAWN OF TIME ITSELF!
FROM THERE HE WILL CHANGE THE COURSE OF ALL TIME!
NO LONGER WILL THERE BE POSITIVE MATTER, ONLY ANTIMATTER WILL PREVAIL!
ALL EARTHS... ALL UNIVERSES... ALL LIFE WILL BE ELIMINATED!
WHILE YOUR FOE REMAINED IN THE ANTIMATTER UNIVERSE, I WAS POWERLESS. BUT I SAW... I OBSERVED!
"THE MONITOR RECRUITED ALL PEOPLE--HEROES AND VILLAINS... NOT TO FIGHT AMONGST THEMSELVES--BUT TO COMBINE THEIR AWESOME POWERS!
"HALF MUST TRAVEL TO THE BEGINNING OF TIME. THE OTHERS MUST GO TO THE PLANET OA, WHERE HISTORY MUST BE CHANGED!
"THERE MUST BE COOPERATION OR ALL LIFE IS DOOMED TO NON-EXISTENCE.
"DECIDE NOW! THERE WILL BE NO SECOND CHANCES!"
10

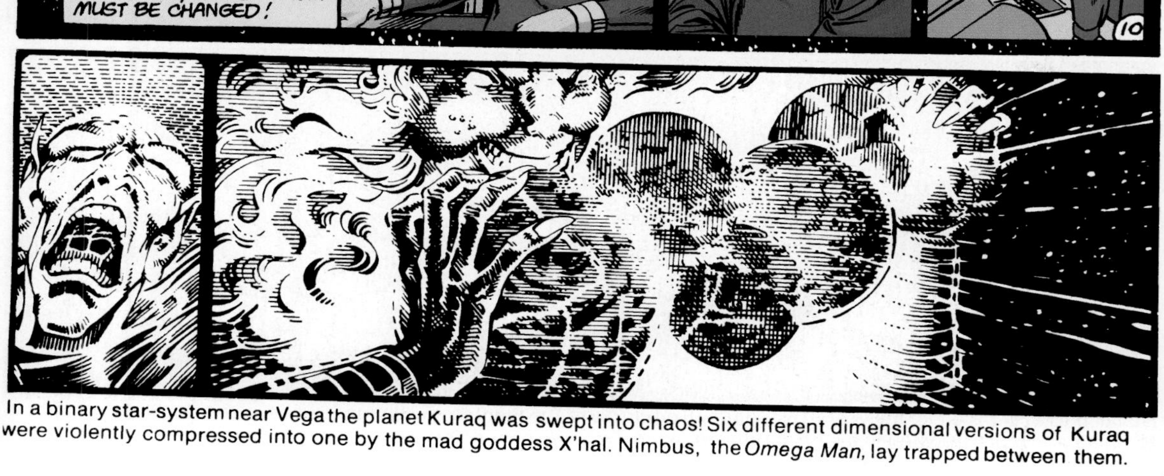

In a binary star-system near Vega the planet Kuraq was swept into chaos! Six different dimensional versions of Kuraq were violently compressed into one by the mad goddess X'hal. Nimbus, the *Omega Man*, lay trapped between them.

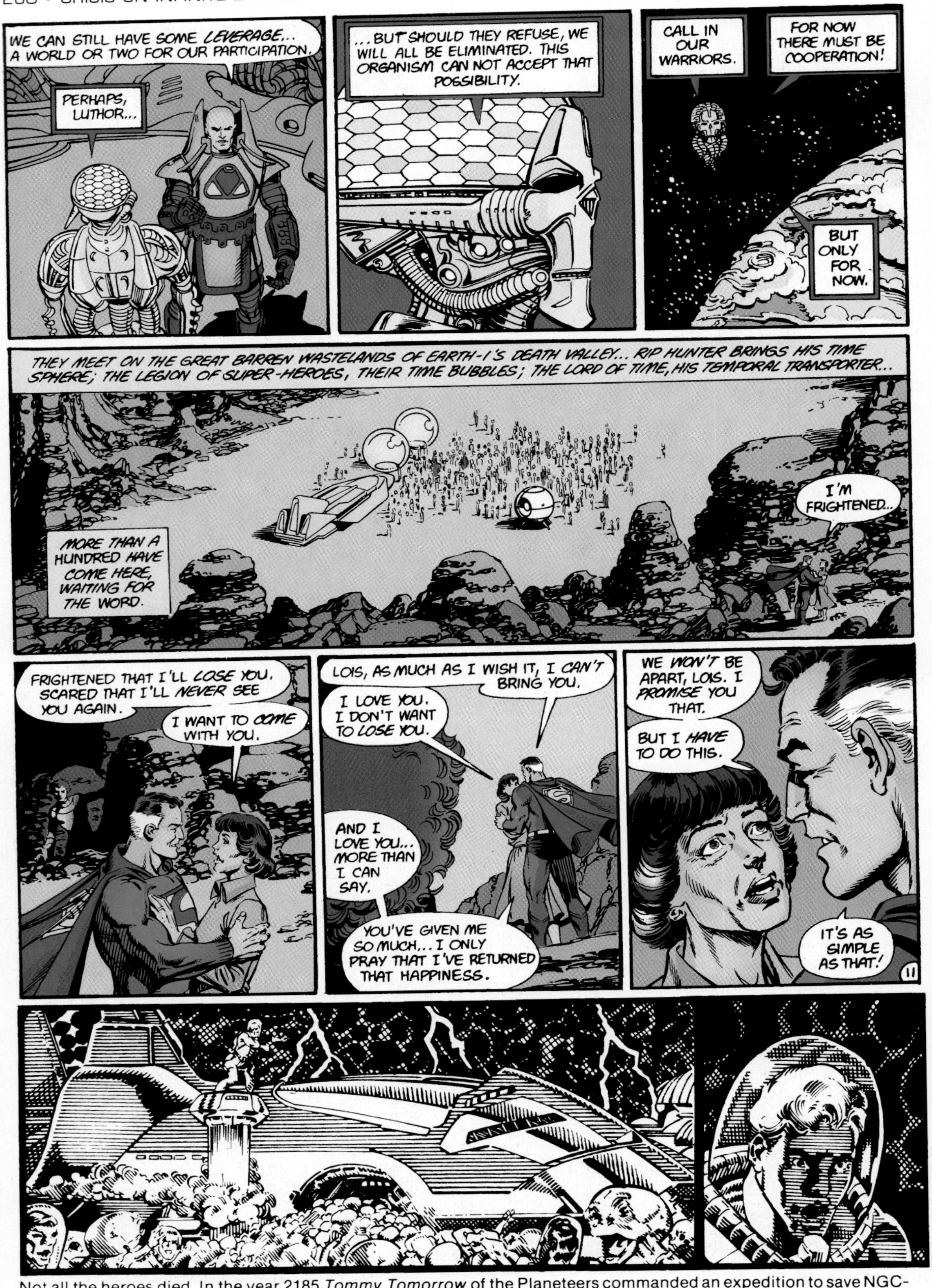
WE CAN STILL HAVE SOME LEVERAGE... A WORLD OR TWO FOR OUR PARTICIPATION.
PERHAPS, LUTHOR...
...BUT SHOULD THEY REFUSE, WE WILL ALL BE ELIMINATED. THIS ORGANISM CAN NOT ACCEPT THAT POSSIBILITY.
CALL IN OUR WARRIORS.
FOR NOW THERE MUST BE COOPERATION!
BUT ONLY FOR NOW.
THEY MEET ON THE GREAT BARREN WASTELANDS OF EARTH-1'S DEATH VALLEY... RIP HUNTER BRINGS HIS TIME SPHERE; THE LEGION OF SUPER-HEROES, THEIR TIME BUBBLES; THE LORD OF TIME, HIS TEMPORAL TRANSPORTER...
MORE THAN A HUNDRED HAVE COME HERE, WAITING FOR THE WORD.
I'M FRIGHTENED...
FRIGHTENED THAT I'LL LOSE YOU. SCARED THAT I'LL NEVER SEE YOU AGAIN.
I WANT TO COME WITH YOU.
LOIS, AS MUCH AS I WISH IT, I CAN'T BRING YOU.
I LOVE YOU. I DON'T WANT TO LOSE YOU.
AND I LOVE YOU... MORE THAN I CAN SAY.
YOU'VE GIVEN ME SO MUCH... I ONLY PRAY THAT I'VE RETURNED THAT HAPPINESS.
WE WON'T BE APART, LOIS. I PROMISE YOU THAT.
BUT I HAVE TO DO THIS.
IT'S AS SIMPLE AS THAT!
11

Not all the heroes died. In the year 2185 *Tommy Tomorrow* of the Planeteers commanded an expedition to save NGC-2683, a star-system threatened by the antimatter cloud. Because of him, the population of sixteen worlds will survive.

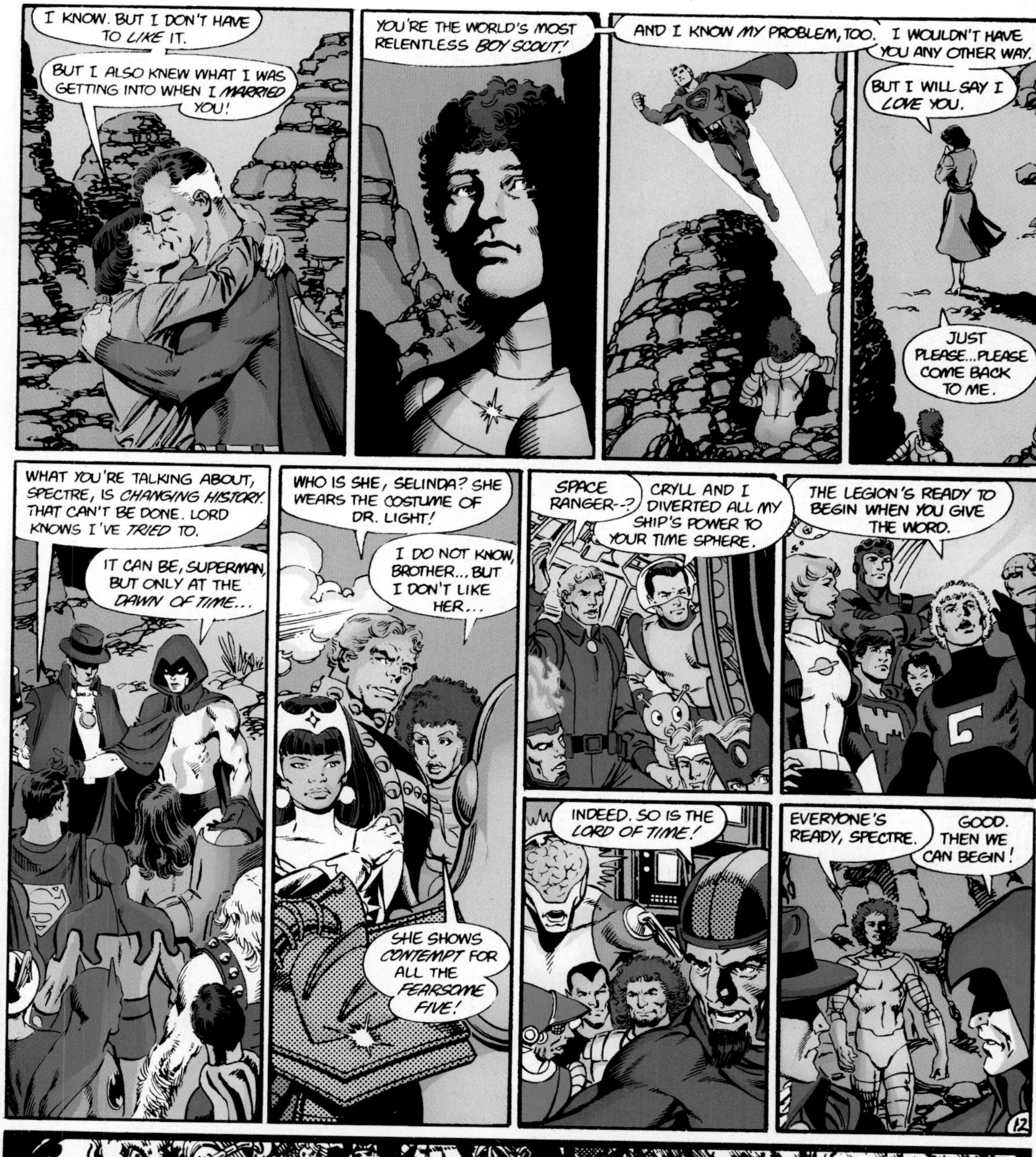
I KNOW. BUT I DON'T HAVE TO LIKE IT.
BUT I ALSO KNEW WHAT I WAS GETTING INTO WHEN I MARRIED YOU!
YOU'RE THE WORLD'S MOST RELENTLESS BOY SCOUT!
AND I KNOW MY PROBLEM, TOO.
I WOULDN'T HAVE YOU ANY OTHER WAY.
BUT I WILL SAY I LOVE YOU.
JUST PLEASE...PLEASE COME BACK TO ME.
WHAT YOU'RE TALKING ABOUT, SPECTRE, IS CHANGING HISTORY. THAT CAN'T BE DONE. LORD KNOWS I'VE TRIED TO.
IT CAN BE, SUPERMAN, BUT ONLY AT THE DAWN OF TIME...
WHO IS SHE, SELINDA? SHE WEARS THE COSTUME OF DR. LIGHT!
I DO NOT KNOW, BROTHER... BUT I DON'T LIKE HER...
SHE SHOWS CONTEMPT FOR ALL THE FEARSOME FIVE!
SPACE RANGER--?
CRYLL AND I DIVERTED ALL MY SHIP'S POWER TO YOUR TIME SPHERE.
THE LEGION'S READY TO BEGIN WHEN YOU GIVE THE WORD.
INDEED. SO IS THE LORD OF TIME!
EVERYONE'S READY, SPECTRE.
GOOD. THEN WE CAN BEGIN!
12

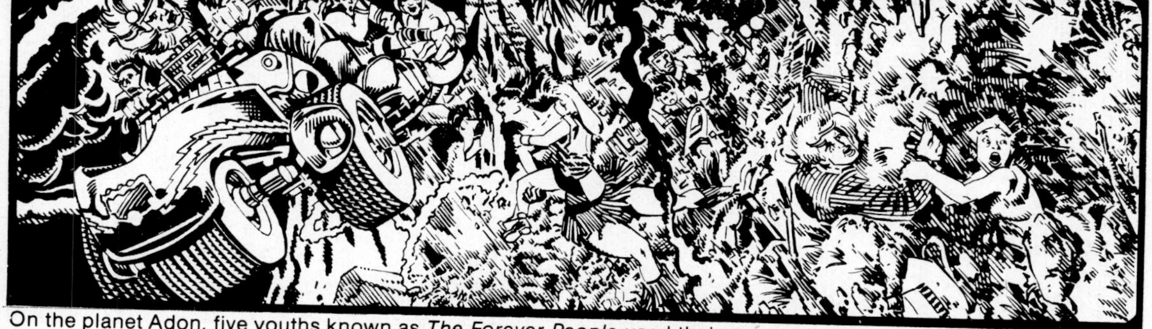

On the planet Adon, five youths known as *The Forever People* used their powers to protect their adopted world from destruction. Across the dimensions, their pursuer, Darkseid the destroyer, cloaked only Apokolips from harm.

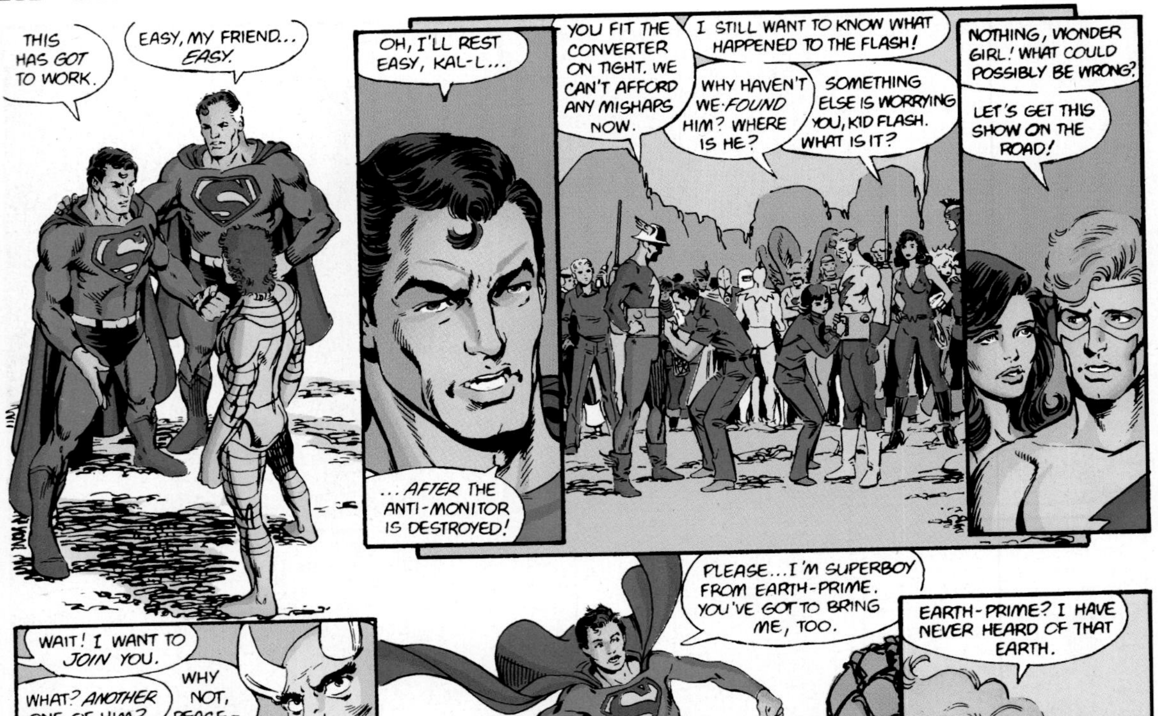
THIS HAS GOT TO WORK.
EASY, MY FRIEND... EASY.
OH, I'LL REST EASY, KAL-L...
...AFTER THE ANTI-MONITOR IS DESTROYED!
YOU FIT THE CONVERTER ON TIGHT. WE CAN'T AFFORD ANY MISHAPS NOW.
I STILL WANT TO KNOW WHAT HAPPENED TO THE FLASH!
WHY HAVEN'T WE FOUND HIM? WHERE IS HE?
SOMETHING ELSE IS WORRYING YOU, KID FLASH. WHAT IS IT?
NOTHING, WONDER GIRL! WHAT COULD POSSIBLY BE WRONG?
LET'S GET THIS SHOW ON THE ROAD!
WAIT! I WANT TO JOIN YOU.
WHAT? ANOTHER ONE OF HIM?
WHY NOT, PEACE-MAKER?
PLEASE... I'M SUPERBOY FROM EARTH-PRIME. YOU'VE GOT TO BRING ME, TOO.
ONLY THIS ONE KINDA SHRUNK IN THE WASHING!
YEAH! ONE GOOD SUPERMAN DESERVES ANOTHER.
EARTH-PRIME? I HAVE NEVER HEARD OF THAT EARTH.
I THOUGHT THERE WERE ONLY FIVE EARTHS LEFT.
THERE ARE-- IT'S BEEN DESTROYED.
I DIDN'T KNOW WHAT HAPPENED TO YOU WHEN YOU VANISHED.*
*DC COMICS PRESENTS #87.--MW
EVEN I DON'T KNOW HOW I DISAPPEARED. BUT I'M HERE.
AND I'M EARTH-PRIME'S LAST SURVIVOR.
I HAVE A REASON TO JOIN WITH YOU GUYS.
BUT IF YOU DON'T LET ME, I'LL DO IT BY MYSELF.
13

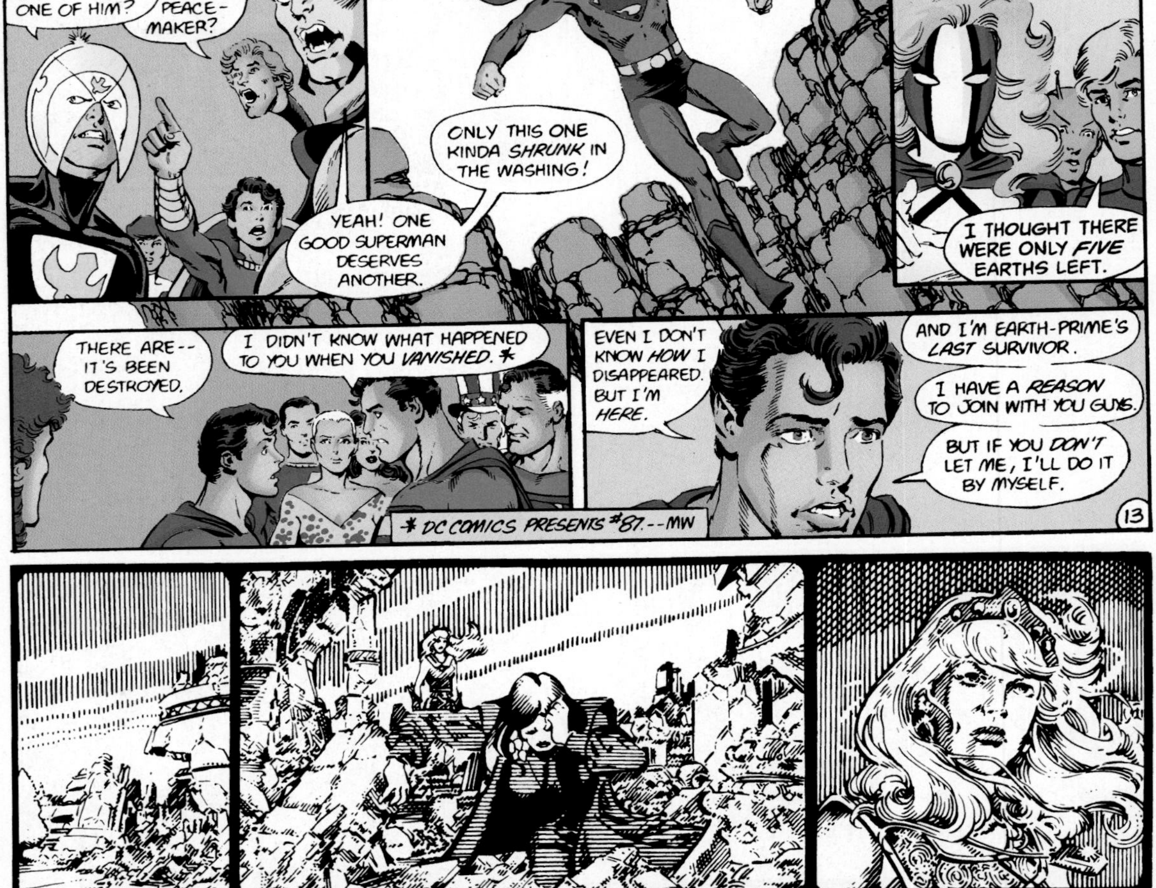

One dimension saved, but another was not so lucky. On *Gemworld* the Citadel of Sapphire was destroyed, people torn and desperate. Only the Earth girl, Amy Winston, who was also their Princess Amethyst, could lead them to triumph!

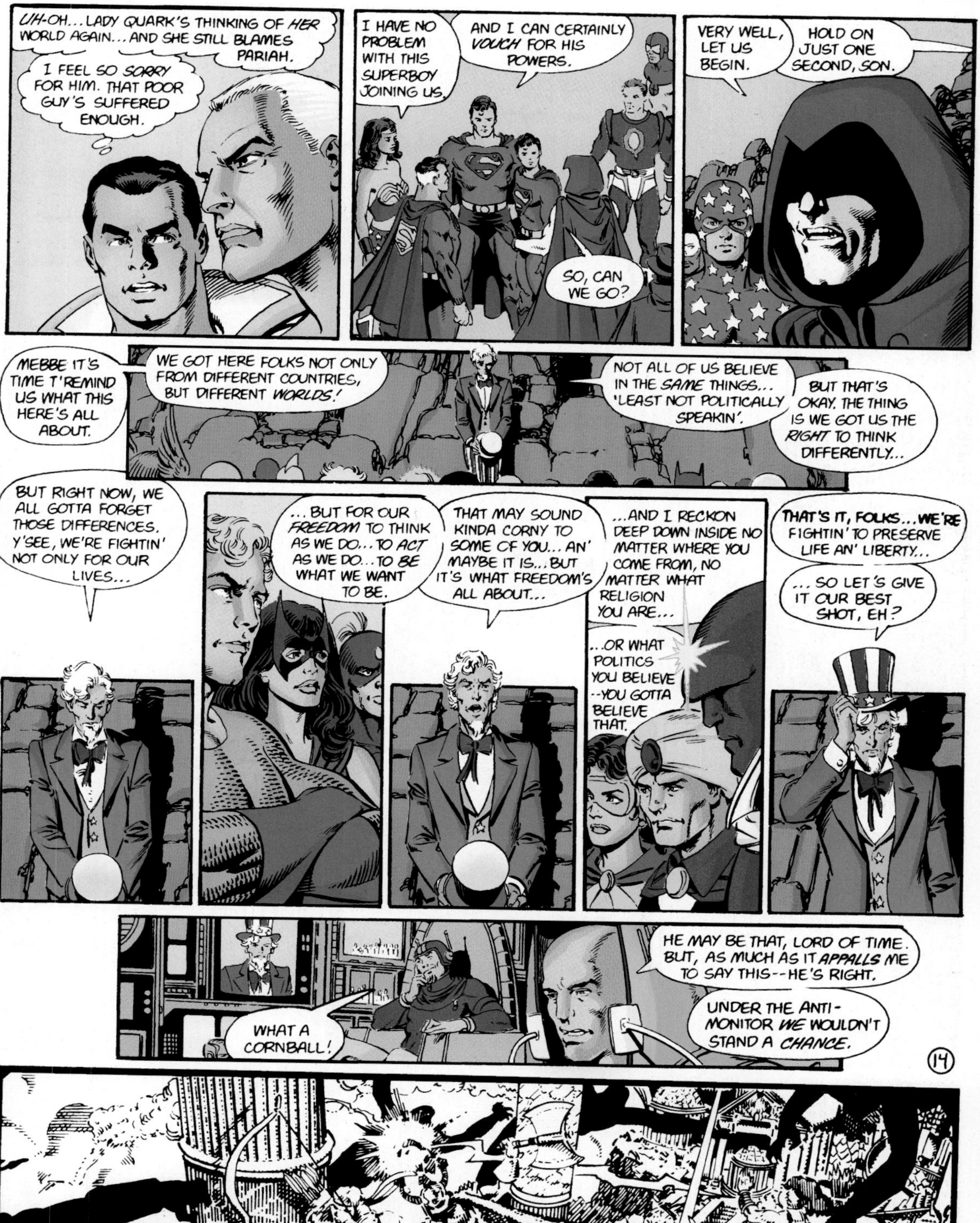
UH-OH... LADY QUARK'S THINKING OF HER WORLD AGAIN... AND SHE STILL BLAMES PARIAH.
I FEEL SO SORRY FOR HIM. THAT POOR GUY'S SUFFERED ENOUGH.
I HAVE NO PROBLEM WITH THIS SUPERBOY JOINING US.
AND I CAN CERTAINLY VOUCH FOR HIS POWERS.
SO, CAN WE GO?
VERY WELL, LET US BEGIN.
HOLD ON JUST ONE SECOND, SON.
MEBBE IT'S TIME T'REMIND US WHAT THIS HERE'S ALL ABOUT.
WE GOT HERE FOLKS NOT ONLY FROM DIFFERENT COUNTRIES, BUT DIFFERENT WORLDS!
NOT ALL OF US BELIEVE IN THE SAME THINGS... 'LEAST NOT POLITICALLY SPEAKIN'.
BUT THAT'S OKAY. THE THING IS WE GOT US THE RIGHT TO THINK DIFFERENTLY...
BUT RIGHT NOW, WE ALL GOTTA FORGET THOSE DIFFERENCES. Y'SEE, WE'RE FIGHTIN' NOT ONLY FOR OUR LIVES...
... BUT FOR OUR FREEDOM TO THINK AS WE DO... TO ACT AS WE DO... TO BE WHAT WE WANT TO BE.
THAT MAY SOUND KINDA CORNY TO SOME OF YOU... AN' MAYBE IT IS... BUT IT'S WHAT FREEDOM'S ALL ABOUT...
...AND I RECKON DEEP DOWN INSIDE NO MATTER WHERE YOU COME FROM, NO MATTER WHAT RELIGION YOU ARE...
...OR WHAT POLITICS YOU BELIEVE --YOU GOTTA BELIEVE THAT.
THAT'S IT, FOLKS... WE'RE FIGHTIN' TO PRESERVE LIFE AN' LIBERTY...
... SO LET'S GIVE IT OUR BEST SHOT, EH?
WHAT A CORNBALL!
HE MAY BE THAT, LORD OF TIME. BUT, AS MUCH AS IT APPALLS ME TO SAY THIS--HE'S RIGHT.
UNDER THE ANTI-MONITOR WE WOULDN'T STAND A CHANCE.
14

No dimension is safe, Monitor—Even the golden halls of *Olympus* itself were bloodied in battle against the forces your brother unleashed. Three of the gods perished, two more are dying. Whoever destroys the gods *must* be mad!

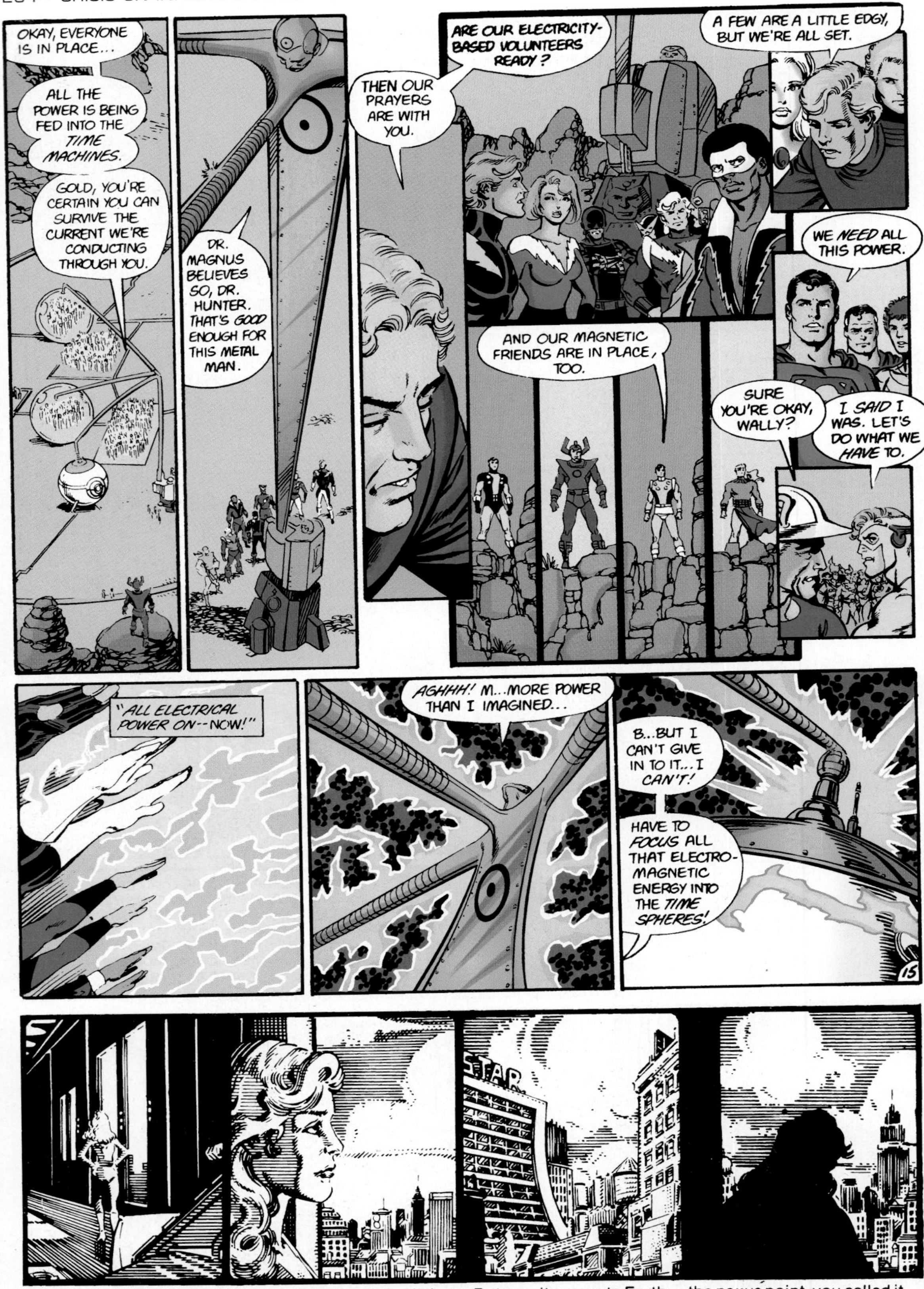
OKAY, EVERYONE IS IN PLACE...
ALL THE POWER IS BEING FED INTO THE TIME MACHINES.
GOLD, YOU'RE CERTAIN YOU CAN SURVIVE THE CURRENT WE'RE CONDUCTING THROUGH YOU.
DR. MAGNUS BELIEVES SO, DR. HUNTER. THAT'S GOOD ENOUGH FOR THIS METAL MAN.
THEN OUR PRAYERS ARE WITH YOU.
ARE OUR ELECTRICITY-BASED VOLUNTEERS READY?
A FEW ARE A LITTLE EDGY, BUT WE'RE ALL SET.
AND OUR MAGNETIC FRIENDS ARE IN PLACE, TOO.
WE NEED ALL THIS POWER.
SURE YOU'RE OKAY, WALLY?
I SAID I WAS. LET'S DO WHAT WE HAVE TO.
"ALL ELECTRICAL POWER ON--NOW!"
AGHHH! M...MORE POWER THAN I IMAGINED...
B...BUT I CAN'T GIVE IN TO IT... I CAN'T!
HAVE TO FOCUS ALL THAT ELECTRO-MAGNETIC ENERGY INTO THE TIME SPHERES!
15
STAR

The Crisis has been universal, striking all worlds in all times. But now it comes to Earth ... the *nexus* point, you called it, Monitor. My homeworld. It's suffered so much already, it seems so unfair that the suffering has to continue.

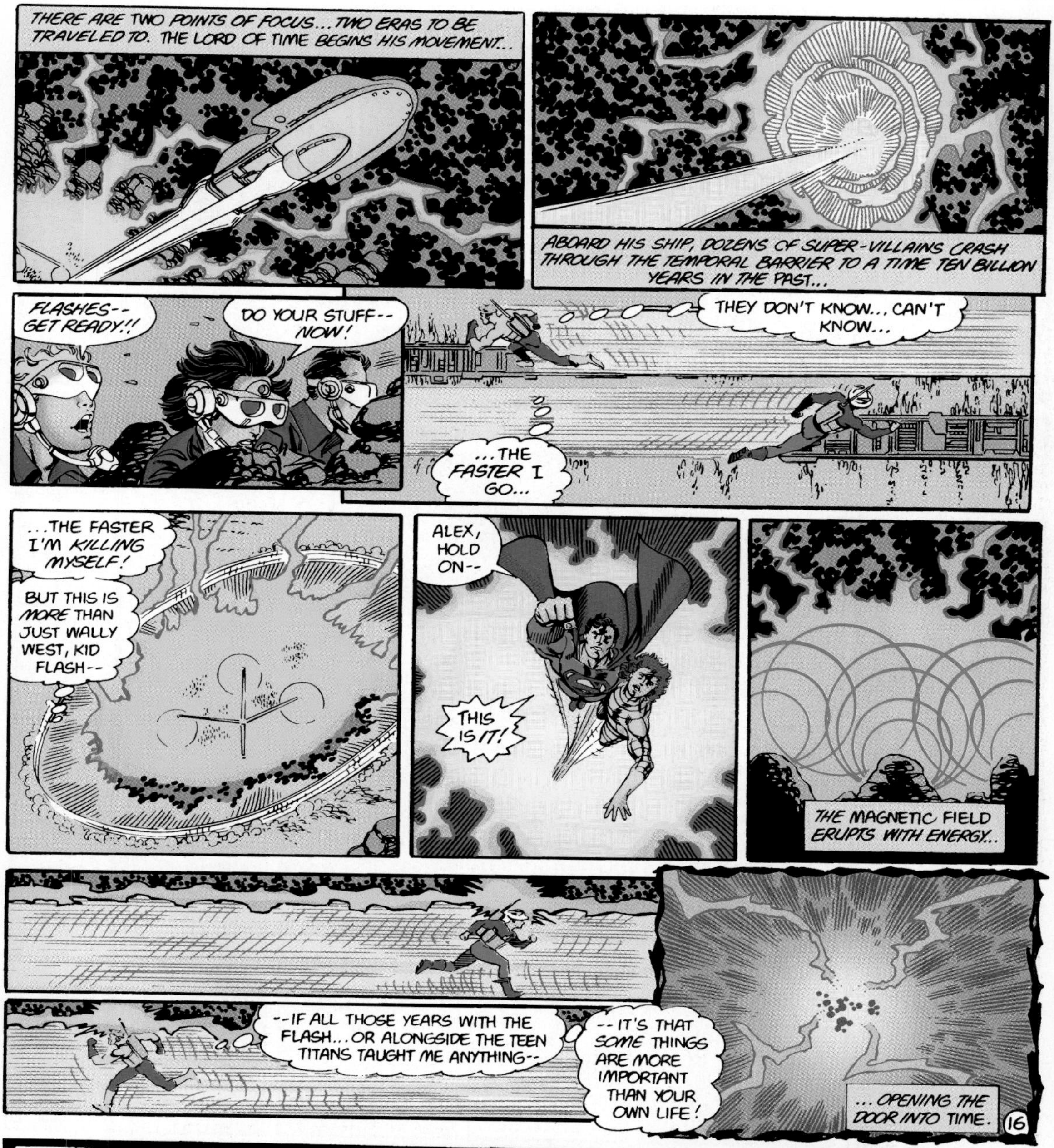
THERE ARE TWO POINTS OF FOCUS... TWO ERAS TO BE TRAVELED TO. THE LORD OF TIME BEGINS HIS MOVEMENT...
ABOARD HIS SHIP, DOZENS OF SUPER-VILLAINS CRASH THROUGH THE TEMPORAL BARRIER TO A TIME TEN BILLION YEARS IN THE PAST...
FLASHES-- GET READY!!
DO YOUR STUFF-- NOW!
THEY DON'T KNOW... CAN'T KNOW...
...THE FASTER I GO...
...THE FASTER I'M KILLING MYSELF!
BUT THIS IS MORE THAN JUST WALLY WEST, KID FLASH--
ALEX, HOLD ON--
THIS IS IT!
THE MAGNETIC FIELD ERUPTS WITH ENERGY..
--IF ALL THOSE YEARS WITH THE FLASH... OR ALONGSIDE THE TEEN TITANS TAUGHT ME ANYTHING--
--IT'S THAT SOME THINGS ARE MORE IMPORTANT THAN YOUR OWN LIFE!
...OPENING THE DOOR INTO TIME.
16

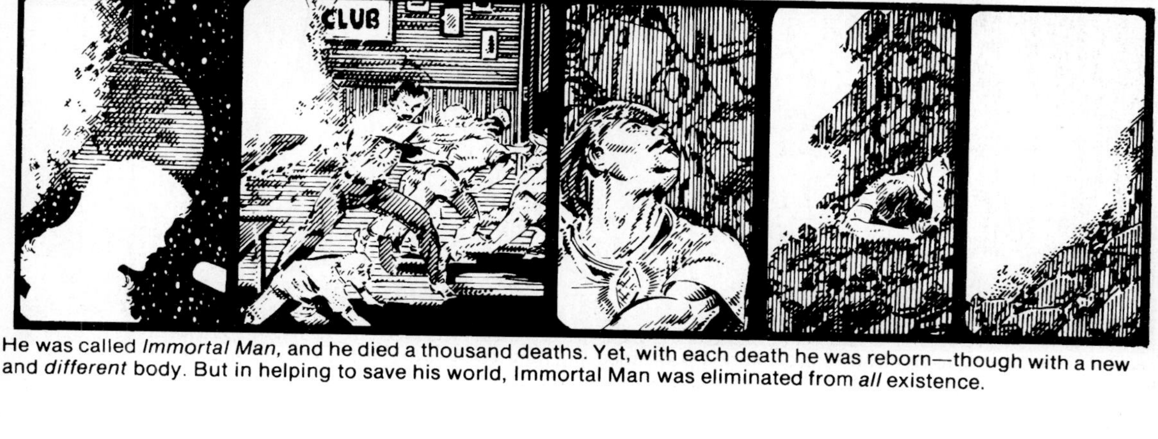
CLUB

He was called *Immortal Man*, and he died a thousand deaths. Yet, with each death he was reborn—though with a new and *different* body. But in helping to save his world, Immortal Man was eliminated from *all* existence.

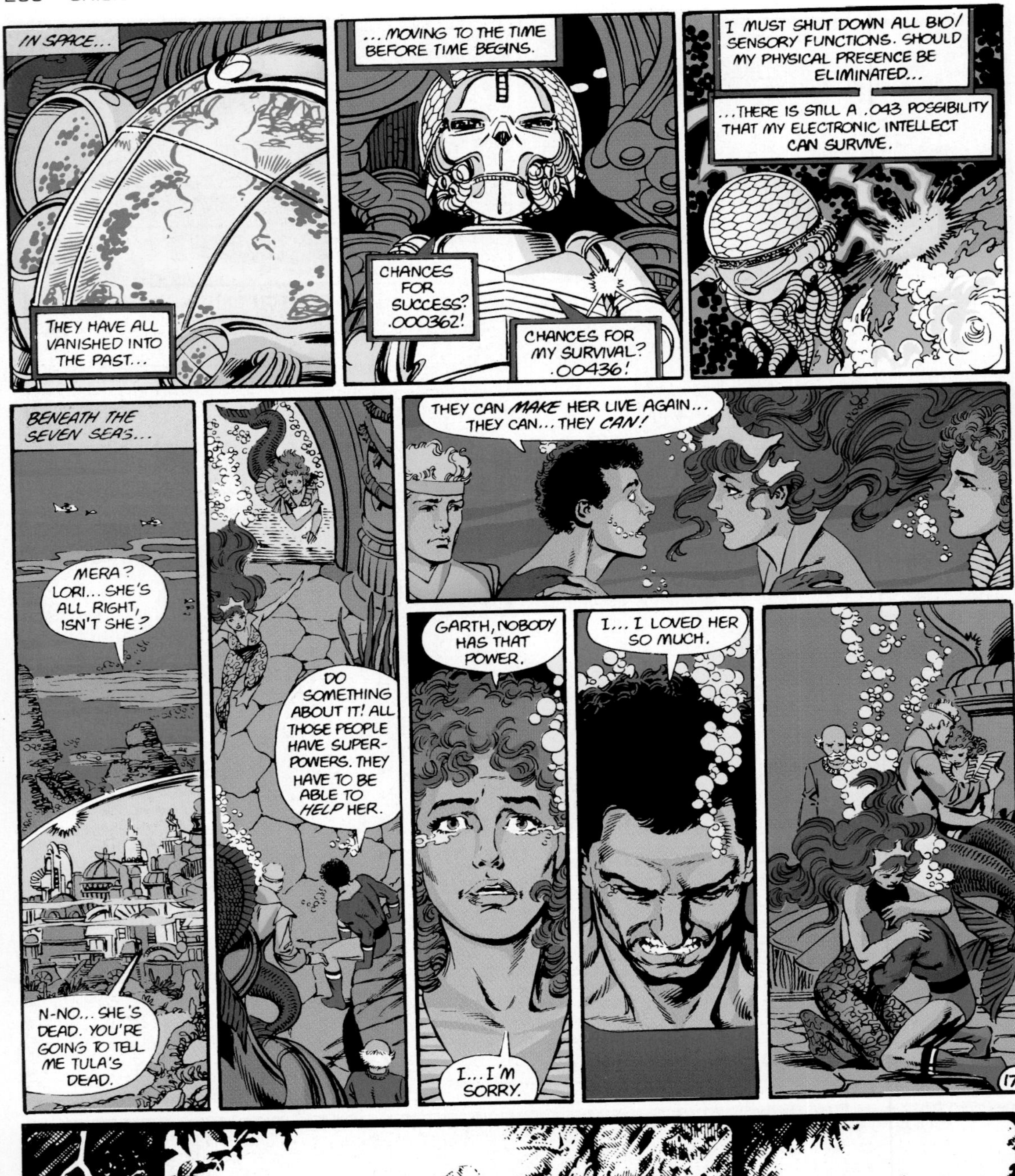
IN SPACE...
THEY HAVE ALL VANISHED INTO THE PAST...
...MOVING TO THE TIME BEFORE TIME BEGINS.
CHANCES FOR SUCCESS? .000362!
CHANCES FOR MY SURVIVAL? .00436!
I MUST SHUT DOWN ALL BIO/SENSORY FUNCTIONS. SHOULD MY PHYSICAL PRESENCE BE ELIMINATED...
...THERE IS STILL A .043 POSSIBILITY THAT MY ELECTRONIC INTELLECT CAN SURVIVE.
BENEATH THE SEVEN SEAS...
MERA? LORI... SHE'S ALL RIGHT, ISN'T SHE?
N-NO... SHE'S DEAD. YOU'RE GOING TO TELL ME TULA'S DEAD.
DO SOMETHING ABOUT IT! ALL THOSE PEOPLE HAVE SUPER-POWERS. THEY HAVE TO BE ABLE TO HELP HER.
THEY CAN MAKE HER LIVE AGAIN... THEY CAN... THEY CAN!
GARTH, NOBODY HAS THAT POWER.
I... I'M SORRY.
I... I LOVED HER SO MUCH.
17

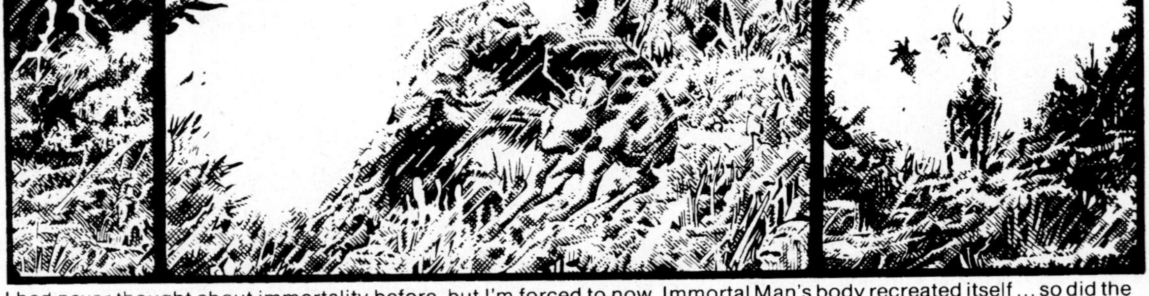

I had never thought about immortality before, but I'm forced to now. Immortal Man's body recreated itself ... so did the body of Alec Holland—now *The Swamp Thing*. But he's not like the Immortal Man—he can't die ... can he?

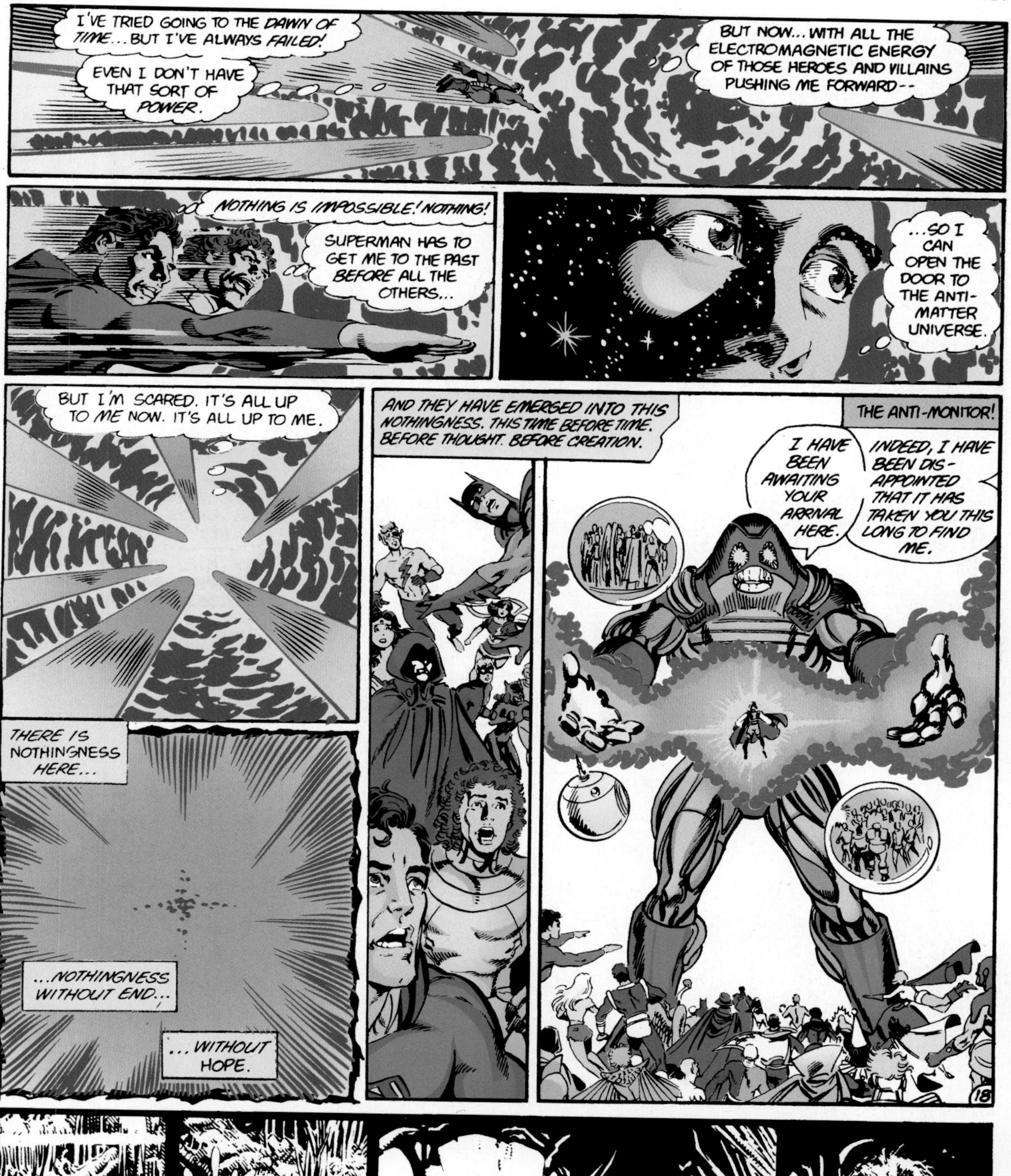
I'VE TRIED GOING TO THE DAWN OF TIME... BUT I'VE ALWAYS FAILED!
EVEN I DON'T HAVE THAT SORT OF POWER.
BUT NOW... WITH ALL THE ELECTROMAGNETIC ENERGY OF THOSE HEROES AND VILLAINS PUSHING ME FORWARD--
NOTHING IS IMPOSSIBLE! NOTHING!
SUPERMAN HAS TO GET ME TO THE PAST BEFORE ALL THE OTHERS...
...SO I CAN OPEN THE DOOR TO THE ANTI-MATTER UNIVERSE.
BUT I'M SCARED. IT'S ALL UP TO ME NOW. IT'S ALL UP TO ME.
THERE IS NOTHINGNESS HERE...
...NOTHINGNESS WITHOUT END...
...WITHOUT HOPE.
AND THEY HAVE EMERGED INTO THIS NOTHINGNESS. THIS TIME BEFORE TIME. BEFORE THOUGHT. BEFORE CREATION.
THE ANTI-MONITOR!
I HAVE BEEN AWAITING YOUR ARRIVAL HERE.
INDEED, I HAVE BEEN DIS-APPOINTED THAT IT HAS TAKEN YOU THIS LONG TO FIND ME.
18

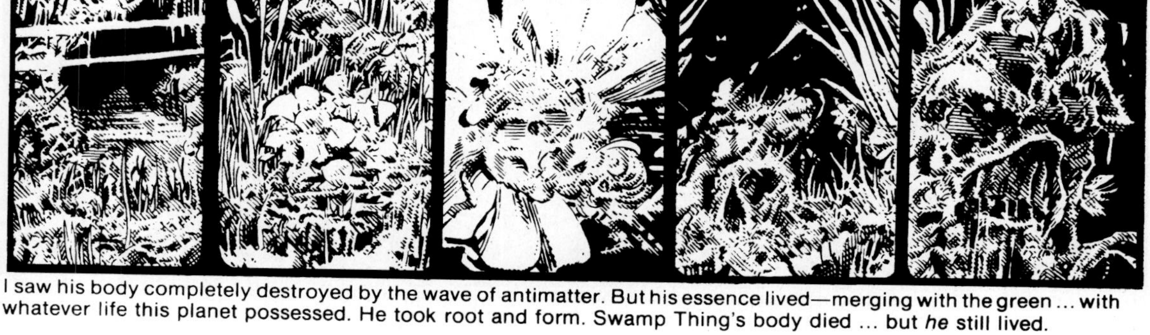

I saw his body completely destroyed by the wave of antimatter. But his essence lived—merging with the green ... with whatever life this planet possessed. He took root and form. Swamp Thing's body died ... but *he* still lived.

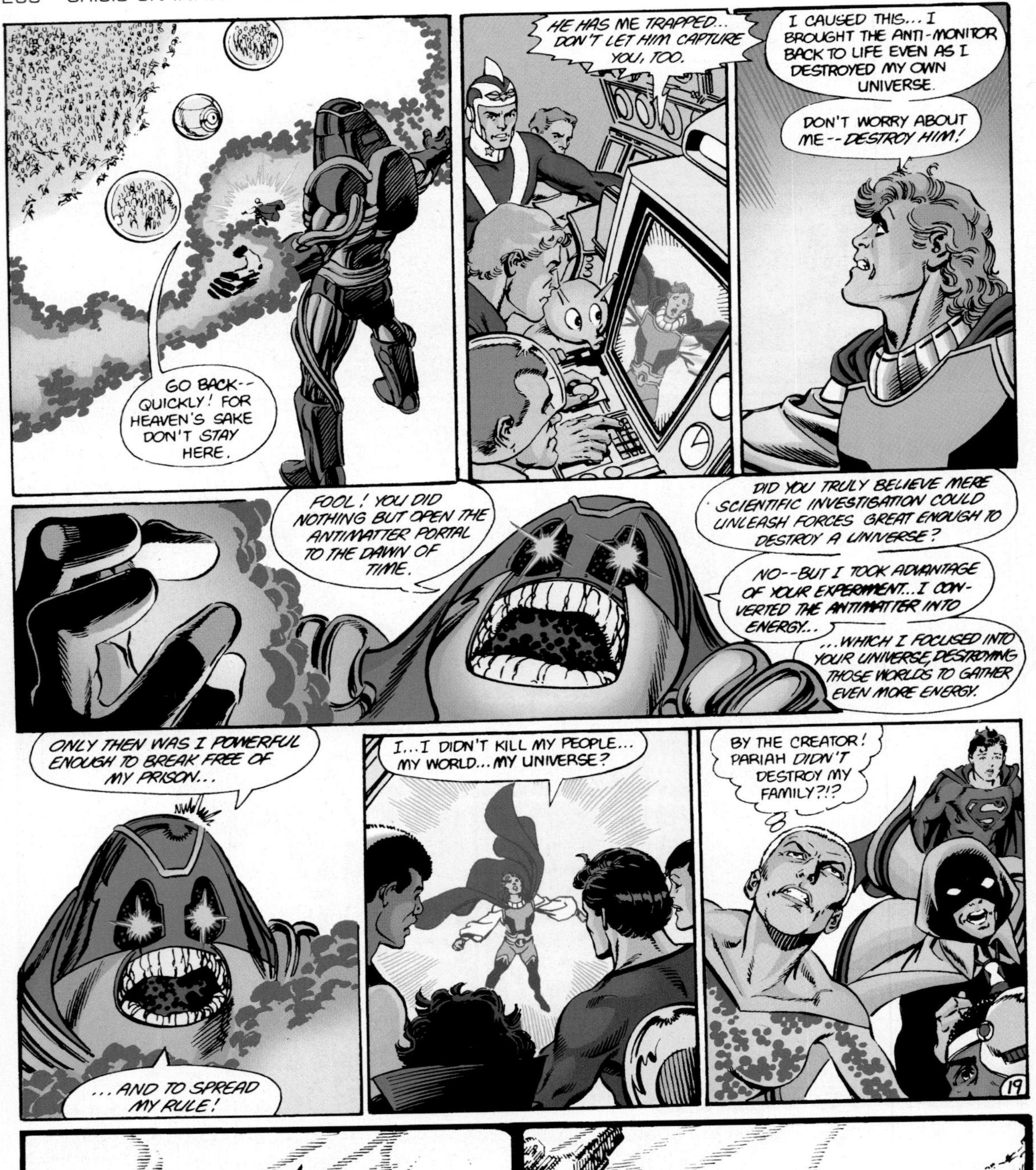
GO BACK--
QUICKLY! FOR HEAVEN'S SAKE DON'T STAY HERE.
HE HAS ME TRAPPED... DON'T LET HIM CAPTURE YOU, TOO.
I CAUSED THIS... I BROUGHT THE ANTI-MONITOR BACK TO LIFE EVEN AS I DESTROYED MY OWN UNIVERSE.
DON'T WORRY ABOUT ME--DESTROY HIM!
FOOL! YOU DID NOTHING BUT OPEN THE ANTIMATTER PORTAL TO THE DAWN OF TIME.
DID YOU TRULY BELIEVE MERE SCIENTIFIC INVESTIGATION COULD UNLEASH FORCES GREAT ENOUGH TO DESTROY A UNIVERSE?
NO--BUT I TOOK ADVANTAGE OF YOUR EXPERIMENT...I CONVERTED THE ANTIMATTER INTO ENERGY...
...WHICH I FOCUSED INTO YOUR UNIVERSE, DESTROYING THOSE WORLDS TO GATHER EVEN MORE ENERGY.
ONLY THEN WAS I POWERFUL ENOUGH TO BREAK FREE OF MY PRISON...
...AND TO SPREAD MY RULE!
I...I DIDN'T KILL MY PEOPLE... MY WORLD... MY UNIVERSE?
BY THE CREATOR! PARIAH DIDN'T DESTROY MY FAMILY?!?
19

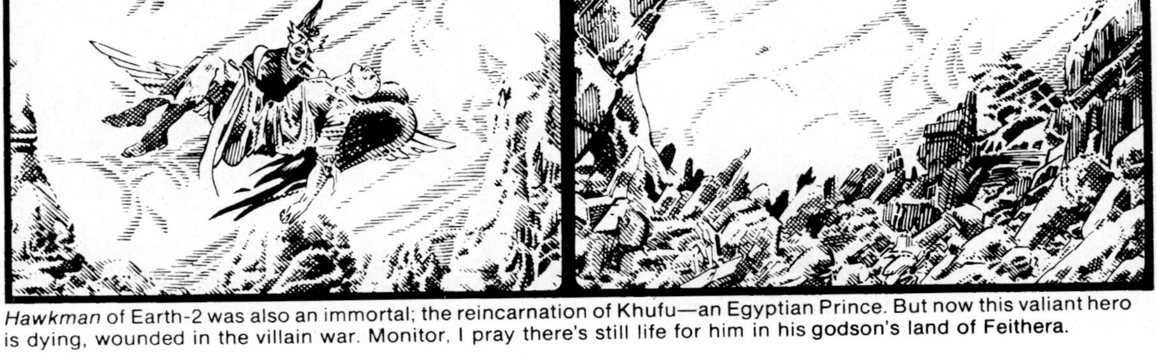

Hawkman of Earth-2 was also an immortal; the reincarnation of Khufu—an Egyptian Prince. But now this valiant hero is dying, wounded in the villain war. Monitor, I pray there's still life for him in his godson's land of Feithera.

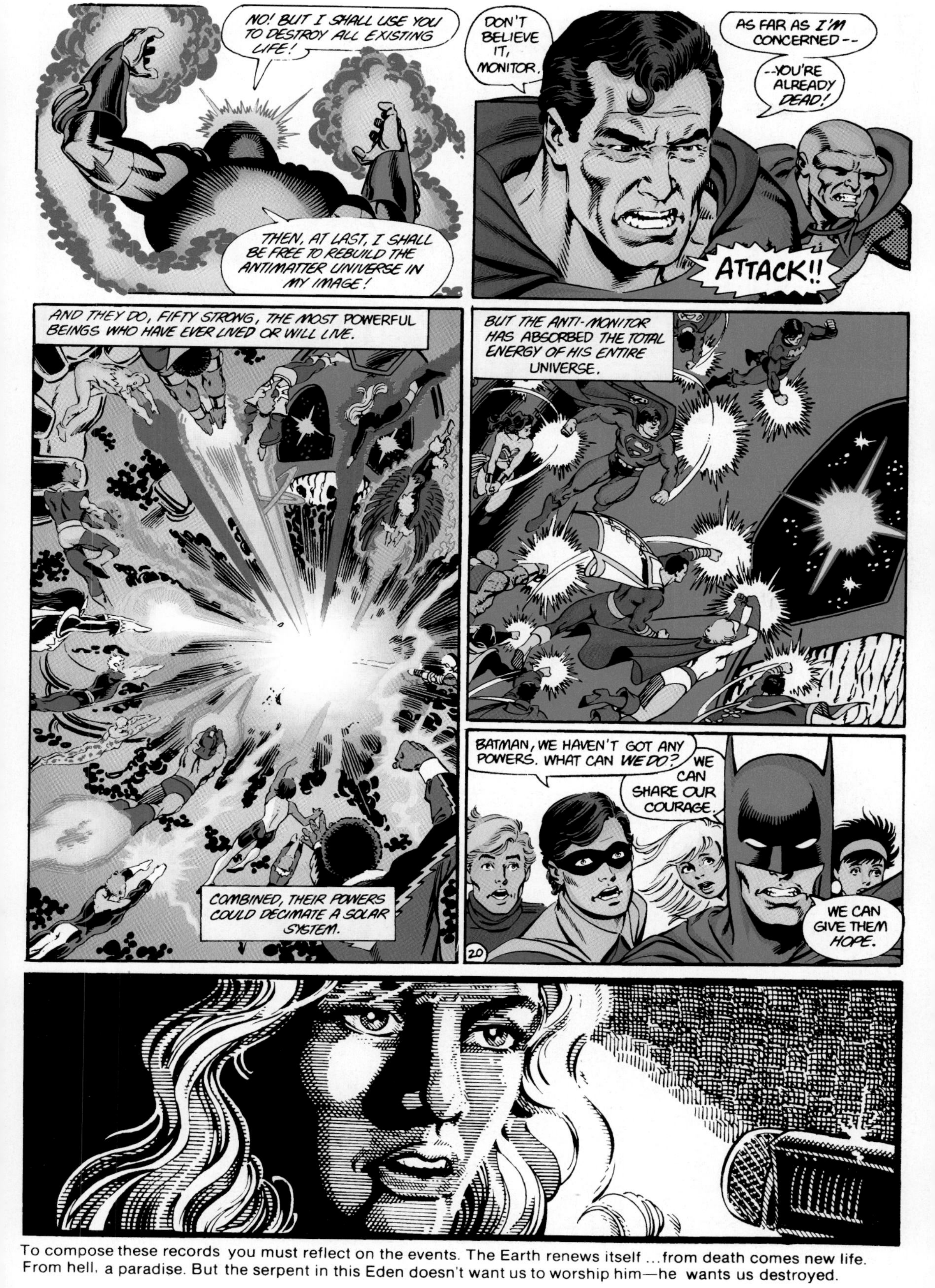
NO! BUT I SHALL USE YOU TO DESTROY ALL EXISTING LIFE!
THEN, AT LAST, I SHALL BE FREE TO REBUILD THE ANTIMATTER UNIVERSE IN MY IMAGE!
DON'T BELIEVE IT, MONITOR.
AS FAR AS I'M CONCERNED --
--YOU'RE ALREADY DEAD!
ATTACK!!
AND THEY DO, FIFTY STRONG, THE MOST POWERFUL BEINGS WHO HAVE EVER LIVED OR WILL LIVE.
COMBINED, THEIR POWERS COULD DECIMATE A SOLAR SYSTEM.
BUT THE ANTI-MONITOR HAS ABSORBED THE TOTAL ENERGY OF HIS ENTIRE UNIVERSE.
BATMAN, WE HAVEN'T GOT ANY POWERS. WHAT CAN WE DO?
WE CAN SHARE OUR COURAGE.
WE CAN GIVE THEM HOPE.
20

To compose these records you must reflect on the events. The Earth renews itself ...from death comes new life. From hell, a paradise. But the serpent in this Eden doesn't want us to worship him—he wants us destroyed.

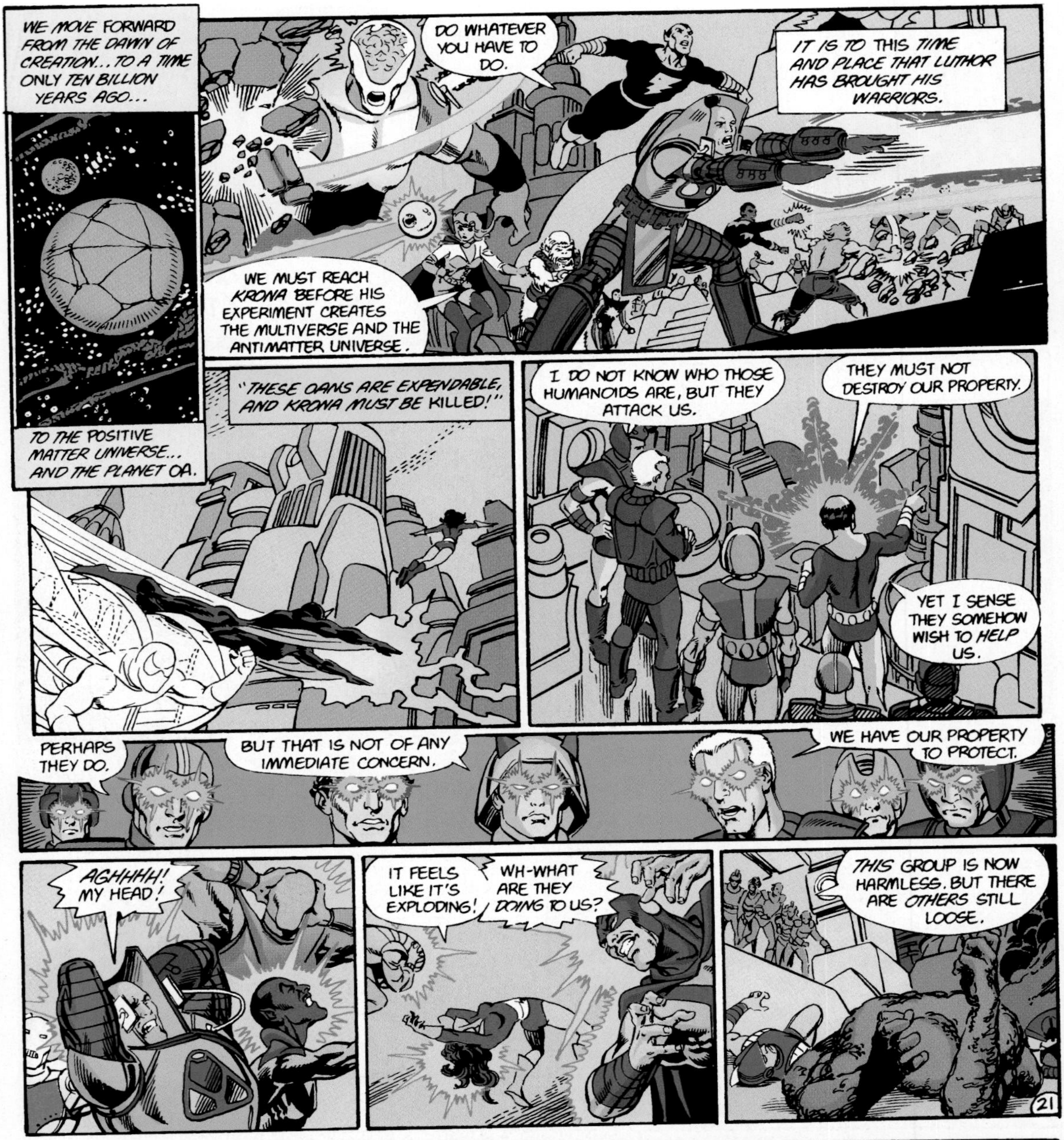
WE MOVE FORWARD FROM THE DAWN OF CREATION... TO A TIME ONLY TEN BILLION YEARS AGO...
DO WHATEVER YOU HAVE TO DO.
IT IS TO THIS TIME AND PLACE THAT LUTHOR HAS BROUGHT HIS WARRIORS.
WE MUST REACH KRONA BEFORE HIS EXPERIMENT CREATES THE MULTIVERSE AND THE ANTIMATTER UNIVERSE.
TO THE POSITIVE MATTER UNIVERSE... AND THE PLANET OA.
"THESE OANS ARE EXPENDABLE, AND KRONA MUST BE KILLED!"
I DO NOT KNOW WHO THOSE HUMANOIDS ARE, BUT THEY ATTACK US.
THEY MUST NOT DESTROY OUR PROPERTY.
YET I SENSE THEY SOMEHOW WISH TO HELP US.
PERHAPS THEY DO.
BUT THAT IS NOT OF ANY IMMEDIATE CONCERN.
WE HAVE OUR PROPERTY TO PROTECT.
AGHHHH! MY HEAD!
IT FEELS LIKE IT'S EXPLODING!
WH-WHAT ARE THEY DOING TO US?
THIS GROUP IS NOW HARMLESS. BUT THERE ARE OTHERS STILL LOOSE.
21

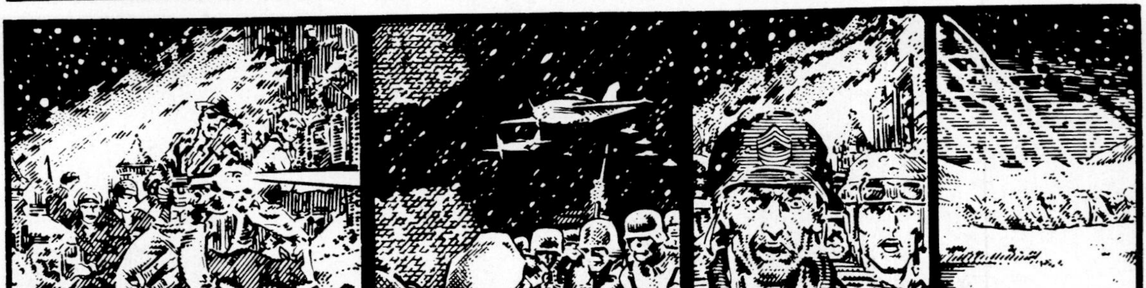

But we refuse to die, don't we...? We struggle for existence ... we race into darkness like *The Losers* did ... not knowing, perhaps never seeing what they fought ... certainly not understanding. Yet they fought for life because they had to.

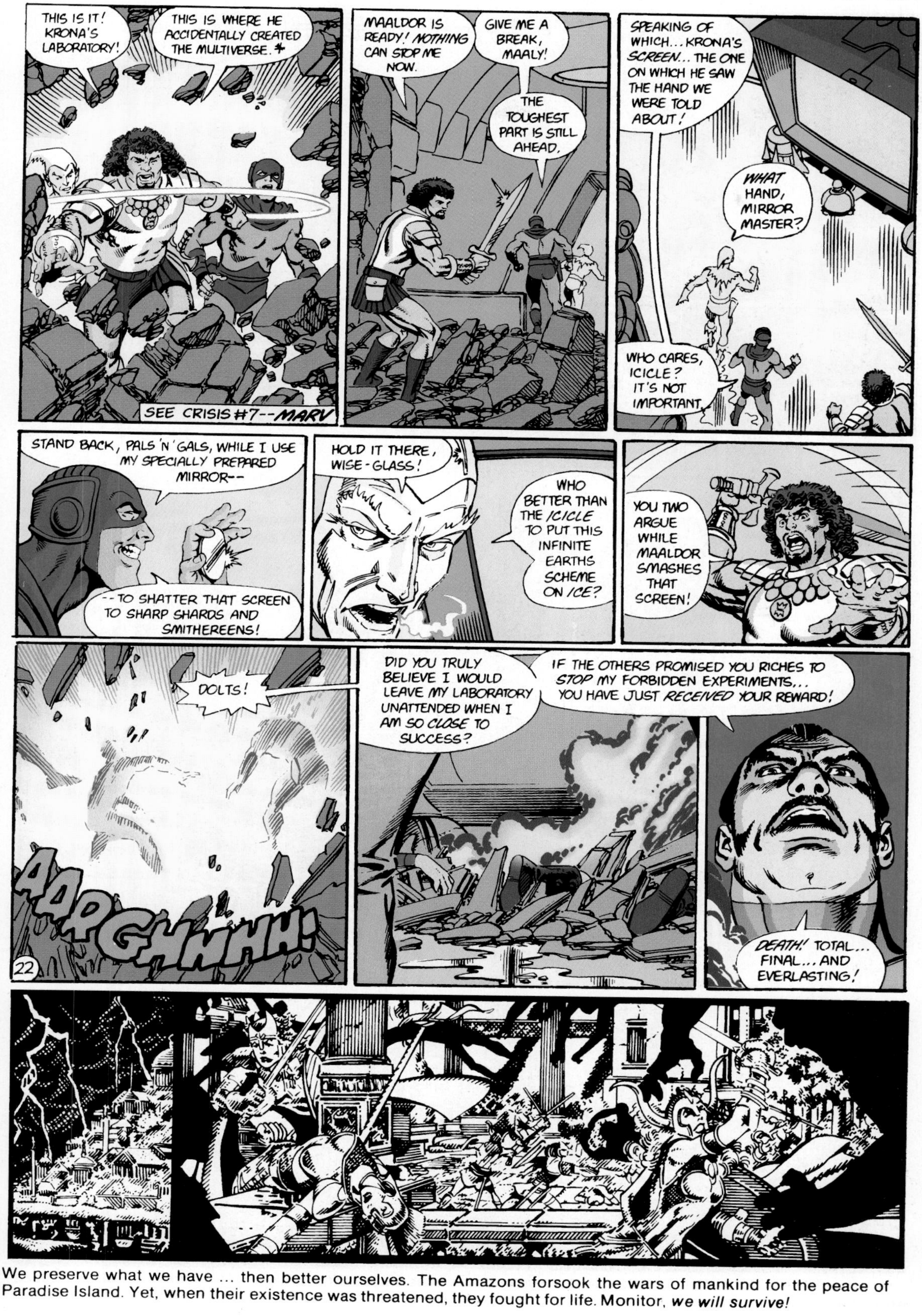
THIS IS IT! KRONA'S LABORATORY!
THIS IS WHERE HE ACCIDENTALLY CREATED THE MULTIVERSE.*
SEE CRISIS #7--MARV
MAALDOR IS READY! NOTHING CAN STOP ME NOW.
GIVE ME A BREAK, MAALY!
THE TOUGHEST PART IS STILL AHEAD.
SPEAKING OF WHICH... KRONA'S SCREEN... THE ONE ON WHICH HE SAW THE HAND WE WERE TOLD ABOUT!
WHAT HAND, MIRROR MASTER?
WHO CARES, ICICLE? IT'S NOT IMPORTANT.
STAND BACK, PALS 'N' GALS, WHILE I USE MY SPECIALLY PREPARED MIRROR--
--TO SHATTER THAT SCREEN TO SHARP SHARDS AND SMITHEREENS!
HOLD IT THERE, WISE-GLASS!
WHO BETTER THAN THE ICICLE TO PUT THIS INFINITE EARTHS SCHEME ON ICE?
YOU TWO ARGUE WHILE MAALDOR SMASHES THAT SCREEN!
DOLTS!
AARGHHHH!
22
DID YOU TRULY BELIEVE I WOULD LEAVE MY LABORATORY UNATTENDED WHEN I AM SO CLOSE TO SUCCESS?
IF THE OTHERS PROMISED YOU RICHES TO STOP MY FORBIDDEN EXPERIMENTS... YOU HAVE JUST RECEIVED YOUR REWARD!
DEATH! TOTAL... FINAL... AND EVERLASTING!

We preserve what we have ... then better ourselves. The Amazons forsook the wars of mankind for the peace of Paradise Island. Yet, when their existence was threatened, they fought for life. Monitor, *we will survive!*

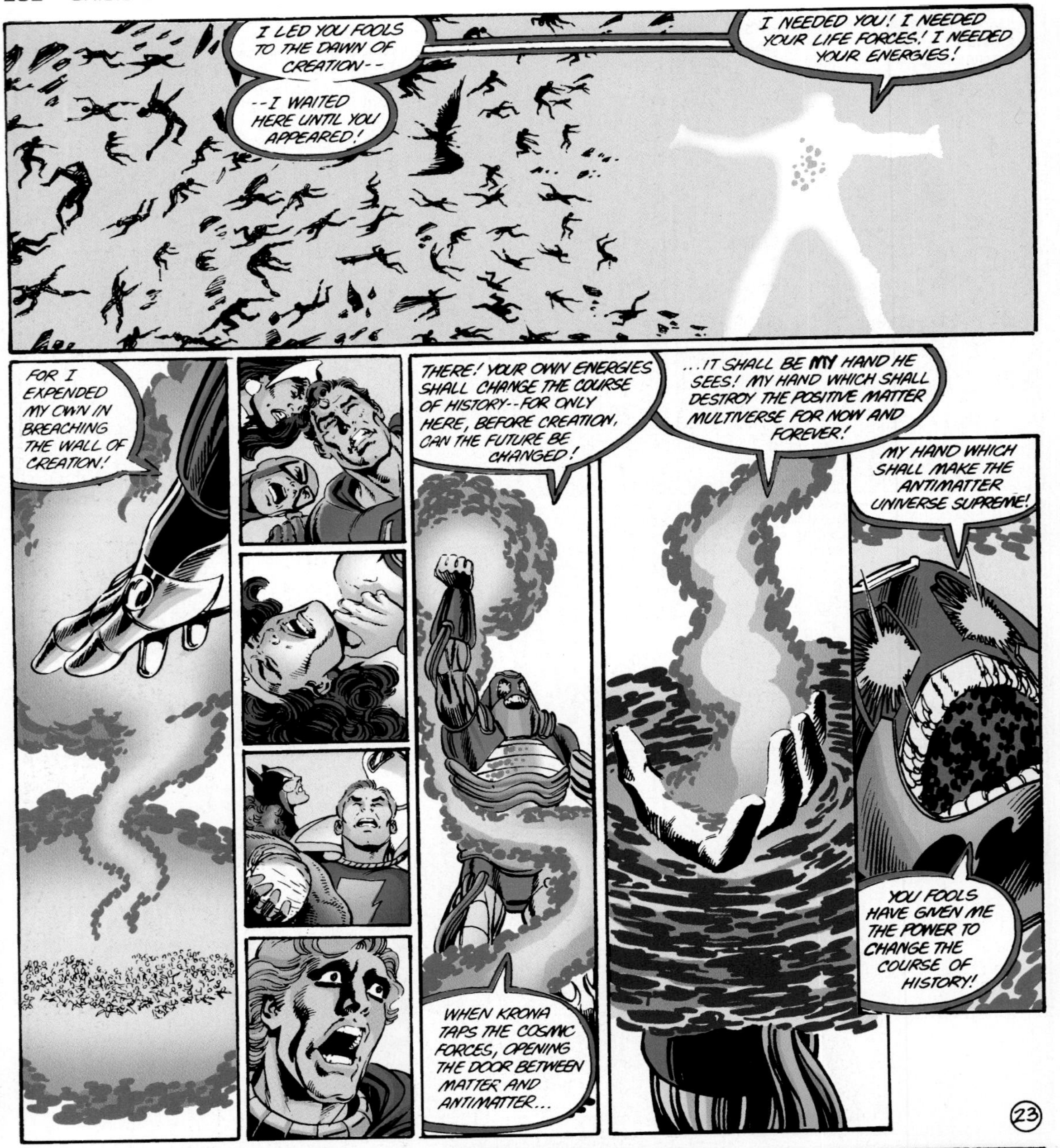
I LED YOU FOOLS TO THE DAWN OF CREATION--
--I WAITED HERE UNTIL YOU APPEARED!
I NEEDED YOU! I NEEDED YOUR LIFE FORCES! I NEEDED YOUR ENERGIES!
FOR I EXPENDED MY OWN IN BREACHING THE WALL OF CREATION!
THERE! YOUR OWN ENERGIES SHALL CHANGE THE COURSE OF HISTORY--FOR ONLY HERE, BEFORE CREATION, CAN THE FUTURE BE CHANGED!
WHEN KRONA TAPS THE COSMIC FORCES, OPENING THE DOOR BETWEEN MATTER AND ANTIMATTER...
...IT SHALL BE MY HAND HE SEES! MY HAND WHICH SHALL DESTROY THE POSITIVE MATTER MULTIVERSE FOR NOW AND FOREVER!
MY HAND WHICH SHALL MAKE THE ANTIMATTER UNIVERSE SUPREME!
YOU FOOLS HAVE GIVEN ME THE POWER TO CHANGE THE COURSE OF HISTORY!
23

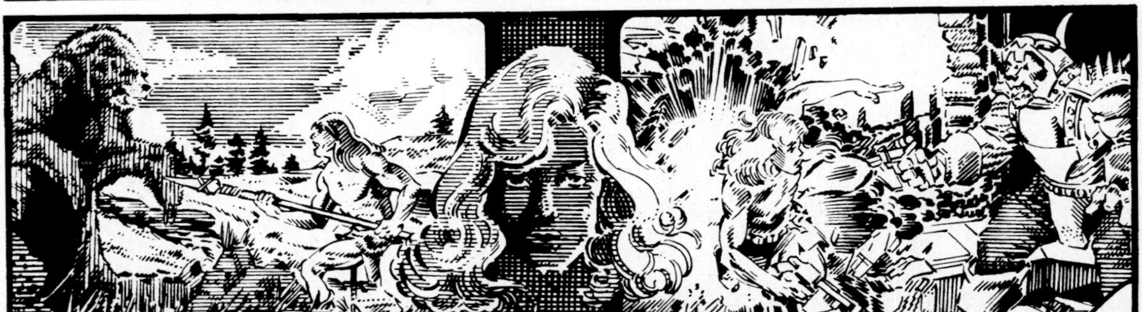

Throughout the history of all worlds, all thinking creatures have fought for survival and freedom—whether in times when they battled with little more than stone, or when their enemies possessed weapons far greater than theirs.

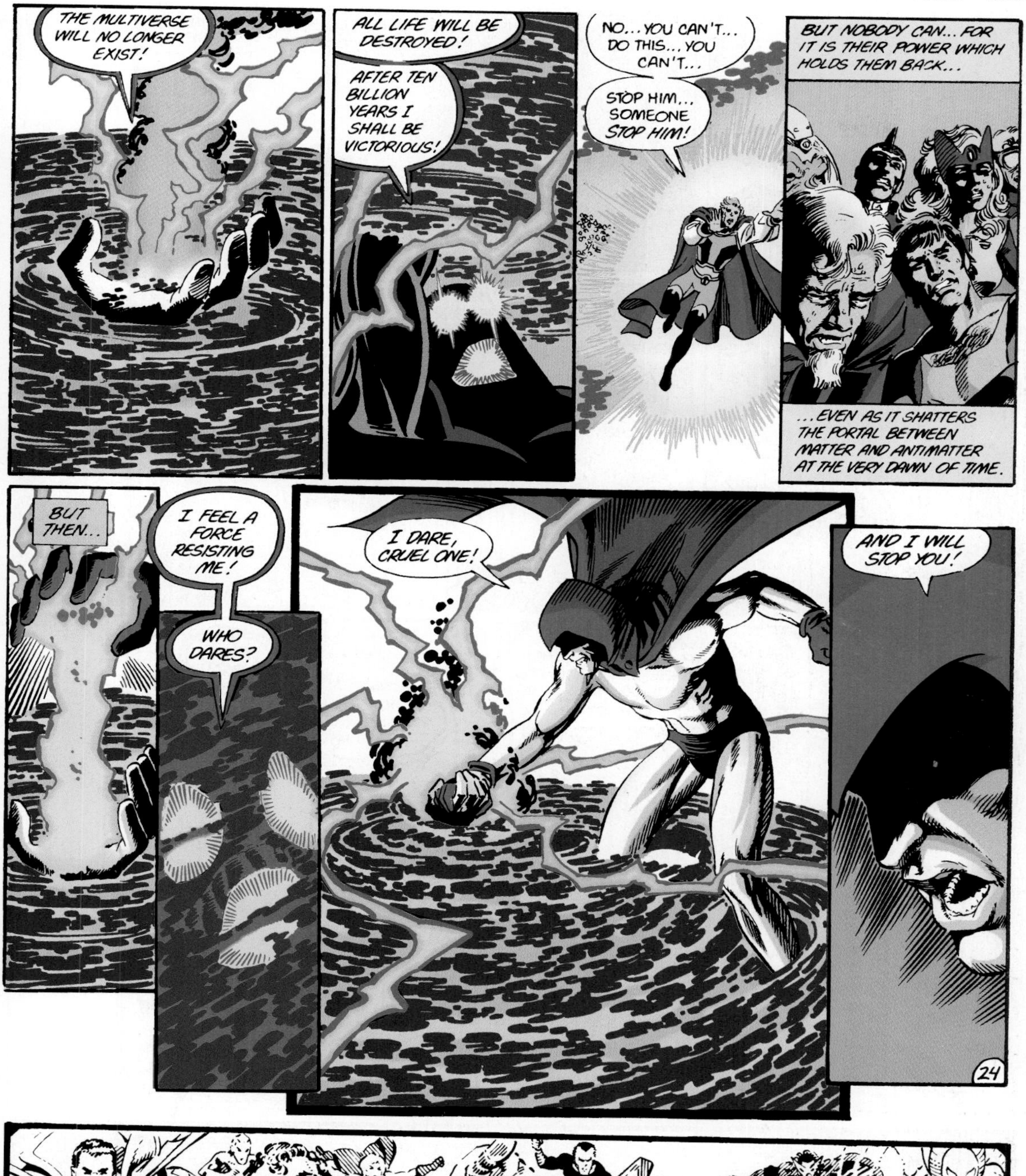
THE MULTIVERSE WILL NO LONGER EXIST!
ALL LIFE WILL BE DESTROYED!
AFTER TEN BILLION YEARS I SHALL BE VICTORIOUS!
NO... YOU CAN'T... DO THIS... YOU CAN'T...
STOP HIM... SOMEONE STOP HIM!
BUT NOBODY CAN... FOR IT IS THEIR POWER WHICH HOLDS THEM BACK...
...EVEN AS IT SHATTERS THE PORTAL BETWEEN MATTER AND ANTIMATTER AT THE VERY DAWN OF TIME.
BUT THEN...
I FEEL A FORCE RESISTING ME!
WHO DARES?
I DARE, CRUEL ONE!
AND I WILL STOP YOU!
24

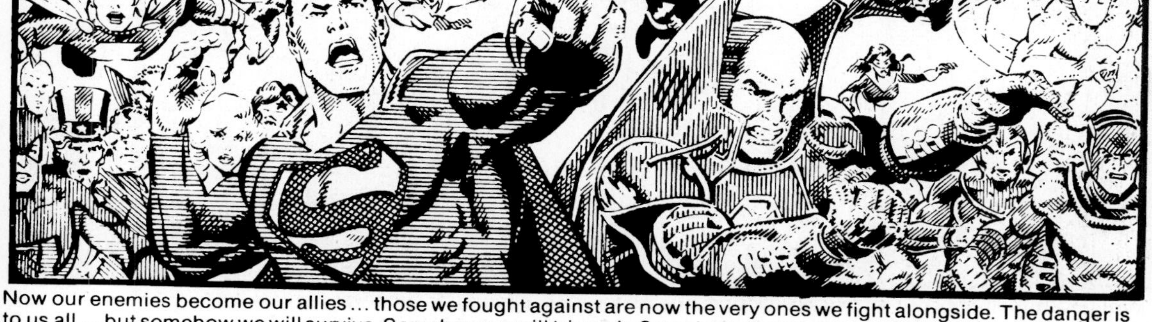

Now our enemies become our allies ... those we fought against are now the very ones we fight alongside. The danger is to us all ... but somehow we will survive. Somehow we will triumph. Somehow we will succeed even in the face of death!

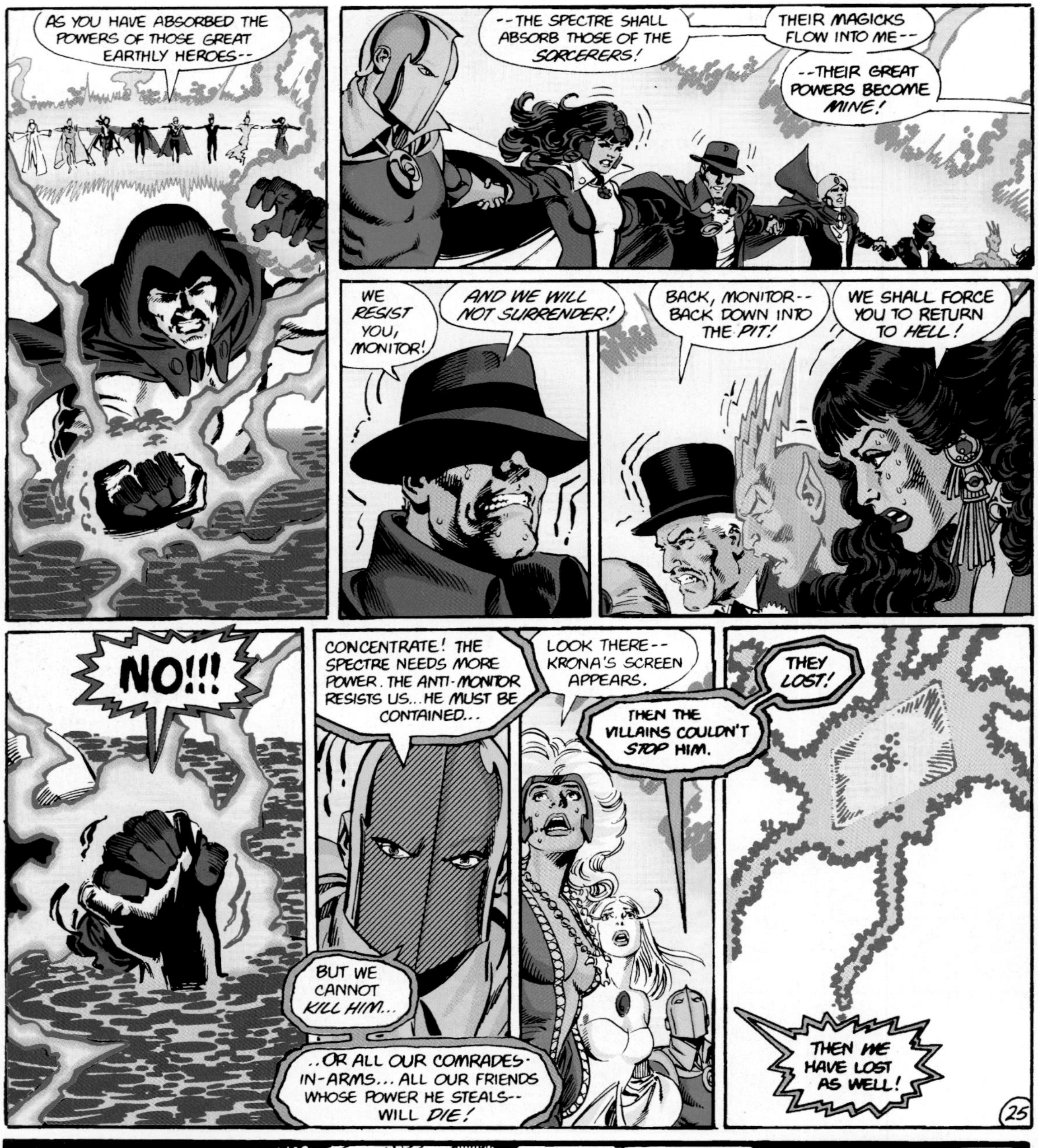
AS YOU HAVE ABSORBED THE POWERS OF THOSE GREAT EARTHLY HEROES--
--THE SPECTRE SHALL ABSORB THOSE OF THE SORCERERS!
THEIR MAGICKS FLOW INTO ME--
--THEIR GREAT POWERS BECOME MINE!
WE RESIST YOU, MONITOR!
AND WE WILL NOT SURRENDER!
BACK, MONITOR-- BACK DOWN INTO THE PIT!
WE SHALL FORCE YOU TO RETURN TO HELL!
NO!!!
CONCENTRATE! THE SPECTRE NEEDS MORE POWER. THE ANTI-MONITOR RESISTS US... HE MUST BE CONTAINED...
LOOK THERE-- KRONA'S SCREEN APPEARS.
THEN THE VILLAINS COULDN'T STOP HIM.
THEY LOST!
BUT WE CANNOT KILL HIM...
..OR ALL OUR COMRADES-IN-ARMS... ALL OUR FRIENDS WHOSE POWER HE STEALS-- WILL DIE!
THEN WE HAVE LOST AS WELL!
25

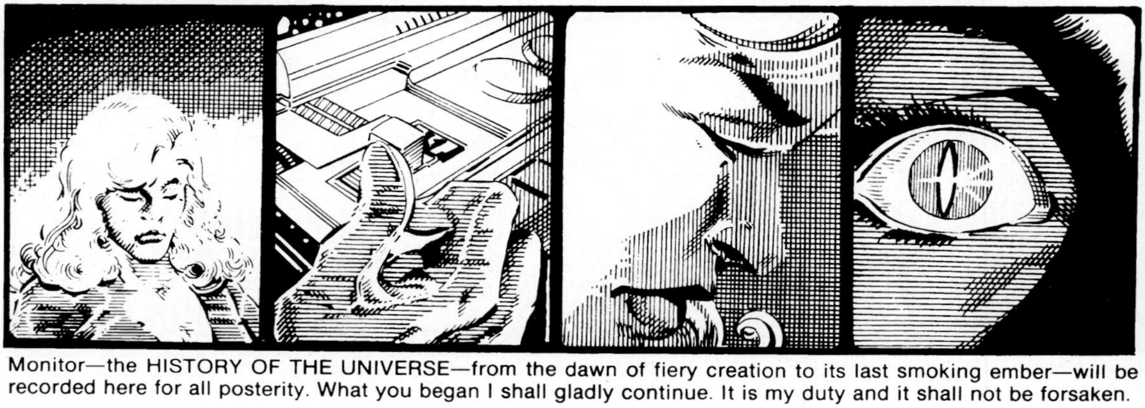
Monitor—the HISTORY OF THE UNIVERSE—from the dawn of fiery creation to its last smoking ember—will be recorded here for all posterity. What you began I shall gladly continue. It is my duty and it shall not be forsaken.

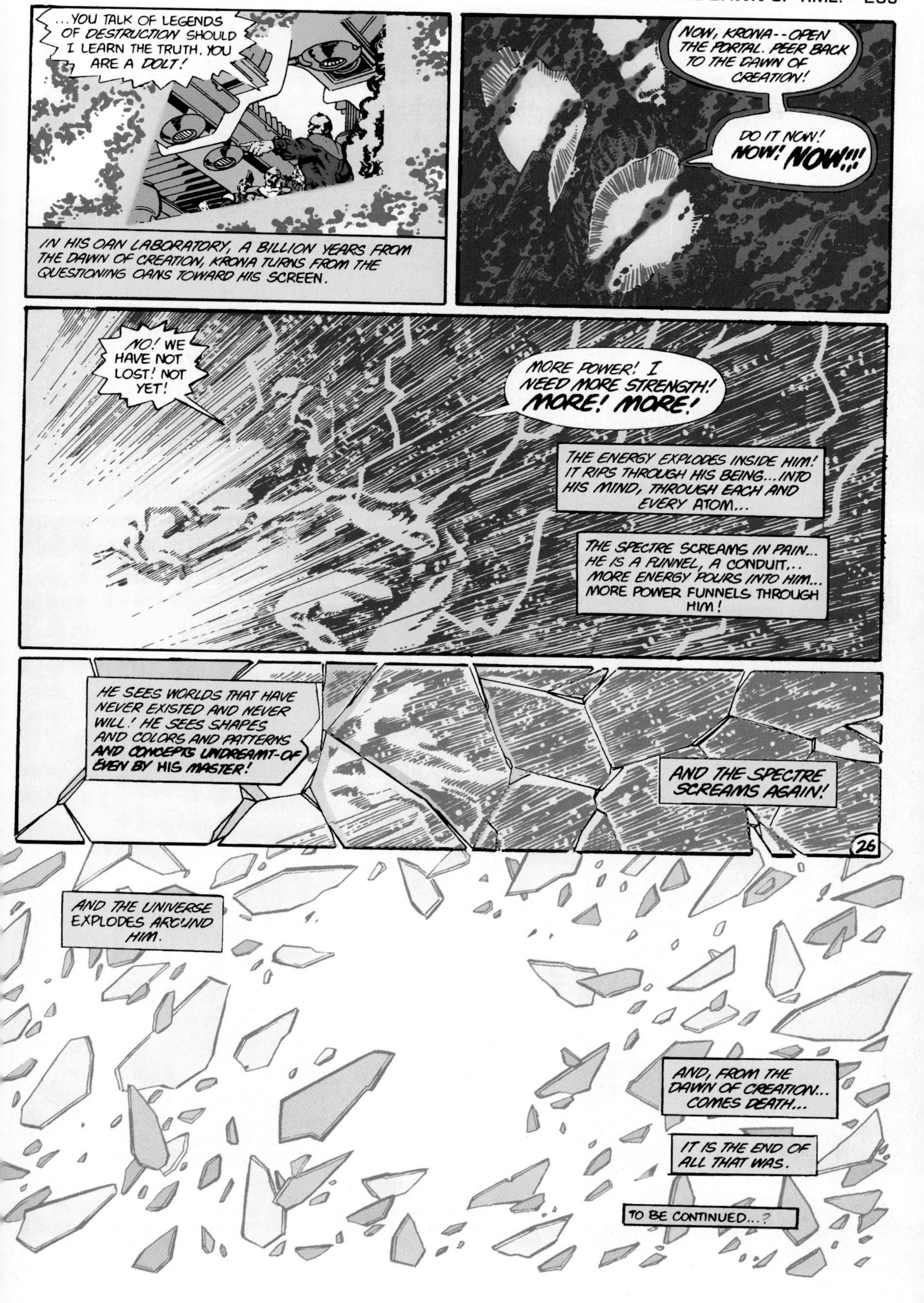
...YOU TALK OF LEGENDS OF DESTRUCTION SHOULD I LEARN THE TRUTH. YOU ARE A DOLT!
IN HIS OAN LABORATORY, A BILLION YEARS FROM THE DAWN OF CREATION, KRONA TURNS FROM THE QUESTIONING OANS TOWARD HIS SCREEN.
NOW, KRONA--OPEN THE PORTAL. PEER BACK TO THE DAWN OF CREATION!
DO IT NOW! NOW! NOW!!!
NO! WE HAVE NOT LOST! NOT YET!
MORE POWER! I NEED MORE STRENGTH! MORE! MORE!
THE ENERGY EXPLODES INSIDE HIM! IT RIPS THROUGH HIS BEING...INTO HIS MIND, THROUGH EACH AND EVERY ATOM...
THE SPECTRE SCREAMS IN PAIN... HE IS A FUNNEL, A CONDUIT,... MORE ENERGY POURS INTO HIM... MORE POWER FUNNELS THROUGH HIM!
HE SEES WORLDS THAT HAVE NEVER EXISTED AND NEVER WILL! HE SEES SHAPES AND COLORS AND PATTERNS AND CONCEPTS UNDREAMT-OF EVEN BY HIS MASTER!
AND THE SPECTRE SCREAMS AGAIN!
26
AND THE UNIVERSE EXPLODES AROUND HIM.
AND, FROM THE DAWN OF CREATION... COMES DEATH...
IT IS THE END OF ALL THAT WAS.
TO BE CONTINUED...?

CRISIS ON INFINITE EARTHS

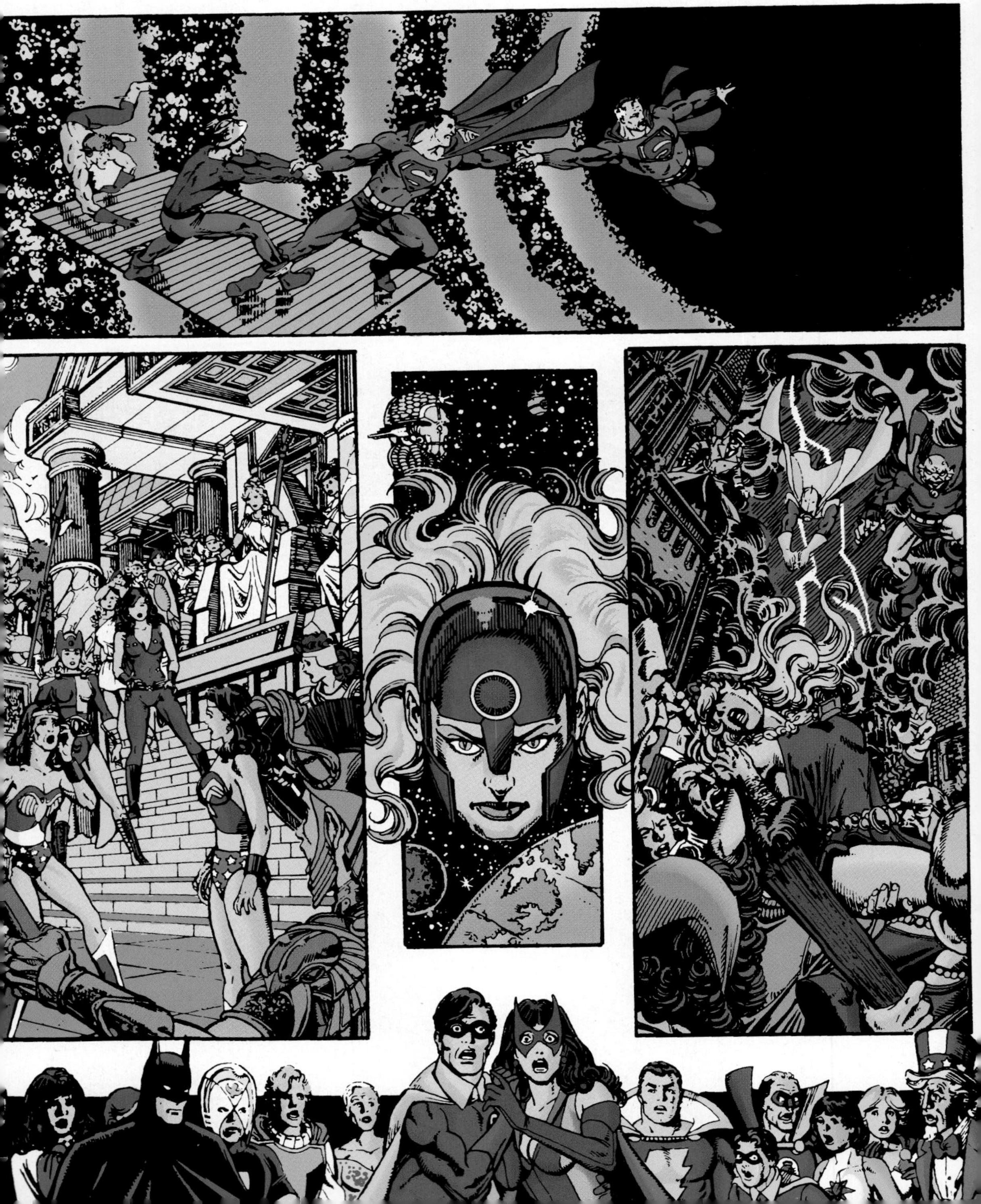

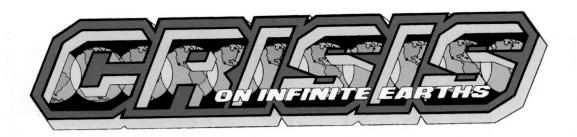

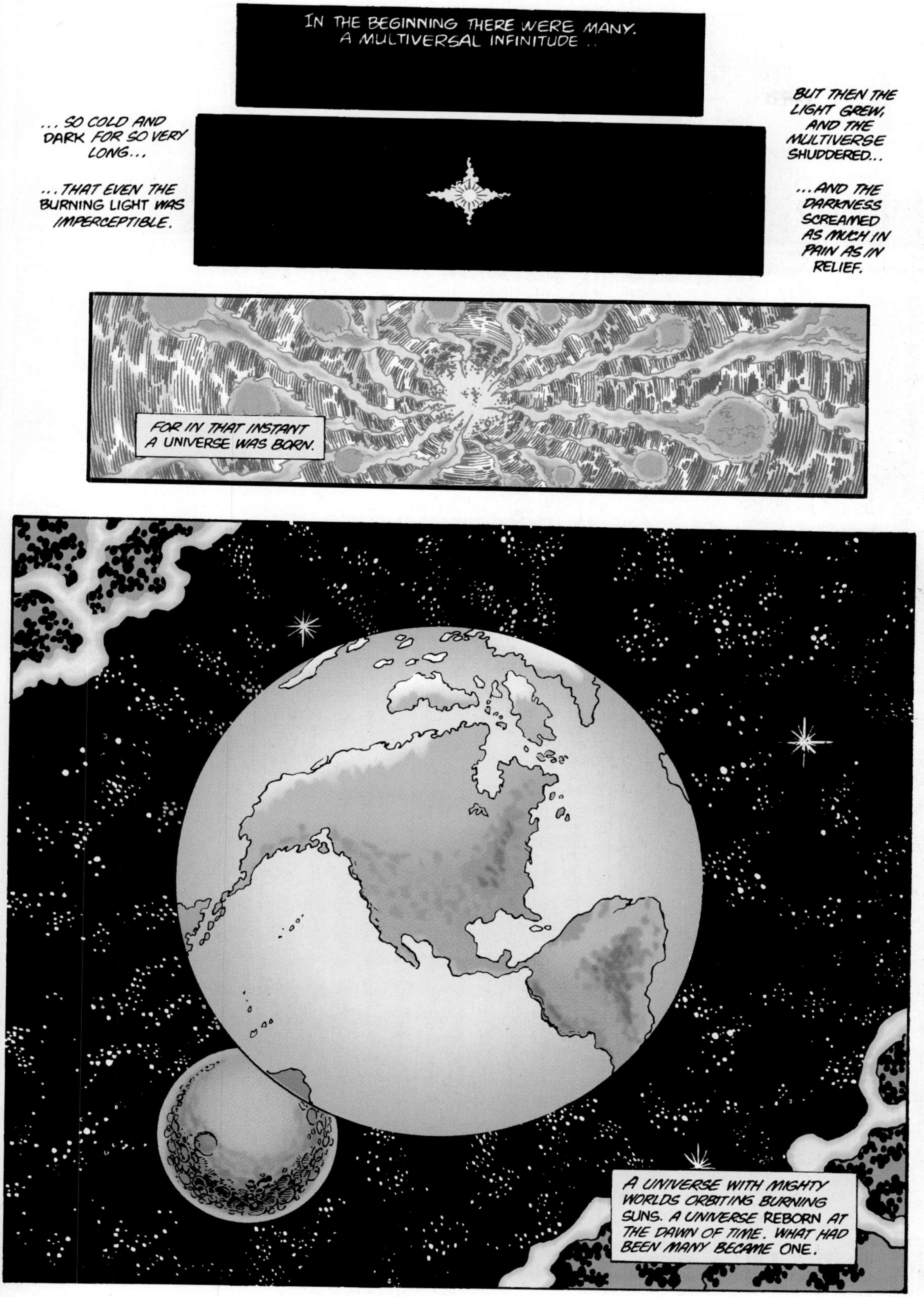
IN THE BEGINNING THERE WERE MANY. A MULTIVERSAL INFINITUDE . .
. . . SO COLD AND DARK FOR SO VERY LONG . . .
. . . THAT EVEN THE BURNING LIGHT WAS IMPERCEPTIBLE.
BUT THEN THE LIGHT GREW, AND THE MULTIVERSE SHUDDERED . . .
. . . AND THE DARKNESS SCREAMED AS MUCH IN PAIN AS IN RELIEF.
FOR IN THAT INSTANT A UNIVERSE WAS BORN.
A UNIVERSE WITH MIGHTY WORLDS ORBITING BURNING SUNS. A UNIVERSE REBORN AT THE DAWN OF TIME. WHAT HAD BEEN MANY BECAME ONE.

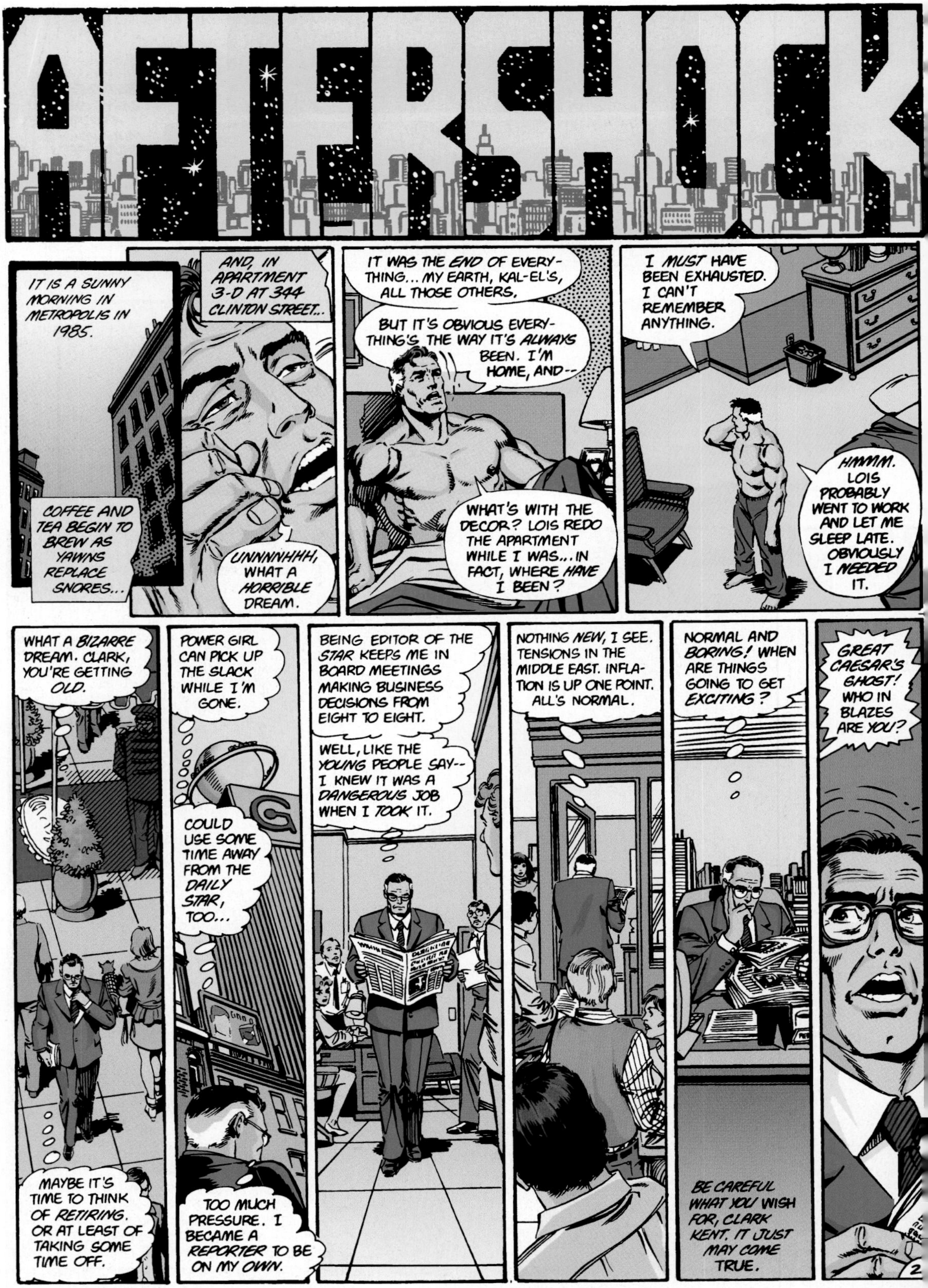
AFTERSHOCK
IT IS A SUNNY MORNING IN METROPOLIS IN 1985.
AND, IN APARTMENT 3-D AT 344 CLINTON STREET...
COFFEE AND TEA BEGIN TO BREW AS YAWNS REPLACE SNORES...
UNNNNHHH, WHAT A HORRIBLE DREAM.
IT WAS THE END OF EVERYTHING... MY EARTH, KAL-EL'S, ALL THOSE OTHERS.
BUT IT'S OBVIOUS EVERYTHING'S THE WAY IT'S ALWAYS BEEN. I'M HOME, AND--
WHAT'S WITH THE DECOR? LOIS REDO THE APARTMENT WHILE I WAS... IN FACT, WHERE HAVE I BEEN?
I MUST HAVE BEEN EXHAUSTED. I CAN'T REMEMBER ANYTHING.
HMMM. LOIS PROBABLY WENT TO WORK AND LET ME SLEEP LATE. OBVIOUSLY I NEEDED IT.
WHAT A BIZARRE DREAM. CLARK, YOU'RE GETTING OLD.
MAYBE IT'S TIME TO THINK OF RETIRING. OR AT LEAST OF TAKING SOME TIME OFF.
POWER GIRL CAN PICK UP THE SLACK WHILE I'M GONE.
COULD USE SOME TIME AWAY FROM THE DAILY STAR, TOO...
TOO MUCH PRESSURE. I BECAME A REPORTER TO BE ON MY OWN.
BEING EDITOR OF THE STAR KEEPS ME IN BOARD MEETINGS MAKING BUSINESS DECISIONS FROM EIGHT TO EIGHT.
WELL, LIKE THE YOUNG PEOPLE SAY-- I KNEW IT WAS A DANGEROUS JOB WHEN I TOOK IT.
NOTHING NEW, I SEE. TENSIONS IN THE MIDDLE EAST. INFLATION IS UP ONE POINT. ALL'S NORMAL.
NORMAL AND BORING! WHEN ARE THINGS GOING TO GET EXCITING?
BE CAREFUL WHAT YOU WISH FOR, CLARK KENT. IT JUST MAY COME TRUE.
GREAT CAESAR'S GHOST! WHO IN BLAZES ARE YOU?
2

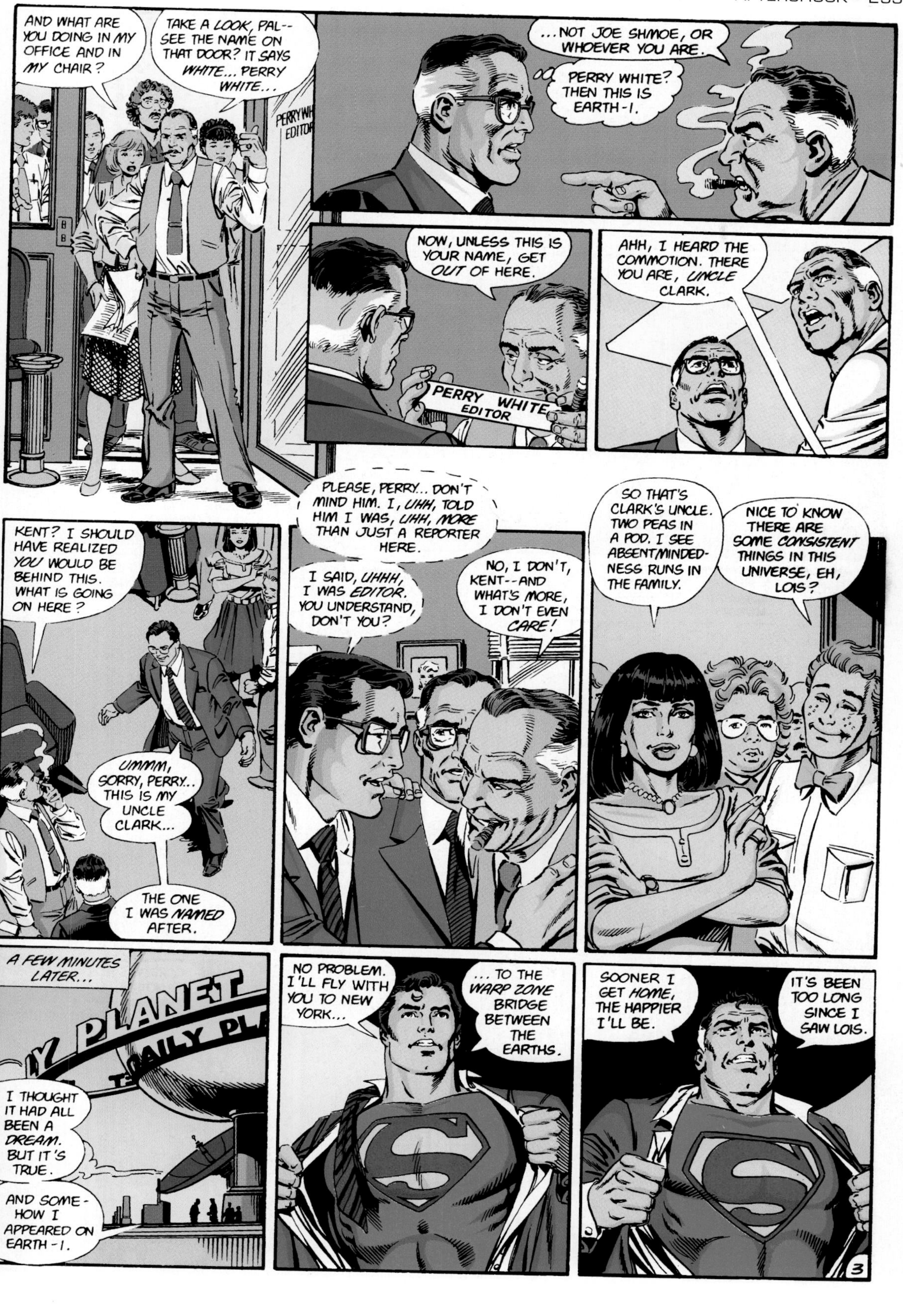
AND WHAT ARE YOU DOING IN MY OFFICE AND IN MY CHAIR?
TAKE A LOOK, PAL-- SEE THE NAME ON THAT DOOR? IT SAYS WHITE... PERRY WHITE...
PERRY WH EDITOR
...NOT JOE SHMOE, OR WHOEVER YOU ARE.
PERRY WHITE? THEN THIS IS EARTH-1.
NOW, UNLESS THIS IS YOUR NAME, GET OUT OF HERE.
PERRY WHITE EDITOR
AHH, I HEARD THE COMMOTION. THERE YOU ARE, UNCLE CLARK.
KENT? I SHOULD HAVE REALIZED YOU WOULD BE BEHIND THIS. WHAT IS GOING ON HERE?
UMMM, SORRY, PERRY... THIS IS MY UNCLE CLARK...
THE ONE I WAS NAMED AFTER.
PLEASE, PERRY... DON'T MIND HIM. I, UHH, TOLD HIM I WAS, UHH, MORE THAN JUST A REPORTER HERE.
I SAID, UHHH, I WAS EDITOR. YOU UNDERSTAND, DON'T YOU?
NO, I DON'T, KENT--AND WHAT'S MORE, I DON'T EVEN CARE!
SO THAT'S CLARK'S UNCLE. TWO PEAS IN A POD. I SEE ABSENTMINDEDNESS RUNS IN THE FAMILY.
NICE TO KNOW THERE ARE SOME CONSISTENT THINGS IN THIS UNIVERSE, EH, LOIS?
A FEW MINUTES LATER...
Y PLANET
DAILY PL
I THOUGHT IT HAD ALL BEEN A DREAM. BUT IT'S TRUE.
AND SOMEHOW I APPEARED ON EARTH-1.
NO PROBLEM. I'LL FLY WITH YOU TO NEW YORK...
...TO THE WARP ZONE BRIDGE BETWEEN THE EARTHS.
SOONER I GET HOME, THE HAPPIER I'LL BE.
IT'S BEEN TOO LONG SINCE I SAW LOIS.
3

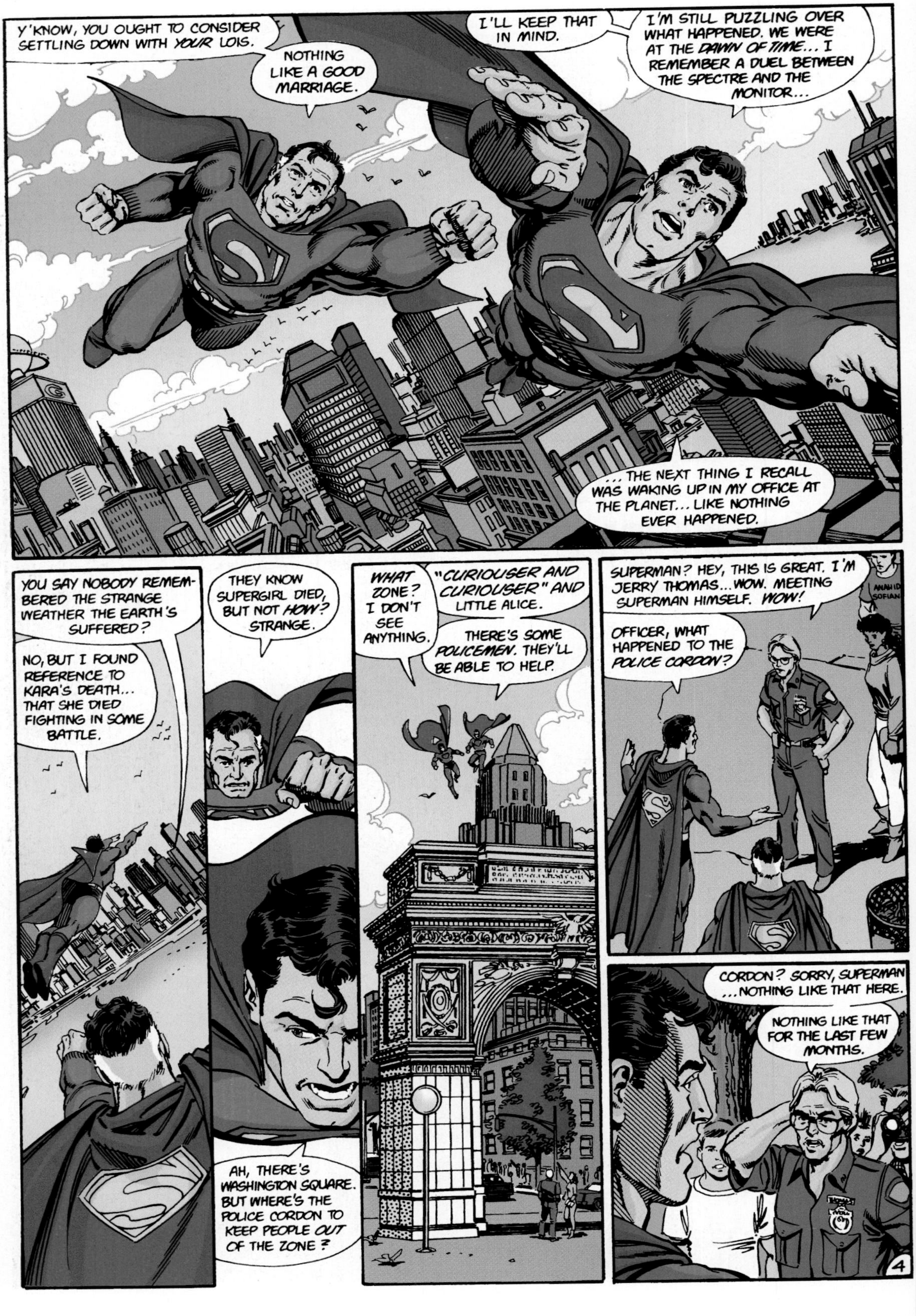
Y'KNOW, YOU OUGHT TO CONSIDER SETTLING DOWN WITH YOUR LOIS.
NOTHING LIKE A GOOD MARRIAGE.
I'LL KEEP THAT IN MIND.
I'M STILL PUZZLING OVER WHAT HAPPENED. WE WERE AT THE DAWN OF TIME... I REMEMBER A DUEL BETWEEN THE SPECTRE AND THE MONITOR...
...THE NEXT THING I RECALL WAS WAKING UP IN MY OFFICE AT THE PLANET... LIKE NOTHING EVER HAPPENED.
YOU SAY NOBODY REMEMBERED THE STRANGE WEATHER THE EARTH'S SUFFERED?
NO, BUT I FOUND REFERENCE TO KARA'S DEATH... THAT SHE DIED FIGHTING IN SOME BATTLE.
THEY KNOW SUPERGIRL DIED, BUT NOT HOW? STRANGE.
AH, THERE'S WASHINGTON SQUARE. BUT WHERE'S THE POLICE CORDON TO KEEP PEOPLE OUT OF THE ZONE?
WHAT ZONE? I DON'T SEE ANYTHING.
"CURIOUSER AND CURIOUSER" AND LITTLE ALICE.
THERE'S SOME POLICEMEN. THEY'LL BE ABLE TO HELP.
SUPERMAN? HEY, THIS IS GREAT. I'M JERRY THOMAS... WOW. MEETING SUPERMAN HIMSELF. WOW!
OFFICER, WHAT HAPPENED TO THE POLICE CORDON?
CORDON? SORRY, SUPERMAN ...NOTHING LIKE THAT HERE.
NOTHING LIKE THAT FOR THE LAST FEW MONTHS.
4

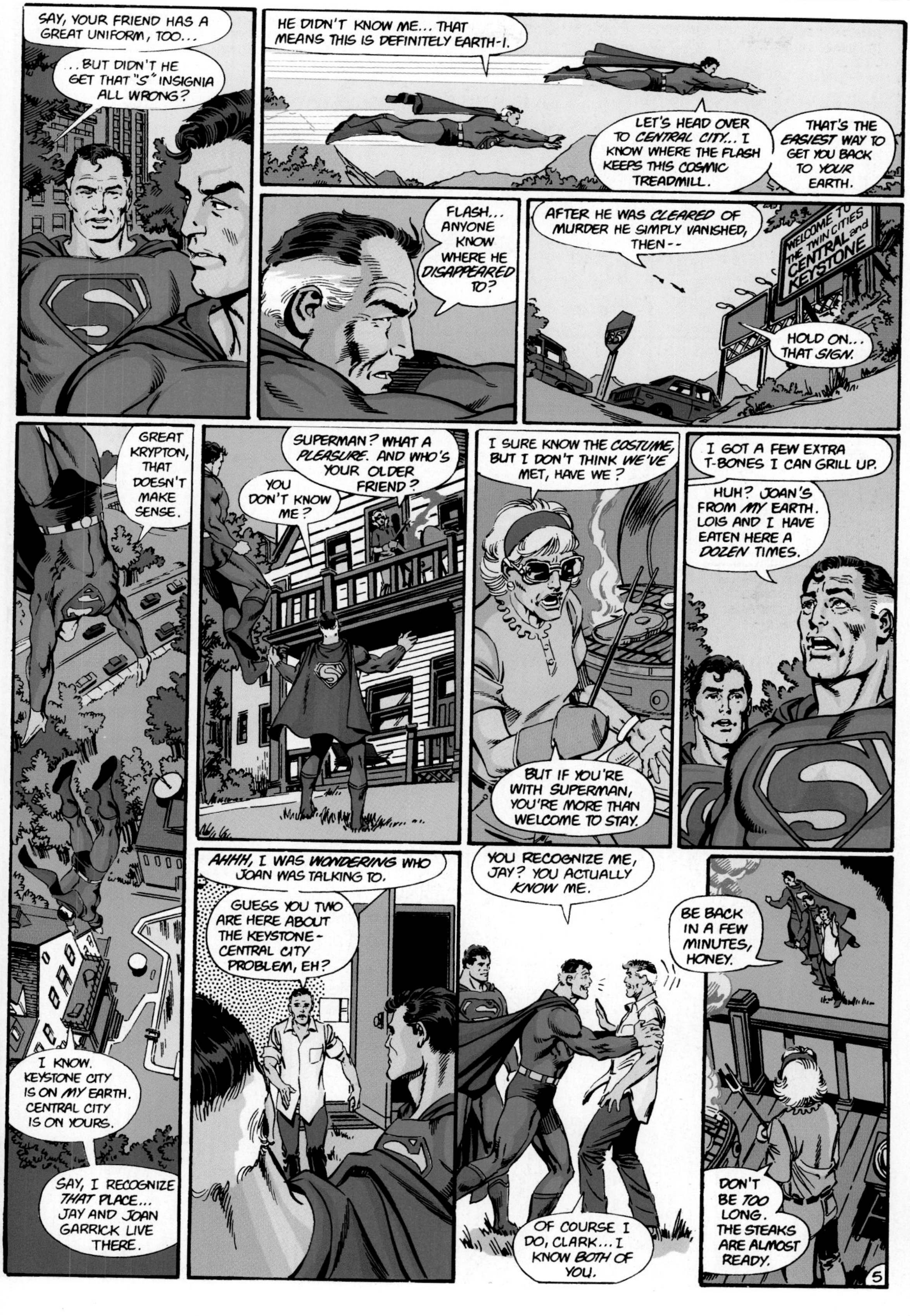
SAY, YOUR FRIEND HAS A GREAT UNIFORM, TOO...
...BUT DIDN'T HE GET THAT "S" INSIGNIA ALL WRONG?
HE DIDN'T KNOW ME... THAT MEANS THIS IS DEFINITELY EARTH-1.
LET'S HEAD OVER TO CENTRAL CITY... I KNOW WHERE THE FLASH KEEPS THIS COSMIC TREADMILL.
THAT'S THE EASIEST WAY TO GET YOU BACK TO YOUR EARTH.
FLASH... ANYONE KNOW WHERE HE DISAPPEARED TO?
AFTER HE WAS CLEARED OF MURDER HE SIMPLY VANISHED, THEN--
WELCOME TO THE TWIN CITIES CENTRAL and KEYSTONE
HOLD ON... THAT SIGN.
GREAT KRYPTON, THAT DOESN'T MAKE SENSE.
I KNOW. KEYSTONE CITY IS ON MY EARTH. CENTRAL CITY IS ON YOURS.
SAY, I RECOGNIZE THAT PLACE... JAY AND JOAN GARRICK LIVE THERE.
SUPERMAN? WHAT A PLEASURE. AND WHO'S YOUR OLDER FRIEND?
YOU DON'T KNOW ME?
I SURE KNOW THE COSTUME, BUT I DON'T THINK WE'VE MET, HAVE WE?
BUT IF YOU'RE WITH SUPERMAN, YOU'RE MORE THAN WELCOME TO STAY.
I GOT A FEW EXTRA T-BONES I CAN GRILL UP.
HUH? JOAN'S FROM MY EARTH. LOIS AND I HAVE EATEN HERE A DOZEN TIMES.
AHHH, I WAS WONDERING WHO JOAN WAS TALKING TO.
GUESS YOU TWO ARE HERE ABOUT THE KEYSTONE-CENTRAL CITY PROBLEM, EH?
YOU RECOGNIZE ME, JAY? YOU ACTUALLY KNOW ME.
OF COURSE I DO, CLARK... I KNOW BOTH OF YOU.
BE BACK IN A FEW MINUTES, HONEY.
DON'T BE TOO LONG. THE STEAKS ARE ALMOST READY.
5

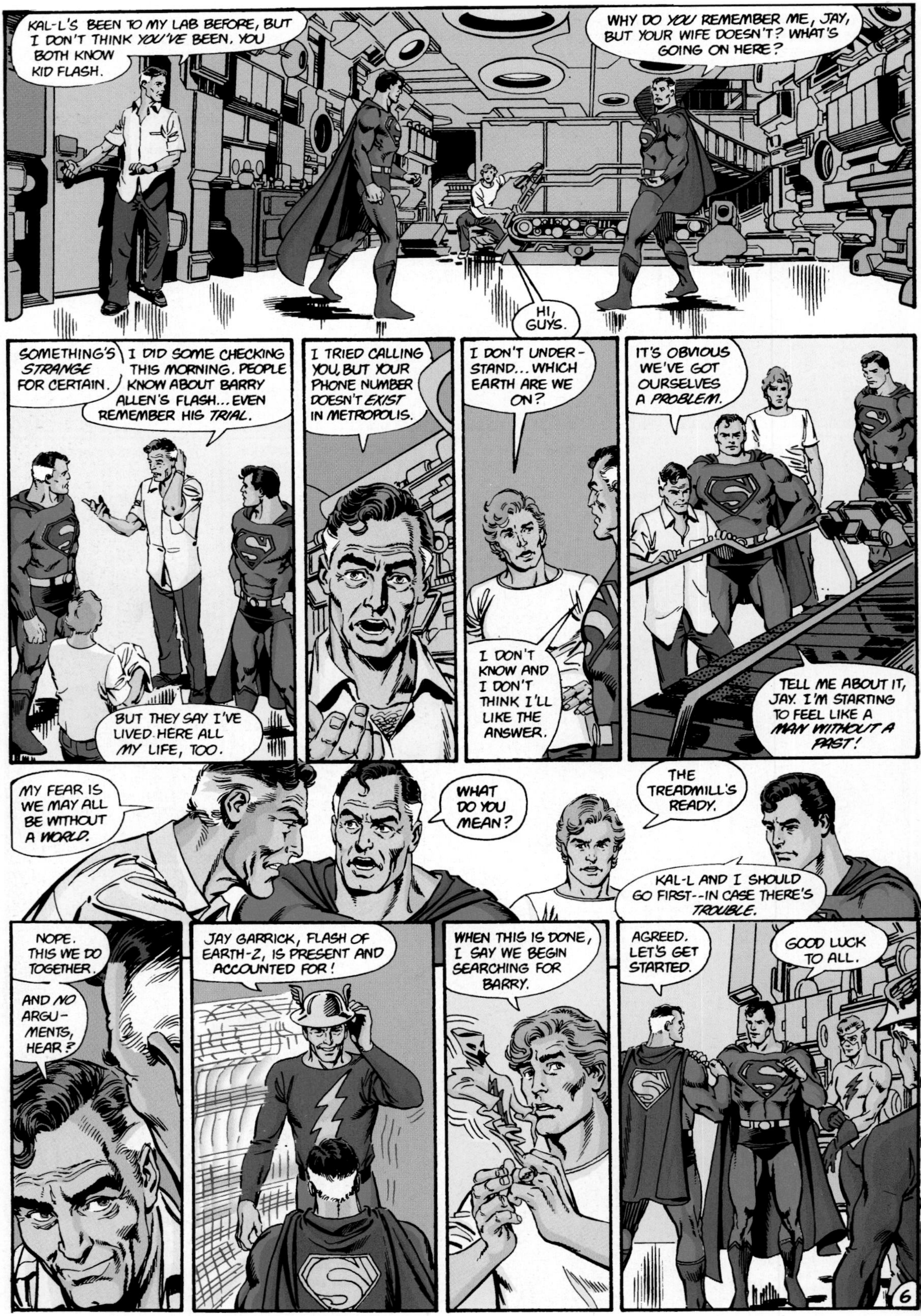

KAL-L'S BEEN TO MY LAB BEFORE, BUT I DON'T THINK YOU'VE BEEN. YOU BOTH KNOW KID FLASH.
WHY DO YOU REMEMBER ME, JAY, BUT YOUR WIFE DOESN'T? WHAT'S GOING ON HERE?
HI, GUYS.
SOMETHING'S STRANGE FOR CERTAIN.
I DID SOME CHECKING THIS MORNING. PEOPLE KNOW ABOUT BARRY ALLEN'S FLASH... EVEN REMEMBER HIS TRIAL.
BUT THEY SAY I'VE LIVED HERE ALL MY LIFE, TOO.
I TRIED CALLING YOU, BUT YOUR PHONE NUMBER DOESN'T EXIST IN METROPOLIS.
I DON'T UNDERSTAND... WHICH EARTH ARE WE ON?
I DON'T KNOW AND I DON'T THINK I'LL LIKE THE ANSWER.
IT'S OBVIOUS WE'VE GOT OURSELVES A PROBLEM.
TELL ME ABOUT IT, JAY. I'M STARTING TO FEEL LIKE A MAN WITHOUT A PAST!
MY FEAR IS WE MAY ALL BE WITHOUT A WORLD.
WHAT DO YOU MEAN?
THE TREADMILL'S READY.
KAL-L AND I SHOULD GO FIRST--IN CASE THERE'S TROUBLE.
NOPE. THIS WE DO TOGETHER.
AND NO ARGUMENTS, HEAR?
JAY GARRICK, FLASH OF EARTH-2, IS PRESENT AND ACCOUNTED FOR!
WHEN THIS IS DONE, I SAY WE BEGIN SEARCHING FOR BARRY.
AGREED. LET'S GET STARTED.
GOOD LUCK TO ALL.
6

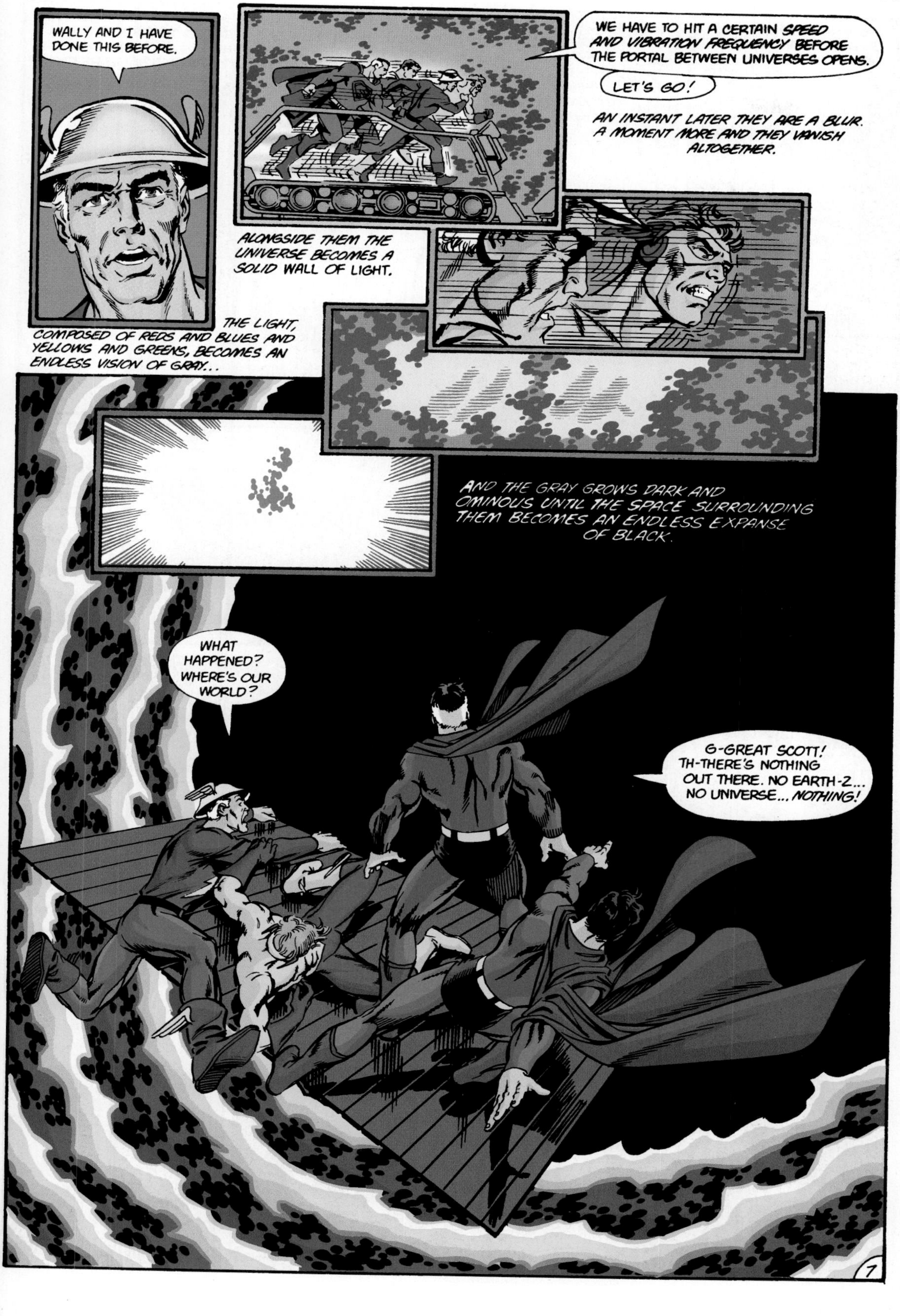
WALLY AND I HAVE DONE THIS BEFORE.
WE HAVE TO HIT A CERTAIN SPEED AND VIBRATION FREQUENCY BEFORE THE PORTAL BETWEEN UNIVERSES OPENS.
LET'S GO!
AN INSTANT LATER THEY ARE A BLUR. A MOMENT MORE AND THEY VANISH ALTOGETHER.
ALONGSIDE THEM THE UNIVERSE BECOMES A SOLID WALL OF LIGHT.
THE LIGHT, COMPOSED OF REDS AND BLUES AND YELLOWS AND GREENS, BECOMES AN ENDLESS VISION OF GRAY...
AND THE GRAY GROWS DARK AND OMINOUS UNTIL THE SPACE SURROUNDING THEM BECOMES AN ENDLESS EXPANSE OF BLACK.
WHAT HAPPENED? WHERE'S OUR WORLD?
G-GREAT SCOTT! TH-THERE'S NOTHING OUT THERE. NO EARTH-2... NO UNIVERSE... NOTHING!
7

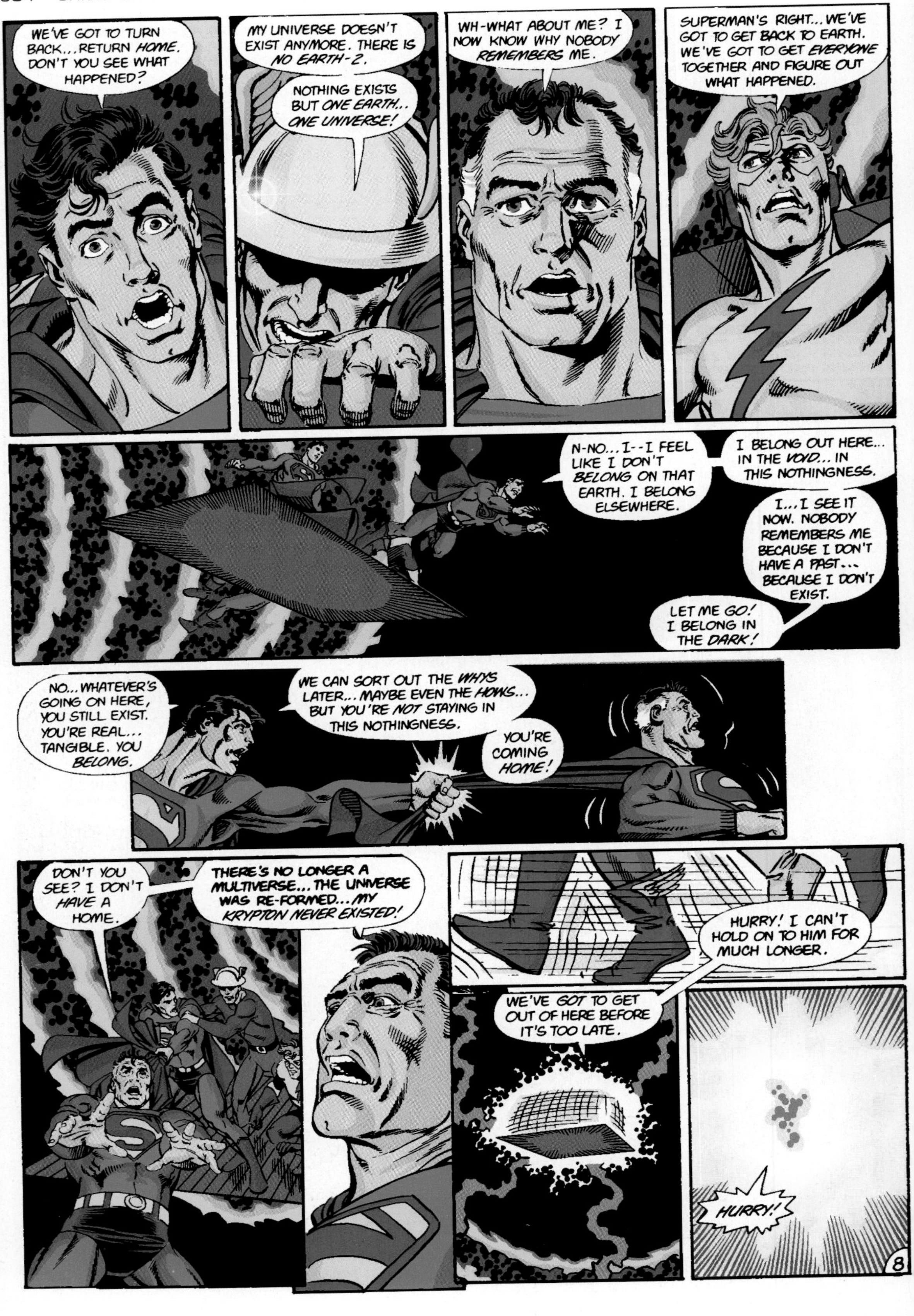
WE'VE GOT TO TURN BACK... RETURN HOME. DON'T YOU SEE WHAT HAPPENED?
MY UNIVERSE DOESN'T EXIST ANYMORE. THERE IS NO EARTH-2.
NOTHING EXISTS BUT ONE EARTH... ONE UNIVERSE!
WH-WHAT ABOUT ME? I NOW KNOW WHY NOBODY REMEMBERS ME.
SUPERMAN'S RIGHT... WE'VE GOT TO GET BACK TO EARTH. WE'VE GOT TO GET EVERYONE TOGETHER AND FIGURE OUT WHAT HAPPENED.
N-NO... I--I FEEL LIKE I DON'T BELONG ON THAT EARTH. I BELONG ELSEWHERE.
I BELONG OUT HERE... IN THE VOID... IN THIS NOTHINGNESS.
I... I SEE IT NOW. NOBODY REMEMBERS ME BECAUSE I DON'T HAVE A PAST... BECAUSE I DON'T EXIST.
LET ME GO! I BELONG IN THE DARK!
NO... WHATEVER'S GOING ON HERE, YOU STILL EXIST. YOU'RE REAL... TANGIBLE. YOU BELONG.
WE CAN SORT OUT THE WHYS LATER... MAYBE EVEN THE HOWS... BUT YOU'RE NOT STAYING IN THIS NOTHINGNESS.
YOU'RE COMING HOME!
DON'T YOU SEE? I DON'T HAVE A HOME.
THERE'S NO LONGER A MULTIVERSE... THE UNIVERSE WAS RE-FORMED... MY KRYPTON NEVER EXISTED!
HURRY! I CAN'T HOLD ON TO HIM FOR MUCH LONGER.
WE'VE GOT TO GET OUT OF HERE BEFORE IT'S TOO LATE.
HURRY!
8

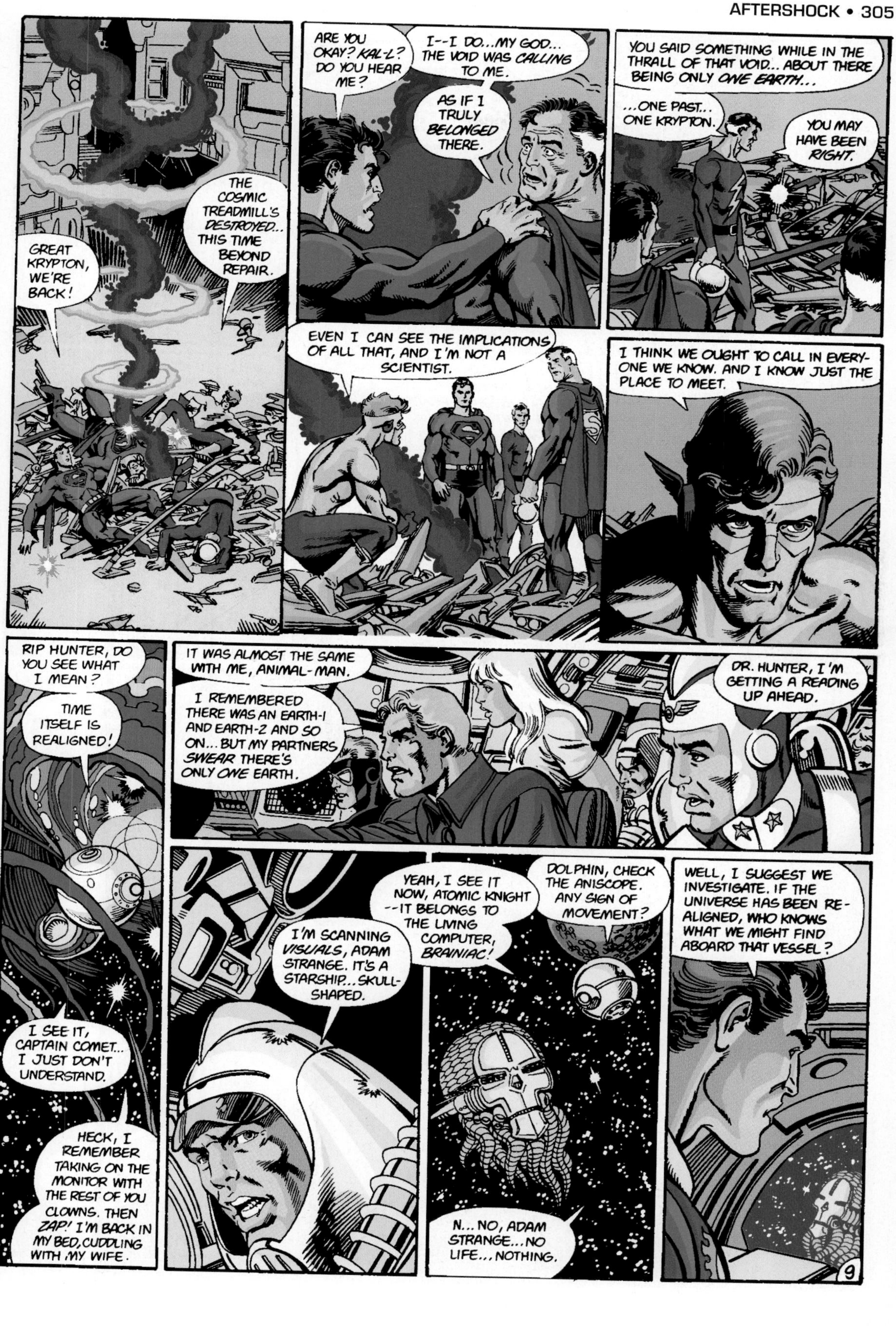
THE COSMIC TREADMILL'S DESTROYED... THIS TIME BEYOND REPAIR.
GREAT KRYPTON, WE'RE BACK!
ARE YOU OKAY? KAL-L? DO YOU HEAR ME?
I--I DO...MY GOD... THE VOID WAS CALLING TO ME.
AS IF I TRULY BELONGED THERE.
YOU SAID SOMETHING WHILE IN THE THRALL OF THAT VOID... ABOUT THERE BEING ONLY ONE EARTH...
...ONE PAST... ONE KRYPTON.
YOU MAY HAVE BEEN RIGHT.
EVEN I CAN SEE THE IMPLICATIONS OF ALL THAT, AND I'M NOT A SCIENTIST.
I THINK WE OUGHT TO CALL IN EVERY-ONE WE KNOW. AND I KNOW JUST THE PLACE TO MEET.
RIP HUNTER, DO YOU SEE WHAT I MEAN?
TIME ITSELF IS REALIGNED!
I SEE IT, CAPTAIN COMET... I JUST DON'T UNDERSTAND.
HECK, I REMEMBER TAKING ON THE MONITOR WITH THE REST OF YOU CLOWNS. THEN ZAP! I'M BACK IN MY BED, CUDDLING WITH MY WIFE.
IT WAS ALMOST THE SAME WITH ME, ANIMAL-MAN.
I REMEMBERED THERE WAS AN EARTH-1 AND EARTH-2 AND SO ON... BUT MY PARTNERS SWEAR THERE'S ONLY ONE EARTH.
DR. HUNTER, I'M GETTING A READING UP AHEAD.
I'M SCANNING VISUALS, ADAM STRANGE. IT'S A STARSHIP... SKULL-SHAPED.
YEAH, I SEE IT NOW, ATOMIC KNIGHT --IT BELONGS TO THE LIVING COMPUTER, BRAINIAC!
DOLPHIN, CHECK THE ANISCOPE. ANY SIGN OF MOVEMENT?
N...NO, ADAM STRANGE...NO LIFE... NOTHING.
WELL, I SUGGEST WE INVESTIGATE. IF THE UNIVERSE HAS BEEN RE-ALIGNED, WHO KNOWS WHAT WE MIGHT FIND ABOARD THAT VESSEL?
9

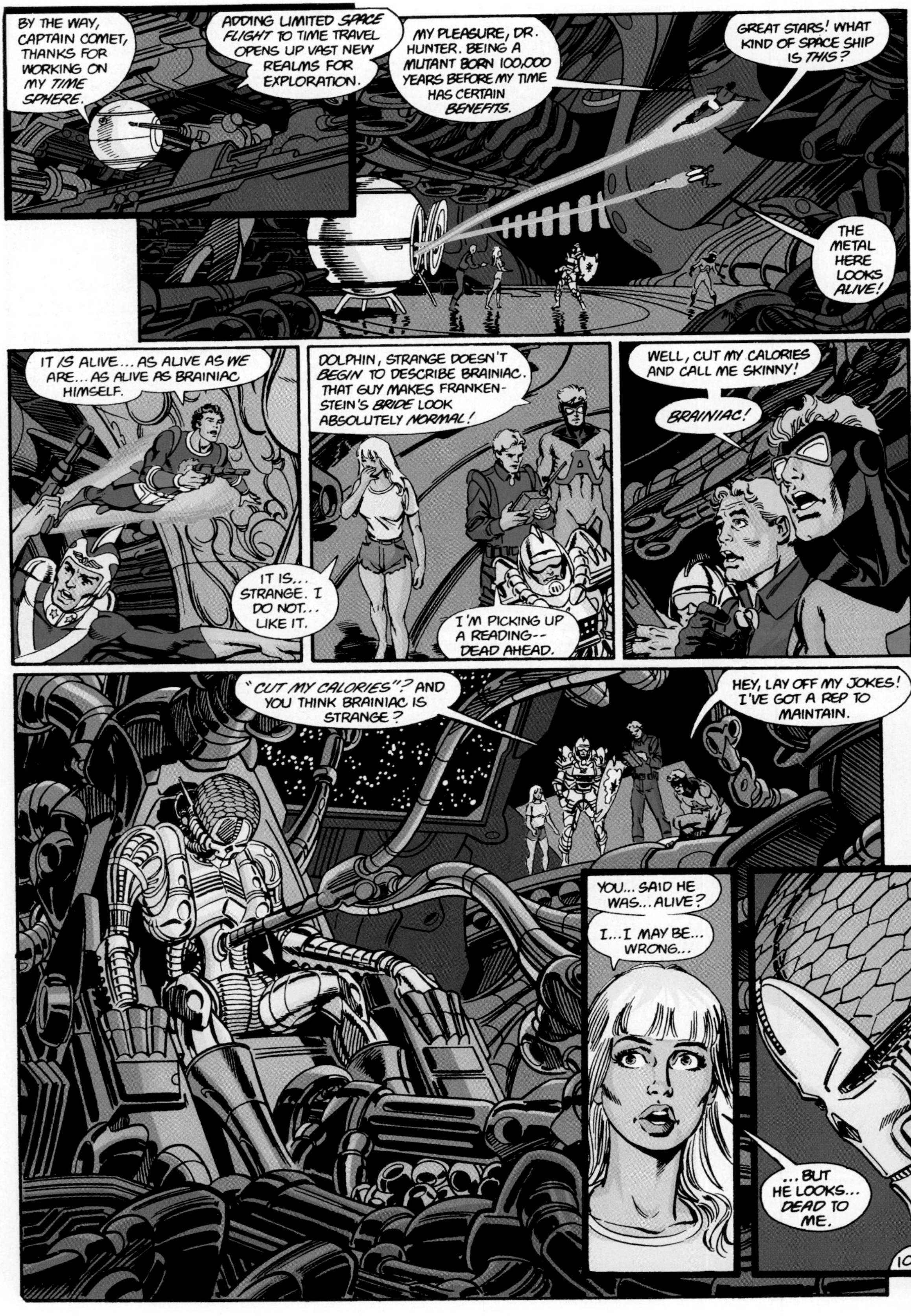
BY THE WAY, CAPTAIN COMET, THANKS FOR WORKING ON MY TIME SPHERE.
ADDING LIMITED SPACE FLIGHT TO TIME TRAVEL OPENS UP VAST NEW REALMS FOR EXPLORATION.
MY PLEASURE, DR. HUNTER. BEING A MUTANT BORN 100,000 YEARS BEFORE MY TIME HAS CERTAIN BENEFITS.
GREAT STARS! WHAT KIND OF SPACE SHIP IS THIS?
THE METAL HERE LOOKS ALIVE!
IT IS ALIVE... AS ALIVE AS WE ARE... AS ALIVE AS BRAINIAC HIMSELF.
IT IS... STRANGE. I DO NOT... LIKE IT.
DOLPHIN, STRANGE DOESN'T BEGIN TO DESCRIBE BRAINIAC. THAT GUY MAKES FRANKEN-STEIN'S BRIDE LOOK ABSOLUTELY NORMAL!
I'M PICKING UP A READING-- DEAD AHEAD.
WELL, CUT MY CALORIES AND CALL ME SKINNY!
BRAINIAC!
"CUT MY CALORIES"? AND YOU THINK BRAINIAC IS STRANGE?
HEY, LAY OFF MY JOKES! I'VE GOT A REP TO MAINTAIN.
YOU... SAID HE WAS... ALIVE?
I... I MAY BE... WRONG...
...BUT HE LOOKS... DEAD TO ME.
10

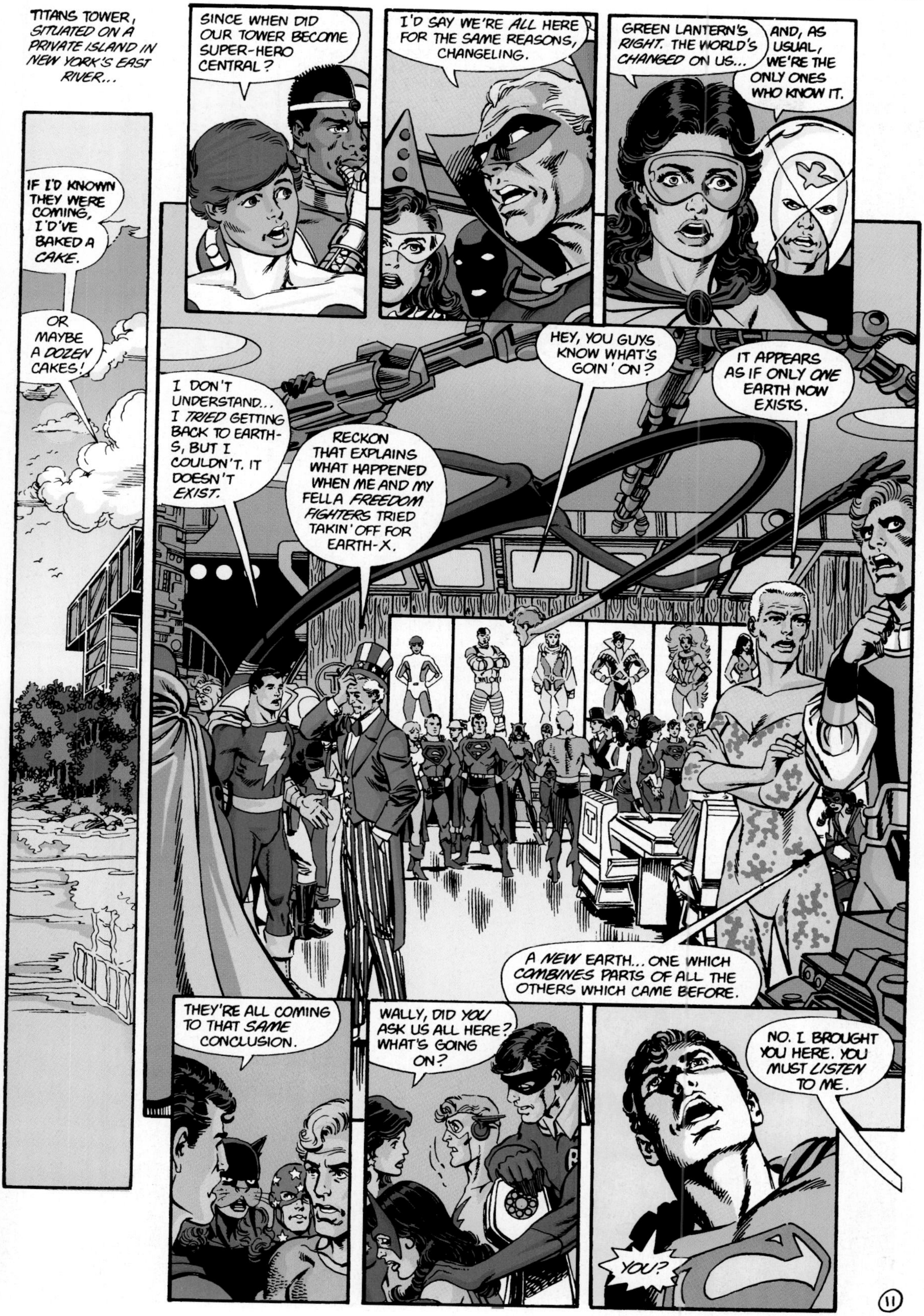
TITANS TOWER, SITUATED ON A PRIVATE ISLAND IN NEW YORK'S EAST RIVER...
IF I'D KNOWN THEY WERE COMING, I'D'VE BAKED A CAKE.
OR MAYBE A DOZEN CAKES!
SINCE WHEN DID OUR TOWER BECOME SUPER-HERO CENTRAL?
I'D SAY WE'RE ALL HERE FOR THE SAME REASONS, CHANGELING.
GREEN LANTERN'S RIGHT. THE WORLD'S CHANGED ON US...
AND, AS USUAL, WE'RE THE ONLY ONES WHO KNOW IT.
I DON'T UNDERSTAND... I TRIED GETTING BACK TO EARTH-S, BUT I COULDN'T. IT DOESN'T EXIST.
RECKON THAT EXPLAINS WHAT HAPPENED WHEN ME AND MY FELLA FREEDOM FIGHTERS TRIED TAKIN' OFF FOR EARTH-X.
HEY, YOU GUYS KNOW WHAT'S GOIN' ON?
IT APPEARS AS IF ONLY ONE EARTH NOW EXISTS.
A NEW EARTH... ONE WHICH COMBINES PARTS OF ALL THE OTHERS WHICH CAME BEFORE.
THEY'RE ALL COMING TO THAT SAME CONCLUSION.
WALLY, DID YOU ASK US ALL HERE? WHAT'S GOING ON?
NO. I BROUGHT YOU HERE. YOU MUST LISTEN TO ME.
YOU?

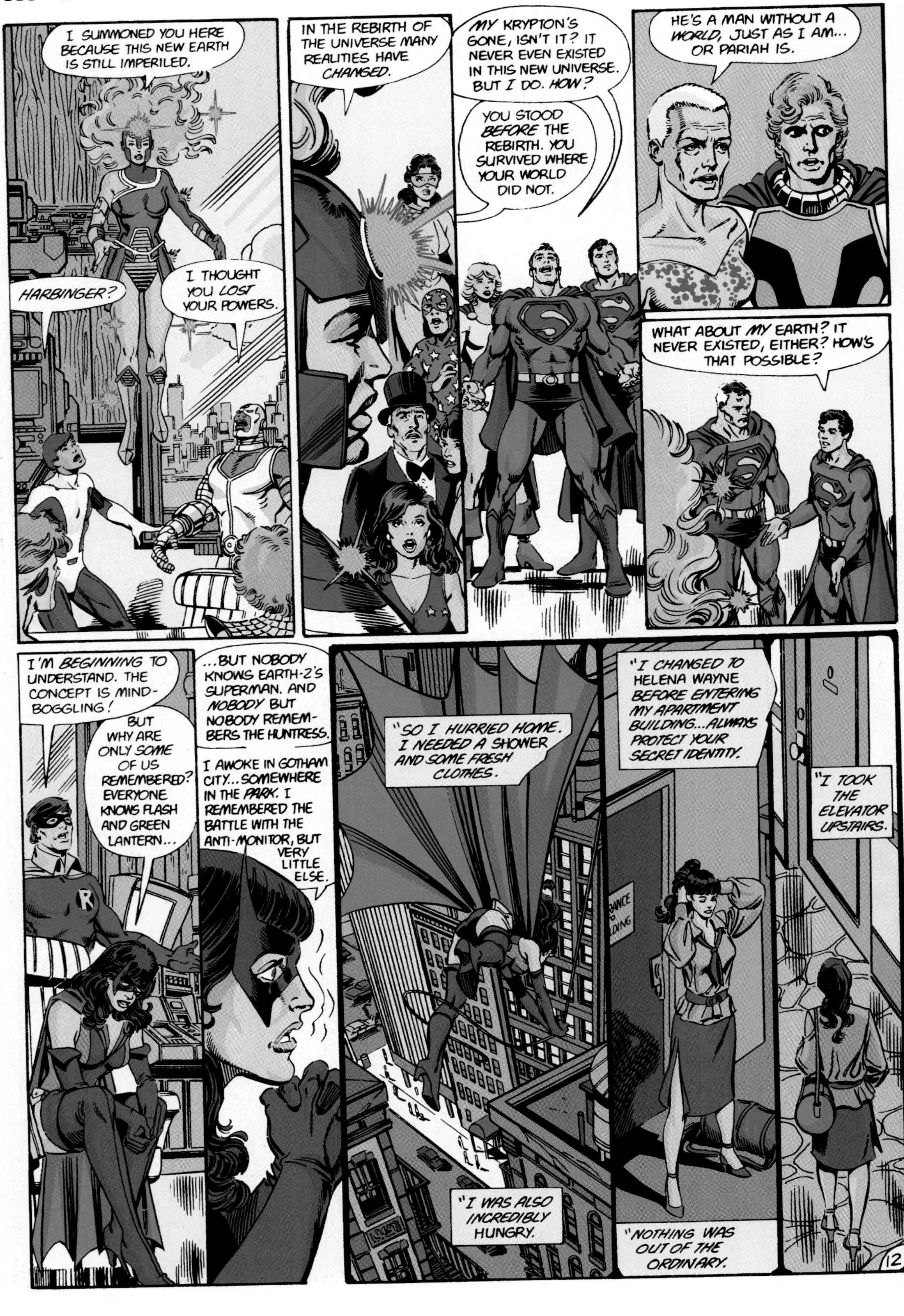

I SUMMONED YOU HERE BECAUSE THIS NEW EARTH IS STILL IMPERILED.
HARBINGER?
I THOUGHT YOU LOST YOUR POWERS.
IN THE REBIRTH OF THE UNIVERSE MANY REALITIES HAVE CHANGED.
MY KRYPTON'S GONE, ISN'T IT? IT NEVER EVEN EXISTED IN THIS NEW UNIVERSE. BUT I DO. HOW?
YOU STOOD BEFORE THE REBIRTH. YOU SURVIVED WHERE YOUR WORLD DID NOT.
HE'S A MAN WITHOUT A WORLD, JUST AS I AM... OR PARIAH IS.
WHAT ABOUT MY EARTH? IT NEVER EXISTED, EITHER? HOW'S THAT POSSIBLE?
I'M BEGINNING TO UNDERSTAND. THE CONCEPT IS MIND-BOGGLING!
BUT WHY ARE ONLY SOME OF US REMEMBERED? EVERYONE KNOWS FLASH AND GREEN LANTERN...
...BUT NOBODY KNOWS EARTH-2'S SUPERMAN. AND NOBODY BUT NOBODY REMEMBERS THE HUNTRESS.
I AWOKE IN GOTHAM CITY... SOMEWHERE IN THE PARK. I REMEMBERED THE BATTLE WITH THE ANTI-MONITOR, BUT VERY LITTLE ELSE.
"SO I HURRIED HOME. I NEEDED A SHOWER AND SOME FRESH CLOTHES.
"I WAS ALSO INCREDIBLY HUNGRY.
"I CHANGED TO HELENA WAYNE BEFORE ENTERING MY APARTMENT BUILDING... ALWAYS PROTECT YOUR SECRET IDENTITY.
"NOTHING WAS OUT OF THE ORDINARY.
"I TOOK THE ELEVATOR UPSTAIRS.
12

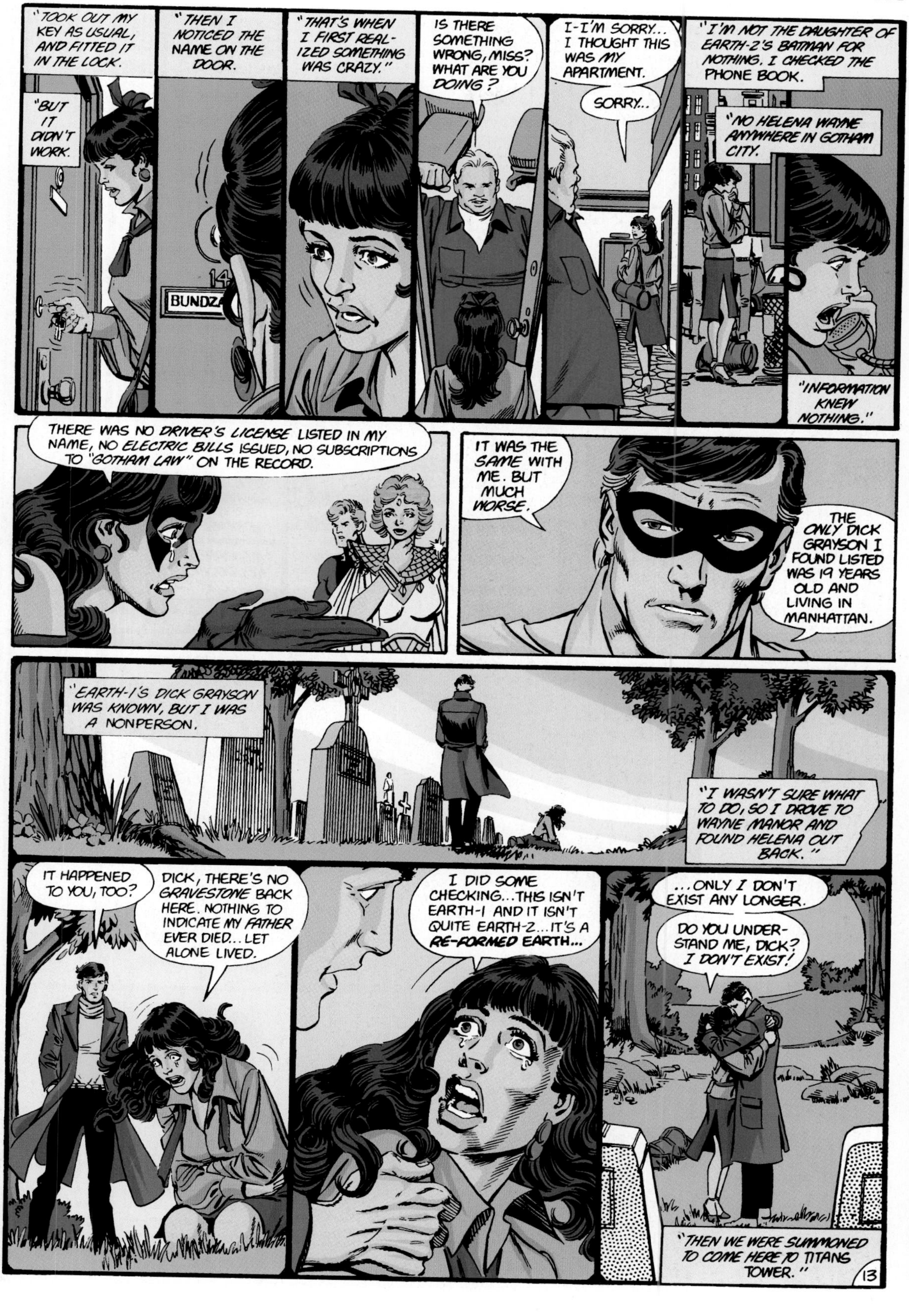
"TOOK OUT MY KEY AS USUAL, AND FITTED IT IN THE LOCK.
"BUT IT DIDN'T WORK.
"THEN I NOTICED THE NAME ON THE DOOR.
BUNDZA
"THAT'S WHEN I FIRST REALIZED SOMETHING WAS CRAZY."
IS THERE SOMETHING WRONG, MISS? WHAT ARE YOU DOING?
I-I'M SORRY... I THOUGHT THIS WAS MY APARTMENT.
SORRY...
"I'M NOT THE DAUGHTER OF EARTH-2'S BATMAN FOR NOTHING. I CHECKED THE PHONE BOOK.
"NO HELENA WAYNE ANYWHERE IN GOTHAM CITY.
"INFORMATION KNEW NOTHING."
THERE WAS NO DRIVER'S LICENSE LISTED IN MY NAME, NO ELECTRIC BILLS ISSUED, NO SUBSCRIPTIONS TO "GOTHAM LAW" ON THE RECORD.
IT WAS THE SAME WITH ME. BUT MUCH WORSE.
THE ONLY DICK GRAYSON I FOUND LISTED WAS 19 YEARS OLD AND LIVING IN MANHATTAN.
"EARTH-1'S DICK GRAYSON WAS KNOWN, BUT I WAS A NONPERSON.
"I WASN'T SURE WHAT TO DO, SO I DROVE TO WAYNE MANOR AND FOUND HELENA OUT BACK."
IT HAPPENED TO YOU, TOO?
DICK, THERE'S NO GRAVESTONE BACK HERE. NOTHING TO INDICATE MY FATHER EVER DIED... LET ALONE LIVED.
I DID SOME CHECKING... THIS ISN'T EARTH-1 AND IT ISN'T QUITE EARTH-2... IT'S A RE-FORMED EARTH...
...ONLY I DON'T EXIST ANY LONGER.
DO YOU UNDERSTAND ME, DICK? I DON'T EXIST!
"THEN WE WERE SUMMONED TO COME HERE TO TITANS TOWER."
13

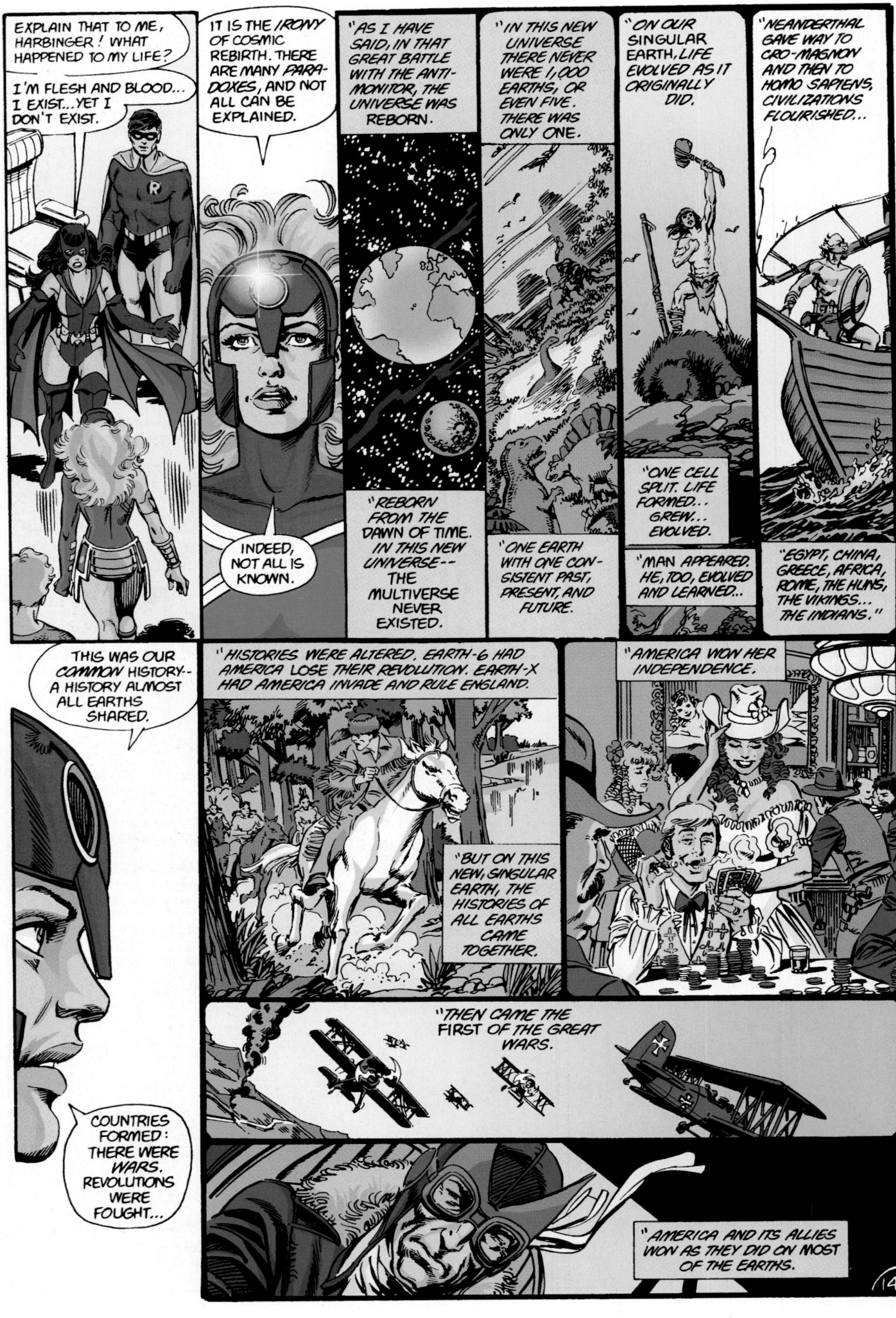
EXPLAIN THAT TO ME, HARBINGER! WHAT HAPPENED TO MY LIFE?
I'M FLESH AND BLOOD... I EXIST...YET I DON'T EXIST.
IT IS THE IRONY OF COSMIC REBIRTH. THERE ARE MANY PARADOXES, AND NOT ALL CAN BE EXPLAINED.
INDEED, NOT ALL IS KNOWN.
"AS I HAVE SAID, IN THAT GREAT BATTLE WITH THE ANTI-MONITOR, THE UNIVERSE WAS REBORN.
"REBORN FROM THE DAWN OF TIME. IN THIS NEW UNIVERSE-- THE MULTIVERSE NEVER EXISTED.
"IN THIS NEW UNIVERSE THERE NEVER WERE 1,000 EARTHS, OR EVEN FIVE. THERE WAS ONLY ONE.
"ONE EARTH WITH ONE CONSISTENT PAST, PRESENT, AND FUTURE.
"ON OUR SINGULAR EARTH, LIFE EVOLVED AS IT ORIGINALLY DID.
"ONE CELL SPLIT. LIFE FORMED... GREW... EVOLVED.
"MAN APPEARED. HE, TOO, EVOLVED AND LEARNED..
"NEANDERTHAL GAVE WAY TO CRO-MAGNON AND THEN TO HOMO SAPIENS, CIVILIZATIONS FLOURISHED...
"EGYPT, CHINA, GREECE, AFRICA, ROME, THE HUNS, THE VIKINGS... THE INDIANS."
THIS WAS OUR COMMON HISTORY-- A HISTORY ALMOST ALL EARTHS SHARED.
COUNTRIES FORMED: THERE WERE WARS. REVOLUTIONS WERE FOUGHT...
"HISTORIES WERE ALTERED. EARTH-6 HAD AMERICA LOSE THEIR REVOLUTION. EARTH-X HAD AMERICA INVADE AND RULE ENGLAND.
"BUT ON THIS NEW, SINGULAR EARTH, THE HISTORIES OF ALL EARTHS CAME TOGETHER.
"AMERICA WON HER INDEPENDENCE.
"THEN CAME THE FIRST OF THE GREAT WARS.
"AMERICA AND ITS ALLIES WON AS THEY DID ON MOST OF THE EARTHS.
14

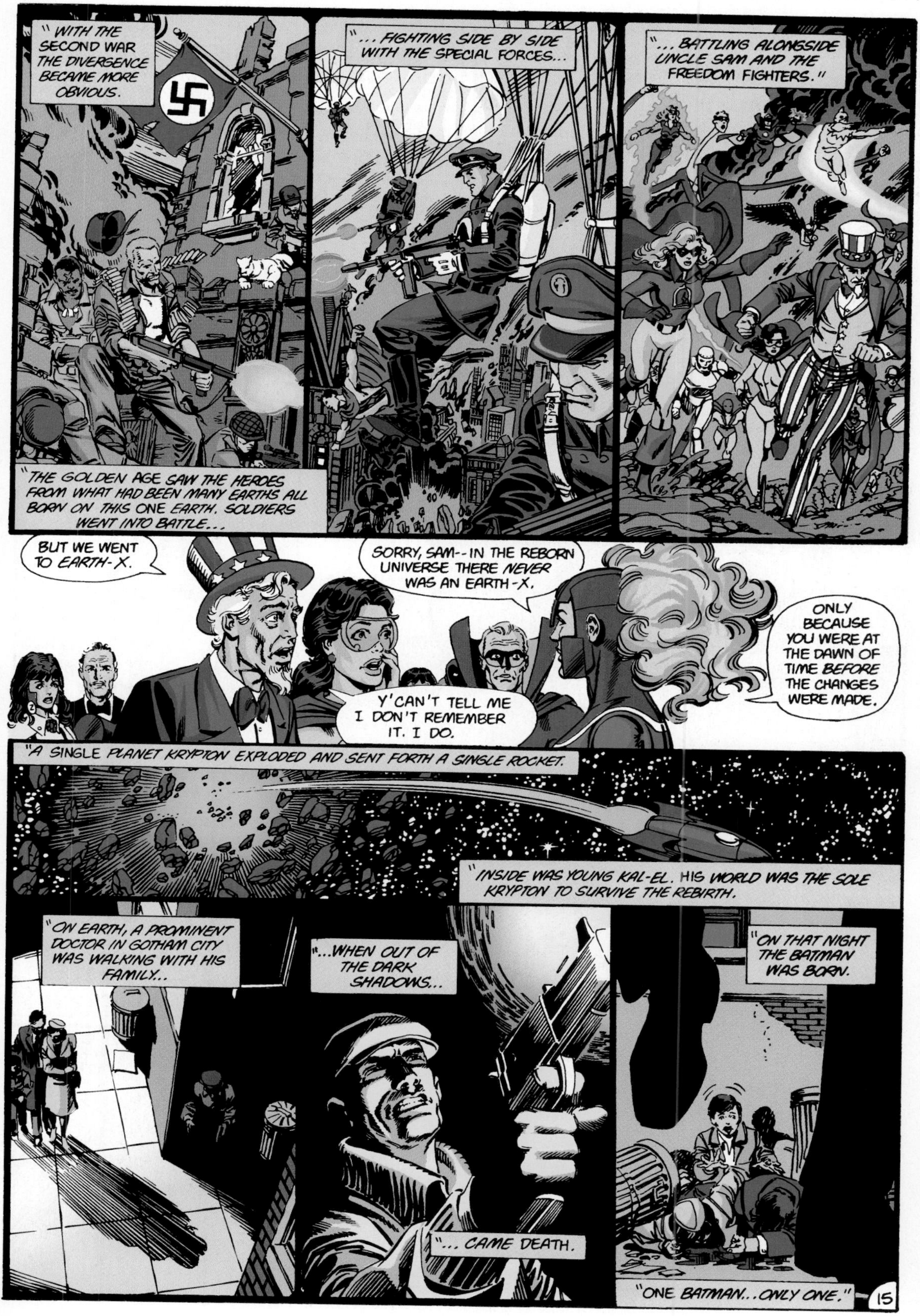
"WITH THE SECOND WAR THE DIVERGENCE BECAME MORE OBVIOUS.
"THE GOLDEN AGE SAW THE HEROES FROM WHAT HAD BEEN MANY EARTHS ALL BORN ON THIS ONE EARTH. SOLDIERS WENT INTO BATTLE...
"...FIGHTING SIDE BY SIDE WITH THE SPECIAL FORCES...
"...BATTLING ALONGSIDE UNCLE SAM AND THE FREEDOM FIGHTERS."
BUT WE WENT TO EARTH-X.
SORRY, SAM--IN THE REBORN UNIVERSE THERE NEVER WAS AN EARTH-X.
Y'CAN'T TELL ME I DON'T REMEMBER IT. I DO.
ONLY BECAUSE YOU WERE AT THE DAWN OF TIME BEFORE THE CHANGES WERE MADE.
"A SINGLE PLANET KRYPTON EXPLODED AND SENT FORTH A SINGLE ROCKET.
"INSIDE WAS YOUNG KAL-EL. HIS WORLD WAS THE SOLE KRYPTON TO SURVIVE THE REBIRTH.
"ON EARTH, A PROMINENT DOCTOR IN GOTHAM CITY WAS WALKING WITH HIS FAMILY...
"...WHEN OUT OF THE DARK SHADOWS...
"...CAME DEATH.
"ON THAT NIGHT THE BATMAN WAS BORN.
"ONE BATMAN...ONLY ONE."
15

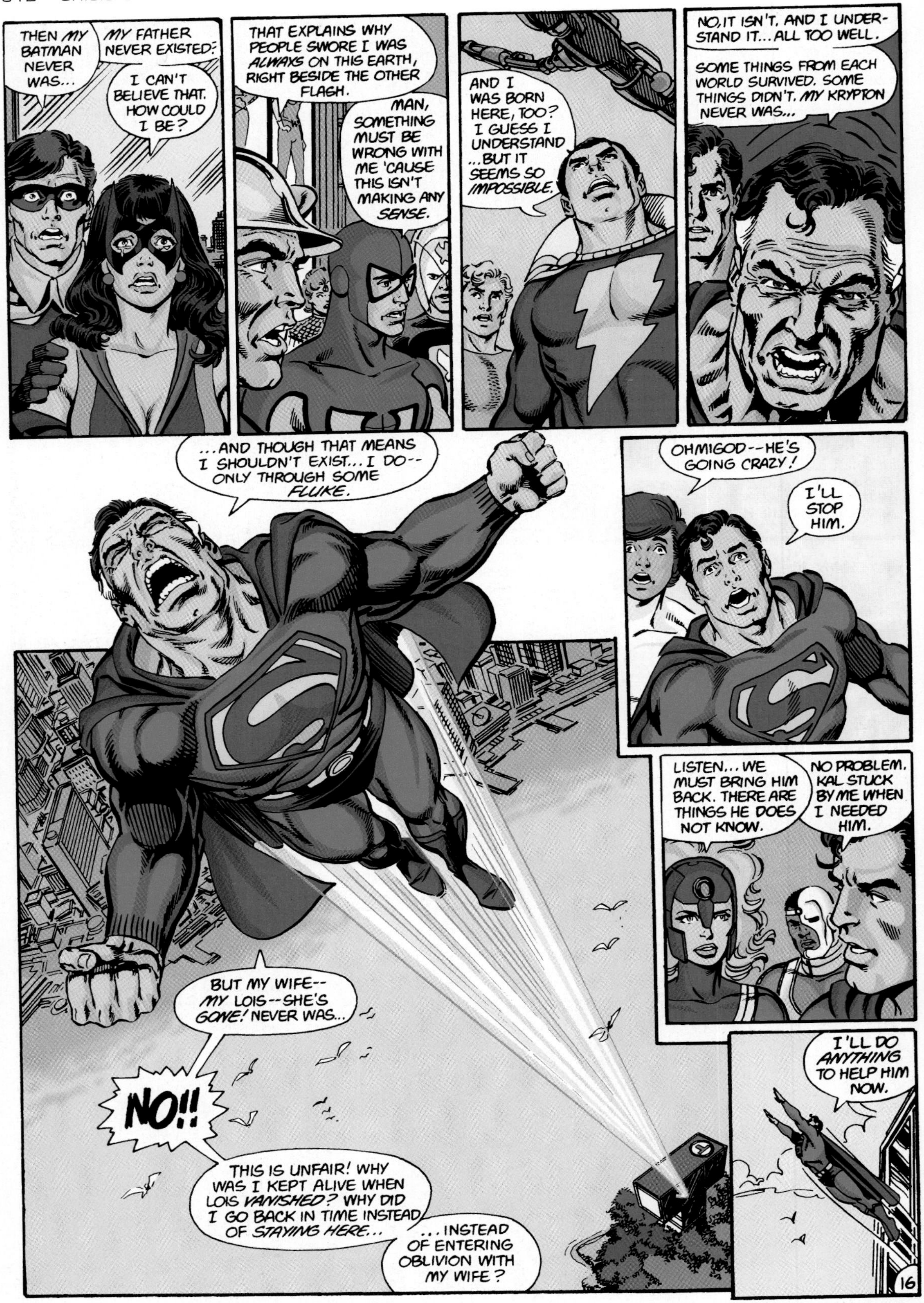
THEN MY BATMAN NEVER WAS...
MY FATHER NEVER EXISTED?
I CAN'T BELIEVE THAT. HOW COULD I BE?
THAT EXPLAINS WHY PEOPLE SWORE I WAS ALWAYS ON THIS EARTH, RIGHT BESIDE THE OTHER FLASH.
MAN, SOMETHING MUST BE WRONG WITH ME 'CAUSE THIS ISN'T MAKING ANY SENSE.
AND I WAS BORN HERE, TOO? I GUESS I UNDERSTAND ...BUT IT SEEMS SO IMPOSSIBLE.
NO, IT ISN'T, AND I UNDERSTAND IT... ALL TOO WELL.
SOME THINGS FROM EACH WORLD SURVIVED. SOME THINGS DIDN'T. MY KRYPTON NEVER WAS...
...AND THOUGH THAT MEANS I SHOULDN'T EXIST... I DO-- ONLY THROUGH SOME FLUKE.
BUT MY WIFE-- MY LOIS--SHE'S GONE! NEVER WAS...
NO!!
THIS IS UNFAIR! WHY WAS I KEPT ALIVE WHEN LOIS VANISHED? WHY DID I GO BACK IN TIME INSTEAD OF STAYING HERE...
...INSTEAD OF ENTERING OBLIVION WITH MY WIFE?
OHMIGOD--HE'S GOING CRAZY!
I'LL STOP HIM.
LISTEN... WE MUST BRING HIM BACK. THERE ARE THINGS HE DOES NOT KNOW.
NO PROBLEM. KAL STUCK BY ME WHEN I NEEDED HIM.
I'LL DO ANYTHING TO HELP HIM NOW.
16

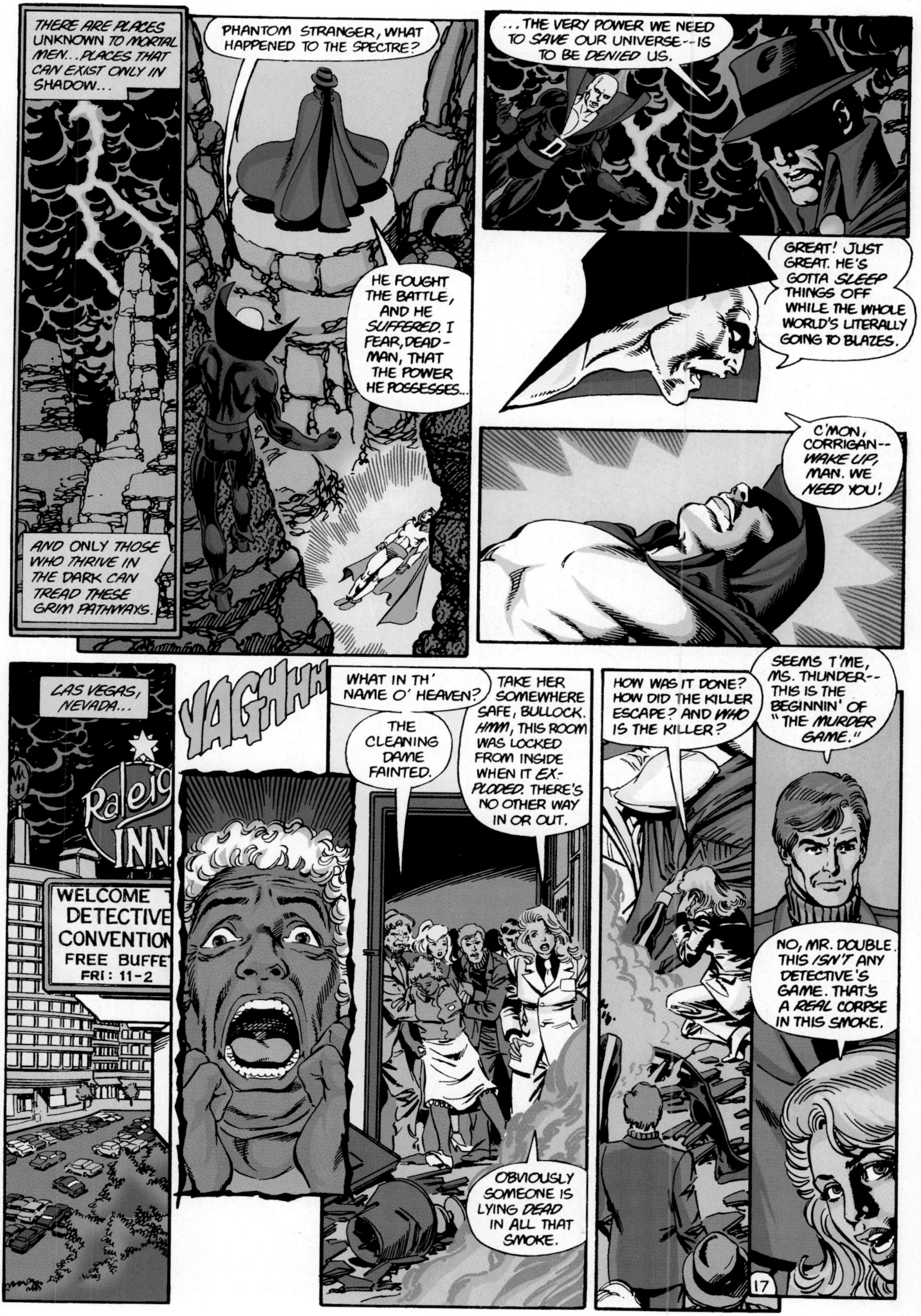
THERE ARE PLACES UNKNOWN TO MORTAL MEN... PLACES THAT CAN EXIST ONLY IN SHADOW...
AND ONLY THOSE WHO THRIVE IN THE DARK CAN TREAD THESE GRIM PATHWAYS.
PHANTOM STRANGER, WHAT HAPPENED TO THE SPECTRE?
HE FOUGHT THE BATTLE, AND HE SUFFERED. I FEAR, DEAD-MAN, THAT THE POWER HE POSSESSES...
...THE VERY POWER WE NEED TO SAVE OUR UNIVERSE--IS TO BE DENIED US.
GREAT! JUST GREAT. HE'S GOTTA SLEEP THINGS OFF WHILE THE WHOLE WORLD'S LITERALLY GOING TO BLAZES.
C'MON, CORRIGAN--WAKE UP, MAN. WE NEED YOU!
LAS VEGAS, NEVADA...
Raleig
INN
WELCOME T
DETECTIVE
CONVENTION
FREE BUFFE
FRI: 11-2
YAGHHH
WHAT IN TH' NAME O' HEAVEN?
THE CLEANING DAME FAINTED.
TAKE HER SOMEWHERE SAFE, BULLOCK. HMM, THIS ROOM WAS LOCKED FROM INSIDE WHEN IT EX-PLODED. THERE'S NO OTHER WAY IN OR OUT.
OBVIOUSLY SOMEONE IS LYING DEAD IN ALL THAT SMOKE.
HOW WAS IT DONE? HOW DID THE KILLER ESCAPE? AND WHO IS THE KILLER?
SEEMS T'ME, MS. THUNDER--THIS IS THE BEGINNIN' OF "THE MURDER GAME."
NO, MR. DOUBLE. THIS ISN'T ANY DETECTIVE'S GAME. THAT'S A REAL CORPSE IN THIS SMOKE.
17

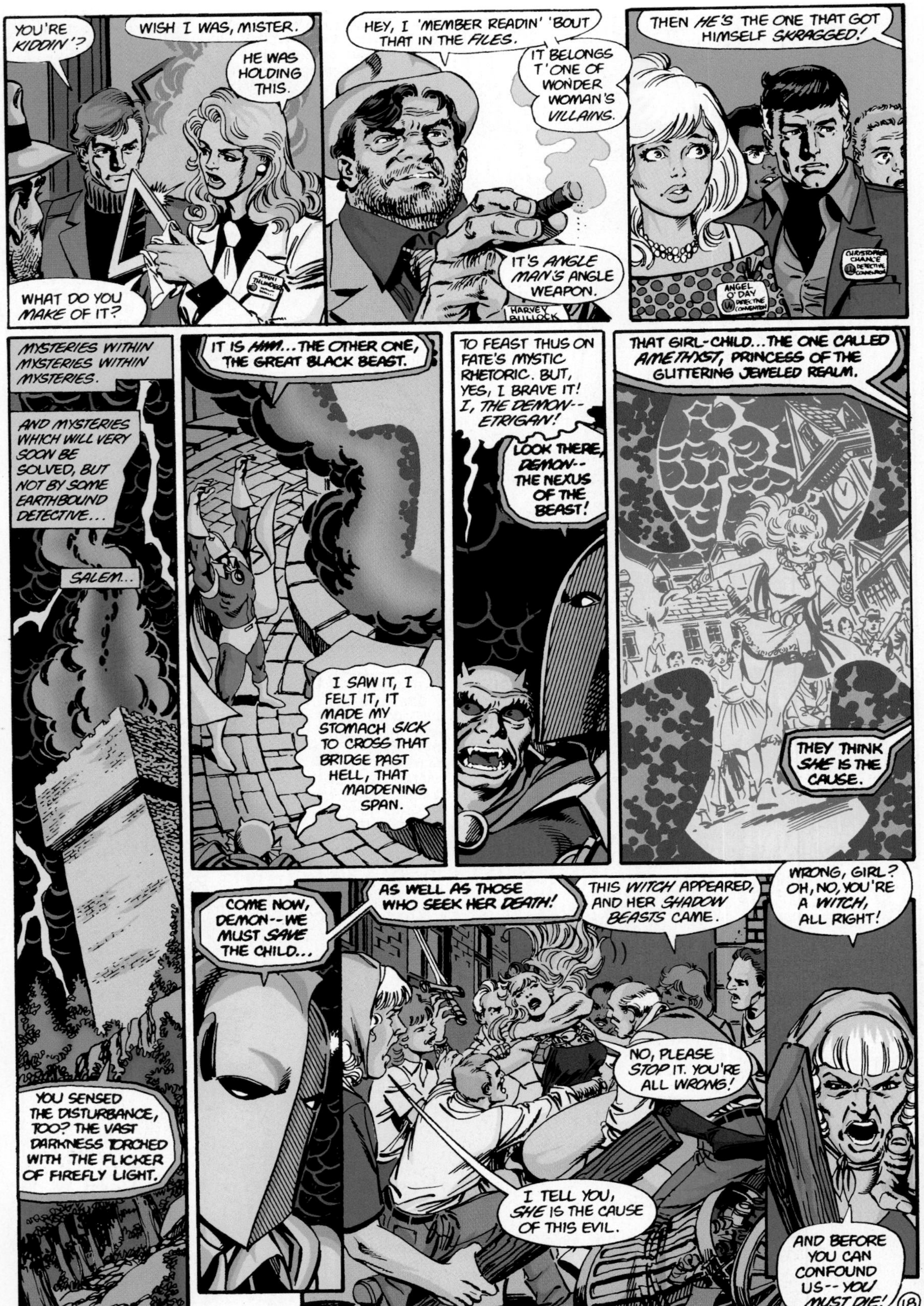
YOU'RE KIDDIN'?
WISH I WAS, MISTER.
HE WAS HOLDING THIS.
WHAT DO YOU MAKE OF IT?
JONNI THUNDER
HEY, I 'MEMBER READIN' 'BOUT THAT IN THE FILES.
IT BELONGS T'ONE OF WONDER WOMAN'S VILLAINS.
IT'S ANGLE MAN'S ANGLE WEAPON.
HARVEY BULLOCK
THEN HE'S THE ONE THAT GOT HIMSELF SKRAGGED!
ANGEL O'DAY
CHRISTOPHER CHANCE
MYSTERIES WITHIN MYSTERIES WITHIN MYSTERIES.
AND MYSTERIES WHICH WILL VERY SOON BE SOLVED, BUT NOT BY SOME EARTHBOUND DETECTIVE...
SALEM...
IT IS HIM... THE OTHER ONE, THE GREAT BLACK BEAST.
I SAW IT, I FELT IT, IT MADE MY STOMACH SICK TO CROSS THAT BRIDGE PAST HELL, THAT MADDENING SPAN.
TO FEAST THUS ON FATE'S MYSTIC RHETORIC. BUT, YES, I BRAVE IT! I, THE DEMON-- ETRIGAN!
LOOK THERE, DEMON-- THE NEXUS OF THE BEAST!
THAT GIRL-CHILD... THE ONE CALLED AMETHYST, PRINCESS OF THE GLITTERING JEWELED REALM.
THEY THINK SHE IS THE CAUSE.
YOU SENSED THE DISTURBANCE, TOO? THE VAST DARKNESS TORCHED WITH THE FLICKER OF FIREFLY LIGHT.
COME NOW, DEMON-- WE MUST SAVE THE CHILD...
AS WELL AS THOSE WHO SEEK HER DEATH!
THIS WITCH APPEARED, AND HER SHADOW BEASTS CAME.
WRONG, GIRL? OH, NO, YOU'RE A WITCH, ALL RIGHT!
NO, PLEASE STOP IT. YOU'RE ALL WRONG!
I TELL YOU, SHE IS THE CAUSE OF THIS EVIL.
AND BEFORE YOU CAN CONFOUND US-- YOU MUST DIE!
18

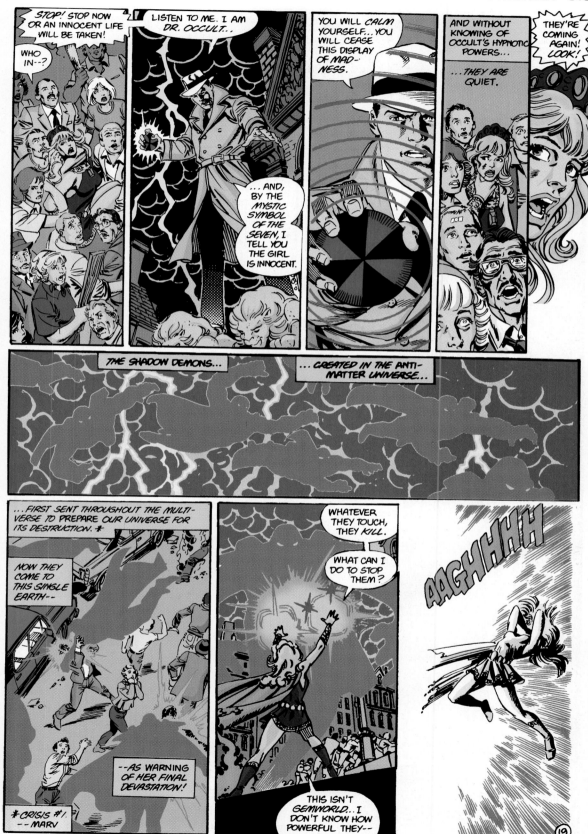

STOP! STOP NOW OR AN INNOCENT LIFE WILL BE TAKEN!

WHO IN--?

LISTEN TO ME. I AM DR. OCCULT...

...AND, BY THE MYSTIC SYMBOL OF THE SEVEN, I TELL YOU THE GIRL IS INNOCENT.

YOU WILL CALM YOURSELF... YOU WILL CEASE THIS DISPLAY OF MADNESS.

AND WITHOUT KNOWING OF OCCULT'S HYPNOTIC POWERS...

...THEY ARE QUIET.

THEY'RE COMING AGAIN! LOOK!

THE SHADOW DEMONS...

...CREATED IN THE ANTI-MATTER UNIVERSE...

...FIRST SENT THROUGHOUT THE MULTI-VERSE TO PREPARE OUR UNIVERSE FOR ITS DESTRUCTION. *

NOW THEY COME TO THIS SINGLE EARTH--

--AS WARNING OF HER FINAL DEVASTATION!

* CRISIS #1. --MARV

WHATEVER THEY TOUCH, THEY KILL.

WHAT CAN I DO TO STOP THEM?

THIS ISN'T GEMWORLD... I DON'T KNOW HOW POWERFUL THEY--

AAGHHHH

⑲

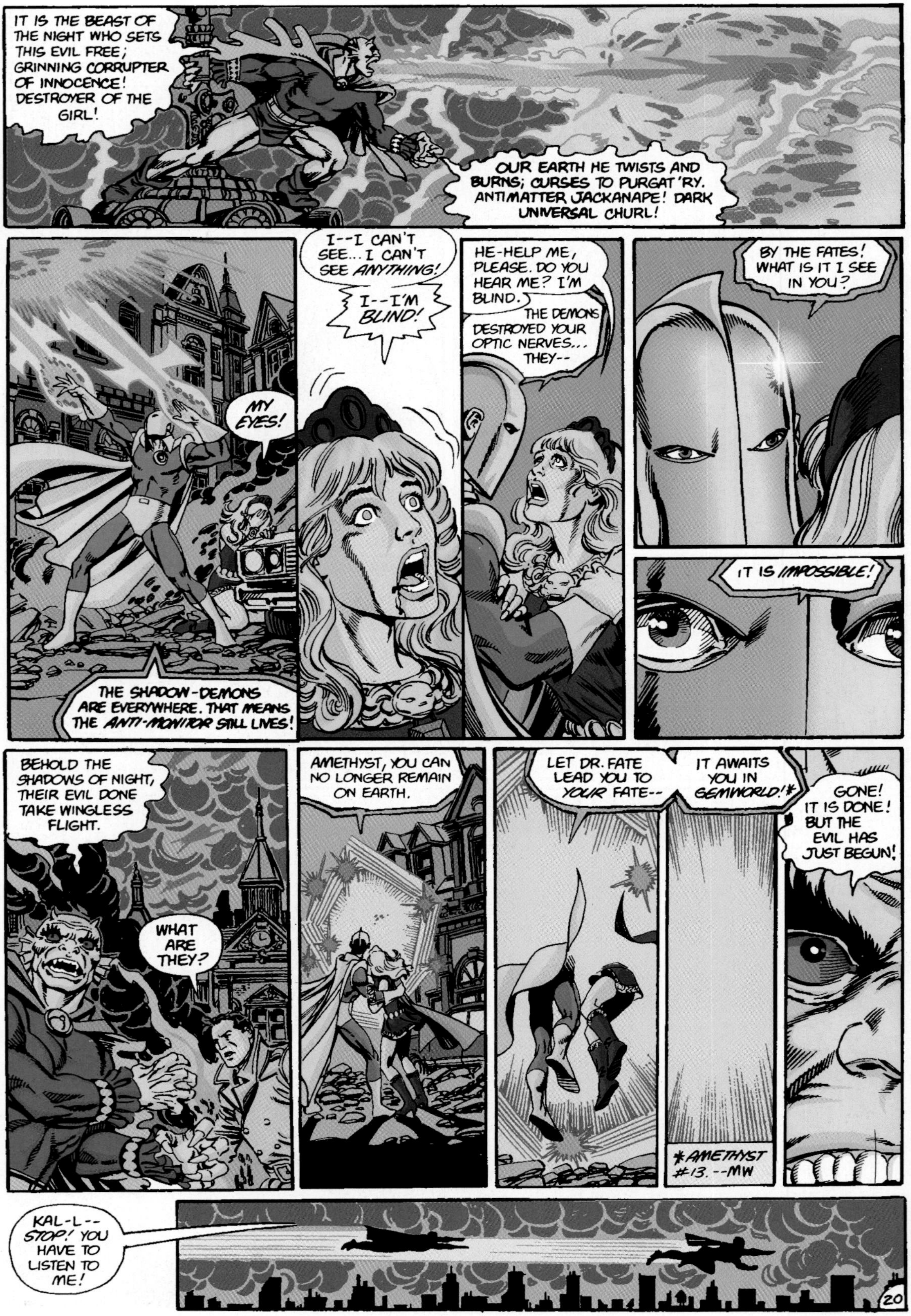
IT IS THE BEAST OF THE NIGHT WHO SETS THIS EVIL FREE; GRINNING CORRUPTER OF INNOCENCE! DESTROYER OF THE GIRL!
OUR EARTH HE TWISTS AND BURNS; CURSES TO PURGAT'RY. ANTIMATTER JACKANAPE! DARK UNIVERSAL CHURL!
MY EYES!
THE SHADOW-DEMONS ARE EVERYWHERE. THAT MEANS THE ANTI-MONITOR STILL LIVES!
I--I CAN'T SEE... I CAN'T SEE ANYTHING!
I--I'M BLIND!
HE-HELP ME, PLEASE. DO YOU HEAR ME? I'M BLIND.
THE DEMONS DESTROYED YOUR OPTIC NERVES... THEY--
BY THE FATES! WHAT IS IT I SEE IN YOU?
IT IS IMPOSSIBLE!
BEHOLD THE SHADOWS OF NIGHT, THEIR EVIL DONE TAKE WINGLESS FLIGHT.
WHAT ARE THEY?
AMETHYST, YOU CAN NO LONGER REMAIN ON EARTH.
LET DR. FATE LEAD YOU TO YOUR FATE--
IT AWAITS YOU IN GEMWORLD!*
*AMETHYST #13. --MW
GONE! IT IS DONE! BUT THE EVIL HAS JUST BEGUN!
KAL-L-- STOP! YOU HAVE TO LISTEN TO ME!

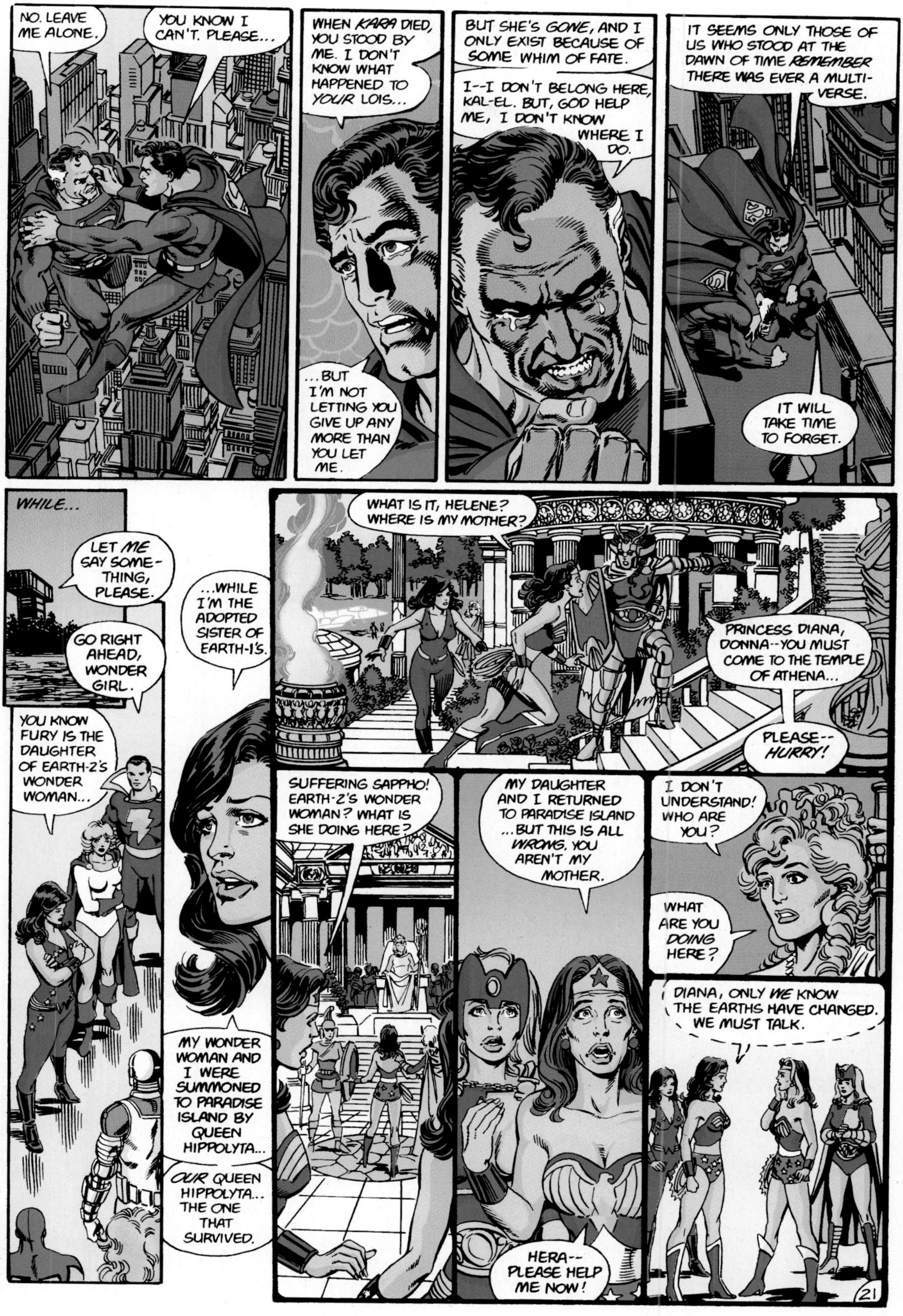
NO. LEAVE ME ALONE.
YOU KNOW I CAN'T. PLEASE...
WHEN KARA DIED, YOU STOOD BY ME. I DON'T KNOW WHAT HAPPENED TO YOUR LOIS...
...BUT I'M NOT LETTING YOU GIVE UP ANY MORE THAN YOU LET ME.
BUT SHE'S GONE, AND I ONLY EXIST BECAUSE OF SOME WHIM OF FATE.
I--I DON'T BELONG HERE, KAL-EL. BUT, GOD HELP ME, I DON'T KNOW WHERE I DO.
IT SEEMS ONLY THOSE OF US WHO STOOD AT THE DAWN OF TIME REMEMBER THERE WAS EVER A MULTI-VERSE.
IT WILL TAKE TIME TO FORGET.
WHILE...
LET ME SAY SOME-THING, PLEASE.
GO RIGHT AHEAD, WONDER GIRL.
...WHILE I'M THE ADOPTED SISTER OF EARTH-1'S.
YOU KNOW FURY IS THE DAUGHTER OF EARTH-2'S WONDER WOMAN...
MY WONDER WOMAN AND I WERE SUMMONED TO PARADISE ISLAND BY QUEEN HIPPOLYTA...
OUR QUEEN HIPPOLYTA... THE ONE THAT SURVIVED.
WHAT IS IT, HELENE? WHERE IS MY MOTHER?
PRINCESS DIANA, DONNA--YOU MUST COME TO THE TEMPLE OF ATHENA...
PLEASE-- HURRY!
SUFFERING SAPPHO! EARTH-2'S WONDER WOMAN? WHAT IS SHE DOING HERE?
MY DAUGHTER AND I RETURNED TO PARADISE ISLAND ...BUT THIS IS ALL WRONG. YOU AREN'T MY MOTHER.
HERA-- PLEASE HELP ME NOW!
I DON'T UNDERSTAND! WHO ARE YOU?
WHAT ARE YOU DOING HERE?
DIANA, ONLY WE KNOW THE EARTHS HAVE CHANGED. WE MUST TALK.
21

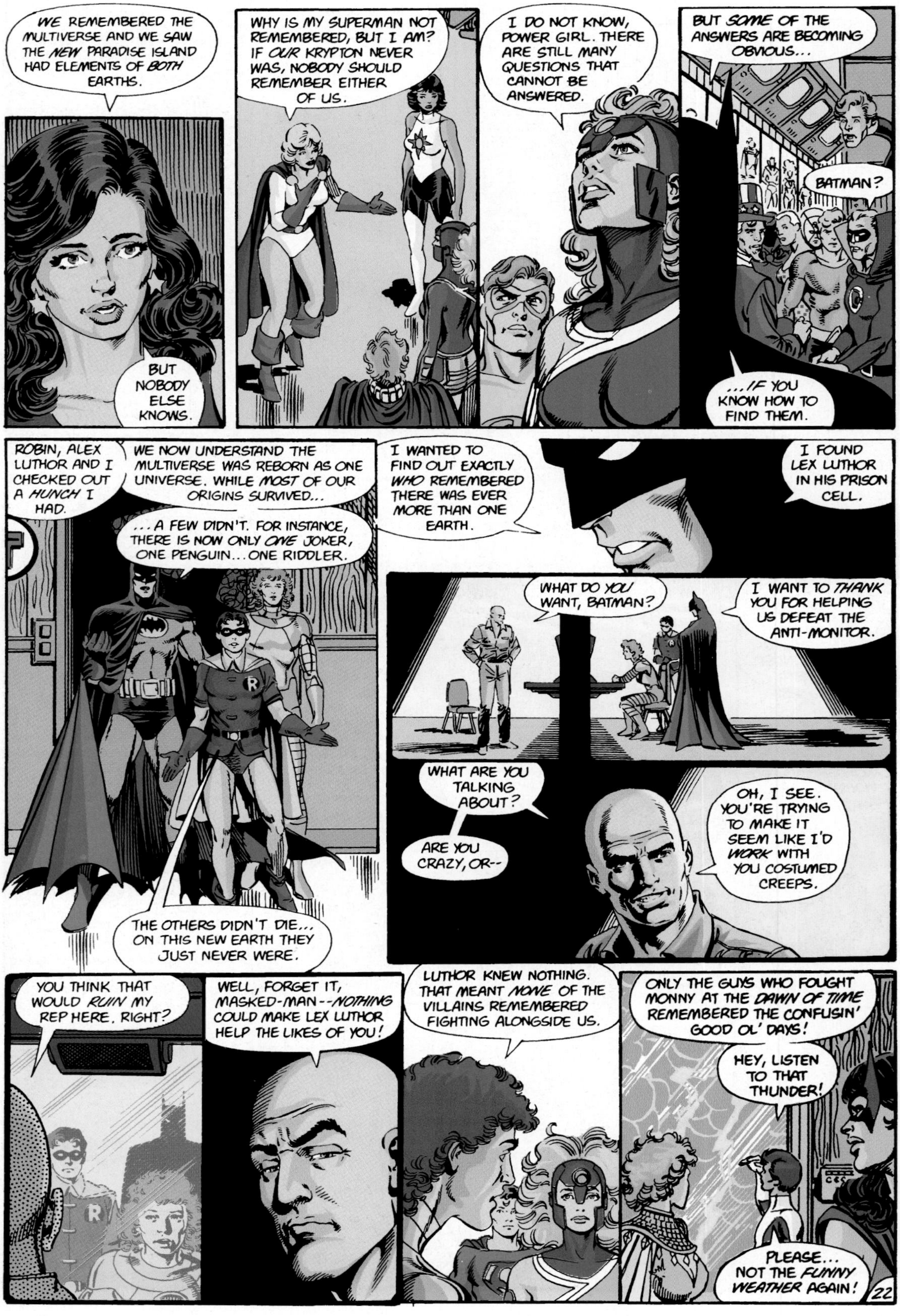

WE REMEMBERED THE MULTIVERSE AND WE SAW THE NEW PARADISE ISLAND HAD ELEMENTS OF BOTH EARTHS.
BUT NOBODY ELSE KNOWS.
WHY IS MY SUPERMAN NOT REMEMBERED, BUT I AM? IF OUR KRYPTON NEVER WAS, NOBODY SHOULD REMEMBER EITHER OF US.
I DO NOT KNOW, POWER GIRL. THERE ARE STILL MANY QUESTIONS THAT CANNOT BE ANSWERED.
BUT SOME OF THE ANSWERS ARE BECOMING OBVIOUS...
BATMAN?
...IF YOU KNOW HOW TO FIND THEM.
ROBIN, ALEX LUTHOR AND I CHECKED OUT A HUNCH I HAD.
WE NOW UNDERSTAND THE MULTIVERSE WAS REBORN AS ONE UNIVERSE. WHILE MOST OF OUR ORIGINS SURVIVED...
...A FEW DIDN'T. FOR INSTANCE, THERE IS NOW ONLY ONE JOKER, ONE PENGUIN...ONE RIDDLER.
THE OTHERS DIDN'T DIE... ON THIS NEW EARTH THEY JUST NEVER WERE.
I WANTED TO FIND OUT EXACTLY WHO REMEMBERED THERE WAS EVER MORE THAN ONE EARTH.
I FOUND LEX LUTHOR IN HIS PRISON CELL.
WHAT DO YOU WANT, BATMAN?
I WANT TO THANK YOU FOR HELPING US DEFEAT THE ANTI-MONITOR.
WHAT ARE YOU TALKING ABOUT?
ARE YOU CRAZY, OR--
OH, I SEE. YOU'RE TRYING TO MAKE IT SEEM LIKE I'D WORK WITH YOU COSTUMED CREEPS.
YOU THINK THAT WOULD RUIN MY REP HERE. RIGHT?
WELL, FORGET IT, MASKED-MAN--NOTHING COULD MAKE LEX LUTHOR HELP THE LIKES OF YOU!
LUTHOR KNEW NOTHING. THAT MEANT NONE OF THE VILLAINS REMEMBERED FIGHTING ALONGSIDE US.
ONLY THE GUYS WHO FOUGHT MONNY AT THE DAWN OF TIME REMEMBERED THE CONFUSIN' GOOD OL' DAYS!
HEY, LISTEN TO THAT THUNDER!
PLEASE... NOT THE FUNNY WEATHER AGAIN!
22

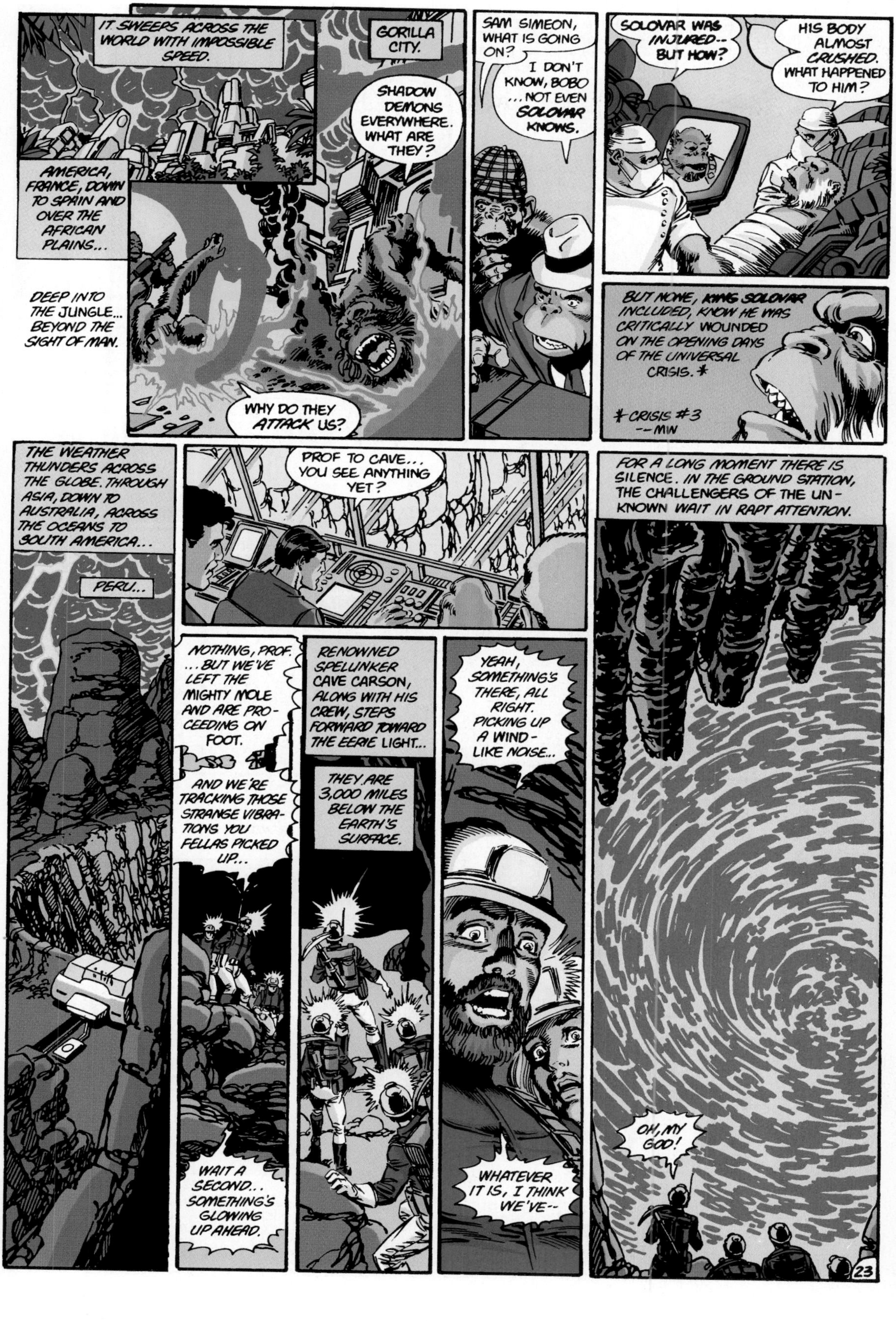
IT SWEEPS ACROSS THE WORLD WITH IMPOSSIBLE SPEED.
AMERICA, FRANCE, DOWN TO SPAIN AND OVER THE AFRICAN PLAINS...
DEEP INTO THE JUNGLE... BEYOND THE SIGHT OF MAN.
GORILLA CITY.
SHADOW DEMONS EVERYWHERE. WHAT ARE THEY?
WHY DO THEY ATTACK US?
SAM SIMEON, WHAT IS GOING ON?
I DON'T KNOW, BOBO ...NOT EVEN SOLOVAR KNOWS.
SOLOVAR WAS INJURED-- BUT HOW?
HIS BODY ALMOST CRUSHED. WHAT HAPPENED TO HIM?
BUT NONE, KING SOLOVAR INCLUDED, KNOW HE WAS CRITICALLY WOUNDED ON THE OPENING DAYS OF THE UNIVERSAL CRISIS.*
*CRISIS #3 --MW
THE WEATHER THUNDERS ACROSS THE GLOBE. THROUGH ASIA, DOWN TO AUSTRALIA, ACROSS THE OCEANS TO SOUTH AMERICA...
PERU...
PROF TO CAVE... YOU SEE ANYTHING YET?
NOTHING, PROF. ...BUT WE'VE LEFT THE MIGHTY MOLE AND ARE PROCEEDING ON FOOT.
AND WE'RE TRACKING THOSE STRANGE VIBRATIONS YOU FELLAS PICKED UP...
WAIT A SECOND.. SOMETHING'S GLOWING UP AHEAD.
RENOWNED SPELUNKER CAVE CARSON, ALONG WITH HIS CREW, STEPS FORWARD TOWARD THE EERIE LIGHT...
THEY ARE 3,000 MILES BELOW THE EARTH'S SURFACE.
YEAH, SOMETHING'S THERE, ALL RIGHT. PICKING UP A WIND-LIKE NOISE...
WHATEVER IT IS, I THINK WE'VE--
FOR A LONG MOMENT THERE IS SILENCE. IN THE GROUND STATION, THE CHALLENGERS OF THE UNKNOWN WAIT IN RAPT ATTENTION.
OH, MY GOD!
23

P-PROF... I'VE NEVER SEEN ANYTHING LIKE IT. IT'S *PURE ENERGY*.

AND IT'S BLOWN ALL OUR INSTRUMENTS RIGHT OFF THE SCALE.

GET IN TOUCH WITH *TITANS TOWER!* THEY'RE *WAITING* FOR THIS.

"AND, PROF... IF YOU KNOW ANY PRAYERS, START SAYING THEM NOW."

"WE'RE GETTING THE SAME ELECTRICAL STORM HERE. THANKS, CAVE."

GET YOURSELF TO SAFETY RIGHT AWAY.

THIS IS *CRAZY!* IT'S LIKE SOMETHING OUTTA *GHOSTBUSTERS*--ONLY WORSE!

HE...HELP ME.

PARIAH! WHAT IS HAPPENING?

I--I FEEL THE *TUG* OF *EVIL* AGAIN...

PULLING AT ME...

B-BUT... BUT I'M NOT DISAPPEARING...

LORD, IT HURTS... SO COLD... SO VERY COLD!

THE ANTIMATTER EFFECT HAS TAKEN OVER ALEX'S BODY AGAIN.

ABOVE THE EARTH, IN THE SCARLET SKIES, THE UNIVERSE SEEMS TO OPEN.

THE YAWNING MAW STARES HUNGRILY AT THE BLUE-GRAY GLOBE WHICH FLOATS BEFORE IT.

...DESPERATELY TRYING TO HOLD ON TO ITS SPACE, TO LAY CLAIM TO ITS ORBIT...

THE EARTH SHAKES AND PROTESTS AND FIGHTS AND SCREAMS...

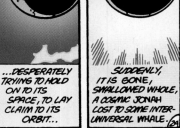

BUT IT FAILS.

SUDDENLY, IT IS GONE, SWALLOWED WHOLE, A COSMIC JONAH LOST TO SOME INTER-UNIVERSAL WHALE.

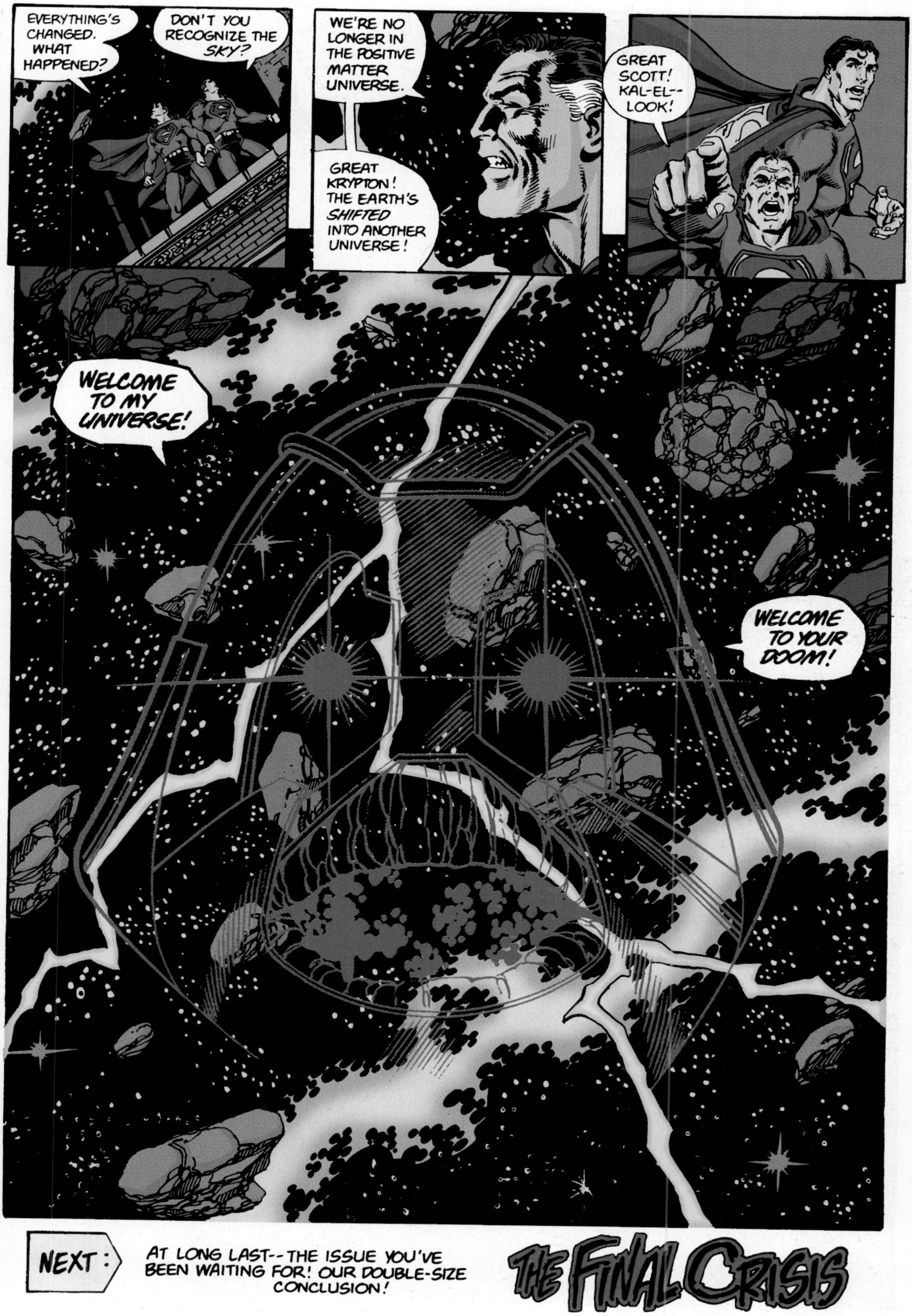
EVERYTHING'S CHANGED. WHAT HAPPENED?
DON'T YOU RECOGNIZE THE SKY?
WE'RE NO LONGER IN THE POSITIVE MATTER UNIVERSE.
GREAT KRYPTON! THE EARTH'S SHIFTED INTO ANOTHER UNIVERSE!
GREAT SCOTT! KAL-EL--LOOK!
WELCOME TO MY UNIVERSE!
WELCOME TO YOUR DOOM!
NEXT:
AT LONG LAST--THE ISSUE YOU'VE BEEN WAITING FOR! OUR DOUBLE-SIZE CONCLUSION!
THE FINAL CRISIS

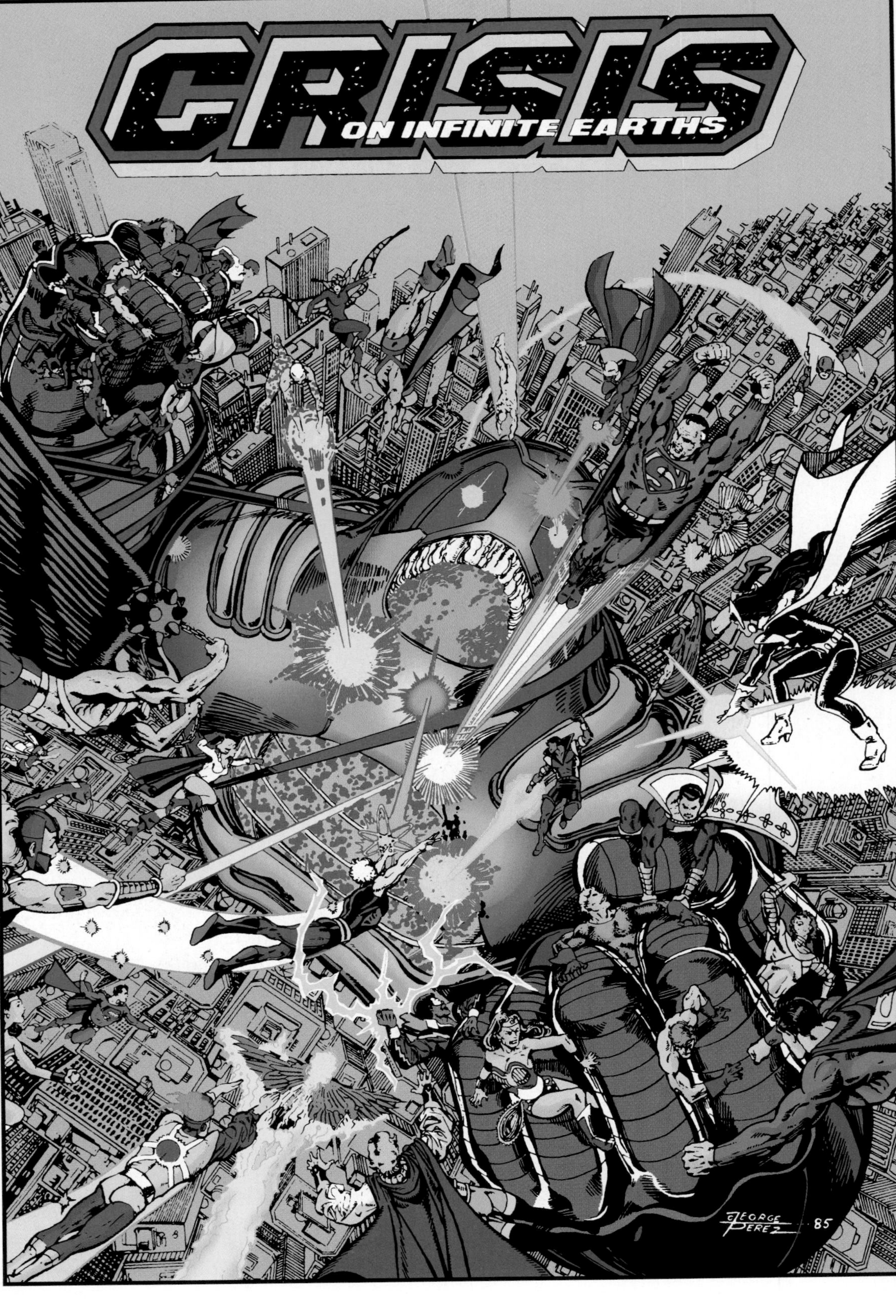
CRISIS
ON INFINITE EARTHS
GEORGE PEREZ 85

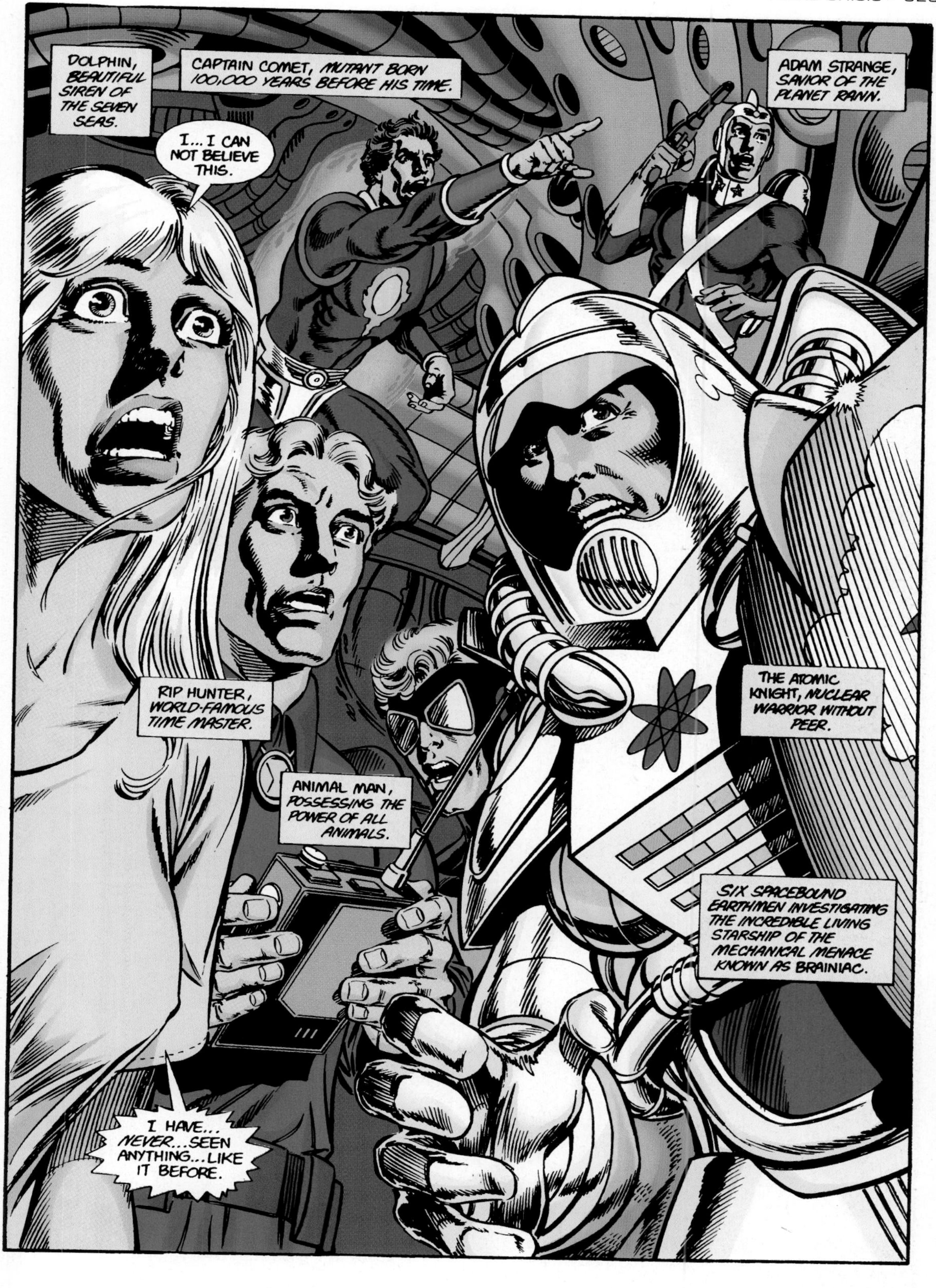
DOLPHIN, BEAUTIFUL SIREN OF THE SEVEN SEAS.
CAPTAIN COMET, MUTANT BORN 100,000 YEARS BEFORE HIS TIME.
ADAM STRANGE, SAVIOR OF THE PLANET RANN.
I... I CAN NOT BELIEVE THIS.
RIP HUNTER, WORLD-FAMOUS TIME MASTER.
ANIMAL MAN, POSSESSING THE POWER OF ALL ANIMALS.
THE ATOMIC KNIGHT, NUCLEAR WARRIOR WITHOUT PEER.
SIX SPACEBOUND EARTHMEN INVESTIGATING THE INCREDIBLE LIVING STARSHIP OF THE MECHANICAL MENACE KNOWN AS BRAINIAC.
I HAVE... NEVER...SEEN ANYTHING...LIKE IT BEFORE.

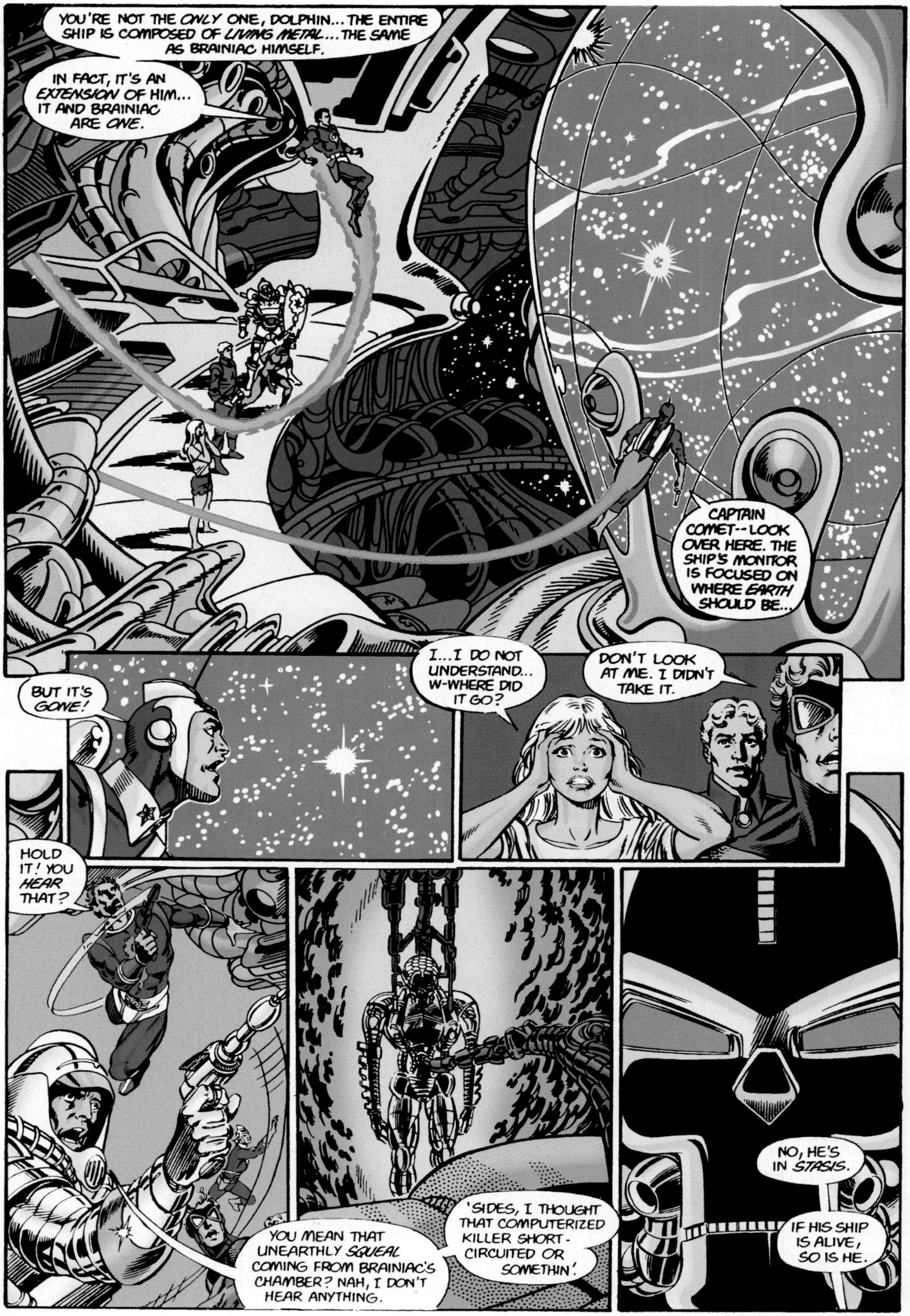

YOU'RE NOT THE ONLY ONE, DOLPHIN... THE ENTIRE SHIP IS COMPOSED OF LIVING METAL... THE SAME AS BRAINIAC HIMSELF.
IN FACT, IT'S AN EXTENSION OF HIM... IT AND BRAINIAC ARE ONE.
CAPTAIN COMET--LOOK OVER HERE. THE SHIP'S MONITOR IS FOCUSED ON WHERE EARTH SHOULD BE...
BUT IT'S GONE!
I...I DO NOT UNDERSTAND... W-WHERE DID IT GO?
DON'T LOOK AT ME. I DIDN'T TAKE IT.
HOLD IT! YOU HEAR THAT?
YOU MEAN THAT UNEARTHLY SQUEAL COMING FROM BRAINIAC'S CHAMBER? NAH, I DON'T HEAR ANYTHING.
'SIDES, I THOUGHT THAT COMPUTERIZED KILLER SHORT-CIRCUITED OR SOMETHIN'.
NO, HE'S IN STASIS.
IF HIS SHIP IS ALIVE, SO IS HE.

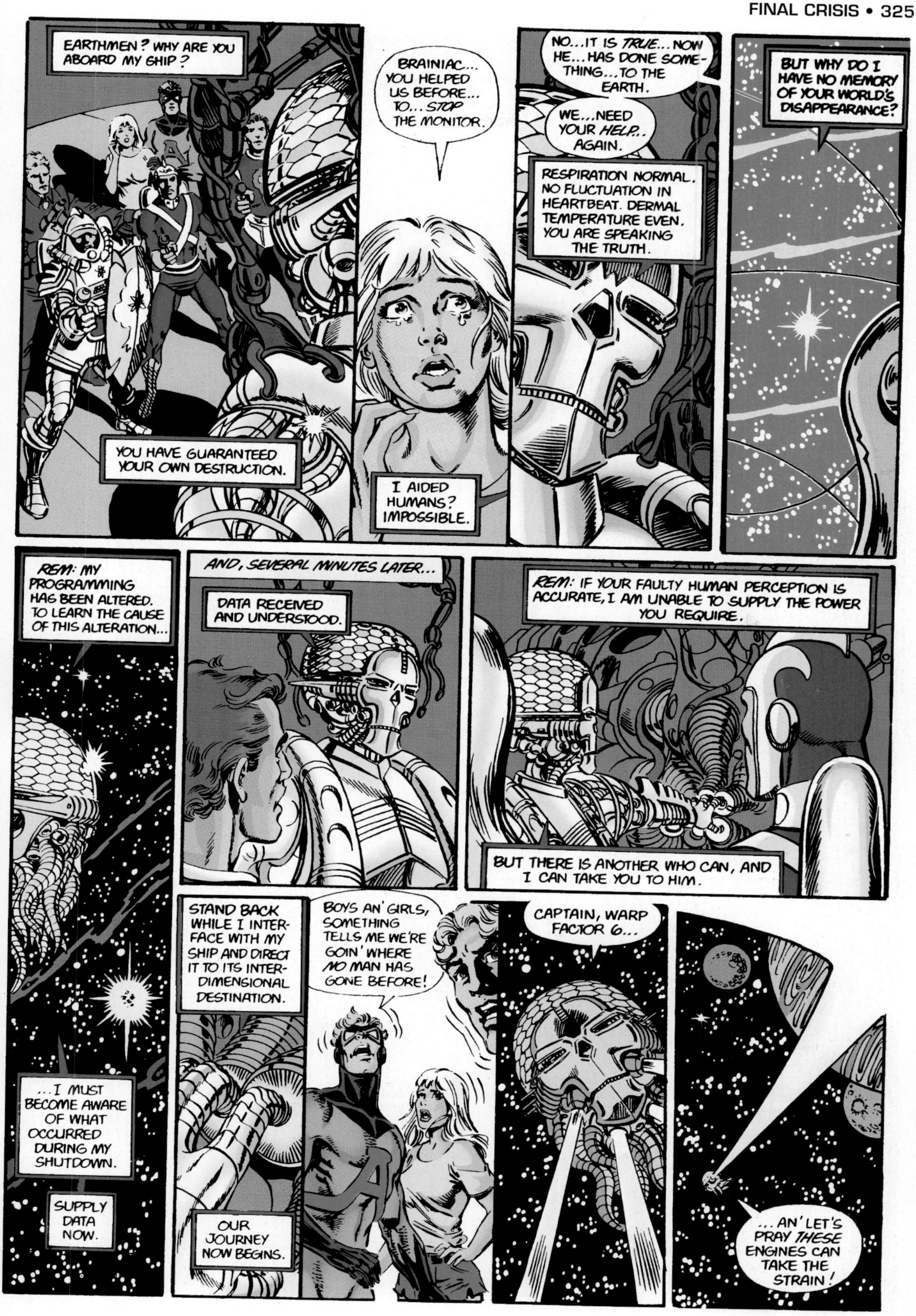
EARTHMEN? WHY ARE YOU ABOARD MY SHIP?
YOU HAVE GUARANTEED YOUR OWN DESTRUCTION.
BRAINIAC... YOU HELPED US BEFORE... TO... STOP THE MONITOR.
I AIDED HUMANS? IMPOSSIBLE.
NO... IT IS TRUE... NOW HE... HAS DONE SOMETHING... TO THE EARTH.
WE... NEED YOUR HELP... AGAIN.
RESPIRATION NORMAL. NO FLUCTUATION IN HEARTBEAT. DERMAL TEMPERATURE EVEN. YOU ARE SPEAKING THE TRUTH.
BUT WHY DO I HAVE NO MEMORY OF YOUR WORLD'S DISAPPEARANCE?
REM: MY PROGRAMMING HAS BEEN ALTERED. TO LEARN THE CAUSE OF THIS ALTERATION...
...I MUST BECOME AWARE OF WHAT OCCURRED DURING MY SHUTDOWN.
SUPPLY DATA NOW.
AND, SEVERAL MINUTES LATER...
DATA RECEIVED AND UNDERSTOOD.
REM: IF YOUR FAULTY HUMAN PERCEPTION IS ACCURATE, I AM UNABLE TO SUPPLY THE POWER YOU REQUIRE.
BUT THERE IS ANOTHER WHO CAN, AND I CAN TAKE YOU TO HIM.
STAND BACK WHILE I INTERFACE WITH MY SHIP AND DIRECT IT TO ITS INTERDIMENSIONAL DESTINATION.
BOYS AN' GIRLS, SOMETHING TELLS ME WE'RE GOIN' WHERE NO MAN HAS GONE BEFORE!
OUR JOURNEY NOW BEGINS.
CAPTAIN, WARP FACTOR 6...
...AN' LET'S PRAY THESE ENGINES CAN TAKE THE STRAIN!

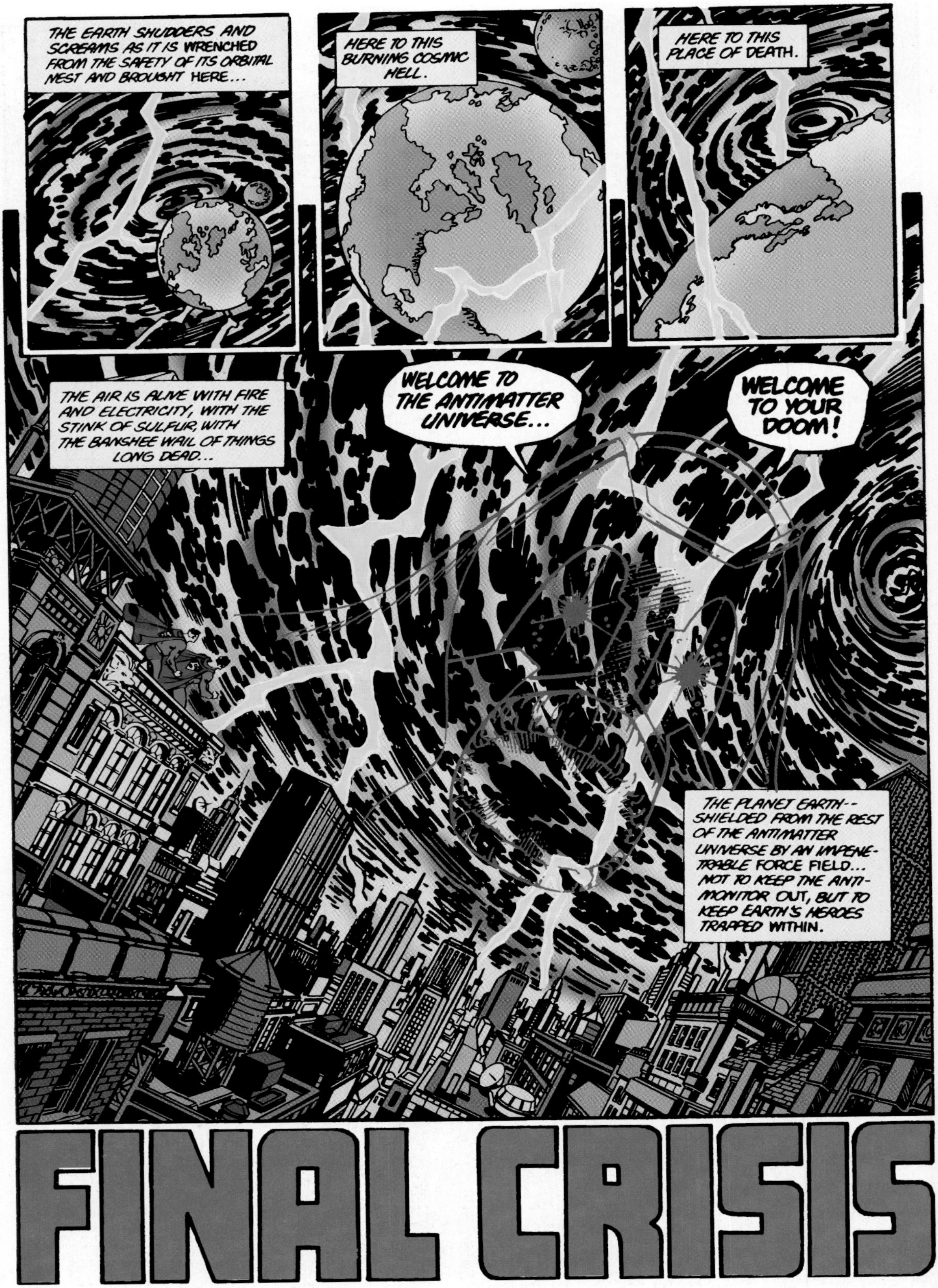
THE EARTH SHUDDERS AND SCREAMS AS IT IS WRENCHED FROM THE SAFETY OF ITS ORBITAL NEST AND BROUGHT HERE...
HERE TO THIS BURNING COSMIC HELL.
HERE TO THIS PLACE OF DEATH.
THE AIR IS ALIVE WITH FIRE AND ELECTRICITY, WITH THE STINK OF SULFUR, WITH THE BANSHEE WAIL OF THINGS LONG DEAD...
WELCOME TO THE ANTIMATTER UNIVERSE...
WELCOME TO YOUR DOOM!
THE PLANET EARTH-- SHIELDED FROM THE REST OF THE ANTIMATTER UNIVERSE BY AN IMPENETRABLE FORCE FIELD... NOT TO KEEP THE ANTI-MONITOR OUT, BUT TO KEEP EARTH'S HEROES TRAPPED WITHIN.
FINAL CRISIS

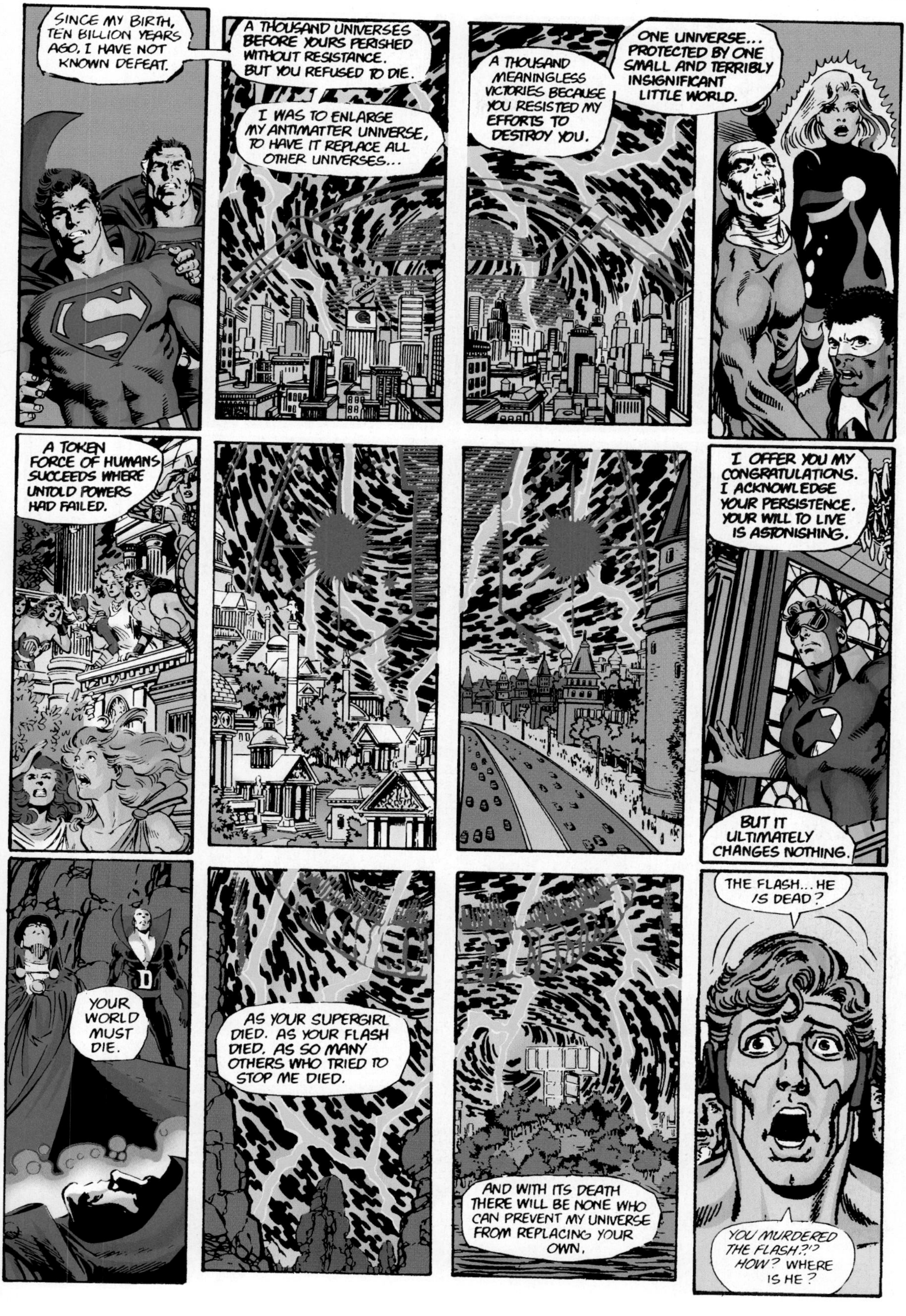
SINCE MY BIRTH, TEN BILLION YEARS AGO, I HAVE NOT KNOWN DEFEAT.
A THOUSAND UNIVERSES BEFORE YOURS PERISHED WITHOUT RESISTANCE. BUT YOU REFUSED TO DIE.
I WAS TO ENLARGE MY ANTIMATTER UNIVERSE, TO HAVE IT REPLACE ALL OTHER UNIVERSES...
A THOUSAND MEANINGLESS VICTORIES BECAUSE YOU RESISTED MY EFFORTS TO DESTROY YOU.
ONE UNIVERSE... PROTECTED BY ONE SMALL AND TERRIBLY INSIGNIFICANT LITTLE WORLD.
A TOKEN FORCE OF HUMANS SUCCEEDS WHERE UNTOLD POWERS HAD FAILED.
I OFFER YOU MY CONGRATULATIONS. I ACKNOWLEDGE YOUR PERSISTENCE. YOUR WILL TO LIVE IS ASTONISHING.
BUT IT ULTIMATELY CHANGES NOTHING.
YOUR WORLD MUST DIE.
AS YOUR SUPERGIRL DIED. AS YOUR FLASH DIED. AS SO MANY OTHERS WHO TRIED TO STOP ME DIED.
AND WITH ITS DEATH THERE WILL BE NONE WHO CAN PREVENT MY UNIVERSE FROM REPLACING YOUR OWN.
THE FLASH... HE IS DEAD?
YOU MURDERED THE FLASH?!? HOW? WHERE IS HE?

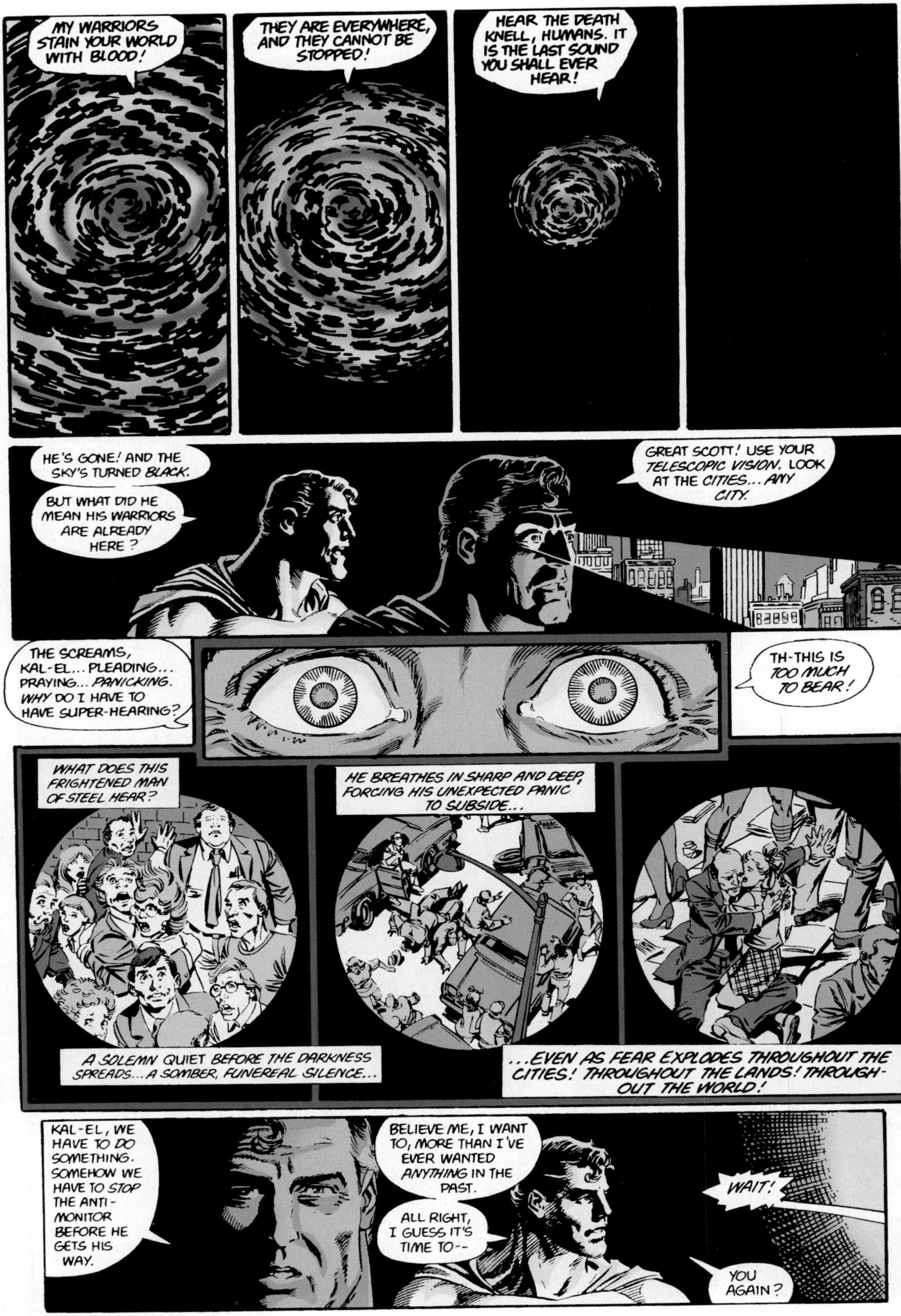
MY WARRIORS STAIN YOUR WORLD WITH BLOOD!
THEY ARE EVERYWHERE, AND THEY CANNOT BE STOPPED!
HEAR THE DEATH KNELL, HUMANS. IT IS THE LAST SOUND YOU SHALL EVER HEAR!
HE'S GONE! AND THE SKY'S TURNED BLACK.
BUT WHAT DID HE MEAN HIS WARRIORS ARE ALREADY HERE?
GREAT SCOTT! USE YOUR TELESCOPIC VISION. LOOK AT THE CITIES... ANY CITY.
THE SCREAMS, KAL-EL... PLEADING... PRAYING... PANICKING. WHY DO I HAVE TO HAVE SUPER-HEARING?
TH-THIS IS TOO MUCH TO BEAR!
WHAT DOES THIS FRIGHTENED MAN OF STEEL HEAR?
HE BREATHES IN SHARP AND DEEP, FORCING HIS UNEXPECTED PANIC TO SUBSIDE...
A SOLEMN QUIET BEFORE THE DARKNESS SPREADS... A SOMBER, FUNEREAL SILENCE...
...EVEN AS FEAR EXPLODES THROUGHOUT THE CITIES! THROUGHOUT THE LANDS! THROUGH-OUT THE WORLD!
KAL-EL, WE HAVE TO DO SOMETHING. SOMEHOW WE HAVE TO STOP THE ANTI-MONITOR BEFORE HE GETS HIS WAY.
BELIEVE ME, I WANT TO, MORE THAN I'VE EVER WANTED ANYTHING IN THE PAST.
ALL RIGHT, I GUESS IT'S TIME TO--
WAIT!
YOU AGAIN?

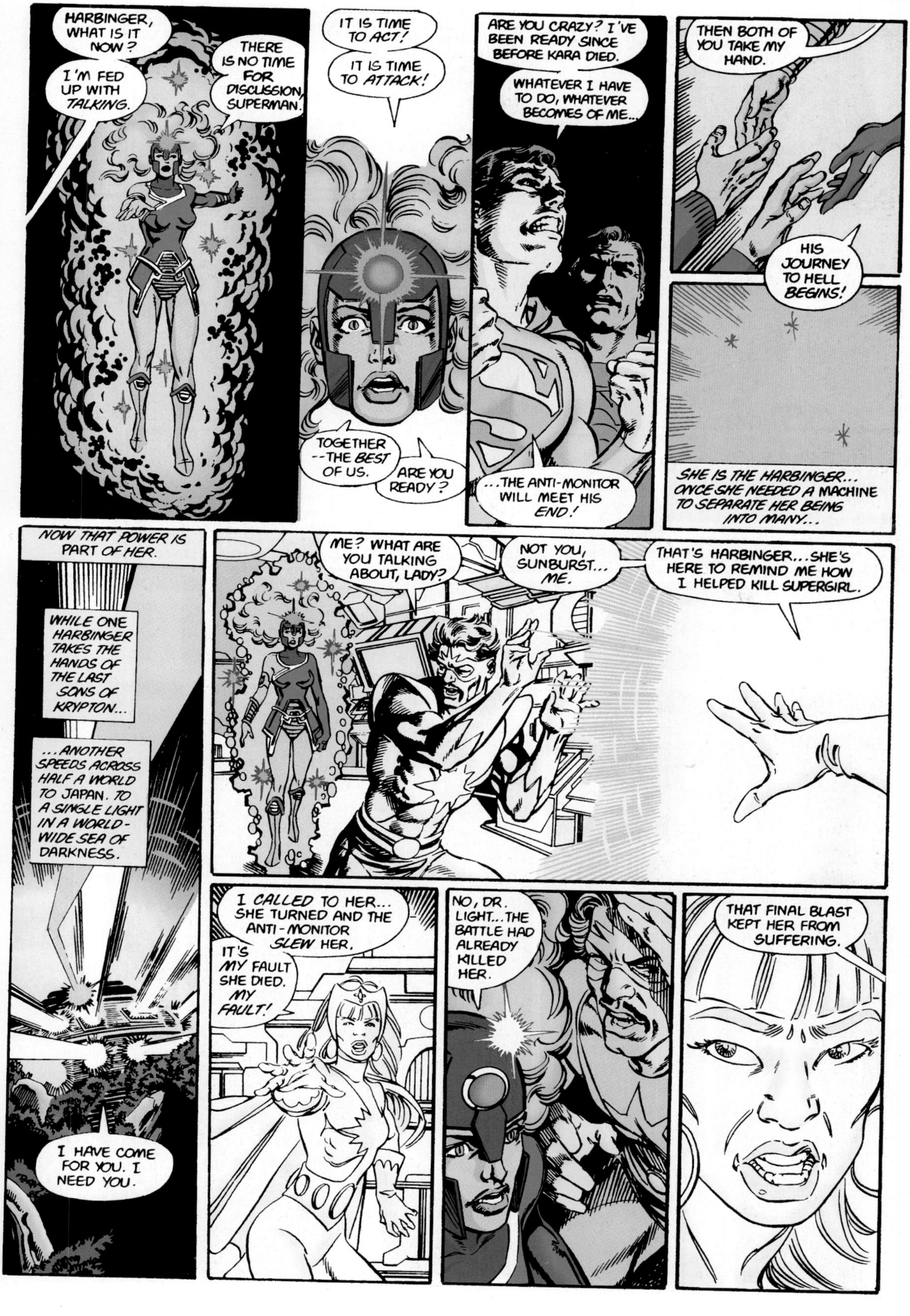
HARBINGER, WHAT IS IT NOW?
I'M FED UP WITH TALKING.
THERE IS NO TIME FOR DISCUSSION, SUPERMAN.
IT IS TIME TO ACT!
IT IS TIME TO ATTACK!
TOGETHER--THE BEST OF US.
ARE YOU READY?
ARE YOU CRAZY? I'VE BEEN READY SINCE BEFORE KARA DIED.
WHATEVER I HAVE TO DO, WHATEVER BECOMES OF ME...
...THE ANTI-MONITOR WILL MEET HIS END!
THEN BOTH OF YOU TAKE MY HAND.
HIS JOURNEY TO HELL BEGINS!
SHE IS THE HARBINGER... ONCE SHE NEEDED A MACHINE TO SEPARATE HER BEING INTO MANY...
NOW THAT POWER IS PART OF HER.
WHILE ONE HARBINGER TAKES THE HANDS OF THE LAST SONS OF KRYPTON...
...ANOTHER SPEEDS ACROSS HALF A WORLD TO JAPAN. TO A SINGLE LIGHT IN A WORLD-WIDE SEA OF DARKNESS.
I HAVE COME FOR YOU. I NEED YOU.
ME? WHAT ARE YOU TALKING ABOUT, LADY?
NOT YOU, SUNBURST... ME.
THAT'S HARBINGER...SHE'S HERE TO REMIND ME HOW I HELPED KILL SUPERGIRL.
I CALLED TO HER... SHE TURNED AND THE ANTI-MONITOR SLEW HER.
IT'S MY FAULT SHE DIED. MY FAULT!
NO, DR. LIGHT...THE BATTLE HAD ALREADY KILLED HER.
THAT FINAL BLAST KEPT HER FROM SUFFERING.

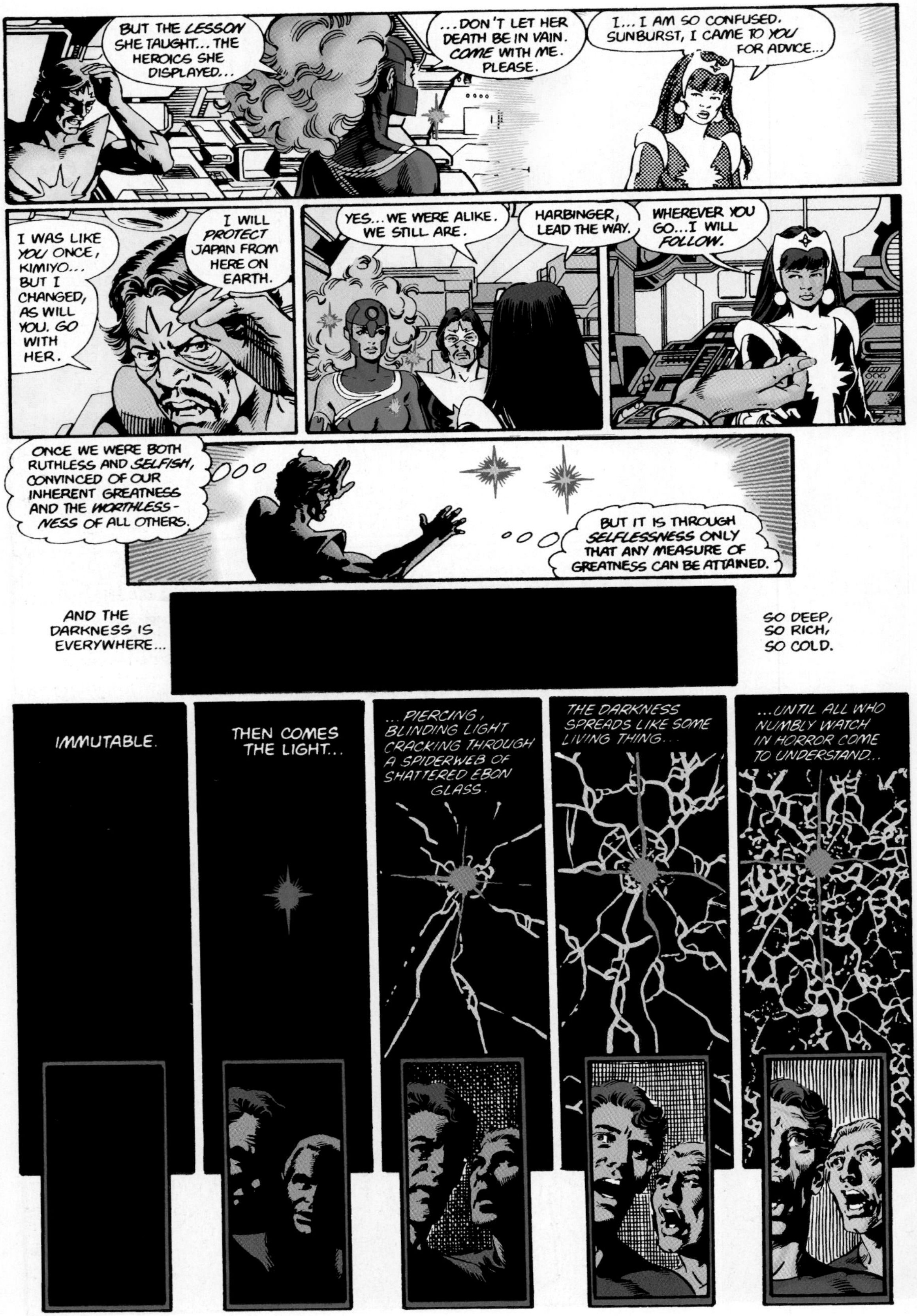
BUT THE LESSON SHE TAUGHT... THE HEROICS SHE DISPLAYED...
...DON'T LET HER DEATH BE IN VAIN. COME WITH ME. PLEASE.
I... I AM SO CONFUSED. SUNBURST, I CAME TO YOU FOR ADVICE...
I WAS LIKE YOU ONCE, KIMIYO... BUT I CHANGED, AS WILL YOU. GO WITH HER.
I WILL PROTECT JAPAN FROM HERE ON EARTH.
YES... WE WERE ALIKE. WE STILL ARE.
HARBINGER, LEAD THE WAY.
WHEREVER YOU GO... I WILL FOLLOW.
ONCE WE WERE BOTH RUTHLESS AND SELFISH, CONVINCED OF OUR INHERENT GREATNESS AND THE WORTHLESS-NESS OF ALL OTHERS.
BUT IT IS THROUGH SELFLESSNESS ONLY THAT ANY MEASURE OF GREATNESS CAN BE ATTAINED.
AND THE DARKNESS IS EVERYWHERE...
SO DEEP, SO RICH, SO COLD.
IMMUTABLE.
THEN COMES THE LIGHT...
...PIERCING, BLINDING LIGHT CRACKING THROUGH A SPIDERWEB OF SHATTERED EBON GLASS.
THE DARKNESS SPREADS LIKE SOME LIVING THING...
...UNTIL ALL WHO NUMBLY WATCH IN HORROR COME TO UNDERSTAND...

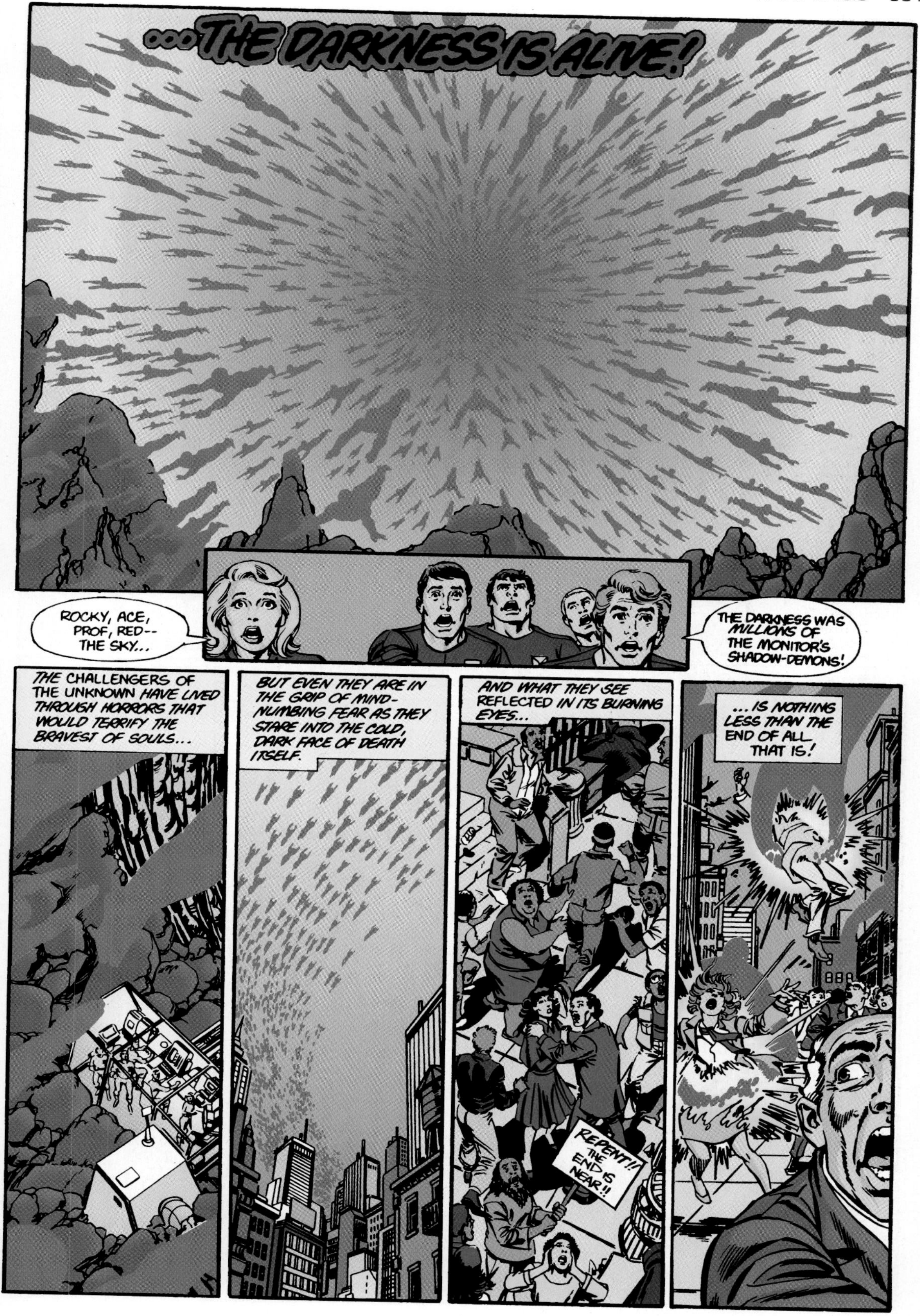
...THE DARKNESS IS ALIVE!
ROCKY, ACE, PROF, RED-- THE SKY...
THE DARKNESS WAS MILLIONS OF THE MONITOR'S SHADOW-DEMONS!
THE CHALLENGERS OF THE UNKNOWN HAVE LIVED THROUGH HORRORS THAT WOULD TERRIFY THE BRAVEST OF SOULS...
BUT EVEN THEY ARE IN THE GRIP OF MIND-NUMBING FEAR AS THEY STARE INTO THE COLD, DARK FACE OF DEATH ITSELF.
AND WHAT THEY SEE REFLECTED IN ITS BURNING EYES...
REPENT!! THE END IS NEAR!!
...IS NOTHING LESS THAN THE END OF ALL THAT IS!

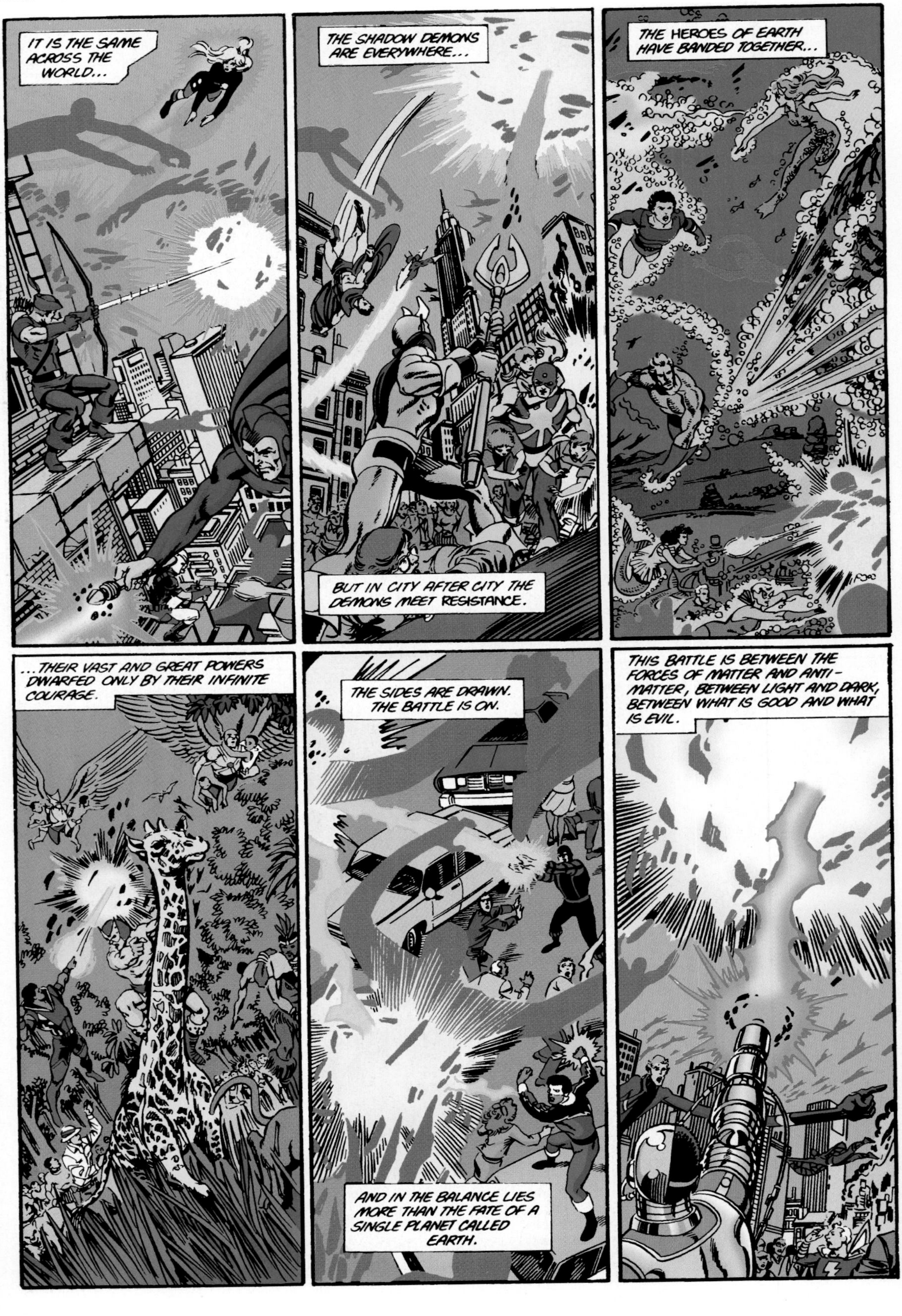
IT IS THE SAME ACROSS THE WORLD...
THE SHADOW DEMONS ARE EVERYWHERE...
BUT IN CITY AFTER CITY THE DEMONS MEET RESISTANCE.
THE HEROES OF EARTH HAVE BANDED TOGETHER...
...THEIR VAST AND GREAT POWERS DWARFED ONLY BY THEIR INFINITE COURAGE.
THE SIDES ARE DRAWN. THE BATTLE IS ON.
AND IN THE BALANCE LIES MORE THAN THE FATE OF A SINGLE PLANET CALLED EARTH.
THIS BATTLE IS BETWEEN THE FORCES OF MATTER AND ANTI-MATTER, BETWEEN LIGHT AND DARK, BETWEEN WHAT IS GOOD AND WHAT IS EVIL.

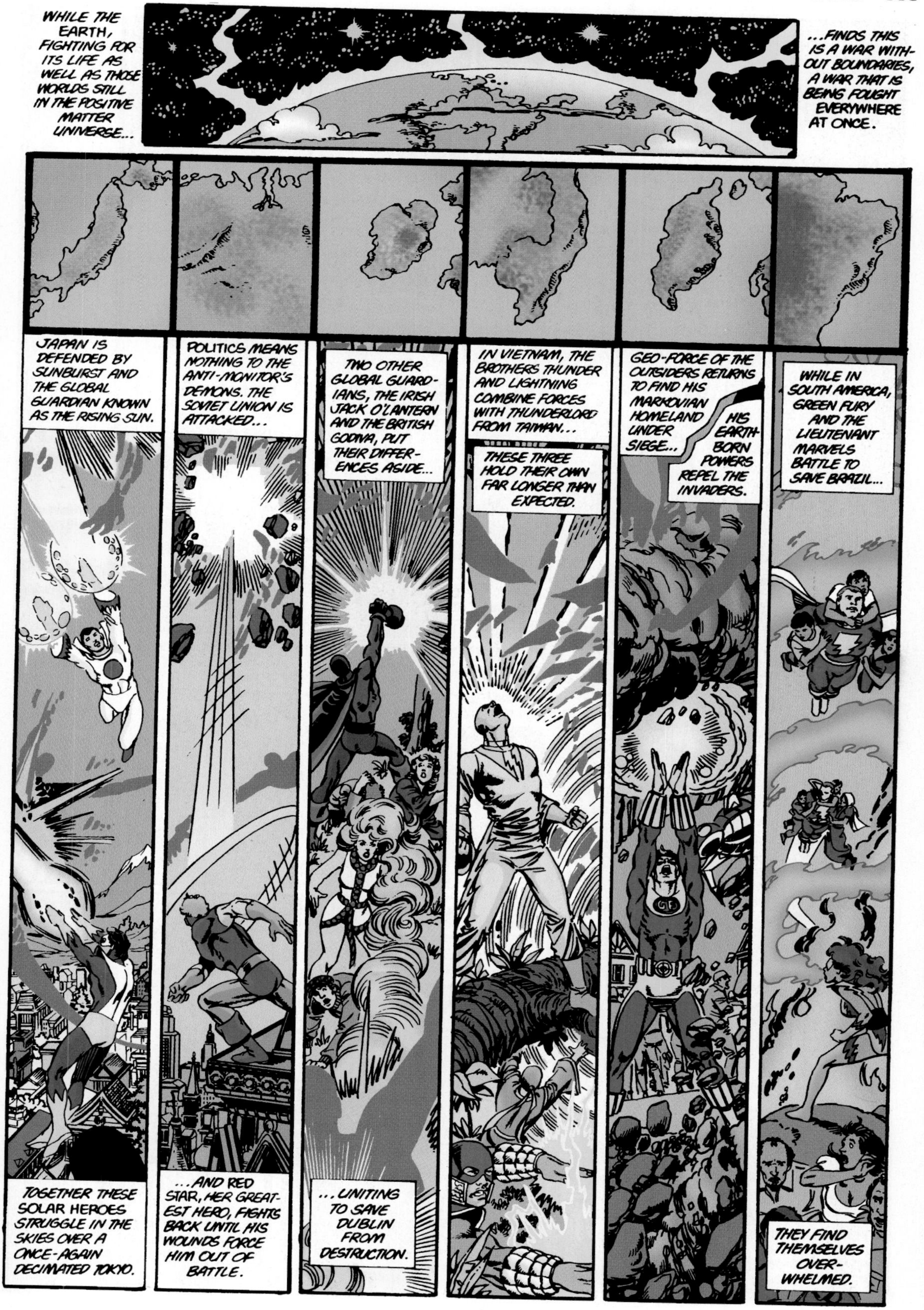
WHILE THE EARTH, FIGHTING FOR ITS LIFE AS WELL AS THOSE WORLDS STILL IN THE POSITIVE MATTER UNIVERSE...
...FINDS THIS IS A WAR WITHOUT BOUNDARIES, A WAR THAT IS BEING FOUGHT EVERYWHERE AT ONCE.
JAPAN IS DEFENDED BY SUNBURST AND THE GLOBAL GUARDIAN KNOWN AS THE RISING SUN.
TOGETHER THESE SOLAR HEROES STRUGGLE IN THE SKIES OVER A ONCE-AGAIN DECIMATED TOKYO.
POLITICS MEANS NOTHING TO THE ANTI-MONITOR'S DEMONS. THE SOVIET UNION IS ATTACKED...
...AND RED STAR, HER GREATEST HERO, FIGHTS BACK UNTIL HIS WOUNDS FORCE HIM OUT OF BATTLE.
TWO OTHER GLOBAL GUARDIANS, THE IRISH JACK O'LANTERN AND THE BRITISH GODIVA, PUT THEIR DIFFERENCES ASIDE...
...UNITING TO SAVE DUBLIN FROM DESTRUCTION.
IN VIETNAM, THE BROTHERS THUNDER AND LIGHTNING COMBINE FORCES WITH THUNDERLORD FROM TAIWAN...
THESE THREE HOLD THEIR OWN FAR LONGER THAN EXPECTED.
GEO-FORCE OF THE OUTSIDERS RETURNS TO FIND HIS MARKOVIAN HOMELAND UNDER SIEGE...
HIS EARTH-BORN POWERS REPEL THE INVADERS.
WHILE IN SOUTH AMERICA, GREEN FURY AND THE LIEUTENANT MARVELS BATTLE TO SAVE BRAZIL...
THEY FIND THEMSELVES OVERWHELMED.

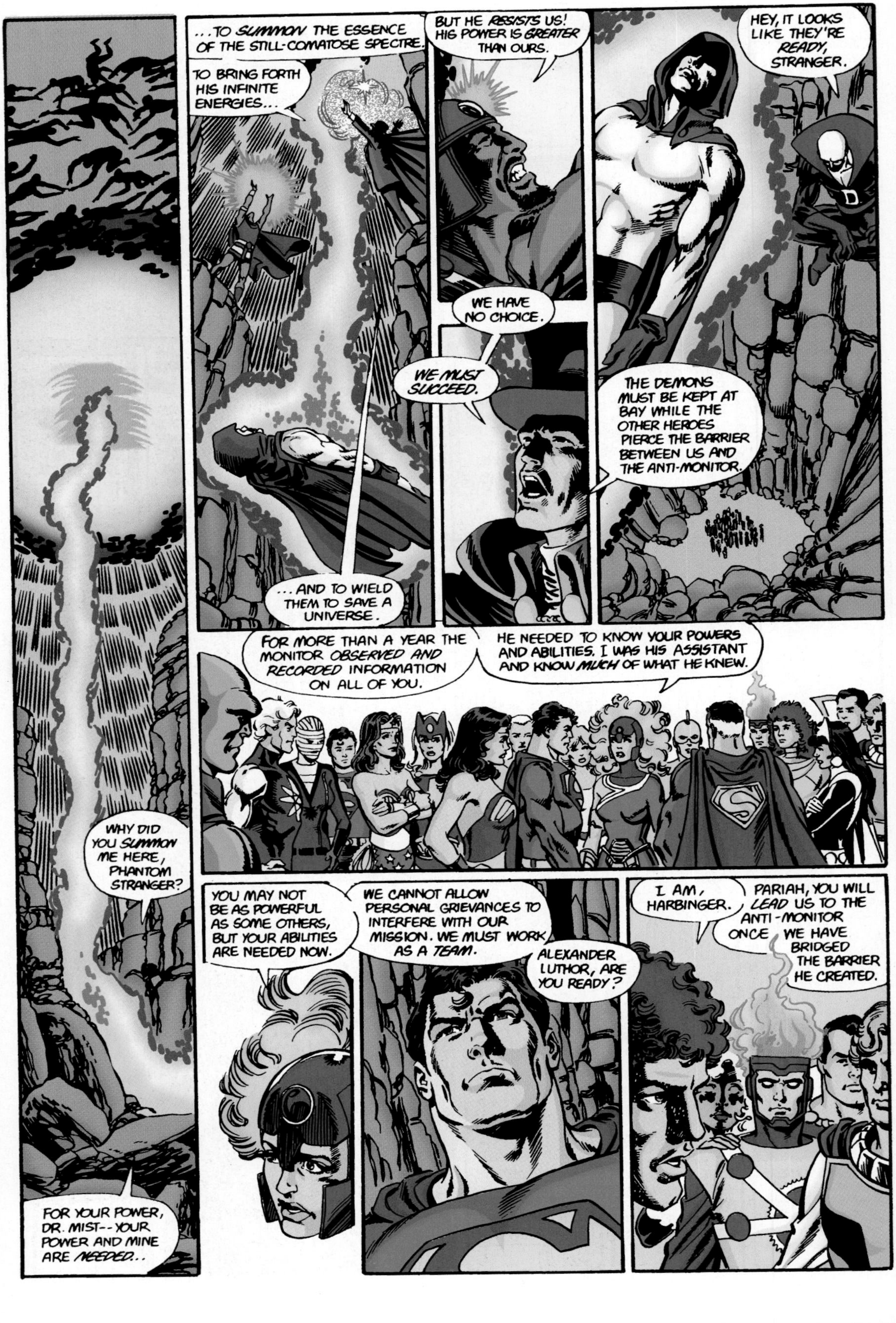
...TO SUMMON THE ESSENCE OF THE STILL-COMATOSE SPECTRE.
TO BRING FORTH HIS INFINITE ENERGIES...
...AND TO WIELD THEM TO SAVE A UNIVERSE.
BUT HE RESISTS US! HIS POWER IS GREATER THAN OURS.
WE HAVE NO CHOICE.
WE MUST SUCCEED.
HEY, IT LOOKS LIKE THEY'RE READY, STRANGER.
THE DEMONS MUST BE KEPT AT BAY WHILE THE OTHER HEROES PIERCE THE BARRIER BETWEEN US AND THE ANTI-MONITOR.
WHY DID YOU SUMMON ME HERE, PHANTOM STRANGER?
FOR YOUR POWER, DR. MIST--YOUR POWER AND MINE ARE NEEDED...
FOR MORE THAN A YEAR THE MONITOR OBSERVED AND RECORDED INFORMATION ON ALL OF YOU.
HE NEEDED TO KNOW YOUR POWERS AND ABILITIES. I WAS HIS ASSISTANT AND KNOW MUCH OF WHAT HE KNEW.
YOU MAY NOT BE AS POWERFUL AS SOME OTHERS, BUT YOUR ABILITIES ARE NEEDED NOW.
WE CANNOT ALLOW PERSONAL GRIEVANCES TO INTERFERE WITH OUR MISSION. WE MUST WORK AS A TEAM.
ALEXANDER LUTHOR, ARE YOU READY?
I AM, HARBINGER.
PARIAH, YOU WILL LEAD US TO THE ANTI-MONITOR ONCE WE HAVE BRIDGED THE BARRIER HE CREATED.

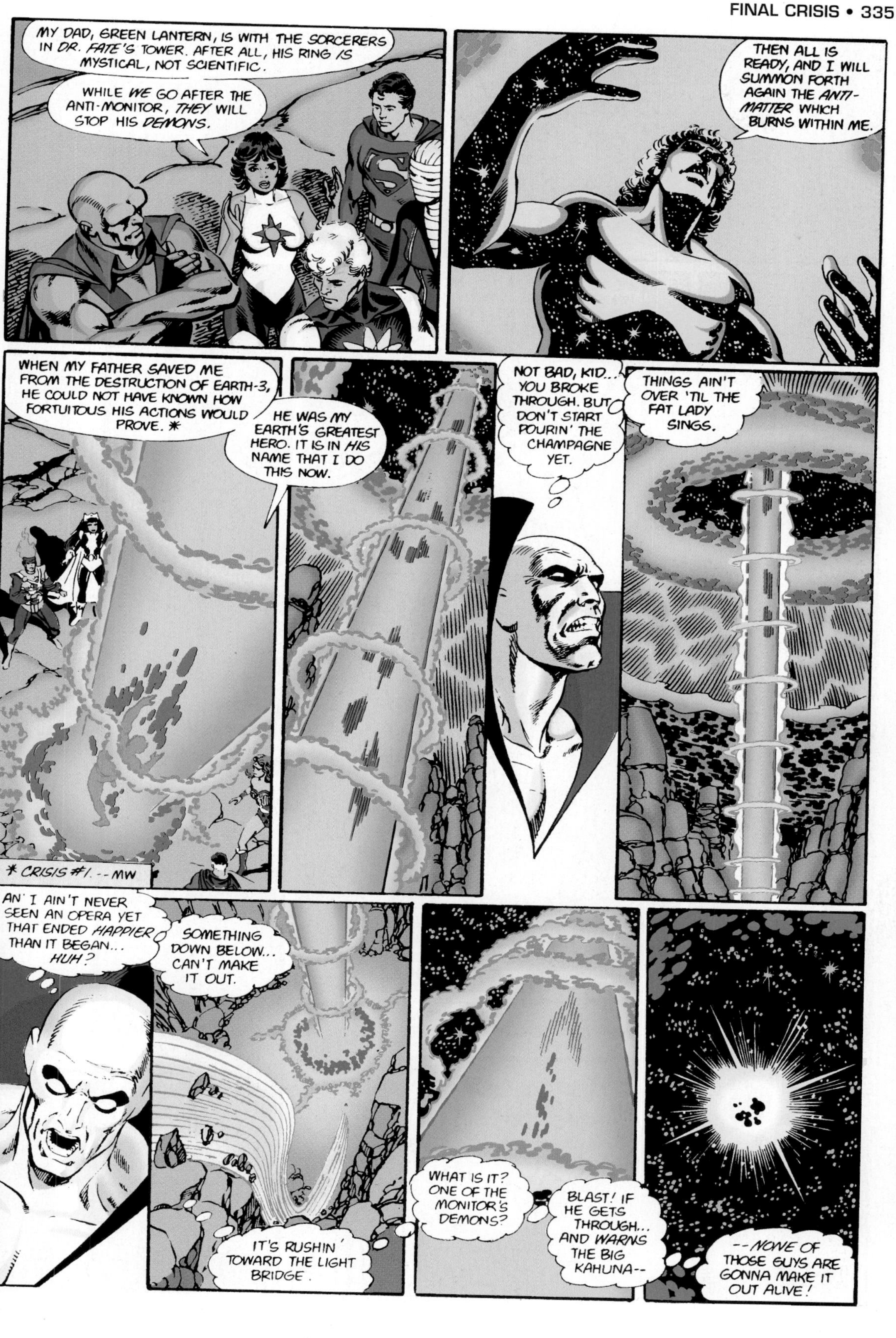
MY DAD, GREEN LANTERN, IS WITH THE SORCERERS IN DR. FATE'S TOWER. AFTER ALL, HIS RING IS MYSTICAL, NOT SCIENTIFIC.
WHILE WE GO AFTER THE ANTI-MONITOR, THEY WILL STOP HIS DEMONS.
THEN ALL IS READY, AND I WILL SUMMON FORTH AGAIN THE ANTI-MATTER WHICH BURNS WITHIN ME.
WHEN MY FATHER SAVED ME FROM THE DESTRUCTION OF EARTH-3, HE COULD NOT HAVE KNOWN HOW FORTUITOUS HIS ACTIONS WOULD PROVE. *
HE WAS MY EARTH'S GREATEST HERO. IT IS IN HIS NAME THAT I DO THIS NOW.
* CRISIS #1. --MW
NOT BAD, KID... YOU BROKE THROUGH. BUT DON'T START POURIN' THE CHAMPAGNE YET.
THINGS AIN'T OVER 'TIL THE FAT LADY SINGS.
AN' I AIN'T NEVER SEEN AN OPERA YET THAT ENDED HAPPIER THAN IT BEGAN... HUH?
SOMETHING DOWN BELOW... CAN'T MAKE IT OUT.
IT'S RUSHIN' TOWARD THE LIGHT BRIDGE.
WHAT IS IT? ONE OF THE MONITOR'S DEMONS?
BLAST! IF HE GETS THROUGH... AND WARNS THE BIG KAHUNA--
--NONE OF THOSE GUYS ARE GONNA MAKE IT OUT ALIVE!

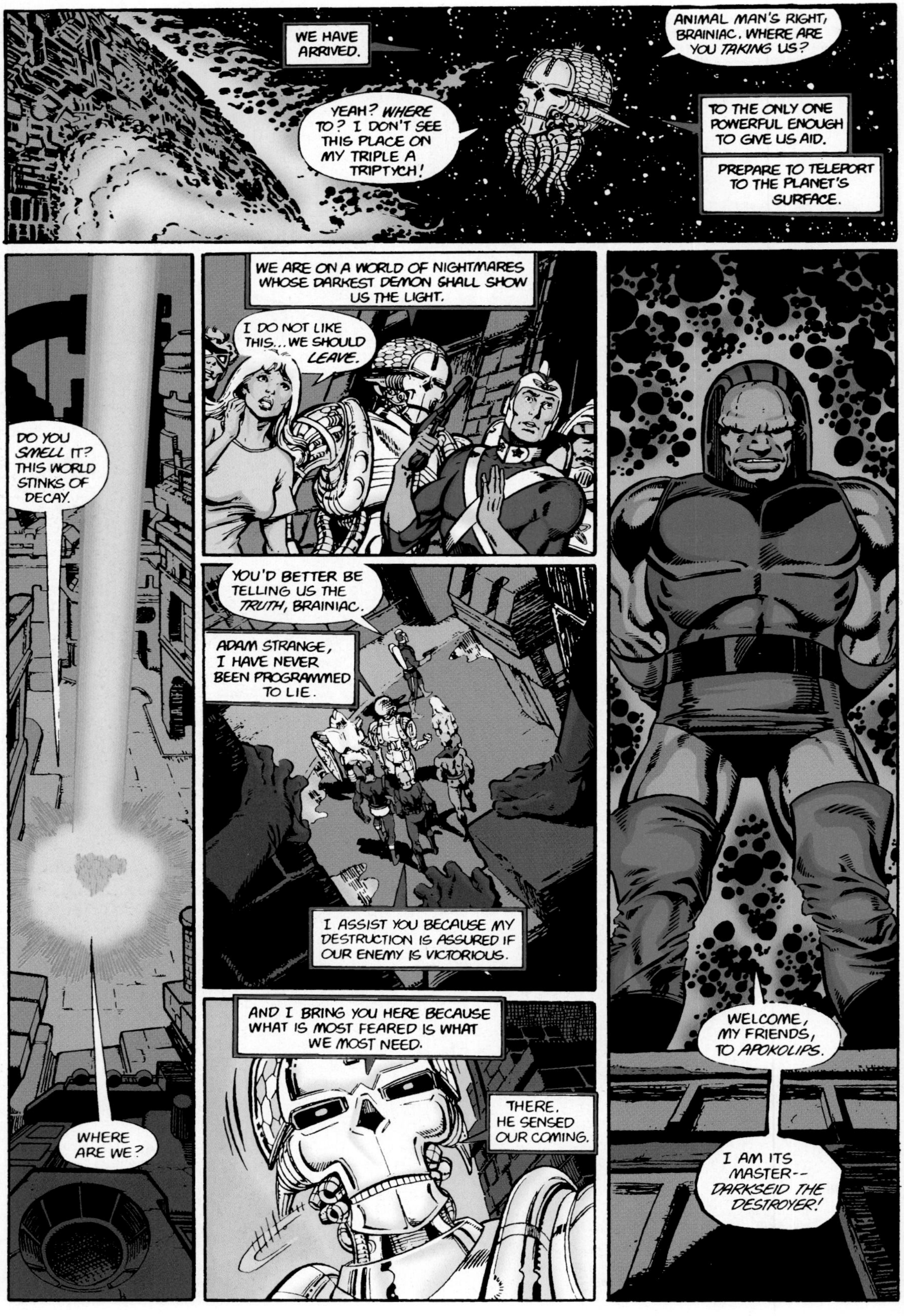
WE HAVE ARRIVED.
ANIMAL MAN'S RIGHT, BRAINIAC. WHERE ARE YOU TAKING US?
YEAH? WHERE TO? I DON'T SEE THIS PLACE ON MY TRIPLE A TRIPTYCH!
TO THE ONLY ONE POWERFUL ENOUGH TO GIVE US AID.
PREPARE TO TELEPORT TO THE PLANET'S SURFACE.
DO YOU SMELL IT? THIS WORLD STINKS OF DECAY.
WHERE ARE WE?
WE ARE ON A WORLD OF NIGHTMARES WHOSE DARKEST DEMON SHALL SHOW US THE LIGHT.
I DO NOT LIKE THIS... WE SHOULD LEAVE.
YOU'D BETTER BE TELLING US THE TRUTH, BRAINIAC.
ADAM STRANGE, I HAVE NEVER BEEN PROGRAMMED TO LIE.
I ASSIST YOU BECAUSE MY DESTRUCTION IS ASSURED IF OUR ENEMY IS VICTORIOUS.
AND I BRING YOU HERE BECAUSE WHAT IS MOST FEARED IS WHAT WE MOST NEED.
THERE. HE SENSED OUR COMING.
WELCOME, MY FRIENDS, TO APOKOLIPS.
I AM ITS MASTER-- DARKSEID THE DESTROYER!

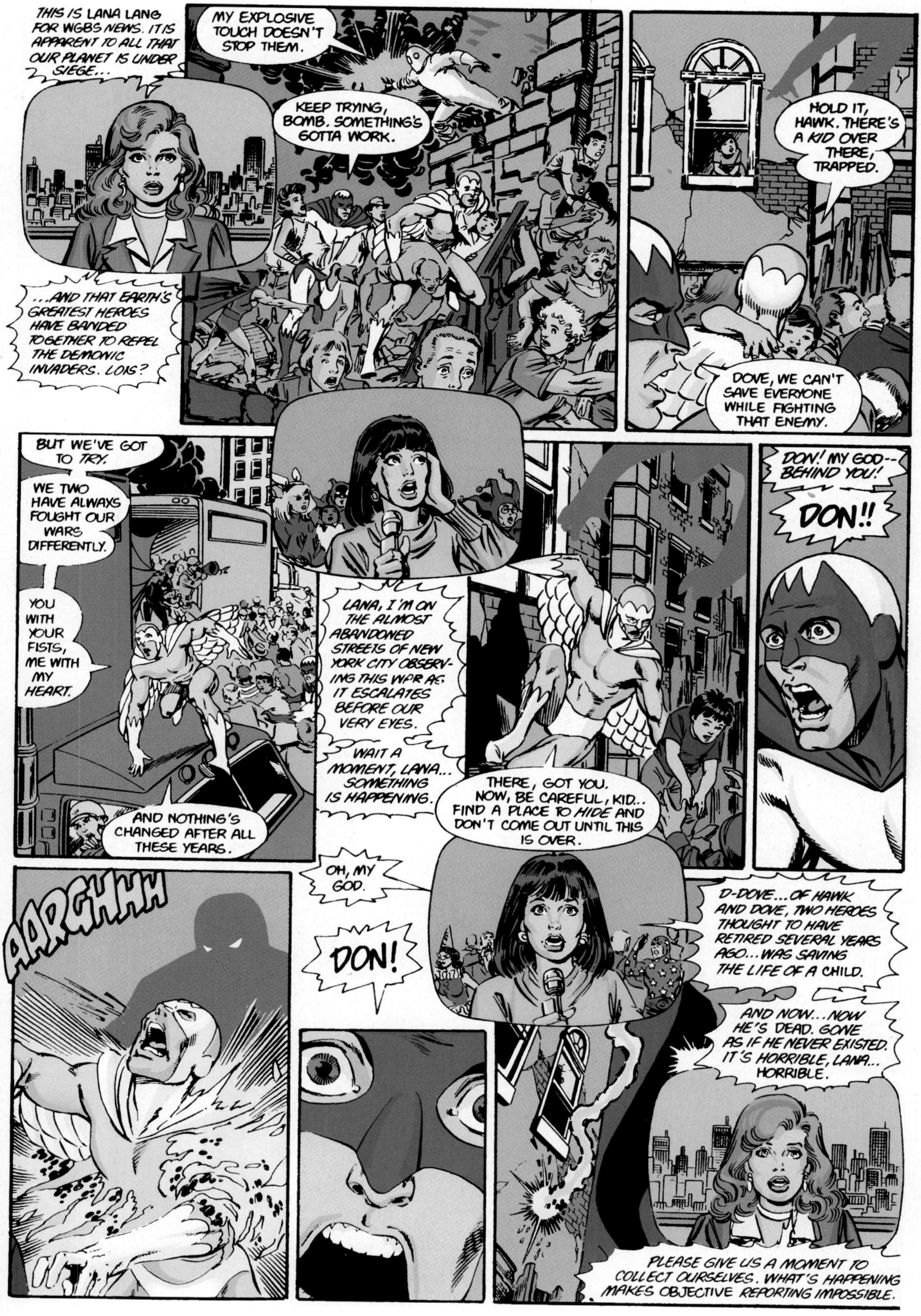
THIS IS LANA LANG FOR WGBS NEWS. IT IS APPARENT TO ALL THAT OUR PLANET IS UNDER SIEGE...
...AND THAT EARTH'S GREATEST HEROES HAVE BANDED TOGETHER TO REPEL THE DEMONIC INVADERS. LOIS?
MY EXPLOSIVE TOUCH DOESN'T STOP THEM.
KEEP TRYING, BOMB. SOMETHING'S GOTTA WORK.
HOLD IT, HAWK. THERE'S A KID OVER THERE, TRAPPED.
DOVE, WE CAN'T SAVE EVERYONE WHILE FIGHTING THAT ENEMY.
BUT WE'VE GOT TO TRY.
WE TWO HAVE ALWAYS FOUGHT OUR WARS DIFFERENTLY.
YOU WITH YOUR FISTS, ME WITH MY HEART.
AND NOTHING'S CHANGED AFTER ALL THESE YEARS.
LANA, I'M ON THE ALMOST ABANDONED STREETS OF NEW YORK CITY OBSERVING THIS WAR AS IT ESCALATES BEFORE OUR VERY EYES.
WAIT A MOMENT, LANA... SOMETHING IS HAPPENING.
THERE, GOT YOU. NOW, BE CAREFUL, KID... FIND A PLACE TO HIDE AND DON'T COME OUT UNTIL THIS IS OVER.
DON! MY GOD-- BEHIND YOU!
DON!!
AARGHHH
OH, MY GOD.
DON!
D-DOVE... OF HAWK AND DOVE, TWO HEROES THOUGHT TO HAVE RETIRED SEVERAL YEARS AGO... WAS SAVING THE LIFE OF A CHILD.
AND NOW... NOW HE'S DEAD. GONE AS IF HE NEVER EXISTED. IT'S HORRIBLE, LANA... HORRIBLE.
PLEASE GIVE US A MOMENT TO COLLECT OURSELVES. WHAT'S HAPPENING MAKES OBJECTIVE REPORTING IMPOSSIBLE.

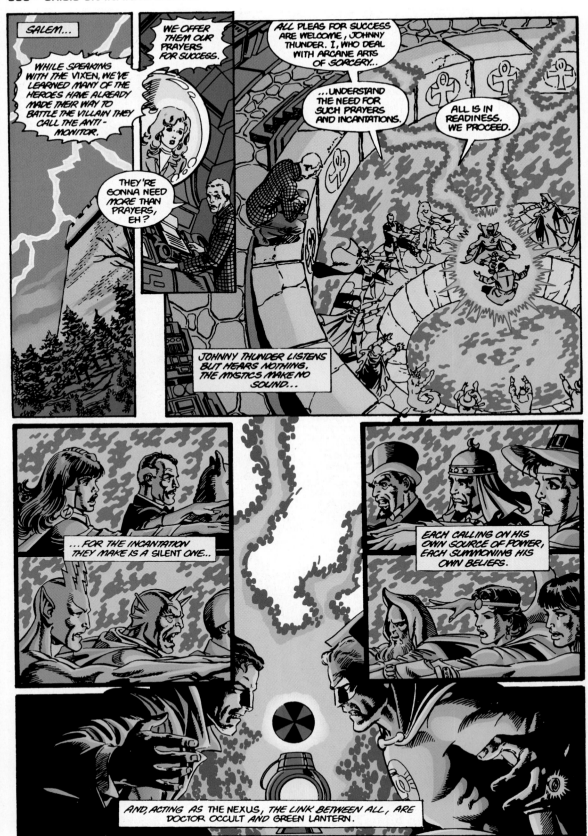

SALEM...

WHILE SPEAKING WITH THE VIXEN, WE'VE LEARNED MANY OF THE HEROES HAVE ALREADY MADE THEIR WAY TO BATTLE THE VILLAIN THEY CALL THE ANTI-MONITOR.

WE OFFER THEM OUR PRAYERS FOR SUCCESS.

THEY'RE GONNA NEED MORE THAN PRAYERS, EH?

ALL PLEAS FOR SUCCESS ARE WELCOME, JOHNNY THUNDER. I, WHO DEAL WITH ARCANE ARTS OF SORCERY...

...UNDERSTAND THE NEED FOR SUCH PRAYERS AND INCANTATIONS.

ALL IS IN READINESS. WE PROCEED.

JOHNNY THUNDER LISTENS BUT HEARS NOTHING. THE MYSTICS MAKE NO SOUND...

....FOR THE INCANTATION THEY MAKE IS A SILENT ONE...

EACH CALLING ON HIS OWN SOURCE OF POWER, EACH SUMMONING HIS OWN BELIEFS.

AND, ACTING AS THE NEXUS, THE LINK BETWEEN ALL, ARE DOCTOR OCCULT AND GREEN LANTERN.

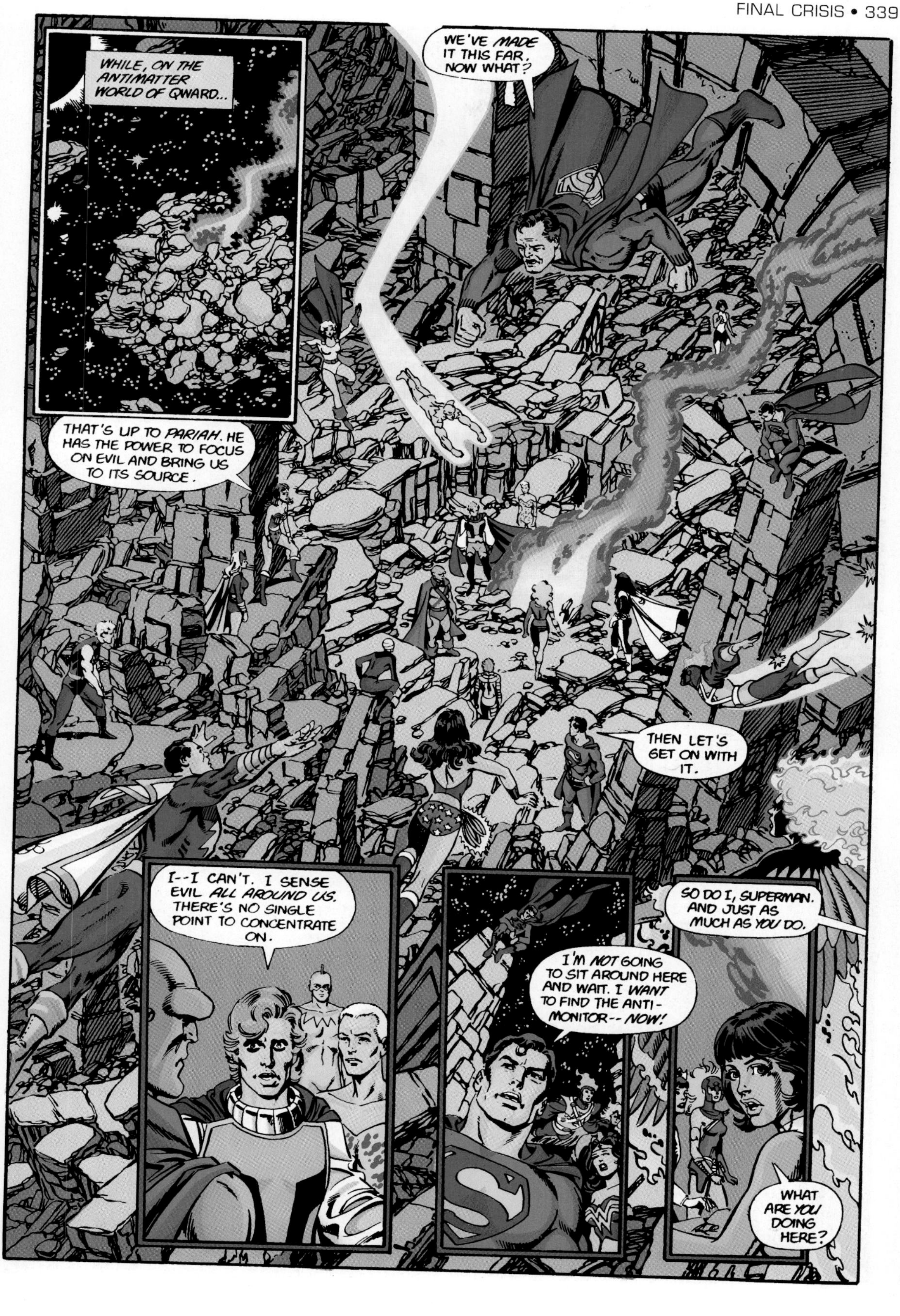
WHILE, ON THE ANTIMATTER WORLD OF QWARD...
WE'VE *MADE* IT THIS FAR, NOW WHAT?
THAT'S UP TO *PARIAH*. HE HAS THE POWER TO FOCUS ON EVIL AND BRING US TO ITS SOURCE.
THEN LET'S GET ON WITH IT.
I--I CAN'T. I SENSE EVIL *ALL AROUND US*. THERE'S NO SINGLE POINT TO CONCENTRATE ON.
I'M *NOT* GOING TO SIT AROUND HERE AND WAIT. I *WANT* TO FIND THE ANTI-MONITOR-- *NOW!*
SO DO I, SUPERMAN. AND JUST AS MUCH AS *YOU* DO.
WHAT ARE *YOU* DOING HERE?

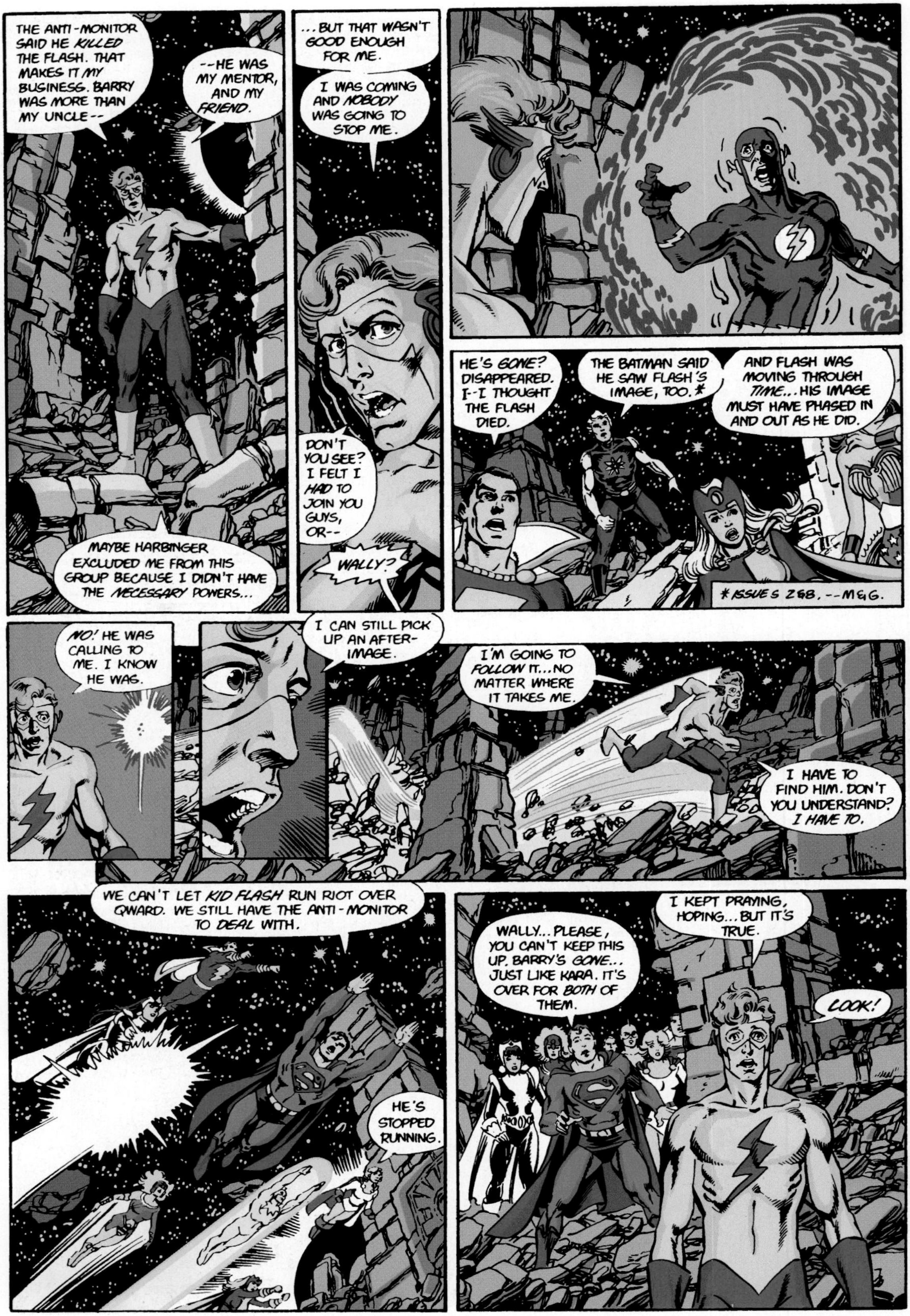
THE ANTI-MONITOR SAID HE KILLED THE FLASH. THAT MAKES IT MY BUSINESS. BARRY WAS MORE THAN MY UNCLE--
--HE WAS MY MENTOR, AND MY FRIEND.
MAYBE HARBINGER EXCLUDED ME FROM THIS GROUP BECAUSE I DIDN'T HAVE THE NECESSARY POWERS...
...BUT THAT WASN'T GOOD ENOUGH FOR ME.
I WAS COMING AND NOBODY WAS GOING TO STOP ME.
DON'T YOU SEE? I FELT I HAD TO JOIN YOU GUYS, OR--
WALLY?
HE'S GONE? DISAPPEARED. I--I THOUGHT THE FLASH DIED.
THE BATMAN SAID HE SAW FLASH'S IMAGE, TOO.*
AND FLASH WAS MOVING THROUGH TIME...HIS IMAGE MUST HAVE PHASED IN AND OUT AS HE DID.
*ISSUES 2&8. --M&G.
NO! HE WAS CALLING TO ME. I KNOW HE WAS.
I CAN STILL PICK UP AN AFTER-IMAGE.
I'M GOING TO FOLLOW IT...NO MATTER WHERE IT TAKES ME.
I HAVE TO FIND HIM. DON'T YOU UNDERSTAND? I HAVE TO.
WE CAN'T LET KID FLASH RUN RIOT OVER QWARD. WE STILL HAVE THE ANTI-MONITOR TO DEAL WITH.
HE'S STOPPED RUNNING.
WALLY... PLEASE, YOU CAN'T KEEP THIS UP. BARRY'S GONE... JUST LIKE KARA. IT'S OVER FOR BOTH OF THEM.
I KEPT PRAYING, HOPING... BUT IT'S TRUE.
LOOK!

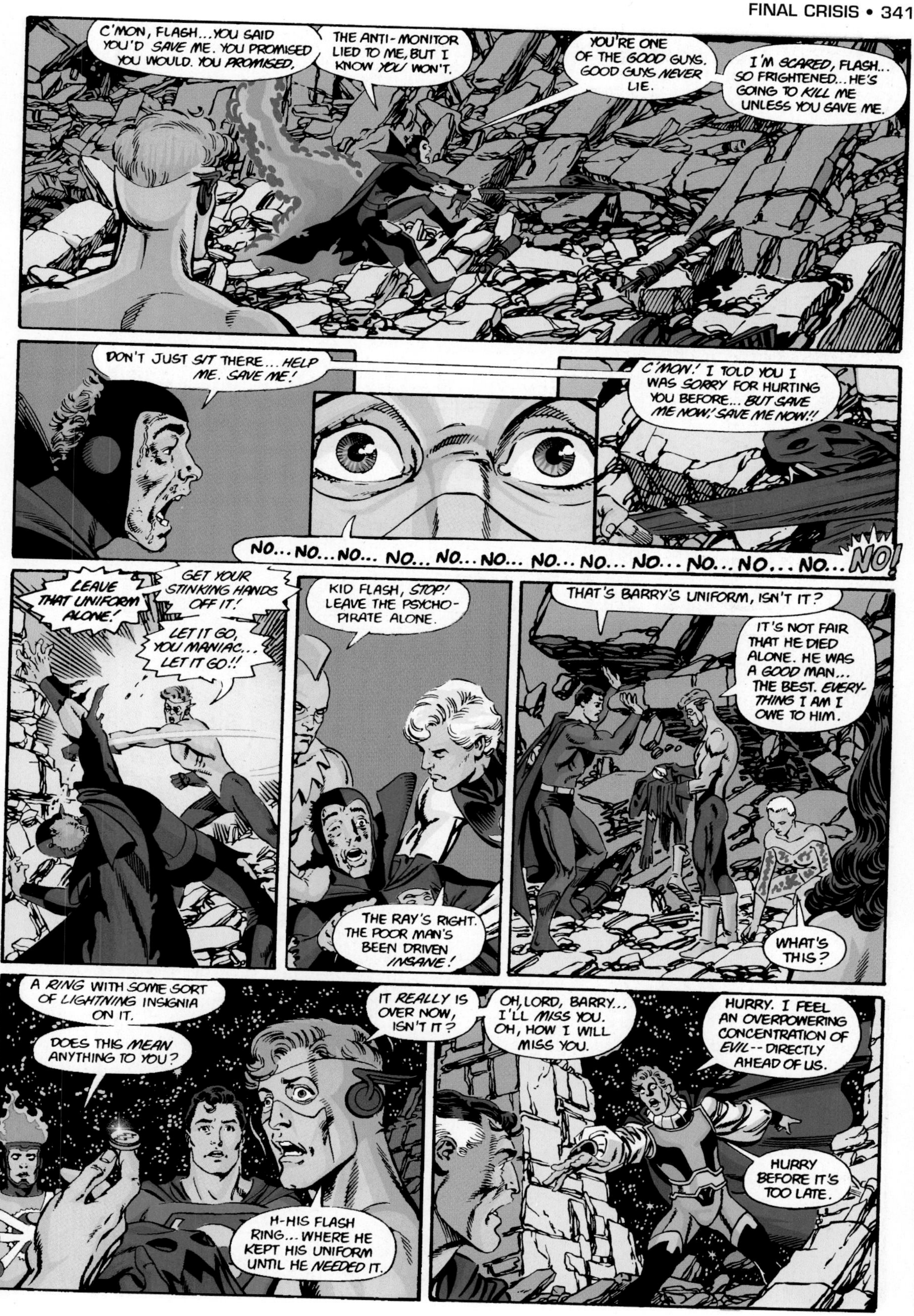
C'MON, FLASH... YOU SAID YOU'D SAVE ME. YOU PROMISED YOU WOULD. YOU PROMISED.
THE ANTI-MONITOR LIED TO ME, BUT I KNOW YOU WON'T.
YOU'RE ONE OF THE GOOD GUYS. GOOD GUYS NEVER LIE.
I'M SCARED, FLASH... SO FRIGHTENED... HE'S GOING TO KILL ME UNLESS YOU GAVE ME.
DON'T JUST SIT THERE... HELP ME. SAVE ME!
C'MON! I TOLD YOU I WAS SORRY FOR HURTING YOU BEFORE... BUT SAVE ME NOW! SAVE ME NOW!!
NO... NO... NO... NO... NO... NO... NO... NO... NO... NO... NO... NO... NO!
LEAVE THAT UNIFORM ALONE!
GET YOUR STINKING HANDS OFF IT!
LET IT GO, YOU MANIAC... LET IT GO!!
KID FLASH, STOP! LEAVE THE PSYCHO-PIRATE ALONE.
THE RAY'S RIGHT. THE POOR MAN'S BEEN DRIVEN INSANE!
THAT'S BARRY'S UNIFORM, ISN'T IT?
IT'S NOT FAIR THAT HE DIED ALONE. HE WAS A GOOD MAN... THE BEST. EVERYTHING I AM I OWE TO HIM.
WHAT'S THIS?
A RING WITH SOME SORT OF LIGHTNING INSIGNIA ON IT.
DOES THIS MEAN ANYTHING TO YOU?
H-HIS FLASH RING... WHERE HE KEPT HIS UNIFORM UNTIL HE NEEDED IT.
IT REALLY IS OVER NOW, ISN'T IT?
OH, LORD, BARRY... I'LL MISS YOU. OH, HOW I WILL MISS YOU.
HURRY. I FEEL AN OVERPOWERING CONCENTRATION OF EVIL-- DIRECTLY AHEAD OF US.
HURRY BEFORE IT'S TOO LATE.

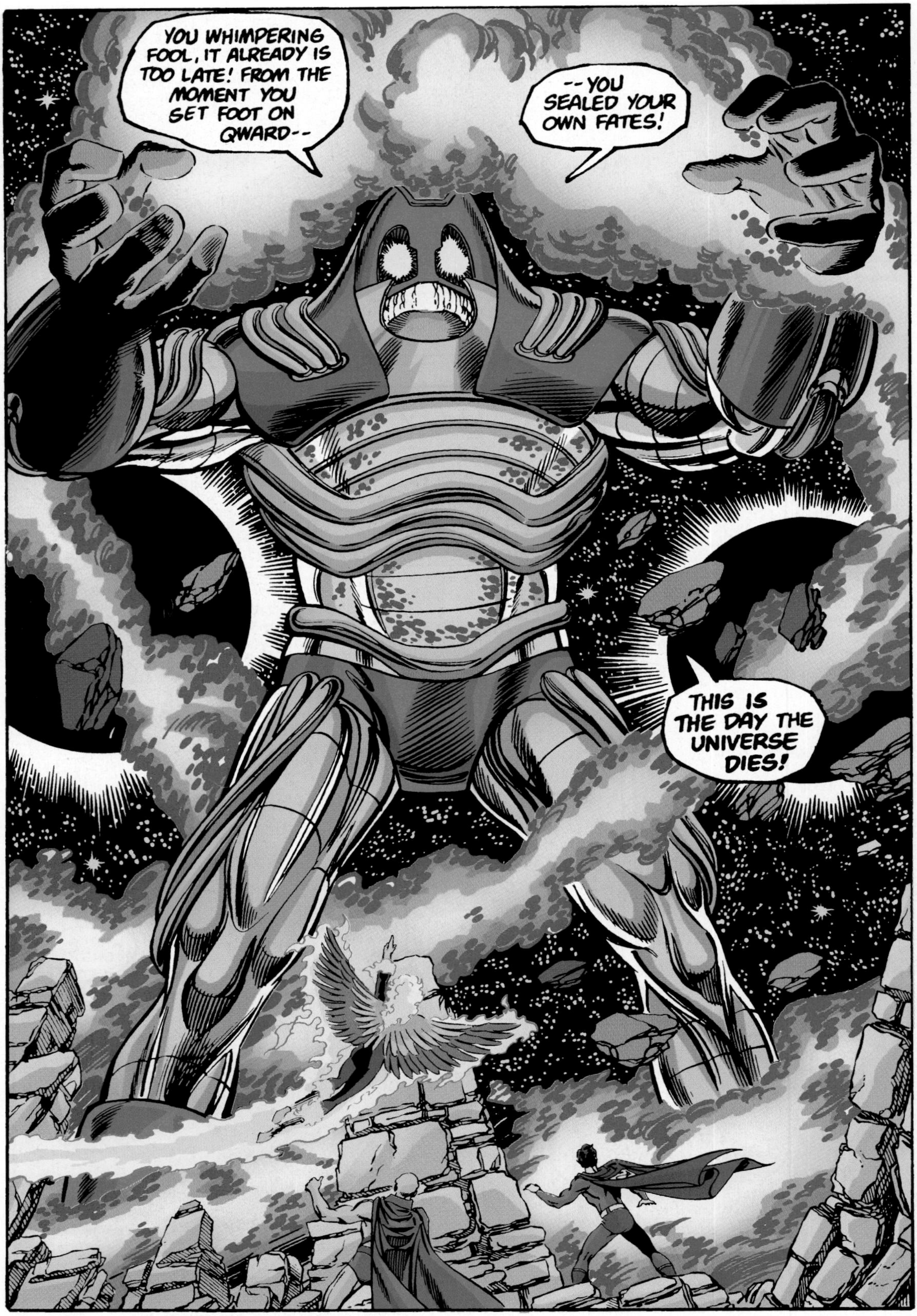
YOU WHIMPERING FOOL, IT ALREADY IS TOO LATE! FROM THE MOMENT YOU SET FOOT ON QWARD--
--YOU SEALED YOUR OWN FATES!
THIS IS THE DAY THE UNIVERSE DIES!

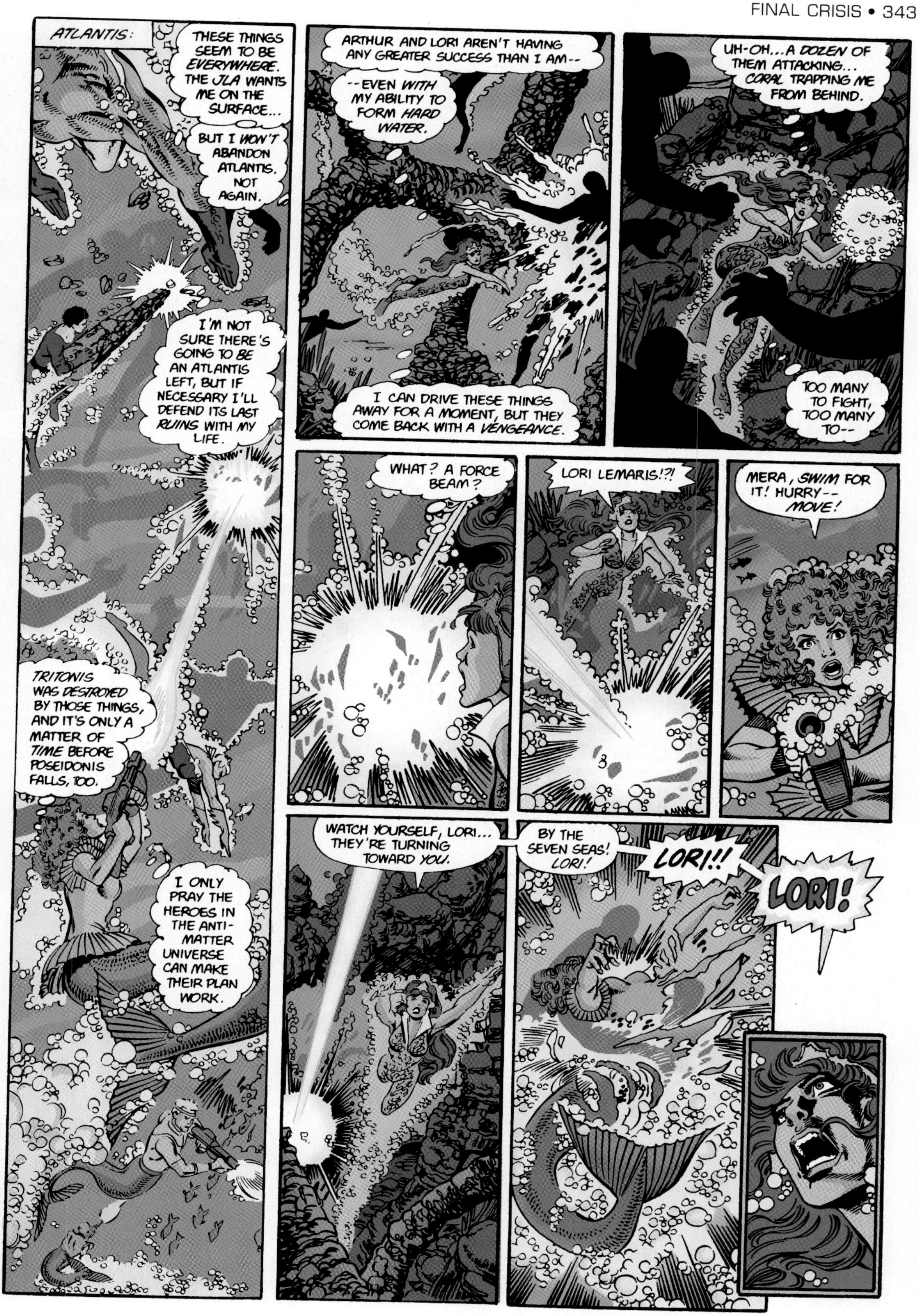
ATLANTIS:
THESE THINGS SEEM TO BE EVERYWHERE. THE JLA WANTS ME ON THE SURFACE...
BUT I WON'T ABANDON ATLANTIS. NOT AGAIN.
I'M NOT SURE THERE'S GOING TO BE AN ATLANTIS LEFT, BUT IF NECESSARY I'LL DEFEND ITS LAST RUINS WITH MY LIFE.
TRITONIS WAS DESTROYED BY THOSE THINGS, AND IT'S ONLY A MATTER OF TIME BEFORE POSEIDONIS FALLS, TOO.
I ONLY PRAY THE HEROES IN THE ANTI-MATTER UNIVERSE CAN MAKE THEIR PLAN WORK.
ARTHUR AND LORI AREN'T HAVING ANY GREATER SUCCESS THAN I AM--
--EVEN WITH MY ABILITY TO FORM HARD WATER.
I CAN DRIVE THESE THINGS AWAY FOR A MOMENT, BUT THEY COME BACK WITH A VENGEANCE.
UH-OH...A DOZEN OF THEM ATTACKING... CORAL TRAPPING ME FROM BEHIND.
TOO MANY TO FIGHT, TOO MANY TO--
WHAT? A FORCE BEAM?
LORI LEMARIS!?!
MERA, SWIM FOR IT! HURRY--MOVE!
WATCH YOURSELF, LORI... THEY'RE TURNING TOWARD YOU.
BY THE SEVEN SEAS! LORI!
LORI!!
LORI!

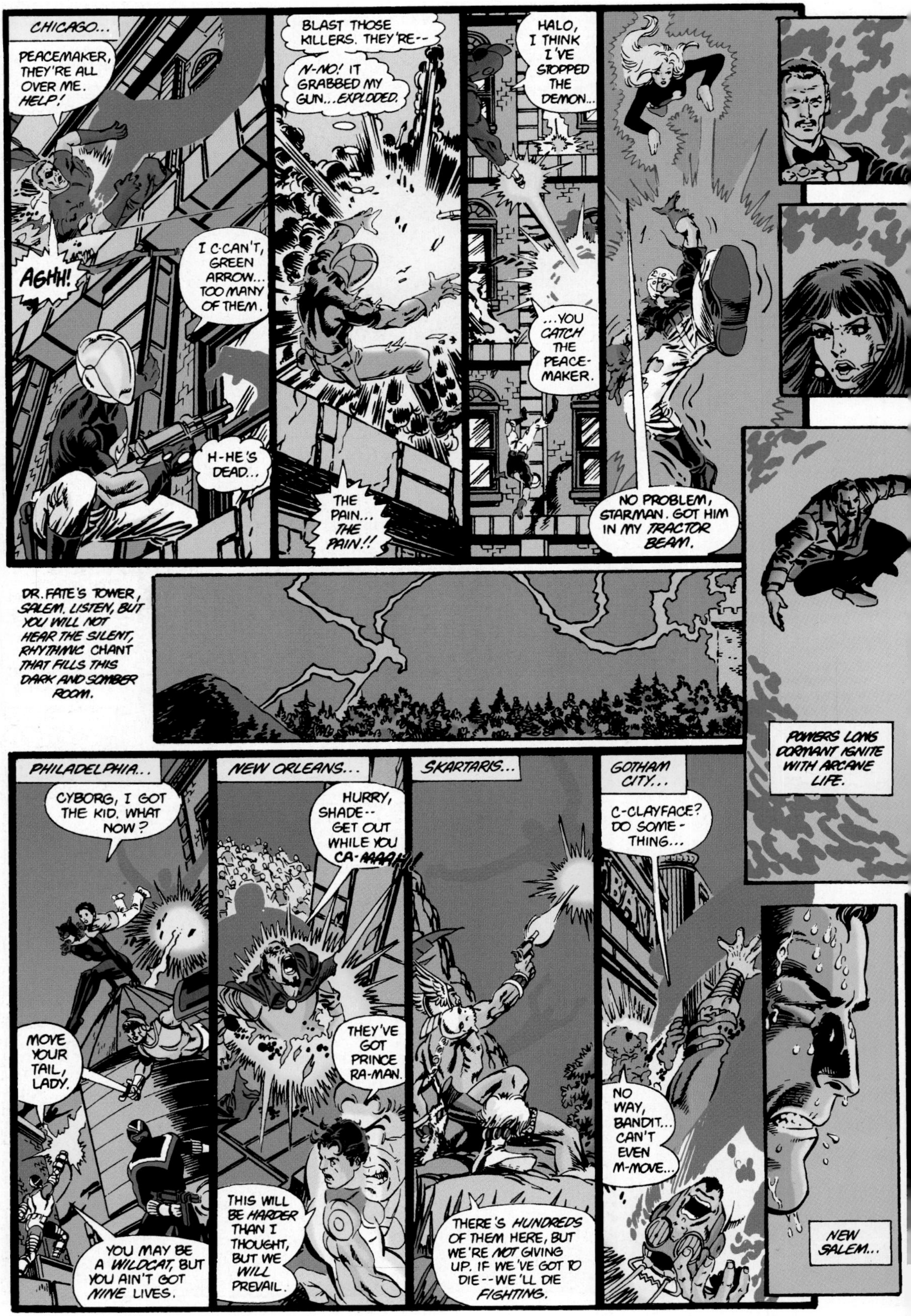
CHICAGO...
PEACEMAKER, THEY'RE ALL OVER ME. HELP!
AGHH!
I C-CAN'T, GREEN ARROW... TOO MANY OF THEM.
H-HE'S DEAD...
BLAST THOSE KILLERS. THEY'RE--
N-NO! IT GRABBED MY GUN... EXPLODED.
THE PAIN... THE PAIN!!
HALO, I THINK I'VE STOPPED THE DEMON...
...YOU CATCH THE PEACEMAKER.
NO PROBLEM, STARMAN. GOT HIM IN MY TRACTOR BEAM.
DR. FATE'S TOWER, SALEM. LISTEN, BUT YOU WILL NOT HEAR THE SILENT, RHYTHMIC CHANT THAT FILLS THIS DARK AND SOMBER ROOM.
POWERS LONG DORMANT IGNITE WITH ARCANE LIFE.
PHILADELPHIA...
CYBORG, I GOT THE KID. WHAT NOW?
MOVE YOUR TAIL, LADY.
YOU MAY BE A WILDCAT, BUT YOU AIN'T GOT NINE LIVES.
NEW ORLEANS...
HURRY, SHADE-- GET OUT WHILE YOU CA-AAAAH!
THEY'VE GOT PRINCE RA-MAN.
THIS WILL BE HARDER THAN I THOUGHT, BUT WE WILL PREVAIL.
SKARTARIS...
THERE'S HUNDREDS OF THEM HERE, BUT WE'RE NOT GIVING UP. IF WE'VE GOT TO DIE--WE'LL DIE FIGHTING.
GOTHAM CITY...
C-CLAYFACE? DO SOME-THING...
NO WAY, BANDIT... CAN'T EVEN M-MOVE...
NEW SALEM...

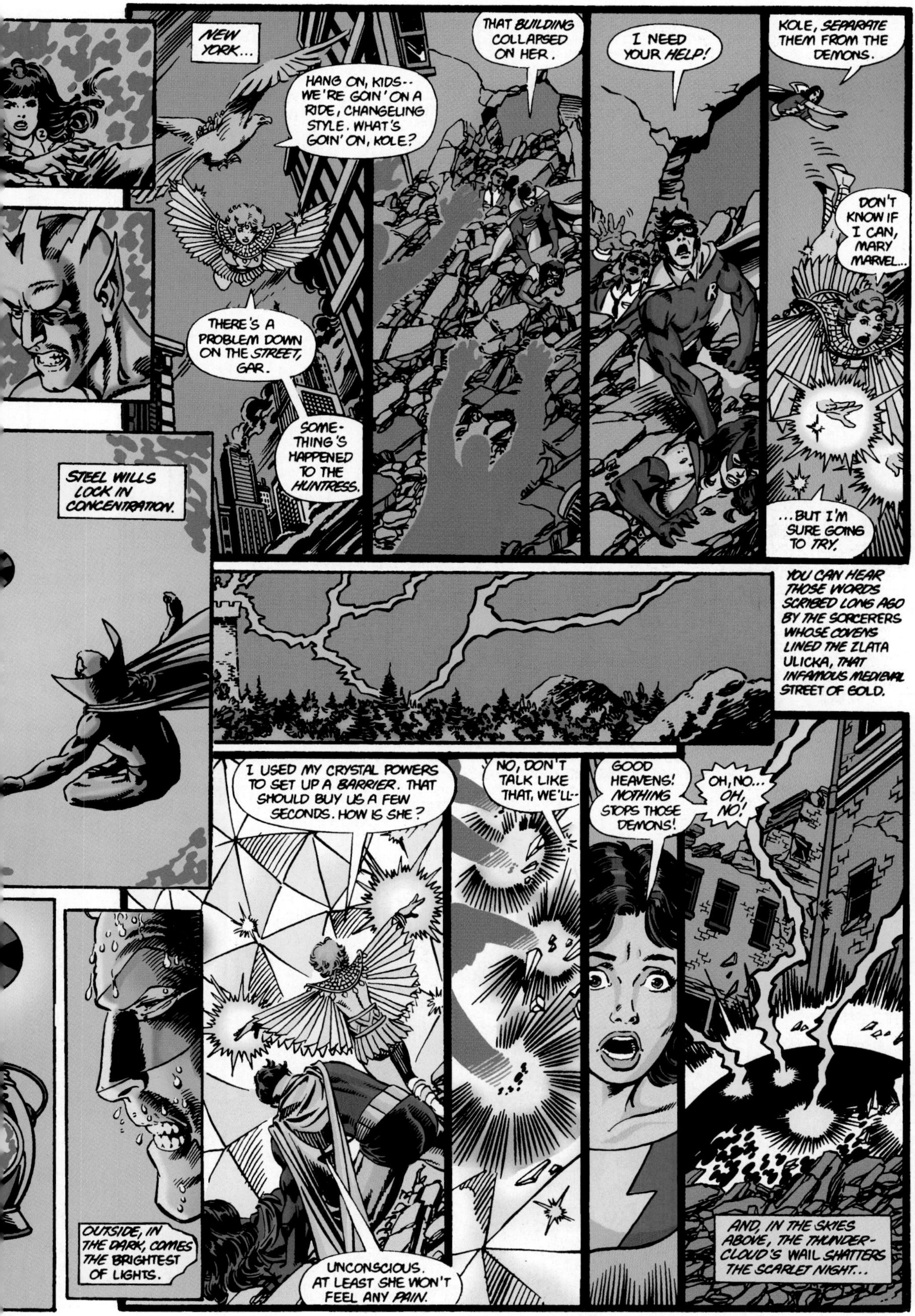
NEW YORK...
HANG ON, KIDS-- WE'RE GOIN' ON A RIDE, CHANGELING STYLE. WHAT'S GOIN' ON, KOLE?
THERE'S A PROBLEM DOWN ON THE STREET, GAR.
SOME-THING'S HAPPENED TO THE HUNTRESS.
THAT BUILDING COLLAPSED ON HER.
I NEED YOUR HELP!
KOLE, SEPARATE THEM FROM THE DEMONS.
DON'T KNOW IF I CAN, MARY MARVEL...
...BUT I'M SURE GOING TO TRY.
STEEL WILLS LOCK IN CONCENTRATION.
YOU CAN HEAR THOSE WORDS SCRIBED LONG AGO BY THE SORCERERS WHOSE COVENS LINED THE ZLATA ULICKA, THAT INFAMOUS MEDIEVAL STREET OF GOLD.
I USED MY CRYSTAL POWERS TO SET UP A BARRIER. THAT SHOULD BUY US A FEW SECONDS. HOW IS SHE?
UNCONSCIOUS. AT LEAST SHE WON'T FEEL ANY PAIN.
NO, DON'T TALK LIKE THAT. WE'LL--
GOOD HEAVENS! NOTHING STOPS THOSE DEMONS!
OH, NO... OH, NO!
OUTSIDE, IN THE DARK, COMES THE BRIGHTEST OF LIGHTS.
AND, IN THE SKIES ABOVE, THE THUNDER-CLOUD'S WAIL SHATTERS THE SCARLET NIGHT...

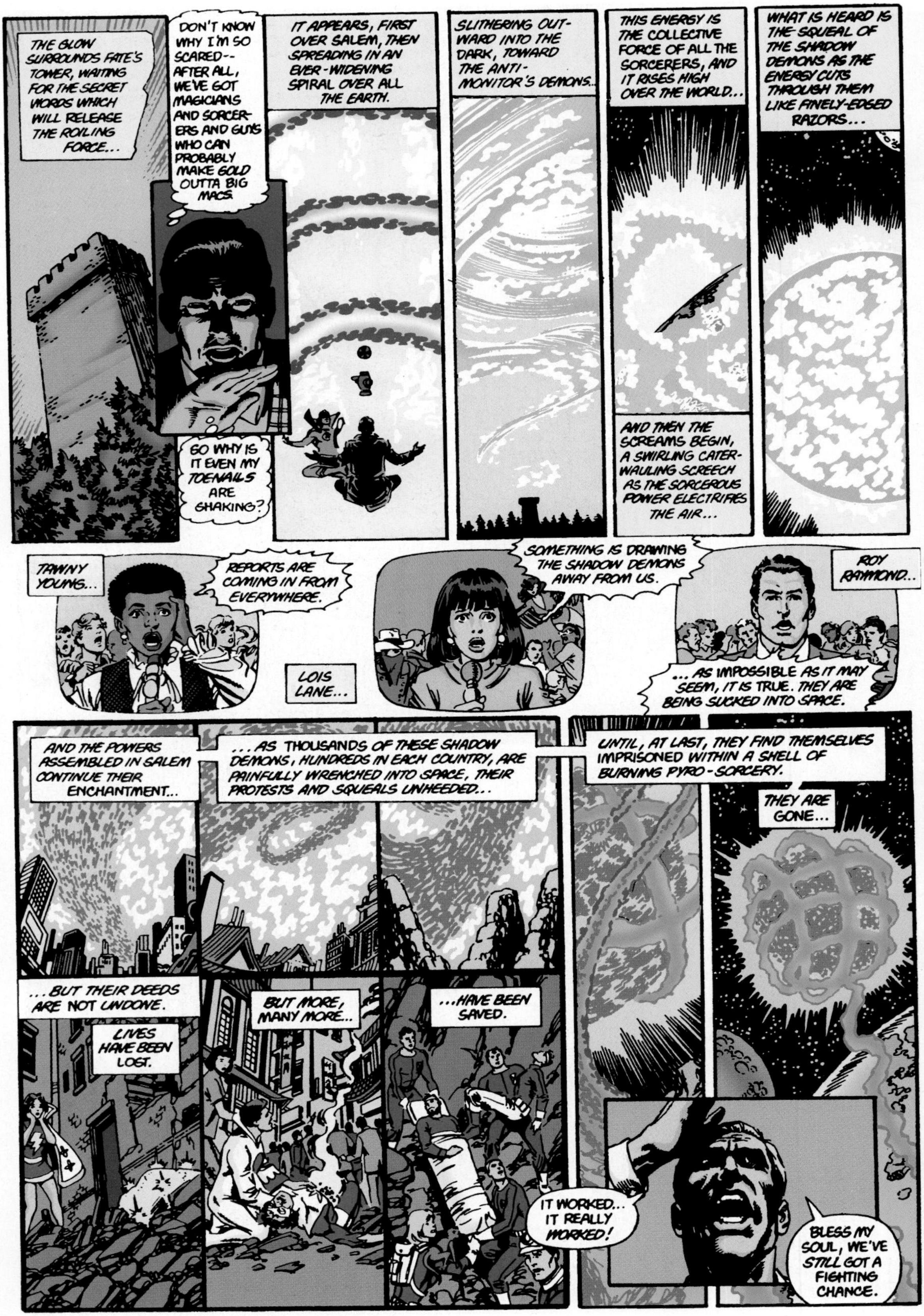
THE GLOW SURROUNDS FATE'S TOWER, WAITING FOR THE SECRET WORDS WHICH WILL RELEASE THE ROILING FORCE...
DON'T KNOW WHY I'M SO SCARED-- AFTER ALL, WE'VE GOT MAGICIANS AND SORCERERS AND GUYS WHO CAN PROBABLY MAKE GOLD OUTTA BIG MACS.
SO WHY IS IT EVEN MY TOENAILS ARE SHAKING?
IT APPEARS, FIRST OVER SALEM, THEN SPREADING IN AN EVER-WIDENING SPIRAL OVER ALL THE EARTH.
SLITHERING OUTWARD INTO THE DARK, TOWARD THE ANTI-MONITOR'S DEMONS...
THIS ENERGY IS THE COLLECTIVE FORCE OF ALL THE SORCERERS, AND IT RISES HIGH OVER THE WORLD...
AND THEN THE SCREAMS BEGIN, A SWIRLING CATERWAULING SCREECH AS THE SORCEROUS POWER ELECTRIFIES THE AIR...
WHAT IS HEARD IS THE SQUEAL OF THE SHADOW DEMONS AS THE ENERGY CUTS THROUGH THEM LIKE FINELY-EDGED RAZORS...
TAWNY YOUNG...
REPORTS ARE COMING IN FROM EVERYWHERE.
LOIS LANE...
SOMETHING IS DRAWING THE SHADOW DEMONS AWAY FROM US.
ROY RAYMOND...
...AS IMPOSSIBLE AS IT MAY SEEM, IT IS TRUE. THEY ARE BEING SUCKED INTO SPACE.
AND THE POWERS ASSEMBLED IN SALEM CONTINUE THEIR ENCHANTMENT...
...AS THOUSANDS OF THESE SHADOW DEMONS, HUNDREDS IN EACH COUNTRY, ARE PAINFULLY WRENCHED INTO SPACE, THEIR PROTESTS AND SQUEALS UNHEEDED...
UNTIL, AT LAST, THEY FIND THEMSELVES IMPRISONED WITHIN A SHELL OF BURNING PYRO-SORCERY.
THEY ARE GONE...
...BUT THEIR DEEDS ARE NOT UNDONE.
LIVES HAVE BEEN LOST.
BUT MORE, MANY MORE...
...HAVE BEEN SAVED.
IT WORKED... IT REALLY WORKED!
BLESS MY SOUL, WE'VE STILL GOT A FIGHTING CHANCE.

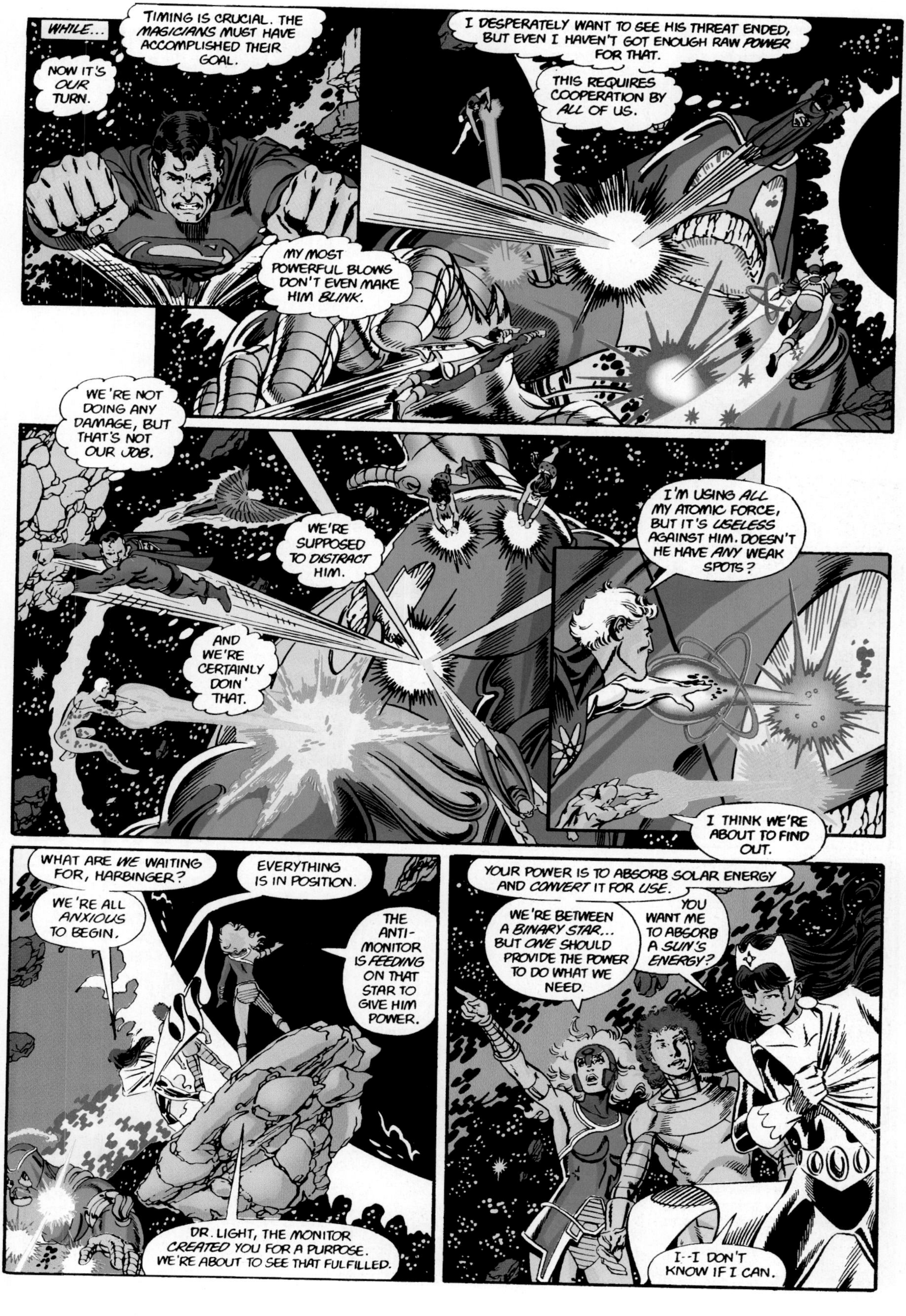
WHILE...
TIMING IS CRUCIAL. THE MAGICIANS MUST HAVE ACCOMPLISHED THEIR GOAL.
NOW IT'S OUR TURN.
I DESPERATELY WANT TO SEE HIS THREAT ENDED, BUT EVEN I HAVEN'T GOT ENOUGH RAW POWER FOR THAT.
THIS REQUIRES COOPERATION BY ALL OF US.
MY MOST POWERFUL BLOWS DON'T EVEN MAKE HIM BLINK.
WE'RE NOT DOING ANY DAMAGE, BUT THAT'S NOT OUR JOB.
WE'RE SUPPOSED TO DISTRACT HIM.
AND WE'RE CERTAINLY DOIN' THAT.
I'M USING ALL MY ATOMIC FORCE, BUT IT'S USELESS AGAINST HIM. DOESN'T HE HAVE ANY WEAK SPOTS?
I THINK WE'RE ABOUT TO FIND OUT.
WHAT ARE WE WAITING FOR, HARBINGER?
WE'RE ALL ANXIOUS TO BEGIN.
EVERYTHING IS IN POSITION.
THE ANTI-MONITOR IS FEEDING ON THAT STAR TO GIVE HIM POWER.
DR. LIGHT, THE MONITOR CREATED YOU FOR A PURPOSE. WE'RE ABOUT TO SEE THAT FULFILLED.
YOUR POWER IS TO ABSORB SOLAR ENERGY AND CONVERT IT FOR USE.
WE'RE BETWEEN A BINARY STAR... BUT ONE SHOULD PROVIDE THE POWER TO DO WHAT WE NEED.
YOU WANT ME TO ABSORB A SUN'S ENERGY?
I--I DON'T KNOW IF I CAN.

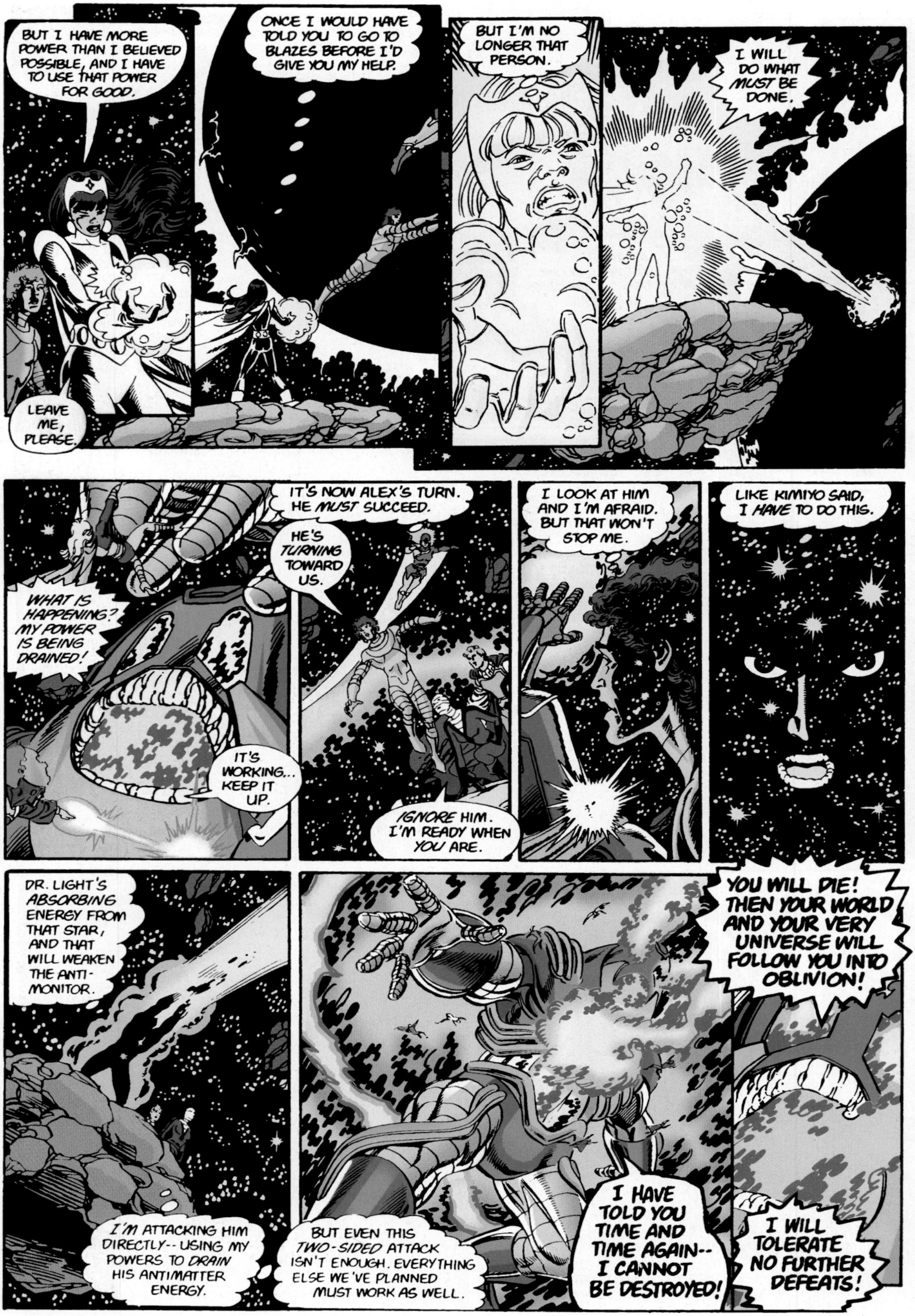

BUT I HAVE MORE POWER THAN I BELIEVED POSSIBLE, AND I HAVE TO USE THAT POWER FOR GOOD.
LEAVE ME, PLEASE.
ONCE I WOULD HAVE TOLD YOU TO GO TO BLAZES BEFORE I'D GIVE YOU MY HELP.
BUT I'M NO LONGER THAT PERSON.
I WILL DO WHAT MUST BE DONE.
WHAT IS HAPPENING? MY POWER IS BEING DRAINED!
IT'S WORKING... KEEP IT UP.
IT'S NOW ALEX'S TURN. HE MUST SUCCEED.
HE'S TURNING TOWARD US.
IGNORE HIM. I'M READY WHEN YOU ARE.
I LOOK AT HIM AND I'M AFRAID. BUT THAT WON'T STOP ME.
LIKE KIMIYO SAID, I HAVE TO DO THIS.
DR. LIGHT'S ABSORBING ENERGY FROM THAT STAR, AND THAT WILL WEAKEN THE ANTI-MONITOR.
I'M ATTACKING HIM DIRECTLY-- USING MY POWERS TO DRAIN HIS ANTIMATTER ENERGY.
BUT EVEN THIS TWO-SIDED ATTACK ISN'T ENOUGH. EVERYTHING ELSE WE'VE PLANNED MUST WORK AS WELL.
YOU WILL DIE! THEN YOUR WORLD AND YOUR VERY UNIVERSE WILL FOLLOW YOU INTO OBLIVION!
I HAVE TOLD YOU TIME AND TIME AGAIN-- I CANNOT BE DESTROYED!
I WILL TOLERATE NO FURTHER DEFEATS!

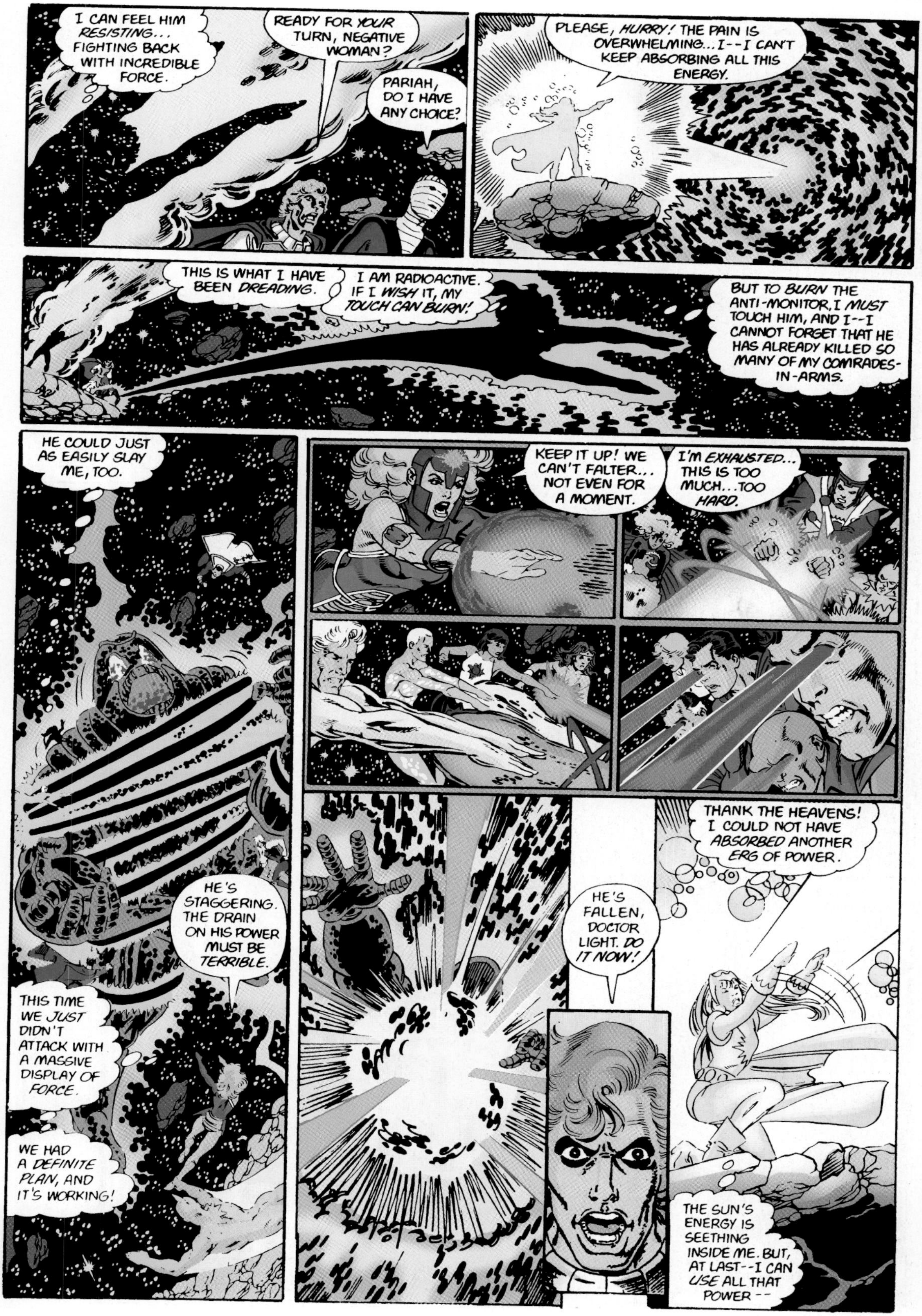
I CAN FEEL HIM RESISTING... FIGHTING BACK WITH INCREDIBLE FORCE.
READY FOR YOUR TURN, NEGATIVE WOMAN?
PARIAH, DO I HAVE ANY CHOICE?
PLEASE, HURRY! THE PAIN IS OVERWHELMING... I--I CAN'T KEEP ABSORBING ALL THIS ENERGY.
THIS IS WHAT I HAVE BEEN DREADING.
I AM RADIOACTIVE. IF I WISH IT, MY TOUCH CAN BURN!
BUT TO BURN THE ANTI-MONITOR, I MUST TOUCH HIM, AND I--I CANNOT FORGET THAT HE HAS ALREADY KILLED SO MANY OF MY COMRADES-IN-ARMS.
HE COULD JUST AS EASILY SLAY ME, TOO.
KEEP IT UP! WE CAN'T FALTER... NOT EVEN FOR A MOMENT.
I'M EXHAUSTED... THIS IS TOO MUCH...TOO HARD.
HE'S STAGGERING. THE DRAIN ON HIS POWER MUST BE TERRIBLE.
THIS TIME WE JUST DIDN'T ATTACK WITH A MASSIVE DISPLAY OF FORCE.
WE HAD A DEFINITE PLAN, AND IT'S WORKING!
HE'S FALLEN, DOCTOR LIGHT. DO IT NOW!
THANK THE HEAVENS! I COULD NOT HAVE ABSORBED ANOTHER ERG OF POWER.
THE SUN'S ENERGY IS SEETHING INSIDE ME. BUT, AT LAST--I CAN USE ALL THAT POWER--

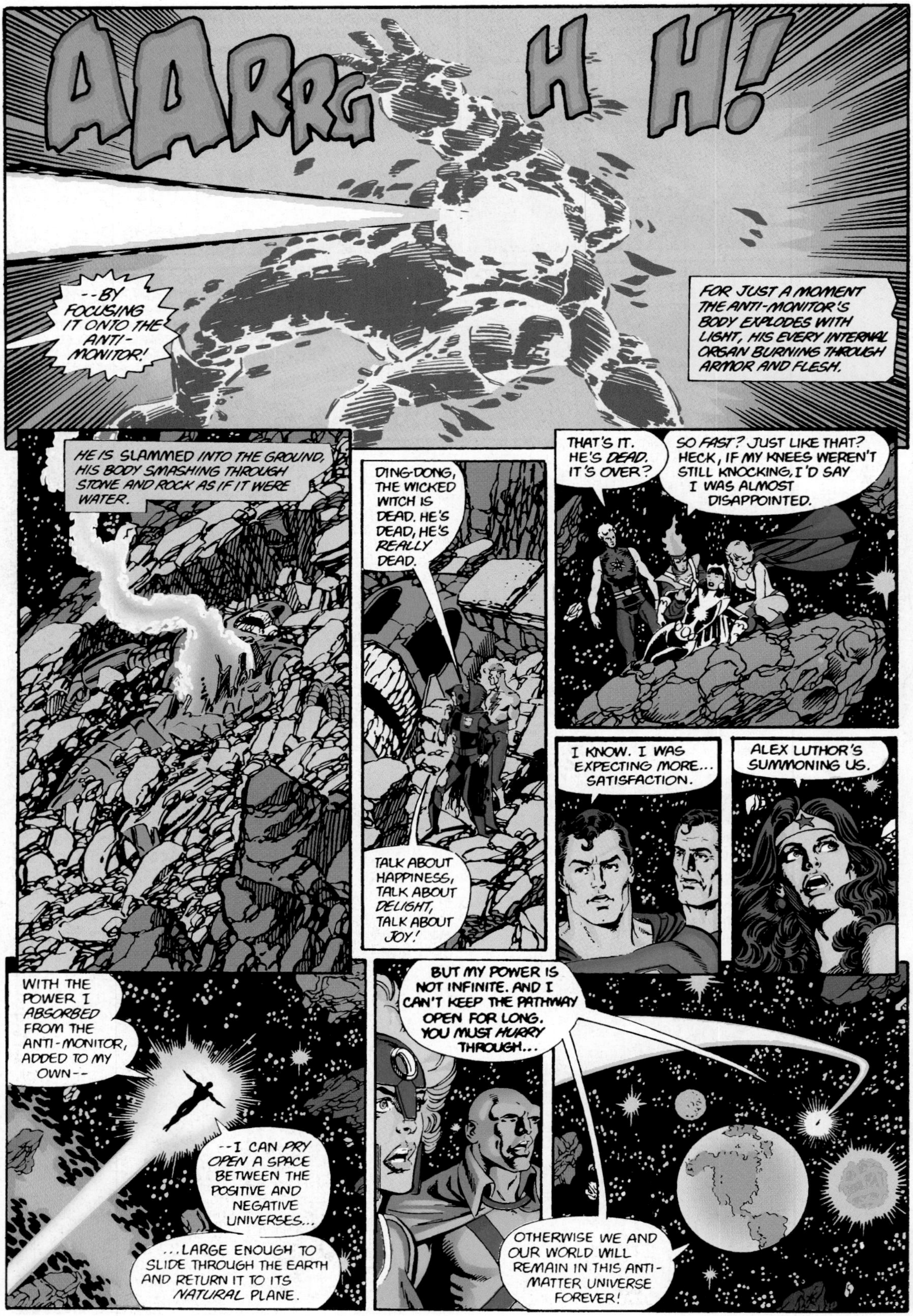
AARRGH H H!
--BY FOCUSING IT ONTO THE ANTI-MONITOR!
FOR JUST A MOMENT THE ANTI-MONITOR'S BODY EXPLODES WITH LIGHT, HIS EVERY INTERNAL ORGAN BURNING THROUGH ARMOR AND FLESH.
HE IS SLAMMED INTO THE GROUND, HIS BODY SMASHING THROUGH STONE AND ROCK AS IF IT WERE WATER.
DING-DONG, THE WICKED WITCH IS DEAD. HE'S DEAD, HE'S REALLY DEAD.
TALK ABOUT HAPPINESS, TALK ABOUT DELIGHT, TALK ABOUT JOY!
THAT'S IT. HE'S DEAD. IT'S OVER?
SO FAST? JUST LIKE THAT? HECK, IF MY KNEES WEREN'T STILL KNOCKING, I'D SAY I WAS ALMOST DISAPPOINTED.
I KNOW. I WAS EXPECTING MORE... SATISFACTION.
ALEX LUTHOR'S SUMMONING US.
WITH THE POWER I ABSORBED FROM THE ANTI-MONITOR, ADDED TO MY OWN--
--I CAN PRY OPEN A SPACE BETWEEN THE POSITIVE AND NEGATIVE UNIVERSES...
...LARGE ENOUGH TO SLIDE THROUGH THE EARTH AND RETURN IT TO ITS NATURAL PLANE.
BUT MY POWER IS NOT INFINITE. AND I CAN'T KEEP THE PATHWAY OPEN FOR LONG. YOU MUST HURRY THROUGH...
OTHERWISE WE AND OUR WORLD WILL REMAIN IN THIS ANTI-MATTER UNIVERSE FOREVER!

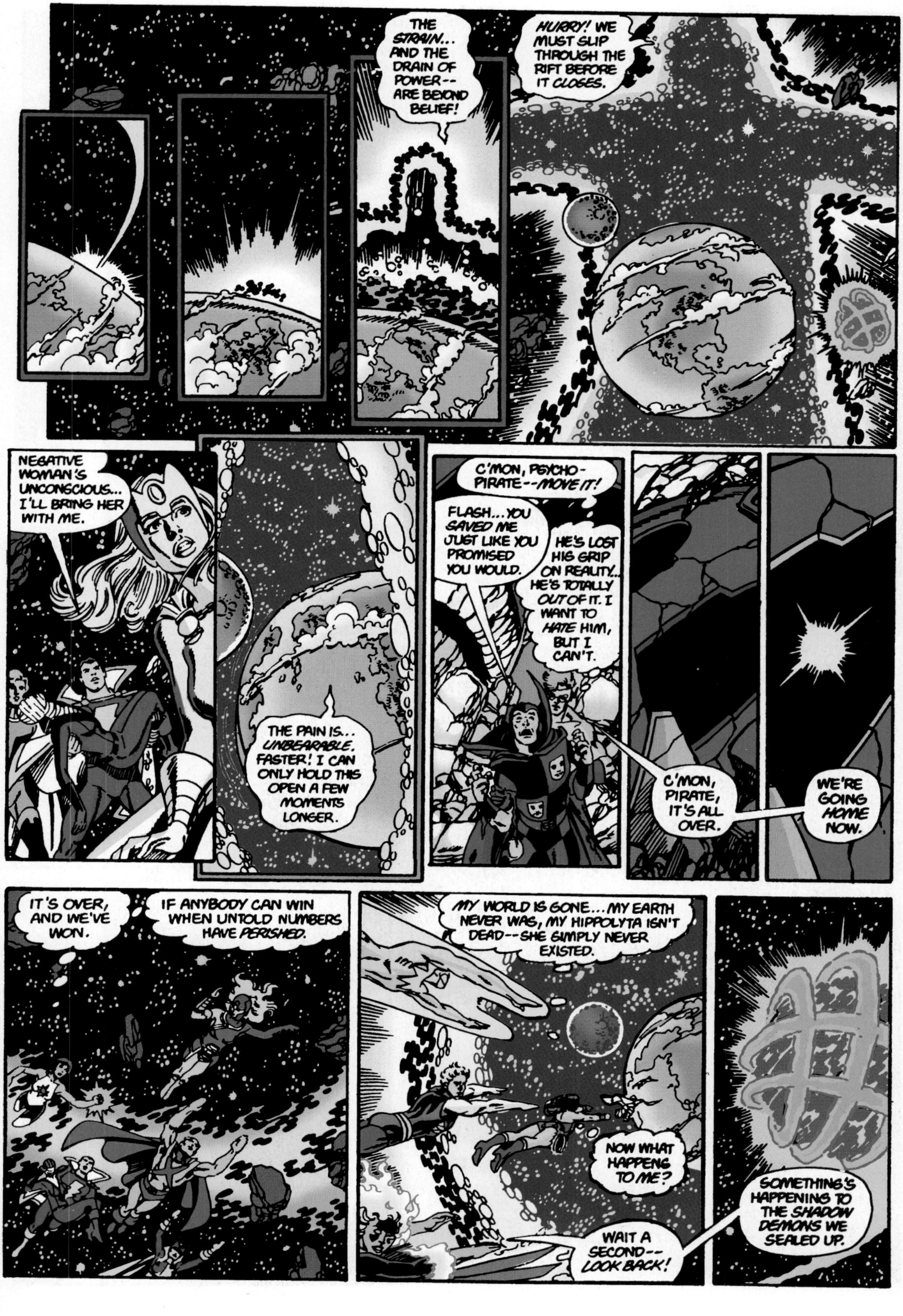
THE STRAIN... AND THE DRAIN OF POWER-- ARE BEYOND BELIEF!
HURRY! WE MUST SLIP THROUGH THE RIFT BEFORE IT CLOSES.
NEGATIVE WOMAN'S UNCONSCIOUS... I'LL BRING HER WITH ME.
THE PAIN IS... UNBEARABLE. FASTER! I CAN ONLY HOLD THIS OPEN A FEW MOMENTS LONGER.
C'MON, PSYCHO-PIRATE--MOVE IT!
FLASH... YOU SAVED ME JUST LIKE YOU PROMISED YOU WOULD.
HE'S LOST HIS GRIP ON REALITY... HE'S TOTALLY OUT OF IT. I WANT TO HATE HIM, BUT I CAN'T.
C'MON, PIRATE, IT'S ALL OVER.
WE'RE GOING HOME NOW.
IT'S OVER, AND WE'VE WON.
IF ANYBODY CAN WIN WHEN UNTOLD NUMBERS HAVE PERISHED.
MY WORLD IS GONE... MY EARTH NEVER WAS, MY HIPPOLYTA ISN'T DEAD--SHE SIMPLY NEVER EXISTED.
NOW WHAT HAPPENG TO ME?
WAIT A SECOND-- LOOK BACK!
SOMETHING'S HAPPENING TO THE SHADOW DEMONS WE SEALED UP.

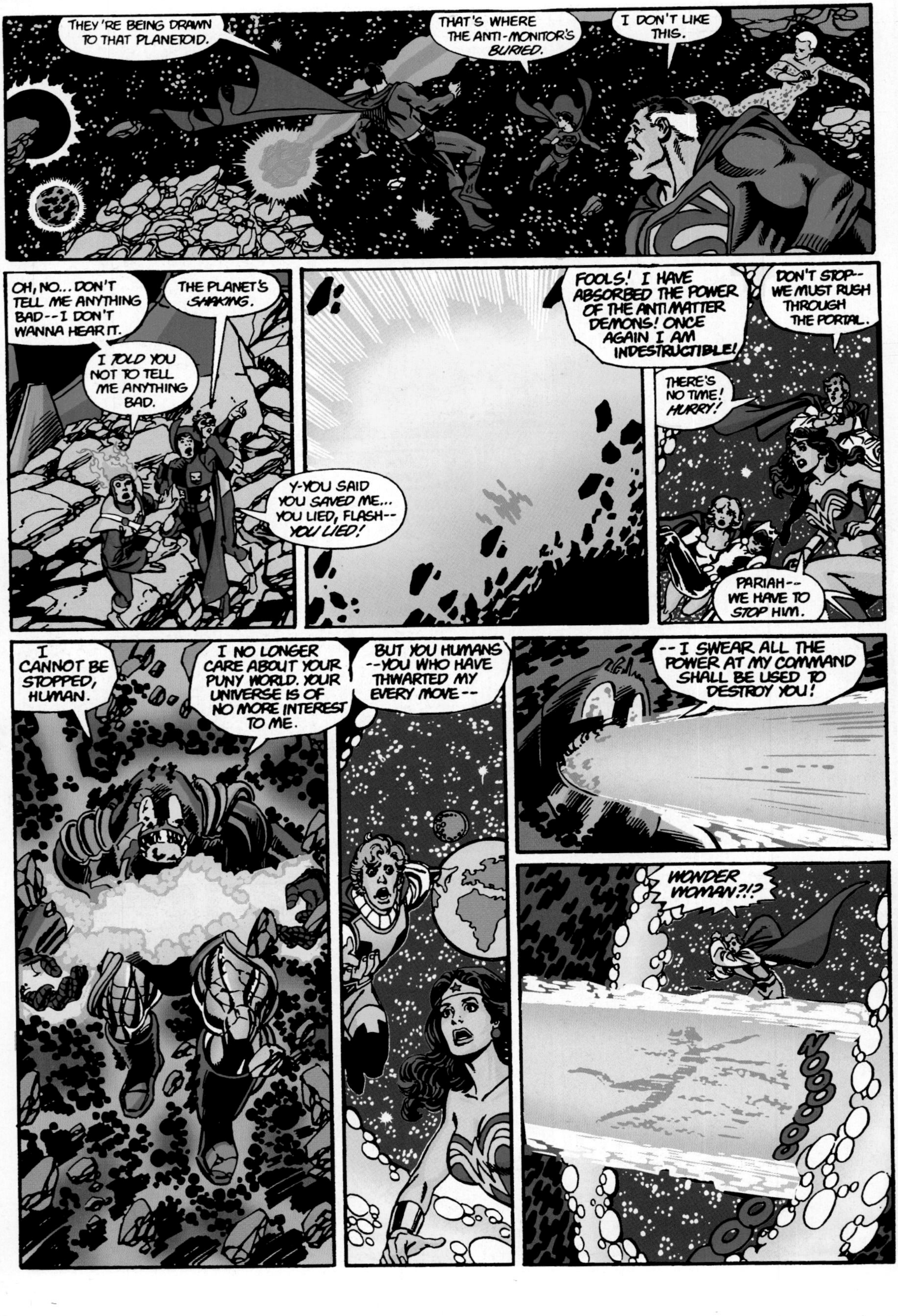
THEY'RE BEING DRAWN TO THAT PLANETOID.
THAT'S WHERE THE ANTI-MONITOR'S BURIED.
I DON'T LIKE THIS.
OH, NO... DON'T TELL ME ANYTHING BAD--I DON'T WANNA HEAR IT.
THE PLANET'S SHAKING.
I TOLD YOU NOT TO TELL ME ANYTHING BAD.
Y-YOU SAID YOU SAVED ME... YOU LIED, FLASH-- YOU LIED!
FOOLS! I HAVE ABSORBED THE POWER OF THE ANTI MATTER DEMONS! ONCE AGAIN I AM INDESTRUCTIBLE!
DON'T STOP-- WE MUST RUSH THROUGH THE PORTAL.
THERE'S NO TIME! HURRY!
PARIAH-- WE HAVE TO STOP HIM.
I CANNOT BE STOPPED, HUMAN.
I NO LONGER CARE ABOUT YOUR PUNY WORLD. YOUR UNIVERSE IS OF NO MORE INTEREST TO ME.
BUT YOU HUMANS --YOU WHO HAVE THWARTED MY EVERY MOVE--
--I SWEAR ALL THE POWER AT MY COMMAND SHALL BE USED TO DESTROY YOU!
WONDER WOMAN?!?
NOOOOO

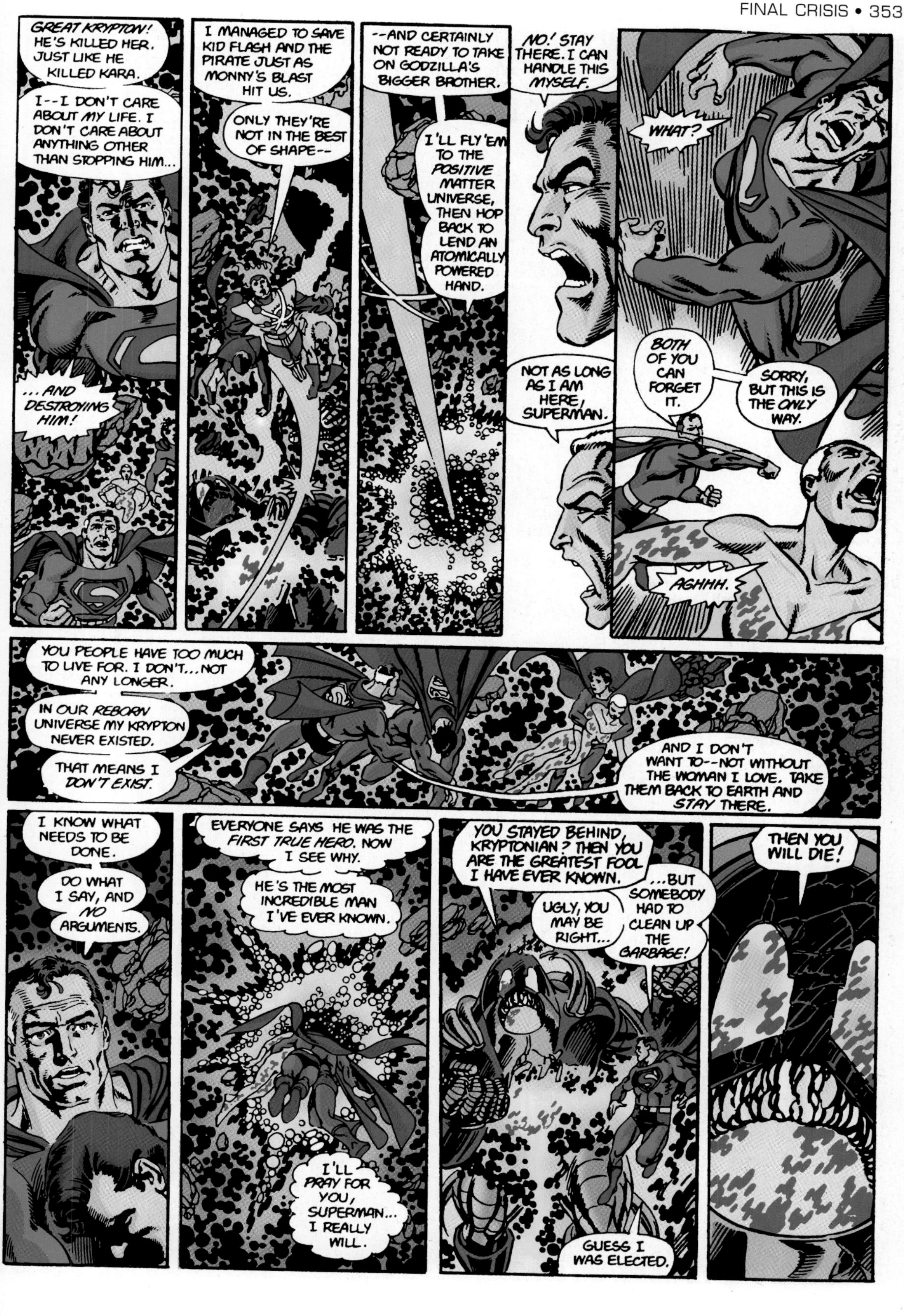
GREAT KRYPTON! HE'S KILLED HER. JUST LIKE HE KILLED KARA.
I--I DON'T CARE ABOUT MY LIFE. I DON'T CARE ABOUT ANYTHING OTHER THAN STOPPING HIM...
...AND DESTROYING HIM!
I MANAGED TO SAVE KID FLASH AND THE PIRATE JUST AS MONNY'S BLAST HIT US.
ONLY THEY'RE NOT IN THE BEST OF SHAPE--
--AND CERTAINLY NOT READY TO TAKE ON GODZILLA'S BIGGER BROTHER.
I'LL FLY 'EM TO THE POSITIVE MATTER UNIVERSE, THEN HOP BACK TO LEND AN ATOMICALLY POWERED HAND.
NO! STAY THERE. I CAN HANDLE THIS MYSELF.
NOT AS LONG AS I AM HERE, SUPERMAN.
WHAT?
BOTH OF YOU CAN FORGET IT.
SORRY, BUT THIS IS THE ONLY WAY.
AGHHH.
YOU PEOPLE HAVE TOO MUCH TO LIVE FOR. I DON'T...NOT ANY LONGER.
IN OUR REBORN UNIVERSE MY KRYPTON NEVER EXISTED.
THAT MEANS I DON'T EXIST.
AND I DON'T WANT TO--NOT WITHOUT THE WOMAN I LOVE. TAKE THEM BACK TO EARTH AND STAY THERE.
I KNOW WHAT NEEDS TO BE DONE.
DO WHAT I SAY, AND NO ARGUMENTS.
EVERYONE SAYS HE WAS THE FIRST TRUE HERO. NOW I SEE WHY.
HE'S THE MOST INCREDIBLE MAN I'VE EVER KNOWN.
I'LL PRAY FOR YOU, SUPERMAN... I REALLY WILL.
YOU STAYED BEHIND, KRYPTONIAN? THEN YOU ARE THE GREATEST FOOL I HAVE EVER KNOWN.
UGLY, YOU MAY BE RIGHT...
...BUT SOMEBODY HAD TO CLEAN UP THE GARBAGE!
GUESS I WAS ELECTED.
THEN YOU WILL DIE!

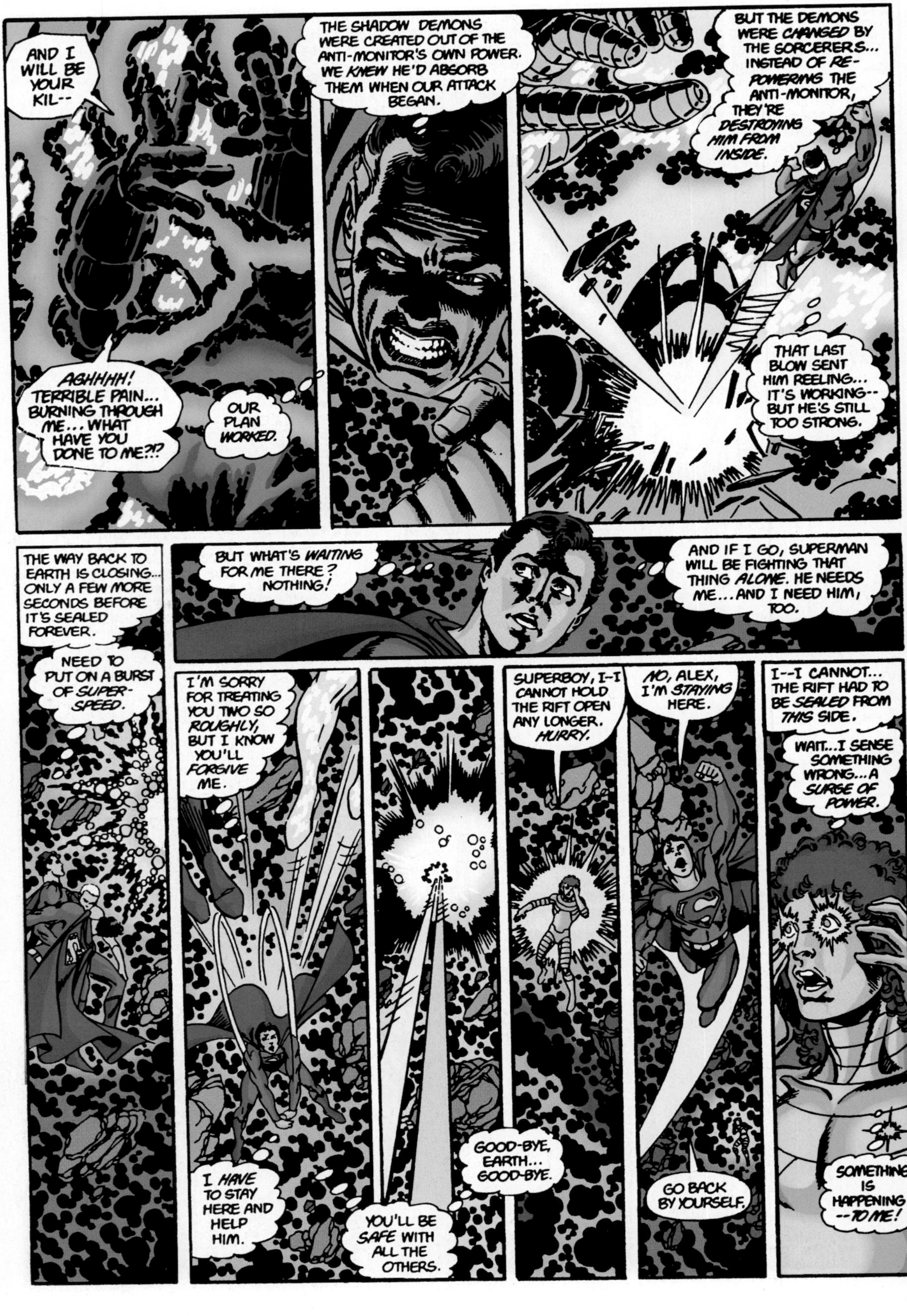
AND I WILL BE YOUR KIL--
AGHHHH! TERRIBLE PAIN... BURNING THROUGH ME... WHAT HAVE YOU DONE TO ME?!?
THE SHADOW DEMONS WERE CREATED OUT OF THE ANTI-MONITOR'S OWN POWER. WE KNEW HE'D ABSORB THEM WHEN OUR ATTACK BEGAN.
OUR PLAN WORKED.
BUT THE DEMONS WERE CHANGED BY THE SORCERERS... INSTEAD OF RE-POWERING THE ANTI-MONITOR, THEY'RE DESTROYING HIM FROM INSIDE.
THAT LAST BLOW SENT HIM REELING... IT'S WORKING-- BUT HE'S STILL TOO STRONG.
THE WAY BACK TO EARTH IS CLOSING... ONLY A FEW MORE SECONDS BEFORE IT'S SEALED FOREVER.
BUT WHAT'S WAITING FOR ME THERE? NOTHING!
AND IF I GO, SUPERMAN WILL BE FIGHTING THAT THING ALONE. HE NEEDS ME... AND I NEED HIM, TOO.
NEED TO PUT ON A BURST OF SUPER-SPEED.
I HAVE TO STAY HERE AND HELP HIM.
I'M SORRY FOR TREATING YOU TWO SO ROUGHLY, BUT I KNOW YOU'LL FORGIVE ME.
YOU'LL BE SAFE WITH ALL THE OTHERS.
GOOD-BYE, EARTH... GOOD-BYE.
SUPERBOY, I--I CANNOT HOLD THE RIFT OPEN ANY LONGER. HURRY.
NO, ALEX, I'M STAYING HERE.
GO BACK BY YOURSELF.
I--I CANNOT... THE RIFT HAD TO BE SEALED FROM THIS SIDE.
WAIT...I SENSE SOMETHING WRONG...A SURGE OF POWER.
SOMETHING IS HAPPENING --TO ME!

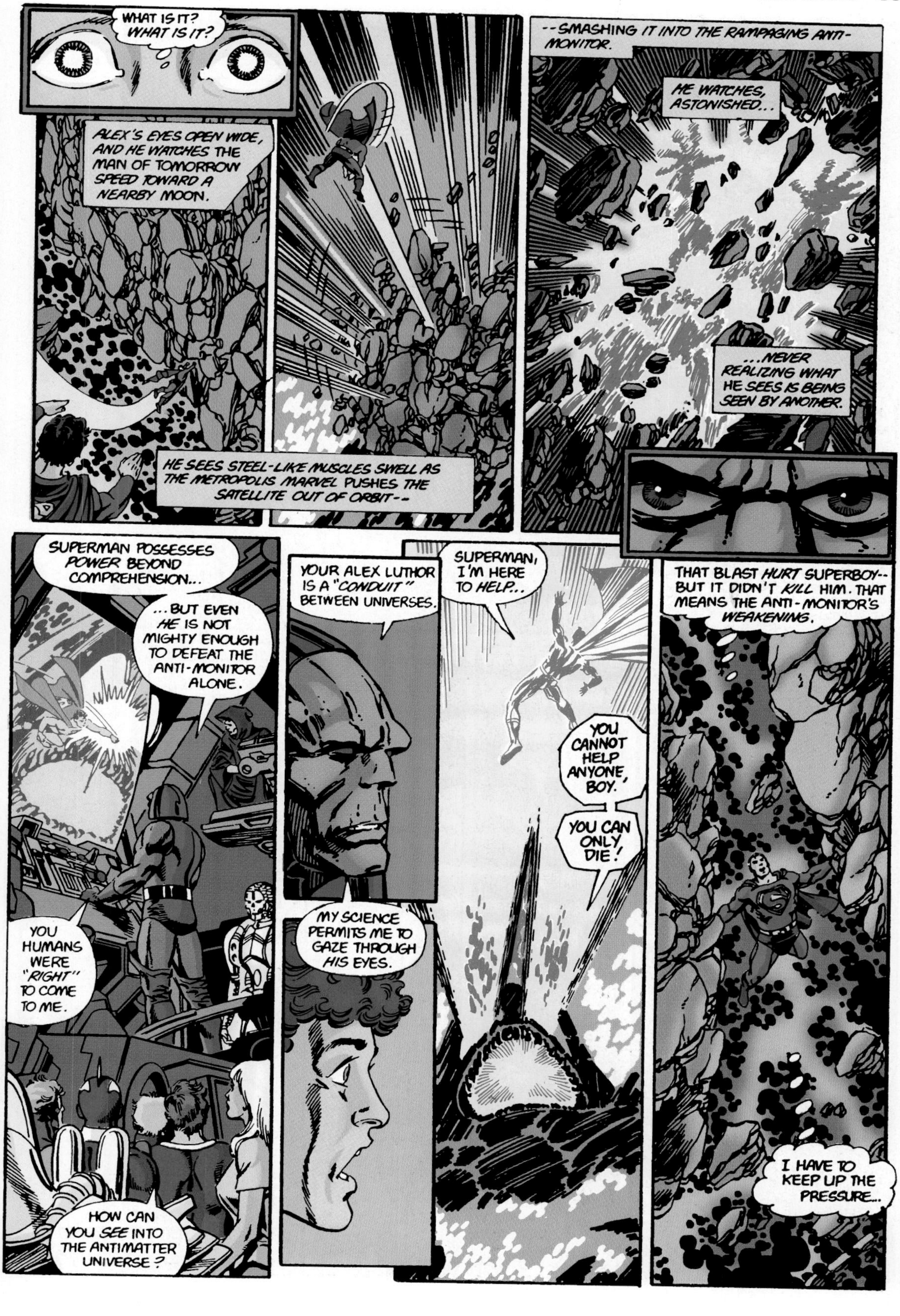
WHAT IS IT? WHAT IS IT?
ALEX'S EYES OPEN WIDE, AND HE WATCHES THE MAN OF TOMORROW SPEED TOWARD A NEARBY MOON.
HE SEES STEEL-LIKE MUSCLES SWELL AS THE METROPOLIS MARVEL PUSHES THE SATELLITE OUT OF ORBIT--
--SMASHING IT INTO THE RAMPAGING ANTI-MONITOR.
HE WATCHES, ASTONISHED...
...NEVER REALIZING WHAT HE SEES IS BEING SEEN BY ANOTHER.
SUPERMAN POSSESSES POWER BEYOND COMPREHENSION...
...BUT EVEN HE IS NOT MIGHTY ENOUGH TO DEFEAT THE ANTI-MONITOR ALONE.
YOU HUMANS WERE "RIGHT" TO COME TO ME.
HOW CAN YOU SEE INTO THE ANTIMATTER UNIVERSE?
YOUR ALEX LUTHOR IS A "CONDUIT" BETWEEN UNIVERSES.
MY SCIENCE PERMITS ME TO GAZE THROUGH HIS EYES.
SUPERMAN, I'M HERE TO HELP...
YOU CANNOT HELP ANYONE, BOY.
YOU CAN ONLY DIE!
THAT BLAST HURT SUPERBOY-- BUT IT DIDN'T KILL HIM. THAT MEANS THE ANTI-MONITOR'S WEAKENING.
I HAVE TO KEEP UP THE PRESSURE...

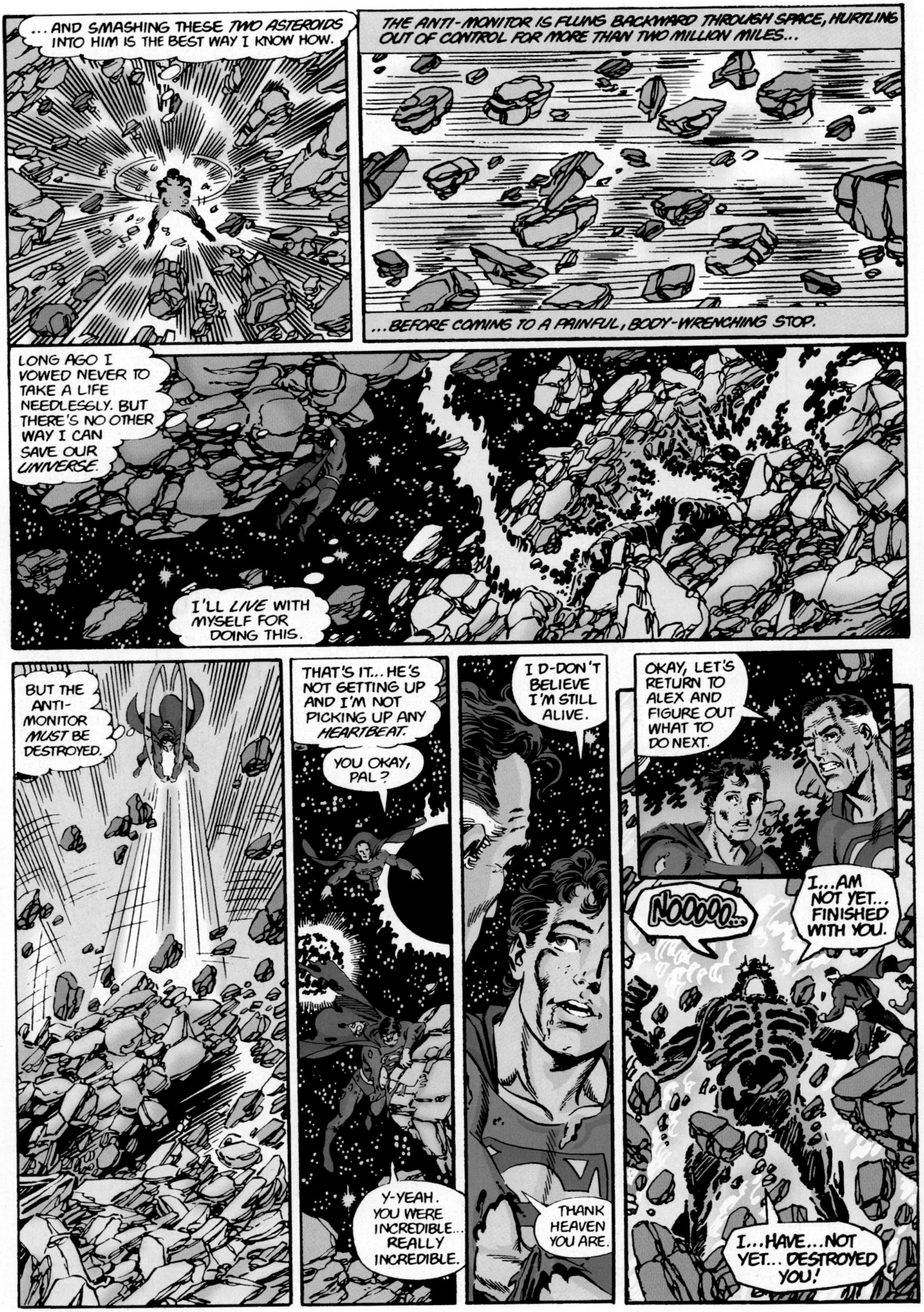
...AND SMASHING THESE TWO ASTEROIDS INTO HIM IS THE BEST WAY I KNOW HOW.
THE ANTI-MONITOR IS FLUNG BACKWARD THROUGH SPACE, HURTLING OUT OF CONTROL FOR MORE THAN TWO MILLION MILES...
...BEFORE COMING TO A PAINFUL, BODY-WRENCHING STOP.
LONG AGO I VOWED NEVER TO TAKE A LIFE NEEDLESSLY. BUT THERE'S NO OTHER WAY I CAN SAVE OUR UNIVERSE.
I'LL LIVE WITH MYSELF FOR DOING THIS.
BUT THE ANTI-MONITOR MUST BE DESTROYED.
THAT'S IT... HE'S NOT GETTING UP AND I'M NOT PICKING UP ANY HEARTBEAT.
YOU OKAY, PAL?
Y-YEAH. YOU WERE INCREDIBLE... REALLY INCREDIBLE.
I D-DON'T BELIEVE I'M STILL ALIVE.
THANK HEAVEN YOU ARE.
OKAY, LET'S RETURN TO ALEX AND FIGURE OUT WHAT TO DO NEXT.
NOOOOO...
I...AM NOT YET... FINISHED WITH YOU.
I...HAVE...NOT YET... DESTROYED YOU!

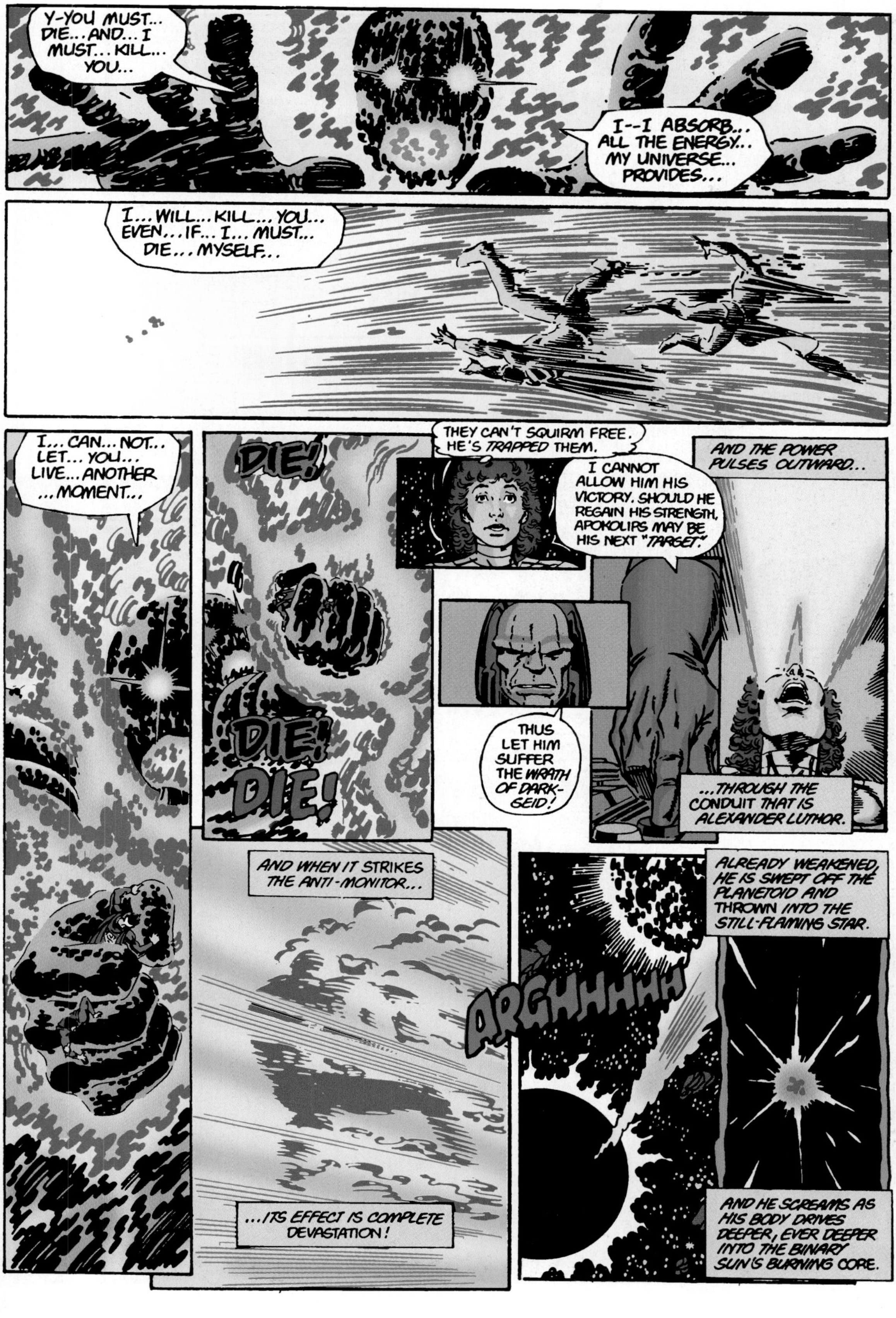
Y-YOU MUST... DIE... AND... I MUST... KILL... YOU...
I--I ABSORB... ALL THE ENERGY... MY UNIVERSE... PROVIDES...
I... WILL... KILL... YOU... EVEN... IF... I... MUST... DIE... MYSELF...
I... CAN... NOT... LET... YOU... LIVE... ANOTHER ...MOMENT...
DIE!
DIE! DIE!
THEY CAN'T SQUIRM FREE. HE'S TRAPPED THEM.
I CANNOT ALLOW HIM HIS VICTORY. SHOULD HE REGAIN HIS STRENGTH, APOKOLIPS MAY BE HIS NEXT "TARGET."
THUS LET HIM SUFFER THE WRATH OF DARK-SEID!
AND THE POWER PULSES OUTWARD...
...THROUGH THE CONDUIT THAT IS ALEXANDER LUTHOR.
AND WHEN IT STRIKES THE ANTI-MONITOR...
...ITS EFFECT IS COMPLETE DEVASTATION!
ALREADY WEAKENED, HE IS SWEPT OFF THE PLANETOID AND THROWN INTO THE STILL-FLAMING STAR.
ARGHHHHH
AND HE SCREAMS AS HIS BODY DRIVES DEEPER, EVER DEEPER INTO THE BINARY SUN'S BURNING CORE.

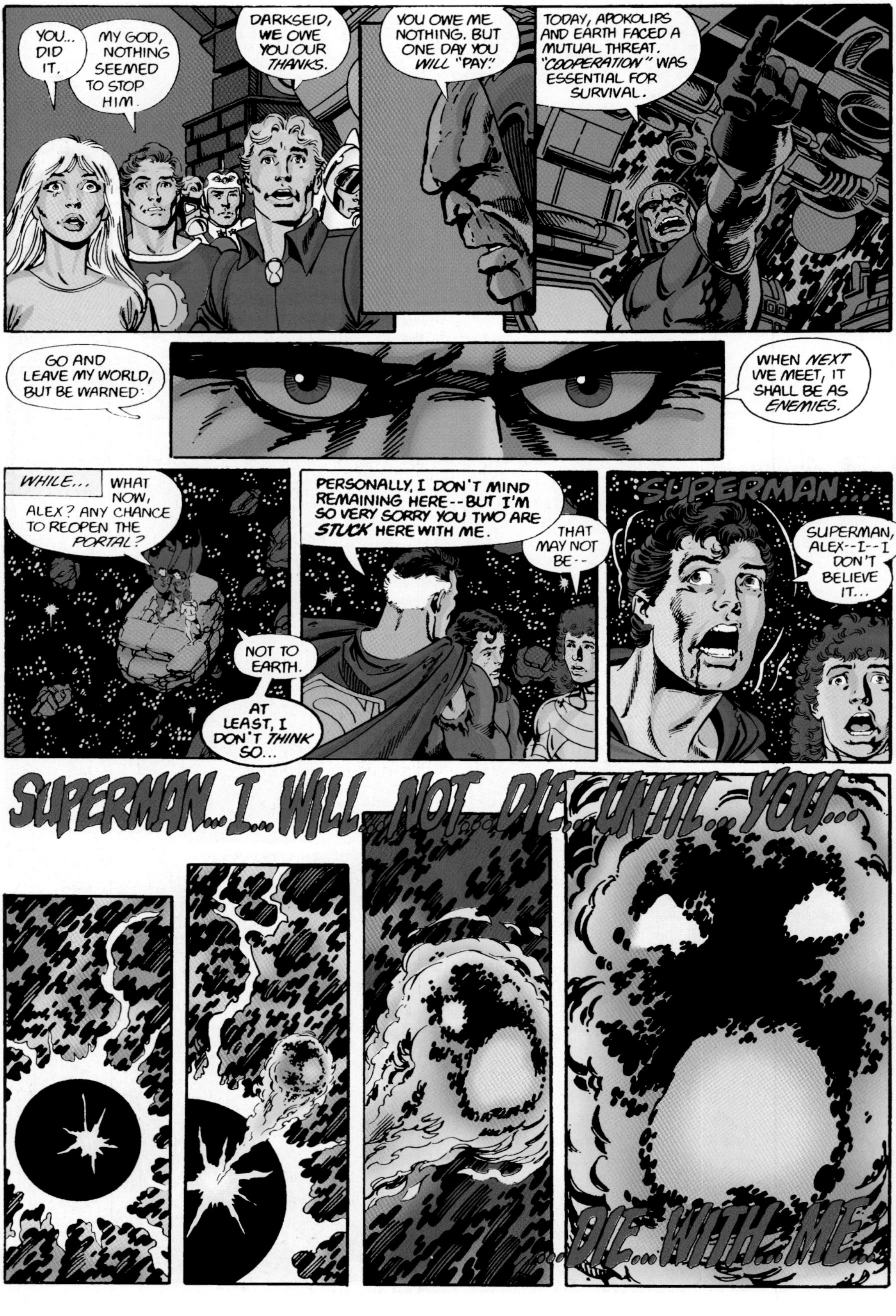
YOU... DID IT.
MY GOD, NOTHING SEEMED TO STOP HIM.
DARKSEID, WE OWE YOU OUR THANKS.
YOU OWE ME NOTHING. BUT ONE DAY YOU WILL "PAY."
TODAY, APOKOLIPS AND EARTH FACED A MUTUAL THREAT. "COOPERATION" WAS ESSENTIAL FOR SURVIVAL.
GO AND LEAVE MY WORLD, BUT BE WARNED:
WHEN NEXT WE MEET, IT SHALL BE AS ENEMIES.
WHILE...
WHAT NOW, ALEX? ANY CHANCE TO REOPEN THE PORTAL?
NOT TO EARTH.
AT LEAST, I DON'T THINK SO...
PERSONALLY, I DON'T MIND REMAINING HERE--BUT I'M SO VERY SORRY YOU TWO ARE STUCK HERE WITH ME.
THAT MAY NOT BE--
SUPERMAN...
SUPERMAN, ALEX--I--I DON'T BELIEVE IT...
SUPERMAN...I...WILL...NOT...DIE...UNTIL...YOU...
...DIE...WITH...ME...

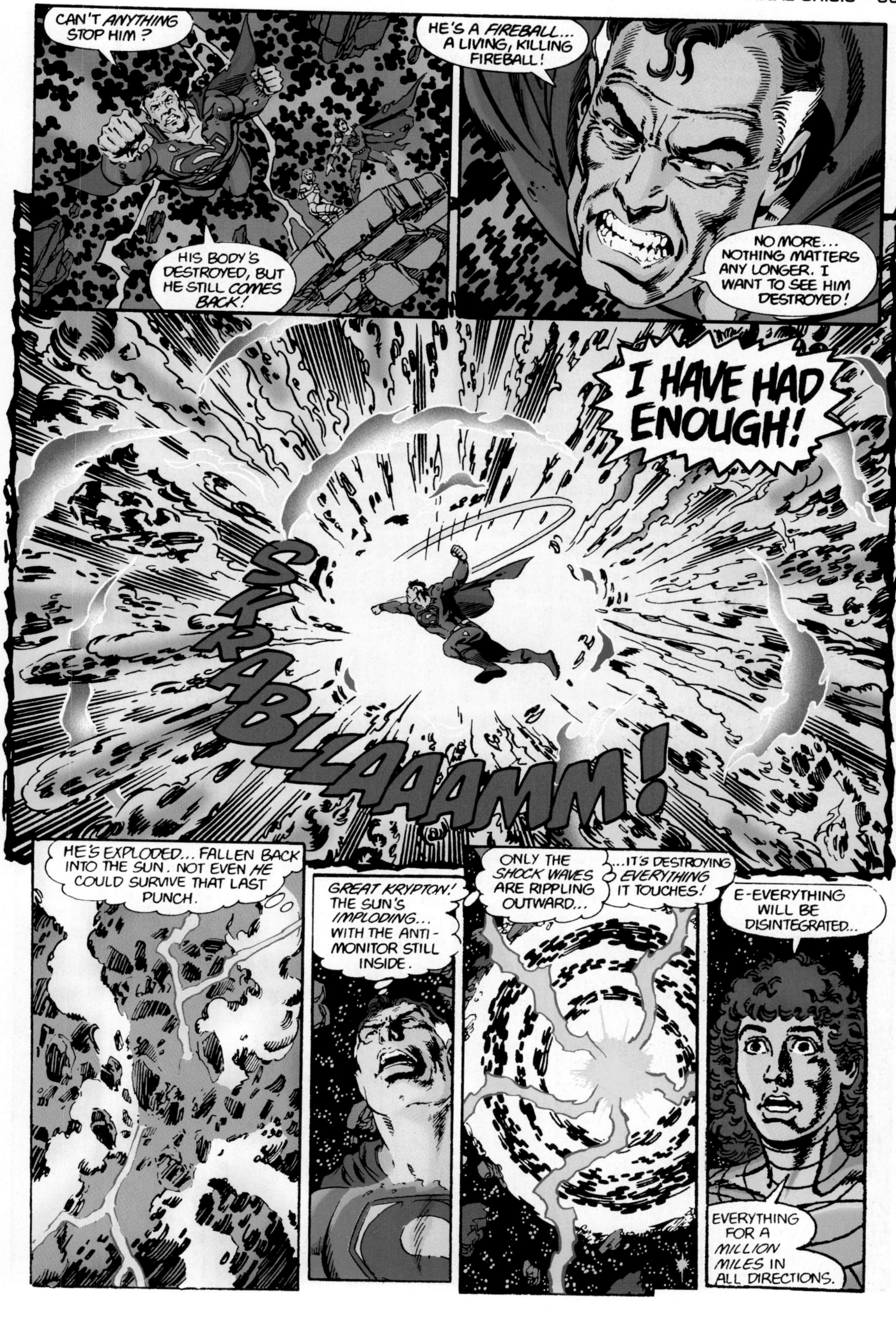
CAN'T *ANYTHING* STOP HIM?
HIS BODY'S DESTROYED, BUT HE STILL *COMES BACK*!
HE'S A *FIREBALL*... A LIVING, KILLING FIREBALL!
NO MORE... NOTHING MATTERS ANY LONGER. I WANT TO SEE HIM DESTROYED!
I HAVE HAD ENOUGH!
SKRABLLAAAMM!
HE'S EXPLODED... FALLEN BACK INTO THE SUN. NOT EVEN *HE* COULD SURVIVE THAT LAST PUNCH.
GREAT KRYPTON! THE SUN'S *IMPLODING*... WITH THE ANTI-MONITOR STILL INSIDE.
ONLY THE *SHOCK WAVES* ARE RIPPLING OUTWARD...
...IT'S DESTROYING *EVERYTHING* IT TOUCHES!
E-EVERYTHING WILL BE DISINTEGRATED...
EVERYTHING FOR A *MILLION MILES* IN ALL DIRECTIONS.

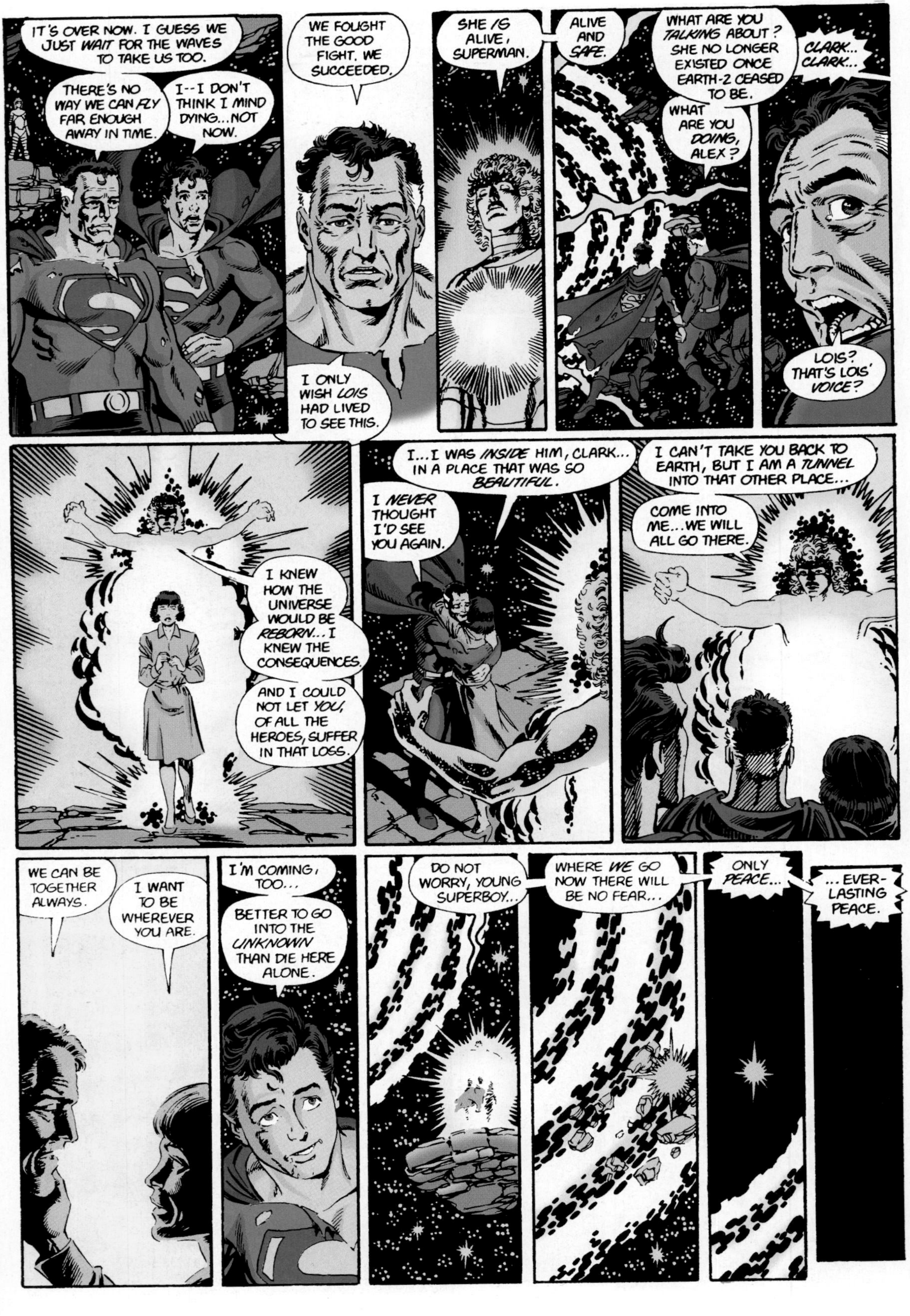
IT'S OVER NOW. I GUESS WE JUST WAIT FOR THE WAVES TO TAKE US TOO.
THERE'S NO WAY WE CAN FLY FAR ENOUGH AWAY IN TIME.
I--I DON'T THINK I MIND DYING...NOT NOW.
WE FOUGHT THE GOOD FIGHT. WE SUCCEEDED.
I ONLY WISH LOIS HAD LIVED TO SEE THIS.
SHE IS ALIVE, SUPERMAN.
ALIVE AND SAFE.
WHAT ARE YOU TALKING ABOUT? SHE NO LONGER EXISTED ONCE EARTH-2 CEASED TO BE.
WHAT ARE YOU DOING, ALEX?
CLARK... CLARK...
LOIS? THAT'S LOIS' VOICE?
I KNEW HOW THE UNIVERSE WOULD BE REBORN... I KNEW THE CONSEQUENCES.
AND I COULD NOT LET YOU, OF ALL THE HEROES, SUFFER IN THAT LOSS.
I...I WAS INSIDE HIM, CLARK... IN A PLACE THAT WAS SO BEAUTIFUL.
I NEVER THOUGHT I'D SEE YOU AGAIN.
I CAN'T TAKE YOU BACK TO EARTH, BUT I AM A TUNNEL INTO THAT OTHER PLACE...
COME INTO ME... WE WILL ALL GO THERE.
WE CAN BE TOGETHER ALWAYS.
I WANT TO BE WHEREVER YOU ARE.
I'M COMING, TOO...
BETTER TO GO INTO THE UNKNOWN THAN DIE HERE ALONE.
DO NOT WORRY, YOUNG SUPERBOY...
WHERE WE GO NOW THERE WILL BE NO FEAR...
ONLY PEACE...
...EVER-LASTING PEACE.

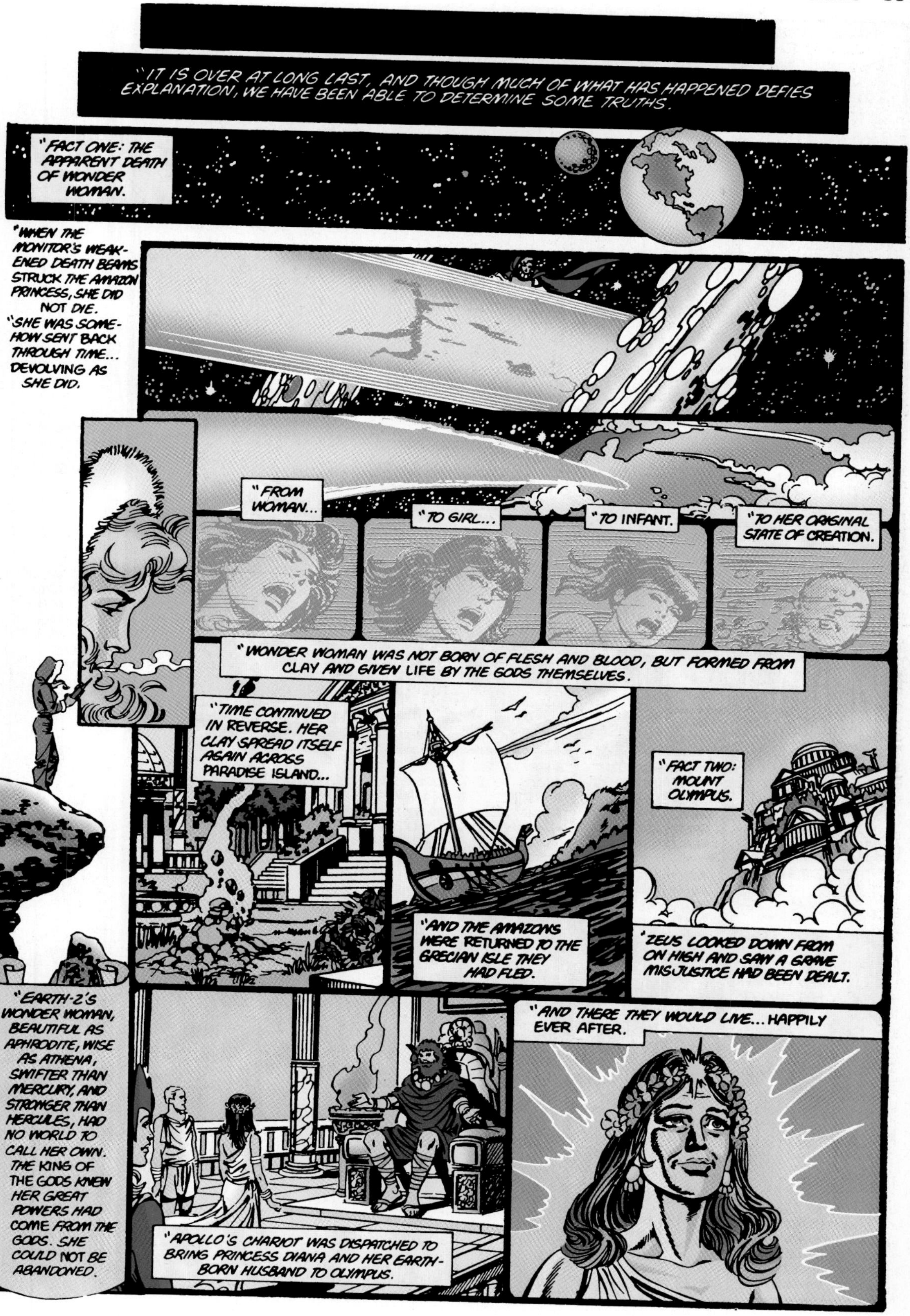
"IT IS OVER AT LONG LAST, AND THOUGH MUCH OF WHAT HAS HAPPENED DEFIES EXPLANATION, WE HAVE BEEN ABLE TO DETERMINE SOME TRUTHS.
"FACT ONE: THE APPARENT DEATH OF WONDER WOMAN.
"WHEN THE MONITOR'S WEAKENED DEATH BEAMS STRUCK THE AMAZON PRINCESS, SHE DID NOT DIE.
"SHE WAS SOMEHOW SENT BACK THROUGH TIME... DEVOLVING AS SHE DID.
"FROM WOMAN...
"TO GIRL...
"TO INFANT.
"TO HER ORIGINAL STATE OF CREATION.
"WONDER WOMAN WAS NOT BORN OF FLESH AND BLOOD, BUT FORMED FROM CLAY AND GIVEN LIFE BY THE GODS THEMSELVES.
"TIME CONTINUED IN REVERSE. HER CLAY SPREAD ITSELF AGAIN ACROSS PARADISE ISLAND...
"AND THE AMAZONS WERE RETURNED TO THE GRECIAN ISLE THEY HAD FLED.
"FACT TWO: MOUNT OLYMPUS.
"ZEUS LOOKED DOWN FROM ON HIGH AND SAW A GRAVE MISJUSTICE HAD BEEN DEALT.
"EARTH-2'S WONDER WOMAN, BEAUTIFUL AS APHRODITE, WISE AS ATHENA, SWIFTER THAN MERCURY, AND STRONGER THAN HERCULES, HAD NO WORLD TO CALL HER OWN. THE KING OF THE GODS KNEW HER GREAT POWERS HAD COME FROM THE GODS. SHE COULD NOT BE ABANDONED.
"APOLLO'S CHARIOT WAS DISPATCHED TO BRING PRINCESS DIANA AND HER EARTH-BORN HUSBAND TO OLYMPUS.
"AND THERE THEY WOULD LIVE... HAPPILY EVER AFTER.

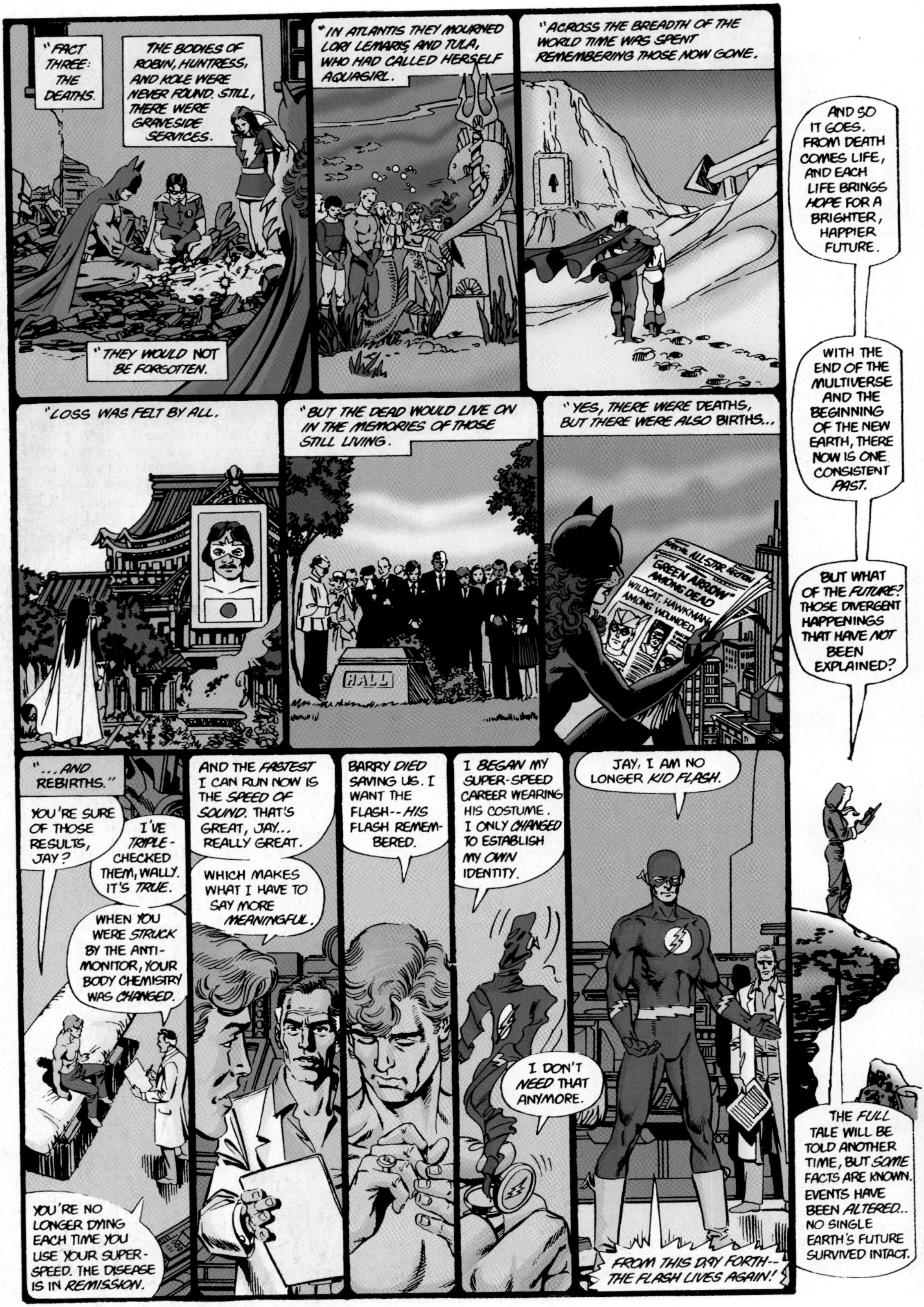
"FACT THREE: THE DEATHS.
THE BODIES OF ROBIN, HUNTRESS, AND KOLE WERE NEVER FOUND. STILL, THERE WERE GRAVESIDE SERVICES.
"THEY WOULD NOT BE FORGOTTEN.
"IN ATLANTIS THEY MOURNED LORI LEMARIS AND TULA, WHO HAD CALLED HERSELF AQUAGIRL.
"ACROSS THE BREADTH OF THE WORLD TIME WAS SPENT REMEMBERING THOSE NOW GONE.
AND SO IT GOES. FROM DEATH COMES LIFE, AND EACH LIFE BRINGS HOPE FOR A BRIGHTER, HAPPIER FUTURE.
WITH THE END OF THE MULTIVERSE AND THE BEGINNING OF THE NEW EARTH, THERE NOW IS ONE CONSISTENT PAST.
BUT WHAT OF THE FUTURE? THOSE DIVERGENT HAPPENINGS THAT HAVE NOT BEEN EXPLAINED?
"LOSS WAS FELT BY ALL.
"BUT THE DEAD WOULD LIVE ON IN THE MEMORIES OF THOSE STILL LIVING.
HALL
"YES, THERE WERE DEATHS, BUT THERE WERE ALSO BIRTHS...
SPECIAL ALL-STAR SECTION
GREEN ARROW AMONG DEAD
WILDCAT, HAWKMAN AMONG WOUNDED
"...AND REBIRTHS."
YOU'RE SURE OF THOSE RESULTS, JAY?
I'VE TRIPLE-CHECKED THEM, WALLY. IT'S TRUE.
WHEN YOU WERE STRUCK BY THE ANTI-MONITOR, YOUR BODY CHEMISTRY WAS CHANGED.
YOU'RE NO LONGER DYING EACH TIME YOU USE YOUR SUPER-SPEED. THE DISEASE IS IN REMISSION.
AND THE FASTEST I CAN RUN NOW IS THE SPEED OF SOUND. THAT'S GREAT, JAY... REALLY GREAT.
WHICH MAKES WHAT I HAVE TO SAY MORE MEANINGFUL.
BARRY DIED SAVING US. I WANT THE FLASH--HIS FLASH REMEMBERED.
I BEGAN MY SUPER-SPEED CAREER WEARING HIS COSTUME. I ONLY CHANGED TO ESTABLISH MY OWN IDENTITY.
I DON'T NEED THAT ANYMORE.
JAY, I AM NO LONGER KID FLASH.
FROM THIS DAY FORTH-- THE FLASH LIVES AGAIN!
THE FULL TALE WILL BE TOLD ANOTHER TIME, BUT SOME FACTS ARE KNOWN. EVENTS HAVE BEEN ALTERED... NO SINGLE EARTH'S FUTURE SURVIVED INTACT.

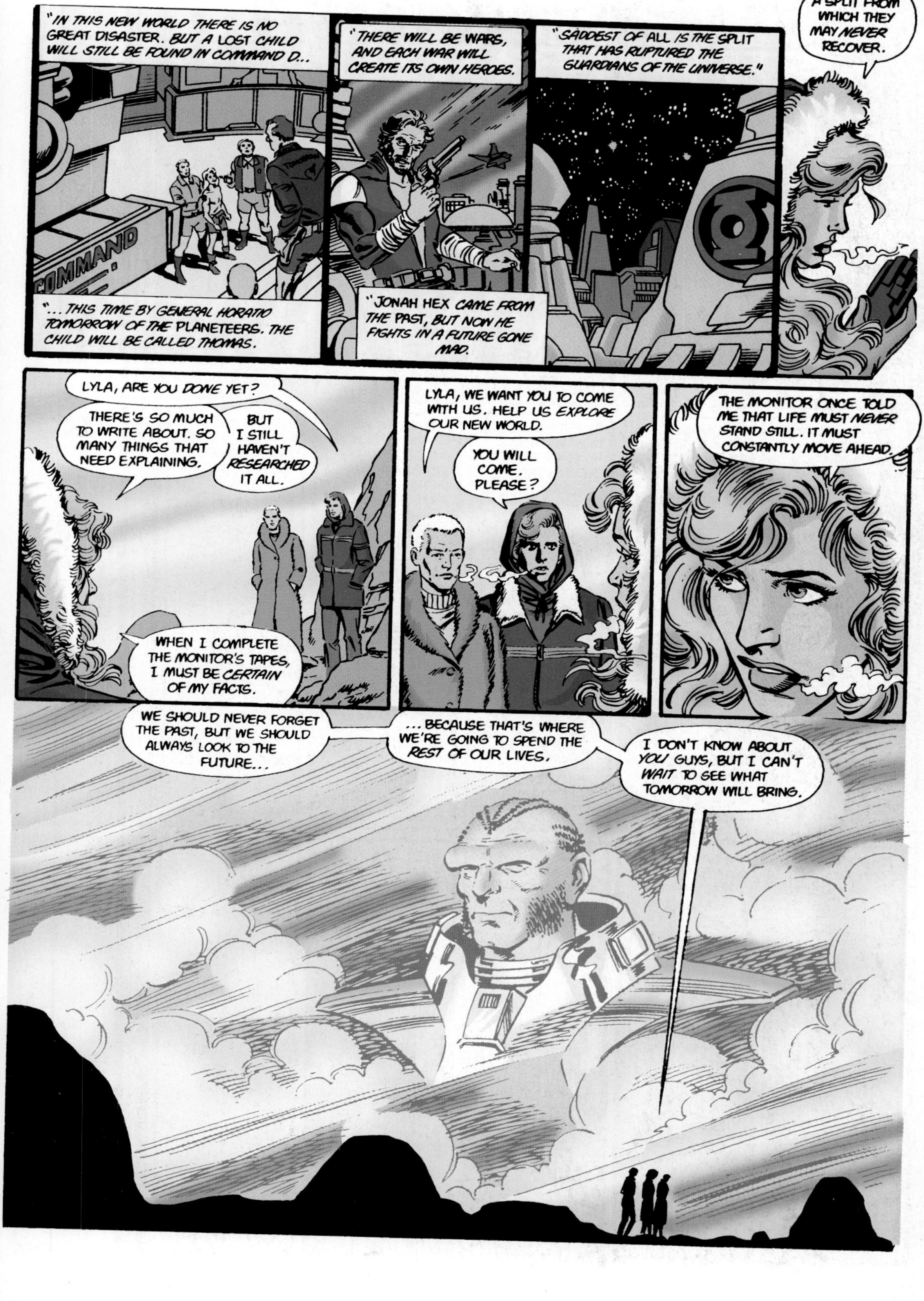
"IN THIS NEW WORLD THERE IS NO GREAT DISASTER. BUT A LOST CHILD WILL STILL BE FOUND IN COMMAND D...
"...THIS TIME BY GENERAL HORATIO TOMORROW OF THE PLANETEERS. THE CHILD WILL BE CALLED THOMAS.
COMMAND
"THERE WILL BE WARS, AND EACH WAR WILL CREATE ITS OWN HEROES.
"JONAH HEX CAME FROM THE PAST, BUT NOW HE FIGHTS IN A FUTURE GONE MAD.
"SADDEST OF ALL IS THE SPLIT THAT HAS RUPTURED THE GUARDIANS OF THE UNIVERSE."
A SPLIT FROM WHICH THEY MAY NEVER RECOVER.
LYLA, ARE YOU DONE YET?
THERE'S SO MUCH TO WRITE ABOUT. SO MANY THINGS THAT NEED EXPLAINING.
BUT I STILL HAVEN'T RESEARCHED IT ALL.
WHEN I COMPLETE THE MONITOR'S TAPES, I MUST BE CERTAIN OF MY FACTS.
LYLA, WE WANT YOU TO COME WITH US. HELP US EXPLORE OUR NEW WORLD.
YOU WILL COME. PLEASE?
THE MONITOR ONCE TOLD ME THAT LIFE MUST NEVER STAND STILL. IT MUST CONSTANTLY MOVE AHEAD.
WE SHOULD NEVER FORGET THE PAST, BUT WE SHOULD ALWAYS LOOK TO THE FUTURE...
...BECAUSE THAT'S WHERE WE'RE GOING TO SPEND THE REST OF OUR LIVES.
I DON'T KNOW ABOUT YOU GUYS, BUT I CAN'T WAIT TO SEE WHAT TOMORROW WILL BRING.

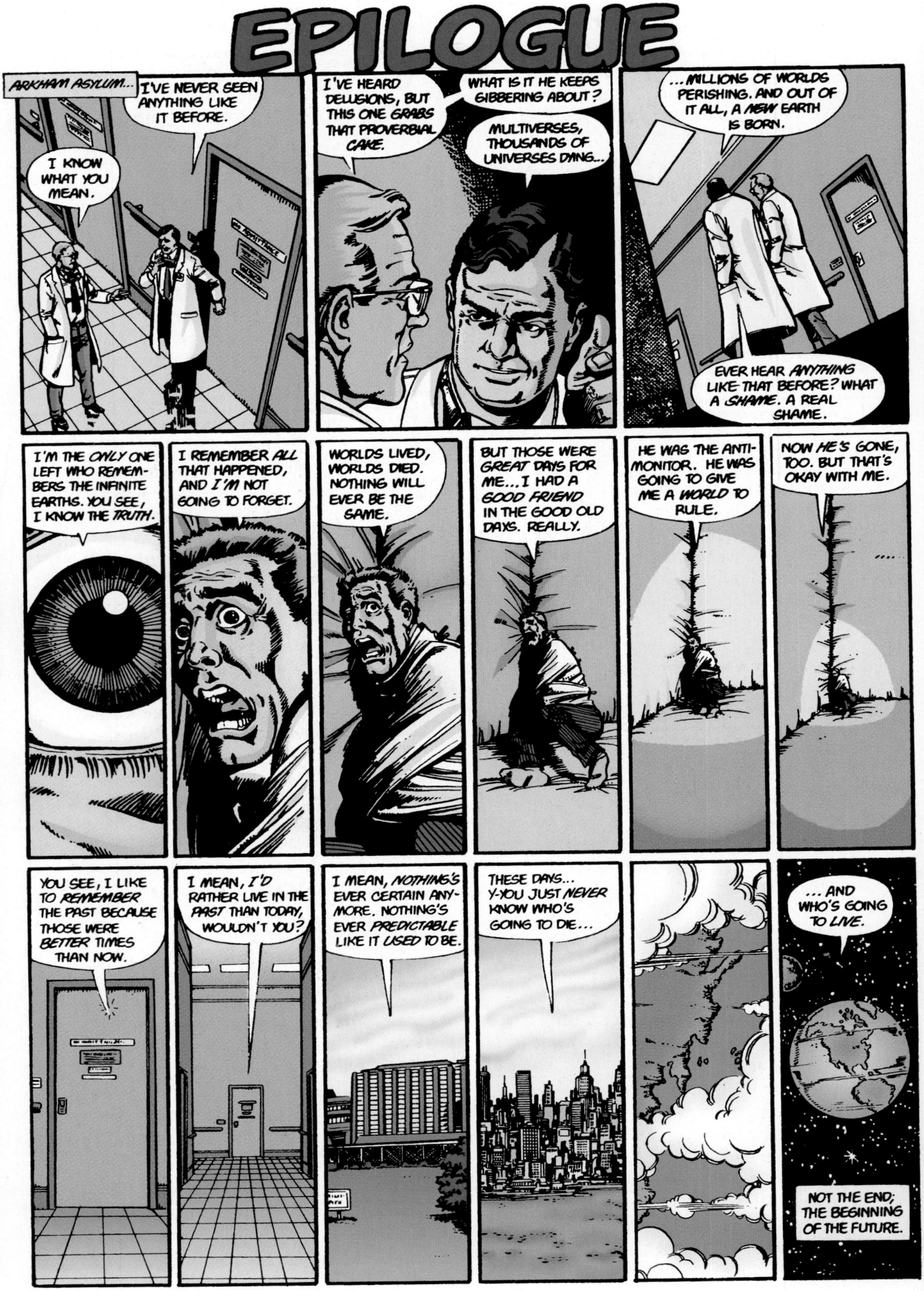
EPILOGUE
ARKHAM ASYLUM...
I'VE NEVER SEEN ANYTHING LIKE IT BEFORE.
I KNOW WHAT YOU MEAN.
I'VE HEARD DELUSIONS, BUT THIS ONE GRABS THAT PROVERBIAL CAKE.
WHAT IS IT HE KEEPS GIBBERING ABOUT?
MULTIVERSES, THOUSANDS OF UNIVERSES DYING...
...MILLIONS OF WORLDS PERISHING. AND OUT OF IT ALL, A NEW EARTH IS BORN.
EVER HEAR ANYTHING LIKE THAT BEFORE? WHAT A SHAME. A REAL SHAME.
I'M THE ONLY ONE LEFT WHO REMEMBERS THE INFINITE EARTHS. YOU SEE, I KNOW THE TRUTH.
I REMEMBER ALL THAT HAPPENED, AND I'M NOT GOING TO FORGET.
WORLDS LIVED, WORLDS DIED. NOTHING WILL EVER BE THE SAME.
BUT THOSE WERE GREAT DAYS FOR ME... I HAD A GOOD FRIEND IN THE GOOD OLD DAYS. REALLY.
HE WAS THE ANTI-MONITOR. HE WAS GOING TO GIVE ME A WORLD TO RULE.
NOW HE'S GONE, TOO. BUT THAT'S OKAY WITH ME.
...
YOU SEE, I LIKE TO REMEMBER THE PAST BECAUSE THOSE WERE BETTER TIMES THAN NOW.
I MEAN, I'D RATHER LIVE IN THE PAST THAN TODAY, WOULDN'T YOU?
I MEAN, NOTHING'S EVER CERTAIN ANYMORE. NOTHING'S EVER PREDICTABLE LIKE IT USED TO BE.
THESE DAYS... Y-YOU JUST NEVER KNOW WHO'S GOING TO DIE...
...AND WHO'S GOING TO LIVE.
NOT THE END; THE BEGINNING OF THE FUTURE.

afterword

WHEW. WHAT A READ, HUH?

That's one of the reasons CRISIS ON INFINITE EARTHS was read avidly by so many readers in its first publication (as a monthly then) in 1985 – it was a *great* super-hero story that stood tall on its own legs, was superbly drawn by the inimitable George Pérez (who painstakingly researched each of the characters that he drew, attaining accuracy not only in their costume details but in their physical attributes and attitudes) and accomplished the herculean task of making the DC Universe more new-reader friendly.

The original publication of CRISIS ON INFINITE EARTHS also served notice to competitors, creators, distributors and retailers (and apparently collectors as well) that DC Comics was serious about keeping its readers happy *and* informed and was a (super-hero) force to be reckoned with. Fan mail poured in, sales boomed, and the door was opened for the many groundbreaking series, formats and projects that sprang forth from that time and have continued unabated, even to this day.

In many ways, CRISIS (as it has always been referred to in DC's offices) became the template for all crossover series that followed its publication – not only by DC Comics, but by other publishers as well. Alas, neither *we* nor *they* have since put together a crossover series that truly challenged the unique nature of CRISIS. (How many others merited this kind of reprinting?) The reason why is simple: none of the crossover series that followed were created by people who viewed producing it as a "calling" (Marv's term) instead of an assignment. And most of the others were constructs, rather than a story that needed telling – a story that made

permanent, irreversible changes in a super-hero universe...a story that made a difference!

From the time Marv and George (and maybe Len Wein, too, if memory serves) made the pitch for CRISIS to when the series concluded at year's end in 1985, Marv and George enjoyed the full and enthusiastic support and encouragement of management – fact is, we three (Paul Levitz, Jenette Kahn and myself) were also a cheering section of sorts. Aside: When Marv and George decided that the advantages (for our brave new DC world) of killing off Supergirl far exceeded the disadvantages, they approached me with the idea. "Sounds right to me," I said. "But, we daren't kill off a main character without Jenette [Kahn]'s approval." It was a tremulous Marv who entered Jenette's lair...it was a stunned Marv who exited. She had listened carefully to his reasons – and given her approval!

Did CRISIS work as a story? Yep! Did it neaten up our universe? You bet! Did it give DC Comics a launch pad to the future? Of course! Did we take advantage of all the opportunities presented by the dramatic conclusion of the landmark series called CRISIS ON INFINITE EARTHS...?

Well... Yes and no. A *full* answer would take too much space here, and I don't want to spoil our celebration. So break out the champagne!

Thank you and good evening*,

Dick Giordano

SEPTEMBER 10, 1998

*see....some things do change.